Horngren's Cost Accounting

A MANAGERIAL EMPHASIS

Seventeenth Edition

Srikant M. Datar
Harvard University

Madhav V. Rajan
University of Chicago

Pearson

Please contact https://support.pearson.com/getsupport/s/contactsupport with any queries on this content.

Cover Image: QQ7/Shutterstock

Acknowledgments of third-party content appear on the appropriate page within the text.

Library of Congress Cataloging-in-Publication Data
Names: Datar, Srikant M., author. | Rajan, Madhav V., author.
Title: Horngren's cost accounting : a managerial emphasis / Srikant M. Datar, Harvard University, Madhav V. Rajan, University of Chicago.
Description: Seventeenth edition. | Hoboken, NJ : Pearson Education, [2021] | Includes index. |
Identifiers: LCCN 2020010431 | ISBN 9780135628478 (hardcover) | ISBN 9780135628508 (paperback) | ISBN 9780135628522 (epub)
Subjects: LCSH: Cost accounting.
Classification: LCC HF5686.C8 H59 2021 | DDC 658.15/11—dc23
LC record available at https://lccn.loc.gov/2020010431

1 2020

Pearson

Access Code Card
ISBN-10: 0-13-562852-0
ISBN-13: 978-0-13-562852-2

Rental
ISBN-10: 0-13-562847-4
ISBN-13: 978-0-13-562847-8

Instructor's Review Copy
ISBN-10: 0-13-562850-4
ISBN-13: 978-0-13-562850-8

Brief Contents

Contents

6 Master Budget and Responsibility Accounting 194

7 Flexible Budgets, Direct-Cost Variances, and Management Control 245

8 Flexible Budgets, Overhead Cost Variances, and Management Control 282

About the Authors

Srikant M. Datar is the Arthur Lowes Dickinson Professor of Business Administration at the Harvard Business School, Faculty Chair of the Harvard University Innovation Labs, and Senior Associate Dean for University Affairs. A graduate with distinction from the University of Bombay, he received gold medals upon graduation from the Indian Institute of Management, Ahmedabad, and the Institute of Cost and Works Accountants of India. A chartered accountant, he holds two master's degrees and a PhD from Stanford University.

Datar has published his research in leading accounting, marketing, and operations management journals, including *The Accounting Review, Contemporary Accounting Research, Journal of Accounting, Auditing and Finance, Journal of Accounting and Economics, Journal of Accounting Research*, and *Management Science*. He has served as an associate editor and on the editorial board of several journals and has presented his research to corporate executives and academic audiences in North America, South America, Asia, Africa, Australia, and Europe. He is a coauthor of two other books: *Managerial Accounting: Making Decisions and Motivating Performance* and *Rethinking the MBA: Business Education at a Crossroads.*

Cited by his students as a dedicated and innovative teacher, Datar received the George Leland Bach Award for Excellence in the Classroom at Carnegie Mellon University and the Distinguished Teaching Award at Stanford University.

Datar is a member of the boards of directors of Novartis A.G., ICF International, T-Mobile US, and Stryker Corporation, and is Senior Strategic Advisor to HCL Technologies. He has worked with many organizations, including Apple Computer, Boeing, DuPont, Ford, General Motors, Morgan Stanley, PepsiCo, Visa, and the World Bank. He is a member of the American Accounting Association and the Institute of Management Accountants.

Madhav V. Rajan is Dean of the University of Chicago Booth School of Business and the George Pratt Shultz Professor of Accounting.

Prior to July 2017, Rajan was the Robert K. Jaedicke Professor of Accounting at Stanford Graduate School of Business and Professor of Law (by courtesy) at Stanford Law School. From 2010 to 2016, he was Senior Associate Dean for Academic Affairs and head of the Stanford MBA program. In April 2017, he received Stanford GSB's Davis Award for Lifetime Achievement and Service.

Rajan received his undergraduate degree in commerce from the University of Madras, India, and his MS in accounting, MBA, and PhD degrees from Carnegie Mellon University. In 1990, his dissertation won the Alexander Henderson Award for Excellence in Economic Theory.

Rajan's research has focused on the economics-based analysis of management accounting issues, especially as they relate to internal control, capital budgeting, supply-chain, and performance systems. His work has been published in a variety of leading journals, including *The Accounting Review, Journal of Accounting and Economics, Journal of Accounting Research, Management Science*, and *Review of Financial Studies*. In 2004, he received the Notable Contribution to Management Accounting Literature award. He is a coauthor of *Managerial Accounting: Making Decisions and Motivating Performance*.

Rajan has served as the Departmental Editor for Accounting at *Management Science* as well as associate editor for both the accounting and operations areas. From 2002 to 2008, Rajan served as an Editor of *The Accounting Review*. He has twice been a plenary speaker at the AAA Management Accounting Conference.

Rajan has received several teaching honors at Wharton and Stanford, including the David W. Hauck Award, the highest undergraduate teaching award at Wharton. He taught in the flagship Stanford Executive Program and was co-director of *Finance and Accounting for the Nonfinancial Executive*. He has participated in custom programs for many companies, including Genentech, Hewlett-Packard, and nVidia, and served as faculty director for the Infosys Global Leadership Program.

Rajan is a director of iShares, Inc., a trustee of the iShares Trust, and a member of the C.M. Capital Investment Advisory Board.

Preface

New to This Edition

Increased Focus on Merchandising and Service Sectors

In keeping with the shifts in the U.S. and world economy, this edition makes great use of merchandising and service sector examples, with corresponding de-emphasis of traditional manufacturing settings. For example, Chapter 10 illustrates linear cost functions in the context of payments for cloud computing services. Chapter 11 describes revenue management using big-data analytics at a company investing in loans. Chapter 21 highlights inventory management in retail organizations and uses an example based on a seller of sunglasses. Chapter 22 incorporates a running example that looks at capital budgeting in the context of a transportation company. Several Concepts in Action boxes focus on the merchandising and service sectors, including achieving cost leadership at Costco (Chapter 1), reducing fixed costs at Lyft (Chapter 2), using activity-based costing to reduce the costs of health care delivery at the Mayo Clinic (Chapter 5), developing Internet-based budgeting at P.F. Chang's (Chapter 6), and analyzing operating income performance at Buffalo Wild Wings (Chapter 13).

Greater Emphasis on Sustainability

This edition places significant emphasis on sustainability as one of the critical managerial challenges of the coming decades. Many managers are promoting the development and implementation of strategies to achieve long-term financial, social, and environmental performance as key imperatives. We highlight this in Chapter 1 and return to the theme in several subsequent chapters. Chapter 13 discusses the benefits to companies from measuring social and environmental performance and how such measures can be incorporated in a balanced scorecard. Chapter 24 provides several examples of companies that mandate disclosures and evaluate managers on environmental and social metrics. A variety of chapters, including Chapters 2, 6, 10, 14, and 22, contain material that stress themes of recognizing and accounting for environmental costs; energy independence; setting stretch targets to motivate greater carbon reductions; using cost analysis, carbon tax, and cap-and-trade auctions to reduce environmental footprints; and constructing "green" homes in a cost-effective manner.

Focus on Innovation

We discuss the role of accounting concepts and systems in fostering and supporting innovation and entrepreneurial activities in firms. In particular, we discuss the challenges posed by recognizing R&D costs as period expenses even though the benefits of innovation accrue in later periods. In Chapter 6, we describe how companies budget for innovation expenses and develop measures to monitor success of the innovation efforts delinked from operational performance in the current period. Chapter 12 presents the importance of nonfinancial measures when making decisions about innovation. Chapter 14 stresses that innovation starts with understanding customer needs while Chapter 20 discusses process innovations for improving quality.

New Cutting-Edge Topics

The pace of change in organizations continues to be rapid. The 17th edition of *Cost Accounting* reflects changes occurring in the role of cost accounting in organizations.

- We have added new material and a new Chapter 11 to explain recent trends in big data and data analytics to manage revenues and predict costs. Companies are increasingly looking for management accountants who can interface with data scientists.
- We introduce sustainability strategies and the methods companies use to implement sustainability and business goals.

- We describe ideas based on academic research regarding the weights to be placed on performance measures in a balanced scorecard. We also have a section on methods to evaluate strategy maps such as the strength of links, differentiators, focal points, and trigger points.
- We provide details on the transfer pricing strategies used by multinational technology firms such as Apple and Google to minimize income taxes.
- We discuss current trends in the regulation of executive compensation.
- We describe the evolution of enterprise resource planning systems and newer simplified costing systems that practice lean accounting.

Solving Learning and Teaching Challenges

Studying cost accounting is one of the best business investments a student can make. Why? Because success in any organization—from the smallest corner store to the largest multinational corporation—requires the use of cost accounting concepts and practices. Cost accounting provides key data to managers for planning and controlling, as well as costing, products, services, and even customers. This book focuses on how cost accounting helps managers make better decisions, as cost accountants increasingly are becoming integral members of their company's decision-making teams. In order to emphasize this prominence in decision making, we use the "different costs for different purposes" theme throughout this book. By focusing on basic concepts, analyses, uses, and procedures instead of procedures alone, we recognize cost accounting as a managerial tool for business strategy and implementation.

We also prepare students for the rewards and challenges they will face in the professional cost accounting world of today and tomorrow. For example, we emphasize both the development of technical skills such as Excel and big-data analytics to leverage available information technology and the values and behaviors that make cost accountants effective in the workplace.

Opening Vignettes

Each chapter opens with a vignette on a real company situation. The vignettes engage the reader in a business situation or dilemma, illustrating why and how the concepts in the chapter are relevant in business. For example, Chapter 2 describes how teen apparel chain Aéropostale was driven into bankruptcy by the relatively high proportion of fixed costs in its operations. Chapter 5 explains the use of activity-based costing by IBM to evaluate the true cost of data breaches. Chapter 9 highlights Under Armor's use of a new internal company system to better manage its inventory and supply chain with efficiency and precision to reduce inventory costs. Chapter 15 shows how Starbucks changed its rewards program to better align rewards with customer spending. Chapter 19 shows the impact on Tesla of the rework costs associated with a drastic ramp-up of production to meet unprecedented customer demand. Chapter 24 describes the misalignment between performance measurement and pay at General Electric.

Concepts in Action Boxes

Found in every chapter, these boxes cover real-world cost accounting issues across a variety of industries, including defense contracting, entertainment, manufacturing, retailing, and sports. New examples include the following:

- Cost Leadership at Costco: Rock-Bottom Prices and Sky-High Profits (Chapter 1)
- Can Cost–Volume–Profit Analysis Help Whole Foods Escape the "Whole Paycheck" Trap? (Chapter 3)
- P.F. Chang's and Internet-Based Budgeting (Chapter 6)
- Can ESPN Avoid the Cord-Cutting "Death Spiral"? (Chapter 9)
- Zara Uses Target Pricing to Become the World's Largest Fashion Retailer (Chapter 14)
- Big Data Joint-Products and Byproducts Create New Business Opportunities (Chapter 17)
- Facebook Works to Overcome Mobile Data Bottlenecks (Chapter 20)

Streamlined Presentation

We continue to try to simplify and streamline our presentation of various topics to make it as easy as possible for students to learn the concepts, tools, and frameworks introduced in different chapters. We have introduced a new chapter, Chapter 11, on data analytics to help management accountants use big data to manage both revenue and costs. This chapter follows Chapter 10 on predicting cost behavior. We received positive feedback for the reorganization of Chapters 12 through 16 in the 16th edition and have maintained that order in the 17th edition as Chapters 13 through 17. Chapter 13 on the balanced scorecard and strategic profitability analysis follows Chapter 12 on decision making and relevant information for operational decisions. Chapter 14 is the first of four chapters on cost allocation. We introduce the purposes of cost allocation in Chapter 14 and discuss cost allocation for long-run product costing and pricing. Continuing the same example, Chapter 15 discusses cost allocation for customer costing. Chapter 16 builds on the Chapter 4 example to discuss cost allocation for support departments. Chapter 17 discusses joint cost allocation.

Other examples of streamlined presentations can be found in the following chapters:

- Chapter 2, in the discussion of fundamental cost concepts and the managerial framework for decision making.
- Chapter 6, where the appendix ties the cash budget to the chapter example.
- Chapter 8, which has a comprehensive chart that lays out all of the variances described in Chapters 7 and 8.
- Chapter 9, which uses a single two-period example to illustrate the impact of various inventory-costing methods and denominator level choices.

Try It! Examples

Found throughout each chapter, Try It! interactive questions give students the opportunity to apply the concept they just learned. Links in the eText allow students to practice in MyLab Accounting without interrupting their interaction with the eText.

Becker Multiple-Choice Questions

Sample problems, assignable in MyLab Accounting, provide an introduction to the CPA Exam format and an opportunity for early practice with CPA exam-style questions.

Hallmark Features of *Cost Accounting*

- Exceptionally strong emphasis on managerial uses of cost information
- Clarity and understandability of the text
- Excellent balance in integrating modern topics with traditional coverage
- Emphasis on human behavior aspects
- Extensive use of real-world examples
- Ability to teach chapters in different sequences
- Excellent quantity, quality, and range of assignment material

The first 13 chapters provide the essence of a one-term (quarter or semester) course. There is ample text and assignment material in the book's 24 chapters for a two-term course. This book can be used immediately after the student has had an introductory course in financial accounting. Alternatively, this book can build on an introductory course in managerial accounting.

Deciding on the sequence of chapters in a textbook is a challenge. Because every instructor has a unique way of organizing his or her course, we utilize a modular, flexible organization that permits a course to be custom tailored. *This organization facilitates diverse approaches to teaching and learning.*

As an example of the book's flexibility, consider our treatment of process costing. Process costing is described in Chapters 17 and 18. Instructors interested in filling out a student's perspective of costing systems can move directly from job-order costing described in Chapter 4 to Chapter 17 without interruption in the flow of material. Other instructors may want their students to delve into activity-based costing and budgeting and more decision-oriented topics early in the course. These instructors may prefer to postpone discussion of process costing.

Acknowledgments

We are indebted to many people for their ideas and assistance. Our primary thanks go to the many academics and practitioners who have advanced our knowledge of cost accounting. The package of teaching materials we present is the work of skillful and valued team members developing some excellent end-of-chapter assignment material. Tommy Goodwin provided outstanding research assistance on technical issues and current developments. Merle Ederhof was enormously helpful with updating the chapter materials and the assignments and brought her health care experience to bear in highlighting new applications for cost accounting in the book.

We would also like to thank the dedicated and hard-working supplement author team and Integra. The book is much better because of the efforts of these colleagues.

In shaping this edition and past editions we would like to thank all the reviewers and colleagues who have worked closely with us and the editorial team. We extend special thanks to those who contributed to the development of Chapter 11, which is new to this edition: Mark Awada, Pascal Bizzaro, Caitlin Bowler, Rachel Caruso, Mahendra Gujarathi, Paul Hamilton, John Harris, Donna McGovern, Tatiana Sandino, and V.G. Narayanan.

We thank the people at Pearson for their hard work and dedication, including Lacey Vitetta, Ellen Geary, Sara Eilert, Christopher DeJohn, Michael Trinchetto, Claudia Fernandes, Stacey Miller, and Martha LaChance. This book and support materials would not have been possible without their dedication and skill. Allison Campbell at Integra expertly managed the production aspects of the manuscript's preparation with superb skill and tremendous dedication. We are deeply appreciative of their good spirits, loyalty, and ability to stay calm in the most hectic of times.

Appreciation also goes to the American Institute of Certified Public Accountants, the Institute of Management Accountants, the Society of Management Accountants of Canada, the Certified General Accountants Association of Canada, the Financial Executive Institute of America, and many other publishers and companies for their generous permission to quote from their publications. Problems from the Uniform CPA examinations are designated (CPA), and problems from the Certified Management Accountant examination are designated (CMA). Many of these problems are adapted to highlight particular points. We are grateful to the professors who contributed assignment material for this edition. Their names are indicated in parentheses at the start of their specific problems. Comments from users are welcome.

SRIKANT M. DATAR
MADHAV V. RAJAN

In memory of Charles T. Horngren 1926–2011

Chuck Horngren revolutionized cost and management accounting. He loved new ideas and introduced many new concepts. He had the unique gift of explaining these concepts in simple and creative ways. He epitomized excellence and never tired of details, whether it was finding exactly the right word or working and reworking assignment materials.

He combined his great intellect with genuine humility and warmth and a human touch that inspired others to do their best. He taught us many lessons about life through his amazing discipline, his ability to make everyone feel welcome, and his love of family.

It was a great privilege, pleasure, and honor to have known Chuck Horngren. Few individuals will have the enormous influence that Chuck had on the accounting profession. Fewer still will be able to do it with the class and style that was his hallmark. He was unique, special, and amazing in many, many ways and, at once, a role model, teacher, mentor, and friend. He is deeply missed.

SRIKANT M. DATAR
Harvard University

MADHAV V. RAJAN
University of Chicago

To Our Families

Swati, Radhika, Gayatri, Sidharth (SD)

Gayathri, Sanjana, Anupama (MVR)

The Manager and Management Accounting

1

All businesses are concerned about revenues and costs.

Managers at companies small and large must understand how revenues and costs behave or risk losing control of the performance of their firms. Managers use cost accounting information to make decisions about research and development, production planning, budgeting, pricing, and the products or services to offer customers. Sometimes these decisions involve tradeoffs. The following article shows how understanding costs and pricing helps companies like Coca-Cola increase profits even as the quantity of products sold decreases.

LEARNING OBJECTIVES

1. Distinguish financial accounting from management accounting
2. Understand how management accountants help firms make strategic decisions
3. Describe the set of business functions in the value chain and identify the dimensions of performance that customers are expecting of companies
4. Explain the five-step decision-making process and its role in management accounting
5. Describe three guidelines management accountants follow in supporting managers
6. Understand how management accounting fits into an organization's structure
7. Understand what professional ethics mean to management accountants

FOR COCA-COLA, SMALLER SIZES MEAN BIGGER PROFITS[1]

Can selling less of something be more profitable than selling more of it? As consumers become more health conscious, they are buying less soda. "Don't want to drink too much?" Get a smaller can. "Don't want so many calories?" Buy a smaller can. "Don't want so much sugar?" Just drink a smaller can. In 2017, while overall sales of soda in the United States declined in terms of volume, industry revenue was higher. How, you ask? Soda companies are charging more for less!

Coca-Cola has been the market leader in selling smaller sizes of soda to consumers. Sales of 7.5-ounce minicans and other smaller packages now account for 10% of Coca-Cola sales by volume. Meanwhile, sales of larger bottles and cans continue to fall. The price per ounce of Coca-Cola sold in smaller cans is higher than the price per ounce of Coca-Cola sold in bulk. The resulting higher profits from the sales of these smaller sizes of soda make up for the decrease in total volume of soda sold. If these trends toward buying smaller cans continue, Coca-Cola will be selling less soda, but making more money, for years to come.

By studying cost accounting, you will learn how successful managers and accountants run their businesses and prepare yourself for leadership roles in the firms you work for. Many large companies, including Nike and the Pittsburgh Steelers, have senior executives with accounting backgrounds.

urbanbuzz/Alamy Stock Photo

[1] *Sources:* Mike Esterl, "Smaller Sizes Add Pop to Soda Sales," *The Wall Street Journal*, January 27, 2016 (http://www.wsj.com/articles/smaller-sizes-add-pop-to-soda-sales-1453890601); John Kell, "Bottled Water Continues to Take the Fizz Out of Diet Soda," *Fortune*, April 19, 2017 (http://fortune.com/2017/04/19/coca-cola-pepsi-dr-pepper-soda-water/); Cara Lombardo, "Coca-Cola Betting Big on Smaller Packages," *The Wall Street Journal*, February 16, 2018 (https://www.wsj.com/articles/coca-cola-betting-big-on-smaller-packages-1518801270).

Financial Accounting, Management Accounting, and Cost Accounting

LEARNING OBJECTIVE 1

Distinguish financial accounting

. . . reporting on past performance to external users

from management accounting

. . . helping managers make decisions

As many of you have already learned in your financial accounting class, accounting systems are used to record economic events and transactions, such as sales and materials purchases, and process the data into information helpful to managers, sales representatives, production supervisors, and others. Processing any economic transaction means collecting, categorizing, summarizing, and analyzing. For example, costs are collected by category, such as materials, labor, and shipping. These costs are then summarized to determine a firm's total costs by month, quarter, or year. Accountants analyze the results and together with managers evaluate, say, how costs have changed relative to revenues from one period to the next. Accounting systems also provide the information found in a firm's income statement, balance sheet, statement of cash flow, and performance reports, such as the cost of serving customers or running an advertising campaign. Managers use this information to make decisions about the activities, businesses, or functional areas they oversee. For example, a report that shows an increase in sales of laptops and iPads at an Apple store may prompt Apple to hire more salespeople at that location. Understanding accounting information is essential for managers to do their jobs.

Individual managers often require the information in an accounting system to be presented or reported differently. Consider, for example, sales order information. A sales manager at Porsche may be interested in the total dollar amount of sales to determine the commissions paid to salespeople. A distribution manager at Porsche may be interested in the sales order quantities by geographic region and by customer-requested delivery dates to ensure vehicles get delivered to customers on time. A manufacturing manager at Porsche may be interested in the quantities of various products and their desired delivery dates so that he or she can develop an effective production schedule.

To simultaneously serve the needs of all three managers, Porsche creates a database, sometimes called a data warehouse or infobarn, consisting of small, detailed bits of information that can be used for multiple purposes. For instance, the sales order database will contain detailed information about a product, its selling price, quantity ordered, and delivery details (place and date) for each sales order. The database stores information in a way that allows different managers to access the information they need. Many companies are building their own enterprise resource planning (ERP) systems. An ERP system is a single database that collects data and feeds them into applications that support a company's business activities, such as purchasing, production, distribution, and sales.

In recent years, managers have begun to use data analytic techniques to gain insights into the data they collect. This is popularly referred to as big data, machine learning, and artificial intelligence. The most common application of machine learning and artificial intelligence is in making predictions. For example, using historical purchase data and other characteristics of a customer, a company like Netflix predicts which movie a particular customer might like and recommends that movie to the customer. Netflix then obtains feedback on whether the customer liked the movie or not and incorporates this feedback into the model, improving and refining it. In this sense the machine learns from its correct and incorrect predictions and is seen as acting intelligently. The vast quantities and variety of data have led to the development of many new prediction techniques. We introduce one such popular technique in Chapter 11 and discuss the role of the management accountant in a data-rich world.

Financial accounting and management accounting have different goals. As you know, **financial accounting** focuses on reporting financial information to external parties such as investors, government agencies, banks, and suppliers based on Generally Accepted Accounting Principles (GAAP). The most important way financial accounting information affects managers' decisions and actions is through compensation, which is often, in part, based on numbers in financial statements.

Management accounting is the process of measuring, analyzing, and reporting financial and nonfinancial information that helps managers make decisions to fulfill the goals of an organization. Managers use management accounting information to

1. develop, communicate, and implement strategies;
2. coordinate design, operations, and marketing decisions and evaluate a company's performance.

EXHIBIT 1-1 Major Differences Between Management and Financial Accounting

	Management Accounting	Financial Accounting
Purpose of information	Help managers make decisions to fulfill an organization's goals	Communicate an organization's financial position to investors, banks, regulators, and other outside parties
Primary users	Managers of the organization	External users such as investors, banks, regulators, and suppliers
Focus and emphasis	Future-oriented (budget for 2020 prepared in 2019)	Past-oriented (reports on 2019 performance prepared in 2020)
Rules of measurement and reporting	Internal measures and reports do not have to follow GAAP but are based on cost-benefit analyses	Financial statements must be prepared in accordance with GAAP and be certified by external, independent auditors
Time span and type of reports	Varies from hourly information to 15 to 20 years, with financial and nonfinancial reports on products, departments, territories, and strategies	Annual and quarterly financial reports, primarily on the company as a whole
Behavioral implications	Designed to influence the behavior of managers and other employees	Primarily reports economic events but also influences behavior because manager's compensation is often based on reported financial results

Management accounting information and reports do not have to follow set principles or rules. The key questions are always (1) how will this information help managers do their jobs better, and (2) do the benefits of producing this information exceed the costs?

Exhibit 1-1 summarizes the major differences between management accounting and financial accounting. Note, however, that reports such as balance sheets, income statements, and statements of cash flows are common to both management accounting and financial accounting.

Cost accounting provides information for both management accounting and financial accounting professionals. **Cost accounting** is the process of measuring, analyzing, and reporting financial and nonfinancial information related to the costs of acquiring or using resources in an organization. For example, calculating the cost of a product is a cost accounting function that meets both the financial accountant's inventory-valuation needs and the management accountant's decision-making needs (such as deciding how to price products and choosing which products to promote). However, today most accounting professionals take the perspective that cost information is part of the management accounting information collected to make management decisions. Thus, the distinction between management accounting and cost accounting is not so clear-cut, and we often use these terms interchangeably in the text.

Businesspeople frequently use the term *cost management*. Unfortunately, the term does not have an exact definition. In this text, we use **cost management** to describe the activities managers undertake to use resources in a way that increases a product's value to customers and achieves an organization's goals. Throughout the text, other than in a manufacturing context, we use the term *product* broadly to also include services. In other words, cost management is not only about reducing costs. Cost management also includes making decisions to incur additional costs—for example, to improve customer satisfaction and quality and to develop new products—with the goal of enhancing revenues and profits. Whether or not to enter new markets, implement new organizational processes, and change product designs are also cost-management decisions. Information from accounting systems helps managers to manage costs, but the information and the accounting systems themselves are not cost management.

DECISION POINT

How is financial accounting different from management accounting?

Strategic Decisions and the Management Accountant

LEARNING OBJECTIVE 2

Understand how management accountants help firms make strategic decisions

. . . they provide information about the sources of competitive advantage

A company's **strategy** specifies how the organization matches its own capabilities with the opportunities in the marketplace. In other words, strategy describes the integrated set of choices an organization makes to create value for its customers while distinguishing itself from its competitors. Businesses follow one of two broad strategies. Some companies, such as Southwest Airlines and Vanguard (the mutual fund company), follow a cost leadership strategy. They profit and grow by providing quality products or services at low prices and by judiciously managing their operations, marketing, customer service, and administration costs. Southwest Airlines, for example, only operates Boeing 737 aircrafts to reduce costs of repairs, maintenance, and spare parts and offers no seat assignments at boarding to reduce the costs of ground staff. Other companies such as Apple and the pharmaceutical giant Johnson & Johnson follow a product differentiation strategy. They generate profits and growth by offering differentiated or unique products or services that appeal to their customers and are often priced higher than the less-popular products or services of their competitors.

Deciding between these strategies is a critical part of what managers do. Management accountants work closely with managers in various departments to formulate strategies by providing information about the sources of competitive advantage, such as (1) the company's cost, productivity, or efficiency advantage relative to competitors or (2) the premium prices a company can charge over its costs from distinctive product or service features. **Strategic cost management** describes cost management that specifically focuses on strategic issues.

Management accounting information helps managers formulate strategy by answering questions such as the following:

- *Who are our most important customers, and what critical capability do we have to be competitive and deliver value to our customers?* After Amazon.com's success selling books online, management accountants at Barnes & Noble outlined the costs and benefits of several alternative approaches for enhancing the company's information technology infrastructure and developing the capability to sell books online. A similar cost–benefit analysis led Toyota to build flexible computer-integrated manufacturing plants that enable it to use the same equipment efficiently to produce a variety of cars in response to changing customer tastes.
- *What is the bargaining power of our customers?* Kellogg Company, for example, uses the reputation of its brand to reduce the bargaining power of its customers and charge higher prices for its cereals.
- *What is the bargaining power of our suppliers?* Management accountants at Dell Computers consider the significant bargaining power of Intel, its supplier of microprocessors, and Microsoft, its supplier of operating system software, when considering how much it must pay to acquire these products.
- *What substitute products exist in the marketplace, and how do they differ from our product in terms of features, price, cost, and quality?* Hewlett-Packard, for example, designs, costs, and prices new printers after comparing the functionality and quality of its printers to other printers available in the marketplace.
- *Will adequate cash be available to fund the strategy, or will additional funds need to be raised?* Procter & Gamble, for example, issued new debt and equity to fund its strategic acquisition of Gillette, a maker of shaving products.

DECISION POINT

How do management accountants support strategic decisions?

The best-designed strategies and the best-developed capabilities are useless unless they are effectively executed. In the next section, we describe how management accountants help managers take actions that create value for their customers.

LEARNING OBJECTIVE 3

Describe the set of business functions in the value chain and identify the dimensions of performance that customers are expecting of companies

. . . R&D, design, production, marketing, distribution, and customer service supported by administration to achieve cost and efficiency, quality, time, and innovation

Value-Chain and Supply-Chain Analysis and Key Success Factors

Customers demand much more than just a fair price; they expect quality products (goods or services) delivered in a timely way. The entire customer experience determines the value a customer derives from a product. In this section, we explore how companies create this value.

Value-Chain Analysis

The **value chain** is the sequence of business functions by which a product (including a service) is made progressively more useful to customers. Exhibit 1-2 shows six primary business functions: research and development, design of products and processes, production, marketing, distribution, and customer service. We illustrate these business functions with Sony Corporation's television division.

1. **Research and development (R&D)**—generating and experimenting with ideas related to new products, services, or processes. At Sony, this function includes research on alternative television signal transmission and on the picture quality of different shapes and thicknesses of television screens.
2. **Design of products and processes**—detailed planning, engineering, and testing of products and processes. Design at Sony includes deciding on the component parts in a television set and determining the effect alternative product designs will have on the set's quality and manufacturing costs. Some representations of the value chain collectively refer to the first two steps as technology development.[2]
3. **Production**—procuring, transporting, and storing ("inbound logistics") and coordinating and assembling ("operations") resources to produce a product or deliver a service. The production of a Sony television set includes the procurement and assembly of the electronic parts, the screen and the packaging used for shipping.
4. **Marketing (including sales)**—promoting and selling products or services to customers or prospective customers. Sony markets its televisions at tradeshows, via advertisements in newspapers and magazines, on the Internet, and through its sales force.
5. **Distribution**—processing orders and shipping products or delivering services to customers ("outbound logistics"). Distribution for Sony includes shipping to retail outlets, catalog vendors, direct sales via the Internet, and other channels through which customers purchase new televisions.
6. **Customer service**—providing after-sales service to customers. Sony provides customer service on its televisions in the form of customer-help telephone lines, support on the Internet, and warranty repair work.

In addition to the six primary business functions, Exhibit 1-2 shows an administration function, which includes accounting and finance, human resource management, and information technology and supports the six primary business functions. When discussing the value chain in subsequent chapters of this text, we include the administration function within the primary functions. For example, included in the marketing function is the function of analyzing, reporting, and accounting for resources spent in different marketing channels, whereas the production function includes the human resource management function of training frontline workers. Each of these business functions is essential to companies satisfying their customers and keeping them satisfied (and loyal) over time.

EXHIBIT 1-2 Different Parts of the Value Chain

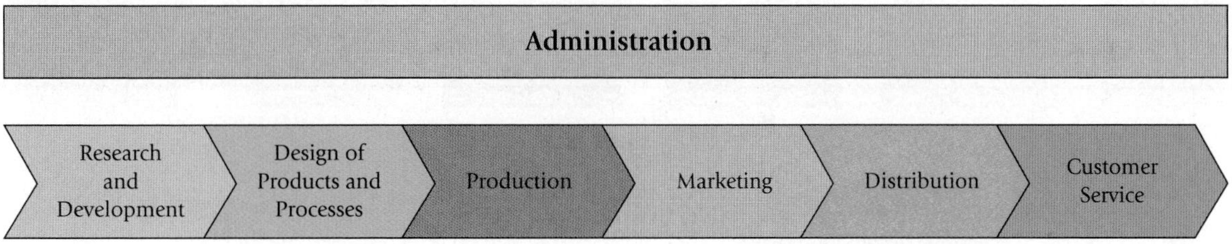

[2] M. Porter, *Competitive Advantage* (New York: Free Press, 1998).

To implement their corporate strategies, companies such as Sony and Procter & Gamble use **customer relationship management (CRM)**, a strategy that integrates people and technology in all business functions to deepen relationships with customers, partners, and distributors. CRM initiatives use technology to coordinate all customer-facing activities (such as marketing, sales calls, distribution, and after-sales support) and the design and production activities necessary to get products and services to customers.

Different companies create value in different ways. As a result, at different times and in different industries, one or more of the value-chain functions are more critical than others. For example, a company such as the biotech and pharmaceutical company Roche emphasizes R&D and the design of products and processes. In contrast, the Italian apparel company, Gucci, focuses on marketing, distribution, and customer service to build its brand.

Exhibit 1-2 depicts the usual order in which different business-function activities physically occur. Do not, however, interpret Exhibit 1-2 to mean that managers should proceed sequentially through the value chain when planning and managing their activities. Companies gain (in terms of cost, quality, and the speed with which new products are developed) if two or more of the individual business functions of the value chain work concurrently as a team. For example, a company's production, marketing, distribution, and customer service personnel can often reduce a company's total costs by providing input for design decisions.

Managers track costs incurred in each value-chain category. Their goal is to reduce costs to improve efficiency or to spend more money to generate even greater revenues. Management accounting information helps managers make cost–benefit tradeoffs. For example, is it cheaper to buy products from a vendor or produce them in-house? How does investing resources in design and manufacturing increase revenues or reduce costs of marketing and customer service?

Supply-Chain Analysis

The parts of the value chain associated with producing and delivering a product or service—production and distribution—are referred to as the *supply chain*. The **supply chain** describes the flow of goods, services, and information from the initial sources of materials and services to the delivery of products to consumers, regardless of whether those activities occur in one organization or in multiple organizations. Consider Coca-Cola and Pepsi: Many companies play a role in bringing these products to consumers as the supply chain in Exhibit 1-3 shows. Cost management requires integrating and coordinating activities across all companies in the supply chain to improve performance and reduce costs. For example, to reduce materials-handling costs, both Coca-Cola and Pepsi require their suppliers (such as plastic and aluminum companies and sugar refiners) to frequently deliver small quantities of materials directly to their production floors. Similarly, to reduce inventory levels in the supply chain, Walmart requires its suppliers, such as Coca-Cola, to directly manage its inventory of products to ensure the right quantities are in its stores at all times.

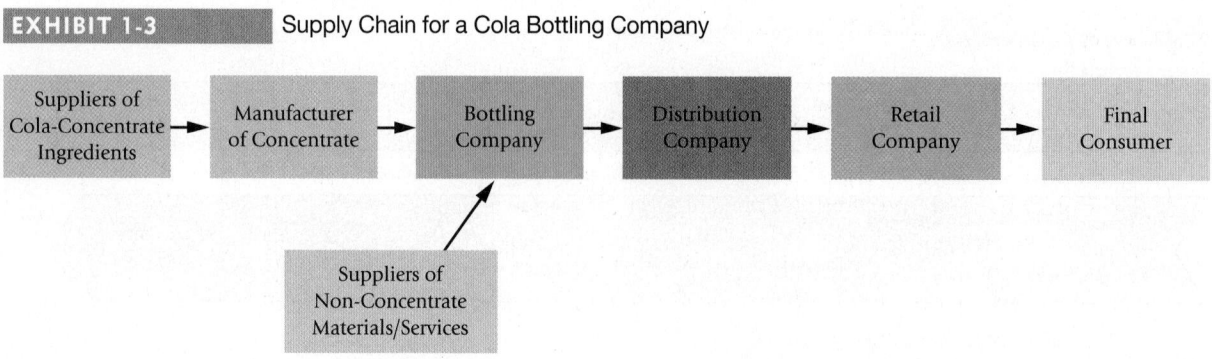

EXHIBIT 1-3 Supply Chain for a Cola Bottling Company

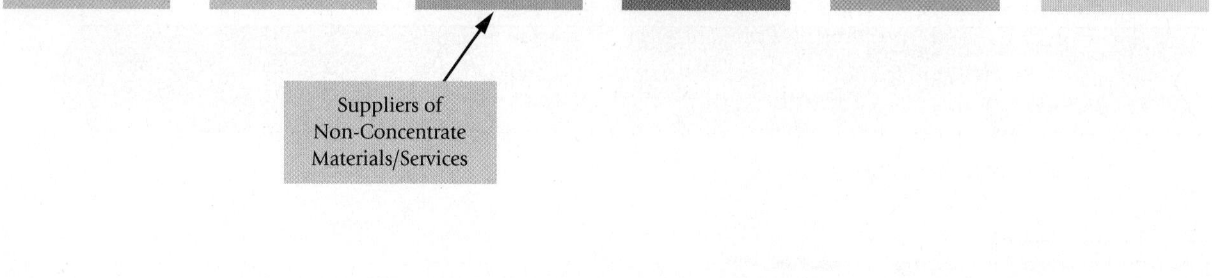

Key Success Factors

Customers want companies to use the value chain and supply chain to deliver ever-improving levels of performance when it comes to several (or even all) of the following:

- **Cost and efficiency**—Companies face continuous pressure to reduce the cost of the products they sell. To calculate and manage the cost of products, managers must first understand the activities (such as setting up machines or distributing products) that cause costs to arise as well as monitor the marketplace to determine the prices customers are willing to pay for the products. Management accounting information helps managers calculate a target cost for a product by subtracting from the "target price" the operating income per unit of product that the company wants to earn. To achieve the target cost, managers eliminate some activities (such as rework) and reduce the costs of performing other activities in all value-chain functions—from initial R&D to customer service (see Concepts in Action: Cost Leadership at Costco: Rock-Bottom Prices and Sky-High Profits). Many U.S. companies have cut costs by outsourcing some of their business functions. Nike, for example, has moved its manufacturing operations to China and Mexico, and Microsoft and IBM are increasingly doing their software development in Spain, Eastern Europe, and India.
- **Quality**—Customers expect high levels of quality. **Total quality management (TQM)** is an integrative philosophy of management for continuously improving the quality of products and processes. Managers who implement TQM believe that every person in the value chain is responsible for delivering products and services that exceed customers' expectations. Using TQM, companies, for example, Toyota, design products to meet customer needs and wants, to make these products with zero (or very few) defects and waste, and to minimize inventories. Managers use management accounting information to evaluate the costs and revenue benefits of TQM initiatives.
- **Time**—Time has many dimensions. Two of the most important dimensions are new-product development time and customer-response time. New-product development time is the time it takes for companies to create new products and bring them to market. The increasing pace of technological innovation has led to shorter product life cycles and more rapid introduction of new products. To make new-product development decisions, managers need to understand the costs and benefits of bringing products to market faster.

  Customer-response time describes the speed at which an organization responds to customer requests. To increase customer satisfaction, organizations need to meet promised delivery dates and reduce delivery times. Bottlenecks are the primary cause of delays. Bottlenecks occur when the work to be performed on a machine or computer exceeds its available capacity. To deliver a product or service quickly, managers need to have adequate capacity. eBay invests in server capacity to create quality experiences for the online auction giant's customers. Management accounting information helps managers quantify the costs and benefits of adding capacity.
- **Innovation**—A constant flow of innovative products or services is the basis for a company's ongoing success. Many companies innovate in their strategies, business models, the services they provide, and the way they market, sell, and distribute their products. Managers at companies such as Novartis, the Swiss pharmaceutical giant, rely on management accounting information to evaluate the costs and benefits of alternative R&D and investment decisions.
- **Sustainability**—Companies are increasingly applying the key success factors of cost and efficiency, quality, time, and innovation to promote **sustainability**—the development and implementation of strategies to achieve long-term financial, social, and environmental goals. The sustainability efforts of the Japanese copier company Ricoh include energy conservation, resource conservation, product recycling, and pollution prevention. By designing products that can be recycled easily, Ricoh simultaneously improves sustainability and the cost and quality of its products.

CONCEPTS IN ACTION

Cost Leadership at Costco: Rock-Bottom Prices and Sky-High Profits[3]

MIHAI ANDRITOIU/Alamy Stock Photo

For decades, Costco has made sky-high profits by selling bulk products at rock-bottom prices. How, you ask? By being laser focused on its cost leadership strategy.

Costco is the world's largest seller of choice and prime beef, organic foods, and rotisserie chicken, and it sells more nuts than Planters. Its private label, Kirkland Signature, which sells everything from beverages to apparel, generates more revenue each year than Coca-Cola. Remarkably, it does all this while refusing to mark up its products by more than 14% (15% for its private-label products). Costco can offer its bulk items at such low prices by judiciously managing its costs.

Costco is a lean company. The warehouse retailer's spending on overhead—selling, general, and administrative costs—is only 10% of revenues, compared with about 20% at Walmart. The company doesn't advertise, has a spartan store environment, and offers a limited selection—only 3,700 products compared with 140,000 at a Walmart superstore and half a billion at Amazon. This allows Costco to drive hard bargains with its suppliers. And Costco's distribution system fills 95% of its freight capacity, an unheard of number in the retail business.

This winning combination of bulk products at low prices delights more than 80 million members around the globe each year. Costco is the third-largest retailer in the world, behind Walmart and Amazon, with $138 billion sales in fiscal 2018.

[3] *Sources:* Neal Babler, "The Magic in the Warehouse," *Fortune*, December 15, 2016 (http://fortune.com/costco-wholesale-shopping/); Uptal M. Dholakia, "When Cost-Plus Pricing Is a Good Idea," *Harvard Business Review* online, July 12, 2018 (https://hbr.org/2018/07/when-cost-plus-pricing-is-a-good-idea).

The interest in sustainability appears to be intensifying among companies. General Electric, Poland Springs (a bottled-water manufacturer), and Hewlett-Packard are among the many companies incorporating sustainability into their decision making. Sustainability is important to these companies for several reasons:

- Many investors care about sustainability. These investors make investment decisions based on a company's financial, social, and environmental performance and raise questions about sustainability at shareholder meetings.
- Companies are finding that sustainability goals attract and inspire employees.
- Customers prefer the products of companies with good sustainability records and boycott companies with poor sustainability records.
- Society and activist nongovernmental organizations, in particular, monitor the sustainability performance of firms and take legal action against those that violate environmental laws. Countries such as China and India are now either requiring or encouraging companies to develop and report on their sustainability initiatives.

DECISION POINT

How do companies add value, and what are the dimensions of performance that customers expect of companies?

Management accountants help managers track the key success factors of their firms and their competitors. Competitive information serves as a *benchmark* managers use to continuously improve operations. Examples of continuous improvement include Southwest Airlines increasing the number of its flights that arrive on time, eBay improving the access its customers have to online auctions, and Lowe's continuously reducing the cost of its home-improvement products. Sometimes, more fundamental changes and innovations in operations, such as redesigning a manufacturing process to reduce costs, may be necessary. To successfully implement their strategies, firms have to do more than analyze their value chains and supply chains and execute key success factors. They also need good decision-making processes.

Decision Making, Planning, and Control: The Five-Step Decision-Making Process

LEARNING OBJECTIVE 4

Explain the five-step decision-making process

. . . identify the problem and uncertainties; obtain information; make predictions about the future; make decisions by choosing among alternatives; implement the decision, evaluate performance, and learn

and its role in management accounting

. . . planning and control of operations and activities

We illustrate a five-step decision-making process using the example of the *Daily News*, a newspaper in Boulder, Colorado. Subsequent chapters of this text describe how managers use this five-step decision-making process to make many different types of decisions.

The *Daily News* differentiates itself from its competitors by using (1) highly respected journalists who write well-researched news articles; (2) color to enhance attractiveness to readers and advertisers; and (3) a Web site that delivers up-to-the-minute news, interviews, and analyses. The newspaper has the following resources to deliver on this strategy: an automated, computer-integrated, state-of-the-art printing facility; a Web-based information technology infrastructure; and a distribution network that is one of the best in the newspaper industry.

To keep up with steadily increasing production costs, Naomi Crawford, manager of the *Daily News*, needs to increase the company's revenues in 2020. As she ponders what she should do in early 2020, Naomi works through the five-step decision-making process.

1. **Identify the problem and uncertainties.** Naomi has two main choices:

   a. increase the selling price of the newspaper or
   b. increase the rate per page charged to advertisers.

   These decisions would take effect in March 2020. The key uncertainty is the effect any increase in prices or advertising rates will have on demand. A decrease in demand could offset the price or rate increases and lead to lower rather than higher revenues.

2. **Obtain information.** Gathering information before making a decision helps managers gain a better understanding of uncertainties. Naomi asks her marketing manager to talk to some representative readers to gauge their reaction to an increase in the newspaper's selling price. She asks her advertising sales manager to talk to current and potential advertisers to assess demand for advertising. She also reviews the effect that past increases in the price of the newspaper had on readership. Ramon Sandoval, management accountant at the *Daily News*, presents information about the effect of past increases or decreases in advertising rates on advertising revenues. He also collects and analyzes information on advertising rates competing newspapers and other media outlets charge.

3. **Make predictions about the future.** Based on this information, Naomi makes predictions about the future. She concludes that increasing prices would upset readers and decrease readership. She has a different view about advertising rates. She expects a marketwide increase in advertising rates and believes that increasing rates will have little effect on the number of advertising pages sold.

   Making predictions requires judgment. Naomi looks for biases in her thinking. Has she correctly judged reader sentiment or is the negative publicity of a price increase overly influencing her decision making? How sure is she that competitors will increase their advertising rates? Is her thinking in this respect biased by how competitors have responded in the past? Have circumstances changed? How confident is she that her sales representatives can convince advertisers to pay higher rates? She retests her assumptions and reviews her thinking. She feels comfortable with her predictions and judgments.

4. **Make decisions by choosing among alternatives.** A company's strategy serves as a vital guidepost for individuals making decisions in different parts of the organization. Consistent strategies provide a common purpose for these disparate decisions. Only if these decisions can be aligned with its strategy will an organization achieve its goals. Without this alignment, the company's decisions will be uncoordinated, pull the organization in different directions, and produce inconsistent results.

   Consistent with a product differentiation strategy, Naomi decides to increase advertising rates by 4% to $5,200 per page in March 2020 but not increase the selling price of the newspaper. She is confident that the *Daily News*'s distinctive style and Web presence will increase readership, creating value for advertisers. She communicates the new advertising rate schedule to the sales department. Ramon estimates advertising revenues of $4,160,000 ($5,200 per page × 800 pages predicted to be sold in March 2020).

Steps 1 through 4 are collectively referred to as *planning*. **Planning** consists of selecting an organization's goals and strategies, predicting results under alternative ways of achieving goals, deciding how to attain the desired goals, and communicating the goals and how to achieve them to the entire organization. Management accountants serve as business partners in planning activities because they understand the key success factors and what creates value.

The most important planning tool when implementing strategy is a *budget*. A **budget** is the quantitative expression of a proposed plan of action by management and is an aid to coordinating what needs to be done to execute that plan. For March 2020, the budgeted advertising revenue of the *Daily News* equals $4,160,000. The full budget for March 2020 includes budgeted circulation revenue and the production, distribution, and customer-service costs to achieve the company's sales goals; the anticipated cash flows; and the potential financing needs. Because multiple departments help prepare the budget, personnel throughout the organization have to coordinate and communicate with one another as well as with the company's suppliers and customers.

5. **Implement the decision, evaluate performance, and learn.** Managers at the *Daily News* take action to implement and achieve the March 2020 budget. Management accountants collect information on how the company's actual performance compares to planned or budgeted performance (also referred to as scorekeeping). The information on actual results is different from the *predecision* planning information Naomi and her staff collected in Step 2 to better understand uncertainties, to make predictions, and to make a decision. Comparing actual performance to budgeted performance is the *control* or *postdecision* role of information. **Control** comprises taking actions that implement the planning decisions, evaluating past performance, and providing feedback and learning to help future decision making.

   Measuring actual performance informs managers how well they and their subunits are doing. Linking rewards to performance helps motivate managers. These rewards are both intrinsic (recognition for a job well done) and extrinsic (salary, bonuses, and promotions linked to performance). We discuss this in more detail in a later chapter (Chapter 23). A budget serves as much as a control tool as a planning tool. Why? Because a budget is a benchmark against which actual performance can be compared.

Consider performance evaluation at the *Daily News*. During March 2020, the newspaper sold advertising, issued invoices, and received payments. The accounting system recorded these invoices and receipts. Exhibit 1-4 shows the *Daily News*'s advertising revenues for March 2020. This performance report indicates that 760 pages of advertising (40 pages fewer than the budgeted 800 pages) were sold. The average rate per page was $5,080, compared with the budgeted $5,200 rate, yielding actual advertising revenues of $3,860,800. The actual advertising revenues were $299,200 less than the budgeted $4,160,000. Observe how

EXHIBIT 1-4 Performance Report of Advertising Revenues at the *Daily News* for March 2020

	Actual Result (1)	Budgeted Amount (2)	Difference: (Actual Result – Budgeted Amount) (3) = (1) – (2)	Difference as a Percentage of Budgeted Amount (4) = (3) ÷ (2)
Advertising pages sold	760 pages	800 pages	40 pages Unfavorable	5.0% Unfavorable
Average rate per page	$5,080	$5,200	$120 Unfavorable	2.3% Unfavorable
Advertising revenues	$3,860,800	$4,160,000	$299,200 Unfavorable	7.2% Unfavorable

managers use both financial and nonfinancial information, such as pages of advertising, to evaluate performance.

The performance report in Exhibit 1-4 spurs investigation and **learning**, which involves examining past performance (the control function) and systematically exploring alternative ways to make better-informed decisions and plans in the future. Learning can lead to changes in goals, strategies, the ways decision alternatives are identified, and the range of information collected when making predictions and sometimes can lead to changes in managers.

The performance report in Exhibit 1-4 would prompt the management accountant to raise several questions directing the attention of managers to problems and opportunities. Is the strategy of differentiating the *Daily News* from other newspapers attracting more readers? Did the marketing and sales department make sufficient efforts to convince advertisers that, even at the higher rate of \$5,200 per page, advertising in the *Daily News* was a good buy? Why was the actual average rate per page (\$5,080) less than the budgeted rate (\$5,200)? Did some sales representatives offer discounted rates? Did economic conditions cause the decline in advertising revenues? Are revenues falling because editorial and production standards have declined? Are more readers getting their news online?

Answers to these questions could prompt the newspaper's publisher to take subsequent actions, including, for example, adding sales personnel, making changes in editorial policy, expanding its presence online and on mobile devices, getting readers to pay for online content, and selling digital advertising. Good implementation requires the marketing, editorial, and production departments to work together and coordinate their actions.

The management accountant could go further by identifying the specific advertisers that cut back or stopped advertising after the rate increase went into effect. Managers could then decide when and how sales representatives should follow up with these advertisers.

Planning and control activities must be flexible enough so that managers can seize opportunities unforeseen at the time the plan was formulated. In no case should control mean that managers cling to a plan when unfolding events (such as a sensational news story) indicate that actions not encompassed by that plan (such as spending more money to cover the story) would offer better results for the company (from higher newspaper sales).

DECISION POINT

How do managers make decisions to implement strategy?

The left side of Exhibit 1-5 provides an overview of the decision-making processes at the *Daily News*. The right side of the exhibit highlights how the management accounting system aids in decision making.

Planning and control activities get more challenging for innovation and sustainability. Consider the problem of how the *Daily News* must innovate as more of its readers migrate to the Web to get their news and apply the five-step process. In Step 1, the uncertainties are much greater. Will there be demand for a newspaper? Will customers look to the *Daily News* to get their information or to other sources? In Step 2, obtaining information is more difficult because there is little history that managers can comfortably rely on. Instead, managers will have to make connections across disparate data, run experiments, engage with diverse experts, and speculate to understand how the world might evolve. In Step 3, making predictions about the future will require developing different scenarios and models. In Step 4, managers must make decisions recognizing that conditions might change in unanticipated ways requiring them to be flexible and adaptable. In Step 5, the learning component is critical. How have the uncertainties evolved and what do managers need to do to respond to these changing circumstances?

Planning and control for sustainability is equally challenging. What should the *Daily News* do about energy consumption in its printing presses, recycling of newsprint, and pollution prevention? Among the uncertainties managers face is whether customers will reward the *Daily News* for these actions by being more loyal and whether investors will react favorably to managers spending resources on sustainability. Information to gauge customer and investor sentiment is not easy to obtain. Predicting how sustainability efforts might pay off in the long run is far from certain. Even as managers make decisions, the sustainability landscape will doubtlessly change with respect to environmental regulations and societal expectations, requiring managers to learn and adapt.

Do these challenges of implementing planning and control systems for innovation and sustainability mean that these systems should not be used for these initiatives? No. Many companies value these systems to manage innovation and sustainability. But, in keeping with the challenges described earlier, companies such as Johnson & Johnson use these systems

EXHIBIT 1-5

How Accounting Aids Decision Making, Planning, and Control at the *Daily News*

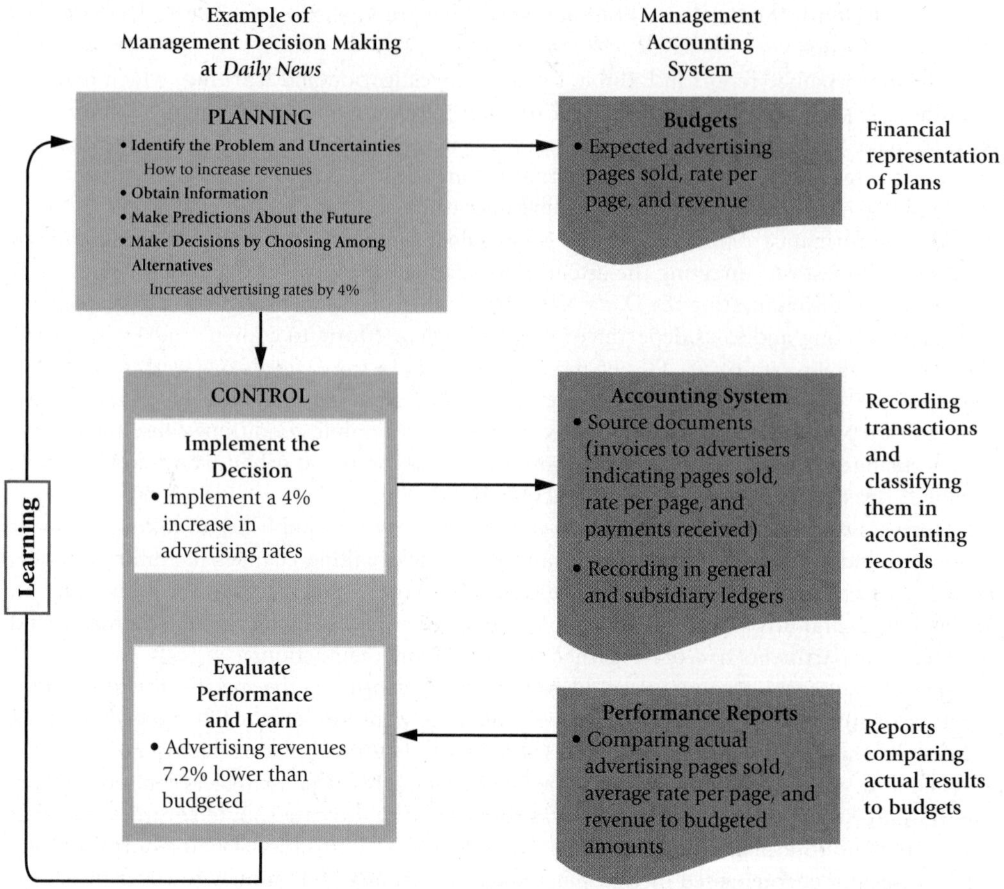

in a different way—to obtain information around key strategic uncertainties, to implement plans while being mindful that circumstances might change, and to evaluate performance in order to learn.

Key Management Accounting Guidelines

LEARNING OBJECTIVE 5

Describe three guidelines management accountants follow in supporting managers

. . . employing a cost–benefit approach, recognizing behavioral as well as technical considerations, and calculating different costs for different purposes

Three guidelines help management accountants add value to strategic and operational decision making in companies: (1) employ a cost–benefit approach, (2) give full recognition to behavioral and technical considerations, and (3) use different costs for different purposes.

Cost–Benefit Approach

Managers continually face resource-allocation decisions, such as whether to purchase a new software package or hire a new employee. They use a **cost–benefit approach** when making these decisions. Managers spend resources if the expected benefits to the company exceed the expected costs. Managers rely on management accounting information to quantify expected benefits and expected costs (although all benefits and costs are not easy to quantify).

Consider the installation of a consulting company's first budgeting system. Previously, the company used historical recordkeeping and little formal planning. A major benefit of installing a budgeting system is that it compels managers to plan ahead, compare actual to budgeted information, learn, and take corrective action. Although the system leads to better decisions and consequently better company performance, the exact benefits are not easy to measure. On the cost side, some costs, such as investments in software and training, are easier to quantify. Others, such as the time spent by managers on the budgeting process, are more difficult to quantify. Regardless, senior managers compare expected benefits and expected costs, exercise judgment, and reach a decision, in this case to install the budgeting system.

Behavioral and Technical Considerations

When utilizing the cost–benefit approach, managers need to keep in mind a number of technical and behavioral considerations. Technical considerations help managers make wise economic decisions by providing desired information (for example, costs in various value-chain categories) in an appropriate format (for example, actual results versus budgeted amounts) and at the preferred frequency (for example, weekly or quarterly). However, management is not only about technical matters. Management is primarily a human activity encouraging individuals to do their jobs better. Budgets have a behavioral effect by motivating and rewarding employees for achieving an organization's goals. So, when workers underperform, for example, behavioral considerations suggest that managers need to explore ways to improve performance rather than just issue a report highlighting underperformance.

Different Costs for Different Purposes

This text emphasizes that managers use alternative ways to compute costs in different decision-making situations because there are different costs for different purposes. A cost concept used for external reporting may not be appropriate for internal, routine reporting.

Consider the advertising costs associated with Microsoft Corporation's launch of a product with a useful life of several years. For external reporting to shareholders, Generally Accepted Accounting Principles require television advertising costs for this product to be fully expensed in the income statement in the year they are incurred. However, for internal reporting, the television advertising costs could be capitalized and then amortized or written off as expenses over several years if Microsoft's management team believes that doing so would more accurately and fairly measure the performance of the managers that launched the new product.

DECISION POINT

What guidelines do management accountants use?

Organization Structure and the Management Accountant

LEARNING OBJECTIVE 6

Understand how management accounting fits into an organization's structure

. . . for example, the responsibilities of the controller

Managers and management accountants have roles and reporting responsibilities within a company's organization structure. We focus first on broad management functions and then look at how the management accounting and finance functions support managers.

Line and Staff Relationships

Organizations distinguish between line management and staff management. **Line management**, such as production, marketing, and distribution management, is directly responsible for achieving the goals of the organization. For example, managers of manufacturing divisions are responsible for meeting particular levels of budgeted operating costs, product quality and safety, and compliance with environmental laws. Similarly, the pediatrics department in a hospital is responsible for quality of service, costs, and patient billings. **Staff management**, such as management accountants and information technology and human-resources management, provides advice, support, and assistance to line management. A plant manager (a line function) may be responsible for investing in new equipment. A management accountant (a staff function) works as a business partner of the plant manager by preparing detailed operating-cost comparisons of alternative pieces of equipment. Organizations operate in teams of line and staff managers so that all inputs into a decision are available simultaneously.

The Chief Financial Officer and the Controller

The **chief financial officer (CFO)**—also called the **finance director** in many countries—is the executive responsible for overseeing the financial operations of an organization. The responsibilities of the CFO vary among organizations, but they usually include the following areas:

- **Controllership**—provides financial information for reports to managers and shareholders and oversees the overall operations of the accounting system.
- **Tax**—plans income taxes, sales taxes, and international taxes.
- **Treasury**—oversees banking, short- and long-term financing, investments, and cash management.
- **Risk management**—manages the financial risk of interest-rate and exchange-rate changes and derivatives management.
- **Investor relations**—communicates with, responds to, and interacts with shareholders.
- **Strategic planning**—defines strategy and allocates resources to implement strategy.

An independent internal audit function reviews and analyzes financial and other records to attest to the integrity of the organization's financial reports and adherence to its policies and procedures.

The **controller** (also called the *chief accounting officer*) is the financial executive primarily responsible for management accounting and financial accounting. This text focuses on the controller as the chief management accounting executive. Modern controllers have no line authority except over their own departments. Yet the controller exercises control over the entire organization in a special way. By reporting and interpreting relevant data, the controller influences the behavior of all employees and helps line managers make better decisions.

Exhibit 1-6 shows an organization chart of the CFO and the corporate controller at Nike, the leading footwear and sports-apparel company. The CFO is a staff manager who reports to and supports the chief executive officer (CEO). As in most organizations, the corporate controller at Nike reports to the CFO. Nike also has regional controllers who support regional managers in the major geographic regions in which the company operates, such as the United States, Asia Pacific, Latin America, and Europe. Because they support the activities of the regional manager, for example, by managing budgets and analyzing costs, regional controllers

EXHIBIT 1-6

Nike: Reporting Relationship for the CFO and the Corporate Controller

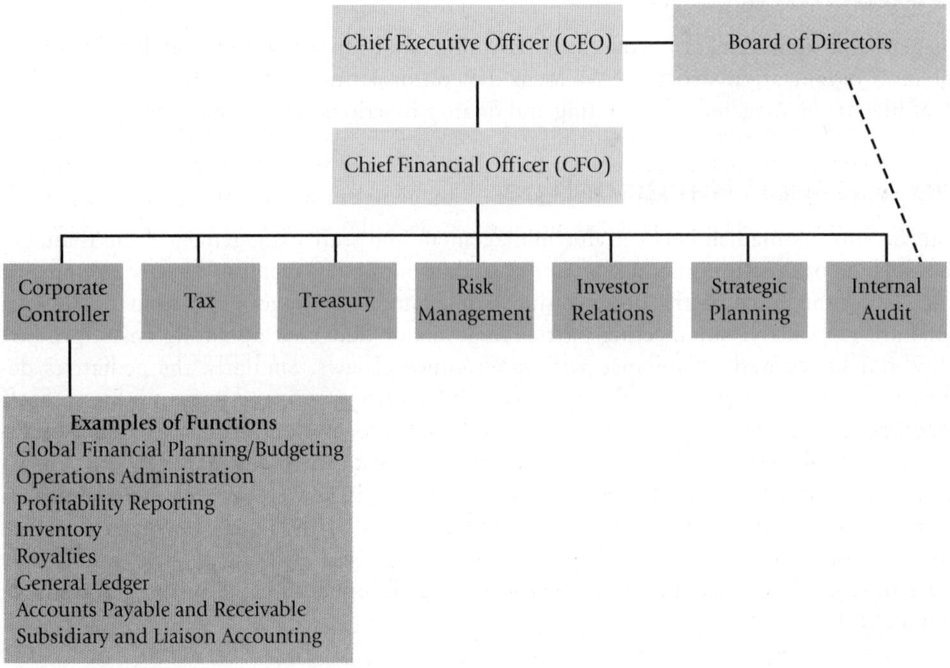

report to the regional manager rather than the corporate controller. At the same time, to align accounting policies and practices for the whole organization, regional controllers have a functional (often called a dotted-line) responsibility to the corporate controller. Individual countries sometimes have a country controller.

Organization charts such as the one in Exhibit 1-6 show formal reporting relationships. In most organizations, there also are informal relationships that must be understood when managers attempt to implement their decisions. Examples of informal relationships are friendships (both professional and personal) among managers and the preferences of top management about the managers they rely on when making decisions.

Think about what managers do to design and implement strategies and the organization structures within which they operate. Then think about the management accountants' and controllers' roles. It should be clear that the successful management accountant must have technical and analytical competence *as well as* behavioral and interpersonal skills.

Management Accounting Beyond the Numbers[4]

To people outside the profession, it may seem like accountants are just "numbers people." It is true that most accountants are adept financial managers, yet their skills do not stop there. The successful management accountant possesses several skills and characteristics that reach well beyond basic analytical abilities.

Management accountants must work well in cross-functional teams and as a business partner. In addition to being technically competent, the best management accountants work well in teams, learn about business issues, understand the motivations of different individuals, respect the views of their colleagues, and show empathy and trust.

Management accountants must promote fact-based analysis and make tough-minded, critical judgments without being adversarial. Management accountants must raise tough questions for managers to consider, especially when preparing budgets. They must do so thoughtfully and with the intent of improving plans and decisions. Before the investment bank JP Morgan lost more than $6 billion on "exotic" financial investments (credit-default swaps), controllers should have raised questions about these risky investments and the fact that the firm was betting on improving economic conditions abroad to earn a large profit.

They must lead and motivate people to change and be innovative. Implementing new ideas, however good they may be, is difficult. When the United States Department of Defense (DoD) began consolidating more than 320 finance and accounting systems into a common platform, the accounting services director and his team of management accountants held meetings to make sure everyone in the agency understood the goal for such a change. Ultimately, the DoD aligned each individual's performance with the transformative change and introduced incentive pay to encourage personnel to adopt the platform and drive innovation within this new framework.

They must communicate clearly, openly, and candidly. Communicating information is a large part of a management accountant's job. When premium car companies such as Rolls Royce and Porsche design new models, management accountants work closely with engineers to ensure that each new car supports a carefully defined balance of commercial, engineering, and financial criteria. To be successful, management accountants must clearly communicate information that multidisciplinary teams need to deliver new innovations profitably.

They must have high integrity. Management accountants must never succumb to pressure from managers to manipulate financial information. Their primary commitment is to the organization and its shareholders. In 2015, Toshiba, the Japanese maker of semiconductors, consumer electronics, and nuclear power plants wrote down $1.9 billion of

DECISION POINT

Where does the management accounting function fit into an organization's structure?

[4] United States Senate Permanent Subcommittee on Investigations. *JPMorgan Chase Whale Trades: A Case History of Derivatives Risks and Abuses.* Washington, DC: Government Printing Office, March 15, 2013; Wendy Garling, "Winning the Transformation Battle at the Defense Finance and Accounting Service," Balanced Scorecard Report, May–June 2007; Bill Nixon, John Burns, and Mostafa Jazayeri, *The Role of Management Accounting in New Product Design and Development Decisions*, Volume 9, Issue 1. London: Chartered Institute of Management Accountants, November 2011; and Eric Pfanner and Magumi Fujikawa, "Toshiba Slashes Earnings for Past Seven Years," *The Wall Street Journal* (September 7, 2015).

earnings that had been overstated over the previous 7 years. The problems stemmed from managers setting aggressive profit targets that subordinates could not meet without inflating divisional results by understating costs, postponing losses, and overstating revenues.

Professional Ethics

LEARNING OBJECTIVE 7

Understand what professional ethics mean to management accountants

. . . for example, management accountants must maintain integrity and credibility in every aspect of their job

In the early 2000s, the ethical conduct of managers came under scrutiny when investors and government regulators discovered that several companies had falsified financial statements to make themselves appear more profitable than they actually were. These companies included Arthur Andersen, a public accounting firm; Countrywide Financial, a home mortgage company; Enron, an oil and gas company; Lehman Brothers, an investment bank; Toshiba, a Japanese conglomerate; and Bernie Madoff Investment Securities have seriously eroded the public's confidence in corporations. All employees in a company must comply with the organization's—and more broadly, society's—expectations of ethical standards.

Ethics are the foundation of a well-functioning economy. When ethics are weak, suppliers bribe executives to win supply contracts rather than invest in improving quality or lowering costs. Without ethical conduct, customers lose confidence in the quality of products produced and become reluctant to buy them, causing markets to fail. Prices of products increase because of higher prices paid to suppliers and fewer products being produced and sold. Investors are unsure about the integrity of financial reports, affecting their ability to evaluate investment decisions, resulting in a reluctance to invest. The scandals at Ahold, an international supermarket operator, and Tyco International, a diversified global manufacturing, company make clear that value is quickly destroyed by unethical behavior.

Institutional Support

Accountants have special ethical obligations, given that they are responsible for the integrity of the financial information provided to internal and external parties. The Sarbanes–Oxley legislation in the United States was passed in 2002 in response to a series of corporate scandals. The act focuses on improving internal control, corporate governance, monitoring of managers, and disclosure practices of public corporations. These regulations impose tough ethical standards and criminal penalties on managers and accountants who don't meet the standards. The regulations also delineate a process for employees to report violations of illegal and unethical acts (these employees are called whistleblowers).

As part of the Sarbanes–Oxley Act, CEOs and CFOs must certify that the financial statements of their firms fairly represent the results of their operations. In order to increase the independence of auditors, the act empowers the audit committee of a company's board of directors (which is composed exclusively of independent directors) to hire, compensate, and terminate the public accounting firm that audits a company. To reduce their financial dependency on their individual clients and increase their independence, the act limits auditing firms from providing consulting, tax, and other advisory services to the companies they are auditing. The act also authorizes the Public Company Accounting Oversight Board to oversee, review, and investigate the work of the auditors.

Professional accounting organizations, which represent management accountants in many countries, offer certification programs indicating that those who have completed them have management accounting and financial management technical knowledge and expertise. These organizations also advocate high ethical standards. In the United States, the Institute of Management Accountants (IMA) has issued ethical guidelines. Exhibit 1-7 presents the IMA's guidance on issues relating to competence, confidentiality, integrity, and credibility. To provide support to its members to act ethically at all times, the IMA runs an ethics hotline service. Members can call professional counselors at the IMA's Ethics Counseling Service to discuss their ethical dilemmas confidentially. The counselors help identify key ethical issues and possible alternative ways of resolving them. The IMA is just one of many institutions that help navigate management accountants through turbulent ethical waters.

EXHIBIT 1-7

Standards of Ethical Behavior for Practitioners of Management Accounting and Financial Management

STATEMENT OF ETHICAL PROFESSIONAL PRACTICE

Members of IMA shall behave ethically. A commitment to ethical professional practice includes overarching principles that express our values and standards that guide member conduct.

PRINCIPLES

IMA's overarching ethical principles include: Honesty, Fairness, Objectivity, and Responsibility. Members shall act in accordance with these principles and shall encourage others within their organizations to adhere to them.

STANDARDS

IMA members have a responsibility to comply with and uphold the standards of Competence, Confidentiality, Integrity, and Credibility. Failure to comply may result in disciplinary action.

I. COMPETENCE

1. Maintain an appropriate level of professional leadership and expertise by enhancing knowledge and skills.
2. Perform professional duties in accordance with relevant laws, regulations, and technical standards.
3. Provide decision support information and recommendations that are accurate, clear, concise, and timely. Recognize and help manage risk.

II. CONFIDENTIALITY

1. Keep information confidential except when disclosure is authorized or legally required.
2. Inform all relevant parties regarding appropriate use of confidential information. Monitor to ensure compliance.
3. Refrain from using confidential information for unethical or illegal advantage.

III. INTEGRITY

1. Mitigate actual conflicts of interest. Regularly communicate with business associates to avoid apparent conflicts of interest. Advise all parties of any potential conflicts of interest.
2. Refrain from engaging in any conduct that would prejudice carrying out duties ethically.
3. Abstain from engaging in or supporting any activity that might discredit the profession.
4. Contribute to a positive ethical culture and place integrity of the profession above personal interests.

IV. CREDIBILITY

1. Communicate information fairly and objectively.
2. Provide all relevant information that could reasonably be expected to influence an intended user's understanding of the reports, analyses, or recommendations.
3. Report any delays or deficiencies in information, timeliness, processing, or internal controls in conformance with organization policy and/or applicable law.
4. Communicate professional limitations or other constraints that would preclude responsible judgment or successful performance of an activity.

Source: IMA Statement of Ethical Professional Practice, 2017. Montvale, NJ: Institute of Management Accountants. Reprinted with permission from the Institute of Management Accountants, Montvale, NJ, www.imanet.org.

Typical Ethical Challenges

Ethical issues can confront management accountants in many ways. Here are two examples:

- **Case A:** A management accountant is concerned about the commercial potential of a software product for which development costs are currently being capitalized as an asset rather than being shown as an expense for internal reporting purposes. The firm's division manager, whose bonus is based, in part, on the division's profits, argues that showing development costs as an asset is justified because the new product will generate profits. However, he presents little evidence to support his argument. The last two products from the division have been unsuccessful. The management accountant wants to make the right decision while avoiding a difficult personal confrontation with his boss, the division manager. (This case is similar to the situation at Toshiba where senior managers set aggressive divisional targets and divisional accountants inflated divisional profits to achieve them.)

- **Case B:** A packaging supplier, bidding for a new contract, offers a management accountant of the purchasing company an all-expenses-paid weekend to the Super Bowl. The supplier does not mention the new contract when extending the invitation. The management accountant is not a personal friend of the supplier. He knows cost issues are critical when it comes to approving the new contract and is concerned that the supplier will ask for details about the bids placed by competing packaging companies.

In each case, the management accountant is faced with an ethical dilemma. Ethical issues are not always clear-cut. Case A involves competence, credibility, and integrity. The management accountant should request that the division manager provide credible evidence that the new product is commercially viable. If the manager does not provide such evidence, expensing development costs in the current period is appropriate.

Case B involves confidentiality and integrity. The supplier in Case B may have no intention of asking questions about competitors' bids. However, the appearance of a conflict of interest in Case B is sufficient for many companies to prohibit employees from accepting "favors" from suppliers.

Exhibit 1-8 presents the IMA's guidance on "Resolving Ethical Issues." For example, if the divisional management accountant in Case A is not satisfied with the response of the division manager regarding the commercial viability of the product, he or she should discuss the issue with the corporate controller. The accountant in Case B should discuss the invitation with his or her immediate supervisor. If the visit is approved, the accountant should inform the supplier that the invitation has been officially approved subject to following corporate policy (which includes not disclosing confidential company information).

DECISION POINT

What are the ethical responsibilities of management accountants?

Most professional accounting organizations around the globe issue statements about professional ethics. These statements include many of the same issues discussed by the IMA in Exhibits 1-7 and 1-8. For example, the Chartered Institute of Management Accountants in the United Kingdom advocates five ethical principles similar to those shown in Exhibit 1-7: professional competence and due care, confidentiality, integrity, objectivity, and professional behavior.

EXHIBIT 1-8

Resolving Ethical Issues

RESOLVING ETHICAL ISSUES

In applying the Standards of Ethical Professional Practice, the member may encounter unethical issues or behavior. In these situations, the member should not ignore them, but rather should actively seek resolution of the issue. In determining which steps to follow, the member should consider all risks involved and whether protections exist against retaliation.

When faced with unethical issues, the member should follow the established policies of his or her organization, including use of an anonymous reporting system if available.

If the organization does not have established policies, the member should consider the following courses of action:

- The resolution process could include a discussion with the member's immediate supervisor. If the supervisor appears to be involved, the issue could be presented to the next level of management.
- IMA offers an anonymous helpline that the member may call to request how key elements of the IMA Statement of Ethical Professional Practice could be applied to the ethical issue.
- The member should consider consulting his or her own attorney to learn of any legal obligations, rights, and risks concerning the issue.

If resolution efforts are not successful, the member may wish to consider disassociating from the organization.

Source: IMA Statement of Ethical Professional Practice, 2017. Montvale, NJ: Institute of Management Accountants. Reprinted with permission from the Institute of Management Accountants, Montvale, NJ, www.imanet.org.

PROBLEM FOR SELF-STUDY

Campbell Soup Company incurs the following costs:

a. Purchase of tomatoes by a canning plant for Campbell's tomato soup products
b. Materials purchased for redesigning Pepperidge Farm biscuit containers to keep biscuits fresh
c. Payment to Backer, Spielvogel, & Bates, the advertising agency, for advertising work on the Healthy Request line of soup products
d. Salaries of food technologists researching a Prego pizza sauce that has minimal calories
e. Payment to Safeway for redeeming coupons on Campbell's food products
f. Cost of a toll-free telephone line for customer inquiries about Campbell's soup products
g. Cost of gloves used by line operators on the Swanson Fiesta breakfast-food production line
h. Cost of handheld computers used by Pepperidge Farm delivery staff serving major supermarket accounts

Classify each cost item (a–h) as one of the business functions in the value chain in Exhibit 1-2 (page 5).

Solution

a. Production
b. Design of products and processes
c. Marketing
d. Research and development
e. Marketing
f. Customer service
g. Production
h. Distribution

DECISION POINTS

The following question-and-answer format summarizes the chapter's learning objectives. Each decision presents a key question related to a learning objective. The guidelines are the answer to that question.

Decision	Guidelines
1. How is financial accounting different from management accounting?	Financial accounting is used to develop reports for external users on past financial performance using GAAP. Management accounting is used to provide future-oriented information to help managers (internal users) make decisions and achieve an organization's goals.
2. How do management accountants support strategic decisions?	Management accountants contribute to strategic decisions by providing information about the sources of competitive advantage.
3. How do companies add value, and what are the dimensions of performance that customers are expecting of companies?	Companies add value through R&D, design of products and processes, production, marketing, distribution, and customer service. Customers want companies to deliver performance through cost and efficiency, quality, timeliness, and innovation.

Decision	Guidelines
4. How do managers make decisions to implement strategy?	Managers use a five-step decision-making process to implement strategy: (1) identify the problem and uncertainties; (2) obtain information; (3) make predictions about the future; (4) make decisions by choosing among alternatives; and (5) implement the decision, evaluate performance, and learn. The first four steps are planning decisions. They include deciding on an organization's goals, predicting results under various alternative ways of achieving those goals, and deciding how to attain the desired goals. Step 5 is the control decision, which includes taking actions to implement the planning decisions, evaluating past performance, and providing feedback that will help future decision making.
5. What guidelines do management accountants use?	Three guidelines that help management accountants increase their value to managers are (1) employing a cost–benefit approach, (2) recognizing behavioral as well as technical considerations, and (3) identifying different costs for different purposes.
6. Where does the management accounting function fit into an organization's structure?	Management accounting is an integral part of the controller's function. In most organizations, the controller reports to the chief financial officer, who is a key member of the top management team.
7. What are the ethical responsibilities of management accountants?	Management accountants have ethical responsibilities that relate to competence, confidentiality, integrity, and credibility.

TERMS TO LEARN

Each chapter will include this section. Like all technical terms, accounting terms have precise meanings. Learn the definitions of new terms when you initially encounter them. The meaning of each of the following terms is given in this chapter and in the Glossary at the end of this text.

budget (**p. 10**)
chief financial officer (CFO) (**p. 14**)
control (**p. 10**)
controller (**p. 14**)
cost accounting (**p. 3**)
cost–benefit approach (**p. 12**)
cost management (**p. 3**)
customer relationship management (CRM) (**p. 6**)
customer service (**p. 5**)
design of products and processes (**p. 5**)
distribution (**p. 5**)
finance director (**p. 14**)
financial accounting (**p. 2**)
learning (**p. 11**)
line management (**p. 13**)
management accounting (**p. 2**)
marketing (**p. 5**)
planning (**p. 10**)
production (**p. 5**)
research and development (R&D) (**p. 5**)
staff management (**p. 13**)
strategic cost management (**p. 4**)
strategy (**p. 4**)
supply chain (**p. 6**)
sustainability (**p. 7**)
total quality management (TQM) (**p. 7**)
value chain (**p. 5**)

ASSIGNMENT MATERIAL

Questions

1-1 How does management accounting differ from financial accounting?
1-2 "Management accounting should not fit the straitjacket of financial accounting." Explain and give an example.
1-3 How can a management accountant help formulate strategy?
1-4 Describe the business functions in the value chain.

1-5 Explain the term *supply chain* and its importance to cost management.

1-6 "Management accounting deals only with costs." Do you agree? Explain.

1-7 How can management accountants help improve quality and achieve timely product deliveries?

1-8 Describe the five-step decision-making process.

1-9 Distinguish planning decisions from control decisions.

1-10 What three guidelines help management accountants provide the most value to managers?

1-11 "Knowledge of technical issues such as computer technology is a necessary but not sufficient condition to becoming a successful management accountant." Do you agree? Why?

1-12 As a new controller, reply to this comment by a plant manager: "As I see it, our accountants may be needed to keep records for shareholders and Uncle Sam, but I don't want them sticking their noses in my day-to-day operations. I do the best I know how. No bean counter knows enough about my responsibilities to be of any use to me."

1-13 Where does the management accounting function fit into an organization's structure?

1-14 Name the four areas in which standards of ethical conduct exist for management accountants in the United States. What organization sets these standards?

1-15 What steps should a management accountant take if established written policies provide insufficient guidance on how to handle an ethical conflict?

Multiple-Choice Questions

In partnership with:
BECKER
PROFESSIONAL EDUCATION®

1-16 Which of the following is not a primary function of the management accountant?

a. Communicates financial results and position to external parties.
b. Uses information to develop and implement business strategy.
c. Aids in the decision making to help an organization meet its goals.
d. Provides input into an entity's production and marketing decisions.

Exercises

1-17 Value chain and classification of costs, computer company. Dell Computer incurs the following costs:

a. Utility costs for the plant assembling the Latitude computer line of products
b. Distribution costs for shipping the Latitude line of products to a retail chain
c. Payment to David Newbury Designs for design of the XPS 2-in-1 laptop
d. Salary of computer scientist working on the next generation of servers
e. Cost of Dell employees' visit to a major customer to demonstrate Dell's products
f. Purchase of competitors' products for testing against potential Dell products
g. Payment to business magazine for running Dell advertisements
h. Cost of cartridges purchased from outside supplier to be used with Dell printers

Required

Classify each of the cost items (**a–h**) into one of the business functions of the value chain shown in Exhibit 1-2 (page 5).

1-18 Value chain and classification of costs, pharmaceutical company. Johnson & Johnson, a health care company, incurs the following costs:

a. Payment of booth registration fee at a medical conference to promote new products to physicians
b. Cost of redesigning an artificial knee to make it easier to implant in patients
c. Cost of a toll-free telephone line used for customer inquiries about its drugs
d. Materials purchased to develop drugs yet to be approved by the government
e. Sponsorship of a professional golfer
f. Labor costs of workers in the tableting area of a production facility
g. Bonus paid to a salesperson for exceeding a monthly sales quota
h. Cost of FedEx courier service to deliver drugs to hospitals

Required

Classify each of the cost items (**a–h**) as one of the business functions of the value chain shown in Exhibit 1-2 (page 5).

1-19 Value chain and classification of costs, fast-food restaurant. Taco Bell, a fast-food restaurant, incurs the following costs:

a. Cost of oil for the deep fryer
b. Wages of the counter help who give customers the food they order
c. Cost of tortillas and lettuce
d. Cost of salsa packets given away with customer orders
e. Cost of the posters indicating the special "two tacos for $2.00"
f. Costs of corporate sponsorship of the World Series
g. Salaries of the food specialists in the corporate test kitchen who create new menu items
h. Cost of "to-go" bags requested by customers who could not finish their meals in the restaurant

Required

Classify each of the cost items (**a–h**) as one of the business functions of the value chain shown in Exhibit 1-2 (page 5).

1-20 Key success factors. Vortex Consulting has issued a report recommending changes for its newest high-tech manufacturing client, Precision Instruments. Precision currently manufactures a single product, a surgical robot that is sold and distributed internationally. The report contains the following suggestions for enhancing business performance:

a. Develop a more advanced cutting tool to stay ahead of competitors.
b. Adopt a TQM philosophy to reduce waste and defects to near zero.
c. Reduce lead times (time from customer order of product to customer receipt of product) by 20% in order to increase customer retention.
d. Redesign the robot to use 25% less energy, as part of Vortex's corporate social responsibility objectives.
e. Benchmark the company's gross margin percentages against its major competitors.

Required

Link each of these changes to the key success factors that are important to managers.

1-21 Key success factors. Phillips Transport Company provides trucking services for major retailers. Managers at the company believe that trucking is a people-management business, and they list the following as factors critical to their success:

a. Increase spending on employee development to streamline processes.
b. Foster cooperative relationships with truck repair providers to allow for less downtime from truck breakdowns.
c. Invest in electric and hybrid vehicles to reduce carbon emissions.
d. Train material-handling employees to reduce errors when loading trucks.
e. Benchmark the company's gross margin percentages against its major competitors.

Required

Match each of the above factors to the key success factors that are important to managers.

1-22 Planning and control decisions. Gregor Company makes and sells brooms and mops. It takes the following actions, not necessarily in the order given. For each action (**a–e**), state whether it is a planning decision or a control decision.

a. Gregor asks its advertising team to develop fresh advertisements to market its newest product.
b. Gregor calculates customer satisfaction scores after introducing its newest product.
c. Gregor compares costs it actually incurred with costs it expected to incur for the production of the new product.
d. Gregor's design team proposes a new product to compete directly with the Swiffer.
e. Gregor estimates the costs it will incur to distribute 30,000 units of the new product in the first quarter of next fiscal year.

1-23 Planning and control decisions. Rachel Mosby is the president of Carolina Landscaping Service. She takes the following actions, not necessarily in the order given. For each action (**a–e**) state whether it is a planning decision or a control decision.

a. Compares payroll costs of the past quarter to budgeted costs.
b. Calculates material costs of a project that was recently completed.
c. Evaluates hiring a marketing professional to grow sales.
d. Estimates the weekly cost of providing landscaping services next year to a local resort.
e. Decides to expand service offerings to include snow removal during the slower winter months.

1-24 Five-step decision-making process, manufacturing. Yukon Foods makes desserts that it sells through grocery stores. Typical products include ice cream sandwiches, sundae cups, and frozen yogurt pops. The managers at Yukon have recently proposed the addition of sugar-free fruit bars. They take the following actions to help decide whether to launch the line.

a. Yukon's test kitchen prepares a number of possible recipes for a consumer focus group.
b. Costs of retooling machinery for the new product are budgeted.
c. The company decides to produce a new line of sugar-free fruit bars.
d. Managers compare actual labor costs of making sugar-free fruit bars with their budgeted costs.
e. Sales managers estimate how much the sales of the new fruit bars will reduce sales of the company's ice cream sandwiches.
f. Managers discuss the possibility of introducing a line of sugar-free fruit bars.
g. To help decide whether to introduce the sugar-free fruit bars, the company researches the price and quality of competing products.

Required

Classify each of the actions (**a–g**) as a step in the five-step decision-making process (identify the problem and uncertainties; obtain information; make predictions about the future; make decisions by choosing among alternatives; implement the decision, evaluate performance, and learn). The actions are not listed in the order they are performed.

1-25 Five-step decision-making process, service firm. Sizemore Landscaping is a firm that provides commercial landscaping and grounds maintenance services. Derek Sizemore, the owner, is trying to find new ways to increase revenues. Mr. Sizemore performs the following actions, not in the order listed.

a. Decides to buy power tilling equipment rather than hire additional landscape workers.
b. Discusses with his employees the possibility of using power equipment instead of manual processes to increase productivity and thus profits.
c. Learns details about a large potential job that is about to go out for bids.
d. Compares the expected cost of buying power equipment to the expected cost of hiring more workers and estimates profits from both alternatives.
e. Estimates that using power equipment will reduce tilling time by 20%.
f. Researches the price of power tillers online.

Required

Classify each of the actions (**a–f**) according to its step in the five-step decision-making process (identify the problem and uncertainties; obtain information; make predictions about the future; make decisions by choosing among alternatives; implement the decision, evaluate performance, and learn).

1-26 Professional ethics and reporting division performance. Maria Mendez is division controller and James Dalton is division manager of the Hestor Shoe Company. Mendez has line responsibility to Dalton, but she also has staff responsibility to the company controller.

Dalton is under severe pressure to achieve the budgeted division income for the year. He has asked Mendez to book $200,000 of revenues on December 31. The customers' orders are firm, but the shoes are still in the production process. They will be shipped on or around January 4. Dalton says to Mendez, "The key event is getting the sales order, not shipping the shoes. You should support me, not obstruct my reaching division goals."

Required

1. Describe Mendez's ethical responsibilities.
2. What should Mendez do if Dalton gives her a direct order to book the sales?

1-27 Professional ethics and reporting division performance. Hannah Gilpin is the controller of Blakemore Auto Glass, a division of Eastern Glass and Window. Blakemore replaces and installs windshields. Her division has been under pressure to improve its divisional operating income. Currently, divisions of Eastern Glass are allocated corporate overhead based on cost of goods sold. Jake Myers, the president of the division, has asked Gilpin to reclassify $50,000 of installation labor, which is included in cost of goods sold, as administrative labor, which is not. Doing so will save the division $20,000 in allocated corporate overhead. The labor costs in question involve installation labor provided by trainee employees. Myers argues, "The trainees are not as efficient as regular employees, so this is unfairly inflating our cost of goods sold. This is really a cost of training (administrative labor), not part of cost of goods sold." Gilpin does not see a reason for reclassification of the costs other than to avoid overhead allocation costs.

Required

1. Describe Gilpin's ethical dilemma.
2. What should Gilpin do if Myers gives her a direct order to reclassify the costs?

Problems

1-28 Planning and control decisions, Internet company. PostNews.com offers its subscribers several services, such as an annotated TV guide and local-area information on weather, restaurants, and movie theaters. Its main revenue sources are fees for banner advertisements and fees from subscribers. Recent data are as follows:

Month/Year	Advertising Revenues	Actual Number of Subscribers	Monthly Fee per Subscriber
June 2018	$ 415,972	29,745	$15.50
December 2018	867,246	55,223	20.50
June 2019	892,134	59,641	20.50
December 2019	1,517,950	87,674	20.50
June 2020	2,976,538	147,921	20.50

The following decisions were made from June through October 2020:

a. June 2020: Raised subscription fee to $25.50 per month from July 2020 onward. The budgeted number of subscribers for this monthly fee is shown in the following table.
b. June 2020: Informed existing subscribers that from July onward, monthly fee would be $25.50.
c. July 2020: Offered e-mail service to subscribers and upgraded other online services.
d. October 2020: Dismissed the vice president of marketing after significant slowdown in subscribers and subscription revenues, based on July through September 2020 data in the following table.
e. October 2020: Reduced subscription fee to $22.50 per month from November 2020 onward.

Results for July–September 2020 are as follows:

Month/Year	Budgeted Number of Subscribers	Actual Number of Subscribers	Monthly Fee per Subscriber
July 2020	145,000	129,250	$25.50
August 2020	155,000	142,726	25.50
September 2020	165,000	145,643	25.50

Required

1. Classify each of the decisions (**a–e**) as a planning or a control decision.
2. Give two examples of other planning decisions and two examples of other control decisions that may be made at PostNews.com.

1-29 Strategic decisions and management accounting. Consider the following series of independent situations in which a firm is about to make a strategic decision.

Decisions

a. Julian Phones is about to decide whether to launch production and sale of a cell phone with standard features.
b. Western Airlines is investigating market demand for a unique design for first-class seating in the form of cabins on its route from Los Angeles to Honolulu.
c. Brandon Coverings is developing window shades that will let light into a room and reduce glare based on the outside brightness. There are no such shades currently on the market.
d. Bledsoe Brands, a manufacturer of breakfast cereal, is developing a line of generic bagged cereals to be sold to a national discount chain.

Required

1. For each decision, state whether the company is following a cost leadership or a product differentiation strategy.
2. For each decision, discuss what information the management accountant can provide about the source of competitive advantage for these firms.

1-30 Strategic decisions and management accounting. Consider the following series of independent situations in which a firm is about to make a strategic decision.

Decisions

a. A running shoe manufacturer is weighing whether to purchase leather from a cheaper supplier in order to compete with lower-priced competitors.
b. An office supply store is considering adding a delivery service that its competitors do not have.
c. A regional retailer is deciding whether to install self-check-out counters. This technology will reduce the number of check-out clerks required in the store.
d. A local florist is considering hiring a horticulture specialist to help customers with gardening questions.

Required

1. For each decision, state whether the company is following a cost leadership or a product differentiation strategy.
2. For each decision, discuss what information the managerial accountant can provide about the source of competitive advantage for these firms.

1-31 Management accounting guidelines. For each of the following items, identify which of the management accounting guidelines applies: cost–benefit approach, behavioral and technical considerations, or different costs for different purposes.

1. Giving constructive feedback when actual performance falls short of the budget.
2. Deciding to give bonuses for superior performance to the employees in a Japanese subsidiary and extra vacation time to the employees in a Swedish subsidiary.
3. Including costs of all the value-chain functions before deciding to launch a new product, but including only its manufacturing costs in determining its inventory valuation.
4. Selecting between a salary plan and a commission plan to compensate sales managers.
5. Signing a lease on a costlier retail location when a lower-cost location had available space.
6. Analyzing whether to keep the billing function within an organization or outsource it.
7. Installing a participatory budgeting system in which managers set their own performance targets, instead of top management imposing performance targets on managers.
8. Recording research costs as an expense for financial reporting purposes (as required by U.S. GAAP) but capitalizing and expensing them over a longer period for management performance-evaluation purposes.
9. Signing a contract to sponsor a basketball star to increase exposure and sales to a younger customer market.

1-32 Management accounting guidelines. For each of the following items, identify which of the management accounting guidelines applies: cost–benefit approach, behavioral and technical considerations, or different costs for different purposes.

1. Changing an employee bonus plan to include additional paid time off in response to a changing employee demographic.
2. Deciding whether to sell products directly to customers in a new overseas market or to hire a distributor.
3. Adding the cost of store operations to merchandise cost when deciding on product pricing, but only including the cost of freight and the merchandise itself when calculating cost of goods sold on the income statement.
4. Introducing a participatory budgeting program that involves lower-level managers.
5. Weighing the cost of increased inspection against the costs associated with customer returns of defective goods.
6. Calculating depreciation cost of new equipment based on expected obsolescence when determining cost of inventory, but using tax depreciation tables for tax reporting.
7. Estimating the loss of future business resulting from bad publicity related to an environmental disaster caused by a company's factory in the Philippines, but estimating cleanup costs for calculating the liability on the balance sheet.

1-33 Role of controller, role of chief financial officer. George Jimenez is the controller at Balkin Electronics, a manufacturer of devices for the computer industry. The company may promote him to chief financial officer.

Required

1. In this table, indicate which executive is *primarily* responsible for each activity.

Activity	Controller	CFO
Managing the company's long-term investments		
Presenting the financial statements to the board of directors		
Strategic review of different lines of businesses		
Budgeting funds for a plant upgrade		
Managing accounts receivable		
Negotiating fees with auditors		
Assessing profitability of various products		
Evaluating the costs and benefits of a new product design		

2. Based on this table and your understanding of the two roles, what types of training or experience will George find most useful for the CFO position?

1-34 Budgeting, ethics, pharmaceutical company. Henry Maddox was recently promoted to Controller of Research and Development for Pharmex, a *Fortune* 500 pharmaceutical company that manufactures prescription drugs and nutritional supplements. The company's total R&D cost for 2020 was expected (budgeted) to be $5 billion. During the company's midyear budget review, Maddox realized that current R&D expenditures were already at $3.5 billion, nearly 40% above the midyear target. At this current rate of expenditure, the R&D division was on track to exceed its total year-end budget by $2 billion!

In a meeting with CFO Emily Alford later that day, Maddox delivered the bad news. Alford was both shocked and outraged that the R&D spending had gotten out of control. Alford wasn't any more understanding when Maddox revealed that the excess cost was entirely related to research and development of a new drug, Amiven, which was expected to go to market next year. The new drug would result in large profits for Pharmex, if the product could be approved by year-end.

Alford had already announced her expectations of third-quarter earnings to Wall Street analysts. If the R&D expenditures weren't reduced by the end of the third quarter, Alford was certain that the targets she had announced publicly would be missed and the company's stock price would tumble. Alford instructed Maddox to make up the budget shortfall by the end of the third quarter using "whatever means necessary."

Maddox was new to the controller's position and wanted to make sure that Alford's orders were followed. Maddox came up with the following ideas for making the third-quarter budgeted targets:

a. Cut planned bonuses to the Amiven R&D team that would be paid in the third quarter, knowing that doing so may result in lower productivity and increased turnover of highly skilled staff.
b. Sell off rights to the drug Centrix. The company had not planned on doing this because, under current market conditions, it would get less than fair value. It would, however, result in a one-time gain that could offset the budget shortfall. Of course, all future profits from Centrix would be lost.
c. Capitalize some of the company's R&D expenditures, reducing R&D expense on the income statement. This transaction would not be in accordance with GAAP, but Maddox thought it was justifiable because the Amiven drug was going to market early next year. Maddox would argue that capitalizing R&D costs this year and expensing them next year would better match revenues and expenses.

Required

1. Referring to the "Standards of Ethical Behavior for Practitioners of Management Accounting and Financial Management," Exhibit 1-7 (page 17), which of the preceding items (**a–c**) are acceptable to use? Which are unacceptable?
2. What would you recommend Maddox do?

1-35 Professional ethics and end-of-year actions. Linda Butler is the new division controller of the snack-foods division of Daniel Foods. Daniel Foods has reported a minimum 15% growth in annual earnings for each of the past 5 years. The snack-foods division has reported annual earnings growth of more than 20% each year in this same period. During the current year, the economy went into a recession. The corporate controller estimates a 10% annual earnings growth rate for Daniel Foods this year. One month before the December 31 fiscal year-end of the current year, Butler estimates the snack-foods division will report an annual earnings growth of only 8%. Rex Ray, the snack-foods division president, is not happy, but he notes that the "end-of-year actions" still need to be taken.

Butler makes some inquiries and is able to compile the following list of end-of-year actions that were more or less accepted by the previous division controller:

a. Deferring December's routine monthly maintenance on packaging equipment by an independent contractor until January of next year.
b. Extending the close of the current fiscal year beyond December 31 so that some sales of next year are included in the current year.
c. Altering dates of shipping documents of next January's sales to record them as sales in December of the current year.
d. Giving salespeople a double bonus to exceed December sales targets.
e. Deferring the current period's advertising by reducing the number of television spots run in December and running more than planned in January of next year.
f. Deferring the current period's reported advertising costs by having Daniel Foods' outside advertising agency delay billing December advertisements until January of next year or by having the agency alter invoices to conceal the December date.
g. Persuading carriers to accept merchandise for shipment in December of the current year even though they normally would not have done so.

Required

1. Why might the snack-foods division president want to take these end-of-year actions?
2. Butler is deeply troubled and reads the "Standards of Ethical Behavior for Practitioners of Management Accounting and Financial Management" in Exhibit 1-7 (page 17). Classify each of the end-of-year actions (**a–g**) as acceptable or unacceptable according to that document.
3. What should Butler do if Ray suggests that these end-of-year actions are taken in every division of Daniel Foods and that she will greatly harm the snack-foods division if she does not cooperate and paint the rosiest picture possible of the division's results?

1-36 Professional ethics and end-of-year actions. Phoenix Press produces consumer magazines. The house and home division, which sells home-improvement and home-decorating magazines, has seen a 20% reduction in operating income over the past 9 months, primarily due to an economic recession and a depressed consumer housing market. The division's controller, Sophie Gellar, has felt pressure from the CFO to improve her division's operating results by the end of the year. Gellar is considering the following options for improving the division's performance by year-end:

a. Cancelling two of the division's least profitable magazines, resulting in the layoff of 25 employees.
b. Changing to a lighter weight paper that would reduce both paper and postage costs by 5%. It is uncertain what effect the lower quality would have on future sales.
c. Recognizing unearned subscription revenue (cash received in advance for magazines that will be delivered in the future) as revenue when cash is received in the current month (just before fiscal year-end) instead of showing it as a liability.
d. Delaying the shipment of January issues, normally shipped on December 20, to January 2, shifting the postage costs to January. Subscription revenue for those issues, however, would be recognized in December.
e. Recognizing advertising revenues that relate to January in December.
f. Switching from declining balance to straight-line depreciation to reduce depreciation expense in the current year.

Required

1. What are the motivations for Gellar to improve the division's year-end operating earnings?
2. From the point of view of the "Standards of Ethical Behavior for Practitioners of Management Accounting and Financial Management," Exhibit 1-7 (page 17), which of the preceding items (**a–f**) are acceptable? Which are unacceptable?
3. What should Gellar do about the pressure to improve performance?

1-37 Ethical challenges, global company environmental concerns. Contemporary Interiors (CI) manufactures high-quality furniture in factories in North Carolina for sale to top American retailers. In 2005, CI purchased a lumber operation in Indonesia, and shifted from using American hardwoods to Indonesian ramin in its products. The ramin proved to be a cheaper alternative, and it was widely accepted by American consumers. CI management credits the early adoption of Indonesian wood for its ability to keep its North Carolina factories open when so many competitors closed their doors. Recently, however, consumers have become increasingly concerned about the sustainability of tropical woods, including ramin. CI has seen sales begin to fall, and the company was even singled out by an environmental group for boycott. It appears that a shift to more sustainable woods before year-end will be necessary, and more costly.

In response to the looming increase in material costs, CEO Geoff Armstrong calls a meeting of upper management. The group generates the following ideas to address customer concerns and/or salvage company profits for the current year:

a. Pay local officials in Indonesia to "certify" the ramin used by CI as sustainable. It is not certain whether the ramin would be sustainable or not. Put highly visible tags on each piece of furniture to inform consumers of the change.
b. Make deep cuts in pricing through the end of the year to generate additional revenue.
c. Record executive year-end bonus compensation accrued for the current year when it is paid in the next year after the December fiscal year-end.
d. Reject the change in materials. Counter the bad publicity with an aggressive ad campaign showing the consumer products as "made in the USA," since manufacturing takes place in North Carolina.
e. Redesign upholstered furniture to replace ramin contained inside with less expensive recycled plastic. The change in materials would not affect the appearance or durability of the furniture. The company would market the furniture as "sustainable."
f. Pressure current customers to take early delivery of goods before the end of the year so that more revenue can be reported in this year's financial statements.
g. Begin purchasing sustainable North American hardwoods and sell the Indonesian lumber subsidiary. Initiate a "plant a tree" marketing program, by which the company will plant a tree for every piece of furniture sold. Material costs would increase 25%, and prices would be passed along to customers.
h. Sell off production equipment prior to year-end. The sale would result in one-time gains that could offset the company's lagging profits. The owned equipment could be replaced with leased equipment at a lower cost in the current year.
i. Recognize sales revenues on orders received but not shipped as of the end of the year.

Required

1. As the management accountant for Contemporary Interiors, evaluate each of the preceding items (**a–i**) in the context of the "Standards of Ethical Behavior for Practitioners of Management Accounting and Financial Management," Exhibit 1-7 (page 17). Which of the items are in violation of these ethics standards and which are acceptable?
2. What should the management accountant do with regard to those items that are in violation of the ethical standards for management accountants?

2 An Introduction to Cost Terms and Purposes

LEARNING OBJECTIVES

1 Define and illustrate a cost object

2 Distinguish between direct costs and indirect costs

3 Explain variable costs and fixed costs

4 Interpret unit costs cautiously

5 Distinguish the financial accounting concepts of inventoriable costs and period costs

6 Illustrate the flow of inventoriable and period costs in financial accounting

7 Explain why product costs are computed in different ways for different purposes

8 Describe a framework for cost accounting and cost management

What does the word *cost* mean to you?

Is it the price you pay for something of value, like a cell phone? A cash outflow, like monthly rent? Something that affects profitability, like salaries? Organizations, like individuals, deal with different types of costs. They incur costs to generate revenues. Unfortunately, when times are bad and revenues decline, companies may find that they are unable to cut costs fast enough, leading to Chapter 11 bankruptcy. This was the case with apparel chain Aéropostale.

HIGH FIXED COSTS BANKRUPT AÉROPOSTALE[1]

In 2015, teen apparel chain Aéropostale announced that it had filed for Chapter 11 bankruptcy. Its high fixed costs—costs that did not decrease as the number of hoodies and t-shirts sold declined—crippled the company.

In the 1990s and early 2000s, Aéropostale saw its logo-centric clothing become a fixture in malls and a favorite of teens who shopped there. During this time, the company rapidly grew to more than 800 stores around the world. This expansion saddled the company with a huge amount of debt. In 2016, as mall traffic tanked and competition from fast-fashion retailers like H&M, Forever 21, and Zara intensified, the company collapsed under the weight of its declining sales and high fixed operating costs—like long-term leases and salaries—and debt-servicing payments. After declaring bankruptcy, Aéropostale quickly closed hundreds of stores and began to feature more non-logoed merchandise to set it apart from competitors such as Abercrombie & Fitch and American Eagle.

Jstone/Shutterstock

As the story of Aéropostale illustrates, managers must understand their firms' costs and closely manage them. Organizations as varied as the United Way, the Mayo Clinic, and Sony generate reports containing a variety of cost concepts and terms managers need to understand to effectively run their businesses. This chapter discusses cost concepts and terms that are the basis of accounting information used for internal and external reporting.

[1] *Sources:* Daphne Howland, "How Aéropostale Crashed and Burned—And What's Next," *Retail Dive*, June 6, 2016 (https://www.retaildive.com/news/how-aeropostale-crashed-and-burnedand-whats-next/420071/); Phil Wahba, "Aéropostale Won't Go Out of Business After All," *Fortune*, September 13, 2016 (http://fortune.com/2016/09/13/aeropostale-bankrupcty/); Riley Griffin, "Move Over Millennials, It's Gen Z's Turn to Kill Industries," *Bloomberg*, August 7, 2018 (https://www.bloomberg.com/news/articles/2018-08-07/move-over-millennials-it-s-gen-z-s-turn-to-kill-industries).

Costs and Cost Terminology

LEARNING OBJECTIVE 1

Define and illustrate a cost object

. . . examples of cost objects are products, services, activities, processes, and customers

A **cost** is the monetary value of resources (such as labor) sacrificed or forgone to achieve a specific objective. A cost is usually measured as the amount that must be paid to acquire the resources consumed. An **actual cost** is a cost that has been incurred (a historical or past cost) and is distinguished from a **budgeted cost**, which is a forecasted, or predicted, cost (a future cost).

When you think of a cost, you invariably think of it in the context of putting a monetary value on a particular thing. We call this "thing" a **cost object**, which is anything for which a cost measurement is desired. Suppose you're a manager at Tesla's car manufacturing plant in Fremont, California (called the "Tesla Factory"). Can you identify some cost objects that would be important to you as a plant manager? Now look at Exhibit 2-1.

You will see that Tesla managers not only want to know the cost of the different products, such as the Model 3, but they also want to know the costs of services, projects, activities, departments, and supporting customers. Managers use their knowledge of these costs to guide decisions about, for example, product innovation, quality, and customer service.

Now think about whether a manager at the Tesla Factory might want to know the *actual cost* or the *budgeted cost* of a cost object. Managers oftentimes need to know both types of costs when making decisions. For example, comparing actual costs to budgeted costs helps managers evaluate how well they controlled costs and learn about how they can do better in the future.

How does a cost measurement system determine the costs of various cost objects? Typically in two stages: accumulation followed by assignment. **Cost accumulation** is the collection of cost data in some organized way by means of an accounting system. For example, at its Fremont car factory, Tesla collects (accumulates) in various categories the costs of different types of materials, different classifications of labor, the costs incurred for supervision, and so on. In the next step, the accumulated costs are then *assigned* to designated cost objects, such as the different models of electric cars that Tesla manufactures at the Tesla Factory. Tesla managers use this cost information in two main ways: (1) to *make* decisions, for example, about how to price different models of cars or how much to invest in R&D and marketing and (2) to *implement* decisions, for example, by providing bonuses to employees to motivate cost reductions.

DECISION POINT

What is a cost object?

Now that we know why it is useful for management accountants to assign costs, we turn our attention to some concepts that will help us do it. Again, think of the different types of costs that we just discussed: materials, labor, and supervision. You are probably thinking that some costs, such as the costs of materials, are easier to assign to a cost object than others, such as the costs of supervision. As you will learn, this is indeed the case.

LEARNING OBJECTIVE 2

Distinguish between direct costs

. . . costs that are traced to the cost object

and indirect costs

. . . costs that are allocated to the cost object

Direct Costs and Indirect Costs

Costs are classified as direct costs or indirect costs. Management accountants use a variety of methods to assign these costs to cost objects.

- **Direct costs of a cost object** are directly related to the particular cost object and can easily and unambiguously be traced to it. For example, the cost of steel or tires is a direct cost of Tesla Model 3s. The cost of steel or tires can easily be traced to or identified with the

EXHIBIT 2-1 Examples of Cost Objects at Tesla

Cost Object	Illustration
Product	A Tesla Model 3 vehicle
Service	Telephone hotline providing information and assistance to Tesla stores and galleries
Project	R&D project on an electric Tesla truck
Customer	The Dubai Road and Transport Authority (RTA), which is building a large fleet of electric taxis in the city
Activity	Setting up machines for production or maintaining production equipment
Department	Worker health and safety department

Tesla Model 3. As workers on the Tesla Model 3 production line request materials from the warehouse, the material requisition document identifies the cost of the materials supplied to the Model 3. Similarly, individual workers record on their time sheets the hours and minutes they spend working on the Model 3. The cost of this labor can also easily be traced to the Model 3 and is another example of a direct cost. The term **cost tracing** is used to describe the assignment of direct costs to a particular cost object.

- **Indirect costs of a cost object** are also related to the particular cost object, but they cannot easily and unambiguously be traced to it. For example, the salaries of plant administrators (including the plant manager) who oversee manufacturing of the different car models produced at the Fremont plant are an indirect cost of the Model 3s. Plant administration costs are related to the cost object (Model 3s) because plant administration is necessary for managing the production of these vehicles. Plant administration costs are indirect costs because plant administrators also oversee the production of other products, such as the Model X. Unlike steel or tires, there is no specific request made by supervisors of the Model 3 production line for plant administration services, and plant administration costs can therefore not easily and unambiguously be traced to the Model 3 line. The term **cost allocation** is used to describe the process of assigning indirect costs to a particular cost object.

Cost assignment is a general term that encompasses both (1) tracing direct costs to a cost object and (2) allocating indirect costs to a cost object. Exhibit 2-2 depicts direct costs and indirect costs and both forms of cost assignment—cost tracing and cost allocation—using the Tesla Model 3 as an example.

Cost Allocation Challenges

Managers want to assign costs accurately to cost objects because inaccurate product costs will mislead managers about the profitability of different products. This could result, for example, in managers unknowingly promoting less-profitable products instead of more-profitable products.

Managers are much more confident about the accuracy of the direct costs of cost objects, such as the cost of steel and tires of the Model 3, because these costs can easily be traced to the cost object. Indirect costs are a different story. Some indirect costs can be assigned to cost objects reasonably accurately. Others are more difficult.

Consider the depreciation cost of the Tesla Factory. This cost is an indirect cost of the Model 3—there is no separate depreciation cost for the area of the plant where the Model 3 is made. Nonetheless, Tesla *allocates* to the Model 3 a part of the depreciation cost of the building—for example, on the basis of a percentage estimate of the building's floor space occupied by the production of the Model 3 relative to the total floor space used to produce all models of cars. This approach measures the building resources used by each car model reasonably and accurately. The more floor space a car model occupies, the greater the depreciation costs assigned to it. Accurately allocating other indirect costs, such as plant administration, to

EXHIBIT 2-2

Cost Assignment to a Cost Object

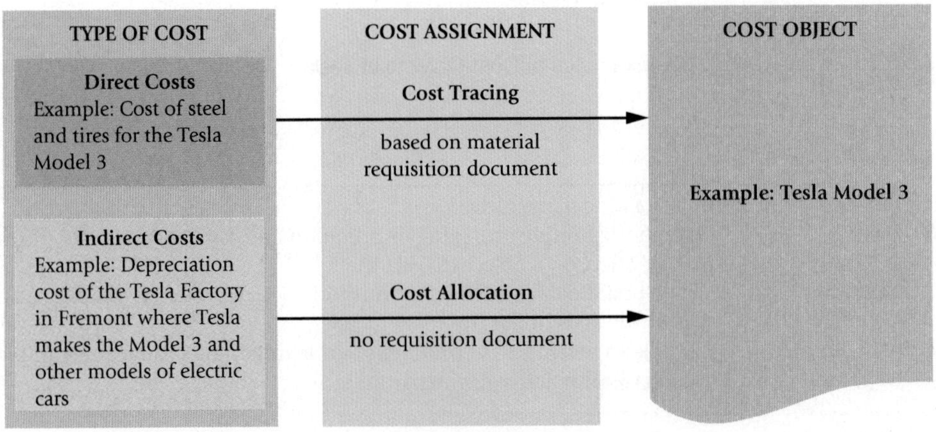

the Model 3, however, is more difficult. For example, should these costs be allocated on the basis of the number of employees working on each car model or the number of cars produced of each model? Measuring the share of plant administration used by each car model is not clear-cut.

Factors Affecting Direct/Indirect Cost Classifications

Several factors affect whether a cost is classified as direct or indirect:

- **The materiality of the cost in question and the availability of information-gathering technology.** The smaller the amount of a cost—that is, the more immaterial the cost is—the more likely it is to be classified as an indirect cost. Consider a mail-order catalog company such as Lands' End and one of their customer orders. Given the amount involved, it is economically worthwhile for the company to trace the courier charge for delivering the package to the customer as a direct cost. In contrast, it may not be worthwhile for Lands' End to trace the cost of the invoice paper included in the package as a direct cost, but rather to classify it as an indirect cost. Why? Although the cost of the paper can be traced to each order, it may not be cost effective to do so. The benefits of knowing that, say, exactly \$0.005 worth of paper is included in each order may not exceed the data processing and administrative costs of tracing the cost to each order. Consider, for example, that the cost tracking is done by the sales administrator who earns a salary of \$60,000 a year. His or her time is better spent organizing customer information to help with the company's marketing efforts than tracking the cost of paper. However, improvements in information-gathering technology make it economically worthwhile to consider smaller and smaller amounts of costs as direct costs. Bar codes, for example, allow manufacturing plants to treat certain low-cost materials such as clips and screws, which were previously classified as indirect costs, as direct costs of products. At Dell, component parts such as the computer chip and the solid-state drive contain bar codes that can be scanned at every point in the production process. Bar codes can be read into a manufacturing cost file by waving a "wand" in the same quick and efficient way supermarket checkout clerks enter the price of each item purchased by a customer.
- **Design of operations.** Classifying a cost as direct is straightforward if a company's facility (or some part of it) is used exclusively for a specific cost object, such as a specific product or a particular customer. For example, General Chemicals can easily classify the cost of its facility entirely dedicated to manufacturing soda ash (sodium carbonate) as a direct cost of the cost object soda ash.

Be aware that a specific cost may be a direct cost of one cost object but an indirect cost of another cost object. *That is, the direct/indirect classification depends on the cost object that one is trying to determine the cost of.* For example, the salary of an assembly department supervisor at Tesla is a direct cost if the cost object is the assembly department. However, because the assembly department assembles different models of electric cars, the supervisor's salary is an indirect cost if the cost object is a specific product such as the Tesla Model 3 sedan. A useful rule to remember is that the broader the cost object definition—the assembly department, rather than the Model 3—the higher the direct cost portion of total costs and the more confident a manager will be about the accuracy of the resulting calculated cost.

DECISION POINT

How do managers decide whether a cost is a direct or an indirect cost?

One final point. A company can incur a cost—sacrifice a resource—without the cost being recorded in the accounting system. For example, certain retirement health benefits are only recorded in the accounting system after an employee retires although the cost is incurred while the employee is actually providing the service. Environmental costs are another example. Many companies, for example General Electric, have had to incur significant costs at a later date to clean up the environmental damage that was caused by actions taken several years earlier. To force managers to consider these costs when making decisions, some companies such as Novartis, the Swiss pharmaceutical giant, are imputing a cost in their cost accounting system for every ton of greenhouse gases emitted to surrogate for future environmental costs. These costs can be a direct cost of a product if they can be traced to a specific product. More commonly, these costs are associated with operating a manufacturing facility and cannot be traced to a specific product. In this case, they are indirect costs.

Cost-Behavior Patterns: Variable Costs and Fixed Costs

LEARNING OBJECTIVE 3

Explain variable costs and fixed costs

. . . the two basic ways in which costs behave

Recall that the definition of a cost is the monetary value of resources (such as labor) sacrificed or forgone to achieve a specific objective, captured by the cost object. Costing systems record the cost of the resources acquired, such as materials, labor, and equipment, and track how those resources are used to achieve the cost object, such as to produce and sell a product or service. Managers can then observe how costs behave by comparing the level of costs to the volume, or the number of units achieved, of the cost object. There are two basic types of cost-behavior patterns. A **variable cost** of a cost object changes *in its total level* in proportion to changes in the volume, or number of units achieved, of the cost object. A **fixed cost** of a cost object remains unchanged *in its total level* for a given time period, despite wide changes in the volume, or number of units achieved, of the cost object. Note that costs are classified as variable or fixed *with respect to a specific cost object* and for *a given time period*. Identifying a cost as variable or fixed provides valuable information for making many management decisions and is an important input when evaluating performance. To illustrate these two basic types of cost-behavior patterns, again consider the costs at the Tesla Factory.

1. **Variable costs.** If Tesla buys a steering wheel at $800 for each of its Tesla Model 3 vehicles, then the total cost of steering wheels is $800 times the number of vehicles produced, as the following table illustrates.

Number of Model 3s Produced (1)	Variable Cost per Steering Wheel (2)	Total Variable Cost of Steering Wheels (3) = (1) × (2)
1	$800	$ 800
1,000	800	800,000
3,000	800	2,400,000

The steering wheel cost is an example of a variable cost with respect to the cost object Model 3 because the *total cost* of steering wheels changes in proportion to changes in the number of Model 3 vehicles produced. Note, however, that the *cost per unit of the cost object* of a variable cost is constant. For example, the cost per steering wheel in column 2 is the same regardless of whether 1,000 or 3,000 Model 3s are produced. As a result, the total cost of steering wheels in column 3 changes proportionately with the number of Model 3s produced in column 1.

Panel A in Exhibit 2-3 shows a graph of the total costs of steering wheels. The costs are represented by the straight line that climbs from the bottom left corner to the top right corner of the graph. The phrases "strictly variable" or "proportionately variable" are sometimes used to describe the variable cost behavior shown in this panel: Zero units of the cost object have a variable cost of $0, and each additional unit of the cost object has the same incremental variable cost.

EXHIBIT 2-3

Graphs of Variable and Fixed Costs

PANEL A: Variable Cost of Steering Wheels at $800 per Tesla Model 3 Assembled

PANEL B: Supervision Costs for the Tesla Model 3 Assembly Line (in millions)

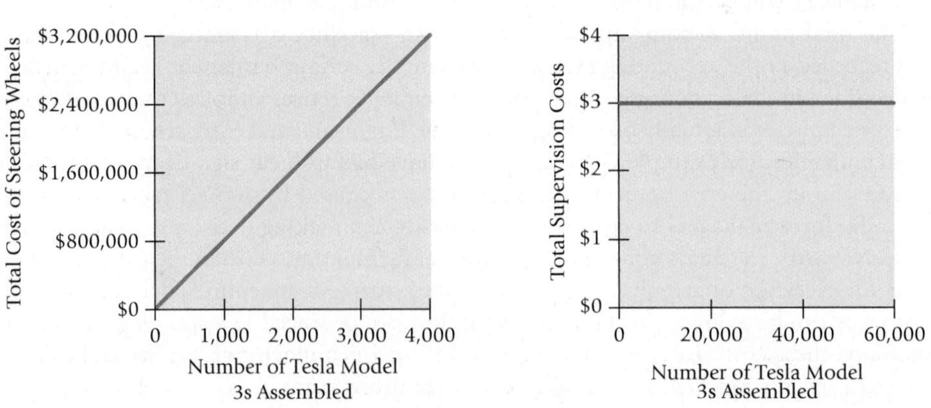

Now consider a different example: At the Tesla Factory, workers are paid a $20 hourly wage to set up machines. Is this cost a variable cost or a fixed cost with respect to the cost object machine setup-hour? The cost is a variable cost since the total wages for the workers change in proportion to the number of machine setup-hours used.

2. **Fixed costs.** Suppose Tesla incurs a total cost of $3,000,000 per year for supervisors who work exclusively on the Model 3 line. These costs are unchanged in total over a designated range of vehicles produced during a given time span (see Exhibit 2-3, Panel B). Note, however, that the fixed costs become smaller and smaller *on a per-unit basis* as the number of vehicles assembled increases, as the following table shows.

Annual Total Fixed Supervision Costs for Tesla Model 3 Assembly Line (1)	Number of Model 3s Produced (2)	Fixed Supervision Cost per Model 3 (3) = (1) ÷ (2)
$3,000,000	10,000	$300
$3,000,000	25,000	$120
$3,000,000	50,000	$ 60

It is precisely because *total* line supervision costs are fixed at $3,000,000 that the fixed supervision cost per Model 3 decreases as the number of Model 3s produced increases; the same fixed costs are spread over a larger number of Model 3s. Be careful not to be misled by the change in fixed cost per unit. While the fixed cost *per unit* decreases as the number of units increases, *total* fixed costs remain unchanged.

Why are some costs variable and other costs fixed? Recall that a cost is usually measured as the amount of money that must be paid to acquire the resources consumed. The cost of steering wheels is a variable cost because Tesla buys the steering wheels only when they are needed. As more Model 3s are produced, proportionately more steering wheels are acquired and proportionately more costs are incurred.

Contrast the variable cost of steering wheels with the $3,000,000 of fixed cost per year incurred for the supervision of the Model 3 assembly line. This level of supervision is acquired and put in place well before Tesla uses it to produce Model 3s and before Tesla even knows how many Model 3s it will produce. Suppose that Tesla puts in place supervisors capable of supervising the production of 60,000 Model 3s each year. If the demand is for only 55,000 Model 3s, there will be idle capacity. Supervisors on the Model 3 line could have supervised the production of 60,000 Model 3s but will supervise only 55,000 Model 3s because of the lower demand. However, Tesla must pay for the unused line supervision capacity because the cost of supervision cannot be reduced in the short run. If demand is even lower—say only 50,000 Model 3s are demanded—the plant's line supervision costs will still be $3,000,000, and its idle capacity will increase.

Unlike variable costs, fixed costs of resources (such as for line supervision) cannot be quickly and easily changed to match changes in their demand. Over time, however, managers can take action to change a company's fixed costs. For example, if the Model 3 line needs to be run for fewer hours because the demand for the vehicles falls, Tesla may lay off supervisors or move them to another production line. Unlike variable costs that go away automatically if resources are not deployed, reducing fixed costs requires active intervention on the part of managers.

Do not assume that individual cost items are inherently variable or fixed. Consider labor costs. Labor costs can be purely variable for units produced when workers are paid on a piece-unit basis (for each unit they make). For example, some companies pay garment workers on a per-shirt-sewed basis, so the firms' labor costs are purely variable. That is, total costs depend on how many shirts workers make. In contrast, other companies negotiate labor union agreements that include set annual salaries and no-layoff clauses for workers. At such a company, the salaries would appropriately be classified as fixed. For example, for decades, Japanese companies provided their workers a lifetime guarantee of employment. Although such a guarantee entails higher fixed labor costs, a firm can benefit because workers are more loyal and dedicated, which can improve productivity. However, during an economic downturn, the company risks losing money if revenues decrease while fixed costs remain unchanged.

CONCEPTS IN ACTION

Lyft Helps Hospitals Reduce Their Fixed Transportation Costs[2]

Roman Tiraspolsky/Shutterstock

Since 2012, more than 1 billion people worldwide have used Lyft—the peer-to-peer on-demand ride-hailing service—to get to the airport or home from a concert. More recently, Lyft has been working with hospital systems and other health care providers to get patients to and from their appointments. By moving from high-fixed-cost shuttle services to Lyft, hospitals are reducing spending while improving patient satisfaction and health outcomes.

What does Lyft mean for hospitals? For some patients, getting to and from health care appointments is difficult and stressful. Every year, 3.6 million Americans miss medical appointments because of transportation challenges, which costs the health care system more than $150 billion annually. As a result, many hospitals operate costly shuttle services. Traditionally, owning and operating these shuttles has involved high fixed costs for hospitals, including buying the assets (vans and busses), maintenance costs, and insurance for a team of drivers.

Now, hospitals can use Lyft for on-demand patient mobility while reducing their transportation and overhead costs. Through the Lyft Concierge platform, hospitals can schedule rides for individuals. The platform pushes a text alert to passengers about the scheduled ride and the hospital covers the cost. For these hospitals, Lyft allows them to convert the fixed costs of owning and operating a shuttle service to variable costs. During slower times, the hospital is not saddled with the fixed costs of shuttle ownership and operation. Of course, when the hospital is busy, they can end up paying more overall than they would have paid if they purchased and maintained the shuttle service themselves.

So far, Lyft Concierge has helped hospitals increase appointment adherence, which helps them avoid lost revenue from missed appointments and no shows, or worse, an expensive trip to the emergency room. As a result, Lyft is now working with a wide range of health care providers including insurance companies and pharmacies to help further reduce barriers to non-emergency health care transportation. For example, Walgreens and CVS are working with Lyft to offer free rides for patients to pick up their prescriptions. The idea is that by helping people pick up their prescriptions, they can boost the rates of people taking their drugs, which improves patient health outcomes and ultimately lowers costs to the health care system.

[2] *Sources:* "How Lyft Improves Patient Experience at Denver's Primary Safety Net Hospital," Lyft customer case study, September 2018 (https://www.lyftbusiness.com/customer-stories/denver-health); Sara Ashley O'Brien, "Lyft Doubles Down on Helping Patients Get Rides to the Doctor," CNN.com, March 5, 2018 (https://money.cnn.com/2018/03/05/technology/lyft-concierge-health-care/index.html); Angelica LaVito, "Blue Cross, Lyft, Walgreens and CVS Partner to Help Patients Get Their Scripts," CNBC.com, March 14, 2018 (https://www.cnbc.com/2018/03/14/blue-cross-lyft-walgreens-and-cvs-partner-to-help-patients-get-their-scripts.html).

Following the global economic crisis of 2007–2009, companies have become very reluctant to lock in fixed costs. Concepts in Action: Lyft Helps Hospitals Reduce Their Fixed Transportation Costs describes how a ride-sharing service offers companies the opportunity to convert the fixed costs of owning corporate cars into variable costs by renting cars on an as-needed basis.

Furthermore, a particular cost item in a company could be variable with respect to one cost object and fixed with respect to another. Consider annual registration and license costs for a fleet of planes owned by an airline. Registration and license costs would be a variable cost with respect to the number of planes owned by the airline since each additional plane requires the airline to pay additional registration and license fees. But the registration and license costs would be a fixed cost with respect to the number of miles flown by one particular plane during a year since the total costs for registration and license remain the same, irrespective of the number of miles flown.

DECISION POINT

How do managers decide whether a cost is a variable or a fixed cost?

Some costs have both fixed and variable elements and are called *mixed* or *semivariable* costs. For example, a company's telephone costs may consist of a fixed monthly base rate and an additional cost for each minute of calling. We discuss mixed costs and techniques to separate out their fixed and variable components in Chapter 10.

Marqet Corporation uses trucks to transport bottles from the warehouse to different retail outlets. Gasoline costs are $0.25 per mile driven. Insurance costs are $5,500 per year. Calculate the total costs and the cost per mile for gasoline and insurance if the truck is driven (a) 25,000 miles per year or (b) 50,000 miles per year.

2-1 TRY IT!

Cost Drivers

Recall that the total level of a variable cost changes, based on the volume, or number of units, of the cost object. Usually, there is a cause-and-effect relationship between a change in the volume of the cost object and a change in the total level of a variable cost. For example, a change in the number of Model 3 vehicles assembled causes a change in the total (variable) cost of steering wheels. In this case, the number of Model 3s is the *cost driver* of the total cost of steering wheels. A **cost driver** is a metric, such as the amount or volume of something or the level of an activity, that causally affects the level of a cost over a given time span. An *activity* is an event, task, or unit of work with a specified purpose—for example, designing products, setting up machines, or testing products. Consider other costs, such as product-design costs. What metric may causally drive the level of total product-design costs? For example, product-design costs may change with the number of parts in the product, which would be considered the product-design costs' cost driver. Or consider distribution costs. The miles driven by trucks to deliver products are a cost driver of distribution costs.

Costs that are fixed in the short run have no cost driver in the short run since they remain unchanged. However, costs that are fixed in the short run may have a cost driver in the long run. Consider the costs of testing, say, 0.1% of the color printers produced at a Hewlett-Packard plant. These costs consist of equipment and staff costs of the testing department, which are difficult to change in the short run. Consequently, they are fixed in the short run regardless of how many color printers are produced at the plant (and hence tested). In this case, the production volume of color printers is not a cost driver of testing costs in the short run. In the long run, however, Hewlett-Packard will increase or decrease the testing department's equipment and staff to the levels needed to support testing of 0.1% of future production volumes. In the long run, production volume of color printers is a cost driver of testing costs. Costing systems that identify the cost of activities such as testing, design, or setup are called *activity-based costing systems*.

Relevant Range

Relevant range is the band or range of the amount or volume of something or the level of an activity in which there is a specific relationship between the volume or the level of an activity, i.e., the cost driver, and the cost in question. For example, a fixed cost is fixed only for a given range of volume or activity (at which the company is expected to operate) and only for a given time period (usually a particular budget period). Suppose Tesla contracts with Thomas Transport Company (TTC) to transport completed Model 3s from the Tesla Factory to Tesla service centers where customers can pick up their new vehicles. TTC rents two trucks, and each truck has an annual fixed rental cost of $40,000. The maximum annual usage of each truck is 120,000 miles. In the current year (2020), the predicted combined total hauling of the two trucks is 170,000 miles.

Exhibit 2-4 shows how annual fixed costs behave at different levels of miles of hauling. Up to 120,000 miles, TTC can operate with one truck; from 120,001 to 240,000 miles, it operates with two trucks; and from 240,001 to 360,000 miles, it operates with three trucks. This pattern will continue as TTC adds trucks to its fleet to provide more miles of hauling. Given the predicted 170,000-mile usage for 2020, the range from 120,001 to 240,000 miles hauled is the range in which TTC expects to operate, resulting in fixed rental costs of $80,000. Within this relevant range, changes in miles hauled will not affect the annual fixed costs.

Fixed costs may change from one year to the next, though. For example, if the total rental fee of the two trucks increases by $2,000 for 2021, the total level of fixed costs will increase to

EXHIBIT 2-4

Fixed-Cost Behavior at Thomas Transport Company

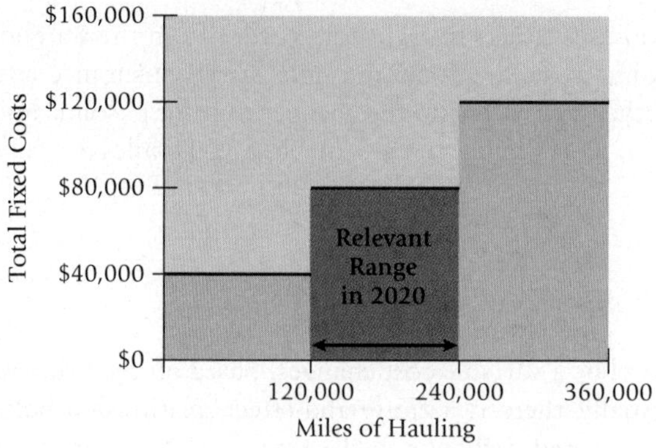

$82,000 (all else remaining the same). If that increase occurs, total rental costs will be fixed at this new level ($82,000) for 2021 for the miles hauled in the 120,001 to 240,000 range.

The relevant range also applies to variable costs. Outside the relevant range, variable costs, such as direct material costs, may no longer change proportionately with changes in the production volume. For example, above a certain volume, the cost of steering wheels may increase at a lower rate because Tesla may be able to negotiate price discounts for purchasing a greater number of steering wheels from its supplier.

Relationships Between Types of Costs

We have introduced two major classifications of costs: direct/indirect and variable/fixed. Costs may simultaneously be as follows:

- Direct and variable
- Direct and fixed
- Indirect and variable
- Indirect and fixed

Exhibit 2-5 shows examples of costs in each of these four cost classifications for the Tesla Model 3.

EXHIBIT 2-5

Examples of Costs in Combinations of the Direct/Indirect and Variable/Fixed Cost Classifications for a Car Manufacturer

		Assignment of Costs to Cost Object	
		Direct Costs	**Indirect Costs**
Cost–Behavior Pattern	**Variable Costs**	• Cost object: Tesla Model 3s produced Example: Tires used in assembly of automobile	• Cost object: Tesla Model 3s produced Example: Power costs at the Tesla Factory. Power usage is metered only to the plant, where multiple products are assembled.
	Fixed Costs	• Cost object: Tesla Model 3s produced Example: Salary of supervisor on Tesla Model 3 assembly line	• Cost object: Tesla Model 3s produced Example: Annual depreciation costs for the Tesla Factory in Fremont. Depreciation costs are for the whole plant, where multiple products are produced.

Total Costs and Unit Costs

LEARNING OBJECTIVE 4

Interpret unit costs cautiously

. . . for many decisions, managers should use total costs, not unit costs

The preceding section concentrated on the behavior patterns of total costs in relation to volume or activity levels. But what about unit costs?

Unit Costs

A **unit cost**, also called an **average cost**, is calculated by dividing the total cost by the related number of units produced. In many decision contexts, calculating a unit cost is essential. Consider the booking agent who has to make the decision to book Taylor Swift to play at Soldier Field. She estimates the cost of the event to be $4,000,000. This knowledge is helpful for the decision, but it is not enough.

Before reaching a decision, the booking agent also must predict the number of people who will attend. Without knowing the number of attendees, she cannot make an informed decision about the admission price she needs to charge to recover the cost of the event or even on whether to have the event at all. So she computes the unit cost of the event by dividing the total cost ($4,000,000) by the expected number of people who will attend. If 50,000 people attend, the unit cost is $80 (4,000,000 ÷ 50,000) per person; if 20,000 attend, the unit cost increases to $200 ($4,000,000 ÷ 20,000). Unless the total cost is "unitized" (that is, averaged by the level of volume or activity), the $4,000,000 cost is difficult to use to make decisions. The unit cost combines the total cost and the number of people in a simple and understandable way.

Accounting systems typically report both total-cost amounts and average-cost-per-unit amounts. The units might be expressed in various ways. Examples are automobiles assembled, packages delivered, or hours worked. Consider Tennessee Products, a manufacturer of speaker systems with a plant in Memphis. Suppose that, in 2020, its first year of operations, the company incurs $40,000,000 of manufacturing costs to produce 500,000 speaker systems. Then the unit cost is $80:

$$\frac{\text{Total manufacturing costs}}{\text{Number of units manufactured}} = \frac{\$40{,}000{,}000}{500{,}000 \text{ units}} = \$80 \text{ per unit}$$

If 480,000 units are sold and 20,000 units remain in ending inventory, the unit-cost concept helps managers determine total costs in the financial statements, i.e., the income statement and balance sheet, which are used to report the company's financial results to shareholders, banks, and the government.

Cost of goods sold in the income statement, 480,000 units × $80 per unit	$38,400,000
Ending inventory in the balance sheet, 20,000 units × $80 per unit	1,600,000
Total manufacturing costs of 500,000 units	$40,000,000

Unit costs are found in all areas of the value chain—for example, the unit cost of a product design, a sales visit, and a customer-service call. By summing unit costs throughout the value chain, managers can calculate the unit costs of the different products or services. Managers use this information, for example, to decide the prices they should charge, or which products they should invest more resources, such as R&D and marketing, in.

Use Unit Costs Cautiously

Although unit costs are regularly used in financial reports and for making product mix and pricing decisions, *for many decisions, managers should think in terms of total costs rather than unit costs*. Consider the manager of the Memphis plant of Tennessee Products. Assume the $40,000,000 in costs incurred in 2020 to produce the 500,000 speaker systems consist of $10,000,000 of fixed costs and $30,000,000 of variable costs (at $60 variable cost per speaker system produced). Suppose the total fixed costs and the variable cost per speaker system in 2021 are expected to be unchanged from 2020. The *budgeted* costs for 2021 at different production levels, calculated on the basis of total variable costs, total fixed costs, and total costs, are as follows:

Units Produced (1)	Variable Cost per Unit (2)	Total Variable Costs (3) = (1) × (2)	Total Fixed Costs (4)	Total Costs (5) = (3) + (4)	Unit Cost (6) = (5) ÷ (1)
100,000	$60	$ 6,000,000	$10,000,000	$16,000,000	$160.00
200,000	$60	$12,000,000	$10,000,000	$22,000,000	$110.00
500,000	$60	$30,000,000	$10,000,000	$40,000,000	$ 80.00
800,000	$60	$48,000,000	$10,000,000	$58,000,000	$ 72.50
1,000,000	$60	$60,000,000	$10,000,000	$70,000,000	$ 70.00

DECISION POINT

How should managers estimate and interpret cost information?

A plant manager who uses the 2020 unit cost of $80 to arrive at the *budgeted* costs for 2021 at different production levels will underestimate the *actual* total costs in 2021 if the plant's 2021 output is below the 2020 level of 500,000 units. If the volume produced falls to 200,000 units due to, say, the presence of a new competitor and less demand, actual costs would be $22,000,000. The unit cost of $80 times 200,000 units equals $16,000,000, which underestimates the actual total costs by $6,000,000 ($22,000,000 - $16,000,000). In other words, *the unit cost of $80 applies only when the company produces 500,000 units.*

An overreliance on the unit cost in this situation could lead to insufficient cash being available to pay the company's costs if volume declines to 200,000 units. As the table indicates, to arrive at the budgeted costs for 2021, managers should think in terms of total variable costs, total fixed costs, and total costs rather than unit cost. As a general rule, first calculate total costs, then compute the unit cost, if it is needed for a particular decision.

Business Sectors, Types of Inventory, Inventoriable Costs, and Period Costs

LEARNING OBJECTIVE 5

Distinguish the financial accounting concepts of inventoriable costs

. . . costs are assets when incurred, then expensed as cost of goods sold when products are sold

and period costs

. . . costs are expenses of the period in which they are incurred

Chapter 1 discussed how cost accounting serves both managerial and financial accountants. In the following two sections, we describe how cost accounting is used to achieve the objectives of *financial* accounting. In this section, we first describe the different sectors of the economy, the different types of inventory that companies hold, and the different classifications of manufacturing costs, and then discuss how these factors affect commonly used classifications of inventoriable and period costs.

Manufacturing-, Merchandising-, and Service-Sector Companies

We define three sectors of the economy and provide examples of companies in each sector.

1. **Manufacturing-sector companies** purchase materials and components and convert them into various finished goods. Examples are automotive companies such as Toyota, cellular-phone producers such as Samsung, food-processing companies such as Heinz, and computer companies such as Lenovo.
2. **Merchandising-sector companies** purchase and then sell tangible products without changing their basic form. This sector includes companies engaged in retailing (for example, electronics stores such as Best Buy and department stores such as Target), distribution (for example, a supplier of hospital products, such as Owens and Minor), or wholesaling (for example, BulbAmerica, which is a wholesale seller of lightbulbs).
3. **Service-sector companies** provide services (intangible products) to their customers. Examples are law firms (e.g., Wachtell, Lipton, Rosen & Katz), accounting firms (e.g., Ernst & Young), banks (e.g., Barclays), mutual fund companies (e.g., Fidelity), insurance companies (e.g., Aetna), transportation companies (e.g., Singapore Airlines), advertising agencies (e.g., Saatchi & Saatchi), television stations (e.g., Turner Broadcasting), Internet service providers (e.g., Comcast), travel agencies (e.g., American Express), healthcare providers (e.g., CommonSpirit Health), and brokerage firms (e.g., Merrill Lynch).

Types of Inventory

Manufacturing-sector companies purchase materials and components and convert them into finished goods. These companies typically have one or more of the following three types of inventory:

1. **Direct materials inventory**. Direct materials in stock that will be used in the manufacturing process (for example, computer chips and components needed to manufacture cellular phones).
2. **Work-in-process inventory**. Goods partially worked on but not yet completed (for example, cellular phones at various stages of completion in the manufacturing process). This is also called **work in progress**.
3. **Finished-goods inventory**. Goods (for example, cellular phones) completed, but not yet sold.

Merchandising-sector companies purchase tangible products and then sell them without changing their basic form. These companies hold only one type of inventory, which is products in their original purchased form, called *merchandise inventory*. Service-sector companies provide only services or intangible products and do not hold inventories of tangible products.

Commonly Used Classifications of Manufacturing Costs

Three terms commonly used when describing manufacturing costs are *direct materials costs, direct manufacturing labor costs*, and *indirect manufacturing costs*. These terms build on the direct versus indirect cost distinction we described earlier, applied to the context of manufacturing costs.

1. **Direct materials costs** are the acquisition costs of all materials that eventually become part of the cost object (work in process and then finished goods); they can easily and unambiguously be traced to the cost object. The steel and tires used to make the Tesla Model 3 and the computer chips used to make cellular phones are examples of direct material costs. Note that direct materials costs include not only the cost of the materials themselves, but the freight-in (inward delivery) charges, sales taxes, and customs duties that must be paid to acquire them.
2. **Direct manufacturing labor costs** include the compensation of all manufacturing labor that can easily and unambiguously be traced to the cost object (work in process and then finished goods). Examples include wages and fringe benefits paid to machine operators and assembly-line workers who convert direct materials into finished goods.
3. **Indirect manufacturing costs** are all manufacturing costs that are related to the cost object (work in process and then finished goods), but that cannot easily and unambiguously be traced to the cost object. Examples include indirect materials such as lubricants, indirect manufacturing labor such as plant maintenance and cleaning labor, plant rent, plant insurance, property taxes on the plant, plant depreciation, and the compensation of plant managers. This cost category is also referred to as **manufacturing overhead costs** or **factory overhead costs**. We use *indirect manufacturing costs* and *manufacturing overhead costs* interchangeably in this text.

We now describe the distinction between inventoriable costs and period costs.

Inventoriable Costs

Inventoriable costs are all costs of a product that are considered assets in a company's balance sheet when the costs are incurred and that are expensed as cost of goods sold only when the product is sold. For manufacturing-sector companies, all manufacturing costs are inventoriable costs. The costs first accumulate as work-in-process inventory assets (in other words, they are "inventoried") and then as finished goods inventory assets. Consider Cellular Products, a manufacturer of cellular phones. The cost of the company's direct materials, such as computer chips, direct manufacturing labor costs, and manufacturing overhead costs create new assets. They are first transformed into work-in-process inventory and eventually become finished-goods inventory (the cellular phones). When the cellular phones are sold, the costs move from being an asset to an expense, i.e., cost of goods sold. This cost is matched against **revenues**, which are inflows of assets (usually cash or accounts receivable) received for products or services customers purchase.

Note that the cost of goods sold includes all manufacturing costs (direct materials, direct manufacturing labor, and manufacturing overhead costs) incurred to produce them. The cellular phones may be sold during a different accounting period than the period in which they were manufactured. Thus, inventorying manufacturing costs in the balance sheet during the accounting period when the phones are manufactured and expensing the manufacturing costs in a later income statement when the phones are sold matches revenues and expenses.

For merchandising-sector companies such as Walmart, inventoriable costs are the costs of goods purchased that are resold in their same form. These costs are made up of the costs of the goods themselves plus any incoming freight, insurance, and handling costs for those goods. Service-sector companies provide only services or intangible products. The absence of inventories of tangible products for sale means service-sector companies have no inventoriable costs.

Period Costs

Period costs are all costs in the income statement other than cost of goods sold. Period costs, such as design costs, marketing, distribution, and customer service costs, are treated as expenses of the accounting period in which they are incurred because managers expect these costs to increase revenues in only that period and not in future periods. For manufacturing-sector companies, all nonmanufacturing costs in the income statement are period costs. For merchandising-sector companies, all costs in the income statement not related to the cost of goods purchased for resale are period costs. Examples of these period costs are labor costs of sales-floor personnel and advertising costs. Because there are no inventoriable costs for service-sector companies, all costs in their income statements are period costs.

An interesting question pertains to the treatment of R&D expenses as period costs.[3] As we saw in Chapter 1, for many companies in industries ranging from machine tools to consumer electronics to telecommunications to pharmaceuticals and biotechnology, innovation is increasingly becoming a key driver of success. The benefits of these innovations and R&D investments will, in most cases, only impact revenues in some future periods. So should R&D expenses still be considered period costs and be matched against revenues of the current period? Yes, because it is highly uncertain whether these innovations will be successful and result in future revenues. Even if the innovations are successful, it is very difficult to determine which future period the innovations will benefit. Some managers believe that treating R&D expenses as period costs dampens innovation because it reduces current period income.

Exhibit 2-5 showed examples of inventoriable costs in direct/indirect and variable/fixed cost classifications for a car manufacturer. Exhibit 2-6 shows examples of period costs in direct/indirect and variable/fixed cost classifications at a bank.

DECISION POINT

What are the differences between the financial accounting concepts of inventoriable and period costs?

EXHIBIT 2-6

Examples of Period Costs in Combinations of the Direct/Indirect and Variable/Fixed Cost Classifications at a Bank

		Assignment of Costs to Cost Object	
		Direct Costs	**Indirect Costs**
Cost-Behavior Pattern	**Variable Costs**	• Cost object: Number of mortgage loans Example: Fees paid to property appraisal company for each mortgage loan	• Cost object: Number of mortgage loans Example: Postage paid to deliver mortgage-loan documents to lawyers/homeowners
	Fixed Costs	• Cost object: Number of mortgage loans Example: Salary paid to executives in mortgage loan department to develop new mortgage-loan products	• Cost object: Number of mortgage loans Example: Cost to the bank of sponsoring annual golf tournament

[3] Under Generally Accepted Accounting Principles (GAAP) in the United States, all R&D costs are expensed for financial accounting. International Financial Reporting Standards permit the capitalization of some development costs for financial accounting.

Illustrating the Flow of Inventoriable Costs and Period Costs

We continue our discussion in section 5 on how cost accounting is used to achieve the objectives of financial accounting. In this section, we illustrate the flow of inventoriable costs and period costs through the income statement of a manufacturing company, where the distinction between inventoriable costs and period costs is most complex.

LEARNING OBJECTIVE 6

Illustrate the flow of inventoriable and period costs in financial accounting

. . . in manufacturing settings, inventoriable costs flow through work in process and finished goods accounts and are expensed when goods are sold; period costs are always expensed as incurred

Manufacturing-Sector Example

Follow the flow of costs for Cellular Products in Exhibits 2-7 and 2-8. Exhibit 2-7 visually highlights the differences in the flow of inventoriable and period costs for a manufacturing-sector company. Note how, as described in the previous section, inventoriable costs go through the balance sheet asset accounts of work-in-process inventory and finished-goods inventory before entering the income statement as the expense item cost of goods sold. Period costs are expensed directly in the income statement. Exhibit 2-8 takes the visual presentation in Exhibit 2-7 and shows how inventoriable costs and period expenses would appear in the income statement and the *schedule of cost of goods manufactured* of a manufacturing company.

We start by tracking the flow of direct materials shown on the left in Exhibit 2-7 and in Panel B in Exhibit 2-8. To keep things simple, all numbers are expressed in thousands, except for the per unit amounts.

Step 1: Cost of direct materials used in 2020. Note how the arrows in Exhibit 2-7 for beginning inventory, $11,000, and direct material purchases, $73,000, "fill up" the direct materials inventory box and how direct materials used, $76,000, "empties out" direct material inventory, leaving an ending inventory of direct materials of $8,000 that becomes the beginning inventory for the next year.

EXHIBIT 2-7 Flow of Revenue and Costs for a Manufacturing-Sector Company, Cellular Products (in thousands)

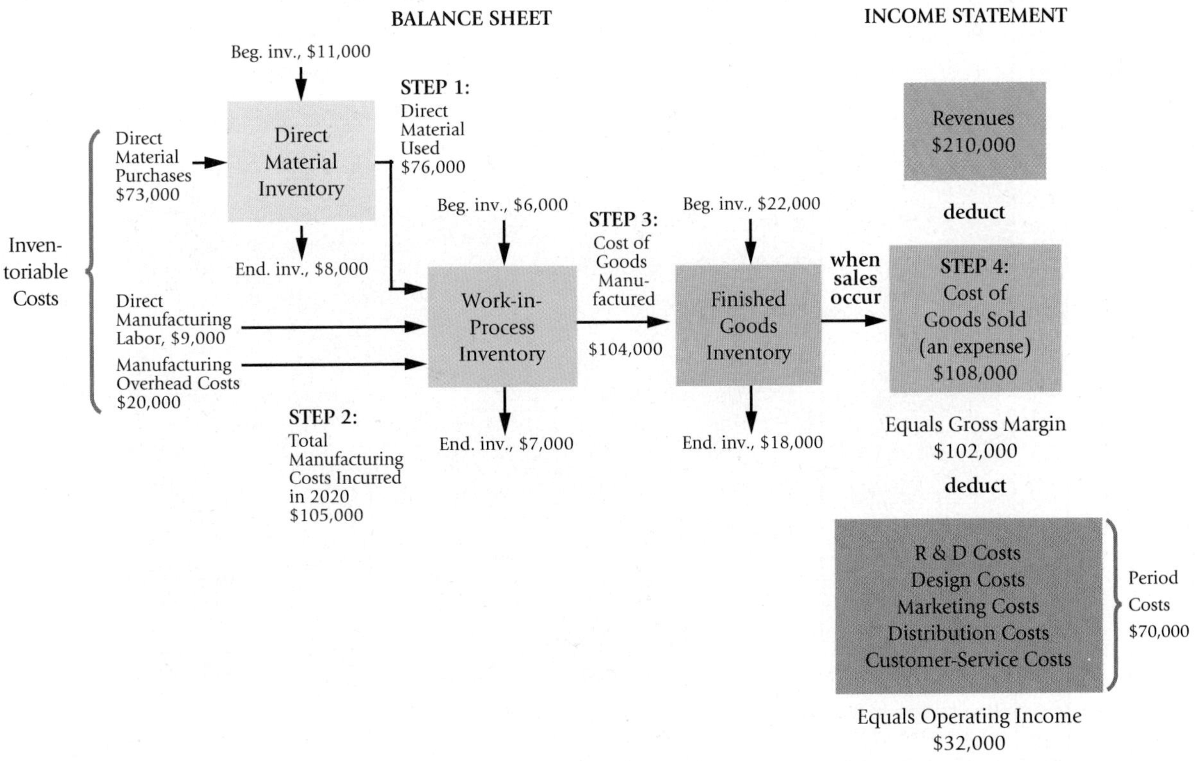

EXHIBIT 2-8 Income Statement and Schedule of Cost of Goods Manufactured of a Manufacturing-Sector Company, Cellular Products

		A	B	C
	1	**PANEL A: INCOME STATEMENT**		
	2	**Cellular Products**		
	3	**Income Statement**		
	4	**For the Year Ended December 31, 2020 (in thousands)**		
	5	Revenues		$210,000
STEP 4	6	Cost of goods sold:		
STEP 4	7	Beginning finished goods inventory, January 1, 2020	$ 22,000	
STEP 4	8	Cost of goods manufactured (see Panel B)	104,000	
STEP 4	9	Cost of goods available for sale	126,000	
STEP 4	10	Ending finished goods inventory, December 31, 2020	18,000	
STEP 4	11	Cost of goods sold		108,000
	12	Gross margin (or gross profit)		102,000
	13	Operating (period) costs:		
	14	R&D, design, mktg., dist., and cust.-service cost	70,000	
	15	Total operating costs		70,000
	16	Operating income		$ 32,000
	17			
	18	**PANEL B: COST OF GOODS MANUFACTURED**		
	19	**Cellular Products**		
	20	**Schedule of Cost of Goods Manufactured[a]**		
	21	**For the Year Ended December 31, 2020 (in thousands)**		
STEP 1	22	Direct materials:		
STEP 1	23	Beginning inventory, January 1, 2020	$ 11,000	
STEP 1	24	Purchases of direct materials	73,000	
STEP 1	25	Cost of direct materials available for use	84,000	
STEP 1	26	Ending inventory, December 31, 2020	8,000	
STEP 1 / STEP 2	27	Direct materials used		$ 76,000
STEP 2	28	Direct manufacturing labor		9,000
STEP 2	29	Manufacturing overhead costs:		
STEP 2	30	Indirect manufacturing labor	$ 7,000	
STEP 2	31	Supplies	2,000	
STEP 2	32	Heat, light, and power	5,000	
STEP 2	33	Depreciation—plant building	2,000	
STEP 2	34	Depreciation—plant equipment	3,000	
STEP 2	35	Miscellaneous	1,000	
STEP 2	36	Total manufacturing overhead costs		20,000
STEP 2 / STEP 3	37	Manufacturing costs incurred during 2020		105,000
STEP 3	38	Beginning work-in-process inventory, January 1, 2020		6,000
STEP 3	39	Total manufacturing costs to account for		111,000
STEP 3	40	Ending work-in-process inventory, December 31, 2020		7,000
STEP 3	41	Cost of goods manufactured (to income statement)		$104,000
	42	[a]Note that this schedule can become a schedule of cost of goods manufactured and sold simply by including the beginning and ending finished goods inventory figures in the supporting schedule rather than in the body of the income statement.		

The cost of direct materials used is calculated in Exhibit 2-8, Panel B (light blue-shaded area), as follows:

Beginning inventory of direct materials, January 1, 2020	$11,000
+ Purchases of direct materials in 2020	73,000
− Ending inventory of direct materials, December 31, 2020	8,000
= Direct materials used in 2020	$76,000

Step 2: Total manufacturing costs incurred in 2020. Total manufacturing costs for 2020 refers to all direct manufacturing costs and manufacturing overhead costs incurred during 2020 for all goods worked on during the year. Cellular Products classifies its manufacturing costs into the three categories described earlier.

(i) Direct materials used in 2020 (shaded light blue in Exhibit 2-8, Panel B)	$ 76,000
(ii) Direct manufacturing labor in 2020 (shaded blue in Exhibit 2-8, Panel B)	9,000
(iii) Manufacturing overhead costs in 2020 (shaded dark blue in Exhibit 2-8, Panel B)	20,000
Total manufacturing costs incurred in 2020	$105,000

Note how in Exhibit 2-7 these costs increase work-in-process inventory.

2-2 TRY IT!

Carolyn Corporation provides the following information for 2020.

Beginning inventory of direct materials, January 1, 2020	$10,000
Purchases of direct materials in 2020	$90,000
Ending inventory of direct materials, December 31, 2020	$ 2,000
Direct manufacturing labor costs in 2020	$32,000
Manufacturing overhead costs in 2020	$39,000

Calculate the total manufacturing costs incurred in 2020

Step 3: Cost of goods manufactured in 2020. **Cost of goods manufactured** refers to the cost of goods brought to completion during the period, regardless of whether they were started before or during the current accounting period.

Note how the work-in-process inventory box in Exhibit 2-7 has a very similar structure to the direct materials inventory box described in Step 1. Beginning work-in-process inventory of $6,000 and total manufacturing costs incurred in 2020 of $105,000 "fill up" the work-in-process inventory box. Some of the manufacturing costs incurred during 2020 are held back as the cost of the ending work-in-process inventory. The ending work-in-process inventory of $7,000 becomes the beginning inventory for the next year, and the $104,000 cost of goods manufactured during 2020 "empties out" the work-in-process inventory while "filling up" the finished-goods inventory box.

The cost of goods manufactured in 2020 (shaded green) is calculated in Exhibit 2-8, Panel B, as follows:

Beginning work-in-process inventory, January 1, 2020	$ 6,000
+ Total manufacturing costs incurred in 2020	105,000
= Total manufacturing costs to account for	111,000
− Ending work-in-process inventory, December 31, 2020	7,000
= Cost of goods manufactured in 2020	$104,000

Step 4: Cost of goods sold in 2020. The cost of goods sold is the cost of finished-goods inventory sold to customers during the current accounting period. Looking at the finished-goods inventory box in Exhibit 2-7, we see that the beginning inventory of finished goods of $22,000 and cost of goods manufactured in 2020 of $104,000 "fill up" the finished-goods inventory box. The ending inventory of finished goods of $18,000 becomes the beginning inventory for the next year, and the $108,000 cost of goods sold during 2020 "empties out" the finished-goods inventory.

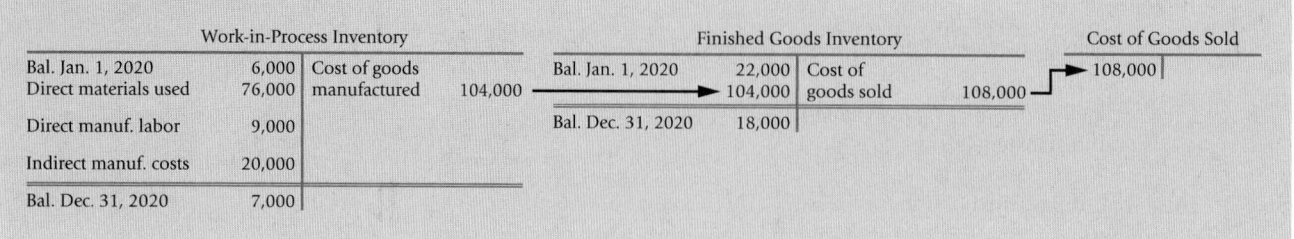

EXHIBIT 2-9 General Ledger T-Accounts for Cellular Products' Manufacturing Cost Flow (in thousands)

Work-in-Process Inventory

Bal. Jan. 1, 2020	6,000	Cost of goods manufactured	104,000
Direct materials used	76,000		
Direct manuf. labor	9,000		
Indirect manuf. costs	20,000		
Bal. Dec. 31, 2020	7,000		

Finished Goods Inventory

Bal. Jan. 1, 2020	22,000	Cost of goods sold	108,000
	104,000		
Bal. Dec. 31, 2020	18,000		

Cost of Goods Sold

108,000	

This cost of goods sold is an expense that is matched against revenues. The cost of goods sold for Cellular Products (shaded olive green) is computed in Exhibit 2-8, Panel A, as follows:

Beginning inventory of finished goods, January 1, 2020	$ 22,000
+ Cost of goods manufactured in 2020	104,000
− Ending inventory of finished goods, December 31, 2020	18,000
= Cost of goods sold in 2020	$108,000

Exhibit 2-9 shows related general ledger T-accounts for Cellular Products' manufacturing cost flow. Note how the cost of goods manufactured ($104,000) is the cost of all goods completed during the accounting period. These costs are all inventoriable costs. Goods completed during the period are transferred to finished-goods inventory. These costs become cost of goods sold in the accounting period when the goods are sold. Also note that the direct materials, direct manufacturing labor, and manufacturing overhead costs of the units in work-in-process inventory ($7,000) and finished-goods inventory ($18,000) as of December 31, 2020, will appear as assets in the balance sheet. These costs will become expenses when the work-in-process inventory is converted to finished goods and the finished goods are sold.

TRY IT! 2-3

Carolyn Corporation provides the following information for 2020.

Beginning work-in-process inventory, January 1, 2020	$ 13,000
Total manufacturing costs incurred in 2020	$169,000
Ending work-in-process inventory, December 31, 2020	$ 6,000
Beginning inventory of finished goods, January 1, 2020	$ 13,000
Ending inventory of finished goods, December 31, 2020	$ 16,000

Calculate (a) Cost of goods manufactured in 2020 and (b) Cost of goods sold in 2020

We can now prepare Cellular Products' income statement for 2020. The income statement of Cellular Products is shown on the right side in Exhibit 2-7 and in Exhibit 2-8, Panel A. Revenues of Cellular Products are (in thousands) $210,000. Inventoriable costs expensed during 2020 equal cost of goods sold of $108,000.

Gross margin = Revenues − Cost of goods sold = $210,000 − $ 108,000 = $102,000.

The $70,000 of operating costs composed of R&D, design, marketing, distribution, and customer-service costs are period costs of Cellular Products. These period costs include, for example, salaries of salespersons, depreciation on computers and other equipment used in marketing, and the cost of leasing warehouse space for distribution. **Operating income** equals total revenues from operations minus cost of goods sold and operating (period) costs (excluding interest expense and income taxes) or, equivalently, gross margin minus period costs. The operating income of Cellular Products is $32,000 (gross margin, $102,000 – period costs, $70,000). Recall from your financial accounting class that period costs are typically summarized under the term *selling, general, and administrative expenses* (SG&A) in the income statement.

Newcomers to cost accounting frequently assume that indirect costs such as rent, telephone, and depreciation are always costs of the period in which they are incurred and are not associated with inventories. When these costs are incurred in marketing or in corporate headquarters, they are period costs. However, when these costs are incurred in manufacturing, they are manufacturing overhead costs and are inventoriable.

Because costs that are inventoried are not expensed until the units associated with them are sold, a manager can produce more units than are expected to be sold in a period without reducing a firm's net income. In fact, building up inventory in this way defers the expensing of (part of) the current period's fixed manufacturing costs as manufacturing costs are inventoried and not expensed until the units are sold in a subsequent period. This in turn actually *increases* the firm's current period gross margin and operating income even though there is no increase in sales, causing outsiders to believe that the company is more profitable than it actually is. We will discuss this risky accounting practice in greater detail in Chapter 9.

Recap of Inventoriable Costs and Period Costs

Exhibit 2-7 highlights the differences between inventoriable costs and period costs for a manufacturing company. The manufacturing costs of finished goods include direct materials; direct manufacturing labor; and manufacturing overhead costs such as supervision, production control, and machine maintenance. All of these costs are inventoriable: They are assigned to work-in-process inventory until the goods are completed, when they are moved to finished-goods inventory until the goods are sold. All nonmanufacturing costs, such as R&D, design, and distribution costs, are period costs.

Inventoriable costs and period costs flow through the income statement at a merchandising company similar to the way costs flow at a manufacturing company. At a merchandising company, however, the flow of costs is much simpler to understand and track. Exhibit 2-10 shows the inventoriable costs and period costs for a retailer or wholesaler that buys goods for resale. The only inventoriable cost is the cost of merchandise. (This corresponds to the cost of finished goods for a manufacturing company.) Purchased goods are held as merchandise inventory, the cost of which is shown as an asset in the balance sheet. As the goods are sold, their costs move to the income statement as the expense item cost of goods sold. A retailer or wholesaler also has a variety of marketing, distribution, and customer-service costs, which are period costs. Period costs are deducted from revenues in the income statement, without ever moving through an inventory asset account.

DECISION POINT

What is the flow of inventoriable and period costs in manufacturing and merchandising settings?

EXHIBIT 2-10 Flow of Revenues and Costs for a Merchandising Company (Retailer or Wholesaler)

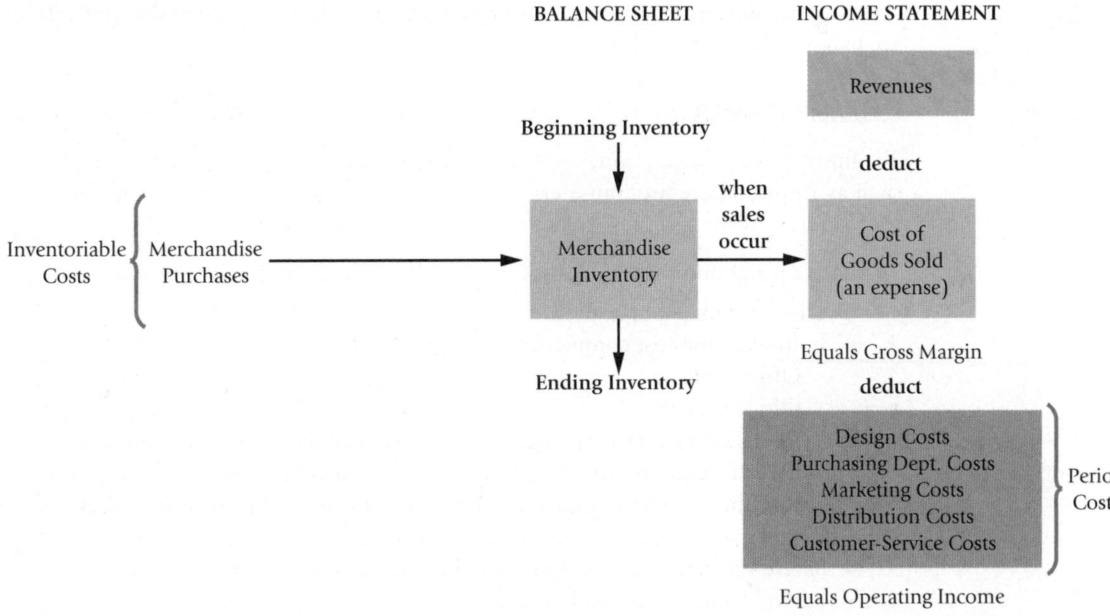

Prime Costs and Conversion Costs

Two terms used to describe cost classifications in manufacturing costing systems are *prime costs* and *conversion costs*. **Prime costs** are all direct manufacturing costs. For Cellular Products,

$$\text{Prime costs} = \text{Direct material costs} + \text{Direct manufacturing labor costs} = \$76{,}000 + \$9{,}000 = \$85{,}000$$

As we have already discussed, the greater the proportion of prime costs (or direct costs) to total costs, the more confident managers can be about the accuracy of the measured costs of products. As information-gathering technology improves, companies can add more and more direct-cost categories. For example, power costs might be metered in specific areas of a plant and identified as a direct cost of specific products. Furthermore, if a production line were dedicated to manufacturing a specific product, the depreciation on the production equipment would be a direct manufacturing cost and would be included in prime costs. Computer software companies often have a "purchased technology" direct manufacturing cost item. This item, which represents payments to suppliers who develop software algorithms for a product, is also included in prime costs. **Conversion costs** are all manufacturing costs other than direct material costs. Conversion costs represent all manufacturing costs incurred to convert direct materials into finished goods. For Cellular Products,

$$\text{Conversion costs} = \begin{matrix}\text{Direct manufacturing}\\ \text{labor costs}\end{matrix} + \begin{matrix}\text{Manufacturing}\\ \text{overhead costs}\end{matrix} = \$9{,}000 + \$20{,}000 = \$29{,}000$$

Note that direct manufacturing labor costs are a part of both prime costs and conversion costs.

Some manufacturing operations, such as computer-integrated manufacturing (CIM) plants, have very few workers. The workers' roles are to monitor the manufacturing process and to maintain the equipment that produces multiple products. The costing systems in CIM plants do not have a direct manufacturing labor cost category because direct manufacturing labor cost is relatively small and because it is difficult to trace this cost to products. In a CIM plant, the only prime cost is the cost of direct materials. The conversion costs for such a plant largely consist of manufacturing overhead costs.

Measuring Costs Requires Judgment

LEARNING OBJECTIVE 7

Explain why product costs are computed in different ways for different purposes

. . . examples are pricing and product-mix decisions, government contracts, and financial statements

We turn our focus back to how cost accounting is used by management accountants. Measuring costs involves a lot of judgment. That is, there are many alternative ways for management accountants to define and classify costs. Generally, the best way to measure a cost depends on the specific situation, purpose, or question that management is trying to address. Moreover, different companies or sometimes even different subunits within the same company may define and classify costs differently. Thus, it is very important to clearly define and understand how costs are measured in a particular situation or company.

Labor Costs

To illustrate the above point, consider labor costs for software programming at companies such as Apple, where programmers work on different software applications for products like the iMac, the iPad, and the iPhone.

- Direct programming labor costs that can be traced to individual products
- Overhead costs (labor related)
  - Indirect labor cost compensation for
    - Office staff
    - Office security
    - Rework labor (time spent by direct laborers correcting software errors)
    - **Overtime premium** (wages paid *in excess* of straight-time rates for overtime work)
    - **Idle time** (wages paid for unproductive time caused by lack of orders, computer breakdowns, delays, poor scheduling, and the like)
  - Salaries for managers, department heads, and supervisors
  - Payroll fringe costs (explained later)

Although labor cost classifications vary among companies, many companies use multiple labor cost categories and subclassifications as above. In general, the salaries of those regarded as management are placed in a separate classification of labor-related overhead and not classified as indirect labor costs.

Benefits of Defining Accounting Terms

Managers, accountants, suppliers, and others will avoid many problems if they clearly define, understand, and agree on how costs are measured when they engage with each other. Consider the classification of programming labor *payroll fringe costs*, which include employer payments for employee benefits such as Social Security, life insurance, health insurance, and pensions. Consider, for example, a software programmer who is paid a wage of $80 an hour with fringe benefits totaling, say, $20 per hour. Some companies classify the $80 as a direct programming labor cost of the product for which the software is being written and the $20 as overhead cost. Other companies classify the entire $100 as direct programming labor cost.

In every situation, it is important for managers and management accountants to clearly define what direct labor includes and what direct labor excludes. This clarity will help prevent disputes regarding cost-reimbursement contracts, income tax payments, and labor union matters, which often can take a substantial amount of time for managers to resolve. Consider that some countries, such as Costa Rica and Mauritius, offer substantial income tax savings to foreign companies that generate employment within their borders. In some cases, to qualify for the tax benefits, the direct labor costs must at least equal a specified percentage of a company's total costs.

When managers do not precisely define direct labor costs, disputes can arise about whether payroll fringe costs should be included as part of direct labor costs when calculating the direct labor percentage for qualifying for such tax benefits. Companies have sought to classify payroll fringe costs as part of direct labor costs to make direct labor costs a higher percentage of total costs. Tax authorities have argued that payroll fringe costs are part of overhead. In addition to payroll fringe costs, other debated items are compensation for training time, idle time, vacations, sick leave, and overtime premium. To prevent disputes, contracts and laws should be as specific as possible about accounting definitions and measurements.

Different Meanings of Product Costs

Many cost terms used by organizations have ambiguous meanings. Consider the term *product cost*. A **product cost** is the sum of the costs assigned to a product for a specific situation, purpose, or question. Different situations may require or result in different measures of product cost, as the brackets on the value chain in Exhibit 2-11 illustrate:

- **Pricing and product-mix decisions.** For the purpose of making decisions about product mix, managers are usually interested in the overall (total) profitability of different products and, consequently, assign costs incurred in all business functions of the value chain to

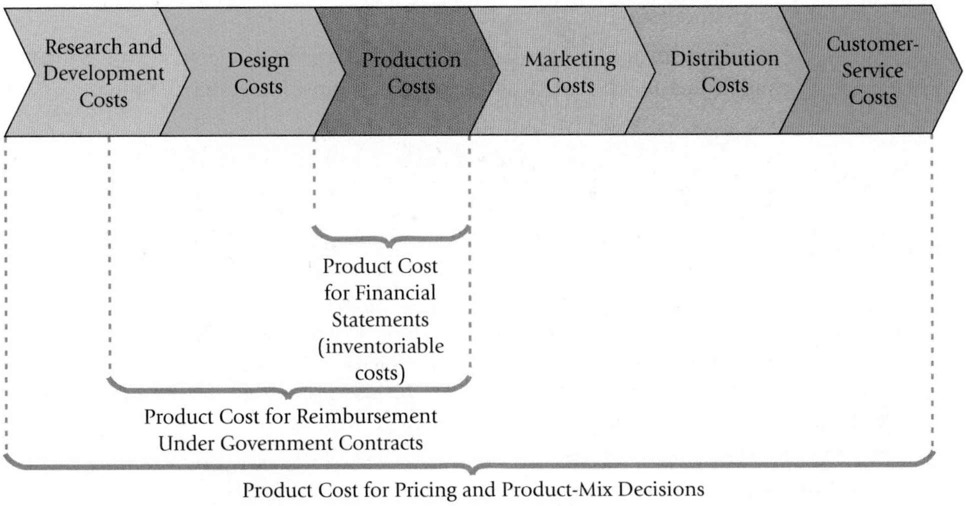

EXHIBIT 2-11

Different Product Costs for Different Purposes

the different products. Similarly, managers typically make decisions about product pricing also based on product costs that include costs incurred in all business functions of the value chain.

- **Reimbursement under government contracts.** Government contracts often reimburse contractors based on the "cost of a product" plus a pre-specified margin of profit. A contract such as this is referred to as a "cost-plus" agreement. Cost-plus agreements are typically used for services and development contracts when it is not easy to predict the amount of money required to design, fabricate, and test items. Because these contracts transfer the risk of cost overruns to the government, agencies such as the Department of Defense and the Department of Energy provide detailed guidelines on the cost items they will allow (and disallow) when calculating the cost of a product. For example, many government agencies explicitly exclude marketing, distribution, and customer-service costs from product costs that qualify for reimbursement, and they may only reimburse R&D costs up to a point. These agencies want to reimburse contractors for only those costs most closely related to delivering products under the contract. The second bracket in Exhibit 2-11 shows how the product-cost calculations for a specific contract may allow for all design and production costs but only part of R&D costs.
- **Preparing financial statements for external reporting under Generally Accepted Accounting Principles (GAAP).** As we discussed in the previous two sections, under GAAP, only manufacturing costs can be assigned to inventories in the financial statements. For the purposes of calculating inventory costs, product costs include only inventoriable (production) costs.

DECISION POINT

Why do managers assign different costs to the same cost objects?

As Exhibit 2-11 illustrates, product-cost measures range from a narrow set of costs for financial statements—a set that includes only production costs—to a broader set of costs for reimbursement under government contracts to a still broader set of costs for pricing and product-mix decisions.

This section focused on how different situations, purposes, and questions result in the inclusion or exclusion of the costs of *different business functions of the value chain* when calculating product costs. The same level of care in terms of clearly defining and understanding how costs are measured should be applied to each cost classification, or cost dimension, introduced in this chapter. Exhibit 2-12 summarizes the key cost classifications. Using the five-step process described in Chapter 1, think about how these different cost classifications help managers make decisions and evaluate performance.

1. **Identify the problem and uncertainties.** Consider a decision about how much to price a product. This decision often depends on how much it costs to make the product.
2. **Obtain information.** Managers identify the direct and indirect costs of a product in each business function. Managers also gather other information about customers, competitors, and the prices of competing products.
3. **Make predictions about the future.** Managers estimate what it will cost to make the product in the future. This requires managers to predict the quantity of the product they expect the company to sell as well as have an understanding of fixed and variable costs.
4. **Make decisions by choosing among alternatives.** Managers choose a price to charge based on a thorough understanding of costs and other information.
5. **Implement the decision, evaluate performance, and learn.** Managers control costs and learn by comparing the actual total costs and unit costs against budgeted amounts.

EXHIBIT 2-12

Alternative Classifications of Costs

1. Business function
   a. Research and development
   b. Design of products and processes
   c. Production
   d. Marketing
   e. Distribution
   f. Customer service
2. Assignment to a cost object
   a. Direct cost
   b. Indirect cost
3. Behavior pattern in relation to the level of activity or volume
   a. Variable cost
   b. Fixed cost
4. Aggregate or average
   a. Total cost
   b. Unit cost
5. Assets or expenses
   a. Inventoriable cost
   b. Period cost

The next section describes how the basic concepts introduced in this chapter lead to a framework for understanding cost accounting and cost management that can then be applied to the study of many topics such as strategy evaluation, quality, and investment decisions.

A Framework for Cost Accounting and Cost Management

LEARNING OBJECTIVE 8

Describe a framework for cost accounting and cost management

. . . three features that help managers make decisions

The following three features of cost accounting and cost management can be used for a wide range of applications:

1. Calculating the cost of products, services, and other cost objects.
2. Obtaining information for planning and control and performance evaluation.
3. Analyzing the relevant information for making decisions.

We develop these ideas in Chapters 3 through 12. The ideas also form the foundation for the study of various topics later in the text.

Calculating the Cost of Products, Services, and Other Cost Objects

You have already learned that costing systems trace direct costs and allocate indirect costs to cost objects. Chapters 4 and 5 describe systems such as job costing and activity-based costing, which are used to calculate total costs and unit costs of products and services. The chapters also discuss how managers use this information to formulate business strategies and make pricing, product-mix, and cost-management decisions.

Obtaining Information for Planning and Control and Performance Evaluation

Budgeting is the most commonly used tool for planning and control. A budget forces managers to look ahead, to translate a company's strategy into plans, to coordinate and communicate within the organization, and to provide a benchmark for evaluating the company's performance. Managers strive to meet their budget targets, so budgeting often affects the behavior of a company's personnel and the decisions they make. Chapter 6 describes budgeting systems.

At the end of a reporting period, managers compare the company's actual results to its planned performance. The managers' tasks are to understand why differences (called variances) between actual and planned performance arise and to use the information provided by these variances as feedback to promote learning and future improvement. Managers also use variances as well as nonfinancial measures, such as defect rates and customer satisfaction ratings, to control and evaluate the performance of various departments, divisions, and managers. Chapters 7 and 8 discuss variance analysis. Chapter 9 describes planning, control, and inventory-costing issues relating to capacity. Chapters 6, 7, 8, and 9 focus on the management accountant's role in implementing strategy.

Analyzing the Relevant Information for Making Decisions

When designing strategies and implementing them, managers must understand which revenues and costs to consider and which ones to ignore. Management accountants help managers identify what information is relevant and what information is irrelevant. Consider a decision about whether to buy a product from an outside vendor or to make it in-house. The costing system indicates that it costs $25 per unit to make the product in-house. A vendor offers to sell the product for $22 per unit. At first glance, it seems it will cost less for the company to buy the product rather than make it. Suppose, however, that of the $25 to make the product in-house, $5 are attributable to plant lease costs that the company has already paid under a lease contract. Furthermore, if the product is bought, the plant will remain idle because it is too costly to retool the plant to make another product. That is, there is no opportunity to use the plant in some other profitable way.

Under these conditions, it will cost less to make the product than to buy it. That's because making the product costs only an *additional* $20 per unit ($25 − $5), compared with an *additional* $22 per unit if it is bought. The $5 per unit of lease cost is irrelevant to the decision because it is a *past* (or *sunk*) cost that has already been incurred regardless of whether the product is made or bought. Analyzing relevant information is a key aspect of making decisions.

When making strategic decisions about which products and how much to produce, managers must know how revenues and costs vary with changes in output levels. For this purpose, managers need to separate fixed costs and variable costs. Chapter 3 analyzes how operating income changes with changes in units sold and how managers use this information to make decisions such as how much to spend on advertising. Chapters 10 and 11 describe methods to estimate the fixed and variable components of costs and to make predictions. Chapter 12 applies the concept of relevance to decision making in many different situations and describes methods managers use to maximize income given the resource constraints they face.

Later chapters in the text discuss topics such as strategy evaluation, customer profitability, quality, just-in-time systems, investment decisions, transfer pricing, and performance evaluation. Each of these topics invariably has product costing, planning and control, and decision-making perspectives. A command of the first 12 chapters will help you master these topics. For example, Chapter 13 on strategy describes the balanced scorecard, a set of financial and nonfinancial measures used to implement strategy that builds on the planning and control functions. The section on strategic analysis of operating income builds on ideas of product costing and variance analysis. The section on downsizing and managing capacity builds on ideas of relevant revenues and relevant costs.

DECISION POINT

What are the three key features of cost accounting and cost management?

PROBLEM FOR SELF-STUDY

Foxwood Company is a metal- and woodcutting manufacturer, selling products to the home-construction market. Consider the following data for 2020:

Sandpaper	$ 2,000
Materials-handling costs	70,000
Lubricants and coolants	5,000
Miscellaneous indirect manufacturing labor	40,000
Direct manufacturing labor	300,000
Direct materials inventory, January 1, 2020	40,000
Direct materials inventory, December 31, 2020	50,000
Finished-goods inventory, January 1, 2020	100,000
Finished-goods inventory, December 31, 2020	150,000
Work-in-process inventory, January 1, 2020	10,000
Work-in-process inventory, December 31, 2020	14,000
Plant-leasing costs	54,000
Depreciation—plant equipment	36,000
Property taxes on plant equipment	4,000
Fire insurance on plant equipment	3,000
Direct materials purchased	460,000
Revenues	1,360,000
Marketing promotions	60,000
Marketing salaries	100,000
Distribution costs	70,000
Customer-service costs	100,000

Required

1. Prepare an income statement with a separate supporting schedule of cost of goods manufactured. For all manufacturing items, classify costs as direct costs or indirect costs and indicate by V or F whether each is a variable cost or a fixed cost (when the cost object is a product unit). If in doubt, decide on the basis of whether the total cost will change substantially over a wide range of units produced.

2. Suppose that both the direct material costs and the plant-leasing costs are for the production of 900,000 units. What is the direct material cost of each unit produced? What is the plant-leasing cost per unit? Assume that the plant-leasing cost is a fixed cost.
3. Suppose Foxwood Company manufactures 1,000,000 units next year. Repeat the computation in requirement 2 for direct materials and plant-leasing costs. Assume the implied cost-behavior patterns persist.
4. As a management consultant, explain concisely to the company president why the unit cost for direct materials did not change in requirements 2 and 3 but the unit cost for plant-leasing costs did change.

Solution

1.

Foxwood Company
Income Statement
For the Year Ended December 31, 2020

Revenues		$ 1,360,000
Cost of goods sold		
Beginning finished-goods inventory, January 1, 2020	$ 100,000	
Cost of goods manufactured (see the following schedule)	960,000	
Cost of goods available for sale	1,060,000	
Deduct ending finished-goods inventory, December 31, 2020	150,000	910,000
Gross margin (or gross profit)		450,000
Operating costs		
Marketing promotions	60,000	
Marketing salaries	100,000	
Distribution costs	70,000	
Customer-service costs	100,000	330,000
Operating income		$ 120,000

Foxwood Company
Schedule of Cost of Goods Manufactured
For the Year Ended December 31, 2020

Direct materials		
Beginning inventory, January 1, 2020		$ 40,000
Purchases of direct materials		460,000
Cost of direct materials available for use		500,000
Ending inventory, December 31, 2020		50,000
Direct materials used		450,000 (V)
Direct manufacturing labor		300,000 (V)
Indirect manufacturing costs		
Sandpaper	$ 2,000 (V)	
Materials-handling costs	70,000 (V)	
Lubricants and coolants	5,000 (V)	
Miscellaneous indirect manufacturing labor	40,000 (V)	
Plant-leasing costs	54,000 (F)	
Depreciation—plant equipment	36,000 (F)	
Property taxes on plant equipment	4,000 (F)	
Fire insurance on plant equipment	3,000 (F)	214,000
Manufacturing costs incurred during 2020		964,000
Beginning work-in-process inventory, January 1, 2020		10,000
Total manufacturing costs to account for		974,000
Ending work-in-process inventory, December 31, 2020		14,000
Cost of goods manufactured (to income statement)		$ 960,000

2. Direct material unit cost = Direct materials used ÷ Units produced
= \$450,000 ÷ 900,000 units = \$0.50 per unit
Plant-leasing unit cost = Plant-leasing costs ÷ Units produced
= \$54,000 ÷ 900,000 units = \$0.06 per unit
3. The direct material costs are variable, so they would increase in total from \$450,000 to \$500,000 (1,000,000 units × \$0.50 per unit). However, their unit cost would be unaffected: \$500,000 ÷ 1,000,000 units = \$0.50 per unit.

   In contrast, the plant-leasing costs of \$54,000 are fixed, so they would not increase in total. However, the plant-leasing cost per unit would decline from \$0.060 to \$0.054: \$54,000 ÷ 1,000,000 units = \$0.054 per unit.
4. The explanation would begin with the answer to requirement 3. As a consultant, you should stress that the unitizing (averaging) of costs that have different behavior patterns can be misleading. A common error is to assume that a total unit cost, which is often a sum of variable unit cost and fixed unit cost, is an indicator that total costs change in proportion to changes in production levels. The next chapter demonstrates the necessity for distinguishing between cost-behavior patterns. You must be wary, especially about unit fixed costs. Too often, unit fixed cost is erroneously regarded as being indistinguishable from unit variable cost.

DECISION POINTS

The following question-and-answer format summarizes the chapter's learning objectives. Each decision presents a key question related to a learning objective. The guidelines are the answer to that question.

Decision	Guidelines
1. What is a cost object?	A cost object is anything for which a manager needs a separate measurement of cost. Examples include a product, a service, a project, a customer, a brand category, an activity, and a department.
2. How do managers decide whether a cost is a direct or an indirect cost?	A direct cost is any cost that is directly related to a particular cost object and that can easily and unambiguously be traced to that cost object. An indirect cost is any cost that is related to a particular cost object but that cannot easily and unambiguously be traced to it. The same cost can be direct with respect to one cost object and indirect with respect to another cost object. This text uses *cost tracing* to describe the assignment of direct costs to a cost object and *cost allocation* to describe the assignment of indirect costs to a cost object.
3. How do managers decide whether a cost is a variable or a fixed cost?	A variable cost changes *in its total level* in proportion to changes in the volume, or number of units achieved, of the cost object. A fixed cost remains unchanged *in its total level* for a given time period, despite wide changes in the volume, or number of units achieved, of the cost object.
4. How should managers estimate and interpret cost information?	In general, focus on total costs, not unit costs. When making total cost estimates, think of variable costs as an amount per unit and fixed costs as a total amount. Interpret the unit cost of a cost object cautiously when it includes a fixed-cost component.
5. What are the differences between the financial accounting concepts of inventoriable and period costs?	Inventoriable costs are all costs of a product that a company regards as an asset in the accounting period in which they are incurred and which become cost of goods sold in the accounting period in which the product is sold. Period costs are expensed in the accounting period in which they are incurred and are all of the costs in an income statement other than cost of goods sold.

Decision	Guidelines
6. What is the flow of inventoriable and period costs in manufacturing and merchandising settings?	In manufacturing settings, inventoriable costs flow through work in process and finished-goods accounts, and are expensed as cost of goods sold when the products are sold. Period costs are expensed as they are incurred. In merchandising settings, only the cost of merchandise is treated as inventoriable; all other costs are treated as period costs.
7. Why do managers assign different costs to the same cost objects?	Managers may assign different costs to the same cost object depending on the specific situation, purpose, or question that management is trying to address. For example, for external reporting purposes in a manufacturing company, the inventoriable cost of a product includes only manufacturing costs. In contrast, costs from all business functions of the value chain are often assigned to a product for pricing and product-mix decisions.
8. What are the three key features of cost accounting and cost management?	Three key features of cost accounting and cost management are (1) calculating the cost of products, services, and other cost objects; (2) obtaining information for planning and control and performance evaluation; and (3) analyzing relevant information for making decisions.

TERMS TO LEARN

This chapter contains more basic terms than any other in this text. Do not proceed before you check your understanding of the following terms. The chapter and the Glossary at the end of the text contain definitions of the following important terms:

actual cost (**p. 29**)
average cost (**p. 37**)
budgeted cost (**p. 29**)
conversion costs (**p. 46**)
cost (**p. 29**)
cost accumulation (**p. 29**)
cost allocation (**p. 30**)
cost assignment (**p. 30**)
cost driver (**p. 35**)
cost object (**p. 29**)
cost of goods manufactured (**p. 43**)
cost tracing (**p. 30**)
direct costs of a cost object (**p. 29**)
direct manufacturing labor costs (**p. 39**)
direct materials costs (**p. 39**)
direct materials inventory (**p. 39**)
factory overhead costs (**p. 39**)
finished-goods inventory (**p. 39**)
fixed cost (**p. 32**)
idle time (**p. 46**)
indirect costs of a cost object (**p. 30**)
indirect manufacturing costs (**p. 39**)
inventoriable costs (**p. 39**)
manufacturing overhead costs (**p. 39**)
manufacturing-sector companies (**p. 38**)
merchandising-sector companies (**p. 38**)
operating income (**p. 44**)
overtime premium (**p. 46**)
period costs (**p. 40**)
prime costs (**p. 46**)
product cost (**p. 47**)
relevant range (**p. 35**)
revenues (**p. 39**)
service-sector companies (**p. 38**)
unit cost (**p. 37**)
variable cost (**p. 32**)
work-in-process inventory (**p. 39**)
work in progress (**p. 39**)

ASSIGNMENT MATERIAL

Questions

2-1 Define cost object and give three examples.
2-2 Define direct costs and indirect costs.
2-3 Why do managers consider direct costs to be more accurate than indirect costs?
2-4 Name three factors that will affect the classification of a cost as direct or indirect.
2-5 Define variable cost and fixed cost. Give an example of each.
2-6 Give an example for each of the following: A cost that is variable and direct, a cost that is variable and indirect, a cost that is fixed and direct, and a cost that is fixed and indirect.
2-7 What is a cost driver? Give one example.

2-8 What is the relevant range? What role does the relevant-range concept play in explaining how costs behave?

2-9 Explain why unit costs must often be interpreted with caution.

2-10 Describe how manufacturing-, merchandising-, and service-sector companies differ from one another.

2-11 What are three different types of inventory that manufacturing companies hold?

2-12 Distinguish between inventoriable costs and period costs.

2-13 Define the following: direct material costs, direct manufacturing-labor costs, manufacturing overhead costs, prime costs, and conversion costs.

2-14 Define product cost. Describe three different purposes for computing product costs.

2-15 What are three features of cost accounting and cost management that can be used for a wide range of applications?

Multiple-Choice Questions

In partnership with: BECKER PROFESSIONAL EDUCATION®

2-16 Applewhite Corporation, a manufacturing company, is analyzing its cost structure in a project to achieve some cost savings. Which of the following statements is/are correct?

I. The cost of the direct materials in Applewhite's products is considered a variable cost.
II. The cost of the depreciation of Applewhite's plant machinery is considered a variable cost because Applewhite uses an accelerated depreciation method for both book and income tax purposes.
III. The cost of electricity for Applewhite's manufacturing facility is considered a fixed cost, even if the cost of the electricity has both variable and fixed components.

1. I, II, and III are correct.
2. I only is correct.
3. II and III only are correct.
4. None of the listed choices is correct.

2-17 Comprehensive Care Nursing Home is required by statute and regulation to maintain a minimum 3:1 ratio of direct service staff to residents to maintain the licensure associated with nursing home beds. The salary expense associated with direct service staff for Comprehensive Care Nursing Home would most likely be classified as

1. Variable cost.
2. Fixed cost.
3. Overhead costs.
4. Inventoriable costs.

2-18 Frisco Corporation is analyzing its fixed and variable costs within its current relevant range. As its cost driver activity changes within the relevant range, which of the following statements is/are correct?

I. As the cost driver level increases, total fixed cost remains unchanged.
II. As the cost driver level increases, unit fixed cost increases.
III. As the cost driver level decreases, unit variable cost decreases.

1. I, II, and III are correct.
2. I and II only are correct.
3. I only is correct.
4. II and III only are correct.

2-19 Year 1 financial data for the ABC Company is as follows:

Sales	$5,000,000
Direct materials	850,000
Direct manufacturing labor	1,700,000
Variable manufacturing overhead	400,000
Fixed manufacturing overhead	750,000
Variable SG&A	150,000
Fixed SG&A	250,000

Under the absorption method, Year 1 cost of goods sold will be

a. $2,550,000 **c.** $3,100,000
b. $2,950,000 **d.** $3,700,000

2-20 The following information was extracted from the accounting records of Roosevelt Manufacturing Company:

Direct materials purchased	80,000
Direct materials used	76,000
Direct manufacturing labor costs	10,000
Indirect manufacturing labor costs	12,000
Sales salaries	14,000
Other plant expenses	22,000
Selling and administrative expenses	20,000

What was the cost of goods manufactured?

1. $124,000
2. $120,000
3. $154,000
4. $170,000

Exercises

2-21 Computing and interpreting manufacturing unit costs. Minnesota Office Products produces three different paper products at its Vaasa lumber plant: Supreme, Deluxe, and Regular. Each product has its own dedicated production line at the plant. It currently uses the following three-part classification for its manufacturing costs: direct materials, direct manufacturing labor, and manufacturing overhead costs. Total manufacturing overhead costs of the plant in July 2020 are $150 million ($15 million of which are fixed). This total amount is allocated to each product line on the basis of the direct manufacturing labor costs of each line. Summary data (in millions) for July 2020 are as follows:

	Supreme	Deluxe	Regular
Direct material costs	$ 89	$ 57	$ 60
Direct manufacturing labor costs	$ 16	$ 26	$ 8
Manufacturing overhead costs	$ 48	$ 78	$ 24
Units produced	125	150	140

Required

1. Compute the manufacturing cost per unit for each product produced in July 2020.
2. Suppose that, in August 2020, production was 150 million units of Supreme, 190 million units of Deluxe, and 220 million units of Regular. Why might the July 2020 information on manufacturing cost per unit be misleading when predicting total manufacturing costs in August 2020?

2-22 Direct, indirect, fixed, and variable costs. Florida Growers Association produces both orange and grapefruit juice that it sells as wholesale products to various grocery suppliers. Each type of juice requires a three-step process. The first step is the preparation department, which cleans the fruit. The second step is the squeezing department, which combines some of the necessary sugars and added flavoring to create the juice. This step also includes quality control using both automated and manual processes. The final step is packaging, which is an entirely automated process.

Required

1. Costs involved in the process are listed next. For each cost, indicate whether it is a direct variable, direct fixed, indirect variable, or indirect fixed cost with respect to the cost object "one gallon of grapefruit juice".

   Costs:

Wages of the operator of the packaging machine	Cost of the oranges and grapefruit
Cartons for the juice	Wages of the fruit cleaners in the first step
Cost of the cleansers used to clean the fruit in step one.	Wages of the machinist running the squeezing machine
Depreciation on packaging machines	Property taxes on the factory building
Wages of the factory cleaning crew	Night security for the factory
Depreciation of the factory building	Sugars and flavorings of the juices
Cost of pest control of the factory	Water and electricity costs of the factory
Hurricane insurance on factory building	Oil, grease, etc. for factory machines
Salary of the production supervisor	Cost of disinfectants to clean the factory

2. If the cost object were the "squeezing department" rather than a gallon of grapefruit juice, which of the preceding costs would now be considered direct rather than indirect?

2-23 Classification of costs, service sector. Market Focus is a marketing research firm that organizes focus groups for consumer-product companies. Each focus group has eight individuals who are paid $60 per session to provide comments on new products. These focus groups meet in hotels and are led by a trained, independent marketing specialist hired by Market Focus. Each specialist is paid a fixed retainer to conduct a minimum number of sessions and a per session fee of $2,200. A Market Focus staff member attends each session to ensure that all the logistical aspects run smoothly.

Required

Classify each cost item **(A–I)** as follows:

a. Direct or indirect (D or I) costs of each individual focus group.

b. Variable or fixed (V or F) costs of how the total costs of Market Focus change as the number of focus groups conducted changes. (If in doubt, select on the basis of whether the total costs will change substantially if there is a large change in the number of groups conducted.)

You will have two answers (D or I; V or F) for each of the following items:

Cost Item	D or I	V or F
A. Payment to individuals in each focus group to provide comments on new products		
B. Annual subscription of Market Focus to *Consumer Reports* magazine		
C. Phone calls made by Market Focus staff member to confirm individuals will attend a focus group session (Records of individual calls are not kept.)		
D. Retainer paid to focus group leader to conduct 18 focus groups per year on new medical products		
E. Recruiting cost to hire marketing specialists		
F. Lease payment by Market Focus for corporate office		
G. Cost of tapes used to record comments made by individuals in a focus group session (These tapes are sent to the company whose products are being tested.)		
H. Gasoline costs of Market Focus staff for company-owned vehicles (Staff members submit monthly bills with no mileage breakdowns.)		
I. Costs incurred to improve the design of focus groups to make them more effective		

2-24 Classification of costs, merchandising sector. Essential College Supplies (ECS) is a store on the campus on a large Midwestern university. The store has both an apparel section (t-shirts with the school logo) and a convenience section. ECS reports revenues for the apparel section separately from the convenience section.

Required

Classify each cost item **(A–H)** as follows:

a. Direct or indirect (D or I) costs of the total number of t-shirts sold.

b. Variable or fixed (V or F) costs of how the total costs of the apparel section change as the total number of t-shirts sold changes. (If in doubt, select on the basis of whether the total costs will change substantially if there is a large change in the total number of t-shirts sold.)

You will have two answers (D or I; V or F) for each of the following items:

Cost Item	D or I	V or F
A. Annual fee for licensing the school logo		
B. Cost of store manager's salary		
C. Costs of t-shirts purchased for sale to customers		
D. Subscription to *College Apparel Trends* magazine		
E. Leasing of computer software used for financial budgeting at the ECS store		
F. Cost of coffee provided free to all customers of the ECS store		
G. Cost of cleaning the store every night after closing		
H. Freight-in costs of t-shirts purchased by ECS		

2-25 Classification of costs, manufacturing sector. The Cooper Furniture Company of Potomac, Maryland, assembles two types of chairs (recliners and rockers). Separate assembly lines are used for each type of chair.

Required

Classify each cost item **(A–I)** as follows:

a. Direct or indirect (D or I) cost for the total number of recliners assembled.

b. Variable or fixed (V or F) cost depending on how total costs change as the total number of recliners assembled changes. (If in doubt, select on the basis of whether the total costs will change substantially if there is a large change in the total number of recliners assembled.)

You will have two answers (D or I; V or F) for each of the following items:

Cost Item	D or I	V or F
A. Cost of fabric used on recliners		
B. Salary of public relations manager for Cooper Furniture		
C. Annual convention for furniture manufacturers; generally Cooper Furniture attends		
D. Cost of lubricant used on the recliner assembly line		
E. Freight costs of recliner frames shipped from Durham, NC, to Potomac, MD		
F. Electricity costs for recliner assembly line (single bill covers entire plant)		
G. Wages paid to temporary assembly-line workers hired in periods of high recliner production (paid on hourly basis)		
H. Annual fire-insurance policy cost for Potomac, MD, plant		
I. Wages paid to plant manager who oversees the assembly lines for both chair types		

2-26 Variable costs, fixed costs, total costs. Bridget Ashton is getting ready to open a small restaurant. She is on a tight budget and must choose between the following long-distance phone plans:

Plan A: Pay $0.10 per minute of long-distance calling.

Plan B: Pay a fixed monthly fee of $15 for up to 240 long-distance minutes and $0.08 per minute thereafter (if she uses fewer than 240 minutes in any month, she still pays $15 for the month).

Plan C: Pay a fixed monthly fee of $22 for up to 510 long-distance minutes and $0.05 per minute thereafter (if she uses fewer than 510 minutes, she still pays $22 for the month).

Required

1. Draw a graph of the total monthly costs of the three plans for different levels of monthly long-distance calling.
2. Which plan should Ashton choose if she expects to make 100 minutes of long-distance calls? 240 minutes? 540 minutes?

2-27 Variable and fixed costs. Consolidated Motors specializes in producing one specialty vehicle. It is called Surfer and is styled to easily fit multiple surfboards in its back area and top-mounted storage racks. Consolidated has the following manufacturing costs:

Plant management costs, $1,992,000 per year

Cost of leasing equipment, $1,932,000 per year

Workers' wages, $800 per Surfer vehicle produced

Direct materials costs: Steel, $1,400 per Surfer; Tires, $150 per tire, each Surfer takes 5 tires (one spare).

City license, which is charged monthly based on the number of tires used in production:

0–500 tires	$ 40,040
501–1,000 tires	$ 65,000
more than 1,000 tires	$249,870

Consolidated currently produces 170 vehicles per month.

Required

1. What is the variable manufacturing cost per vehicle? What is the fixed manufacturing cost per month?
2. Plot a graph for the variable manufacturing costs and a second for the fixed manufacturing costs per month. How does the concept of relevant range relate to your graphs? Explain.
3. What is the total manufacturing cost of each vehicle if 80 vehicles are produced each month? 205 vehicles? How do you explain the difference in the manufacturing cost per unit?

Required

2-28 Cost behavior. Compute the missing amounts.

	Variable Costs		Fixed Costs	
	Per Unit	Total	Per Unit	Total
If 10,000 units are produced	$5	?	$3	?
If 20,000 units are produced	?	?	?	?
If 50,000 units are produced	?	?	?	?

2-29 Variable costs, fixed costs, relevant range. Gummy Land Candies manufactures jawbreaker candies in a fully automated process. The machine that produces candies was purchased recently and can make 5,000 jawbreakers per month. The machine cost $6,500 and is depreciated using straight-line depreciation over 10 years assuming zero residual value. Rent for the factory space and warehouse and other fixed manufacturing overhead costs total $1,200 per month.

Gummy Land currently makes and sells 3,900 jawbreakers per month. Gummy Land buys just enough materials each month to make the jawbreakers it needs to sell. Materials cost $0.40 per jawbreaker.

Next year Gummy Land expects demand to increase by 100%. At this volume of materials purchased, it will get a 10% discount on price. Rent and other fixed manufacturing overhead costs will remain the same.

Required

1. What is Gummy Land's current annual relevant range of output?
2. What is Gummy Land's current annual fixed manufacturing cost within the relevant range? What is the annual variable manufacturing cost?
3. What will Gummy Land's relevant range of output be next year? How, if at all, will total annual fixed and variable manufacturing costs change next year? Assume that if it needs to, Gummy Land could buy an identical machine at the same cost as the one it already has.

2-30 Cost drivers and value chain. American Technology Company (ATC) is developing a new camera/security home system to compete with other security systems in the industry. The company will sell the cameras to wholesalers that will, in turn, sell them in retail stores to the final customer. ATC has undertaken the following activities in its value chain to bring its product to market:

A. Perform market research on competing brands
B. Design a prototype of the phone app and the security camera
C. Test the compatibility of the phone app and the security camera
D. Make necessary design changes to the prototype based on testing performed in C above.
E. Manufacture the security cameras
F. Attend trade shows to make wholesalers aware of the camera
G. Process orders from the trade show orders and wholesalers
H. Deliver the security cameras to the wholesalers
I. Provide online assistance to the security camera users
J. Make additional design changes to the security camera based on customer feedback

During the process of product development, production, marketing, distribution, and customer service, ATC has kept track of the following cost drivers:

Number of security cameras shipped by ATC
Number of design changes
Number of deliveries made to wholesalers
Engineering hours spent on initial product design
Hours spent researching competing market brands
Customer-service hours
Number of security camera orders processed
Machine-hours required to run the production equipment
Number of product tests conducted
FTEs spent on attending trade shows

Required

1. Identify each value-chain activity listed at the beginning of the exercise with one of the following value-chain categories:
   a. Design of products and processes
   b. Production
   c. Marketing
   d. Distribution
   e. Customer service
2. Use the list of preceding cost drivers to find one or more reasonable cost drivers for each of the activities in ATC's value chain.

2-31 Cost drivers and functions. The representative cost drivers in the right column of this table are randomized so they do not match the list of functions in the left column.

Function	Representative Cost Driver
1. Accounts payable	A. Number of invoices sent
2. Human resources	B. Number of purchase orders
3. Equipment maintenance	C. Number of customers
4. Catalog mailings	D. Number of machines
5. Purchasing	E. Number of employees
6. Warehousing	F. Number of bills received from vendors
7. Accounts receivable	G. Number of pallets moved

Required

1. Match each function with its representative cost driver.
2. Give a second example of a cost driver for each function.

2-32 Total costs and unit costs, service setting. National Training recently started a business providing training events for corporations. In order to better understand the profitability of the business, the owners asked you for an analysis of costs—what costs are fixed, what costs are variable, and so on, for each training session. You have the following cost information:

Trainer: $11,000 per session

Materials: $2,500 per session and $35 per attendee

Catering Costs (subcontracted):

Food: $75 per attendee

Setup/cleanup: $25 per attendee

Fixed fee: $5,000 per training session

National Training is pleased with the service they use for the catering and have allowed them to place brochures on each dinner table as a form of advertising. In exchange, the caterer gives National Training a $1,000 discount per session.

Required

1. Draw a graph depicting fixed costs, variable costs, and total costs for each training session versus the number of guests.
2. Suppose 100 persons attend the next event. What is National Training's total net cost and the cost per attendee?
3. Suppose instead that 175 persons attend. What is National Training's total net cost and the cost per attendee?
4. How should National Training charge customers for their services? Explain briefly.

2-33 Total and unit cost, decision making. Gayle's Glassworks makes glass flanges for scientific use. Materials cost $1 per flange, and the glass blowers are paid a wage rate of $28 per hour. A glass blower blows 10 flanges per hour. Fixed manufacturing costs for flanges are $28,000 per period. Period (nonmanufacturing) costs associated with flanges are $10,000 per period and are fixed.

Required

1. Graph the fixed, variable, and total manufacturing cost for flanges, using units (number of flanges) on the *x*-axis.
2. Assume Gayle's Glassworks manufactures and sells 5,000 flanges this period. Its competitor, Flora's Flasks, sells flanges for $10 each. Can Gayle sell below Flora's price and still make a profit on the flanges?
3. How would your answer to requirement 2 differ if Gayle's Glassworks made and sold 10,000 flanges this period? Why? What does this indicate about the use of unit cost in decision making?

2-34 Inventoriable costs versus period costs. Each of the following cost items pertains to one of these companies: Home Depot (a merchandising-sector company), Apple (a manufacturing-sector company), and Rent a Nanny (a service-sector company):

A. Cost of lumber and plumbing supplies available for sale at Home Depot
B. Electricity used to provide lighting for assembly-line workers at an Apple manufacturing plant
C. Depreciation on store shelving in Home Depot
D. Mileage paid to nannies traveling to clients for Rent a Nanny
E. Wages for personnel responsible for quality testing of the Apple products during the assembly process
F. Salaries of Rent a Nanny marketing personnel planning local-newspaper advertising campaigns
G. Lunches provided to the nannies for Rent a Nanny
H. Salaries of employees at Apple retail stores
I. Shipping costs for Apple to transport products to retail stores

Required

1. Distinguish between manufacturing-, merchandising-, and service-sector companies.
2. Distinguish between inventoriable costs and period costs.
3. Classify each of the cost items (**A–I**) as an inventoriable cost or a period cost. Explain your answers.

Problems

2-35 Computing cost of goods purchased and cost of goods sold. The following data are for Murray Department Store. The account balances (in thousands) are for 2020.

Marketing, distribution, and customer-service costs	$ 35,000
Merchandise inventory, January 1, 2020	22,000
Utilities	18,000
General and administrative costs	40,000
Merchandise inventory, December 31, 2020	33,000
Purchases	150,000
Miscellaneous costs	3,000
Transportation-in	5,000
Purchase returns and allowances	2,000
Purchase discounts	8,000
Revenues	290,000

Required

1. Compute **(a)** the cost of goods purchased and **(b)** the cost of goods sold.
2. Prepare the income statement for 2020.

2-36 Cost of goods purchased, cost of goods sold, and income statement. The following data are for Mama Retail Outlet Stores. The account balances (in thousands) are for 2020.

Marketing and advertising costs	$ 54,000
Merchandise inventory, January 1, 2020	94,000
Shipping of merchandise to customers	10,000
Depreciation on store fixtures	8,800
Purchases	521,000
General and administrative costs	63,000
Merchandise inventory, December 31, 2020	101,000
Merchandise freight-in	21,000
Purchase returns and allowances	25,000
Purchase discounts	22,000
Revenues	690,000

Required

1. Compute **(a)** the cost of goods purchased and **(b)** the cost of goods sold.
2. Prepare the income statement for 2020.

2-37 Flow of Inventoriable Costs. Stewart Tables' selected data for March 2020 are presented here (in millions):

Direct materials inventory, March 1, 2020	$ 90
Direct materials purchased	345
Direct materials used	365
Total manufacturing overhead costs	485
Variable manufacturing overhead costs	270
Total manufacturing costs incurred during March 2020	1,570
Work-in-process inventory, March 1, 2020	215
Cost of goods manufactured	1,640
Finished-goods inventory, March 1, 2020	160
Cost of goods sold	1,740

Required

Calculate the following costs:

1. Direct materials inventory, March 31, 2020
2. Fixed manufacturing overhead costs for March 2020
3. Direct manufacturing labor costs for March 2020
4. Work-in-process inventory, March 31, 2020
5. Cost of finished goods available for sale in March 2020
6. Finished goods inventory, March 31, 2020

2-38 Cost of goods manufactured, income statement, manufacturing company. Consider the following account balances (in thousands) for the Peterson Company:

Peterson Company	Beginning of 2020	End of 2020
Direct materials inventory	21,000	23,000
Work-in-process inventory	26,000	25,000
Finished-goods inventory	13,000	20,000
Purchases of direct materials		74,000
Direct manufacturing labor		22,000
Indirect manufacturing labor		17,000
Plant insurance		7,000
Depreciation—plant, building, and equipment		11,000
Repairs and maintenance—plant		3,000
Marketing, distribution, and customer-service costs		91,000
General and administrative costs		24,000

Required

1. Prepare a schedule for the cost of goods manufactured for 2020.
2. Revenues for 2020 were $310 million. Prepare the income statement for 2020.

2-39 Cost of goods manufactured, income statement, manufacturing company. The following information is available for the McCain Manufacturing Company for 2020.

Accounts receivable, January 1, 2020	$120,000
Accounts payable, January 1, 2020	?
Raw materials, January 1, 2020	10,000
Work in process, January 1, 2020	25,000
Finished goods, January 1, 2020	75,000
Accounts receivable, December 31, 2020	80,000
Accounts payable, December 31, 2020	200,000
Raw materials, December 31, 2020	?
Work in process, December 31, 2020	60,000
Finished goods, December 31, 2020	50,000
Raw materials used in production	100,000
Raw materials purchased	130,000
Accounts receivable collections	?
Accounts payable payments	80,000
Sales	?
Total manufacturing costs	?
Cost of goods manufactured	?
Cost of goods sold	60% of Sales
Gross margin	400,000

Required

Assume that all raw materials are purchased on credit and all sales are credit sales. Compute the missing amounts above.

2-40 Income statement and schedule of cost of goods manufactured. The Howell Corporation has the following account balances (in millions):

For Specific Date		For Year 2020	
Direct materials inventory, January 1, 2020	$15	Purchases of direct materials	$325
Work-in-process inventory, January 1, 2020	10	Direct manufacturing labor	100
Finished goods inventory, January 1, 2020	70	Depreciation—plant and equipment	80
Direct materials inventory, December 31, 2020	20	Plant supervisory salaries	5
Work-in-process inventory, December 31, 2020	5	Miscellaneous plant overhead	35
Finished goods inventory, December 31, 2020	55	Revenues	950
		Marketing, distribution, and customer-service costs	240
		Plant supplies used	10
		Plant utilities	30
		Indirect manufacturing labor	60

Required

Prepare an income statement and a supporting schedule of cost of goods manufactured for the year ended December 31, 2020. (For additional questions regarding these facts, see the next problem.)

2-41 Interpretation of statements (continuation of 2-40).

Required

1. How would the answer to Problem 2-40 be modified if you were asked for a schedule of cost of goods manufactured and sold instead of a schedule of cost of goods manufactured? Be specific.
2. Would the sales manager's salary (included in marketing, distribution, and customer-service costs) be accounted for any differently if the Howell Corporation were a merchandising-sector company instead of a manufacturing-sector company?
3. Using the flow of manufacturing costs outlined in Exhibit 2-9 (page 44), describe how the wages of an assembler in the plant would be accounted for in this manufacturing company.
4. Plant supervisory salaries are usually regarded as manufacturing overhead costs. When might some of these costs be regarded as direct manufacturing costs? Give an example.
5. Suppose that both the direct materials used and the plant and equipment depreciation are related to the manufacture of 1 million units of product. What is the unit cost for the direct materials assigned to those units? What is the unit cost for plant and equipment depreciation? Assume that yearly plant and equipment depreciation is computed on a straight-line basis.
6. Assume that the implied cost-behavior patterns in requirement 5 persist. That is, direct material costs behave as a variable cost and plant and equipment depreciation behaves as a fixed cost. Repeat the computations in requirement 5, assuming that the costs are being predicted for the manufacture of 1.2 million units of product. How would the total costs be affected?
7. As a management accountant, explain concisely to the president why the unit costs differed in requirements 5 and 6.

2-42 Income statement and schedule of cost of goods manufactured. Chan's manufacturing costing system uses a three-part classification of direct materials, direct manufacturing labor, and manufacturing overhead costs. The following items (in millions) pertain to Chan Corporation:

For Specific Date		For Year 2020	
Work-in-process inventory, January 1, 2020	$15	Plant utilities	$ 9
Direct materials inventory, December 31, 2020	10	Indirect manufacturing labor	24
Finished-goods inventory, December 31, 2020	20	Depreciation—plant and equipment	5
Accounts payable, December 31, 2020	28	Revenues	352
Accounts receivable, January 1, 2020	51	Miscellaneous manufacturing overhead	12
Work-in-process inventory, December 31, 2020	8	Marketing, distribution, and customer-service costs	92
Finished-goods inventory, January 1, 2020	40	Direct materials purchased	83
Accounts receivable, December 31, 2020	37	Direct manufacturing labor	48
Accounts payable, January 1, 2020	42	Plant supplies used	3
Direct materials inventory, January 1, 2020	31	Property taxes on plant	7

Required

Prepare an income statement and a supporting schedule of cost of goods manufactured. (For additional questions regarding these facts, see the next problem.)

2-43 Terminology, interpretation of statements (continuation of 2-42).

Required

1. Calculate total prime costs and total conversion costs.
2. Calculate total inventoriable costs and period costs.
3. Design costs and R&D costs are not considered product costs for financial statement purposes. When might some of these costs be regarded as product costs? Give an example.
4. Suppose that both the direct materials used and the depreciation on plant and equipment are related to the manufacture of 1 million units of product. Determine the unit cost for the direct materials assigned to those units and the unit cost for depreciation on plant and equipment. Assume that yearly depreciation is computed on a straight-line basis.
5. Assume that the implied cost-behavior patterns in requirement 4 persist. That is, direct material costs behave as a variable cost and depreciation on plant and equipment behaves as a fixed cost. Repeat the computations in requirement 4, assuming that the costs are being predicted for the manufacture of 2 million units of product. Determine the effect on total costs.
6. Assume that depreciation on the equipment (but not the plant) is computed based on the number of units produced because the equipment deteriorates with units produced. The depreciation rate on equipment is $6.00 per unit. Calculate the depreciation on equipment assuming (a) 1 million units of product are produced and (b) 2 million units of product are produced.

2-44 Different meanings of product costs. There are at least three different purposes for which we measure product costs. They are (1) product mix decisions, (2) determining the appropriate charge for a government contract, and (3) preparing financial statements for external reporting following GAAP. In the following table, indicate whether the respective type of cost would be included or excluded for the particular purpose. If your answer is not definitive (include or exclude), provide a short explanation of why.

Required

Type of Cost	Purpose: Product Mix	Purpose: Government Contract	Purpose: Financial Statement (using GAAP)
Direct material			
Direct manufacturing labor			
Manufacturing overhead			
Distribution costs			
Product design costs			
R&D costs			
Customer service			

2-45 Missing records, computing inventory costs. Sam Wright recently took over as the controller of Osborn Brothers Manufacturing. Last month, the previous controller left the company with little notice and left the accounting records in disarray. Sam needs the ending inventory balances to report first-quarter numbers.

For the previous month (March 2020), Sam was able to piece together the following information:

Direct materials purchased	$ 90,000
Work-in-process inventory, March 1, 2020	$ 30,000
Direct materials inventory, March 1, 2020	$ 13,500
Finished-goods inventory, March 1, 2020	$190,000
Conversion costs	$340,000
Total manufacturing costs added during the period	$400,000
Cost of goods manufactured	5 times direct materials used
Gross margin as a percentage of revenues	30%
Revenues	$640,000

Calculate the cost of

Required

1. Finished-goods inventory, March 31, 2020
2. Work-in-process inventory, March 31, 2020
3. Direct materials inventory, March 31, 2020

2-46 Comprehensive problem on unit costs, product costs. Atlanta Office Equipment manufactures and sells metal shelving. It began operations on January 1, 2020. Costs incurred for 2020 are as follows (V stands for variable; F stands for fixed):

Direct materials used	$140,000 V
Direct manufacturing labor costs	22,000 V
Plant energy costs	5,000 V
Indirect manufacturing labor costs	18,000 V
Indirect manufacturing labor costs	14,000 F
Other indirect manufacturing costs	8,000 V
Other indirect manufacturing costs	26,000 F
Marketing, distribution, and customer-service costs	120,000 V
Marketing, distribution, and customer-service costs	43,000 F
Administrative costs	54,000 F

Variable manufacturing costs are variable with respect to units produced. Variable marketing, distribution, and customer-service costs are variable with respect to units sold.

Inventory data are as follows:

	Beginning: January 1, 2020	Ending: December 31, 2020
Direct materials	0 lb	2,300 lbs
Work in process	0 units	0 units
Finished goods	0 units	? units

Production in 2020 was 100,000 units. Two pounds of direct materials are used to make one unit of finished product.

Revenues in 2020 were $473,200. The selling price per unit and the purchase price per pound of direct materials were stable throughout the year. The company's ending inventory of finished goods is carried at the average unit manufacturing cost for 2020. Finished-goods inventory on December 31, 2020, was $20,970.

Required

1. Calculate direct materials inventory, total cost, December 31, 2020.
2. Calculate finished-goods inventory, total units, December 31, 2020.
3. Calculate selling price in 2020.
4. Calculate operating income for 2020.

2-47 Cost classification; ethics. Paul Howard, the new plant manager of Garden Scapes Manufacturing Plant Number 7, has just reviewed a draft of his year-end financial statements. Howard receives a year-end bonus of 11.5% of the plant's operating income before tax. The year-end income statement provided by the plant's controller was disappointing to say the least. After reviewing the numbers, Howard demanded that his controller go back and "work the numbers" again. Howard insisted that if he didn't see a better operating income number the next time around, he would be forced to look for a new controller.

Garden Scapes Manufacturing classifies all costs directly related to the manufacturing of its product as product costs. These costs are inventoried and later expensed as costs of goods sold when the product is sold. All other expenses, including finished-goods warehousing costs of $3,640,000, are classified as period expenses. Howard had suggested that warehousing costs be included as product costs because they are "definitely related to our product." The company produced 260,000 units during the period and sold 240,000 units.

As the controller reworked the numbers, he discovered that if he included warehousing costs as product costs, he could improve operating income by $280,000. He was also sure these new numbers would make Howard happy.

Required

1. Show numerically how operating income would improve by $280,000 just by classifying the preceding costs as product costs instead of as period expenses.
2. Is Howard correct in his justification that these costs are "definitely related to our product"?
3. By how much will Howard profit personally if the controller makes the adjustments in requirement 1?
4. What should the plant controller do?

2-48 Finding unknown amounts. An auditor for the Internal Revenue Service is trying to reconstruct some partially destroyed records of two taxpayers. For each of the cases in the accompanying list, find the unknowns designated by the letters A and B for Case 1 and C and D for Case 2.

Required

	Case 1	Case 2
	(in thousands)	
Accounts receivable, December 31	$10,000	$ 3,560
Cost of goods sold	A	31,000
Accounts payable, January 1	4,800	2,450
Accounts payable, December 31	3,300	1,920
Finished-goods inventory, December 31	B	8,600
Gross margin	14,500	C
Work-in-process inventory, January 1	2,600	600
Work-in-process inventory, December 31	0	4,000
Finished-goods inventory, January 1	10,000	3,000
Direct materials used	16,000	22,000
Direct manufacturing labor	4,100	7,900
Manufacturing overhead costs	5,500	D
Purchases of direct materials	11,600	13,500
Revenues	45,000	49,600
Accounts receivable, January 1	2,500	2,000

Cost–Volume–Profit Analysis

3

All managers want to know how profits will change as the units sold, selling price, or the cost per unit of a product or service changes.

Home Depot managers, for example, might wonder how many units of a new power drill must be sold to break even or make a certain amount of profit. Procter & Gamble managers might ask how expanding their business in Nigeria would affect costs, revenues, and profits. These questions have a common "what if" theme: What if we sold more power drills? What if we started selling in Nigeria? Examining these what-if possibilities and alternatives helps managers make better decisions.

The following article explains how Goldenvoice, the organizer of the Coachella music festival in California, generated additional revenues to cover its fixed costs and turn a loss into a profit.

LEARNING OBJECTIVES

1. Explain the features of cost–volume–profit (CVP) analysis
2. Determine the breakeven point and output level needed to achieve a target operating income
3. Understand how income taxes affect CVP analysis
4. Explain how managers use CVP analysis to make decisions
5. Explain how sensitivity analysis helps managers cope with uncertainty
6. Use CVP analysis to plan variable and fixed costs
7. Apply CVP analysis to a company producing multiple products
8. Apply CVP analysis in service and not-for-profit organizations
9. Distinguish contribution margin from gross margin

HOW COACHELLA TUNES UP THE SWEET SOUND OF PROFITS[1]

Each year, the Coachella music festival in California features more than 150 of the biggest names in rock, hip-hop, and electronic dance music. Putting on this annual music extravaganza is costly. Headlining acts such as Beyoncé command as much as $4 million to perform, and production—including stagehands, insurance, and security—costs up to $12 million before the first note is played.

To cover its high fixed costs and make a profit, Coachella needs to sell a lot of tickets. After struggling for years to turn a profit, Goldenvoice expanded Coachella to two identical editions on consecutive weekends—same venue, same lineup, and same ticket price—and Stagecoach, a country music festival at the same venue 1 week later. This allowed temporary infrastructure costs such as stages and fencings to be shared across all events. With tickets prices from $429 to $9,500, the 2017 Coachella festival sold $114 million in tickets, while Stagecoach grossed more than $22 million in ticket sales. By expanding Coachella's volume, Goldenvoice was able to recover its fixed costs and tune up the sweet sound of profits.

WENN Ltd/Alamy Stock Photo

[1] *Sources:* Chris Parker, "The Economics of Music Festivals: Who's Getting Rich? Who's Going Broke?" *L.A. Weekly*, April 17, 2013 (http://www.laweekly.com/music/the-economics-of-music-festivals-whos-getting-rich-whos-going-broke-4167927); Anil Patel, "Coachella: A Lesson in Strategic Growth," Anil Patel's blog, LinkedIn, April 17, 2015 (https://www.linkedin.com/pulse/coachella-lesson-strategic-growth-anil-patel); Dave Brooks, "Coachella Grossed Record-Breaking $114 Million This Year," *Billboard*, October 18, 2017 (https://www.billboard.com/articles/business/8005736/coachella-festival-2017-114-million-gross); Mikael Wood, "How Beyoncé Changed Coachella's Temperature," *Los Angeles Times*, April 15, 2018 (http://www.latimes.com/entertainment/music/la-et-ms-coachella-2018-review-20180415-story.html).

High fixed cost businesses, such as American Airlines and General Motors, pay particular attention to "what ifs" behind decisions because these companies need significant revenues just to break even. In the airline industry, for example, the profits most airlines make come from the last two to five passengers who board each flight! Consequently, when revenues at American Airlines dropped, it was forced to declare bankruptcy. In this chapter, you will see how cost–volume–profit (CVP) analysis helps managers minimize such risks.

Essentials of CVP Analysis

LEARNING OBJECTIVE 1

Explain the features of cost–volume–profit (CVP) analysis

. . . how operating income changes with changes in output level, selling prices, variable costs, or fixed costs

In Chapter 2, we discussed total revenues, total costs, and income. Managers use **cost–volume–profit (CVP) analysis** to study the behavior of and relationship among these elements as changes occur in the number of units sold, the selling price, the variable cost per unit, or the fixed costs of a product. Consider this example:

> Emma Jones is a young entrepreneur who recently used *GMAT Success*, a test-prep book and software package for the business school admission test. Emma loved the book and program so much that after graduating she signed a contract with *GMAT Success*'s publisher to sell the learning materials. She recently sold them at a college fair in Boston and is now thinking of selling them at a college fair in Chicago. Emma can purchase each package (book and software) from the publisher for $120 per package, with the privilege of returning all unsold packages and receiving a full $120 refund per package. She must pay $2,000 to rent a booth at the fair. She will incur no other costs. Should she rent the booth or not?

Emma, like most managers who face such a situation, works through the series of steps introduced in Chapter 1 to make the most profitable decisions.

1. **Identify the problem and uncertainties.** Every managerial decision involves selecting a course of action. The problem of whether or not to rent the booth hinges on how Emma resolves two important uncertainties: the price she can charge and the number of packages she can sell at that price. Emma must decide knowing that the outcome of the action she chooses is uncertain. The more confident she is about selling a large number of packages at a high price, the more willing she will be to rent the booth.
2. **Obtain information.** To better understand the uncertainties, Emma obtains information, for example, about the type of individuals likely to attend the fair and other test-prep packages that might be sold at the fair. She also collects data from the Boston fair.
3. **Make predictions about the future.** Emma predicts she can charge $200 for the *GMAT Success* package. At that price, she is reasonably confident that she will be able to sell at least 30 packages and possibly as many as 60. Emma must be realistic and exercise judgment when making these predictions. If they are too optimistic, she will rent the booth when she should not. If they are too pessimistic, she will not rent the booth when she should.

   Emma believes that her experience at the Chicago fair will be similar to her experience at the Boston fair 4 months earlier. Yet Emma is uncertain about several aspects of her prediction. Are the fairs truly comparable? For example, will attendance at the two fairs be the same? Have market conditions changed over the past 4 months? Are biases creeping into her thinking? Is her keenness to sell at the Chicago fair because of lower-than-expected sales in the last couple of months leading to overly optimistic predictions? Has she ignored some competitive risks? Will other test-prep vendors at the fair reduce their prices? If they do, should she? How many packages can she expect to sell if she does?

   Emma rethinks her plan and retests her assumptions. She obtains data about student attendance and sales of similar products in past years. She feels confident that her predictions are reasonable, accurate, and carefully thought through.

4. **Make decisions by choosing among alternatives.** Emma uses the CVP analysis that follows and decides to rent the booth at the Chicago fair.
5. **Implement the decision, evaluate performance, and learn.** At the end of the Chicago fair, Emma compares actual performance to predicted performance to understand why things worked out the way they did. For example, Emma evaluates whether her predictions about price and the number of packages she could sell were correct. This helps her learn and make better decisions about renting booths at future fairs.

As we described in Chapter 1, machine learning and data analytics can help Emma in several of these steps. Emma can store information on multiple factors, such as details about individuals who have attended similar fairs, the number of test-prep packages sold at different prices at these fairs, and characteristics such as weather, market conditions, number of competitive vendors, and location. Using this information, a data-analytic model can predict how many packages Emma might expect to sell at different prices. The model is free of some human bias because lower-than-expected sales in the last 2 months is not a feature of the model. The experience from the Chicago fair (how well the model predicted actual outcomes) becomes an input into the model and helps to improve and refine it. The machine and the model learn from each experience.

But how does Emma use CVP analysis in Step 4 to make her decision? She begins by identifying which costs are fixed and which costs are variable and then calculates *contribution margin.*

Contribution Margin

The booth-rental cost of $2,000 is a fixed cost because it is the same no matter how many packages Emma sells. The cost of the packages is a variable cost because it increases in proportion to the number of packages sold. Emma returns whatever she doesn't sell for a full refund.

To understand how operating income will change with different quantities of packages sold, Emma calculates operating income for sales of 5 packages and 40 packages.

	5 Packages Sold		40 Packages Sold	
Revenues	$ 1,000	($200 per package × 5 packages)	$8,000	($200 per package × 40 packages)
Variable purchase costs	600	($120 per package × 5 packages)	4,800	($120 per package × 40 packages)
Fixed costs	2,000		2,000	
Operating income	$(1,600)		$1,200	

The only numbers that change as a result of selling different quantities of packages are *total revenues* and *total variable costs*. The difference between total revenues and total variable costs is called **contribution margin.** That is,

$$\text{Contribution margin} = \text{Total revenues} - \text{Total variable costs}$$

Contribution margin explains why operating income increases by $2,800 from a loss of $(1,600) to income of $1,200 as the number of units sold increases from 5 packages to 40 packages. The contribution margin when Emma sells 5 packages is $400 ($1,000 in total revenues minus $600 in total variable costs); the contribution margin when Emma sells 40 packages is $3,200 ($8,000 in total revenues minus $4,800 in total variable costs), an increase of $2,800 ($3,200 − $400). When calculating the contribution margin, be sure to subtract all variable costs. For example, if Emma incurs variable selling costs from commissions paid to salespeople for each package sold at the fair, variable costs would include the cost of each package plus the sales commission paid on it.

Contribution margin per unit is a useful tool for calculating contribution margin and operating income. It is defined as:

$$\text{Contribution margin per unit} = \text{Selling price} - \text{Variable cost per unit}$$

In the *GMAT Success* example, the contribution margin per package, or per unit, is \$200 − \$120 = \$80. Contribution margin per unit recognizes the tight coupling of selling price and variable cost per unit. Unlike fixed costs, Emma will only incur the variable cost per unit of \$120 when she sells a package of *GMAT Success*.

Contribution margin per unit provides a second way to calculate contribution margin:

$$\text{Contribution margin} = \text{Contribution margin per unit} \times \text{Number of units sold}$$

For example, when Emma sells 40 packages, contribution margin = \$80 per unit × 40 units = \$3,200.

Even before she gets to the fair, Emma incurs \$2,000 in fixed costs. Because the contribution margin per unit is \$80, Emma will recover \$80 for each package that she sells at the fair. Emma hopes to sell enough packages to fully recover the \$2,000 she spent renting the booth and to then make a profit.

To get a feel for how operating income will change for different quantities of packages sold, Emma can prepare a contribution income statement as in Exhibit 3-1. The income statement in Exhibit 3-1 is called a **contribution income statement** because it groups costs into variable costs and fixed costs to highlight contribution margin.

$$\text{Operating income} = \text{Contribution margin} - \text{Fixed costs}$$

Each additional package sold from 0 to 1 to 5 increases contribution margin by \$80 per package and helps Emma recover more and more of her fixed costs and reduce her operating loss. If Emma sells 25 packages, contribution margin equals \$2,000 (\$80 per package × 25 packages). This quantity exactly recovers her fixed costs and results in \$0 operating income. If Emma sells 40 packages, contribution margin increases by another \$1,200 (\$3,200 − \$2,000), all of which becomes operating income. As you look across Exhibit 3-1 from left to right, you see that the increase in contribution margin exactly equals the increase in operating income (or the decrease in operating loss).

When companies such as Samsung and Prada sell multiple products, calculating contribution margin per unit is cumbersome. Instead of expressing contribution margin in dollars per unit, these companies express it as a percentage called **contribution margin percentage** (or **contribution margin ratio**):

$$\text{Contribution margin percentage (or contribution margin ratio)} = \frac{\text{Contribution margin}}{\text{Revenues}}$$

Consider a sales level such as the 40 units sold in Exhibit 3-1:

$$\text{Contribution margin percentage} = \frac{\$3{,}200}{\$8{,}000} = 0.40\text{, or } 40\%$$

Contribution margin percentage is the contribution margin per dollar of revenue. Emma earns 40% for each dollar of revenue (40¢) she takes in. Contribution margin percentage is a handy way to calculate contribution margin for different dollar amounts of revenue. Rearranging terms in the equation defining contribution margin percentage, we get

$$\text{Contribution margin} = \text{Contribution margin percentage} \times \text{Revenues (in dollars)}$$

EXHIBIT 3-1

Contribution Income Statement for Different Quantities of *GMAT Success* Packages Sold

Home Insert Page Layout Formulas Data Review View

	A	B	C	D	E	F	G	H
1				Number of Packages Sold				
2				0	1	5	25	40
3	Revenues	\$ 200	per package	\$ 0	\$ 200	\$ 1,000	\$5,000	\$8,000
4	Variable costs	\$ 120	per package	0	120	600	3,000	4,800
5	Contribution margin	\$ 80	per package	0	80	400	2,000	3,200
6	Fixed costs	\$2,000		2,000	2,000	2,000	2,000	2,000
7	Operating income			\$(2,000)	\$(1,920)	\$(1,600)	\$ 0	\$1,200

To derive the relationship between operating income and contribution margin percentage, recall that

$$\text{Operating income} = \text{Contribution margin} - \text{Fixed costs}$$

Substituting for contribution margin in the above equation:

$$\text{Operating income} = \text{Contribution margin percentage} \times \text{Revenues} - \text{Fixed costs}$$

For example, in Exhibit 3-1, if Emma sells 40 packages,

Revenues	$8,000
Contribution margin percentage	40%
Contribution margin, 40% × $8,000	$3,200
Fixed costs	2,000
Operating income	$1,200

When there is only one product, as in our example, we can divide both the numerator and denominator of the contribution margin percentage equation by the quantity of units sold and calculate contribution margin percentage as follows:

$$\text{Contribution margin percentage} = \frac{\text{Contribution margin/Quantity of units sold}}{\text{Revenues/Quantity of units sold}}$$

$$= \frac{\text{Contribution margin per unit}}{\text{Selling price}}$$

In our example,

$$\text{Contribution margin percentage} = \frac{\$80}{\$200} = 0.40\text{, or } 40\%$$

Contribution margin percentage is a useful tool for calculating how a change in revenues changes contribution margin. As Emma's revenues increase by $3,000 from $5,000 to $8,000, her contribution margin increases from $2,000 to $3,200 (by $1,200):

Contribution margin at revenue of $8,000, 0.40 × $8,000	$3,200
Contribution margin at revenue of $5,000, 0.40 × $5,000	2,000
Change in contribution margin when revenue increases by $3,000, 0.40 × $3,000	$1,200

$$\text{Change in contribution margin} = \text{Contribution margin percentage} \times \text{Change in revenues}$$

Contribution margin analysis is a widely used technique. For example, managers at Home Depot use contribution margin analysis to evaluate how sales fluctuations during a recession will affect the company's profitability.

Expressing CVP Relationships

How was the Excel spreadsheet in Exhibit 3-1 constructed? Underlying the exhibit are equations that express the CVP relationships and influence the structure of the contribution income statement in Exhibit 3-1. There are three related ways (we will call them "methods") to model CVP relationships:

1. The equation method
2. The contribution margin method
3. The graph method

Different methods are useful for different decisions. The equation method and the contribution margin method are most useful when managers want to determine operating income at a few specific sales levels (for example, 5, 15, 25, and 40 units sold). The graph method helps managers visualize the relationship between units sold and operating income over a wide range of quantities.

Equation Method

Each column in Exhibit 3-1 is expressed as an equation.

$$\text{Revenues} - \text{Variable costs} - \text{Fixed costs} = \text{Operating income}$$

How are revenues in each column calculated?

$$\text{Revenues} = \text{Selling price } (SP) \times \text{Quantity of units sold } (Q)$$

How are variable costs in each column calculated?

$$\text{Variable costs} = \text{Variable cost per unit } (VCU) \times \text{Quantity of units sold } (Q)$$

So,

$$\left[\begin{pmatrix}\text{Selling}\\ \text{price}\end{pmatrix} \times \begin{pmatrix}\text{Quantity of}\\ \text{units sold}\end{pmatrix} - \begin{pmatrix}\text{Variable cost}\\ \text{per unit}\end{pmatrix} \times \begin{pmatrix}\text{Quantity of}\\ \text{units sold}\end{pmatrix}\right] - \begin{matrix}\text{Fixed}\\ \text{costs}\end{matrix} = \begin{matrix}\text{Operating}\\ \text{income}\end{matrix} \qquad \text{(Equation 1)}$$

Equation 1 becomes the basis for calculating operating income for different quantities of units sold. For example, if you go to cell F7 in Exhibit 3-1, the calculation of operating income when Emma sells 5 packages is

$$(\$200 \times 5) - (\$120 \times 5) - \$2{,}000 = \$1{,}000 - \$600 - \$2{,}000 = -\$1{,}600$$

Contribution Margin Method

Rearranging equation 1,

$$\left[\begin{pmatrix}\text{Selling}\\ \text{price}\end{pmatrix} - \begin{matrix}\text{Variable cost}\\ \text{per unit}\end{matrix}\right) \times \begin{pmatrix}\text{Quantity of}\\ \text{units sold}\end{pmatrix}\Bigg] - \begin{matrix}\text{Fixed}\\ \text{costs}\end{matrix} = \begin{matrix}\text{Operating}\\ \text{income}\end{matrix}$$

$$\begin{pmatrix}\text{Contribution margin}\\ \text{per unit}\end{pmatrix. \times \begin{matrix}\text{Quantity of}\\ \text{units sold}\end{matrix}\Bigg) - \begin{matrix}\text{Fixed}\\ \text{costs}\end{matrix} = \begin{matrix}\text{Operating}\\ \text{income}\end{matrix} \qquad \text{(Equation 2)}$$

The contribution margin per unit is \$80 (\$200 − \$120), so when Emma sells 5 packages,

$$\text{Operating income} = (\$80 \times 5) - \$2{,}000 = -\$1{,}600$$

Equation 2 expresses the basic idea we described earlier—each unit sold helps Emma recover \$80 (in contribution margin) of the \$2,000 in fixed costs.

TRY IT! 3-1

Best Windows is a small company that installs windows. Its cost structure is as follows:

Selling price from each window installation	\$ 700
Variable cost of each window installation	\$ 600
Annual fixed costs	\$160,000

Use (a) the equation method and (b) the contribution method to calculate operating income if Best installs 4,000 windows.

Graph Method

The graph method helps managers visualize the relationships between total revenues and total costs. Exhibit 3-2 illustrates the graph method for *GMAT Success*. Because we have assumed that total costs and total revenues change linearly with units sold, the graph shows each relationship as a line. We need only two points to plot each line.

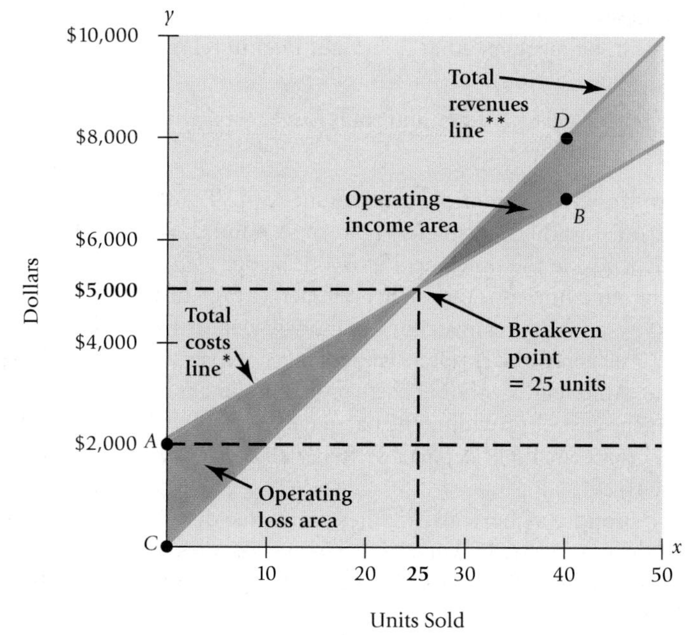

*Slope of the total costs line is the variable cost per unit = $120
**Slope of the total revenues line is the selling price = $200

EXHIBIT 3-2

Cost–Volume Graph for *GMAT Success*

1. **Total costs line.** The total costs line is the sum of fixed costs and variable costs. Fixed costs are $2,000 for all quantities of units sold within the relevant range. To plot the total costs line, use as one point the $2,000 fixed costs at zero units sold (point A) because variable costs are $0 when no units are sold. Select a second point by choosing any other output level (say, 40 units sold) and determine the corresponding total costs. Total variable costs at this output level are $4,800 (40 units × $120 per unit). Remember, fixed costs are $2,000 for all quantities of units sold within the relevant range, so total costs at 40 units sold equal $6,800 ($2,000 + $4,800), which is point B in Exhibit 3-2. The total costs line is the straight line from point A through point B.
2. **Total revenues line.** One convenient starting point is $0 revenues at 0 units sold, which is point C in Exhibit 3-2. Select a second point by choosing any other convenient output level and determining the corresponding total revenues. At 40 units sold, total revenues are $8,000 ($200 per unit × 40 units), which is point D in Exhibit 3-2. The total revenues line is the straight line from point C through point D.

The profit or loss at any sales level can be determined by the vertical distance between the two lines at that level in Exhibit 3-2. For quantities fewer than 25 units sold, total costs exceed total revenues, and the purple area indicates operating losses. For quantities greater than 25 units sold, total revenues exceed total costs, and the blue-green area indicates operating incomes. At 25 units sold, total revenues equal total costs. Emma will break even by selling 25 packages.

DECISION POINT

How can CVP analysis help managers?

Cost–Volume–Profit Assumptions

Now that you know how CVP analysis works, think about the following assumptions we made during the analysis:

1. Changes in revenues and costs result solely from changes in the number of product (or service) units sold. That is, the number of units sold is the only revenue driver and the only cost driver. Just as a cost driver is any factor that affects costs, a **revenue driver** is a variable, such as number of units sold, that causally affects revenues.
2. Total costs can be separated into two components: a fixed component that does not vary with units sold (such as Emma's $2,000 booth fee) and a variable component that changes based on units sold (such as the $120 cost per *GMAT Success* package).

3. When represented graphically, the behaviors of total revenues and total costs are linear (meaning they can be represented as a straight line) in relation to units sold within a relevant range (and time period).
4. Selling price, variable cost per unit, and total fixed costs (within a relevant range and time period) are known and constant.

As you can tell from these assumptions, to conduct a CVP analysis, you need to correctly distinguish fixed from variable costs. Always keep in mind, however, that whether a cost is variable or fixed depends on the time period for a decision.

The shorter the time horizon, the higher the percentage of total costs considered fixed. For example, suppose an American Airlines plane will depart from its gate in the next hour and currently has 20 seats unsold. A potential passenger arrives with a transferable ticket from a competing airline. American's variable costs of placing one more passenger in an otherwise empty seat (such as the cost of providing the passenger with a free beverage) is negligible. With only an hour to go before the flight departs, virtually all costs (such as crew costs and baggage-handling costs) are fixed.

Alternatively, suppose American Airlines must decide whether to continue to offer this particular flight next year. If American Airlines decides to cancel this flight because very few passengers during the last year have taken it, many more of its costs, including crew costs, baggage-handling costs, and airport fees for the flight, would be considered variable: Over this longer 1-year time period, American Airlines would not have to incur these costs if the flight were no longer operating. Always consider the relevant range, the length of the time horizon, and the specific decision situation when classifying costs as variable or fixed.

Breakeven Point and Target Operating Income

LEARNING OBJECTIVE 2

Determine the breakeven point and output level needed to achieve a target operating income

...compare contribution margin and fixed costs

In previous sections, we used the number of packages sold as an input to the contribution income statement, the equation method, the contribution margin method, and the graph method to calculate Emma's operating income for different quantities of packages sold. In this section, we use the same tools to reverse the logic. We use as input the amount of operating income Emma wants to earn and then compute the number of packages Emma must sell to earn this income. We first consider how much Emma must sell to avoid a loss.

Breakeven Point

The **breakeven point (BEP)** is that quantity of output sold at which total revenues equal total costs—that is, the quantity of output sold that results in \$0 of operating income. You have already learned how to use the graph method to calculate the breakeven point. Also, recall from Exhibit 3-1 that operating income was \$0 when Emma sold 25 units; this is the breakeven point. But by understanding the equations underlying the calculations in Exhibit 3-1, we can calculate the breakeven point directly for *GMAT Success* rather than trying out different quantities and checking when operating income equals \$0.

Recall the equation method (equation 1):

$$\left[\left(\begin{matrix}\text{Selling}\\\text{price}\end{matrix}\times\begin{matrix}\text{Quantity of}\\\text{units sold}\end{matrix}\right)-\left(\begin{matrix}\text{Variable cost}\\\text{per unit}\end{matrix}\times\begin{matrix}\text{Quantity of}\\\text{units sold}\end{matrix}\right)\right]-\begin{matrix}\text{Fixed}\\\text{costs}\end{matrix}=\begin{matrix}\text{Operating}\\\text{income}\end{matrix}$$

Setting operating income to \$0 and denoting quantity of output units sold by Q,

$$(\$200 \times Q) - (\$120 \times Q) - \$2{,}000 = \$0$$
$$\$80 \times Q = \$2{,}000$$
$$Q = \$2{,}000 \div \$80 \text{ per unit} = 25 \text{ units}$$

If Emma sells fewer than 25 units, she will incur a loss; if she sells 25 units, she will break even; and if she sells more than 25 units, she will make a profit. Although this breakeven point is expressed in units, it can also be expressed in revenues: 25 units × \$200 selling price = \$5,000.

Recall the contribution margin method (equation 2):

$$\left(\begin{array}{c}\text{Contribution}\\ \text{margin per unit}\end{array} \times \begin{array}{c}\text{Quantity of}\\ \text{units sold}\end{array}\right) - \text{Fixed costs} = \text{Operating income}$$

At the breakeven point, operating income is by definition \$0, and so,

$$\text{Contribution margin per unit} \times \text{Breakeven quantity of units} = \text{Fixed costs} \qquad \text{(Equation 3)}$$

Rearranging equation 3 and entering the data,

$$\begin{array}{c}\text{Breakeven}\\ \text{quantity of units}\end{array} = \frac{\text{Fixed costs}}{\text{Contribution margin per unit}} = \frac{\$2{,}000}{\$80\text{ per unit}} = 25\text{ units}$$

$$\begin{aligned}\text{Breakeven revenues} &= \text{Breakeven quantity of units} \times \text{Selling price}\\ &= 25\text{ units} \times \$200\text{ per unit} = \$5{,}000\end{aligned}$$

In practice (because companies have multiple products), management accountants usually calculate the breakeven point directly in terms of revenues using contribution margin percentages. Recall that in the *GMAT Success* example, at revenues of \$8,000, contribution margin is \$3,200:

$$\begin{array}{c}\text{Contribution margin}\\ \text{percentage}\end{array} = \frac{\text{Contribution margin}}{\text{Revenues}} = \frac{\$3{,}200}{\$8{,}000} = 0.40\text{, or }40\%$$

That is, 40% of each dollar of revenue, or 40¢, is the contribution margin. To break even, contribution margin must equal Emma's fixed costs, which are \$2,000. To earn \$2,000 of contribution margin, when \$1 of revenue results in a \$0.40 contribution margin, revenues must equal \$2,000 ÷ 0.40 = \$5,000.

$$\begin{array}{c}\text{Breakeven}\\ \text{revenues}\end{array} = \frac{\text{Fixed costs}}{\text{Contribution margin\%}} = \frac{\$2{,}000}{0.40} = \$5{,}000$$

While the breakeven point tells managers how much they must sell to avoid a loss, managers are equally interested in how they will achieve the operating income targets underlying their strategies and plans. In our example, selling 25 units at a price of \$200 (equal to revenue of \$5,000) assures Emma that she will not lose money if she rents the booth. While this news is comforting, how does Emma determine how much she needs to sell to achieve a targeted amount of operating income?

Target Operating Income

Suppose Emma wants to earn an operating income of \$1,200? How many units must she sell? One approach is to keep plugging in different quantities into Exhibit 3-1 and check when operating income equals \$1,200. Exhibit 3-1 shows that operating income is \$1,200 when 40 packages are sold. A more convenient approach is to use equation 1 from page 70.

$$\left[\left(\begin{array}{c}\text{Selling}\\ \text{price}\end{array}\right) \times \left(\begin{array}{c}\text{Quantity of}\\ \text{units sold}\end{array}\right) - \left(\begin{array}{c}\text{Variable cost}\\ \text{per unit}\end{array}\right) \times \left(\begin{array}{c}\text{Quantity of}\\ \text{units sold}\end{array}\right)\right] - \begin{array}{c}\text{Fixed}\\ \text{costs}\end{array} = \begin{array}{c}\text{Operating}\\ \text{income}\end{array} \qquad \text{(Equation 1)}$$

We denote by Q the unknown quantity of units Emma must sell to earn an operating income of \$1,200. Selling price is \$200, variable cost per package is \$120, fixed costs are \$2,000, and target operating income is \$1,200. Substituting these values into equation 1, we have

$$\begin{aligned}(\$200 \times Q) - (\$120 \times Q) - \$2{,}000 &= \$1{,}200\\ \$80 \times Q &= \$2{,}000 + \$1{,}200 = \$3{,}200\\ Q &= \$3{,}200 \div \$80\text{ per unit} = 40\text{ units}\end{aligned}$$

Alternatively, we could use equation 2,

$$\left(\begin{array}{c}\text{Contribution margin}\\ \text{per unit}\end{array} \times \begin{array}{c}\text{Quantity of}\\ \text{units sold}\end{array}\right) - \begin{array}{c}\text{Fixed}\\ \text{costs}\end{array} = \begin{array}{c}\text{Operating}\\ \text{income}\end{array} \qquad \textbf{(Equation 2)}$$

Given a target operating income ($1,200 in this case), we can rearrange terms to get equation 4.

$$\text{Quantity of units required to be sold} = \frac{\text{Fixed costs} + \text{Target operating income}}{\text{Contribution margin per unit}} \qquad \text{(Equation 4)}$$

$$\text{Quantity of units required to be sold} = \frac{\$2{,}000 + \$1{,}200}{\$80 \text{ per unit}} = 40 \text{ units}$$

Proof:

Revenues, $200 per unit × 40 units	$8,000
Variable costs, $120 per unit × 40 units	4,800
Contribution margin, $80 per unit × 40 units	3,200
Fixed costs	2,000
Operating income	$1,200

The revenues needed to earn an operating income of $1,200 can also be calculated directly by recognizing (1) that $3,200 of contribution margin must be earned (to cover the fixed costs of $2,000 plus earn an operating income of $1,200) and (2) that $1 of revenue earns $0.40 (40¢) of contribution margin (the contribution margin percentage is 40%). To earn a contribution margin of $3,200, revenues must equal $3,200 ÷ 0.40 = $8,000. That is,

$$\text{Revenues needed to earn target operating income} = \frac{\text{Fixed costs} + \text{Target operating income}}{\text{Contribution margin percentage}}$$

$$\text{Revenues needed to earn operating income of } \$1{,}200 = \frac{\$2{,}000 + \$1{,}200}{0.40} = \frac{\$3{,}200}{0.40} = \$8{,}000$$

TRY IT! 3-2

Best Windows is a small company that installs windows. Its cost structure is as follows:

Selling price from each window installation	$ 700
Variable cost of each window installation	$ 600
Annual fixed costs	$160,000

Calculate (a) the breakeven point in units and revenues and (b) the number of windows Best Windows must install and the revenues needed to earn a target operating income of $180,000.

Could we use the graph method and the graph in Exhibit 3-2 to figure out how many units Emma must sell to earn an operating income of $1,200? Yes, but it is not as easy to determine the precise point at which the difference between the total revenues line and the total costs line equals $1,200. Recasting Exhibit 3-2 in the form of a profit–volume (PV) graph, however, makes it easier to answer this question.

A **PV graph** shows how changes in the quantity of units sold affect operating income. Exhibit 3-3 is the PV graph for *GMAT Success* (fixed costs, $2,000; selling price, $200; and variable cost per unit, $120). The PV line can be drawn using two points. One convenient point (M) is the operating loss at 0 units sold, which is equal to the fixed costs of $2,000 and is shown at −$2,000 on the vertical axis. A second convenient point (N) is the breakeven point, which is 25 units in our example (see page 73). The PV line is the straight line from point M through point N. To find the number of units Emma must sell to earn an operating income of $1,200, draw a horizontal line parallel to the *x*-axis corresponding to $1,200 on the vertical axis (the *y*-axis). At the point where this line intersects the PV line, draw a vertical line down to the horizontal axis (the *x*-axis). The vertical line intersects the *x*-axis at 40 units, indicating that by selling 40 units Emma will earn an operating income of $1,200.

DECISION POINT

How can managers determine the breakeven point or the output needed to achieve a target operating income?

Just like Emma, managers at larger companies such as California Pizza Kitchen use profit–volume analyses to understand how profits change with sales volumes. They use this understanding to target the sales levels they need to achieve to meet their profit plans.

So far, we have ignored the effect of income taxes in CVP analysis. In many companies, boards of directors want top executives and managers to consider the effect their decisions have on the company's operating income *after* income taxes because this is the measure that drives shareholders' dividends and returns. Some decisions might not result in a large operating income, but their favorable tax consequences make them attractive over other investments

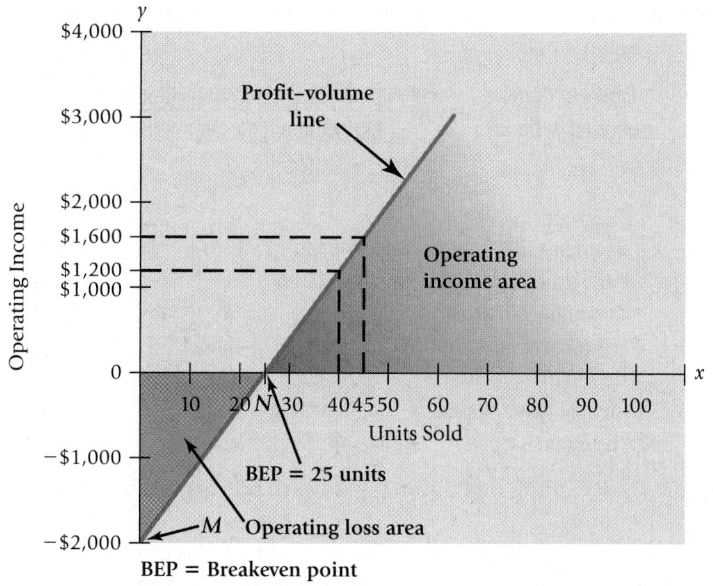

EXHIBIT 3-3

Profit–Volume Graph for *GMAT Success*

that have larger operating incomes but attract much higher taxes. CVP analysis can easily be adapted to consider the effect of taxes.

Income Taxes and Target Net Income

LEARNING OBJECTIVE 3

Understand how income taxes affect CVP analysis

. . .focus on net income

Net income is operating income plus nonoperating revenues (such as interest revenue) minus nonoperating costs (such as interest cost) minus income taxes. For simplicity, throughout this chapter we assume nonoperating revenues and nonoperating costs are zero. So, the net income equation is:

$$\text{Net income} = \text{Operating income} - \text{Income taxes}$$

To make net income evaluations, CVP calculations for target income must be stated in terms of target net income instead of target operating income. For example, Emma may be interested in knowing the quantity of units of *GMAT Success* she must sell to earn a net income of \$1,120, assuming an income tax rate of 30%.

$$\text{Target net income} = \left(\begin{array}{c}\text{Target}\\ \text{operating income}\end{array}\right) - \left(\begin{array}{c}\text{Target}\\ \text{operating income}\end{array} \times \text{Tax rate}\right)$$

$$\text{Target net income} = (\text{Target operating income}) \times (1 - \text{Tax rate})$$

$$\text{Target operating income} = \frac{\text{Target net income}}{1 - \text{Tax rate}} = \frac{\$1{,}120}{1 - 0.30} = \$1{,}600$$

In other words, to earn a target net income of \$1,120, Emma's target operating income is \$1,600.

Proof:		
	Target operating income	\$1,600
	Tax at 30% (0.30 × \$1,600)	480
	Target net income	\$1,120

The key step is to take the target net income number and convert it into the corresponding target operating income number. We can then use equation 1 to determine the target operating income and substitute numbers from our *GMAT Success* example.

$$\left[\left(\begin{array}{c}\text{Selling}\\ \text{price}\end{array}\right) \times \left(\begin{array}{c}\text{Quantity of}\\ \text{units sold}\end{array}\right) - \left(\begin{array}{c}\text{Variable cost}\\ \text{per unit}\end{array}\right) \times \left(\begin{array}{c}\text{Quantity of}\\ \text{units sold}\end{array}\right)\right] - \begin{array}{c}\text{Fixed}\\ \text{costs}\end{array} = \begin{array}{c}\text{Operating}\\ \text{income}\end{array} \quad \text{(Equation 1)}$$

$$(\$200 \times Q) - (\$120 \times Q) - \$2{,}000 = \$1{,}600$$

$$\$80 \times Q = \$3{,}600$$

$$Q = \$3{,}600 \div \$80 \text{ per unit} = 45 \text{ units}$$

Alternatively, we can calculate the number of units Emma must sell by using the contribution margin method and equation 4:

$$\text{Quantity of units required to be sold} = \frac{\text{Fixed costs} + \text{Target operating income}}{\text{Contribution margin per unit}}$$

$$= \frac{\$2{,}000 + \$1{,}600}{\$80 \text{ per unit}} = 45 \text{ units}$$

Proof:

Revenues, \$200 per unit × 45 units	\$9,000
Variable costs, \$120 per unit × 45 units	5,400
Contribution margin	3,600
Fixed costs	2,000
Operating income	1,600
Income taxes, \$1,600 × 0.30	480
Net income	\$1,120

DECISION POINT

How can managers incorporate income taxes into CVP analysis?

Emma can also use the PV graph in Exhibit 3-3. To earn the target operating income of \$1,600, Emma needs to sell 45 units.

Focusing the analysis on target net income instead of target operating income will not change the breakeven point because, by definition, operating income at the breakeven point is \$0 and no income taxes are paid when there is no operating income.

TRY IT! 3-3

Best Windows is a small company that installs windows. Its cost structure is as follows:

Selling price from each window installation	\$ 700
Variable cost of each window installation	\$ 600
Annual fixed costs	\$160,000
Tax rate	30%

Calculate the number of windows Best Windows must install and the revenues needed to earn a target net income of \$63,000.

Using CVP Analysis for Decision Making

LEARNING OBJECTIVE 4

Explain how managers use CVP analysis to make decisions

. . . choose the alternative that maximizes operating income

A manager can also use CVP analysis to make other strategic decisions such as choosing the product features of engine size, transmission system, or steering system for a new car model. Different choices will affect the vehicle's selling price, variable cost per unit, fixed costs, and units sold. CVP analysis helps managers estimate the expected profitability of different choices. In our *GMAT Success* example, Emma uses CVP analysis to make decisions about advertising and selling price.

Decision to Advertise

Suppose Emma anticipates selling 40 units of the *GMAT Success* package at the fair. Exhibit 3-3 indicates that Emma's operating income will be \$1,200. Emma is considering advertising the product and its features in the fair brochure. The advertisement will be a fixed cost of \$500. Emma thinks that advertising will increase sales by 10% to 44 packages. Should Emma advertise? The following table presents the CVP analysis.

	40 Packages Sold with No Advertising (1)	44 Packages Sold with Advertising (2)	Difference (3) = (2) − (1)
Revenues (\$200 × 40; \$200 × 44)	\$8,000	\$8,800	\$ 800
Variable costs (\$120 × 40; \$120 × 44)	4,800	5,280	480
Contribution margin (\$80 × 40; \$80 × 44)	3,200	3,520	320
Fixed costs	2,000	2,500	500
Operating income	\$1,200	\$1,020	\$ (180)

Operating income will decrease from $1,200 to $1,020, so Emma should not advertise. Note that Emma could focus only on the difference column and come to the same conclusion: If Emma advertises, contribution margin will increase by $320 (revenues, $800 − variable costs, $480) and fixed costs will increase by $500, resulting in a $180 decrease in operating income.

When using CVP analysis, try evaluating your decisions based on differences rather than mechanically working through the contribution income statement. What if advertising costs were $400 or $600 instead of $500? Analyzing differences allows managers to get to the heart of CVP analysis and sharpens their intuition by focusing only on the revenues and costs that will change as a result of a decision.

Decision to Reduce the Selling Price

Having decided not to advertise, Emma is contemplating whether to reduce the selling price to $175. At this price, she thinks she will sell 50 units. At this quantity, the test-prep package company that supplies *GMAT Success* will sell the packages to Emma for $115 per unit instead of $120. Should Emma reduce the selling price?

Contribution margin from lowering price to $175: ($175 − $115) per unit × 50 units	$3,000
Contribution margin from maintaining price at $200: ($200 − $120) per unit × 40 units	3,200
Change in contribution margin from lowering price	$ (200)

Decreasing the price will reduce contribution margin by $200 and, because the fixed costs of $2,000 will not change, will also reduce Emma's operating income by $200. Emma should not reduce the selling price.

Determining Target Prices

Emma could also ask, "At what price can I sell 50 units (purchased at $115 per unit) and still earn an operating income of $1,200?" The answer is $179, as the following calculations show:

	Target operating income	$1,200
	Add fixed costs	2,000
	Target contribution margin	$3,200
	Divided by number of units sold	÷ 50 units
	Target contribution margin per unit	$ 64
	Add variable cost per unit	115
	Target selling price	$ 179
Proof:	Revenues, $179 per unit × 50 units	$8,950
	Variable costs, $115 per unit × 50 units	5,750
	Contribution margin	3,200
	Fixed costs	2,000
	Operating income	$1,200

Emma should also examine the effects of other decisions, such as simultaneously increasing advertising costs and raising or lowering the price of *GMAT Success*. In each case, Emma compares the changes in contribution margin (through the effects on selling prices, variable costs, and quantities of units sold) to the changes in fixed costs and chooses the alternative that provides the highest operating income. Concepts in Action: Can Cost–Volume–Profit Analysis Help Whole Foods Escape the "Whole Paycheck" Trap? describes how Whole Foods, the supermarket chain, reduced prices of its products to increase contribution margin and operating income.

DECISION POINT

How do managers use CVP analysis to make decisions?

Strategic decisions invariably entail risk. Managers can use CVP analysis to evaluate how the operating income of their companies will be affected if the outcomes they predict are not achieved—say, if sales are 10% lower than they estimated. Evaluating this risk affects the strategic decisions a manager might make. For example, if the probability of a decline in sales is high, a manager may choose a cost structure with higher variable costs and fewer fixed costs, even if this cost structure results in lower operating income.

CONCEPTS IN ACTION

Can Cost–Volume–Profit Analysis Help Whole Foods Escape the "Whole Paycheck" Trap?[2]

photocritical/Shutterstock

For many years, Whole Foods—the American supermarket chain—has been criticized for the high prices of its organic groceries. While it has the highest profit margin in the industry, Whole Foods has struggled to shake its "whole paycheck" reputation as a grocery store for wealthy people who are willing to pay top dollar for asparagus water and ornamental kale.

In 2017, Amazon purchased Whole Foods for $13.7 billion. Its first order of business was to cut prices on more than 500 groceries, including bananas, avocados, and eggs. Why? Amazon believed that lower prices would drive new customers to Whole Foods and boost its profits.

"We're determined to make healthy and organic food affordable for everyone. Everybody should be able to eat Whole Foods quality—we will lower prices without compromising Whole Foods' long-held commitment to the highest standards," said Amazon executive Jeff Wilke.

Amazon also rolled out special discounts at Whole Foods for its Amazon Prime members, including 10% off hundreds of sale items and rotating weekly specials such as $10 per pound off halibut steaks. It also began selling Whole Foods' private-label brands through its Web site and its Amazon Fresh, Prime Pantry, and Prime Now programs. One year after Amazon acquired Whole Foods, annual revenue grew approximately 7% and the number of items purchased per transaction increased.

[2] *Sources:* Abha Bhattarai, "Whole Foods Has Tried to Lower Prices Before. Can Amazon Make It Work?" *The Washington Post*, August 25, 2017 (https://www.washingtonpost.com/business/capitalbusiness/whole-foods-has-tried-lower-prices-before-can-amazon-make-it-work/2017/08/25/2b2d1308-89a1-11e7-a50f-e0d4e6ec070a_story.html); Tonya Garcia, "Amazon Prime Members Are Adopting Whole Foods Benefits Faster Than Previous Perks," MarketWatch.com, July 31, 2018 (https://www.marketwatch.com/story/amazon-prime-members-are-adopting-whole-foods-benefits-faster-than-previous-perks-2018-07-27); Christian Hetrick, "A Year After Amazon Takeover, Whole Foods Still Hasn't Shed Its Whole Paycheck Status," *The Philadelphia Inquirer*, August 20, 2018 (http://www2.philly.com/philly/business/consumer_news/amazon-whole-foods-prices-prime-wegman-20180820.html); Lisa Baertlein and Jeffrey Dastin, "Amazon Cuts Whole Foods Prices for Prime Members in New Grocery Showdown," *Reuters*, May 16, 2018 (https://www.reuters.com/article/us-amazon-com-whole-foods/amazon-cuts-whole-foods-prices-for-prime-members-in-new-grocery-showdown-idUSKCN1IH0BM).

Sensitivity Analysis and Margin of Safety

LEARNING OBJECTIVE 5

Explain how sensitivity analysis helps managers cope with uncertainty

...determine the effect on operating income of different assumptions

Sensitivity analysis is a "what if" technique managers use to examine how an outcome will change if the original predicted data are not achieved or if an underlying assumption changes. The analysis answers questions such as "What will operating income be if the quantity of units sold decreases by 5% from the original prediction?" and "What will operating income be if variable cost per unit increases by 10%?" For example, companies such as Boeing and Airbus use CVP analysis to evaluate how many airplanes they need to sell in order to recover the multibillion-dollar costs of designing and developing new ones. The managers then do a sensitivity analysis to test how sensitive their conclusions are to different assumptions, such as the size of the market for the airplane, its selling price, and the market share they think it can capture. The analysis helps visualize the possible outcomes and risks *before* the company commits to funding a project.

Electronic spreadsheets, such as Excel, enable managers to systematically and efficiently conduct CVP-based sensitivity analyses and to examine the effect and interaction of changes in selling price, variable cost per unit, and fixed costs on target operating income. Exhibit 3-4 displays a spreadsheet for the *GMAT Success* example.

Using the spreadsheet, Emma can immediately see how many units she needs to sell to achieve particular operating-income levels, given alternative levels of fixed costs and variable cost per unit that she may face. For example, she must sell 32 units to earn an operating income of $1,200 if fixed costs are $2,000 and variable cost per unit is $100. Emma can also use cell C13 of Exhibit 3-4 to determine that she needs to sell 56 units to break even if the fixed cost of the booth rental at the Chicago fair is raised to $2,800 and if the variable cost per unit charged by the test-prep package supplier increases to $150. Emma can use this information along with sensitivity analysis and her predictions about how much she can sell to decide if she should rent the booth.

EXHIBIT 3-4

Spreadsheet Analysis of CVP Relationships for *GMAT Success*

Home | Insert | Page Layout | Formulas | Data | Review | View

D5 ▼ *fx* =($A5+D$3)/(F1-$B5)

	A	B	C	D	E	F
1			Number of Units Required to Be Sold at $200			
2			Selling Price to Earn Target Operating Income of			
3		Variable Costs	$0	$1,200	$1,600	$2,000
4	Fixed Costs	per Unit	(Breakeven point)			
5	$2,000	$100	20	32[a]	36	40
6	$2,000	$120	25	40	45	50
7	$2,000	$150	40	64	72	80
8	$2,400	$100	24	36	40	44
9	$2,400	$120	30	45	50	55
10	$2,400	$150	48	72	80	88
11	$2,800	$100	28	40	44	48
12	$2,800	$120	35	50	55	60
13	$2,800	$150	56	80	88	96
14						

[a]Number of units required to be sold $= \dfrac{\text{Fixed costs + Target operating income}}{\text{Contribution margin per unit}} = \dfrac{\$2{,}000 + \$1{,}200}{\$200 - \$100} = 32$

An important aspect of sensitivity analysis is **margin of safety**:

$$\text{Margin of safety} = \text{Budgeted (or actual) revenues} - \text{Breakeven revenues}$$
$$\text{Margin of safety (in units)} = \text{Budgeted (or actual) sales quantity} - \text{Breakeven quantity}$$

The margin of safety answers the "what if" question: If budgeted revenues are above the breakeven point and drop, how far can they fall below budget before the breakeven point is reached? Sales might decrease as a result of factors such as a poorly executed marketing program or a competitor introducing a better product. Assume that Emma has fixed costs of $2,000, a selling price of $200, and variable cost per unit of $120. From Exhibit 3-1, if Emma sells 40 units, budgeted revenues are $8,000 and budgeted operating income is $1,200. The breakeven point is 25 units or $5,000 in total revenues.

$$\text{Margin of safety} = \begin{array}{c}\text{Budgeted}\\\text{revenues}\end{array} - \begin{array}{c}\text{Breakeven}\\\text{revenues}\end{array} = \$8{,}000 - \$5{,}000 = \$3{,}000$$
$$\begin{array}{c}\text{Margin of}\\\text{safety (in units)}\end{array} = \begin{array}{c}\text{Budgeted}\\\text{sales (units)}\end{array} - \begin{array}{c}\text{Breakeven}\\\text{sales (units)}\end{array} = 40 - 25 = 15 \text{ units}$$

Sometimes margin of safety is expressed as a percentage:

$$\text{Margin of safety percentage} = \frac{\text{Margin of safety in dollars}}{\text{Budgeted (or actual) revenues}}$$

In our example, margin of safety percentage $= \dfrac{\$3{,}000}{\$8{,}000} = 37.5\%$

That is, revenues would have to decrease substantially, by 37.5%, to reach breakeven revenues. The high margin of safety gives Emma confidence that she is unlikely to suffer a loss.

If, however, Emma expects to sell only 30 units, budgeted revenues would be $6,000 ($200 per unit × 30 units) and the margin of safety would equal

$$\text{Budgeted revenues} - \text{Breakeven revenues} = \$6{,}000 - \$5{,}000 = \$1{,}000$$
$$\begin{array}{c}\text{Margin of}\\\text{safety percentage}\end{array} = \frac{\text{Margin of safety in dollars}}{\text{Budgeted (or actual) revenues}} = \frac{\$1{,}000}{\$6{,}000} = 16.67\%$$

That is, if revenues fall by more than 16.67%, Emma would suffer a loss. A low margin of safety increases the risk of a loss. Emma would need to look for ways to lower the breakeven point by reducing fixed costs or increasing contribution margin. For example, could she charge a higher price without reducing demand or could she purchase the software at a lower cost? If Emma can neither reduce her fixed costs nor increase contribution margin and if she cannot tolerate this level of risk, she will prefer not to rent a booth at the fair.

DECISION POINT

What can managers do to cope with uncertainty or changes in underlying assumptions?

Sensitivity analysis gives managers a good feel for a decision's risks. It is a simple approach to recognizing **uncertainty**, which is the possibility that an actual amount will deviate from an expected amount. The appendix to this chapter describes a more comprehensive approach to modeling uncertainty using probability distributions.

TRY IT! 3-4

Best Windows is a small company that installs windows. Its cost structure is as follows:

Selling price from each window installation	$ 700
Variable cost of each window installation	$ 600
Annual fixed costs	$160,000

Calculate the margin of safety in units and dollars and the margin of safety percentage if Best Windows expects to sell 4,000 windows in the year.

Cost Planning and CVP

LEARNING OBJECTIVE 6

Use CVP analysis to plan variable and fixed costs

...compare risk of losses versus higher returns

Managers have the ability to choose the levels of fixed and variable costs in their cost structures. This is a strategic decision that affects risk and returns. In this section, we describe how managers and management accountants think through this decision.

Alternative Fixed-Cost/Variable-Cost Structures

CVP-based sensitivity analysis highlights the risks and returns as fixed costs are substituted for variable costs in a company's cost structure. In Exhibit 3-4, compare line 6 and line 11.

	Fixed Costs	Variable Cost per Unit	Number of Units Required to Be Sold at $200 Selling Price to Earn Target Operating Income of $0 (breakeven point)	$2,000
Line 6	$2,000	$120	25	50
Line 11	$2,800	$100	28	48

Line 11, which has higher fixed costs and lower variable cost per unit than line 6, has a higher breakeven point but requires fewer units to be sold (48 vs. 50) to earn an operating income of $2,000. CVP analysis helps managers evaluate various fixed-cost/variable-cost structures. Suppose the Chicago fair organizers offer Emma three rental alternatives:

Option 1: $2,000 fixed fee

Option 2: $800 fixed fee plus 15% of *GMAT Success* revenues

Option 3: 25% of *GMAT Success* revenues with no fixed fee

Exhibit 3-5 graphically depicts the profit–volume relationship and risks for each option.

- The line representing the relationship between units sold and operating income for Option 1 is the same as the line in the PV graph shown in Exhibit 3-3 (fixed costs of $2,000 and contribution margin per unit of $80).
- The line representing Option 2 shows fixed costs of $800 and a contribution margin per unit of $50 [selling price, $200, minus variable cost per unit, $120, minus variable rental fees per unit, $30 (0.15 × $200)].
- The line representing Option 3 shows fixed costs of $0 and a contribution margin per unit of $30 [selling price, $200, minus variable cost per unit, $120, minus variable rental fees per unit, $50 (0.25 × $200)].

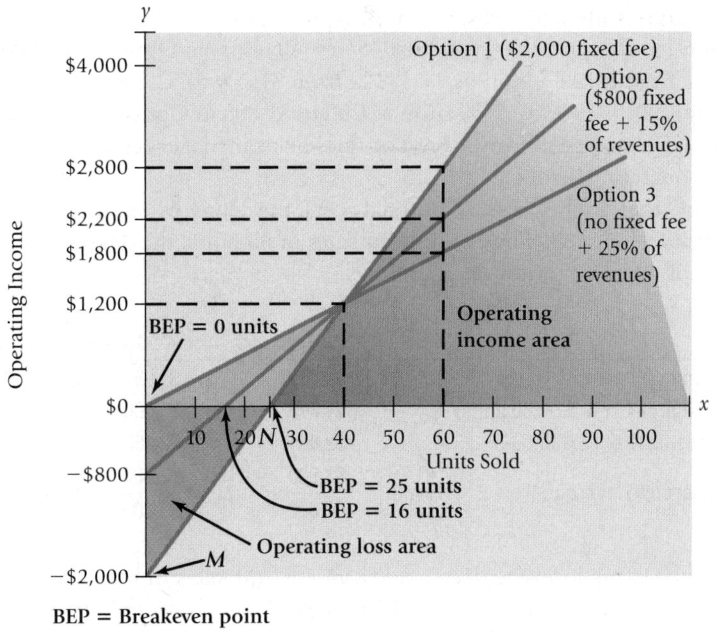

EXHIBIT 3-5

Profit–Volume Graph for Alternative Rental Options for *GMAT Success*

Option 3 has the lowest breakeven point (0 units), and Option 1 has the highest breakeven point (25 units). Option 1 is associated with the highest risk of loss if sales are low, but it also has the highest contribution margin per unit ($80) and therefore the highest operating income when sales are high (greater than 40 units).

The choice among Options 1, 2, and 3 is a strategic decision. Emma's decision will significantly affect her operating income (or loss), depending on the demand for the product. Faced with this uncertainty, Emma's choice will depend on her confidence in the demand for *GMAT Success* and her willingness to risk losses if demand is low. For example, if Emma's tolerance for risk is high, she will choose Option 1 with its high potential rewards. If Emma is risk averse, she will prefer Option 3, with smaller rewards if sales are high but with no risk of loss if sales are low.

Operating Leverage

Operating leverage measures the risk-return tradeoff across alternative cost structures. **Operating leverage** describes the effects that fixed costs have on changes in operating income as changes occur in units sold and contribution margin. Organizations with a high proportion of fixed costs in their cost structures, as is the case with Option 1, have high operating leverage. The line representing Option 1 in Exhibit 3-5 is the steepest of the three lines. Small increases in sales lead to large increases in operating income. Small decreases in sales result in large decreases in operating income and greater risk of losses. *At any given level of sales,*

$$\text{Degree of operating leverage} = \frac{\text{Contribution margin}}{\text{Operating income}}$$

The following table shows the **degree of operating leverage** at sales of 40 units for the three rental options.

	Option 1	Option 2	Option 3
1. Contribution margin per unit (see page 80)	$ 80	$ 50	$ 30
2. Contribution margin (row 1 × 40 units)	$3,200	$2,000	$1,200
3. Operating income (from Exhibit 3-5)	$1,200	$1,200	$1,200
4. Degree of operating leverage (row 2 ÷ row 3)	$\frac{\$3,200}{\$1,200} = 2.67$	$\frac{\$2,000}{\$1,200} = 1.67$	$\frac{\$1,200}{\$1,200} = 1.00$

These results indicate that, when sales are 40 units, a 1% change in sales and contribution margin will result in 2.67% change in operating income for Option 1 and a 1% change in operating income for Option 3. Consider, for example, a sales increase of 50% from 40 to 60 units.

Contribution margin will increase by 50% under each option (from \$3,200 to \$4,800 (\$80 × 60 units) in Option 1 and from \$2,000 to \$3,000 [\$50 × 60 units] in Option 3). Operating income, however, will increase by 2.67 × 50% = 133% from \$1,200 to \$2,800 in Option 1, but it will increase by only 1.00 × 50% = 50% from \$1,200 to \$1,800 in Option 3 (see Exhibit 3-5). The degree of operating leverage at a given level of sales helps managers calculate the effect of sales fluctuations on operating income.

Keep in mind that, in the presence of fixed costs, the degree of operating leverage is different at different levels of sales. For example, at sales of 60 units, the degree of operating leverage under each of the three options is as follows:

	Option 1	Option 2	Option 3
1. Contribution margin per unit (page 80)	\$ 80	\$ 50	\$ 30
2. Contribution margin (row 1 × 60 units)	\$4,800	\$3,000	\$1,800
3. Operating income (from Exhibit 3-5)	\$2,800	\$2,200	\$1,800
4. Degree of operating leverage (row 2 ÷ row 3)	$\frac{\$4,800}{\$2,800} = 1.71$	$\frac{\$3,000}{\$2,200} = 1.36$	$\frac{\$1,800}{\$1,800} = 1.00$

The degree of operating leverage decreases from 2.67 (at sales of 40 units) to 1.71 (at sales of 60 units) under Option 1 and from 1.67 to 1.36 under Option 2. In general, whenever there are fixed costs, the degree of operating leverage decreases as the level of sales increases beyond the breakeven point. If fixed costs are \$0 as they are in Option 3, contribution margin equals operating income and the degree of operating leverage equals 1.00 at all sales levels.

It is important for managers to monitor operating leverage carefully. Consider companies such as General Motors and American Airlines. Their high operating leverage was a major reason for their financial problems. Anticipating high demand for their services, these companies borrowed money to acquire assets, resulting in high fixed costs. As sales declined, they suffered losses and could not generate enough cash to service interest and debt, causing them to seek bankruptcy protection. Managers and management accountants must manage the level of fixed costs and variable costs to balance the risk-return tradeoff.

What can managers do to reduce fixed costs? Nike, the shoe and apparel company, does no manufacturing and incurs no fixed costs of operating manufacturing plants. Instead, it outsources production and buys its products from suppliers in countries such as China, Indonesia, and Vietnam. As a result, all of Nike's production costs are variable costs. Nike reduces its risk of loss by increasing variable costs and reducing fixed costs.

Companies that continue to do their own manufacturing are moving their facilities from the United States to lower-cost countries, such as Mexico and China, to reduce both fixed costs and variable costs. Other companies, such as General Electric and Hewlett-Packard, have shifted service functions, such as after-sales customer service, to their customer call centers in countries such as India. These decisions by companies are often controversial. Some economists argue that outsourcing or building plants in other countries helps keep costs, and therefore prices, low and enables U.S. companies to remain globally competitive. Others argue that outsourcing and setting up manufacturing in other countries reduces job opportunities in the United States and hurts working-class families.

DECISION POINT

How should managers choose among different variable-cost/fixed-cost structures?

TRY IT! 3-5

Best Windows is a small company that installs windows. Its cost structure is as follows:

Selling price from each window installation	\$ 700
Variable cost of each window installation	\$ 600
Annual fixed costs	\$160,000
Number of window units sold	3,400

Best Windows is considering changing its sales compensation for next year. Best Windows would pay salespeople a 3% commission next year and reduce fixed selling costs by \$67,000.

Calculate the degree of operating leverage at sales of 3,400 units under the two options. Comment briefly on the result.

Effects of Sales Mix on Income

LEARNING OBJECTIVE 7

Apply CVP analysis to a company producing multiple products

...assume sales mix of products remains constant as total units sold changes

Companies sell multiple products, each of which are drivers of revenues and costs. **Sales mix** is the quantities (or proportion) of various products (or services) that constitute a company's total unit sales. Suppose Emma is now budgeting for another college fair in New York. She plans to sell two different test-prep packages—*GMAT Success* and *GRE Guarantee*—and budgets the following:

	GMAT Success	***GRE Guarantee***	**Total**
Expected sales	60	40	100
Revenues, $200 and $100 per unit	$12,000	$4,000	$16,000
Variable costs, $120 and $70 per unit	7,200	2,800	10,000
Contribution margin, $80 and $30 per unit	$ 4,800	$1,200	6,000
Fixed costs			4,500
Operating income			$ 1,500

What is the breakeven point for Emma's business now? The total number of units that must be sold to break even in a multiproduct company depends on the sales mix. For Emma, this is the combination of the number of units of *GMAT Success* sold and the number of units of *GRE Guarantee* sold. We assume that the budgeted sales mix (60 units of *GMAT Success* sold for every 40 units of *GRE Guarantee* sold, that is, a ratio of 3:2) will not change at different levels of total unit sales. That is, we think of Emma selling a bundle of 3 units of *GMAT Success* and 2 units of *GRE Guarantee*. (Note that this does not mean that Emma physically bundles the two products together into one big package.)

Each bundle yields a contribution margin of $300, calculated as follows:

	Number of Units of *GMAT Success* and *GRE Guarantee* in Each Bundle	**Contribution Margin per Unit for *GMAT Success* and *GRE Guarantee***	**Contribution Margin of the Bundle**
GMAT Success	3	$80	$240
GRE Guarantee	2	30	60
Total			$300

To compute the breakeven point, we calculate the number of bundles Emma needs to sell.

$$\text{Breakeven point in bundles} = \frac{\text{Fixed costs}}{\text{Contribution margin per bundle}} = \frac{\$4{,}500}{\$300 \text{ per bundle}} = 15 \text{ bundles}$$

The breakeven point in units of *GMAT Success* and *GRE Guarantee* is as follows:

GMAT Success: 15 bundles × 3 units per bundle	45 units
GRE Guarantee: 15 bundles × 2 units per bundle	30 units
Total number of units to break even	75 units

The breakeven point in dollars for *GMAT Success* and *GRE Guarantee* is as follows:

GMAT Success: 45 units × $200 per unit	$ 9,000
GRE Guarantee: 30 units × $100 per unit	3,000
Breakeven revenues	$12,000

When there are multiple products, it is often convenient to use the contribution margin percentage. Under this approach, Emma also calculates the revenues from selling a bundle of 3 units of *GMAT Success* and 2 units of *GRE Guarantee*:

	Number of Units of *GMAT Success and GRE Guarantee* in Each Bundle	**Selling Price for *GMAT Success* and *GRE Guarantee***	**Revenue of the Bundle**
GMAT Success	3	$200	$600
GRE Guarantee	2	100	200
Total			$800

$$\text{Contribution margin percentage for the bundle} = \frac{\text{Contribution margin of the bundle}}{\text{Revenue of the bundle}} = \frac{\$300}{\$800} = 0.375, \text{ or } 37.5\%$$

$$\text{Breakeven revenues} = \frac{\text{Fixed costs}}{\text{Contribution margin \% for the bundle}} = \frac{\$4,500}{0.375} = \$12,000$$

$$\text{Number of bundles required to be sold to break even} = \frac{\text{Breakeven revenues}}{\text{Revenue per bundle}} = \frac{\$12,000}{\$800 \text{ per bundle}} = 15 \text{ bundles}$$

The breakeven point in units and dollars for *GMAT Success* and *GRE Guarantee* are as follows:

GMAT Success: 15 bundles × 3 units per bundle = 45 units × $200 per unit = $9,000

GRE Guarantee: 15 bundles × 2 units per bundle = 30 units × $100 per unit = $3,000

Recall that the breakeven point calculations assume the same budgeted sales mix (3 units of *GMAT Success* for every 2 units of *GRE Guarantee*) at different levels of total unit sales.

Of course, there are many different sales mixes (in units) that can result in a contribution margin of $4,500 that leads to Emma breaking even, as the following table shows:

Sales Mix (Units)		**Contribution Margin from**		
GMAT Success **(1)**	***GRE Guarantee*** **(2)**	***GMAT Success*** **(3) = $80 × (1)**	***GRE Guarantee*** **(4) = $30 × (2)**	**Total Contribution Margin (5) = (3) + (4)**
48	22	$3,840	$ 660	$4,500
36	54	2,880	1,620	4,500
30	70	2,400	2,100	4,500

If, for example, the sales mix changes to 3 units of *GMAT Success* for every 7 units of *GRE Guarantee*, the breakeven point increases from 75 units to 100 units, composed of 30 units of *GMAT Success* and 70 units of *GRE Guarantee*. The breakeven quantity increases because the sales mix has shifted toward the lower-contribution-margin product, *GRE Guarantee* ($30 per unit compared to *GMAT Success*'s $80 per unit). In general, for any given total quantity of units sold, a shift in sales mix towards units with lower contribution margins, decreases operating income.

TRY IT! 3-6

Best Windows plans to sell two different brands of windows—Chad and Musk—and budgets the following:

	Chad Windows	**Musk Windows**	**Total**
Expected sales	3,000	1,500	4,500
Revenues, $700 and $300 per unit	$2,100,000	$450,000	$2,550,000
Variable costs, $600 and $250 per unit	1,800,000	375,000	2,175,000
Contribution margin, $100 and $50 per unit	$ 300,000	$ 75,000	375,000
Fixed costs			160,000
Operating income			$ 215,000

Calculate the breakeven point for Best Windows in terms of (a) the number of units sold and (b) revenues.

How do companies choose their sales mix? They adjust their mix to respond to demand changes. For example, when gasoline prices increased and customers wanted smaller cars, auto companies, such as Ford, Nissan, and Toyota, shifted their production mix to produce smaller cars. This shift to smaller cars increased the breakeven point because the sales mix had shifted toward lower-contribution-margin products. Despite this increase in the breakeven point, shifting the sales mix to smaller cars was the correct decision because the demand for larger cars had fallen. At no point should a manager focus on changing the sales mix to lower the breakeven point without taking into account customer preferences and demand.

DECISION POINT

How can managers apply CVP analysis to a company producing multiple products?

CVP Analysis in Service and Not-for-Profit Organizations

LEARNING OBJECTIVE 8

Apply CVP analysis in service and not-for-profit organizations

...define appropriate output measures

So far, CVP analysis has focused on Emma's merchandising company. Of course, managers at manufacturing companies such as BMW, service companies such as Bank of America, and not-for-profit organizations such as the United Way also use CVP analysis to make decisions. To apply CVP analysis in service and not-for-profit organizations, we need measures of output, which are different from the tangible units sold by manufacturing and merchandising companies. Examples of output measures in various service industries (for example, airlines, hotels/motels, and hospitals) and not-for-profit organizations (for example, universities) are as follows:

Industry	Measure of Output
Airlines	Passenger miles
Hotels/motels	Room-nights occupied
Hospitals	Patient days
Universities	Student credit-hours

CVP analysis is based on variable and fixed costs defined with respect to these output measures. Consider Highbridge Consulting, a boutique management consulting firm. Highbridge measures output in terms of person-days of consulting services. It hires consultants to match the demand for consulting services.

Highbridge hires and trains new consultants before consultants are deployed on assignments. In 2020, Highbridge has a recruiting budget of \$1,250,000. This budget covers the costs of hiring consultants at an average annual cost of \$100,000 and fixed costs of recruiting and training (including administrative salaries and expenses of the recruiting department) of \$250,000. How many consultants can Highbridge recruit in 2020? Highbridge uses CVP analysis to answer this question by setting the recruiting department's operating income to \$0. Let Q be the number of consultants hired:

$$\text{Recruiting budget} - \text{Variable costs} - \text{Fixed costs} = 0$$
$$\$1{,}250{,}000 - \$100{,}000\,Q - \$250{,}000 = 0$$
$$\$100{,}000\,Q = \$1{,}250{,}000 - \$250{,}000 = \$1{,}000{,}000$$
$$Q = \$1{,}000{,}000 \div \$100{,}000 \text{ per consultant} = 10 \text{ consultants}$$

Suppose Highbridge anticipates reduced demand in 2021. It reduces its recruiting budget by 40% to \$1,250,000 × (1 − 0.40) = \$750,000, expecting to hire 6 consultants (40% fewer than 2020). Assuming the cost per consultant and the recruiting department's fixed costs remain the same as in 2020, is this budget correct? No, as the following calculation shows:

$$\$750{,}000 - \$100{,}000\,Q - \$250{,}000 = 0$$
$$\$100{,}000\,Q = \$750{,}000 - \$250{,}000 = \$500{,}000$$
$$Q = \$500{,}000 \div \$100{,}000 \text{ per consultant} = 5 \text{ consultants}$$

Highbridge will only be able to recruit 5 consultants. Note the following two characteristics of the CVP relationships in this service company situation:

1. The percentage decrease in the number of consultants hired, (10 − 5) ÷ 10, or 50%, is greater than the 40% reduction in the recruiting budget. It is greater because the \$250,000 in fixed costs still must be paid, leaving a proportionately lower budget to hire consultants.

In other words, the percentage drop in consultants hired exceeds the percentage drop in the recruiting budget because of the fixed costs.

2. Given the reduced recruiting budget of \$750,000 in 2021, the manager can adjust recruiting activities to hire 6 consultants in one or more of the following ways: (1) by reducing the variable cost per person (the average compensation) from the current \$100,000 per consultant, or (2) by reducing the recruiting department's total fixed costs from the current \$250,000. For example if the recruiting department's fixed costs were reduced to \$210,000 and the cost per consultant were reduced to \$90,000, Highbridge would be able to hire the 6 consultants it needs, (\$750,000 − \$210,000) ÷ \$90,000 = 6 consultants.

DECISION POINT

How do managers apply CVP analysis in service and not-for-profit organizations?

If the fixed costs of the recruiting department remain \$250,000 and Highbridge wants to hire 6 consultants at an average cost of \$100,000, it would have to set the recruiting budget at \$850,000 [(\$100,000 × 6) + \$250,000] instead of \$750,000. Again the percentage decrease in the number of consultants hired 40% [(10 − 6) ÷ 10] is greater than the 32% [(\$1,250,000 − \$850,000) ÷ \$1,250,000] reduction in the recruiting budget because of the fixed costs of the recruiting department.

Contribution Margin Versus Gross Margin

LEARNING OBJECTIVE 9

Distinguish contribution margin

...revenues minus all variable costs

from gross margin

...revenues minus cost of goods sold

So far, we have developed two important concepts relating to profit margin—contribution margin, which was introduced in this chapter, and gross margin, which was discussed in Chapter 2. Is there a relationship between these two concepts? In the following equations, we clearly distinguish contribution margin, which provides information for CVP and risk analysis, from gross margin, a measure of competitiveness, described in Chapter 2.

$$\text{Gross margin} = \text{Revenues} - \text{Cost of goods sold}$$
$$\text{Contribution margin} = \text{Revenues} - \text{All variable costs}$$

The gross margin measures how much a company can charge for its products over and above the cost of acquiring or producing them. Companies, such as brand-name pharmaceuticals producers, have high gross margins because their products are often patented and provide unique and distinctive benefits to consumers. In contrast, manufacturers of generic medicines and basic chemicals have low gross margins because the market for these products is highly competitive. Contribution margin indicates how much of a company's revenues are available to cover fixed costs. It helps in assessing the risk of losses. For example, the risk of loss is low if the contribution margin exceeds a company's fixed costs even when sales are low. Gross margin and contribution margin are related but give different insights. For example, a company operating in a competitive market with a low gross margin will have a low risk of loss if its fixed costs are small.

Consider the distinction between gross margin and contribution margin in the manufacturing sector. The concepts differ in two ways: fixed manufacturing costs and variable operating (nonmanufacturing) costs. The following example (figures assumed) illustrates this difference:

Contribution Income Statement Emphasizing Contribution Margin (in thousands)			Financial Accounting Income Statement Emphasizing Gross Margin (in thousands)	
Revenues		\$1,000	Revenues	\$1,000
Variable manufacturing costs	\$250		Cost of goods sold (variable manufacturing costs, \$250 + fixed manufacturing costs, \$160)	410
Variable operating (nonmanuf.) costs	270	520		
Contribution margin		480	Gross margin	590
Fixed manufacturing costs	160			
Fixed operating (nonmanuf.) costs	138	298	Operating (nonmanuf.) costs (variable, \$270 + fixed, \$138)	408
Operating income		\$ 182	Operating income	\$ 182

Fixed manufacturing costs of \$160,000 are not deducted from revenues when computing the contribution margin but are deducted when computing the gross margin. The cost of goods sold in a manufacturing company includes all variable manufacturing costs and all fixed manufacturing costs ($250,000 + $160,000). The company's variable operating (nonmanufacturing) costs (such as commissions paid to salespersons) of $270,000 are deducted from revenues when computing the contribution margin (because these are variable costs), but are not deducted when computing gross margin (because cost of goods sold only includes manufacturing costs).

Like contribution margin, gross margin can be expressed as a total, as an amount per unit, or as a percentage. For example, the **gross margin percentage** is the gross margin divided by revenues—59% ($590 ÷ $1,000) in our manufacturing-sector example.

One reason why managers sometimes confuse gross margin and contribution margin with each other is that the two are often identical in the case of merchandising companies because the cost of goods sold equals the variable cost of goods purchased (and subsequently sold).

DECISION POINT

What is the difference between contribution margin and gross margin?

PROBLEM FOR SELF-STUDY

Wembley Travel Agency specializes in flights between Los Angeles and London. It books passengers on United Airlines at $900 per round-trip ticket. Until last month, United paid Wembley a commission of 10% of the ticket price paid by each passenger. This commission was Wembley's only source of revenues. Wembley's fixed costs are $14,000 per month (for salaries, rent, and so on), and its variable costs, such as sales commissions and bonuses, are $20 per ticket purchased for a passenger.

United Airlines has just announced a revised payment schedule for all travel agents. It will now pay travel agents a 10% commission per ticket up to a maximum of $50. Any ticket costing more than $500 generates only a $50 commission, regardless of the ticket price. Wembley's managers are concerned about how United's new payment schedule will affect its breakeven point and profitability.

1. Under the old 10% commission structure, how many round-trip tickets must Wembley sell each month (a) to break even and (b) to earn an operating income of $7,000 per month?
2. How does United's revised payment schedule affect your answers to (a) and (b) in requirement 1?

Solution

1. Wembley receives a 10% commission on each ticket: 10% × $900 = $90. Thus,

$$\text{Selling price} = \$90 \text{ per ticket}$$
$$\text{Variable cost per unit} = \$20 \text{ per ticket}$$
$$\text{Contribution margin per unit} = \$90 - \$20 = \$70 \text{ per ticket}$$
$$\text{Fixed costs} = \$14{,}000 \text{ per month}$$

a. $$\frac{\text{Breakeven number}}{\text{of tickets}} = \frac{\text{Fixed costs}}{\text{Contribution margin per unit}} = \frac{\$14{,}000}{\$70 \text{ per ticket}} = 200 \text{ tickets}$$

b. When target operating income = $7,000 per month,

$$\frac{\text{Quantity of tickets}}{\text{required to be sold}} = \frac{\text{Fixed costs} + \text{Target operating income}}{\text{Contribution margin per unit}}$$
$$= \frac{\$14{,}000 + \$7{,}000}{\$70 \text{ per ticket}} = \frac{\$21{,}000}{\$70 \text{ per ticket}} = 300 \text{ tickets}$$

2. Under the new system, Wembley would receive only $50 on the $900 ticket. Thus,

$$\text{Selling price} = \$50 \text{ per ticket}$$
$$\text{Variable cost per unit} = \$20 \text{ per ticket}$$
$$\text{Contribution margin per unit} = \$50 - \$20 = \$30 \text{ per ticket}$$
$$\text{Fixed costs} = \$14{,}000 \text{ per month}$$

a. $$\frac{\text{Breakeven number}}{\text{of tickets}} = \frac{\$14{,}000}{\$30 \text{ per ticket}} = 467 \text{ tickets (rounded up)}$$

b. $$\frac{\text{Quantity of tickets}}{\text{required to be sold}} = \frac{\$21{,}000}{\$30 \text{ per ticket}} = 700 \text{ tickets}$$

The $50 cap on the commission paid per ticket causes the breakeven point to more than double (from 200 to 467 tickets) and the tickets required to be sold to earn $7,000 per month to also more than double (from 300 to 700 tickets). As would be expected, managers at Wembley reacted very negatively to the United Airlines announcement to change commission payments.

DECISION POINTS

The following question-and-answer format summarizes the chapter's learning objectives. Each decision presents a key question related to a learning objective. The guidelines are the answer to that question.

Decision	Guidelines
1. How can CVP analysis help managers?	CVP analysis assists managers in understanding the behavior of a product's or service's total costs, total revenues, and operating income as changes occur in the output level, selling price, variable costs, or fixed costs.
2. How can managers determine the breakeven point or the output needed to achieve a target operating income?	The breakeven point is the quantity of output at which total revenues equal total costs. The three methods for computing the breakeven point and the quantity of output to achieve target operating income are the equation method, the contribution margin method, and the graph method. Each method is merely a restatement of the others. Managers often select the method they find easiest to use in a specific decision situation.
3. How can managers incorporate income taxes into CVP analysis?	Income taxes can be incorporated into CVP analysis by using the target net income to calculate the target operating income. The breakeven point is unaffected by income taxes because no income taxes are paid when operating income equals zero.
4. How do managers use CVP analysis to make decisions?	Managers compare how revenues, costs, and contribution margins change across various alternatives. They then choose the alternative that maximizes operating income.
5. What can managers do to cope with uncertainty or changes in underlying assumptions?	Sensitivity analysis is a "what if" technique that examines how an outcome will change if the original predicted data are not achieved or if an underlying assumption changes. When making decisions, managers use CVP analysis to compare contribution margins and fixed costs under different assumptions. Managers also calculate the margin of safety equal to budgeted revenues minus breakeven revenues.
6. How should managers choose among different variable-cost/fixed-cost structures?	Choosing the variable-cost/fixed-cost structure is a strategic decision for companies. CVP analysis helps managers compare the risk of losses when revenues are low and the upside profits when revenues are high for different proportions of variable and fixed costs in a company's cost structure.
7. How can managers apply CVP analysis to a company producing multiple products?	Managers apply CVP analysis in a multiple product company by assuming the sales mix of products sold remains constant as the total quantity of units sold changes.
8. How do managers apply CVP analysis in service and not-for-profit organizations?	Managers define output measures such as passenger-miles in the case of airlines or patient-days in the context of hospitals and identify costs that are fixed and those that vary with these measures of output.
9. What is the difference between contribution margin and gross margin?	Contribution margin is revenues minus all variable costs, whereas gross margin is revenues minus cost of goods sold. Contribution margin measures the risk of a loss, whereas gross margin measures the competitiveness of a product.

APPENDIX

Decision Models and Uncertainty[3]

This appendix explores the characteristics of uncertainty, describes an approach managers can use to make decisions in a world of uncertainty, and illustrates the insights gained when uncertainty is recognized in CVP analysis. In the face of uncertainty, managers rely on decision models to help them make the right choices.

Role of a Decision Model

Uncertainty is the possibility that an actual amount will deviate from an expected amount. In the *GMAT Success* example, Emma might forecast sales at 42 units, but actual sales might turn out to be 30 units or 60 units. A decision model helps managers deal with such uncertainty. It is a formal method for making a choice, commonly involving both quantitative and qualitative analyses. This appendix focuses on the quantitative analysis that usually includes the following steps:

Step 1: Identify a choice criterion. A **choice criterion** is an objective that can be quantified, such as maximize income or minimize costs. Managers use the choice criterion to choose the best alternative action. Emma's choice criterion is to maximize expected operating income at the Chicago college fair.

Step 2: Identify the set of alternative actions that can be taken. We use the letter *a* with subscripts $_{1,2,}$ and $_3$ to distinguish each of Emma's three possible actions:

a_1 = Pay \$2,000 fixed fee

a_2 = Pay \$800 fixed fee plus 15% of *GMAT Success* revenues

a_3 = Pay 25% of *GMAT Success* revenues with no fixed fee

Step 3: Identify the set of events that can occur. An **event** is a possible relevant occurrence, such as the actual number of *GMAT Success* packages Emma might sell at the fair. The set of events should be mutually exclusive and collectively exhaustive. Events are mutually exclusive if they cannot occur at the same time. Events are collectively exhaustive if, taken together, they make up the entire set of possible relevant occurrences (no other event can occur). Examples of mutually exclusive and collectively exhaustive events are growth, decline, or no change in industry demand and increase, decrease, or no change in interest rates. Only one event out of the entire set of mutually exclusive and collectively exhaustive events will actually occur.

Suppose Emma's only uncertainty is the number of units of *GMAT Success* that she can sell. For simplicity, suppose Emma estimates that sales will be either 30 or 60 units. This set of events is mutually exclusive because clearly sales of 30 units and 60 units cannot both occur at the same time. It is collectively exhaustive because under our assumptions sales cannot be anything other than 30 or 60 units. We use the letter *x* with subscripts $_1$ and $_2$ to distinguish the set of mutually exclusive and collectively exhaustive events:

x_1 = 30 units

x_2 = 60 units

Step 4: Assign a probability to each event that can occur. A **probability** is the likelihood or chance that an event will occur. The decision model approach to coping with uncertainty assigns probabilities to events. A **probability distribution** describes the likelihood, or the

[3] *Source:* Based on teaching notes prepared by R. Williamson.

probability, that each of the mutually exclusive and collectively exhaustive set of events will occur. In some cases, there will be much evidence to guide the assignment of probabilities. For example, the probability of obtaining heads in the toss of a coin is 1/2 and that of drawing a particular playing card from a standard, well-shuffled deck is 1/52. In business, the probability of having a specified percentage of defective units may be assigned with great confidence on the basis of production experience with thousands of units. In other cases, there will be little evidence supporting estimated probabilities—for example, expected sales of a new pharmaceutical product next year. Suppose that Emma, on the basis of past experience, assesses a 60% chance, or a 6/10 probability, that she will sell 30 units and a 40% chance, or a 4/10 probability, that she will sell 60 units. Using $P(x)$ as the notation for the probability of an event, the probabilities are:

$$P(x_1) = 6/10 = 0.60$$
$$P(x_2) = 4/10 = 0.40$$

The sum of these probabilities must equal 1.00 because these events are mutually exclusive and collectively exhaustive.

Step 5: Identify the set of possible outcomes. **Outcomes** specify, in terms of the choice criterion, the predicted economic results of the various possible combinations of actions and events. In the *GMAT Success* example, the outcomes are the six possible operating incomes displayed in the decision table in Exhibit 3-6. A **decision table** is a summary of the alternative actions, events, outcomes, and probabilities of events.

Distinguish among actions, events, and outcomes. Actions are decision choices available to managers—for example, the particular rental alternatives that Emma can choose. Events are the set of all relevant occurrences that can happen—for example, the different quantities of *GMAT Success* packages that may be sold at the fair. The outcome is operating income, which depends both on the action the manager selects (rental alternative chosen) and the event that occurs (the quantity of packages sold).

Exhibit 3-7 presents an overview of relationships among a decision model, the implementation of a chosen action, its outcome, and subsequent performance evaluation. Thoughtful managers step back and evaluate what happened and learn from their experiences. This learning serves as feedback for adapting the decision model for future actions.

EXHIBIT 3-6 Decision Table for *GMAT Success*

Home Insert Page Layout Formulas Data Review View

	A	B	C	D	E	F	G	H	I
1	Selling price =	$200			Operating Income				
2	Package cost =	$120			Under Each Possible Event				
3			Percentage						
4		Fixed	of Fair	Event x_1: Units Sold =	30		Event x_2: Units Sold =	60	
5	Actions	Fee	Revenues	Probability(x_1) =	0.60		Probability(x_2) =	0.40	
6	a_1: Pay $2,000 fixed fee	$2,000	0%	$400[l]			$2,800[m]		
7	a_2: Pay $800 fixed fee plus 15% of revenues	$ 800	15%	$700[n]			$2,200[p]		
8	a_3:Pay 25% of revenues with no fixed fee	$ 0	25%	$900[q]			$1,800[r]		
9									
10	[l]Operating income = ($200 – $120)(30) – $2,000	=	$ 400						
11	[m]Operating income = ($200 – $120)(60) – $2,000	=	$2,800						
12	[n]Operating income = ($200 – $120 – 15% × $200)(30) – $800	=	$ 700						
13	[p]Operating income = ($200 – $120 – 15% × $200)(60) – $800	=	$2,200						
14	[q]Operating income = ($200 – $120 – 25% × $200)(30)	=	$ 900						
15	[r]Operating income = ($200 – $120 – 25% × $200)(60)	=	$1,800						

EXHIBIT 3-7 A Decision Model and Its Link to Performance Evaluation

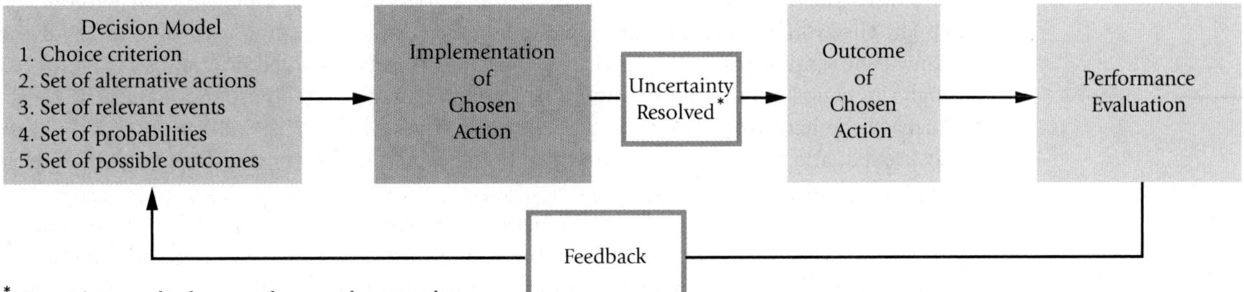

*Uncertainty resolved means the event becomes known.

Expected Value

An **expected value** is the weighted average of the outcomes, with the probability of each outcome serving as the weight. When the outcomes are measured in monetary terms, expected value is often called **expected monetary value**. Using information in Exhibit 3-6, the expected monetary value of each booth-rental alternative denoted by $E(a_1)$, $E(a_2)$, and $E(a_3)$ is as follows:

Pay \$2,000 fixed fee:	$E(a_1) = (0.60 \times \$400) + (0.40 \times \$2{,}800) = \$1{,}360$
Pay \$800 fixed fee plus 15% of revenues:	$E(a_2) = (0.60 \times \$700) + (0.40 \times \$2{,}200) = \$1{,}300$
Pay 25% of revenues with no fixed fee:	$E(a_3) = (0.60 \times \$900) + (0.40 \times \$1{,}800) = \$1{,}260$

To maximize expected operating income, Emma should select action a_1—pay the Chicago fair organizers a \$2,000 fixed fee.

To interpret the expected value of selecting action a_1, imagine that Emma attends many fairs, each with the probability distribution of operating incomes given in Exhibit 3-6. For a specific fair, Emma will earn operating income of either \$400, if she sells 30 units, or \$2,800, if she sells 60 units. But if Emma attends 100 fairs, she will expect to earn \$400 operating income 60% of the time (at 60 fairs) and \$2,800 operating income 40% of the time (at 40 fairs), for a total operating income of \$136,000 (\$400 × 60 + \$2,800 × 40). The expected value of \$1,360 is the operating income per fair that Emma will earn when averaged across all fairs (\$136,000 ÷ 100). Of course, in many real-world situations, managers must make one-time decisions under uncertainty. Even in these cases, expected value is a useful tool for choosing among alternatives.

Consider the effect of uncertainty on the preferred action choice. If Emma were certain she would sell only 30 units (that is, $P(x_1) = 1$), she would prefer alternative a_3—pay 25% of revenues with no fixed fee. To follow this reasoning, examine Exhibit 3-6. When 30 units are sold, alternative a_3 yields the maximum operating income of \$900. Because fixed costs are \$0, booth-rental costs are lower, equal to \$1,500 (25% of revenues = 0.25 × \$200 per unit × 30 units), when sales are low.

However, if Emma were certain she would sell 60 packages (that is, $P(x_2) = 1$), she would prefer alternative a_1—pay a \$2,000 fixed fee. Exhibit 3-6 indicates that when 60 units are sold, alternative a_1 yields the maximum operating income of \$2,800. That's because, when 60 units are sold, rental payments under a_2(\$800 + 0.15 × \$200 per unit × 60 units = \$2,600) and a_3 (0.25 × \$200 per unit × 60 units = \$3,000) are more than the fixed \$2,000 fee under a_1.

Despite the high probability of selling only 30 units, Emma still prefers to take action a_1, which is to pay a fixed fee of \$2,000. That's because the high risk of low operating income (the 60% probability of selling only 30 units) is more than offset by the high return from selling 60 units, which has a 40% probability. If Emma were more averse to risk (measured in our example by the difference between operating incomes when 30 versus 60 units are sold), she might have preferred action a_2 or a_3. For example, action a_2 ensures an operating income of at least \$700, greater than the operating income of \$400 that she would earn under action a_1 if only 30 units were sold. Of course, choosing a_2 limits the upside potential to \$2,200 relative to \$2,800 under a_1, if 60 units are sold. If Emma is very concerned about downside risk, however, she may be willing to forgo some upside benefits to protect against a \$400 outcome by choosing a_2.[4]

[4] For more formal approaches, refer to Jeffrey H. Moore and Larry R. Weatherford, *Decision Modeling with Microsoft Excel*, 6th ed. (Upper Saddle River, NJ: Prentice Hall, 2001).

Good Decisions and Good Outcomes

Always distinguish between a good decision and a good outcome. One can exist without the other. Suppose you are offered a one-time-only gamble tossing a coin. You will win $20 if the outcome is heads, but you will lose $1 if the outcome is tails. As a decision maker, you proceed through the logical phases: gathering information, assessing outcomes, and making a choice. You accept the bet. Why? Because the expected value is $9.50 $[0.5(\$20) + 0.5(-\$1)]$. The coin is tossed, and the outcome is tails. You lose. From your viewpoint, this was a good decision but a bad outcome.

A decision can be made only on the basis of information that is available at the time of evaluating and making the decision. By definition, uncertainty rules out guaranteeing that the best outcome will always be obtained. As in our example, it is possible that bad luck will produce bad outcomes even when good decisions have been made. A bad outcome does not mean a bad decision was made. The best protection against a bad outcome is a good decision.

TERMS TO LEARN

This chapter and the Glossary at the end of the text contain definitions of the following important terms:

breakeven point (BEP) (**p. 72**)
choice criterion (**p. 89**)
contribution income statement (**p. 68**)
contribution margin (**p. 67**)
contribution margin per unit (**p. 67**)
contribution margin percentage (**p. 68**)
contribution margin ratio (**p. 68**)
cost–volume–profit (CVP) analysis (**p. 66**)
decision table (**p. 90**)
degree of operating leverage (**p. 81**)
event (**p. 89**)
expected monetary value (**p. 91**)
expected value (**p. 91**)
gross margin percentage (**p. 87**)
margin of safety (**p. 79**)
net income (**p. 75**)
operating leverage (**p. 81**)
outcomes (**p. 90**)
probability (**p. 89**)
probability distribution (**p. 89**)
PV graph (**p. 74**)
revenue driver (**p. 71**)
sales mix (**p. 83**)
sensitivity analysis (**p. 78**)
uncertainty (**p. 80**)

ASSIGNMENT MATERIAL

Note: To underscore the basic CVP relationships, the assignment material ignores income taxes unless stated otherwise.

Questions

3-1 Define cost–volume–profit analysis.

3-2 Describe the assumptions underlying CVP analysis.

3-3 Distinguish between operating income and net income.

3-4 Define contribution margin, contribution margin per unit, and contribution margin percentage.

3-5 Describe three methods that managers can use to express CVP relationships.

3-6 Why is it more accurate to describe the subject matter of this chapter as CVP analysis rather than as breakeven analysis?

3-7 "CVP analysis is both simple and simplistic. If you want realistic analysis to underpin your decisions, look beyond CVP analysis." Do you agree? Explain.

3-8 How does an increase in the income tax rate affect the breakeven point?

3-9 Describe sensitivity analysis. How has the advent of the electronic spreadsheet affected the use of sensitivity analysis?

3-10 Give an example of how a manager can decrease variable costs while increasing fixed costs.

3-11 Give an example of how a manager can increase variable costs while decreasing fixed costs.

3-12 What is operating leverage? How is the degree of operating leverage helpful to managers?

3-13 "There is no such thing as a fixed cost. All costs can be 'unfixed' given sufficient time." Do you agree? What is the implication of your answer for CVP analysis?

3-14 How can a company with multiple products compute its breakeven point?

3-15 "In CVP analysis, gross margin is a less-useful concept than contribution margin." Do you agree? Explain briefly.

Multiple-Choice Questions

In partnership with:

BECKER PROFESSIONAL EDUCATION

3-16 Jack's Jax has total fixed costs of $25,000. If the company's contribution margin is 60%, the income tax rate is 25% and the selling price of a box of Jax is $20, how many boxes of Jax would the company need to sell to produce a net income of $15,000?

a. 5,625 **b.** 4,445
c. 3,750 **d.** 3,333

3-17 During the current year, XYZ Company increased its variable SG&A expenses while keeping fixed SG&A expenses the same. As a result, XYZ's

a. Contribution margin and gross margin will be lower.
b. Contribution margin will be higher, while its gross margin will remain the same.
c. Operating income will be the same under both the financial accounting income statement and contribution income statement.
d. Inventory amounts booked under the financial accounting income statement will be lower than under the contribution income statement.

3-18 Under the contribution income statement, a company's contribution margin will be

a. Higher if fixed SG&A costs decrease.
b. Higher if variable SG&A costs increase.
c. Lower if fixed manufacturing overhead costs decrease.
d. Lower if variable manufacturing overhead costs increase.

3-19 A company needs to sell 10,000 units of its only product in order to break even. Fixed costs are $110,000, and the per unit selling price and variable costs are $20 and $9, respectively. If total sales are $220,000, the company's margin of safety will be equal to

a. $0 **b.** $20,000
c. $110,000 **d.** $200,000

3-20 Once a company exceeds its breakeven level, operating income can be calculated by multiplying

a. The sales price by unit sales in excess of breakeven units.
b. Unit sales by the difference between the sales price and fixed cost per unit.
c. The contribution margin ratio by the difference between unit sales and breakeven sales.
d. The contribution margin per unit by the difference between unit sales and breakeven sales.

Exercises

3-21 CVP computations. Fill in the blanks for each of the following independent cases.

Case	Revenues	Variable Costs	Fixed Costs	Total Costs	Operating Income	Contribution Margin Percentage
a.		$600		$800	$1,600	
b.	$2,500		$200		$ 900	
c.	$ 500	$300		$500		
d.	$1,200		$200			25%

3-22 CVP computations. Davidson Manufacturing sold 435,000 units of its product for $74 per unit in 2020. Variable cost per unit is $62, and total fixed costs are $1,940,000.

Required

1. Calculate (a) contribution margin and (b) operating income.
2. Davidson's current manufacturing process is labor intensive. Kate Schmidt, Davidson's production manager, has proposed investing in state-of-the-art manufacturing equipment, which will increase the

annual fixed costs to $5,655,000. The variable costs are expected to decrease to $54 per unit. Davidson expects to maintain the same sales volume and selling price next year. How would acceptance of Schmidt's proposal affect your answers to (a) and (b) in requirement 1?
3. Should Davidson's executives accept Schmidt's proposal? Explain.

3-23 CVP analysis, changing revenues and costs. Sunset Travel Agency specializes in flights between Toronto and Jamaica. It books passengers on Hamilton Air. Sunset's fixed costs are $23,500 per month. Hamilton Air charges passengers $1,500 per round-trip ticket.

Calculate the number of tickets Sunset must sell each month to (a) break even and (b) make a target operating income of $10,000 per month in each of the following independent cases.

Required

1. Sunset's variable costs are $43 per ticket. Hamilton Air pays Sunset 6% commission on ticket price.
2. Sunset's variable costs are $40 per ticket. Hamilton Air pays Sunset 6% commission on ticket price.
3. Sunset's variable costs are $40 per ticket. Hamilton Air pays $60 fixed commission per ticket to Sunset. Comment on the results.
4. Sunset's variable costs are $40 per ticket. It receives $60 commission per ticket from Hamilton Air. It charges its customers a delivery fee of $5 per ticket. Comment on the results.

3-24 CVP exercises. The Deli-Sub Shop owns and operates six stores in and around Minneapolis. You are given the following corporate budget data for next year:

Revenues	$11,000,000
Fixed costs	$ 3,000,000
Variable costs	$ 7,500,000

Variable costs change based on the number of subs sold.
Compute the budgeted operating income for each of the following deviations from the original budget data. (Consider each case independently.)

Required

1. A 10% increase in contribution margin, holding revenues constant
2. A 10% decrease in contribution margin, holding revenues constant
3. A 5% increase in fixed costs
4. A 5% decrease in fixed costs
5. A 5% increase in units sold
6. A 5% decrease in units sold
7. A 10% increase in fixed costs and a 10% increase in units sold
8. A 5% increase in fixed costs and a 5% decrease in variable costs
9. Which of these alternatives yields the highest budgeted operating income? Explain why this is the case.

3-25 CVP exercises. The Doral Company manufactures and sells pens. Currently, 5,000,000 units are sold per year at $0.50 per unit. Fixed costs are $900,000 per year. Variable costs are $0.30 per unit. (Consider each case separately.)

Required

1. **a.** What is the current annual operating income?
   b. What is the current breakeven point in revenues?

Compute the new operating income for each of the following changes:

2. A $0.04 per unit increase in variable costs
3. A 10% increase in fixed costs and a 10% increase in units sold
4. A 20% decrease in fixed costs, a 20% decrease in selling price, a 10% decrease in variable cost per unit, and a 40% increase in units sold

Compute the new breakeven point in units for each of the following changes:

5. A 10% increase in fixed costs
6. A 10% increase in selling price and a $20,000 increase in fixed costs

3-26 CVP relationships. The McNamara Company has a maximum production capacity of 20,000 units per year. For that capacity level, fixed costs are $280,000 per year. Variable costs per unit are $30.

In the coming year, the company has orders for 24,000 units at $50. The company wants to make a minimum overall operating income of $148,000 on these 24,000 units.

Required

What maximum unit purchase price would McNamara Company be willing to pay to a subcontractor for the additional 4,000 units it cannot manufacture itself to earn an operating income of $148,000.

3-27 CVP analysis, income taxes. The Express Meal has two restaurants that are open 24 hours a day. Fixed costs for the two restaurants together total $400,000 per year. Service varies from a cup of coffee to full meals. The average sales check per customer is $8.50. The average cost of food and other variable costs for each customer is $3.50. The income tax rate is 30%. Target net income is $140,000.

Required

1. Compute the revenues needed to earn the target net income.
2. How many customers are needed to break even? To earn net income of $140,000?
3. Compute net income if the number of customers is 150,000.

3-28 CVP analysis, sensitivity analysis. Right Fit Jeans Co. sells blue jeans wholesale to major retailers across the country. Each pair of jeans has a selling price of $40 with $30 in variable costs of goods sold. The company has fixed manufacturing costs of $1,050,000 and fixed marketing costs of $150,000. Sales commissions are paid to the wholesale sales reps at 10% of revenues. The company has an income tax rate of 20%.

Required

1. How many jeans must Right Fit sell in order to break even?
2. How many jeans must the company sell in order to reach
   a. A target operating income of $300,000?
   b. A net income of $300,000?
3. How many jeans would Right Fit have to sell to earn the net income in requirement 2b if (Consider each requirement independently.)
   a. The contribution margin per unit increases by 20%.
   b. The selling price is increased to $45.
   c. The company outsources manufacturing to an overseas company, increasing variable costs per unit by $1.00 and saving 60% of fixed manufacturing costs.

3-29 CVP analysis, margin of safety. Suppose Morrison Corp.'s breakeven point is revenues of $1,100,000. Fixed costs are $660,000.

Required

1. Compute the contribution margin percentage.
2. Compute the selling price if variable costs are $16 per unit.
3. Suppose 75,000 units are sold. Compute the margin of safety in units and dollars.
4. What does this tell you about the risk of Morrison making a loss? What are the most likely reasons for this risk to increase?

3-30 Choosing most profitable production volume. Answer the following questions.

1. Blanchard Company manufactures and sells dresses at a variable cost of $30 each and a fixed cost of *x*. It can sell 6,000 dresses at a selling price of $50 to earn an operating income of $20,000 or it can sell 3,500 dresses at a selling price of $60 and another 2,000 dresses at a selling price of $40. Which alternative should Blanchard choose?
2. Canta Corporation manufactures and sells a special kind of ball bearing. Its cost structure depends on the number of bearings it produces. Its fixed costs and variable manufacturing cost per unit for different ranges of production are described in the following table:

Production Range in Units	Fixed Costs	Variable Manufacturing Cost per Unit
1–3,000	$250,000	$75
3,001–6000	$350,000	$50
6,001–10,000	$750,000	$25

Canta's sales director believes the company can sell 2,500 units at a selling price of $300; or 5,000 units at a price of $200; or 8,000 units at a price of $175. If it chose to sell 8,000 units, however, it would incur additional advertising costs of $50,000 and variable selling costs of $5 per unit.

Should Canta Corporation plan to produce and sell (a) 2,500 units (b) 5,000 units or (c) 8,000 units?

Required

3-31 Operating leverage. Cover Rugs is holding a 2-week carpet sale at Josh's Club, a local warehouse store. Cover Rugs plans to sell carpets for $950 each. The company will purchase the carpets from a local distributor for $760 each, with the privilege of returning any unsold units for a full refund. Josh's Club has offered Cover Rugs two payment alternatives for the use of space.

- Option 1: A fixed payment of $7,410 for the sale period
- Option 2: 10% of total revenues earned during the sale period

Assume Cover Rugs will incur no other costs.

Required

1. Calculate the breakeven point in units for (a) Option 1 and (b) Option 2.
2. At what level of revenues will Cover Rugs earn the same operating income under either option?
   a. For what range of unit sales will Cover Rugs prefer Option 1?
   b. For what range of unit sales will Cover Rugs prefer Option 2?
3. Calculate the degree of operating leverage at sales of 65 units for the two rental options.
4. Briefly explain and interpret your answer to requirement 3.

3-32 CVP analysis, international cost structure differences. Rugs-R-Us, Inc., is considering three possible countries for the sole manufacturing site of its newest area rug: Brazil, Italy, and France. All area rugs are to be sold to retail outlets in the United States for $250 per unit. These retail outlets add their own markup when selling to final customers. Fixed costs and variable cost per unit (area rug) differ in the three countries.

Country	Sales Price to Retail Outlets	Annual Fixed Costs	Variable Manufacturing Cost per Area Rug	Variable Marketing & Distribution Cost per Area Rug
Brazil	$250.00	$7,500,000	$45.00	$10.00
Italy	250.00	5,000,000	65.00	15.00
France	250.00	9,000,000	55.00	20.00

Required

1. Compute the breakeven point for Rugs-R-Us, Inc., in each country in (a) units sold and (b) revenues.
2. If Rugs-R-Us, Inc., plans to produce and sell 80,000 rugs in 2020, what is the budgeted operating income for each of the three manufacturing locations? Comment on the results.

3-33 Sales mix, new and upgrade customers. Chartz 1-2-3 is a top-selling electronic spreadsheet product. Chartz is about to release version 5.0. It divides its customers into two groups: new customers and upgrade customers (those who previously purchased Chartz 1-2-3 4.0 or earlier versions). Although the same physical product is provided to each customer group, sizable differences exist in selling prices and variable marketing costs:

	New Customers		Upgrade Customers	
Selling price		$195		$115
Variable costs				
Manufacturing	$15		$15	
Marketing	50	65	20	35
Contribution margin		$130		$ 80

The fixed costs of Chartz 1-2-3 5.0 are $16,500,000. The planned sales mix in units is 60% new customers and 40% upgrade customers.

Required

1. What is the Chartz 1-2-3 5.0 breakeven point in units, assuming that the planned 60%/40% sales mix is attained?
2. If the sales mix is attained, what is the operating income when 170,000 total units are sold?
3. Show how the breakeven point in units changes with the following customer mixes:
   a. New 40% and upgrade 60%
   b. New 80% and upgrade 20%
   c. Comment on the results.

3-34 Sales mix, three products. The Kenosha Company has three product lines of beer mugs—A, B, and C—with contribution margins of $5, $4, and $3, respectively. The president foresees sales of 175,000 units in the coming period, consisting of 25,000 units of A, 100,000 units of B, and 50,000 units of C. The company's fixed costs for the period are $351,000.

Required

1. What is the company's breakeven point in units, assuming that the given sales mix is maintained?
2. If the sales mix is maintained, what is the total contribution margin when 175,000 units are sold? What is the operating income?
3. What would operating income be if the company sold 25,000 units of A, 75,000 units of B, and 75,000 units of C? What is the new breakeven point in units if these relationships persist in the next period?
4. Comparing the breakeven points in requirements 1 and 3, is it always better for a company to choose the sales mix that yields the lower breakeven point? Explain.

3-35 Contribution margin, decision making. Welch Men's Clothing's revenues and cost data for 2020 are as follows:

Revenues		$600,000
Cost of goods sold (all variable costs)		300,000
Gross margin		300,000
Operating costs:		
Salaries fixed	$140,000	
Sales commissions (12% of sales)	72,000	
Depreciation of equipment and fixtures	10,000	
Store rent ($3,500 per month)	42,000	
Other operating costs	45,000	309,000
Operating income (loss)		$ (9,000)

Mr. Welch, the owner of the store, is unhappy with the operating results. An analysis of other operating costs reveals that it includes $30,000 variable costs, which vary with sales volume, and $15,000 (fixed) costs.

Required

1. Compute the contribution margin of Welch Men's Clothing.
2. Compute the contribution margin percentage.
3. Mr. Welch estimates that he can increase units sold, and hence revenues by 25% by incurring additional advertising costs of $8,000. Calculate the impact of the additional advertising costs on operating income.
4. What other actions can Mr. Welch take to improve operating income?

3-36 Contribution margin, gross margin, and margin of safety. Bella Beauty manufactures and sells a face cream to small specialty stores in the greater Los Angeles area. It presents the monthly operating income statement shown here to George Sanchez, a potential investor in the business. Help Mr. Sanchez understand Bella Beauty's cost structure.

	A	B	C	D
1	**Bella Beauty**			
2	**Operating Income Statement June 2020**			
3	Units sold			10,000
4	Revenues			$120,000
5	Cost of goods sold			
6	Variable manufacturing costs		$50,000	
7	Fixed manufacturing costs		19,920	
8	Total cost of goods sold			69,920
9	Gross margin			50,080
10	Operating costs:			
11	Variable marketing costs		$22,000	
12	Fixed marketing & admin. costs		18,000	
13	Total operating costs			40,000
14	Operating income			$ 10,080

Required

1. Recast the income statement to emphasize contribution margin.
2. Calculate the contribution margin percentage and breakeven point in units and revenues for June 2020.
3. What is the margin of safety (in units) for June 2020?
4. If sales in June were only 9,500 units and Bella Beauty's tax rate is 30%, calculate its net income.

3-37 Uncertainty and expected costs. Kindmart is an international retail store. Kindmart's managers are considering implementing a new business-to-business (B2B) information system for processing merchandise orders. The current system costs Kindmart $2,000,000 per month and $55 per order. Kindmart has two options, a partially automated B2B and a fully automated B2B system. The partially automated B2B system will have a fixed cost of $6,000,000 per month and a variable cost of $45 per order. The fully automated B2B system has a fixed cost of $14,000,000 per month and a variable cost of $25 per order.

Based on data from the past 2 years, Kindmart has determined the following distribution on monthly orders:

Monthly Number of Orders	Probability
300,000	0.25
500,000	0.45
700,000	0.30

Required

1. Prepare a table showing the cost of each plan for each quantity of monthly orders.
2. What is the expected cost of each plan?
3. In addition to the information system's costs, what other factors should Kindmart consider before deciding to implement a new B2B system?

Problems

3-38 CVP analysis, service firm. Safari Escapes generates average revenue of $6,250 per person on its 5-day package tours to wildlife parks in Kenya. The variable costs per person are as follows:

Airfare	$1,300
Hotel accommodations	2,450
Meals	900
Ground transportation	100
Park tickets and other costs	500
Total	$5,250

Annual fixed costs total $590,000.

Required

1. Calculate the number of package tours that must be sold to break even.
2. Calculate the revenue needed to earn a target operating income of $92,000.
3. If fixed costs increase by $29,500, what decrease in variable cost per person must be achieved to maintain the breakeven point calculated in requirement 1?
4. The general manager at Safari Escapes proposes to increase the price of the package tour to $7,750 to decrease the breakeven point in units. Using information in the original problem, calculate the new breakeven point in units. What factors should the general manager consider before deciding to increase the price of the package tour?

3-39 CVP, target operating income, service firm. Spotted Turtle provides day care for children Mondays through Fridays. Its monthly variable costs per child are as follows:

Lunch and snacks	$130
Educational supplies	75
Other supplies (paper products, toiletries, etc.)	35
Total	$240

Monthly fixed costs consist of the following:

Rent	$2,100
Utilities	400
Insurance	250
Salaries	1,400
Miscellaneous	650
Total	$4,800

Spotted Turtle charges each parent $640 per child per month.

Required

1. Calculate the breakeven point.
2. Spotted Turtle's target operating income is $10,800 per month. Compute the number of children who must be enrolled to achieve the target operating income.
3. Spotted Turtle lost its lease and had to move to another building. Monthly rent for the new building is $3,500. In addition, at the suggestion of parents, Spotted Turtle plans to take children on field trips. Monthly costs of the field trips are $2,500. By how much should Spotted Turtle increase fees per child to meet the target operating income of $10,800 per month, assuming the same number of children as in requirement 2?

3-40 CVP analysis, margin of safety. Dynamic Docs prepares marketing plans for growing businesses. For 2020, budgeted revenues are $3,500,000 based on 700 marketing plans at an average rate per plan of $5,000. The company would like to achieve a margin of safety percentage of at least 25%. The company's current fixed costs are $1,800,000 and variable costs average $2,000 per marketing plan. (Consider each of the following separately.)

Required

1. Calculate Dynamic Docs' breakeven point and margin of safety in units.
2. Which of the following changes would help Dynamic Docs achieve its desired margin of safety?
   a. The average revenue per customer increases to $5,600.
   b. The planned number of marketing plans prepared increases by 8%.
   c. Dynamic Docs purchases new software that results in a $48,000 increase to fixed costs but reduces variable costs by $300 per marketing plan.

3-41 CVP analysis, income taxes. (CMA, adapted) J.T. Brooks and Company, a manufacturer of quality handmade walnut bowls, has had a steady growth in sales for the past 5 years. However, increased competition has led Mr. Brooks, the president, to believe that an aggressive marketing campaign will be necessary next year to maintain the company's present growth. To prepare for next year's marketing campaign, the company's controller has prepared and presented Mr. Brooks with the following data for the current year, 2020:

Variable cost (per bowl)	
Direct materials	$ 3.00
Direct manufacturing labor	8.00
Variable overhead (manufacturing, marketing, distribution, and customer service)	7.50
Total variable cost per bowl	$ 18.50
Fixed costs	
Manufacturing	$ 20,000
Marketing, distribution, and customer service	194,500
Total fixed costs	$214,500
Selling price	$ 35.00
Expected sales, 22,000 units	$770,000
Income tax rate	40%

Required

1. What is the projected net income for 2020?
2. What is the breakeven point in units for 2020?
3. Mr. Brooks has set the revenue target for 2021 at a level of $875,000 (or 25,000 bowls). He believes an additional marketing cost of $16,500 for advertising in 2021, with all other costs remaining constant, will be necessary to attain the revenue target. What is the net income for 2021 if the additional $16,500 is spent and the revenue target is met?
4. What is the breakeven point in revenues for 2021 if the additional $16,500 is spent for advertising?
5. If the additional $16,500 is spent, what are the required 2021 revenues for 2021 net income to equal 2020 net income?
6. At a sales level of 25,000 units, what maximum amount can be spent on advertising if a 2021 net income of $108,450 is desired?

3-42 CVP, sensitivity analysis. Jan's Ornaments sells handmade ornaments for $35.00 per ornament. Operating information for 2020 is as follows:

Sales revenue ($35 per ornament)	$420,000
Variable cost ($20 per ornament)	240,000
Contribution margin	180,000
Fixed costs	160,000
Operating income	$ 20,000

Jan, the owner of the company, wants to increase operating income over the next year by at least $20,000. To do so, the company is considering the following options:

Required

1. Spend $25,000 on advertising, which should result in a 15% increase in sales.
2. Increase selling price to $39 per ornament, which is expected to decrease sales by 10%.
3. Automate some steps in the manufacturing process, which would increase fixed costs by $30,000 and decrease variable cost to $18.00 per unit. Sales would remain the same.
4. Increase the selling price to $36 and decrease variable costs to $19. This alternative would result in a 5% decrease in sales.

Evaluate each of the alternatives considered by Jan's Ornaments separately. Do any of the options meet or exceed Jan's targeted increase in operating income of $20,000? What should Jan do?

3-43 CVP analysis, shoe stores. The HighStep Shoe Company operates a chain of shoe stores that sell 10 different styles of inexpensive men's shoes with identical unit costs and selling prices. A unit is defined as a pair of shoes. Each store has a store manager who is paid a fixed salary. Individual salespeople receive a fixed salary and a sales commission. HighStep is considering opening another store that is expected to have the revenue and cost relationships shown here. (Consider each question independently.)

	A	B	C	D	E
1	Unit Variable Data (per pair of shoes)			Annual Fixed Costs	
2	Selling price	$60.00		Rent	$ 30,000
3	Cost of shoes	$37.00		Salaries	100,000
4	Sales commission	3.00		Advertising	40,000
5	Variable cost per unit	$40.00		Other fixed costs	10,000
6				Total fixed costs	$180,000

Required

1. What is the annual breakeven point in (a) units sold and (b) revenues?
2. If 8,000 units are sold, what will be the store's operating income (loss)?
3. If sales commissions are discontinued and fixed salaries are raised by a total of $15,500, what would be the annual breakeven point in (a) units sold and (b) revenues?
4. Refer to the original data. If, in addition to his fixed salary, the store manager is paid a commission of $2.00 per unit sold, what would be the annual breakeven point in (a) units sold and (b) revenues?
5. Refer to the original data. If, in addition to his fixed salary, the store manager is paid a commission of $2.00 *per unit in excess of the breakeven point*, what would be the store's operating income if 12,000 units were sold?

3-44 CVP analysis, shoe stores (continuation of 3-43). Refer to requirement 3 of Problem 3-43. In this problem, assume the role of the owner of HighStep.

Required

1. As owner, which sales compensation plan would you choose if forecasted annual sales of the new store were at least 10,000 units? What do you think of the motivational aspect of your chosen compensation plan?
2. Suppose the target operating income is $69,000. How many units must be sold to reach the target operating income under (a) the original salary-plus-commissions plan and (b) the higher-fixed-salaries-only plan? Which method would you prefer? Explain briefly.
3. You open the new store on January 1, 2020, with the original salary-plus-commission compensation plan in place. Because you expect the cost of the shoes to rise due to inflation, you place a firm bulk order for 11,000 shoes and lock in the $37 price per unit. But toward the end of the year, only 9,500 shoes are sold, and you authorize a markdown of the remaining inventory to $50 per unit. Finally, all units are sold. Salespeople, as usual, get paid a commission of 5% of revenues. What is the annual operating income for the store?

3-45 Alternate cost structures, uncertainty, and sensitivity analysis. Corporate Printing Company currently leases its only copy machine for $1,500 a month. The company is considering replacing this leasing agreement with a new contract that is entirely commission based. Under the new agreement, Corporate would pay a commission for its printing at a rate of $20 for every 500 pages printed. The company currently charges $0.20 per page to its customers. The paper used in printing costs the company $0.05 per page and other variable costs, including hourly labor, amount to $0.10 per page.

Required

1. What is the company's breakeven point under the current leasing agreement? What is it under the new commission-based agreement?
2. For what range of sales levels will Corporate prefer (a) the fixed lease agreement and (b) the commission agreement?
3. Do this question only if you have covered the chapter appendix in your class. Corporate estimates that the company is equally likely to sell 20,000, 30,000, 40,000, 50,000, or 60,000 pages of print. Using information from the original problem, prepare a table that shows the expected profit at each sales level under the fixed leasing agreement and under the commission-based agreement. What is the expected value of each agreement? Which agreement should Corporate choose?

3-46 CVP, alternative cost structures. Glamour Accessories operates a kiosk at the local mall, selling cell phone covers for $30 each. Glamour Accessories currently pays $1,000 a month to rent the space and pays two full-time employees to each work 160 hours a month at $10 per hour. The store shares a manager with a neighboring kiosk and pays 50% of the manager's annual salary of $60,000 and benefits of $12,000. The wholesale cost of the cell phone covers to the company is $10.

Required

1. How many cell phone covers does Glamour Accessories need to sell each month to break even?
2. If Glamour Accessories wants to earn an operating income of $5,300 per month, how many cell phone covers does the store need to sell?
3. If the store's hourly employees agreed to a 15% sales-commission-only pay structure, instead of their hourly pay, how many cell phone covers would Glamour Accessories need to sell to earn an operating income of $5,300?

4. Assume Glamour Accessories pays its employees hourly under the original pay structure but is able to pay the mall 10% of its monthly revenue instead of monthly rent. At what sales levels would Glamour Accessories prefer to pay a fixed amount of monthly rent, and at what sales levels would it prefer to pay 10% of its monthly revenue as rent?

3-47 CVP analysis, income taxes, sensitivity. (CMA, adapted) Thompson Engine Company manufactures and sells diesel engines for use in small farming equipment. For its 2020 budget, Thompson Engine Company estimates the following:

Selling price	$ 7,000
Variable cost per engine	$ 2,000
Annual fixed costs	$5,560,000
Net income	$ 900,000
Income tax rate	40%

The first-quarter income statement, as of March 31, reported that sales were not meeting expectations. During the first quarter, only 300 units had been sold at the current price of $7,000. The income statement showed that variable and fixed costs were as planned, which meant that the 2020 annual net income projection would not be met unless management took action. A management committee was formed and presented the following mutually exclusive alternatives to the president:

a. Reduce the selling price by 15%. The sales organization forecasts that at this significantly reduced price, 1,400 units can be sold during the remainder of the year. Total fixed costs and variable cost per unit will stay as budgeted.
b. Lower variable cost per unit by $750 through the use of less-expensive direct materials. The selling price will also be reduced by $800, and sales of 1,130 units are expected for the remainder of the year.
c. Reduce fixed costs by 5% and lower the selling price by 25%. Variable cost per unit will be unchanged. Sales of 1,500 units are expected for the remainder of the year.

Required

1. If no changes are made to the selling price or cost structure, determine the number of units that Thompson Engine Company must sell (a) to break even and (b) to achieve its net income objective.
2. Determine which alternative Thompson Engine Company should select to achieve its net income objective. Show your calculations.

3-48 Choosing between compensation plans, operating leverage. (CMA, adapted) Zahner Corporation manufactures housewares products that are sold through a network of external sales agents. The agents are paid a commission of 20% of revenues. Zahner is considering replacing the sales agents with its own salespeople, who would be paid a commission of 10% of revenues and total salaries of $3,520,000. The income statement for the year ending December 31, 2020, under the two scenarios is shown here.

	A	B	C	D	E
1		**Zahner Corporation**			
2		**Income Statement**			
3		**For the Year Ended December 2020**			
4		**Using Sales Agents**		**Using Own Sales Force**	
5	Revenues		$35,200,000		$35,200,000
6	Cost of goods sold				
7	Variable	$13,375,000		$13,375,000	
8	Fixed	4,125,000	17,500,000	4,125,000	17,500,000
9	Gross margin		17,700,000		17,700,000
10	Marketing costs				
11	Commissions	$ 7,040,000		$ 3,520,000	
12	Fixed costs	4,025,000	11,065,000	7,545,000	11,065,000
13	Operating income		$ 6,635,000		$ 6,635,000

Required

1. Calculate Zahner's 2020 contribution margin percentage, breakeven revenue, and degree of operating leverage under the two scenarios.
2. Describe the advantages and disadvantages of each type of sales alternative.
3. In 2021, Zahner uses its own salespeople, who demand a 15% commission. If all other cost-behavior patterns are unchanged, how much revenue must the salespeople generate in order to earn the same operating income as in 2020?

3-49 Sales mix, three products. The Ronowski Company has three product lines of belts—A, B, and C—with contribution margins of $3, $2, and $1, respectively. The president foresees sales of 200,000 units in the coming period, consisting of 20,000 units of A, 100,000 units of B, and 80,000 units of C. The company's fixed costs for the period are $255,000.

Required

1. What is the company's breakeven point in units, assuming that the given sales mix is maintained?
2. If the sales mix is maintained, what is the total contribution margin when 200,000 units are sold? What is the operating income?
3. What would operating income be if 20,000 units of A, 80,000 units of B, and 100,000 units of C were sold? What is the new breakeven point in units if these relationships persist in the next period?

3-50 Multiproduct CVP and decision making. Clear Waters produces two types of water filters. One attaches to the faucet and cleans all water that passes through the faucet. The other is a pitcher-cum-filter that only purifies water meant for drinking.

The unit that attaches to the faucet is sold for $72 and has variable costs of $20.

The pitcher-cum-filter sells for $88 and has variable costs of $16.

Clear Waters sells two faucet models for every three pitchers sold. Fixed costs equal $960,000.

Required

1. What is the breakeven point in unit sales and dollars for each type of filter at the current sales mix?
2. Clear Waters is considering buying new production equipment. The new equipment will increase fixed cost by $166,400 per year and will decrease the variable cost of the faucet and the pitcher units by $4 and $8, respectively. Assuming the same sales mix, how many of each type of filter does Clear Waters need to sell to break even?
3. Assuming the same sales mix, at what total sales level would Clear Waters be indifferent between using the old equipment and buying the new production equipment? If total sales are expected to be 23,000 units, should Clear Waters buy the new production equipment?

3-51 Sales mix, two products. The Stackpole Company retails two products: a standard and a deluxe version of a luggage carrier. The budgeted income statement for next period is as follows:

	Standard Carrier	Deluxe Carrier	Total
Units sold	187,500	62,500	250,000
Revenues at $28 and $50 per unit	$5,250,000	$3,125,000	$8,375,000
Variable costs at $18 and $30 per unit	3,375,000	1,875,000	5,250,000
Contribution margins at $10 and $20 per unit	$1,875,000	$1,250,000	3,125,000
Fixed costs			2,250,000
Operating income			$ 875,000

Required

1. Compute the breakeven point in units, assuming that the company achieves its planned sales mix.
2. Compute the breakeven point in units (a) if only standard carriers are sold and (b) if only deluxe carriers are sold.
3. Suppose 250,000 units are sold but only 50,000 of them are deluxe. Compute the operating income. Compute the breakeven point in units. Compare your answer with the answer to requirement 1. What is the major lesson of this problem?

3-52 Gross margin and contribution margin. The Museum of Fine Art is preparing for its annual appreciation dinner for contributing members. Last year, 500 members attended the dinner. Tickets for the dinner were $30 per attendee. The profit report for last year's dinner follows.

Ticket sales	$15,000
Cost of dinner	16,000
Gross margin	(1,000)
Invitations and paperwork	2,500
Profit (loss)	$ (3,500)

This year the dinner committee does not want to lose money on the dinner. To help achieve its goal, the committee analyzed last year's costs. Of the $16,000 cost of the dinner, $8,500 were fixed costs and $7,500 were variable costs. Of the $2,500 cost of invitations and paperwork, $1,750 were fixed and $750 were variable.

Required

1. Prepare last year's profit report using the contribution margin format.
2. The committee is considering expanding this year's dinner invitation list to include volunteer members (in addition to contributing members). If the committee expands the dinner invitation list, it expects attendance to double. Calculate the effect this will have on the profitability of the dinner assuming fixed costs will be the same as last year.

3-53 Ethics, CVP analysis. Megaphone Corporation produces a molded plastic casing, M&M101, for many cell phones currently on the market. Summary data from its 2020 income statement are as follows:

Revenues	$5,000,000
Variable costs	3,250,000
Fixed costs	1,890,000
Operating income	$ (140,000)

Joshua Kirby, Megaphone's president, is very concerned about Megaphone Corporation's poor profitability. He asks Leroy Gibbs, production manager, and Tony DiNunzo, controller, to see if there are ways to reduce costs.

After 2 weeks, Leroy returns with a proposal to reduce variable costs to 55% of revenues by reducing the costs Megaphone currently incurs for safe disposal of wasted plastic. Tony is concerned that this would expose the company to potential environmental liabilities. He tells Leroy, "We would need to estimate some of these potential environmental costs and include them in our analysis." "You can't do that," Leroy replies. "We are not violating any laws. There is some possibility that we may have to incur environmental costs in the future, but if we bring it up now, this proposal will not go through because our senior management always assumes these costs to be larger than they turn out to be. The market is very tough, and we are in danger of shutting down the company and costing all of us our jobs. The only reason our competitors are making money is because they are doing exactly what I am proposing."

Required

1. Calculate Megaphone Corporation's breakeven revenues for 2020.
2. Calculate Megaphone Corporation's breakeven revenues if variable costs are 55% of revenues.
3. Calculate Megaphone Corporation's operating income for 2020 if variable costs had been 55% of revenues.
4. Given Leroy Gibbs's comments, what should Tony DiNunzo do?

3-54 Deciding where to produce. (CMA, adapted) Portal Corporation produces the same power generator in two Illinois plants, a new plant in Peoria and an older plant in Moline. The following data are available for the two plants:

	A	B	C	D	E
1		Peoria		Moline	
2	Selling price		$150.00		$150.00
3	Variable manufacturing cost per unit	$72.00		$88.00	
4	Fixed manufacturing cost per unit	30.00		15.00	
5	Variable marketing and distribution cost per unit	14.00		14.00	
6	Fixed marketing and distribution cost per unit	19.00		14.50	
7	Total cost per unit		135.00		131.50
8	Operating income per unit		$ 15.00		$ 18.50
9	Production rate per day	400	units	320	units
10	Normal annual capacity usage	240	days	240	days
11	Maximum annual capacity	300	days	300	days

All fixed costs per unit are calculated based on a normal capacity usage consisting of 240 working days. When the number of working days exceeds 240, overtime charges raise the variable manufacturing costs of additional units by $3.00 per unit in Peoria and $8.00 per unit in Moline.

Portal Corporation is expected to produce and sell 192,000 power generators during the coming year. Wanting to take advantage of the higher operating income per unit at Moline, the company's production manager has decided to manufacture 96,000 units at each plant, resulting in a plan in which Moline operates at maximum capacity (320 units per day × 300 days) and Peoria operates at its normal volume (400 units per day × 240 days).

Required

1. Calculate the breakeven point in units for the Peoria plant and for the Moline plant.
2. Calculate the operating income that would result from the production manager's plan to produce 96,000 units at each plant.
3. Determine how the production of 192,000 units should be allocated between the Peoria and Moline plants to maximize operating income for Portal Corporation. Show your calculations.

4 Job Costing

LEARNING OBJECTIVES

1. Describe the building-block concepts of costing systems
2. Distinguish job costing from process costing
3. Describe the approaches to evaluating and implementing job-costing systems
4. Outline the seven-step approach to normal costing
5. Distinguish actual costing from normal costing
6. Track the flow of costs in a job-costing system
7. Adjust for under- or overallocated manufacturing overhead costs at the end of the fiscal year using alternative methods
8. Understand variations of normal costing

No one likes to lose money.

Whether a company is a new startup venture providing marketing consulting services or an established manufacturer of custom-built motorcycles, knowing how to job cost—that is, knowing how much it costs to produce an individual product—is critical if a company is to generate a profit. As the following article shows, Mortenson | Clark knows this all too well.

JOB COSTING AND THE NEW GOLDEN STATE WARRIORS ARENA[1]

Mortenson | Clark was responsible for costing, pricing, and constructing the new home of Steph Curry and the Golden State Warriors, the Chase Center in San Francisco. Completed in 2019, the $1.2 billion state-of-the-art arena anchors a new development featuring restaurants, cafes, two office towers, public plazas, and a new public waterfront park along San Francisco Bay.

To construct the Chase Center, Mortenson | Clark managers used historical data and marketplace information to carefully estimate all costs associated with the project: direct costs, indirect costs, and general administrative costs. Direct costs included the 9,000 tons of structural steel, 100,000 cubic yards of concrete, and 450 construction workers per day required for construction. Indirect costs included the cost of supervisory labor, company-owned equipment, and safety equipment. Finally, general administrative costs allocated to the Chase Center project included office rent, utilities, and insurance.

Throughout the 3-year construction process, job costing was critical as onsite managers reported on the status of the new arena. Managers used a 200-page monthly "playbook" to identify potential problems with the project and took corrective action to ensure the Chase Center was delivered within the original project budget and on time to start the 2019–2020 NBA season.

Kevin McGovern/Shutterstock

[1] *Sources*: Carol Eaton, "Innovative Chase Center Taking Shape in San Francisco," *California Constructor*, September–October 2018 (http://www.modernpubsonline.com/CA-Constructor/CCSeptOct2018/html/print/CC%20S-O%2018_DL.pdf); Christine Kirkpatrick, "Warriors Basketball Arena Stays in Lead at Halftime," *Engineering News-Record*, July 23, 2018 (https://www.enr.com/articles/44887-warriors-basketball-arena-stays-in-lead-at-halftime); Cindy Riley, "$1B Arena Awaits Warriors' Return to Frisco," ConstructionEquipmentGuide.com, March 14, 2018 (https://www.constructionequipmentguide.com/1b-arena-awaits-warriors-return-to-frisco/39470).

Building-Block Concepts of Costing Systems

LEARNING OBJECTIVE 1

Describe the building-block concepts of costing systems

. . . the building blocks are cost object, direct costs, indirect costs, cost pools, and cost-allocation bases

Before we begin our discussion of costing systems, let's review the cost-related terms from Chapter 2 and introduce some new terms.

1. A *cost object* is anything for which a measurement of costs is desired—for example, a product, such as an iMac computer, or a service, such as the cost of providing a knee replacement surgery.
2. The *direct costs of a cost object* are costs that are directly related to a particular cost object and that can easily and unambiguously be traced to it —for example, the implants needed for a knee replacement surgery.
3. The *indirect costs of a cost object* are costs that are related to a particular cost object but that cannot easily and unambiguously be traced to it —for example, the salaries of supervisors who oversee multiple products, only one of which is the iMac, or the depreciation of a hospital facility where many different types of healthcare services are performed. Indirect costs are allocated to the cost object using a cost-allocation method. Recall that *cost assignment* is a general term for assigning costs, whether direct or indirect, to a cost object. *Cost tracing* is the process of assigning direct costs. *Cost allocation* is the process of assigning indirect costs. The relationship among these three concepts can be graphically represented as

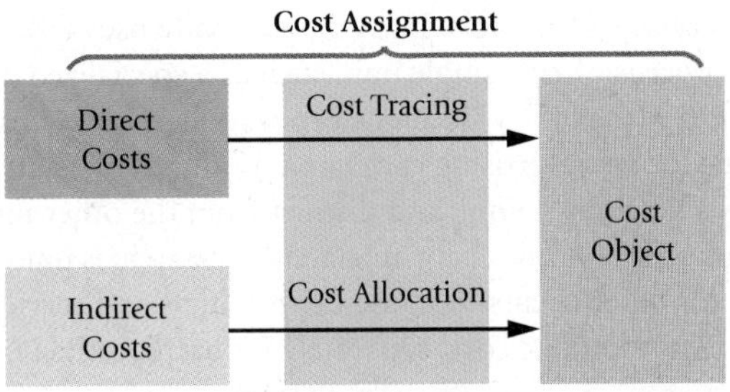

We also need to introduce and explain two more terms to understand costing systems:

4. **Cost pool.** A **cost pool** is a grouping of individual indirect cost items. Cost pools can range from broad, such as all manufacturing-plant costs, to narrow, such as the costs of operating metal-cutting machines. The cost items in a cost pool have the same cost-allocation base and they are grouped together and allocated to cost objects. Cost pools thus simplify the allocation of indirect costs because the separate cost items do not have to be allocated individually.
5. **Cost-allocation base.** How should a company allocate the costs of operating metal-cutting machines among the different products that are manufactured on them? One way is to determine the number of machine-hours that are used to manufacture the different products. The **cost-allocation base** (number of machine-hours) is a systematic way to link an indirect cost or group of indirect costs (operating costs of all metal-cutting machines) to cost objects (different products). For example, if the indirect costs of operating metal-cutting machines is \$500,000 based on running these machines for 10,000 hours, the cost-allocation rate is \$500,000 ÷ 10,000 hours = \$50 per machine-hour, where machine-hours is the cost-allocation base. If a product uses 800 machine-hours, it will be allocated \$50 per machine-hour × 800 machine-hours = \$40,000. The ideal cost-allocation base is the cost driver of the indirect costs because there is a cause-and-effect relationship between the cost driver and the indirect costs. A cost-allocation base can be either financial (such as direct labor costs) or nonfinancial (such as the number of machine-hours).

Sometimes a cost may need to be allocated in a situation where the cause-and-effect relationship is not clear-cut. Consider a corporate-wide advertising program that promotes the general image of a company and its various divisions and products, rather than the image of an individual product. Many companies, such as PepsiCo, allocate costs like these to their individual divisions and products on the basis of revenues: The higher a division's revenue, the higher the allocated costs of the advertising program. Allocating costs this way is based on the criterion of *benefits received* rather than cause-and-effect. Divisions with higher revenues benefit from the advertising program more than divisions with lower revenues and, therefore, are allocated more of the advertising costs.

Another criterion for allocating some costs is the cost object's *ability to bear* the costs allocated to it. The city government of Houston, Texas, for example, distributes the costs of the city manager's office to other city departments—including the police department, fire department, library system, and others—based on the size of their budgets. The city's rationale is that larger departments should absorb a larger share of the overhead costs. Organizations generally use the cause-and-effect criterion to allocate costs, followed by benefits received, and finally, and more rarely, by ability to bear.

The concepts represented by these five terms constitute the building blocks we will use to design the costing systems described in this chapter.

DECISION POINT

What are the building-block concepts of a costing system?

Job-Costing and Process-Costing Systems

LEARNING OBJECTIVE 2

Distinguish job costing

. . . job costing is used to cost a distinct product or service

from process costing

. . . process costing is used to cost masses of identical or similar units of products or services

Management accountants use two basic types of costing systems to assign costs to products or services.

1. **Job-costing system.** In a job-costing system, the cost object is a unit or multiple units of a distinct product or service called a **job**. Each job generally uses different amounts of resources. The product or service is often a single unit, such as a specialized machine made at Hitachi, a construction project managed by Bechtel Corporation, a heart transplant surgery performed at the Mayo Clinic, or an advertising campaign produced by Saatchi & Saatchi. Each special machine made by Hitachi is unique and distinct from the other machines made at the plant. An advertising campaign for one client at Saatchi & Saatchi is unique and distinct from advertising campaigns for other clients. Because the products and services are distinct, job-costing systems are used to accumulate costs separately for each product or service.
2. **Process-costing system.** In a process-costing system, the cost object is masses of identical or similar units of a product or service. For example, Citibank provides the same service to all its customers when processing customer deposits. Intel provides the same product (say, a Core i9 chip) to each of its customers. All Minute Maid consumers receive the same frozen orange juice product. In each period, process-costing systems divide the total costs of producing an identical or similar product or service by the total number of units produced to obtain a per-unit cost. This per-unit cost is the average unit cost that applies to each of the identical or similar units produced in that period.

Exhibit 4-1 presents examples of job costing and process costing in the service, merchandising, and manufacturing sectors. These two types of costing systems lie at opposite ends of a continuum; in between, one type of system can blur into the other to some degree.

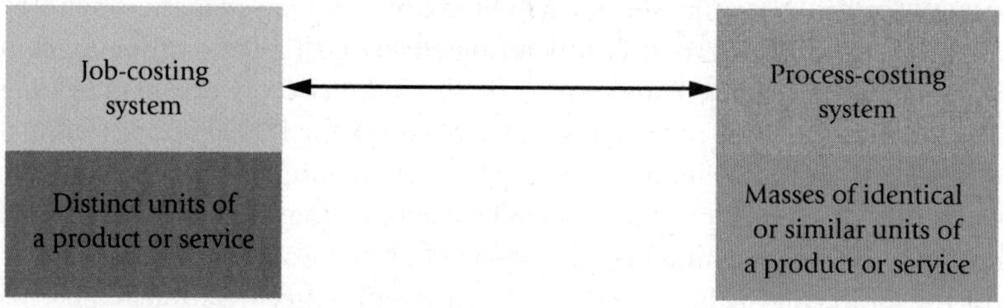

Many companies have costing systems that are neither pure job-costing systems nor pure process-costing systems but—instead—have elements of both, tailored to the underlying operations. For example, Kellogg Corporation uses job costing to calculate the total cost to manufacture each of its different and distinct types of products—such as Corn Flakes, Crispix, and Froot Loops—and process costing to calculate the per-unit cost of producing each identical box of Corn Flakes, each identical box of Crispix, and so on. In this chapter, we focus on job-costing systems. Chapters 18 and 19 discuss process-costing systems.

DECISION POINT

How do you distinguish job costing from process costing?

EXHIBIT 4-1

Examples of Job Costing and Process Costing in the Service, Merchandising, and Manufacturing Sectors

	Service Sector	Merchandising Sector	Manufacturing Sector
Job Costing	• Audit engagements done by PricewaterhouseCoopers • Consulting engagements done by McKinsey & Co. • Advertising-agency campaigns run by Ogilvy & Mather • Legal cases argued by Hale & Dorr • Movies produced by Netflix	• The Home Depot delivering individual appliances ordered online • Special promotion of new products by Walmart	• Assembly of individual aircrafts at Boeing • Construction of ships at Litton Industries
Process Costing	• Bank-check clearing at Bank of America • Standard physical therapy session at ATI Physical Therapy	• Grain dealing by Arthur Daniel Midlands • Lumber dealing by Weyerhauser	• Oil refining by Shell Oil • Beverage production by PepsiCo

Job Costing: Evaluation and Implementation

LEARNING OBJECTIVE 3

Describe the approaches to evaluating and implementing job-costing systems

. . . to determine costs of jobs in a timely manner

We will illustrate job costing using the example of the Robinson Company, which manufactures and installs specialized machinery for the paper-making industry. In early 2020, Robinson receives a request to bid on the manufacturing and installation of a new paper-making machine for the Western Pulp and Paper Company (WPP). Robinson has never made a machine quite like this one, and its managers wonder what to bid for the job. In order to make decisions about the job, Robinson's management team works through the five-step decision-making process.

1. **Identify the problems and uncertainties.** The decision of whether and how much to bid for the WPP job depends on how management resolves two critical uncertainties: (1) what it will cost to complete the job and (2) the prices Robinson's competitors are likely to bid.

2. **Obtain information.** Robinson's managers first evaluate whether doing the WPP job is consistent with the company's strategy. Do they want to do more of these kinds of jobs? Is this an attractive segment of the market? Will Robinson be able to develop a competitive advantage over its competitors and satisfy customers such as WPP? After completing their research, Robinson's managers conclude that the WPP job fits well with the company's strategy and capabilities.

   Robinson's managers study the drawings and engineering specifications provided by WPP and decide on the technical details of the machine. They compare the specifications of this machine to similar machines they have made in the past, identify competitors that might bid on the job, and gather information on what these bids might be.

3. **Make predictions about the future.** Robinson's managers estimate the cost of direct materials, direct manufacturing labor, and overhead for the WPP job. They also consider qualitative factors and risk factors and evaluate any biases they might have. For example, do engineers and employees working on the WPP job have the necessary skills and technical competence? Would they find the experience valuable and challenging? How

accurate are the cost estimates, and what is the likelihood of cost overruns? What biases do Robinson's managers have to be careful about?

4. **Make decisions by choosing among alternatives.** Robinson's managers consider several alternative bids based on what they believe competing firms will bid, the technical expertise needed for the job, business risks, and other qualitative factors. Ultimately Robinson decides to bid $15,000. The manufacturing cost estimate is $9,800, which yields a markup of more than 50% on the manufacturing costs.
5. **Implement the decision, evaluate performance, and learn.** Robinson wins the bid for the WPP job. As Robinson works on the job, management accountants carefully track all of the costs incurred (which are detailed later in this chapter). Ultimately, Robinson's managers will compare the predicted costs against actual costs to evaluate how well the company did on the WPP job.

In its job-costing system, Robinson accumulates the costs incurred for a job in different parts of the value chain, such as manufacturing, marketing, and customer service. We focus here on Robinson's manufacturing function (which also includes the installation of the paper-making machine at the customer site). To make a machine, Robinson purchases some components from outside suppliers and makes other components itself. Each of Robinson's jobs also has a service element: installing a machine at a customer's site and integrating it with the customer's other machines and processes.

One form of job-costing that Robinson can use is **actual costing** where direct costs are traced to a cost object based on the *actual direct-cost rates* times the actual quantities of the direct-cost inputs used. Indirect costs are allocated based on the *actual indirect-cost rates* times the actual quantities of the cost-allocation bases used or incurred. An actual indirect-cost rate is calculated by dividing the actual annual indirect costs by the actual (total) annual quantity of the cost-allocation base.

$$\text{Actual indirect cost rate} = \frac{\text{Actual annual indirect costs}}{\text{Actual annual quantity of the cost-allocation base}}$$

As its name suggests, actual costing systems calculate the actual costs of jobs. Yet actual costing systems are not commonly found in practice because actual costs can usually not be computed in a *timely* manner.[2] The problem is not with computing direct-cost rates for direct materials and direct manufacturing labor. For example, Robinson records the actual prices paid for materials. As it uses these materials, the prices paid serve as actual direct-cost rates for charging material costs to jobs. As we discuss next, calculating actual indirect-cost rates on a timely basis each week or each month is, however, a problem. Robinson can only calculate accurate actual indirect-cost rates at the end of the fiscal year. However, the firm's managers are unwilling to wait that long to learn the costs of various jobs because they need cost information to monitor and manage the costs of jobs while they are in progress. Ongoing cost information about current jobs also helps managers estimate the costs of and prepare competitive bids for *new* jobs.

Time Period Used to Compute Indirect-Cost Rates

There are two reasons for using longer periods, such as a year, to calculate indirect-cost rates.

1. **The numerator reason (indirect-cost pool).** The shorter the period, the greater the influence of seasonal patterns on the amount of costs in a cost pool. For example, if indirect-cost rates were calculated each month, the costs of heating (included in the numerator) would be charged to production only during the winter months. Collecting indirect costs over an annual period incorporates the effects of all four seasons into a single, annual indirect-cost rate.

   Levels of total indirect costs are also affected by nonseasonal erratic costs. Nonseasonal erratic costs are costs incurred in a particular month that benefit operations

[2] Actual costing is presented in more detail on pages 115–117.

in future months, such as equipment-repair costs and the costs of vacation and holiday pay for employees. If monthly indirect-cost rates were calculated, the jobs done in a month in which there were high, nonseasonal erratic costs would be charged with these higher costs. Pooling all indirect costs together over the course of a full year and calculating a single annual indirect-cost rate helps smooth some of the erratic short-term bumps in costs.

2. **The denominator reason (quantity of the cost-allocation base).** Another reason for calculating indirect-cost rates over longer periods is to avoid spreading monthly fixed indirect costs over fluctuating levels of monthly output and fluctuating quantities of the cost-allocation base. Consider the following example.

Reardon and Pane is a firm of tax accountants whose work follows a highly seasonal pattern. Tax season (January–April) is very busy. Other times of the year are less busy. The firm has both variable indirect costs and fixed indirect costs. Variable indirect costs (such as supplies, power, and indirect support labor) vary with the quantity of the cost-allocation base (direct professional labor-hours). Monthly fixed indirect costs (depreciation and general administrative support) do not vary with short-run fluctuations in the quantity of the cost-allocation base:

	Indirect Costs			Direct Professional Labor-Hours	Variable Indirect Cost Rate per Direct Professional Labor-Hour	Fixed Indirect Cost Rate per Direct Professional Labor-Hour	Total Allocation Rate per Direct Professional Labor-Hour
	Variable (1)	Fixed (2)	Total (3)	(4)	(5) = (1) ÷ (4)	(6) = (2) ÷ (4)	(7) = (3) ÷ (4)
High-output month	$40,000	$60,000	$100,000	3,200	$12.50	$18.75	$31.25
Low-output month	10,000	60,000	70,000	800	$12.50	$75.00	87.50

Variable indirect costs change in proportion to changes in the number of direct professional labor-hours worked. Therefore, the variable indirect-cost rate is the same in both the high-output months and the low-output months ($12.50 in both as the table shows). (At times, overtime payments could cause the monthly variable indirect-cost rate to be higher in high-output months.)

Now consider the fixed costs of $60,000. Reardon and Pane chooses this level of monthly fixed costs for the year recognizing that it needs to support higher professional labor-hours during some periods of the year and lower professional labor-hours during other periods. The fixed costs cause monthly total indirect-cost rates to vary considerably—from $31.25 per hour to $87.50 per hour. Few managers believe that identical jobs done in different months should be allocated such significantly different indirect-cost charges per hour ($87.50 ÷ $31.25 = 2.80, or 280%). Furthermore, if fees for preparing tax returns are based on calculated costs, fees would be *high* in low-output months leading to lost business, when in fact management wants to accept more business to use the idle capacity during these months (for more details, see Chapter 9). Reardon and Pane chose a specific level of capacity based on a time horizon far beyond a mere month. An average, annualized indirect-cost rate based on the total annual indirect costs and the total annual level of output smoothes the effect of monthly variations in output levels. This rate is more representative of the total costs and total output the company's managers considered when choosing the level of capacity and, therefore, the level of fixed costs.

Another denominator reason for using annual indirect-cost rates is that the number of Monday-to-Friday workdays in a month affects the calculation of monthly indirect-cost rates. The number of workdays per month varies from 20 to 23 during a year. Because February has the fewest workdays (and consequently labor-hours), if separate rates are computed each month, jobs done in February would bear a greater share of the firm's fixed indirect costs (such as depreciation and property taxes) than identical jobs done in other months. Calculating indirect-cost rates over an annual period reduces the effect of the number of workdays per month on calculated unit costs.

DECISION POINT

What is the main challenge of implementing job-costing systems?

Normal Costing

As we indicated, because it's hard to calculate accurate actual indirect-cost rates on a weekly or monthly basis, managers cannot calculate the actual costs of jobs as they are completed. Nonetheless, managers have a need for a close approximation of the costs of various jobs as they are being completed during the year, not just at the end of the fiscal year. Managers want to know a job's timely manufacturing costs (and other costs, such as marketing costs) to price jobs, monitor and manage costs, evaluate the success of jobs, learn about what did and did not work, bid on new jobs, and prepare interim financial statements. In order to facilitate immediate job cost approximations, a *predetermined* or *budgeted* indirect-cost rate is calculated for each cost pool at the beginning of a fiscal year and used to allocate overhead costs to jobs as they are being completed. For the numerator and denominator reasons described above, the **budgeted indirect-cost rate** for each cost pool is computed as

$$\text{Budgeted indirect cost rate} = \frac{\text{Budgeted annual indirect costs}}{\text{Budgeted annual quantity of the cost-allocation base}}$$

Using budgeted indirect-cost rates gives rise to normal costing.

Normal costing is a costing system that (1) traces direct costs to a cost object by using the actual direct-cost rates times the actual quantities of the direct-cost inputs and (2) allocates indirect costs based on the *budgeted* indirect-cost rates times the actual quantities of the cost-allocation bases.

General Approach to Job Costing Using Normal Costing

LEARNING OBJECTIVE 4

Outline the seven-step approach to normal costing

. . . the seven-step approach is used to compute direct and indirect costs of a job

We illustrate normal costing for the Robinson Company example using the following seven steps to assign costs to an individual job. This approach is commonly used by companies in the manufacturing, merchandising, and service sectors.

Step 1: Identify the Job That Is the Chosen Cost Object. The cost object in the Robinson Company example is Job WPP 298, manufacturing a paper-making machine for Western Pulp and Paper (WPP) in 2020. Robinson's managers and management accountants gather information to cost jobs through source documents. A **source document** is an original record (such as a labor time card on which an employee's work hours are recorded) that supports journal entries in an accounting system. The main source document for Job WPP 298 is a job-cost record. A **job-cost record**, also called a **job-cost sheet**, is used to record and accumulate all the costs assigned to a specific job, starting when work begins. Exhibit 4-2 shows the job-cost record for the paper-making machine ordered by WPP. Follow the various steps in costing Job WPP 298 on the job-cost record in Exhibit 4-2.

Step 2: Identify the Direct Costs of the Job. Robinson identifies two direct-manufacturing cost categories: direct materials and direct manufacturing labor.

- **Direct materials:** On the basis of the engineering specifications and drawings provided by WPP, a manufacturing engineer orders materials from the storeroom using a basic source document called a **materials-requisition record**, which contains information about the cost of direct materials used on a specific job and in a specific department. Exhibit 4-3, Panel A, shows a materials-requisition record for the Robinson Company. See how the record specifies the job for which the material is requested (WPP 298) and describes the material (Part Number MB 468-A, metal brackets), the actual quantity (8), the actual unit cost ($14), and the actual total cost ($112). The $112 actual total cost also appears on the job-cost record in Exhibit 4-2. If we add the cost of all materials requisitions, the total actual direct materials cost is $4,606, which is shown in the Direct Materials panel of the job-cost record in Exhibit 4-2.
- **Direct manufacturing labor:** Accounting for direct manufacturing labor is similar to accounting for direct materials. The source document for direct manufacturing labor is a **labor-time sheet**, which contains information about the amount of labor time used

EXHIBIT 4-2 Source Documents at Robinson Company: Job-Cost Record

	A	B	C	D	E	F
1			JOB-COST RECORD			
2	JOB NO:	WPP 298		CUSTOMER:	Western Pulp and Paper	
3	Date Started:	Feb. 10, 2020		Date Completed	Feb. 28, 2020	
4						
5						
6	**DIRECT MATERIALS**					
7	Date	Materials		Quantity	Unit	Total
8	Received	Requisition No.	Part No.	Used	Cost	Costs
9	Feb. 10, 2020	2020: 198	MB 468-A	8	$14	$ 112
10	Feb. 10, 2020	2020: 199	TB 267-F	12	63	756
11						•
12						•
13	Total					$ 4,606
14						
15	**DIRECT MANUFACTURING LABOR**					
16	Period	Labor Time	Employee	Hours	Hourly	Total
17	Covered	Record No.	No.	Used	Rate	Costs
18	Feb. 10–16, 2020	LT 232	551-87-3076	25	$18	$ 450
19	Feb. 10–16, 2020	LT 247	287-31-4671	5	19	95
20	•	•	•	•	•	•
21	•	•	•	•	•	•
22	Total			88		$ 1,579
23						
24	**MANUFACTURING OVERHEAD***					
25		Cost Pool		Allocation Base	Allocation-	Total
26	Date	Category	Allocation Base	Quantity Used	Base Rate	Costs
27	Feb. 28, 2020	Manufacturing	Direct Manufacturing	88 hours	$40	$ 3,520
28			Labor-Hours			
29						
30	Total					$ 3,520
31	**TOTAL MANUFACTURING COST OF JOB**					$ 9,705
32						
33						
34	*The Robinson Company uses a single manufacturing-overhead cost pool. The use of multiple overhead cost pools					
35	would mean multiple entries in the "Manufacturing Overhead" section of the job-cost record.					
36						

for a specific job in a specific department. Exhibit 4-3, Panel B, shows a typical weekly labor-time sheet for a particular employee (G. L. Cook). Each day Cook records the time spent on individual jobs (in this case WPP 298 and JL 256), as well as the time spent on other tasks, such as the maintenance of machines and cleaning, that are not related to a specific job.

The 25 hours that Cook spent on Job WPP 298 appears on the job-cost record in Exhibit 4-2 at a cost of \$450 (25 hours × \$18 per hour). Similarly, the job-cost record for Job JL 256 will show a cost of \$216 (12 hours × \$18 per hour). The 3 hours of time spent on maintenance and cleaning at \$18 per hour equals \$54. This cost is part of indirect manufacturing costs because it is not traceable to any particular job. This indirect cost is included as part of the manufacturing-overhead cost pool allocated to jobs. The total direct manufacturing labor costs of \$1,579 for the paper-making machine that appears in

EXHIBIT 4-3 Source Documents at Robinson Company: Materials-Requisition Record and Labor-Time Sheet

PANEL A:

MATERIALS-REQUISITION RECORD

Materials-Requisition Record No. 2020: 198
Job No. WPP 298 Date: FEB. 10, 2020

Part No.	Part Description	Quantity	Unit Cost	Total Cost
MB 468-A	Metal Brackets	8	$14	$112

Issued By: B. Clyde Date: Feb. 10, 2020
Received By: L. Daley Date: Feb. 10, 2020

PANEL B:

LABOR-TIME SHEET

Labor-Time Record No: LT 232
Employee Name: G. L. Cook Employee No: 551-87-3076
Employee Classification Code: Grade 3 Machinist
Hourly Rate: $18
Week Start: Feb. 10, 2020 Week End: Feb. 16, 2020

Job. No.	M	T	W	Th	F	S	Su	Total
WPP 298	4	8	3	6	4	0	0	25
JL 256	3	0	4	2	3	0	0	12
Maintenance	1	0	1	0	1	0	0	3
Total	8	8	8	8	8	0	0	40

Supervisor: R. Stuart Date: Feb. 16, 2020

the Direct Manufacturing Labor panel of the job-cost record in Exhibit 4-2 is the sum of all the direct manufacturing labor costs charged by different employees for producing and installing Job WPP 298.

All costs other than direct materials and direct manufacturing labor are classified as indirect costs.

Step 3: Select the Cost-Allocation Bases to Use for Allocating Indirect Costs to the Job. Recall that indirect manufacturing costs are those costs that are necessary to do a job, but that cannot easily and unambiguously be traced to a specific job. It would be impossible to complete a job without incurring indirect costs such as supervision, manufacturing engineering, utilities, and machine depreciation and repairs. Moreover, different jobs require different quantities of indirect resources. Because these costs cannot be traced to a specific job, managers must allocate them to jobs in a systematic way.

Companies often use multiple cost-allocation bases to allocate indirect costs because different indirect costs have different cost drivers. For example, some indirect costs such as depreciation and repairs of machines are more closely related to machine-hours. Other indirect costs such as supervision and production support are more closely related to direct manufacturing labor-hours. Robinson, however, chooses direct manufacturing labor-hours as the sole allocation base for assigning all indirect manufacturing costs to jobs. The managers do so because, in Robinson's labor-intensive environment, they believe the number of direct manufacturing labor-hours largely drives the manufacturing overhead resources required by individual jobs. (We will see in Chapter 5 that managers in many manufacturing environments often need to broaden the set of cost-allocation bases.) In 2020, Robinson budgets 28,000 direct manufacturing labor-hours.

Step 4: Identify the Indirect Costs Associated with Each Cost-Allocation Base. Because Robinson believes that a single cost-allocation base—direct manufacturing labor-hours—can be used to allocate indirect manufacturing costs to jobs, Robinson creates a single cost pool called manufacturing overhead costs. This pool represents all indirect costs of the Manufacturing Department that are difficult to trace directly to individual jobs. In 2020, budgeted manufacturing overhead costs total $1,120,000.

As we can see in this step and Step 3 above, managers first identify cost-allocation bases and then identify the costs related to each cost-allocation base, not the other way around. They choose this order because the creation of cost pools (the number of cost pools, and the grouping of specific indirect cost items into certain cost pools) must be guided by an understanding of the companies' cost drivers (the reasons why indirect costs are being incurred). Of course, Steps 3 and 4 are often done almost simultaneously.

Step 5: Compute the Indirect-Cost Rate for Each Cost-Allocation Base. For each cost pool, the budgeted indirect-cost rate is calculated by dividing the budgeted total indirect costs in the pool (determined in Step 4) by the budgeted total quantity of the cost-allocation base (determined in Step 3). Robinson calculates the rate for its single cost-allocation base and manufacturing overhead cost pool as follows:

$$\text{Budgeted manufacturing overhead rate} = \frac{\text{Budgeted manufacturing overhead costs}}{\text{Budgeted total quantity of cost-allocation base}}$$

$$= \frac{\$1{,}120{,}000}{28{,}000 \text{ direct manufacturing labor-hours}}$$

$$= \$40 \text{ per direct manufacturing labor-hour}$$

Step 6: Compute the Indirect Costs Allocated to the Job. The indirect costs of a job are calculated by multiplying the *actual* quantity of each allocation base (one allocation base for each cost pool) associated with the job by the *budgeted* indirect cost rate of each allocation base (computed in Step 5). Recall that Robinson's managers selected direct manufacturing labor-hours as the only cost-allocation base. Robinson uses 88 direct manufacturing labor-hours on the WPP 298 job. Consequently, the manufacturing overhead costs allocated to WPP 298 equal \$3,520 (\$40 per direct manufacturing labor-hour × 88 hours) and appear in the Manufacturing Overhead panel of the WPP 298 job-cost record in Exhibit 4-2.

Step 7: Compute the Total Cost of the Job by Adding All Direct and Indirect Costs Assigned to the Job. Exhibit 4-2 shows that the total manufacturing costs of the WPP job are \$9,705.

Direct manufacturing costs		
Direct materials	\$4,606	
Direct manufacturing labor	1,579	\$ 6,185
Manufacturing overhead costs		
(\$40 per direct manufacturing labor-hour × 88 hours)		3,520
Total manufacturing costs of job WPP 298		\$9,705

Recall that Robinson bid a price of \$15,000 for the job. At that revenue, the normal-costing system shows that the job's gross margin is \$5,295 (\$15,000 − \$9,705) and its gross-margin percentage is 35.3% (\$5,295 ÷ \$15,000 = 0.353).

CONCEPTS IN ACTION

Better Job Costing Through Big Data and Data Analytics[3]

LaineN/Shutterstock

Across the globe, companies are looking to glean meaningful intelligence from large data sets and translate that into competitive advantage. Among Fortune 1000 companies, 73% are currently leveraging big data to decrease their expenses. One way companies can achieve this is by using big data and data analytics to improve their job costing.

Thanks to big data, companies can now analyze millions of internal and external data points to identify the costs and revenues associated with various activities. By aggregating all this data and benchmarking it against historical performance and current activities, it is possible to extract meaningful information about the profitability of doing certain work. Using big data, it is possible to accurately answer specific questions like whether a construction company should bid on a job or whether a consulting firm should hire another business development person.

Companies effectively leveraging data-driven decision making are, on average, 5% more productive and 6% more profitable than their competitors. As a result, new software programs are using big data to help companies improve their job costing capabilities to ensure that each new job is a profitable job.

[3] *Sources*: Andrew McAfee and Erik Brynjolfsson, "Big Data: The Management Revolution," *Harvard Business Review*, October 2012 (https://hbr.org/2012/10/big-data-the-management-revolution); Randy Bean, "How Companies Say They're Using Big Data," *Harvard Business Review* online, April 28, 2017 (https://hbr.org/2017/04/how-companies-say-theyre-using-big-data); "How To Make Job Costing More Accurate With Big Data," Datafloq.com, June 14, 2016 (https://datafloq.com/read/how-to-make-job-costing-more-accurate-big-data/2119); "New Partnership to Launch Big Data Scope & Costing Tool to Australian Agencies," Virtu Group press release, Sydney, Australia, January 20, 2017 (https://www.thevirtugroup.com/2017/01/20/tangram-partnership/).

TRY IT! 4-1

Huckvale Corporation manufactures custom cabinets for kitchens. It uses a normal-costing system with two direct-cost categories—direct materials and direct manufacturing labor—and one indirect-cost pool, manufacturing overhead costs. It provides the following information for 2020:

Budgeted manufacturing overhead costs	$1,160,000
Budgeted direct manufacturing labor-hours	29,000 hours
Actual manufacturing overhead costs	$1,260,000
Actual direct manufacturing labor-hours	28,000 hours

Calculate the total manufacturing costs of a job at 32 Pioneer Drive using normal costing based on the following information:

Actual direct materials costs	$ 3,600
Actual direct manufacturing labor	180 hours
Actual direct manufacturing labor rate	$ 18 per hour

Robinson's manufacturing and sales managers can use the gross margin and gross-margin percentage calculations to compare the profitability of different jobs. A job-cost analysis provides the information managers need to gauge the manufacturing and sales performance of their firms and to answer questions about why some jobs are not as profitable as others. Were direct materials wasted? Was the direct manufacturing labor cost of the job too high? Was the job simply underpriced? With the explosion in the availability of data and analytic tools, the ability of companies to use job costing to improve profitability has grown significantly (see Concepts in Action: Better Job Costing Through Big Data and Data Analytics).

Exhibit 4-4 is an overview of Robinson Company's job-costing system. The exhibit illustrates the five building blocks of job-costing systems introduced at the beginning of this

EXHIBIT 4-4

Job-Costing Overview for Determining Manufacturing Costs of Jobs at Robinson Company

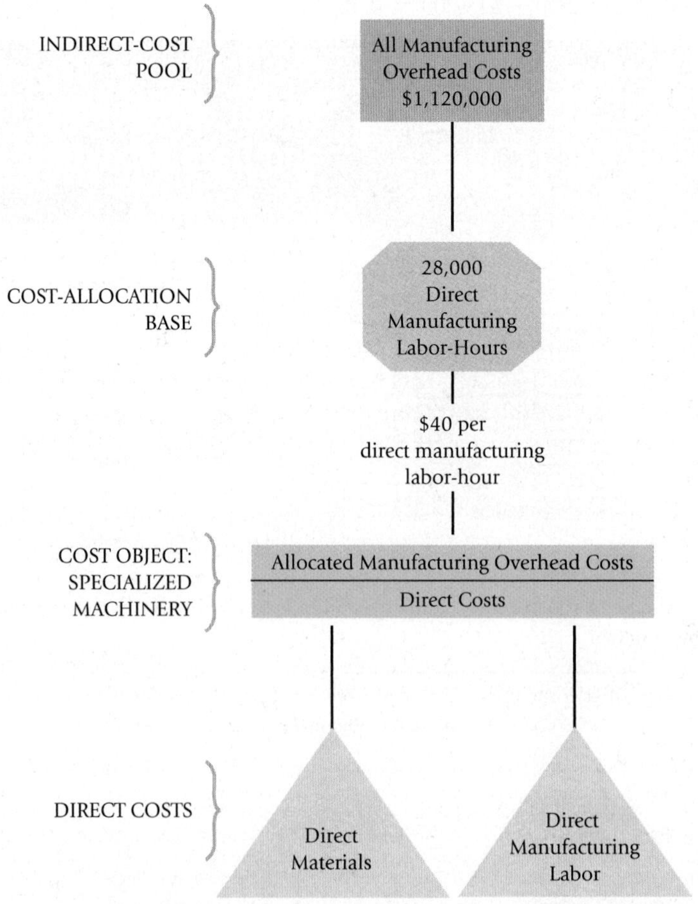

chapter: (1) cost objects, (2) direct costs of a cost object, (3) indirect (overhead) costs of a cost object, (4) indirect-cost pools, and (5) cost-allocation bases. (The symbols in the exhibit are used consistently in the costing-system overviews presented in this text. A triangle always identifies a direct cost, a rectangle represents an indirect-cost pool, and an octagon describes a cost-allocation base.) Costing-system overviews such as Exhibit 4-4 are important learning tools. We urge you to sketch one when you need to understand a costing system.

Note the similarities between Exhibit 4-4 and the cost of the WPP 298 job described in Step 7. Exhibit 4-4 shows two direct-cost categories (direct materials and direct manufacturing labor) and one indirect-cost category (manufacturing overhead). Step 7 also describes two direct-cost categories and one indirect-cost category.

DECISION POINT

How do you implement a normal-costing system?

The Role of Technology

Information technology gives managers quick and accurate job-costing information, making it easier for them to manage and control jobs. Consider, for example, the direct materials charged to jobs. Managers control these costs as materials are purchased and used. Using Electronic Data Interchange (EDI) technology, companies like Robinson order materials from their suppliers by clicking a few keys on a computer keyboard. EDI, an electronic computer link between a company and its suppliers, ensures that the order is transmitted quickly and accurately with minimal paperwork and costs. A bar code scanner records the receipt of incoming materials, and a computer matches the receipt with the order, arranges for payment to the supplier, and records the materials received. When an operator on the production floor transmits a request for materials via a computer terminal, the computer prepares a materials-requisition record, instantly recording the issue of materials in the materials and job-cost records. Each day, the computer sums the materials-requisition records charged to a particular job or manufacturing department. A performance report is then prepared monitoring the actual costs of direct materials. The use of direct materials can be reported hourly if managers believe the benefits exceed the cost of such frequent reporting.

Similarly, information about direct manufacturing labor is obtained as employees log into computer terminals and key in job numbers, their employee numbers, and the start and end times of their work on different jobs. The computer automatically prints the labor time record and, using hourly rates stored for each employee, calculates the direct manufacturing labor costs of individual jobs. Information technology can also give managers instant feedback to help them control manufacturing overhead costs, jobs in process, jobs completed, and jobs shipped and installed at customer sites.

Actual Costing

LEARNING OBJECTIVE 5

Distinguish actual costing

. . . actual costing uses actual indirect-cost rates

from normal costing

. . . normal costing uses budgeted indirect-cost rates

How would the cost of Job WPP 298 change if Robinson used actual costing rather than normal costing? Both actual costing and normal costing trace direct costs to jobs in the same way because source documents identify the actual quantities and actual rates of direct materials and direct manufacturing labor for a job as the work is being done. The only difference between normal costing and actual costing is that normal costing uses *budgeted* indirect-cost rates calculated at the beginning of the year, whereas actual costing uses *actual* indirect-cost rates calculated at the end of the year. Exhibit 4-5 distinguishes actual costing from normal costing.

The following actual data for 2020 are for Robinson's manufacturing operations:

	Actual
Total manufacturing overhead costs	$1,215,000
Total direct manufacturing labor-hours	27,000

Steps 1 and 2 are the same in both normal and actual costing: Step 1 identifies WPP 298 as the cost object; Step 2 calculates actual direct materials costs of $4,606 and actual direct manufacturing labor costs of $1,579. Recall from Step 3 that Robinson uses a single cost-allocation base, direct manufacturing labor-hours, to allocate all manufacturing overhead costs to jobs. The actual quantity of direct manufacturing labor-hours for 2020 is 27,000

EXHIBIT 4-5

Actual Costing and Normal Costing Methods

	Actual Costing	Normal Costing
Direct Costs	*Actual direct-cost rates* × actual quantities of direct-cost inputs	*Actual direct-cost rates* × actual quantities of direct-cost inputs
Indirect Costs	*Actual indirect-cost rates* × actual quantities of cost-allocation bases	*Budgeted indirect-cost rates* × actual quantities of cost-allocation bases

hours. In Step 4, Robinson groups all actual indirect manufacturing costs of $1,215,000 into a single manufacturing overhead cost pool. In Step 5, the **actual indirect-cost rate** is calculated by dividing actual total indirect costs in the pool (determined in Step 4) by the actual total quantity of the cost-allocation base (determined in Step 3). Robinson calculates the actual manufacturing overhead rate in 2020 for its single manufacturing overhead cost pool as follows:

$$\text{Actual manufacturing overhead rate} = \frac{\text{Actual annual manufacturing overhead costs}}{\text{Actual annual quantity of the cost-allocation base}}$$

$$= \frac{\$1{,}215{,}000}{27{,}000 \text{ direct manufacturing labor-hours}}$$

$$= \$45 \text{ per direct manufacturing labor-hour}$$

In Step 6, under an actual-costing system,

$$\text{Manufacturing overhead costs allocated to WPP 298} = \text{Actual manufacturing overhead rate} \times \text{Actual quantity of direct manufacturing labor-hours}$$

$$= \$45 \text{ per direct manuf. labor-hour} \times 88 \text{ direct manufacturing labor-hours}$$

$$= \$3{,}960$$

In Step 7, the cost of the job under actual costing is $10,145, calculated as follows:

Direct manufacturing costs		
Direct materials	$4,606	
Direct manufacturing labor	1,579	$ 6,185
Manufacturing overhead costs		
($45 per direct manufacturing labor-hour × 88 actual direct manufacturing labor-hours)		3,960
Total manufacturing costs of job		$10,145

DECISION POINT

How do you distinguish actual costing from normal costing?

The calculated manufacturing cost of the WPP 298 job is higher by $440 under actual costing than under normal costing ($10,145 vs. $9,705) because the actual indirect-cost rate is $45 per hour, whereas the budgeted indirect-cost rate is $40 per hour. That is, ($45 − $40) × 88 actual direct manufacturing labor-hours = $440.

As we discussed previously, the manufacturing costs of a job are available much earlier in a normal-costing system than in an actual costing system. Consequently, Robinson's manufacturing and sales managers can evaluate the profitability and the adequacy of the pricing of the different jobs, and the efficiency with which the jobs are done, as soon as they are completed, while the experience is still fresh in everyone's mind. Another advantage of normal costing is that it provides managers with cost information at a point when there is still time to take corrective actions, such as improving the company's labor efficiency or reducing the company's overhead costs.

Costs allocated using normal costing will not, in general, equal costs allocated using actual costing based on actual indirect cost rates calculated at the end of the year. For financial accounting purposes, if the differences between normal and actual costing are significant, adjustments will need to be made so that the cost of goods sold and the costs in various inventory accounts are based on actual rather than normal costing. Companies have to prepare financial statements based on what actually happened rather than on what was expected to happen at the beginning of the year. We describe these adjustments later in the chapter.

The next section describes in detail how a normal job-costing system is used within the financial accounting framework in order to achieve the costing objectives of financial accounting. *Instructors and students who do not wish to explore these details can go directly to page 125 to the section "Budgeted Indirect Costs and End-of-Accounting-Year Adjustments."*

4-2 TRY IT!

Huckvale Corporation manufactures custom cabinets for kitchens. It uses an actual costing system with two direct-cost categories—direct materials and direct manufacturing labor—and one indirect-cost pool, manufacturing overhead costs. It provides the following information for 2020.

Budgeted manufacturing overhead costs	$1,160,000
Budgeted direct manufacturing labor-hours	29,000 hours
Actual manufacturing overhead costs	$1,260,000
Actual direct manufacturing labor-hours	28,000 hours

Calculate the cost of the 32 Pioneer Drive job using actual costing based on the following information:

Actual direct materials costs	$3,600
Actual direct manufacturing labor	180 hours
Actual direct manufacturing labor rate	$ 18 per hour

A Normal Job-Costing System in Manufacturing

LEARNING OBJECTIVE 6

Track the flow of costs in a job-costing system

. . . from purchase of materials to sale of finished goods

The following example looks at events that occurred at Robinson Company in February 2020. Before getting into the details of how normal costing is used within the financial accounting framework, study Exhibit 4-6, which provides an overview for understanding the flow of costs.

The upper part of Exhibit 4-6 shows the flow of inventoriable costs from the purchase of materials and other manufacturing inputs to their conversion into work in process and finished goods, to the sale of finished goods.

Direct materials and direct manufacturing labor can be easily traced to jobs. They become part of the work-in-process inventory asset on the balance sheet once work on the jobs has commenced. Robinson also incurs manufacturing overhead costs (including indirect materials and indirect manufacturing labor) to convert direct materials into work-in-process inventory. Overhead (indirect) costs, however, cannot be easily traced to individual jobs. As we described earlier in this chapter, manufacturing overhead costs are first accumulated in a manufacturing overhead account and then allocated to individual jobs. As manufacturing overhead costs are allocated, they become part of work-in-process inventory.

As we described in Chapter 2, when individual jobs are completed, work-in-process inventory becomes another balance sheet asset, finished-goods inventory. Only when finished goods are sold is the expense of cost of goods sold recognized in the income statement and matched against revenues earned.

The lower part of Exhibit 4-6 shows the period costs—marketing and customer-service costs. These costs do not create any assets on the balance sheet because they are not incurred to transform materials into a finished product. Instead, they are expensed in the income statement in the period that they are incurred.

We next describe the entries made in the general ledger.

EXHIBIT 4-6 Flow of Costs in Job Costing

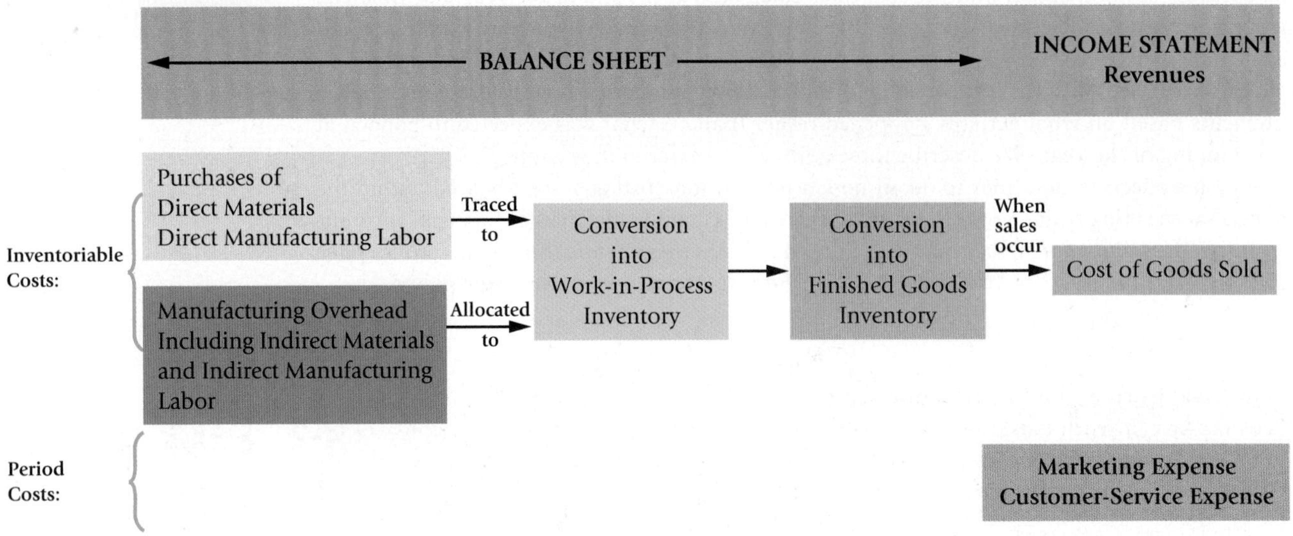

General Ledger

You know by this point that a job-costing system has a separate job-cost record for each job. A summary of the job-cost record is typically found in a subsidiary ledger. The general ledger account—Work-in-Process Control—presents the total of these separate job-cost records pertaining to all unfinished jobs. The job-cost records and Work-in-Process Control account track job costs from when jobs start until they are complete. When jobs are completed or sold, they are recorded in the finished-goods inventory records of jobs in the subsidiary ledger. The general ledger account Finished Goods Control records the total of these separate job-cost records for all jobs completed and subsequently for all jobs sold.

Exhibit 4-7 shows T-account relationships for Robinson Company's general ledger. The general ledger gives a "bird's-eye view" of the costing system. The amounts shown in Exhibit 4-7 are based on the monthly transactions and respective journal entries. As you go through each of the journal entries below, use Exhibit 4-7 to see how the various entries being made come together. General ledger accounts with "Control" in their titles (for example, Materials Control and Accounts Payable Control) have underlying subsidiary ledgers that contain additional details, such as each type of material in inventory and individual suppliers Robinson must pay.

Some companies simultaneously make entries in the general ledger and subsidiary ledger accounts. Others, such as Robinson, simplify their accounting by making entries in the subsidiary ledger when transactions occur and entries in the general ledger less frequently, often on a monthly basis, when monthly financial statements are prepared.

A general ledger should be viewed as only one of many tools managers can use for planning and control. To control operations, managers rely on not only the source documents used to record amounts in the subsidiary ledgers, but also on nonfinancial information such as the percentage of jobs requiring rework or that are behind schedule.

Explanations of Transactions

We next look at a summary of Robinson Company's transactions for February 2020 and the corresponding journal entries for those transactions.

1. Purchases of materials (direct and indirect) on credit, $89,000

Materials Control	89,000	
Accounts Payable Control		89,000

EXHIBIT 4-7 Manufacturing Job-Costing System Using Normal Costing: Diagram of General Ledger Relationships for February 2020

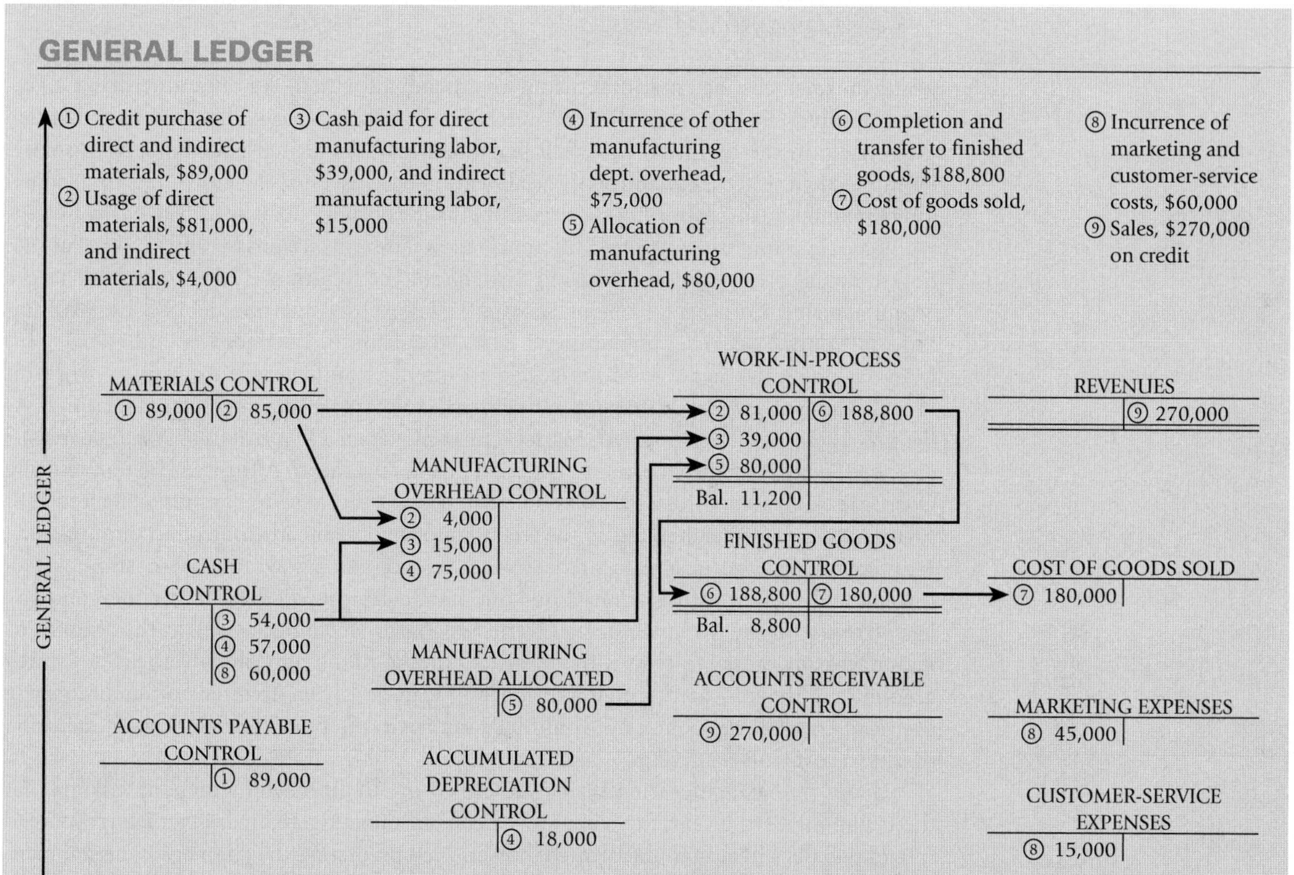

The debit balance of $11,200 in the Work-in-Process Control account represents the total cost of all jobs that have not been completed as of the end of February 2020. There were no incomplete jobs as of the beginning of February 2020.

The debit balance of $8,800 in the Finished Goods Control account represents the cost of all jobs that have been completed but not sold as of the end of February 2020. There were no jobs completed but not sold as of the beginning of February 2020.

2. Usage of direct materials, $81,000, and indirect materials, $4,000

Work-in-Process Control	81,000	
Manufacturing Overhead Control	4,000	
Materials Control		85,000

3. Manufacturing payroll for February: direct labor, $39,000, and indirect labor, $15,000, paid in cash

Work-in-Process Control	39,000	
Manufacturing Overhead Control	15,000	
Cash Control		54,000

4. Other manufacturing overhead costs incurred during February, $75,000, consisting of
   - supervision and engineering salaries, $44,000 (paid in cash),
   - plant utilities, repairs, and insurance, $13,000 (paid in cash),
   - plant depreciation, $18,000

Manufacturing Overhead Control	75,000	
Cash Control		57,000
Accumulated Depreciation Control		18,000

5. Allocation of manufacturing overhead to jobs, $80,000

Work-in-Process Control	80,000	
Manufacturing Overhead Allocated		80,000

Under normal costing, **manufacturing overhead allocated**—or **manufacturing overhead applied**—is the amount of manufacturing overhead costs allocated to individual jobs based on the budgeted rate, $40 per direct manufacturing labor-hour in this case, multiplied by the actual quantity of the allocation base used for each job. (The total actual direct manufacturing labor-hours across all jobs in February 2020 are 2,000.)

Keep in mind the distinct difference between transactions 4 and 5. In transaction 4, actual overhead costs incurred throughout the month are added (debited) to the Manufacturing Overhead Control account. These costs are not debited to Work-in-Process Control because, unlike direct costs, they cannot be traced to individual jobs. Manufacturing overhead costs are added (debited) to individual jobs and to Work-in-Process Control *only when* manufacturing overhead costs are allocated in transaction 5. At the time these costs are allocated, Manufacturing Overhead Control is, *in effect*, decreased (credited) via its contra account, Manufacturing Overhead Allocated. Manufacturing Overhead Allocated is referred to as a *contra account* because the amounts debited to it represent the amounts credited to the Manufacturing Overhead Control account. Having Manufacturing Overhead Allocated as a contra account allows the job-costing system to separately retain information about the manufacturing overhead costs the company has *incurred* (in the Manufacturing Overhead Control account) as well as the amount of manufacturing overhead costs it has *allocated* (in the Manufacturing Overhead Allocated account). If the allocated manufacturing overhead had been credited to manufacturing overhead control, the company would lose information about the actual manufacturing overhead costs it is incurring.

Under the normal-costing system described in our Robinson Company example, at the beginning of the year, the company calculated the budgeted manufacturing overhead rate of $40 per direct manufacturing labor-hour by predicting the company's annual manufacturing overhead costs and the annual quantity of the cost-allocation base. Almost certainly, the total of the amounts allocated using the budgeted manufacturing rate will differ from the predicted total manufacturing overhead costs. We discuss what to do with this difference later in the chapter.

6. The sum of all individual jobs completed and transferred to finished goods in February 2020 is $188,800

Finished Goods Control	188,800	
Work-in-Process Control		188,800

7. Cost of goods sold, $180,000

Cost of Goods Sold	180,000	
Finished Goods Control		180,000

8. Marketing costs for February 2020, $45,000, and customer-service costs for February 2020, $15,000, paid in cash

Marketing Expenses	45,000	
Customer-Service Expenses	15,000	
Cash Control		60,000

9. Sales revenues from all jobs sold and delivered in February 2020, all on credit, $270,000

Accounts Receivable Control	270,000	
Revenues		270,000

4-3 TRY IT!

Huckvale Corporation manufactures custom cabinets for kitchens. It uses a normal-costing system with two direct-cost categories—direct materials and direct manufacturing labor—and one indirect-cost pool, manufacturing overhead costs. It provides the following information for April 2020:

Actual direct materials used	$20,000
Actual direct manufacturing labor costs paid in cash	50,000
Indirect materials used	$2,000
Supervision and engineering salaries paid in cash	$49,000
Plant utilities and repairs paid in cash	7,000
Plant depreciation	$20,000
Actual direct manufacturing labor-hours	3,000
Cost of individual jobs completed and transferred to finished goods	$230,000
Cost of goods sold	$225,000

The following information is also available for 2020:

Budgeted manufacturing overhead costs	$1,160,000
Direct manufacturing labor-hours	29,000 hours

Present journal entries for (a) usage of direct and indirect materials, (b) manufacturing labor incurred, (c) manufacturing overhead costs incurred, (d) allocation of manufacturing overhead costs to jobs, (e) cost of jobs completed and transferred to finished goods, and (f) cost of goods sold.

Subsidiary Ledgers

Exhibits 4-8 and 4-9 present subsidiary ledgers that contain the underlying details—the "worm's-eye view"—of the "bird's-eye view" of the general ledger. Subsidiary ledgers help Robinson's managers track individual jobs such as the WPP 298 job. The sum of all entries in the underlying subsidiary ledgers equals the total amounts in the corresponding general ledger control accounts.

Materials Records by Type of Material

The subsidiary ledger for materials at Robinson Company—called *Materials Records*—is used to continuously record the quantity of materials received, issued to jobs, and the inventory balances for each type of material. Panel A of Exhibit 4-8 shows the Materials Record for Metal Brackets (Part No. MB 468-A). In many companies, the source documents supporting the receipt and issue of materials (the material requisition record in Exhibit 4-3, Panel A, page 112) are scanned into a computer. Software programs then automatically update the Materials Records and make all the necessary accounting entries in the subsidiary and general ledgers. The cost of materials received across all types of direct and indirect material records at the Robinson Company for February 2020 is $89,000 (Exhibit 4-8, Panel A). The cost of materials issued across all types of direct and indirect material records for February 2020 is $85,000 (Exhibit 4-8, Panel A).

As direct materials are used, they are recorded as issued in the Materials Records (see Exhibit 4-8, Panel A, for a record of the Metal Brackets issued for the WPP machine job). Direct materials are also charged to Work-in-Process Inventory Records for Jobs, which are the subsidiary ledger accounts for the Work-in-Process Control account in the general ledger. For example, the metal brackets used in the WPP machine job appear as direct material costs of $112 in the subsidiary ledger under the work-in-process inventory record for WPP 298 (Exhibit 4-9, Panel A, which is based on the job-cost record source document in Exhibit 4-2, page 111). The cost of direct materials used across all job-cost records for February 2020 is $81,000 (Exhibit 4-9, Panel A).

As indirect materials (for example, lubricants) are used, they are charged to the Manufacturing Department overhead records (Exhibit 4-8, Panel C), which comprise the subsidiary ledger for the Manufacturing Overhead Control account. The Manufacturing

EXHIBIT 4-8 Subsidiary Ledgers for Materials, Labor, and Manufacturing Department Overhead[1]

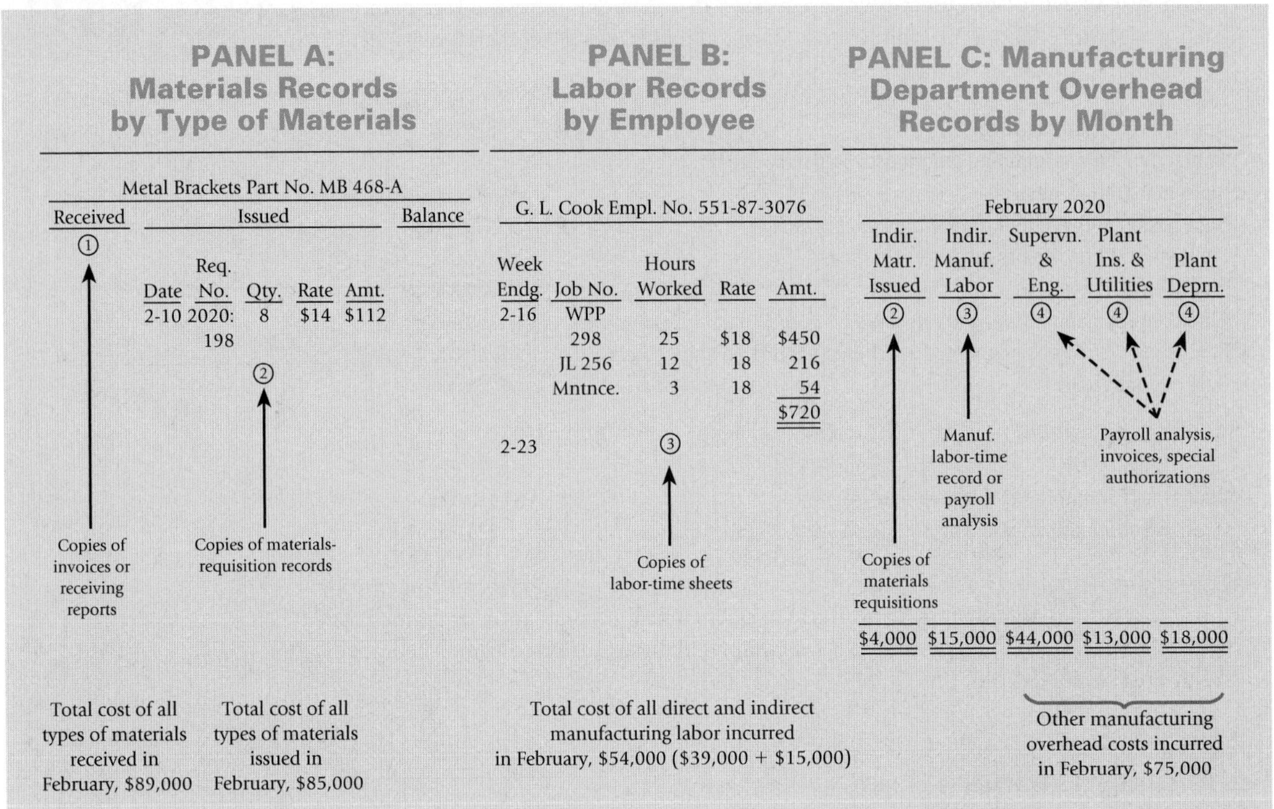

[1]The arrows show how the supporting documentation (for example, copies of materials requisition records) results in the journal entry number shown in circles (for example, journal entry number 2) that corresponds to the entries in Exhibit 4-7.

Department overhead records are used to accumulate actual costs in individual overhead categories by each indirect-cost-pool account in the general ledger. Recall that Robinson has only one indirect-cost pool: Manufacturing Overhead. The cost of indirect materials used is not added directly to individual job records. Instead, this cost is allocated to individual job records as a part of manufacturing overhead.

Labor Records by Employee

Labor records by employee (see Exhibit 4-8, Panel B, for G. L. Cook) are used to trace the costs of direct manufacturing labor to individual jobs and to accumulate the costs of indirect manufacturing labor in the Manufacturing Department overhead records (Exhibit 4-8, Panel C). The labor records are based on the labor-time sheet source documents (see Exhibit 4-3, Panel B, page 112). The subsidiary ledger for employee labor records (Exhibit 4-8, Panel B) shows the different jobs that G. L. Cook, Employee No. 551-87-3076, worked on and the $720 of wages owed to Cook, for the week ending February 16. The sum of total wages owed to all employees for February 2020 is $54,000. The job-cost record for WPP 298 shows direct manufacturing labor costs of $450 for the time Cook spent on the WPP machine job during that week (Exhibit 4-9, Panel A). Total direct manufacturing labor costs recorded in all job-cost records (the subsidiary ledger for Work-in-Process Control) for February 2020 is $39,000.

G. L. Cook's employee record shows $54 for maintenance, which is an indirect manufacturing labor cost. The total indirect manufacturing labor costs of $15,000 for February 2020 appear in the Manufacturing Department overhead records in the subsidiary ledger (Exhibit 4-8, Panel C). These costs, by definition, cannot be traced to an individual job. Instead, they are allocated to individual jobs as a part of manufacturing overhead.

EXHIBIT 4-9 Subsidiary Ledgers for Individual Jobs[1]

PANEL A: Work-in-Process Inventory Records by Jobs

Job No. WPP 298

	In-Process				Completed		Balance	
Date	Direct Materials	Direct Manuf. Labor	Allocated Manuf. Overhead	Total Cost	Date	Total Cost	Date	Total Cost
2-10	$ 112			$ 112				
2-16		$ 450		$ 450				
	•	•		•				
2-28	$4,606	$1,579	$3,520	$9,705	2-28	$9,705	2-28	$0
	②	③	⑤			⑥		
	Copies of materials-requisition records	Copies of labor-time sheets	Budgeted rate × actual direct manuf. labor-hours			Completed job-cost record		
	Total cost of direct materials issued to all jobs in Feb., $81,000	Total cost of direct manuf. labor used on all jobs in Feb., $39,000	Total manuf. overhead allocated to all jobs in Feb., $80,000			Total cost of all jobs completed and transferred to finished goods in Feb., $188,800		

PANEL B: Finished Goods Inventory Records by Job

Job No. WPP 298

Received		Issued		Balance	
Date	Amt.	Date	Amt.	Date	Amt.
2-28	$9,705	2-28	$9,705	2-28	$0
	⑥				
	Completed job-cost record		Costed sales invoice		
	Total cost of all jobs transferred to finished goods in Feb., $188,800		Total cost of all jobs sold and invoiced in Feb., $180,000		

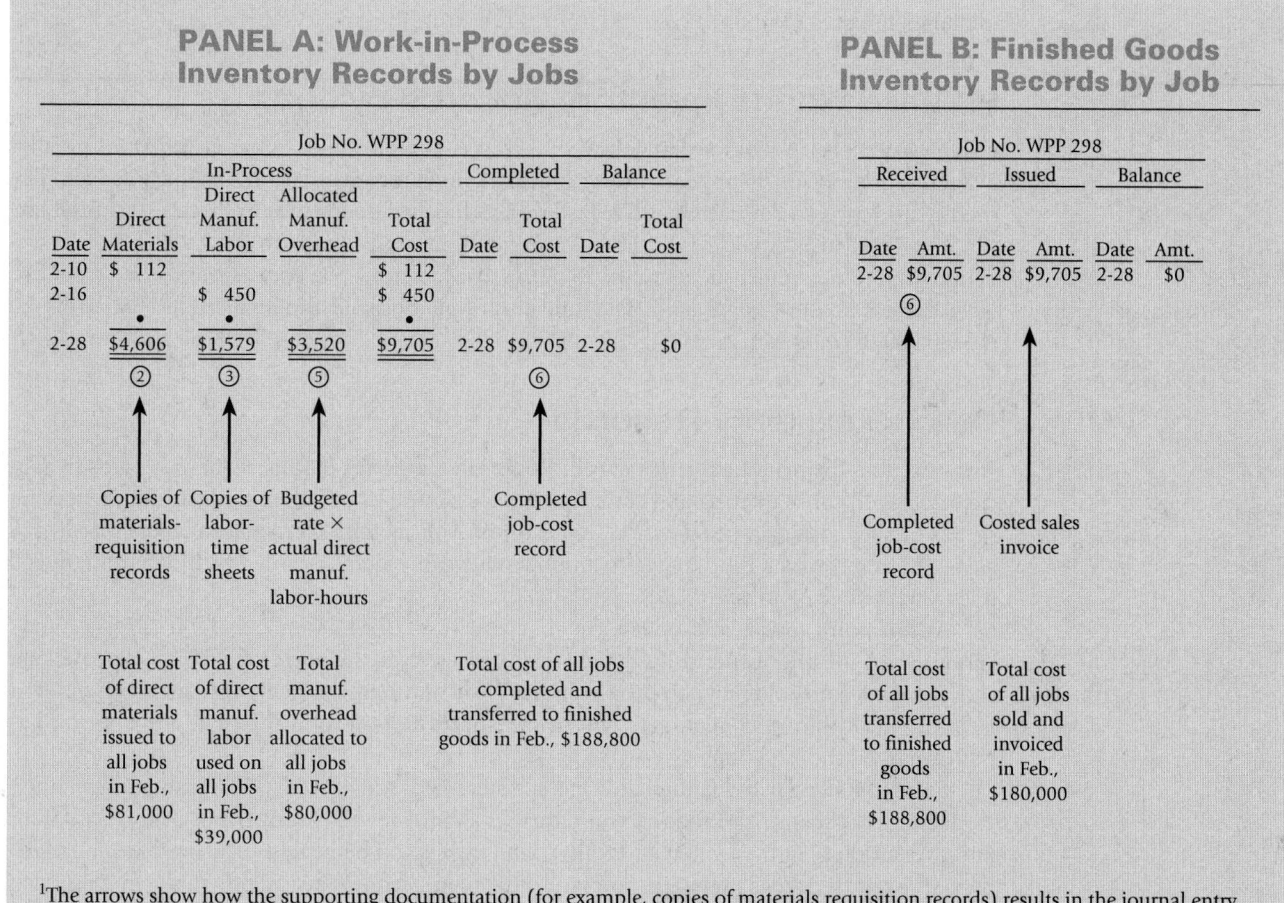

[1]The arrows show how the supporting documentation (for example, copies of materials requisition records) results in the journal entry number shown in circles (for example, journal entry number 2) that corresponds to the entries in Exhibit 4-7.

Manufacturing Department Overhead Records by Month

The Manufacturing Department overhead records (see Exhibit 4-8, Panel C) that make up the subsidiary ledger for the Manufacturing Overhead Control account show details of different categories of overhead costs such as indirect materials, indirect manufacturing labor, supervision and engineering, plant insurance and utilities, and plant depreciation. The source documents for these entries include invoices (for example, a utility bill) and special schedules (for example, a depreciation schedule) from the responsible accounting officer. Manufacturing department overhead for February 2020 is indirect materials, $4,000; indirect manufacturing labor, $15,000; and other manufacturing overhead, $75,000 (Exhibit 4-8, Panel C).

Work-in-Process Inventory Records by Jobs

As we have discussed, the job-cost record for each individual job in the subsidiary ledger is debited by the actual cost of direct materials and direct manufacturing labor used by individual jobs. In Robinson's normal-costing system, the job-cost record for each individual job in the subsidiary ledger is also debited for manufacturing overhead allocated based on the budgeted manufacturing overhead rate times the actual direct manufacturing labor-hours used in that job. For example, the job-cost record for Job WPP 298 (Exhibit 4-9, Panel A) shows Manufacturing Overhead Allocated of $3,520 (the budgeted rate of $40 per labor-hour × 88 actual direct manufacturing labor-hours used). For the

2,000 actual direct manufacturing labor-hours used for all jobs in February 2020, the total manufacturing overhead allocated equals \$40 per labor-hour × 2,000 direct manufacturing labor-hours = \$80,000.

Finished Goods Inventory Records by Jobs

Exhibit 4-9, Panel A, shows that Job WPP 298 was completed at a cost of \$9,705. Job WPP 298 also simultaneously appears in the finished-goods records of the subsidiary ledger. The total cost of all jobs completed and transferred to finished goods in February 2020 is \$188,800 (Exhibit 4-9, Panels A and B). Exhibit 4-9, Panel B, indicates that Job WPP 298 was sold and delivered to the customer on February 28, 2020, at which time \$9,705 was transferred from finished goods to cost of goods sold. The total cost of all jobs sold and invoiced in February 2020 is \$180,000 (Exhibit 4-9, Panel B).

Other Subsidiary Records

Just as it does for manufacturing payroll, Robinson maintains employee labor records in subsidiary ledgers for marketing and customer-service payroll as well as records for different types of advertising costs (print, television, and radio). An accounts receivable subsidiary ledger is also used to record the February 2020 amounts due from each customer, including the \$15,000 due from the sale of Job WPP 298.

At this point, pause and review the nine entries in this example. Exhibit 4-7 is a handy summary of all nine general-ledger entries presented in the form of T-accounts. Be sure to trace each journal entry, step by step, to T-accounts in the general ledger presented in Exhibit 4-7. Robinson's managers will use this information to evaluate how Robinson has performed on the WPP job.

Exhibit 4-10 provides Robinson's income statement for February 2020 using information from entries 7, 8, and 9. Managers could further subdivide the cost of goods sold calculations and present them in the format of Exhibit 2-8 (page 42). The benefit of using the subdivided format is that it allows managers to discern detailed performance trends that can help them improve the efficiency on future jobs.

Nonmanufacturing Costs and Job Costing

In Chapter 2 (pages 47–49), you learned that companies use product costs for different purposes. The product costs reported as inventoriable costs to shareholders may differ from the product costs reported to managers to guide their pricing and product-mix decisions. Managers must keep in mind that even though marketing and customer-service costs are expensed when incurred for financial accounting purposes, companies often trace or allocate these costs to individual jobs for pricing, product-mix, and cost-management decisions.

EXHIBIT 4-10

Robinson Company Income Statement for the Month Ending February 2020

Revenues		\$270,000
Cost of goods sold (\$180,000 + \$14,000[1])		194,000
Gross margin		76,000
Operating costs		
Marketing costs	\$45,000	
Customer-service costs	15,000	
Total operating costs		60,000
Operating income		\$ 16,000

[1]Cost of goods sold has been increased by \$14,000, the difference between the Manufacturing overhead control account (\$94,000) and the Manufacturing overhead allocated (\$80,000). In a later section of this chapter, we discuss this adjustment, which represents the amount by which actual manufacturing overhead cost exceeds the manufacturing overhead allocated to jobs during February 2020.

Robinson can trace direct marketing costs and customer-service costs to jobs the same way in which it traces direct manufacturing costs to jobs. What about indirect marketing and customer-service costs? Assume these costs have the same cost-allocation base, revenues, and are included in a single cost pool. Robinson can then calculate a budgeted indirect-cost rate by dividing budgeted indirect marketing costs plus budgeted indirect customer-service costs by budgeted revenues. Robinson can use this rate to allocate these indirect costs to jobs. For example, if this rate were 15% of revenues, Robinson would allocate $2,250 to Job WPP 298 (0.15 × $15,000, the revenue from the job). By assigning both manufacturing costs and nonmanufacturing costs to jobs, Robinson can compare all costs against the revenues of different jobs.

DECISION POINT

How are transactions recorded in a manufacturing job-costing system?

Budgeted Indirect Costs and End-of-Accounting-Year Adjustments

LEARNING OBJECTIVE 7

Adjust for under- or overallocated manufacturing overhead costs at the end of the fiscal year using alternative methods

. . . for example, writing the amount off to the Cost of Goods Sold account

Managers try to closely approximate actual manufacturing overhead costs and the actual total quantities of the cost-allocation base(s) when calculating the budgeted indirect cost rate(s). However, for the numerator and denominator reasons explained earlier in the chapter, under normal costing, a company's actual overhead costs incurred each month are likely to not equal its overhead costs allocated each month. Even at the end of the year, total allocated overhead costs are unlikely to equal total actual overhead costs incurred because allocated costs are based on estimates made up to 12 months before actual costs are incurred. For financial accounting purposes, companies are required under Generally Accepted Accounting Principles to report results in the financial statements based on *actual* costs. We now describe adjustments that accountants need to make when, at the end of the fiscal year, indirect costs allocated differ from actual indirect costs incurred.

Underallocated and Overallocated Indirect Costs

Underallocated indirect costs occur when the allocated amount of indirect costs in an accounting period is less than the actual overhead amount incurred for the period. **Overallocated indirect costs** occur when the allocated amount of indirect costs in an accounting period is greater than the actual overhead amount incurred for the period.

$$\text{Underallocated (overallocated) indirect costs} = \text{Actual indirect costs incurred} - \text{Indirect costs allocated}$$

Underallocated (overallocated) indirect costs are also called **underapplied (overapplied) indirect costs** and **underabsorbed (overabsorbed) indirect costs.**

Consider the manufacturing overhead cost pool at Robinson Company. There are two indirect-cost accounts in the general ledger related to manufacturing overhead:

1. Manufacturing Overhead Control, which records the actual costs in all the individual overhead categories (such as indirect materials, indirect manufacturing labor, supervision, engineering, utilities, and plant depreciation).
2. Manufacturing Overhead Allocated, which records the manufacturing overhead allocated to individual jobs on the basis of the budgeted indirect cost rate multiplied by actual direct manufacturing labor-hours.

At the end of the year, the overhead accounts show the following amounts.

Manufacturing Overhead Control	
Bal. Dec. 31, 2020	1,215,000

Manufacturing Overhead Allocated	
Bal. Dec. 31, 2020	1,080,000

The $1,080,000 credit balance in Manufacturing Overhead Allocated results from multiplying the 27,000 actual direct manufacturing labor-hours worked on all jobs in 2020 by the budgeted rate of $40 per direct manufacturing labor-hour.

The $135,000 ($1,215,000 − $1,080,000) difference (a net debit) is an underallocated amount because actual manufacturing overhead costs incurred are greater than the allocated amount. This difference arises for two reasons related to the computation of the $40 budgeted hourly rate:

1. **Numerator reason (indirect-cost pool).** Actual manufacturing overhead costs of $1,215,000 are greater than the budgeted amount of $1,120,000.
2. **Denominator reason (quantity of allocation base).** Total actual direct manufacturing labor-hours of 27,000 are fewer than the budgeted 28,000 hours.

There are three main approaches to accounting for the $135,000 underallocated manufacturing overhead costs caused by Robinson underestimating manufacturing overhead costs and overestimating the total quantity of the cost-allocation base: (1) adjusted allocation-rate approach, (2) proration approach, and (3) write-off to cost of goods sold approach.

Adjusted Allocation-Rate Approach

The **adjusted allocation-rate approach** restates all overhead entries in the general ledger and subsidiary ledgers using actual overhead cost rates rather than budgeted overhead cost rates. First, the actual manufacturing overhead rate is computed at the end of the fiscal year. Then the manufacturing overhead costs allocated to every job during the year are re-computed using the actual manufacturing overhead rate (rather than the budgeted manufacturing overhead rate). Finally, end-of-year closing entries are made. The result is that at year-end, every job-cost record and finished-goods record—as well as the ending Work-in-Process Control, Finished Goods Control, and Cost of Goods Sold accounts—represent actual manufacturing overhead costs incurred.

The widespread adoption of computerized accounting systems has greatly reduced the cost of using the adjusted allocation-rate approach. In our Robinson example, the actual manufacturing overhead rate ($45 per direct manufacturing labor-hour, see page 116) exceeds the budgeted manufacturing overhead rate ($40 per direct manufacturing labor-hour) by 12.5% [($45 − $40) ÷ $40]. At year-end, Robinson could increase the manufacturing overhead allocated to each job in 2020 by 12.5% using a single software command. The command would adjust both the subsidiary ledgers and the general ledger.

Consider the Western Pulp and Paper machine job, WPP 298. Under normal costing, the manufacturing overhead cost allocated to the job is $3,520 (the budgeted rate of $40 per direct manufacturing labor-hour × 88 hours). Increasing the manufacturing overhead allocated by 12.5%, or $440 ($3,520 × 0.125), means the adjusted amount of manufacturing overhead cost allocated to Job WPP 298 is $3,960 ($3,520 + $440). Note from page 116 that using actual costing, manufacturing overhead allocated to this job is $3,960 (the actual rate of $45 per direct manufacturing labor-hour × 88 hours). Making this adjustment to normal costing for each job in the subsidiary ledgers ensures that the actual total manufacturing overhead costs of $1,215,000 are allocated to jobs.

The adjusted allocation-rate approach offers the benefits of both the *timeliness and convenience of normal costing during the year and the allocation of the entire actual manufacturing overhead costs at year-end.* Each individual job-cost record and the end-of-year account balances for inventories and cost of goods sold are adjusted to actual costs. These adjustments, in turn, will affect the income Robinson reports. Knowing the actual profitability of individual jobs after they are completed provides managers with accurate and useful insights for future decisions about which jobs to undertake, how to price them, and how to manage their costs.

Proration Approach

The **proration** approach spreads under- or overallocated overhead among ending work-in-process inventory, finished-goods inventory, and cost of goods sold. No overhead costs are prorated to the materials inventory account because no manufacturing overhead costs have been allocated to it. We illustrate end-of-year proration in the Robinson Company example. Assume the following actual results for Robinson Company in 2020:

	A	B	C
1	Account	Account Balance (Before Proration)	Manufacturing Overhead in Each Account Balance Allocated in the Current Year (Before Proration)
2	Work-in-process control	$ 50,000	$ 16,200
3	Finished goods control	75,000	31,320
4	Cost of goods sold	2,375,000	1,032,480
5		$2,500,000	$1,080,000

How should Robinson prorate the underallocated $135,000 of manufacturing overhead at the end of 2020?

On the basis of the total amount of manufacturing overhead allocated in 2020 (before proration) included in the ending balances of Work-in-Process Control, Finished Goods Control, and Cost of Goods Sold accounts. In the following table, the $135,000 underallocated overhead is prorated over the three accounts in proportion to the total amount of manufacturing overhead allocated (before proration) in column 2, resulting in the ending balances (after proration) in column 5.

	A	B	C	D	E	F	G
10		Account Balance (Before Proration)	Manufacturing Overhead in Each Account Balance Allocated in the Current Year (Before Proration)	Manufacturing Overhead in Each Account Balance Allocated in the Current Year as a Percent of Total	Proration of $135,000 of Underallocated Manufacturing Overhead		Account Balance (After Proration)
11	Account	(1)	(2)	(3) = (2) / $1,080,000	(4) = (3) × $135,000		(5) = (1) + (4)
12	Work-in-process control	$ 50,000	$ 16,200	1.5%	0.015 × $135,000 =	$ 2,025	$ 52,025
13	Finished goods control	75,000	31,320	2.9%	0.029 × 135,000 =	3,915	78,915
14	Cost of goods sold	2,375,000	1,032,480	95.6%	0.956 × 135,000 =	129,060	2,504,060
15	Total	$2,500,000	$1,080,000	100.0%		$135,000	$2,635,000

Robinson's actual manufacturing overhead costs ($1,215,000) in 2020 exceed its allocated manufacturing overhead costs ($1,080,000) in 2020 by 12.5%. The prorated amounts in column 4 can also be derived by multiplying the balances in column 2 by 12.5%. For example, the $3,915 prorated manufacturing overhead to Finished Goods is 12.5% × $31,320. Adding the prorated amounts effectively results in Robinson allocating manufacturing overhead at 112.5% of what had been allocated before, and thus in Robinson using the actual manufacturing overhead rate. (Recall that Robinson's actual manufacturing overhead rate ($45 per direct manufacturing labor-hour) exceeds the budgeted manufacturing overhead rate ($40 per direct manufacturing labor-hour) by 12.5%.) The journal entry to record this proration is

Work-in-Process Control	2,025	
Finished Goods Control	3,915	
Cost of Goods Sold	129,060	
Manufacturing Overhead Allocated	1,080,000	
Manufacturing Overhead Control		1,215,000

If manufacturing overhead had been overallocated, the Work-in-Process Control, Finished Goods Control, and Cost of Goods Sold accounts would be decreased (credited) instead of increased (debited).

This journal entry closes (brings to zero) the manufacturing overhead-related accounts and restates the 2020 ending balances for Work-in-Process Control, Finished Goods Control, and Cost of Goods Sold to what they would have been if actual manufacturing overhead rates had been used rather than budgeted manufacturing overhead rates. This method reports the same 2020 ending balances in the general ledger as the adjusted allocation-rate approach discussed above. However, unlike the adjusted allocation-rate approach, the sum of the amounts shown in the subsidiary ledgers will not match the amounts shown in the general ledger after proration because no adjustments are made to the budgeted manufacturing overhead rates used in the individual job-cost records. The objective of the proration approach is to only adjust the general ledger to actual manufacturing overhead rates for purposes of financial reporting. The increase in the cost of goods sold expense by $129,060 as a result of the proration causes Robinson's reported operating income to decrease by the same amount.

Some companies use the proration approach, but base it on the ending balances of Work-in-Process Control, Finished Goods Control, and Cost of Goods Sold accounts prior to proration (see column 1 of the preceding table). The following table shows that prorations based on ending account balances are not the same as the more accurate prorations calculated earlier based on the amount of manufacturing overhead allocated (before proration) to the accounts because the ratios of allocated manufacturing overhead costs to total costs in these accounts are not the same.

	A	B	C	D	E	F
1		Account Balance (Before Proration)	Account Balance as a Percent of Total	Proration of $135,000 of Underallocated Manufacturing Overhead		Account Balance (After Proration)
2	Account	(1)	(2) = (1) / $2,500,000	(3) = (2) × $135,000		(4) = (1) + (3)
3	Work-in-process control	$ 50,000	2.0%	0.02 × $135,000 =	$ 2,700	$ 52,700
4	Finished goods control	75,000	3.0%	0.03 × 135,000 =	4,050	79,050
5	Cost of goods sold	2,375,000	95.0%	0.95 × 135,000 =	128,250	2,503,250
6	Total	$2,500,000	100.0%		$135,000	$2,635,000

However, proration based on ending balances is frequently justified as being an expedient way of approximating the more accurate results one would obtain by using allocated manufacturing overhead costs.

Write-Off to Cost of Goods Sold Approach

Under the write-off approach, the total under- or overallocated manufacturing overhead is included in this year's Cost of Goods Sold expense. For Robinson, the journal entry would be as follows:

Cost of Goods Sold	135,000	
Manufacturing Overhead Allocated	1,080,000	
Manufacturing Overhead Control		1,215,000

Robinson's two Manufacturing Overhead accounts—Manufacturing Overhead Control and Manufacturing Overhead Allocated—are closed with the difference between them included in Cost of Goods Sold. The Cost of Goods Sold account after the write-off equals $2,510,000, the balance before the write-off of $2,375,000 *plus the underallocated* manufacturing overhead amount of $135,000. This results in operating income decreasing by $135,000.

4-4 TRY IT!

Huckvale Corporation manufactures custom cabinets for kitchens. It uses a normal-costing system with two direct-cost categories—direct materials and direct manufacturing labor—and one indirect-cost pool, manufacturing overhead costs. It provides the following information about manufacturing overhead costs for 2020.

Budgeted manufacturing overhead costs	$1,160,000
Budgeted direct manufacturing labor-hours	29,000 hours
Actual manufacturing overhead costs	$1,260,000
Actual direct manufacturing labor-hours	28,000 hours

The following information is available as of December 31, 2020.

Account	Account Balance (Before Proration)	Manufacturing Overhead in Each Account Balance Allocated in the Current Year (Before Proration)
Work-in-Process Control	$ 45,000	$ 29,000
Finished Goods Control	65,000	63,800
Cost of Goods Sold	1,600,000	1,067,200
	$1,710,000	$1,160,000

Calculate the underallocated or overallocated manufacturing overhead at the end of 2020 and prorate it to Work-in-Process Control, Finished Goods Control, and Cost of Goods Sold accounts based on the allocated manufacturing overhead in each account balance using normal costing.

Choosing Among Approaches

Which of the three approaches of dealing with under- or overallocated overhead is the best one to use? When making this decision, managers should consider the amount of the under- or overallocated overhead costs and the purpose of the adjustment, as the following table indicates.

If the purpose of the adjustment is to . . .	and the total amount of underallocation or overallocation is . . .	then managers prefer to use the . . .
state the balance sheet and income statements based on actual rather than budgeted manufacturing overhead rates	big, relative to total operating income, and inventory levels are high	proration method because it is the most accurate method of allocating actual manufacturing overhead costs to the general ledger accounts.
state the balance sheet and income statements based on actual rather than budgeted manufacturing overhead rates	small, relative to total operating income, or inventory levels are low	write-off to cost of goods sold approach because it is a good approximation of the more accurate proration method.
provide an accurate record of actual individual job costs in order to conduct a profitability analysis, learn how to better manage the costs of jobs, and bid on future jobs	big, relative to total operating income	adjusted allocation-rate method because it makes adjustments in individual job records in addition to the general ledger accounts.

Many management accountants and managers argue that *to the extent that the underallocated overhead cost reflects inefficiency during the period*, it should be written off to the Cost of Goods Sold account instead of being prorated to the Work-in-Process and Finished-Goods inventory accounts. This line of reasoning suggests applying a combination of the write-off and proration methods. For example, the portion of the underallocated overhead cost that is due to inefficiency (say, because of excessive spending or idle capacity) and that could have been avoided should be written off to the Cost of Goods Sold account, whereas the portion that is unrelated to inefficiency and that is unavoidable should be prorated. Unlike full proration, this approach avoids including part of the cost of current-period inefficiencies in inventory assets.

As our discussion suggests, choosing which method to use and determining the amount to be written off is often a matter of judgment. The method managers choose affects the operating income a company reports. In the case of underallocated overhead, the method of writing off to cost of goods sold results in lower operating income compared to proration. In the case of overallocated overhead, proration results in lower operating income compared to writing the overhead off to cost of goods sold.

Do managers prefer to report lower or higher operating income? Reporting lower operating income lowers the company's taxes, saving the company cash and increasing company value. But managers are often compensated based on operating income and so favor reporting higher operating incomes even if it results in higher taxes. Managers of companies in financial difficulty also tend to report higher incomes to avoid violating financial covenants. Shareholders and boards of directors seek to motivate managerial actions that increase company value. For this reason, many compensation plans include metrics such as after-tax cash flow, in addition to operating income. At no time should managers make choices that are illegal or unethical. We discuss these issues in more detail in Chapter 24.

DECISION POINT

How should managers adjust for under- or overallocated manufacturing overhead costs at the end of the accounting year?

Robinson's managers believed that a single manufacturing overhead cost pool with direct manufacturing labor-hours as the cost-allocation base was appropriate for allocating all manufacturing overhead costs to jobs. Had Robinson's managers felt that different manufacturing departments (for example, machining and assembly) used overhead resources differently, they would have assigned overhead costs to each department and calculated a separate overhead allocation rate for each department based on the cost driver of the overhead costs in each department. The general ledger would contain Manufacturing Overhead Control and Manufacturing Overhead Allocated accounts for each department, resulting in end-of-year adjustments for under- or overallocated overhead costs for each department.

Instructors and students interested in exploring these more detailed allocations can go to Chapter 16, where we continue the Robinson Company example.

Variations of Normal Costing: A Service-Sector Example

LEARNING OBJECTIVE 8

Understand variations of normal costing

. . . some variations of normal costing use budgeted direct-cost rates

Job costing is also very useful in service organizations such as accounting and consulting firms, advertising agencies, auto repair shops, and hospitals. In an accounting firm, each audit is a job. The costs of each audit are accumulated in a job-cost record, much like the document used by Robinson Company, based on the seven-step approach described earlier. On the basis of labor-time sheets, direct labor costs of the professional staff—audit partners, audit managers, and audit staff—are traced to individual jobs. Other direct costs, such as travel, out-of-town meals, and lodging are also traced to jobs. The costs of secretarial support, office staff, rent, and depreciation of furniture and equipment are indirect costs because these costs cannot easily be traced to jobs. Indirect costs are allocated to jobs, for example, using a cost-allocation base such as number of professional labor-hours.

In some service organizations, a variation of normal costing is helpful because actual direct-labor costs, the largest component of total costs in many service organizations, can be difficult to trace to jobs as they are completed. For example, the actual direct-labor costs of an audit may include bonuses that become known only at the end of the year (a numerator reason). Also, the hours worked each period might vary significantly depending on the number of working days each month and the demand for services (a denominator reason) while the direct-labor costs remain largely fixed. It would be inappropriate to charge a job with higher actual direct labor costs simply because a month had fewer working days or demand for services was low in that month. Using budgeted rates gives a better picture of the direct labor cost per hour that the company had planned when it hired the workers. In situations like these, a company needing timely cost information during the progress of an audit will use budgeted rates for some *direct* costs in addition to the budgeted rates for indirect costs. All budgeted rates are calculated at the start of the fiscal year. Recall that "pure" normal costing uses actual cost rates for all direct costs and budgeted cost rates only for indirect costs.

The mechanics of using budgeted rates for direct costs are similar to the methods employed when using budgeted rates for indirect costs. We illustrate this for Donahue and Associates, a public accounting firm. For 2020, Donahue budgets total direct-labor costs of $14,400,000, total indirect costs of $12,960,000, and total direct (professional) labor-hours of 288,000. In this case,

$$\text{Budgeted direct-labor cost rate} = \frac{\text{Budgeted total direct-labor costs}}{\text{Budgeted total direct-labor hours}}$$

$$= \frac{\$14{,}400{,}000}{288{,}000 \text{ direct labor-hours}} = \$50 \text{ per direct labor-hour}$$

Assuming only one indirect-cost pool and total direct-labor costs as the cost-allocation base,

$$\text{Budgeted indirect cost rate} = \frac{\text{Budgeted total costs in indirect cost pool}}{\text{Budgeted total quantity of cost-allocation base (direct-labor costs)}}$$

$$= \frac{\$12{,}960{,}000}{\$14{,}400{,}000} = 0.90, \text{ or } 90\% \text{ of direct-labor costs}$$

Suppose that in March 2020, an audit of Hanley Transport, a client of Donahue, uses 800 direct labor-hours. Donahue calculates the direct-labor costs of the audit by multiplying the budgeted direct-labor cost rate, $50 per direct labor-hour, by 800, the actual quantity of direct labor-hours. The indirect costs allocated to the Hanley Transport audit are determined by multiplying the budgeted indirect-cost rate (90%) by the direct-labor costs assigned to the job ($40,000). Assuming no other direct costs for travel and the like, the cost of the Hanley Transport audit is

Direct-labor costs, $50 × 800	$40,000
Indirect costs allocated, 90% × $40,000	36,000
Total	$76,000

At the end of the fiscal year, the direct costs traced to jobs using budgeted rates will generally not equal actual direct costs because the actual rate and the budgeted rate are developed at different times using different information. End-of-year adjustments for under- or overallocated direct costs would need to be made in the same way that adjustments are made for under- or overallocated indirect costs.

The Donahue and Associates example illustrates that most costing systems used in practice do not exactly match either the actual-costing system or the normal-costing system described earlier in the chapter. As another example, engineering consulting firms, such as Tata Consulting Engineers in India and Terracon Consulting Engineers in the United States, often use budgeted rates to allocate indirect costs (such as engineering and office-support costs) as well as some direct costs (such as professional labor-hours) and trace some actual direct costs (such as the cost of making blueprints and fees paid to outside experts). Users of costing systems should be aware that they may encounter different systems.

DECISION POINT

What are some variations of normal costing?

PROBLEM FOR SELF-STUDY

Your manager asks you to bring the following incomplete accounts of Endeavor Printing, Inc., up to date through January 31, 2020. Consider the data that appear in the T-accounts as well as the following information in items (a) through (j).

Endeavor's normal-costing system has two direct-cost categories (direct material costs and direct manufacturing labor costs) and one indirect-cost pool (manufacturing overhead costs, which are allocated using direct manufacturing labor costs).

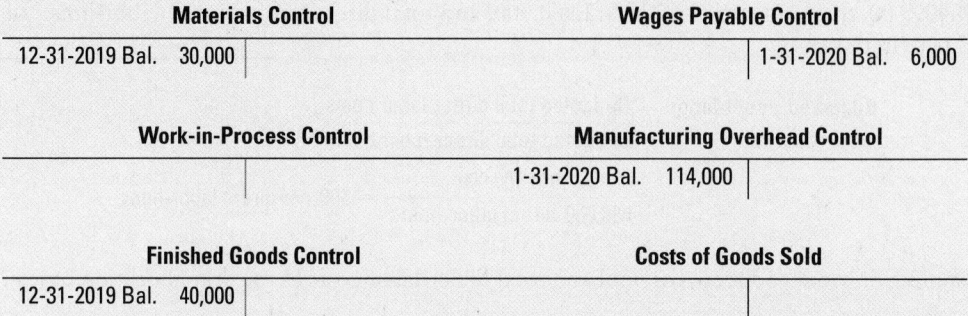

Materials Control		Wages Payable Control	
12-31-2019 Bal. 30,000			1-31-2020 Bal. 6,000

Work-in-Process Control		Manufacturing Overhead Control	
		1-31-2020 Bal. 114,000	

Finished Goods Control		Costs of Goods Sold	
12-31-2019 Bal. 40,000			

Additional information follows:

a. Manufacturing overhead is allocated using a budgeted rate that is set every December. You forecast next year's manufacturing overhead costs and next year's direct manufacturing labor costs. The budget for 2020 is $1,200,000 for manufacturing overhead costs and $800,000 for direct manufacturing labor costs.
b. The only job unfinished on January 31, 2020, is No. 419, on which direct manufacturing labor costs are $4,000 (250 direct manufacturing labor-hours) and direct material costs are $16,000.
c. Total direct materials issued to production during January 2020 are $180,000.
d. Cost of goods completed during January is $360,000.
e. Materials inventory as of January 31, 2020, is $40,000.
f. Finished-goods inventory as of January 31, 2020, is $30,000.
g. All plant workers earn the same wage rate. Direct manufacturing labor-hours used for January total 5,000 hours. Other labor costs total $20,000.
h. The gross plant payroll paid in January equals $104,000. Ignore withholdings.
i. All "actual" manufacturing overhead costs incurred during January have already been posted.
j. All materials are direct materials.

Calculate the following:

1. Materials purchased during January
2. Cost of Goods Sold during January
3. Direct manufacturing labor costs incurred during January
4. Manufacturing Overhead Allocated during January
5. Balance, Wages Payable Control, December 31, 2019
6. Balance, Work-in-Process Control, January 31, 2020
7. Balance, Work-in-Process Control, December 31, 2019
8. Manufacturing Overhead Underallocated or Overallocated for January 2020

Solution

Amounts from the T-accounts are labeled "(T)."

1. From Materials Control T-account, Materials purchased:
   $180,000 (c) + $40,000 (e) − 30,000 (T) = $190,000
2. From Finished Goods Control T-account, Cost of Goods Sold:
   $40,000 (T) + $360,000 (d) − $30,000 (f) = $370,000

3. Direct manufacturing wage rate: $4,000 (b) ÷ 250 direct manufacturing labor-hours (b) = $16 per direct manufacturing labor-hour
   Direct manufacturing labor costs: 5,000 direct manufacturing labor-hours (g) × $16 per direct manufacturing labor-hour = $80,000
4. Manufacturing overhead rate: $1,200,000 (a) ÷ $800,000 (a) = 150%
   Manufacturing Overhead Allocated: 150% of $80,000 (see 3) = 1.50 × $80,000 = $120,000
5. From Wages Payable Control T-account, Wages Payable Control, December 31, 2019: $104,000 (h) + $6,000 (T) − $80,000 (see 3) − $20,000 (g) = $10,000
6. Work-in-Process Control, January 31, 2020: $16,000 (b) + $4,000 (b) + 150% of $4,000 (b) = $26,000 (This answer is used in item 7.)
7. From Work-in-Process Control T-account, Work-in-Process Control, December 31, 2019: $360,000 (d) + $26,000 (see 6) − $180,000 (c) − $80,000 (see 3) − $120,000 (see 4) = $6,000
8. Manufacturing overhead overallocated: $120,000 (see 4) − $114,000 (T) = $6,000.

Letters alongside entries in T-accounts correspond to letters in the preceding additional information. Numbers alongside entries in T-accounts correspond to numbers in the preceding requirements.

Materials Control

December 31, 2019, Bal.	(given)	30,000			
	(1)	190,000*		(c)	180,000
January 31, 2020, Bal.	(e)	40,000			

Work-in-Process Control

December 31, 2019, Bal.	(7)	6,000		(d)	360,000
Direct materials	(c)	180,000			
Direct manufacturing labor	(b) (g) (3)	80,000			
Manufacturing overhead allocated	(3) (a) (4)	120,000			
January 31, 2020, Bal.	(b) (6)	26,000			

Finished Goods Control

December 31, 2019, Bal.	(given)	40,000		(2)	370,000
	(d)	360,000			
January 31, 2020, Bal.	(f)	30,000			

Wages Payable Control

	(h)	104,000	December 31, 2019, Bal.	(5)	10,000
				(g) (3)	80,000
				(g)	20,000
			January 31, 2020	(given)	6,000

Manufacturing Overhead Control

Total January charges	(given)	114,000			

Manufacturing Overhead Allocated

				(3) (a) (4)	120,000

Cost of Goods Sold

	(d) (f) (2)	370,000			

*Can be computed only after all other postings in the account have been made.

DECISION POINTS

The following question-and-answer format summarizes the chapter's learning objectives. Each decision presents a key question related to a learning objective. The guidelines are the answer to that question.

Decision	Guidelines
1. What are the building-block concepts of a costing system?	The building-block concepts of a costing system are cost object, direct costs of a cost object, indirect costs of a cost object, cost pool, and cost-allocation base. Costing-system overview diagrams represent these five concepts in a systematic way. Costing systems aim to report cost numbers that reflect the way cost objects (such as products or services) use the resources of an organization.
2. How do you distinguish job costing from process costing?	Job-costing systems assign costs to distinct units of a product or service. Process-costing systems assign costs to masses of identical or similar units of a product or service and compute unit costs on an average basis. These two costing systems represent opposite ends of a continuum. The costing systems of many companies combine some elements of both job costing and process costing.
3. What is the main challenge of implementing job-costing systems?	The main challenge of implementing job-costing systems is estimating actual costs of jobs in a timely manner.
4. How do you implement a normal-costing system?	A general seven-step approach to normal costing requires identifying (1) the job, (2) the actual direct costs, (3) the cost-allocation bases, (4) the budgeted indirect costs associated with each cost allocation base, i.e., the indirect-cost pools, (5) the budgeted cost-allocation rates, (6) the allocated indirect costs (budgeted rates times actual quantities of the cost-allocation bases), and (7) the total costs (direct costs + indirect costs) of a job.
5. How do you distinguish actual costing from normal costing?	Actual costing and normal costing differ in the indirect-cost rates used: (see table below) Both systems use actual quantities of inputs for tracing direct costs and actual quantities of the cost-allocation bases for allocating indirect costs.
6. How are transactions recorded in a manufacturing job-costing system?	A manufacturing job-costing system records the flow of inventoriable costs in the general and subsidiary ledgers for (1) acquisition of materials and other manufacturing inputs, (2) their conversion into work in process, (3) their conversion into finished goods, and (4) the sale of finished goods. The job-costing system expenses period costs, such as marketing costs, as they are incurred.

	Actual Costing	Normal Costing
Direct-cost rates	Actual rates	Actual rates
Indirect-cost rates	Actual rates	Budgeted rates

Decision	Guidelines
7. How should managers adjust for under- or overallocated manufacturing overhead costs at the end of the accounting year?	The two standard approaches of adjusting for under- or overallocated manufacturing overhead costs at the end of the accounting year for the purposes of stating balance sheet and income statement amounts at actual costs are (1) to adjust the allocation rate and (2) to prorate on the basis of the total amount of the allocated manufacturing overhead cost in the ending balances of Work-in-Process Control, Finished Goods Control, and Cost of Goods Sold accounts. Many companies write off amounts of under- or overallocated manufacturing overhead costs to Cost of Goods Sold when the amounts are immaterial or when the underallocated overhead costs are the result of inefficiencies.
8. What are some variations of normal costing?	In some variations of normal costing, organizations use budgeted rates to assign direct costs, as well as indirect costs, to jobs.

TERMS TO LEARN

This chapter and the Glossary at the end of the text contain definitions of the following important terms:

actual costing **(p. 108)**
actual indirect-cost rate **(p. 116)**
adjusted allocation-rate approach **(p. 126)**
budgeted indirect-cost rate **(p. 110)**
cost-allocation base **(p. 105)**
cost pool **(p. 105)**
job **(p. 106)**
job-cost record **(p. 110)**
job-cost sheet **(p. 110)**
job-costing system **(p. 106)**
labor-time sheet **(p. 110)**
manufacturing overhead allocated **(p. 120)**
manufacturing overhead applied **(p. 120)**
materials-requisition record **(p. 110)**
normal costing **(p. 110)**
overabsorbed indirect costs **(p. 125)**
overallocated indirect costs **(p. 125)**
overapplied indirect costs **(p. 125)**
process-costing system **(p. 106)**
proration **(p. 126)**
source document **(p. 110)**
underabsorbed indirect costs **(p. 125)**
underallocated indirect costs **(p. 125)**
underapplied indirect costs **(p. 125)**

ASSIGNMENT MATERIAL

Questions

4-1 Define cost pool, cost tracing, cost allocation, and cost-allocation base.

4-2 How does a job-costing system differ from a process-costing system?

4-3 Why might an advertising agency use job costing for an advertising campaign by PepsiCo, whereas a bank might use process costing to determine the cost of checking account deposits?

4-4 Describe the seven steps in job costing.

4-5 Give examples of two cost objects in companies using job costing.

4-6 Describe three major source documents used in job-costing systems.

4-7 What is the advantage of using computerized source documents to prepare job-cost records?

4-8 Give two reasons why most organizations use an annual period rather than a weekly or monthly period to compute budgeted indirect-cost rates.

4-9 Distinguish between actual costing and normal costing.

4-10 Describe two ways in which a house-construction company may use job-cost information.

4-11 Comment on the following statement: "In a normal-costing system, the amounts in the Manufacturing Overhead Control account will always equal the amounts in the Manufacturing Overhead Allocated account."

4-12 Describe three different debit entries to the Work-in-Process Control T-account under normal costing.

4-13 Describe three alternative ways to adjust for under- or overallocated overhead costs.

4-14 When might a company use budgeted costs rather than actual costs to compute direct-labor rates?

4-15 Describe briefly why Electronic Data Interchange (EDI) is helpful to managers.

Multiple-Choice Questions

In partnership with:

BECKER PROFESSIONAL EDUCATION®

4-16 Which of the following does not accurately describe the application of job costing?

a. Finished goods that are purchased by customers will directly impact cost of goods sold.

b. Indirect manufacturing labor and indirect materials are part of the actual manufacturing costs incurred.

c. Direct materials and direct manufacturing labor are included in total manufacturing costs.

d. Manufacturing overhead costs incurred is used to determine total manufacturing costs.

4-17 Sturdy Manufacturing Co. assembled the following cost data for job #23:

Direct manufacturing labor	$80,000
Indirect manufacturing labor	12,000
Equipment depreciation	1,000
Other indirect manufacturing costs	1,500
Direct materials	95,000
Indirect materials	4,000
Manufacturing overhead overapplied	2,000

What are the total manufacturing costs for job #23 if the company uses normal job costing?

a. $191,500 **b.** $193,500

c. $194,500 **d.** $195,500

4-18 For which of the following industries would job costing most likely not be appropriate?

a. Small business printing. **b.** Cereal production.

c. Home construction. **d.** Aircraft assembly.

4-19 ABC Company uses job costing and has assembled the following cost data for the production and assembly of item X:

Direct manufacturing labor wages	$35,000
Direct material used	70,000
Indirect manufacturing labor	4,000
Utilities	400
Fire insurance	500
Manufacturing overhead applied	11,000
Indirect materials	6,000
Depreciation on equipment	600

Based on the above cost data, the manufacturing overhead for item X is

a. $500 overallocated.

b. $600 underallocated.

c. $500 underallocated

d. $600 overallocated.

4-20 Under Stanford Corporation's job-costing system, manufacturing overhead is applied to work in process using a predetermined annual overhead rate. During November, Year 1, Stanford's transactions included the following:

Direct materials issued to production	$180,000
Indirect materials issued to production	16,000
Manufacturing overhead incurred	250,000
Manufacturing overhead applied	226,000
Direct manufacturing labor costs	214,000

Stanford had neither beginning nor ending work-in-process inventory. What was the cost of jobs completed and transferred to finished goods in November 20X1?

1. $604,000
2. $644,000
3. $620,000
4. $660,000

Exercises

4-21 (10 min) **Job costing, process costing.**

Required

In each of the following situations, determine whether job costing or process costing would be more appropriate.

a. A CPA firm
b. An oil refinery
c. A custom furniture manufacturer
d. A tire manufacturer
e. A textbook publisher
f. A home builder
g. An advertising agency
h. A dairy
i. A flour mill
j. A paint manufacturer
k. A nursing home
l. A landscaping company
m. An orange juice concentrate producer
n. A movie studio
o. A law firm
p. A commercial aircraft manufacturer
q. A management consulting firm
r. A cell phone battery manufacturer
s. A catering service
t. A paper mill
u. A computer repair shop

4-22 Actual costing, normal costing, accounting for manufacturing overhead. Dakota Products uses a job-costing system with two direct-cost categories (direct materials and direct manufacturing labor) and one manufacturing overhead cost pool. Dakota allocates manufacturing overhead costs using direct manufacturing labor costs. Dakota provides the following information:

	Budget for 2020	Actual Results for 2020
Direct material costs	$2,250,000	$2,150,000
Direct manufacturing labor costs	1,700,0000	1,650,000
Manufacturing overhead costs	3,060,000	3,217,500

Required

1. Compute the actual and budgeted manufacturing overhead rates for 2020.
2. During March, the job-cost record for Job 626 contained the following information:

Direct materials used	$55,000
Direct manufacturing labor costs	$45,000

   Compute the cost of Job 626 using (a) actual costing and (b) normal costing.
3. At the end of 2020, compute the under- or overallocated manufacturing overhead under normal costing. Why is there no under- or overallocated manufacturing overhead under actual costing?
4. Why might managers at Dakota Products prefer to use normal costing?

4-23 Job costing, normal and actual costing. Atkinson Construction assembles residential houses. It uses a job-costing system with two direct-cost categories (direct materials and direct labor) and one indirect-cost pool (assembly support). Direct labor-hours is the allocation base for assembly support costs. In December 2019, Atkinson budgets 2020 assembly-support costs to be $8,800,000 and 2020 direct labor-hours to be 220,000.

At the end of 2020, Atkinson is comparing the costs of several jobs that were started and completed in 2020.

	Laguna Model	Mission Model
Construction period	Feb–June 2020	May–Oct 2020
Direct material costs	$106,550	$127,450
Direct labor costs	$ 36,250	$ 41,130
Direct labor-hours	970	1,000

Direct materials and direct labor are paid for on a contract basis. The costs of each are known when direct materials are used or when direct labor-hours are worked. The 2020 actual assembly-support costs were $8,400,000, and the actual direct labor-hours were 200,000.

Required

1. Compute the (a) budgeted indirect-cost rate and (b) actual indirect-cost rate. Why do they differ?
2. What are the job costs of the Laguna Model and the Mission Model using (a) normal costing and (b) actual costing?
3. Why might Atkinson Construction prefer normal costing over actual costing?

4-24 Budgeted manufacturing overhead rate, allocated manufacturing overhead. Taylor Company uses normal costing. It allocates manufacturing overhead costs using a budgeted rate per machine-hour. The following data are available for 2020:

Budgeted manufacturing overhead costs	$3,800,000
Budgeted machine-hours	200,000
Actual manufacturing overhead costs	$3,660,000
Actual machine-hours	196,000

Required

1. Calculate the budgeted manufacturing overhead rate.
2. Calculate the manufacturing overhead allocated during 2020.
3. Calculate the amount of under- or overallocated manufacturing overhead. Why do Taylor's managers need to calculate this amount?

4-25 Job costing, accounting for manufacturing overhead, budgeted rates. The Lulu Company uses a normal job-costing system at its Minneapolis plant. The plant has a machining department and an assembly department. Its job-costing system has two direct-cost categories (direct materials and direct manufacturing labor) and two manufacturing overhead cost pools (the machining department overhead, allocated to jobs based on actual machine-hours, and the assembly department overhead, allocated to jobs based on actual direct manufacturing labor costs). The 2020 budget for the plant is as follows:

	Machining Department	Assembly Department
Manufacturing overhead	$1,800,000	$4,000,000
Direct manufacturing labor costs	$1,400,000	$2,000,000
Direct manufacturing labor-hours	180,000	250,000
Machine-hours	50,000	250,000

Required

1. Identify the components of the overview diagram of Lulu's job-costing system. Compute the budgeted manufacturing overhead rate for each department.
2. During February, the job-cost record for Job 494 contained the following:

	Machining Department	Assembly Department
Direct materials used	$45,000	$74,000
Direct manufacturing labor costs	$19,000	$20,000
Direct manufacturing labor-hours	1,400	1,800
Machine-hours	2,100	1,100

Compute the total manufacturing overhead costs allocated to Job 494.
3. At the end of 2020, the actual manufacturing overhead costs were $2,000,000 in machining and $4,100,000 in assembly. Assume that 54,000 actual machine-hours were used in machining and that actual direct manufacturing labor costs in assembly were $2,300,000. Compute the under- or overallocated manufacturing overhead for each department.

4-26 Job costing, consulting firm. Wilson Partners, a management consulting firm, has the following condensed budget for 2020:

Revenues		$19,250,000
Total costs:		
Direct costs		
Professional labor	$ 4,375,000	
Indirect costs		
Client support	12,950,000	17,325,000
Operating income		$ 1,925,000

Wilson has a single direct-cost category (professional labor) and a single indirect-cost pool (client support). Indirect costs are allocated to jobs on the basis of professional labor costs.

Required

1. Identify the components of the overview diagram of the job-costing system. Calculate the 2020 budgeted indirect-cost rate for Wilson Partners.
2. The markup rate for pricing jobs is intended to produce operating income equal to 10% of revenues. Calculate the markup rate as a percentage of professional labor costs.
3. Wilson is bidding on a consulting job for Guardian, a wireless communications company. The budgeted breakdown of professional labor on the job is as follows:

Professional Labor Category	Budgeted Rate per Hour	Budgeted Hours
Director	$204	4
Partner	103	18
Associate	51	45
Assistant	32	155

Calculate the budgeted cost of the Guardian job. How much will Wilson bid for the job if it is to earn its target operating income of 10% of revenues?

4-27 Time period used to compute indirect cost rates. Capitola Manufacturing produces surfboards. The company uses a normal-costing system and allocates manufacturing overhead on the basis of direct manufacturing labor-hours. Most of the company's production and sales occur in the first and second quarters of the year. The company is in danger of losing one of its larger customers, Pacific Wholesale, due to large fluctuations in price. The owner of Capitola has requested an analysis of the manufacturing cost per unit in the second and third quarters. You have been provided the following budgeted information for the coming year:

	Quarter			
	1	2	3	4
Surfboards manufactured and sold	500	400	100	250

It takes 2 direct manufacturing labor-hours to make each board. The actual direct material cost is $65.00 per board. The actual direct manufacturing labor rate is $20 per hour. The budgeted variable manufacturing overhead rate is $16 per direct manufacturing labor-hour. Budgeted fixed manufacturing overhead costs are $20,000 each quarter.

Required

1. Calculate the total manufacturing cost per unit for the second and third quarter assuming the company allocates manufacturing overhead costs based on the budgeted manufacturing overhead rate determined for each quarter.
2. Calculate the total manufacturing cost per unit for the second and third quarter assuming the company allocates manufacturing overhead costs based on an annual budgeted manufacturing overhead rate.
3. Capitola Manufacturing prices its surfboards at manufacturing cost plus 20%. Why might Pacific Wholesale be seeing large fluctuations in the prices of boards? Which of the methods described in requirements 1 and 2 would you recommend Capitola use? Explain.

4-28 Accounting for manufacturing overhead. Seaway Woodworking uses normal costing and allocates manufacturing overhead to jobs based on a budgeted labor-hour rate and actual direct labor-hours. Under- or overallocated overhead, if immaterial, is written off to Cost of Goods Sold. During 2020, Seaway recorded the following:

Budgeted manufacturing overhead costs	$4,080,000
Budgeted direct labor-hours	170,000
Actual manufacturing overhead costs	$4,261,000
Actual direct labor-hours	178,000

Required

1. Compute the budgeted manufacturing overhead rate.
2. Prepare the summary journal entry to record the allocation of manufacturing overhead.
3. Compute the amount of under- or overallocated manufacturing overhead. Is the amount significant enough to warrant proration of overhead costs, or should Seaway Woodworking write it off to cost of goods sold? Prepare the journal entry to adjust for the under- or overallocated overhead.

4-29 Job costing, journal entries. The University of Chicago Press is wholly owned by the university. It performs the bulk of its work for other university departments, which pay as though the press were an outside business enterprise. The press also publishes and maintains a stock of books for general sale. The press uses normal costing to cost each job. Its job-costing system has two direct-cost categories (direct materials and direct manufacturing labor) and one indirect-cost pool (manufacturing overhead, allocated on the basis of direct manufacturing labor costs).

The following data (in thousands) pertain to 2020:

Direct materials and supplies purchased on credit	$ 800
Direct materials used	710
Indirect materials issued to various production departments	100
Direct manufacturing labor	1,300
Indirect manufacturing labor incurred by various production departments	900
Depreciation on building and manufacturing equipment	400
Miscellaneous manufacturing overhead[4] incurred by various production departments (ordinarily would be detailed as repairs, photocopying, utilities, etc.)	550
Manufacturing overhead allocated at 160% of direct manufacturing labor costs	?
Cost of goods manufactured	4,120
Revenues	8,000
Cost of goods sold (before adjustment for under- or overallocated manufacturing overhead)	4,020
Inventories, December 31, 2019 (not 2020):	
Materials Control	100
Work-in-Process Control	60
Finished Goods Control	500

Required

1. Prepare an overview diagram of the job-costing system at the University of Chicago Press.
2. Prepare journal entries to summarize the 2020 transactions. As your final entry, adjust for the year-end under- or overallocated manufacturing overhead as a write-off to Cost of Goods Sold. Number your entries. Explanations for each entry may be omitted.
3. Show posted T-accounts for all inventories, Cost of Goods Sold, Manufacturing Overhead Control, and Manufacturing Overhead Allocated.
4. How did the University of Chicago Press perform in 2020?

4-30 Journal entries, T-accounts, and source documents. Virtual Company produces gadgets for the coveted small appliance market. The following data reflect activity for the year 2020:

Costs incurred:	
Purchases of direct materials (net) on credit	$125,000
Direct manufacturing labor cost	88,000
Indirect labor	54,700
Depreciation, factory equipment	36,000
Depreciation, office equipment	7,300
Maintenance, factory equipment	26,000
Miscellaneous factory overhead	9,600
Rent, factory building	70,000
Advertising expense	92,000
Sales commissions	36,000

Inventories:

	January 1, 2020	December 31, 2020
Direct materials	$ 9,700	$13,000
Work in process	6,200	24,000
Finished goods	66,000	32,000

Virtual Co. uses a normal-costing system and allocates overhead to work in process at a rate of $2.50 per direct manufacturing labor dollar. Indirect materials are insignificant so there is no inventory account for indirect materials.

Required

1. Prepare journal entries to record the transactions for 2020, including an entry to close out under- or overallocated overhead to cost of goods sold. For each journal entry indicate the source document that

[4] The term *manufacturing overhead* is not used uniformly. Other terms that are often encountered in printing companies include *job overhead* and *shop overhead*.

would be used to authorize each entry. Also note which subsidiary ledger, if any, should be referenced as backup for the entry.

2. Post the journal entries to T-accounts for all of the inventories, Cost of Goods Sold, the Manufacturing Overhead Control Account, and the Manufacturing Overhead Allocated Account.

4-31 Job costing, journal entries. Docks Transport assembles prestige manufactured homes. Its job-costing system has two direct-cost categories (direct materials and direct manufacturing labor) and one indirect-cost pool (manufacturing overhead allocated at a budgeted $21 per machine-hour in 2020). The following data (in millions) show operation costs for 2020:

Materials Control, beginning balance, January 1, 2020	$ 13
Work-in-Process Control, beginning balance, January 1, 2020	4
Finished Goods Control, beginning balance, January 1, 2020	7
Materials and supplies purchased on credit	154
Direct materials used	147
Indirect materials (supplies) issued to various production departments	19
Direct manufacturing labor	90
Indirect manufacturing labor incurred by various production departments	32
Depreciation on plant and manufacturing equipment	26
Miscellaneous manufacturing overhead incurred (ordinarily would be detailed as repairs, utilities, etc., with a corresponding credit to various liability accounts)	14
Manufacturing overhead allocated, 4,000,000 actual machine-hours	?
Cost of goods manufactured	295
Revenues	400
Cost of goods sold	293

Required

1. Identify the components of the overview diagram of Docks Transport's job-costing system.
2. Prepare journal entries. Number your entries. Explanations for each entry may be omitted. Post to T-accounts. What is the ending balance of Work-in-Process Control?
3. Show the journal entry for adjusting for under- or overallocated manufacturing overhead directly as a year-end writeoff to Cost of Goods Sold. Post the entry to T-accounts.
4. How did Docks Transport perform in 2020?

4-32 Job costing, unit cost, ending work in process. Robert Company produces pipes for concert-quality organs. Each job is unique. In April 2019, it completed all outstanding orders, and then, in May 2019, it worked on only two jobs, M1 and M2:

	A	B	C
1	**Robert Company, May 2019**	**Job M1**	**Job M2**
2	Direct materials	$ 79,000	$ 58,000
3	Direct manufacturing labor	273,000	208,000

Direct manufacturing labor is paid at the rate of $26 per hour. Manufacturing overhead costs are allocated at a budgeted rate of $16 per direct manufacturing labor-hour. Only Job M1 was completed in May.

Required

1. Calculate the total cost for Job M1.
2. 1,000 pipes were produced for Job M1. Calculate the cost per pipe.
3. Prepare the journal entry transferring Job M1 to finished goods.
4. What is the ending balance in the Work-in-Process Control account?

4-33 Job costing; actual, normal, and variation of normal costing. Chico & Partners, a Quebec-based public accounting partnership, specializes in audit services. Its job-costing system has a single direct-cost category (professional labor) and a single indirect-cost pool (audit support, which contains all costs of the Audit Support Department). Audit support costs are allocated to individual jobs using actual professional labor-hours. Chico & Partners employs 10 professionals to perform audit services.

Budgeted and actual amounts for 2020 are as follows:

	A	B	C
1	**Chico & Partners**		
2	**Budget for 2020**		
3	Professional labor compensation	$990,000	
4	Audit support department costs	774,000	
5	Professional labor-hours billed to clients	18,000	hours
6			
7	**Actual results for 2020**		
8	Audit support department costs	$735,000	
9	Professional labor-hours billed to clients	17,500	hours
10	Actual professional labor cost rate	$ 58	per hour

Required

1. Compute the direct-cost rate and the indirect-cost rate per professional labor-hour for 2020 under (a) actual costing, (b) normal costing, and (c) the variation of normal costing that uses budgeted rates for direct costs.
2. Which job-costing system would you recommend Chico & Partners use? Explain.
3. Chico's 2020 audit of Pierre & Co. was budgeted to take 160 hours of professional labor time. The actual professional labor time spent on the audit was 180 hours. Compute the cost of the Pierre & Co. audit using (a) actual costing, (b) normal costing, and (c) the variation of normal costing that uses budgeted rates for direct costs. Explain any differences in the job cost.

4-34 Job costing; variation on actual, normal, and variation of normal costing. Clayton Solutions designs Web pages for clients in the education sector. The company's job-costing system has a single direct cost category (Web-designing labor) and a single indirect cost pool composed of all overhead costs. Overhead costs are allocated to individual jobs based on direct labor-hours. The company employs six Web designers. Budgeted and actual information regarding Clayton Solutions follows:

Budget for 2020:	
Direct labor costs	$280,000
Direct labor-hours	10,000
Overhead costs	$180,000
Actual results for 2020:	
Direct labor costs	$260,000
Direct labor-hours	10,000
Overhead costs	$200,000

Required

1. Compute the direct-cost rate and the indirect-cost rate per Web-designing labor-hour for 2020 under (a) actual costing, (b) normal costing, and (c) the variation of normal costing that uses budgeted rates for direct costs.
2. Which method would you suggest Clayton Solutions use? Explain.
3. Clayton Solutions' Web design for Greenville Day School was budgeted to take 95 direct labor-hours. The actual time spent on the project was 80 hours. Compute the cost of the Greenville Day School job using (a) actual costing, (b) normal costing, and (c) the variation of normal costing that uses budgeted rates for direct costs.

4-35 Proration of overhead. The Row-On-Watershed Company (ROW) produces a line of non-motorized boats. ROW uses a normal-costing system and allocates manufacturing overhead using direct manufacturing labor cost. The following data are for 2020:

Budgeted manufacturing overhead cost	$110,000
Budgeted direct manufacturing labor cost	$220,000
Actual manufacturing overhead cost	$117,000
Actual direct manufacturing labor cost	$230,000

Inventory balances on December 31, 2020, were as follows:

Account	Ending balance	2020 direct manufacturing labor cost in ending balance
Work in process	$ 41,500	$ 23,000
Finished goods	232,400	66,700
Cost of goods sold	556,100	140,300

Required

1. Calculate the manufacturing overhead allocation rate.
2. Compute the amount of under- or overallocated manufacturing overhead.
3. Calculate the ending balances in work in process, finished goods, and cost of goods sold if under- or overallocated manufacturing overhead is as follows:
   a. Written off to cost of goods sold
   b. Prorated based on ending balances (before proration) in each of the three accounts
   c. Prorated based on the overhead allocated in 2020 in the ending balances (before proration) in each of the three accounts
4. Which method would you choose? Justify your answer.

Problems

4-36 Job costing, accounting for manufacturing overhead, budgeted rates. The Carlson Company uses a job-costing system at its Dover, Delaware, plant. The plant has a machining department and a finishing department. Carlson uses normal costing with two direct-cost categories (direct materials and direct manufacturing labor) and two manufacturing overhead cost pools (the machining department with machine-hours as the allocation base and the finishing department with direct manufacturing labor costs as the allocation base). The 2020 budget for the plant is as follows:

	Machining Department	Finishing Department
Manufacturing overhead costs	$10,560,000	$8,181,000
Direct manufacturing labor costs	$ 970,000	$4,050,000
Direct manufacturing labor-hours	36,000	175,000
Machine-hours	220,000	34,000

Required

1. Identify the components of the overview diagram of Carlson's job-costing system.
2. What is the budgeted manufacturing overhead rate in the machining department? In the finishing department?
3. During the month of January, the job-cost record for Job 431 shows the following:

	Machining Department	Finishing Department
Direct materials used	$15,000	$ 2,000
Direct manufacturing labor costs	$ 700	$ 1,200
Direct manufacturing labor-hours	40	50
Machine-hours	130	25

   Compute the total manufacturing overhead cost allocated to Job 431.
4. Assuming that Job 431 consisted of 100 units of product, what is the cost per unit?
5. Amounts at the end of 2020 are as follows:

	Machining Department	Finishing Department
Manufacturing overhead incurred	$11,190,000	$7,982,000
Direct manufacturing labor costs	$ 990,000	$4,100,000
Machine-hours	230,000	33,000

   Compute the under- or overallocated manufacturing overhead for each department and for the Dover plant as a whole.
6. Why might Carlson use two different manufacturing overhead cost pools in its job-costing system?

4-37 Service industry, job costing, law firm. Kidman & Associates is a law firm specializing in labor relations and employee-related work. It employs 30 professionals (5 partners and 25 associates) who work directly with its clients. The average budgeted total compensation per professional for 2020 is $97,500. Each professional is budgeted to have 1,500 billable hours to clients in 2020. All professionals work for clients to their maximum 1,500 billable hours available. All professional labor costs are included in a single direct-cost category and are traced to jobs on a per-hour basis. All costs of Kidman & Associates other than professional labor costs are included in a single indirect-cost pool (legal support) and are allocated to jobs using professional labor-hours as the allocation base. The budgeted level of indirect costs in 2020 is $2,475,000.

Required

1. Prepare an overview diagram of Kidman's job-costing system.
2. Compute the 2020 budgeted direct-cost rate per hour of professional labor.
3. Compute the 2020 budgeted indirect-cost rate per hour of professional labor.
4. Kidman & Associates is considering bidding on two jobs:
   a. Litigation work for Richardson, Inc., which requires 120 budgeted hours of professional labor.
   b. Labor contract work for Punch, Inc., which requires 160 budgeted hours of professional labor.
   Prepare a cost estimate for each job.

4-38 Service industry, job costing, two direct- and two indirect-cost categories, law firm (continuation of 4-37). Kidman has just completed a review of its job-costing system. This review included a detailed analysis of how past jobs used the firm's resources and interviews with personnel about what factors drive the level of indirect costs. Management concluded that a system with two direct-cost categories (professional partner labor and professional associate labor) and two indirect-cost categories (general support and secretarial support) would yield more accurate job costs. Budgeted information for 2020 related to the two direct-cost categories is as follows:

	Professional Partner Labor	Professional Associate Labor
Number of professionals	5	25
Hours of billable time per professional	1,500 per year	1,500 per year
Total compensation (average per professional)	$210,000	$75,000

Budgeted information for 2020 relating to the two indirect-cost categories is as follows:

	General Support	Secretarial Support
Total costs	$2,025,000	$450,000
Cost-allocation base	Professional labor-hours	Partner labor-hours

Required

1. Compute the 2020 budgeted direct-cost rates for (a) professional partners and (b) professional associates.
2. Compute the 2020 budgeted indirect-cost rates for (a) general support and (b) secretarial support.
3. Compute the budgeted costs for the Richardson and Punch jobs, given the following information:

	Richardson, Inc.	Punch, Inc.
Professional partners	48 hours	32 hours
Professional associates	72 hours	128 hours

4. Comment on the results in requirement 3. Why are the job costs different from those computed in Problem 4-37?
5. Would you recommend Kidman & Associates use the job-costing system in Problem 4-37 or the job-costing system in this problem? Explain.

4-39 Proration of overhead. (Z. Iqbal, adapted) The Zaf Radiator Company uses a normal-costing system with a single manufacturing overhead cost pool and machine-hours as the cost-allocation base. The following data are for 2020:

Budgeted manufacturing overhead costs	$4,800,000
Overhead allocation base	Machine-hours
Budgeted machine-hours	80,000
Manufacturing overhead costs incurred	$4,900,000
Actual machine-hours	75,000

Machine-hours data and the ending balances (before proration of under- or overallocated overhead) are as follows:

	Actual Machine-Hours	2020 End-of-Year Balance
Cost of Goods Sold	60,000	$8,000,000
Finished Goods Control	11,000	1,250,000
Work-in-Process Control	4,000	750,000

Required

1. Compute the budgeted manufacturing overhead rate for 2020.
2. Compute the under- or overallocated manufacturing overhead of Zaf Radiator in 2020. Adjust for this amount using the following:
   a. Write-off to Cost of Goods Sold
   b. Proration based on ending balances (before proration) in Work-in-Process Control, Finished Goods Control, and Cost of Goods Sold
   c. Proration based on the overhead allocated in 2020 (before proration) in the ending balances of Work-in-Process Control, Finished Goods Control, and Cost of Goods Sold
3. Which method do you prefer in requirement 2? Explain.

4-40 Normal costing, overhead allocation, working backward. Gardi Manufacturing uses normal costing for its job-costing system, which has two direct-cost categories (direct materials and direct manufacturing labor) and one indirect-cost category (manufacturing overhead). The following information is obtained for 2020:

- Total manufacturing costs, $8,300,000
- Manufacturing overhead allocated, $4,100,000 (allocated at a rate of 250% of direct manufacturing labor costs)
- Work-in-process inventory on January 1, 2020, $420,000
- Cost of finished goods manufactured, $8,100,000

Required

1. Use information in the first two bullet points to calculate (a) direct manufacturing labor costs in 2020 and (b) cost of direct materials used in 2020.
2. Calculate the ending work-in-process inventory on December 31, 2020.

4-41 General ledger relationships, under- and overallocation. (S. Sridhar, adapted) Walworth Company uses normal costing in its job-costing system. Partially completed T-accounts and additional information for Walworth for 2020 are as follows:

Direct Materials Control

1-1-2020	44,000	233,000
	140,000	

Work-in-Process Control

1-1-2020	43,000	
Dir. manuf. labor	354,000	

Finished Goods Control

1-1-2020	11,000	667,800
	923,920	

Manufacturing Overhead Control

509,000	

Manufacturing Overhead Allocated

Cost of Goods Sold

Additional information:

a. Direct manufacturing labor wage rate was $12 per hour.
b. Manufacturing overhead was allocated at $16 per direct manufacturing labor-hour.
c. During the year, sales revenues were $1,080,000, and marketing and distribution costs were $129,000.

Required

1. What was the amount of direct materials issued to production during 2020?
2. What was the amount of manufacturing overhead allocated to jobs during 2020?
3. What was the total cost of jobs completed during 2020?
4. What was the balance of work-in-process inventory on December 31, 2020?
5. What was the cost of goods sold before proration of under- or overallocated overhead?
6. What was the under- or overallocated manufacturing overhead in 2020?
7. Adjust for the under- or overallocated manufacturing overhead using the following:
   a. Write-off to Cost of Goods Sold
   b. Proration based on ending balances (before proration) in Work-in-Process Control, Finished Goods Control, and Cost of Goods Sold
8. Using each of the approaches in requirement 7, calculate Walworth's operating income for 2020.
9. Which approach in requirement 7 do you recommend Walworth use? Explain your answer briefly.

4-42 Proration of overhead. Oregon Outfitters, a manufacturer of fly fishing flies, uses a normal-costing system with a single overhead cost pool and direct labor cost as the cost-allocation base. The following data are for 2020:

Budgeted manufacturing overhead costs	$1,210,000
Overhead allocation base	Direct Labor Cost
Budgeted direct labor cost	$550,000
Actual manufacturing overhead costs incurred	$1,200,500
Actual direct labor cost	$562,200

Manufacturing overhead allocated data and the ending balances (before proration of under- or overallocated overhead) in each account are as follows:

	Mfg OH Allocated	2020 End-of-Year Balance
Cost of Goods Sold	$841,051	$2,100,000
Finished Goods Control	272,105	600,000
Work-in-Process Control	123,684	300,000

Required

1. Compute the budgeted manufacturing overhead rate for 2020.
2. Compute the under- or overallocated manufacturing overhead of Oregon Outfitters in 2020. Adjust for this amount using the following:
   a. Write-off to Cost of Goods Sold
   b. Proration based on ending balances (before proration) in Work-in-Process Control, Finished Goods Control, and Cost of Goods Sold
   c. Proration based on the overhead allocated in 2020 (before proration) in the ending balances of Work-in-Process Control, Finished Goods Control, and Cost of Goods Sold
3. Which method do you prefer in requirement 2? Explain.

4-43 Overview of general ledger relationships. Brane Company uses normal costing in its job-costing system. The company produces custom bikes for toddlers. The beginning balances (December 1) and ending balances (as of December 30) in their inventory accounts are as follows:

	Beginning Balance 12/1	Ending Balance 12/30
Materials Control	$ 2,200	$ 8,600
Work-in-Process Control	6,800	9,100
Manufacturing Department Overhead Control	—	94,500
Finished Goods Control	4,500	19,500

Additional information:

a. Direct materials purchased during December were $66,400.
b. Cost of goods manufactured for December was $235,000.
c. No direct materials were returned to suppliers.
d. No units were started or completed on December 31 and no direct materials were requisitioned on December 31.
e. The manufacturing labor costs for the December 31 working day: direct manufacturing labor, $4,350, and indirect manufacturing labor, $1,450.
f. Manufacturing overhead has been allocated at 140% of direct manufacturing labor costs through December 31.

Required

1. Prepare journal entries for the December 31 payroll.
2. Use T-accounts to compute the following:
   a. The total amount of materials requisitioned into work in process during December
   b. The total amount of direct manufacturing labor recorded in work in process during December (Hint: You have to solve requirements **2b** and **2c** simultaneously)
   c. The total amount of manufacturing overhead recorded in work in process during December
   d. Ending balance in work in process, December 31
   e. Cost of goods sold for December before adjustments for under- or overallocated manufacturing overhead
3. Prepare closing journal entries related to manufacturing overhead. Assume that all under- or overallocated manufacturing overhead is closed directly to Cost of Goods Sold.

4-44 Allocation and proration of overhead. Grade A prints custom training material for corporations. The business was started January 1, 2020. The company uses a normal-costing system. It has two direct-cost pools, materials and labor, and one indirect-cost pool, overhead. Overhead is charged to printing jobs on the basis of direct labor cost. The following information is available for 2020.

Budgeted direct labor costs	$270,000
Budgeted overhead costs	$324,000
Costs of actual material used	$138,000
Actual direct labor costs	$257,000
Actual overhead costs	$310,800

There were two jobs in process on December 31, 2020: Job 11 and Job 12. Costs added to each job as of December 31 are as follows:

	Direct Materials	Direct Labor
Job 11	$4,360	$5,300
Job 12	$5,720	$6,000

Grade A has no finished-goods inventories because all printing jobs are transferred to cost of goods sold when completed.

Required

1. Compute the overhead allocation rate.
2. Calculate the balance in ending work in process and cost of goods sold before any adjustments for under- or overallocated overhead.
3. Calculate under- or overallocated overhead.
4. Calculate the ending balances in work in process and cost of goods sold if the under- or overallocated overhead amount is as follows:
   a. Written off to cost of goods sold
   b. Prorated using the overhead allocated in 2020 (before proration) in the ending balances of cost of goods sold and work-in-process control accounts
5. Which of the methods in requirement 4 would you choose? Explain.

4-45 Job costing, ethics. Beth Bledsoe joined Baker Brothers, Inc. as controller in October 2019. Baker Brothers manufactures and installs custom kitchen countertops. The company uses a normal-costing system with two direct-cost pools, direct materials and direct manufacturing labor, and one indirect-cost pool, manufacturing overhead. In 2019, manufacturing overhead was allocated to jobs at 150% of direct manufacturing labor cost. At the end of 2019, an immaterial amount of underallocated overhead was closed out to cost of goods sold, and the company showed a small loss.

Bledsoe is eager to impress her new employer, and she knows that in 2020, Baker Brothers' upper management is under pressure to show a profit in a challenging competitive environment because they are hoping to be acquired by a large private equity firm sometime in 2021. At the end of 2019, Bledsoe decides to adjust the manufacturing overhead rate to 160% of direct labor cost. She explains to the company president that, because overhead was underallocated in 2019, this adjustment is necessary. Information for 2020 follows:

Actual direct manufacturing labor, 2020	$890,000
Actual manufacturing overhead costs, 2020	$1,250,000

The ending balances (before proration of under- or overallocated overhead) in each account are as follows:

	Balance 12/31/2020
Cost of Goods Sold	$2,950,000
Finished Goods Control	300,000
Work-in-Process Control	244,000

Baker Brothers' revenue for 2020 was $5,580,000, and the company's selling and administrative expenses were $2,790,000.

Required

1. Calculate the amount of under- or overallocated manufacturing overhead in 2020.
2. Calculate Baker Brothers' net operating income for 2020 under the following:
   a. Under- or overallocated manufacturing overhead is written off to cost of goods sold.
   b. Under- or overallocated manufacturing overhead is prorated based on the ending balances in work in process, finished goods, and cost of goods sold.
3. In your own words, describe how you expect net operating income in *future* periods to compare under scenarios 2a and 2b above.
4. Bledsoe chooses option 2a above, stating that the amount is immaterial. Comment on the ethical implications of her choice. Do you think that there were any ethical issues when she established the manufacturing overhead rate for 2020 back in late 2019? Refer to the IMA Statement of Ethical Professional Practice.

4-46 Job costing, service industry. Emerson Associates (EA) provides market analysis services for clients. Consultants contract with clients to perform jobs for predetermined fees. All jobs feature the work of one professional consultant, and some larger jobs include additional support labor. Because of this, EA's normal-costing system includes two direct cost pools, professional labor and support labor, and one indirect cost pool, overhead. EA charges $80/hour to jobs for professional labor and charges $50/hour for support labor. Overhead is applied to jobs at a rate of $30 per labor-hour, whether professional or support. This rate was determined based on an annual estimated overhead cost of $600,000 and estimated labor-hours of 20,000 (10,000 professional hours and 10,000 support hours). Actual overhead in May was $50,000. EA tracks job costs in an account titled Jobs in Process (JIP). When the job is completed, costs are closed out to Cost of Completed Jobs (COCJ). Following is cost information for May 2020:

	From Beginning JIP			Incurred in May	
Client	**Professional Labor**	**Support Labor**	**Overhead Allocated**	**Professional Labor Hrs.**	**Support Labor Hrs.**
Peterson Products	$40,000	$22,000	$28,200	140 hrs.	150 hrs.
Jacobson, Inc.	$12,000		$ 4,500	600 hrs.	
Best Foods				450 hrs.	360 hrs.

As of May 1, there were two jobs in progress: Peterson Products and Jacobson, Inc.. The job for Best Foods was started and completed in May.

Required

1. Calculate JIP at the end of May.
2. Calculate COCJ for May.
3. Calculate under- or overallocated overhead in May.
4. Calculate the ending balances in JIP and COCJ if the under- or overallocated overhead amount is prorated based on the ending balances (before proration) in JIP and COCJ.
5. Ann Baker, the controller of Emerson Associates, is concerned about the validity of allocating overhead equally for professional and support hours. She believes that overhead related to professional labor is approximately twice as costly as overhead related to support labor. Calculate new overhead rates per professional labor-hour and per support labor-hour that would address this issue. How would the cost of the Best Foods job be affected by this change? (Ignore the impact of under- or overallocated overhead.)

Activity-Based Costing and Activity-Based Management

5

A good mystery never fails to capture the imagination.

Business and organizations are like a good mystery. Their costing systems are often filled with unresolved questions: Why are we bleeding red ink? Are we pricing our products accurately? Activity-based costing can help unravel the mystery and result in improved operations. IBM uses activity-based costing to evaluate the true cost of data breaches.

LEARNING OBJECTIVES

1. Explain how broad averaging undercosts and overcosts products or services
2. Present three guidelines for refining a costing system
3. Distinguish between simple and activity-based costing systems
4. Describe a four-part cost hierarchy
5. Cost products or services using activity-based costing
6. Evaluate the benefits and costs of implementing activity-based costing systems
7. Explain how managers use activity-based costing systems in activity-based management

ACTIVITY-BASED COSTING AND THE TRUE COST OF DATA BREACHES[1]

Another day, another data breach. In 2017 alone, significant data breaches hit more than 1,300 U.S. companies, government agencies, and other organizations.

- But how much do these data breaches cost the companies impacted? Along with expensive technical investigations and regulatory filings, data breaches also have hidden costs such as lost business, negative impact on reputation, and employee time spent on recovery. To determine the true cost of data breaches, IBM turned to activity-based costing (ABC). ABC analysis found that company expenditures on data breaches fell within four activity-cost centers:
  - **Detection and escalation**—Detecting the breach of personal data and reporting it to the appropriate personnel
  - **Notification**—Notifying affected individuals, regulators, and the media
  - **Post-data breach response**—Setting up services for affected individuals and paying regulatory fines and penalties
  - **Lost business:**—Losing customers and managing business disruption, system downtime, and costs associated with new customer acquisition and revenue loss

Using ABC, IBM concluded that the average cost of a data breach globally is \$3.86 million, or \$148 for each lost record. "Knowing where the costs lie, and how to reduce them, can help companies invest their resources more strategically and lower the huge financial risks at state," said IBM executive Wendi Whitmore.

In this chapter, we show how ABC systems help managers make cost-management decisions by improving product designs, processes, and efficiency.

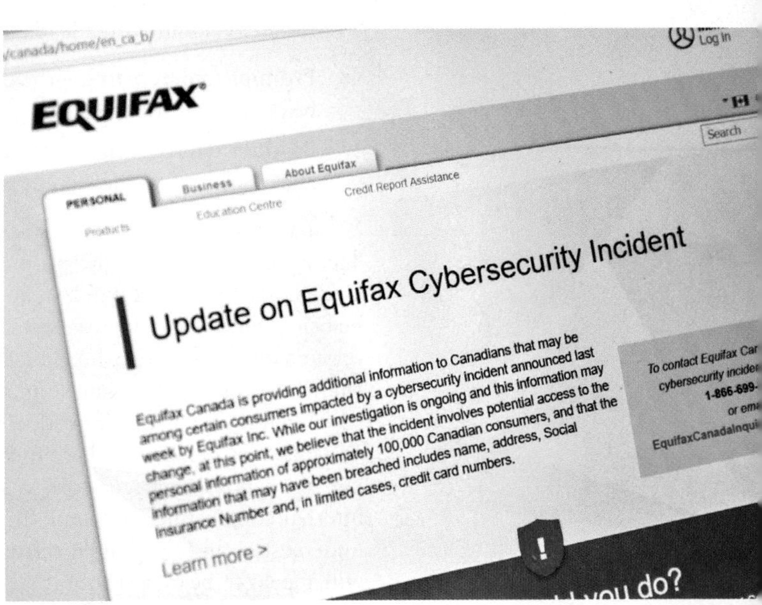

dennizn/Shutterstock

[1] *Sources:* IBM, *2018 Cost of a Data Breach Study: Global Overview*, July 2018 (https://www-01.ibm.com/common/ssi/cgi-bin/ssialias?htmlfid=55017055USEN&); "IBM Study: Hidden Costs of Data Breaches Increase Expenses for Businesses," IBM press release, Cambridge, Massachusetts, July 11, 2018 (https://newsroom.ibm.com/2018-07-11-IBM-Study-Hidden-Costs-of-Data-Breaches-Increase-Expenses-for-Businesses); Herb Weisbaum, "The Total Cost of a Data Breach—Including Lost Business—Keeps Growing," NBCnews.com, July 30, 2018 (https://www.nbcnews.com/business/consumer/total-cost-data-breach-including-lost-business-keeps-growing-n895826); Victor Reklaitis, "How the Number of Data Breaches Is Soaring—in One Chart," MarketWatch.com, May 25, 2018 (https://www.marketwatch.com/story/how-the-number-of-data-breaches-is-soaring-in-one-chart-2018-02-26).

Broad Averaging and Its Consequences

LEARNING OBJECTIVE 1

Explain how broad averaging undercosts and overcosts products or services

...it does not measure the different resources consumed by different products and services

Historically, companies (such as television and automobile manufacturers) produced a limited variety of products. These companies used relatively few overhead resources to support their operations, so indirect (or overhead) costs were a relatively small percentage of total costs. Managers used simple costing systems to allocate overhead costs broadly in an easy, inexpensive, and reasonably accurate way. But as product diversity and the proportion of indirect costs increased, broad averaging led to inaccurate product costs. That's because simple *peanut-butter costing* (yes, that's what it's called) broadly averages or spreads the cost of resources uniformly to cost objects (such as products or services) when, in fact, the individual products or services use those resources in nonuniform ways.

Undercosting and Overcosting

The following example illustrates how averaging can result in inaccurate and misleading cost data. Consider the cost of a restaurant bill for four colleagues who meet monthly to discuss business developments. Each diner orders separate entrees, desserts, and drinks. The restaurant bill for the most recent meeting is as follows.

	Emma	James	Jessica	Matthew	Total	Average
Entree	$11	$20	$15	$14	$ 60	$15
Dessert	0	8	4	4	16	4
Drinks	4	14	8	6	32	8
Total	$15	$42	$27	$24	$108	$27

If the $108 total restaurant bill is divided evenly, $27 is the average cost per diner. This cost-averaging approach treats each diner the same. When costs are averaged across all four diners, both Emma and Matthew are overcosted (the cost allocated to them is higher than their individual cost), James is undercosted (the cost allocated to him is lower than his individual cost), and Jessica is (by coincidence) accurately costed. Emma, especially, may object to paying the average bill of $27 because her individual bill is only $15.

Broad averaging often leads to undercosting or overcosting of products or services:

- **Product undercosting**—the cost measurement system reports a cost for a product that is below the cost of the resources the product consumes (James's dinner).
- **Product overcosting**— the cost measurement system reports a cost for a product that is above the cost of the resources the product consumes (Emma's dinner).

What are the strategic consequences of product undercosting and overcosting? Suppose a manager uses the product cost reported by the cost measurement system to guide pricing decisions. Undercosted products will be underpriced. The revenue from undercosted products may even be below the cost of the resources that are used to produce them, thus leading to losses for the organization. Overcosted products will be overpriced, potentially leading to losses in market share to competitors selling similar products at lower prices.

What if sale prices of products, such as refrigerators, are determined by the market based on consumer demand and competition among companies? Consider a company manufacturing two types of refrigerators, a simple one and a complex one with a number of different internal compartments, temperature settings, and vents. Suppose the complex refrigerator is undercosted and the simple refrigerator is overcosted. In this case, the complex refrigerator will appear to be more profitable than it actually is while the simple refrigerator will appear to be less profitable than it actually is. Managers may strategically promote the complex undercosted refrigerators, thinking they are highly profitable, when in fact these refrigerators consume large amounts of resources and may be far less profitable than they appear. Managers may, in turn, underinvest in the simple overcosted refrigerator, which shows low profits when in fact the profits from this refrigerator may be considerably higher. Alternatively, they may focus on trying to reduce the cost of the simple refrigerator to make it more profitable when, in fact, this refrigerator is reasonably profitable and the opportunities to reduce its costs may be quite limited.

Product-Cost Cross-Subsidization

Product-cost cross-subsidization means that if a company undercosts one of its products, it will overcost at least one of its other products. Similarly, if a company overcosts one of its products, it will undercost at least one of its other products. Product-cost cross-subsidization is very common when a cost is uniformly spread—meaning it is broadly averaged—across multiple products without managers recognizing the amount of resources each product consumes.

In the restaurant-bill example, the amount of cost cross-subsidization of each diner can be readily computed because all cost items can be traced as direct costs to each diner. If all diners pay $27, Emma is paying $12 more than her actual cost of $15. She is cross-subsidizing James who is paying $15 less than his actual cost of $42. Calculating the amount of cost cross-subsidization takes more work when there are indirect costs to be considered. Why? Because when two or more diners use the resources represented by indirect costs, we need to find a way to allocate costs to each diner. Consider, for example, a $40 bottle of wine whose cost is shared equally. Each diner would pay $10 ($40 ÷ 4). Suppose Matthew drinks two glasses of wine, while Emma, James, and Jessica drink one glass each for a total of five glasses. Allocating the cost of the bottle of wine on the basis of the glasses of wine that each diner drinks would result in Matthew paying $16 ($40 × 2/5) and each of the others paying $8 ($40 × 1/5). In this case, by sharing the cost equally, Emma, James, and Jessica are each paying $2 ($10 − $8) more and are cross-subsidizing Matthew who is paying $6($16 − $10) less for his wine for the night.

To see the effects of broad averaging on direct and indirect costs, we next consider Plastim Corporation's costing system.

DECISION POINT

When does product undercosting or overcosting occur?

Simple Costing System at Plastim Corporation

Plastim Corporation manufactures lenses for the rear taillights of automobiles. A lens, made from black, red, orange, or white plastic, is the part of the taillight visible on the automobile's exterior. Lenses are made by injecting molten plastic into a mold, which gives the lens its desired shape. The mold is cooled to allow the molten plastic to solidify, and the lens is removed.

Plastim sells all its lenses to Giovanni Motors, a major automobile manufacturer. Under the contract, Plastim manufactures two types of lenses for Giovanni: a simple lens called S3 and a complex lens called C5. The complex lens is large and has special features, such as multicolor molding (when more than one color is injected into the mold) and a complex shape that wraps around the corner of the car. Manufacturing C5 lenses is complicated because various parts in the mold must align and fit precisely. The S3 lens is simpler to make because it has a single color and few special features.

Design, Manufacturing, and Distribution Processes

Whether lenses are simple or complex, Plastim follows this sequence of steps to design, produce, and distribute them:

- **Design products and processes.** Each year Giovanni Motors specifies details of the simple and complex lenses it needs for its new models of cars. Plastim's design department designs the new molds and specifies the manufacturing process to make the lenses.
- **Manufacture lenses.** The lenses are molded, finished, cleaned, and inspected.
- **Distribute lenses.** Finished lenses are packed and sent to Giovanni Motors' plants.

Plastim is operating at capacity and incurs very low marketing costs. Because of its high-quality products, Plastim has minimal customer-service costs. Plastim competes with several other companies that also manufacture simple lenses. At a recent meeting, Giovanni's purchasing manager informed Plastim's sales manager that Bandix, which makes only simple lenses, is offering to supply the S3 lens to Giovanni at a price of $53, well below the $63 price that Plastim is currently projecting and budgeting for 2020. Unless Plastim can lower its selling price, it will lose the Giovanni business for the simple lens for the upcoming model year. Fortunately, the same competitive pressures do not exist for the complex lens, which Plastim currently sells to Giovanni at $137 per lens.

Plastim's managers have two primary options:

- Give up the Giovanni business in simple lenses if selling them is unprofitable. Bandix makes only simple lenses and perhaps, therefore, uses simpler technology and processes than Plastim. The simpler operations may give Bandix a cost advantage that Plastim cannot match. If so, it is better for Plastim to not supply the S3 lens to Giovanni.
- Reduce the price of the simple lens and either accept a lower margin or aggressively seek to reduce costs.

To make these long-run strategic decisions, managers first need to understand the costs to design, make, and distribute the S3 and C5 lenses.

Bandix makes only simple lenses and can fairly accurately calculate the cost of a lens by dividing total costs by the number of simple lenses produced. Plastim's costing environment is more challenging because the manufacturing overhead costs support the production of both simple and complex lenses. Plastim's managers and management accountants need to find a way to allocate overhead costs to each type of lens.

In computing costs, Plastim assigns both variable costs and costs that are fixed in the short run to the S3 and C5 lenses. Managers cost products and services to guide long-run strategic decisions such as what mix of products and services to produce and sell and what prices to charge for them. In the long run, managers have the ability to influence all costs. The firm will only survive in the long run if revenues exceed total costs, regardless of whether these costs are variable or fixed in the short run.

To guide pricing and cost-management decisions, Plastim's managers need to consider all costs and therefore assign both manufacturing and nonmanufacturing costs to the S3 and C5 lenses. If managers had wanted to calculate the cost of inventory, Plastim's management accountants would have assigned only manufacturing costs to the lenses, as required by Generally Accepted Accounting Principles. Surveys of company practice across the globe indicate that the vast majority of companies use costing systems not just for inventory costing but also for strategic purposes, such as pricing and product-mix decisions and decisions about cost reduction, process improvement, design, and planning and budgeting. Managers of these companies assign all costs to products and services. Even merchandising-sector companies (for whom inventory costing is straightforward) and service-sector companies (who have no inventory) expend considerable resources in designing and operating their costing systems to allocate costs for strategic purposes.

Simple Costing System Using a Single Indirect-Cost Pool

Plastim currently has a simple costing system that allocates indirect costs using a single indirect-cost rate, the type of system described in Chapter 4. The only difference between these two chapters is that Chapter 4 focuses on jobs while here the cost objects are products. Exhibit 5-1 shows an overview of Plastim's simple costing system. Use this exhibit as a guide as you study the following steps, each of which is marked in Exhibit 5-1.

Step 1: Identify the Products That Are the Chosen Cost Objects. The cost objects are the 60,000 simple S3 lenses and the 15,000 complex C5 lenses that Plastim will produce in 2020. Plastim's management accountants first calculate the total costs and then the unit cost of designing, manufacturing, and distributing lenses.

Step 2: Identify the Direct Costs of the Products. The direct costs are direct materials and direct manufacturing labor. Exhibit 5-2 shows the direct and indirect costs for the S3 and the C5 lenses using the simple costing system. The direct-cost calculations appear on lines 5, 6, and 7 in Exhibit 5-2. Plastim's simple costing system classifies all costs other than direct materials and direct manufacturing labor as indirect costs.

Step 3: Select the Cost-Allocation Bases to Use for Allocating Indirect (or Overhead) Costs to the Products. A majority of the indirect costs consists of salaries paid to supervisors, engineers, manufacturing support, and maintenance staff who support direct manufacturing labor. Plastim's managers use direct manufacturing labor-hours as the only allocation base

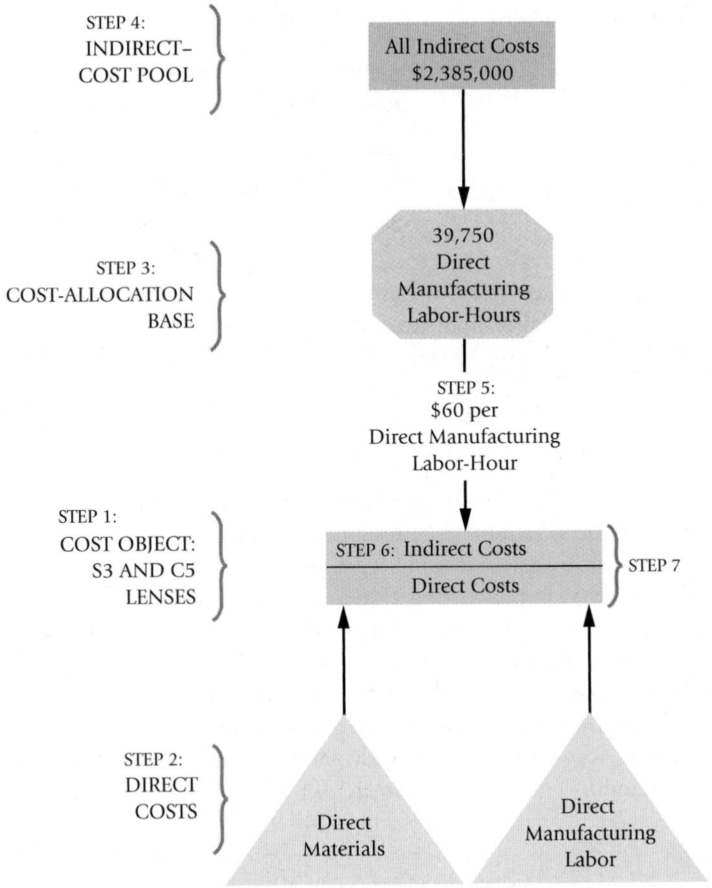

EXHIBIT 5-1

Overview of Plastim's Simple Costing System

to allocate all manufacturing and nonmanufacturing indirect costs to S3 and C5. Historically, many companies used such simple costing systems because overhead costs were only a small component of costs and because a single cost driver accurately reflected how overhead resources were used. In 2020, Plastim's managers budget 39,750 direct manufacturing labor-hours.

Step 4: Identify the Indirect Costs Associated With Each Cost-Allocation Base. Because Plastim uses only a single cost-allocation base, Plastim's management accountants group all budgeted indirect costs of $2,385,000 for 2020 into a single overhead cost pool.

EXHIBIT 5-2 Plastim's Product Costs Using the Simple Costing System

	A	B	C	D	E	F	G
1		60,000			15,000		
2		Simple Lenses (S3)			Complex Lenses (C5)		
3		Total	per Unit		Total	per Unit	Total
4		(1)	(2) = (1) ÷ 60,000		(3)	(4) = (3) ÷ 15,000	(5) = (1) + (3)
5	Direct materials	$1,125,000	$18.75		$ 675,000	$45.00	$1,800,000
6	Direct manufacturing labor	600,000	10.00		195,000	13.00	795,000
7	Total direct costs (Step 2)	1,725,000	28.75		870,000	58.00	2,595,000
8	Indirect costs allocated (Step 6)	1,800,000	30.00		585,000	39.00	2,385,000
9	Total costs (Step 7)	$3,525,000	$58.75		$1,455,000	$97.00	$4,980,000
10							

Step 5: Compute the Rate per Unit of Each Cost-Allocation Base.

$$\text{Budgeted indirect-cost rate} = \frac{\text{Budgeted total costs in indirect-cost pool}}{\text{Budgeted total quantity of cost-allocation base}}$$

$$= \frac{\$2{,}385{,}000}{39{,}750 \text{ direct manufacturing labor-hours}}$$

$$= \$60 \text{ per direct manufacturing labor-hour}$$

Step 6: Compute the Indirect Costs Allocated to the Products. Plastim's managers budget 30,000 total direct manufacturing labor-hours to make the 60,000 S3 lenses and 9,750 total direct manufacturing labor-hours to make the 15,000 C5 lenses. Exhibit 5-2 shows indirect costs of $1,800,000 ($60 per direct manufacturing labor-hour × 30,000 direct manufacturing labor-hours) allocated to the simple lens and $585,000 ($60 per direct manufacturing labor-hour × 9,750 direct manufacturing labor-hours) allocated to the complex lens.

Step 7: Compute the Total Cost of the Products by Adding All Direct and Indirect Costs Assigned to the Products. Exhibit 5-2 presents the product costs for the simple and complex lenses. The direct costs are calculated in Step 2 and the indirect costs in Step 6. Be sure you see the parallel between the simple costing system overview diagram (Exhibit 5-1) and the costs calculated in Step 7. Exhibit 5-1 shows two direct-cost categories and one indirect-cost category. Therefore, the budgeted cost of each type of lens in Step 7 (Exhibit 5-2) has three line items: two for direct costs and one for allocated indirect costs. It is very helpful to draw overview diagrams to see the big picture of costing systems before getting into the detailed costing of products and services. The budgeted cost per S3 lens is $58.75, well above the $53 selling price quoted by Bandix. The budgeted cost per C5 lens is $97.

TRY IT! 5-1

Vanderbilt Metal Works produces two types of metal lamps. Vanderbilt manufactures 24,640 basic lamps and 6,250 designer lamps. Its simple costing system uses a single indirect-cost pool and allocates costs to the two lamps on the basis of direct manufacturing labor-hours. It provides the following budgeted cost information:

	Basic Lamps	Designer Lamps	Total
Direct materials per lamp	$ 5	$19	
Direct manufacturing labor per lamp	0.4 hours	0.5 hours	
Direct manufacturing labor rate per hour	$30	$30	
Indirect manufacturing costs			$220,677

Calculate the total budgeted costs of the basic and designer lamps using Vanderbilt's simple costing system.

Applying the Five-Step Decision-Making Process at Plastim

To decide how it should respond to the threat that Bandix poses to its S3 lens business, Plastim's managers work through the five-step decision-making process introduced in Chapter 1.

1. **Identify the problem and uncertainties.** The problem is clear: If Plastim wants to retain the Giovanni business for S3 lenses and make a profit, it must find a way to reduce the price and costs of the S3 lens. The two major uncertainties Plastim faces are (1) whether its technology and processes for the S3 lens are competitive with Bandix's and (2) whether Plastim's S3 lens is overcosted by the simple costing system.

2. **Obtain information.** Senior management asks a team of design and process engineers to analyze and evaluate the design, manufacturing, and distribution operations for the S3 lens. The team is very confident that the technology and processes for the S3 lens are not inferior

to those of Bandix and other competitors because Plastim has many years of experience in manufacturing and distributing the S3 lens with a history and culture of continuous process improvements. The team is less certain about Plastim's capabilities in manufacturing and distributing complex lenses because it only recently started making this type of lens. Given these doubts, senior management is happy that Giovanni Motors considers the price of the C5 lens to be competitive. Plastim's managers are puzzled, though, by how, at the currently budgeted prices, Plastim is expected to earn a very large profit margin percentage (operating income ÷ revenues) on the C5 lenses and a small profit margin percentage on the S3 lenses:

	60,000 Simple Lenses (S3)		15,000 Complex Lenses (C5)		
	Total (1)	per Unit (2) = (1) ÷ 60,000	Total (3)	per Unit (4) = (3) ÷ 15,000	Total (5) = (1) + (3)
Revenues	$3,780,000	$63.00	$2,055,000	$137.00	$5,835,000
Total costs	3,525,000	58.75	1,455,000	97.00	4,980,000
Operating income	$ 255,000	$ 4.25	$ 600,000	$ 40.00	$ 855,000
Profit margin percentage		6.75%		29.20%	

As they continue to gather information, Plastim's managers begin to ponder why the profit margins are under so much pressure for the S3 lens, where the company has strong capabilities, but not on the newer, less-established C5 lens. Plastim is not deliberately charging a low price for S3, so managers begin to evaluate the costing system. Plastim's simple costing system may be overcosting the simple S3 lens (assigning too much cost to it) and undercosting the complex C5 lens (assigning too little cost to it).

3. **Make predictions about the future.** Plastim's key challenge is to get a better estimate of what it will cost to design, make, and distribute the S3 and C5 lenses. Managers are fairly confident about the direct material and direct manufacturing labor cost of each lens because these costs are easily traced to the lenses. Of greater concern is how accurately the simple costing system measures the indirect resources used by each type of lens. The managers believe the costing system can be substantially improved.

   Even as they come to this conclusion, managers want to avoid biased thinking. In particular, they want to be careful that the desire to be competitive on the S3 lens does not lead to assumptions that bias them in favor of lowering costs of the S3 lens.

4. **Make decisions by choosing among alternatives.** On the basis of predicted costs and taking into account how Bandix might respond, Plastim's managers must decide whether they should bid for Giovanni Motors' S3 lens business and, if they do bid, what price they should offer.

5. **Implement the decision, evaluate performance, and learn.** If Plastim bids and wins Giovanni's S3 lens business, it must compare actual costs as it makes and ships the S3 lenses to predicted costs and learn why actual costs deviate from predicted costs. Such evaluation and learning form the basis for future improvements.

The next few sections focus on Steps 3, 4, and 5: (3) how Plastim improves the allocation of indirect costs to the S3 and C5 lenses; (4) how it uses these predictions to bid for the S3 lens business; and (5) how it evaluates performance, makes product design and process improvements, and learns using the new system.

LEARNING OBJECTIVE 2

Present three guidelines for refining a costing system

...classify more costs as direct costs, expand the number of indirect-cost pools, and identify cost drivers

Refining a Costing System

In a **refined costing system**, the use of broad averages for assigning the cost of resources to cost objects (such as jobs, products, and services) is replaced by better measurement of the costs of indirect resources used by different cost objects, even if the various cost objects use the indirect resources to highly varying degrees. Refining a costing system helps managers make better decisions, such as how to price products and which products to produce.

Developments That Have Increased the Demand for Refining Costing Systems

Three key developments have accelerated the demand for refinements to costing systems.

1. **Increase in product diversity.** The growing demand for customized products has led managers to increase the variety of products and services their companies offer. Kanthal, a Swedish manufacturer of heating elements, for example, produces more than 10,000 different types of electrical heating wires and thermostats. Banks, such as Barclays Bank in the United Kingdom, offer many different types of accounts and services: special passbook accounts, ATMs, credit cards, and electronic banking products. Producing these products places different demands on resources because of differences in volume, process, technology, and complexity. For example, the computer and network resources needed to support electronic banking products are much greater than the computer and network resources needed to support a passbook savings account. The use of broad averages fails to capture these differences in demand and leads to distorted and inaccurate cost information.
2. **Increase in indirect costs with different cost drivers.** The use of product and process technology such as computer-integrated manufacturing (CIM) and flexible manufacturing systems (FMS) has led to an increase in indirect costs and a decrease in direct costs, particularly direct manufacturing labor costs. In CIM and FMS, computers on the manufacturing floor instruct equipment to set up and run quickly and automatically. The computers accurately measure hundreds of production parameters and directly control the manufacturing processes to achieve high-quality output. Managing complex technology and producing diverse products also require additional support function resources for activities such as production scheduling, product and process design, and engineering. Because direct manufacturing labor is not a cost driver of these costs, allocating indirect costs on the basis of direct manufacturing labor (as in Plastim's simple costing system) does not accurately measure how resources are being used by different products.
3. **Increase in product market competition.** As markets have become more competitive, managers have felt the need to obtain more accurate cost information to help them make important strategic decisions, such as how to price products and which products to sell. Making correct decisions about pricing and product mix is critical in competitive markets because competitors quickly capitalize on a manager's mistakes. For example, if Plastim overcosts the S3 lens and charges a higher price, a competitor aware of the true costs of making the lens could charge a lower price and gain the S3 business as Bandix is attempting to do.

The preceding developments explain why managers have an increasing need to refine cost systems. Refining costing systems requires gathering, validating, analyzing, and storing vast quantities of data. Advances in information technology have drastically reduced the costs of performing these activities.

Guidelines for Refining a Costing System

There are three main guidelines for refining a costing system:

1. **Trace more costs as direct costs.** Identify as many direct costs as is economically feasible. This guideline aims to reduce the amount of costs classified as indirect, thereby minimizing the extent to which costs have to be allocated rather than traced.
2. **Increase the number of indirect-cost pools.** Expand the number of indirect-cost pools until each pool is fairly homogeneous. All costs in a *homogeneous cost pool* have the same or similar cause-and-effect or benefits-received relationship with a single cost driver or metric that is used as the cost-allocation base. Consider, for example, a single indirect-cost pool, containing both indirect machining costs and indirect distribution costs, that is allocated to products using machine-hours. This pool is not homogeneous because machine-hours are a cost driver of machining costs but not of distribution costs, which have a different cost driver: cubic feet of product delivered. If, instead, machining costs and distribution costs are separated into two indirect-cost pools, with machine-hours as the cost-allocation base for the machining-cost pool and cubic feet of product delivered as the cost-allocation base for the distribution-cost pool, each indirect-cost pool would become homogeneous.

DECISION POINT

What are the main guidelines for refining a costing system?

3. **Identify cost drivers.** As we describe later in the chapter, whenever possible, managers should use the cost driver (the cause of indirect costs) as the cost-allocation base for each homogeneous indirect-cost pool (the effect).

Activity-Based Costing Systems

LEARNING OBJECTIVE 3

Distinguish between simple and activity-based costing systems

. . . unlike simple systems, activity-based costing systems calculate costs of individual activities in order to cost products

One of the best tools for refining a costing system is *activity-based costing*. **Activity-based costing (ABC)** refines a costing system by identifying individual activities as the fundamental source of indirect costs. An **activity** is an event, task, or unit of work with a specified purpose—for example, designing products, setting up machines, operating machines, or distributing products. More informally, activities are verbs; they are things that a firm does. ABC systems identify activities in all functions of the value chain, calculate costs of individual activities, and assign costs to cost objects such as products and services on the basis of the mix of activities needed to produce each product or service.[2]

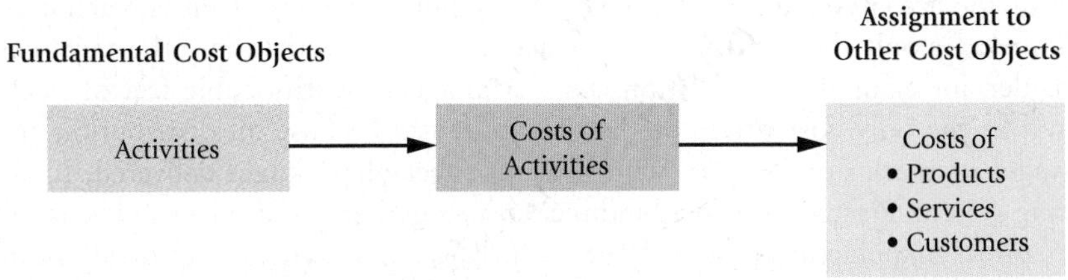

Plastim's ABC System

After reviewing its simple costing system and the potential miscosting of products inherent in it, Plastim's managers decide to implement an ABC system. Direct material costs and direct manufacturing labor costs can be traced to products easily, so the ABC system focuses on refining the assignment of *indirect costs* to departments, processes, products, or other cost objects. To identify activities, Plastim organizes a team of managers from design, manufacturing, distribution, accounting, and administration. In the next step, Plastim's ABC system breaks down its current single indirect-cost pool into finer pools of costs related to the different activities that have been identified.

Identifying activities is difficult. The team evaluates hundreds of tasks performed at Plastim. It must decide which tasks should be classified as separate activities and which should be combined. For example, should maintenance of molding machines, operations of molding machines, and process control be regarded as separate activities or combined into a single activity? An activity-based costing system with many activities may become overly detailed and unwieldy to operate. An activity-based costing system with too few activities may not be refined enough to accurately capture cause-and-effect relationships between cost drivers and various indirect costs. To achieve an effective balance, Plastim's team focuses on activities that account for a sizable fraction of indirect costs and combines activities that have the same cost driver into a single activity. For example, the team decides to combine maintenance of molding machines, operations of molding machines, and process control into a single activity—molding machine operations—because all these activities have the same cost driver: molding machine-hours.

The team identifies the following seven activities based on the steps and processes needed to design, manufacture, and distribute S3 and C5 lenses.

a. Design products and processes
b. Set up molding machines to ensure that the molds are properly held in place and parts are properly aligned before manufacturing starts
c. Operate molding machines to manufacture lenses

[2] For more details on ABC systems, see R. Cooper and R. S. Kaplan, *The Design of Cost Management Systems* (Upper Saddle River, NJ: Prentice Hall, 1999); G. Cokins, *Activity-Based Cost Management: An Executive's Guide* (Hoboken, NJ: John Wiley & Sons, 2001); and R. S. Kaplan and S. Anderson, *Time-Driven Activity-Based Costing: A Simpler and More Powerful Path to Higher Profits* (Boston: Harvard Business School Press, 2007).

d. Clean and maintain the molds after lenses are manufactured
e. Prepare batches of finished lenses for shipment
f. Distribute lenses to customers
g. Administer and manage all processes at Plastim

These activity descriptions (or *activity list* or *activity dictionary*) form the basis of the activity-based costing system. Compiling the list of activities, however, is only the first step in implementing activity-based costing systems. Plastim must also identify the cost of each activity and the related cost driver by using the three guidelines for refining a costing system described on pages 156–157.

1. **Trace more costs as direct costs.** Plastim's ABC system subdivides the single indirect-cost pool into seven smaller cost pools related to the different activities that have been identified. The costs in the cleaning and maintenance activity-cost pool (item d) consist of salaries and wages paid to workers who clean the mold. These costs are direct costs because they can be economically traced to a specific mold and lens.
2. **Increase the number of indirect-cost pools.** The remaining six activity-cost pools are indirect-cost pools. Unlike the single indirect-cost pool of Plastim's simple costing system, each of the activity-related cost pools is fairly homogeneous. That is, each activity-cost pool includes only those narrow and focused sets of costs that have the same cost driver. Consider, for example, distribution costs. Managers identify cubic feet of packages delivered as the only cost driver of distribution costs because all distribution costs (such as wages of truck drivers) vary with the cubic feet of packages delivered. In the simple costing system, Plastim pooled all indirect costs together and used a single cost-allocation base, direct manufacturing labor-hours, which was not a cost driver of all indirect costs such as distribution costs. Managers were therefore unable to accurately capture how different cost objects (the S3 and C5 lenses) used resources.

   To determine the costs of activity pools, managers assign costs accumulated in various account classifications (such as salaries, wages, maintenance, and electricity) to each of the activity-cost pools. This process is commonly called *first-stage allocation*. For example, as we will see later in the chapter, of the $2,385,000 in the total indirect-cost pool, Plastim identifies setup costs of $300,000. Setup costs include depreciation and maintenance costs of setup equipment, wages of setup workers, and allocated salaries of design engineers, process engineers, and supervisors. We discuss *first-stage allocation* in more detail in Chapters 15 and 16. We focus here on the *second-stage allocation*, the allocation of costs of activity-cost pools to cost objects such as products or services.
3. **Identify cost drivers.** ABC systems are developed by identifying the activities that are the source of indirect costs. In many instances, the volume or number of units of an activity performed can be measured in different ways, and managers must decide which metric best captures the cause-and-effect relationship between the activity and the costs in the activity pool. Plastim's managers consider various alternatives and use their knowledge of operations to choose among them. For example, Plastim's managers choose setup-hours rather than the number of setups as the cost driver of setup costs because Plastim's managers believe that the more complex setups of C5 lenses take more time and are more costly than the simpler setups of S3 lenses. Over time, Plastim's managers can use data to test their choices of cost drivers. (Chapter 10 discusses several methods to estimate the relationship between a cost driver and the associated costs.)

The logic of ABC systems is twofold. First, when managers structure activity-cost pools more finely, it leads to more precise costing of the individual activities. Second, allocating the costs in the activity pools to products by measuring the units of the cost-allocation bases of the various activities used by different products leads to more accurate product costs. We illustrate this logic by focusing on the setup activity at Plastim.

Setting up molding machines frequently entails trial runs, fine-tuning, and adjustments. Improper setups cause quality problems such as scratches on the surface of the lens. The resources needed for each setup depend on the complexity of the manufacturing operation. Complex lenses require more setup resources (setup-hours) per setup than simple lenses. Furthermore, complex lenses can be produced only in small batches because the molds for complex lenses need to be cleaned more often than molds for simple lenses. Relative to simple lenses, complex lenses therefore not only use more setup-hours per setup, but also require more frequent setups.

Setup data for the simple S3 lens and the complex C5 lens are as follows.

		Simple S3 Lens	Complex C5 Lens	Total
1	Quantity of lenses produced	60,000	15,000	
2	Number of lenses produced per batch	240	50	
3 = (1) ÷ (2)	Number of batches	250	300	
4	Setup time per batch	2 hours	5 hours	
5 = (3) × (4)	Total setup-hours	500 hours	1,500 hours	2,000 hours

Recall that in its simple costing system, Plastim uses direct manufacturing labor-hours to allocate all $2,385,000 of indirect costs (which includes $300,000 of indirect setup costs) to products. The following table compares how setup costs allocated to simple and complex lenses will be different if Plastim allocates setup costs to lenses based on setup-hours rather than direct manufacturing labor-hours. Of the $60 total rate per direct manufacturing labor-hour (page 154), the setup cost per direct manufacturing labor-hour amounts to $7.54717 ($300,000 ÷ 39,750 total direct manufacturing labor-hours). The setup cost per setup-hour equals $150 ($300,000 ÷ 2,000 total setup-hours).

	Simple S3 Lens	Complex C5 Lens	Total
Setup cost allocated using direct manufacturing labor-hours:			
$7.54717 × 30,000; $7.54717 × 9,750	$226,415	$ 73,585	$300,000
Setup cost allocated using setup-hours:			
$150 × 500; $150 × 1,500	$ 75,000	$225,000	$300,000

ABC systems that use available time (setup-hours in our example) to allocate activity costs to cost objects are sometimes called *time-driven activity-based costing (TDABC) systems.* Following guidelines 2 and 3, Plastim should use setup-hours, the cost driver of setup costs, and not direct manufacturing labor-hours, to allocate setup costs to products. The C5 lens uses substantially more setup-hours than the S3 lens (1,500 hours ÷ 2,000 hours = 75% of the total setup-hours) because the C5 requires a greater number of setups (batches) and each setup is more challenging and requires more setup-hours.

The ABC system therefore allocates significantly more setup costs to C5 than to S3. When direct manufacturing labor-hours rather than setup-hours are used to allocate setup costs in the simple costing system, the S3 lens is allocated a very large share of the setup costs because the S3 lens uses a larger proportion of direct manufacturing labor-hours (30,000 ÷ 39,750 = 75.47%). As a result, the simple costing system overcosts the S3 lens with regard to setup costs.

As we will see later in the chapter, ABC systems provide valuable information to managers beyond more accurate product costs. For example, identifying setup-hours as the cost driver correctly orients managers' cost-reduction efforts on reducing setup-hours and cost per setup-hour. Note that setup-hours are related to batches (or groups) of lenses made, not the number of individual lenses. Activity-based costing attempts to identify the most relevant cause-and-effect relationship for each activity-cost pool without restricting the cost driver to be units of the cost objects or metrics related to units of the cost objects (such as direct manufacturing labor-hours). As our discussion of setups illustrates, limiting cost-allocation bases to only units of cost objects may weaken the cause-and-effect relationship between the cost-allocation base and the costs in a cost pool. Broadening cost drivers to batches (or groups) of lenses, not just individual lenses, leads us to *cost hierarchies*.

DECISION POINT

What is the difference between the design of a simple costing system and an activity-based costing (ABC) system?

Cost Hierarchies

LEARNING OBJECTIVE 4

Describe a four-part cost hierarchy

...a four-part cost hierarchy is used to categorize costs based on different types of cost drivers—for example, costs that vary with each unit of a product versus costs that vary with each batch of products

A **cost hierarchy** categorizes various activity-cost pools on the basis of the different types of cost drivers or cost-allocation bases, or different degrees of difficulty in determining cause-and-effect (or benefits-received) relationships. ABC systems commonly use a cost hierarchy with four levels that reflect the cost drivers of the activity-cost pools: (1) output unit–level costs, (2) batch-level costs, (3) product-sustaining costs, and (4) facility-sustaining costs.

Output unit–level costs are the costs of activities performed that vary with each individual unit of the cost object, such as a product or service. Machine operations costs (such as the cost of energy, machine depreciation, and repair) related to the activity of running the automated molding machines are output unit–level costs because, over time, the cost of this activity increases with additional units of output produced (or machine-hours used). Plastim's ABC system uses molding machine-hours, an output unit–level cost-allocation base, to allocate machine operations costs to products.

Batch-level costs are the costs of activities that vary with a group of units of the cost object, such as a product or service, rather than with each individual unit of the cost object. In the Plastim example, setup costs are batch-level costs because, over time, the cost of this setup activity varies with the setup-hours needed to produce batches (groups) of lenses regardless of the number of lenses included in each batch. For example, if Plastim produces 20% fewer lenses using the same number of setup hours, would setup costs change? No, because setup-hours, not the number of lenses produced, drive setup costs.

As described in the table on page 159, the S3 lens requires 500 setup-hours (2 setup-hours per batch × 250 batches). The C5 lens requires 1,500 setup-hours (5 setup-hours per batch × 300 batches). The total setup costs allocated to S3 and C5 depend on the total setup-hours required by each type of lens, not on the number of lenses of S3 and C5 produced. Plastim's ABC system uses setup-hours, a batch-level cost-allocation base, to allocate setup costs to products. Other examples of batch-level costs are material-handling and quality-inspection costs associated with batches (not the quantities) of products produced and costs of placing purchase orders, receiving materials, and paying invoices related to the number of purchase orders placed rather than the quantity or value of materials purchased.

Product-sustaining costs (service-sustaining costs) are the costs of activities undertaken to support individual products or services regardless of the number of units or batches of the product produced or services provided. In the Plastim example, design costs are product-sustaining costs. Design costs depend largely on the time designers spend on designing and modifying the product, mold, and process, not on the number of lenses subsequently produced or the number of batches in which the lenses are produced using the mold. These design costs are a function of the complexity of the mold, measured by the number of parts in the mold multiplied by the area (in square feet) over which the molten plastic must flow (12 parts × 2.5 square feet, or 30 parts-square feet for the S3 lens; and 14 parts × 5 square feet, or 70 parts-square feet for the C5 lens). Plastim's ABC system uses parts-square feet, a product-sustaining cost-allocation base, to allocate design costs to products. Other examples of product-sustaining costs are product research and development costs, costs of making engineering changes, and marketing costs to launch new products.

Facility-sustaining costs are the costs of activities that managers cannot trace to individual cost objects, such as products or services, but that support the organization as a whole. In the Plastim example and at companies such as Volvo, Samsung, and General Electric, the general administration costs (including top management compensation, rent, and building security) are facility-sustaining costs. It is usually difficult to find a good cost-allocation base that reflects a cause-and-effect relationship between these costs and the cost objects, so some companies deduct facility-sustaining costs as a separate lump-sum amount from operating income rather than allocate these costs to products. Managers who follow this approach need to keep in mind that when making decisions based on costs (such as pricing), some lump-sum costs have not been allocated. They must set prices that are higher than the allocated costs to recover some of the unallocated facility-sustaining costs. Other companies, such as Plastim, allocate facility-sustaining costs to products on some basis—for example, direct manufacturing labor-hours—because management believes that all costs should be allocated to products even if it's done in a somewhat arbitrary way. Allocating all costs to products or services ensures that managers take into account all costs when making decisions based on costs. As long as managers are aware of the nature of facility-sustaining costs and the pros and cons of allocating them, which method a manager chooses is a matter of personal preference or company custom.

DECISION POINT

What is a cost hierarchy?

Implementing Activity-Based Costing

LEARNING OBJECTIVE 5

Cost products or services using activity-based costing

...use cost rates for different activities to compute indirect costs of a product

Now that you understand the basic concepts of ABC, let's see how Plastim's managers develop an ABC system by refining the simple costing system. We will also compare the two systems, and identify the factors to consider when deciding whether to develop an ABC system.

Implementing ABC at Plastim

To implement ABC, Plastim's managers follow the seven-step approach to costing and the three guidelines for refining costing systems (trace more costs as direct costs, increase the number of homogenous indirect-cost pools, and identify cost drivers of the costs in the cost pools). Exhibit 5-3 shows an overview of Plastim's ABC system. Use this exhibit as a guide as you study the following steps, each of which is marked in Exhibit 5-3.

Step 1: Identify the Products That Are the Chosen Cost Objects. The cost objects are the 60,000 S3 and the 15,000 C5 lenses that Plastim will produce in 2020. Plastim's managers want to determine the total costs and then the per-unit cost of designing, manufacturing, and distributing these lenses.

Step 2: Identify the Direct Costs of the Products. The managers identify the following direct costs of the lenses because these costs can be easily and unambiguously traced to a specific mold and lens: direct material costs, direct manufacturing labor costs, and mold cleaning and maintenance costs.

Exhibit 5-5 shows the direct and indirect costs for the S3 and C5 lenses using the ABC system. The direct costs calculations appear on lines 6, 7, 8, and 9 in Exhibit 5-5. Plastim's managers classify all other costs as indirect costs, as we will see in Exhibit 5-4.

Step 3: Select the Activities and Cost-Allocation Bases to Use for Allocating Indirect Costs to the Products. Following guideline 2 (increase the number of homogenous indirect-cost pools)

EXHIBIT 5-3 Overview of Plastim's Activity-Based Costing System

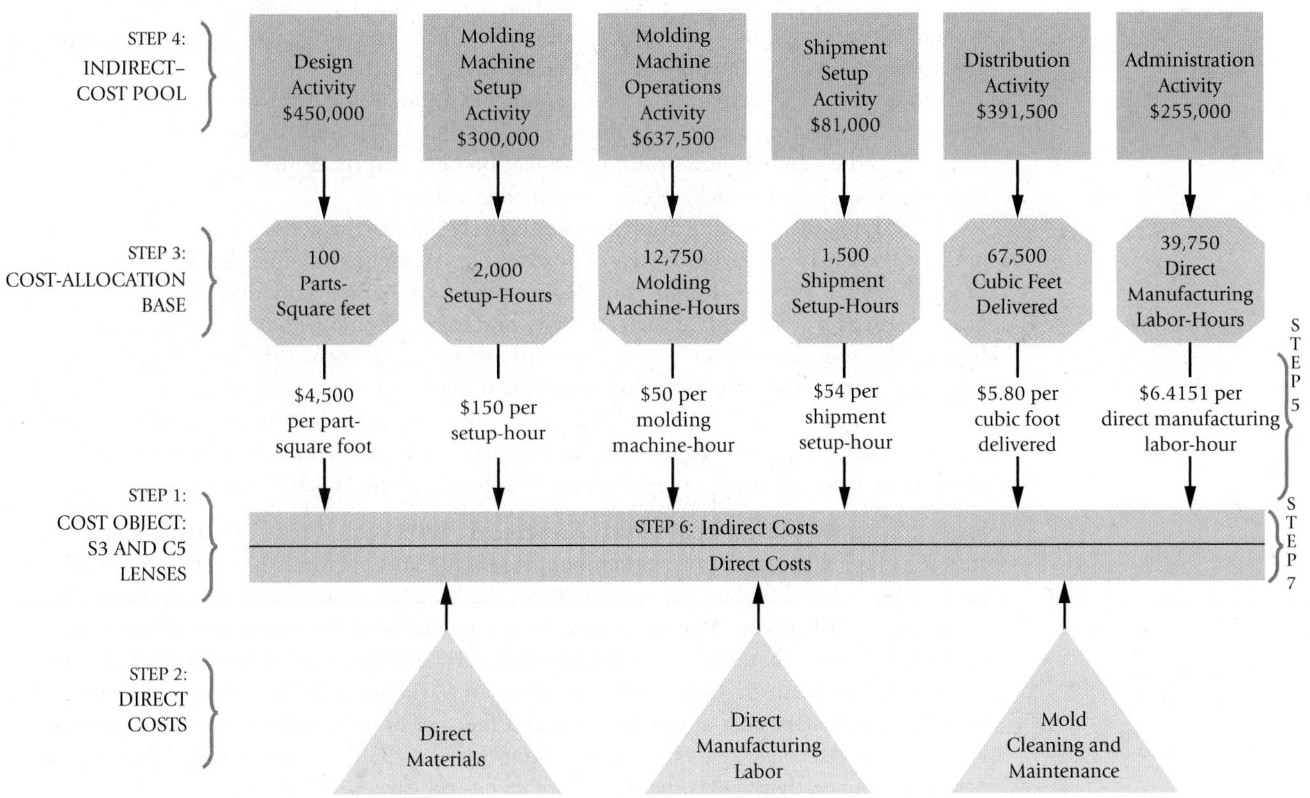

EXHIBIT 5-4 Activity-Cost Rates for Indirect-Cost Pools

	A	B	C	D	E	F	G	H
1			(Step 4)	(Step 3)		(Step 5)		
2	Activity	Cost Hierarchy Category	Total Budgeted Indirect Costs	Budgeted Quantity of Cost-Allocation Base		Budgeted Indirect Cost Rate		Cause-and-Effect Relationship Between Allocation Base and Activity Cost
3	(1)	(2)	(3)	(4)		(5) = (3) ÷ (4)		(6)
4	Design	Product sustaining	$450,000	100	parts-square feet	$ 4,500	per part-square foot	Design Department indirect costs increase with more complex molds (more parts, larger surface area).
5	Molding machine setup	Batch-level	$300,000	2,000	setup-hours	$ 150	per setup-hour	Indirect setup costs increase with setup-hours.
6	Machine operations	Output unit-level	$637,500	12,750	molding machine-hours	$ 50	per molding machine-hour	Indirect costs of operating molding machines increase with molding machine-hours.
7	Shipment setup	Batch-level	$ 81,000	1,500	shipment setup-hours	$ 54	per shipment setup-hour	Shipping costs incurred to prepare batches for shipment increase with the number of shipment setup-hours.
8	Distribution	Output unit-level	$391,500	67,500	cubic feet delivered	$ 5.80	per cubic foot delivered	Distribution costs increase with the cubic feet of packages delivered.
9	Administration	Facility sustaining	$255,000	39,750	direct manuf. labor-hours	$6.4151	per direct manuf. labor-hour	The demand for administrative resources increases with direct manufacturing labor-hours.

and guideline 3 (identify cost drivers of the costs in the cost pools) for refining a costing system (pages 156–157), Plastim's managers identify six activities in order to allocate indirect costs to products: (1) design, (2) molding machine setup, (3) machine operations, (4) shipment setup, (5) distribution, and (6) administration. Exhibit 5-4, column 2, shows the cost hierarchy category, and column 4 shows the cost-allocation base and the budgeted total quantity of the cost-allocation base for each activity described in column 1.

Identifying the cost-allocation bases effectively defines the activity pools into which costs must be grouped in an ABC system. For example, rather than define the design activities of product design, process design, and prototyping as separate activities, Plastim's managers group them as a combined "design" activity and form a homogenous design-cost pool. Why? Because the same cost driver—the complexity of the mold—drives the cost of each design activity. In contrast, the manufacturing department identifies two activity-cost pools—a molding machine setup-cost pool and a machine operations-cost pool—instead of a single manufacturing overhead cost pool, because each activity has a different cost driver: setup-hours for the molding machine setup-cost pool and machine-hours for the machine operations-cost pool.

Step 4: Identify the Indirect Costs Associated With Each Cost-Allocation Base. In this step, Plastim's managers try to assign budgeted indirect costs for 2020 to the activities identified in Step 3 (see Exhibit 5-4, column 3) on the basis of a cause-and-effect relationship between the identified cost-allocation base for an activity and the individual indirect costs. For example, all costs that have a cause-and-effect relationship to cubic feet of packages moved are assigned to the distribution-cost pool. Of course, the strength of the cause-and-effect relationship between the cost-allocation base and the cost of an activity varies across cost pools. For example, the cause-and-effect relationship between direct manufacturing labor-hours and administration activity costs, which, as we discussed earlier, is somewhat arbitrary, is not as strong as the relationship between setup-hours and setup activity costs, where setup-hours is the cost driver of setup costs.

Some indirect costs can be directly identified with a particular activity. For example, salaries paid to design engineers and depreciation of equipment used in the design department are directly identified with the design activity. Other indirect costs need to be *allocated across activities*. For example, on the basis of interviews or time records, manufacturing engineers and supervisors estimate the time they will spend on design, molding machine setup, and molding machine operations. If a manufacturing engineer spends 15% of her time on design, 45% of her time managing molding machine setups, and 40% of her time on molding operations, the company will allocate the manufacturing engineer's salary to each of these activities in proportion to the time spent. Another example is rent costs that are allocated to activity-cost pools on the basis of square-feet area used by the different activities.

As you will see, most costs do not fit neatly into activity categories. Often, costs first need to be allocated to activities (Stage 1 of the two-stage cost-allocation model) before the costs of the activities can then be allocated to cost objects such as products (Stage 2).

The following table shows the assignment of indirect costs to the seven activities identified in Step 3. Recall that Plastim's management accountants reclassify mold-cleaning costs as a direct cost because these costs can be easily traced to a specific mold and lens.

	Design	Molding Machine Setup	Molding Operations	Mold Cleaning	Shipment Setup	Distribution	Administration	Total
Salaries (supervisors, design engineers, process engineers)	$320,000	$105,000	$137,500	$ 0	$21,000	$ 61,500	$165,000	$ 810,000
Wages of support staff	65,000	115,000	70,000	234,000	34,000	125,000	40,000	683,000
Depreciation	24,000	30,000	290,000	18,000	11,000	140,000	15,000	528,000
Maintenance	13,000	16,000	45,000	12,000	6,000	25,000	5,000	122,000
Power and fuel	18,000	20,000	35,000	6,000	5,000	30,000	10,000	124,000
Rent	10,000	14,000	60,000	0	4,000	10,000	20,000	118,000
Total	$450,000	$300,000	$637,500	$270,000	$81,000	$391,500	$255,000	$2,385,000

Step 5: Compute the Rate per Unit of Each Cost-Allocation Base. Exhibit 5-4, column 5, summarizes the calculation of the budgeted indirect-cost rates using the budgeted total quantity of each cost-allocation base from Step 3 and the total budgeted indirect costs of each activity from Step 4.

Step 6: Compute the Indirect Costs Allocated to the Individual Products. Exhibit 5-5 shows total budgeted indirect costs of $1,153,953 allocated to the simple lens and $961,047 allocated to the complex lens. Follow the budgeted indirect-cost calculations for each lens in Exhibit 5-5. For each activity, Plastim's operations personnel budget the total quantity of the cost-allocation base that will be used by each type of lens (recall that Plastim operates at capacity). For example, lines 15 and 16 in Exhibit 5-5 show that of the 2,000 total setup-hours, the S3 lens is budgeted to use 500 hours and the C5 lens 1,500 hours. The budgeted indirect-cost rate is $150 per setup-hour (Exhibit 5-4, column 5, line 5). Therefore, the total budgeted cost of the setup activity allocated to the S3 lens is $75,000 (500 setup-hours × 150 per setup-hour) and to the C5 lens is $225,000 (1,500 setup-hours × 150 per setup-hour). The budgeted setup cost *per unit* equals $1.25 ($75,000 ÷ 60,000 units) for the S3 lens and $15 ($225,000 ÷ 15,000 units) for the C5 lens.

Next consider shipment setup costs. Plastim supplies its S3 and C5 lenses to two different Giovanni plants. One of these is an international plant in Mexico. Preparing for these shipments is more time consuming than preparing shipments to the local plant in Indiana because of additional documents related to customs, taxes, and insurance. The following table shows the budgeted number of shipments of S3 and C5 lenses to each plant.

	Mexico Plant Shipments	Indiana Plant Shipments	Total Shipments
Simple S3 lens shipments	10	100	110
Complex C5 lens shipments	30	60	90
			200

EXHIBIT 5-5 Plastim's Product Costs Using an Activity-Based Costing System

Home Insert Page Layout Formulas Data Review View

	A	B	C	D	E	F	G
1		60,000			15,000		
2		Simple Lenses (S3)			Complex Lenses (C5)		
3		Total	per Unit		Total	per Unit	Total
4	**Cost Description**	(1)	(2) = (1) ÷ 60,000		(3)	(4) = (3) ÷ 15,000	(5) = (1) + (3)
5	Direct costs						
6	Direct materials	$1,125,000	$18.75		$ 675,000	$ 45.00	$1,800,000
7	Direct manufacturing labor	600,000	10.00		195,000	13.00	795,000
8	Direct mold cleaning and maintenance costs	120,000	2.00		150,000	10.00	270,000
9	Total direct costs (Step 2)	1,845,000	30.75		1,020,000	68.00	2,865,000
10	Indirect Costs of Activities						
11	Design						
12	S3, 30 parts-sq.ft. × $4,500	135,000	2.25				} 450,000
13	C5, 70 parts-sq.ft. × $4,500				315,000	21.00	
14	Setup of molding machines						
15	S3, 500 setup-hours × $150	75,000	1.25				} 300,000
16	C5, 1,500 setup-hours × $150				225,000	15.00	
17	Machine operations						
18	S3, 9,000 molding machine-hours × $50	450,000	7.50				} 637,500
19	C5, 3,750 molding machine-hours × $50				187,500	12.50	
20	Shipment setup						
21	S3, 750 shipment setup hours × $54	40,500	0.67				} 81,000
22	C5, 750 shipment setup hours × $54				40,500	2.70	
23	Distribution						
24	S3, 45,000 cubic feet delivered × $5.80	261,000	4.35				} 391,500
25	C5, 22,500 cubic feet delivered × $5.80				130,500	8.70	
26	Administration						
27	S3, 30,000 dir. manuf. labor-hours × $6.4151	192,453	3.21				} 255,000
28	C5, 9,750 dir. manuf. labor-hours × $6.4151				62,547	4.17	
29	Total indirect costs allocated (Step 6)	1,153,953	19.23		961,047	64.07	2,115,000
30	Total Costs (Step 7)	$2,998,953	$49.98		$1,981,047	$132.07	$4,980,000
31							

Each shipment to the Mexico plant requires 12.5 hours of the shipment department personnel's time, while each shipment to the Indiana plant requires half that time, 6.25 hours. The following table indicates the budgeted shipping setup-hours for the S3 and C5 lenses.

	Shipment Setup-Hours for Mexico Plant	Shipment Setup-Hours for Indiana Plant	Total Shipment Setup-Hours
Simple S3 lens shipment setup-hours (12.5 hours × 10; 6.25 hours × 100)	125	625	750
Complex C5 lens shipment setup-hours (12.5 hours × 30; 6.25 hours × 60)	375	375	750
			1,500

The budgeted indirect-cost rate is $54 per shipment setup-hour (Exhibit 5-4, column 5, line 7). Therefore, lines 21 and 22 in Exhibit 5-5 show that the total budgeted cost of the shipment setup activity allocated to the S3 lens is $40,500 (750 shipment setup-hours × $54 per shipment setup-hour) and to the C5 lens is $40,500 (750 shipment setup-hours × $54 per shipment setup-hour). Budgeted setup cost per unit equals $0.67 ($40,500 ÷ 60,000 units) for the S3 lens and $2.70 ($40,500 ÷ 15,000 units) for the C5 lens.

Costing for shipment setups using shipment setup-hours as the cost driver is another example of time-driven activity-based costing (TDABC) because available time is used to allocate the costs in the activity pool. TDABC allows Plastim's managers to account for the varying complexity in the shipments of S3 and C5 lenses. Notice that if Plastim had ignored the complexity of different shipments and allocated costs to lenses based only on the number of shipments, it would have calculated a budgeted indirect-cost rate of $405 per shipment in Exhibit 5-4 ($81,000 ÷ 200 shipments). Using this rate the total budgeted cost of the shipment setup activity allocated to the S3 lens is $44,550 (110 shipments × $405 per shipment) and to the C5 lens is $36,450 (90 shipments × $54 per shipment). The budgeted setup cost per unit equals $0.74 ($44,550 ÷ 60,000 units) for the S3 lens and $2.43 ($36,450 ÷ 15,000 units) for the C5 lens. Using the number of shipments, rather than shipment setup-hours, as the cost driver would overcost the simple S3 lens and undercost the complex C5 lens.

Step 7: Compute the Total Cost of the Products by Adding All Direct and Indirect Costs Assigned to the Products. Exhibit 5-5 presents the product costs for the simple and complex lenses. The direct costs are calculated in Step 2, and the indirect costs are calculated in Step 6. The ABC system overview in Exhibit 5-3 shows three direct-cost categories and six indirect-cost categories. The budgeted cost of each lens type in Exhibit 5-5 has nine line items, three for direct costs and six for indirect costs. The differences between the ABC product costs of S3 and C5 calculated in Exhibit 5-5 highlight how each of these products uses different amounts of direct and indirect costs related to each of the activities.

5-2 TRY IT!

Vanderbilt Metal Works produces two types of metal lamps. Vanderbilt manufactures 24,640 basic lamps and 6,250 designer lamps. Its activity-based costing system uses two indirect-cost pools. One cost pool is for setup costs and the other for general manufacturing overhead. Vanderbilt allocates setup costs to the two lamps based on setup labor-hours and general manufacturing overhead costs on the basis of direct manufacturing labor-hours. It provides the following budgeted cost information:

	Basic Lamps	Designer Lamps	Total
Direct materials per lamp	$ 5	$19	
Direct manufacturing labor-hours per lamp	0.4 hours	0.5 hours	
Direct manufacturing labor rate per hour	$30	$30	
Setup costs			$130,800
Lamps produced per batch	320	50	
Setup-hours per batch	1 hour	2 hours	
General manufacturing overhead costs			$ 89,877

Calculate the total budgeted costs of the basic and designer lamps using Vanderbilt's activity-based costing system.

We emphasize two features of ABC systems. First, these systems identify all costs used by products, whether the costs are variable or fixed in the short run. Thus, ABC systems lend themselves to making long-run strategic decisions where managers want revenues to exceed total costs. Otherwise, a company will make losses and will be unable to continue in business. Second, recognizing the hierarchy of costs is critical when allocating costs to products. Management accountants use the cost hierarchy to first calculate the total costs of each product. They then derive per-unit costs by dividing total costs by the number of units produced.

DECISION POINT

How do managers cost products or services using ABC systems?

Comparing Alternative Costing Systems

Exhibit 5-6 compares the simple costing system using a single indirect-cost pool (Exhibits 5-1 and 5-2) that Plastim had been using and the newly developed ABC system (Exhibits 5-3 and 5-5). Note three points in Exhibit 5-6, consistent with the guidelines for refining a costing system: (1) ABC systems classify more costs as direct costs; (2) ABC systems have more indirect-cost pools that reflect homogenous costs of the different activities; and (3) for each activity-cost pool, ABC systems seek a cost-allocation base that has a cause-and-effect relationship with costs in the cost pool (cost driver).

The increased number and homogeneous nature of cost pools and the choice of cost-allocation bases, tied to the cost hierarchy, give Plastim's managers greater confidence in the activity and product cost numbers from the ABC system.

The bottom part of Exhibit 5-6 shows that allocating costs to lenses using the simple costing system with just a single indirect-cost pool and a single output unit-level allocation base—direct manufacturing labor-hours—overcosts the simple S3 lens by \$8.77 per unit and undercosts the complex C5 lens by \$35.07 per unit. The C5 lens uses a disproportionately larger amount of indirect costs than is represented by the direct manufacturing labor-hour cost-allocation base. The S3 lens uses a disproportionately smaller amount of these costs.

The benefit of an ABC system is that it provides more accurate information that leads to better decisions. But managers must weigh this benefit against the measurement and implementation costs of an ABC system.

EXHIBIT 5-6 Comparing Alternative Costing Systems

	Simple Costing System Using a Single Indirect-Cost Pool (1)	ABC System (2)	Difference (3) = (2) − (1)
Direct-cost categories	2 Direct materials Direct manufacturing labor	3 Direct materials Direct manufacturing labor Direct mold cleaning and maintenance labor	1
Total direct costs	\$2,595,000	\$2,865,000	\$270,000
Indirect-cost pools	1 Single indirect-cost pool allocated using direct manufacturing labor-hours	6 Design (parts-square feet)[1] Molding machine setup (setup-hours) Machine operations (molding machine-hours) Shipment setup (shipment setup-hours) Distribution (cubic feet delivered) Administration (direct manufacturing labor-hours)	5
Total indirect costs	\$2,385,000	\$2,115,000	(\$270,000)
Total costs assigned to simple (S3) lens	\$3,525,000	\$2,998,953	(\$526,047)
Cost per unit of simple (S3) lens	\$ 58.75	\$ 49.98	(\$ 8.77)
Total costs assigned to complex (C5) lens	\$1,455,000	\$1,981,047	\$526,047
Cost per unit of complex (C5) lens	\$ 97.00	\$ 132.07	\$ 35.07

[1]Cost drivers for the various indirect-cost pools are shown in parentheses.

Considerations in Implementing Activity-Based Costing Systems

Managers choose the level of detail of a costing system by evaluating the expected costs of the system against the expected benefits of better decisions that result from more accurate cost information.

LEARNING OBJECTIVE 6

Evaluate the benefits and costs of implementing activity-based costing systems

...more accurate costs that aid in decision making when products make diverse demands on indirect resources versus costs incurred for measurement and implementation

Benefits and Costs of Activity-Based Costing Systems

Here are some of the telltale signs that implementing an ABC system is likely to provide significant benefits and improvements over an existing costing system:

- Significant amounts of indirect costs are allocated using only one or two cost pools.
- All or most indirect costs are identified as output unit–level costs (few indirect costs are described as batch-level costs, product-sustaining costs, or facility-sustaining costs).
- Products make diverse demands on resources because of differences in volume, process steps, batch size, or complexity.
- Products that a company is well suited to make and sell show small profits, whereas products that a company is less suited to make and sell show large profits.
- Operations staff has substantial disagreement with the reported costs of manufacturing and marketing products and services.

When managers decide to implement ABC, they must make important choices about the level of detail to use. Should managers choose many finely specified activities, cost drivers, and cost pools, or would a few suffice? For example, Plastim's managers could identify a different molding machine-hour rate for each of the different types of molding machines. In making such choices, managers weigh the benefits against the costs and limitations of implementing a more detailed costing system.

The main costs and limitations of an ABC system are the measurements necessary to implement it. ABC systems require managers to estimate costs of activity pools and to identify and measure cost drivers for these pools to serve as cost-allocation bases. Even basic ABC systems require many calculations to determine costs of products and services. These measurements are costly. Activity-cost rates also need to be updated regularly.

As ABC systems get very detailed and more cost pools are created, more allocations are necessary to calculate activity costs for each cost pool, which increases the chances of misidentifying the costs of different activity-cost pools. For example, supervisors are more prone to incorrectly identify the time they spend on different activities if they have to allocate their time over five activities rather than only two activities.

Occasionally, managers are forced to use allocation bases for which data are readily available rather than allocation bases they would have liked to use but for which data are difficult to obtain. For example, in its ABC system, Plastim's managers measure mold complexity in terms of the number of parts in the mold and the surface area of the mold (parts-square feet). If these data are difficult to obtain or measure, Plastim's managers may be forced to use some other measure of complexity, such as the amount of material flowing through the mold, that may only be weakly related to the cost of the design activity.

When incorrect or imprecise cost-allocation bases are used, activity-cost information can be inaccurate and even misleading. For example, if the cost per load moved decreases, a company may conclude that it has become more efficient in its materials-handling operations. In fact, the lower cost per load moved may have resulted solely from moving many lighter loads over shorter distances.

Many companies, such as Kanthal, a Swedish heating elements manufacturer, have found the strategic and operational benefits of a less-detailed ABC system to be good enough to not warrant incurring the costs and challenges of operating a more detailed system. Other organizations, such as Hewlett-Packard, have implemented ABC in only certain divisions (such as the Roseville Networks Division, which manufactures printed circuit boards) or functions (such as procurement and production). As improvements in information technology and accompanying declines in measurement costs continue, more detailed ABC systems have become a practical alternative in many companies. With these advancements, more detailed ABC systems are able to pass the cost–benefit test.

Global surveys of company practices suggest that ABC implementation varies among companies. Nevertheless, the framework and the ideas underlying ABC provide a standard for judging whether any simple costing system is good enough for a particular management purpose. ABC thinking can help managers improve any simple costing system.

ABC in Service and Merchandising Companies

Although many early examples of ABC originated in manufacturing, managers also use ABC in service and merchandising companies. For instance, the Plastim example includes the application of ABC to a service activity—design—and to a merchandising activity—distribution. Companies such as Braintree Hospital, BCTel, Charles Schwab, and Union Pacific (Railroad) have implemented some form of ABC system to identify profitable product mixes, improve efficiency, and satisfy customers. Similarly, many retail and wholesale companies—for example, Supervalu, a retailer and distributor of grocery store products, and Owens and Minor, a medical supplies distributor—have used ABC systems. As we describe in Chapter 15, a large number of financial services companies (as well as other companies) employ variations of ABC systems to analyze and improve the profitability of their customer interactions.

The widespread use of ABC systems in service and merchandising companies reinforces the idea that ABC systems are used by managers for strategic decisions rather than for inventory valuation. (Inventory valuation is fairly straightforward in merchandising companies and not needed in service companies.) Service companies, in particular, find great value from ABC because a vast majority of their cost structure is composed of indirect costs. After all, there are few direct costs when a bank makes a loan or when a representative answers a phone call at a call center. As we have seen, a major benefit of ABC is its ability to assign indirect costs to cost objects by identifying activities and cost drivers. As a result, ABC systems provide greater insight into the management of these indirect costs than do traditional costing systems. The general approach to ABC in service and merchandising companies is similar to the ABC approach in manufacturing organizations.

USAA Federal Savings Bank followed the approach described in this chapter when it implemented ABC in its banking operations. Managers calculated the cost rates of various activities, such as performing ATM transactions, opening and closing accounts, administering mortgages, and processing Visa transactions, by dividing the cost of these activities by the time available to do them. Managers used these time-based rates to cost individual products, such as checking accounts, mortgages, and Visa cards, and to calculate the costs of supporting different types of customers. Information from this time-driven ABC system helped USAA Federal Savings Bank to improve its processes and identify profitable products and customer segments. Concepts in Action: Mayo Clinic Uses Time-Driven Activity-Based Costing to Reduce Costs and Improve Care describes how the Mayo Clinic has similarly benefited from ABC analysis.

Activity-based costing raises some interesting issues when it is applied to a public service institution such as the U.S. Postal Service. The costs of delivering mail to remote locations are far greater than the costs of delivering mail within urban areas. However, for fairness and community-building reasons, the Postal Service does not charge higher prices to customers in remote areas. In this case, activity-based costing is valuable for understanding, managing, and reducing costs but not for pricing decisions.

Behavioral Issues in Implementing Activity-Based Costing Systems

Successfully implementing ABC systems requires more than an understanding of the technical details. ABC implementation often represents a significant change in the costing system and, as the chapter discusses, requires a manager to choose the level of detail and how to define activities. What then are some of the behavioral issues to which managers and management accountants must be sensitive when implementing an ABC system?

1. **Gaining support of top management and creating a sense of urgency for the ABC effort.** This requires managers and management accountants to clearly communicate the

CONCEPTS IN ACTION

Mayo Clinic Uses Time-Driven Activity-Based Costing to Reduce Costs and Improve Care[3]

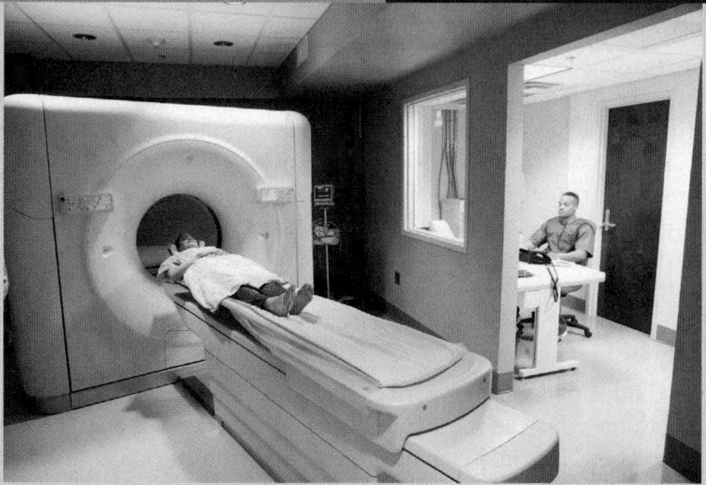

Fuse/Corbis/Getty Images

Nearly $1 of every $5 spent in the United States is on health care. Several medical centers, such as the Mayo Clinic in Rochester, Minnesota, are using time-driven activity-based costing (TDABC) to help bring accurate cost and value measurement practices into the health care delivery system.

TDABC assigns all of the organization's resource costs to cost objects using a framework that requires two sets of estimates. TDABC first calculates the cost of supplying resource capacity, such as a doctor's time. The total cost of resources—including personnel, supervision, insurance, space occupancy, technology, and supplies—is divided by the available capacity—the time available for doctors to do their work—to obtain the capacity cost rate. Next, TDABC uses the capacity cost rate to drive resource costs to cost objects, such as the number of patients seen, by estimating the demand for resource capacity (time) that the cost object requires.

Medical centers implementing TDABC have succeeded in reducing costs. For orthopedic procedures at the Mayo Clinic, the TDABC-modified process resulted in shorter stays for patients, a 24% decrease in patients discharged to expensive skilled nursing facilities, and a 15% decrease in cost. Similarly, the Mayo Clinic redesigned its stroke-recovery practice to reduce costs by 25% with no adverse impact on patient outcomes.

More broadly, health care providers implementing TDABC have found that better outcomes for patients often go hand in hand with lower total costs. For example, spending more on early detection and better diagnosis of disease reduces patient suffering and often leads to less-complex and less-expensive care. With the insights from TDABC, health care providers can utilize medical staff, equipment, facilities, and administrative resources far more efficiently; streamline the path of patients through the system; and select treatment approaches that improve outcomes while eliminating services that do not.

[3] *Sources:* W. David Freeman, Kevin M. Barrett, Lisa Nordan, Aaron C. Spaulding, Borert S. Kaplan, and Meredith Karney, "Lessons from Mayo Clinic's Redesign of Stroke Care," *Harvard Business Review*, October 19, 2018 (https://hbr.org/2018/10/lessons-from-mayo-clinics-redesign-of-stroke-care); Derek A. Haas, Richard A. Helmers, March Rucci, Meredith Brady, and Robert S. Kaplan, "The Mayo Clinic Model for Running a Value-Improvement Program," *Harvard Business Review*, October 22, 2015 (https://hbr.org/2015/10/the-mayo-clinic-model-for-running-a-value-improvement-program); Robert S. Kaplan and Michael E. Porter, "How to Solve the Cost Crisis in Health Care," *Harvard Business Review*, September 2011 (https://hbr.org/2011/09/how-to-solve-the-cost-crisis-in-health-care); Robert S. Kaplan and Steven R. Anderson, "The Innovation of Time-Driven Activity-Based Costing," *Journal of Cost Management 21*, 2 (March–April 2007): 5–15.

strategic and operational benefits of ABC, such as improvements in product and process design. For example, at USAA Federal Savings Bank, managers calculated the cost of individual activities such as opening and closing accounts and demonstrated how the information gained from ABC provided insights into ways of improving the efficiency of bank operations that were previously unavailable.

2. **Creating a guiding coalition of managers throughout the value chain for the ABC effort.** ABC systems measure how the resources of an organization are used. Managers responsible for these resources have the best knowledge about the underlying activities and their cost drivers. Getting managers to cooperate and take the initiative for implementing ABC is essential for gaining the required expertise, the proper credibility, greater commitment, valuable coordination, and the necessary leadership.

3. **Educating and training employees in ABC as a basis for employee empowerment.** Management accountants must disseminate information about ABC throughout the organization to enable employees in all areas of the business to use their knowledge of ABC to make improvements. For example, WS Industries, an Indian manufacturer of insulators, not only shared ABC information with its workers but also established an incentive plan that gave them a percentage of the cost savings. The results were dramatic because employees were empowered and motivated to implement numerous cost-saving projects.
4. **Seeking small short-run successes as proof that the ABC implementation is yielding results.** Too often, managers and management accountants seek big improvements far too quickly. In many situations, achieving a significant change overnight is difficult. However, showing how ABC information has helped improve a process and save costs, even if only in small ways, motivates the team to stay on course and build momentum. The credibility gained from small victories leads to additional improvements involving larger numbers of people and other parts of the organization. Eventually ABC becomes rooted in the culture of the organization. Sharing short-term successes also helps motivate employees to be innovative. At USAA Federal Savings Bank, managers created a "process improvement" Slack channel to facilitate the sharing of process improvement ideas.
5. **Recognizing that ABC information is not perfect.** The management accountant must help managers recognize both the value and the limitations of ABC. Open and honest communication about the tradeoffs inherent in designing an ABC system ensures that managers use the information thoughtfully to make sound decisions and can question its output without sounding adversarial.

DECISION POINT

What are the main benefits and costs of implementing an ABC system?

Activity-Based Management

LEARNING OBJECTIVE 7

Explain how managers use activity-based costing systems in activity-based management

...such as pricing decisions, product-mix decisions, and cost-reduction efforts

The emphasis of this chapter so far has been on the role of ABC systems in obtaining better, or more accurate, product costs. However, Plastim's managers must now use this information to make decisions (Step 4 of the five-step decision process, page 155) and to implement the decision, evaluate performance, and learn (Step 5, page 155). **Activity-based management (ABM)** is a method of management decision making that uses activity-based costing information to improve customer satisfaction and profitability. We define ABM broadly to include decisions about pricing and product mix, cost reduction, process improvement, and product and process design.

Pricing and Product-Mix Decisions

An ABC system gives managers information about the costs of making and selling diverse products. With this information, managers can make pricing and product-mix decisions. For example, the ABC system indicates that Plastim can match its competitor's price of $53 for the S3 lens and still make a profit because the ABC cost of S3 is $49.98 (see Exhibit 5-5).

Plastim's managers offer Giovanni Motors a price of $52 for the S3 lens. Plastim's managers are confident that they can use the deeper understanding of costs that the ABC system provides to improve efficiency and further reduce the cost of the S3 lens. Without information from the ABC system, Plastim managers might have erroneously concluded that they would incur an operating loss on the S3 lens at a price of $53. This incorrect conclusion would have probably caused Plastim to reduce or exit its business in simple lenses and focus instead on complex lenses, where its single indirect-cost-pool system indicated it was very profitable.

Focusing on complex lenses would have been a mistake. The ABC system indicates that the cost of making the complex lens is much higher—$132.07 versus $97 indicated by the direct manufacturing labor-hour-based costing system Plastim had been using. As Plastim's operations staff had thought all along, Plastim has no competitive advantage in making C5 lenses. At a price of $137 per lens for C5, the profit margin is very small ($137.00 − $132.07 = $4.93).

As Plastim reduces its prices on simple lenses, it would need to negotiate a higher price for complex lenses while also reducing costs in order to generate a higher profit margin.

Cost Reduction and Process Improvement Decisions

Managers use ABC systems to focus on how and where to reduce costs. They set cost reduction targets for the cost per unit of the cost-allocation base in different activity areas. For example, the supervisor of the distribution activity area at Plastim could have a performance target of decreasing distribution cost per cubic foot of products delivered from \$5.80 to \$5.40 by reducing distribution labor and warehouse rental costs. The goal is to reduce these costs by improving the way work is done without compromising customer service or the actual or perceived value (usefulness) customers obtain from the product or service. That is, the supervisor will attempt to take out only those costs that are *nonvalue added.*

Controlling cost drivers, such as setup-hours or cubic feet delivered, is another fundamental way that operating personnel manage costs. For example, the distribution department can decrease distribution costs by packing the lenses in a way that reduces the bulkiness of the packages delivered.

The following table shows the reduction in distribution costs of the S3 and C5 lenses as a result of actions that lower cost per cubic foot delivered (from \$5.80 to \$5.40) and total cubic feet of deliveries (from 45,000 to 40,000 for S3 and 22,500 to 20,000 for C5).

	60,000 (S3) Lenses		15,000 (C5) Lenses	
	Total (1)	per Unit (2) = (1) ÷ 60,000	Total (3)	per Unit (4) = (3) ÷ 15,000
Distribution costs (from Exhibit 5-5)				
S3: 45,000 cubic feet × \$5.80/cubic feet	\$261,000	\$4.35		
C5: 22,500 cubic feet × \$5.80/cubic feet			\$130,500	\$8.70
Distribution costs as a result of process improvements				
S3: 40,000 cubic feet × \$5.40/cubic feet	216,000	3.60		
C5: 20,000 cubic feet × \$5.40/cubic feet			108,000	7.20
Savings in distribution costs from process improvements	\$ 45,000	\$0.75	\$ 22,500	\$1.50

In the long run, total distribution costs will decrease from \$391,500 (\$261,000 + \$130,500) to \$324,000 (\$216,000 + \$108,000). In the short run, however, distribution costs may be fixed and may not decrease. Suppose all \$391,500 of distribution costs are fixed costs in the short run. The efficiency improvements (using less distribution labor and space) mean that the same \$391,500 of distribution costs can now be used to distribute $72{,}500\left(= \frac{\$391{,}500}{\$5.40 \text{ per cubic feet}}\right)$ cubic feet of lenses compared to the 67,500 cubic feet of lenses it currently distributes (see Exhibit 5-4). In this case, how should costs be allocated to the S3 and C5 lenses?

ABC systems distinguish costs incurred from resources used to design, manufacture, and deliver products and services. For the distribution activity, after process improvements,

Costs incurred = \$391,500

Resources used = \$216,000 (for S3 lens) + \$108,000 (for C5 lens) = \$324,000

On the basis of the resources used by each product, Plastim's ABC system allocates \$216,000 to S3 and \$108,000 to C5 for a total of \$324,000. The difference of \$67,500 (\$391,500 − \$324,000) is shown as costs of unused but available distribution capacity. Plastim's ABC system does not allocate the costs of unused capacity to products so as not to burden the product costs of S3 and C5 with the cost of resources not used by these products. Instead, the system highlights the amount of unused capacity as a separate line item to alert managers to reduce these costs, such as by redeploying labor to other uses or laying off workers.

Design Decisions

ABC systems help managers to evaluate the effect of current product and process design choices on activities and, as a result, costs and to identify design changes that reduce costs. For example, design decisions that decrease the complexity of the mold reduce costs of design, but also materials, labor, machine setups, machine operations, and mold cleaning and maintenance because a less-complex design reduces scrap and the time for setup and operation of the molding machine. Plastim's customers may be willing to give up some features of the lens in exchange for a lower price. Note that Plastim's previous costing system, which used direct manufacturing labor-hours as the cost-allocation base for all indirect costs, would have mistakenly signaled that Plastim should choose designs that most reduce direct manufacturing labor-hours. In fact, there is a weak cause-and-effect relationship between direct manufacturing labor-hours and indirect costs.

Planning and Managing Activities

Most managers implementing ABC systems for the first time start by analyzing actual costs to identify activity-cost pools, cost-allocation bases, and activity-cost rates. Managers then calculate budgeted rates (as in the Plastim example) that they use for planning, making decisions, and managing activities. At year-end, managers compare budgeted costs and actual costs to evaluate how well activities were managed. Management accountants make adjustments for underallocated or overallocated indirect costs for each activity using methods described in Chapter 4. As activities and processes change, managers calculate new activity-cost rates.

We return to activity-based management in later chapters. Management decisions that use activity-based costing information are described in Chapter 6, where we discuss activity-based budgeting; in Chapter 12, where we discuss outsourcing and adding or dropping business segments; in Chapter 13, where we present reengineering and downsizing; in Chapter 14, where we evaluate alternative design choices to improve efficiency and reduce nonvalue-added costs; in Chapter 15, where we explore managing customer profitability; in Chapter 20, where we explain quality improvements; and in Chapter 21, where we describe how to evaluate suppliers.

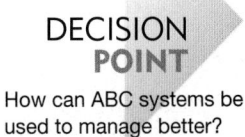

DECISION POINT

How can ABC systems be used to manage better?

PROBLEM FOR SELF-STUDY

Family Supermarkets (FS) has decided to increase the size of its Memphis store. It wants information about the profitability of individual product lines: soft drinks, fresh produce, and packaged food. FS provides the following data for 2020 for each product line:

	Soft Drinks	Fresh Produce	Packaged Food
Revenues	$317,400	$840,240	$483,960
Cost of goods sold	$240,000	$600,000	$360,000
Cost of bottles returned	$ 4,800	$ 0	$ 0
Number of purchase orders placed	144	336	144
Number of deliveries received	120	876	264
Hours of shelf-stocking time	216	2,160	1,080
Items sold	50,400	441,600	122,400

FS also provides the following information for 2020:

Activity (1)	Description of Activity (2)	Total Support Costs (3)	Cost-Allocation Base (4)
1. Bottle returns	Returning of empty bottles to store	$ 4,800	Direct tracing to soft-drink line
2. Ordering	Placing of orders for purchases	$ 62,400	624 purchase orders
3. Delivery	Physical delivery and receipt of merchandise	$100,800	1,260 deliveries
4. Shelf stocking	Stocking of merchandise on store shelves and ongoing restocking	$ 69,120	3,456 hours of shelf-stocking time
5. Customer support	Assistance provided to customers, including checkout and bagging	$122,880	614,400 items sold
Total		$360,000	

Required

1. Family Supermarkets currently allocates store support costs (all costs other than cost of goods sold) to product lines on the basis of cost of goods sold of each product line. Calculate the operating income and operating income as a percentage of revenues for each product line.
2. If Family Supermarkets allocates store support costs (all costs other than cost of goods sold) to product lines using an ABC system, calculate the operating income and operating income as a percentage of revenues for each product line.
3. Comment on your answers in requirements 1 and 2.

Solution

1. The following table shows the operating income and operating income as a percentage of revenues for each product line. All store support costs (all costs other than cost of goods sold) are allocated to product lines using cost of goods sold of each product line as the cost-allocation base. Total store support costs equal $360,000 (cost of bottles returned, $4,800 + cost of purchase orders, $62,400 + cost of deliveries, $100,800 + cost of shelf stocking, $69,120 + cost of customer support, $122,880). The allocation rate for store support costs = $360,000 ÷ $1,200,000 (soft drinks $240,000 + fresh produce $600,000 + packaged food, $360,000) = 30% of cost of goods sold. To allocate support costs to each product line, FS multiplies the cost of goods sold of each product line by 0.30.

	Soft Drinks	Fresh Produce	Packaged Food	Total
Revenues	$317,400	$840,240	$483,960	$1,641,600
Cost of goods sold	240,000	600,000	360,000	1,200,000
Store support cost				
($240,000; $600,000; $360,000) × 0.30	72,000	180,000	108,000	360,000
Total costs	312,000	780,000	468,000	1,560,000
Operating income	$ 5,400	$ 60,240	$ 15,960	$ 81,600
Operating income ÷ Revenues	1.70%	7.17%	3.30%	4.97%

2. The ABC system identifies bottle-return costs as a direct cost because these costs can be traced to the soft-drink product line. FS then calculates cost-allocation rates for each activity area (as in Step 5 of the seven-step costing system, described earlier on page 163). The activity rates are as follows:

Activity (1)	Cost Hierarchy (2)	Total Costs (3)	Quantity of Cost-Allocation Base (4)	Overhead Allocation Rate (5) = (3) ÷ (4)
Ordering	Batch-level	$ 62,400	624 purchase orders	$100 per purchase order
Delivery	Batch-level	$100,800	1,260 deliveries	$80 per delivery
Shelf stocking	Output unit–level	$ 69,120	3,456 shelf-stocking hours	$20 per stocking-hour
Customer support	Output unit–level	$122,880	614,400 items sold	$0.20 per item sold

Store support costs for each product line by activity are obtained by multiplying the total quantity of the cost-allocation base for each product line by the activity-cost rate. Operating income and operating income as a percentage of revenues for each product line are as follows:

	Soft Drinks	Fresh Produce	Packaged Food	Total
Revenues	$317,400	$840,240	$483,960	$1,641,600
Cost of goods sold	240,000	600,000	360,000	1,200,000
Bottle-return costs	4,800	0	0	4,800
Ordering costs	14,400	33,600	14,400	62,400
(144; 336; 144) purchase orders × $100				
Delivery costs				
(120; 876; 264) deliveries × $80	9,600	70,080	21,120	100,800
Shelf-stocking costs				
(216; 2,160; 1,080) stocking-hours × $20	4,320	43,200	21,600	69,120
Customer-support costs				
(50,400; 441,600; 122,400) items sold × $0.20	10,080	88,320	24,480	122,880
Total costs	283,200	835,200	441,600	1,560,000
Operating income	$ 34,200	$ 5,040	$ 42,360	$ 81,600
Operating income ÷ Revenues	10.78%	0.60%	8.75%	4.97%

3. Managers believe the ABC system is more credible than the simple costing system. The ABC system distinguishes the different types of activities at FS more precisely. It also tracks more accurately how individual product lines use resources. Rankings of relative profitability—operating income as a percentage of revenues—of the three product lines under the simple costing system and under the ABC system are as follows:

Simple Costing System		ABC System	
1. Fresh produce	7.17%	1. Soft drinks	10.78%
2. Packaged food	3.30%	2. Packaged food	8.75%
3. Soft drinks	1.70%	3. Fresh produce	0.60%

The percentage of revenues, cost of goods sold, and activity costs for each product line are as follows:

	Soft Drinks	Fresh Produce	Packaged Food
Revenues	19.34%	51.18%	29.48%
Cost of goods sold	20.00	50.00	30.00
Bottle returns	100.00	0	0
Activity areas:			
Ordering	23.08	53.84	23.08
Delivery	9.53	69.52	20.95
Shelf stocking	6.25	62.50	31.25
Customer support	8.20	71.88	19.92

Soft drinks have fewer deliveries and require less shelf-stocking time and customer support than either fresh produce or packaged food. Most major soft-drink suppliers deliver merchandise to the store shelves and stock the shelves themselves. In contrast, the fresh produce area has the most deliveries and consumes a large percentage of shelf-stocking time. It also has the highest number of individual sales items and so requires the most customer support. The simple costing system assumed that each product line used the resources in each activity area in the same ratio as their respective individual cost of goods sold to total cost of goods sold. Clearly, this assumption is incorrect. Relative to cost of goods sold, soft drinks and packaged food use fewer resources, while fresh produce uses more resources. As a result, the ABC system reduces the costs assigned to soft drinks and packaged food and increases the costs assigned to fresh produce. The simple costing system is an example of averaging that is too broad.

FS managers can use the ABC information to guide decisions such as how to allocate a planned increase in floor space. An increase in the percentage of space allocated to soft drinks is warranted. Note, however, that ABC information is only one input into decisions about shelf-space allocation. In many situations, companies cannot make product decisions in isolation but must consider the effect that dropping or de-emphasizing a product might have on customer demand for other products. For example, FS will have a minimum limit on the shelf space allocated to fresh produce because reducing the choice of fresh produce will lead to customers not shopping at FS, resulting in loss of sales of other, more profitable products.

Pricing decisions can also be made in a more informed way with ABC information. For example, suppose a competitor announces a 5% reduction in soft-drink prices. Given the 10.78% margin FS currently earns on its soft-drink product line, it has flexibility to reduce prices and still make a profit on this product line. In contrast, the simple costing system erroneously implied that soft drinks only had a 1.70% margin, leaving little room to counter a competitor's pricing initiatives.

DECISION POINTS

The following question-and-answer format summarizes the chapter's learning objectives. Each decision presents a key question related to a learning objective. The guidelines are the answer to that question.

Decision	Guidelines
1. When does product undercosting or overcosting occur?	Product undercosting (overcosting) occurs when the cost measurement system produces a cost for a product that is below (above) the cost of the resources that the product consumes. Broad averaging, or peanut-butter costing, a common cause of undercosting or overcosting, is the result of using broad averages that uniformly assign, or spread, the cost of resources to products when, in fact, the individual products use those resources in a nonuniform way. Product-cost cross-subsidization means that one undercosted (overcosted) product results in at least one other product being overcosted (undercosted).
2. What are the main guidelines for refining a costing system?	Refining a costing system means making changes to better measure the costs of indirect resources used by different cost objects such as products or services. These changes can require classifying more costs as direct costs, increasing the number of indirect-cost pools so that each pool is fairly homogenous, or using cost drivers as cost-allocation bases.
3. What is the difference between the design of a simple costing system and an activity-based costing (ABC) system?	The ABC system differs from the simple system by its fundamental focus on activities. The ABC system typically has more homogeneous indirect-cost pools than the simple costing system, and more cost drivers are used as cost-allocation bases.
4. What is a cost hierarchy?	A cost hierarchy categorizes activity-cost pools on the basis of the different types of cost drivers, cost-allocation bases, or different degrees of difficulty in determining cause-and-effect (or benefits-received) relationships. ABC systems commonly use a cost hierarchy with the following four levels: output unit–level costs, batch-level costs, product-sustaining costs, and facility-sustaining costs.

Decision	Guidelines
5. How do managers cost products or services using ABC systems?	In ABC, costs of individual activities are identified and then assigned to the cost objects, such as products or services, based on the activities the products or services consume.
6. What are the main benefits and costs of implementing an ABC system?	The main benefit of an ABC system is more accurate cost information, particularly in situations where indirect costs are a high percentage of total costs and where products and services make diverse demands on indirect resources. The main costs of ABC systems are the difficulties of the measurements necessary to implement and update the systems.
7. How can ABC systems be used to manage better?	Activity-based management (ABM) is a management method of decision making that uses ABC information to satisfy customers and improve profits. ABC systems are used for such management decisions as pricing, product-mix, cost reduction, process improvement, product and process redesign, and planning and managing activities.

TERMS TO LEARN

This chapter and the Glossary at the end of this text contain definitions of the following important terms:

activity (**p. 157**)
activity-based costing (ABC) (**p. 157**)
activity-based management (ABM) (**p. 170**)
batch-level costs (**p. 160**)
cost hierarchy (**p. 159**)
facility-sustaining costs (**p. 160**)
output unit–level costs (**p. 160**)
product-cost cross-subsidization (**p. 151**)
product overcosting (**p. 150**)
product-sustaining costs (**p. 160**)
product undercosting (**p. 150**)
refined costing system (**p. 155**)
service-sustaining costs (**p. 160**)

ASSIGNMENT MATERIAL

Questions

5-1 What is broad averaging, and what consequences can it have on costs?

5-2 Why should managers worry about product overcosting or undercosting?

5-3 What is costing system refinement? Describe three guidelines for refinement.

5-4 What is an activity-based approach to designing a costing system?

5-5 Describe four levels of a cost hierarchy.

5-6 Why is it important to classify costs into a cost hierarchy?

5-7 What are the key reasons for product cost differences between simple costing systems and ABC systems?

5-8 Describe four decisions for which ABC information is useful.

5-9 What are five behavioral issues to consider in implementing ABC systems?

5-10 Describe four signs that help indicate when ABC systems are likely to provide the most benefits.

5-11 What are the main costs and limitations of implementing ABC systems?

5-12 "ABC systems only apply to manufacturing companies." Do you agree? Explain.

5-13 "Activity-based costing is the wave of the present and the future. All companies should adopt it." Do you agree? Explain.

5-14 "Increasing the number of indirect-cost pools is guaranteed to sizably increase the accuracy of product or service costs." Do you agree? Why?

5-15 The controller of a retail company has just had a $50,000 request to implement an ABC system quickly turned down. A senior vice president, in rejecting the request, noted, "Given a choice, I will always prefer a $50,000 investment in improving things a customer sees or experiences, such as our shelves or our store layout. How does a customer benefit by our spending $50,000 on a supposedly better accounting system?" How should the controller respond?

Multiple-Choice Questions

In partnership with:

BECKER PROFESSIONAL EDUCATION®

5-16 Conroe Company is reviewing the data provided by its management accounting system. Which of the following statements is/are correct?

I. A cost driver is a causal factor that increases the total cost of a cost object.
II. Cost drivers may be volume based or activity based.
III. Cost drivers are normally the largest cost in the manufacturing process.

1. I, II, and III are correct.
2. I and II only are correct.
3. I only is correct.
4. II and III only are correct.

5-17 Nobis Company uses an ABC system. Which of the following statements is/are correct with respect to ABC?

I. All cost allocation bases used in ABC systems are cost drivers.
II. ABC systems are useful in manufacturing, but not in merchandising or service industries.
III. ABC systems can eliminate cost distortions because ABC develops cost drivers that have a cause-and-effect relationship with the activities performed.

1. I, II, and III are correct.
2. II and III only are correct.
3. III only is correct.
4. None of the listed choices is correct.

Exercises

5-18 Cost hierarchy. Roberta, Inc., manufactures elliptical machines for several well-known companies. The machines differ significantly in their complexity and their manufacturing batch sizes. The following costs were incurred in 2020:

a. Indirect manufacturing labor costs such as supervision that supports direct manufacturing labor, $935,000
b. Procurement costs of placing purchase orders, receiving materials, and paying suppliers related to the number of purchase orders placed, $650,000
c. Cost of indirect materials, $234,000
d. Costs incurred to set up machines each time a different product needs to be manufactured, $392,000
e. Designing processes, drawing process charts, and making engineering process changes for products, $236,900
f. Machine-related overhead costs such as depreciation, maintenance, and production engineering, $865,000 (These resources relate to the activity of running the machines.)
g. Plant management, plant rent, and plant insurance, $498,000

Required

1. Classify each of the preceding costs as output unit–level, batch-level, product sustaining, or facility sustaining. Explain each answer.
2. Consider two types of elliptical machines made by Roberta, Inc. One machine, designed for professional use, is complex to make and is produced in many batches. The other machine, designed for home use, is simple to make and is produced in few batches. Suppose that Roberta needs the same number of machine-hours to make each type of elliptical machine and that Roberta allocates all overhead costs using machine-hours as the only allocation base. How, if at all, would the machines be miscosted? Briefly explain why.
3. How is the cost hierarchy helpful to Roberta in managing its business?

5-19 ABC, cost hierarchy, service. (CMA, adapted) Vineyard Test Laboratories does heat testing (HT) and stress testing (ST) on materials and operates at capacity. Under its current simple costing system, Vineyard aggregates all operating costs of $1,190,000 into a single overhead cost pool. Vineyard calculates a rate per test-hour of $17 ($1,190,000 ÷ 70,000 total test-hours). HT uses 40,000 test-hours, and ST uses 30,000 test-hours. Gary Celeste, Vineyard's controller, believes that there is enough variation in test procedures and cost structures to establish separate costing and billing rates for HT and ST. The market for test services is becoming competitive. Without this information, any miscosting and mispricing of its services could cause Vineyard to lose business. Celeste divides Vineyard's costs into four activity-cost categories.

a. Direct-labor costs, $146,000. These costs can be directly traced to HT, $100,000, and ST, $46,000.
b. Equipment-related costs (rent, maintenance, energy, and so on), $350,000. These costs are allocated to HT and ST on the basis of test-hours.
c. Setup costs, $430,000. These costs are allocated to HT and ST on the basis of the number of setup-hours required. HT requires 13,600 setup-hours, and ST requires 3,600 setup-hours.
d. Costs of designing tests, $264,000. These costs are allocated to HT and ST on the basis of the time required for designing the tests. HT requires 3,000 hours, and ST requires 1,400 hours.

Required

1. Classify each activity cost as output unit–level, batch-level, product or service sustaining, or facility sustaining. Explain each answer.
2. Calculate the cost per test-hour for HT and ST. Explain briefly the reasons why these numbers differ from the $17 per test-hour that Vineyard calculated using its simple costing system.
3. Explain the accuracy of the product costs calculated using the simple costing system and the ABC system. How might Vineyard's management use the cost hierarchy and ABC information to better manage its business?

5-20 Alternative allocation bases for a professional services firm. The Walliston Group (WG) provides tax advice to multinational firms. WG charges clients for (a) direct professional time (at an hourly rate) and (b) support services (at 30% of the direct professional costs billed). The three professionals in WG and their rates per professional hour are as follows:

Professional	Billing Rate per Hour
Max Walliston	$640
Alexa Boutin	220
Jacob Abbington	100

WG has just prepared the May 2020 bills for two clients. The hours of professional time spent on each client are as follows:

	Hours per Client	
Professional	San Antonio Dominion	Amsterdam Enterprises
Walliston	26	4
Boutin	5	14
Abbington	39	52
Total	70	70

Required

1. What amounts did WG bill to San Antonio Dominion and Amsterdam Enterprises for May 2020?
2. Suppose support services were billed at $75 per professional labor-hour (instead of 30% of professional labor costs). How would this change affect the amounts WG billed to the two clients for May 2020? Comment on the differences between the amounts billed in requirements 1 and 2.
3. How would you determine whether professional labor costs or professional labor-hours is the more appropriate allocation base for WG's support services?

5-21 Plantwide, department, and ABC indirect cost rates. Roadster Company (RC) designs and produces automotive parts. In 2020, actual variable manufacturing overhead is $280,000. RC's simple costing system allocates variable manufacturing overhead to its three customers based on machine-hours and prices its contracts based on full costs. One of its customers has regularly complained of being charged noncompetitive prices, so RC's controller Matthew Draper realizes that it is time to examine the consumption of overhead resources more closely. He knows that there are three main departments that consume overhead resources: design, production, and engineering. Interviews with the department personnel and examination of time records yield the following detailed information:

	A	B	C	D	E	F
1				Usage of Cost Drivers by Customer Contract		
2	Department	Cost Driver	Manufacturing Overhead in 2020	Southern Motors	Caesar Motors	Jupiter Auto
3	Design	CAD–design–hours	$ 35,000	150	250	100
4	Production	Engineering–hours	25,000	130	100	270
5	Engineering	Machine–hours	220,000	300	3,700	1,000
6	Total		$280,000			

Required

1. Compute the manufacturing overhead allocated to each customer in 2020 using the simple costing system that uses machine-hours as the allocation base.
2. Compute the manufacturing overhead allocated to each customer in 2020 using department-based manufacturing overhead rates.
3. Comment on your answers in requirements 1 and 2. Which customer do you think was complaining about being overcharged in the simple system? If the new department-based rates are used to price contracts, which customer(s) will be unhappy? How would you respond to these concerns?
4. How else might RC use the information available from its department-by-department analysis of manufacturing overhead costs?
5. RC's managers are wondering if they should further refine the department-by-department costing system into an ABC system by identifying different activities within each department. Under what conditions would it not be worthwhile to further refine the department costing system into an ABC system?

5-22 Plantwide, department, and activity-cost rates. Trendy Inc. makes two styles of trophies, basic and deluxe, and operates at capacity. Trendy does large custom orders. Trendy budgets to produce 10,000 basic trophies and 5,000 deluxe trophies. Manufacturing takes place in two production departments: forming and assembly. In the forming department, indirect manufacturing costs are accumulated in two cost pools, setup and general overhead. In the assembly department, all indirect manufacturing costs are accumulated in one general overhead cost pool. The basic trophies are formed in batches of 200 but because of the more intricate detail of the deluxe trophies, they are formed in batches of 50.

The controller has asked you to compare plantwide, department, and activity-based cost allocation.

Trendy Budgeted Information for the Year Ended November 30, 2020

Forming Department	Basic	Deluxe	Total
Direct materials	$25,000	$19,800	$44,800
Direct manufacturing labor	24,000	25,000	49,000
Overhead costs			
Setup			36,750
General overhead			31,850

Assembly Department	Basic	Deluxe	Total
Direct materials	$ 5,000	$ 4,450	$ 9,450
Direct manufacturing labor	15,500	19,500	35,000
Overhead costs			
General overhead			42,000

Required

1. Calculate the budgeted unit cost of basic and deluxe trophies based on a single plantwide overhead rate, if total overhead is allocated based on total direct costs. (Don't forget to include direct material and direct manufacturing labor cost in your unit cost calculation.)
2. Calculate the budgeted unit cost of basic and deluxe trophies based on departmental overhead rates, where forming department overhead costs are allocated based on direct manufacturing labor costs of the forming department and assembly department overhead costs are allocated based on total direct manufacturing labor costs of the assembly department.
3. Calculate the budgeted unit cost of basic and deluxe trophies if Trendy allocates overhead costs in each department using activity-based costing, where setup costs are allocated based on number of batches and general overhead costs for each department are allocated based on direct manufacturing labor costs of each department.
4. Explain briefly why plantwide, department, and activity-based costing systems show different costs for the basic and deluxe trophies. Which system would you recommend and why?

5-23 ABC, process costing. Walsh Company produces mathematical and financial calculators and operates at capacity. Data related to the two products are presented here:

	Mathematical	Financial
Annual production in units	25,000	50,000
Direct material costs	$75,000	$150,000
Direct manufacturing labor costs	$25,000	$ 50,000
Direct manufacturing labor-hours	1,250	2,500
Machine-hours	40,000	70,000
Number of production runs	50	50
Inspection-hours	1,200	800

Total manufacturing overhead costs are as follows:

	Total
Machining costs	$440,000
Setup costs	110,000
Inspection costs	120,000

Required

1. Choose a cost driver for each overhead cost pool and calculate the manufacturing overhead cost per unit for each product.
2. Compute the manufacturing cost per unit for each product.
3. How might Walsh's managers use the new cost information from its activity-based costing system to better manage its business?

5-24 Department costing, service company. DLN is an architectural firm that designs and builds buildings. It prices each job on a cost plus 20% basis. Overhead costs in 2020 are $8,100,000. DLN's simple costing system allocates overhead costs to its jobs based on number of jobs. There were three jobs in 2020. One customer, Chandler, has complained that the cost and price of its building in Chicago was not competitive. As a result, the controller has initiated a detailed review of the overhead allocation to determine whether overhead costs should be charged to jobs in proportion to consumption of overhead resources by jobs. She gathers the following information:

			Quantity of Cost Drivers Used by Each Project		
Department	Cost Driver	Overhead Costs in 2020	Chandler	Henry	Manley
Design	Design department hours	$3,000,000	2,000	10,000	8,000
Engineering	Number of engineering hours	1,000,000	4,000	4,000	4,500
Construction	Labor-hours	4,100,000	29,000	27,000	26,000
		$8,100,000			

Required

1. Compute the overhead allocated to each project in 2020 using the simple costing system that allocates overhead costs to jobs based on the number of jobs.
2. Compute the overhead allocated to each project in 2020 using department overhead cost rates.
3. Do you think Chandler had a valid reason for dissatisfaction with the cost and price of its building? How does the allocation based on department rates change costs for each project?
4. What value, if any, would DLN get by allocating costs of each department based on the activities done in that department?

5-25 Activity-based costing, service company. Aniline Corporation owns a small printing press that prints leaflets, brochures, and advertising materials. Aniline classifies its various printing jobs as standard jobs or special jobs. Aniline's simple job-costing system has two direct-cost categories (direct materials and direct labor) and a single indirect-cost pool. Aniline operates at capacity and allocates all indirect costs using printing machine-hours as the allocation base.

Aniline is concerned about the accuracy of the costs assigned to standard and special jobs and therefore is planning to implement an activity-based costing system. Aniline's ABC system would have the same direct-cost categories as its simple costing system. However, instead of a single indirect-cost pool, there would now be six categories for assigning indirect costs: design, purchasing, setup, printing machine operations, marketing, and administration. To see how activity-based costing would affect the costs of standard and special jobs, Aniline collects the following information for the fiscal year 2020 that just ended.

Home Insert Page Layout Formulas Data Review View

	A	B	C	D	E	F	G	H
1		Standard Job	Special Job	Total	Cause-and-Effect Relationship Between Allocation Base and Activity Cost			
2	Number of printing jobs	2,400	1,200					
3	Price per job	$ 1,700	$ 2,000					
4	Cost of supplies per job	$ 210	$ 310					
5	Direct labor costs per job	$ 170	$ 220					
6	Printing machine-hours per job	10	10					
7	Cost of printing machine operations			$ 1,008,000	Indirect costs of operating printing machines			
8					increase with printing machine-hours			
9	Setup-hours per job	6	9					
10	Setup costs			$ 781,200	Indirect setup costs increase with setup-hours			
11	Total number of purchase orders	330	430					
12	Purchase order costs			$ 27,360	Indirect purchase order costs			
13					increase with number of purchase orders			
14	Design costs	$ 7,000	$ 35,000	$ 42,000	Design costs are allocated to standard and special			
15					jobs based on a special study of the design department			
16	Marketing costs as a percentage of revenues	4%	4%	$ 259,200				
17	Administration costs			$ 309,120	Demand for administrative resources increases with direct labor costs			

Required

1. Calculate the cost of a standard job and a special job under the simple costing system.
2. Calculate the cost of a standard job and a special job under the activity-based costing system.
3. Compare the costs of a standard job and a special job in requirements 1 and 2. Why do the simple and activity-based costing systems differ in the cost of a standard job and a special job?
4. How might Aniline use the new cost information from its activity-based costing system to better manage its business?

5-26 Activity-based costing, manufacturing. Decorative Doors, Inc., produces two types of doors, interior and exterior. The company's simple costing system has two direct-cost categories (materials and labor) and one indirect-cost pool. The simple costing system allocates indirect costs on the basis of machine-hours. Recently, the owners of Decorative Doors have been concerned about a decline in the market share for their interior doors, usually their biggest seller. Information related to Decorative Doors production for the most recent year follows:

	Interior	Exterior
Units sold	3,200	1,800
Selling price	$ 125	$ 200
Direct material cost per unit	$ 30	$ 45
Direct manufacturing labor cost per hour	$ 16	$ 16
Direct manufacturing labor-hours per unit	1.50	2.25
Production runs	40	85
Material moves	72	168
Machine setups	45	155
Machine-hours	5,500	4,500
Number of inspections	250	150

The owners have heard of other companies in the industry that are now using an activity-based costing system and are curious how an ABC system would affect their product costing decisions. After analyzing the indirect-cost pool for Decorative Doors, the owners identify six activities as generating indirect costs: production scheduling, material handling, machine setup, assembly, inspection, and marketing. Decorative Doors collected the following data related to the indirect-cost activities:

Activity	Activity Cost	Activity-Cost Driver
Production scheduling	$95,000	Production runs
Material handling	$45,000	Material moves
Machine setup	$25,000	Machine setups
Assembly	$60,000	Machine-hours
Inspection	$ 8,000	Number of inspections

Marketing costs were determined to be 3% of the sales revenue for each type of door.

Required

1. Calculate the cost of an interior door and an exterior door under the existing simple costing system.
2. Calculate the cost of an interior door and an exterior door under an activity-based costing system.
3. Compare the costs of the doors in requirements 1 and 2. Why do the simple and activity-based costing systems differ in the cost of an interior door and an exterior door?
4. How might Decorative Doors, Inc., use the new cost information from its activity-based costing system to address the declining market share for interior doors?

5-27 ABC, retail product-line profitability. Fitzgerald Supermarkets operates at capacity and decides to apply ABC analysis to three product lines: baked goods, milk and fruit juice, and frozen foods. It identifies four activities and their activity-cost rates as follows:

Ordering	$95 per purchase order
Delivery and receipt of merchandise	$76 per delivery
Shelf stocking	$19 per hour
Customer support and assistance	$0.15 per item sold

The revenues, cost of goods sold, store support costs, activities that account for the store support costs, and activity-area usage of the three product lines are as follows:

	Baked Goods	Milk and Fruit Juice	Frozen Foods
Financial data			
Revenues	$60,000	$66,500	$50,500
Cost of goods sold	$41,000	$51,000	$32,000
Store support	$12,300	$15,300	$ 9,600
Activity-area usage (cost-allocation base)			
Ordering (purchase orders)	44	24	14
Delivery (deliveries)	120	60	36
Shelf stocking (hours)	170	150	20
Customer support (items sold)	15,400	20,200	7,960

Under its simple costing system, Fitzgerald Supermarkets allocated support costs to products at the rate of 30% of cost of goods sold.

Required

1. Use the simple costing system to prepare a product-line profitability report for Fitzgerald Supermarkets.
2. Use the ABC system to prepare a product-line profitability report for Fitzgerald Supermarkets.
3. What new insights does the ABC system in requirement 2 provide to Fitzgerald Supermarkets managers?

5-28 ABC, wholesale, customer profitability. Ruiz Wholesalers operates at capacity and sells furniture items to four department-store chains (customers). Mr. Ruiz commented, "We apply ABC to determine product-line profitability. The same ideas apply to customer profitability, and we should find out our customer profitability as well." Ruiz Wholesalers sends catalogs to corporate purchasing departments on a monthly basis. The customers are entitled to return unsold merchandise within a 6-month period from the purchase date and receive a full purchase price refund. The following data were collected from last year's operations:

	Chain			
	1	2	3	4
Gross sales	$45,000	$35,000	$120,000	$80,000
Sales returns:				
Number of items	107	41	55	51
Amount	$ 9,000	$ 5,500	$ 8,400	$ 7,000
Number of orders:				
Regular	35	155	60	80
Rush	9	52	15	35

Ruiz has calculated the following activity rates:

Activity	Cost-Driver Rate
Regular order processing	$22 per regular order
Rush order processing	$110 per rush order
Returned items processing	$10 per item
Catalogs and customer support	$1,400 per customer

Customers pay the transportation costs. The cost of goods sold averages 80% of net sales.

Required

Determine the contribution to profit from each customer last year. Comment on your solution.

5-29 Activity-based costing. The job-costing system at Shirley's Custom Framing has five indirect-cost pools (purchasing, material handling, machine maintenance, product inspection, and packaging). The company is in the process of bidding on two jobs: Job 215, an order of 16 intricate personalized frames, and Job 325, an order of six standard personalized frames. The controller wants you to compare overhead allocated under the current simple job-costing system and a newly designed activity-based job-costing system. Total budgeted costs in each indirect-cost pool and the budgeted quantity of each activity driver are as follows.

	Budgeted Overhead	Activity Driver	Budgeted Quantity of Activity Driver
Purchasing	$ 25,600	Purchase orders processed	1,600
Material handling	32,900	Material moves	4,700
Machine maintenance	150,000	Machine-hours	10,000
Product inspection	11,200	Inspections	1,600
Packaging	12,400	Units produced	3,100
	$232,100		

Information related to Job 215 and Job 325 follows. Job 215 incurs more batch-level costs because it uses more types of materials that need to be purchased, moved, and inspected relative to Job 325.

	Job 215	Job 325
Number of purchase orders	26	5
Number of material moves	14	3
Machine-hours	20	80
Number of inspections	12	5
Units produced	16	6

Required

1. Compute the total overhead allocated to each job under a simple costing system, where overhead is allocated based on machine-hours.
2. Compute the total overhead allocated to each job under an activity-based costing system using the appropriate activity drivers.
3. Explain why Shirley's Custom Framing might favor the ABC job-costing system over the simple job-costing system, especially in its bidding process.

5-30 ABC, product costing at banks, cross-subsidization. United Savings Bank (USB) is examining the profitability of its Premier Account, a combined savings and checking account. Depositors receive a 2% annual interest rate on their average deposit. USB earns an interest rate spread of 3% (the difference between the rate at which it lends money and the rate it pays depositors) by lending money for home-loan purposes at 5%. Thus, USB would gain $60 on the interest spread if a depositor had an average Premier Account balance of $2,000 in 2020 ($\$2,000 \times 3\% = \$60$).

The Premier Account allows depositors unlimited use of services such as deposits, withdrawals, checking accounts, and foreign currency drafts. Depositors with Premier Account balances of $1,000 or more receive unlimited free use of services. Depositors with minimum balances of less than $1,000 pay a $22-a-month service fee for their Premier Account.

USB recently conducted an activity-based costing study of its services. It assessed the following costs for six individual services. The use of these services in 2020 by three customers is as follows:

	Activity-Based Cost per "Transaction"	Account Usage		
		Lindell	Welker	Colston
Deposit/withdrawal with teller	$ 2.50	44	49	4
Deposit/withdrawal with automatic teller machine (ATM)	0.80	12	24	13
Deposit/withdrawal on prearranged monthly basis	0.50	0	14	58
Bank checks written	8.20	8	2	3
Foreign currency drafts	12.10	6	1	5
Inquiries about account balance	1.70	7	16	6
Average Premier Account balance for 2020		$1,200	$700	$24,900

Assume Lindell and Colston always maintain a balance above $1,000, whereas Welker always has a balance below $1,000.

Required

1. Compute the 2020 profitability of the Lindell, Welker, and Colston Premier Accounts at USB.
2. Why might USB worry about the profitability of individual customers if the Premier Account product offering is profitable as a whole?
3. What changes would you recommend for USB's Premier Account?

Problems

5-31 Job costing with single direct-cost category, single indirect-cost pool, law firm. Timlin Associates is a recently formed law partnership. Rachel Hamilton, the managing partner of Timlin Associates, has just finished a tense phone call with Phil Lopez, president of Lopez Enterprises. Phil strongly complained about the price Timlin charged for some legal work done for his company.

Hamilton also received a phone call from Timlin's only other client, Clinical Inc., which was very pleased with both the quality of the work and the price charged on its most recent job.

Timlin Associates operates at capacity and uses a cost-based approach to pricing (billing) each job. Currently it uses a simple costing system with a single direct-cost category (professional labor-hours) and a single indirect-cost pool (general support). Indirect costs are allocated to cases on the basis of professional labor-hours per case. The job files show the following:

	Lopez Enterprises	Clinical Inc.
Professional labor	2,500 hours	2,500 hours

Professional labor costs at Timlin Associates are $250 an hour. Indirect costs are allocated to cases at $125 an hour. Total indirect costs in the most recent period were $625,000.

Required

1. Why is it important for Timlin Associates to understand the costs associated with individual jobs?
2. Compute the costs of the Lopez Enterprises and Clinical Inc. jobs using Timlin's simple costing system.

5-32 Job costing with multiple direct-cost categories, single indirect-cost pool, law firm (continuation of 5-31). Rachel Hamilton, the managing partner of Timlin Associates, asks her assistant to collect details on those costs included in the $625,000 indirect-cost pool that can be traced to each individual job. After analysis, Timlin is able to reclassify $450,000 of the $625,000 as direct costs:

Other Direct Costs	Lopez Enterprises	Clinical Inc.
Research support labor	$41,000	$232,500
Computer time	4,000	31,000
Travel and allowances	14,000	81,000
Telephones/faxes	4,500	21,000
Photocopying	6,500	14,500
Total	$70,000	$380,000

Hamilton decides to calculate the costs of each job as if Timlin had used six direct-cost pools and a single indirect-cost pool. The single indirect-cost pool would have $175,000 of costs and would be allocated to each case using the professional labor-hours base.

Required

1. Calculate the revised indirect-cost allocation rate per professional labor-hour for Timlin Associates when total indirect costs are $175,000.
2. Compute the costs of the Lopez Enterprises and Clinical Inc. jobs if Timlin Associates had used its refined costing system with multiple direct-cost categories and one indirect-cost pool.
3. Compare the costs of Lopez Enterprises and Clinical Inc. jobs in requirement 2 with those calculated using the simple costing system. Comment on the results.

5-33 Job costing with multiple direct-cost categories, multiple indirect-cost pools, law firm (continuation of 5-31 and 5-32). Timlin has two classifications of professional staff: partners and associates. Hamilton asks her assistant to examine the relative use of partners and associates on the recent Lopez Enterprises and Clinical Inc. jobs. The Lopez Enterprises job used 1,400 partner-hours and 1,100 associate-hours. The Clinical Inc. job used 1,100 partner-hours and 1,400 associate-hours. Therefore, totals of the two jobs together were 2,500 partner-hours and 2,500 associate-hours. Hamilton decides to examine how using separate direct-cost rates for partners and associates and using separate indirect-cost pools for partners and associates would have affected the costs of the Lopez Enterprises and Clinical Inc. jobs. Indirect costs in each indirect-cost pool would be allocated on the basis of total hours of that category of professional labor. From the total indirect-cost pool of $175,000, $100,000 is attributable to the activities of partners and $75,000 is attributable to the activities of associates.

The rates per category of professional labor are as follows:

Category of Professional Labor	Direct Cost per Hour	Indirect Cost per Hour
Partner	$200	$100,000 ÷ 2,500 hours = $40
Associate	$150	$ 75,000 ÷ 2,500 hours = $30

Required

1. Compute the costs of the Lopez Enterprises and Clinical Inc. jobs using Timlin's further refined system, with multiple direct-cost categories and multiple indirect-cost pools.
2. For what decisions might Timlin Associates find it more useful to use this job-costing approach rather than the approaches of a simple costing system or a refined costing system with multiple direct-cost categories and one indirect-cost pool?

5-34 First-stage allocation, time-driven activity-based costing, manufacturing sector. Marshall Devices manufactures metal products and uses activity-based costing to allocate overhead costs to customer orders for pricing purposes. Many customer orders are won through competitive bidding based on costs. Direct material and direct manufacturing labor costs are traced directly to each order. Marshall's direct manufacturing labor rate is $20 per hour. The company reports the following budgeted yearly overhead costs:

Wages and salaries	$480,000
Depreciation	60,000
Rent	120,000
Other overhead	240,000
Total overhead costs	$900,000

Marshall has established four activity-cost pools and the following budgeted activity for each cost pool:

Activity-Cost Pool	Activity Measure	Budgeted Total Activity for the Year
Direct manufacturing labor support	Number of direct manufacturing labor-hours	30,000 direct manufacturing labor-hours
Order processing	Number of customer orders	500 orders
Design support	Number of custom design-hours	2,490 custom design-hours
Other	Facility-sustaining costs allocated to orders based on direct manufacturing labor-hours	30,000 direct manufacturing labor-hours

Some customer orders require more complex designs, while others need simple designs. Marshall estimates that it will do 120 complex designs during a year, which will each take 11.75 hours for a total of 1,410 design-hours. It estimates it will do 180 simple designs, which will each take 6 hours for a total of 1,080 design-hours.

Paul Napoli, Marshall's controller, has prepared the following estimates for distribution of the overhead costs across the four activity-cost pools:

	Direct Manufacturing Labor Support	Order Processing	Design Support	Other	Total
Wages and salaries	40%	25%	30%	5%	100%
Depreciation	25%	10%	15%	50%	100%
Rent	30%	25%	10%	35%	100%
Other overhead	20%	30%	35%	15%	100%

Order 277100 consists of four different metal products. Three products require a complex design and one requires a simple design. Order 277100 requires $4,550 of direct materials and 80 direct manufacturing labor-hours.

Required

1. Allocate the overhead costs to each activity-cost pool. Calculate the activity rate for each pool.
2. Determine the cost of Order 277100.
3. How does activity-based costing enhance Marshall's ability to price its orders? Suppose Marshall used a simple costing system to allocate all overhead costs to orders on the basis of direct manufacturing labor-hours. How might this have affected Marshall's pricing decision for Order 227100?
4. When designing its activity-based costing system, Marshall uses time-driven activity-based costing (TDABC) for its design department. What does this approach allow Marshall to do? How would the cost of Order 277100 have been different if Marshall had used the number of customer designs rather than the number of custom design-hours to allocate costs to different customer orders? Which cost driver do you prefer for design support? Why?

5-35 First-stage allocation, time-driven activity-based costing, service sector. LawnCare USA provides lawn care and landscaping services to commercial clients. LawnCare USA uses activity-based costing to bid on jobs and to evaluate their profitability. LawnCare USA reports the following budgeted annual costs:

Wages and salaries	$360,000
Depreciation	72,000
Supplies	120,000
Other overhead	288,000
Total overhead costs	$840,000

John Gilroy, controller of LawnCare USA, has established four activity-cost pools and the following budgeted activity for each cost pool:

Activity-Cost Pool	Activity Measure	Total Activity for the Year
Estimating jobs	Number of job estimates	250 estimates
Lawn care	Number of direct labor-hours	10,000 direct labor-hours
Landscape design	Number of design hours	500 design hours
Other	Facility-sustaining costs that are not allocated to jobs	Not applicable

Gilroy estimates that LawnCare USA's costs are distributed to the activity-cost pools as follows:

	Estimating Jobs	Lawn Care	Landscape Design	Other	Total
Wages and salaries	5%	70%	15%	10%	100%
Depreciation	10%	65%	10%	15%	100%
Supplies	0%	100%	0%	0%	100%
Other overhead	15%	50%	20%	15%	100%

Sunset Office Park, a new development in a nearby community, has contacted LawnCare USA to provide an estimate on landscape design and annual lawn maintenance. The job is estimated to require a single landscape design requiring 40 design hours in total and 250 direct labor-hours annually. LawnCare USA has a policy of pricing estimates at 150% of cost.

Required

1. Allocate LawnCare USA's costs to the activity-cost pools and determine the activity rate for each pool.
2. Estimate total cost for the Sunset Office Park job. How much would LawnCare USA bid to perform the job?
3. LawnCare USA does 30 landscape designs for its customers each year. Estimate the total cost for the Sunset Office park job if LawnCare USA allocated costs of the Landscape Design activity based on the number of landscape designs rather than the number of landscape design-hours. How much would LawnCare USA bid to perform the job? Which cost driver do you prefer for the Landscape Design activity? Why?
4. Sunset Office Park asks LawnCare USA to give an estimate for providing its services for a 2-year period. What are the advantages and disadvantages for LawnCare USA to provide a 2-year estimate?

5-36 Department and activity-cost rates, service sector. Raynham's Radiology Center (RRC) performs X-rays, ultrasounds, computer tomography (CT) scans, and magnetic resonance imaging (MRI). RRC has developed a reputation as a top radiology center in the state. RRC has achieved this status because it constantly reexamines its processes and procedures. RRC has been using a single, facilitywide overhead allocation rate. The vice president of finance believes that RRC can make better process improvements if it uses more disaggregated cost information. She says, "We have state-of-the-art medical imaging technology. Can't we have state-of-the-art accounting technology?"

Raynham's Radiology Center Budgeted Information for the Year Ended May 31, 2020

	X-rays	Ultrasound	CT Scan	MRI	Total
Technician labor	$ 62,000	$101,000	$155,000	$ 103,000	$ 421,000
Depreciation	42,240	256,000	424,960	876,800	1,600,000
Materials	22,600	16,400	23,600	31,500	94,100
Administration					20,000
Maintenance					250,000
Sanitation					252,500
Utilities					151,100
	$126,840	$373,400	$603,560	$1,011,300	$2,788,700
Number of procedures	3,842	4,352	2,924	2,482	
Minutes to clean after each procedure	5	5	15	35	
Minutes for each procedure	5	15	25	40	

RRC operates at capacity. The proposed allocation bases for overhead are:

Administration	Number of procedures
Maintenance (including parts)	Capital cost of the equipment (use Depreciation)
Sanitation	Total cleaning minutes
Utilities	Total procedure minutes

Required

1. Calculate the budgeted cost per service for X-rays, ultrasounds, CT scans, and MRI using direct technician labor costs as the allocation basis.
2. Calculate the budgeted cost per service of X-rays, ultrasounds, CT scans, and MRI if RRC allocated overhead costs using activity-based costing.
3. Explain how the disaggregation of information could be helpful to RRC's intention to continuously improve its services.

5-37 Activity-based costing, merchandising. Pharmassist, Inc., a distributor of special pharmaceutical products, operates at capacity and has three main market segments:

a. General supermarket chains
b. Drugstore chains
c. Mom-and-pop single-store pharmacies

Rick Flair, the new controller of Pharmassist, reported the following data for 2020.

	A	B	C	D	E
1					
2	Pharmassist, 2020	General			
3		Supermarket	Drugstore	Mom-and-Pop	Total for
4		Chains	Chains	Single Stores	Pharmassist
5	Revenues	$3,704,000	$3,145,000	$1,988,000	$8,837,000
6	Cost of goods sold	3,612,000	2,990,000	1,804,000	8,406,000
7	Gross margin	$ 92,000	$ 155,000	$ 184,000	431,000
8	Other operating costs				313,075
9	Operating income				$ 117,925

For many years, Pharmassist has used gross margin percentage to evaluate the relative profitability of its market segments. But Flair recently attended a seminar on activity-based costing and is considering using it at Pharmassist to analyze and allocate "other operating costs." He meets with all the key managers and several of his operations and sales staff, and they agree that there are five key activities that drive other operating costs at Pharmassist:

Activity Area	Cost Driver
Order processing	Number of customer purchase orders
Line-item processing	Number of line items ordered by customers
Delivering to stores	Number of store deliveries
Cartons shipped to store	Number of cartons shipped
Stocking of customer store shelves	Hours of shelf stocking

Each customer order consists of one or more line items. A line item represents a single product (such as Extra-Strength Tylenol Tablets). Each product line item is delivered in one or more separate cartons. Each store delivery entails the delivery of one or more cartons of products to a customer. Pharmassist's staff stacks cartons directly onto display shelves in customers' stores. Currently, there is no additional charge to the customer for shelf stocking and not all customers use Pharmassist for this activity. The level of each activity in the three market segments and the total cost incurred for each activity in 2020 is as follows:

	A	B	C	D	E
13					
14	**Activity-Based Cost Data**		**Activity Level**		
15	**Pharmassist, 2020**	**General**			**Total Cost**
16		**Supermarket**	**Drugstore**	**Mom-and-Pop**	**of Activity**
17	**Activity**	**Chains**	**Chains**	**Single Stores**	**in 2020**
18	Orders processed (number)	200	500	1,800	$ 87,500
19	Line-items ordered (number)	2,100	4,800	15,600	67,500
20	Store deliveries made (number)	110	280	990	67,620
21	Cartons shipped to stores (number)	34,000	23,000	23,000	80,000
22	Shelf stocking (hours)	310	210	95	10,455
23					$313,075

Required

1. Compute the 2020 gross-margin percentage for each of Pharmassist's three market segments.
2. Compute the cost driver rates for each of the five activity areas.
3. Use the activity-based costing information to allocate the $313,075 of "other operating costs" to each of the market segments. Compute the operating income for each market segment.
4. Comment on the results. What new insights are available with the activity-based costing information?

5-38 Choosing cost drivers, activity-based costing, activity-based management. Pastel Bags (PB) is a designer of high-quality backpacks and purses. Each design is made in small batches. Each spring, PB comes out with new designs for the backpack and the purse. The company uses these designs for a year and then moves on to the next trend. The bags are all made on the same fabrication equipment that is expected to operate at capacity. The equipment must be switched over to a new design and set up to prepare for the production of each new batch of products. When completed, each batch of products is immediately shipped to a wholesaler. Shipping costs vary with the number of shipments. Budgeted information for the year is as follows:

Pastel Bags
Budget for Costs and Activities
for the Year Ended February 29, 2020

Direct materials—purses	$ 319,155
Direct materials—backpacks	454,995
Direct manufacturing labor—purses	99,000
Direct manufacturing labor—backpacks	113,000
Setup	64,000
Shipping	73,000
Design	169,000
Plant utilities and administration	221,000
Total	$1,513,150

Other budget information follows:

	Backpacks	Purses	Total
Number of bags	6,175	3,075	9,250
Hours of production	1,665	2,585	4,250
Number of batches	120	80	200
Number of designs	2	2	4

Required

1. Identify the cost hierarchy level for each cost category.
2. Identify the most appropriate cost driver for each cost category. Explain briefly your choice of cost driver.
3. Calculate the budgeted cost per unit of cost driver for each cost category.
4. Calculate the budgeted total costs and cost per unit for each product line.
5. Explain how you could use the information in requirement 4 to reduce costs.

5-39 ABC, health care. Phoenix Medical Associates operates a walk-in medical clinic in Tempe, Arizona. The clinic includes two different departments, Urgent Care, which serves patients with minor to moderate acute illnesses and injuries, and Living Well, which administers vaccines, school and work physicals, and conducts workshops on healthy living topics. The center's budget for 2020 follows.

Professional salaries:		
4 physicians × $200,000	$800,000	
2 X-ray technicians × $50,000	100,000	
12 nurses × $60,000	720,000	
1 nutritionist × $50,000	50,000	$1,670,000
Medical supplies		600,000
Rent and clinic maintenance		180,000
Laboratory services		216,000
General overhead, including administrative staff		540,000
Total		$3,206,000

Anita Alvarez, the director of the clinic, is keen on determining the cost of each department. Alvarez compiles the following data describing employee allocations to individual departments:

	Urgent Care	Living Well	Total
Physicians	3	1	4
X-ray technicians	2		2
Nurses	7	5	12
Nutritionist		1	1

Alvarez has recently become aware of activity-based costing as a method to refine costing systems. She asks her accountant, David Burke, how she should apply this technique. Burke obtains the following budgeted information for 2020:

	Urgent Care	Living Well	Total
Square feet of clinic space	6,000	10,000	16,000
Patient visits	17,500	22,500	40,000
Number of laboratory tests	15,000	3,000	18,000

Required

1. a. Selecting cost-allocation bases that you believe are the most appropriate for allocating indirect costs to departments, calculate the budgeted indirect cost rates for medical supplies, rent and clinic maintenance, laboratory services, and general overhead.
   b. Using an activity-based costing approach to cost analysis, calculate the budgeted cost of each department and the budgeted cost per patient visit of each department.
   c. What benefits can Phoenix Medical Associates obtain by implementing the ABC system?
2. What factors, other than cost, do you think Phoenix Medical Associates should consider in allocating resources to its departments?

5-40 Unused capacity, activity-based costing, activity-based management. Zarson's Netballs is a manufacturer of high-quality basketballs and volleyballs. Setup costs are driven by the number of setups. Equipment and maintenance costs increase with the number of machine-hours, and lease rent is paid per square foot. Capacity of the facility is 14,000 square feet, and Zarson is using only 80% of this capacity. Zarson records the cost of unused capacity as a separate line item and not as a product cost. The following is the budgeted information for Zarson:

Zarson's Netballs
Budgeted Costs and Activities
for the Year Ended December 31, 2020

Direct materials—basketballs	$ 168,100
Direct materials—volleyballs	303,280
Direct manufacturing labor—basketballs	111,800
Direct manufacturing labor—volleyballs	100,820
Setup	157,500
Equipment and maintenance costs	115,200
Lease rent	210,000
Total	$1,166,700

Other budget information follows:

	Basketballs	Volleyballs
Number of balls	58,000	85,000
Machine-hours	13,500	10,500
Number of setups	450	300
Square footage of production space used	3,200	8,000

Required

1. Calculate the budgeted cost per unit of cost driver for each indirect-cost pool.
2. What is the budgeted cost of unused capacity?
3. What is the budgeted total cost and the cost per unit of resources used to produce (a) basketballs and (b) volleyballs?
4. Why might excess capacity be beneficial for Zarson? What are some of the issues Zarson should consider before increasing production to use the space?

5-41 Unused capacity, activity-based costing, activity-based management. Huntington Boards manufactures two models of surfboards, Basic and Competition, in a facility in Southern California. In fabrication, machine setup costs are driven by the number of setups, and machine maintenance and utility costs increase with the number of machine hours, and indirect labor costs increase with direct labor hours. Facility rent and machine depreciation are fixed, and are the basis of manufacturing capacity. Fixed costs are allocated equally to each unit produced, regardless of model. Currently, Huntington uses 80% of its manufacturing capacity. The cost of unused capacity is not assigned to products, but is expensed as a separate line item. For 2020, Huntington has budgeted the following:

Huntington Boards
Budgeted Costs for the
Year Ended December 31, 2020

Direct materials—Basic boards	$260,000
Direct materials—Competition boards	450,000
Direct manufacturing labor—Basic boards	307,500
Direct manufacturing labor—Competition boards	512,500
Machine setup costs	90,000
Machine maintenance and utility costs	251,100
Indirect labor costs	330,000
Facility rent	254,000
Machine depreciation	63,500

Other information:

	Basic	Competition
Units produced	5,200	7,500
Machine hours	31,200	52,500
Number of setups	400	800
Direct labor-hours	15,000	25,000

Required

1. Calculate the cost-allocation rate for each of the activity-cost pools for variable and fixed overhead costs.
2. Calculate the cost of unused capacity for the year.
3. Calculate the total cost for each model, and the cost per unit for each model.
4. Huntington has the opportunity to sublease the unused factory space to a startup company that will be manufacturing surf apparel. None of Huntington's machinery will be used. Is there a minimum annual rent that Huntington should charge? Are there any other considerations that Huntington's management should make prior to offering the space?

5-42 ABC, implementation, ethics. (CMA, adapted) Plum Electronics, a division of Berry Corporation, manufactures two large-screen television models: the Mammoth, which has been produced since 2016 and sells for $990, and the Maximum, a newer model introduced in early 2018 that sells for $1,254. Based on the following income statement for the year ended November 30, 2020, senior management at Berry have decided to concentrate Plum's marketing resources on the Maximum model and to begin to phase out the Mammoth model because Maximum generates much higher operating income per unit.

Plum Electronics
Income Statement for the
Fiscal Year Ended November 30, 2020

	Mammoth	Maximum	Total
Revenues	$21,780,000	$5,016,000	$26,796,000
Cost of goods sold	13,794,000	3,511,200	17,305,200
Gross margin	7,986,000	1,504,800	9,490,800
Selling and administrative expense	6,413,000	1,075,800	7,488,800
Operating income	$ 1,573,000	$ 429,000	$ 2,002,000
Units produced and sold	22,000	4,000	
Operating income per unit sold	$ 71.50	$ 107.25	

Details for cost of goods sold for Mammoth and Maximum are as follows:

	Mammoth		Maximum	
	Total	Per Unit	Total	Per Unit
Direct materials	$ 5,033,600	$ 228.80	$2,569,600	$642.40
Direct manufacturing labor[a]	435,600	19.80	184,800	46.20
Machine costs[b]	3,484,800	158.40	316,800	79.20
Total direct costs	$ 8,954,000	$ 407.00	$3,071,200	$767.80
Manufacturing overhead costs[c]	$ 4,840,000	$ 220.00	$ 440,000	$110.00
Total cost of goods sold	$13,794,000	$ 627.00	$3,511,200	$877.80

[a] Mammoth requires 1.5 hours per unit and Maximum requires 3.5 hours per unit. The direct manufacturing labor cost is $13.20 per hour.
[b] Machine costs include lease costs of the machine, repairs, and maintenance. Mammoth requires 8 machine-hours per unit and Maximum requires 4 machine-hours per unit. The machine-hour rate is $19.80 per hour.
[c] Manufacturing overhead costs are allocated to products based on machine-hours at the rate of $27.50 per hour.

Plum's controller, Steve Jacobs, is advocating the use of activity-based costing and activity-based management and has gathered the following information about the company's manufacturing overhead costs for the year ended November 30, 2020.

		Units of the Cost-Allocation Base		
Activity Center (Cost-Allocation Base)	**Total Activity Costs**	**Mammoth**	**Maximum**	**Total**
Soldering (number of solder points)	$1,036,200	1,185,000	385,000	1,570,000
Shipments (number of shipments)	946,000	16,200	3,800	20,000
Quality control (number of inspections)	1,364,000	56,200	21,300	77,500
Purchase orders (number of orders)	1,045,440	80,100	109,980	190,080
Machine power (machine-hours)	63,360	176,000	16,000	192,000
Machine setups (number of setups)	825,000	16,000	14,000	30,000
Total manufacturing overhead	$5,280,000			

After completing his analysis, Jacobs shows the results to Charles Clark, the Plum division president. Clark does not like what he sees. "If you show headquarters this analysis, they are going to ask us to phase out the Maximum line, which we have just introduced. This whole costing stuff has been a major problem for us. First Mammoth was not profitable and now Maximum isn't.

"Looking at the ABC analysis, I see two problems. First, we do many more activities than the ones you have listed. If you had included all activities, maybe your conclusions would be different. Second, you used number of setups and number of inspections as allocation bases. The numbers would be different had you used setup-hours and inspection-hours instead. I know that measurement problems precluded you from using these other cost-allocation bases, but I believe you ought to make some adjustments to our current numbers to compensate for these issues. I know you can do better. We can't afford to phase out either product."

Jacobs knows that his numbers are fairly accurate. As a quick check, he calculates the profitability of Maximum and Mammoth using more and different allocation bases. The set of activities and activity rates he had used results in numbers that closely approximate those based on more detailed analyses. He is confident that headquarters, knowing that Maximum was introduced only recently, will not ask Plum to phase it out. He is also aware that a sizable portion of Clark's bonus is based on division revenues. Phasing out either product would adversely affect his bonus. Still, he feels some pressure from Clark to do something.

Required

1. Using activity-based costing, calculate the gross margin per unit of the Maximum and Mammoth models.
2. Explain briefly why these numbers differ from the gross margin per unit of the Maximum and Mammoth models calculated using Plum's existing simple costing system.
3. Comment on Clark's concerns about the accuracy and limitations of ABC.
4. How might Plum find the ABC information helpful in managing its business?
5. What should Steve Jacobs do in response to Clark's comments?

5-43 Activity-based costing, activity-based management, merchandising. Pet World operates a pet supply superstore in Atlanta with three main product lines: food, toys, and accessories. Pet World allocates common selling, general, and administration (SG&A) costs to each product line using the cost of merchandise of each product line. Department manager salaries, while considered SG&A, are direct and are assigned directly to each product line. The company wants to optimize the pricing and cost management of each product line and is wondering whether its accounting system is providing it with the best information for making such decisions. Store manager Jason Wu gathers the following information regarding the three product lines:

Pet World
Product Line Information
for the Year Ended December 31, 2020

	Food	Toys	Accessories	Total
Revenues	$1,600,000	$900,000	$1,000,000	$3,500,000
Cost of merchandise	$ 900,000	$500,000	$ 600,000	$2,000,000
Salary of department manager	$ 48,000	$ 54,000	$ 52,000	$ 154,000
Number of purchase orders placed	600	950	1,500	3,050
Number of boxes received	2,400	2,500	4,500	9,400
Square feet of store space	12,000	2,000	4,000	18,000

For 2020, Pet World budgets the following selling, general, and administration costs:

Pet World
SG&A Costs
for the Year Ended December 31, 2020

Purchasing department expense	$ 186,000
Receiving department expense	160,500
Selling expense	310,000
Rent	432,000
Store manager's salary	120,000
Utilities	62,000
Total	$1,270,500

Required

1. Prepare an income statement for Pet World, by product line and in total, allocating common SG&A expenses using cost of merchandise. Calculate the profit per square foot of store space for each product line.
2. Identify an improved method for allocating costs to the three product lines. Explain. Use the method for allocating SG&A costs that you propose to prepare new product-line income statements. Calculate the profit per square foot of store space for each product line. Compare your results to the results in requirement 1.
3. What recommendations would you make to the store manager based on the results of the activity-based costing analysis?

6 Master Budget and Responsibility Accounting

LEARNING OBJECTIVES

1. Describe the master budget and explain its benefits
2. Describe the advantages and challenges of implementing budgets
3. Prepare the operating budget and its supporting schedules
4. Use computer-based financial planning models for sensitivity analysis
5. Describe responsibility centers and responsibility accounting
6. Recognize the human aspects of budgeting
7. Appreciate the special challenges of budgeting in multinational companies

No one likes to run out of cash.

To manage their spending, businesses, like individuals, need budgets. Budgets help managers and their employees know whether they're on target for their growth and spending goals. Budgets are important for all types of companies: large financial institutions such as Citigroup, which suffered big financial losses after the housing bubble burst in the mid-2000s; large retailers such as Home Depot, whose profit margins are thin; profitable computer companies such as Apple, which sell high-dollar-value goods; and luxury hotels such as the Ritz-Carlton, which sell high-dollar-value services.

"SCRIMPING" AT THE RITZ: MASTER BUDGETS

"Ladies and gentlemen serving ladies and gentlemen." That's the motto of the Ritz-Carlton. However, the aura of the chain's old-world elegance stands in contrast to its emphasis—behind the scenes, of course—on cost control and budgets. From Boston to Beijing, a Ritz hotel's performance is the responsibility of its general manager and controller at each location. Local forecasts and budgets are prepared annually and are the basis of subsequent performance evaluations for the hotel and people who work there. The budget comprises revenue forecasts and standard costs for hotel rooms, conventions, weddings, meeting facilities, merchandise, and food and beverages. Managers monitor the revenue budget daily, review occupancy rates and adjust prices if necessary. Corporate headquarters monitors actual performance each month against the approved budget and other Ritz hotels. Any ideas for boosting revenues and reducing costs are regularly shared among hotels.

Why do successful companies budget? Because, as the Ritz-Carlton example illustrates, budgeting is a critical function in an organization's decision-making process. Southwest Airlines, for example, uses budgets to monitor and manage fluctuating fuel costs. Walmart depends on its budget to maintain razor-thin margins as it competes with Target. Gillette uses budgets to plan marketing campaigns for its razors and blades.

Even though budgeting is essential for businesses, many managers are often frustrated by the budgeting process. They find it difficult to predict the future and dislike superiors challenging them to improve the performance of their departments. They also dislike being personally evaluated on targets that are challenging and prefer to develop budgets that they can beat. We discuss these issues and the ways thoughtful executives deal with them later in this chapter. For now, we highlight some of the benefits managers get from budgeting.

Suzanne Porter/Rough Guides/Dorling Kindersley, Ltd.

Budgets help managers accomplish the following:

1. Communicate directions and goals to different departments of a company to help them coordinate the actions they must pursue to satisfy customers and succeed in the marketplace.
2. Judge performance by measuring financial results against planned objectives, activities, and timelines and learn about potential problems.
3. Motivate employees to achieve their goals.

Interestingly, even when it comes to entrepreneurial activities, research shows that business planning increases a new venture's probability of survival, as well as its product development and venture-organizing activities.[1] As the old adage goes: "If you fail to plan, you plan to fail."

In this chapter, you will see that a budget is based on an organization's strategy and expresses its operating and financial plans. Most importantly, you will see that budgeting is a human activity that requires judgment and wise interpretation.

Budgets and the Budgeting Cycle

A *budget* is (1) the quantitative expression of a proposed plan of action by management for a specified period and (2) an aid to coordinate what needs to be done to implement that plan. The budget generally includes both the plan's financial and nonfinancial aspects and serves as a road map for the company to follow in an upcoming period. A financial budget quantifies managers' expectations regarding a company's income, cash flows, and financial position in a future period via a budgeted income statement, a budgeted statement of cash flows, and a budgeted balance sheet. Managers develop financial budgets using supporting information from nonfinancial budgets for, say, units manufactured or sold, number of employees, and number of new products being introduced to the marketplace.

LEARNING OBJECTIVE 1

Describe the master budget

...the master budget is the initial budget prepared before the start of a period

and explain its benefits

...benefits include planning, coordination, and control

Strategic Plans and Operating Plans

Budgeting is most useful when it is integrated with a company's strategy. *Strategy* specifies how an organization matches its capabilities with the opportunities in the marketplace to accomplish its objectives. To develop successful strategies, managers must consider questions such as the following:

- What are our objectives?
- What set of integrated choices can we make along the value chain (for example, in product and service design, operations, and marketing) to create value for our customers while distinguishing ourselves from our competitors?
- What organizational and financial structures serve us best?
- What are the risks and opportunities of alternative strategies, and what are our contingency plans if our preferred plan fails?

A company, such as Home Depot, can have a strategy of providing quality products or services at a low price. Another company, such as Porsche or the Ritz-Carlton, can have a strategy of providing a unique product or service that is priced higher than the products or services of competitors. Exhibit 6-1 shows that strategic plans are expressed through long-run budgets and operating plans are expressed via short-run budgets. But there is more to the story! The exhibit shows arrows pointing backward as well as forward. The backward arrows show that budgets can lead to changes in plans and strategies. Budgets help managers assess strategic risks and opportunities by providing them with feedback about the likely effects of their strategies and plans. Sometimes that feedback prompts managers to revise their plans and possibly their strategies.

[1] For more details, see Frederic Delmar and Scott Shane, "Does Business Planning Facilitate the Development of New Ventures?" *Strategic Management Journal* (December 2003).

EXHIBIT 6-1

Strategy, Planning, and Budgets

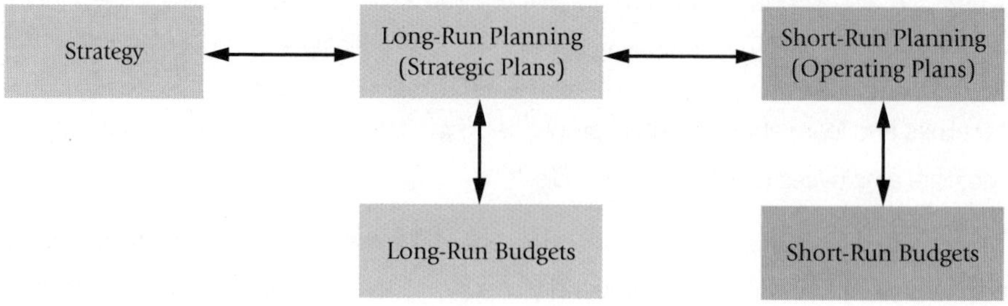

Boeing's experience with the 747-8 program illustrates how budgets can help managers rework their operating plans. Boeing believed that utilizing some of the design concepts it was implementing in its 787 Dreamliner program would be a relatively inexpensive way to reconfigure its 747-8 jet. However, continued cost overruns and delays undermined that strategy: In early 2012, the 747-8 program was already $2 billion over budget and a year behind schedule. As a result, the company expected to earn no profit on any of the more than 100 orders for 747-8 planes it had on its books. And with the budget revealing higher-than-expected costs in design and production, Boeing postponed production plans for the 747-8 program until it could rework its plans.

Budgeting Cycle and Master Budget

Well-managed companies usually cycle through the following annual budgeting steps:

1. Before the start of the fiscal year, managers at all levels take into account the company's past performance, market feedback, and anticipated future changes to initiate plans for the next period. For example, an anticipated economic recovery from a recession may cause managers to plan for sales increases, higher production, and greater promotion expenses. Managers and management accountants work together to develop plans for the company as a whole and its subunits such as departments or divisions.
2. At the beginning of the fiscal year, senior managers give subordinate managers a frame of reference, a set of specific financial or nonfinancial expectations against which they will compare actual results.
3. During the course of the year, management accountants help managers investigate any deviations from the plans, such as an unexpected decline in sales. If necessary, corrective action follows—changes in a product's features, a reduction in prices to boost sales, or cutting of costs to maintain profitability.

The preceding three steps describe the ongoing budget-related processes. The working document at the core of this process is called the *master budget*. The **master budget** expresses management's operating and financial plans for a specified period, usually a fiscal year, and it includes a set of budgeted financial statements. The master budget is the initial plan of what the company intends to accomplish in the period and evolves from both the operating and financing decisions managers make as they prepare the budget.

- Operating decisions deal with how best to use the limited resources of an organization.
- Financing decisions deal with how to obtain the funds to acquire those resources.

The terminology used to describe budgets varies among companies. For example, budgeted financial statements are sometimes called **pro forma statements**. Some companies, such as Hewlett-Packard, refer to budgeting as *targeting*. And many companies, such as Nissan Motor Company and Owens Corning, refer to the budget as a *profit plan*. Microsoft refers to goals as *commitments* and distributes firm-level goals across the company, connecting them to organizational, team, and—ultimately—individual commitments.

This text focuses on how management accounting helps managers make operating decisions, which is why operating budgets are emphasized here. Managers spend a significant part of their time preparing and analyzing budgets because budgeting yields many advantages.

DECISION POINT

What is the master budget, and why is it useful?

Advantages and Challenges of Implementing Budgets

LEARNING OBJECTIVE 2

Describe the advantages

...coordination, communication, performance evaluation, and managerial motivation

and challenges of implementing budgets

...time-consuming back and forth debates

Budgets are an integral part of management control systems. As we discussed at the start of this chapter, when administered thoughtfully by managers, budgets do the following:

- Promote coordination and communication among subunits within the company
- Provide a framework for judging performance and facilitating learning
- Motivate managers and other employees

Promoting Coordination and Communication

Coordination is meshing and balancing all aspects of production or service and all departments in a company in the best way for the company to meet its goals. *Communication* is making sure all employees understand those goals. Coordination forces executives to think about the relationships among individual departments within the company, as well as between the company and its supply-chain partners.

Consider budgeting at Pace, a United Kingdom–based manufacturer of electronic products. A key product is Pace's digital set-top box for decoding satellite broadcasts. The marketing team coordinates and communicates with Pace's customers, such as BSkyB, to understand new services they plan to launch and to predict future demand. The production manager coordinates and communicates with the marketing department and with the materials procurement group to plan the production of set-top boxes as needed by customers.

Providing a Framework for Judging Performance and Facilitating Learning

Budgets enable a company's managers to measure actual performance against predicted performance. Budgets can overcome two limitations of using past performance as a basis for judging actual results. One limitation is that past results often incorporate past miscues and substandard performance. Suppose the cellular telephone company Mobile Communications is budgeting sales for the current year (2020). The 2019 performance was poor because of a weak sales force, many of whom have since left the company. The president of Mobile said of those salespeople, "They could not sell ice cream in a heat wave." Using 2019 sales would set the performance bar for 2020 much too low.

The other limitation of using past performance is that future conditions may differ from the past. Suppose, in 2020, Mobile had a 20% revenue increase, compared with a 10% revenue increase in 2019. Does this increase indicate outstanding sales performance? Not if the forecasted and actual 2020 industry growth rate was 40%. The 40% budgeted growth rate for the industry provides Mobile Communications with a better benchmark against which to evaluate its 2020 sales performance than using the 2019 actual growth rate of 10%. Many companies evaluate managers based on how well they perform relative to their peers.

One of the most valuable benefits of budgeting is that it helps managers gather information for improving future performance. When actual outcomes fall short of budgeted or planned results, it prompts thoughtful senior managers to ask questions about what happened and why and how this knowledge can be used to ensure that such shortfalls do not occur again. This probing and learning is one of the most important reasons why budgeting helps improve performance.

Motivating Managers and Other Employees

Research shows that the performance of employees improves when they receive a challenging budget. Why? Because they view not meeting it as a failure. Most employees are motivated to work more intensely to avoid failure than to achieve success (they are loss-averse). As employees get closer to a goal, they work harder to achieve it. Creating a little anxiety improves performance. However, overly ambitious and unachievable budgets can de-motivate employees because they see little chance of avoiding failure. As a result, many executives like to set demanding, but achievable, goals for their subordinate managers and employees.[2] General Electric's former chief executive officer (CEO) Jack Welch describes challenging, yet achievable, budgets as energizing, motivating, and satisfying for managers and other employees and capable of unleashing out-of-the-box and creative thinking.

Challenges in Administering Budgets

The budgeting process involves all levels of management. Top managers want lower-level managers to participate in the budgeting process because they have more specialized knowledge and firsthand experience with the day-to-day aspects of running the business. This is the *information* benefit of bottom-up participatory budgeting. Participation also creates greater commitment and accountability toward the budget among lower-level managers. But bottom-up budgeting creates *incentive* problems. Because subordinate managers are evaluated against the budget, they tend to set targets that are easier to achieve. To counterbalance this incentive, senior managers probe and debate the budgets submitted by subordinates to make them demanding but achievable. This is the top-down feature of budgeting.

The back-and-forth between superior and subordinate managers at all levels makes budgeting a time-consuming process. Estimates suggest that senior managers spend about 10–20% of their time on budgeting, and financial planning departments up to 50%.[3] For most organizations, the annual budget process is a months-long exercise that consumes a tremendous amount of resources.

The widespread use of budgets in companies ranging from major multinational corporations to small local businesses indicates that the advantages of budgeting systems outweigh the costs. To gain the benefits of budgeting, management at all levels of a company, particularly senior managers, should support the budget. Lower-level managers who feel that top managers do not "believe" in budgets are unlikely to be active participants in the formulation and successful administration of budgets.

Budgets should not be administered rigidly. A manager may commit to a budget, but unplanned events may require managers to deviate from the budget. For example, Chipotle, devastated by food-safety issues that sickened about 500 diners in the second half of 2015 and resulted in a halving of its stock price, responded with a new marketing campaign and the largest media buy in its history in an effort to woo customers back. The dramatic decline in consumer demand during the 2007–2009 recession led designers such as Gucci to slash their ad budgets and put on hold planned new boutiques. Macy's and other retailers, stuck with shelves of merchandise ordered before the financial crisis, slashed prices and cut their workforces.

DECISION POINT

When should a company prepare budgets? What are the advantages and challenges of implementing budgets?

Developing an Operating Budget

LEARNING OBJECTIVE 3

Prepare the operating budget

...the budgeted income statement

and its supporting schedules

...such as cost of goods sold and operating (nonmanufacturing) costs

Budgets are typically developed for a set period, such as a month, quarter, or year, which can be then broken into subperiods. For example, a 12-month cash budget may be broken into 12 monthly periods so that cash inflows and outflows can be better coordinated.

Time Coverage of Budgets

The motive for creating a budget should guide a manager in choosing the period for the budget. For example, consider budgeting for a new Harley-Davidson 500-cc motorcycle. If the purpose is to budget for the total profitability of this new model, a 5-year period (or more) may be necessary to cover the product from design to manufacturing, sales, and after-sales support. In contrast, for a seasonal theater production, a 6-month cash budget from the planning stage to the final performance should suffice.

Managers frequently use a 1-year budget period, subdivided into quarters and months. They revise and update the budget during the year. For example, at the end of the second quarter, management may change the budget for the next two quarters in light of new information obtained during the first 6 months.

---

[2] For a detailed discussion and several examples of the merits of setting specific hard goals, see Gary P. Latham, "The Motivational Benefits of Goal-Setting," *Academy of Management Executive 18*, 4 (2004).

[3] See Peter Horvath and Ralf Sauter, "Why Budgeting Fails: One Management System Is Not Enough," *Balanced Scorecard Report* (September 2004).

Some companies use *rolling budgets*. A **rolling budget**, also called a **continuous budget** or **rolling forecast**, is a budget that is always available for a specified future period. It is created by continually adding a month, quarter, or year to the period that just ended. Consider Electrolux, a global appliance company, which has a 3- to 5-year strategic plan and a 4-quarter rolling budget. A 4-quarter rolling budget for the April 2019 to March 2020 period is superseded in the next quarter—that is, in June 2019—by a 4-quarter rolling budget for July 2019 to June 2020, and so on. There is always a 12-month budget (for the next year) in place. Rolling budgets constantly force Electrolux's management to think dynamically about the forthcoming 12 months, regardless of the quarter at hand. The disadvantage is the time it takes to prepare fresh forecasts. Some companies, such as Borealis, Europe's leading polyolefin plastics manufacturer, and Nordea, the largest financial services group in the Nordic and Baltic Sea region, prepare rolling financial forecasts that look ahead five quarters.

Steps in Preparing an Operating Budget

Consider Stylistic Furniture, a company that makes two types of granite-top coffee tables: Casual and Deluxe. It is late 2019 and Stylistic's CEO, Rex Jordan, is very concerned about how to respond to the board of directors' mandate to increase profits by 10% in the coming year. Jordan goes through the five-step decision-making process introduced in Chapter 1.

1. **Identify the problem and uncertainties.** The problem is to identify a strategy and to build a budget to achieve 10% profit growth. There are several uncertainties. Can Stylistic dramatically increase the sales of its more profitable Deluxe tables? What price pressures will Stylistic face? Will cost of materials increase? Can Stylistic reduce costs through efficiency improvements?
2. **Obtain information.** Stylistic's managers gather information about sales of tables in the current year. Sales of Deluxe tables have been stronger than expected. A key competitor in Stylistic's Casual tables' line has had quality problems that are likely to persist through 2020. The prices of direct materials have increased slightly during 2019 compared to 2018.
3. **Make predictions about the future.** Stylistic's managers feel confident that, with a little more marketing, they will be able to grow the Deluxe tables' business in 2020 and even increase prices moderately relative to 2019. They also do not expect significant price pressures on Casual tables during the year because of the quality problems faced by a key competitor.

   The purchasing manager anticipates that prices of direct materials in 2020 will remain unchanged from 2019. The manufacturing manager believes that manufacturing costs of tables will be the same as in 2019 with efficiency improvements offsetting price increases in other inputs. Achieving these efficiency improvements is important if Stylistic is to maintain its 12% operating margin (that is, operating income ÷ sales = 12%) and to grow sales and operating income.
4. **Make decisions by choosing among alternatives.** Jordan and his managers feel confident about their strategy to increase the sales of Deluxe tables. This decision has some risks, but is the best option available for Stylistic to increase its profits by 10%.
5. **Implement the decision, evaluate performance, and learn.** As we will discuss in Chapters 7 and 8, managers compare actual performance to predicted performance to learn why things turned out the way they did and how to do better. Stylistic's managers would want to know: Were their predictions about the prices of Casual and Deluxe tables correct? Did prices of inputs increase more or less than anticipated? Did efficiency improvements occur? Such learning would help when building budgets in subsequent years.

Stylistic's managers begin work on the 2020 budget. Exhibit 6-2 shows various parts of the master budget, comprising financial projections for Stylistic's operating and financial budgets for 2020. The light, medium, and dark green boxes in Exhibit 6-2 show the **operating budget**, consisting of the budgeted income statement and its supporting budget schedules.

The light green revenues budget box is the starting point of the operating budget. The supporting schedules—shown in medium green—quantify the budgets for various business

EXHIBIT 6-2

Overview of the Master Budget for Stylistic Furniture

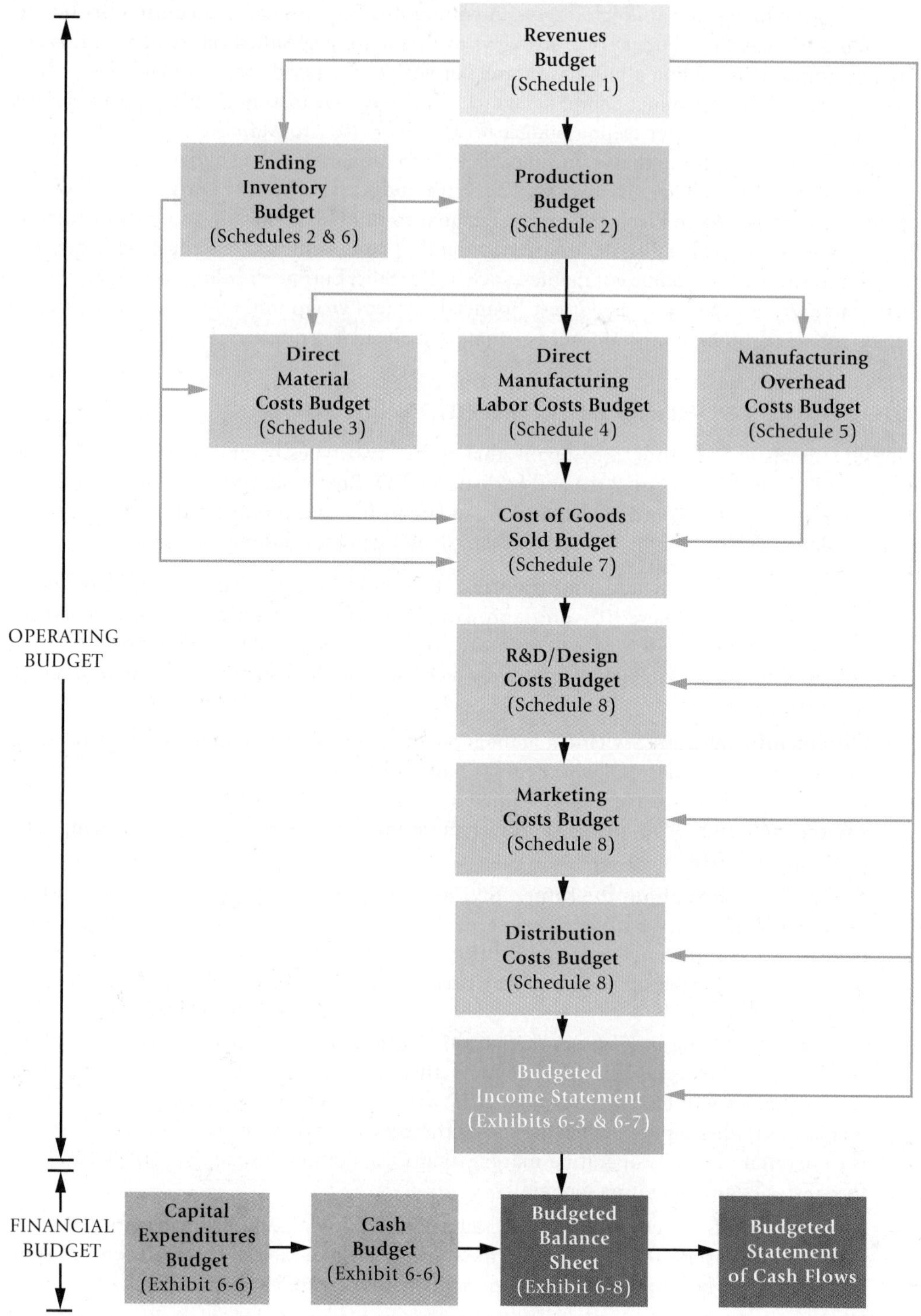

functions of the value chain, from research and development to distribution costs. These schedules build up to the budgeted income statement—the key summary statement in the operating budget—shown in dark green.

The orange and purple boxes in the exhibit are the **financial budget**, which is the part of the master budget made up of the capital expenditures budget, the cash budget, the budgeted balance sheet, and the budgeted statement of cash flows. A financial budget focuses on how operations and planned capital outlays affect cash—shown in orange. Management accountants use the cash budget and the budgeted income statement to prepare two other summary financial statements—the budgeted balance sheet and the budgeted statement of cash flows, which are shown in purple.

The steps for preparing an operating budget for Stylistic Furniture for 2020 follow, using Exhibit 6-2 as a guide. The chapter appendix presents Stylistic's cash budget and budgeted balance sheet. The following are details of Stylistic's operations:

- Stylistic sells two models of granite-top coffee tables: Casual and Deluxe. Revenue unrelated to sales, such as interest income, is zero.
- Work-in-process inventory is negligible and is ignored.
- Direct materials inventory and finished-goods inventory are costed using the first-in, first-out (FIFO) method. The unit costs of direct materials purchased and unit costs of finished-goods sold remain unchanged throughout each budget year, but can change from year to year.
- There are two types of direct materials: red oak and granite slabs. The direct material costs are variable with respect to units of output—coffee tables.
- Direct manufacturing labor is hired on an hourly basis; no overtime is worked.
- Manufacturing overhead costs have two cost drivers—direct manufacturing labor-hours and setup labor-hours, and two manufacturing overhead cost pools—manufacturing operations overhead and machine setup overhead.
- Direct manufacturing labor-hours are the cost driver for the variable portion of manufacturing operations overhead costs. The fixed component of manufacturing operations overhead costs is tied to the manufacturing capacity of 300,000 direct manufacturing labor-hours Stylistic has planned for 2020.
- Setup labor-hours are the cost driver for the variable portion of machine setup overhead costs. The fixed component of machine setup overhead costs is tied to the setup capacity of 15,000 setup labor-hours Stylistic has planned for 2020.
- For computing inventoriable costs of finished goods, Stylistic allocates all (variable and fixed) manufacturing operations overhead costs using direct manufacturing labor-hours and machine setup overhead costs using setup labor-hours.
- Operating (nonmanufacturing) costs consist of product design, marketing, and distribution costs. All product design costs are fixed costs for 2020. The variable component of marketing costs is the 6.5% sales commission on revenues paid to salespeople. The variable portion of distribution costs varies with cubic feet of tables sold and shipped.

The following data are available for the 2020 budget:

Direct materials	
Red oak	$ 7 per board foot (b.f.) (same as in 2019)
Granite	$10 per square foot (sq. ft.) (same as in 2019)
Direct manufacturing labor	$20 per hour

	Content of Each Product Unit	
	Casual Granite Table	Deluxe Granite Table
Red oak	12 board feet	12 board feet
Granite	6 square feet	8 square feet
Direct manufacturing labor	4 hours	6 hours

	Product	
	Casual Granite Table	Deluxe Granite Table
Expected sales in units	50,000	10,000
Selling price	$ 600	$ 800
Target ending inventory in units	11,000	500
Beginning inventory in units	1,000	500
Beginning inventory in dollars	$384,000	$262,000

	Direct Materials	
	Red Oak	Granite
Beginning inventory	70,000 b.f.	60,000 sq. ft.
Target ending inventory	80,000 b.f.	20,000 sq. ft.

Stylistic budgets costs to support the revenues budget, taking into account efficiency improvements it expects to make in 2020. Recall from Step 3 of the decision-making process (page 199) that efficiency improvements are critical to offset the anticipated increases in the cost of inputs and to maintain Stylistic's 12% operating margin.

The budget manual contains instructions and information for preparing budgets. Although the details differ among companies, the following basic steps are common for developing the operating budget of a manufacturing company. Beginning with the revenues budget, each of the other budgets follows step by step in logical fashion. As you go through the details for preparing a budget, think about two things: (1) the information needed to prepare each budget and (2) the actions managers plan to take to improve performance.

Step 1: Prepare the Revenues Budget. Stylistic's managers plan to sell two models of granite-top coffee tables, Casual and Deluxe, in 2020. The revenues budget describes the quantities and prices for each table.

A revenues budget is the usual starting point for the operating budget. Why? Because the forecasted level of unit sales or revenues has a major impact on the production capacity and the inventory levels planned for 2020—and, therefore, manufacturing and operating (nonmanufacturing) costs. Many factors affect the sales forecast, including the sales volume in recent periods, general economic and industry conditions, market research studies, pricing policies, advertising and sales promotions, competition, and regulatory policies. The key to Stylistic achieving its goal of growing its profits by 10% is to grow its sales of Deluxe tables from 8,000 tables in 2019 to 10,000 tables in 2020.

Managers use customer relationship management (CRM) or sales management systems to gather information. Statistical, machine learning, and data-analytic models, such as regression, trend analysis, decision-tree, and gradient-boosting, use indicators of economic activity and past sales data to forecast future sales. The models improve and learn from past experiences in predicting sales. Sales managers and sales representatives debate how best to position, price, and promote Casual and Deluxe tables relative to competitors' products. Together with top management, they consider various actions, such as adding product features, digital advertising, and changing sales incentives, to increase revenues, taking into account related costs. The sales forecast represents the output of models, collective experience, and judgment of managers.

Top managers decide on the budgeted sales quantities and prices to determine the revenues budget of $38,000,000 shown in Schedule 1. These are challenging targets designed to motivate the organization to achieve higher levels of performance.

Schedule 1: Revenues Budget
for the Year Ending December 31, 2020

	Units	Selling Price	Total Revenues
Casual	50,000	$600	$30,000,000
Deluxe	10,000	800	8,000,000
Total			$38,000,000

Revenues budgets are usually based on market conditions and expected demand because these factors drive revenues. Occasionally, other factors, such as available production capacity (being less than demand) or a manufacturing input in short supply, limit revenues. In these cases, managers base the revenues budget on the maximum units that can be produced.

Step 2: Prepare the Production Budget (in Units). The next step in the budgeting process is to plan the production quantities of Casual and Deluxe tables. The only new information managers need to prepare the production budget is the desired level of finished goods inventory. High inventory levels increase the cost of carrying inventory, the costs of quality, and shrinkage costs. Low inventory levels increase setup costs and result in lost sales because of product unavailability. Stylistic's management decides to maintain the inventory of Deluxe tables but increase the inventory of Casual tables to avoid the supply shortages that hurt the company in 2019.

The manufacturing manager prepares the production budget, shown in Schedule 2. She calculates the units of finished goods to be produced as follows:

$$\text{Budget production (units)} = \text{Budget sales (units)} + \text{Target ending finished goods inventory (units)} - \text{Beginning finished goods inventory (units)}$$

Schedule 2: Production Budget (in Units)
for the Year Ending December 31, 2020

	Product	
	Casual	Deluxe
Budgeted sales in units (Schedule 1)	50,000	10,000
Add target ending finished-goods inventory	11,000	500
Total required units	61,000	10,500
Deduct beginning finished-goods inventory	1,000	500
Units of finished goods to be produced	60,000	10,000

The production budget drives budgeted production costs (for example, direct materials, direct manufacturing labor, and manufacturing overhead) after considering efficiency improvements planned for 2020. Costs are also influenced by actions such as product redesign needed to achieve the revenues budget.

Managers are always looking to reduce costs, for example, by improving processes, streamlining manufacturing, and reducing the time to complete various activities such as setting up machines or transporting materials. Making these changes improves a company's competitiveness, but also requires investment. The budgeting exercise is an ideal time for managers to evaluate plans and request the needed financial resources.

6-1 TRY IT!

Firelight Corporation manufactures and sells two types of decorative lamps, Knox and Ayer. The following data are available for the year 2020.

	Product	
	Knox	Ayer
Expected sales in units	22,100	15,000
Selling price	$ 29	$ 39
Target ending inventory in units	2,200	1,200
Beginning inventory in units	3,300	1,200

Calculate the revenues budget (label it Schedule 1) and the production budget in units (label it Schedule 2) for year ending December 31, 2020.

Step 3: Prepare the Direct Materials Usage Budget and Direct Materials Purchases Budget. The budgeted production, calculated in Schedule 2, and the efficiency with which workers use materials determine the quantities and dollars of direct materials used. In determining the direct materials usage budget, senior managers consider process improvements planned to improve quality and reduce waste. The budget motivates production managers to reduce direct material costs.

Like many companies, Stylistic has a *bill of materials* stored in its computer systems that it constantly updates for efficiency improvements. This document identifies how each product is manufactured, specifying all materials (and components), the sequence in which the materials are used, the quantity of materials in each finished unit, and the work centers where the operations are performed. For example, the bill of materials would indicate that 12 board feet of red oak and 6 square feet of granite are needed for a Casual coffee table and 12 board feet of red oak and 8 square feet of granite are needed for a Deluxe coffee table. Direct materials inventories are costed using the first-in, first-out (FIFO) method. The management accountant uses this information to calculate the direct materials usage budget in Schedule 3A.

Schedule 3A: Direct Materials Usage Budget in Quantity and Dollars for the Year Ending December 31, 2020

	Material		
	Red Oak	Granite	Total
Physical Units Budget			
Direct materials required for Casual tables (60,000 units × 12 b.f. and 6 sq. ft.)	720,000 b.f.	360,000 sq. ft.	
Direct materials required for Deluxe tables (10,000 units × 12 b.f. and 8 sq. ft.)	120,000 b.f.	80,000 sq. ft.	
Total quantity of direct materials to be used	840,000 b.f.	440,000 sq. ft.	
Cost Budget			
Available from beginning direct materials inventory (under a FIFO cost-flow assumption) (Given)			
Red oak: 70,000 b.f. × $7 per b.f.	$ 490,000		
Granite: 60,000 sq. ft. × $10 per sq. ft.		$ 600,000	
To be purchased and used this period			
Red oak: (840,000 − 70,000) b.f. × $7 per b.f.	5,390,000		
Granite: (440,000 − 60,000) sq. ft. × $10 per sq. ft.		3,800,000	
Direct materials to be used this period	$5,880,000	$4,400,000	$10,280,000

The only new information needed to prepare the direct materials purchases budget is the desired levels of direct materials inventory. During 2020, Stylistic's managers plan to increase the inventory of red oak but reduce the inventory of granite as described on page 201. The purchasing manager then prepares the budget for direct material purchases, shown in Schedule 3B:

Schedule 3B: Direct Materials Purchases Budget for the Year Ending December 31, 2020

	Material		
	Red Oak	Granite	Total
Physical Units Budget			
To be used in production (from Schedule 3A)	840,000 b.f.	440,000 sq. ft.	
Add target ending inventory	80,000 b.f.	20,000 sq. ft.	
Total requirements	920,000 b.f.	460,000 sq. ft.	
Deduct beginning inventory	70,000 b.f.	60,000 sq. ft.	
Purchases to be made	850,000 b.f.	400,000 sq. ft.	
Cost Budget			
Red oak: 850,000 b.f. × $7 per b.f.	$5,950,000		
Granite: 400,000 sq. ft. × $10 per sq. ft.		$4,000,000	
Direct materials to be purchased this period	$5,950,000	$4,000,000	$9,950,000

Step 4: Prepare the Direct Manufacturing Labor Costs Budget. To create the budget for direct manufacturing labor costs, Stylistic's managers estimate wage rates, production methods, process and efficiency improvements, and hiring plans. The company hires direct manufacturing labor workers on an hourly basis. Workers do not work overtime. Manufacturing managers use *labor standards*, the time allowed per unit of output, to calculate the direct manufacturing labor costs budget in Schedule 4 based on information on pages 201–203.

Schedule 4: Direct Manufacturing Labor Costs Budget for the Year Ending December 31, 2020

	Output Units Produced (Schedule 2)	Direct Manufacturing Labor-Hours per Unit	Total Hours	Hourly Wage Rate	Total
Casual	60,000	4	240,000	$20	$4,800,000
Deluxe	10,000	6	60,000	20	1,200,000
Total			300,000		$6,000,000

6-2 TRY IT!

Firelight Corporation manufactures and sells two types of decorative lamps, Knox and Ayer. It expects to manufacture 21,000 Knox lamps and 15,000 Ayer lamps in 2020. The following data are available for the year 2020.

Direct materials	
Metal	$ 2 per pound (same as in 2019)
Fabric	$ 3 per yard (same as in 2019)
Direct manufacturing labor	$18 per hour

Content of Each Product Unit

	Product	
	Knox	Ayer
Metal	6 pounds	7 pounds
Fabric	1 yard	3 yards
Direct manufacturing labor	0.1 hours	0.2 hours
	Direct Materials	
	Metal	**Fabric**
Beginning inventory	10,000 pounds	3,000 yards
Target ending inventory	8,000 pounds	1,000 yards

Calculate (a) the direct materials usage budget in quantity and dollars (label it Schedule 3A), (b) the direct materials purchase budget in quantity and dollars (label it Schedule 3B), and (c) the direct manufacturing labor costs budget (label it Schedule 4) for the year ending December 31, 2020.

Step 5: Prepare the Manufacturing Overhead Costs Budget. Stylistic's managers next budget for manufacturing overhead costs such as supervision, depreciation, maintenance, supplies, and power. To manage overhead costs, managers need to understand the various activities needed to manufacture products and the cost drivers of those activities. As described on page 201, Stylistic's managers identify two activities for manufacturing overhead costs in its activity-based costing system: manufacturing operations and machine setups. The following table presents the activities and their cost drivers.

Manufacturing Overhead Costs	Cost Driver of Variable Component of Overhead Costs	Cost Driver of Fixed Component of Overhead Costs	Manufacturing and Setup Capacity in 2020
Manufacturing operations overhead costs	Direct manufacturing labor-hours	Manufacturing capacity	300,000 direct manufacturing labor-hours
Machine setup overhead costs	Setup labor-hours	Setup capacity	15,000 setup labor-hours

The use of activity-based cost drivers gives rise to **activity-based budgeting (ABB)**, a budgeting method that focuses on the budgeted cost of the activities necessary to produce and sell products and services.

In its activity-based costing system, Stylistic's manufacturing managers estimate various line items of overhead costs that comprise manufacturing operations overhead (that is, all costs for which direct manufacturing labor-hours is the cost driver). Managers identify opportunities for process and efficiency improvements, such as reducing defect rates and the time to manufacture a table, and then calculate budgeted manufacturing operations overhead costs in the operating department. They also determine the resources that they will need from the two support departments—kilowatt-hours of energy from the power department and hours of maintenance service from the maintenance department. The support department managers, in turn, plan the costs of personnel and supplies that they will need in order to provide the operating department with the support services it requires. The costs of the support departments are then allocated (first-stage cost allocation) as part of manufacturing operations overhead. Chapter 15 describes the allocation of support department costs to operating departments when support departments provide services to each other and to operating departments. The first half of Schedule 5 (page 207) shows the various line items of costs that constitute manufacturing operations overhead costs—that is, all variable and fixed overhead costs (in the operating and support departments) that are caused by the 300,000 direct manufacturing labor-hours (the cost driver).

Stylistic budgets costs differently for variable and fixed overhead costs. Consider variable overhead costs of supplies: Stylistic's managers use past historical data and their knowledge of operations to estimate the cost of supplies per direct manufacturing labor-hour of \$5. The total budgeted cost of supplies for 2020 is \$5 multiplied by 300,000 budgeted direct manufacturing labor-hours, equal to \$1,500,000. The total variable manufacturing operations overhead cost equals \$21.60 (\$5 + \$5.60 + \$7 + \$4) per direct manufacturing labor-hour multiplied by 300,000 budgeted direct manufacturing labor-hours, equal to \$6,480,000.

Stylistic measures manufacturing operations capacity in terms of the direct manufacturing labor-hours that the facility is configured to support. It currently has a capacity of 300,000 direct manufacturing labor-hours. To support this level of capacity, and taking into account potential cost improvements, managers estimate total fixed manufacturing operations overhead costs of \$2,520,000. (Note that, unlike 2020, Stylistic may not operate at full capacity each year, but fixed manufacturing operations costs will still be \$2,520,000.) Fixed manufacturing overhead cost is \$2,520,000 ÷ 300,000 = \$8.40 per direct manufacturing labor-hour (regardless of the budgeted direct manufacturing labor-hours, which may be less than 300,000 in a particular year). That is, each direct manufacturing labor-hour will absorb \$21.60 of variable manufacturing operations overhead plus \$8.40 of fixed manufacturing operations overhead for a total of \$30 of manufacturing operations overhead cost per direct manufacturing labor-hour.

Next, Stylistic's managers determine how setups will be done for the Casual and Deluxe line of tables, taking into account past experiences and potential improvements in setup efficiency.

For example, managers consider the following:

- Increasing the number of tables produced per batch so fewer batches (and therefore fewer setups) are needed for the budgeted production of tables
- Decreasing the setup time per batch
- Reducing the supervisory time needed, for example by increasing the skill base of workers

Stylistic's managers forecast the following setup information for the Casual and Deluxe tables:

	Casual Tables	Deluxe Tables	Total
1. Quantity of tables to be produced	60,000 tables	10,000 tables	
2. Number of tables to be produced per batch	50 tables/batch	40 tables/batch	
3. Number of batches (1) ÷ (2)	1,200 batches	250 batches	
4. Setup time per batch	10 hours/batch	12 hours/batch	
5. Total setup-hours (3) × (4)	12,000 hours	3,000 hours	15,000 hours
6. Setup-hours per table (5) ÷ (1)	0.2 hour	0.3 hour	

Using an approach similar to the one described for manufacturing operations overhead costs, Stylistic's managers estimate various line items of costs that comprise variable machine setup overhead costs (supplies, indirect manufacturing labor, and power)—that is, all costs caused by the 15,000 setup labor-hours (the cost driver) and fixed machine setup overhead costs such as depreciation and supervision. The bottom half of Schedule 5 summarizes (1) total variable machine setup overhead costs per setup labor-hour = \$88(\$26 + \$56 + \$6) × the budgeted 15,000 setup labor-hours = \$1,320,000 and (2) fixed machine setup overhead costs of \$1,680,000 needed to support the planned 15,000 setup labor-hours of capacity.

(Stylistic may not operate at full capacity each year but fixed machine setup costs will still be $1,680,000.) The fixed machine setup cost is $1,680,000 ÷ 15,000 = $112 per setup labor-hour (regardless of the budgeted setup labor-hours, which may be less than 15,000 in a particular year). That is, each setup labor-hour will absorb $88 of variable machine setup overhead cost plus $112 of fixed machine setup overhead cost for a total of $200 of machine setup overhead cost per setup labor-hour.

Schedule 5: Manufacturing Overhead Costs Budget for the Year Ending December 31, 2020

Manufacturing Operations Overhead Costs		
Variable costs (for 300,000 direct manufacturing labor-hours)		
Supplies ($5 per direct manufacturing labor-hour)	$1,500,000	
Indirect manufacturing labor ($5.60 per direct manufacturing labor-hour)	1,680,000	
Power (support department costs) ($7 per direct manufacturing labor-hour)	2,100,000	
Maintenance (support department costs) ($4 per direct manufacturing labor-hour)	1,200,000	$6,480,000
Fixed costs (to support capacity of 300,000 direct manufacturing labor-hours)		
Depreciation	1,020,000	
Supervision	390,000	
Power (support department costs)	630,000	
Maintenance (support department costs)	480,000	2,520,000
Total manufacturing operations overhead costs		$9,000,000
Machine Setup Overhead Costs		
Variable costs (for 15,000 setup labor-hours)		
Supplies ($26 per setup labor-hour)	$ 390,000	
Indirect manufacturing labor ($56 per setup labor-hour)	840,000	
Power (support department costs) ($6 per setup labor-hour)	90,000	$ 1,320,000
Fixed costs (to support capacity of 15,000 setup labor-hours)		
Depreciation	603,000	
Supervision	1,050,000	
Power (support department costs)	27,000	1,680,000
Total machine setup overhead costs		$ 3,000,000
Total manufacturing overhead costs		$12,000,000

Note how using activity-based cost drivers provides additional and detailed information that improves decision making compared with budgeting based solely on output-based cost drivers. Of course, managers must always evaluate whether the expected benefit of adding more cost drivers exceeds the expected cost.[4]

Note that Stylistic is scheduled to operate at capacity. Therefore, the budgeted quantity of the cost allocation base/cost driver is the same for variable overhead costs and fixed overhead costs—300,000 direct manufacturing labor-hours for manufacturing operations overhead costs and 15,000 setup labor-hours for machine setup overhead costs. In this case, the budgeted rate for the manufacturing operations overhead cost does not have to be calculated separately for variable costs and for fixed costs as we did earlier. Instead, it can be calculated directly by estimating total budgeted manufacturing operations overhead: $9,000,000 ÷ 300,000 direct manufacturing labor-hours = $30 per direct manufacturing labor-hour. Similarly, the budgeted rate for machine setup overhead cost can be calculated as total budgeted machine setup overhead: $3,000,000 ÷ 15,000 budgeted setup hours = $200 per setup-hour.

[4] The Stylistic example illustrates ABB using manufacturing operations and setup costs included in Stylistic's manufacturing overhead costs budget. ABB implementations in practice include costs in many parts of the value chain. For an example, see Sofia Borjesson, "A Case Study on Activity-Based Budgeting," *Journal of Cost Management 10*, 4 (Winter 1997): 7–18.

TRY IT! 6-3

Firelight Corporation manufactures and sells two types of decorative lamps, Knox and Ayer. The following data are available for the year 2020. Machine setup-hours is the only driver of manufacturing overhead costs. Firelight has a setup capacity of 660 hours.

	Knox	Ayer
1. Quantity of lamps to be produced	21,000 lamps	15,000 lamps
2. Number of lamps to be produced per batch	200 lamps/batch	100 lamps/batch
3. Setup time per batch	2 hours/batch	3 hours/batch

Variable cost = $80 per setup-hour

Fixed cost = $71,000

Calculate the manufacturing overhead costs budget (label it Schedule 5).

Step 6: Prepare the Ending Inventories Budget. Schedule 6A shows the computation of the unit cost of coffee tables started and completed in 2020. Stylistic uses these calculations for the ending inventories budget and the budgeted cost of goods sold. In accordance with Generally Accepted Accounting Principles, inventoriable (product) costs include direct costs and both variable and fixed manufacturing overhead. Stylistic allocates to finished-goods inventory manufacturing operations overhead costs at the budgeted rate of $30 per direct manufacturing labor-hour and machine setup overhead costs at the budgeted rate of $200 per setup-hour.

Schedule 6A: Budgeted Unit Costs of Ending Finished-Goods Inventory December 31, 2020

		Product			
		Casual Tables		Deluxe Tables	
	Cost per Unit of Input	Input per Unit of Output	Total	Input per Unit of Output	Total
Red oak	$ 7	12 b.f.	$ 84	12 b.f.	$ 84
Granite	10	6 sq. ft.	60	8 sq. ft.	80
Direct manufacturing labor	20	4 hrs.	80	6 hrs.	120
Manufacturing operations overhead	30	4 hrs.	120	6 hrs.	180
Machine setup overhead	200	0.2 hrs.	40	0.3 hrs.	60
Total			$384		$524

Under the FIFO method, managers use this unit cost to calculate the cost of target ending inventories of finished goods in Schedule 6B.

Schedule 6B: Ending Inventories Budget December 31, 2020

	Quantity	Cost per Unit		Total
Direct materials				
Red oak	80,000*	$ 7	$ 560,000	
Granite	20,000*	10	200,000	$ 760,000
Finished goods				
Casual	11,000*	$384**	$4,224,000	
Deluxe	500*	524**	262,000	4,486,000
Total ending inventory				$5,246,000

*Data are from page 201. **From Schedule 6A, this is based on 2020 costs of manufacturing finished goods because under the FIFO costing method, the units in finished-goods ending inventory consists of units that are produced during 2020.

6-4 TRY IT!

Firelight Corporation manufactures and sells two types of decorative lamps, Knox and Ayer. The following data are available for the year 2020.

	Product	
	Knox	Ayer
Target ending inventory in units	2,200	1,200

Metal	$ 2 per pound (same as in 2019)
Fabric	$ 3 per yard (same as in 2019)
Direct manufacturing labor	$ 18 per hour
Machine setup overhead	$140 per hour

	Content of Each Product Unit	
	Knox	Ayer
Metal	6 pounds	7 pounds
Fabric	1 yard	3 yards
Direct manufacturing labor	0.1 hours	0.2 hours
Machine setup overhead	0.01 hours	0.015 hours

	Direct Materials	
	Metal	Fabric
Target ending inventory	8,000 pounds	1,000 yards

Calculate (a) the budgeted unit costs of ending finished-goods inventory on December 31, 2020 (label it Schedule 6A) and (b) the ending inventories budget on December 31, 2020 (label it Schedule 6B).

Step 7: Prepare the Cost of Goods Sold Budget. The manufacturing and purchase managers, together with the management accountant, use information from Schedules 3–6 to prepare Schedule 7—the cost of goods sold expense budget that will be subtracted from revenues to calculate Stylistic's budgeted gross margin for 2020.

Schedule 7: Cost of Goods Sold Budget for the Year Ending December 31, 2020

	From Schedule		Total
Beginning finished-goods inventory, January 1, 2020	Given*		$ 646,000
Direct materials used	3A	$10,280,000	
Direct manufacturing labor	4	6,000,000	
Manufacturing overhead	5	12,000,000	
Cost of goods manufactured			28,280,000
Cost of goods available for sale			28,926,000
Deduct ending finished-goods inventory, December 31, 2020	6B		4,486,000
Cost of goods sold			$24,440,000

*Based on beginning inventory values in 2020 for Casual tables, $384,000, and Deluxe tables, $262,000 (page 201).

Step 8: Prepare the Operating (Nonmanufacturing) Costs Budget. Schedules 2–7 represent budgets for Stylistic's manufacturing costs. Stylistic also incurs operating (nonmanufacturing) costs in other parts of the value chain—product design, marketing, and distribution. Just as in the case of manufacturing costs, the key to managing operating overhead costs is to understand the various activities and quantities of cost drivers to efficiently design, market, and distribute Deluxe and Casual tables in 2020.

The number of design changes is the cost driver for product design costs. Product design costs of $1,024,000 are fixed costs for 2020 and adjusted at the start of the year based on the number of design changes planned for 2020.

Total revenue is the cost driver for the variable portion of marketing (and sales) costs. The commission paid to salespeople equals \$0.065 per dollar (or 6.5%) of revenues. Managers budget the fixed component of marketing costs, \$1,330,000, at the start of the year based on budgeted revenues for 2020.

Cubic feet of tables sold and shipped (Casual: 18 cubic feet × 50,000 tables + Deluxe: 24 cubic feet × 10,000 tables = 1,140,000 cubic feet) is the cost driver of the variable component of budgeted distribution costs. Variable distribution costs equal \$2 per cubic foot. The fixed component of budgeted distribution costs equal to \$1,596,000 varies with the company's distribution capacity, which in 2020 is 1,140,000 cubic feet (to support the distribution of 50,000 Casual tables and 10,000 Deluxe tables). For brevity, Schedule 8 shows the product design, marketing, and distribution costs budget for 2020 in a single schedule.

Schedule 8: Operating (Nonmanufacturing) Costs Budget for the Year Ending December 31, 2020

Business Function	Variable Costs	Fixed Costs	Total Costs
Product design	—	\$1,024,000	\$1,024,000
Marketing (Variable cost: \$38,000,000 × 0.065)	\$2,470,000	1,330,000	3,800,000
Distribution (Variable cost: \$2 × 1,140,000 cu. ft.)	2,280,000	1,596,000	3,876,000
	\$4,750,000	\$3,950,000	\$8,700,000

Innovation is an important item on the agenda of most companies. Sometimes, as in the case of Stylistic, the product design innovations are incremental or small, with the benefits of the innovation generating revenues within the same year. In other cases, the innovations, such as developing new medicines, are radical or breakthrough innovations. Research and development (R&D) costs may have to be incurred for several years before any revenues are realized.[5] Management accountants separately budget for and track breakthrough innovations to isolate operational performance for the year from investments in innovation for subsequent years. They develop project milestones, such as expert evaluations, intellectual property creation, patents received, and customer engagement, to monitor progress and value creation of the innovation projects.

Step 9: Prepare the Budgeted Operating Income Statement. The CEO and managers of various business functions, with help from the management accountant, use information in Schedules 1, 7, and 8 to finalize the budgeted operating income statement, shown in Exhibit 6-3. The style used in Exhibit 6-3 is typical, but managers and accountants could include more details in the income statement. As more details are put in the income statement, fewer supporting schedules are needed.

EXHIBIT 6-3

Budgeted Operating Income Statement for Stylistic Furniture

	A	B	C	D
1	**Budgeted Income Statement for Stylistic Furniture**			
2	**For the Year Ending December 31, 2020**			
3	Revenues	Schedule 1		\$38,000,000
4	Cost of goods sold	Schedule 7		24,440,000
5	Gross margin			13,560,000
6	Operating costs			
7	Product design costs	Schedule 8	\$1,024,000	
8	Marketing costs	Schedule 8	3,800,000	
9	Distribution costs	Schedule 8	3,876,000	8,700,000
10	Operating income			\$ 4,860,000

[5] Some critics argue that the short-term costs and uncertain long-term benefits of breakthrough innovations result in companies underinvesting in these innovations. Others argue that companies overspend on these innovations without creating value. How much to spend on these innovations is always a matter of management judgment.

Budgeting is a cross-functional activity. The strategies developed by top managers for achieving a company's revenue and operating income goals affect the costs planned for the different business functions of the value chain. For example, the budgeted increase in sales at Stylistic is based on spending more for marketing and must be matched with higher production costs to ensure there is an adequate supply of tables and with higher distribution costs to ensure the timely delivery of tables to customers.

Rex Jordan, the CEO of Stylistic Furniture, is very pleased with the 2020 budget and the plans to increase operating income by 10% compared with 2019. The keys to achieving higher operating income are a significant increase in sales of Deluxe tables and process improvements and efficiency gains throughout the value chain. As Jordan studies the budget more carefully, he is struck by two comments appended to the budget: First, changes in the competitive environment may require Stylistic to reduce selling prices by 3% to \$582 for Casual tables and to \$776 for Deluxe tables to achieve the budgeted number of tables sold. Second, supply shortages of direct materials may result in prices of direct materials (red oak and granite) to be 5% higher than budgeted. In this second scenario, selling prices are anticipated to remain unchanged. He asks Tina Larsen, a management accountant, to use Stylistic's financial planning model to evaluate how these events will affect budgeted operating income.

DECISION POINT

What is the operating budget, and what are its components?

6-5 TRY IT!

Firelight Corporation manufactures and sells two types of decorative lamps, Knox and Ayer. The following data are available for the year 2020. The numbers below represent the calculations from the previous Try It! examples (6-1 through 6-4) together with the relevant schedule numbers from those examples.

Revenues (Schedule 1)	\$1,125,900
Beginning inventory of finished goods (1-1-2020)	94,500
Ending inventory of finished goods, 12-31-2020 (Schedule 6B)	77,000
Direct materials used (Schedule 3A)	660,000
Direct manufacturing labor (Schedule 4)	91,800
Manufacturing overhead (Schedule 5)	123,800
Variable marketing costs (2% of revenues)	
Fixed marketing costs	42,000
Variable distribution costs (\$3.00 per cu. ft. for 35,000 cu. ft.)	
Fixed distribution costs	47,000
Fixed administration costs	79,000

Calculate (a) the cost of goods sold budget (label it Schedule 7); (b) the operating (nonmanufacturing) costs budget (label it Schedule 8); and (c) the operating income budget for the year ending December 31, 2020.

Financial Planning Models and Sensitivity Analysis

LEARNING OBJECTIVE 4

Use computer-based financial planning models for sensitivity analysis

. . . for example, understand the effects of changes in selling prices and direct material prices on budgeted income

Financial planning models are mathematical representations of the relationships among operating activities, financing activities, and other factors that affect the master budget. Computer-based enterprise resource planning (ERP) systems store vast quantities of information about the materials, machines and equipment, labor, power, maintenance, and setups needed to produce different products. Budgeting tools within ERP systems simplify budgeting, reduce the need to re-input data, and reduce the time required to prepare budgets. Managers identify sales quantities for different products and the software quickly computes the budgeted costs for manufacturing these products. ERP systems also help managers budget for operating costs. Many service companies, such as banks, hospitals, airlines, and restaurants, also use ERP systems to manage their operations. The Concepts in Action: P.F. Chang's and Internet-Based Budgeting is an example of a service company using a software platform to coordinate and manage its budgets across multiple restaurants.

CONCEPTS IN ACTION

P.F. Chang's and Internet-Based Budgeting[6]

David Tonelson/Shutterstock

P.F. Chang's China Bistro is an Asian-themed casual dining restaurant chain, with more than 300 locations globally and approximately $900 million in annual revenues. The company uses Adaptive Insights Business Planning Cloud, an Internet-based software platform, to manage its planning and budgeting process. P.F. Chang's develops a budget for revenue, food cost, labor cost, and overhead expenses for each location. The Adaptive software consolidates those budgets to quickly create a companywide budget. The system has reduced budget and forecasting cycle times by 80%. As one P.F. Chang's manager concluded, "In the time it takes me to make a lettuce wrap, I'm able to put together a budget!"

Managers measure key performance indicators in real-time at each location to better understand costs, improve profit margins, and fund growth. Restaurant managers can gauge the success of marketing campaigns and the impact of menu changes. Managers can work with each other and perform "what if?" budget scenario analysis from anywhere in the world. Recently, chief financial officer Jim Bell examined how kitchen staff cuts at the company's Boston restaurants affected profitability while on a flight from Spokane, Washington, to Phoenix, Arizona.

[6] *Sources*: "Cooking Up a Modern FP&A Environment for a Global Dining Empire," Adaptive Insights customer case study, June 2017 (https://www.adaptiveinsights.com/customer-stories/p-f-changs); Tatyana Shumsky, "Corporate Finance Cuts Back on Excel," *The Wall Street Journal*, November 24, 2017, (https://www.wsj.com/articles/stop-using-excel-finance-chiefs-tell-staffs-1511346601).

As they prepare budgets, managers do not focus only on what they can achieve. They also identify the risks they face such as a potential decline in demand for the company's products, the entry of a new competitor, or an increase in the prices of different inputs. Managers use sensitivity analysis to evaluate these risks. *Sensitivity analysis* is a "what-if" technique that examines how a result will change if the original predicted data are not achieved or if an underlying assumption changes.

To see how sensitivity analysis works, we consider two scenarios identified as possibly affecting Stylistic Furniture's budget model for 2020. Either of the two scenarios could happen, but not both together.

Scenario 1: A 3% decrease in the selling price of the Casual table and a 3% decrease in the selling price of the Deluxe table.

Scenario 2: A 5% increase in the price per board foot of red oak and a 5% increase in the price per square foot of granite.

Exhibit 6-4 presents the budgeted operating income for the two scenarios.

EXHIBIT 6-4 Effect of Changes in Budget Assumptions on Budgeted Operating Income for Stylistic Furniture

	A	B	C	D	E	F	G	H	I
1	Key Assumptions								
2		Units Sold		Selling Price		Direct Material Cost		Budgeted Operating Income	
3	What-If Scenario	Casual	Deluxe	Casual	Deluxe	Red Oak	Granite	Dollars	Change from Master Budget
4	Master budget	50,000	10,000	$600	$800	$7.00	$10.00	$4,860,000	
5	Scenario 1	50,000	10,000	582	776	$7.00	$10.00	3,794,100	22% decrease
6	Scenario 2	50,000	10,000	600	800	$7.35	$10.50	4,418,000	9% decrease

In the case of Scenario 1, note that a change in the selling price per table affects revenues (Schedule 1) as well as variable marketing costs (sales commissions, Schedule 8). The Problem for Self-Study at the end of the chapter shows the revised schedules for Scenario 1. Similarly, a change in the price of direct materials affects the direct material usage budget (Schedule 3A), the unit cost of ending finished-goods inventory (Schedule 6A), the ending finished-goods inventories budget (Schedule 6B), and the cost of goods sold budget (Schedule 7).

Exhibit 6-4 shows that operating income decreases substantially if selling prices decrease by 3%, but declines much less if direct materials prices increase by 5%. The sensitivity analysis prompts Stylistic's managers to put in place contingency plans. For example, if selling prices decline in 2020, Stylistic may need to reduce costs even more than planned. More generally, when the success or viability of a venture is highly dependent on attaining a certain income target, managers should frequently update their budgets as uncertainty is resolved. These updated budgets can help managers adjust expenditure levels as circumstances change.

DECISION POINT

How can managers plan for changes in the assumptions underlying the budget and manage risk?

Earlier in this chapter we described a rolling budget as a budget that is always available for a specified future period. Rolling budgets are constantly updated to reflect the latest cost and revenue information and make managers responsive to changing conditions and market needs.

Instructors and students who, at this point, want to explore the cash budget and the budgeted balance sheet for the Stylistic Furniture example can skip ahead to the appendix on page 221.

Budgeting and Responsibility Accounting

To attain the goals described in the master budget, top managers must coordinate the efforts of all of the firm's employees—from senior executives through middle levels of management to every supervised worker. To coordinate the company's efforts, top managers assign a certain amount of responsibility to lower-level managers and then hold them accountable for how they perform. Consequently, how each company structures its organization significantly shapes how it coordinates its actions.

LEARNING OBJECTIVE 5

Describe responsibility centers

...a part of an organization that a manager is accountable for

and responsibility accounting

...measurement of plans and actual results that a manager is accountable for

Organization Structure and Responsibility

Organization structure is an arrangement of lines of responsibility within an organization. A company such as Exxon Mobil is organized by business function—refining, marketing, and so on—with the president of each business function having decision-making authority over his or her function. Functional organizations develop strong competencies within each function but are generally less focused on particular markets or customers. To respond to this concern, other companies, such as Procter & Gamble, the household-products giant, are organized primarily by product line or brand. The managers of the individual divisions (toothpaste, soap, and so on) have decision-making authority concerning all the business functions (manufacturing, marketing, and so on) within that division. This results in some inefficiencies as support functions get duplicated in different divisions without sufficient scale or competence. Some companies, such as Swiss pharmaceutical firm Novartis, combine functional and divisional structures, for example leaving marketing within divisions but having manufacturing organized as a business function to supply products to different divisions. There is no perfect organization structure. Companies choose the structure that best meets their needs at that time, making the tradeoff between efficiency and end-to-end business authority.

Each manager, regardless of level, is in charge of a responsibility center. A **responsibility center** is a part, segment, or subunit of an organization whose manager is accountable for a specified set of activities. Higher-level managers supervise centers with broader responsibility and larger numbers of subordinates. **Responsibility accounting** is a system that measures the plans, budgets, actions, and actual results of each responsibility center. There are four types of responsibility centers:

1. **Cost center**—The manager is accountable for costs only.
2. **Revenue center**—The manager is accountable for revenues only.
3. **Profit center**—The manager is accountable for revenues and costs.
4. **Investment center**—The manager is accountable for investments, revenues, and costs.

The maintenance department of a Marriott hotel is a cost center because the maintenance manager is responsible only for costs and the budget is based only on costs. The sales department is a revenue center because the sales manager is responsible primarily for revenues, and the department's budget is primarily based on revenues. The hotel manager is in charge of a profit center because the manager is accountable for both revenues and costs, and the hotel's budget is based on revenues and costs. The regional manager responsible for determining the amount to be invested in new hotel projects and for revenues and costs generated from these investments is in charge of an investment center. So, this center's budget is based on revenues, costs, and the investment base.

A responsibility center can be structured to promote better alignment of individual and company goals. For example, until recently, OPD, an office products distributor, operated its sales department solely as a revenue center. Each salesperson received a commission of 3% of the revenues per order, regardless of its size, the cost of processing it, or the cost of delivering the office products. Upon analyzing customer profitability, OPD found that many customers were unprofitable. The main reason was the high ordering and delivery costs of small orders. OPD's managers decided to make the sales department a profit center, accountable for revenues and costs, and to change the incentive system for salespeople to 15% of the monthly profits of their customers. The costs for each customer included the manufacturing, ordering, and delivery costs. The effect of this change was immediate. The sales department began charging customers for ordering and delivery, and salespeople at OPD actively encouraged customers to consolidate their purchases into fewer orders. As a result, each order began producing larger revenues. The profitability of customers increased because of a 40% reduction in ordering and delivery costs in 1 year.

Feedback

Budgets coupled with responsibility accounting provide feedback to top managers about the performance relative to the budget of different responsibility center managers.

Differences between actual results and budgeted amounts—called *variances*—can help managers implement strategies and evaluate them in three ways:

1. **Early warning.** Variances alert managers early to events not easily or immediately evident. Managers can then take corrective actions or exploit the available opportunities. For example, after observing a small decline in sales during a period, managers may want to investigate whether this is an indication of an even steeper decline to come later in the year.
2. **Performance evaluation.** Variances prompt managers to probe how well the company has implemented its strategies. Were materials and labor used efficiently? Was R&D spending increased as planned? Did product warranty costs decrease as planned?
3. **Evaluating strategy.** Variances sometimes signal to managers that their strategies are ineffective. For example, a company seeking to compete by reducing costs and improving quality may find that it is achieving these goals but that it is having little effect on sales and profits. Top management may then want to reevaluate the strategy.

Responsibility and Controllability

Controllability is the degree of influence a specific manager has over costs, revenues, or related items for which he or she is responsible. A **controllable cost** is any cost primarily subject to the influence of a given *responsibility center manager* for a given *period*. A responsibility accounting system could either exclude all uncontrollable costs from a manager's performance report or segregate such costs from the controllable costs. For example, a machining supervisor's performance report might be confined to direct materials, direct manufacturing labor, power, and machine maintenance costs and might exclude costs such as rent and taxes paid on the plant.

In practice, controllability is difficult to pinpoint for two main reasons:

1. Few costs are clearly under the sole influence of one manager. For example, purchasing managers are able to affect the prices their firms pay for direct materials, but these prices also depend on market conditions beyond the managers' control. Similarly, the decisions production managers make can affect the quantities of direct materials used but also

depend on the quality of materials purchased. Moreover, managers often work in teams. Think about how difficult it is to evaluate individual responsibility in a team situation.

2. With a long enough time span, all costs will come under somebody's control. However, most performance reports focus on periods of a year or less. A current manager may benefit from a predecessor's accomplishments or may inherit a predecessor's problems and inefficiencies. For example, managers may have to work with undesirable contracts with suppliers or labor unions negotiated by their predecessors. How can we separate what the current manager actually controls from the results of decisions other managers made? Exactly what is the current manager accountable for? The answers may not be clear-cut.

Executives differ in how they embrace the controllability notion when evaluating people reporting to them. Some CEOs regard the budget as a firm commitment subordinates must meet and that "numbers always tell the story." Failing to meet the budget is viewed unfavorably. An executive once noted, "You can miss your plan once, but you wouldn't want to miss it twice." Such an approach forces managers to learn to perform under adverse circumstances and to deliver consistent results year after year. It removes the need to discuss which costs are controllable and which are uncontrollable because it does not matter whether the performance was due to controllable or uncontrollable factors. The disadvantage of this approach is that it subjects a manager's compensation to greater risk. It also de-motivates managers when uncontrollable factors adversely affect their performance evaluations even though they performed well in terms of factors they could control.

Other CEOs believe that focusing on making the numbers in a budget puts excessive pressure on managers. These CEOs adjust for uncontrollable factors and evaluate managers only on what they can control, such as their performance relative to competitors. Using relative performance measures takes out the effects of favorable or unfavorable business conditions that are outside the manager's control and affect all competing managers in the same way. The challenge is in finding the correct benchmarks. Relative performance measures, however, reduce the pressure on managers to perform when circumstances are difficult.

Managers should avoid thinking about controllability only in the context of performance evaluation. Responsibility accounting is more far-reaching. It focuses on gaining *information and knowledge*, not only on control. *Responsibility accounting helps managers to first focus on whom they should ask to obtain information and not on whom they should blame.* Comparing the shortfall of actual revenues to budgeted revenues is certainly relevant when evaluating the performance of the sales managers of Ritz-Carlton hotels. But the more fundamental purpose of responsibility accounting is to gather information from the sales managers to enable future improvement. Holding them accountable for sales motivates them to learn about market conditions and dynamics outside of their personal control but which are relevant for deciding the actions the hotels might take to increase future sales. Similarly, purchasing managers may be held accountable for total purchase costs, not because of their ability to control market prices, but because of their ability to predict and respond to uncontrollable prices and understand their causes.

Performance reports for responsibility centers are sometimes designed to change managers' behavior in the direction top managers desire even if the reports decrease controllability. Consider a manufacturing department. If the department is designated as a cost center, the manufacturing manager may emphasize efficiency and de-emphasize the pleas of sales personnel for faster service and rush orders that reduce efficiency and increase costs. Evaluating the department as a profit center decreases the manufacturing manager's controllability (because the manufacturing manager has limited influence on sales) but it motivates the manager to look more favorably at rush orders that benefit sales. She will weigh the impact of decisions on costs and revenues rather than on costs alone.

Call centers provide another example. If designated as a cost center, the call-center manager will focus on controlling operating costs, for example, by decreasing the time customer representatives spend on each call. If designed as a profit center, the call-center manager will cause customer-service representatives to balance efficiency against better customer service and lead to efforts to upsell and cross-sell other products. Hewlett-Packard, Microsoft, Oracle, and others offer software platforms designed to prompt and help call-center personnel turn their cost centers into profit centers. The new adage is "Every service call is a sales call."

DECISION POINT

How do companies use responsibility centers? Should performance reports of responsibility center managers include only costs the manager can control?

Many managers regard budgets negatively. To them, the word *budget* is about as popular as, say, *downsizing*, *layoff*, or *strike*. Top managers must convince their subordinates that the budget is a tool designed to help them set and reach goals. As with all tools of management, it has its benefits and challenges. Budgets must be used thoughtfully and wisely, but whatever the manager's perspective on budgets—pro or con—they are not remedies for weak management talent, faulty organization, or a poor accounting system.

Human Aspects of Budgeting

LEARNING OBJECTIVE 6

Recognize the human aspects of budgeting

...to engage subordinate managers in the budgeting process

Why did we discuss the master budget and responsibility accounting in the same chapter? Primarily to emphasize that human factors are crucial in budgeting. Too often, budgeting is thought of as a mechanical tool because the budgeting techniques themselves are free of emotion. However, the administration of budgeting requires education, persuasion, and intelligent interpretation.

Budgetary Slack

As we discussed earlier in this chapter, budgeting is most effective when lower-level managers actively participate and meaningfully engage in the budgeting process. Participation adds credibility to the budgeting process and makes employees more committed and accountable for meeting the budget. But participation requires "honest" communication about the business from subordinates and lower-level managers to their bosses.

At times, subordinates may try to "play games" and build in *budgetary slack*. **Budgetary slack** is the practice of underestimating budgeted revenues or overestimating budgeted costs to make budgeted targets easier to achieve. This practice frequently occurs when budget variances (the differences between actual results and budgeted amounts) are used to evaluate the performance of line managers and their subordinates. Line managers are also unlikely to be fully honest in their budget communications if top managers mechanically institute across-the-board cost reductions (say, a 10% reduction in all areas) in the face of projected revenue reductions.

Budgetary slack provides managers with a hedge against unexpected adverse circumstances. But budgetary slack also misleads top managers about the true profit potential of the company, which leads to inefficient resource planning and allocation and poor coordination of activities across different parts of the company.

To avoid the problems of budgetary slack, some companies use budgets primarily for planning and to a lesser extent for performance evaluation. They evaluate the performance of managers using multiple indicators that take into account various factors that become known during the course of the year, such as the prevailing business environment and the performance of their industry or their competitors. Evaluating performance in this way takes time and requires careful judgment.

One approach to dealing with budgetary slack is to obtain good benchmark data when setting the budget. Consider the plant manager of a beverage bottler. Suppose top managers could purchase a consulting firm's study of productivity levels—such as the number of bottles filled per hour—at a number of comparable plants owned by other bottling companies. The managers could then share this independent information with the plant manager and use it to set the operations budget. Using external benchmark performance measures reduces a manager's ability to set budget levels that are easy to achieve.

Rolling budgets are another approach to reducing budgetary slack. As we discussed earlier in the chapter, companies that use rolling budgets always have a budget for a defined period, say 12 months, by adding, at the end of each quarter, a budget for one more quarter to replace the quarter just ended. The continuous updating of budget information and the richer information it provides reduce the opportunity to create budgetary slack relative to when budgeting is done only annually.

Some companies, such as IBM, have designed innovative performance evaluation measures that reward managers based on the subsequent accuracy of the forecasts used in preparing budgets. For example, the *higher and more accurate* the budgeted profit forecasts of division managers, the higher their incentive bonuses.[7] Another approach to reducing budgetary slack is for managers to become knowledgeable about what subordinates do by having in-depth dialogues about budgets and performance goals. Managers should not dictate decisions and actions of subordinates. Rather, managers should provide support, challenge assumptions to motivate performance, and enhance mutual learning. Subsequently, managers evaluate performance using both objective measures and subjective judgment. Of course, using subjective judgment requires that subordinates trust their managers to evaluate them fairly.

In addition to developing their organization's strategies, top managers are responsible for defining a company's core values and norms and building employee commitment to adhere to them. Norms and values describe acceptable and unacceptable behavior. For example, Johnson & Johnson (J&J) has a credo that describes its responsibilities to doctors, patients, employees, communities, and shareholders. Employees are trained in the credo to help them understand the behavior that is expected of them. J&J has a strong culture of mentoring subordinates. J&J's values and employee practices create an environment where managers know their subordinates well, which helps to reduce budgetary slack.

Stretch Targets

Many of the best performing companies, such as General Electric, Microsoft, and Novartis, set "stretch" targets. Stretch targets are challenging but achievable levels of expected performance, intended to create a little discomfort. Creating some performance anxiety motivates employees to exert extra effort and attain better performance, but setting targets that are very difficult or impossible to accomplish hurts performance because employees don't try to achieve them. Organizations such as Goldman Sachs also use "horizontal" stretch goal initiatives. The aim is to enhance professional development of employees by asking them to take on significantly different responsibilities or roles outside their comfort zone.

A major rationale for stretch targets is their psychological motivation. Consider the following two compensation arrangements offered to a salesperson:

- In the first arrangement, the salesperson is paid $80,000 for achieving a sales target of $1,000,000 and $0.08 for every dollar of sales above $1,000,000 up to $1,100,000.
- In the second arrangement, the salesperson is paid $88,000 for achieving a sales target of $1,100,000 (a stretch target) with a reduction in compensation of $0.08 for every dollar of sales less than $1,100,000 up to $1,000,000.

For simplicity we assume that sales will be between $1,000,000 and $1,100,000.

The salesperson receives the same level of compensation under the two arrangements for all levels of sales between $1,000,000 and $1,100,000. The question is whether the psychological motivation is the same in the two compensation arrangements. Many executives who favor stretch targets point to the asymmetric way in which salespeople psychologically perceive the two compensation arrangements. In the first arrangement, achieving the sales target of $1,000,000 is seen as good and everything above it as a bonus. In the second arrangement, not reaching the stretch sales target of $1,100,000 is seen as a failure. If salespeople are loss averse, that is, they feel the pain of loss more than the joy of success, they will work harder under the second arrangement to achieve sales of $1,100,000 and not fail.

At no point should the pressure for performance embedded in stretch targets push employees to engage in illegal or unethical practices. The more a company tries to push performance, the greater the emphasis it must place on training employees to follow its code of conduct (for example, no bribery, side payments, or dishonest dealings) and its norms and values (for example, putting customers first and not compromising quality).

[7] For an excellent discussion of these issues, see Chapter 14 ("Formal Models in Budgeting and Incentive Contracts") in Robert S. Kaplan and Anthony A. Atkinson, *Advanced Management Accounting*, 3rd ed. (Upper Saddle River, NJ: Prentice Hall, 1998).

Some ethical questions are subtle and not clear-cut. Consider, for example, a division manager, faced with the choice of doing maintenance on a machine at the end of 2019 or early in 2020. It is preferable to do the maintenance in 2019 because delaying maintenance increases the probability of the machine breaking down. But a manager may not do so if it means that he will not reach his 2019 operating income target and may lose his bonus. If the risks of a breakdown and loss are substantial, many observers would view delaying maintenance as unethical. If the risks are minimal, there may be more debate whether delaying maintenance is unethical.

Kaizen Budgeting

Chapter 1 noted the importance of continuous improvement, or *kaizen* in Japanese. **Kaizen budgeting** explicitly incorporates continuous improvement anticipated during the budget period into the budget numbers. A number of companies that focus on cost reduction, including General Electric in the United States and Toyota in Japan, use Kaizen budgeting to continuously reduce costs. Much of the cost reduction associated with Kaizen budgeting arises from many small improvements rather than "quantum leaps." The improvements tend to come from employee suggestions as a result of a culture that values, recognizes, and rewards these suggestions.

As an example, throughout our nine budgeting steps for Stylistic Furniture, we assumed 4 hours of direct labor time were required to manufacture each Casual coffee table. A Kaizen budgeting approach would incorporate continuous improvement based on 4.00 direct manufacturing labor-hours per table for the first quarter of 2020, 3.95 hours for the second quarter, 3.90 hours for the third quarter, and so on. The implications: lower direct manufacturing labor costs and lower variable manufacturing operations overhead costs (because direct manufacturing labor is the cost driver of variable manufacturing operations overhead). If continuous improvement targets are not met, managers adjust the targets or work with employees to identify process improvements.

Managers can also apply Kaizen budgeting to activities such as setups to reduce setup time and costs per set up or distribution to reduce the cubic feet of each shipment or shipping cost per cubic foot. Kaizen budgeting for specific activities is a key building block of the master budget for companies that use the Kaizen approach.

A growing number of agencies in the United States, such as the Environmental Protection Agency and the Department of Defense, are using Kaizen techniques to bring together government employees, regulators, and end users to reduce inefficiencies and eliminate bureaucratic procedures. The U.S. Postal Service has identified many different programs to reduce its costs. The success of these efforts will depend heavily on human factors such as the commitment and engagement of managers and employees to make these changes.

DECISION POINT

Why are human factors crucial in budgeting?

Budgeting for Reducing Carbon Emissions

In response to pressures from consumers, investors, governments, and nongovernmental organizations, many companies proactively manage and report on environmental performance. Budgeting is a very effective tool to motivate managers to lessen carbon emissions. Several companies, such as British Telecom and Unilever, set science-based carbon reduction goals based on climate models.

These science-based targets are stretched to spur innovation, prompt the development of new technologies and business models, and prepare companies for future regulatory and policy changes. What is the effect of stretched targets on actual emission reduction? Some recent research shows that companies that set more difficult targets (to be achieved over several years) complete a higher percentage of such targets. This is particularly true for carbon reduction projects in high-polluting industries that require more innovation.[8]

---

[8] See Ioannis Ioannou, Shelley Xin Li, and George Serafeim, "The Effect of Target Difficulty on Target Completion: The Case of Reducing Carbon Emissions," *The Accounting Review* (2016).

Budgeting in Multinational Companies

LEARNING OBJECTIVE 7

Appreciate the special challenges of budgeting in multinational companies

...exposure to currency fluctuations and to different legal, political, and economic environments

Multinational companies, such as FedEx, Kraft, and Pfizer, have operations in many countries. An international presence has benefits—access to new markets and resources—and drawbacks—operating in less-familiar business environments and exposure to currency fluctuations. When preparing budgets, managers of multinational companies need to understand the political, legal, tax, and economic environments of the different countries in which they operate. They budget revenues and expenses in different currencies but also budget foreign exchange rates to convert these earnings into their home currency (say, U.S. dollars). In some countries, such as Turkey and Zimbabwe, where annual inflation rates are very high, the value of the local currency can decline sharply. To reduce the negative impact of unfavorable exchange rate movements, finance managers frequently use techniques such as forward, future, and option contracts to minimize the impact of foreign currency fluctuations (see Chapter 12).

When there is considerable business and exchange rate uncertainty related to global operations, a natural question to ask is: "Do managers of multinational companies find budgeting to be a helpful tool?" The answer is yes. When conditions are volatile, budgeting is not useful for evaluating performance. Instead, managers use budgets to help them adapt their plans and coordinate their actions as circumstances change. Senior managers evaluate performance more subjectively, based on how well subordinate managers have managed in these constantly shifting and volatile environments.

DECISION POINT

What are the special challenges involved in budgeting at multinational companies?

PROBLEM FOR SELF-STUDY

Consider the Stylistic Furniture example described earlier. Suppose that to maintain its sales quantities, Stylistic needs to decrease selling prices by 3% to \$582 per Casual table and \$776 per Deluxe table. All other data are unchanged.

Required

Prepare a budgeted income statement, including all necessary detailed supporting budget schedules that are different from the schedules presented in the chapter. Indicate those schedules that will remain unchanged.

Solution

Schedules 1 and 8 will change. Schedule 1 changes because a change in selling price affects revenues. Schedule 8 changes because revenues are a cost driver of marketing costs (sales commissions). The remaining Schedules 2–7 will not change because a change in selling price has no effect on manufacturing costs. The revised schedules and the new budgeted income statement follow.

Schedule 1: Revenues Budget
for the Year Ending December 31, 2020

	Selling Price	Units	Total Revenues
Casual tables	\$582	50,000	\$29,100,000
Deluxe tables	776	10,000	7,760,000
Total			\$36,860,000

Schedule 8: Operating (nonmanufacturing) Costs Budget
for the Year Ending December 31, 2020

Business Function	Variable Costs	Fixed Costs (as in Schedule 8, page 210)	Total Costs
Product design		\$1,024,000	\$1,024,000
Marketing (Variable cost: \$36,860,000 × 0.065)	\$2,395,900	1,330,000	3,725,900
Distribution (Variable cost: \$2 × 1,140,000 cu. ft.)	2,280,000	1,596,000	3,876,000
	\$4,675,900	\$3,950,000	\$8,625,900

Stylistic Furniture Budgeted Income Statement for the Year Ending December 31, 2020

Revenues	Schedule 1		$36,860,000
Cost of goods sold	Schedule 7		24,440,000
Gross margin			12,420,000
Operating costs			
Product design	Schedule 8	$1,024,000	
Marketing costs	Schedule 8	3,725,900	
Distribution costs	Schedule 8	3,876,000	8,625,900
Operating income			$ 3,794,100

DECISION POINTS

The following question-and-answer format summarizes the chapter's learning objectives. Each decision presents a key question related to a learning objective. The guidelines are the answer to that question.

Decision	Guidelines
1. What is the master budget, and why is it useful?	The master budget summarizes the financial projections of all the company's budgets. It expresses management's operating and financing plans—the formalized outline of the company's financial objectives and how they will be attained. Budgets are tools that, by themselves, are neither good nor bad. Budgets are useful when administered skillfully.
2. When should a company prepare budgets? What are the advantages and challenges of implementing budgets?	Budgets should be prepared when their expected benefits exceed their expected costs. There are four key advantages of budgets: (1) they compel strategic analysis and planning, (2) they promote coordination and communication among subunits of the company, (3) they provide a framework for judging performance and facilitating learning, and (4) they motivate managers and other employees. The challenges are the time-consuming back-and-forth debates between senior and subordinate managers to set budgets.
3. What is the operating budget, and what are its components?	The operating budget is the budgeted income statement and its supporting budget schedules. The starting point for the operating budget is generally the revenues budget. The following supporting schedules are derived from the activities needed to support the revenues budget: production budget, direct materials usage budget, direct materials purchases budget, direct manufacturing labor cost budget, manufacturing overhead costs budget, ending inventories budget, cost of goods sold budget, and R&D/product design, marketing, distribution, and customer-service budgets.
4. How can managers plan for changes in the assumptions underlying the budget and manage risk?	Managers can use financial planning models—-mathematical statements of the relationships among operating activities, financing activities, and other factors that affect the budget. These models make it possible for managers to conduct a what-if (sensitivity) analysis of the risks that changes in the original predicted data or changes in underlying assumptions would have on the master budget and to develop plans to respond to changed conditions.

Decision	Guidelines
5. How do companies use responsibility centers? Should performance reports of responsibility center managers include only costs the manager can control?	A responsibility center is a part, segment, or subunit of an organization whose manager is accountable for a specified set of activities. Four types of responsibility centers are cost centers, revenue centers, profit centers, and investment centers. Responsibility accounting systems are useful because they measure the plans, budgets, actions, and actual results of each responsibility center. Controllable costs are costs primarily subject to the influence of a given responsibility center manager for a given time period. Performance reports of responsibility center managers often include costs, revenues, and investments that the managers cannot control. Responsibility accounting associates financial items with managers on the basis of which manager has the most knowledge and information about specific items, regardless of the manager's ability to exercise full control.
6. Why are human factors crucial in budgeting?	The administration of budgets requires education, participation, persuasion, and intelligent interpretation. When wisely administered, budgets create commitment, accountability, and honest communication among employees and can be used as the basis for continuous improvement efforts. When badly managed, budgeting can lead to game-playing and budgetary slack—the practice of making budget targets more easily achievable.
7. What are the special challenges involved in budgeting at multinational companies?	Budgeting is a valuable tool for multinational companies but is challenging because of the uncertainties posed by operating in multiple countries. In addition to budgeting in different currencies, managers in multinational companies also need to budget for foreign exchange rates and consider the political, legal, tax, and economic environments of the different countries in which they operate. In times of high uncertainty, managers use budgets to help the organization learn and adapt to its circumstances rather than to evaluate performance.

APPENDIX

The Cash Budget

The chapter illustrated the operating budget, which is one part of the master budget. The other part is the financial budget, which is composed of the capital expenditures budget, the cash budget, the budgeted balance sheet, and the budgeted statement of cash flows. This appendix focuses on the cash budget and the budgeted balance sheet. We discuss capital budgeting in Chapter 22. The budgeted statement of cash flows is beyond the scope of this text and generally is covered in financial accounting and corporate finance courses.

Why should Stylistic's managers want a cash budget in addition to the operating income budget presented in the chapter? Recall that Stylistic's management accountants prepared the operating budget on an accrual accounting basis consistent with how the company reports its actual operating income. But Stylistic's managers also need to plan cash flows to ensure that the company has adequate cash to pay vendors, meet payroll, and pay operating expenses as these payments come due. Stylistic could be very profitable, but the pattern of cash receipts from revenues might be delayed and result in insufficient cash being available to make scheduled payments. Stylistic's managers may then need to initiate a plan to borrow money to finance any shortfall. Building a profitable operating plan does not guarantee that adequate cash will be available, so Stylistic's managers need to prepare a cash budget in addition to an operating income budget.

Exhibit 6-5 shows Stylistic Furniture's balance sheet for the year ended December 31, 2019. The budgeted cash flows for 2020 are as follows:

	Quarters			
	1	2	3	4
Collections from customers	$9,136,600	$10,122,000	$10,263,200	$8,561,200
Disbursements				
Direct materials	3,031,400	2,636,967	2,167,900	2,242,033
Direct manufacturing labor payroll	1,888,000	1,432,000	1,272,000	1,408,000
Manufacturing overhead costs	3,265,296	2,476,644	2,199,924	2,435,136
Operating (nonmanufacturing) costs	2,147,750	2,279,000	2,268,250	2,005,000
Machinery purchase	—	—	758,000	—
Income taxes	725,000	400,000	400,000	400,000

The quarterly data are based on the budgeted cash effects of the operations formulated in Schedules 1–8 in the chapter, but the details of that formulation are not shown here to keep this illustration as brief and as focused as possible.

Stylistic wants to maintain a $320,000 minimum cash balance at the end of each quarter. The company can borrow or repay money at an interest rate of 12% per year. Management does not want to borrow any more short-term cash than is necessary. By special arrangement with the bank, Stylistic pays interest when repaying the principal. Assume, for simplicity, that borrowing takes place at the beginning and repayment at the end of the quarter under consideration (in multiples of $1,000). Interest is computed to the nearest dollar.

Suppose a management accountant at Stylistic receives the preceding data and the other data contained in the budgets in the chapter (pages 200–211). Her manager asks her to:

1. Prepare a cash budget for 2020 by quarter. That is, prepare a statement of cash receipts and disbursements by quarter, including details of borrowing, repayment, and interest.

EXHIBIT 6-5

Balance Sheet for Stylistic Furniture, December 31, 2019

Home | Insert | Page Layout | Formulas | Data | Review | View

	A	B	C	D
1	Stylistic Furniture Balance Sheet			
2	December 31, 2019			
3	Assets			
4	Current assets			
5	Cash		$ 300,000	
6	Accounts receivable		1,711,000	
7	Direct materials inventory		1,090,000	
8	Finished goods inventory		646,000	$ 3,747,000
9	Property, Plant, and equipment			
10	Land		2,000,000	
11	Building and equipment	$ 22,000,000		
12	Accumulated depreciation	(6,900,000)	15,100,000	17,100,000
13	Total			$20,847,000
14	Liabilities and Stockholders' Equity			
15	Current liabilities			
16	Accounts payable		$ 904,000	
17	Income taxes payable		325,000	$ 1,229,000
18	Stockholders' equity			
19	Common stock, no-par 25,000 shares outstanding		3,500,000	
20	Retained earnings		16,118,000	19,618,000
21	Total			$20,847,000

2. Prepare a budgeted income statement for the year ending December 31, 2020. This statement should include interest expense and income taxes (federal, state, and local at a rate of 35% of operating income).
3. Prepare a budgeted balance sheet on December 31, 2020.

Preparation of Budgets

1. The **cash budget** is a schedule of expected cash receipts and cash disbursements. It predicts the effects on the cash position at the given level of operations. Exhibit 6-6 presents the cash budget by quarters to show the impact of cash flow timing on bank loans and their repayment. In practice, monthly—and sometimes weekly or even daily—cash budgets are critical for cash planning and control. Cash budgets help avoid unnecessary idle cash and unexpected cash deficiencies. They thus keep cash balances in line with needs. Ordinarily, the cash budget has these main sections:
   a. **Cash available for needs (before any financing).** The beginning cash balance plus cash receipts equals the total cash available for needs before any financing. Cash receipts

EXHIBIT 6-6 Cash Budget for Stylistic Furniture for the Year Ending December 31, 2020

Home Insert Page Layout Formulas Data Review View

	A	B	C	D	E	F
1	**Stylistic Furniture**					
2	**Cash Budget**					
3	**For Year Ending December 31, 2020**					
4		**Quarter 1**	**Quarter 2**	**Quarter 3**	**Quarter 4**	**Year as a Whole**
5	Cash balance, beginning	$ 300,000	$ 320,154	$ 320,783	$ 324,359	$ 300,000
6	Add receipts					
7	Collections from customers	9,136,600	10,122,000	10,263,200	8,561,200	38,083,000
8	Total cash available for needs (x)	9,436,600	10,442,154	10,583,983	8,885,559	38,383,000
9	Cash disbursements					
10	Direct materials	3,031,400	2,636,967	2,167,900	2,242,033	10,078,300
11	Direct Manufacturing labor payroll	1,888,000	1,432,000	1,272,000	1,408,000	6,000,000
12	Manufacturing overhead costs	3,265,296	2,476,644	2,199,924	2,435,136	10,377,000
13	Nonmanufacturing costs	2,147,750	2,279,000	2,268,250	2,005,000	8,700,000
14	Machinery purchase			758,000		758,000
15	Income taxes	725,000	400,000	400,000	400,000	1,925,000
16	Total cash disbursements (y)	11,057,446	9,224,611	9,066,074	8,490,169	37,838,300
17	Minimum cash balance desired	320,000	320,000	320,000	320,000	320,000
18	Total cash needed	11,377,446	9,544,611	9,386,074	8,810,169	38,158,300
19	Cash excess (deficiency)*	$ (1,940,846)	$ 897,543	$ 1,197,909	$ 75,390	$ 224,700
20	Financing					
21	Borrowing (at beginning)	$ 1,941,000	$ 0	$ 0	$ 0	$ 1,941,000
22	Repayment (at end)	0	(846,000)	(1,095,000)	0	(1,941,000)
23	Interest (at 12% per year)**	0	(50,760)	(98,550)	0	(149,310)
24	Total effects of financing (z)	1,941,000	(896,760)	(1,193,550)	0	(149,310)
25	Cash balance, ending***	$ 320,154	$ 320,783	$ 324,359	$ 395,390	$ 395,390
26	*Excess of total cash available − Total cash needed before financing					
27	**Note that the short-term interest payments pertain only to the amount of principal being repaid at the end of a quarter. The specific computations regarding interest are $846,000 × 0.12 × 0.5 = $50,760; $1,095,000 × 0.12 × 0.75 = $98,550. Also note that *depreciation does not require a cash outlay.*					
28	***Ending cash balance = Total cash available for needs (x) − Total disbursements (y) + Total effects of financing (z)					

depend on collections of accounts receivable, cash sales, and miscellaneous recurring sources, such as rental or royalty receipts. Information on the expected collectability of accounts receivable is needed for accurate predictions. Key factors include bad-debt (uncollectible accounts) experience (not an issue in the Stylistic case) and average time lag between sales and collections.

b. **Cash disbursements.** Cash disbursements by Stylistic Furniture include the following:

   i. *Direct materials purchases.* Suppliers are paid in full in the month after the goods are delivered.

   ii. *Direct manufacturing labor and other wage and salary outlays.* All payroll-related costs are paid in the month in which the labor effort occurs.

   iii. *Other costs.* These depend on timing and credit terms. (In the Stylistic case, all other costs are paid in the month in which the cost is incurred.) *Note that depreciation does not require a cash outlay.*

   iv. *Other cash disbursements.* These include outlays for property, plant, equipment, and other long-term investments.

   v. Income tax payments as shown each quarter.

c. **Financing effects.** Short-term financing requirements depend on how the total cash available for needs [keyed as (*x*) in Exhibit 6-6] compares with the total cash disbursements [keyed as (*y*)], plus the minimum ending cash balance desired. The financing plans will depend on the relationship between total cash available for needs and total cash needed. If there is a deficiency of cash, Stylistic obtains loans. If there is excess cash, Stylistic repays any outstanding loans.

d. **Ending cash balance.** The cash budget in Exhibit 6-6 shows the pattern of short-term "self-liquidating" cash loans. In quarter 1, Stylistic budgets a $1,940,846 cash deficiency. The company therefore undertakes short-term borrowing of $1,941,000 that it pays off over the course of the year. Seasonal peaks of production or sales often result in heavy cash disbursements for purchases, payroll, and other operating outlays as the company produces and sells products. Cash receipts from customers typically lag behind sales. The loan is *self-liquidating* in the sense that the company uses the borrowed money to acquire resources that it uses to produce and sell finished goods and uses the proceeds from sales to repay the loan. This self-liquidating cycle is the movement from cash to inventories to receivables and back to cash.

2. The budgeted income statement is presented in Exhibit 6-7. It is merely the budgeted operating income statement in Exhibit 6-3 (page 210) expanded to include interest expense and income taxes.

EXHIBIT 6-7

Budgeted Income Statement for Stylistic Furniture for the Year Ending December 31, 2020

	A	B	C	D
1		**Stylistic Furniture**		
2		**Budgeted Income Statement**		
3		**for the Year Ending December 31, 2020**		
4	Revenues	Schedule 1		$38,000,000
5	COGS	Schedule 7		24,440,000
6	Gross margin			13,560,000
7	Operating costs			
8	Product design costs	Schedule 8	$1,024,000	
9	Marketing costs	Schedule 8	3,800,000	
10	Distribution costs	Schedule 8	3,876,000	8,700,000
11	Operating income			4,860,000
12	Interest expense	Exhibit 6-6		149,310
13	Income before income taxes			4,710,690
14	Income taxes (at 35%)			1,648,742
15	Net income			$ 3,061,948

3. The budgeted balance sheet is presented in Exhibit 6-8. Each item is projected in light of the details of the business plan as expressed in all the previous budget schedules. For example, the ending balance of accounts receivable of $1,628,000 is computed by adding the budgeted revenues of $38,000,000 (from Schedule 1 on page 202) to the beginning balance of accounts receivable of $1,711,000 (from Exhibit 6-5) and subtracting cash receipts of $38,083,000 (from Exhibit 6-6).

For simplicity, this example explicitly gave the cash receipts and disbursements. Usually, the receipts and disbursements are calculated based on the lags between the items reported on the accrual basis of accounting in an income statement and balance sheet and their related cash receipts and disbursements. Consider accounts receivable.

EXHIBIT 6-8 Budgeted Balance Sheet for Stylistic Furniture, December 31, 2020

Home Insert Page Layout Formulas Data Review View

	A	B	C	D
1	**Stylistic Furniture**			
2	**Budgeted Balance Sheet**			
3	**December 31, 2020**			
4	**Assets**			
5	Current assets			
6	Cash (from Exhibit 6-6)		$ 395,390	
7	Accounts receivable (1)		1,628,000	
8	Direct materials inventory (2)		760,000	
9	Finished goods inventory (2)		4,486,000	$ 7,269,390
10	Property, plant, and equipment			
11	Land (3)		2,000,000	
12	Building and equipment (4)	$22,758,000		
13	Accumulated depreciation (5)	(8,523,000)	14,235,000	16,235,000
14	Total			$23,504,390
15	**Liabilities and Stockholders' Equity**			
16	Current liabilities			
17	Accounts payable (6)		$ 775,700	
18	Income taxes payable (7)		48,742	$ 824,442
19	Stockholders' equity			
20	Common stock, no-par, 25,000 shares outstanding (8)		3,500,000	
21	Retained earnings (9)		19,179,948	22,679,948
22	Total			$23,504,390
23				
24	Notes:			
25	Beginning balances are used as the starting point for most of the following computations			
26	(1) $1,711,000 + $38,000,000 revenues − $38,083,000 receipts (Exhibit 6-6) = $1,628,000			
27	(2) From Schedule 6B, p. 208			
28	(3) From opening balance sheet (Exhibit 6-5)			
29	(4) $22,000,000 (Exhibit 6-5) + $758,000 purchases (Exhibit 6-6) = $22,758,000			
30	(5) $6,900,000 (Exhibit 6-5) + $1,020,000 + $603,000 depreciation from Schedule 5, p. 207			
31	(6) $904,000 (Exhibit 6-5) + $9,950,000 (Schedule 3B) − $10,078,300 (Exhibit 6-6) = $775,300			
32	There are no other current liabilities. From Exhibit 6-6: Cash flows for direct manufacturing labor = $6,000,000 from Schedule 4 Cash flows for manufacturing overhead costs = $10,377,000 ($12,000,000 − depreciation $1,623,000) from Schedule 5 Cash flows for nonmanufacturing costs = $8,700,000 from Schedule 8.			
33	(7) $325,000 (Exhibit 6-5) + $1,648,742 (from Exhibit 6-7) − $1,925,000 payment (Exhibit 6-6) = $48,742			
34	(8) From opening balance sheet (Exhibit 6-5)			
35	(9) $16,118,000 (Exhibit 6-5) + net income $3,061,948 (Exhibit 6-7) = $19,179,948			

The budgeted sales for the year are broken down into sales budgets for each month and quarter. For example, Stylistic Furniture budgets sales by quarter of $9,282,000, $10,332,000, $10,246,000, and $8,140,000, which equal 2020 budgeted sales of $38,000,000.

	Quarter 1		Quarter 2		Quarter 3		Quarter 4	
	Casual	Deluxe	Casual	Deluxe	Casual	Deluxe	Casual	Deluxe
Budgeted sales in units	12,270	2,400	13,620	2,700	13,610	2,600	10,500	2,300
Selling price	$ 600	$ 800	$ 600	$ 800	$ 600	$ 800	$ 600	$ 800
Budgeted revenues	$7,362,000	$1,920,000	$8,172,000	$2,160,000	$8,166,000	$2,080,000	$6,300,000	$1,840,000
	$9,282,000		$10,332,000		$10,246,000		$8,140,000	

Notice that sales are expected to be higher in the second and third quarters relative to the first and fourth quarters when weather conditions limit the number of customers shopping for furniture.

Once Stylistic's managers determine the sales budget, a management accountant prepares a schedule of cash collections that serves as an input for the preparation of the cash budget. Stylistic estimates that 80% of all sales made in a quarter are collected in the same quarter and 20% are collected in the following quarter. Estimated collections from customers each quarter are calculated in the following table:

Schedule of Cash Collections

	Quarters			
	1	2	3	4
Accounts receivable balance on January 1, 2020 (Fourth-quarter sales from prior year collected in first quarter of 2020)	$1,711,000			
From first-quarter 2020 sales ($9,282,000 × 0.80; $9,282,000 × 0.20)	7,425,600	$ 1,856,400		
From second-quarter 2020 sales ($10,332,000 × 0.80; $10,332,000 × 0.20)		8,265,600	$ 2,066,400	
From third-quarter 2020 sales ($10,246,000 × 0.80; $10,246,000 × 0.20)			8,196,800	$2,049,200
From fourth-quarter 2020 sales ($8,140,000 × 0.80)				6,512,000
Total collections	$9,136,600	$10,122,000	$10,263,200	$8,561,200

Uncollected fourth-quarter 2020 sales of $1,628,000 ($ 8,140,000 × 0.20) appear as accounts receivable in the budgeted balance sheet of December 31, 2020 (see Exhibit 6-8). Note that the quarterly cash collections from customers calculated in this schedule equal the cash collections by quarter shown on page 222.

TRY IT! 6-6

Firelight Corporation manufactures and sells two types of decorative lamps, Knox and Ayer. The following data are available for the year 2020.

Accounts receivable (January 1, 2020)	$105,000
Budgeted sales in Quarter 1 (January 1 to March 31, 2020)	315,900
Budgeted sales in Quarter 2 (April 1 to June 30, 2020)	340,000
Budgeted sales in Quarter 3 (July 1 to September 30, 2020)	280,000
Budgeted sales in Quarter 4 (October 1 to December 31, 2020)	290,000

All sales are made on account with 65% of sales made in a quarter collected in the same quarter and 35% collected in the following quarter.

Calculate the cash collected from receivables in each of the four quarters of 2020.

EXHIBIT 6-9 Sensitivity Analysis: Effects of Key Budget Assumptions in Exhibit 6-4 on 2020 Short-Term Borrowing for Stylistic Furniture

	A	B	C	D	E	F	G	H	I	J
1				Direct Material			Short-Term Borrowing and Repayment by Quarter			
2		Selling Price		Purchase Costs		Budgeted	Quarters			
3	Scenario	Casual	Deluxe	Red Oak	Granite	Operating Income	1	2	3	4
4	1	$582	$776	$7.00	$10.00	$3,794,100	$2,146,000	$(579,000)	$(834,000)	$170,000
5	2	$600	$800	7.35	10.50	4,483,800	2,048,000	$(722,000)	$(999,000)	$ 41,000

Sensitivity Analysis and Cash Flows

Exhibit 6-4 (page 212) shows how differing assumptions about selling prices of coffee tables and direct material prices led to differing amounts for budgeted operating income for Stylistic Furniture. A key use of sensitivity analysis is to budget cash flow. Exhibit 6-9 outlines the short-term borrowing implications of the two combinations examined in Exhibit 6-4. Scenario 1, with the lower selling prices per table ($582 for the Casual table and $776 for the Deluxe table), requires $2,146,000 of short-term borrowing in quarter 1 that cannot be fully repaid as of December 31, 2020. Scenario 2, with the 5% higher direct material costs, requires $2,048,000 borrowing by Stylistic Furniture that also cannot be repaid by December 31, 2020. Sensitivity analysis helps managers anticipate such outcomes and take steps to minimize the effects of expected reductions in cash flows from operations.

TERMS TO LEARN

This chapter and the Glossary at the end of the text contain definitions of the following important terms:

activity-based budgeting (ABB) (**p. 205**)
budgetary slack (**p. 216**)
cash budget (**p. 223**)
continuous budget (**p. 199**)
controllability (**p. 214**)
controllable cost (**p. 214**)
cost center (**p. 213**)
financial budget (**p. 200**)
financial planning models (**p. 211**)
investment center (**p. 213**)
Kaizen budgeting (**p. 218**)
master budget (**p. 196**)
operating budget (**p. 199**)
organization structure (**p. 213**)
pro forma statements (**p. 196**)
profit center (**p. 213**)
responsibility accounting (**p. 213**)
responsibility center (**p. 213**)
revenue center (**p. 213**)
rolling budget (**p. 199**)
rolling forecast (**p. 199**)

ASSIGNMENT MATERIAL

Questions

6-1 What are the four elements of the budgeting cycle?
6-2 Define master budget.
6-3 "Strategy, plans, and budgets are unrelated to one another." Do you agree? Explain.
6-4 "Budgeted performance is a better criterion than past performance for judging managers." Do you agree? Explain.
6-5 "Production managers and marketing managers are like oil and water. They just don't mix." How can a budget assist in reducing conflicts between these two areas?
6-6 "Budgets meet the cost–benefit test by pushing managers to act differently." Do you agree? Explain.
6-7 Define rolling budget. Give an example.
6-8 Outline the steps in preparing an operating budget.
6-9 "The sales forecast is the cornerstone for budgeting." Do you agree? Explain.

6-10 How can sensitivity analysis be used to increase the benefits of budgeting?

6-11 Define Kaizen budgeting.

6-12 Describe how nonoutput-based cost drivers can be incorporated into budgeting.

6-13 Explain how the choice of the type of responsibility center (cost, revenue, profit, or investment) affects behavior.

6-14 What are some additional considerations when budgeting in multinational companies?

6-15 "Cash budgets must be prepared before the operating income budget." Do you agree? Explain.

Multiple-Choice Questions

In partnership with:
BECKER PROFESSIONAL EDUCATION®

6-16 Master budget. Which of the following statements is correct regarding the components of the master budget?

a. The cash budget is used to create the capital budget.
b. Operating budgets are used to create cash budgets.
c. The manufacturing overhead budget is used to create the production budget.
d. The cost of goods sold budget is used to create the selling and administrative expense budget.

6-17 Operating and financial budgets. Which of the following statements is correct regarding the drivers of operating and financial budgets?

a. The sales budget will drive the cost of goods sold budget.
b. The cost of goods sold budget will drive the units of production budget.
c. The production budget will drive the selling and administrative expense budget.
d. The cash budget will drive the production and selling and administrative expense budgets.

6-18 Production budget. Superior Industries' sales budget shows quarterly sales for the next year as follows: Quarter 1, 10,000; Quarter 2, 8,000; Quarter 3, 12,000; Quarter 4, 14,000. Company policy is to have a target finished-goods inventory at the end of each quarter equal to 20% of the next quarter's sales. What would be the budgeted production for the second quarter of next year?

1. 7,200 units;
2. 8,800 units;
3. 12,000 units;
4. 10,400 units

6-19 Responsibility centers. Elmhurst Corporation is considering changes to its responsibility accounting system. Which of the following statements is/are correct for a responsibility accounting system.

i. In a cost center, managers are responsible for controlling costs but not revenue.
ii. The idea behind responsibility accounting is that a manager should be held responsible for those items that the manager can control to a significant extent.
iii. To be effective, a good responsibility accounting system must help managers to plan and to control.
iv. Costs that are allocated to a responsibility center are normally controllable by the responsibility center manager.

1. I and II only are correct.
2. II and III only are correct.
3. I, II, and III are correct.
4. I, II, and IV are correct.

6-20 Cash budget. Mary Jacobs, the controller of the Jenks Company is working on Jenks' cash budget for year 2. She has information on each of the following items:

i. Wages due to workers accrued as of December 31, year 1.
ii. Limits on a line of credit that may be used to fund Jenks' operations in year 2.
iii. The balance in accounts payable as of December 31, year 1, from credit purchases made in year 1.

Which of the items above should Jacobs take into account when building the cash budget for year 2?

a. I and II **b.** I and III
c. II and III **d.** I, II, and III

Exercises

6-21 Sales budget, service setting. In 2020, Rouse & Sons, a small environmental-testing firm, performed 10,800 radon tests for $310 each and 15,400 lead tests for $220 each. Because newer homes are being built with lead-free pipes, lead-testing volume is expected to decrease by 13% next year. However, awareness of radon-related health hazards is expected to result in a 6% increase in radon-test volume each year in the near future. Jim Rouse feels that if he lowers his price for lead testing to $210 per test, he will have to face only a 5% decline in lead-test sales in 2021.

Required

1. Prepare a 2021 sales budget for Rouse & Sons assuming that Rouse holds prices at 2020 levels.
2. Prepare a 2021 sales budget for Rouse & Sons assuming that Rouse lowers the price of a lead test to $210. Should Rouse lower the price of a lead test in 2021 if the company's goal is to maximize sales revenue?

6-22 Sales and production budget. The Coby Company expects sales in 2021 of 201,000 units of serving trays. Coby's beginning inventory for 2021 is 13,000 trays, and its target ending inventory is 29,000 trays. Compute the number of trays budgeted for production in 2021.

6-23 Direct material budget. Hartley Co. produces wine. The company expects to produce 2,510,000 two-liter bottles of Chablis in 2021. Hartley purchases empty glass bottles from an outside vendor. Its target ending inventory of such bottles is 80,000; its beginning inventory is 55,000. For simplicity, ignore breakage. Compute the number of bottles to be purchased in 2021.

6-24 Material purchases budget. The McGrath Company has prepared a sales budget of 42,000 finished units for a 3-month period. The company has an inventory of 13,000 units of finished goods on hand at December 31 and has a target finished-goods inventory of 15,000 units at the end of the succeeding quarter.

It takes 3 gallons of direct materials to make one unit of finished product. The company has an inventory of 61,000 gallons of direct materials at December 31 and has a target ending inventory of 53,000 gallons at the end of the succeeding quarter. How many gallons of direct materials should McGrath Company purchase during the 3 months ending March 31?

6-25 Revenues, production, and purchases budgets. The Yucatan Co. in Mexico has a division that manufactures bicycles. Its budgeted sales for Model XG in 2021 are 95,000 units. Yucatan's target ending inventory is 7,000 units, and its beginning inventory is 11,000 units. The company's budgeted selling price to its distributors and dealers is 3,500 pesos per bicycle.

Yucatan buys all its wheels from an outside supplier. No defective wheels are accepted. A separate division of the company orders the extra wheels Yucatan needs for replacement parts. The company's target ending inventory is 14,000 wheels, and its beginning inventory is 16,000 wheels. The budgeted purchase price is 400 pesos per wheel.

Required

1. Compute the budgeted revenues in pesos.
2. Compute the number of bicycles that Yucatan should produce.
3. Compute the budgeted purchases of wheels in units and in pesos.
4. What actions can Yucatan's managers take to reduce budgeted purchasing costs of wheels assuming the same budgeted sales for Model XG?

6-26 Revenues and production budget. Saphire, Inc., bottles and distributes mineral water from the company's natural springs in northern Oregon. Saphire markets two products: 12-ounce disposable plastic bottles and 1-gallon reusable plastic containers.

Required

1. For 2021, Saphire marketing managers project monthly sales of 500,000 12-ounce bottles and 130,000 1-gallon containers. Average selling prices are estimated at $0.30 per 12-ounce bottle and $1.60 per 1-gallon container. Prepare a revenues budget for Saphire, Inc., for the year ending December 31, 2021.
2. Saphire begins 2021 with 980,000 12-ounce bottles in inventory. The vice president of operations requests that ending inventory of 12-ounce bottles on December 31, 2021, be no less than 660,000 bottles. Based on sales projections as budgeted previously, what is the minimum number of 12-ounce bottles Saphire must produce during 2021?
3. The VP of operations requests that ending inventory of 1-gallon containers on December 31, 2021, be 300,000 units. If the production budget calls for Saphire to produce 1,200,000 1-gallon containers during 2021, what is the beginning inventory of 1-gallon containers on January 1, 2021?

6-27 Budgeting; direct material usage, manufacturing cost, and gross margin. Xander Manufacturing Company manufactures blue rugs using wool and dye as direct materials. One rug is budgeted to use 36 skeins of wool at a cost of $2 per skein and 0.8 gallons of dye at a cost of $6 per gallon. All other materials are indirect. At the beginning of the year, Xander has an inventory of 458,000 skeins of wool at a cost of $961,800 and 4,000 gallons of dye at a cost of $23,680. Target ending inventory of wool and dye is zero. Xander uses the FIFO inventory cost-flow method.

Xander blue rugs are very popular and demand is high, but because of capacity constraints the firm will produce only 200,000 blue rugs per year. The budgeted selling price is $2,000 each. There are no rugs in beginning inventory. Target ending inventory of rugs is also zero.

Xander makes rugs by hand, but uses a machine to dye the wool. Thus, overhead costs are accumulated in two cost pools—one for dyeing and the other for weaving. Dyeing overhead is allocated to products based on machine-hours (MH). Weaving overhead is allocated to products based on direct manufacturing labor-hours (DMLH).

Xander budgets 0.2 machine-hours to dye each skein in the dyeing process. There is no direct manufacturing labor cost for dyeing. Xander budgets 62 direct manufacturing labor-hours to weave a rug at a budgeted rate of $13 per hour.

The following table presents the budgeted overhead costs for the dyeing and weaving cost pools:

	Dyeing (based on 1,440,000 MH)	Weaving (based on 12,400,000 DMLH)
Variable costs		
Indirect materials	$ 0	$15,400,000
Maintenance	6,560,000	5,540,000
Utilities	7,550,000	2,890,000
Fixed costs		
Indirect labor	347,000	1,700,000
Depreciation	2,100,000	274,000
Other	723,000	5,816,000
Total budgeted costs	$17,280,000	$31,620,000

Required

1. Prepare a direct materials usage budget in both units and dollars.
2. Calculate the budgeted overhead allocation rates for dyeing and weaving.
3. Calculate the budgeted unit cost of a blue rug for the year.
4. Prepare a revenues budget for blue rugs for the year, assuming Xander sells (a) 200,000 or (b) 185,000 blue rugs (that is, at two different sales levels).
5. Calculate the budgeted cost of goods sold for blue rugs under each sales assumption.
6. Find the budgeted gross margin for blue rugs under each sales assumption.
7. What actions might you take as a manager to improve profitability if sales drop to 185,000 blue rugs?
8. How might top management at Xander use the budget developed in requirements 1–6 to better manage the company?

6-28 Budgeting, service company. Stevens Snow Removal (SSR) Company provides snow removal services to commercial clients. The company has enjoyed considerable growth in recent years due to a successful marketing campaign and new relationships with commercial real-estate developers. SSR owner Jason Stevens makes sales calls himself and quotes on jobs based on square feet of plowed surface. SSR hires freelance truck owners to plow the parking lots using SSR snowplow attachments, and pays them $40 per hour. A part-time bookkeeper takes care of billing customers and other office tasks. Overhead is allocated based on direct labor-hours (DLH).

Jason Stevens estimates that his snow removers will work a total of 2,000 jobs during the year. Each job averages 5,000 square feet of plowed surface and requires 6 direct labor-hours. The following table presents the budgeted overhead costs for 2021:

Variable costs	
Supplies and maintenance ($10 per DLH)	$120,000
Fixed costs (to support capacity of 12,000 DLH)	
Indirect labor	30,000
Depreciation	6,000
Other	24,000
Total budgeted costs	$180,000

Required

1. Prepare a direct labor budget in both hours and dollars.
2. Calculate the budgeted overhead allocation rate based on the budgeted quantity of the cost drivers.
3. Calculate the budgeted total cost of all jobs for the year and the budgeted cost of an average 5,000-square-feet snow-removal job.
4. Prepare a revenues budget for the year, assuming that SSR charges customers $0.08 per square foot.
5. Calculate the budgeted operating income.
6. What actions can Stevens take if sales should decline to 1,800 jobs annually?

6-29 Budgets for production and direct manufacturing labor. (CMA, adapted) DeWitt Company makes and sells artistic frames for pictures of weddings, graduations, and other special events. Ron Bahar, the controller, is responsible for preparing DeWitt's master budget and has accumulated the following information for 2021:

	2021				
	January	February	March	April	May
Estimated sales in units	12,000	13,000	6,000	11,000	11,000
Selling price	$ 53.00	$ 52.00	$52.00	$ 52.00	$ 52.00
Direct manufacturing labor-hours per unit	3.0	3.0	2.0	2.0	2.0
Wage per direct manufacturing labor-hour	$ 11.00	$ 11.00	$11.00	$ 12.00	$ 12.00

In addition to wages, direct manufacturing labor-related costs include pension contributions of $0.40 per hour, worker's compensation insurance of $0.10 per hour, employee medical insurance of $0.50 per hour, and Social Security taxes. Assume that as of January 1, 2021, the Social Security tax rates are 7.5% for employers and 7.5% for employees. The cost of employee benefits paid by DeWitt on its direct manufacturing employees is treated as a direct manufacturing labor cost.

DeWitt has a labor contract that calls for a wage increase to $12 per hour on April 1, 2021. New labor-saving machinery has been installed and will be fully operational by March 1, 2021. DeWitt expects to have 16,000 frames on hand at December 31, 2020, and it has a policy of carrying an end-of-month inventory of 100% of the following month's sales plus 50% of the second following month's sales.

Required

1. Prepare a production budget and a direct manufacturing labor cost budget for DeWitt Company by month and for the first quarter of 2021. You may combine both budgets in one schedule. The direct manufacturing labor cost budget should include labor-hours and show the details for each labor-cost category.
2. What actions has the budget process prompted DeWitt's management to take?
3. How might DeWitt's managers use the budget developed in requirement 1 to better manage the company?

6-30 Activity-based budgeting. The Jerico store of Jiffy Mart, a chain of small neighborhood convenience stores, is preparing its activity-based budget for January 2021. Jiffy Mart has three product categories: soft drinks (35% of cost of goods sold [COGS]), fresh produce (25% of COGS), and packaged food (40% of COGS). The following table shows the four activities that consume indirect resources at the Jerico store, the cost drivers and their rates, and the cost-driver amount budgeted to be consumed by each activity in January 2021.

			January 2021 Budgeted Amount of Cost Driver Used		
Activity	Cost Driver	January 2021 Budgeted Cost-Driver Rate	Soft Drinks	Fresh Snacks	Packaged Food
Ordering	Number of purchase orders	$ 45	14	24	14
Delivery	Number of deliveries	$ 41	12	62	19
Shelf stocking	Hours of stocking time	$10.50	16	172	94
Customer support	Number of items sold	$ 0.09	4,600	34,200	10,750

Required

1. What is the total budgeted indirect cost at the Jerico store in January 2021? What is the total budgeted cost of each activity at the Jerico store for January 2021? What is the budgeted indirect cost of each product category for January 2021?
2. Which product category has the largest fraction of total budgeted indirect costs?
3. Given your answer in requirement 2, what advantage does Jiffy Mart gain by using an activity-based approach to budgeting over, say, allocating indirect costs to products based on cost of goods sold?

6-31 Kaizen approach to activity-based budgeting (continuation of 6-30). Jiffy Mart has a Kaizen (continuous improvement) approach to budgeting monthly activity costs for each month of 2021. Each successive month, the budgeted cost-driver rate decreases by 0.4% relative to the preceding month. So, for example, February's budgeted cost-driver rate is 0.996 times January's budgeted cost-driver rate, and March's budgeted cost-driver rate is 0.996 times the budgeted February rate. Jiffy Mart assumes that the budgeted amount of cost-driver usage remains the same each month.

Required

1. What are the total budgeted cost for each activity and the total budgeted indirect cost for March 2021?
2. What are the benefits of using a Kaizen approach to budgeting? What are the limitations of this approach, and how might Jiffy Mart management overcome them?

6-32 Responsibility and controllability. Consider each of the following independent situations for Prestige Fountains. Prestige manufactures and sells decorative fountains for commercial properties. The company also contracts to service both its own and other brands of fountains. Prestige has a manufacturing plant, a supply warehouse that supplies both the manufacturing plant and the service technicians (who often need parts to repair fountains), and 12 service vans. The service technicians drive to customer sites to service the fountains. Prestige owns the vans, pays for the gas, and supplies fountain parts, but the technicians own their own tools.

1. In the manufacturing plant, the production manager is not happy with the motors that the purchasing manager has been purchasing. In May, the production manager stops requesting motors from the supply warehouse and starts purchasing them directly from a different motor manufacturer. Actual materials costs in May are higher than budgeted.
2. Utility costs in the supply warehouse for August are higher than budgeted. Investigation reveals that the air conditioners were left on each evening and on weekends, in violation of company policy. When approached about the issue, the manager complained that the warehouse is too hot in the mornings during the summer if the air conditioners are not allowed to run continually.
3. Gasoline costs for each van are budgeted based on the service area of the van and the amount of driving expected for the month. The driver of van 3 routinely has monthly gasoline costs exceeding the budget for van 3. After investigating, the service manager finds that the driver has been driving the van for personal use.
4. Regency Mall, one of Prestige's fountain service customers, calls the service people only for emergencies and not for routine maintenance. Thus, the materials and labor costs for these service calls exceeds the monthly budgeted costs for a contract customer.
5. Prestige's sales representatives have recently written contracts with five new customers in a city 50 miles away. Currently, Prestige does not bill for travel time to maintenance jobs. A recent profitability analysis shows that when a single client in that city is serviced, the company loses money on that call.
6. The cost of health insurance for service technicians has increased by 40% this year, which caused the actual health insurance costs to greatly exceed the budgeted health insurance costs for the service technicians.

Required

For each situation described, determine where (that is, with whom) (a) responsibility and (b) controllability lie. Suggest ways to solve the problem or to improve the situation.

6-33 Responsibility, controllability, and stretch targets. Consider each of the following independent situations for Sunshine Tours, a company owned by David Bartlett that sells motor coach tours to schools and other groups. Sunshine Tours owns a fleet of 10 motor coaches and employs 12 drivers, 1 maintenance technician, 3 sales representatives, and an office manager. Sunshine Tours pays for all fuel and maintenance on the coaches. Drivers are paid $0.50 per mile while in transit, plus $15 per hour while idle (time spent waiting while tour groups are visiting their destinations). The maintenance technician and office manager are both full-time salaried employees. The sales representatives work on straight commission.

1. One of the motor coach drivers seems to be reaching his destinations more quickly than any of the other drivers and is reporting longer idle time.
2. Sunshine Tours allows motor coach drivers to select meal stops on long distance trips. Drivers are encouraged to discuss the stop locations with the client's trip contact in advance to ensure that the restaurant meets customer expectations. A recent investigation has shown that one driver only stops at a particular restaurant chain. Customer satisfaction surveys for that driver's trips have shown decreased satisfaction regarding the meal stops. It is suspected that the driver is receiving kickbacks from the restaurant in return for steering customers to them.
3. Regular preventive maintenance of the motor coaches has been proven to improve fuel efficiency and reduce overall operating costs by averting costly repairs. During busy months, however, it is difficult for the maintenance technician to complete all of the maintenance tasks within his 40-hour workweek.
4. David Bartlett has read about stretch targets, and he believes that a change in the compensation structure of the sales representatives may improve sales. Rather than a straight commission of 10% of sales, he is considering a system where each representative is given a monthly goal of 50 contracts. If the goal is met, the representative is paid a 12% commission. If the goal is not met, the commission falls to 8%. Currently, each sales representative averages 45 contracts per month.
5. Fuel consumption has increased significantly in recent months. David Bartlett is considering ways to promote improved fuel efficiency and reduce harmful emissions using stretch environmental targets, where drivers and the maintenance mechanic would receive a bonus if fuel consumption falls below 90% of budgeted fuel usage per mile driven.

Required

For situations 1–3, discuss which employee has responsibility for the related costs and the extent to which costs are controllable and by whom. What are the risks or costs to the company? What can be done to solve the problem or improve the situation? For situations 4 and 5, describe the potential benefits and costs of establishing stretch targets.

6-34 Cash flow analysis, sensitivity analysis. HealthMart is a retail store selling home oxygen equipment. HealthMart also services home oxygen equipment, for which the company bills customers monthly. HealthMart has budgeted for increases in service revenue of $200 each month due to a recent advertising campaign. The forecast of sales and service revenue for March–June 2021 is as follows:

Sales and Service Revenues Budget, March–June 2021

Month	Expected Sales Revenue	Expected Service Revenue	Total Revenue
March	$6,000	$4,000	$10,000
April	8,000	4,200	12,200
May	7,500	4,400	11,900
June	9,000	4,600	13,600

Almost all of the sales revenues of the oxygen equipment are credit card sales; cash sales are negligible. The credit card company deposits 97% of the revenues recorded each day into HealthMart's account overnight. For the servicing of home oxygen equipment, 60% of oxygen services billed each month is collected in the month of the service, and 40% is collected in the month following the service.

Required

1. Calculate the cash that HealthMart expects to collect in April, May, and June 2021 from sales and service revenues. Show calculations for each month.
2. HealthMart has budgeted expenditures for May of $11,000 and requires a minimum cash balance of $250 at the end of each month. It has a cash balance on May 1 of $400.
   a. Given your answer to requirement 1, will HealthMart need to borrow cash to cover its payments for May and maintain a minimum cash balance of $250 at the end of May?
   b. Assume (independently for each situation) that (1) May total revenues might be 10% lower or that (2) total costs might be 5% higher. Under each of those two scenarios, show the total net cash for May and the amount HealthMart would have to borrow to cover its cash payments for May and maintain a minimum cash balance of $250 at the end of May. (Again, assume a balance of $400 on May 1.)
3. Why do HealthMart's managers prepare a cash budget in addition to the revenue, expenses, and operating income budget? Has preparing the cash budget been helpful? Explain briefly.

Problems

6-35 Budget schedules for a manufacturer. Hale Specialties manufactures, among other things, woolen blankets for the athletic teams of the two local high schools. The company sews the blankets from fabric and sews on a logo patch purchased from the licensed logo store site. The teams are as follows:

- Broncos, with red blankets and the Broncos logo
- Rams, with black blankets and the Rams logo

Also, the black blankets are slightly larger than the red blankets.

The budgeted direct-cost inputs for each product in 2020 are as follows:

	Broncos Blanket	Rams Blanket
Red wool fabric	5 yards	0 yards
Black wool fabric	0 yards	6 yards
Broncos logo patches	1	0
Rams logo patches	0	1
Direct manufacturing labor	4 hours	5 hours

Data pertaining to the direct materials for March 2020 are as follows:

Actual Beginning Direct Materials Inventory, March 1, 2020

	Broncos Blanket	Rams Blanket
Red wool fabric	40 yards	0 yards
Black wool fabric	0 yards	20 yards
Broncos logo patches	50	0
Rams logo patches	0	65

Target Ending Direct Materials Inventory, March 31, 2020

	Broncos Blanket	Rams Blanket
Red wool fabric	30 yards	0 yards
Black wool fabric	0 yards	20 yards
Broncos logo patches	30	0
Rams logo patches	0	30

Unit cost data for direct-cost inputs pertaining to February 2020 and March 2020 are as follows:

	February 2020 (Actual)	March 2020 (Budgeted)
Red wool fabric (per yard)	$10	$11
Black wool fabric (per yard)	14	13
Broncos logo patches (per patch)	8	8
Rams logo patches (per patch)	7	9
Manufacturing labor cost per hour	27	28

Manufacturing overhead (both variable and fixed) is allocated to each blanket on the basis of budgeted direct manufacturing labor-hours per blanket. The budgeted variable manufacturing overhead rate for March 2020 is $17 per direct manufacturing labor-hour. The budgeted fixed manufacturing overhead for March 2020 is $14,625. Both variable and fixed manufacturing overhead costs are allocated to each unit of finished goods.

Data relating to finished-goods inventory for March 2020 are as follows:

	Broncos Blankets	Rams Blankets
Beginning inventory in units	14	19
Beginning inventory in dollars (cost)	$1,960	$2,945
Target ending inventory in units	24	29

Budgeted sales for March 2020 are 140 units of the Broncos blankets and 195 units of the Rams blankets. The budgeted selling prices per unit in March 2020 are $305 for the Broncos blankets and $378 for the Rams blankets. Assume the following in your answer:

- Work-in-process inventories are negligible and ignored.
- Direct materials inventory and finished-goods inventory are costed using the FIFO method.
- Unit costs of direct materials purchased and finished goods are constant in March 2020.

Required

1. Prepare the following budgets for March 2020:
   a. Revenues budget
   b. Production budget in units
   c. Direct material usage budget and direct materials purchases budget
   d. Direct manufacturing labor costs budget
   e. Manufacturing overhead costs budget
   f. Ending inventories budget (direct materials and finished goods)
   g. Cost of goods sold budget
2. Suppose Hale Specialties decides to incorporate continuous improvement into its budgeting process. Describe two areas where it could incorporate continuous improvement into the budget schedules in requirement 1.

6-36 Budgeted costs, Kaizen improvements, environmental costs. US Apparel (USA) manufactures plain white and solid-colored T-shirts. Budgeted inputs include the following:

	Price	Quantity	Cost per unit of output
Fabric	$ 8 per yard	0.75 yard per unit	$6 per unit
Labor	$ 16 per DMLH	0.25 DMLH per unit	$4 per unit
Dye*	$0.50 per ounce	4 ounces per unit	$2 per unit

*For colored T-shirts only

Budgeted sales and selling price per unit are as follows:

	Budgeted Sales	Selling Price per Unit
White T-shirts	10,000 units	$12 per T-shirt
Colored T-shirts	50,000 units	$15 per T-shirt

USA has the opportunity to switch from using the dye it currently uses to using an environmentally friendly dye that costs $1.25 per ounce. The company would still need 4 ounces of dye per shirt. USA is reluctant to change because of the increase in costs (and decrease in profit), but the Environmental Protection Agency has threatened to fine the company $130,000 if it continues to use the harmful but less expensive dye.

Required

1. Given the preceding information, would USA be better off financially by switching to the environmentally friendly dye? (Assume all other costs would remain the same.)
2. If USA chooses to be environmentally responsible and switches to the new dye, the changes in the process will allow production managers to implement Kaizen costing. If USA can reduce fabric and labor costs each by 1% per month on all the shirts it manufactures, by how much will overall costs decrease at the end of 12 months? (Round to the nearest dollar for calculating cost reductions.)
3. Refer to requirement 2. How could the reduction in material and labor costs be accomplished? Are there any problems with this plan?

6-37 Revenue and production budgets. (CPA, adapted) The Chen Corporation manufactures and sells two products: Thingone and Thingtwo. In July 2019, Chen's budget department gathered the following data to prepare budgets for 2020:

2020 Projected Sales

Product	Units	Price
Thingone	69,000	$160
Thingtwo	44,000	$258

2020 Inventories in Units

	Expected	Target
Product	January 1, 2020	December 31, 2020
Thingone	24,000	29,000
Thingtwo	7,000	8,000

The following direct materials are used in the two products:

	Amount Used per Unit		
Direct Material	Unit	Thingone	Thingtwo
A	pound	6	7
B	pound	4	5
C	each	0	3

Projected data for 2020 for direct materials are:

Direct Material	Anticipated Purchase Price	Expected Inventories January 1, 2020	Target Inventories December 31, 2020
A	$13	36,000 lb.	38,000 lb.
B	8	31,000 lb.	34,000 lb.
C	7	9,000 units	12,000 units

Projected direct manufacturing labor requirements and rates for 2020 are:

Product	Hours per Unit	Rate per Hour
Thingone	4	$13
Thingtwo	5	18

Manufacturing overhead is allocated at the rate of $24 per direct manufacturing labor-hour.

Required

Based on the preceding projections and budget requirements for Thingone and Thingtwo, prepare the following budgets for 2020:

1. Revenues budget (in dollars)
2. What questions might the CEO ask the marketing manager when reviewing the revenues budget? Explain briefly.
3. Production budget (in units)

4. Direct material purchases budget (in quantities)
5. Direct material purchases budget (in dollars)
6. Direct manufacturing labor budget (in dollars)
7. Budgeted finished-goods inventory at December 31, 2020 (in dollars)
8. What questions might the CEO ask the production manager when reviewing the production, direct materials, and direct manufacturing labor budgets?
9. How does preparing a budget help Chen Corporation's top management better manage the company?

6-38 Budgeted income statement. (CMA, adapted) Spin Cycle Company is a manufacturer of commercial-grade exercise bikes that are sold to hotels and health clubs. Maintaining the bikes is an important area of customer satisfaction. Because of increased industry competition, Spin Cycle's financial performance has suffered. However, the introduction of a new model and a predicted upturn in the economy are leading Spin Cycle's managers to predict improved performance in 2021. The following income statement shows results for 2020:

Spin Cycle Company Income Statement for the Year Ended December 31, 2020 (in Thousands)

Revenues		
Equipment	$12,000	
Maintenance contracts	4,000	
Total revenues		$16,000
Cost of goods sold		10,000
Gross margin		6,000
Operating costs		
Marketing	800	
Distribution	200	
Customer maintenance	300	
Administration	900	
Total operating costs		2,200
Operating income		$ 3,800

Spin Cycle's management team is preparing the 2021 budget and is studying the following information:

1. Selling prices of bikes are expected to increase by 15% due to the introduction of the new model. The selling price of each maintenance contract is expected to remain unchanged from 2020.
2. Bike sales in units are expected to increase by 10%, with a corresponding 10% growth in units of maintenance contracts.
3. Cost of each unit sold is expected to increase by 8% to pay for the necessary technology and quality improvements for the new model.
4. Marketing costs are expected to increase by $200,000.
5. Distribution costs vary in proportion to the number of bikes sold.
6. One additional maintenance technician is to be hired at a total cost of $60,000, which covers wages and related travel costs. The objective is to improve customer service and shorten response time.
7. There are no anticipated changes to administration costs.
8. There is no beginning or ending inventory of equipment.

Required

1. Prepare a budgeted income statement for the year ending December 31, 2021.
2. How well does the budget align with Spin Cycle's strategy?
3. How does preparing the budget help Spin Cycle's management team better manage the company?

6-39 Responsibility in a restaurant. Janet Jefferson operates a group of 10 Fresh Stop food trucks that serve lunch to busy workers in the business center of a large Midwest city. One of the most popular items on the menu is a quinoa salad made with organic vegetables. The ingredients of the salad, as well as other menu items, are prepped in a central kitchen each morning, under the supervision of the company's chef, Marie Beck, and loaded onto the trucks. The food truck operators assemble the salads as the orders are placed to ensure maximum freshness. Janet employs a purchasing agent, Bruce Atkins, who orders produce directly from local farmers. Bruce places produce orders at the beginning of each week, based on projected demand, and the farmers make deliveries every 2 days. In September 2020, an unexpected early freeze destroys the local farmer's arugula that is a key ingredient of the quinoa salad. Bruce decides to replace the arugula order with baby spinach. Unhappy that Bruce made the change without her approval, Chef Marie sends a kitchen helper out to a retail organic grocer to purchase imported arugula at a significantly higher price. Her argument is that the spinach is not an acceptable substitution, and that the change will be noticed by the company's many regular customers. By the following week, Bruce is able to purchase arugula from a southern grower that serves the company in the off-season. Janet is displeased with Bruce for not securing replacement wholesale arugula in time to avoid the substitution, and with Marie for making the unauthorized purchase at the much higher price.

Required

Who is responsible for the cost of the arugula? At what level is the cost controllable? Do you agree that Janet should be angry with the purchasing agent Bruce? With Marie? Why or why not?

6-40 Comprehensive problem with ABC costing. Animal Gear Company makes two pet carriers, the Cat-allac and the Dog-eriffic. They are both made of plastic with metal doors, but the Cat-allac is smaller. Information for the two products for the month of April is given in the following tables:

Input Prices

Direct materials	
Plastic	$ 5 per pound
Metal	$ 4 per pound
Direct manufacturing labor	$10 per direct manufacturing labor-hour

Input Quantities per Unit of Output

	Cat-allac	Dog-eriffic
Direct materials		
Plastic	4 pounds	6 pounds
Metal	0.5 pound	1 pound
Direct manufacturing labor-hours	3 hours	5 hours
Machine-hours (MH)	11 MH	19 MH

Inventory Information, Direct Materials

	Plastic	Metal
Beginning inventory	290 pounds	70 pounds
Target ending inventory	410 pounds	65 pounds
Cost of beginning inventory	$1,102	$217

Animal Gear accounts for direct materials using a FIFO cost-flow assumption.

Sales and Inventory Information, Finished Goods

	Cat-allac	Dog-eriffic
Expected sales in units	530	225
Selling price	$ 205	$ 310
Target ending inventory in units	30	10
Beginning inventory in units	10	19
Beginning inventory in dollars	$1,000	$4,650

Animal Gear uses a FIFO cost-flow assumption for finished-goods inventory.

Animal Gear uses an activity-based costing system and classifies overhead into three activity pools: Setup, Processing, and Inspection. Activity rates for these activities are $105 per setup-hour, $10 per machine-hour, and $15 per inspection-hour, respectively. Other information follows:

Cost-Driver Information

	Cat-allac	Dog-eriffic
Number of units per batch	25	9
Setup time per batch	1.50 hours	1.75 hours
Inspection time per batch	0.5 hour	0.7 hour

If necessary, round up to calculate number of batches.

Operating (nonmanufacturing) fixed costs for March equal $32,000, half of which are salaries. Salaries are expected to increase 5% in April. Other operating fixed costs will remain the same. The only variable operating cost is sales commission, equal to 1% of sales revenue.

Required

Prepare the following for April:

1. Revenues budget
2. Production budget in units
3. Direct material usage budget and direct material purchases budget
4. Direct manufacturing labor cost budget
5. Manufacturing overhead cost budgets for each of the three activities
6. Budgeted unit cost of ending finished-goods inventory and ending inventories budget
7. Cost of goods sold budget
8. Operating (nonmanufacturing) costs budget
9. Budgeted income statement (ignore income taxes)
10. How does preparing the budget help Animal Gear's management team better manage the company?

6-41 Cash budget (continuation of 6-40). Refer to the information in Problem 6-40.

Assume the following: Animal Gear (AG) does not make any sales on credit. AG sells only to the public and accepts cash and credit cards; 90% of its sales are to customers using credit cards, for which AG gets the cash right away, less a 2% transaction fee.

Purchases of materials are on account. AG pays for half the purchases in the period of the purchase and the other half in the following period. At the end of March, AG owes suppliers $8,000.

AG plans to replace a machine in April at a net cash cost of $13,000.

Labor, other manufacturing costs, and operating (nonmanufacturing) costs are paid in cash in the month incurred except of course depreciation, which is not a cash flow. Depreciation is $25,000 of the manufacturing cost and $10,000 of the operating (nonmanufacturing) cost for April.

AG currently has a $2,000 loan at an annual interest rate of 12%. The interest is paid at the end of each month. If AG has more than $7,000 cash at the end of April, it will pay back the loan. AG owes $5,000 in income taxes that need to be remitted in April. AG has cash of $5,900 on hand at the end of March.

Required

1. Prepare a cash budget for April for Animal Gear.
2. Why do Animal Gear's managers prepare a cash budget in addition to the revenue, expenses, and operating income budget?

6-42 Comprehensive operating budget. Skulas, Inc., manufactures and sells snowboards. Skulas manufactures a single model, the Pipex. In late 2020, Skulas's management accountant gathered the following data to prepare budgets for January 2021:

Materials and Labor Requirements	
Direct materials	
Wood	9 board feet (b.f.) per snowboard
Fiberglass	10 yards per snowboard
Direct manufacturing labor	5 hours per snowboard

Skulas's CEO expects to sell 2,900 snowboards during January 2021 at an estimated retail price of $650 per board. Further, the CEO expects a 2021 beginning inventory of 500 snowboards and would like to end January 2021 with 200 snowboards in stock.

Direct Materials Inventories	Beginning Inventory, January 1, 2021	Ending Inventory, January 31, 2021
Wood	2,040 b.f.	1,540 b.f.
Fiberglass	1,040 yards	2,040 yards

Variable manufacturing overhead is $7 per direct manufacturing labor-hour. There are also $81,000 in fixed manufacturing overhead costs budgeted for January 2021. Skulas combines both variable and fixed manufacturing overhead into a single rate based on direct manufacturing labor-hours. Variable marketing costs are allocated at the rate of $250 per sales visit. The marketing plan calls for 38 sales visits during January 2021. Finally, there are $35,000 in fixed operating (nonmanufacturing) costs budgeted for January 2021.

Other data include the following:

	2020 Unit Price	2021 Unit Price
Wood	$32.00 per b.f.	$34.00 per b.f.
Fiberglass	$ 8.00 per yard	$ 9.00 per yard
Direct manufacturing labor	$28.00 per hour	$29.00 per hour

The inventoriable unit cost for ending finished-goods inventory on December 31, 2020, is $374.80. Assume Skulas uses a FIFO inventory method for both direct materials and finished goods. Ignore work in process in your calculations.

Required

1. Prepare the January 2021 revenues budget (in dollars).
2. Prepare the January 2021 production budget (in units).
3. Prepare the direct material usage and purchases budgets for January 2021.
4. Prepare a direct manufacturing labor costs budget for January 2021.
5. Prepare a manufacturing overhead costs budget for January 2021.
6. What is the budgeted manufacturing overhead rate for January 2021?
7. What is the budgeted manufacturing overhead cost per output unit in January 2021?
8. Calculate the cost of a snowboard manufactured in January 2021.
9. Prepare an ending inventory budget for both direct materials and finished goods for January 2021.
10. Prepare a cost of goods sold budget for January 2021.
11. Prepare the budgeted operating income statement for Skulas, Inc., for January 2021.
12. What questions might the CEO ask the management team when reviewing the budget? Should the CEO set stretch targets? Explain briefly.
13. How does preparing the budget help Skulas's management team better manage the company?

6-43 Cash budgeting, budgeted balance sheet (continuation of 6-42) (Appendix).
Refer to the information in Problem 6-42.
Budgeted balances at January 31, 2021, are as follows:

Cash	?
Accounts receivable	?
Inventory	?
Property, plant and equipment (net)	$1,175,600
Accounts payable	?
Long-term liabilities	182,000
Stockholders' equity	?

Selected budget information for December 2020 follows:

Cash balance, December 31, 2020	$ 124,000
Budgeted sales	1,650,000
Budgeted materials purchases	820,000

Customer invoices are payable within 30 days. From past experience, Skulas's accountant projects 40% of invoices will be collected in the month invoiced, and 60% will be collected in the following month.

Accounts payable relates only to the purchase of direct materials. Direct materials are purchased on credit with 50% of direct materials purchases paid during the month of the purchase, and 50% paid in the month following purchase.

Fixed manufacturing overhead costs include $64,000 of depreciation costs and fixed operating (non-manufacturing) overhead costs include $10,000 of depreciation costs. Direct manufacturing labor and the remaining manufacturing and operating (nonmanufacturing) overhead costs are paid monthly.

All property, plant, and equipment acquired during January 2021 were purchased on credit and did not entail any outflow of cash.

There were no borrowings or repayments with respect to long-term liabilities in January 2021.

On December 15, 2020, Skulas's board of directors voted to pay a $160,000 dividend to stockholders on January 31, 2021.

Required

1. Prepare a cash budget for January 2021. Show supporting schedules for the calculation of collection of receivables and payments of accounts payable, and for disbursements for fixed manufacturing and operating (nonmanufacturing) overhead.
2. Skulas is interested in maintaining a minimum cash balance of $120,000 at the end of each month. Will Skulas be in a position to pay the $160,000 dividend on January 31?
3. Why do Skulas's managers prepare a cash budget in addition to the revenue, expenses, and operating income budget?
4. Prepare a budgeted balance sheet for January 31, 2021, by calculating the January 31, 2021, balances in (a) cash, (b) accounts receivable, (c) inventory, (d) accounts payable, and (e) plugging in the balance for stockholders' equity.

6-44 Comprehensive problem; ABC manufacturing, two products. Butler, Inc., operates at capacity and makes wooden playground equipment. Although Butler's swing sets and play forts are a matching set, they are sold individually and so the sales mix is not 1:1. Butler's management is planning its annual budget for fiscal year 2021. Here is information for 2021:

Input Prices

Direct materials	
Wood	$2.00 per b.f.
Chain	$5.00 per ft.
Direct manufacturing labor	$ 20 per direct manufacturing labor-hour

Input Quantities per Unit of Output

	Swing Sets	Play Forts
Direct materials		
Wood	120 b.f.	200 b.f.
Chain	40 ft.	–
Direct manufacturing labor	12 hours	15 hours
Machine-hours (MH)	2 MH	5 MH

Inventory Information, Direct Materials

	Wood	Chain
Beginning inventory	20,000 b.f.	2,000 ft.
Target ending inventory	18,000 b.f.	1,800 ft.
Cost of beginning inventory	$38,500	$9,000

Butler accounts for direct materials using a FIFO cost flow assumption.

Sales and Inventory Information, Finished Goods

	Swing Sets	Play Forts
Expected sales in units	980	1,480
Selling price	$ 1,000	$ 1,200
Target ending inventory in units	100	120
Beginning inventory in units	80	100
Beginning inventory in dollars	$61,000	$90,000

Butler uses a FIFO cost-flow assumption for finished-goods inventory.

Swing sets are manufactured in batches of 20, and play forts are manufactured in batches of 10. It takes 2 hours to set up for a batch of swing sets and 1 hour to set up for a batch of play forts.

Butler uses activity-based costing and has classified all overhead costs as shown in the following table. Budgeted fixed overhead costs vary with capacity. Butler operates at capacity so budgeted fixed overhead cost per unit equals the budgeted fixed overhead costs divided by the budgeted quantities of the cost allocation base.

Cost Type	Budgeted Variable	Budgeted Fixed	Cost Driver/Allocation Base
Manufacturing			
Materials handling	$ 13,600	$ 20,000	Number of b.f. of wood used
Setup	2,600	4,900	Setup-hours
Processing	180,000	200,000	Machine-hours
Inspection	10,000	5,000	Number of units produced
Operating (nonmanufacturing)			
Marketing	$ 82,680	$192,920	Sales revenue
Distribution	0	295,500	Number of deliveries

Delivery trucks transport either 10 swing sets or 5 play forts in each delivery.

Required

Do the following for the year 2021:

1. Prepare the revenues budget.
2. Use the revenues budget to do the following:
   a. Find the budgeted allocation rate for marketing costs.
   b. Find the budgeted number of deliveries and allocation rate for distribution costs.
3. Prepare the production budget in units.
4. Use the production budget to find the following:
   a. The budgeted number of setups and setup-hours and the allocation rate for setup costs.
   b. The budgeted total machine-hours and the allocation rate for processing costs.
   c. The budgeted total units produced and the allocation rate for inspection costs.
5. Prepare the direct material usage budget and the direct material purchases budget in both units and dollars; round to whole dollars.
6. Use the direct material usage budget to find the budgeted allocation rate for materials-handling costs.
7. Prepare the direct manufacturing labor cost budget.
8. Prepare the manufacturing overhead cost budget for materials handling, setup, processing, and inspection costs.
9. Prepare the budgeted unit cost of ending finished-goods inventory and ending inventories budget.
10. Prepare the cost of goods sold budget.
11. Prepare the operating (nonmanufacturing) overhead costs budget for marketing and distribution.
12. Prepare a budgeted operating income statement (ignore income taxes).
13. How does preparing the budget help Butler's management team better manage the company?

6-45 Cash budget (continuation of 6-44) (Appendix). Refer to the information in Problem 6-44.

All purchases made in a given month are paid for in the following month, and direct material purchases make up all of the accounts payable balance and are reflected in the accounts payable balances at the beginning and the end of the year.

Sales are made to customers with terms net 45 days. Fifty percent of a month's sales are collected in the month of the sale, 25% are collected in the month following the sale, and 25% are collected 2 months after the sale and are reflected in the accounts receivables balances at the beginning and the end of the year.

Direct manufacturing labor, variable manufacturing overhead, and variable marketing costs are paid as they are incurred. Fifty percent of fixed manufacturing overhead costs, 60% of fixed marketing costs, and 100% of fixed distribution costs are depreciation expenses. The remaining fixed manufacturing overhead and marketing costs are paid as they are incurred.

Selected balances for December 31, 2020, follow:

Cash	$ 40,000
Accounts payable	85,000
Accounts receivable	170,000

Selected budget information for December 2021 follows:

Accounts payable	$ 90,000
Accounts receivable	168,000

Butler has budgeted to purchase equipment costing $610,000 for cash during 2021. Butler desires a minimum cash balance of $25,000. The company has a line of credit from which it may borrow in increments of $1,000 at an interest rate of 10% per year. By special arrangement, with the bank, Butler pays interest when repaying the principal, which only needs to be repaid in 2022.

Required

1. Prepare a cash budget for 2021. If Butler must borrow cash to meet its desired ending cash balance, show the amount that must be borrowed.
2. Does the cash budget for 2021 give Butler's managers all of the information necessary to manage cash in 2021? How might that be improved?
3. What insight does the cash budget give to Butler's managers that the budgeted operating income statement does not?

6-46 Budgeting and ethics. Jayzee Company manufactures a variety of products in a variety of departments and evaluates departments and departmental managers by comparing actual cost and output relative to the budget. Departmental managers help create the budgets and usually provide information about input quantities for materials, labor, and overhead costs.

Kurt Jackson is the manager of the department that produces product Z. Kurt has estimated these inputs for product Z:

Input	Budget Quantity per Unit of Output
Direct material	8 pounds
Direct manufacturing labor	30 minutes
Machine time	24 minutes

The department produces about 100 units of product Z each day. Kurt's department always gets excellent evaluations, sometimes exceeding budgeted production quantities. For each 100 units of product Z produced, the company uses, on average, about 48 hours of direct manufacturing labor (eight people working 6 hours each), 790 pounds of material, and 39.5 machine-hours.

Top management of Jayzee Company has decided to implement budget standards that will challenge the workers in each department, and it has asked Kurt to design more challenging input standards for product Z. Kurt provides top management with the following input quantities:

Input	Budget Quantity per Unit of Output
Direct material	7.9 pounds
Direct manufacturing labor	29 minutes
Machine time	23.6 minutes

Required

Discuss the following:

1. Are these budget standards challenging for the department that produces product Z?
2. Why do you suppose Kurt picked these particular standards?
3. What steps can Jayzee Company's top management take to make sure Kurt's standards really meet the goals of the firm?

6-47 Kaizen budgeting for carbon emissions. Angler Chemical Company currently operates three manufacturing plants in Colorado, Utah, and Arizona. Annual carbon emissions for these plants in the first quarter of 2021 are140,000 metric tons per quarter (or 560,000 metric tons in 2021). Angler management is investigating improved manufacturing techniques that will reduce annual carbon emissions to below 505,000 metric tons so that the company can meet Environmental Protection Agency guidelines in 2022. Costs and benefits are as follows:

Total cost to reduce carbon emissions	$14 per metric ton reduced in 2022 below 560,000 metric tons
Fine in 2022 if EPA guidelines are not met	$800,000

Angler Management has chosen to use Kaizen budgeting to achieve its goal for carbon emissions.

Required

1. If Angler reduces emissions by 2% each quarter, beginning with the second quarter of 2021, will the company reach its goal of 505,000 metric tons in 2022?
2. What would be the net financial cost or benefit of their plan? Ignore the time value of money.
3. What factors other than cost might weigh into Angler's decision to carry out this plan? What do you recommend Angler to do?

6-48 Comprehensive budgeting problem; activity-based costing, operating and financial budgets. Tyva makes a very popular undyed cloth sandal in one style, but in Regular and Deluxe. The Regular sandals have cloth soles and the Deluxe sandals have cloth-covered wooden soles. Tyva is preparing its budget for June 2021 and has estimated sales based on past experience. Other information for the month of June follows:

Input Prices	
Direct materials	
Cloth	$5.25 per yard
Wood	$7.50 per board foot
Direct manufacturing labor	$15 per direct manufacturing labor-hour

Input Quantities per Unit of Output (per Pair of Sandals)

	Regular	Deluxe
Direct materials		
Cloth	1.3 yards	1.5 yards
Wood	0	2 b.f.
Direct manufacturing labor-hours (DMLH)	5 hours	7 hours
Setup-hours per batch	2 hours	3 hours

Inventory Information, Direct Materials

	Cloth	Wood
Beginning inventory	610 yards	800 b.f.
Target ending inventory	386 yards	295 b.f.
Cost of beginning inventory	$3,219	$6,060

Tyva accounts for direct materials using a FIFO cost-flow assumption.

Sales and Inventory Information, Finished Goods

	Regular	Deluxe
Expected sales in units (pairs of sandals)	2,000	3,000
Selling price	$ 120	$ 195
Target ending inventory in units	400	600
Beginning inventory in units	250	650
Beginning inventory in dollars	$23,250	$92,625

Tyva uses a FIFO cost-flow assumption for finished-goods inventory.

All the sandals are made in batches of 50 pairs of sandals. Tyva incurs manufacturing overhead costs, marketing and general administration, and shipping costs. Besides materials and labor, manufacturing costs include setup, processing, and inspection costs. Tyva ships 40 pairs of sandals per shipment. Tyva uses activity-based costing and has classified all overhead costs for the month of June as shown in the following chart:

Cost Type	Denominator Activity	Rate
Manufacturing		
Setup	Setup-hours	$ 18 per setup-hour
Processing	Direct manufacturing labor-hours (DMLH)	$1.80 per DMLH
Inspection	Number of pairs of sandals	$1.35 per pair
Operating (nonmanufacturing)		
Marketing and general administration	Sales revenue	8%
Shipping	Number of shipments	$ 15 per shipment

Required

1. Prepare each of the following for June:
   a. Revenues budget
   b. Production budget in units
   c. Direct material usage budget and direct material purchases budget in both units and dollars; round to dollars
   d. Direct manufacturing labor cost budget
   e. Manufacturing overhead cost budgets for setup, processing, and inspection activities
   f. Budgeted unit cost of ending finished-goods inventory and ending inventories budget
   g. Cost of goods sold budget
   h. Marketing and general administration and shipping costs budget

2. Tyva's balance sheet for May 31 follows.

Tyva Balance Sheet as of May 31

Assets		
Cash		$ 9,435
Accounts receivable	$324,000	
Less: Allowance for bad debts	16,200	307,800
Inventories		
Direct materials		9,279
Finished goods		115,875
Fixed assets	$870,000	
Less: Accumulated depreciation	136,335	733,665
Total assets		$1,176,054

Liabilities and Equity	
Accounts payable	$ 15,600
Taxes payable	10,800
Interest payable	750
Long-term debt	150,000
Common stock	300,000
Retained earnings	698,904
Total liabilities and equity	$1,176,054

Use the balance sheet and the following information to prepare a cash budget for Tyva for June. Round to dollars.

- All sales are on account; 60% are collected in the month of the sale, 38% are collected the following month, and 2% are never collected and written off as bad debts.
- All purchases of materials are on account. Tyva pays for 80% of purchases in the month of purchase and 20% in the following month.
- All other costs are paid in the month incurred, including the declaration and payment of a $15,000 cash dividend in June.
- Tyva is making monthly interest payments of 0.5% (6% per year) on a $150,000 long-term loan.
- Tyva plans to pay the $10,800 of taxes owed as of May 31 in the month of June. Income tax expense for June is $25,107, which will be paid in July.
- 30% of processing, setup, and inspection costs and 10% of marketing and general administration and shipping costs are depreciation.

3. Prepare a budgeted income statement for June and a budgeted balance sheet for Tyva as of June 30, 2021.

Flexible Budgets, Direct-Cost Variances, and Management Control

7

LEARNING OBJECTIVES

1. Understand static budgets and static-budget variances
2. Examine the concept of a flexible budget and learn how to develop one
3. Calculate flexible-budget variances and sales-volume variances
4. Explain why standard costs are often used in variance analysis
5. Compute price variances and efficiency variances for direct-cost categories
6. Understand how managers use variances
7. Describe benchmarking and explain its role in cost management

Every organization, regardless of its profitability or growth, has to maintain control over its expenses.

And when customers are cautious with their spending, the need for managers to use budgeting and variance analysis tools for cost control becomes especially critical. By studying variances, managers can focus on where specific performances have fallen short and make corrective adjustments to achieve significant savings for their companies. The drive to achieve cost reductions might seem at odds with the growing push for organizations to pursue environmentally sound business practices. To the contrary, managers looking to be more efficient in their operations have found that cornerstones of the sustainability movement, such as reducing waste and power usage, offer fresh ways to help them manage risk and control costs, as the following article shows.

WALMART'S FLEET GOES GREEN TO REDUCE STANDARD COSTS[1]

Shipping goods is both costly and one of the biggest sources of carbon emissions in the United States and globally. Walmart, the world's largest retailer, found a way to deliver more goods to its stores while driving fewer miles, reducing greenhouse gas emissions and the company's standard (budgeted) costs of transporting products.

In 2005, Walmart established a goal to double the efficiency of its fleet of 6,000 trucks by 2015. This encouraged the company to add more cargo to its trailers and change its driving routes to eliminate unproductive miles. It also began collaborating with tractor and trailer manufacturers on new green technologies for its trucks, such as hybrid powertrains and carbon fiber trailers. Walmart achieved its efficiency goal 6 months ahead of schedule, and today the company delivers one billion more cases of goods than it did in 2005 while driving 460 million fewer miles. This has reduced the company's carbon dioxide emissions by 650,000 metric tons annually.

Higher fleet efficiency also significantly reduced Walmart's standard transportation costs.

Frontpage/Shutterstock

[1] *Sources*: Walmart Inc., 2018 Global Responsibility Report, Bentonville, AR, 2018 (https://corporate.walmart.com/media-library/document/2018-grr-summary/_proxyDocument?id=00000162-e4a5-db25-a97f-f7fd785a0001); Jim Mele, "Green Fleet of the Year: Walmart," *FleetOwner*, May 2, 2017 (https://www.fleetowner.com/running-green/green-fleet-year-walmart); "Walmart Marks Fulfillment of Key Global Responsibility Commitments," Walmart Inc. press release, Bentonville, AR, November 17, 2015 (https://news.walmart.com/news-archive/2015/11/17/walmart-marks-fulfillment-of-key-global-responsibility-commitments).

Each year, Walmart saves more than $1 billion annually compared to its 2005 baseline, showing that a cleaner environment and lower costs can go hand in hand.

In Chapter 6, you saw how budgets help managers with their planning function. We now explain how budgets, specifically flexible budgets, are used to compute variances, which assist managers in their control function. Variance analysis supports the critical final function in the five-step decision-making process by enabling managers to *evaluate performance and learn* after decisions are implemented. In this chapter and the next, we explain how.

Static Budgets and Variances

LEARNING OBJECTIVE 1

Understand static budgets

...the master budget based on output planned at start of period

and static-budget variances

...the difference between the actual result and the corresponding budgeted amount in the static budget

A **variance** is the difference between actual results and expected performance. The expected performance is also called **budgeted performance**, which is a point of reference for making comparisons.

The Use of Variances

Variances bring together the planning and control functions of management and facilitate management by exception. **Management by exception** is a practice whereby managers focus more closely on areas that are not operating as expected and less closely on areas that are. Consider the scrap and rework costs at a Maytag appliances plant. If actual costs are much higher than originally budgeted, variances prompt managers to find out why and correct the problem to reduce future scrap and rework. If a positive variance occurs, such as lower-than-planned costs, managers try to understand the reasons for the decrease (better operator training or changes in manufacturing methods, for example) so these practices can be continued and implemented by other divisions.

Variances are also used for evaluating performance and to motivate managers. For example, production-line managers at Maytag may have incentives linked to achieving a budgeted amount of operating costs.

Sometimes variances suggest that the company should consider a change in strategy. For example, large negative variances caused by excessive defect rates for a new product may cause managers to investigate and modify the product design or withdraw the product from the market. Variances also help managers make more informed predictions about the future and thereby improve the quality of the five-step decision-making process.

The benefits of variance analysis are not restricted to companies. Public officials have realized that the ability to make timely tactical changes based on variance information can result in making fewer draconian adjustments later. For example, the city of Scottsdale, Arizona, monitors its tax and fee performance against expenditures monthly. Why? One of the city's goals is to keep its water usage rates stable. By monitoring the extent to which the city's water revenues are matching its current expenses, Scottsdale can avoid sudden spikes in the rate it charges residents for water as well as finance water-related infrastructure projects.[2]

How important is variance analysis as a decision-making tool? Very! A survey by the United Kingdom's Chartered Institute of Management Accountants found that it was easily the most popular costing tool used by organizations of all sizes.

Static Budgets and Static-Budget Variances

As you study the exhibits in this chapter, note that "level" followed by a number denotes the amount of detail shown by a variance analysis. Level 1 reports the least detail, level 2 offers more information, and so on.

Consider Webb Company, a firm that manufactures and sells jackets. The jackets require tailoring and many other hand operations. Webb sells exclusively to distributors, who in turn sell to independent clothing stores and retail chains. For simplicity, we assume the following:

1. Webb's only costs are in the manufacturing function; Webb incurs no costs in other value-chain functions such as marketing and distribution.
2. All units manufactured in April 2020 are sold in April 2020.
3. There is no beginning or ending direct materials, work-in-process, or finished-goods inventories.

[2] For an excellent discussion and other related examples from governmental settings, see S. Kavanagh and C. Swanson, "Tactical Financial Management: Cash Flow and Budgetary Variance Analysis," *Government Finance Review* (October 1, 2009); Adam Khan, *Cost and Optimization in Government: An Introduction to Cost Accounting*. New York: Routledge, 2017.

Webb has three variable-cost categories. The budgeted variable cost per jacket is as follows:

Cost Category	Variable Cost per Jacket
Direct materials costs	$60
Direct manufacturing labor costs	16
Variable manufacturing overhead costs	12
Total variable costs	$88

The *number of units manufactured* is the cost driver for direct materials, direct manufacturing labor, and variable manufacturing overhead. The relevant range for the cost driver is from 0 to 12,000 jackets. Budgeted and actual data for April 2020 are shown below:

Budgeted fixed costs for production between 0 and 12,000 jackets	$276,000
Budgeted selling price	$ 120 per jacket
Budgeted production and sales	12,000 jackets
Actual production and sales	10,000 jackets

The **static budget**, or master budget, is based on the level of output planned at the start of the budget period. The master budget is called a static budget because the budget for the period is developed around a single (static) planned output level. Exhibit 7-1, column 3, presents the static budget for Webb Company for April 2020 that was prepared at the end of 2019. For each line item in the income statement, Exhibit 7-1, column 1, displays data for the actual April results. The following table presents more details for some of the differences between actual and budgeted outcomes:

	Actual Revenues and Costs (1)	Actual Jackets Produced and Sold (2)	Actual Price/Cost per Jacket (3) = (1) ÷ (2)	Budgeted Price/ Cost per Jacket (4)
Revenues	$1,250,000	10,000	$125.00	$120.00
Direct material costs	$ 621,600	10,000	$ 62.16	$ 60.00

We describe potential reasons and explanations for these differences as we discuss different variances throughout the chapter.

The **static-budget variance** (see Exhibit 7-1, column 2) is the difference between the actual result and the corresponding budgeted amount in the static budget.

Level 1 Analysis

	Actual Results (1)	Static-Budget Variances (2) = (1) − (3)	Static Budget (3)
Units sold	10,000	2,000 U	12,000
Revenues	$1,250,000	$190,000 U	$1,440,000
Variable costs			
Direct materials	621,600	98,400 F	720,000
Direct manufacturing labor	198,000	6,000 U	192,000
Variable manufacturing overhead	130,500	13,500 F	144,000
Total variable costs	950,100	105,900 F	1,056,000
Contribution margin	299,900	84,100 U	384,000
Fixed costs	285,000	9,000 U	276,000
Operating income	$ 14,900	$ 93,100 U	$ 108,000

$ 93,100 U
Static-budget variance

[a]F = favorable effect on operating income; U = unfavorable effect on operating income.

EXHIBIT 7-1

Static-Budget-Based Variance Analysis for Webb Company for April 2020[a]

A **favorable variance**—denoted F in this text—has the effect, when considered in isolation, of increasing operating income relative to the budgeted amount. For revenue items, F means actual revenues exceed budgeted revenues. For cost items, F means actual costs are less than budgeted costs. An **unfavorable variance**—denoted U in this text—has the effect, when viewed in isolation, of decreasing operating income relative to the budgeted amount. Unfavorable variances are also called *adverse variances* in some countries, such as the United Kingdom.

The unfavorable static-budget variance for operating income of $93,100 in Exhibit 7-1 is calculated by subtracting static-budget operating income of $108,000 from actual operating income of $14,900:

$$\begin{aligned}\text{Static-budget variance for operating income} &= \text{Actual result} - \text{Static-budget amount}\\ &= \$14{,}900 - \$108{,}000\\ &= \$93{,}100\text{ U.}\end{aligned}$$

The analysis in Exhibit 7-1 provides managers with additional information on the static-budget variance for operating income of $93,100 U. The more detailed breakdown indicates how the line items that comprise operating income—revenues, individual variable costs, and fixed costs—add up to the static-budget variance of $93,100.

Recall that Webb produced and sold only 10,000 jackets, although managers anticipated an output of 12,000 jackets in the static budget. *Managers want to know how much of the static-budget variance is due to Webb inaccurately forecasting what it expected to produce and sell and how much is due to how it actually performed manufacturing and selling 10,000 jackets.* Managers, therefore, create a flexible budget, which enables a more in-depth understanding of deviations from the static budget.

DECISION POINT

What are static budgets and static-budget variances?

TRY IT! 7-1

Jay Draperies makes and sells curtains. Information related to its performance in 2020 is given below:

	Actual	Budgeted
Units made and sold	1,500	1,400
Selling price	$ 190 per curtain	$ 200 per curtain
Variable costs	$162,750	$ 110 per curtain
Fixed costs	$ 75,000	$77,000

Calculate Jay Draperies' static-budget variance for (a) revenues, (b) variable costs, (c) fixed costs, and (d) operating income.

Flexible Budgets

LEARNING OBJECTIVE 2

Examine the concept of a flexible budget

...the budget that is adjusted (flexed) to recognize the actual output level

and learn how to develop one

...proportionately increase variable costs; keep fixed costs the same

A **flexible budget** calculates budgeted revenues and budgeted costs based on *the actual output in the budget period*. The flexible budget is prepared at the end of the period (April 2020 for Webb), after managers know the actual output of 10,000 jackets. The flexible budget is the *hypothetical* budget that Webb *would have* prepared at the start of the budget period if it had correctly forecast that actual output for April would be 10,000 jackets. Webb planned for an output of 12,000 jackets so the flexible budget is not the plan Webb initially had in mind for April 2020. In preparing Webb's flexible budget, all costs are either completely variable or completely fixed with respect to the number of jackets produced. Note the following:

- The budgeted selling price is the same $120 per jacket used in the static budget.
- The budgeted unit variable cost is the same $88 per jacket used in the static budget.
- Budgeted contribution margin per unit = Budgeted selling price − Budgeted variable cost per unit = $120 per jacket − $88 per jacket = $32 per jacket
- The budgeted *total* fixed costs are the same static-budget amount of $276,000. Why? Because the 10,000 jackets produced falls within the relevant range of 0 to 12,000 jackets for which budgeted fixed costs are $276,000.

The *only* difference between the static budget and the flexible budget is that the static budget is prepared for the planned output of 12,000 jackets, whereas the flexible budget is prepared retroactively based on the actual output of 10,000 jackets. In other words, the static budget is being "flexed," or adjusted, from 12,000 jackets to 10,000 jackets.[3]

Webb develops its flexible budget in three steps.

Step 1: Identify the Actual Quantity of Output. In April 2020, Webb produced and sold 10,000 jackets.

Step 2: Calculate the Flexible Budget for Revenues Based on the Budgeted Selling Price and Actual Quantity of Output.

$$\text{Flexible-budget revenues} = \$120 \text{ per jacket} \times 10{,}000 \text{ jackets}$$
$$= \$1{,}200{,}000$$

Step 3: Calculate the Flexible Budget for Costs Based on the Budgeted Variable Cost per Output Unit, Actual Quantity of Output, and Budgeted Fixed Costs.

Flexible-budget variable costs	
Direct materials, $60 per jacket × 10,000 jackets	$ 600,000
Direct manufacturing labor, $16 per jacket × 10,000 jackets	160,000
Variable manufacturing overhead, $12 per jacket × 10,000 jackets	120,000
Total flexible-budget variable costs	880,000
Flexible-budget fixed costs	276,000
Flexible-budget total costs	$1,156,000

These three steps enable Webb to prepare a flexible budget, as shown in Exhibit 7-2, column 3. The flexible budget allows for a more detailed analysis of the $93,100 unfavorable static-budget variance for operating income.

DECISION POINT

How can managers develop a flexible budget, and why is it useful to do so?

EXHIBIT 7-2 Level 2 Flexible-Budget-Based Variance Analysis for Webb Company for April 2020[a]

Level 2 Analysis

	Actual Results (1)	Flexible-Budget Variances (2) = (1) − (3)	Flexible Budget (3)	Sales-Volume Variances (4) = (3) − (5)	Static Budget (5)
Units sold	10,000	0	10,000	2,000 U	12,000
Revenues	$1,250,000	$50,000 F	$1,200,000	$240,000 U	$1,440,000
Variable costs					
Direct materials	621,600	21,600 U	600,000	120,000 F	720,000
Direct manufacturing labor	198,000	38,000 U	160,000	32,000 F	192,000
Variable manufacturing overhead	130,500	10,500 U	120,000	24,000 F	144,000
Total variable costs	950,100	70,100 U	880,000	176,000 F	1,056,000
Contribution margin	299,900	20,100 U	320,000	64,000 U	384,000
Fixed manufacturing costs	285,000	9,000 U	276,000	0	276,000
Operating income	$ 14,900	$29,100 U	$ 44,000	$ 64,000 U	$ 108,000

Level 2: $29,100 U Flexible-budget variance; $ 64,000 U Sales-volume variance

Level 1: $93,100 U Static-budget variance

[a]F = favorable effect on operating income; U = unfavorable effect on operating income.

[3] Suppose Webb, when preparing its annual budget for 2020 at the end of 2019, had perfectly anticipated that its output in April 2020 would equal 10,000 jackets. Then the flexible budget for April 2020 would be identical to the static budget.

TRY IT! 7-2

Consider Jay Draperies. With the same information for 2020 as provided in Try It! 7-1, calculate Jay Draperies's flexible budget for (a) revenues, (b) variable costs, (c) fixed costs, and (d) operating income.

LEARNING OBJECTIVE 3

Calculate flexible-budget variances

...each flexible-budget variance is the difference between an actual result and a flexible-budget amount

and sales-volume variances

...each sales-volume variance is the difference between a flexible-budget amount and a static-budget amount

Flexible-Budget Variances and Sales-Volume Variances

Exhibit 7-2 shows the flexible-budget-based variance analysis for Webb, which subdivides the \$93,100 unfavorable static-budget variance for operating income into two parts: a flexible-budget variance of \$29,100 U and a sales-volume variance of \$64,000 U. The **sales-volume variance** is the difference between a flexible-budget amount and the corresponding static-budget amount. The **flexible-budget variance** is the difference between an actual result and the corresponding flexible-budget amount.

Sales-Volume Variances

Keep in mind that the flexible-budget amounts in column 3 of Exhibit 7-2 and the static-budget amounts in column 5 are both computed using budgeted selling prices, budgeted variable cost per jacket, and budgeted fixed costs. The difference between the static-budget and the flexible-budget amounts is called the sales-volume variance because it arises *solely* from the difference between the 10,000 actual quantity (or volume) of jackets sold and the 12,000 quantity of jackets expected to be sold in the static budget.

$$\begin{array}{c}\text{Sales-volume}\\ \text{variance for}\\ \text{operating income}\end{array} = \begin{array}{c}\text{Flexible-budget}\\ \text{amount}\end{array} - \begin{array}{c}\text{Static-budget}\\ \text{amount}\end{array}$$

$$= \$44{,}000 - \$108{,}000$$

$$= \$64{,}000\text{ U}$$

The sales-volume variance in operating income for Webb measures the change in the budgeted contribution margin because Webb sold 10,000 jackets rather than the budgeted 12,000.

$$\begin{array}{c}\text{Sales-volume}\\ \text{variance for}\\ \text{operating income}\end{array} = \left(\begin{array}{c}\text{Budgeted contribution}\\ \text{margin per unit}\end{array}\right) \times \left(\begin{array}{c}\text{Actual units}\\ \text{sold}\end{array} - \begin{array}{c}\text{Static-budget}\\ \text{units sold}\end{array}\right)$$

$$= \$32\text{ per jacket} \times (10{,}000\text{ jackets} - 12{,}000\text{ jackets})$$

$$= \$32\text{ per jacket} \times (-2{,}000\text{ jackets}) = \$64{,}000\text{ U}$$

Exhibit 7-2, column 4, shows the components of this overall variance by identifying the sales-volume variance for each line item in the income statement. The unfavorable sales-volume variance in operating income arises because of one or more of the following reasons:

1. Failure of Webb's managers to execute the sales plans
2. Weaker-than-anticipated overall demand for jackets
3. Competitors taking away market share from Webb
4. Unexpected changes in customer tastes and preferences away from Webb's designs
5. Quality problems leading to customer dissatisfaction with Webb's jackets

How Webb responds to the unfavorable sales-volume variance will depend on what its managers believe caused the variance. For example, if Webb's managers believe the unfavorable sales-volume variance was caused by market-related reasons (reasons 1, 2, 3, or 4), the sales manager would be in the best position to explain what happened and suggest corrective actions that may be needed, such as sales promotions, market studies, changes to advertising plans, or changes in design. If, however, managers believe the unfavorable sales-volume variance was caused by quality problems (reason 5), the production manager would be in the best position to analyze the causes and suggest strategies for improvement, such as changes in the manufacturing process or investments in new machines.

The static-budget variances compare actual revenues and costs for 10,000 jackets against budgeted revenues and costs for 12,000 jackets. A portion of this difference, the sales-volume variance, reflects the effects of selling fewer units or inaccurate forecasting of sales. By removing this component from the static-budget variance, managers can compare their firm's revenues earned and costs incurred for April 2020 against the flexible budget—the revenues and costs Webb would have budgeted for the 10,000 jackets actually produced and sold. *Flexible-budget variances are a better measure of sales price and cost performance than static-budget variances because they compare actual revenues to budgeted revenues and actual costs to budgeted costs for the same 10,000 jackets of output.*

Flexible-Budget Variances

The first three columns of Exhibit 7-2 compare actual results with flexible-budget amounts. Column 2 shows the flexible-budget variances for each line item in the income statement:

$$\text{Flexible-budget variance} = \text{Actual result} - \text{Flexible-budget amount}$$

The operating income line in Exhibit 7-2 shows the flexible-budget variance is \$29,100 U (\$14,900 − \$44,000). The \$29,100 U arises because the actual selling price, actual variable cost per unit, and actual fixed costs differ from the budgeted amounts. The actual results and budgeted amounts for the selling price and variable cost per unit are as follows:

	Actual Result	Budgeted Amount
Selling price	\$125.00 (\$1,250,000 ÷ 10,000 jackets)	\$120.00 (\$1,200,000 ÷ 10,000 jackets)
Variable cost per jacket	\$ 95.01 (\$ 950,100 ÷ 10,000 jackets)	\$ 88.00 (\$ 880,000 ÷ 10,000 jackets)

The flexible-budget variance for revenues is called the **selling-price variance** because it arises solely from the difference between the actual selling price and the budgeted selling price:

$$\begin{aligned}\text{Selling-price variance} &= \left(\text{Actual selling price} - \text{Budgeted selling price}\right) \times \text{Actual units sold}\\ &= (\$125 \text{ per jacket} - \$120 \text{ per jacket}) \times 10{,}000 \text{ jackets}\\ &= \$50{,}000\text{ F}\end{aligned}$$

Webb has a favorable selling-price variance because the \$125 actual selling price exceeds the \$120 budgeted amount, which increases operating income. Marketing managers are generally in the best position to understand and explain the reason for a selling price difference. For example, was the difference due to better quality? Or was it due to an overall increase in market prices? Webb's managers concluded it was due to a general increase in prices.

$$\begin{aligned}\text{Flexible-budget variance for total variable costs} &= \left(\text{Actual variable cost per unit} - \text{Budgeted variable cost per unit}\right) \times \text{Actual units sold}\\ &= (\$95.10 \text{ per jacket} - \$88 \text{ per jacket}) \times 10{,}000 \text{ jackets}\\ &= \$70{,}100\text{ U}\end{aligned}$$

It's unfavorable because of one or both of the following:

- Webb used greater quantities of inputs (such as direct manufacturing labor-hours) compared to the budgeted quantities of inputs.
- Webb incurred higher prices per unit for the inputs (such as the wage rate per direct manufacturing labor-hour) compared to the budgeted prices per unit of the inputs.

Higher input quantities and/or higher input prices relative to the budgeted amounts could be the result of Webb deciding to produce a better product than planned or the result of inefficiencies related to Webb's manufacturing and purchasing operations, or both. *Think of variance analysis as providing suggestions for further investigation rather than as establishing conclusive evidence of good or bad performance.*

DECISION POINT

How are flexible-budget and sales-volume variances calculated?

The actual fixed costs of $285,000 are $9,000 more than the budgeted amount of $276,000. This unfavorable flexible-budget variance reflects unplanned increases in the cost of fixed indirect resources, such as the factory's rent or supervisors' salaries.

In the rest of this chapter, we will focus on variable direct-cost input variances. Chapter 8 emphasizes indirect (overhead) cost variances.

TRY IT! 7-3

Consider Jay Draperies again. With the same information for 2020 as provided in Try It! 7-1, calculate Jay Draperies's flexible-budget and sales-volume variances for (a) revenues, (b) variable costs, (c) fixed costs, and (d) operating income.

Standard Costs for Variance Analysis

LEARNING OBJECTIVE 4

Explain why standard costs are often used in variance analysis

...standard costs exclude past inefficiencies and take into account expected future changes

To gain further insight, a company will subdivide the flexible-budget variance for its direct-cost inputs into two more-detailed variances:

1. A price variance that reflects the difference between an actual input price and a budgeted input price
2. An efficiency variance that reflects the difference between an actual input quantity and a budgeted input quantity

We will call these level 3 variances. Managers generally have more control over efficiency variances than price variances because the quantity of inputs used is primarily affected by factors inside the company (such as the efficiency with which operations are performed), whereas changes in materials prices or wage rates are heavily influenced by external market forces.

Obtaining Budgeted Input Prices and Budgeted Input Quantities

To calculate price and efficiency variances, Webb needs to obtain budgeted input prices and budgeted input quantities. Webb's three main sources for this information are (1) past data, (2) data from similar companies, and (3) standards. Each source has its advantages and disadvantages.

1. **Actual input data from past periods.** Most companies have past data on actual input prices and actual input quantities. These historical data could be analyzed for trends or patterns using techniques we will discuss in Chapters 10 and 11 to estimate budgeted prices and quantities. Machine learning and artificial intelligence models use sophisticated algorithms to make these predictions.

   Advantages: Past data represent quantities and prices that are real rather than hypothetical benchmarks. Moreover, past data are typically easy to collect at a low cost.

   Disadvantages: A firm's inefficiencies, such as the wastage of direct materials, are incorporated in past data. Consequently, the data do not represent the performance the firm could have ideally attained, only the performance it achieved in the past. Past data also do not incorporate any changes expected for the budget period, such as improvements resulting from new investments in technology.

2. **Data from other companies that have similar processes.** Another source of information is data from peer companies or companies that have similar processes, which can serve as a benchmark. For example, Baptist Healthcare System in Louisville, Kentucky, benchmarks its labor performance data against those of similar top-ranked hospitals.

   Advantages: Data from other companies can provide a firm useful information about how it is performing relative to its competitors.

   Disadvantages: Input-price and input-quantity data from other companies often are not available or may not be comparable to a particular company's situation. Consider

Costco, which pays hourly workers an average of more than $20 per hour, well above the national average of $11.50 for a retail sales worker. Costco also provides the vast majority of its workforce with company-sponsored health care. Costco believes that higher wages and benefits increase employee satisfaction, improve productivity, and reduce turnover. But these wage rates are not a relevant benchmark for a company that follows a different labor strategy.

3. **Standards developed by the firm itself.** A **standard** is a carefully determined price, cost, or quantity that is used as a benchmark for judging performance. Standards are usually expressed on a per-unit basis. Consider how Webb determines its direct manufacturing labor standards. Webb conducts engineering studies to obtain a detailed breakdown of the steps required to make a jacket. Each step is assigned a standard time based on work performed by a *skilled* worker using equipment operating in an *efficient* manner. Similarly, Webb determines the standard quantity of square yards of cloth based on what is required by a skilled operator to make a jacket.

   Advantages: Standard times (1) aim to exclude past inefficiencies and (2) take into account changes expected to occur in the budget period. An example of the latter would be a decision by Webb's managers to lease new, faster, and more accurate sewing machines. Webb would then incorporate higher levels of efficiency into the new standards.

   Disdvantages: Because they are not based on realized benchmarks, the standards might not be achievable, and workers could get discouraged trying to meet them.

The term *standard* refers to many different things:

- A **standard input** is a carefully determined quantity of input, such as square yards of cloth or direct manufacturing labor-hours, required for one unit of output, such as a jacket.
- A **standard price** is a carefully determined price a company expects to pay for a unit of input. In the Webb example, the standard wage rate the firm expects to pay its operators is an example of a standard price of a direct manufacturing labor-hour.
- A **standard cost** is a carefully determined cost of a unit of output, such as the standard direct manufacturing labor cost of a jacket at Webb.

$$\frac{\text{Standard cost per output unit for}}{\text{each variable direct-cost input}} = \frac{\text{Standard input allowed}}{\text{for one output unit}} \times \frac{\text{Standard price}}{\text{per input unit}}$$

Standard direct material cost per jacket: 2 square yards of cloth input allowed per output unit (jacket) manufactured, at $30 standard price per square yard

$$\text{Standard direct material cost per jacket} = 2 \text{ square yards} \times \$30 \text{ per square yard} = \$60$$

Standard direct manufacturing labor cost per jacket: 0.8 manufacturing labor-hour of input allowed per output unit manufactured, at $20 standard price per hour

$$\text{Standard direct manufacturing labor cost per jacket} = 0.8 \text{ labor-hour} \times \$20 \text{ per labor-hour} = \$16$$

How are the words *budget* and *standard* related? Budget is the broader term. To clarify, budgeted input prices, input quantities, and costs need *not* be based on standards. As we saw previously, they could be based on past data or competitive benchmarks. However, when standards *are* used to obtain budgeted input quantities and prices, the terms *standard* and *budget* are used interchangeably. For example, the *standard-cost* computations shown previously for direct materials and direct manufacturing labor result in the *budgeted* direct material cost per jacket of $60 and the *budgeted* direct manufacturing labor cost of $16 referred to earlier.

In its standard costing system, Webb uses standards that are attainable by operating efficiently but that allow for normal disruptions. A normal disruption could include, for example, a short delay in the receipt of materials needed to produce the jackets or a production hold-up because a piece of equipment needed a minor repair. An alternative is to set more-challenging standards that are more difficult to attain. As we discussed in Chapter 6, challenging standards can increase the motivation of employees and a firm's performance. However, if workers believe the standards are unachievable, they can become frustrated and the firm's performance could suffer.

DECISION POINT

What is a standard cost, and what are its purposes?

Price Variances and Efficiency Variances for Direct-Cost Inputs

LEARNING OBJECTIVE 5

Compute price variances

. . . each price variance is the difference between an actual input price and a budgeted input price

and efficiency variances

. . . each efficiency variance is the difference between an actual input quantity and a budgeted input quantity for actual output

for direct-cost categories

Consider Webb's two direct-cost categories. The actual cost for each of these categories for the 10,000 jackets manufactured and sold in April 2020 is as follows:

Direct Materials Purchased and Used[4]	
1. Square yards of cloth purchased and used	22,200
2. Actual price incurred per square yard	$ 28
3. Direct material costs (22,200 × $28) [shown in Exhibit 7-2, column 1]	$621,600

Direct Manufacturing Labor Used	
1. Direct manufacturing labor-hours used	9,000
2. Actual price incurred per direct manufacturing labor-hour	$ 22
3. Direct manufacturing labor costs (9,000 × $22) [shown in Exhibit 7-2, column 1]	$198,000

Let's use the Webb Company data to illustrate the price variance and the efficiency variance for direct-cost inputs.

A **price variance** is the difference between actual price and budgeted price, multiplied by the actual input quantity such as direct materials purchased. A price variance is sometimes called a **rate variance**, especially when it's used to describe the price variance for direct manufacturing labor. An **efficiency variance** is the difference between the actual input quantity used (such as square yards of cloth) and the budgeted input quantity allowed for actual output, multiplied by budgeted price. An efficiency variance is sometimes called a **usage variance**. Let's explore price and efficiency variances in greater detail.

Price Variances

The formula for computing the price variance is as follows:

$$\text{Price variance} = \left(\text{Actual price of input} - \text{Budgeted price of input}\right) \times \text{Actual quantity of input}$$

The price variances for Webb's two direct-cost categories are as follows:

Direct-Cost Category	(**Actual price of input**	−	**Budgeted price of input**)	×	**Actual quantity of input**	=	**Price Variance**
Direct materials	($28 per sq. yard)	−	$30 per sq. yard)	×	22,200 square yards	=	$44,400 F
Direct manufacturing labor	($22 per hour	−	$20 per hour)	×	9,000 hours	=	$18,000 U

The direct materials price variance is favorable because the actual price of cloth is less than the budgeted price, resulting in an increase in operating income. The direct manufacturing labor price variance is unfavorable because the actual wage rate paid to labor is more than the budgeted rate, resulting in a decrease in operating income.

Managers should always consider a broad range of possible causes for a price variance. For example, Webb's favorable direct materials price variance could be due to one or more of the following:

- Webb's purchasing manager skillfully negotiated lower direct materials prices.
- The purchasing manager switched to a lower-priced supplier.
- The purchasing manager obtained quantity discounts by ordering larger quantities.

[4] The Problem for Self-Study (pages 263–264) relaxes the assumption that the quantity of direct materials used equals the quantity of direct materials purchased.

- Direct materials prices decreased unexpectedly due to an oversupply of materials.
- The budgeted purchase prices of direct materials were set too high because managers did not carefully analyze market conditions.
- The purchasing manager negotiated favorable prices because he was willing to accept unfavorable terms on factors other than prices (such as agreeing to lower-quality material).

How Webb's managers respond to the direct materials price variance depends on what they believe caused it. For example, if the purchasing manager received quantity discounts by ordering a larger amount of materials than budgeted, Webb's management accountants would investigate whether the quantity discounts exceeded the higher storage and inventory holding costs. A favorable price variance does not mean Webb benefited from the purchase manager's actions—this can only be determined after evaluating the effect of the manager's actions on other parts of the business or in future periods.

Efficiency Variance

For any actual level of output, the efficiency variance is the difference between the actual quantity of input used and the budgeted quantity of input allowed for that output level, multiplied by the budgeted input price:

$$\text{Efficiency variance} = \left(\begin{array}{c}\text{Actual}\\ \text{quantity of}\\ \text{input used}\end{array} - \begin{array}{c}\text{Budgeted quantity}\\ \text{of input allowed}\\ \text{for actual output}\end{array}\right) \times \begin{array}{c}\text{Budgeted price}\\ \text{of input}\end{array}$$

The idea here is that, given a certain output level, a company is inefficient if it uses a larger quantity of input than budgeted. Conversely, a company is efficient if it uses a smaller input quantity than was budgeted for that output level.

The efficiency variances for each of Webb's direct-cost categories are as follows:

Direct-Cost Category	(Actual quantity of input used − Budgeted quantity of input allowed for actual output)	× Budgeted price of input	= Efficiency variance
Direct materials	[22,200 sq. yds. − (10,000 units × 2 sq. yds. / unit)]	× $30 per sq. yard	
	= (22,200 sq. yds. − 20,000 sq. yds.)	× $30 per sq. yard	= $66,000 U
Direct manufacturing labor	[9,000 hours − (10,000 units × 0.8 hour / unit)]	× $20 per hour	
	= (9,000 hours − 8,000 hours)	× $20 per hour	= $20,000 U

The two manufacturing efficiency variances—the direct materials efficiency variance and the direct manufacturing labor efficiency variance—are each unfavorable. Why? Because given the firm's actual output, more inputs were used than the budgeted quantity allowed. This lowered Webb's operating income.

As with price variances, there is a broad range of possible causes for these efficiency variances. For example, Webb's unfavorable efficiency variance for direct manufacturing labor could be due to one or more of the following:

- Workers working more slowly or making poor-quality jackets that require reworking.
- The personnel manager hiring underskilled workers.
- Inefficient production scheduling resulting in idle and lost time.
- Improper maintenance leading to equipment failures.
- Inaccurately evaluating the skill levels of employees and the environment in which they operate and consequently setting standards that are too tight.

Suppose Webb's managers determine that the unfavorable variance is due to poor machine maintenance. They would then establish a team consisting of plant engineers and machine operators to develop a maintenance schedule to reduce future breakdowns and prevent adverse effects on labor time and product quality.[5]

Exhibit 7-3 provides an alternative way to calculate price and efficiency variances. It shows how the price variance and the efficiency variance subdivide the flexible-budget variance. Consider direct materials. The direct materials flexible-budget variance of $21,600 U is the difference between the actual costs incurred (actual input quantity × actual price) of $621,600 shown in column 1 and the flexible budget (budgeted input quantity allowed for actual output × budgeted price) of $600,000 shown in column 3. Column 2 (actual input quantity × budgeted price) is inserted between column 1 and column 3. Then:

- The difference between columns 1 and 2 is the price variance of $44,400 F. This is a price variance because the same actual input quantity (22,200 sq. yds.) is multiplied by the *actual price* ($28) in column 1 and the *budgeted price* ($30) in column 2.
- The difference between columns 2 and 3 is the efficiency variance of $66,000 U. This is an efficiency variance because the same budgeted price ($30) is multiplied by the *actual input quantity* (22,200 sq. yds.) in column 2 and the *budgeted input quantity allowed for actual output* (20,000 sq. yds.) in column 3.
- The sum of the direct materials price variance, $44,400 F, and the direct materials efficiency variance, $66,000 U, equals the direct materials flexible budget variance, $21,600 U.

Exhibit 7-4 provides a summary of the different variances. Note how the variances at each higher level provide disaggregated and more detailed information for evaluating performance.

We now present Webb's journal entries under its standard costing system.

EXHIBIT 7-3 Columnar Presentation of Variance Analysis: Direct Costs for Webb Company for April 2020[a]

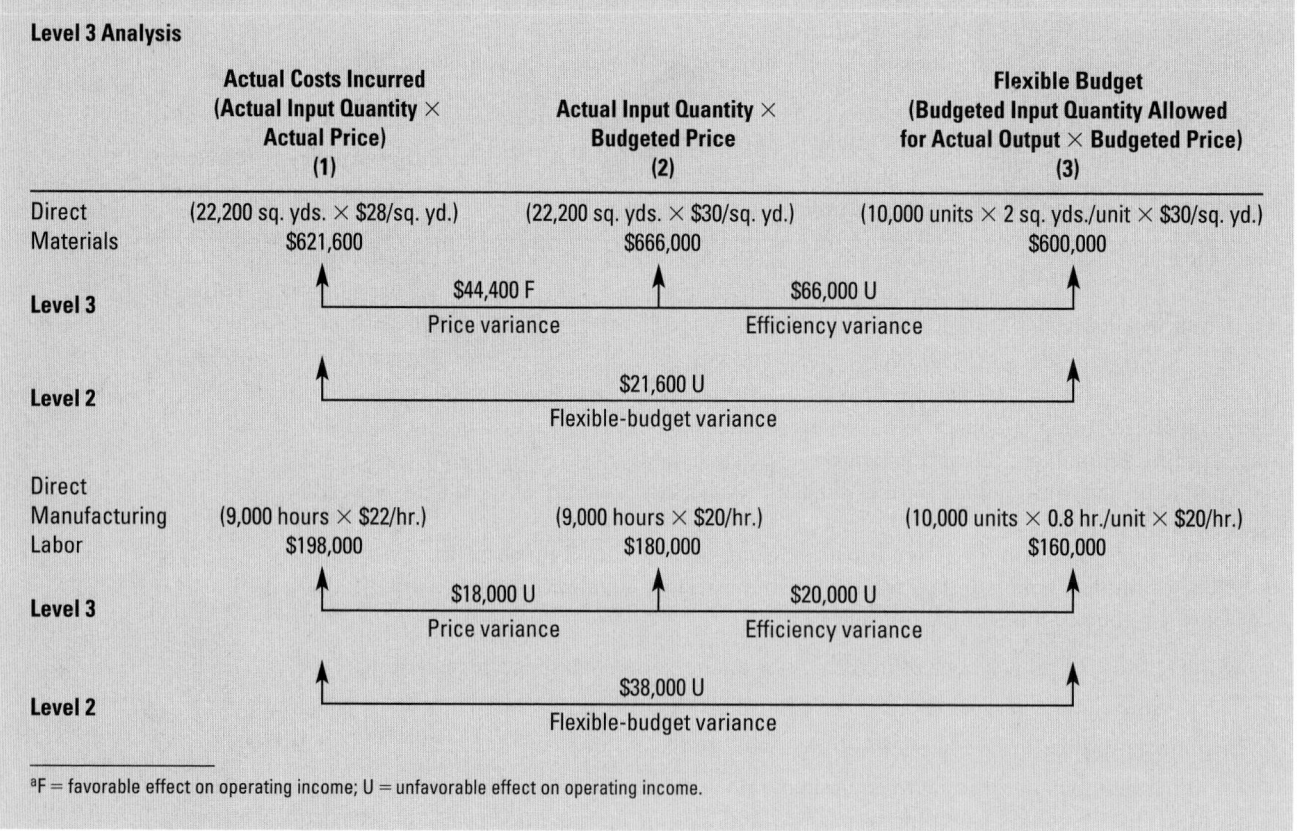

Level 3 Analysis

	Actual Costs Incurred (Actual Input Quantity × Actual Price) (1)		**Actual Input Quantity × Budgeted Price (2)**		**Flexible Budget (Budgeted Input Quantity Allowed for Actual Output × Budgeted Price) (3)**
Direct Materials	(22,200 sq. yds. × $28/sq. yd.) $621,600		(22,200 sq. yds. × $30/sq. yd.) $666,000		(10,000 units × 2 sq. yds./unit × $30/sq. yd.) $600,000
Level 3		$44,400 F Price variance		$66,000 U Efficiency variance	
Level 2			$21,600 U Flexible-budget variance		
Direct Manufacturing Labor	(9,000 hours × $22/hr.) $198,000		(9,000 hours × $20/hr.) $180,000		(10,000 units × 0.8 hr./unit × $20/hr.) $160,000
Level 3		$18,000 U Price variance		$20,000 U Efficiency variance	
Level 2			$38,000 U Flexible-budget variance		

[a]F = favorable effect on operating income; U = unfavorable effect on operating income.

[5] When there are multiple inputs, such as different types of materials, that can be substituted for one another, the efficiency variance can be further decomposed into mix and yield variances. The appendix to this chapter describes how these variances are calculated.

EXHIBIT 7-4

Summary of Level 1, 2, and 3 Variance Analyses

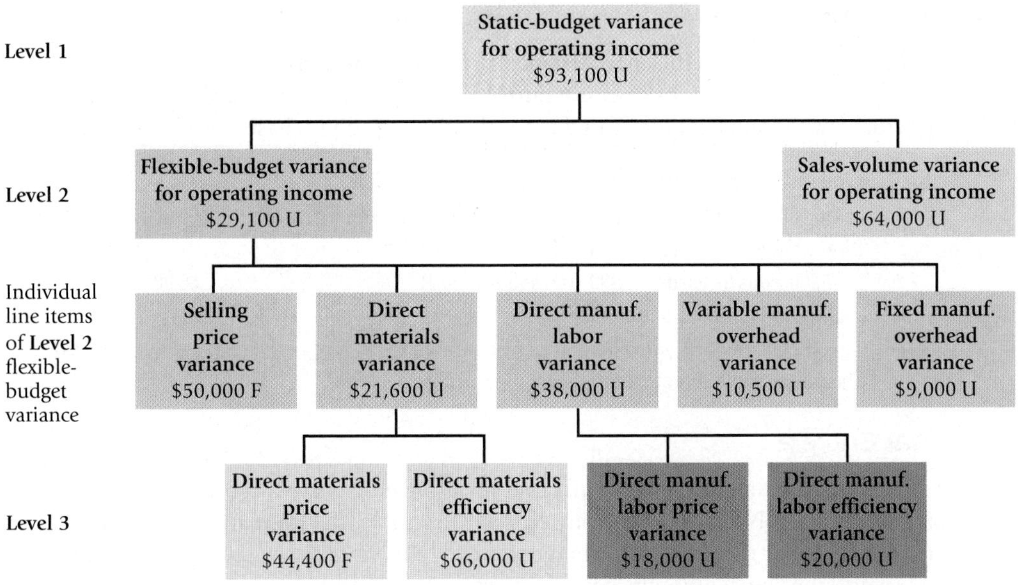

7-4 TRY IT!

Jay Draperies manufactures curtains. To complete a curtain, Jay requires the following inputs:

Direct materials standard:	10 square yards at $5 per yard
Direct manufacturing labor standard:	5 hours at $12 per hour

During the second quarter, Jamie Draperies made 1,500 curtains and used 14,000 square yards of fabric costing $67,200. Direct manufacturing labor totaled 7,800 hours for $95,550.

a. Compute the direct materials price and efficiency variances for the quarter.
b. Compute the direct manufacturing labor price and efficiency variances for the quarter.

Journal Entries Using Standard Costs

We next illustrate journal entries for Webb Company using standard costing. Our focus is on direct materials and direct manufacturing labor. All the numbers in the following journal entries are found in Exhibit 7-3.

Note: In each of the following entries, unfavorable variances are always debits (they decrease operating income), and favorable variances are always credits (they increase operating income).

Journal Entry 1A

Isolate the direct materials price variance at the time the materials are purchased by increasing (debiting) the Direct Materials Control account by the standard price for materials. This is the earliest time possible to isolate this variance.

1a.	Direct Materials Control		
	(22,200 square yards × $30 per square yard)	666,000	
	Direct Materials Price Variance		
	(22,200 square yards × $2 per square yard)		44,400
	Accounts Payable Control		
	(22,200 square yards × $28 per square yard)		621,600
	This records the direct materials purchased.		

Journal Entry 1B

Isolate the direct materials efficiency variance at the time the direct materials are used by increasing (debiting) the Work-in-Process Control account. Use the standard quantities allowed for the actual output units manufactured times their standard purchase prices.

1b.	Work-in-Process Control		
	(10,000 jackets × 2 yards per jacket × $30 per square yard)	600,000	
	Direct Materials Efficiency Variance		
	(2,200 square yards × $30 per square yard)	66,000	
	Direct Materials Control		
	(22,200 square yards × $30 per square yard)		666,000
	This records the direct materials used.		

Journal Entry 2

Isolate the direct manufacturing labor price variance and efficiency variance at the time labor is used by increasing (debiting) the Work-in-Process Control by the standard hours and standard wage rates allowed for the actual units manufactured. Note that the Wages Payable Control account measures the actual amounts payable to workers based on the actual hours they worked and their actual wage rate.

2.	Work-in-Process Control		
	(10,000 jackets × 0.80 hour per jacket × $20 per hour)	160,000	
	Direct Manufacturing Labor Price Variance		
	(9,000 hours × $2 per hour)	18,000	
	Direct Manufacturing Labor Efficiency Variance		
	(1,000 hours × $20 per hour)	20,000	
	Wages Payable Control		
	(9,000 hours × 22 per hour)		198,000
	This records the liability for Webb's direct manufacturing labor costs.		

Standard costing and variance analysis focus managerial attention on areas not operating as expected. The journal entries point to another advantage of standard costing systems: They simplify product costing. As each unit is manufactured, costs are assigned to it using the standard cost of direct materials, the standard cost of direct manufacturing labor, and, as you will see in a later chapter (Chapter 8), the standard manufacturing overhead cost.

From the perspective of control, variances are isolated at the earliest possible time. For example, the direct materials price variance is calculated at the time materials are purchased. Managers take corrective actions—such as negotiating cost reductions from current suppliers or obtaining price quotes from new suppliers—soon after purchases are made and the unfavorable variance is known. If managers only learn about the variances after materials are used in production, it would delay these actions.

Suppose variance amounts are immaterial at the end of the fiscal year. For simplicity, assume that the balances in the different direct-cost variance accounts as of April 2020 are also the balances at the end of 2020. Webb would record the following journal entry to write off the direct-cost variance accounts to the Cost of Goods Sold account.

Cost of Goods Sold	59,600	
Direct Materials Price Variance	44,400	
Direct Materials Efficiency Variance		66,000
Direct Manufacturing Labor Price Variance		18,000
Direct Manufacturing Labor Efficiency Variance		20,000

Alternatively, assume Webb has inventories at the end of the fiscal year and that the variances are material. The variance accounts will be prorated among the cost of goods sold and various inventory accounts using the methods described in Chapter 4 (pages 125–128). For example, the Direct Materials Price Variance will be prorated among Materials Control, Work-in-Process

Control, Finished Goods Control, and Cost of Goods Sold on the basis of the standard costs of direct materials in each account's ending balance. Direct Materials Efficiency Variance is prorated among Work-in-Process Control, Finished Goods Control, and Cost of Goods Sold on the basis of the direct material costs in each account's ending balance (after proration of the direct materials price variance).

As discussed in Chapter 4, many accountants, industrial engineers, and managers argue that to the extent variances measure inefficiency during the year, they should be written off against income for that period instead of being prorated among inventories and the cost of goods sold. They believe it is better to apply a combination of the write-off and proration methods for each individual variance so that, unlike full proration, the firm does not end up carrying the costs of inefficiency as part of its inventoriable costs. Consider the efficiency variance: The portion of the variance due to avoidable inefficiencies should be written off to cost of goods sold. In contrast, the portion that is unavoidable should be prorated. Likewise, if a portion of the direct materials price variance is unavoidable because it is entirely caused by general market conditions, it too should be prorated.

Implementing Standard Costing

Standard costing provides valuable information that is used for the management and control of materials, labor, and other activities related to production.

Standard Costing and Information Technology

Both large and small firms are increasingly using computerized standard costing systems. For example, companies such as Sandoz (a maker of generic drugs) and Dell store standard prices and standard quantities in their computer systems. A bar code scanner records the receipt of materials, immediately costing each material using its stored standard price. The receipt of materials is then matched with the firm's purchase orders and recorded in accounts payable to isolate the direct material price variance.

The direct materials efficiency variance is calculated as output is completed by comparing the standard quantity of direct materials that should have been used with the computerized request for direct materials submitted by an operator on the production floor. Labor variances are calculated as employees log into production-floor terminals and punch in their employee numbers, start and end times, and the quantity of product they helped produce. Enterprise resource planning (ERP) systems (see Chapter 6) have made it easy for firms to track standard, average, and actual costs and assess variances in real time. Managers use this instantaneous feedback to immediately detect and correct cost-related problems.

Wide Applicability of Standard Costing

Manufacturing firms as well as firms in the service sector find standard costing to be a useful tool. Companies implementing total quality management programs use standard costing to control materials costs. Service-sector companies such as McDonald's use standard costs to control labor costs. Companies implementing computer-integrated manufacturing (CIM), such as Toyota, use flexible budgeting and standard costing to manage activities such as materials handling and setups. Variance information helps managers identify areas of the firm's manufacturing or purchasing process that most need attention.

DECISION POINT

Why should a company calculate price and efficiency variances?

Management's Use of Variances

LEARNING OBJECTIVE 6

Understand how managers use variances

...managers use variances to improve future performance

Managers and management accountants use variances to evaluate performance after decisions are implemented, to trigger organization learning, and to make continuous improvements. Variances serve as an early warning system to alert managers to existing problems or to prospective opportunities. When done well, variance analysis enables managers to evaluate the effectiveness of the actions and performance of personnel in the current period, as well as to fine-tune strategies for achieving improved performance in the future. Concepts in Action: Can Chipotle Wrap Up Its Materials-Cost Increases? shows the importance of direct-cost variance analyses to the fast casual dining giant.

CONCEPTS IN ACTION

Can Chipotle Wrap Up Its Materials-Cost Increases?[6]

Patrick T. Fallon/Bloomberg/Getty Images

Along with burritos, Chipotle cooked up profitable growth for many years. The company's build-your-own-meal model and focus on organic and naturally raised ingredients successfully attracted millions of customers in the United States and beyond. With competition and operating costs on the rise, however, Chipotle's success going forward will depend on its ability to wrap up materials costs.

For Chipotle, profitability depends on making each burrito at the lowest possible cost. The two key direct costs are labor and materials costs. Labor costs include wages for restaurant managers and staff, along with benefits such as health insurance. Materials costs include the "critical seven" expensive food ingredients—steak, carnitas, barbacoa, chicken, cheese, guacamole, and sour cream—and items such as foil, paper bags, and plastic silverware.

To reduce labor costs, Chipotle makes subtle recipe and preparation shifts to find the right balance between taste and cost. For example, it washes and cuts some produce items, such as tomatoes and romaine lettuce, and shreds cheese in central kitchens to ensure food safety and reduce in-store labor costs. Since 2010, these actions have helped limit growth in labor costs from 25.4% of revenues in 2010 to 26.9% in 2017. Materials costs rose from 30.5% of revenue to 34.3% due to the focus on naturally raised ingredients and food safety. Responsibly raised meat and fresh local produce cost Chipotle more than conventional ingredients. To reduce material usage Chipotle aggressively manages portion control. While employees gladly oblige customers asking for extra rice, beans, or salsa, they control the "critical seven" food ingredients.

In 2018, to further manage its materials costs while driving environmental sustainability, Chipotle introduced new measures to reduce food waste during the preparation process. It also began cooking food to match sales to reduce food waste at the end of each day. With future profitability dependent on lowering materials costs, variance analysis will be a critical ingredient for Chipotle to deliver on its promise of "food with integrity."

[6] *Sources*: Sarah Nassauer, "Inside Chipotle's Kitchen: What's Really Handmade," *The Wall Street Journal*, February 24, 2015 (https://www.wsj.com/articles/inside-chipotles-kitchen-whats-really-handmade-1424802150); "New Chipotle Food Safety Procedures Largely in Place; Company Will Share Learnings from 2015 Outbreaks at All-Team Meeting," Chipotle Mexican Grill press release, Denver, CO, January 19, 2016 (https://ir.chipotle.com/news-releases?item=122453).

Multiple Causes of Variances

To interpret variances correctly and to make appropriate decisions, managers need to understand the multiple causes of variances. They also must not interpret a variance in isolation. A variance in one part of the value chain may result from decisions made in the same or another part of the value chain. Consider an unfavorable direct materials efficiency variance on Webb's production line. Possible operational causes of this variance across the value chain are shown below:

1. Poor design of products or processes
2. Poor work on the production line because of underskilled workers or faulty machines
3. Inappropriate assignment of labor or machines to specific jobs
4. Congestion caused by scheduling rush orders placed by Webb's sales representatives
5. Webb's cloth suppliers not manufacturing materials of uniformly high quality

Item 5 offers an even broader reason for the unfavorable direct materials efficiency variance—inefficiencies in the supply chain of cloth suppliers for Webb's jackets. Whenever possible, managers must attempt to understand root causes of variances.

When to Investigate Variances

A standard is not a single measure but rather a range of acceptable input quantities, costs, output quantities, or prices. Often, a variance within an acceptable range is considered to be an "in-control occurrence" and calls for no investigation or action. So how do managers decide when to investigate variances? They use subjective judgments or rules of thumb. For critical items such as product defects, even a small variance can prompt an investigation. For other items such as direct material costs, labor costs, and repair costs, companies generally have rules such as "investigate all variances exceeding $5,000 or 20% of the budgeted cost, whichever is lower." Why? Because a 4% variance in direct materials costs of $1 million—a $40,000 variance—deserves more attention than a 15% variance in repair costs of $10,000—a $1,500 variance. In other words, variance analysis is subject to the same cost–benefit test as all other phases of a management control system.

Using Variances for Performance Measurement

Managers often use variance analysis to evaluate the performance of their employees or business units. Suppose a purchasing manager for Starbucks has just negotiated a deal that results in a favorable price variance for direct materials. As our earlier discussion suggests, a favorable direct materials price variance needs further investigation before reaching conclusions about the purchasing manager's performance. If the purchasing manager bargained effectively with suppliers, it would support a positive evaluation. If, however, (1) the purchasing manager secured a discount by placing larger orders, leading to higher inventory costs, or (2) accepted a bid from a low-priced supplier by sacrificing quality, it is not so clear. The gains from the favorable direct materials price variance could be offset by higher inventory storage costs or higher inspection costs and defect rates, resulting in an unfavorable direct materials efficiency variance (using more inputs than budgeted to produce a given level of output).

Bottom line: Managers should not automatically interpret a favorable variance as "good news" or assume it means their subordinates performed well.

Firms benefit from variance analysis because it highlights individual aspects of performance. However, if any single performance measure (for example, achieving a certain labor efficiency variance or a certain consumer rating) is overemphasized, managers will tend to make decisions that will cause the particular performance measure to look good. These actions may conflict with the company's overall goals, inhibiting the goals from being achieved. This faulty perspective on performance usually arises when top management designs a performance evaluation and reward system that does not emphasize total company objectives or overall *effectiveness*, such as sales, market share, or overall profitability.

Using Variances for Organization Learning

The goal of variance analysis is for managers to understand why variances arise, to learn, and to improve their firm's future performance. For instance, to reduce the unfavorable direct materials efficiency variance, Webb's managers may attempt to improve the design of its jackets, the commitment of its workers to do the job right the first time, and the quality of the materials. Sometimes an unfavorable direct materials efficiency variance may signal a need to change the strategy related to a product, perhaps because it cannot be made at a low enough cost. Variance analysis should not be used to "play the blame game" (find someone to blame for every unfavorable variance) but to help managers learn about what happened and how to perform better in the future.

Companies need to strike a delicate balance between using variances to evaluate performance and to promote organizational learning. If performance evaluation is overemphasized, managers will focus on setting and meeting targets that are easy to attain rather than targets that are challenging, require creativity and resourcefulness, and lead to learning. For example, Webb's manufacturing manager will prefer an easy standard that allows workers ample time to manufacture a jacket. But doing so will weaken the drive to learn and to come up with new ways to produce. Overemphasizing performance might have other negative consequences—the manufacturing manager might push workers to produce jackets within the time allowed, even if this leads to poorer quality, which would later hurt revenues. Negative effects such as these can be minimized if variance analysis is seen as a way to promote learning.

Using Variances for Continuous Improvement

One form of learning is continuous improvement. Managers can use variance analysis for continuous improvement. How? By repeatedly identifying causes of variances, taking corrective actions, and evaluating results. Some companies use Kaizen budgeting (Chapter 6, p. 218) to specifically target reductions in budgeted costs over successive periods. The advantage of Kaizen budgeting is that it makes continuous improvement goals explicit.

Continuous improvement goals need to be implemented thoughtfully. In a research or design setting, injecting too much discipline and focusing on incremental improvement may dissuade creativity and truly innovative approaches. Overly relying on gaining efficiencies should not deter employees from taking risky approaches or from challenging basic assumptions about products and processes.

Financial and Nonfinancial Performance Measures

Almost all companies use a combination of financial and nonfinancial performance measures for planning and control rather than relying exclusively on one or the other. To control a production process, supervisors cannot wait for an accounting report with variances reported in dollars. Instead, they use timely nonfinancial performance measures to exercise control. For example, Nissan and other manufacturers display real-time defect rates and production levels on large screens throughout their plants to monitor performance.

DECISION POINT

How do managers use variances?

In Webb's cutting room, cloth is laid out and cut into pieces, which are then matched and assembled. Managers exercise control in the cutting room by observing workers and by focusing on *nonfinancial measures*, such as number of square yards of cloth used to produce 1,000 jackets or the percentage of jackets started and completed without requiring any rework. Webb's production workers find these nonfinancial measures easy to understand. Webb's managers also use *financial measures* to evaluate the overall cost efficiency with which operations are being run and to help guide decisions about, say, changing the mix of inputs used in manufacturing jackets. Financial measures are critical in a company because they indicate the economic impact of diverse physical activities. This knowledge allows managers to make trade-offs, such as increasing the costs of one physical activity (say, cutting) to reduce the costs of another physical measure (say, defects).

Benchmarking and Variance Analysis

LEARNING OBJECTIVE 7

Describe benchmarking and explain its role in cost management

...benchmarking compares actual performance against the best levels of performance

Webb Company based its budgeted amounts on an analysis of its own operations. Companies sometimes develop standards based on the operations of other companies. **Benchmarking** is the continuous process of comparing one company's performance levels against the best levels of performance in competing companies or in companies having similar processes. When benchmarks are used as standards, managers and management accountants know that the company will be competitive in the marketplace if it can meet or beat those standards.

Companies develop benchmarks and calculate variances on items that are the most important to their businesses. A common unit of measurement used to compare the efficiency of airlines is cost per available seat mile. Available seat mile (ASM) is a measure of airline size and equals the total seats in a plane multiplied by the distance traveled. Consider the cost per available seat mile for United relative to five competing U.S. airlines. Summary data are in Exhibit 7-5. The benchmark companies are in alphabetical order in column A. Also reported in Exhibit 7-5 are operating cost per ASM, operating revenue per ASM, operating income per ASM, fuel cost per ASM, labor cost per ASM, and total available seat miles for each airline. All airlines have positive operating income.

How well did United manage its costs? The answer depends on which specific benchmark is being used for comparison. United's actual operating cost of 14.60 cents per ASM is above the average operating cost of 13.08 cents per ASM of the five other airlines. Moreover, United's operating cost per ASM is 35.8% higher than Jet Blue, the lowest-cost competitor at 10.75 cents per ASM $[(14.60 - 10.75) \div 10.75 = 0.358]$. So why is United's operating cost per ASM so high? Column (6) suggests that labor cost is one important reason, alerting United management to become more cost competitive in using labor inputs.

Finding appropriate benchmarks is not easy. Many companies purchase benchmark data from consulting firms. Another problem is identifying comparable benchmarks—to make an "apples to apples" comparison. Differences exist across companies in their strategies,

EXHIBIT 7-5 Available Seat Mile (ASM) Benchmark Comparison of United Airlines with Five Other Airlines

	A	B	C	D	E	F	G
1		Operating Cost	Operating Revenue	Operating Income	Fuel Cost	Labor Cost	Total ASMs
2		(cents per ASM)	(cents per ASM)	(cents per ASM)	(cents per ASM)	(cents per ASM)	(Millions)
3	**Airline**	(1)	(2)	(3) = (2) – (1)	(4)	(5)	(6)
4	United	14.60	16.09	1.49	2.40	4.99	234,547
5	Airlines used as benchmarks:						
6	Alaska	12.05	15.16	3.11	2.04	3.65	41,468
7	American	15.65	17.31	1.66	2.42	5.14	243,824
8	Delta	15.47	18.16	2.69	2.49	5.10	228,416
9	JetBlue	10.75	12.52	1.77	2.34	3.58	56,039
10	Southwest	11.47	13.75	2.28	2.43	5.03	153,966
11	Average of airlines used as benchmarks	13.08	15.38	2.30	2.35	4.50	144,743
12							
13	*Source: 2017 data from the MIT Airline Data Project*						

inventory costing methods, depreciation methods, and so on. For example, JetBlue serves fewer cities and flies mostly long-haul routes compared with United, which serves almost all major U.S. cities and several international cities and flies both long-haul and short-haul routes. Southwest Airlines differs from United because it specializes in short-haul direct flights and offers fewer services on board its planes. Because United's strategy is different from JetBlue and Southwest, its cost per ASM is also likely to be different. United's strategy is more comparable to American and Delta, and its cost per ASM is lower than these airlines. But United competes head to head with Alaska, JetBlue, and Southwest in several cities and markets, so it needs to benchmark against these carriers as well.

United's management accountants can use benchmarking data to address several questions. How do factors such as plane size and type or duration of flights affect the cost per ASM? Do airlines differ in their fixed cost/variable cost structures? To what extent can United's performance be improved by rerouting flights, changing the frequency or timing of flights, or using different types of aircraft? What explains revenue differences per ASM across airlines? Is it differences in perceived service quality or differences in competitive power at specific airports? Management accountants are more valuable to managers when they use benchmarking data to provide insight into *why* costs or revenues differ across companies or plants, rather than simply reporting the magnitude of the differences.

DECISION POINT
What is benchmarking, and why is it useful?

PROBLEM FOR SELF-STUDY

O'Shea Company manufactures ceramic vases. It uses its standard costing system when developing its flexible-budget amounts. In September 2020, O'Shea produced 2,000 finished units. The following information relates to its two direct manufacturing cost categories: direct materials and direct manufacturing labor.

Direct materials used were 4,400 kilograms (kg). The standard direct materials input allowed for one output unit is 2 kilograms at $15 per kilogram. O'Shea purchased 5,000 kilograms of materials at $16.50 per kilogram, a total of $82,500. (This Problem for Self-Study illustrates how to calculate direct materials variances when the quantity of materials purchased in a period differs from the quantity of materials used in that period.)

Actual direct manufacturing labor-hours were 3,250, at a total cost of $66,300. Standard manufacturing labor time allowed is 1.5 hours per output unit, and the standard direct manufacturing labor cost is $20 per hour.

Required

1. Calculate the direct materials price variance and efficiency variance and the direct manufacturing labor price variance and efficiency variance. Base the direct materials price variance on a flexible budget for *actual quantity purchased*, but base the direct materials efficiency variance on a flexible budget for *actual quantity used*.
2. Prepare journal entries for a standard costing system that isolates variances at the earliest possible time.

Solution

1. Exhibit 7-6 shows how the columnar presentation of variances introduced in Exhibit 7-3 can be adjusted for the difference in timing between purchase and use of materials. Note, in particular, the two sets of computations in column 2 for direct materials—the $75,000 for direct materials purchased and the $66,000 for direct materials used. The direct materials price variance is calculated on purchases so that managers responsible for the purchase can immediately identify and isolate reasons for the variance and initiate any desired corrective action. The efficiency variance is the responsibility of the production manager, so this variance is identified only at the time materials are used.

EXHIBIT 7-6 Columnar Presentation of Variance Analysis for O'Shea Company: Direct Materials and Direct Manufacturing Labor for September 2020[a]

Level 3 Analysis

	Actual Costs Incurred (Actual Input Quantity × Actual Price) (1)	Actual Input Quantity × Budgeted Price (2)		Flexible Budget (Budgeted Input Quantity Allowed for Actual Output × Budgeted Price) (3)
Direct Materials	(5,000 kg × $16.50/kg) $82,500	(5,000 kg × $15.00/kg) $75,000	(4,400 kg × $15.00/kg) $66,000	(2,000 units × 2 kg/unit × $15.00/kg) $60,000
	$7,500 U Price variance		$6,000 U Efficiency variance	
Direct Manufacturing Labor	(3,250 hrs. × $20.40/hr.) $66,300	(3,250 hrs. × $20.00/hr.) $65,000		(2,000 units × 1.50 hrs./unit × $20.00/hr.) $60,000
	$1,300 U Price variance		$5,000 U Efficiency variance	

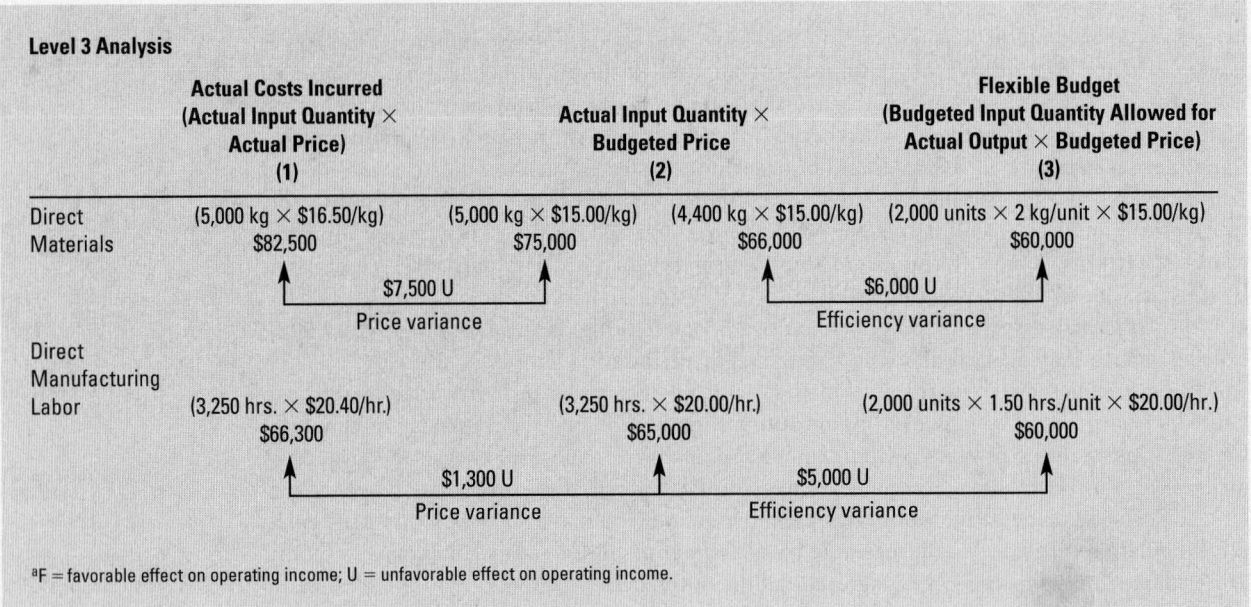

[a]F = favorable effect on operating income; U = unfavorable effect on operating income.

2.

Materials Control (5,000 kg × $15 per kg)	75,000	
Direct Materials Price Variance (5,000 kg × $1.50 per kg)	7,500	
Accounts Payable Control (5,000 kg × $16.50 per kg)		82,500
Work-in-Process Control (2,000 units × 2 kg per unit × $15 per kg)	60,000	
Direct Materials Efficiency Variance (400 kg × $15 per kg)	6,000	
Materials Control (4,400 kg × $15 per kg)		66,000
Work-in-Process Control (2,000 units × 1.5 hours per unit × $20 per hour)	60,000	
Direct Manufacturing Labor Price Variance (3,250 hours × $0.40 per hour)	1,300	
Direct Manufacturing Labor Efficiency Variance (250 hours × $20 per hour)	5,000	
Wages Payable Control (3,250 hours × $20.40 per hour)		66,300

Note: All the variances are debits because they are unfavorable and therefore reduce operating income.

DECISION POINTS

The following question-and-answer format summarizes the chapter's learning objectives. Each decision presents a key question related to a learning objective. The guidelines are the answer to that question.

Decision	Guidelines
1. What are static budgets and static-budget variances?	A static budget is based on the level of output planned at the start of the budget period. The static-budget variance is the difference between the actual result and the corresponding budgeted amount in the static budget.
2. How can managers develop a flexible budget, and why is it useful to do so?	A flexible budget is adjusted (flexed) to calculate what the budget would have been for the actual output level. When all costs are either variable or fixed with respect to output, the flexible budget requires information about the budgeted selling price, budgeted variable cost per output unit, budgeted fixed costs, and actual quantity of output units. Flexible budgets help managers gain more insight into the causes of variances than is available from static budgets.
3. How are flexible-budget and sales-volume variances calculated?	The static-budget variance can be subdivided into a flexible-budget variance (the difference between the actual result and the corresponding flexible-budget amount) and a sales-volume variance (the difference between the flexible-budget amount and the corresponding static-budget amount).
4. What is a standard cost, and what are its purposes?	A standard cost is a carefully determined cost used as a benchmark for judging performance. The purposes of a standard cost are to exclude past inefficiencies and to take into account changes expected to occur in the budget period.
5. Why should a company calculate price and efficiency variances?	Price and efficiency variances help managers gain insight into two different—but not independent—aspects of performance. The price variance focuses on the difference between the actual input price and the budgeted input price. The efficiency variance focuses on the difference between the actual quantity of input and the budgeted quantity of input allowed for actual output.
6. How do managers use variances?	Managers use variances for control, decision making, performance evaluation, organization learning, and continuous improvement. When using variances, managers should consider several variances together rather than focus only on an individual variance.
7. What is benchmarking, and why is it useful?	Benchmarking compares a firm's performance against the best levels of performance in competing companies or companies with similar processes to measure how well a company and its managers are doing.

APPENDIX

Mix and Yield Variances for Substitutable Inputs

The Webb Company example illustrates how to calculate price and efficiency variances when there is a single form of each input: one direct material (cloth) and one type of direct labor. But what if managers have leeway in combining and substituting inputs? For example, Del Monte Foods can combine material inputs (such as pineapples, cherries, and grapes) in varying proportions for its cans of fruit cocktail. Within limits, these individual fruits are *substitutable inputs* in making the fruit cocktail.

We illustrate how the efficiency variance (pages 255–256) can be subdivided into variances that highlight the financial impact of input mix and input yield when inputs are substitutable. We focus on multiple direct manufacturing labor inputs and substitution among these inputs. The same approach can be used for substitutable direct materials inputs.

Mode Company also manufactures jackets but, unlike Webb, employs workers of different skill (or experience) levels. Workers are of Low, Medium, or High skill. Higher-skill workers focus on more complicated aspects of the jacket, such as adding darts and fancy seam lines. They are compensated accordingly. Mode's production standards require 0.80 labor-hours to produce 1 jacket; 50% of the hours are budgeted to be Low skill, 30% Medium, and 20% High. The direct manufacturing labor inputs budgeted to produce 1 jacket are:

0.40 (50% of 0.80) hours of Low-skill workers at $12 per hour	$ 4.80
0.24 (30% of 0.80) hours of Medium-skill workers at $20 per hour	4.80
0.16 (20% of 0.80) hours of High-skill workers at $40 per hour	6.40
Total budgeted direct manufacturing labor cost of 1 jacket	$16.00

The budgeted $16 labor cost for a jacket that requires 0.80 labor hours, implies a weighted average labor rate of $20 per hour ($16 ÷ 0.80 hours).

In April 2020, Mode produced 10,000 jackets using 9,000 labor-hours as follows:

4,500	hours of Low-skill workers at actual cost of $12 per hour	$ 54,000
3,150	hours of Medium-skill workers at actual cost of $26 per hour	81,900
1,350	hours of High-skill workers at actual cost of $46 per hour	62,100
9,000	hours of direct manufacturing labor	198,000
Budgeted cost of 8,000 direct manufacturing labor-hours at $20 per hour		160,000
Flexible-budget variance for direct manufacturing labor		$ 38,000 U

The actual labor mix percentage is Low skill, 50% (4,500 ÷ 9,000); Medium skill, 35% (3,150 ÷ 9,000); and High skill, 15% (1,350 ÷ 9,000).

Direct Manufacturing Labor Price and Efficiency Variances

Exhibit 7-7 presents in columnar format the analysis of Mode's flexible-budget variance for direct manufacturing labor. The labor price and efficiency variances are calculated separately for each category of direct manufacturing labor and then added together. The variance analysis

EXHIBIT 7-7 Direct Manufacturing Labor Price and Efficiency Variances for Mode Company for April 2020[a]

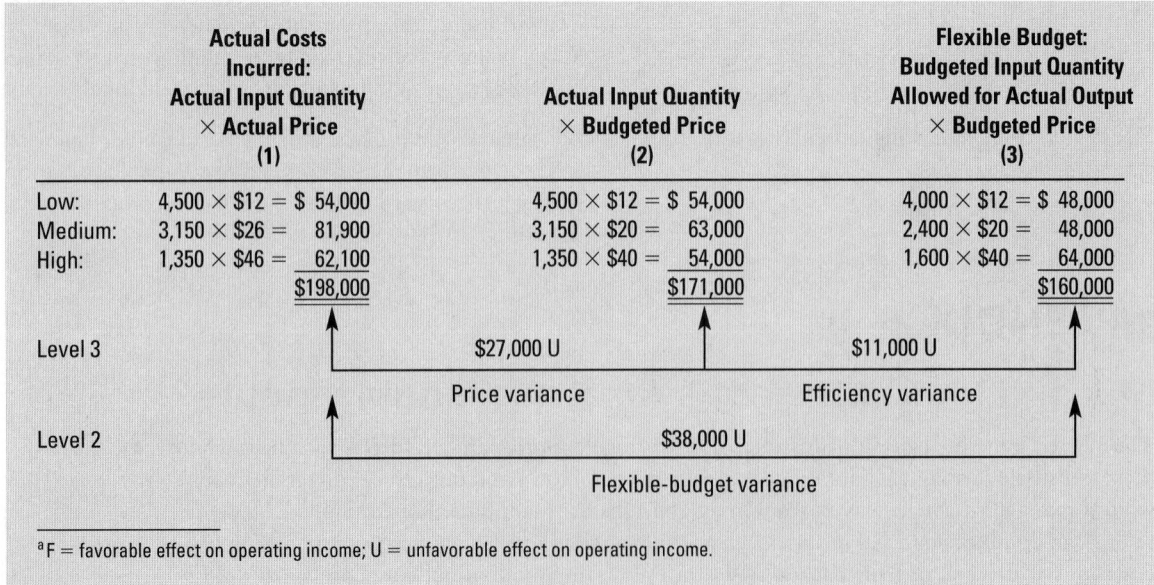

	Actual Costs Incurred: Actual Input Quantity × Actual Price (1)	Actual Input Quantity × Budgeted Price (2)	Flexible Budget: Budgeted Input Quantity Allowed for Actual Output × Budgeted Price (3)
Low:	4,500 × $12 = $ 54,000	4,500 × $12 = $ 54,000	4,000 × $12 = $ 48,000
Medium:	3,150 × $26 = 81,900	3,150 × $20 = 63,000	2,400 × $20 = 48,000
High:	1,350 × $46 = 62,100	1,350 × $40 = 54,000	1,600 × $40 = 64,000
	$198,000	$171,000	$160,000

Level 3: $27,000 U Price variance (between (1) and (2)); $11,000 U Efficiency variance (between (2) and (3))

Level 2: $38,000 U Flexible-budget variance (between (1) and (3))

[a]F = favorable effect on operating income; U = unfavorable effect on operating income.

prompts Webb to investigate the unfavorable price and efficiency variances in each category. Why did it pay more for certain types of labor and use more hours than it had budgeted? Were actual wage rates higher, in general, or could the personnel department have negotiated lower rates? Did the additional labor costs result from inefficiencies in processing?

Direct Manufacturing Labor Mix and Yield Variances

Managers sometimes have discretion to substitute one input for another. The manager of Mode's operations has some leeway in combining Low-, Medium-, and High-skill workers without affecting the quality of the jackets. We assume that to maintain quality, mix percentages of each type of labor can only vary up to 5% from standard mix. For example, the percentage of Low-skill labor in the mix can vary between 45% and 55% (50% ± 5%). When inputs are substitutable, direct manufacturing labor efficiency improvement relative to budgeted costs can come from two sources: (1) using a cheaper mix to produce a given quantity of output, measured by the mix variance, and (2) using less input to achieve a given quantity of output, measured by the yield variance.

Holding actual total quantity of all direct manufacturing labor used constant, the total **direct manufacturing labor mix variance** is the difference between:

1. budgeted cost for actual mix of actual total quantity of direct manufacturing labor used and
2. budgeted cost of budgeted mix of actual total quantity of direct manufacturing labor used.

Holding budgeted input mix constant, the **direct manufacturing labor yield variance** is the difference between:

1. budgeted cost of direct manufacturing labor based on actual total quantity of direct manufacturing labor used and
2. flexible-budget cost of direct manufacturing labor based on budgeted total quantity of direct manufacturing labor allowed for actual output produced.

Exhibit 7-8 presents the direct manufacturing labor mix and yield variances for Mode Company. Note that column (1) in this exhibit is identical to column (2) in Exhibit 7-7, and column (3) is the same in both exhibits.

EXHIBIT 7-8 Direct Manufacturing Labor Yield and Mix Variances for Mode Company for April 2020[a]

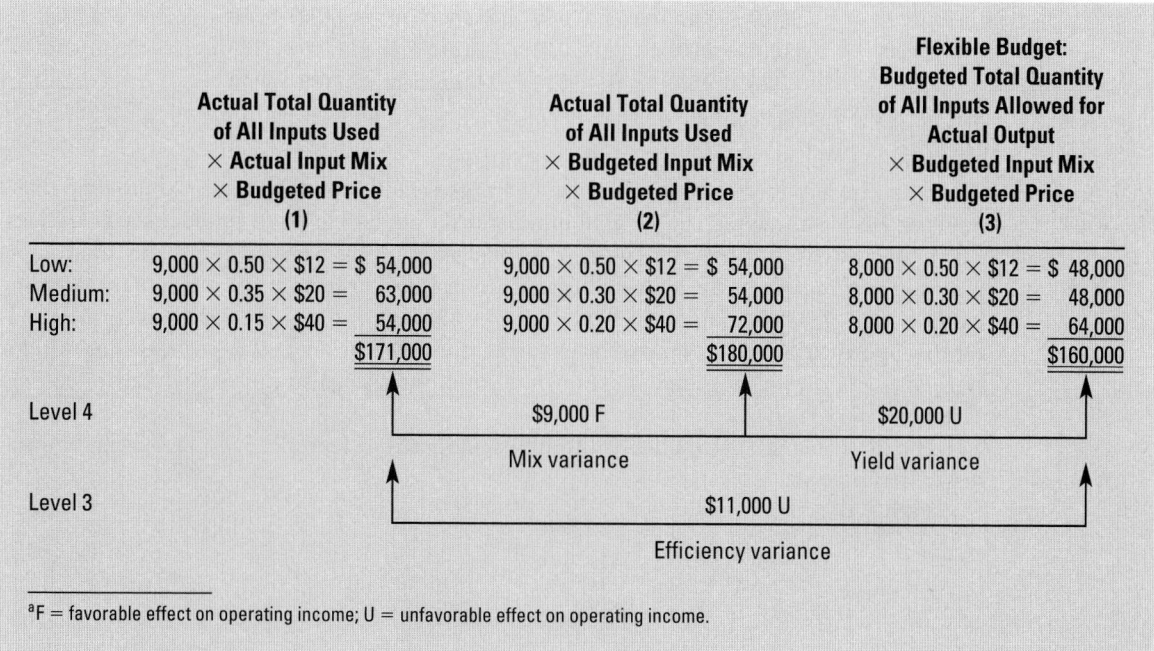

	Actual Total Quantity of All Inputs Used × Actual Input Mix × Budgeted Price (1)	Actual Total Quantity of All Inputs Used × Budgeted Input Mix × Budgeted Price (2)	Flexible Budget: Budgeted Total Quantity of All Inputs Allowed for Actual Output × Budgeted Input Mix × Budgeted Price (3)
Low:	9,000 × 0.50 × $12 = $ 54,000	9,000 × 0.50 × $12 = $ 54,000	8,000 × 0.50 × $12 = $ 48,000
Medium:	9,000 × 0.35 × $20 = 63,000	9,000 × 0.30 × $20 = 54,000	8,000 × 0.30 × $20 = 48,000
High:	9,000 × 0.15 × $40 = 54,000	9,000 × 0.20 × $40 = 72,000	8,000 × 0.20 × $40 = 64,000
	$171,000	$180,000	$160,000

Level 4: $9,000 F Mix variance (between (1) and (2)); $20,000 U Yield variance (between (2) and (3))

Level 3: $11,000 U Efficiency variance (between (1) and (3))

[a]F = favorable effect on operating income; U = unfavorable effect on operating income.

Direct Manufacturing Labor Mix Variance

The total direct manufacturing labor mix variance is the sum of the direct manufacturing labor mix variances for each input:

$$\begin{matrix}\text{Direct} \\ \text{labor} \\ \text{mix variance} \\ \text{for each input}\end{matrix} = \begin{matrix}\text{Actual total} \\ \text{quantity of all} \\ \text{direct labor} \\ \text{inputs used}\end{matrix} \times \left(\begin{matrix}\text{Actual} \\ \text{direct labor} \\ \text{input mix} \\ \text{percentage}\end{matrix} - \begin{matrix}\text{Budgeted} \\ \text{direct labor} \\ \text{input mix} \\ \text{percentage}\end{matrix}\right) \times \begin{matrix}\text{Budgeted} \\ \text{price of} \\ \text{direct labor} \\ \text{input}\end{matrix}$$

The direct manufacturing labor mix variances are as follows:

Low:	9,000 hours × (0.50 − 0.50) × \$12 per hour = 9,000 × 0.00 × \$12 =	\$ 0
Medium:	9,000 hours × (0.35 − 0.30) × \$20 per hour = 9,000 × 0.05 × \$20 =	9,000 U
High:	9,000 hours × (0.15 − 0.20) × \$40 per hour = 9,000 × −0.05 × \$40 =	18,000 F
Total direct manufacturing labor mix variance		\$ 9,000 F

The total direct manufacturing labor mix variance is favorable because, relative to the budgeted mix, Mode substitutes 5% of the cheaper Medium-skill labor for 5% of the more-expensive High-skill labor.

Direct Manufacturing Labor Yield Variance

The yield variance is the sum of the direct manufacturing labor yield variances for each input:

$$\begin{matrix}\text{Direct} \\ \text{labor} \\ \text{yield variance} \\ \text{for each input}\end{matrix} = \left(\begin{matrix}\text{Actual total} \\ \text{quantity of} \\ \text{all direct} \\ \text{labor} \\ \text{inputs used}\end{matrix} - \begin{matrix}\text{Budgeted total} \\ \text{quantity of all} \\ \text{direct labor} \\ \text{input allowed} \\ \text{for actual output}\end{matrix}\right) \times \begin{matrix}\text{Budgeted} \\ \text{direct labor} \\ \text{input mix} \\ \text{percentage}\end{matrix} \times \begin{matrix}\text{Budgeted} \\ \text{price of} \\ \text{direct labor} \\ \text{input}\end{matrix}$$

The direct manufacturing labor yield variances are as follows:

Low:	(9,000 − 8,000) hours × 0.50 × \$12 per hour = 1,000 × 0.50 × \$12 =	\$ 6,000 U
Medium:	(9,000 − 8,000) hours × 0.30 × \$20 per hour = 1,000 × 0.30 × \$20 =	6,000 U
High:	(9,000 − 8,000) hours × 0.20 × \$40 per hour = 1,000 × 0.20 × \$40 =	8,000 U
Total direct manufacturing labor yield variance		\$20,000 U

The total direct manufacturing labor yield variance is unfavorable because Mode used 9,000 hours of labor rather than the 8,000 hours that it should have used to produce 10,000 jackets. The budgeted cost per hour of labor in the budgeted mix is \$20 per hour. The unfavorable yield variance represents the budgeted cost of using 1,000 more hours of direct manufacturing labor, (9,000 − 8,000) hours × \$20 per hour = \$20,000 U. Mode should investigate reasons for the unfavorable yield variance. For example, did substitution of cheaper Medium-skill for High-skill labor, which resulted in the favorable mix variance, also cause the unfavorable yield variance?

The direct manufacturing labor variances computed in Exhibits 7-7 and 7-8 can be summarized as follows:

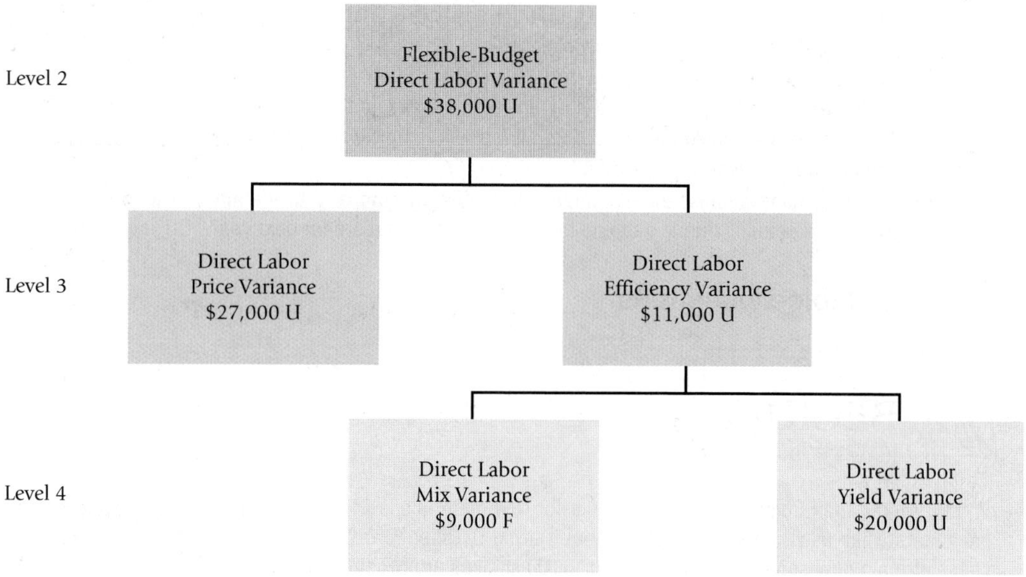

TERMS TO LEARN

This chapter and the Glossary at the end of the text contain definitions of the following important terms:

benchmarking (**p. 262**)
budgeted performance (**p. 246**)
direct manufacturing labor mix variance (**p. 267**)
direct manufacturing labor yield variance (**p. 267**)
efficiency variance (**p. 254**)
favorable variance (**p. 248**)
flexible budget (**p. 248**)
flexible-budget variance (**p. 250**)
management by exception (**p. 246**)
price variance (**p. 254**)
rate variance (**p. 254**)
sales-volume variance (**p. 250**)
selling-price variance (**p. 251**)
standard (**p. 253**)
standard cost (**p. 253**)
standard input (**p. 253**)
standard price (**p. 253**)
static budget (**p. 247**)
static-budget variance (**p. 247**)
unfavorable variance (**p. 248**)
usage variance (**p. 254**)
variance (**p. 246**)

ASSIGNMENT MATERIAL

Questions

7-1 What is the relationship between management by exception and variance analysis?

7-2 What are two possible sources of information a company might use to compute the budgeted amount in variance analysis?

7-3 Distinguish between a favorable variance and an unfavorable variance.

7-4 What is the key difference between a static budget and a flexible budget?

7-5 Why might a flexible-budget analysis be more informative than a static-budget analysis?

7-6 Describe the steps in developing a flexible budget.

7-7 List four reasons for using standard costs.

7-8 How might a manager get insight into the causes of a direct materials flexible-budget variance?

7-9 List three causes of a favorable direct materials price variance.

7-10 Describe three reasons for an unfavorable direct manufacturing labor efficiency variance.

7-11 How does variance analysis help in continuous improvement?

7-12 Why might an analyst examining variances in the production area look beyond that business function for explanations of those variances?

7-13 Comment on the following statement by a plant manager: "Meetings with my plant accountant are frustrating. All he wants to do is pin the blame on someone for the variances he reports."

7-14 When inputs are substitutable, how can the direct materials efficiency variance be decomposed further to obtain useful information?

7-15 "Benchmarking against other companies enables a company to identify the lowest-cost producer. This amount should become the performance measure for next year." Do you agree?

Multiple-Choice Questions

In partnership with:

BECKER PROFESSIONAL EDUCATION®

7-16 Metal Shelf Company's standard cost for raw materials is $4.00 per pound and it is expected that each metal shelf uses two pounds of material. During October Year 2, 25,000 pounds of materials are purchased from a new supplier for $97,000 and 13,000 shelves are produced using 27,000 pounds of materials. Which statement is a possible explanation concerning the direct materials variances?

a. The production department had to use more materials since the quality of the materials was inferior.
b. The purchasing manager paid more than expected for materials.
c. Production workers were more efficient than anticipated.
d. The overall materials variance is positive; no further analysis is necessary.

7-17 All of the following statements regarding standards are accurate except:

a. Standards allow management to budget at a per-unit level.
b. Ideal standards account for a minimal amount of normal spoilage.
c. Participative standards usually take longer to implement than authoritative standards.
d. Currently attainable standards take into account the level of training available to employees.

7-18 Amalgamated Manipulation Manufacturing's (AMM) standards anticipate that there will be 3 pounds of raw material used for every unit of finished goods produced. AMM began the month of May with 5,000 pounds of raw material, purchased 15,000 pounds for $19,500 and ended the month with 4,000 pounds on hand. The company produced 5,000 units of finished goods. The company estimates standard costs at $1.50 per pound. The materials price and efficiency variances for the month of May were as follows:

	Price Variance	Efficiency Variance
1.	$3,000 U	$1,500 F
2.	$3,000 F	$ 0
3.	$3,000 F	$1,500 U
4.	$3,200 F	$1,500 U

7-19 Atlantic Company has a manufacturing facility in Brooklyn that manufactures robotic equipment for the auto industry. For Year 1, Atlantic collected the following information from its main production line:

Actual quantity purchased	200 units
Actual quantity used	110 units
Standard quantity for units produced	100 units
Actual price paid	$ 8 per unit
Standard price	$ 10 per unit

Atlantic isolates price variances at the time of purchase. What is the materials price variance for Year 1?

1. $400 favorable
2. $400 unfavorable
3. $220 favorable
4. $220 unfavorable

7-20 Basix Inc. calculates direct manufacturing labor variances and has the following information:

1. Actual hours worked: 200
2. Standard hours allowed for actual output: 250
3. Actual rate per hour: $12
4. Standard rate per hour: $10

Given the information above, which of the following is correct regarding direct manufacturing labor variances?

a. The price and efficiency variances are favorable.
b. The price and efficiency variances are unfavorable.
c. The price variance is favorable, while the efficiency variance is unfavorable.
d. The price variance is unfavorable, while the efficiency variance is favorable.

Exercises

7-21 Flexible budget. Brabham Enterprises manufactures tires for the Formula I motor racing circuit. For August 2020, it budgeted to manufacture and sell 3,000 tires at a variable cost of $73 per tire and total fixed costs of $57,000. The budgeted selling price was $111 per tire. Actual results in August 2020 were 2,700 tires manufactured and sold at a selling price of $113 per tire. The actual total variable costs were $218,700, and the actual total fixed costs were $53,500.

Required

1. Prepare a performance report (akin to Exhibit 7-2, page 249) with a flexible budget and a static budget.
2. Comment on the results in requirement 1.

7-22 Flexible budget. Bryant Company's budgeted prices for direct materials, direct manufacturing labor, and direct marketing (distribution) labor per attaché case are $43, $6, and $13, respectively. The president is pleased with the following performance report:

	Actual Costs	Static Budget	Variance
Direct materials	$438,000	$473,000	$35,000 F
Direct manufacturing labor	63,600	66,000	2,400 F
Direct marketing (distribution) labor	133,500	143,000	9,500 F

Actual output was 10,000 attaché cases. Assume all three direct-cost items shown are variable costs.

Required

Is the president's pleasure justified? Prepare a revised performance report that uses a flexible budget and a static budget.

7-23 Flexible-budget preparation and analysis. Bank Management Printers, Inc., produces luxury checkbooks with three checks and stubs per page. Each checkbook is designed for an individual customer and is ordered through the customer's bank. The company's operating budget for September 2020 included these data:

Number of checkbooks	15,000
Selling price per book	$ 20
Variable cost per book	$ 8
Fixed costs for the month	$145,000

The actual results for September 2020 were as follows:

Number of checkbooks produced and sold	12,000
Average selling price per book	$ 21
Variable cost per book	$ 7
Fixed costs for the month	$150,000

The executive vice president of the company observed that the operating income for September was much lower than anticipated, despite a higher-than-budgeted selling price and a lower-than-budgeted variable cost per unit. As the company's management accountant, you have been asked to provide explanations for the disappointing September results.

Bank Management develops its flexible budget on the basis of budgeted per-output-unit revenue and per-output-unit variable costs without detailed analysis of budgeted inputs.

Required

1. Prepare a static-budget-based variance analysis of the September performance.
2. Prepare a flexible-budget-based variance analysis of the September performance.
3. Why might Bank Management find the flexible-budget-based variance analysis more informative than the static-budget-based variance analysis? Explain your answer.

7-24 Flexible budget, working backward. The Edinburgh Company produces engine parts for car manufacturers. A new accountant intern at Edinburgh has accidentally deleted the company's variance analysis calculations for the year ended December 31, 2020. The following table is what remains of the data.

Performance Report, Year Ended December 31, 2020

	Actual Results	Flexible-Budget Variances	Flexible Budget	Sales-Volume Variances	Static Budget
Units sold	101,000				93,000
Revenues	$681,750				$334,800
Variable costs	404,000				167,400
Contribution margin	277,750				167,400
Fixed costs	220,350				110,000
Operating income	$ 57,400				$ 57,400

Required

1. Calculate all the variances in the preceding table. (If your work is accurate, you will find that the total static-budget variance is $0.)
2. What are the actual and budgeted selling prices? What are the actual and budgeted variable costs per unit?
3. Review the variances you have calculated and discuss possible causes and potential problems. What is the important lesson learned here?

7-25 Flexible-budget and sales volume variances. Cascade, Inc., produces the basic fillings used in many popular frozen desserts and treats—vanilla and chocolate ice creams, puddings, meringues, and fudge. Cascade uses standard costing and carries over no inventory from one month to the next. The ice-cream product group's results for June 2020 were as follows:

Performance Report, June 2020

	Actual Results	Static Budget
Units (pounds)	460,000	447,000
Revenues	$2,626,600	$ 2,592,600
Variable manufacturing costs	1,651,400	1,564,500
Contribution margin	$ 975,200	$ 1,028,100

Jeff Geller, the business manager for ice-cream products, is pleased that more pounds of ice cream were sold than budgeted and that revenues were up. Unfortunately, variable manufacturing costs went up, too. The bottom line is that contribution margin declined by $52,900, which is just over 2% of the budgeted revenues of $2,592,600. Overall, Geller feels that the business is running fine.

Required

1. Calculate the static-budget variance in units, revenues, variable manufacturing costs, and contribution margin. What percentage is each static-budget variance relative to its static-budget amount?
2. Break down each static-budget variance into a flexible-budget variance and a sales-volume variance.
3. Calculate the selling-price variance.
4. Assume the role of management accountant at Cascade. How would you present the results to Jeff Geller? Should he be more concerned? If so, why?

7-26 Price and efficiency variances. Sunshine Foods manufactures pumpkin scones. For January 2020, it budgeted to purchase and use 14,750 pounds of pumpkin at $0.92 a pound. Actual purchases and usage for January 2020 were 16,000 pounds at $0.85 a pound. Sunshine budgeted for 59,000 pumpkin scones. Actual output was 59,200 pumpkin scones.

Required

1. Compute the flexible-budget variance.
2. Compute the price and efficiency variances.
3. Comment on the results for requirements 1 and 2 and provide a possible explanation for them.

7-27 Materials and manufacturing labor variances. Consider the following data collected for Great Homes, Inc.:

	Direct Materials	Direct Manufacturing Labor
Cost incurred: Actual inputs × actual prices	$200,000	$90,000
Actual inputs × standard prices	214,000	86,000
Standard inputs allowed for actual output × standard prices	225,000	80,000

Required

Compute the price, efficiency, and flexible-budget variances for direct materials and direct manufacturing labor.

7-28 Direct materials and direct manufacturing labor variances. Rugged Life, Inc., designs and manufactures fleece quarter-zip jackets. It sells its jackets to brand-name outdoor outfitters in lots of one dozen. Rugged Life's May 2020 static budget and actual results for direct inputs are as follows:

Static Budget	
Number of jacket lots (1 lot = 1 dozen)	300
Per Lot of Jackets:	
Direct materials	18 yards at $4.65 per yard = $83.70
Direct manufacturing labor	2.4 hours at $12.50 per hour = $30.00
Actual Results	
Number of jacket lots sold	325
Total Direct Inputs:	
Direct materials	6,500 yards at $4.85 per yard = $31,525
Direct manufacturing labor	715 hours at $12.60 per hour = $9,009

Rugged Life has a policy of analyzing all input variances when they add up to more than 8% of the total cost of materials and labor in the flexible budget, and this is true in May 2020. The production manager discusses the sources of the variances: "A new type of material was purchased in May. This led to faster cutting and sewing, but the workers used more material than usual as they learned to work with it. For now, the standards are fine."

Required

1. Calculate the direct materials and direct manufacturing labor price and efficiency variances in May 2020. What is the total flexible-budget variance for both inputs (direct materials and direct manufacturing labor) combined? What percentage is this variance of the total cost of direct materials and direct manufacturing labor in the flexible budget?
2. Comment on the May 2020 results. Would you continue the "experiment" of using the new material?

7-29 Price and efficiency variances, journal entries. The Schuyler Corporation manufactures lamps. It has set up the following standards per finished unit for direct materials and direct manufacturing labor:

Direct materials: 10 lb. at $4.50 per lb.	$45.00
Direct manufacturing labor: 0.5 hour at $30 per hour	15.00

The number of finished units budgeted for January 2020 was 10,000; 9,850 units were actually produced.

Actual results in January 2020 were as follows:

Direct materials: 98,055 lb. used	
Direct manufacturing labor: 4,900 hours	$154,350

Assume that there was no beginning inventory of either direct materials or finished units.

During the month, materials purchased amounted to 100,000 lb., at a total cost of $465,000. Input price variances are isolated upon purchase. Input-efficiency variances are isolated at the time of usage.

Required

1. Compute the January 2020 price and efficiency variances of direct materials and direct manufacturing labor.
2. Prepare journal entries to record the variances in requirement 1.
3. Comment on the January 2020 price and efficiency variances of Schuyler Corporation.
4. Why might Schuyler calculate direct materials price variances and direct materials efficiency variances with reference to different points in time?

7-30 Materials and manufacturing labor variances, standard costs. Dawson, Inc., is a privately held furniture manufacturer. For August 2020, Dawson had the following standards for one of its products, a wicker chair:

	Standards per Chair
Direct materials	3 square yards of input at $5.50 per square yard
Direct manufacturing labor	0.5 hour of input at $10.50 per hour

The following data were compiled regarding *actual performance*: actual output units (chairs) produced, 2,200; square yards of input purchased and used, 6,200; price per square yard, $5.70; direct manufacturing labor costs, $9,844; actual hours of input, 920; labor price per hour, $10.70.

Required

1. Show computations of price and efficiency variances for direct materials and direct manufacturing labor. Give a plausible explanation of why each variance occurred.
2. Suppose 8,700 square yards of materials were purchased (at $5.70 per square yard), even though only 6,200 square yards were used. Suppose further that variances are identified at their most timely control point; accordingly, direct materials price variances are isolated and traced at the time of purchase to the purchasing department rather than to the production department. Compute the price and efficiency variances under this approach.

7-31 Journal entries and T-accounts (continuation of 7-30). Prepare journal entries and post them to T-accounts for all transactions in Exercise 7-30, including requirement 2. Summarize how these journal entries differ from the normal-costing entries described in Chapter 4, pages 117–120.

7-32 Price and efficiency variances, benchmarking. Jacinta Enterprises manufactures insulated cold beverage cups printed with college and corporate logos, which it distributes nationally in lots of 12 dozen cups. In June 2020, Jacinta produced 5,000 lots of its most popular line of cups, the 24-ounce lidded tumbler, at its plant in Peoria. The production manager, Sophie Barrett, asks her assistant, John Hardy, to find out the precise per-unit actual variable costs at the Peoria plant and the variable costs of a competitor, Beverage King, who offers similar-quality tumblers at cheaper prices. Hardy pulls together the following information for each lot:

Per lot	Peoria Plant	Beverage King
Direct materials	72 lbs. @ $3.20 per lb.	70 lbs. @ $2.90 per lb.
Direct manufacturing labor	2.5 hrs. @ $11 per hr.	2.4 hrs. @ $10 per hr.
Variable overhead	$21 per lot	$20 per lot

Required

1. What is the actual variable cost per lot at the Peoria Plant and at Beverage King?
2. Using the Beverage King data as the standard, calculate the direct materials and direct manufacturing labor price and efficiency variances for the Peoria plant.
3. What advantage does Jacinta get by using Beverage King's benchmark data as standards in calculating its variances? Identify two issues that Barrett should keep in mind in using the Beverage King data as the standards.

7-33 Static and flexible budgets, service sector. Student Finance (StuFi) is a start-up that aims to use the power of social communities to transform the student loan market. It connects participants through a dedicated lending pool, enabling current students to borrow from a school's alumni community. StuFi's revenue model is to take an upfront fee of 40 basis points (0.40%) *each* from the alumni investor and the student borrower for every loan originated on its platform.

StuFi hopes to go public in the near future and is keen to ensure that its financial results are in line with that ambition. StuFi's budgeted and actual results for the third quarter of 2020 are presented below.

	Static Budget		Actual Results	
New loans originated	8,200		10,250	
Average amount of loan	$ 145,000		$ 162,000	
Variable costs per loan:				
Professional labor	$ 360	(8 hrs at $45 per hour)	$ 475	(9.5 hrs at $50 per hour)
Credit verification	$ 100		$ 100	
Federal documentation fees	$ 120		$ 125	
Courier services	$ 50		$ 54	
Administrative costs (fixed)	$ 800,000		$ 945,000	
Technology costs (fixed)	$1,300,000		$1,415,000	

Required

1. Prepare StuFi's static budget of operating income for the third quarter of 2020.
2. Prepare an analysis of variances for the third quarter of 2020 along the lines of Exhibit 7-2; identify the sales volume and flexible budget variances for operating income.
3. Compute the professional labor price and efficiency variances for the third quarter of 2020.
4. What factors would you consider in evaluating the effectiveness of professional labor in the third quarter of 2020?

Problems

7-34 Flexible budget, direct materials, and direct manufacturing labor variances. Emerald Statuary manufactures bust statues of famous historical figures. All statues are the same size. Each unit requires the same amount of resources. The following information is from the static budget for 2020:

Expected production and sales	7,000 units
Expected selling price per unit	$ 680
Total fixed costs	$1,400,000

Standard quantities, standard prices, and standard unit costs follow for direct materials and direct manufacturing labor:

	Standard Quantity	Standard Price	Standard Unit Cost
Direct materials	10 pounds	$ 8 per pound	$ 80
Direct manufacturing labor	3.7 hours	$50 per hour	$185

During 2020, actual number of units produced and sold was 4,800, at an average selling price of $720. Actual cost of direct materials used was $392,700 (66,000 pounds at $5.95 per pound). Actual direct manufacturing labor costs were $878,400 (18,300 actual direct manufacturing labor-hours at $48 per hour). Actual fixed costs were $1,170,000. There were no beginning or ending inventories.

Required

1. Calculate the sales-volume variance and flexible-budget variance for operating income.
2. Compute price and efficiency variances for direct materials and direct manufacturing labor.

7-35 Variance analysis, nonmanufacturing setting. Joyce Brown has run Medical Maids, a specialty cleaning service for medical and dental offices, for the past 10 years. Her static budget and actual results for April 2020 are shown below. Joyce has one employee who has been with her for all 10 years that she has been in business. In addition, at any given time she also employs two other less-experienced workers. It usually takes each employee 2 hours to clean an office, regardless of his or her experience. Brown pays her experienced employee $30 per office and the other two employees $15 per office. There were no wage increases in April.

Medical Maids Actual and Budgeted Income Statements for the Month Ended April 30, 2020

	Budget	Actual
Offices cleaned	140	160
Revenue	$26,600	$36,000
Variable costs:		
Costs of supplies	630	680
Labor	3,360	4,200
Total variable costs	3,990	4,880
Contribution margin	22,610	31,120
Fixed costs	4,900	4,900
Operating income	$17,710	$26,220

Required

1. How many offices, on average, did Brown budget for each employee? How many offices did each employee actually clean?
2. Prepare a flexible budget for April 2020.
3. Compute the sales price variance and the labor efficiency variance for each labor type.
4. What information, in addition to that provided in the income statements, would you want Brown to gather, if you wanted to improve operational efficiency?

7-36 Comprehensive variance analysis review. Edgar Animal Health, Inc., produces a generic medication used to treat cats with feline diabetes. The liquid medication is sold in 100ml vials. Edgar employs a team of sales representatives who are paid commissions.

Given the narrow margins in the generic veterinary drugs industry, Edgar relies on tight standards and cost controls to manage its operations. Edgar has the following budgeted amounts for the month of October 2020:

Average selling price per vial	$ 8.00
Total direct materials cost per vial	$ 3.50
Direct manufacturing labor cost per hour	$ 15.00
Average labor productivity rate (vials per hour)	100
Sales commission cost per vial	$ 0.70
Fixed administrative and manufacturing overhead	$900,000

Edgar budgeted sales of 750,000 vials for October. At the end of the month, the controller revealed that actual results for October were as follows:

- Unit sales and production were 80% of plan.
- Actual average selling price decreased to $8.10.
- Productivity increased to 120 vials per hour.
- Actual direct manufacturing labor cost was $15.10 per hour.
- Actual total direct material cost per unit increased to $3.60.
- Actual sales commissions were $0.75 per vial.
- Fixed overhead costs were $100,000 above budget.

Calculate the following amounts for Edgar for October 2020:

Required

1. Static-budget and actual operating income
2. Static-budget variance for operating income
3. Flexible-budget operating income
4. Flexible-budget variance for operating income
5. Sales-volume variance for operating income
6. Price and efficiency variances for direct manufacturing labor
7. Flexible-budget variance for direct manufacturing labor

7-37 Possible causes for price and efficiency variances. You have been invited to interview for an internship with an international food manufacturing company. When you arrive for the interview, you are given the following information related to a fictitious chocolatier for the month of June. The chocolatier manufactures truffles in 12-piece boxes. The production is labor intensive, and the delicate nature of the chocolate requires a high degree of skill.

Actual	
Boxes produced	10,000
Direct materials used in production	13,000 pounds (lbs.)
Actual direct material cost	$78,000
Actual direct manufacturing labor-hours	2,400
Actual direct manufacturing labor cost	$31,200

Standards	
Purchase price of direct materials	$ 7 per pound
Direct materials per box	0.90 pounds
Wage rate	$ 15 per hour
Boxes per hour	6

Please respond to the following questions as if you were in an interview situation:

Required

1. Calculate the direct materials efficiency and price variances and the direct manufacturing labor price and efficiency variances for the month of June.
2. Discuss some possible causes of the variances you have calculated. Can you make any possible connection between the material and labor variances? What recommendations do you have for future improvement?

7-38 Material-cost variances, use of variances for performance evaluation. Katharine Johnson is the owner of Best Bikes, a company that produces high-quality cross-country bicycles. Best Bikes participates in a supply chain that consists of suppliers, manufacturers, distributors, and elite bicycle shops. For several years Best Bikes has purchased titanium from suppliers in the supply chain. Best Bikes uses titanium for the bicycle frames because it is stronger and lighter than other metals and therefore increases the quality of the bicycle. Earlier this year, Best Bikes hired Michael Bentfield, a recent graduate from State University, as purchasing manager. Michael believed that he could reduce costs if he purchased titanium from an online marketplace at a lower price.

Best Bikes established the following standards based upon the company's experience with previous suppliers. The standards are as follows:

Cost of titanium	$18 per pound
Titanium used per bicycle	8 lbs.

Actual results for the first month using the online supplier of titanium are as follows:

Bicycles produced	400
Titanium purchased	5,200 lb. for $88,400
Titanium used in production	4,700 lb.

Required

1. Compute the direct materials price and efficiency variances.
2. What factors can explain the variances identified in requirement 1? Could any other variances be affected?
3. Was switching suppliers a good idea for Best Bikes? Explain why or why not.
4. Should Michael Bentfield's performance evaluation be based solely on price variances? Should the production manager's evaluation be based solely on efficiency variances? Why is it important for Katharine Johnson to understand the causes of a variance before she evaluates performance?
5. Other than performance evaluation, what reasons are there for calculating variances?
6. What future problems could result from Best Bikes' decision to buy a lower quality of titanium from the online marketplace?

7-39 Direct manufacturing labor and direct materials variances, missing data. (CMA, heavily adapted) Oyster Bay Surfboards manufactures fiberglass surfboards. The standard cost of direct materials and direct manufacturing labor is $248 per board. This includes 35 pounds of direct materials, at the budgeted price of $3 per pound, and 11 hours of direct manufacturing labor, at the budgeted rate of $13 per hour. Following are additional data for the month of July:

Units completed	5,600 units
Direct material purchases	230,000 pounds
Cost of direct material purchases	$759,000
Actual direct manufacturing labor-hours	43,000 hours
Actual direct manufacturing labor cost	$623,500
Direct materials efficiency variance	$ 1,200 F

There were no beginning inventories.

Required

1. Compute direct manufacturing labor variances for July.
2. Compute the actual pounds of direct materials used in production in July.
3. Calculate the actual price per pound of direct materials purchased.
4. Calculate the direct materials price variance.

7-40 Direct materials efficiency, mix, and yield variances. Sandy's Snacks produces snack mixes for the gourmet and natural foods market. Its most popular product is Tempting Trail Mix, a mixture of peanuts, dried cranberries, and chocolate pieces. For each batch, the budgeted quantities and budgeted prices are as follows:

	Quantity per Batch	Price per Cup
Peanuts	60 cups	$1
Dried cranberries	30 cups	$2
Chocolate pieces	10 cups	$3

Small changes to the standard mix of direct materials reflected in the above quantities do not significantly affect the overall end product. In addition, not all ingredients added to production end up in the finished product, as some are rejected during inspection.

In the current period, Sandy's Snacks made 100 batches of Tempting Trail Mix with the following actual quantity, cost, and mix of inputs:

	Actual Quantity	Actual Cost	Actual Mix
Peanuts	6,720 cups	$ 5,712	64%
Dried cranberries	2,625 cups	5,775	25%
Chocolate pieces	1,155 cups	3,350	11%
Total actual	10,500 cups	$14,837	100%

Required

1. What is the budgeted cost of direct materials for the 100 batches?
2. Calculate the total direct materials efficiency variance.
3. Calculate the total direct materials mix and yield variances.
4. How do the variances calculated in requirement 3 relate to those calculated in requirement 2? What do the variances calculated in requirement 3 tell you about the 100 batches produced this period? Are the variances large enough to investigate?

7-41 Direct materials and manufacturing labor variances, solving unknowns. (CPA, adapted) On May 1, 2020, Barron Company began the manufacture of a new paging machine known as Sleek. The company installed a standard costing system to account for manufacturing costs. The standard costs for a unit of Sleek follow:

Direct materials (2 lb. at $? per lb.)	$10.00
Direct manufacturing labor (? hour at $15 per hour)	12.00
Manufacturing overhead (?% of direct manufacturing labor costs)	3.00
Standard cost per unit	$?

The following data were obtained from Barron's records for the month of May:

	Debit	Credit
Revenues		$180,000
Direct materials price variance	$1,048	
Direct materials efficiency variance	2,400	
Direct manufacturing labor price variance	1,925	
Direct manufacturing labor efficiency variance		2,250

Actual production in May was 5,000 units of Sleek, and actual sales in May were 3,000 units.

The amount shown for direct materials price variance applies to materials purchased and used during May. There was no beginning inventory of materials on May 1, 2020.

Compute each of the following items for Barron Company for the month of May. Show your computations.

Required

1. (a) Standard cost per pound of direct materials, (b) Standard hours per unit of direct manufacturing labor, (c) Standard manufacturing overhead cost expressed as a percentage of standard direct manufacturing labor cost, (d) Standard cost per unit (paging machine)
2. Standard direct manufacturing labor-hours allowed for actual output produced
3. Actual direct manufacturing labor-hours worked
4. Actual direct manufacturing labor wage rate
5. Standard quantity of direct materials allowed (in pounds)
6. Actual quantity of direct materials purchased and used (in pounds)
7. Actual direct materials price per pound

7-42 Direct materials and manufacturing labor variances, journal entries. Varsity Corn Hole is a small business that Manny Mercado developed while in college. He began building wooden corn hole game sets for friends, hand painted with college colors and logos. As demand grew, he hired some workers and began to manage the operation. Varsity Corn Hole maintains two departments: construction and painting. In the construction department, workers use wood to make the game sets. Varsity Corn Hole has some employees who have been with the company for a very long time and others who are new and inexperienced. Because of the nature of the wood, workers must work around flaws in the materials. Manny does not store inventory, and buys the wood as he receives an order.

Actual and standard data for the construction department for September 2020 are shown below:

Actual	
Game sets produced	80
Direct materials used in production	1,800 sq. ft. of wood
Actual direct material cost	$7,020
Actual direct manufacturing labor-hours	300
Actual direct manufacturing labor cost	$4,650

Standards	
Purchase price of direct materials	$ 4 per sq. ft. of wood
Direct materials per game set	20 sq. ft. of wood
Wage rate in construction department	$ 15 per hour
Construction department direct labor hours per game set	4 hours

Required

1. For the construction department, calculate the price and efficiency variances for the wood and the price and efficiency variances for direct manufacturing labor.
2. Record the journal entries for the variances incurred.
3. Discuss logical explanations for the combination of variances that the construction department of Varsity Corn Hole experienced.

7-43 Use of materials and manufacturing labor variances for benchmarking. You are a new junior accountant at Clearvision Corporation, maker of lenses for eyeglasses. Your company sells generic-quality lenses for a moderate price. Your boss, the controller, has given you the latest month's report for the lens trade association. This report includes information related to operations for your firm and your closest competitor for September 2020. The report also includes information related to the industry benchmark for lens manufacturers for each line item in the report. You are Firm A and your closest competitor is Firm B.

	Firm A	Firm B	Industry Benchmark
Materials input	2.25	1.80	2.00 oz. of glass
Materials price	$ 4.80	$ 5.25	$ 5.00 per oz.
Labor-hours used per lens	0.80	1.20	1.0 hours
Wage rate	$ 14.00	$11.00	$12.00 per direct manuf. labor-hour
Variable overhead rate	$ 16.00	$12.00	$15.00 per direct manuf. labor-hour

Required

1. Calculate the total variable cost per unit for each firm. Compute the percent of total for the material, labor, and variable overhead components.
2. Using Firm B as a benchmark, calculate direct materials and direct manufacturing labor price and efficiency variances for Firm A for one lens.
3. Write a brief memo to your boss outlining the advantages and disadvantages of belonging to this trade association for benchmarking purposes. Include a few ideas to improve productivity that you want your boss to take to the department heads' meeting.

7-44 Direct manufacturing labor variances: price, efficiency, mix, and yield. Elena Martinez employs two workers in her wedding cake bakery. The first worker, Gabrielle, has been making wedding cakes for 20 years and is paid $25 per hour. The second worker, Joseph, is less experienced and is paid $15 per hour. One wedding cake requires, on average, 6 hours of labor. The budgeted direct manufacturing labor quantities for one cake are as follows:

	Quantity
Gabrielle	3 hours
Joseph	3 hours
Total	6 hours

That is, each cake is budgeted to require 6 hours of direct manufacturing labor, composed of 50% of Gabrielle's labor and 50% of Joseph's, although sometimes Gabrielle works more hours on a particular cake and Joseph less, or vice versa, with no obvious change in the quality of the cake.

During the month of May, the bakery produces 50 cakes. Actual direct manufacturing labor costs are as follows:

Gabrielle (140 hours)	$3,500
Joseph (165 hours)	2,475
Total actual direct labor cost	$5,975

Required

1. What is the budgeted cost of direct manufacturing labor for 50 cakes?
2. Calculate the total direct manufacturing labor price and efficiency variances.
3. For the 50 cakes, what is the total actual amount of direct manufacturing labor used? What is the actual direct manufacturing labor input mix percentage? What is the budgeted amount of Gabrielle's and Joseph's labor that should have been used for the 50 cakes?
4. Calculate the total direct manufacturing labor mix and yield variances. How do these numbers relate to the total direct manufacturing labor efficiency variance? What do these variances tell you?

7-45 Direct materials and direct manufacturing labor variances with missing data. The Shirt Company produces cotton/polyester blend T-shirts to supply a custom T-shirt customer. The company experienced a computer failure and some of the data were lost and could not be recovered. The data the company were able to recover are shown below:

Direct materials used	800,000 sq. yds.
Direct materials purchased	820,000 sq. yds.
Direct materials price variance	$ 24,600 F
Direct materials efficiency variance	$ 16,000 U
Direct manufacturing labor price variance	$ 26,500 U
Direct manufacturing labor efficiency variance	$ 30,000 U
Standard price of direct materials	$ 2 per sq. yd.
Standard quantity of direct materials per T-shirt	1.2 sq. yds.
Actual direct manufacturing labor cost	$7,976,500
Actual direct manufacturing labor rate	$ 15.05/hr

Calculate the following:

Required

1. Actual price per square yard of direct materials
2. Actual quantity of shirts produced
3. Actual direct manufacturing labor hours worked
4. Standard direct manufacturing labor rate
5. Standard direct manufacturing labor hours per shirt

7-46 Mix and yield variances in the service sector. Cathy Jeffries operates Relaxing Day, a day spa with 15 employees. Jim Ryan has recently been hired by Jeffries as a controller. Relaxing Day's previous accountant had done very little in the area of variance analysis, but Ryan believes that the company could benefit from a greater understanding of its business processes. Because of the labor-intensive nature of the business, he decides to focus on calculating labor variances.

Ryan examines past accounting records, and establishes some standards for the price and quantity of labor. While Relaxing Day's employees earn a range of hourly wages, they fall into two general categories: skilled labor, with an average wage of $30 per hour, and unskilled labor, with an average wage of $12 per hour. The average spa treatment requires 5 hours and typically requires a combination of 4 skilled hours and 1 unskilled hour.

Actual data from last month, when 800 spa treatments were completed, are as follows:

Skilled (3,318 hours)	$ 99,540
Unskilled (632 hours)	6,952
Total actual direct labor cost	$106,492

Looking over last month's data, Ryan determines that Relaxing Day's labor price variance was $632 favorable, but the labor efficiency variance was $1,524 unfavorable. When Ryan presents his findings to Jeffries, the latter is furious. "Do you mean to tell me that my employees wasted $1,524 worth of time last month? At closer look, the skilled labor wasted more time than the unskilled labor who are paid less. I've had enough. They had better shape up, or else!" Ryan tries to calm her down, saying that in this case the efficiency variance does not necessarily mean that employees were wasting time. Ryan tells her that he is going to perform a more detailed analysis, and will get back to her with more information soon.

Required

1. What is the budgeted cost of direct labor for 800 spa treatments?
2. How were the $632 favorable price variance and the $1,524 unfavorable labor efficiency variance calculated? What was the company's flexible-budget variance?
3. What do you think Ryan meant when he said that "in this case the efficiency variance does not necessarily mean that employees were wasting time"?
4. For the 800 spa treatments performed last month, what is the actual direct labor input mix percentage? What was the standard mix for direct labor?
5. Calculate the total direct labor mix and yield variances.
6. How could these variances be interpreted? Did the employees waste time? Upon further investigation, Ryan discovers that there were some unfilled vacancies last month in the unskilled labor positions that have recently been filled. How will this new information likely impact the variances going forward?

7-47 Price and efficiency variances, benchmarking and ethics. Sunto Scientific manufactures GPS devices for a chain of retail stores. Its most popular model, the Magellan XS, is assembled in a dedicated facility in Savannah, Georgia. Sunto is keenly aware of the competitive threat from smartphones that use Google Maps and has put in a standard cost system to manage production costs of the Magellan XS. It has also implemented a just-in-time system so the Savannah facility operates with no inventory of any kind.

Producing the Magellan XS involves combining a navigation system (imported from Sunto's plant in Dresden at a fixed price), an LCD screen made of polarized glass, and a casing developed from specialty plastic. The budgeted and actual amounts for Magellan XS for July 2020 were as follows:

	Budgeted Amounts	Actual Amounts
Magellan XS units produced	4,000	4,400
Navigation systems cost	$81,600	$89,000
Navigation systems used	4,080	4,450
Polarized glass cost	$40,000	$40,300
Sheets of polarized glass used	800	816
Plastic casing cost	$12,000	$12,500
Ounces of specialty plastic used	4,000	4,250
Direct manufacturing labor costs	$36,000	$37,200
Direct manufacturing labor-hours	2,000	2,040

The controller of the Savannah plant, Jim Williams, is disappointed with the standard costing system in place. The standards were developed on the basis of a study done by an outside consultant at the start of the year. Williams points out that he has rarely seen a significant unfavorable variance under this system. He observes that even at the present level of output, workers seem to have a substantial amount of idle time. Moreover, he is concerned that the production supervisor, John Kelso, is aware of the issue but is unwilling to tighten the standards because the current lenient benchmarks make his performance look good.

Required

1. Compute the price and efficiency variances for the three categories of direct materials and for direct manufacturing labor in July 2020.
2. Describe the types of actions the employees at the Savannah plant may have taken to reduce the accuracy of the standards set by the outside consultant. Why would employees take those actions? Is this behavior ethical?
3. If Williams does nothing about the standard costs, will his behavior violate any of the standards of ethical conduct for practitioners described in the IMA Statement of Ethical Professional Practice (see Exhibit 1-7 on page 17)?
4. What actions should Williams take?
5. Williams can obtain benchmarking information about the estimated costs of Sunto's competitors such as Garmin and TomTom from the Competitive Intelligence Institute (CII). Discuss the pros and cons of using the CII information to compute the variances in requirement 1.

8 Flexible Budgets, Overhead Cost Variances, and Management Control

LEARNING OBJECTIVES

1. Explain the similarities and differences in planning variable overhead costs and fixed overhead costs
2. Develop budgeted variable overhead cost rates and budgeted fixed overhead cost rates
3. Compute the variable overhead flexible-budget variance, the variable overhead efficiency variance, and the variable overhead spending variance
4. Compute the fixed overhead flexible-budget variance, the fixed overhead spending variance, and the fixed overhead production-volume variance
5. Show how the 4-variance analysis approach reconciles the actual overhead incurred with the overhead amounts allocated during the period
6. Explain the relationship between the sales-volume variance and the production-volume variance
7. Calculate variances in activity-based costing
8. Examine the use of overhead variances in nonmanufacturing settings

Matt Rakowski/Shutterstock

What do this week's weather forecast and an organization's performance have in common?

Much of the time, reality doesn't match what people expect. Rain that results in a little league game being cancelled may suddenly give way to sunshine. Business owners expecting to "whistle their way to the bank" may change their tune after tallying their monthly bills and discovering that skyrocketing operational costs have significantly reduced their profits. Differences, or variances, are all around us.

Analyzing variances is a valuable activity for firms because the process highlights the areas where performance most lags expectations. By using this information to make corrective adjustments, companies can achieve significant savings. Furthermore, the process of setting up standards requires firms to have a thorough understanding of their fixed and variable overhead costs, which brings its own benefits, as the following article shows.

MANAGING OVERHEAD COSTS AT WEWORK[1]

WeWork, one of the world's richest startups, is a global shared office space provider. WeWork takes on long-term leases for raw office space and builds out the interior with flexible spaces and unique designs that it then subleases to both startups and established companies. WeWork has grown its community to more than 150,000 individuals and companies renting space starting at $190 per month.

WeWork's business model has significant overhead costs. With more than 170 locations globally, the company makes up-front, fixed-cost investments designed to benefit the company for many years. Fixed overhead costs at each location include costs of long-term leases as well as materials costs for office build-outs, including glass, wood flooring, aluminum, and modern light fixtures. Variable overhead costs at WeWork include some employee salaries, utilities, office supplies, and micro-roasted coffee available to members at each location.

Understanding its fixed and variable overhead costs allows WeWork's management accountants to develop budgeted fixed and variable overhead costs for each desk and office it rents out. It also influences its preferred customer mix. Around a quarter of the company's revenue comes from large companies such as Microsoft, Facebook, and General Electric. The long-term commitments of these companies allow for more revenue certainty to recover overhead costs. In November 2019, however, WeWork had to withdraw its initial public offering because it had not been able to turn a profit.

[1] *Sources*: Eliot Brown, "A $20 Billion Startup Fueled by Silicon Valley Pixie Dust," *The Wall Street Journal*, October 20, 2017 (https://www.wsj.com/articles/wework-a-20-billion-startup-fueled-by-silicon-valley-pixie-dust-1508424483); Ellen Huet, "WeWork, with $900 Million in Sales, Finds Cheaper Ways to Expand," Bloomberg.com, February 26, 2018 (https://www.bloomberg.com/news/articles/2018-02-26/wework-with-900-million-in-sales-finds-cheaper-ways-to-expand); John Havel, "Why Is WeWork Worth So Much?" TheHustle.com, March 11, 2016 (https://thehustle.co/why-wework-is-worth-so-much); WeWork Cos., "WeWork Pricing & Membership Plans," https://www.wework.com/workspace, accessed December 2018.

In Chapter 7, you learned how managers use flexible budgets and variance analysis to help plan and control the direct-cost categories of direct materials and direct manufacturing labor. In this chapter, you will learn how managers plan for and control the indirect-cost categories of variable manufacturing overhead and fixed manufacturing overhead.

Planning of Variable and Fixed Overhead Costs

LEARNING OBJECTIVE 1

Explain the similarities and differences in planning variable overhead costs and fixed overhead costs

. . . for both, plan only essential activities and be efficient; fixed overhead costs are usually determined well before the budget period begins

We use the Webb Company example to illustrate the planning and control of variable and fixed overhead costs. Webb manufactures jackets it sells to distributors, who in turn sell them to independent clothing stores and retail chains. Because we assume Webb's only costs are manufacturing costs, for simplicity we use the term "overhead costs" instead of "manufacturing overhead costs" in this chapter. Webb's variable overhead costs include energy, machine maintenance, engineering support, and indirect materials. Webb's fixed overhead costs include plant leasing costs, depreciation on plant equipment, and the salaries of the plant managers.

Planning Variable Overhead Costs

To effectively plan variable overhead costs, managers focus on activities that create a superior product or service for their customers and eliminate activities that do not add value. For example, customers expect Webb's jackets to last, so Webb's managers consider sewing to be an essential activity and plan variable overhead costs to maintain the sewing machines. To reduce costs of maintenance, managers schedule periodic equipment maintenance rather than wait for sewing machines to break down. Many companies use sensors embedded in machines to gather data about machine performance and feed these data into machine learning algorithms to schedule the precise preventive maintenance each machine needs at exactly the right time. Many companies are also seeking ways to reduce energy consumption, both to cut variable overhead costs and to be environmentally friendly. Webb installs smart meters in order to monitor energy use in real time and steer production operations away from peak consumption periods.

Planning Fixed Overhead Costs

Planning fixed overhead costs is similar to planning variable overhead costs—only spend on essential activities and be efficient. But there is an additional strategic issue when planning fixed overhead costs: choosing the appropriate level of capacity or investment that will benefit the company in the long run. Consider Webb's leasing of sewing machines, each of which has a fixed cost per year. Leasing too many machines will result in overcapacity and unnecessary fixed leasing costs. Leasing too few machines will result in an inability to meet demand, lost sales of jackets, and unhappy customers. Consider AT&T, which did not initially foresee the iPhone's appeal or the proliferation of "apps" and consequently did not upgrade its network sufficiently to handle the resulting data traffic. AT&T subsequently had to impose limits on how customers could use the iPhone (such as by curtailing tethering and the streaming of Webcasts). This explains why, at one point following the iPhone's release, AT&T had the lowest customer satisfaction ratings among all major carriers.

The planning of fixed overhead costs differs from the planning of variable overhead costs in another regard as well: timing. At the start of a budget period, management will have made most of the decisions determining the level of fixed overhead costs to be incurred. But it's the day-to-day, ongoing operating decisions that mainly determine the level of variable overhead costs in a period. For example, the variable overhead costs of hospitals, which include the costs of disposable supplies, doses of medication, suture packets, and medical waste disposal, are a function of the number and nature of procedures carried out, as well as the practice patterns of the physicians. However, most of the costs of providing hospital service are fixed overhead costs—those related to buildings, equipment, and salaried labor. These costs are determined at the start of a period and are unrelated to a hospital's volume of activity.[2]

DECISION POINT

How do managers plan variable overhead costs and fixed overhead costs?

[2] Free-standing surgery centers have thrived because they have lower fixed overhead costs compared to traditional hospitals. For an enlightening summary of costing issues in health care, see A. Macario, "What Does One Minute of Operating Room Time Cost?" *Journal of Clinical Anesthesia*, June 2010.

Standard Costing at Webb Company

LEARNING OBJECTIVE 2

Develop budgeted variable overhead cost rates

...budgeted variable costs divided by quantity of cost-allocation base

and budgeted fixed overhead cost rates

...budgeted fixed costs divided by quantity of cost-allocation base

Webb uses standard costing. Chapter 7 explained how the standards for Webb's direct manufacturing costs are developed. This chapter explains how the standards for Webb's manufacturing overhead costs are developed. **Standard costing** is a costing system that (1) traces direct costs to output produced by multiplying the standard prices or rates by the standard quantities of inputs allowed for actual outputs produced, and (2) allocates overhead costs on the basis of the standard overhead cost rates times the standard quantities of the allocation bases allowed for the actual outputs produced.

The standard cost of Webb's jackets can be computed at the start of the budget period. This feature of standard costing simplifies recordkeeping because no record is needed of the actual overhead costs or of the actual quantities of the cost-allocation bases used for making the jackets. What managers *do* need are the standard overhead cost rates for Webb's variable and fixed overhead based on the planned amounts of variable and fixed overhead and the standard quantities of the allocation bases. We describe these computations next. Once managers set these standards, the costs of using standard costing are low relative to the costs of using actual costing or normal costing.

Developing Budgeted Variable Overhead Rates

Budgeted variable overhead cost-allocation rates can be developed in four steps. Throughout the chapter, we use the broader term *budgeted rate* rather than *standard rate* to be consistent with the term used to describe normal costing in earlier chapters. When standard costing is used, as is the case with Webb, the budgeted rates are standard rates.

Step 1: Choose the Period to Be Used for the Budget. Webb uses a 12-month budget period. Chapter 4 (pages 108–109) provided two reasons for using annual overhead rates rather than, say, monthly rates. The first relates to the numerator, such as reducing the influence of seasonality on the firm's cost structure. The second relates to the denominator, such as reducing the effect of varying output and number of days in a month. In addition, setting overhead rates once a year rather than 12 times a year saves managers' time.

Step 2: Select the Cost-Allocation Bases to Use in Allocating the Variable Overhead Costs to the Output Produced. Webb's operating managers select machine-hours as the cost-allocation base because they believe that the number of machine-hours is the sole cost driver of variable overhead. Based on an engineering study, Webb estimates it will take 0.40 of a machine-hour per actual output unit. For its budgeted output of 144,000 jackets in 2020, Webb budgets 57,600 $(0.40 \times 144{,}000)$ machine-hours.

Step 3: Identify the Variable Overhead Costs Associated With Each Cost-Allocation Base. Webb groups all of its variable overhead costs, including the costs of energy, machine maintenance, engineering support, indirect materials, and indirect manufacturing labor, in a single cost pool. Webb's total budgeted variable overhead costs for 2020 are $1,728,000.

Step 4: Compute the Rate per Unit of Each Cost-Allocation Base Used to Allocate the Variable Overhead Costs to the Output Produced. Dividing the amount in Step 3 ($1,728,000) by the amount in Step 2 (57,600 machine-hours), Webb estimates a rate of $30 per standard machine-hour for allocating its variable overhead costs.

When standard costing is used, the variable overhead rate per unit of the cost-allocation base ($30 per machine-hour for Webb) is generally expressed as a standard rate per output unit. Webb calculates the budgeted variable overhead cost rate per output unit as follows:

$$\begin{aligned}\text{Budgeted variable overhead cost rate per output unit} &= \text{Budgeted input allowed per output unit} \times \text{Budgeted variable overhead cost rate per input unit}\\ &= 0.40 \text{ hour per jacket} \times \$30 \text{ per hour}\\ &= \$12 \text{ per jacket}\end{aligned}$$

The $12-per-jacket rate is the budgeted variable overhead cost rate in Webb's static budget for 2020 as well as in the monthly performance reports the firm prepares during 2020. If Webb had multiple cost-allocation bases (for example machine hours and direct manufacturing labor-hours) and corresponding variable overhead cost pools, Webb would repeat Steps 1 to 4 for each cost pool.

The $12-per-jacket rate represents the amount by which managers expect Webb's variable overhead costs to change when the output changes. As the number of jackets manufactured increases, the variable overhead costs allocated to output (for inventory costing) increase at the rate of $12 per jacket. The $12 per jacket constitutes the firm's total variable overhead costs per unit of output, including the costs of energy, repairs, indirect labor, and so on. Managers control variable overhead costs by setting a budget for each of these line items and then investigating the possible causes of any significant variances.

Developing Budgeted Fixed Overhead Rates

Fixed overhead costs are, by definition, a lump sum of costs that remains unchanged for a given period, despite wide changes in a firm's level of activity or output. Fixed costs are included in flexible budgets, but they remain the same within the relevant range of activity regardless of the output level chosen to "flex" the variable costs and revenues. Recall from Exhibit 7-2 and the steps in developing a flexible budget that Webb's monthly fixed overhead costs of $276,000 are the same in the static budget as they are in the flexible budget. Do not assume, however, that these costs can never be changed. Managers can reduce them by selling equipment or laying off employees, for example. But the costs are fixed in the sense that, unlike variable costs such as direct material costs, fixed costs do not *automatically* increase or decrease with the level of activity within the relevant range.

The process of developing the budgeted fixed overhead rate is the same as the one for calculating the budgeted variable overhead rate. The steps are as follows:

Step 1: Choose the Period to Use for the Budget. As with variable overhead costs, the budget period for fixed overhead costs is typically 1 year, to help smooth out seasonal effects.

Step 2: Select the Cost-Allocation Bases to Use in Allocating the Fixed Overhead Costs to the Output Produced. Webb uses machine-hours as the only cost-allocation base for the firm's fixed overhead costs. Why? Because Webb's managers believe that, in the long run, the company's fixed overhead costs will increase or decrease to the levels needed to support the amount of machine-hours. Therefore, in the long run, the number of machine-hours used is the only cost driver of fixed overhead costs. The number of machine-hours is the denominator in the budgeted fixed overhead rate computation and is called the **denominator level**. For simplicity, we assume Webb expects to operate at capacity in fiscal year 2020, with a budgeted usage of 57,600 machine-hours for a budgeted output of 144,000 jackets.[3]

Step 3: Identify the Fixed Overhead Costs Associated With Each Cost-Allocation Base. Because Webb identifies a single cost-allocation base—machine-hours—to allocate fixed overhead costs, it groups all such costs into a single cost pool. Costs in this pool include depreciation on plant and equipment, plant and equipment leasing costs, and the plant manager's salary. Webb's fixed overhead budget for 2020 is $3,312,000.

Step 4: Compute the Rate per Unit of Each Cost-Allocation Base Used to Allocate Fixed Overhead Costs to the Output Produced. By dividing the $3,312,000 from Step 3 by the 57,600 machine-hours from Step 2, Webb estimates a fixed overhead cost rate of $57.50 per machine-hour:

$$\begin{array}{c}\text{Budgeted fixed}\\ \text{overhead cost per}\\ \text{unit of cost-allocation}\\ \text{base}\end{array} = \frac{\begin{array}{c}\text{Budgeted total costs}\\ \text{in fixed overhead cost pool}\end{array}}{\begin{array}{c}\text{Budgeted total quantity of}\\ \text{cost-allocation base}\end{array}} = \frac{\$3{,}312{,}000}{57{,}600} = \$57.50 \text{ per machine-hour}$$

[3] Because Webb plans its capacity over multiple periods, anticipated demand in 2020 could be such that budgeted output for 2020 is less than Webb's capacity. Companies vary in the denominator levels they choose. Some choose budgeted output and others choose capacity. In either case, the approach and analysis presented in this chapter is unchanged. Chapter 9 discusses in more detail the implications of choosing a denominator level.

Under standard costing, the $57.50 fixed overhead cost per machine-hour is usually expressed as a standard cost per output unit. Recall that Webb's engineering study estimates that it will take 0.40 machine-hour per output unit. Webb can now calculate the budgeted fixed overhead cost per output unit as follows:

$$\text{Budgeted fixed overhead cost per output unit} = \text{Budgeted quantity of cost-allocation base allowed per output unit} \times \text{Budgeted fixed overhead cost per unit of cost-allocation base}$$

$$= 0.40 \text{ of a machine-hour per jacket} \times \$57.50 \text{ per machine-hour}$$

$$= \$23.00 \text{ per jacket}$$

DECISION POINT

How are budgeted variable overhead and budgeted fixed overhead cost rates calculated?

When preparing monthly budgets for 2020, Webb divides the $3,312,000 annual total fixed costs into 12 equal monthly amounts of $276,000. If Webb had multiple cost-allocation bases and corresponding fixed overhead cost pools, Webb would repeat Steps 1 to 4 for each cost pool.

Variable Overhead Cost Variances

LEARNING OBJECTIVE 3

Compute the variable overhead flexible-budget variance,

...difference between actual variable overhead costs and flexible-budget variable overhead amounts

the variable overhead efficiency variance,

...difference between actual quantity of cost-allocation base and budgeted quantity of cost-allocation base

and the variable overhead spending variance

...difference between actual variable overhead cost rate and budgeted variable overhead cost rate

We now illustrate how management accountants use the budgeted variable overhead rate to compute Webb's variable overhead cost variances. The following data are for April 2020, when Webb produced and sold 10,000 jackets:

	Actual Result	Flexible-Budget Amount
1. Output units (jackets)	10,000	10,000
2. Machine-hours per output unit	0.45	0.40
3. Machine-hours (1 × 2)	4,500	4,000
4. Variable overhead costs	$130,500	$120,000
5. Variable overhead costs per machine-hour (4 ÷ 3)	$ 29.00	$ 30.00
6. Variable overhead costs per output unit (4 ÷ 1)	$ 13.05	$ 12.00

As we saw in Chapter 7, the flexible budget enables Webb to highlight the differences between actual costs and actual quantities versus budgeted costs and budgeted quantities for the actual output level of 10,000 jackets.

Flexible-Budget Analysis

The **variable overhead flexible-budget variance** measures the difference between actual variable overhead costs incurred and flexible-budget variable overhead amounts.

$$\text{Variable overhead flexible-budget variance} = \text{Actual costs incurred} - \text{Flexible-budget amount}$$

$$= \$130{,}500 - \$120{,}000$$

$$= \$10{,}500 \text{ U}$$

This $10,500 unfavorable flexible-budget variance means Webb's actual variable overhead exceeded the flexible-budget amount by $10,500 for the 10,000 jackets actually produced and sold. Webb's managers would want to know why. Did Webb use more machine-hours than planned to produce the 10,000 jackets? If so, was it because workers were less skilled than expected in using machines? Or did Webb spend more on variable overhead costs, such as maintenance?

Just as we illustrated in Chapter 7 with the flexible-budget variance for direct-cost items, Webb's managers can get further insight into the reason for the $10,500 unfavorable variance (denoted U in this text) by subdividing it into the efficiency variance and spending variance.

Variable Overhead Efficiency Variance

The **variable overhead efficiency variance** is the difference between the actual quantity of the cost-allocation base used and budgeted quantity of the cost-allocation base that should have been used to produce the actual output, multiplied by the budgeted variable overhead cost per unit of the cost-allocation base.

$$\begin{matrix}\text{Variable}\\ \text{overhead}\\ \text{efficiency}\\ \text{variance}\end{matrix} = \left(\begin{matrix}\text{Actual quantity of}\\ \text{variable overhead}\\ \text{cost-allocation base}\\ \text{used for actual}\\ \text{output}\end{matrix} - \begin{matrix}\text{Budgeted quantity of}\\ \text{variable overhead}\\ \text{cost-allocation base}\\ \text{allowed for}\\ \text{actual output}\end{matrix}\right) \times \begin{matrix}\text{Budgeted variable}\\ \text{overhead cost per unit}\\ \text{of cost-allocation base}\end{matrix}$$

$$= (4{,}500 \text{ hours} - 0.40 \text{ hr./unit} \times 10{,}000 \text{ units}) \times \$30 \text{ per hour}$$

$$= (4{,}500 \text{ hours} - 4{,}000 \text{ hours}) \times \$30 \text{ per hour}$$

$$= \$15{,}000 \text{ U}$$

Columns 2 and 3 of Exhibit 8-1 depict the variable overhead efficiency variance. The variance arises solely because of the difference between the actual quantity (4,500 hours) and budgeted quantity (4,000 hours) of the cost-allocation base. The variable overhead efficiency variance is computed the same way the efficiency variance for direct-cost items is (Chapter 7, pages 255–256). However, the interpretation of the variance is different. The efficiency variances for direct-cost items are based on the differences between the actual inputs used and the budgeted inputs allowed for the actual output produced. For example, a forensic laboratory (the kind popularized by television shows such as *CSI* and *Dexter*) would calculate a direct labor efficiency variance based on whether the lab used more or fewer hours than the standard hours allowed for the actual number of DNA tests. In contrast, the efficiency variance for variable overhead is based on the efficiency with which *the cost-allocation base* is used. Webb's unfavorable variable overhead efficiency variance of $15,000 means that the actual machine-hours (the cost-allocation base) of 4,500 hours was higher than the budgeted machine-hours of 4,000 hours allowed to manufacture 10,000 jackets and this, because machine-hours are a cost driver for variable overhead, pushed up the potential spending on variable overhead.

EXHIBIT 8-1 Columnar Presentation of Variable Overhead Variance Analysis: Webb Company for April 2020[a]

	Actual Costs Incurred: Actual Input Quantity × Actual Rate (1)		**Actual Input Quantity × Budgeted Rate (2)**		**Flexible Budget: Budgeted Input Quantity Allowed for Actual Output × Budgeted Rate (3)**
	(4,500 hrs. × $29/hr.) = $130,500		(4,500 hrs. × $30/hr.) = $135,000		(0.40 hr./unit × 10,000 units × $30/hr.) 4,000 hrs. × $30/hr. $120,000
Level 3		$4,500 F Spending variance		$15,000 U Efficiency variance	
Level 2			$10,500 U Flexible-budget variance		

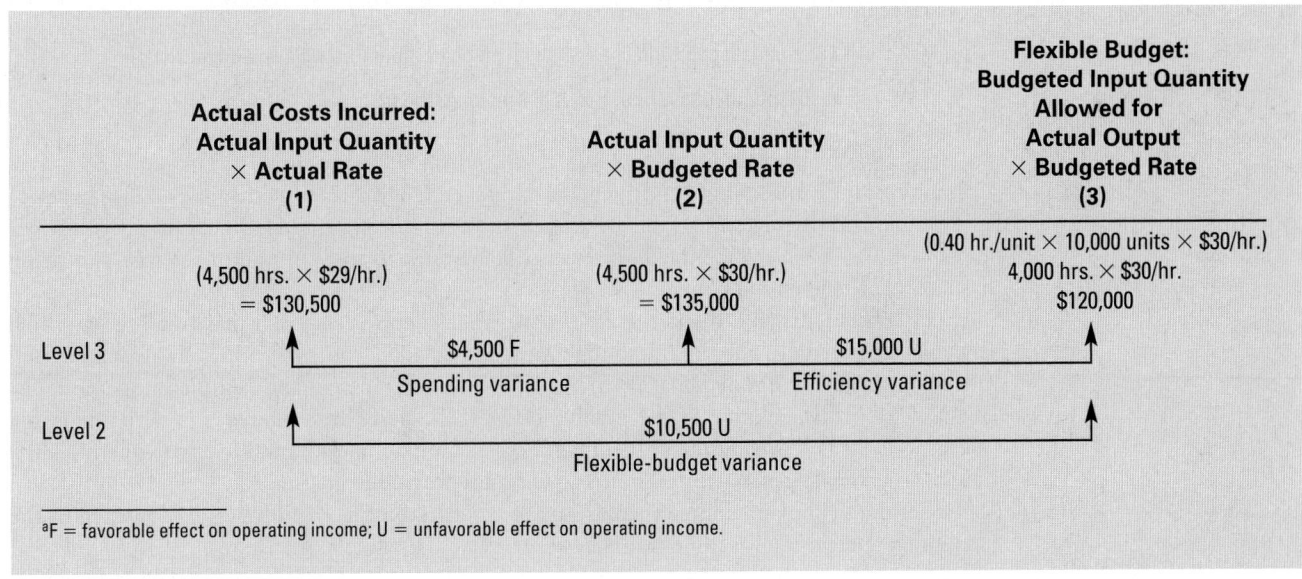

[a]F = favorable effect on operating income; U = unfavorable effect on operating income.

The following table shows possible causes for Webb's actual machine-hours exceeding the budgeted machine-hours and Webb's potential responses to each of these causes.

Possible Causes for Exceeding Budget	Potential Management Responses
1. Workers were under-skilled and so less efficient than expected in using machines.	1. Encourage the human resources department to implement better employee-hiring practices and training procedures.
2. The production scheduler inefficiently scheduled jobs, resulting in more machine-hours used than budgeted.	2. Improve plant operations by installing production-scheduling software.
3. Machines were not maintained in good operating condition.	3. Ensure preventive maintenance is done on all machines.
4. Webb's sales staff promised a distributor a rush delivery, which resulted in more machine-hours used than budgeted.	4. Coordinate production schedules with sales staff and distributors and share information with them.
5. Budgeted machine time standards were set too tight.	5. Commit more resources to develop appropriate standards.

Note how, depending on the cause(s) of the \$15,000 U variance, corrective actions may need to be taken not just in manufacturing but also in other business functions of the value chain, such as sales and distribution.

As we discussed in Chapter 6, managers should not focus on meeting short-run cost targets if they are likely to result in harmful long-run consequences. In the Webb example, machines may not have been in good working condition in April 2020 because preventive maintenance had not been done in prior months to meet monthly cost targets in those months. Many companies have internal maintenance procedures so that failure to do monthly maintenance as needed raises a "red flag."

Variable Overhead Spending Variance

The **variable overhead spending variance** is the difference between the actual variable overhead cost per unit of the cost-allocation base and the budgeted variable overhead cost per unit of the cost-allocation base, multiplied by the actual quantity of variable overhead cost-allocation base used.

$$\begin{aligned}\text{Variable overhead spending variance} &= \left(\begin{array}{c}\text{Actual variable}\\\text{overhead cost per unit}\\\text{of cost-allocation base}\end{array} - \begin{array}{c}\text{Budgeted variable}\\\text{overhead cost per unit}\\\text{of cost-allocation base}\end{array}\right) \times \begin{array}{c}\text{Actual quantity of}\\\text{variable overhead}\\\text{cost-allocation base}\\\text{used}\end{array}\\ &= (\$29 \text{ per machine-hour} - \$30 \text{ per machine-hour}) \times 4{,}500 \text{ machine-hours}\\ &= (-\$1 \text{ per machine-hour}) \times 4{,}500 \text{ machine-hours}\\ &= \$4{,}500 \text{ F}\end{aligned}$$

Columns 1 and 2 in Exhibit 8-1 depict this variance. The variable overhead spending variance is favorable because *actual* variable overhead cost per unit of the cost-allocation base (\$29 per machine-hour) is *lower* than the *budgeted* variable overhead cost per unit of the cost-allocation base (\$30 per machine-hour).

To understand why this is the case, recall that Webb used 4,500 machine-hours, which is 12.5% greater than the flexible-budget amount of 4,000 machine-hours. However, actual variable overhead costs of \$130,500 are only 8.75% greater than the flexible-budget amount of \$120,000. Thus, relative to the flexible budget, the percentage increase in actual variable overhead costs is less than the percentage increase in machine-hours. Hence, the actual variable overhead cost per machine-hour is lower than the budgeted amount.

Why might the percentage increase in actual variable overhead costs be lower than the percentage increase in machine-hours? There are two possible reasons:

1. The actual prices of the individual inputs included in variable overhead costs, such as the price of energy, indirect materials, or indirect labor, are lower than budgeted prices of

these inputs. For example, the actual price of electricity may only be $0.09 per kilowatt-hour, compared with a price of $0.10 per kilowatt-hour in the flexible budget.

2. Relative to the flexible budget, the percentage increase in the actual use of individual items in the variable overhead-cost pool is less than the percentage increase in machine-hours. Compared with the flexible-budget amount of 30,000 kilowatt-hours, suppose the actual energy use was 32,400 kilowatt-hours, or 8% higher. The fact that this is a smaller percentage increase than the 12.5% increase in machine-hours (4,500 actual machine-hours versus a flexible budget of 4,000 machine-hours) will lead to a favorable variable overhead spending variance (denoted F in this text) representing more efficient use of energy.

In the last stage of the five-step decision-making process, Webb's managers examine signals provided by the variable overhead variances to *evaluate the firm's performance and learn.* Learning leads to better predictions and, as we describe next, actions to improve results in future periods.

Consider potential reasons for actual prices of variable overhead cost items to be lower than budgeted prices (reason 1 above), such as skillful negotiation on the part of the purchasing manager, oversupply in the market, or lower quality of inputs such as indirect materials. Webb's response depends on what managers believe to be the cause of the variance. If, for example, prices are lower because of low input quality, managers might put in place new quality management systems.

Consider potential reasons for the efficiency with which variable overhead resources are used (reason 2 above), such as the skill levels of workers, maintenance of machines, and the efficiency of the manufacturing process. If, for example, efficiency gains stem from manufacturing process improvements, managers might organize cross-functional teams to achieve more process improvements.

We emphasize, as we have before, that a manager should not always view a favorable variable overhead spending variance as desirable. The variable overhead spending variance would be favorable if Webb's managers purchased lower-priced, poor-quality indirect materials; hired less-skilled indirect workers; or performed less machine maintenance. These decisions reduce costs in the short run but are likely to hurt product quality and the business in the long run.

To clarify the concepts of variable overhead efficiency variance and variable overhead spending variance, consider the following example. Suppose that (1) energy is the only item of variable overhead cost and machine-hours is the cost-allocation base, (2) actual machine-hours used equals the number of machine-hours under the flexible budget, and (3) the actual price of energy equals the budgeted price. What is the efficiency variance? Zero, because the company has been efficient with respect to the number of machine-hours (the cost-allocation base) used to produce the actual output. Will there be a spending variance? Yes because (3) only eliminates reason 1 above. The energy consumed *per machine-hour* could be higher than budgeted (reason 2 above), for example, because the machines have not been maintained correctly. The cost of this higher energy usage would be reflected in an unfavorable spending variance.

8-1 TRY IT!

Duvet Company manufactures pillows. The 2020 operating budget was based on production of 20,000 pillows, with 0.75 machine-hours allowed per pillow. Budgeted variable overhead per hour was $25.

Actual production for 2020 was 18,000 pillows using 13,000 machine-hours. Actual variable costs were $26 per machine-hour.

Calculate the following:

a. The budgeted variable overhead for 2020
b. The variable overhead spending variance
c. The variable overhead efficiency variance

Journal Entries for Variable Overhead Costs and Variances

We now prepare journal entries for the Variable Overhead Control account and the contra account Variable Overhead Allocated.

Entries for variable overhead for April 2020 (data from Exhibit 8-1) are as follows:

1. Variable Overhead Control	130,500	
Accounts Payable and various other accounts		130,500
To record actual variable overhead costs incurred.		
2. Work-in-Process Control	120,000	
Variable Overhead Allocated		120,000
To record variable overhead cost allocated (0.40 machine-hour / unit × 10,000 units × $30 / machine-hour). (The costs accumulated in Work-in-Process Control are transferred to Finished-Goods Control when production is completed and to Cost of Goods Sold when the products are sold.)		
3. Variable Overhead Allocated	120,000	
Variable Overhead Efficiency Variance	15,000	
Variable Overhead Control		130,500
Variable Overhead Spending Variance		4,500
This records the variances for the accounting period.		

These variances are the underallocated or overallocated variable overhead costs. At the end of the fiscal year, the variance accounts are written off to cost of goods sold if immaterial in amount. If the variances are material in amount, they are prorated among the Work-in-Process Control, Finished-Goods Control, and Cost of Goods Sold accounts on the basis of the variable overhead allocated to these accounts, as described in Chapter 4, pages 126–128. As we discussed in Chapter 4, only unavoidable costs are prorated. Any part of the variances attributable to avoidable inefficiency is written off in the period. Assume that the balances in the variable overhead variance accounts as of April 2020 are also the balances at the end of the 2020 fiscal year and are immaterial in amount. The following journal entry records the write-off of the variance accounts to the Cost of Goods Sold:

Cost of Goods Sold	10,500	
Variable Overhead Spending Variance	4,500	
Variable Overhead Efficiency Variance		15,000

DECISION POINT

What variances can be calculated for variable overhead costs?

Next we demonstrate how to calculate fixed overhead cost variances.

LEARNING OBJECTIVE 4

Compute the fixed overhead flexible-budget variance,

...difference between actual fixed overhead costs and flexible-budget fixed overhead amounts

the fixed overhead spending variance,

...same as the preceding explanation

and the fixed overhead production-volume variance

...difference between budgeted fixed overhead and fixed overhead allocated on the basis of actual output produced

Fixed Overhead Cost Variances

The flexible-budget amount for a fixed-cost item is also the amount included in the static budget prepared at the start of the period. No adjustment is required for differences between actual output and budgeted output for fixed costs because fixed costs are unaffected by changes in the output level within the relevant range. At the start of 2020, Webb budgeted its fixed overhead costs to be $276,000 per month. The actual amount for April 2020 turned out to be $285,000. The **fixed overhead flexible-budget variance** is the difference between actual fixed overhead costs and fixed overhead costs in the flexible budget:

$$\text{Fixed overhead flexible-budget variance} = \text{Actual costs incurred} - \text{Flexible-budget amount}$$

$$= \$285{,}000 - \$276{,}000$$

$$= \$9{,}000\text{ U}$$

The variance is unfavorable because the $285,000 actual fixed overhead costs exceed the $276,000 budgeted for April 2020, which decreases that month's operating income by $9,000.

The variable overhead flexible-budget variance described earlier in this chapter was subdivided into a spending variance and an efficiency variance. There is no efficiency variance for fixed overhead costs. That's because a given lump sum of fixed overhead costs will be unaffected by how efficiently machine-hours are used to produce output in a given budget period. As Exhibit 8-2 shows, because there is no efficiency variance, the **fixed overhead spending variance** is the same amount as the fixed overhead flexible-budget variance:

$$\text{Fixed overhead spending variance} = \text{Actual costs incurred} - \text{Flexible-budget amount}$$
$$= \$285{,}000 - \$276{,}000$$
$$= \$9{,}000\text{ U}$$

Reasons for the unfavorable spending variance could be higher equipment-leasing costs, higher depreciation on plant and equipment, or higher administrative costs, such as a higher-than-budgeted salary paid to the plant manager. If equipment-leasing costs were higher, for example, managers might look to lease equipment from other suppliers.

Production-Volume Variance

The **production-volume variance** arises only for fixed costs. It is the difference between the budgeted fixed overhead and the fixed overhead allocated on the basis of actual output produced. Recall that at the start of the year, Webb calculated a budgeted fixed overhead rate of $57.50 per machine-hour based on monthly budgeted fixed overhead costs of $276,000. Under standard costing, Webb's fixed overhead costs are allocated to the actual output produced during each period at the rate of $57.50 per standard machine-hour, which is equivalent to a rate of $23 per jacket (0.40 machine-hour per jacket × $57.50 per machine-hour). If Webb produces 1,000 jackets, $23,000 ($23 per jacket × 1,000 jackets) out of April's budgeted fixed overhead costs of $276,000 will be allocated to the jackets. If Webb produces 10,000 jackets, $230,000 ($23 per jacket × 10,000 jackets) will be allocated. Only if Webb produces 12,000 jackets (that is, operates, as budgeted, at capacity) will all $276,000 ($23 per jacket × 12,000 jackets) of the budgeted fixed overhead costs be allocated to the jacket output. The key point here is that even though Webb budgeted its fixed overhead costs to be $276,000, it does not necessarily allocate all these costs to output. The reason is that Webb budgets $276,000 of fixed costs to support its planned production of 12,000 jackets. If Webb produces fewer than 12,000 jackets, it only allocates the budgeted cost of capacity actually needed and used to produce the jackets.

EXHIBIT 8-2 Columnar Presentation of Fixed Overhead Variance Analysis: Webb Company for April 2020[a]

	Actual Costs Incurred (1)	Flexible Budget: Same Budgeted Lump Sum (as in Static Budget) Regardless of Output Level (2)	Allocated: Budgeted Input Quantity Allowed for Actual Output × Budgeted Rate (3)
			(0.40 hr./unit × 10,000 units × $57.50/hr.)
			(4,000 hrs. × $57.50/hr.)
	$285,000	$276,000	$230,000

Level 3: (1) to (2): $9,000 U — Spending variance; (2) to (3): $46,000 U — Production-volume variance

Level 2: (1) to (2): $9,000 U — Flexible-budget variance

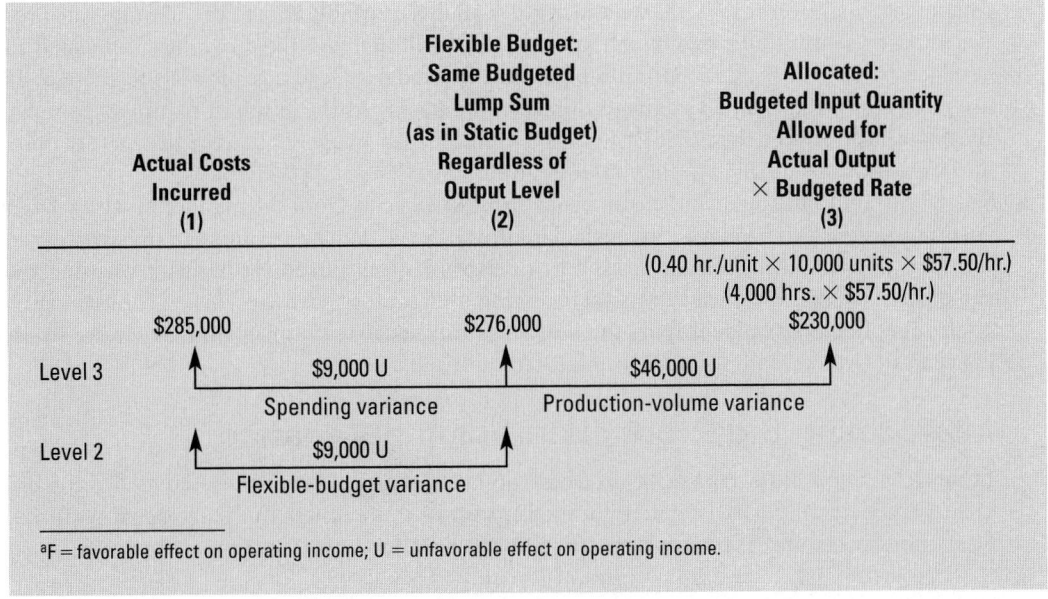

[a]F = favorable effect on operating income; U = unfavorable effect on operating income.

EXHIBIT 8-3

Behavior of Fixed Manufacturing Overhead Costs: Budgeted for Planning and Control Purposes and Allocated for Inventory Costing Purposes for Webb Company for April 2020

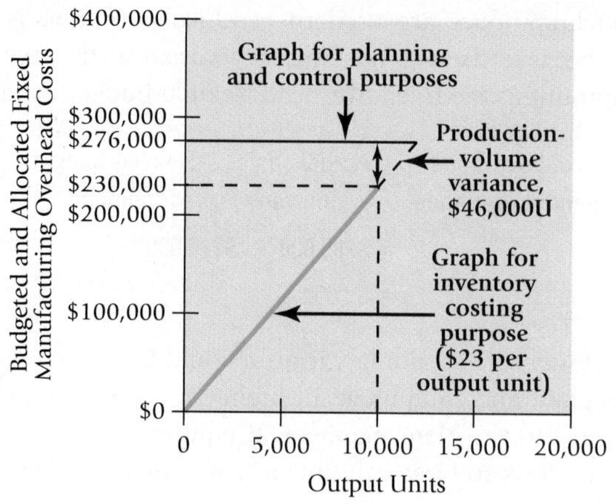

The production-volume variance, also referred to as the **denominator-level variance**, is the difference between the budgeted and allocated fixed overhead amounts. Note that the allocated overhead can be expressed in terms of the budgeted fixed cost per unit of the allocation base (machine-hours for Webb) or in terms of the budgeted fixed cost per unit:

$$\text{Production volume variance} = \text{Budgeted fixed overhead} - \text{Fixed overhead allocated for actual output units produced}$$

$$= \$276{,}000 - (0.40 \text{ hour per jacket} \times \$57.50 \text{ per hour} \times 10{,}000 \text{ jackets})$$

$$= \$276{,}000 - (\$23 \text{ per jacket} \times 10{,}000 \text{ jackets})$$

$$= \$276{,}000 - \$230{,}000$$

$$= \$46{,}000 \text{ U}$$

As shown in Exhibit 8-2, the budgeted fixed overhead ($276,000) will be the lump sum shown in the static budget and also in any flexible budget within the relevant range. The fixed overhead allocated ($230,000) is calculated by multiplying the number of output units produced during the budget period (10,000 units) by the budgeted cost per output unit ($23). The $46,000 U production-volume variance can also be thought of as $23 per jacket × 2,000 jackets that were *not* produced.

Exhibit 8-3 shows Webb's production-volume variance. For planning and control purposes, Webb's fixed (manufacturing) overhead costs do not change in the 0- to 12,000-unit relevant range. Contrast this behavior of fixed costs with how costs are depicted for the purpose of inventory costing in Exhibit 8-3. Under Generally Accepted Accounting Principles, fixed (manufacturing) overhead costs are allocated as an inventoriable cost to the output units produced. Every output unit that Webb manufactures will increase fixed overhead allocated to products by $23. That is, for purposes of allocating fixed overhead costs to jackets, these costs are viewed *as if* they had a variable-cost behavior pattern. As the graph in Exhibit 8-3 shows, the difference between the $276,000 in fixed overhead costs budgeted and the $230,000 of costs allocated is the $46,000 U production-volume variance.

Be careful to distinguish the true behavior of fixed costs from the manner in which fixed costs are assigned to products. In particular, although fixed costs are unitized (i.e., converted into per-unit amounts) and allocated for inventory-costing purposes, be wary of using the same per-unit fixed overhead costs for planning and control purposes. When forecasting or controlling fixed costs, identifying the best ways to use capacity, or when making decisions, concentrate on total lump-sum costs instead of unitized costs.

Interpreting the Production-Volume Variance

Lump-sum fixed costs represent the costs of acquiring capacity. These costs do not decrease automatically if the capacity needed turns out to be less than the capacity acquired. Sometimes costs are fixed for a specific time period for contractual reasons, such as an annual lease contract for equipment. At other times, costs are fixed because capacity has to be acquired or disposed of in fixed increments, or lumps. For example, suppose that acquiring a sewing machine gives Webb the ability to produce 1,000 jackets. If it is not possible to buy or lease a fraction of a machine, Webb can add capacity only in increments of 1,000 jackets. That is, Webb may choose capacity levels of 10,000, 11,000, or 12,000 jackets, but nothing in between.

What explains the $46,000 U production-volume variance? Why did this overcapacity occur? Why were 10,000 jackets produced instead of 12,000? Is demand weak? Should Webb reevaluate its product and marketing strategies? Is there a quality problem? Or did Webb make a strategic mistake by acquiring too much capacity? The causes of the $46,000 U production-volume variance will determine the actions Webb's managers take in response to the variance.

In contrast, a favorable production-volume variance indicates an overallocation of fixed overhead costs. That is, the overhead costs allocated to the actual output produced exceed the budgeted fixed overhead costs of $276,000. The favorable production-volume variance represents fixed costs allocated in excess of $276,000.

Be careful when drawing conclusions about Webb's capacity planning on the basis of an unfavorable production-volume variance. Consider why Webb sold only 10,000 jackets in April. Suppose a new competitor gained market share by pricing its jackets lower than Webb's. To sell the budgeted 12,000 jackets, Webb might have had to reduce its own selling price on all 12,000 jackets. Suppose it decided that selling 10,000 jackets at a higher price yielded higher operating income than selling 12,000 jackets at a lower price. This would be a good decision even though it would mean Webb would not utilize all its capacity. The production-volume variance cannot take into account such information. We should not interpret the $46,000 U amount as the total economic cost of selling 2,000 jackets fewer than the 12,000 jackets budgeted.

Companies plan their plant capacity strategically on the basis of market information about how much capacity will be needed over some future time horizon. For 2020, Webb's budgeted quantity of output is equal to the maximum capacity of the plant for that budget period. Actual demand (and quantity produced) turned out to be below the budgeted quantity of output, so Webb reports an unfavorable production-volume variance for April 2020. However, it would be incorrect to conclude that Webb's management made a poor planning decision regarding its plant capacity. The demand for Webb's jackets might be highly uncertain. Given this uncertainty and the cost of not having sufficient capacity to meet sudden demand surges (including lost contribution margins as well as reduced repeat business), Webb's management may have made a wise capacity choice for 2020.

So what should Webb's managers ultimately do about the unfavorable variance in April? Should they try to reduce capacity, increase sales, or do nothing? Suppose Webb's managers anticipate they will not need 12,000 jackets of capacity in future years. They will then cancel leases on some machines but continue to maintain some excess capacity to accommodate unexpected surges in demand. Concepts in Action: Variance Analysis and Standard Costing Help Sandoz Manage Its Overhead Costs highlights another example of managers using variances to help guide their decisions.

We next describe journal entries to record fixed overhead costs using standard costing.

8-2 TRY IT!

Duvet Company manufactures pillows. For 2020, the company expects fixed overhead costs of $300,000. Duvet uses machine-hours to allocate fixed overhead costs and anticipates 15,000 hours during the year to manufacture 20,000 pillows.

During 2020, Duvet manufactured 18,000 pillows and spent $290,000 on fixed overhead costs.

Calculate the following:

a. The fixed overhead rate for 2020
b. The fixed overhead spending variance for 2020
c. The production-volume variance for 2020

CONCEPTS IN ACTION

Variance Analysis and Standard Costing Help Sandoz Manage Its Overhead Costs[4]

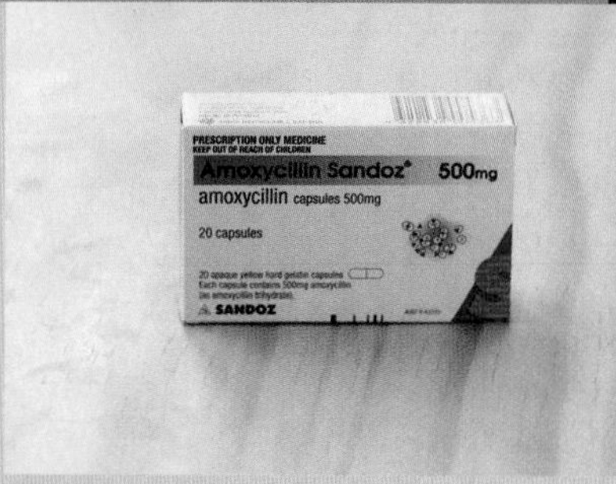

Fir Mamat/Alamy Stock Photo

Sandoz, the $10.1 billion generics division of Swiss-based Novartis AG, is the world's third largest generic drug manufacturer. As products lose patents, multiple manufacturers enter the market and prices drop. How much? Very significantly. In the United States, for example, 90% of all prescription drugs dispensed were generics, but they account for only 23% of total drug costs. To compete, generics companies must carefully control costs.

To manage overhead costs, Sandoz prepares an overhead budget based on a detailed production plan, planned overhead spending, and other factors. Sandoz uses activity-based costing to assign budgeted overhead costs to different work centers (for example, mixing, blending, tableting, testing, and packaging). Finally, overhead costs are assigned to products based on the activity levels required by each product at each work center.

Each month, Sandoz compares actual costs to the standard costs of products made to evaluate whether costs are in line with the budget. If not, reasons are examined and accountable managers are notified. Manufacturing overhead variances are examined at the work center level. These variances help determine when equipment is not running as expected so it can be repaired or replaced. Variances also help to identify inefficiencies in processing and setup and cleaning times, which leads to more efficient ways to use equipment. Sometimes, the manufacturing overhead variance analysis leads to the review and improvement of the standards themselves—a critical element in planning the level of plant capacity. Management also reviews current and future capacity on a monthly basis to identify constraints and future capital needs.

[4] *Sources*: Novartis AG, 2018 Form 20-F (Basel, Switzerland: Novartis AG, 2019) (https://www.novartis.com/sites/www.novartis.com/files/novartis-20-f-2018.pdf); Association for Accessible Medicines, *2018 Generic Drug Access and Savings in the U.S.*, Washington, DC: Association for Accessible Medicines, 2018 (https://accessiblemeds.org/resources/blog/2018-generic-drug-access-and-savings-report); conversations with, and documents prepared by, Tobias Hestler and Chris Lewis of Sandoz, 2016.

Journal Entries for Fixed Overhead Costs and Variances

We illustrate journal entries for fixed overhead costs for April 2020 using the Fixed Overhead Control account and the contra account Fixed Overhead Allocated (data from Exhibit 8-2).

1. Fixed Overhead Control	285,000	
Salaries Payable, Accumulated Depreciation, and various other accounts		285,000
To record actual fixed overhead costs incurred.		
2. Work-in-Process Control	230,000	
Fixed Overhead Allocated		230,000
To record fixed overhead costs allocated.		
(0.40 machine-hour/unit × 10,000 units × $57.50/machine-hour). (The costs accumulated in Work-in-Process Control are transferred to Finished-Goods Control when production is completed and to the Cost of Goods Sold when the products are sold.)		
3. Fixed Overhead Allocated	230,000	
Fixed Overhead Spending Variance	9,000	
Fixed Overhead Production-Volume Variance	46,000	
Fixed Overhead Control		285,000
To record variances for the accounting period.		

Overall, $285,000 of fixed overhead costs were incurred during April, but only $230,000 were allocated to jackets. The difference of $55,000 is precisely the underallocated fixed overhead costs we introduced when studying normal costing in Chapter 4. The third entry illustrates how the fixed overhead spending variance of $9,000 and the fixed overhead production-volume variance of $46,000 together record this amount in a standard costing system.

At the end of the fiscal year, the fixed overhead spending variance is written off to the Cost of Goods Sold if it is immaterial in amount or prorated among Work-in-Process Control, Finished-Goods Control, and Cost of Goods Sold on the basis of the fixed overhead allocated to these accounts as described in Chapter 4, pages 126–128. Some companies combine the write-off and proration methods—that is, they write off the portion of the variance that is due to inefficiency and could have been avoided and prorate the portion of the variance that is unavoidable. Assume that the balance in the Fixed Overhead Spending Variance account as of April 2020 is also the balance at the end of 2020 and is immaterial in amount. The following journal entry records the write-off to Cost of Goods Sold.

Cost of Goods Sold	9,000	
Fixed Overhead Spending Variance		9,000

We now consider the production-volume variance. Assume that the balance in the Fixed Overhead Production-Volume Variance account as of April 2020 is also the balance at the end of 2020. Also assume that some of the jackets manufactured during 2020 are in work-in-process and finished-goods inventory at the end of the year. Many management accountants make a strong argument for writing off to Cost of Goods Sold and not prorating an unfavorable production-volume variance. Proponents of this argument contend that the unfavorable production-volume variance of \$46,000 measures the cost of resources expended for 2,000 jackets that were not produced (\$23 per jacket × 2,000 jackets = \$46,000). Prorating these costs would inappropriately allocate the fixed overhead costs incurred for the 2,000 jackets not produced to the jackets that were produced. The jackets produced already bear their representative share of fixed overhead costs of \$23 per jacket. Therefore, this argument favors charging the unfavorable production-volume variance against the year's revenues so that fixed costs of unused capacity are not carried in work-in-process inventory and finished-goods inventory.

There is, however, an alternative view. This view regards the denominator level as a "soft" rather than a "hard" measure of the fixed resources required to produce each jacket. Suppose that, either because of the design of the jacket or the functioning of the machines, it took more machine-hours than previously thought to manufacture each jacket. Consequently, Webb could make only 10,000 jackets rather than the planned 12,000 in April. In this case, the \$276,000 of budgeted fixed overhead costs supports the production of the 10,000 jackets manufactured. Under this reasoning, prorating the fixed overhead production-volume variance would appropriately spread the fixed overhead costs among the Work-in-Process Control, Finished-Goods Control, and Cost of Goods Sold accounts.

What about a favorable production-volume variance? Suppose Webb manufactured 13,800 jackets in April 2020.

$$\text{Production-volume variance} = \begin{pmatrix}\text{Budgeted}\\ \text{fixed}\\ \text{overhead}\end{pmatrix} - \begin{pmatrix}\text{Fixed overhead allocated using}\\ \text{budgeted cost per output unit overhead}\\ \text{allowed for actual output produced}\end{pmatrix}$$

$$= \$276{,}000 - (\$23 \text{ per jacket} \times 13{,}800 \text{ jackets})$$

$$= \$276{,}000 - \$317{,}400 = \$41{,}400 \text{ F}$$

Because actual production exceeded the planned capacity level, clearly the fixed overhead costs of \$276,000 supported the production of all 13,800 jackets and should therefore be allocated to them. Prorating the favorable production-volume variance achieves this outcome and reduces the amounts in the Work-in-Process Control, Finished-Goods Control, and Cost of Goods Sold accounts. Proration is also the more conservative approach in the sense that it results in a lower operating income than if the entire favorable production-volume variance were credited to Cost of Goods Sold.

Another argument for not always writing off variances is that such a policy might invite gaming behavior. If variances are always written off to Cost of Goods Sold, a company could set standards to either increase (for financial reporting purposes) or decrease (for tax purposes) its operating income. For example, Webb could generate a favorable production-volume variance by setting the denominator level used to allocate the firm's fixed overhead costs low and thereby increase its operating income. Or the firm could do just the opposite if it wanted to decrease its operating income to lower its taxes. The proration method has the effect of approximating the allocation of fixed costs based on actual costs and actual output, so it is not susceptible to this type of manipulation.

There is no clear-cut or preferred approach for closing out the production-volume variance. The appropriate accounting procedure is a matter of judgment and depends on the circumstances of each case. Variations of the proration method may be desirable. For example, a company may choose to write off a portion of the production-volume variance and prorate the rest. The goal is to write off that part of the production-volume variance that represents the cost of capacity not used to support the production of output during the period. The rest of the production-volume variance is prorated to Work-in-Process Control, Finished-Goods Control, and Cost of Goods Sold.

DECISION POINT

What variances can be calculated for fixed overhead costs?

If Webb were to write off the production-volume variance to Cost of Goods Sold, it would make the following journal entry.

Cost of Goods Sold	46,000	
Fixed Overhead Production-Volume Variance		46,000

Integrated Analysis of Overhead Cost Variances

LEARNING OBJECTIVE 5

Show how the 4-variance analysis approach reconciles the actual overhead incurred with the overhead amounts allocated during the period

...the 4-variance analysis approach identifies spending and efficiency variances for variable overhead costs and spending and production-volume variances for fixed overhead costs

As our discussion indicates, the variance calculations for variable overhead and fixed overhead differ:

- Variable overhead has no production-volume variance.
- Fixed overhead has no efficiency variance.

Exhibit 8-4 presents an integrated summary of the variable overhead variances and the fixed overhead variances computed using standard costs for April 2020. Panel A shows the variances for variable overhead, whereas Panel B contains the fixed overhead variances. As you study Exhibit 8-4, note how the columns in Panels A and B are aligned to measure the different variances. In both Panels A and B,

- the difference between columns 1 and 2 measures the spending variance.
- the difference between columns 2 and 3 measures the efficiency variance (if applicable).
- the difference between columns 3 and 4 measures the production-volume variance (if applicable).

Panel A contains an efficiency variance; Panel B has no efficiency variance for fixed overhead. As we discussed, a lump-sum amount of fixed costs will be unaffected by the degree of operating efficiency in a given budget period.

Panel A does not have a production-volume variance because the amount of variable overhead allocated is always the same as the flexible-budget amount. Variable costs never have any unused capacity. When production and sales decline from 12,000 jackets to 10,000 jackets, budgeted variable overhead costs proportionately decline. Fixed costs are different. Panel B has a production-volume variance (see Exhibit 8-3) because Webb did not use some of the fixed overhead capacity it had acquired when it planned to produce 12,000 jackets.

4-Variance Analysis

When all of the overhead variances are presented together as in Exhibit 8-4, we refer to it as a 4-variance analysis:

	4-Variance Analysis		
	Spending Variance	**Efficiency Variance**	**Production-Volume Variance**
Variable overhead	$4,500 F	$15,000 U	Never a variance
Fixed overhead	$9,000 U	Never a variance	$46,000 U

EXHIBIT 8-4 Columnar Presentation of Integrated 4-Variance Analysis: Webb Company for April 2020[a]

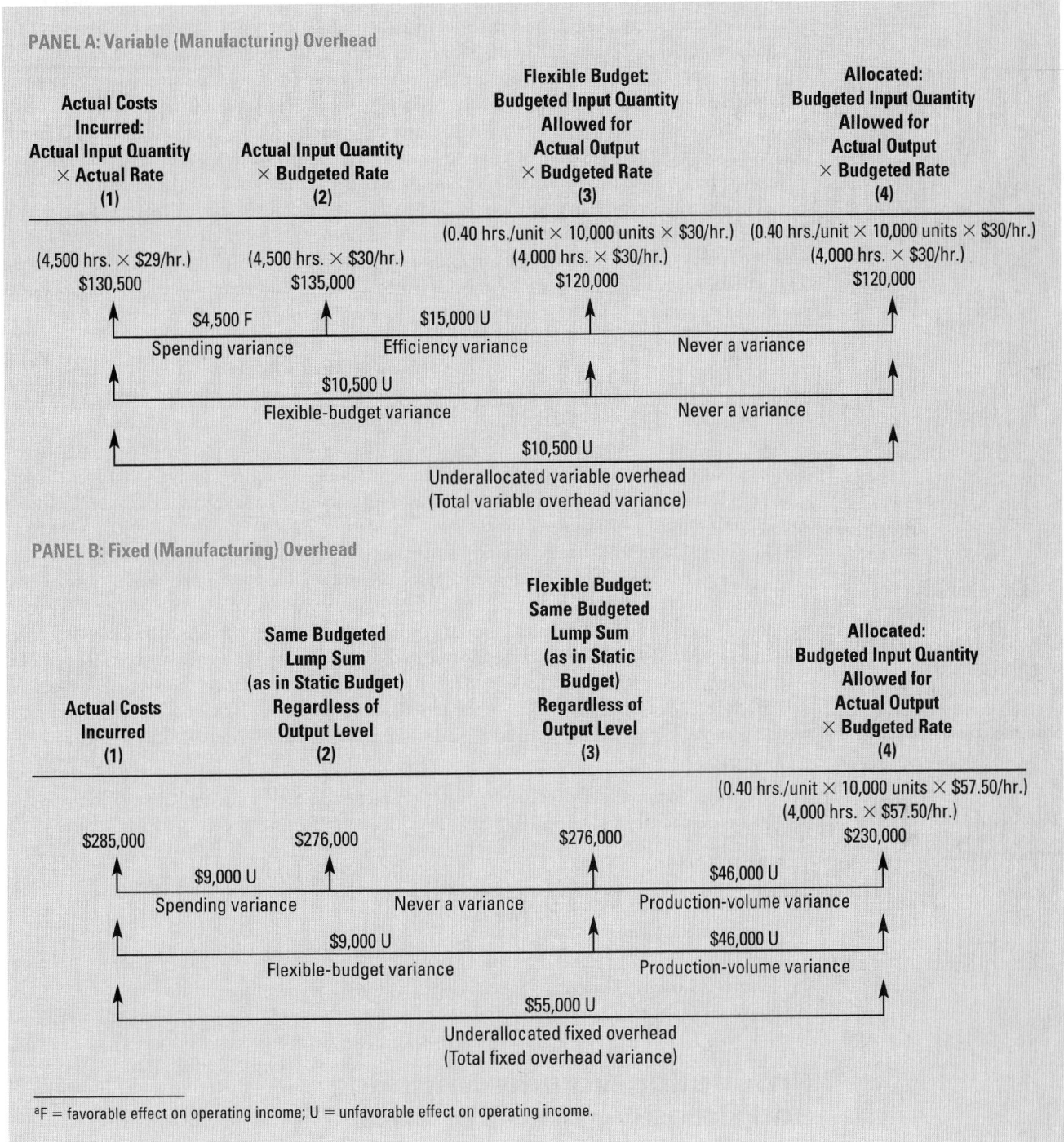

PANEL A: Variable (Manufacturing) Overhead

Actual Costs Incurred: Actual Input Quantity × Actual Rate (1)	Actual Input Quantity × Budgeted Rate (2)	Flexible Budget: Budgeted Input Quantity Allowed for Actual Output × Budgeted Rate (3)	Allocated: Budgeted Input Quantity Allowed for Actual Output × Budgeted Rate (4)
		(0.40 hrs./unit × 10,000 units × $30/hr.)	(0.40 hrs./unit × 10,000 units × $30/hr.)
(4,500 hrs. × $29/hr.)	(4,500 hrs. × $30/hr.)	(4,000 hrs. × $30/hr.)	(4,000 hrs. × $30/hr.)
$130,500	$135,000	$120,000	$120,000

(1) to (2): $4,500 F — Spending variance; (2) to (3): $15,000 U — Efficiency variance; (3) to (4): Never a variance

(1) to (3): $10,500 U — Flexible-budget variance; (3) to (4): Never a variance

(1) to (4): $10,500 U — Underallocated variable overhead (Total variable overhead variance)

PANEL B: Fixed (Manufacturing) Overhead

Actual Costs Incurred (1)	Same Budgeted Lump Sum (as in Static Budget) Regardless of Output Level (2)	Flexible Budget: Same Budgeted Lump Sum (as in Static Budget) Regardless of Output Level (3)	Allocated: Budgeted Input Quantity Allowed for Actual Output × Budgeted Rate (4)
			(0.40 hrs./unit × 10,000 units × $57.50/hr.)
			(4,000 hrs. × $57.50/hr.)
$285,000	$276,000	$276,000	$230,000

(1) to (2): $9,000 U — Spending variance; (2) to (3): Never a variance; (3) to (4): $46,000 U — Production-volume variance

(1) to (3): $9,000 U — Flexible-budget variance; (3) to (4): $46,000 U — Production-volume variance

(1) to (4): $55,000 U — Underallocated fixed overhead (Total fixed overhead variance)

[a]F = favorable effect on operating income; U = unfavorable effect on operating income.

The 4-variance analysis provides the same level of information as the variance analysis for variable overhead and fixed overhead separately (in Exhibits 8-1 and 8-2, respectively) but does so in a unified presentation that also indicates those variances that are never present.

As with other variances, overhead variances are not necessarily independent of each other. For example, Webb may purchase lower-quality machine fluids (leading to a favorable variable overhead spending variance), which results in the machines taking longer to operate than budgeted (causing an unfavorable variable overhead efficiency variance), and producing less than budgeted output (causing an unfavorable production-volume variance).

Combined Variance Analysis

Different companies use variance analysis differently. Managers in large, complex businesses, such as General Electric and Disney, use detailed 4-variance analysis to keep track of areas that are and are not operating as expected. Managers of small businesses rely more on personal observations and nonfinancial measures. They find less value from the additional measurements required for 4-variance analyses. As we saw in Chapter 2 and will see in Chapter 10, many costs such as supervision, quality control, and materials handling have both variable- and fixed-cost components that may not be easy to separate. Managers use less detailed analysis that *combines* the variable overhead and fixed overhead into a single total overhead cost.

When a single total overhead cost category is used, it can still be analyzed in depth. Managers still need to estimate variable-overhead costs and fixed-overhead costs to subdivide the total overhead variance into spending, efficiency, and production-volume variances. The variances are now the sums of the variable overhead and fixed overhead variances, as computed in Exhibit 8-4. The combined variance analysis follows:

	Combined 3-Variance Analysis		
	Spending Variance	**Efficiency Variance**	**Production-Volume Variance**
Total overhead	$4,500 U	$15,000 U	$46,000 U

The accounting for 3-variance analysis is simpler than for 4-variance analysis, but some information is lost because the variable and fixed overhead spending variances are combined into a single total overhead spending variance.

DECISION POINT

What is the most detailed way for a company to reconcile actual overhead incurred with the amount allocated during a period?

The overall **total-overhead variance** is the sum of the preceding variances. In the Webb example, this equals $65,500 U. This amount aggregates the flexible-budget and production-volume variances and equals the underallocated (or underapplied) overhead costs. (Recall our discussion of underallocated overhead costs in normal costing from Chapter 4, pages 125–126.) Using figures from Exhibit 8-4, the $65,500 U total-overhead variance is the difference between (1) the total actual overhead incurred ($130,500 + $285,000 = $415,500) and (2) the overhead allocated ($120,000 + $230,000 = $350,000) to the actual output produced. If the total-overhead variance were favorable, it would equal the overallocated (or overapplied) overhead costs.

TRY IT! 8-3

Consider again the Duvet Company. Complete the following table based on your answers to Try It! 8-1 and Try It! 8-2.

Variances	Spending	Efficiency	Production-Volume
Variable manufacturing overhead			
Fixed manufacturing overhead			

a. In a combined 3-variance analysis, what is the total spending variance?
b. What is the total overhead variance?

Production-Volume Variance and Sales-Volume Variance

LEARNING OBJECTIVE 6

Explain the relationship between the sales-volume variance and the production-volume variance

...the production-volume and operating-income volume variances together comprise the sales-volume variance

As we complete our study of variance analysis for Webb Company, it helps to step back to see the "big picture" and to link the accounting and performance evaluation functions of standard costing. Exhibit 7-1, page 247, first identified a static-budget variance of $93,100 U as the difference between the static budget operating income of $108,000 and the actual operating income of $14,900. Exhibit 7-2, page 249, then subdivided the static-budget variance of $93,100 U into a flexible-budget variance of $29,100 U and a sales-volume variance of $64,000 U. In both Chapter 7 and this chapter, we presented more detailed variances that subdivided the flexible budget variance of $29,100 U, whenever possible, into individual flexible-budget variances for the selling price, direct materials, direct manufacturing labor, and variable overhead. For the fixed overhead, we noted that the flexible-budget variance is the same as the spending variance. Where does the production-volume variance belong then? As we shall see, the production-volume variance is a component of the sales-volume variance. Under our assumption of actual production and sales of 10,000 jackets, Webb's costing system debits to Work-in-Process Control the standard costs of the 10,000 jackets produced. These amounts are then transferred to Finished Goods and finally to Cost of Goods Sold:

Direct materials (Chapter 7, page 258, entry 1b)	
($60 per jacket × 10,000 jackets)	$ 600,000
Direct manufacturing labor (Chapter 7, page 258, entry 2)	
($16 per jacket × 10,000 jackets)	160,000
Variable overhead (Chapter 8, page 290, entry 2)	
($12 per jacket × 10,000 jackets)	120,000
Fixed overhead (Chapter 8, page 294, entry 2)	
($23 per jacket × 10,000 jackets)	230,000
Cost of goods sold at standard cost	
($111 per jacket × 10,000 jackets)	$1,110,000

Webb's costing system also records revenues from the 10,000 jackets sold at the budgeted selling price of $120 per jacket. The net effect on Webb's budgeted operating income is shown below:

Revenues at budgeted selling price	
($120 per jacket × 10,000 jackets)	$1,200,000
Cost of goods sold at standard cost	
($111 per jacket × 10,000 jackets)	1,110,000
Operating income based on budgeted profit per jacket	
($9 per jacket × 10,000 jackets)	$ 90,000

A crucial point to keep in mind is that under standard costing, fixed overhead costs are allocated to finished goods as each jacket is produced and so appear as if they are a variable cost. That is, in determining the budgeted operating income of $90,000, only $230,000 ($23 per jacket × 10,000 jackets) of the fixed overhead costs are considered, whereas the budgeted fixed overhead costs are $276,000. Webb's accountants then record the $46,000 unfavorable production-volume variance (the difference between the budgeted fixed overhead costs, $276,000, and allocated fixed overhead costs, $230,000, page 294, entry 2), as well as the various flexible-budget variances (including the fixed overhead spending variance) that total $29,100 U (see Exhibit 7-2, page 249). This results in actual operating income of $14,900 as follows:

Operating income based on budgeted profit per jacket	
($9 per jacket × 10,000 jackets)	$ 90,000
Unfavorable production-volume variance	(46,000)
Flexible-budget operating income (Exhibit 7-2)	44,000
Unfavorable flexible-budget variance for operating income (Exhibit 7-2)	(29,100)
Actual operating income (Exhibit 7-2)	$ 14,900

In contrast, the static-budget operating income of $108,000 (page 248) never appears in Webb's costing system because standard costing records budgeted revenues, standard costs, and variances only for the 10,000 jackets actually produced and sold, not for the 12,000 jackets that were *planned* to be produced and sold. As a result, the sales-volume variance of $64,000 U, which is the difference between the static-budget operating income of $108,000 and the flexible-budget operating income of $44,000 (Exhibit 7-2, page 249), is never actually recorded under standard costing. Nevertheless, the sales-volume variance is useful because it helps managers understand the lost contribution margin from selling 2,000 fewer jackets (the sales-volume variance assumes fixed costs remain at the budgeted level of $276,000).

The sales-volume variance has two components:

1. A difference between the operating income reported in the standard-costing system of $90,000 and the flexible-budget operating income of $44,000 (Exhibit 7-2, page 249) for the 10,000 actual units produced. This difference arises because Webb's costing system allocates fixed costs to each unit produced (as if they behave in a variable manner) and so allocates $230,000 ($23 per unit × 10,000 units), rather than the budgeted fixed costs of $276,000. This difference is the production-volume variance of $46,000 U, *which is recorded in Webb's standard costing system.*

EXHIBIT 8-5 Summary of Levels 1, 2, and 3 Variance Analysis: Webb Company for April 2020

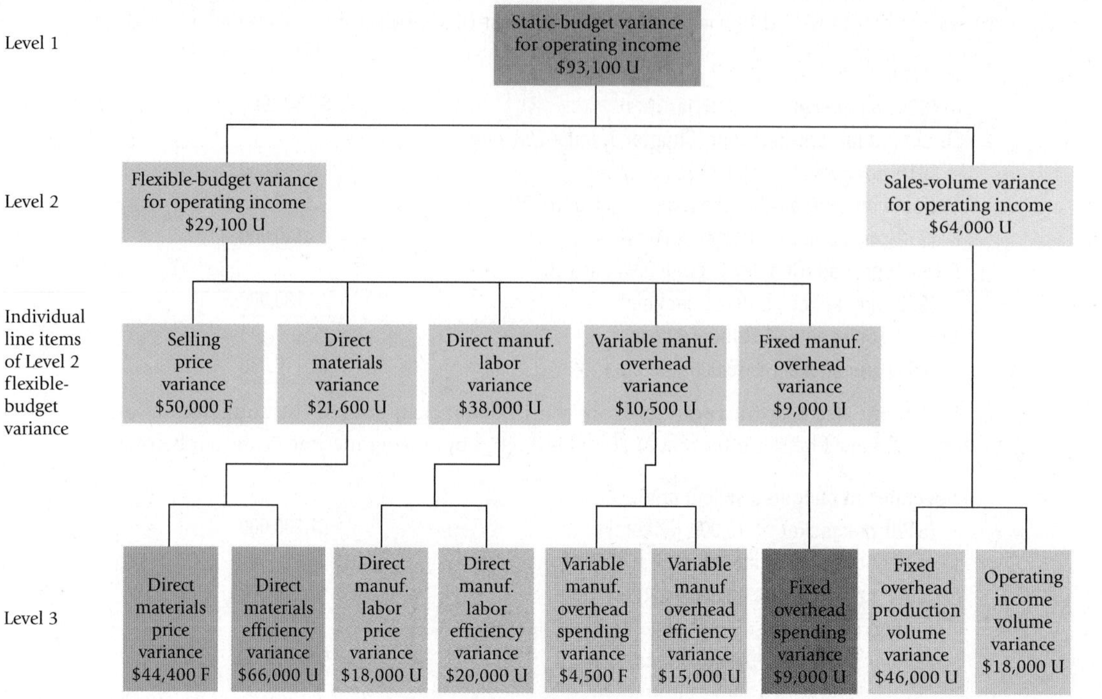

2. A difference between the static-budget operating income of $108,000 for 12,000 jackets and the budgeted operating income of $90,000 for 10,000 jackets. This is the **operating-income volume variance** of $18,000 U ($108,000 − $90,000). It reflects the fact that Webb produced and sold 2,000 fewer units than budgeted. *This part of the sales volume variance does not appear in Webb's standard costing system.*

In summary, we have the following:

	Production-volume variance	$46,000 U
(+)	Operating-income volume variance	18,000 U
Equals	Sales-volume variance	$64,000 U

DECISION POINT

How is the sales-volume variance related to the production-volume variance?

Although useful from a managerial point of view, the sales-volume variance and the operating-income volume variance are not part of the standard-costing system. The production-volume variance is part of the standard-costing system because Webb must account for the fixed overheads incurred that were not allocated to products. We can now provide a summary (see Exhibit 8-5) that formally disaggregates the static-budget variance of $93,100 U into its components. Note how the comprehensive chart incorporates all of the variances you have studied in Chapters 7 and 8.

We next describe the use of variance analysis in activity-based costing systems.

Variance Analysis and Activity-Based Costing

LEARNING OBJECTIVE 7

Calculate variances in activity-based costing

...compare budgeted and actual overhead costs of activities

Activity-based costing (ABC) systems focus on individual activities as the fundamental cost objects. ABC systems classify the costs of various activities into a cost hierarchy—output unit-level costs, batch-level costs, product-sustaining costs, and facility-sustaining costs (see pages 159–160). In this section, we show how a company that has an ABC system and batch-level costs can benefit from variance analysis. Batch-level costs are the costs of activities related to a group of units of products or services rather than to each individual unit of product or service. We illustrate variance analysis for variable batch-level direct costs and fixed batch-level overhead costs.[5]

[5] The techniques we demonstrate can be applied to analyze variable batch-level overhead costs as well.

Consider Lyco Brass Works, which manufactures many different types of faucets and brass fittings. Because of the wide range of products it produces, Lyco uses an activity-based costing system. In contrast, Webb uses a simple costing system because it makes only one type of jacket. One of Lyco's products is Elegance, a decorative brass faucet for home spas.

Lyco produces Elegance in batches. It uses dedicated materials-handling labor to bring materials to the production floor, transport items in process from one work center to the next, and take the finished goods to the shipping area. Therefore, materials-handling labor costs for Elegance are direct costs of Elegance. Because the materials for a batch are moved together, materials-handling labor costs vary with the number of batches rather than with the number of units in a batch. Materials-handling labor costs are variable direct batch-level costs.

To manufacture a batch of Elegance, Lyco must set up machines and molds using highly skilled labor from a separate setup department. Setup costs are overhead costs. For simplicity, assume that setup costs are fixed costs of salaries paid to engineers and supervisors and the costs of leasing setup equipment. In the long run, number of setup-hours is the cost driver of setup costs.

Information regarding Elegance for 2020 follows:

	Actual Result	Static-Budget Amount
1. Units of Elegance produced and sold	151,200	180,000
2. Batch size (units per batch)	140	150
3. Number of batches (line 1 ÷ line 2)	1,080	1,200
4. Materials-handling labor-hours per batch	5.25	5
5. Total materials-handling labor-hours (line 3 × line 4)	5,670	6,000
6. Cost per materials-handling labor-hour	$ 14.50	$ 14
7. Total materials-handling labor costs (line 5 × line 6)	$ 82,215	$ 84,000
8. Setup-hours per batch	6.25	6
9. Total setup-hours (line 3 × line 8)	6,750	7,200
10. Total fixed setup overhead costs	$220,000	$216,000

Flexible Budget and Variance Analysis for Direct Materials-Handling Labor Costs

To prepare the flexible budget for the materials-handling labor costs, Lyco starts with the actual units of output produced, 151,200 units, and proceeds with the following steps.

Step 1: Using the Budgeted Batch Size, Calculate the Number of Batches That Should Have Been Used to Produce the Actual Output. At the budgeted batch size of 150 units, Lyco should have produced the 151,200 units of output in 1,008 batches (151,200 units ÷ 150 units per batch).

Step 2: Using the Budgeted Materials-Handling Labor-Hours per Batch, Calculate the Number of Materials-Handling Labor-Hours That Should Have Been Used. At the budgeted 5 labor-hours per batch, 1,008 batches should have required 5,040 materials-handling labor-hours (1,008 batches × 5 hours per batch).

Step 3: Using the Budgeted Cost per Materials-Handling Labor-Hour, Calculate the Flexible-Budget Amount for Materials-Handling Labor-Hours. The flexible-budget amount is 5,040 materials-handling labor-hours × $14 budgeted cost per materials-handling labor hour = $70,560.

Note how the flexible-budget calculations for the materials-handling labor costs focus on batch-level quantities (materials-handling labor-hours per batch rather than per unit). If a cost had been a product-sustaining cost—such as product design cost—the flexible-budget quantity computations would focus at the product-sustaining level by, for example, evaluating the actual complexity of the product's design relative to the budget.

The flexible-budget variance for the materials-handling labor costs can now be calculated as follows:

$$\begin{aligned}\text{Flexible-budget variance} &= \text{Actual costs} - \text{Flexible-budget costs}\\ &= (5{,}670 \text{ hours} \times \$14.50 \text{ per hour}) - (5{,}040 \text{ hours} \times \$14 \text{ per hour})\\ &= \$82{,}215 - \$70{,}560\\ &= \$11{,}655 \text{ U}\end{aligned}$$

The unfavorable variance indicates that materials-handling labor costs were $11,655 higher than the flexible-budget target. We can get some insight into the possible reasons for this unfavorable outcome by examining the price and efficiency components of the flexible-budget variance. Exhibit 8-6 presents the variances in columnar form.

$$\begin{aligned}\text{Price variance} &= \left(\text{Actual price of input} - \text{Budgeted price of input}\right) \times \text{Actual quantity of input}\\ &= (\$14.50 \text{ per hour} - \$14 \text{ per hour}) \times 5{,}670 \text{ hours}\\ &= \$0.50 \text{ per hour} \times 5{,}670 \text{ hours}\\ &= \$2{,}835 \text{ U}\end{aligned}$$

The unfavorable price variance for materials-handling labor indicates that the $14.50 actual cost per materials-handling labor-hour exceeds the $14.00 budgeted cost per materials-handling labor-hour. This variance could be the result of Lyco's human resources manager negotiating wage rates less skillfully or of wage rates increasing unexpectedly due to a scarcity of labor.

$$\begin{aligned}\text{Efficiency variance} &= \left(\text{Actual quantity of input used} - \text{Budgeted quantity of input allowed for actual output}\right) \times \text{Budgeted price of input}\\ &= (5{,}670 \text{ hours} - 5{,}040 \text{ hours}) \times \$14 \text{ per hour}\\ &= 630 \text{ hours} \times \$14 \text{ per hour}\\ &= \$8{,}820 \text{ U}\end{aligned}$$

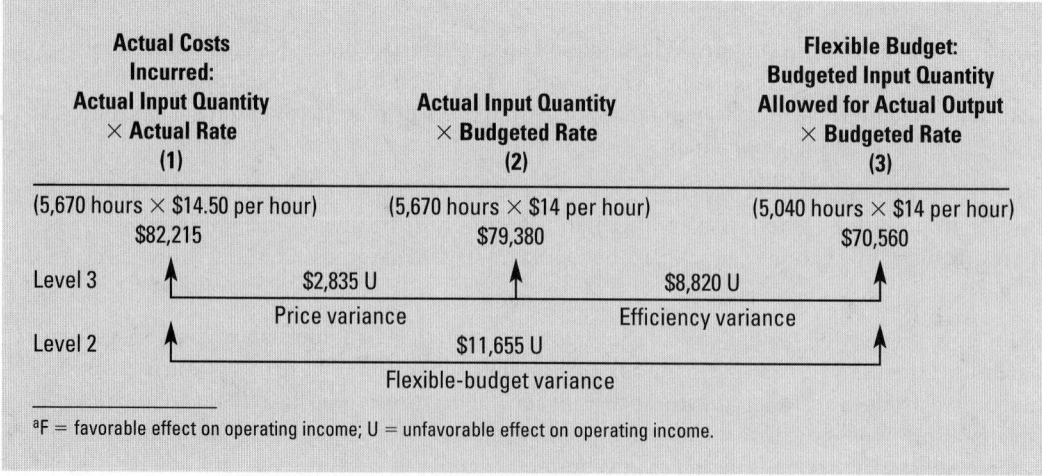

EXHIBIT 8-6 Columnar Presentation of Variance Analysis for Direct Materials-Handling Labor Costs: Lyco Brass Works for 2020[a]

Actual Costs Incurred: Actual Input Quantity × Actual Rate (1)	Actual Input Quantity × Budgeted Rate (2)	Flexible Budget: Budgeted Input Quantity Allowed for Actual Output × Budgeted Rate (3)
(5,670 hours × $14.50 per hour) $82,215	(5,670 hours × $14 per hour) $79,380	(5,040 hours × $14 per hour) $70,560

Level 3: $2,835 U Price variance (between (1) and (2)); $8,820 U Efficiency variance (between (2) and (3))

Level 2: $11,655 U Flexible-budget variance (between (1) and (3))

[a]F = favorable effect on operating income; U = unfavorable effect on operating income.

The unfavorable efficiency variance indicates that the 5,670 actual materials-handling labor-hours exceeded the 5,040 budgeted materials-handling labor-hours for the actual output. Possible reasons for the unfavorable efficiency variance are as follows:

- Smaller actual batch sizes of 140 units, instead of the budgeted batch sizes of 150 units, resulted in Lyco producing the 151,200 units in 1,080 batches instead of 1,008 (151,200 ÷ 150) batches
- The actual materials-handling labor-hours per batch (5.25 hours) were higher than the budgeted materials-handling labor-hours per batch (5 hours)

Reasons for smaller-than-budgeted batch sizes could include quality problems when batch sizes exceed 140 faucets and higher costs of carrying inventory.

Possible reasons for the larger actual materials-handling labor-hours per batch are:

- Inefficient layout of the Elegance production line
- Materials-handling labor having to wait at work centers for pickup or delivery of materials
- Unmotivated, inexperienced, and underskilled employees
- Very tight standards for materials-handling time

Identifying the reasons for the efficiency variance helps Lyco's managers develop a plan for improving its materials-handling labor efficiency and take corrective action.

We now consider fixed setup overhead costs.

Flexible Budget and Variance Analysis for Fixed Setup Overhead Costs

Exhibit 8-7 presents the variances for fixed setup overhead costs in columnar form.

Lyco's fixed setup overhead flexible-budget variance is calculated as follows:

$$\begin{aligned}\text{Fixed-setup overhead flexible-budget variance} &= \text{Actual costs incurred} - \text{Flexible-budget costs}\\ &= \$220{,}000 - \$216{,}000\\ &= \$4{,}000\text{ U}\end{aligned}$$

EXHIBIT 8-7 Columnar Presentation of Fixed Setup Overhead Variance Analysis: Lyco Brass Works for 2020[a]

	Actual Costs Incurred (1)		**Flexible Budget: Same Budgeted Lump Sum (as in Static Budget) Regardless of Output Level (2)**		**Allocated: Budgeted Input Quantity Allowed for Actual Output × Budgeted Rate (3)**
					(1,008[b] batches × 6 hours/batch × $30/hour)
					(6,048 hours × $30/hour)
	$220,000		$216,000		$181,440
Level 3		$4,000 U Spending variance		$34,560 U Production-volume variance	
Level 2		$4,000 U Flexible-budget variance			

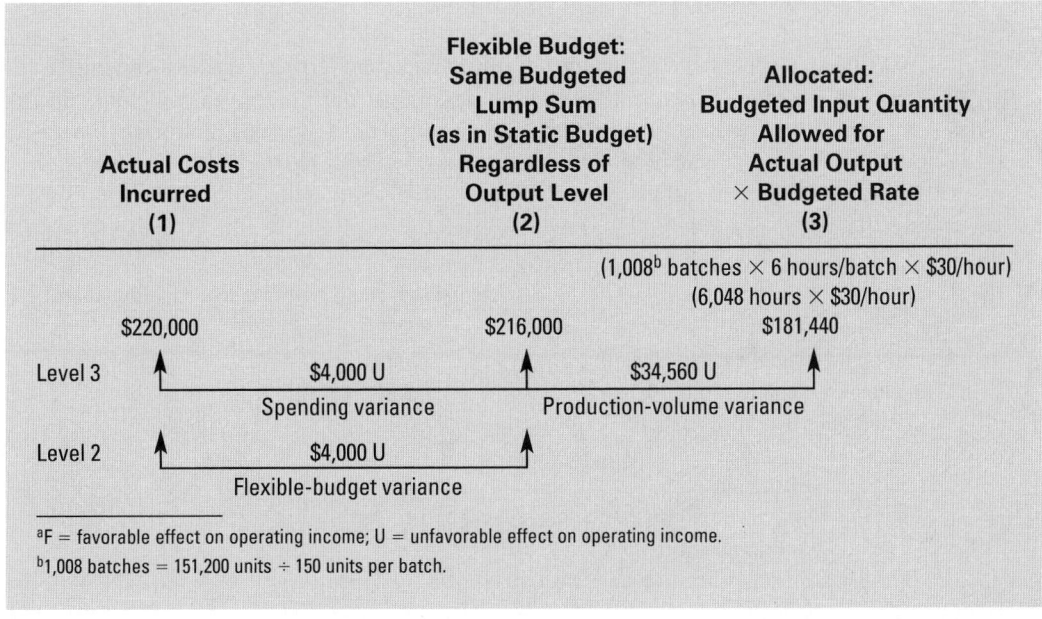

[a]F = favorable effect on operating income; U = unfavorable effect on operating income.

[b]1,008 batches = 151,200 units ÷ 150 units per batch.

Note that the flexible-budget amount for the fixed setup overhead costs equals the static-budget amount of $216,000. That's because there is no "flexing" of fixed costs. Moreover, because the fixed overhead costs have no efficiency variance, the fixed setup overhead spending variance is the same as the fixed overhead flexible-budget variance. The spending variance could be unfavorable because of higher leasing costs of new setup equipment or higher salaries paid to engineers and supervisors.

To calculate the production-volume variance, Lyco first computes the budgeted cost-allocation rate for the fixed setup overhead costs using the same four-step approach described on page 285.

Step 1: Choose the Period to Use for the Budget. Lyco uses 12 months (the year 2020).

Step 2: Select the Cost-Allocation Base to Use in Allocating the Fixed Overhead Costs to the Output Produced. Lyco uses the 7,200 budgeted setup-hours (equal to the setup capacity) as the cost-allocation base for fixed setup overhead costs.

Step 3: Identify the Fixed Overhead Costs Associated with the Cost-Allocation Base. Lyco's fixed setup overhead cost budget for 2020 is $216,000.

Step 4: Compute the Rate per Unit of the Cost-Allocation Base Used to Allocate the Fixed Overhead Costs to the Output Produced. Dividing the $216,000 from Step 3 by the 7,200 setup-hours from Step 2, Lyco estimates a fixed setup overhead cost rate of $30 per setup-hour.

The production-volume variance for fixed setup overhead costs is calculated as:

$$\begin{aligned}\text{Production-volume variance for fixed setup overhead costs} &= \text{Budgeted fixed setup overhead costs} - \text{Fixed setup overhead allocated using budgeted input allowed for actual output units produced}\\ &= \$216{,}000 - (1{,}008 \text{ batches} \times 6 \text{ hours / batch} \times \$30/\text{hour})\\ &= \$216{,}000 - (6{,}048 \text{ hours} \times \$30/\text{hour})\\ &= \$216{,}000 - \$181{,}440\\ &= \$34{,}560 \text{ U}\end{aligned}$$

DECISION POINT

How can variance analysis be used in an activity-based costing system?

During 2020, Lyco planned to produce 180,000 units of Elegance but actually produced 151,200 units. The unfavorable production-volume variance measures the amount of extra fixed setup costs Lyco incurred for setup capacity it did not use. One interpretation is that the $34,560 U production-volume variance represents an inefficient use of the company's setup capacity. However, Lyco may have earned higher operating income by selling 151,200 units at a higher price than 180,000 units at a lower price. As a result, Lyco's managers should interpret the production-volume variance cautiously because it does not consider the effect of output on selling prices and operating income.

TRY IT! 8-4

Trivor, Inc., produces a special line of toy racing cars. Trivor produces the cars in batches. To manufacture each batch of cars, Trivor must set up the machines and molds. Setup costs are fixed batch-level costs. In the long run, number of setup-hours is the cost driver of setup costs. A separate Setup Department is responsible for setting up machines and molds for each style of car. The following information pertains to July 2020:

	Actual Amounts	Static-Budget Amounts
Units produced and sold	13,000	15,000
Batch size (number of units per batch)	260	250
Setup-hours per batch	5.4	5
Total fixed setup overhead costs	$12,150	$12,000

Calculate the following:

a. The spending variance for fixed setup overhead costs
b. The budgeted fixed setup overhead rate
c. The production-volume variance for fixed overhead setup costs

Overhead Variances in Nonmanufacturing Settings

LEARNING OBJECTIVE 8

Examine the use of overhead variances in nonmanufacturing settings

...analyze nonmanufacturing variable overhead costs for decision making and cost management; fixed overhead variances are especially important in service settings

Our Webb Company example examined variable and fixed manufacturing overhead costs. Managers can also use variance analysis to examine the overhead costs of the nonmanufacturing areas of the company. For example, when product distribution costs are high, as they are in the automobile, consumer durables, cement, and steel industries, standard costing can provide managers with reliable and timely information on variable distribution overhead spending variances and efficiency variances.

What about service-sector companies such as airlines, hospitals, hotels, and railroads? How can they benefit from variance analyses? The output measures these companies commonly use are passenger-miles flown, patient-days provided, room-days occupied, and ton-miles of freight hauled. Few costs can be traced to these outputs in a cost-effective way. Most of the costs are fixed overhead costs, such as the costs of equipment, buildings, and staff. Using capacity effectively is the key to profitability, and fixed overhead variances can help managers in this task. Retail businesses such as Kmart also have high-capacity–related fixed costs (lease and occupancy costs). In the case of Kmart, sales declines resulted in unused capacity and unfavorable fixed-cost variances. Kmart reduced its fixed costs by closing some of its stores, but it also had to file for Chapter 11 bankruptcy.

Consider the following data for United Airlines for selected years from the past 18 years. Available seat miles (ASMs) are the actual seats in an airplane multiplied by the distance the plane traveled.

Year	Total ASMs (Millions) (1)	Operating Revenue per ASM (2)	Operating Cost per ASM (3)	Operating Income per ASM (4) = (2) − (3)
2000	175,493	10.2 cents	10.0 cents	0.2 cents
2003	136,566	8.6 cents	9.8 cents	−1.2 cents
2006	143,085	10.6 cents	10.8 cents	−0.2 cents
2008	135,859	11.9 cents	13.6 cents	−1.7 cents
2011	118,973	13.1 cents	13.5 cents	−0.4 cents
2015	219,956	13.1 cents	12.2 cents	0.9 cents
2018	234,547	16.1 cents	14.6 cents	1.5 cents

When air travel declined after the events of September 11, 2001, United's revenues fell. However, most of the company's fixed costs—for its airport facilities, equipment, personnel, and so on—did not decrease. United had a large unfavorable production-volume variance because its capacity was underutilized. As column 1 of the table indicates, United responded by reducing its capacity substantially. Available seat miles (ASMs) declined from 175,493 million in 2000 to 136,566 million in 2003. Yet United was unable to fill even the planes it had kept, so its revenue per ASM declined (column 2) and its cost per ASM stayed roughly the same (column 3). United filed for Chapter 11 bankruptcy in December 2002 and began seeking government guarantees to obtain the loans it needed. Subsequently, strong demand for airline travel, as well as productivity improvements from more efficient use of resources and networks, led to increased traffic and higher average ticket prices. United's disciplined approach to capacity and tight control over growth led to an increase of more than 20% in its revenue per ASM between 2003 and 2006. United came out of bankruptcy on February 1, 2006. Subsequently, however, the global recession and soaring jet fuel prices negatively impacted United's performance, leading to losses and further reduction in capacity. In 2011, United acquired Continental Airlines, resulting in 85% growth in ASM between 2011 and 2015. The revenue benefits from a stronger economy and a plunge in fuel prices led United to even greater profitability per ASM through 2018.

Financial and Nonfinancial Performance Measures

The overhead variances discussed in this chapter are examples of financial performance measures. As the preceding examples illustrate, nonfinancial measures such as those related to capacity utilization and physical measures of input usage also provide useful information. The nonfinancial measures that managers of Webb would likely find helpful in planning and controlling its overhead costs include the following:

1. Quantity of actual indirect materials used per machine-hour, relative to the quantity of budgeted indirect materials used per machine-hour
2. Actual energy used per machine-hour, relative to the budgeted energy used per machine-hour
3. Actual machine-hours per jacket, relative to the budgeted machine-hours per jacket

These performance measures, like the financial variances discussed in this chapter and Chapter 7, alert managers to problems and are reported daily or hourly on the production floor. Overhead variances capture the financial effects of factors such as the three listed. An especially interesting example along these lines comes from Japan: Some Japanese companies have begun reining in their CO_2 emissions in part by doing a budgeted-to-actual variance analysis of the emissions. The goal is to make employees aware of the emissions and reduce them in advance of greenhouse-gas reduction plans being drawn up by the Japanese government.

DECISION POINT

How are overhead variances useful in nonmanufacturing settings?

Both financial and nonfinancial performance measures are used to evaluate the performance of managers. Exclusive reliance on either is always too simplistic because each gives a different perspective on performance. Nonfinancial measures (such as those described) provide feedback on individual aspects of a manager's performance, whereas financial measures evaluate the overall effect of and tradeoffs among different nonfinancial performance measures. We discuss these issues further in Chapters 12, 19, and 23.

PROBLEM FOR SELF-STUDY

Nina Garcia is the newly appointed president of Aerospace Products Division (APD), which manufactures solar arrays for satellites. Garcia is concerned about manufacturing overhead costs at APD. APD allocates variable and fixed overhead costs to solar arrays on the basis of laser-cutting-hours. The budget information for May 2020 is as follows:

Budgeted variable overhead rate	$200 per hour
Budgeted fixed overhead rate	$240 per hour
Budgeted laser-cutting time per solar array	1.5 hours
Budgeted production and sales for May 2020	5,000 solar arrays
Budgeted fixed overhead costs for May 2020	$1,800,000

Actual results for May 2020 are as follows:

Solar arrays produced and sold	4,800 units
Laser-cutting-hours used	8,400 hours
Variable overhead costs	$1,478,400
Fixed overhead costs	$1,832,200

Required

1. Compute the spending variance and the efficiency variance for variable overhead.
2. Compute the spending variance and the production-volume variance for fixed overhead.
3. Give two explanations for each of the variances calculated in requirements 1 and 2.

Solution

1 and 2. See Exhibit 8-8.

3. a. Variable overhead spending variance, $201,600 F. Possible reasons for this variance are (1) actual prices of individual items included in variable overhead (such as cutting fluids) are lower than budgeted prices; (2) the percentage increase in the actual quantity usage of individual items in the variable overhead cost pool is less than the percentage increase in laser-cutting-hours compared to the flexible budget.

b. Variable overhead efficiency variance, $240,000 U. Possible reasons for this variance are (1) inadequate maintenance of laser machines, causing them to take more laser-cutting time per solar array; (2) undermotivated, inexperienced, or underskilled workers operating the laser-cutting machines, resulting in more laser-cutting time per solar array.

c. Fixed overhead spending variance, $32,200 U. Possible reasons for this variance are (1) actual prices of individual items in the fixed-cost pool (for example, cost of leasing machines) are unexpectedly higher than the prices budgeted; (2) APD had to lease more machines or hire more supervisors than had been budgeted.

d. Production-volume variance, $72,000 U. Actual production of solar arrays is 4,800 units, compared with 5,000 units budgeted. Possible reasons for this variance are (1) demand factors, such as a decline in an aerospace program that led to a decline in demand for satellites; (2) supply factors such as a production stoppage due to labor problems or machine breakdowns.

EXHIBIT 8-8 Columnar Presentation of Integrated Variance Analysis: Laser Products for May 2020[a]

PANEL A: Variable (Manufacturing) Overhead

Actual Costs Incurred: Actual Input Quantity × Actual Rate (1)	Actual Input Quantity × Budgeted Rate (2)	Flexible Budget: Budgeted Input Quantity Allowed for Actual Output × Budgeted Rate (3)	Allocated: Budgeted Input Quantity Allowed for Actual Output × Budgeted Rate (4)
		(1.5 hrs./unit × 4,800 units × $200/hr.)	(1.5 hrs./unit × 4,800 units × $200/hr.)
(8,400 hrs. × $176/hr.)	(8,400 hrs. × $200/hr.)	(7,200 hrs. × $200/hr.)	(7,200 hrs. × $200/hr.)
$1,478,400	$1,680,000	$1,440,000	$1,440,000

- (1)–(2): $201,600 F Spending variance; (2)–(3): $240,000 U Efficiency variance; (3)–(4): Never a variance
- (1)–(3): $38,400 U Flexible-budget variance; (3)–(4): Never a variance
- (1)–(4): $38,400 U Underallocated variable overhead (Total variable overhead variance)

PANEL B: Fixed (Manufacturing) Overhead

Actual Costs Incurred (1)	Same Budgeted Lump Sum (as in Static Budget) Regardless of Output Level (2)	Flexible Budget: Same Budgeted Lump Sum (as in Static Budget) Regardless of Output Level (3)	Allocated: Budgeted Input Quantity Allowed for Actual Output × Budgeted Rate (4)
			(1.5 hrs./unit × 4,800 units × $240/hr.)
			(7,200 hrs. × $240/hr.)
$1,832,200	$1,800,000	$1,800,000	$1,728,000

- (1)–(2): $32,200 U Spending variance; (2)–(3): Never a variance; (3)–(4): $72,000 U Production-volume variance
- (1)–(3): $32,200 U Flexible-budget variance; (3)–(4): $72,000 U Production-volume variance
- (1)–(4): $104,200 U Underallocated fixed overhead (Total fixed overhead variance)

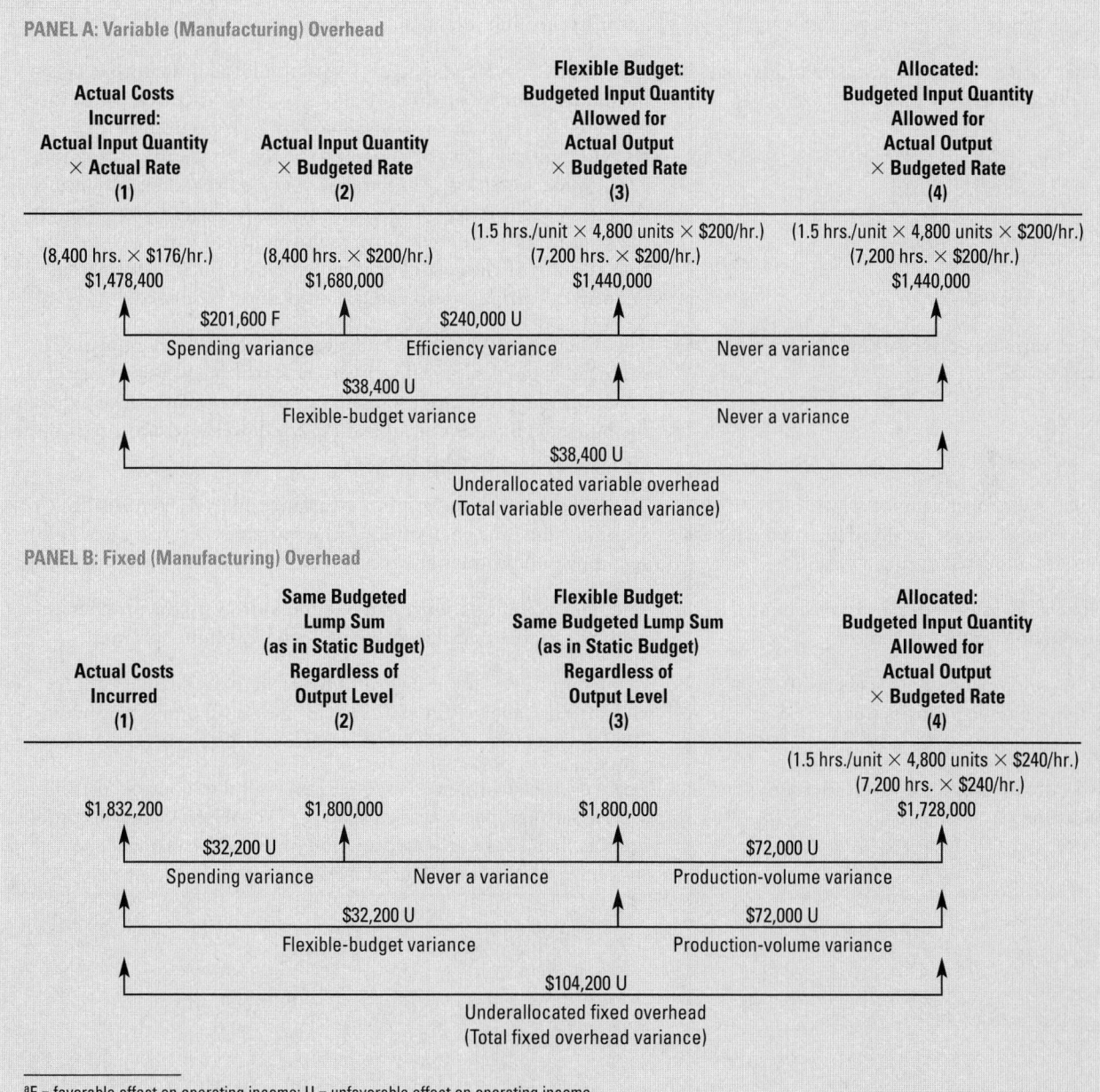

[a]F = favorable effect on operating income; U = unfavorable effect on operating income.

DECISION POINTS

The following question-and-answer format summarizes the chapter's learning objectives. Each decision presents a key question related to a learning objective. The guidelines are the answer to that question.

Decision	Guidelines
1. How do managers plan variable overhead costs and fixed overhead costs?	Planning of both variable and fixed overhead costs involves efficiently undertaking activities that add value. For variable-cost planning, managers plan costs throughout the budget period; for fixed-cost planning, most key decisions are made before the start of the period.
2. How are budgeted variable overhead and budgeted fixed overhead cost rates calculated?	The budgeted variable (fixed) overhead cost rate is calculated by dividing the budgeted variable (fixed) overhead costs by the denominator level of the cost-allocation base.
3. What variances can be calculated for variable overhead costs?	The variable overhead efficiency variance is the difference between the actual quantity of the cost-allocation base used relative to the budgeted quantity of the cost-allocation base to produce the actual output, multiplied by the budgeted variable overhead cost per unit of the allocation base. The variable overhead spending variance is the difference between the actual variable overhead cost per unit of the cost-allocation base relative to the budgeted variable overhead cost per unit of the cost-allocation base multiplied by the actual quantity of variable overhead cost-allocation base used.
4. What variances can be calculated for fixed overhead costs?	The difference between the budgeted and actual amount of fixed overhead is the flexible-budget variance, which equals the spending variance. The production-volume variance is the difference between the budgeted fixed overhead and the fixed overhead allocated on the basis of actual output produced.
5. What is the most detailed way for a company to reconcile actual overhead incurred with the amount allocated during a period?	The most detailed analysis is a 4-variance analysis comprising spending and efficiency variances for variable overhead costs and spending and production-volume variances for fixed overhead costs.
6. How is the sales-volume variance related to the production-volume variance?	The sales-volume variance can be subdivided into the production-volume variance and the operating-income volume variance.
7. How can variance analysis be used in an activity-based costing system?	Using output and input measures for an activity, flexible budgets and variance analysis in ABC systems give insight into why actual activity costs differ from budgeted activity costs.
8. How are overhead variances useful in nonmanufacturing settings?	Fixed overhead variances are especially useful to control costs in service settings, where using capacity effectively is the key to profitability. In all cases, the information provided by variances are supplemented by nonfinancial metrics.

TERMS TO LEARN

The chapter and the Glossary at the end of the text contain definitions of the following important terms:

denominator level (**p. 285**)
denominator-level variance (**p. 292**)
fixed overhead flexible-budget variance (**p. 290**)
fixed overhead spending variance (**p. 291**)
operating-income volume variance (**p. 300**)
production-volume variance (**p. 291**)
standard costing (**p. 284**)
total-overhead variance (**p. 298**)
variable overhead efficiency variance (**p. 287**)
variable overhead flexible-budget variance (**p. 286**)
variable overhead spending variance (**p. 288**)

ASSIGNMENT MATERIAL

Questions

8-1 How do managers plan for variable overhead costs?

8-2 How does planning of fixed overhead costs differ from planning of variable overhead costs?

8-3 How does standard costing differ from actual costing?

8-4 What are the steps in developing a budgeted variable overhead cost-allocation rate?

8-5 What are the factors that affect the spending variance for variable manufacturing overhead?

8-6 Assume variable manufacturing overhead is allocated using machine-hours. Give three possible reasons for a favorable variable overhead efficiency variance.

8-7 Describe the difference between a direct materials efficiency variance and a variable manufacturing overhead efficiency variance.

8-8 What are the steps in developing a budgeted fixed overhead rate?

8-9 Why is the flexible-budget variance the same amount as the spending variance for fixed manufacturing overhead?

8-10 Explain how the analysis of fixed manufacturing overhead costs differs for (a) planning and control and (b) inventory costing for financial reporting.

8-11 Provide one caveat that will affect whether a production-volume variance is a good measure of the economic cost of unused capacity.

8-12 "The production-volume variance should always be written off to Cost of Goods Sold." Do you agree? Explain.

8-13 What are the variances in a 4-variance analysis?

8-14 "Overhead variances are interdependent rather than independent." Give an example.

8-15 How can flexible-budget variance analysis be used to control costs of activity areas?

Multiple-Choice Questions

In partnership with: BECKER PROFESSIONAL EDUCATION®

8-16 Each of the following statements is correct regarding overhead variances except

a. Actual overhead greater than applied overhead is unfavorable.
b. The efficiency overhead variance ignores the standard variable overhead rate.
c. Variable overhead rates are not a factor in the production-volume variance calculation.
d. Favorable spending and efficiency variances imply that the flexible budget variance must be favorable.

8-17 Steed Co. budgets production of 150,000 units in the next year. Steed's chief financial officer expects that each unit will take 8 hours to produce at an hourly wage rate of $10 per hour. If factory (manufacturing) overhead is applied on the basis of direct labor hours at $6 per hour, the budget for factory (manufacturing) overhead will total

a. $7,200,000 **b.** $9,000,000
c. $12,000,000 **d.** $19,200,000

8-18 As part of her annual review of her company's budgets versus actuals, Mary Gerard isolates unfavorable variances with the hope of getting a better understanding of what caused them and how to avoid them next year. The variable overhead efficiency variance (with direct labor-hours as the cost-allocation base) was the most unfavorable over the previous year, which Gerard will specifically be able to trace to

a. Actual variable overhead costs below allocated variable overhead costs.
b. Actual production units below budgeted production units.
c. Standard direct labor-hours below actual direct labor-hours.
d. The standard variable overhead rate below the actual variable overhead rate.

8-19 Culpepper Corporation had the following inventories at the beginning and end of January:

	January 1	January 31
Finished goods	$125,000	$117,000
Work in process	235,000	251,000
Direct materials	134,000	124,000

The following additional manufacturing data were available for the month of January.

Direct materials purchased	$189,000
Transportation in	3,000
Direct manufacturing labor	400,000
Actual factory (manufacturing) overhead	175,000

Culpepper Corporation applies factory (manufacturing) overhead at a rate of 40% of direct manufacturing labor cost, and any overallocated or underallocated factory overhead is deferred until the end of the year. Culpepper's balance in its factory overhead control account at the end of January was

1. $15,000 overallocated. **3.** $5,000 underallocated.
2. $15,000 underallocated. **4.** $5,000 overallocated.

8-20 Fordham Corporation produces a single product. The standard costs for one unit of its Concourse product are as follows:

Direct materials (6 pounds at $0.50 per pound)	$ 3
Direct manufacturing labor (2 hours at $10 per hour)	20
Variable manufacturing overhead (2 hours at $5 per hour)	10
Total	33

During November Year 2, 4,000 units of Concourse were produced. The costs associated with November operations were as follows:

Material purchased (36,000 pounds at $0.60 per pound)	$21,600
Material used in production (28,000 pounds)	
Direct manufacturing labor (8,200 hours at $9.75 per hour)	79,950
Variable manufacturing overhead incurred	41,820

What is the variable overhead efficiency variance for Concourse for November Year 2?

1. $2,000 favorable **3.** $1,000 favorable
2. $2,000 unfavorable **4.** $1,000 unfavorable

Exercises

8-21 Variable manufacturing overhead, variance analysis. Esquire Clothing is a manufacturer of designer suits. The cost of each suit is the sum of three variable costs (direct material costs, direct manufacturing labor costs, and manufacturing overhead costs) and one fixed-cost category (manufacturing overhead costs). Variable manufacturing overhead cost is allocated to each suit on the basis of budgeted direct manufacturing labor-hours per suit. For June 2020, each suit is budgeted to take 4 labor-hours. Budgeted variable manufacturing overhead cost per labor-hour is $12. The budgeted number of suits to be manufactured in June 2020 is 1,040.

Actual variable manufacturing costs in June 2020 were $52,164 for 1,080 suits started and completed. There were no beginning or ending inventories of suits. Actual direct manufacturing labor-hours for June were 4,536.

Required

1. Compute the flexible-budget variance, the spending variance, and the efficiency variance for variable manufacturing overhead.
2. Comment on the results.

8-22 Fixed manufacturing overhead, variance analysis (continuation of 8-21). Esquire Clothing allocates fixed manufacturing overhead to each suit using budgeted direct manufacturing labor-hours per suit. Data pertaining to fixed manufacturing overhead costs for June 2020 are budgeted, $62,400, and actual, $63,916.

Required

1. Compute the spending variance for fixed manufacturing overhead. Comment on the results.
2. Compute the production-volume variance for June 2020. What inferences can Esquire Clothing draw from this variance?

8-23 Variable manufacturing overhead variance analysis. The Sourdough Bread Company bakes baguettes for distribution to upscale grocery stores. The company has two direct-cost categories: direct materials and direct manufacturing labor. Variable manufacturing overhead is allocated to products on the basis of standard direct manufacturing labor-hours. Following are some budget data for the Sourdough Bread Company:

Direct manufacturing labor use	0.02 hours per baguette
Variable manufacturing overhead	$10.00 per direct manufacturing labor-hour

The Sourdough Bread Company provides the following additional data for the year ended December 31, 2020:

Planned (budgeted) output	3,100,000 baguettes
Actual production	2,600,000 baguettes
Direct manufacturing labor	46,800 hours
Actual variable manufacturing overhead	$617,760

Required

1. What is the denominator level used for allocating variable manufacturing overhead? (That is, for how many direct manufacturing labor-hours is Sourdough Bread budgeting?)
2. Prepare a variance analysis of variable manufacturing overhead. Use Exhibit 8-4 (page 297) for reference.
3. Discuss the variances you have calculated and give possible explanations for them.

8-24 Fixed manufacturing overhead variance analysis (continuation of 8-23). The Sourdough Bread Company also allocates fixed manufacturing overhead to products on the basis of standard direct manufacturing labor-hours. For 2020, fixed manufacturing overhead was budgeted at $3.00 per direct manufacturing labor-hour. Actual fixed manufacturing overhead incurred during the year was $294,000.

Required

1. Prepare a variance analysis of fixed manufacturing overhead cost. Use Exhibit 8-4 (page 297) as a guide.
2. Is fixed overhead underallocated or overallocated? By what amount?
3. Comment on your results. Discuss the variances and explain what may be driving them.

8-25 Manufacturing overhead, variance analysis. The Revolutions Corporation is a manufacturer of centrifuges. Fixed and variable manufacturing overheads are allocated to each centrifuge using budgeted assembly-hours. Budgeted assembly time is 2 hours per unit. The following table shows the budgeted amounts and actual results related to overhead for June 2020.

	Actual Results	Static-Budget Amounts
Number of centrifuges assembled and sold	120	125
Hours of assembly time	225	
Variable manufacturing overhead cost per hour of assembly time		$ 32
Variable manufacturing overhead costs	$ 7,650	
Fixed manufacturing overhead costs	$13,500	$12,500

Required

1. Prepare an analysis of all variable manufacturing overhead and fixed manufacturing overhead variances using the columnar approach in Exhibit 8-4 (page 297).
2. Prepare journal entries for Revolutions' June 2020 variable and fixed manufacturing overhead costs and variances; write off these variances to Cost of Goods Sold for the quarter ending June 30, 2020.
3. How does the planning and control of variable manufacturing overhead costs differ from the planning and control of fixed manufacturing overhead costs?

8-26 4-variance analysis, fill in the blanks. Tytler, Inc., produces chemicals for large biotech companies. It has the following data for manufacturing overhead costs during August 2020:

	Variable	Fixed
Actual costs incurred	$33,500	$16,000
Costs allocated to products	30,000	14,200
Flexible budget	———	15,000
Actual input × budgeted rate	32,200	———

Fill in the blanks. Use F for favorable and U for unfavorable:

	Variable	Fixed
(1) Spending variance	$____	$____
(2) Efficiency variance	____	____
(3) Production-volume variance	____	____
(4) Flexible-budget variance	____	____
(5) Underallocated (overallocated) manufacturing overhead	____	____

8-27 Straightforward 4-variance overhead analysis. The Ramirez Company uses standard costing in its manufacturing plant for auto parts. The standard cost of a particular auto part, based on a denominator level of 4,000 output units per year, included 5 machine-hours of variable manufacturing overhead at $7 per hour and 5 machine-hours of fixed manufacturing overhead at $14 per hour. Actual output produced was 4,200 units. Variable manufacturing overhead incurred was $170,000. Fixed manufacturing overhead incurred was $303,000. Actual machine-hours were 22,000.

Required

1. Prepare an analysis of all variable manufacturing overhead and fixed manufacturing overhead variances, using the 4-variance analysis in Exhibit 8-4 (page 297).
2. Prepare journal entries using the 4-variance analysis.
3. Describe how individual fixed manufacturing overhead items are controlled from day to day.
4. Discuss possible causes of the fixed manufacturing overhead variances.

8-28 Straightforward coverage of manufacturing overhead, standard-costing system. The Brazil division of an American telecommunications company uses standard costing for its machine-paced production of telephone equipment. Data regarding production during June are as follows:

Variable manufacturing overhead costs incurred	$537,470
Variable manufacturing overhead cost rate	$7 per standard machine-hour
Fixed manufacturing overhead costs incurred	$146,101
Fixed manufacturing overhead costs budgeted	$136,000
Denominator level in machine-hours	68,000
Standard machine-hour allowed per unit of output	1.2
Units of output	66,500
Actual machine-hours used	75,700
Ending work-in-process inventory	0

Required

1. Prepare an analysis of all manufacturing overhead variances. Use the 4-variance analysis framework illustrated in Exhibit 8-4 (page 297).
2. Prepare journal entries for manufacturing overhead costs and their variances.
3. Describe how individual variable manufacturing overhead items are controlled from day to day.
4. Discuss possible causes of the variable manufacturing overhead variances.

8-29 Overhead variances, service sector. Family Meals Now (FMN) operates a meal home-delivery service. It has agreements with 20 restaurants to pick up and deliver meals to customers who place orders on FMN's website. FMN allocates variable and fixed overhead costs on the basis of delivery time. FMN's owner, Thomas Stewart, obtains the following information for May 2020 overhead costs:

	Actual Results	Static-Budget Amounts
Output units (number of deliveries)	8,300	9,000
Hours per delivery		0.70
Hours of delivery time	5,680	
Variable overhead cost per hour of delivery time		$ 1.60
Variable overhead costs	$10,224	
Fixed overhead costs	$39,400	$37,800

Required

1. Compute spending and efficiency variances for FMN's variable overhead costs in May 2020.
2. Compute the spending variance and production-volume variance for FMN's fixed overhead costs in May 2020.
3. Comment on FMN's overhead variances and suggest how Thomas Stewart might manage FMN's variable overhead costs differently from its fixed overhead costs.

8-30 Total overhead, 3-variance analysis, working backward. Stained Glass, Inc., makes jewelry boxes out of scrap stained glass material. Budget and actual information for July 2020, follows first for direct manufacturing labor and then for manufacturing overhead costs.

Direct manufacturing labor	
Actual direct manufacturing labor costs	$178,125
Direct manufacturing labor efficiency variance	$7,500 U
Direct manufacturing labor flexible-budget variance	$1,875 F
Budgeted price of direct manufacturing labor	$15 per hour
Manufacturing overhead	
Total actual manufacturing overhead costs	$133,000
Budgeted variable manufacturing overhead rate	$7 per direct manufacturing labor-hour
Budgeted fixed manufacturing overhead rate	$5 per direct manufacturing labor-hour
Budgeted fixed manufacturing overhead costs	$44,000

Required

1. For July 2020, calculate (a) the direct manufacturing labor price variance, (b) the actual number of direct manufacturing labor-hours used, (c) the flexible-budget amount for direct manufacturing labor, and (d) the direct manufacturing labor-hours allowed for the actual output produced.
2. Calculate the spending and efficiency variances for total overhead.
3. Describe how individual variable overhead items are controlled from day to day. Also, describe how individual fixed overhead items are controlled.

8-31 Production-volume variance analysis and sales-volume variance. Chart Hills Company makes customized golf shirts for sale to golf courses. Each shirt requires 3 direct manufacturing labor-hours to produce because of the customized logo for each golf course. Chart Hills uses direct manufacturing labor-hours to allocate the overhead cost to production. Fixed overhead costs, including rent, depreciation, supervisory salaries, and other production expenses, are budgeted at $28,500 per month. The facility currently used is large enough to produce 5,000 shirts per month.

During March, Chart Hills produced 4,200 shirts and actual fixed costs were $28,000.

Required

1. Calculate the fixed overhead spending variance and indicate whether it is favorable (F) or unfavorable (U).
2. If Chart Hills uses direct manufacturing labor-hours available at capacity to calculate the budgeted fixed overhead rate, what is the production-volume variance? Indicate whether it is favorable (F) or unfavorable (U).
3. An unfavorable production-volume variance could be interpreted as the economic cost of unused capacity. Why would Chart Hills be willing to incur this cost?
4. Chart Hills' budgeted variable cost per unit is $18, and it expects to sell its shirts for $35 apiece. Compute the sales-volume variance and reconcile it with the production-volume variance calculated in requirement 2. What does each concept measure?

8-32 Overhead variances, service setting. Jones Equity Company offers financial services to its clients. Recently, Jones has experienced rapid growth and has increased both its client base and the variety of services it offers. The company is becoming concerned about its rising costs, however, particularly related to technology overhead.

Jones' measure of output is the number of client interactions in a given period. After some study, Jones determines that its variable and fixed technology overhead costs are both driven by CPU units of processing time for client interactions.

The technology budget for Jones for the first quarter of 2020 was as follows:

Client interactions	13,000
CPU units per client interaction	0.4
Fixed overhead costs	$16,120
Variable overhead rate	$2.20 per CPU unit

The actual results for the first quarter of 2020 are given below:

Client interactions	14,200
Fixed overhead costs	$15,900
Variable overhead costs	$12,000
CPU units used	5,700

Required

1. Calculate the variable overhead spending and efficiency variances, and indicate whether each is favorable (F) or unfavorable (U).
2. Calculate the fixed overhead spending and production-volume variances, and indicate whether each is favorable (F) or unfavorable (U).
3. Comment on Jones Equity's overhead variances. In your view, is the firm right to be worried about its control over technology spending?

8-33 Identifying favorable and unfavorable variances. Tred-America, Inc., manufactures tires for large auto companies. It uses standard costing and allocates variable and fixed manufacturing overhead based on machine-hours. For each independent scenario given, indicate whether each of the manufacturing variances will be favorable or unfavorable or, in case of insufficient information, indicate "CBD" (cannot be determined).

Scenario	Variable Overhead Spending Variance	Variable Overhead Efficiency Variance	Fixed Overhead Spending Variance	Fixed Overhead Production-Volume Variance
Production output is 8% more than budgeted, and actual fixed manufacturing overhead costs are 7% less than budgeted				
Production output is 11% more than budgeted, and actual machine-hours are 5% less than budgeted				
Production output is 15% less than budgeted				
Actual machine-hours are 18% greater than flexible-budget machine-hours				
Relative to the flexible budget, actual machine-hours are 10% greater, and actual variable manufacturing overhead costs are 15% less				

8-34 Flexible-budget variances, review of Chapters 7 and 8. Eric Williams is a cost accountant and business analyst for Diamond Design Company (DDC), which manufactures expensive brass doorknobs. DDC uses two direct-cost categories: direct materials and direct manufacturing labor. Williams feels that manufacturing overhead is most closely related to material usage. Therefore, DDC allocates manufacturing overhead to production based upon pounds of materials used.

At the beginning of 2020, DDC budgeted annual production of 420,000 doorknobs and adopted the following standards for each doorknob:

	Input	Cost/Doorknob
Direct materials (brass)	0.3 lb. at $10/lb.	$ 3.00
Direct manufacturing labor	1.2 hours at $17/hour	20.40
Manufacturing overhead:		
Variable	$5 / lb. × 0.3 lb.	1.50
Fixed	$15 / lb. × 0.3 lb.	4.50
Standard cost per doorknob		$29.40

Actual results for April 2020 are as follows:

Production	29,000 doorknobs
Direct materials purchased	12,400 lb. at $11/lb.
Direct materials used	8,500 lbs.
Direct manufacturing labor	29,200 hours for $671,600
Variable manufacturing overhead	$ 65,100
Fixed manufacturing overhead	$158,000

Required

1. For the month of April, compute the following variances, indicating whether each is favorable (F) or unfavorable (U):
   a. Direct materials price variance (based on purchases)
   b. Direct materials efficiency variance
   c. Direct manufacturing labor price variance
   d. Direct manufacturing labor efficiency variance
   e. Variable manufacturing overhead spending variance
   f. Variable manufacturing overhead efficiency variance
   g. Production-volume variance
   h. Fixed manufacturing overhead spending variance
2. Can Williams use any of the variances to help explain any of the other variances? Give examples.

Problems

8-35 Comprehensive variance analysis. Cooking Whiz manufactures premium food processors. The following are some manufacturing overhead data for Cooking Whiz for the year ended December 31, 2020:

Manufacturing Overhead	Actual Results	Flexible Budget	Allocated Amount
Variable	$ 71,808	$ 80,640	$ 80,640
Fixed	360,672	351,360	368,640

Budgeted number of output units: 915
Planned allocation rate: 2 machine-hours per unit
Actual number of machine-hours used: 1,632

Static-budget variable manufacturing overhead costs: $76,860

Required

Compute the following quantities (you should be able to do so in the prescribed order):

1. Budgeted number of machine-hours planned
2. Budgeted fixed manufacturing overhead costs per machine-hour
3. Budgeted variable manufacturing overhead costs per machine-hour
4. Budgeted number of machine-hours allowed for actual output produced
5. Actual number of output units
6. Actual number of machine-hours used per output unit

8-36 Journal entries (continuation of 8-35).

Required

1. Prepare journal entries for variable and fixed manufacturing overhead (you will need to calculate the various variances to accomplish this).
2. Overhead variances are written off to the Cost of Goods Sold (COGS) account at the end of the fiscal year. Show how COGS is adjusted through journal entries.

8-37 Graphs and overhead variances. Best Around, Inc., is a manufacturer of vacuums and uses standard costing. Manufacturing overhead (both variable and fixed) is allocated to products on the basis of budgeted machine-hours. In 2020, budgeted fixed manufacturing overhead cost was $17,000,000. Budgeted variable manufacturing overhead was $10 per machine-hour. The denominator level was 1,000,000 machine-hours.

Required

1. Prepare a graph for fixed manufacturing overhead. The graph should display how Best Around, Inc.'s fixed manufacturing overhead costs will be depicted for the purposes of (a) planning and control and (b) inventory costing.
2. Suppose that 1,125,000 machine-hours were allowed for actual output produced in 2020, but 1,200,000 actual machine-hours were used. Actual manufacturing overhead was $12,075,000, variable, and $17,100,000, fixed. Compute (a) the variable manufacturing overhead spending and efficiency variances and (b) the fixed manufacturing overhead spending and production-volume variances. Use the columnar presentation illustrated in Exhibit 8-4 (page 297).
3. What is the amount of the under- or overallocated variable manufacturing overhead and the under- or overallocated fixed manufacturing overhead? Why are the flexible-budget variance and the under- or overallocated overhead amount always the same for variable manufacturing overhead but rarely the same for fixed manufacturing overhead?
4. Suppose the denominator level was 1,700,000 rather than 1,000,000 machine-hours. What variances in requirement 2 would be affected? Recompute them.

8-38 Overhead variance, missing information. Consider the following two situations—cases A and B—independently. Data refer to operations for April 2020. For each situation, assume standard costing. Also assume the use of a flexible budget for control of variable and fixed manufacturing overhead based on machine-hours.

		Cases	
		A	**B**
(1)	Fixed manufacturing overhead incurred	$27,000	$132,900
(2)	Variable manufacturing overhead incurred	$10,511	—
(3)	Denominator level in machine-hours	—	45,000
(4)	Standard machine-hours allowed for actual output achieved	4,700	—
(5)	Fixed manufacturing overhead (per standard machine-hour)	—	—
Flexible-Budget Data:			
(6)	Variable manufacturing overhead (per standard machine-hour)	—	$ 2.10
(7)	Budgeted fixed manufacturing overhead	$23,375	$130,500
(8)	Budgeted variable manufacturing overhead[a]	—	—
(9)	Total budgeted manufacturing overhead[a]	—	—
Additional Data:			
(10)	Standard variable manufacturing overhead allocated	$10,340	—
(11)	Standard fixed manufacturing overhead allocated	$19,975	—
(12)	Production-volume variance	—	$ 580 F
(13)	Variable manufacturing overhead spending variance	$ 457 U	$ 1,490 F
(14)	Variable manufacturing overhead efficiency variance	—	$ 1,680 F
(15)	Fixed manufacturing overhead spending variance	—	—
(16)	Actual machine-hours used	—	—

[a]For standard machine-hours allowed for actual output produced.

Required

Fill in the blanks under each case. [*Hint*: Prepare a worksheet similar to that in Exhibit 8-4 (page 297). Fill in the knowns and then solve for the unknowns.]

8-39 Flexible budgets, 4-variance analysis. (CMA, adapted) Grant Manufacturing uses standard costing. It allocates manufacturing overhead (both variable and fixed) to products on the basis of standard direct manufacturing labor-hours (DMLH). Grant develops its manufacturing overhead rate from the current annual budget. The manufacturing overhead budget for 2020 is based on budgeted output of 576,000 units, requiring 2,304,000 DMLH. The company is able to schedule production uniformly throughout the year.

A total of 46,000 output units requiring 193,200 DMLH was produced during August 2020. Manufacturing overhead (MOH) costs incurred for August amounted to $329,100. The actual costs, compared with the annual budget and 1/12 of the annual budget, are as follows:

Annual Manufacturing Overhead Budget 2020

	Total Amount	Per Output Unit	Per DMLH Input Unit	Monthly MOH Budget August 2020	Actual MOH Costs for August 2020
Variable MOH					
Indirect manufacturing labor	$ 921,600	$1.60	$0.40	$ 76,800	$ 76,800
Supplies	576,000	1.00	0.25	48,000	89,400
Fixed MOH					
Supervision	691,200	1.20	0.30	57,600	47,100
Utilities	345,600	0.60	0.15	28,800	39,900
Depreciation	806,400	1.40	0.35	67,200	75,900
Total	$3,340,800	$5.80	$1.45	$278,400	$329,100

Required

Calculate the following amounts for Grant Manufacturing for August 2020:

1. Total manufacturing overhead costs allocated
2. Variable manufacturing overhead spending variance
3. Fixed manufacturing overhead spending variance
4. Variable manufacturing overhead efficiency variance
5. Production-volume variance

Be sure to identify each variance as favorable (F) or unfavorable (U).

8-40 Activity-based costing, batch-level variance analysis. Audrina's Fleet Feet, Inc., produces dance shoes for stores all over the world. While the pairs of shoes are boxed individually, they are crated and shipped in batches. The shipping department records both variable direct batch-level costs and fixed batch-level overhead costs. The following information pertains to shipping department costs for 2020.

	Static-Budget Amounts	Actual Results
Pairs of shoes shipped	225,000	180,000
Average number of pairs of shoes per crate	15	10
Packing hours per crate	0.9 hours	1.1 hour
Variable direct cost per hour	$18	$16
Fixed overhead cost	$54,000	$56,500

Required

1. What is the static budget number of crates for 2020?
2. What is the flexible budget number of crates for 2020?
3. What is the actual number of crates shipped in 2020?
4. Assuming fixed overhead is allocated using crate-packing hours, what is the predetermined fixed overhead allocation rate?
5. For variable direct batch-level costs, compute the price and efficiency variances.
6. For fixed overhead costs, compute the spending and the production-volume variances.

8-41 Overhead variances and sales-volume variance. Johns Manufacturing Company manufactures and sells rolling suitcases. After several years of increased sales, Johns experiences a drop in sales in 2020 from increased competition. Johns uses machine-hours as the cost-allocation base for variable and fixed manufacturing costs. Budgeted and actual costs for 2020 are as follows:

	Actual Results	Static-Budget Amounts
Suitcases produced and sold	120,000	150,000
Selling price	$ 72	$ 80
Machine-hours	310,000	375,000
Variable direct materials costs	$20 per unit	$20 per unit
Variable direct manufacturing labor costs	$18 per unit	$18 per unit
Variable overhead cost per machine-hour		$1.80 per mach.-hr
Variable overhead costs	$527,000	
Fixed overhead costs	$532,400	$525,000

Required

1. Calculate the variable overhead and fixed overhead variances (spending, efficiency, spending, and volume).
2. Create a chart like that in Exhibit 7-2 showing Flexible Budget Variances and Sales-Volume Variances for revenues, costs, contribution margin, and operating income.
3. Calculate the operating income based on budgeted profit per suitcase.
4. Reconcile the budgeted operating income from requirement 3 to the actual operating income from your chart in requirement 2.
5. Calculate the operating income volume variance and show how the sales-volume variance is composed of the production-volume variance and the operating income volume variance.

8-42 Activity-based costing, batch-level variance analysis. The Cotton Shop (TCS) specializes in making fraternity and sorority tote bags for the college market. TCS produces bags in batch sizes of 100. For rush orders, TCS will produce smaller batches for an additional charge of $180 per setup.

Budgeted and actual costs for the production process for 2020 are as follows:

	Static-Budget Amounts	Actual Results
Number of bags produced	125,000	114,000
Average number of bags per setup	100	95
Hours to set up machines	6	5.80
Direct variable cost per setup-hour	$ 25	$ 27
Total fixed setup overhead costs	$60,000	$62,640

Required

1. What is the static budget number of setups for 2020?
2. What is the flexible-budget number of setups for 2020?
3. What is the actual number of setups in 2020?
4. Assuming fixed setup overhead costs are allocated using setup-hours, what is the predetermined fixed setup overhead allocation rate?
5. Does TCS's charge of $180 cover the budgeted direct variable cost of an order? The budgeted total cost?
6. For direct variable setup costs, compute the price and efficiency variances.
7. For fixed setup overhead costs, compute the spending and the production-volume variances.
8. What qualitative factors should TCS consider before accepting or rejecting a special order?

8-43 Comprehensive review of Chapters 7 and 8, working backward from given variances. The Gallo Company uses a flexible budget and standard costs to aid planning and control of its machining manufacturing operations. Its costing system for manufacturing has two direct-cost categories (direct materials and direct manufacturing labor—both variable) and two overhead-cost categories (variable manufacturing overhead and fixed manufacturing overhead, both allocated using direct manufacturing labor-hours).

At the 50,000 budgeted direct manufacturing labor-hour level for August, budgeted direct manufacturing labor is $1,250,000, budgeted variable manufacturing overhead is $500,000, and budgeted fixed manufacturing overhead is $1,000,000.

The following actual results are for August:

Direct materials price variance (based on purchases)	$179,300 F
Direct materials efficiency variance	75,900 U
Direct manufacturing labor costs incurred	535,500
Variable manufacturing overhead flexible-budget variance	10,400 U
Variable manufacturing overhead efficiency variance	18,100 U
Fixed manufacturing overhead incurred	957,550

The standard cost per pound of direct materials is $11.50. The standard allowance is 6 pounds of direct materials for each unit of product. During August, 20,000 units of product were produced. There was no beginning inventory of direct materials. There was no beginning or ending work in process. In August, the direct materials price variance was $1.10 per pound.

In July, labor unrest caused a major slowdown in the pace of production, resulting in an unfavorable direct manufacturing labor efficiency variance of $40,000. There was no direct manufacturing labor price variance. Labor unrest persisted into August. Some workers quit. Their replacements had to be hired at higher wage rates, which had to be extended to all workers. The actual average wage rate in August exceeded the standard average wage rate by $0.50 per hour.

Required

1. Compute the following for August:
   a. Total pounds of direct materials purchased
   b. Total number of pounds of excess direct materials used
   c. Variable manufacturing overhead spending variance
   d. Total number of actual direct manufacturing labor-hours used
   e. Total number of standard direct manufacturing labor-hours allowed for the units produced
   f. Production-volume variance
2. Describe how Gallo's control of variable manufacturing overhead items differs from its control of fixed manufacturing overhead items.

8-44 Review of Chapters 7 and 8, 3-variance analysis. (CPA, adapted) The Beal Manufacturing Company's costing system has two direct-cost categories: direct materials and direct manufacturing labor. Manufacturing overhead (both variable and fixed) is allocated to products on the basis of standard direct manufacturing labor-hours (DMLH). At the beginning of 2020, Beal adopted the following standards for its manufacturing costs:

	Input	Cost per Output Unit
Direct materials	5 lb. at $4 per lb.	$ 20.00
Direct manufacturing labor	4 hrs. at $16 per hr.	64.00
Manufacturing overhead:		
Variable	$8 per DLH	32.00
Fixed	$9 per DLH	36.00
Standard manufacturing cost per output unit		$152.00

The denominator level for total manufacturing overhead per month in 2020 is 37,000 direct manufacturing labor-hours. Beal's budget for January 2020 was based on this denominator level. The records for January indicated the following:

Direct materials purchased	40,300 lb. at $3.80 per lb.
Direct materials used	37,300 lb.
Direct manufacturing labor	31,400 hrs. at $16.25 per hr.
Total actual manufacturing overhead (variable and fixed)	$650,000
Actual production	7,600 output units

Required

1. Prepare a schedule of total standard manufacturing costs for the 7,600 output units in January 2020.
2. For the month of January 2020, compute the following variances, indicating whether each is favorable (F) or unfavorable (U):
   a. Direct materials price variance, based on purchases
   b. Direct materials efficiency variance
   c. Direct manufacturing labor price variance
   d. Direct manufacturing labor efficiency variance
   e. Total manufacturing overhead spending variance
   f. Variable manufacturing overhead efficiency variance
   g. Production-volume variance

8-45 Nonfinancial variances. Kathy's Kettle Potato Chips produces gourmet chips distributed to chain sub shops throughout California. To ensure that their chips are of the highest quality and have taste appeal, Kathy has a rigorous inspection process. For quality control purposes, Kathy has a standard based on the number of pounds of chips inspected per hour and the number of pounds that pass or fail the inspection.

Kathy expects that for every 1,000 pounds of chips produced, 200 pounds of chips will be inspected. Inspection of 200 pounds of chips should take 1 hour. Kathy also expects that 1% of the chips inspected will fail the inspection. During the month of May, Kathy produced 113,000 pounds of chips and inspected 22,300 pounds of chips in 120 hours. Of the 22,300 pounds of chips inspected, 215 pounds of chips failed to pass the inspection.

Required

1. Compute two variances that help determine whether the time spent on inspections was more or less than expected. (Follow a format similar to the one used for the variable overhead spending and efficiency variances, but without prices.)
2. Compute two variances that can be used to evaluate the percentage of the chips that fail the inspection.

8-46 Overhead variances, service sector, working backward. NWI is a service provider that offers computing resources measured in RAM (random-access memory)-hours to handle enterprise-wide applications. Information about variable overhead costs for March 2020 are as follows:

Budgeted variable overhead rate	$6 per RAM-hour
Flexible budget RAM-hours for actual services provided	14,850 RAM-hours
Actual RAM-hours for actual services provided	15,000 RAM hours
Variable overhead spending variance	$500 F

Information about fixed overhead costs for March 2020 are as follows:

Actual fixed overhead costs	$30,375
Fixed overhead spending variance	$1,575 U
Budgeted hours (denominator level) for fixed overhead costs	18,000 RAM-hours

Required

1. For variable overhead costs in March 2020, prepare an exhibit like Exhibit 8-1 and fill in the following (a) the flexible budget in column 3 (budgeted RAM-hours allowed for actual services provided), (b) actual RAM-hours used for the services provided times the budgeted variable overhead rate in column 2, (c) use the variable overhead spending variance, to calculate actual variable costs in column 1, (d) calculate the variable overhead efficiency variance, and (e) calculate the variable overhead flexible-budget variance. (f) Will variable overhead be over- or underallocated? By how much?
2. For fixed overhead costs in March 2020, prepare an exhibit like Exhibit 8-2 and complete the following: (a) use the fixed overhead spending variance to calculate the flexible budget in column 2, (b) calculate the budgeted fixed overhead allocation rate, (c) calculate the allocated amount of fixed overhead in column 3, (d) calculate the production-volume variance for fixed overhead costs, and (e) calculate the fixed overhead flexible budget variance. (f) Will fixed overhead be over- or underallocated? By how much?

8-47 Direct-cost and overhead variances, income statement. The Manzano Company started business on January 1, 2020. The company adopted a standard costing system for the production of backpacks. Manzano chose direct manufacturing labor as the allocation base for overhead. Budgeted and actual costs for 2020 are as follows:

	Actual Results	Static-Budget Amounts
Backpacks produced	180,000	160,000
Backpacks sold	144,000	160,000
Selling price	$ 17	$17
Direct material fabric per backpack		1.5 yards
Price par yard of fabric		$2 per yard
Direct material fabric used in yards	280,000 yards	
Variable direct materials costs	$ 574,000	
Direct manufacturing labor-hours per backpack		0.5 labor-hour
Direct manufacturing labor wage rate		$12 per labor-hour
Direct manufacturing labor-hours used	100,000 hours	
Direct manufacturing labor costs	$1,260,000	
Fixed manufacturing overhead costs	$ 875,000	$800,000

Required

1. Calculate the following variances for 2020, and indicate whether each is favorable (F) or unfavorable (U):
   a. Direct materials efficiency variance
   b. Direct materials price variance
   c. Direct manufacturing labor efficiency variance
   d. Direct manufacturing labor price variance
   e. Fixed overhead flexible-budget variance
   f. Fixed overhead production-volume variance
   g. Calculate the total variances for the period representing the amounts by which costs are overallocated or underallocated for the year.
2. (a) Calculate standard production cost per backpack; (b) Calculate Manzano Company's gross margin for 2020 based on selling 144,000 backpacks, after prorating the total variance calculated in requirement 1-g between cost of goods sold and finished goods inventory. Manzano has no direct materials or work-in-process inventory.

8-48 Overhead variances, ethics. Butler Company uses standard costing. The company has a manufacturing plant in Portland, Oregon. Firm management has always used variance analysis as a performance measure for the plant.

John Mack has just been hired as a new controller for Butler Company. John is good friends with the Portland plant manager and wants him to get a favorable review. To help him out, John underestimates production, and budgets annual output of 800,000 units for 2020. His explanation for this is that the economy is slowing and sales are likely to decrease. Budgeted and actual costs for 2020 are as follows:

	Actual Results	Static-Budget Amounts
Units produced and sold	1,000,000	800,000
Direct manufacturing labor-hours per unit		0.5 labor-hour
Direct manufacturing labor-hours	510,000	
Variable overhead rate		$3.50 per labor-hour
Variable overhead costs	$1,800,000	
Fixed overhead costs	$1,240,000	$1,200,000

Required

1. Compute the budgeted fixed cost per labor-hour for the fixed overhead.
2. Compute the variable overhead spending variance and the variable overhead efficiency variance.
3. Compute the fixed overhead spending and volume variances.
4. Compute the budgeted fixed cost per labor-hour for the fixed overhead if John Mack had estimated production more realistically at the expected sales level of 1,000,000 units.
5. Summarize the fixed overhead variance based on both the projected level of production of 800,000 units and 1,000,000 units.
6. Did John Mack's attempt to make his friend, the plant manager, look better work? Why or why not?
7. What do you think of John Mack's behavior overall?

9 Inventory Costing and Capacity Analysis

LEARNING OBJECTIVES

1. Identify what distinguishes variable costing from absorption costing
2. Compute operating income under absorption costing and under variable costing, and explain the difference in operating income
3. Understand how absorption costing can provide undesirable incentives for managers to build up inventory
4. Differentiate throughput costing from variable costing and from absorption costing
5. Describe the different capacity concepts that can be used in absorption costing
6. Examine the key factors managers use to choose a capacity level to compute the budgeted fixed manufacturing cost rate
7. Understand issues that play an important role in capacity planning and control

Few numbers capture the attention of managers and shareholders more than operating profits reported in the firm's income statement.

In industries that require significant upfront investments in capacity, two key decisions have a substantial impact on a company's financial accounting profits: (1) the amount of money a firm spends on fixed investments and (2) the extent to which the firm eventually utilizes capacity to meet customer demand. Unfortunately, the compensation and reward systems of a firm, as well as the choice of inventory-costing methods used to prepare the financial statements, may induce managers to make decisions that benefit short-term reported earnings at the expense of a firm's long-term financial health. It may take a significant threat to motivate managers to make the right capacity and inventory choices, as the following article illustrates.

UNDER ARMOUR RACES TO DEFEAT ITS INVENTORY BACKLOG[1]

Can you have too much of a good thing? When the good thing in question is excess inventory, the answer is a resounding "Yes!"

Under Armour, the athletic-apparel retailer, discovered this in 2017 when a software glitch caused inventory levels to soar. The company could not get its products to wholesalers on time, which caused inventory to swell by 22% year over year. To clear out its inventory, Under Armour had to slash prices to clear its backlog before it could get newer products on the shelves of its retail partners. This caused company revenue and profitability to drop for more than a year.

To better manage its inventory going forward, Under Armour implemented a new internal company system that ensures the company is managing its inventory and supply chain with efficiency and precision. Under Armour reduced its vendors by 25% and its products by 40% to better manage its existing operations and product line. By 2018, it was then able to cut its promotional days when products were on sale by one third, which increased revenue and helped stabilize operations in the competitive athletic-apparel marketplace.

JHVEPhoto/Shutterstock

[1] *Sources:* Angus Loten and Sara Germano, "Under Armour Links Sales Decline to Software Upgrade," *CIO Journal* (blog), *The Wall Street Journal*, October 31, 2017 (https://blogs.wsj.com/cio/2017/10/31/under-armour-links-sales-decline-to-software-upgrade/); Jacob Sonenshine, "Under Armour's Newest Executive is Zeroing in on Its Biggest Problem," *Business Insider*, June 20, 2018 (https://markets.businessinsider.com/news/stocks/under-armour-stock-price-newest-executive-is-zeroing-in-on-its-biggest-problem-2018-6-1027263545); Holden Wilen, "Kevin Plank Warns Competitors: Under Armour Will Soon Be 'Something to Deal With' Again," *Baltimore Business Journal*, October 30, 2018 (https://www.bizjournals.com/baltimore/news/2018/10/30/kevin-plank-warns-competitors-under-armour-will.html).

Managers in industries with high fixed costs, like manufacturing, must manage capacity levels and make decisions about how to use available capacity. Managers must also decide on management approaches to production and inventory (as Under Armour did). These decisions and the accounting choices managers make affect the operating profits reported in the income statements of manufacturing companies. This chapter focuses on two types of choices:

1. *The inventory-costing choice* is an important application of how choices in the costing system impact the results reported in a firm's financial statements. The inventory-costing choice determines which manufacturing costs are treated as inventoriable costs. Recall from Chapter 2 (page 39) that *inventoriable costs* are all costs of a product that are regarded as assets on the company's balance sheet when they are incurred and expensed as cost of goods sold in the income statement when the product is sold. There are three types of inventory costing methods: variable costing, absorption costing, and throughput costing.
2. *The denominator-level capacity choice* focuses on the capacity level used to calculate budgeted fixed manufacturing cost rates used in costing systems. There are four possible choices of capacity levels: theoretical capacity, practical capacity, normal capacity utilization, and master-budget capacity utilization.

The chapter also discusses the factors that managers should consider when choosing among these different capacity levels when costing is done for managerial accounting purposes such as product costing, product pricing, or performance evaluation, and for financial or tax accounting purposes.

Variable and Absorption Costing

LEARNING OBJECTIVE 1

Identify what distinguishes variable costing

...fixed manufacturing costs excluded from inventoriable costs

from absorption costing

...fixed manufacturing costs included in inventoriable costs

The two most common methods used by manufacturing companies to cost inventories are *variable costing* and *absorption costing*. We describe each of the methods in this section and then discuss them in detail, using a hypothetical telescope-manufacturing company as an example.

Variable Costing

Variable costing is a method of inventory costing in which all *variable* manufacturing costs (direct and indirect) are included in inventoriable costs. All fixed manufacturing costs are excluded from inventoriable costs and are instead treated as costs of the period in which they are incurred. Note that *variable costing* is an imprecise term in the sense that only variable *manufacturing* costs are inventoried; variable nonmanufacturing costs are still treated as period costs and are expensed. Another commonly used term to describe this method is **direct costing**. This term is also imprecise because variable manufacturing overhead (an indirect cost) is considered inventoriable under variable costing, whereas fixed direct costs, such as marketing costs, are considered period costs.

Absorption Costing

Absorption costing is a method of inventory costing in which *all* manufacturing costs, variable and fixed, are included as inventoriable costs. That is, inventory "absorbs" all manufacturing costs. The job costing system you studied in Chapter 4 is an example of absorption costing.

Under both variable costing and absorption costing, all variable manufacturing costs are inventoriable costs and all nonmanufacturing costs in the value chain (such as research and development and marketing), whether variable or fixed, are period costs and are recorded as expenses when they are incurred.

Comparing Variable and Absorption Costing

The easiest way to understand the difference between variable costing and absorption costing is with an example. In this chapter, we will study Stassen Company, an optical consumer-products manufacturer, and focus on its product line of high-end telescopes for aspiring astronomers.

Stassen uses standard costing:

- Direct costs are traced to products using standard prices and standard inputs allowed for actual outputs produced.
- Indirect (overhead) manufacturing costs are allocated using standard indirect rates times standard inputs allowed for actual outputs produced.

Stassen's management wants to prepare an income statement for 2020 (the fiscal year just ended) to evaluate the performance of the telescope product line. The operating information for the year is as follows:

	A	B
1		**Units**
2	Beginning inventory	0
3	Production	8,000
4	Sales	6,000
5	Ending inventory	2,000

Actual price and cost data for 2020 are as follows:

	A	B
10	Selling price	$ 1,000
11	Variable manufacturing cost per unit:	
12	Direct materials cost per unit	$ 110
13	Direct manufacturing labor cost per unit	40
14	Manufacturing overhead cost per unit	50
15	Total variable manufacturing cost per unit	$ 200
16	Variable marketing cost per unit sold	$ 185
17	Fixed manufacturing costs (all indirect)	$1,080,000
18	Fixed marketing costs (all indirect)	$1,380,000

For simplicity and to focus on the main ideas, we assume the following about Stassen:

- Stassen incurs manufacturing and marketing costs only. The cost driver for all variable manufacturing costs is units produced; the cost driver for variable marketing costs is units sold. There are no batch-level costs and no product-sustaining costs.
- There are no price variances, efficiency variances, or spending variances. Therefore, the *budgeted* (standard) price and cost data for 2020 are the same as the *actual* price and cost data.
- Work-in-process inventory is zero.
- Stassen budgeted sales of 6,000 units for 2020, which is the same as the actual sales for 2020.
- Stassen budgeted production of 8,000 units for 2020. This was used to calculate the budgeted fixed manufacturing cost per unit of $135 ($1,080,000/8,000 units).[2]
- The actual production for 2020 is 8,000 units. As a result, there is no production-volume variance for manufacturing costs in 2020. A later example, based on data for 2021, does include production-volume variances. However, even in that case, the income statement contains no variances other than the production-volume variance.
- Variances are written off to cost of goods sold in the period (year) in which they occur.

[2] Throughout this section, we use budgeted *output* as the basis for calculating the fixed manufacturing cost per unit for ease of exposition. In the latter half of this chapter, we consider the relative merits of alternative denominator-level choices for calculating this unit cost.

Based on the preceding information, Stassen's inventoriable costs per unit produced in 2020 under the two inventory costing methods are as follows:

	Variable Costing		Absorption Costing	
Variable manufacturing cost per unit produced:				
Direct materials	$110		$110	
Direct manufacturing labor	40		40	
Manufacturing overhead	50	$200	50	$200
Fixed manufacturing cost per unit produced		—		135
Total inventoriable cost per unit produced		$200		$335

To summarize, the main difference between variable costing and absorption costing is the accounting for fixed manufacturing costs:

- Under variable costing, fixed manufacturing costs are not inventoried; they are treated as a period expense.
- Under absorption costing, fixed manufacturing costs are inventoried. In our example, the standard fixed manufacturing cost is $135 per unit ($1,080,000 ÷ 8,000 units) produced.

DECISION POINT

How does variable costing differ from absorption costing?

9-1 TRY IT!

Cowan Auto makes and sells batteries. In 2020, it made 50,000 batteries and sold 35,000 of them, at an average selling price of $40 per unit. The following additional information relates to Cowan Auto for 2020:

Direct materials	$ 24.00 per unit
Direct manufacturing labor	$ 8.00 per unit
Variable manufacturing costs	$ 0.50 per unit
Sales commissions	$ 3.50 per part
Fixed manufacturing costs	$325,000 per year
Administrative expenses, all fixed	$250,000 per year

What is Cowan Auto's inventoriable cost per unit using (1) variable costing and (2) absorption costing?

Variable Versus Absorption Costing: Operating Income and Income Statements

LEARNING OBJECTIVE 2

Compute operating income under absorption costing

...using the gross-margin format

and variable costing,

...using the contribution-margin format

and explain the difference in operating income

...income is affected by the unit level of production and the unit level of sales under absorption costing, but only by the unit level of sales under variable costing

When comparing variable and absorption costing, we must take the length of the time horizon over which we are comparing the two systems into account. How do the data produced by variable and absorption costing differ over a 1-year period? How do they differ over a 2-year period?

Comparing Income Statements for One Year

What will Stassen's operating income be if it uses variable costing or absorption costing? The differences between these methods are illustrated in Exhibit 9-1. Panel A shows the variable costing income statement and Panel B the absorption-costing income statement for Stassen's telescope product line for 2020. The variable-costing income statement uses the contribution-margin format introduced in Chapter 3; the absorption-costing income statement uses the gross-margin format introduced in Chapter 2. Why these different formats? The distinction between variable costs and fixed costs is central to variable costing, and it is highlighted by the contribution-margin format. In contrast, the distinction between manufacturing and non-manufacturing costs is central to absorption costing, and it is highlighted by the gross-margin format.

EXHIBIT 9-1 Comparison of Variable Costing and Absorption Costing for Stassen Company: Telescope Product-Line Income Statements for 2020

	A	B	C	D	E	F	G
1	**Panel A: VARIABLE COSTING**				**Panel B: ABSORPTION COSTING**		
2	Revenues: \$1,000 × 6,000 units		\$6,000,000		Revenues: \$1,000 × 6,000 units		\$6,000,000
3	Variable cost of goods sold:				Cost of goods sold:		
4	Beginning inventory	\$ 0			Beginning inventory	\$ 0	
5	Variable manufacturing costs: \$200 × 8,000 units	1,600,000			Variable manufacturing costs: \$200 × 8,000 units	1,600,000	
6					Allocated fixed manufacturing costs: \$135 × 8,000 units	1,080,000	
7	Cost of goods available for sale	1,600,000			Cost of goods available for sale	2,680,000	
8	Deduct ending inventory: \$200 × 2,000 units	(400,000)			Deduct ending inventory: \$335 × 2,000 units	(670,000)	
9	Variable cost of goods sold		1,200,000		Cost of goods sold		2,010,000
10	Variable marketing costs: \$185 × 6,000 units sold		1,110,000				
11	Contribution margin		3,690,000		Gross Margin		3,990,000
12	Fixed manufacturing costs		1,080,000		Variable marketing costs: \$185 × 6,000 units sold		1,110,000
13	Fixed marketing costs		1,380,000		Fixed marketing costs		1,380,000
14	Operating income		\$1,230,000		Operating Income		\$1,500,000
15							
16	Manufacturing costs expensed:				Manufacturing costs expensed:		
17	Variable cost of goods sold		\$1,200,000				
18	Fixed manufacturing costs		1,080,000				
19	Total		\$2,280,000		Cost of goods sold		\$2,010,000

Absorption-costing income statements do not need to differentiate between variable and fixed costs. However, we will make this distinction between variable and fixed costs in the Stassen example in order to illustrate how individual line items are classified differently under variable costing and absorption costing. In Exhibit 9-1, Panel B, note that inventoriable cost is \$335 per unit under absorption costing: allocated fixed manufacturing costs of \$135 per unit plus variable manufacturing costs of \$200 per unit.

Notice how the fixed manufacturing costs of \$1,080,000 are accounted for under variable costing and absorption costing in Exhibit 9-1. The income statement under variable costing deducts the \$1,080,000 lump sum as an expense for 2020. In contrast, under absorption costing, the \$1,080,000 (\$135 per unit × 8,000 units) is initially treated as an inventoriable cost in 2020. Of this \$1,080,000, \$810,000 (\$135 per unit × 6,000 units) subsequently becomes a part of cost of goods sold in 2020, and \$270,000 (\$135 per unit × 2,000 units) remains an asset—part of ending finished goods inventory on December 31, 2020.

Operating income is \$270,000 higher under absorption costing compared with variable costing because only \$810,000 of fixed manufacturing costs are expensed under absorption costing, whereas all \$1,080,000 of fixed manufacturing costs are expensed under variable costing. Note that the variable manufacturing cost of \$200 per unit is accounted for the same way in both income statements in Exhibit 9-1.

These points can be summarized as follows:

	Variable Costing	**Absorption Costing**
Variable manufacturing costs: \$200 per telescope produced	Inventoriable	Inventoriable
Fixed manufacturing costs: \$1,080,000 per year	Deducted as an expense of the period	Inventoriable at \$135 per telescope produced using budgeted denominator level of 8,000 units produced per year (\$1,080,000 ÷ 8,000 units = \$135 per unit)

The basis of the difference between variable costing and absorption costing is how fixed manufacturing costs are accounted for. If inventory levels change, operating income will differ between the two methods because of the difference in accounting for fixed manufacturing costs. To see this difference, let's compare telescope sales of 6,000, 7,000, and 8,000 units by Stassen in 2020, when 8,000 units were produced. Of the $1,080,000 total fixed manufacturing costs, the amount expensed in the 2020 income statement under each of these scenarios would be as follows:

	A	B	C	D	E	G	H
1			Variable Costing			Absorption Costing	
2							
3	Units	Ending	Fixed Manufacturing Costs			Fixed Manufacturing Costs	
4	Sold	Inventory	Included in Inventory	Amount Expensed		Included in Inventory[a]	Amount Expensed[b]
5	6,000	2,000	$0	$1,080,000		$270,000	$ 810,000
6	7,000	1,000	$0	$1,080,000		$135,000	$ 945,000
7	8,000	0	$0	$1,080,000		$ 0	$1,080,000
8							
9	[a]$135 × Ending Inventory						
10	[b]$135 × Units Sold						

In the last scenario, where 8,000 units are produced and sold, both variable and absorption costing report the same net income because inventory levels are unchanged. This chapter's appendix describes how the choice of variable costing or absorption costing affects the breakeven quantity of sales when inventory levels are allowed to vary.

9-2 TRY IT!

SW Toys started 2020 with no inventories. During the year, their expected and actual production was 34,000 units, of which they sold 23,800 units at $80 each. Cost data for the year is as follows:

Manufacturing costs incurred:	
Variable	$520,000
Fixed	$425,000
Marketing costs incurred:	
Variable	$162,100
Fixed	$ 81,600

Calculate SW Toys' operating income under (1) variable costing and (2) absorption costing. Explain why operating income differs under the two approaches.

Comparing Income Statements for Multiple Years

To get a more comprehensive view of the effects of variable costing and absorption costing, Stassen's management accountants prepare income statements for 2 years of operations, starting with 2020. The operating data, in units, are given in the following table:

	E	F	G
1		2020	2021
2	Budgeted production	8,000	8,000
3	Beginning inventory	0	2,000
4	Actual production	8,000	5,000
5	Sales	6,000	6,500
6	Ending inventory	2,000	500

All other 2020 data given earlier for Stassen also apply for 2021.

In 2021, Stassen has a production-volume variance because actual telescope production differs from the budgeted level of production of 8,000 units per year used to calculate the budgeted fixed manufacturing cost per unit. The actual quantity sold for 2021 is 6,500 units, which is the same as the sales quantity budgeted for that year.

Exhibit 9-2 presents the income statements for 2020 and 2021, under variable costing in Panel A, and under absorption costing in Panel B. As you study Exhibit 9-2, note that the 2020 columns in both Panels A and B show the same figures as Exhibit 9-1. The 2021 column is similar to 2020 *except for the production-volume variance line item under absorption costing in Panel B*. Keep in mind the following points about absorption costing as you study Panel B of Exhibit 9-2:

1. The $135 fixed manufacturing cost rate is based on the budgeted denominator capacity level of 8,000 units in 2020 and 2021 ($1,080,000 ÷ 8,000 units = $135 per unit). Whenever production (the quantity produced, not the quantity sold) deviates from the denominator level, there will be a production-volume variance. The amount of Stassen's production-volume variance is determined by multiplying $135 per unit by the difference between the denominator level and the actual level of production.

EXHIBIT 9-2 Comparison of Variable Costing and Absorption Costing for Stassen Company: Telescope Product-Line Income Statements for 2020 and 2021

	A	B	C	D	E
1	**Panel A: VARIABLE COSTING**				
2		**2020**		**2021**	
3	Revenues: $1,000 × 6,000; 6,500 units		$6,000,000		$6,500,000
4	Variable cost of goods sold:				
5	Beginning inventory: $200 × 0; 2,000 units	$ 0		$ 400,000	
6	Variable manufacturing costs: $200 × 8,000; 5,000 units	1,600,000		1,000,000	
7	Cost of goods available for sale	1,600,000		1,400,000	
8	Deduct ending inventory: $200 × 2,000; 500 units	(400,000)		(100,000)	
9	Variable cost of goods sold		1,200,000		1,300,000
10	Variable marketing costs: $185 × 6,000; 6,500 units		1,110,000		1,202,500
11	Contribution margin		3,690,000		3,997,500
12	Fixed manufacturing costs		1,080,000		1,080,000
13	Fixed marketing costs		1,380,000		1,380,000
14	Operating income		$1,230,000		$1,537,500
15					
16	**Panel B: ABSORPTION COSTING**				
17		**2020**		**2021**	
18	Revenues: $1,000 × 6,000; 6,500 units		$6,000,000		$6,500,000
19	Cost of goods sold:				
20	Beginning inventory: $335 × 0; 2,000 units	0		670,000	
21	Variable manufacturing costs: $200 × 8,000; 5,000 units	1,600,000		1,000,000	
22	Allocated fixed manufacturing costs: $135 × 8,000; 5,000 units	1,080,000		675,000	
23	Cost of goods available for sale	2,680,000		2,345,000	
24	Deduct ending inventory: $335 × 2,000; 500 units	(670,000)		(167,500)	
25	Adjustment for production-volume variance[a]	$ 0		$ 405,000	U
26	Cost of goods sold		2,010,000		2,582,500
27	Gross Margin		3,990,000		3,917,500
28	Variable marketing costs: $185 × 6,000; 6,500 units		1,110,000		1,202,500
29	Fixed marketing costs		1,380,000		1,380,000
30	Operating Income		$1,500,000		$1,335,000
31					
32	[a]Production-volume variance = Budgeted fixed manufacturing costs − Fixed manufacturing overhead allocated using budgeted cost per output unit allowed for actual output produced (Panel B, line 22)				
33	2020: $1,080,000 − ($135 × 8,000) = $1,080,000 − $1,080,000 = $0				
34	2021: $1,080,000 − ($135 × 5,000) = $1,080,000 − $675,000 = $405,000 U				
35					
36	Production-volume variance can also be calculated as follows:				
37	Fixed manufacturing cost per unit × (Denominator level − Actual output units produced)				
38	2020: $135 × (8,000 − 8,000) units = $135 × 0 = $0				
39	2021: $135 × (8,000 − 5,000) units = $135 × 3,000 = $405,000 U				

Recall how standard costing works under absorption costing. Each time a unit is manufactured, \$135 of fixed manufacturing costs is included in the cost of goods manufactured and available for sale. In 2021, when 5,000 units are manufactured, \$675,000 (\$135 per unit × 5,000 units) of fixed manufacturing costs is included in the cost of goods available for sale (see Exhibit 9-2, Panel B, line 22). Total fixed manufacturing costs for 2021 are \$1,080,000. The production-volume variance of \$405,000 U (unfavorable) equals the difference between \$1,080,000 and \$675,000. In Panel B, note how, for each year, the fixed manufacturing costs included in the cost of goods available for sale plus the production-volume variance always equals \$1,080,000.

2. As a result of the production-volume variance, the absorption costing income is lower in 2021 than in 2020 even though Stassen sold 500 more units. We explore the impact of production levels on income under absorption costing in greater detail later in this chapter.
3. The production-volume variance, which relates only to fixed manufacturing overhead, exists under absorption costing but not under variable costing. Under variable costing, fixed manufacturing costs of \$1,080,000 are always treated as a period expense, regardless of the level of production (and sales).

Here's a summary (using information from Exhibit 9-2) of the operating-income differences for Stassen Company for 2020 and 2021:

	2020	2021
1. Absorption-costing operating income	\$1,500,000	\$1,335,000
2. Variable-costing operating income	\$1,230,000	\$1,537,500
3. Difference: (1) – (2)	\$ 270,000	\$ (202,500)

The sizeable differences in the preceding table illustrate why managers whose performance is measured by reported income are concerned about the choice between variable costing and absorption costing.

Why do variable costing and absorption costing report different operating income numbers? In general, if inventory increases during an accounting period, less operating income will be reported under variable costing than under absorption costing. Conversely, if inventory decreases, more operating income will be reported under variable costing than under absorption costing. The difference in reported operating income is due solely to the fact that, under absorption costing, (1) fixed manufacturing costs are moved into inventories as inventories increase and (2) fixed manufacturing costs are moved out of inventories as inventories decrease.

The difference between operating income under absorption costing and variable costing can be computed by formula 1, which focuses on fixed manufacturing costs in beginning inventory and ending inventory:

	A	B	C	D	E	F	G	H
1	Formula 1							
2						Fixed manufacturing		Fixed manufacturing
3		Absorption-costing	–	Variable-costing	=	costs in ending inventory	–	costs in beginning inventory
4		operating income		operating income		under absorption costing		under absorption costing
5	2020	\$1,500,000	–	\$1,230,000	=	(\$135 × 2,000 units)	–	(\$135 × 0 units)
6		\$270,000			=	\$270,000		
7								
8	2021	\$1,335,000	–	\$1,537,500	=	(\$135 × 500 units)	–	(\$135 × 2,000 units)
9		(\$202,500)			=	(\$202,500)		

Fixed manufacturing costs in ending inventory are deferred to a future period under absorption costing. For example, \$270,000 of fixed manufacturing overhead is deferred to 2021 on December 31, 2020. In contrast, under variable costing, all \$1,080,000 of fixed manufacturing costs are treated as an expense of 2020.

Recall that

$$\text{Beginning inventory} + \text{Cost of goods manufactured} = \text{Cost of goods sold} + \text{Ending Inventory}$$

Therefore, instead of focusing on fixed manufacturing costs in ending and beginning inventory (as in formula 1), we could alternatively look at fixed manufacturing costs in units produced and units sold. The latter approach (see formula 2) highlights how fixed manufacturing costs move between units produced and units sold during the fiscal year.

Home Insert Page Layout Formulas Data Review View

	A	B	C	D	E	F	G	H
12	**Formula 2**							
13						**Fixed manufacturing costs**		**Fixed manufacturing costs**
14		**Absorption-costing**	–	**Variable-costing**	=	**inventoried in units produced**	–	**in cost of goods sold**
15		**operating income**		**operating income**		**under absorption costing**		**under absorption costing**
16	**2020**	$1,500,000	–	$1,230,000	=	($135 × 8,000 units)	–	($135 × 6,000 units)
17		$270,000			=	$270,000		
18								
19	**2021**	$1,335,000	–	$1,537,500	=	($135 × 5,000 units)	–	($135 × 6,500 units)
20		($202,500)			=	($202,500)		

Managers face increasing pressure to reduce inventory levels. Some companies are achieving steep reductions in inventory levels using management approaches such as just-in-time production—a production system under which products are manufactured only when needed. Formula 1 illustrates that, as Stassen reduces its inventory levels, operating income differences between absorption costing and variable costing become smaller, and even immaterial. Consider, for example, the formula for 2020. If instead of 2,000 units in ending inventory, Stassen had only two units in ending inventory, the difference between absorption-costing operating income and variable-costing operating income would drop from $270,000 to just $270.

Variable Costing and the Effect of Sales and Production on Operating Income

Given a constant contribution margin per unit and constant fixed costs, the period-to-period change in operating income under variable costing is *driven solely by changes in the quantity of units actually sold*. Consider the variable-costing operating income of Stassen in 2021 versus 2020. Recall the following:

$$\text{Contribution margin per unit} = \text{Selling price} - \text{Variable manufacturing cost per unit} - \text{Variable marketing cost per unit}$$
$$= \$1{,}000 \text{ per unit} - \$200 \text{ per unit} - \$185 \text{ per unit}$$
$$= \$615 \text{ per unit}$$

$$\text{Change in variable-costing operating income} = \text{Contribution margin per unit} \times \text{Change in quantity of units sold}$$

$$\text{2021 vs. 2020: } \$1{,}537{,}500 - \$1{,}230{,}000 = \$615 \text{ per unit} \times (6{,}500 \text{ unit} - 6{,}000 \text{ units})$$
$$\$\ 307{,}500 = \$307{,}500$$

DECISION POINT

How does operating income differ under variable and absorption costing?

Under variable costing, Stassen managers cannot increase operating income by "producing for inventory." Why not? Because, as you can see from the preceding computations, when using variable costing, only the quantity of units sold drives operating income. We'll explain later in this chapter that absorption costing enables managers to increase operating income by increasing both the unit level of sales and the unit level of production. Before you proceed to the next section, make sure that you examine Exhibit 9-3 for a detailed comparison of the differences between variable costing and absorption costing.

EXHIBIT 9-3 Comparative Income Effects of Variable Costing and Absorption Costing

Question	Variable Costing	Absorption Costing	Comment
Are fixed manufacturing costs inventoried?	No	Yes	Basic theoretical question of when these costs should be expensed
Is there a production-volume variance?	No	Yes	Choice of denominator level affects measurement of operating income under absorption costing only
Are classifications between variable and fixed costs routinely made?	Yes	Infrequently	Absorption costing can be easily modified to obtain subclassifications for variable and fixed costs, if desired (for example, see Exhibit 9-1, Panel B)
How do changes in unit inventory levels affect operating income?[a]			Differences are attributable to the timing of when fixed manufacturing costs are expensed
Production = sales	Equal	Equal	
Production > sales	Lower[b]	Higher[c]	
Production < sales	Higher	Lower	
What are the effects on cost-volume-profit relationship (for a given level of fixed costs and a given contribution margin per unit)?	Driven by unit level of sales	Driven by (a) unit level of sales, (b) unit level of production, and (c) chosen denominator level	Management control benefit: Effects of changes in output level on operating income are easier to understand under variable costing

[a]Assuming that all manufacturing variances are written off as period costs, no change occurs in work-in-process inventory, and no change occurs in the budgeted fixed manufacturing cost rate between accounting periods.
[b]That is, lower operating income than under absorption costing.
[c]That is, higher operating income than under variable costing.

Absorption Costing and Performance Measurement

LEARNING OBJECTIVE 3

Understand how absorption costing can provide undesirable incentives for managers to build up inventory

...producing more units for inventory absorbs fixed manufacturing costs and increases operating income

Absorption costing is the required inventory costing method for external financial reporting in most countries (we provide potential reasons for this rule later in the chapter). Many companies use absorption costing for internal accounting as well for several reasons:

- It is cost-effective and less confusing for managers to use one common method of inventory costing for both external and internal reporting and performance evaluation.
- It can help prevent managers from taking actions that make their performance measure look good, but that hurt the income the company reports to shareholders.
- It measures the cost of all manufacturing resources, whether variable or fixed, necessary to produce inventory. Many companies use inventory-costing information for long-run decisions, such as pricing and choosing a product mix. For these long-run decisions, inventory costs should include both variable *and* fixed costs.

An important attribute of absorption costing is that it enables a manager to increase margins and operating income by producing more ending inventory. Producing for inventory is justified when a firm's managers anticipate rapid growth in demand and want to produce and store additional units to deal with possible production shortages in the next year. For example, with expectations that global solar power capacity will triple over the next 5 years, manufacturers of solar panels are stepping up production in order to take advantage of an anticipated high demand. But, under absorption costing, managers may be tempted to produce inventory even when they *do not* anticipate customer demand to grow. The reason is that this production leads to higher operating income, which can benefit managers in two ways: directly, because higher incomes typically result in a higher bonus for the manager, and indirectly, because greater income levels have a positive effect on stock price, which increases managers' stock-based compensation. But higher income results in the company paying higher taxes. Shareholders and supporters of good corporate governance would also argue that it is unethical for managers to take actions that are intended solely to increase their compensation rather than to improve the company. Producing for inventory is a risky strategy, especially in industries with volatile demand or high risk of product obsolescence because of the pace at which innovation is occurring. For example, tablet sales have been sliding since 2014 and even newer models such as the iPad Pro are being sold at deeply discounted prices in an attempt to spur sales and reduce inventories.

To mitigate the undesirable incentives to build up inventories that absorption costing provides, a number of companies use variable costing for internal reporting. Variable costing focuses attention on distinguishing variable manufacturing costs from fixed manufacturing costs. This distinction is important for short-run decision making (as in cost–volume–profit analysis in Chapter 3 and in planning and control in Chapters 6, 7, and 8).

Companies that use both methods for internal reporting—variable costing for short-run decisions and performance evaluation and absorption costing for long-run decisions—benefit from the relative advantages of each. Surveys sponsored by Chartered Institute of Management Accountants (United Kingdom), the world's largest professional body of management accountants, have shown that while most organizations employ absorption-costing systems, more than 75% indicate the use of variable-costing information as either the most important or second most important measure for decision-making purposes.

In the next section, we explore in more detail the challenges that arise from absorption costing.

Undesirable Buildup of Inventories

A manager whose bonus is based on reported absorption-costing income may be motivated to build up an undesirable level of inventory. Assume that Stassen's managers have such a bonus plan. Exhibit 9-4 shows how Stassen's absorption-costing operating income for 2021 changes as the production level changes. This exhibit assumes that the production-volume variance is written off to cost of goods sold at the end of each year. Beginning inventory of 2,000 units and sales of 6,500 units for 2021 are unchanged from the case shown in Exhibit 9-2. *As you review* Exhibit 9-4, *keep in mind that the computations are basically the same as those in* Exhibit 9-2.

Exhibit 9-4 shows that production of 4,500 units meets the 2021 sales budget of 6,500 units (2,000 units from beginning inventory + 4,500 units produced). Operating income at this production level is $1,267,500. By producing more than 4,500 units, commonly referred to as *producing for inventory*, Stassen increases absorption-costing operating income. Each additional unit in 2021 ending inventory will increase operating income by $135. For example, if 9,000 units are produced (column H in Exhibit 9-4), ending inventory will be 4,500 units and operating income increases to $1,875,000. This amount is $607,500 more than the operating income with zero ending inventory ($1,875,000 − $1,267,500, or 4,500 units × $135 per unit = $607,500). By producing 4,500 units for inventory, the company using absorption costing includes $607,500 of fixed manufacturing costs in finished-goods inventory, so those costs are not expensed in 2021.

The scenarios outlined in Exhibit 9-4 raise three other important points. First, column D is the base-case setting and just restates the 2021 absorption costing results from Panel B of Exhibit 9-2. Second, column F highlights that when inventory levels are unchanged, that is, production equals sales, absorption-costing income equals the income under variable costing (see Panel A of Exhibit 9-2 for comparison). Third, the example in Exhibit 9-4 focuses on 1 year, 2021. A Stassen manager who built up an inventory of 4,500 telescopes at the end of 2021 would have to further increase ending inventories in 2022 to increase that year's operating income by producing for inventory. There are limits to how much inventory levels can be increased over time because of physical constraints on storage space and management controls. Such limits reduce the likelihood of incurring some of absorption costing's undesirable effects. Nevertheless, managers do have the ability and incentive to move costs in and out of inventory in order to manage operating income under absorption costing.

Top management can implement checks and balances that limit managers from producing for inventory under absorption costing. However, the practice cannot be completely

EXHIBIT 9-4 Effect on Absorption-Costing Operating Income of Different Production Levels for Stassen Company: Telescope Product-Line Income Statement for 2021 at Sales of 6,500 Units

Home Insert Page Layout Formulas Data Review View

	A	B	C	D	E	F	G	H	I
1	**Unit Data**								
2	Beginning inventory	2,000		2,000		2,000		2,000	
3	Production	4,500		5,000		6,500		9,000	
4	Goods available for sale	6,500		7,000		8,500		11,000	
5	Sales	6,500		6,500		6,500		6,500	
6	Ending inventory	0		500		2,000		4,500	
7									
8	**Income Statement**								
9	Revenues	$6,500,000		$6,500,000		$6,500,000		$6,500,000	
10	Cost of goods sold:								
11	Beginning inventory: $335 × 2,000	670,000		670,000		670,000		670,000	
12	Variable manufacturing costs: $200 × production	900,000		1,000,000		1,300,000		1,800,000	
13	Allocated fixed manufacturing costs: $135 × production	607,500		675,000		877,500		1,215,000	
14	Cost of goods available for sale	2,177,500		2,345,000		2,847,500		3,685,000	
15	Deduct ending inventory: $335 × ending inventory	0		(167,500)		(670,000)		(1,507,500)	
16	Adjustment for production-volume variance[a]	472,500	U	405,000	U	202,500	U	(135,000)	F
17	Cost of goods sold	2,650,000		2,582,500		2,380,000		2,042,500	
18	Gross Margin	3,850,000		3,917,500		4,120,000		4,457,500	
19	Marketing costs: $1,380,000 + ($185 per unit × 6,500 units sold)	2,582,500		2,582,500		2,582,500		2,582,500	
20	Operating Income	$1,267,500		$1,335,000		$1,537,500		$1,875,000	
21									
22	[a]Production-volume variance = Budgeted fixed manufacturing costs − Allocated fixed manufacturing costs (Income Statement, line 13)								
23	At production of 4,500 units: $1,080,000 − $607,500 = $472,500 U								
24	At production of 5,000 units: $1,080,000 − $675,000 = $405,000 U								
25	At production of 6,500 units: $1,080,000 − $877,500 = $202,500 U								
26	At production of 9,000 units: $1,080,000 − $1,215,000 = ($135,000) F								

prevented. There are many subtle ways a manager can produce for inventory that may not be easy to detect. For example, consider the following scenarios:

- A plant manager may switch to manufacturing products that absorb the highest amount of fixed manufacturing costs, regardless of the customer demand for these products (called "cherry-picking" the production line). Delaying the production of items that absorb the least or lower amount of fixed manufacturing costs could lead to failure to meet promised customer delivery dates (which, over time, can result in a loss of customers).
- A plant manager may accept a particular order to increase production, even though another plant in the same company is better suited to handle that order.
- To increase production, a manager may defer maintenance of equipment beyond the current period. Although operating income in this period may increase as a result, future operating income could decrease by a larger amount if repair costs increase and equipment becomes less efficient.

Proposals for Revising Performance Evaluation

Top management, with help from the controller and management accountants, can take several steps to reduce the undesirable incentives of absorption costing:

- Focus on careful budgeting and inventory planning to reduce management's freedom to build up excess inventory. For example, include in the budgeted monthly balance sheets estimates of the dollar amount of inventories. If actual inventories exceed these dollar amounts, top management can investigate the inventory buildups.
- Incorporate a carrying charge for inventory in the internal accounting system. For example, the company could assess an inventory carrying charge of 1% per month on the investment tied up in inventory and for spoilage and obsolescence when it evaluates a manager's performance. An increasing number of companies are beginning to adopt this practice.

- Change the period used to evaluate performance. Critics of absorption costing give examples in which managers take actions that maximize quarterly or annual income at the potential expense of long-run income. When their performance is evaluated over a 3- to 5-year period, managers will be less tempted to produce for inventory.
- Include nonfinancial as well as financial variables in performance evaluation schemes. Examples of nonfinancial measures that can be used to monitor the performance of Stassen's managers in 2021 (see column H of Exhibit 9-4) are as follows:

$$(a)\ \frac{\text{Ending inventory in units in 2021}}{\text{Beginning inventory in units in 2021}} = \frac{4{,}500}{2{,}000} = 2.25$$

$$(b)\ \frac{\text{Units produced in 2021}}{\text{Units sold in 2021}} = \frac{9{,}000}{6{,}500} = 1.38$$

DECISION POINT

Why might managers build up finished-goods inventory if the company uses absorption costing?

Top management would want to see production equal to sales and relatively stable levels of inventory. Companies that manufacture or sell several products could report these two measures for each of the products they manufacture and sell.

Besides the formal performance measurement systems, companies develop codes of conduct to discourage behavior that benefits managers but not the company and to build values and cultures that focus on behaving ethically. We discuss these topics in Chapter 24.

Comparing Inventory Costing Methods

LEARNING OBJECTIVE 4

Differentiate throughput costing

...direct materials costs are inventoried

from variable costing

...variable manufacturing costs are inventoried

and from absorption costing

...variable and fixed manufacturing costs are inventoried

Before we begin our discussion of capacity, we will look at *throughput costing*, a variation of variable costing, and compare the three inventory costing methods.

Throughput Costing

Some managers believe that even variable costing promotes an excessive amount of costs being inventoried. They argue that only direct materials, such as the lenses, casing, scope, and mount in the case of Stassen's telescopes, are "truly variable" in output. **Throughput costing**, which is also called **super-variable costing**, is an extreme form of variable costing in which only direct materials costs are included in inventoriable costs. All other costs are costs of the period in which they are incurred. In particular, variable direct manufacturing labor costs and variable manufacturing overhead costs are regarded as period costs and are deducted as expenses of the period.

Exhibit 9-5 is the throughput-costing income statement for Stassen Company for 2020 and 2021. *Throughput margin* equals revenues minus all direct materials costs of the goods sold. Compare the operating income amounts reported in Exhibit 9-5 with those for absorption costing and variable costing:

	2020	2021
Absorption-costing operating income	$1,500,000	$1,335,000
Variable-costing operating income	$1,230,000	$1,537,500
Throughput-costing operating income	$1,050,000	$1,672,500

Only the $110 direct materials cost per unit is inventoriable under throughput costing, compared with $335 per unit under absorption costing and $200 per unit under variable costing. When the production quantity exceeds sales, as in 2020, throughput costing results in the largest amount of expenses in the current period's income statement. Advocates of throughput costing say it provides managers less incentive to produce for inventory than either variable costing or, especially, absorption costing. Throughput costing is a more recent phenomenon in comparison with variable costing and absorption costing and has avid supporters, but so far it has not been widely adopted.[3]

[3] See E. Goldratt, *The Theory of Constraints* (New York: North River Press, 1990); E. Noreen, D. Smith, and J. Mackey, *The Theory of Constraints and Its Implications for Management Accounting* (New York: North River Press, 1995).

EXHIBIT 9-5

Throughput Costing for Stassen Company: Telescope Product-Line Income Statements for 2020 and 2021

	A	B	C
1		**2020**	**2021**
2	Revenues: $1,000 × 6,000; 6,500 units	$6,000,000	$6,500,000
3	Direct materials cost of goods sold:		
4	Beginning inventory: $110 × 0; 2,000 units	0	220,000
5	Direct materials: $110 × 8,000; 5,000 units	880,000	550,000
6	Cost of goods available for sale	880,000	770,000
7	Deduct ending inventory: $110 × 2,000; 500 units	(220,000)	(55,000)
8	Direct materials cost of goods sold	660,000	715,000
9	Throughput margin[a]	5,340,000	5,785,000
10	Manufacturing costs (other than direct materials)[b]	1,800,000	1,530,000
11	Marketing costs[c]	2,490,000	2,582,500
12	Operating income	$1,050,000	$1,672,500
13			
14	[a]Throughput margin equals revenues minus direct materials cost of goods sold		
15	[b]Fixed manuf. costs + [(variable manuf. labor cost per unit + variable manuf. overhead cost per unit) × units produced]; $1,080,000 + [($40 + $50) × 8,000; 5,000 units]		
16	[c]Fixed marketing costs + (variable marketing cost per unit × units sold); $1,380,000 + ($185 × 6,000; 6,500 units)		

9-3 TRY IT!

Greer Replica produces a specialty statue for sale to collectors. In 2020, Greer's expected and actual output was 17,000 statues. Greer sold 13,600 statues at an average selling price of $330. Other information for Greer for 2020 is given below:

Direct materials	$83 per unit
Variable manufacturing costs	$60 per unit
Fixed manufacturing costs	$64 per unit
Variable administrative costs	$40 per unit

Calculate Greer Replica's cost per statue under (1) absorption costing, (2) variable costing, and (3) throughput costing. What is Greer's throughput margin for 2020?

A Comparison of Alternative Inventory-Costing Methods

Variable costing and absorption costing may be combined with actual, normal, or standard costing. Exhibit 9-6 compares product costing under these six alternative inventory-costing systems.

Variable costing has been controversial among accountants because of how it affects *external reporting*, not because of disagreement about the need to delineate between variable and fixed costs for internal planning and control. Accountants who argue that variable costing should be allowed for external financial reporting maintain that the fixed portion of manufacturing costs is more closely related to the capacity to produce than to the actual production of specific units. Fixed costs should therefore be expensed, not inventoried, they argue.

Accountants who support absorption costing for *external reporting* maintain that inventories should carry a fixed-manufacturing-cost component because both variable manufacturing costs and fixed manufacturing costs are necessary to produce goods. Therefore, both types of costs should be inventoried in order to match all manufacturing costs to revenues, regardless of their different behavior patterns. For external reporting to shareholders, companies around the globe tend to follow the current generally accepted accounting principle (GAAP) that all manufacturing costs, including fixed costs, are inventoriable. This also eases the burden on firms and auditors to attempt to disentangle fixed and variable costs of production, a distinction that is not always clear-cut in practice.

EXHIBIT 9-6 Comparison of Alternative Inventory-Costing Systems

			Actual Costing	Normal Costing	Standard Costing
Absorption Costing	Variable Costing	Variable Direct Manufacturing Costs	Actual prices × Actual quantity of inputs used	Actual prices × Actual quantity of inputs used	Standard prices × Standard quantity of inputs allowed for actual output achieved
Absorption Costing	Variable Costing	Variable Manufacturing Overhead Costs	Actual variable overhead rates × Actual quantity of cost-allocation bases used	Budgeted variable overhead rates × Actual quantity of cost-allocation bases used	Standard variable overhead rates × Standard quantity of cost-allocation bases allowed for actual output achieved
Absorption Costing		Fixed Direct Manufacturing Costs	Actual prices × Actual quantity of inputs used	Actual prices × Actual quantity of inputs used	Standard prices × Standard quantity of inputs allowed for actual output achieved
Absorption Costing		Fixed Manufacturing Overhead Costs	Actual fixed overhead rates × Actual quantity of cost-allocation bases used	Budgeted fixed overhead rates × Actual quantity of cost-allocation bases used	Standard fixed overhead rates × Standard quantity of cost-allocation bases allowed for actual output achieved

DECISION POINT

How does throughput costing differ from variable costing and from absorption costing?

Similarly, for tax reporting in the United States, managers must take direct production costs, as well as fixed and variable indirect production costs, into account in the computation of inventoriable costs in accordance with the "full absorption" method of inventory costing. Indirect production costs include items such as rent, utilities, maintenance, repair expenses, indirect materials, and indirect labor. For other indirect cost categories (including depreciation, insurance, taxes, officers' salaries, factory administrative expenses, and strike-related costs), the portion of the cost that is "incident to and necessary for production or manufacturing operations or processes" is inventoriable for tax purposes *only* if it is treated as inventoriable for the purposes of financial reporting. Accordingly, managers must often allocate costs between those portions related to manufacturing activities and those not related to manufacturing.[4]

Denominator-Level Capacity Concepts and Fixed-Cost Capacity Analysis

LEARNING OBJECTIVE 5

Describe the different capacity concepts that can be used in absorption costing

...supply perspective: theoretical and practical capacity; demand perspective: normal and master-budget capacity utilization

We have seen that the difference between variable and absorption costing arises solely from the treatment of fixed manufacturing costs. Spending on fixed manufacturing costs enables firms to obtain the scale or capacity needed to satisfy the expected market demand from customers. Determining the "right" amount of spending, or the appropriate level of capacity, is one of the most difficult decisions managers face. Having more capacity than is needed to meet market demand means firms will have unused capacity and will incur costs associated with the unused capacity. Having less capacity than is needed to meet market demand means that demand from some customers will be unfilled. These customers may go to other sources of supply and never return. Both managers and accountants must understand these issues related to capacity costs.

We start this section by analyzing a key question in absorption costing: Given a firm's level of spending on fixed manufacturing costs, what capacity level should managers and accountants use to compute the fixed manufacturing cost per unit produced? We then study the broader question of how a firm should decide on its level of capacity investment.

[4] Details regarding tax rules can be found in Section 1.471-11 of the U.S. Internal Revenue Code: Inventories of Manufacturers (see http://ecfr.gpoaccess.gov). Recall from Chapter 2 that costs not related to production, such as marketing, distribution, or research expenses, are treated as period expenses for financial reporting. Under U.S. tax rules, a firm can still consider these costs as inventoriable for tax purposes provided that it does so consistently.

Absorption Costing and Alternative Denominator-Level Capacity Concepts

Earlier chapters, especially Chapters 4, 5, and 8, highlighted how normal and standard costing report costs in an ongoing timely manner throughout a fiscal year. The choice of the capacity level used to allocate budgeted fixed manufacturing costs to products can greatly affect the product-cost information available to managers and the operating income reported under normal or standard costing.

Consider the Stassen Company example again. Recall that the annual fixed manufacturing costs of the production facility are $1,080,000. Stassen currently uses absorption costing with standard costs for external reporting purposes, and calculates its budgeted fixed manufacturing rate on a per unit basis. We will now examine four different capacity levels that could be used as the denominator to compute the budgeted fixed manufacturing cost rate: theoretical capacity, practical capacity, normal capacity utilization, and master-budget capacity utilization.

Theoretical Capacity and Practical Capacity

In business and accounting, capacity ordinarily means a "constraint," or an "upper limit." **Theoretical capacity** is the level of capacity based on producing at full efficiency all the time. Stassen can produce 25 units per shift when the production lines are operating at maximum speed. If we assume 360 days per year, the theoretical annual capacity for 2 shifts per day is as follows:

$$25 \text{ units per shift} \times 2 \text{ shifts per day} \times 360 \text{ days} = 18{,}000 \text{ units}$$

Theoretical capacity is theoretical in the sense that it does not allow for any slowdowns or downtimes due to plant maintenance, shutdown periods, or interruptions on the assembly lines. Theoretical capacity levels are unattainable in the real world, but they represent an idealized aspiration for capacity utilization.

Practical capacity is the level of capacity that is achieved when theoretical capacity is reduced by considering unavoidable production interruptions such as scheduled maintenance time and shutdowns for holidays. Assume that practical capacity is the practical production rate of 20 units per shift (as opposed to 25 units per shift under theoretical capacity) for 2 shifts per day for 300 days a year (as opposed to 360 days a year under theoretical capacity). The practical annual capacity is as follows:

$$20 \text{ units per shift} \times 2 \text{ shifts per day} \times 300 \text{ days} = 12{,}000 \text{ units}$$

Engineering and human resource factors are both important when estimating theoretical or practical capacity. Engineers at the Stassen facility can provide input on the technical capabilities of machines for cutting and polishing lenses. Human resources can evaluate employee safety factors such as increased injury risk when the line operates at faster speeds.

Normal Capacity Utilization and Master-Budget Capacity Utilization

Both theoretical capacity and practical capacity measure capacity levels in terms of what a plant can *supply*—available capacity. In contrast, normal capacity utilization and master-budget capacity utilization measure capacity levels in terms of *demand* for the output of the plant, that is, the amount of capacity the plant expects to use based on the demand for its products. In many cases, budgeted demand is well below production capacity available.

Normal capacity utilization is the level of capacity utilization that satisfies average customer demand over a period (say, 2 to 3 years) that includes seasonal, cyclical, and trend factors. **Master-budget capacity utilization** is the level of capacity utilization that managers expect for the current budget period, which is typically 1 year. These two capacity utilization levels can differ quite significantly in industries that face cyclical demand patterns. For example:

- The automobile industry may expect a period of high demand when interest rates are low or a period of low demand when a recession is forecast.
- Vendors of health care information technology systems may experience a period of high demand when Medicare, the largest payer of health care services in the United States, has increased its payment rates or a period of low demand when reimbursement rates for health care services are cut.

Consider Stassen's master budget for 2020, based on production of 8,000 telescopes per year. Despite using this master-budget capacity utilization level of 8,000 telescopes for 2020, top management believes that over the next 3 years the normal (average) annual production level will be 10,000 telescopes per year. It views 2020's budgeted production level of 8,000 telescopes to be "abnormally" low because a major competitor has been sharply reducing its selling price and spending a lot of money on advertising. Stassen expects that the competitor's lower price and advertising blitz will not be a long-run phenomenon and that, by 2021 and beyond, Stassen's production and sales will increase.

Effect on Budgeted Fixed Manufacturing Cost Rate

We now illustrate how each of these four denominator levels affects the budgeted fixed manufacturing cost rate. Stassen has budgeted (standard) fixed manufacturing overhead costs of $1,080,000 for 2020. This lump sum is incurred to provide the capacity to produce telescopes. The amount includes, among other costs, leasing costs for the facility and the compensation of the facility managers. The budgeted fixed manufacturing cost rates for 2020 for each of the four capacity-level concepts are depicted in column (4) below:

	A	B	C	D	E	F
1		Budgeted Fixed	Budgeted	Budgeted Fixed	Budgeted Variable	Budgeted Total
2	Denominator-Level	Manufacturing	Capacity Level	Manufacturing	Manufacturing	Manufacturing
3	Capacity Concept	Costs per Year	(in units)	Cost per Unit	Cost per Unit	Cost per Unit
4	(1)	(2)	(3)	(4) = (2)/(3)	(5)	(6) = (4) + (5)
5	Theoretical capacity	$1,080,000	18,000	$ 60	$200	$260
6	Practical capacity	$1,080,000	12,000	$ 90	$200	$290
7	Normal capacity utilization	$1,080,000	10,000	$108	$200	$308
8	Master-budget capacity utilization	$1,080,000	8,000	$135	$200	$335

The significant difference in cost rates in column (4) (from $60 to $135) arises because of large differences in budgeted capacity levels under the different capacity concepts.

Budgeted (standard) variable manufacturing costs, in column (5), are constant at $200 per unit, leading to the total budgeted (standard) manufacturing cost per unit for alternative capacity-level concepts in column (6).

Because different denominator-level capacity concepts yield different budgeted manufacturing costs per unit, Stassen must decide which capacity level to use. Stassen is not required to use the same capacity-level concept, say, for management planning and control, external reporting to shareholders, and income tax purposes.

DECISION POINT

What are the different capacity levels a company can use to compute the budgeted fixed manufacturing cost rate?

TRY IT! 9-4

Allbirds can produce 900 pairs of sneakers per hour at maximum efficiency. There are two 12-hour shifts each day. Due to unavoidable operating interruptions, production averages 500 units per hour. The plant actually operates only 26 days per month. Based on the current month's budget, Allbirds estimates that it will be able to sell only 306,000 units due to the entry of a competitor with high personalization capabilities. But demand is unlikely to be affected in the future and will average around 311,000 units each month.

Assuming 30 days per month, calculate Allbirds' monthly (1) theoretical capacity, (2) practical capacity, (3) normal capacity utilization, and (4) master-budget capacity utilization.

Choosing a Capacity Level

At the start of each fiscal year, managers must determine the budgeted fixed manufacturing cost rates to be used for different purposes, including (1) product costing and capacity management, (2) pricing decisions, (3) performance evaluation, (4) financial reporting, and (5) tax requirements. We now discuss how to choose among the different denominator levels related to the various capacity concepts.

LEARNING OBJECTIVE 6

Examine the key factors managers use to choose a capacity level to compute the budgeted fixed manufacturing cost rate

...managers must consider the effect a capacity level has on product costing, pricing decisions, performance evaluation, and financial and tax statements

Product Costing and Capacity Management

As the Stassen example illustrates, use of theoretical capacity results in an unrealistically small fixed manufacturing cost per unit because it is based on an idealistic and unattainable level of capacity utilization. Theoretical capacity is rarely used to calculate budgeted fixed manufacturing cost per unit because it departs significantly from the capacity that is effectively available to a company.

Instead, many companies favor practical capacity as the denominator to calculate the budgeted fixed manufacturing cost per unit. Practical capacity in the Stassen example represents the maximum number of units (12,000) that Stassen can reasonably expect to produce per year for the \$1,080,000 it will spend annually on capacity. If Stassen had consistently planned to produce fewer units, say 6,000 telescopes each year, it would have built a smaller plant and incurred lower fixed manufacturing costs.

Stassen budgets \$90 in fixed manufacturing cost per unit based on the \$1,080,000 it costs to acquire the capacity to produce 12,000 units. This level of plant capacity is an important strategic decision that managers make well before Stassen uses the capacity and even before Stassen knows how much of the capacity it will actually use. That is, the budgeted fixed manufacturing cost of \$90 per unit measures the *cost per unit of supplying the capacity*.

Demand for Stassen's telescopes in 2020 is expected to be 8,000 units, which is 4,000 units lower than the practical capacity of 12,000 units. However, it costs Stassen \$1,080,000 per year to acquire the capacity to make 12,000 units, so the cost of *supplying* the capacity needed to make 12,000 units is still \$90 per unit. The capacity and its cost are fixed *in the short run*; unlike variable costs, the capacity supplied does not automatically reduce to match the capacity needed in 2020. As a result, not all of the capacity supplied at \$90 per unit will be needed or used in 2020. Using practical capacity as the denominator level, managers can subdivide the cost of resources supplied into used and unused components. At the supply cost of \$90 per unit, the manufacturing resources that Stassen will use equal \$720,000 (\$90 per unit × 8,000 units). Manufacturing resources that Stassen will not use are \$360,000 [\$90 per unit × (12,000 − 8,000) units].

Using practical capacity as the denominator level sets the cost of capacity at the cost of supplying the capacity, regardless of the demand for the capacity. Highlighting the cost of capacity acquired but not used directs managers' attention toward managing unused capacity, perhaps by designing new products to fill unused capacity, by leasing unused capacity to others, or by eliminating unused capacity. In contrast, using either of the capacity levels based on the demand for Stassen's telescopes—master-budget capacity utilization or normal capacity utilization—hides the amount of unused capacity. For example, if Stassen had used master-budget capacity utilization as the capacity level, it would have calculated budgeted fixed manufacturing cost per unit as \$135 (\$1,080,000 ÷ 8,000 units). This calculation does not use data about practical capacity, so it does not separately identify the cost of unused capacity. Note, however, that the cost of \$135 per unit includes a charge for unused capacity: It is composed of the \$90 fixed manufacturing resource that would be used to produce each unit at the practical capacity utilization level of 12,000 units plus the cost of unused capacity allocated to each unit, \$45 per unit (\$360,000 ÷ 8,000 units).

From the perspective of long-run product costing, which cost of capacity should Stassen use for pricing purposes and for benchmarking its product cost structure against competitors: \$90 per unit based on practical capacity or \$135 per unit based on master-budget capacity utilization? Probably the \$90 per unit based on practical capacity. Why? Because \$90 per unit represents the budgeted cost per unit of only the capacity used to produce the product, and it explicitly excludes the cost of any unused capacity. Stassen's customers will be willing to pay a price that covers the cost of the capacity actually used but will not want to pay for unused capacity that provides no benefits to them. Customers expect Stassen to manage its unused capacity or to bear the cost of unused capacity, not pass it along to them. Moreover, if Stassen's competitors manage unused capacity more effectively, the cost of capacity in the competitors' cost structures (which guides competitors' pricing decisions) is likely to approach $90. In the next section, we illustrate how using normal capacity utilization or master-budget capacity utilization can result in managers setting selling prices that are not competitive.

Pricing Decisions and the Downward Demand Spiral

The **downward demand spiral** for a company is the continuing reduction in the demand for its products that occurs when competitor prices are not met; as demand drops further, higher and higher unit costs produced by costing systems based on normal and master-budget capacity utilization result in greater reluctance to meet competitors' prices.

The easiest way to understand the downward demand spiral is with an example. Assume Stassen uses master-budget capacity utilization of 8,000 units for product costing in 2020. The resulting manufacturing cost is $335 per unit ($200 variable manufacturing cost per unit + $135 fixed manufacturing cost per unit). Assume that in December 2019, a competitor offers to supply a major customer of Stassen (a customer who was expected to purchase 2,000 units in 2020) telescopes at $300 per unit. The Stassen manager doesn't want to show a loss on the account and wants to recoup all costs in the long run, so the manager declines to match the competitor's price. The account is lost. The loss of the customer means budgeted fixed manufacturing costs of $1,080,000 will now be spread over the remaining master-budget volume of 6,000 units at a rate of $180 per unit ($1,080,000 ÷ 6,000 units).

Suppose yet another Stassen customer, who also accounts for 2,000 units of budgeted volume, receives a bid from a competitor at a price of $350 per unit. The Stassen manager compares this bid with his revised unit cost of $380 ($200 + $180) and declines to match the competition, and the account is lost. Planned output would shrink further to 4,000 units. Budgeted fixed manufacturing cost per unit for the remaining 4,000 telescopes would now be $270 ($1,080,000 ÷ 4,000 units). The following table shows the effect of spreading fixed manufacturing costs over a shrinking level of master-budget capacity utilization:

	A	B	C	D
1	Master-Budget		Budgeted Fixed	
2	Capacity Utilization	Budgeted Variable	Manufacturing	Budgeted Total
3	Denominator Level	Manufacturing Cost	Cost per Unit	Manufacturing
4	(Units)	per Unit	[$1,080,000 ÷ (1)]	Cost per Unit
5	(1)	(2)	(3)	(4) = (2) + (3)
6	8,000	$200	$135	$335
7	6,000	$200	$180	$380
8	4,000	$200	$270	$470
9	3,000	$200	$360	$560

Practical capacity, by contrast, is a stable measure. The use of practical capacity as the denominator to calculate budgeted fixed manufacturing cost per unit avoids the recalculation of unit costs when expected demand levels change because the fixed cost rate is calculated based on *capacity available* rather than *capacity used to meet demand*. Managers who use reported unit costs in a mechanical way to set prices are less likely to promote a downward demand spiral when they use practical capacity than when they use normal capacity utilization or master-budget capacity utilization.

Using practical capacity as the denominator level also gives the manager a more accurate idea of the resources needed and used to produce a unit when the cost of unused capacity is excluded. As discussed earlier, the cost of manufacturing resources supplied to produce a telescope is $290 ($200 variable manufacturing cost per unit plus $90 fixed manufacturing cost per unit). This cost is lower than the prices Stassen's competitors offer and would have correctly led the manager to match the prices and retain the accounts (assuming for purposes of this discussion that Stassen has no other costs). If, however, the prices competitors offered were lower than $290 per unit, the Stassen manager would not recover the cost of resources used to supply telescopes. This would signal to the manager that Stassen was noncompetitive even if it had no unused capacity. The only way for Stassen to be profitable and retain customers in the long run would be to reduce its manufacturing cost per unit.

The downward demand spiral is currently at work in the traditional landline phone industry. As more telephone customers shift services to wireless or Internet-based options, Verizon and AT&T, the two largest telephone service providers in the United States, are reducing their focus on providing copper-wire telephone service to homes and business. As AT&T told the U.S. Federal Communications Commission, "The business model for legacy phone services is in a death spiral." Concepts in Action: Can ESPN Avoid the Cord-Cutting "Death Spiral"? illustrates a similar phenomenon affecting cable networks.

CONCEPTS IN ACTION

Can ESPN Avoid the Cord-Cutting "Death Spiral"?[5]

Web Pix/Alamy Stock Photo

For years, ESPN has dominated the sports-broadcasting airwaves in the United States and around the world. Consisting of eight cable-television networks, a website, a magazine, and various international operations, ESPN is an $8 billion business unit within The Walt Disney Company. As recently as 2015, ESPN contributed about half of all revenue to Disney's media networks business, the company's biggest segment, and had operating margins of 40%, good for a $4.4 billion profit.

But the game has changed for ESPN. From 2012 to 2018 ESPN lost more than 16 million subscribers. With new entertainment options from Netflix, Hulu, Amazon Prime, and others, many television viewers are cancelling their costly cable subscriptions (people known as "cord cutters") or never signing up for cable to begin with ("cord nevers"). With subscriber fees to ESPN's networks costing around $8 per month, cord cutting cost ESPN more than $1.5 billion in 2018 revenue at a time when its fixed costs are rising. Since 2013, the fees paid by ESPN to sports leagues to carry live events have more than doubled to $4.7 billion annually. In 2015, ESPN signed a new deal with the NBA that will cost the network $1.4 billion per year over 9 years to show live professional basketball games. In 2018, ESPN inked a similar deal with the Ultimate Fighting Championship to pay $300 million per year for 5 years for broadcast and streaming rights.

Some observers have wondered whether cord cutting will lead to a downward demand spiral for ESPN and other cable networks, better known as a "death spiral." Under this scenario, a further reduction in subscribers would force ESPN to raise its subscription rates to make up for the lost revenue to cover its high fixed costs. The higher unit costs, in turn, would encourage even more subscribers to cut the cord, further slashing revenues and making ESPN's model unsustainable.

As a result, ESPN managers have taken aggressive action to reduce its costs where possible. From 2015 to 2017, ESPN laid off more than 450 on-air and behind-the-scenes employees. The company is also pursuing new revenue opportunities, including its new ESPN+ streaming service. For $4.99 per month, subscribers get access to thousands of Major League Baseball, National Hockey League, Major League Soccer, and Professional Golf Association events, as well as popular international sports, including soccer, cricket, and rugby. While many sports fans are still tuning in, will enough of them pay for ESPN in the years ahead to ensure it avoids a "death spiral"? That remains to be seen.

---

[5] *Sources:* Jeremy Bowman, "Don't Expect ESPN to Cut the Cord Anytime Soon," *The Motley Fool*, January 24, 2016 (https://www.fool.com/investing/general/2016/01/24/dont-expect-espn-to-cut-the-cord-anytime-soon.aspx); Kevin Draper, "ESPN Is Laying Off 150 More Employees," *The New York Times*, November 29, 2017 (https://www.nytimes.com/2017/11/29/sports/espn-layoffs.html); Todd Spangle, "ESPN+ Launches With a Ton of Live Sports – and Limited Ads," *Variety*, April 12, 2018 (https://variety.com/2018/digital/news/espn-plus-subscription-sports-streaming-limited-ads-1202751319/); Trefis Team, "With Subscriber Declines Continuing, How Much is ESPN Worth?" Forbes.com, March 15, 2018 (https://www.forbes.com/sites/greatspeculations/2018/03/15/with-subscriber-declines-continuing-how-much-is-espn-worth/); Shalini Ramachandran, "Adding to ESPN's Struggles: Politics," *The Wall Street Journal*, May 25, 2018 (https://www.wsj.com/articles/how-a-weakened-espn-became-consumed-by-politics-1527176425); Cynthia Littleton, "ESPN Loses 2 Million Subscribers in Fiscal 2018," *Variety*, November 21, 2018 (https://variety.com/2018/biz/news/espn-disney-channel-subscriber-losses-2018-1203035003/).

Performance Evaluation

Consider how the choice among normal capacity utilization, master-budget capacity utilization, and practical capacity affects how a company evaluates its marketing manager. Normal capacity utilization is often used as a basis for long-run plans. Normal capacity utilization depends on the time span selected and the forecasts made for each year. *However, normal capacity utilization is an average that provides no meaningful feedback to the marketing manager for a particular year.* Using normal capacity utilization to judge current performance of a marketing manager is an example of a company misusing a long-run measure for a short-run purpose. The company should use master-budget capacity utilization, rather than normal capacity utilization or practical capacity, to evaluate a marketing manager's performance in the current year because the master budget is the principal short-run planning and control tool. Managers feel more obligated to reach the levels specified in the master budget, which the company should have carefully set in relation to the maximum opportunities for sales in the current year.

When large differences exist between practical capacity and master-budget capacity utilization, several companies (such as Texas Instruments, Polysar, and Sandoz) classify the difference as *planned unused capacity*. One reason for this approach is performance evaluation. Consider our Stassen telescope example. The managers in charge of capacity planning usually do not make pricing decisions. Top management decided to build a production facility with 12,000 units of practical capacity, focusing on demand over the next 5 years. But Stassen's marketing managers, who are mid-level managers, make the pricing decisions. These marketing managers believe they should be held accountable only for the manufacturing overhead costs related to their potential customer base in 2020. The master-budget capacity utilization suggests a potential customer base in 2020 of 8,000 units (2/3 of the 12,000 practical capacity). Using responsibility accounting principles (see Chapter 6, pages 213–216), only 2/3 of the budgeted total fixed manufacturing costs ($1,080,000 × 2/3) would be attributed to the fixed capacity costs of meeting 2020 demand. The remaining 1/3 of the numerator ($1,080,000 × 1/3 = $360,000) would be separately shown as the capacity cost related to increases in long-run demand expected to occur beyond 2020.[6]

Financial Reporting

The magnitude of the favorable/unfavorable production-volume variance under absorption costing is affected by the choice of the denominator level used to calculate the budgeted fixed manufacturing cost per unit. Assume the following actual operating information for Stassen in 2020:

	A	B	C
1	Beginning inventory	0	
2	Production	8,000	units
3	Sales	6,000	units
4	Ending inventory	2,000	units
5	Selling price	$ 1,000	per unit
6	Variable manufacturing cost	$ 200	per unit
7	Fixed manufacturing costs	$ 1,080,000	
8	Variable marketing cost	$ 185	per unit sold
9	Fixed marketing costs	$ 1,380,000	

Note that this is the same data used to calculate the income under variable and absorption costing for Stassen in Exhibit 9-1. As before, we assume that there are no price, spending, or efficiency variances in manufacturing costs.

[6] For further discussion, see T. Klammer, *Capacity Measurement and Improvement* (Chicago: Irwin, 1996). This research was facilitated by CAM-I, an organization promoting innovative cost management practices. CAM-I's research on capacity costs explores how companies can identify types of capacity costs that can be reduced (or eliminated) without affecting the required output to meet customer demand. An example is improving processes to successfully eliminate the costs of capacity held in anticipation of handling difficulties due to imperfect coordination with suppliers and customers.

Recall from Chapter 8 the equation used to calculate the production-volume variance:

$$\text{Production-volume variance} = \begin{pmatrix}\text{Budgeted}\\ \text{fixed}\\ \text{manufacturing}\\ \text{overhead}\end{pmatrix} - \begin{pmatrix}\text{Fixed manufacturing overhead allocated using}\\ \text{budgeted cost per output unit}\\ \text{allowed for actual output produced}\end{pmatrix}$$

The four different capacity-level concepts result in four different budgeted fixed manufacturing overhead cost rates. The different rates will result in different amounts of fixed manufacturing overhead costs allocated to the 8,000 units actually produced and in different production-volume variances. Using the budgeted fixed manufacturing costs of $1,080,000 (equal to actual fixed manufacturing costs) and the rates calculated on page 338 for different denominator levels, the production-volume variance computations are as follows:

Production-volume variance (theoretical capacity)	= $1,080,000 − (8,000 units × $60 per unit)
	= $1,080,000 − 480,000
	= $600,000 U
Production-volume variance (practical capacity)	= $1,080,000 − (8,000 units × $90 per unit)
	= $1,080,000 − 720,000
	= $360,000 U
Production-volume variance (normal capacity utilization)	= $1,080,00 − (8,000 units × $108 per unit)
	= $1,080,000 − 864,000
	= $216,000 U
Production-volume variance (master-budget capacity utilization)	= $1,080,000 − (8,000 units × $135 per unit)
	= $1,080,000 − 1,080,000
	= $0

How Stassen treats its production-volume variance at the end of the fiscal year will determine the effect this variance has on the company's operating income. We now discuss the three alternative approaches Stassen can use to treat the production-volume variance. These approaches were first discussed in Chapter 4 (pages 126–130).

1. **Adjusted allocation-rate approach.** This approach restates all amounts in the general and subsidiary ledgers using recalculated actual cost rates. Given that actual fixed manufacturing costs are $1,080,000 and actual production is 8,000 units, the recalculated fixed manufacturing cost is $135 per unit ($1,080,000 ÷ 8,000 actual units). Under the adjusted allocation-rate approach, the choice of the capacity level used to calculate the budgeted fixed manufacturing cost per unit has no impact on year-end financial statements. In effect, actual costing is adopted at the end of the fiscal year.
2. **Proration approach.** This approach spreads the under- or overallocated overhead among ending balances in Work-in-Process Control, Finished Goods Control, and Cost of Goods Sold. The proration restates the ending balances in these accounts to what they would have been if actual cost rates had been used rather than budgeted cost rates. Under this approach, the choice of the capacity level used to calculate the budgeted fixed manufacturing cost per unit also has no effect on the year-end financial statements.
3. **Write-off variances to cost of goods sold approach.** Exhibit 9-7 shows how this approach affects Stassen's operating income for 2020. Recall that the ending inventory on December 31, 2020, is 2,000 units. Using master-budget capacity utilization as the denominator level results in assigning the highest amount of fixed manufacturing cost per unit to the 2,000 units in ending inventory (see the line item "deduct ending inventory" in Exhibit 9-7). Accordingly, operating income is highest using master-budget capacity utilization. The differences in operating income for the four denominator-level concepts in Exhibit 9-7 are

due to the different amounts of fixed manufacturing overhead being inventoried at the end of 2020:

Fixed Manufacturing Overhead in December 31, 2020, Inventory		
Theoretical capacity	2,000 units × $60 per unit	= $120,000
Practical capacity	2,000 units × $90 per unit	= $180,000
Normal capacity utilization	2,000 units × $108 per unit	= $216,000
Master-budget capacity utilization	2,000 units × $135 per unit	= $270,000

In Exhibit 9-7, for example, the $54,000 difference ($1,500,000 − $1,446,000) in operating income between master-budget capacity utilization and normal capacity utilization is due to the difference in fixed manufacturing overhead inventoried ($270,000 − $216,000).

To summarize, the common factor behind the increasing operating-income numbers in the columns from left to right in Exhibit 9-4 (page 333) and Exhibit 9-7 is the increasing amount of fixed manufacturing costs incurred that is included in ending inventory. The amount of fixed manufacturing costs inventoried depends on two factors: the number of units in ending inventory and the rate at which fixed manufacturing costs are allocated to each unit. Exhibit 9-4 shows the effect on operating income of increasing the number of units in ending inventory (by increasing production). Exhibit 9-7 shows the effect on operating income of increasing the fixed manufacturing cost allocated per unit (by decreasing the denominator level used to calculate the rate).

EXHIBIT 9-7 Income-Statement Effects of Using Alternative Capacity-Level Concepts: Stassen Company for 2020

Home Insert Page Layout Formulas Data Review View

	A	B	C	D	E	F	G	H	I
1		Theoretical Capacity		Practical Capacity		Normal Capacity Utilization		Master-Budget Capacity Utilization	
2	Denominator level in units	18,000		12,000		10,000		8,000	
3	Revenues[a]	$6,000,000		$6,000,000		$6,000,000		$6,000,000	
4	Cost of goods sold:								
5	Beginning inventory	0		0		0		0	
6	Variable manufacturing costs[b]	1,600,000		1,600,000		1,600,000		1,600,000	
7	Fixed manufacturing costs[c]	480,000		720,000		864,000		1,080,000	
8	Cost of goods available for sale	2,080,000		2,320,000		2,464,000		2,680,000	
9	Deduct ending inventory[d]	(520,000)		(580,000)		(616,000)		(670,000)	
10	Cost of goods sold (at standard cost)	1,560,000		1,740,000		1,848,000		2,010,000	
11	Adjustment for production-volume variance	600,000	U	360,000	U	216,000	U	0	
12	Cost of goods sold	2,160,000		2,100,000		2,064,000		2,010,000	
13	Gross margin	3,840,000		3,900,000		3,936,000		3,990,000	
14	Marketing costs[e]	2,490,000		2,490,000		2,490,000		2,490,000	
15	Operating income	$1,350,000		$1,410,000		$1,446,000		$1,500,000	
16									
17	[a]$1,000 × 6,000 units = $6,000,000			[d]Ending inventory costs:					
18	[b]$200 × 8,000 units = $1,600,000			($200 + $60) × 2,000 units = $520,000					
19	[c]Fixed manufacturing overhead costs:			($200 + $90) × 2,000 units = $580,000					
20	$60 × 8,000 units = $ 480,000			($200 + $108) × 2,000 units = $616,000					
21	$90 × 8,000 units = $ 720,000			($200 + $135) × 2,000 units = $670,000					
22	$108 × 8,000 units = $ 864,000			[e]Marketing costs:					
23	$135 × 8,000 units = $1,080,000			$1,380,000 + ($185 × 6,000 units) = $2,490,000					

Chapter 8 (pages 294–295) discusses the various issues managers and management accountants must consider when deciding whether to prorate the production-volume variance among inventories and cost of goods sold or to simply write off the variance to cost of goods sold. The objective is to write off the portion of the production-volume variance that represents the cost of capacity not used to support the production of output during the period. Determining this amount is almost always a matter of judgment.

For financial reporting, SFAS 151 provides greater clarity by requiring that the allocation of fixed manufacturing overheads to production be based on the normal capacity of the facilities. In this case, normal capacity refers to a *range* of production levels expected to be achieved over a number of periods or seasons under normal circumstances. With abnormally high production, fixed overhead allocated to each unit produced is decreased so that inventories are not measured above cost. When production is below the range of expected variation in output, the unallocated fixed overhead costs are recognized as an expense in the period in which they are incurred. The provisions of SFAS 151 need not be applied to immaterial items. Moreover, the rule does not require disclosure of the dollar amount of any adjustment necessary for compliance, that is, the amount of fixed overhead costs associated with unused productive capacity that is currently expensed to cost of goods sold, rather than included in the ending work-in-process and finished-goods inventories.

Tax Requirements

For tax reporting purposes in the United States, the Internal Revenue Service (IRS) requires companies to assign inventoriable indirect production costs by a "method of allocation which fairly apportions such costs among the various items produced." The IRS accepts approaches that involve the use of either overhead rates (which the IRS terms the "manufacturing burden rate method") or standard costs. Under either approach, U.S. tax reporting requires end-of-period reconciliation between actual and applied indirect costs using the adjusted allocation-rate method or the proration method.[7] More interestingly, under either approach, the IRS permits the use of practical capacity to calculate budgeted fixed manufacturing cost per unit. Further, the production-volume variance generated this way can be deducted for tax purposes in the year in which the cost is incurred. The tax benefits from this policy are evident from Exhibit 9-7. Note that the operating income when the denominator is set to practical capacity (column D, where the production volume variance of $360,000 is written off to cost of goods sold) is lower than those under normal capacity utilization (column F) or master-budget capacity utilization (column H).

DECISION POINT

What are the major factors managers consider in choosing the capacity level to compute the budgeted fixed manufacturing cost rate?

Planning and Control of Capacity Costs

LEARNING OBJECTIVE 7

Understand issues that play an important role in capacity planning and control

. . . uncertainty regarding the expected spending on capacity costs and the demand for installed capacity, the role of capacity-related issues in nonmanufacturing areas, and the possible use of activity-based costing techniques in allocating capacity costs

In addition to the accounting-related issues previously discussed in this chapter, managers must take a variety of other factors into account when planning capacity levels and in deciding how best to control and assign capacity costs. These factors include the level of uncertainty about both the expected costs and the expected demand for the installed capacity, the presence of capacity-related issues in the nonmanufacturing parts of the value chain, and the potential use of activity-based costing techniques in allocating capacity costs.

Difficulties in Forecasting Chosen Capacity Levels

Practical capacity measures the available supply of capacity. Managers can usually use engineering studies and human resource considerations (such as worker safety) to obtain a reliable estimate of this denominator level for the budget period.

[7] For example, Section 1.471-11 of the U.S. Internal Revenue Code states, "The proper use of the standard cost method . . . requires that a taxpayer must reallocate to the goods in ending inventory a pro rata portion of any net negative or net positive overhead variances." Of course, variances that are not material in amount can be expensed (i.e., written off to cost of goods sold), provided the same treatment is carried out in the firm's financial reports.

It is more difficult to obtain reliable estimates of demand-side denominator levels, especially longer-term normal capacity utilization figures. For example, many U.S. steel companies in the 1980s believed they were in the downturn of a demand cycle that would be followed by an upturn within 2 or 3 years. After all, steel had been a cyclical business in which upturns followed downturns, making the notion of normal capacity utilization appear reasonable. Unfortunately, the steel demand cycle did not turn up in the 1980s, resulting in numerous plants and some companies closing.

The recent global economic issues, including tensions in the trading relationship between the U.S. and China, demonstrate the extent to which demand projections can be inaccurate. Consider that Apple Inc. in January 2019 revised its forecast for first-quarter revenue for fiscal year 2019 down to $84 billion from $91.5 billion forecast just 2 months earlier. Similarly, citing growing international trade worries, Marriot International in November 2018 revised its growth forecast for revenue per available room for the fourth quarter of fiscal year 2018 down to 2% from the previous estimate of 2.5–3% made earlier in 2018.

In addition to dealing with economic cycles and inaccurate forecasts, companies also face the problem of marketing managers who may overestimate their ability to regain lost sales and market share. Their estimate of "normal" demand for their product may consequently be based on an overly optimistic outlook. Master-budget capacity utilization focuses only on the expected demand for the next year. Therefore, companies can more reliably estimate master-budget capacity utilization than normal capacity utilization. However, master-budget capacity utilization is still just a forecast, and the true demand realization could be either higher or lower than this estimate.

It is important to understand that costing systems, such as normal costing or standard costing, do not recognize uncertainty the way managers recognize it. A single amount, rather than a range of possible amounts, is used as the denominator level when calculating the budgeted fixed manufacturing cost per unit in absorption costing. Consider Stassen's facility, which has an estimated practical capacity of 12,000 units. The estimated master-budget capacity utilization for 2020 is 8,000 units. However, there is still substantial doubt about the actual number of units Stassen will have to manufacture in 2020 and in future years. In contrast, managers do recognize uncertainty in their capacity-planning decisions. Stassen built its current plant with a 12,000-unit practical capacity in part to provide the capability to meet possible demand surges. Even if such surges do not occur in a given period, do not conclude that unused capacity in a given period is necessarily a wasted resource. The gains from meeting sudden demand surges may well outweigh the costs of having unused capacity in some periods.

Difficulties in Forecasting Fixed Manufacturing Costs

The fixed manufacturing cost rate is based on a numerator (budgeted fixed manufacturing costs) and a denominator (some measure of capacity or capacity utilization). Our discussion so far has emphasized issues concerning the choice of the denominator. Challenging issues also arise in measuring the numerator. For example, the move toward renewable energy has resulted in many conventional energy companies becoming unprofitable and having to write-down the value of assets such as their power plants. The write-downs reduce the numerator because there is less depreciation expense included in the calculation of fixed capacity cost per kilowatt-hour of electricity produced. The difficulty that managers face in this situation is that the amount of write-downs is not clear-cut but, rather, a matter of judgment. On the other hand, infrastructure costs for information technology have continued to plummet and have moved from fixed to variable costs in many cases because of the cloud capabilities offered by providers such as Amazon Web Services.

Nonmanufacturing Costs

Capacity costs also arise in nonmanufacturing parts of the value chain. Stassen may acquire a fleet of vehicles capable of distributing the practical capacity of its production facility. When actual production is below practical capacity, there will be unused-capacity costs related to the distribution function, as well as unused-capacity costs related to the manufacturing function.

As you saw in Chapter 8, capacity cost issues are prominent in many service-sector companies—such as airlines, hospitals, and railroads—even though these companies carry no inventory and so have no inventory costing problems. For example, in calculating the fixed overhead cost per patient-day in its obstetrics and gynecology department, a hospital must decide which denominator level to use: practical capacity, normal capacity utilization, or master-budget capacity utilization. The hospital's decision may have implications for capacity management as well as pricing and performance evaluation.

Activity-Based Costing

To maintain simplicity, the Stassen example in this chapter assumed that all costs were either variable or fixed. In particular, there were no batch-level costs and no product-sustaining costs. It is easy to see that the distinction between variable and absorption costing carries over directly into activity-based costing systems, with batch-level costs acting as variable costs and product-sustaining ones as fixed costs.

In order to focus on the choice of denominator to calculate the budgeted fixed manufacturing cost rate, our Stassen example assumed that all fixed manufacturing costs had a single cost driver: telescope units produced. As you saw in Chapter 5, activity-based costing systems have multiple overhead cost pools at the output-unit, batch, product-sustaining, and facility-sustaining levels—each with its own cost driver. In calculating activity cost rates (for fixed costs of setups and material handling, say), management must choose a capacity level for the quantity of the cost driver (such as setup-hours or loads moved). Should management use practical capacity, normal capacity utilization, or master-budget capacity utilization? For all the reasons described in this chapter (such as pricing and capacity management), most proponents of activity-based costing argue that managers should use practical capacity as the denominator level to calculate activity cost rates.

DECISION POINT

What issues must managers take into account when planning capacity levels and when assigning capacity costs?

PROBLEM FOR SELF-STUDY

Assume Stassen Company on January 1, 2020, decides to contract with another company to preassemble a large percentage of the components of its telescopes. The revised manufacturing cost structure for Stassen during the 2020–2021 period is as follows:

Variable manufacturing cost per unit produced:	
Direct materials	$ 250
Direct manufacturing labor	20
Manufacturing overhead	5
Total variable manufacturing cost per unit produced	$ 275
Fixed manufacturing costs	$480,000

Under the revised cost structure, a larger percentage of Stassen's manufacturing costs are variable for units produced. The denominator level of production used to calculate budgeted fixed manufacturing cost per unit in 2020 and 2021 is 8,000 units. Assume no other change from the data underlying Exhibits 9-1 and 9-2. Summary information pertaining to absorption-costing operating income and variable-costing operating income with this revised cost structure are as follows:

	2020	2021
Absorption-costing operating income	$1,500,000	$1,560,000
Variable-costing operating income	1,380,000	1,650,000
Difference	$ 120,000	$ (90,000)

Required

1. Compute the budgeted fixed manufacturing cost per unit in 2020 and 2021.
2. Explain the difference between absorption-costing operating income and variable-costing operating income in 2020 and 2021, focusing on fixed manufacturing costs in beginning and ending inventory.
3. Why are these differences smaller than the differences in Exhibit 9-2?

4. Assume the same preceding information, except that for 2020, the master-budget capacity utilization is 10,000 units instead of 8,000. How would Stassen's absorption-costing income for 2020 differ from the $1,500,000 shown previously? Show your computations.

Solution

1. $$\text{Budgeted fixed manufacturing cost per unit} = \frac{\text{Budgeted fixed manufacturing cost}}{\text{Budgeted production units}}$$

$$= \frac{\$480{,}000}{8{,}000 \text{ units}}$$

$$= \$60 \text{ per unit}$$

2. $$\text{Absorption-costing operating income} - \text{Variable-costing operating income} = \text{Fixed manufacturing costs in ending inventory under absorption costing} - \text{Fixed manufacturing costs in beginning inventor under absorption costing}$$

2020: $1,500,000 − $1,380,000 = ($60 per unit × 2,000 units) − ($60 per unit × 0 units)
$120,000 = $120,000

2021: $1,560,000 − $1,650,000 = ($60 per unit × 500 units) − ($60 per unit × 2,000 units)
−$90,000 = −$90,000

3. Subcontracting a large part of manufacturing has greatly reduced the magnitude of fixed manufacturing costs. This reduction, in turn, means differences between absorption costing and variable costing are much smaller than in Exhibit 9-2.
4. Given the higher master-budget capacity utilization level of 10,000 units, the budgeted fixed manufacturing cost rate for 2020 is now as follows:

$$\frac{\$480{,}000}{10{,}000 \text{ units}} = \$48 \text{ per unit}$$

The manufacturing cost per unit is $323 ($275 + $48). So, the production-volume variance for 2020 is

$$(10{,}000 \text{ units} - 8{,}000 \text{ units}) \times \$48 \text{ per unit} = \$96{,}000 \text{ U}$$

The absorption-costing income statement for 2020 is as follows:

Revenues: $1,000 per unit × 6,000 units	$6,000,000
Cost of goods sold:	
Beginning inventory	0
Variable manufacturing costs: $275 per unit × 8,000 units	2,200,000
Fixed manufacturing costs: $48 per unit × 8,000 units	384,000
Cost of goods available for sale	2,584,000
Deduct ending inventory: $323 per unit × 2,000 units	(646,000)
Cost of goods sold (at standard costs)	1,938,000
Adjustment for production-volume variance	96,000 U
Cost of goods sold	2,034,000
Gross margin	3,966,000
Marketing costs: $1,380,000 fixed + ($185 per unit × 6,000 units sold)	2,490,000
Operating income	$1,476,000

The higher denominator level used to calculate the budgeted fixed manufacturing cost per unit means that fewer fixed manufacturing costs are inventoried ($48 per unit × 2,000 units = $96,000) than when the master-budget capacity utilization was 8,000 units ($60 per unit × 2,000 units = $120,000). This difference of $24,000 ($120,000 − $96,000) results in operating income being lower by $24,000 relative to the prior calculated income level of $1,500,000.

DECISION POINTS

The following question-and-answer format summarizes the chapter's learning objectives. Each decision presents a key question related to a learning objective. The guidelines are the answer to that question.

Decision	Guidelines
1. How does variable costing differ from absorption costing?	Variable costing and absorption costing differ in only one respect: how to account for fixed manufacturing costs. Under variable costing, fixed manufacturing costs are excluded from inventoriable costs and are a cost of the period in which they are incurred. Under absorption costing, fixed manufacturing costs are inventoriable and become a part of cost of goods sold in the period when sales occur.
2. How does operating income differ under variable and absorption costing?	The variable-costing income statement is based on the contribution-margin format. Under it, operating income is driven by the unit level of sales. Under absorption costing, the income statement follows the gross-margin format. Operating income is driven by the unit level of production, the unit level of sales, and the denominator level used for assigning fixed manufacturing costs.
3. Why might managers build up finished-goods inventory if the company uses absorption costing?	When absorption costing is used, managers can increase current period operating income by producing more units for inventory. Producing for inventory absorbs more fixed manufacturing costs into inventory and reduces costs expensed in the income statement in the current period. Critics of absorption costing characterize this possible manipulation of income as the major negative consequence of treating fixed manufacturing costs as inventoriable costs.
4. How does throughput costing differ from variable costing and from absorption costing?	Throughput costing treats all costs except direct materials as costs of the period in which they are incurred. Throughput costing results in a lower amount of manufacturing costs being inventoried than either variable or absorption costing.
5. What are the different capacity levels a company can use to compute the budgeted fixed manufacturing cost rate?	Capacity levels can be measured in terms of capacity supplied—theoretical capacity or practical capacity. Capacity can also be measured in terms of output demanded—normal capacity utilization or master-budget capacity utilization.
6. What are the major factors managers consider in choosing the capacity level to compute the budgeted fixed manufacturing cost rate?	The major factors managers consider in choosing the capacity level to compute the budgeted fixed manufacturing cost rate are (a) effect on product costing and capacity management, (b) effect on pricing decisions, (c) effect on performance evaluation, (d) effect on financial statements, and (e) tax requirements.
7. What issues must managers take into account when planning capacity levels and when assigning capacity costs?	Critical factors when planning capacity levels and for assigning capacity costs include the uncertainty about the expected spending on capacity costs and the demand for the installed capacity; the role of capacity-related issues in nonmanufacturing areas; and the possible use of activity-based costing techniques in allocating capacity costs.

APPENDIX

Breakeven Points in Variable Costing and Absorption Costing

Chapter 3 introduced cost–volume–profit analysis. If variable costing is used, the breakeven point (that's where operating income is $0) is computed in the usual manner. There is only one breakeven point in this case, and it depends on (1) fixed (manufacturing and operating) costs and (2) contribution margin per unit.

The formula for computing the breakeven point under variable costing is a special case of the more general target operating income formula from Chapter 3 (page 73):

$$\text{Let } Q = \text{Number of units sold to earn the target operating income}$$

$$\text{Then } Q = \frac{\text{Total fixed costs} + \text{Target operating income}}{\text{Contribution margin per unit}}$$

Breakeven occurs when the target operating income is $0. In our Stassen illustration for 2020 (see Exhibit 9-1, page 326):

$$Q = \frac{(\$1{,}080{,}000 + \$1{,}380{,}000) + \$0}{(\$1{,}000 - (\$200 + \$185))} = \frac{\$2{,}460{,}000}{\$615}$$

$$= 4{,}000 \text{ units}$$

We now verify that Stassen will achieve breakeven under variable costing by selling 4,000 units:

Revenues, $1,000 × 4,000 units	$4,000,000
Variable costs, $385 × 4,000 units	1,540,000
Contribution margin, $615 × 4,000 units	2,460,000
Fixed costs	2,460,000
Operating income	$ 0

If absorption costing is used, the required number of units to be sold to earn a specific target operating income is not unique because of the number of variables involved. The following formula shows the factors that will affect the target operating income under absorption costing:

$$Q = \frac{\begin{matrix}\text{Total}\\\text{fixed}\\\text{costs}\end{matrix} + \begin{matrix}\text{Target}\\\text{operating}\\\text{income}\end{matrix} + \left[\begin{matrix}\text{Fixed}\\\text{manufacturing}\\\text{cost rate}\end{matrix} \times \left(\begin{matrix}\text{Breakeven}\\\text{sales}\\\text{in units}\end{matrix} - \begin{matrix}\text{Units}\\\text{produced}\end{matrix}\right)\right]}{\text{Contribution margin per unit}}$$

In this formula, the numerator is the sum of three terms (from the perspective of the two " + " signs), compared with two terms in the numerator of the variable-costing formula stated earlier. The additional term in the numerator under absorption costing is as follows:

$$\left[\begin{matrix}\text{Fixed manufacturing}\\\text{cost rate}\end{matrix} \times \left(\begin{matrix}\text{Breakeven sales}\\\text{in untis}\end{matrix} - \begin{matrix}\text{Units}\\\text{produced}\end{matrix}\right)\right]$$

This term reduces the fixed costs that need to be recovered when units produced exceed the breakeven sales quantity. When production exceeds the breakeven sales quantity, some of the fixed manufacturing costs that are expensed under variable costing are not expensed under absorption costing; they are instead included in finished-goods inventory. The breakeven sales quantity under absorption costing is correspondingly lower than under variable costing.[8]

[8] The reverse situation, where production is lower than the breakeven sales quantity, is not possible unless the firm has opening inventory. In that case, provided the variable manufacturing cost per unit and the fixed manufacturing cost rate are constant over time, the breakeven formula given is still valid. The breakeven sales quantity under absorption costing would then exceed that under variable costing.

For Stassen Company in 2020, suppose that actual production is 5,280 units. Then one breakeven point, Q, under absorption costing is as follows:

$$Q = \frac{(\$1{,}080{,}000 + \$1{,}380{,}000) + \$0 + [\$135 \times (Q - 5{,}280)]}{(\$1{,}000 - (\$200 + \$185))}$$

$$= \frac{(\$2{,}460{,}000 + \$135Q - \$712{,}800)}{\$615}$$

$$\$615Q = \$1{,}747{,}200 + \$135Q$$

$$\$480Q = \$1{,}747{,}200$$

$$Q = 3{,}640$$

We next verify that production of 5,280 units and sales of 3,640 units will lead Stassen to break even under absorption costing:

Revenues, $1,000 × 3,640 units		$3,640,000
Cost of goods sold:		
Cost of goods sold at standard cost, $335 × 3,640 units	$1,219,400	
Production-volume variance, $135 × (8,000 − 5,280) units	367,200 U	1,586,600
Gross margin		2,053,400
Marketing costs:		
Variable marketing costs, $185 × 3,640 units	673,400	
Fixed marketing costs	1,380,000	2,053,400
Operating income		$ 0

The breakeven point under absorption costing depends on (1) fixed manufacturing costs, (2) fixed operating (marketing) costs, (3) contribution margin per unit, (4) unit level of production, and (5) the capacity level chosen as the denominator to set the fixed manufacturing cost rate. For Stassen in 2020, a combination of 3,640 units sold, fixed manufacturing costs of $1,080,000, fixed marketing costs of $1,380,000, contribution margin per unit of $615, an 8,000-unit denominator level, and production of 5,280 units would result in an operating income of $0. *Note, however, that there are many combinations of these five factors that would give an operating income of $0.* For example, holding all other factors constant, a combination of 6,240 units produced and 3,370 units sold also results in an operating income of $0 under absorption costing. We provide verification of this alternative breakeven point next:

Revenues, $1,000 × 3,370 units		$3,370,000
Cost of goods sold:		
Cost of goods sold at standard cost, $335 × 3,370 units	$1,128,950	
Production-volume variance, $135 × (8,000 − 6,240) units	237,600 U	1,366,550
Gross margin		2,003,450
Marketing costs:		
Variable marketing costs, $185 × 3,370 units	623,450	
Fixed marketing costs	1,380,000	2,003,450
Operating income		$ 0

Suppose actual production in 2020 was equal to the denominator level, 8,000 units, and there were no units sold and no fixed marketing costs. All the units produced would be placed in inventory, so all the fixed manufacturing costs would be included in inventory. There would be no production-volume variance. Under these conditions, the company could break even under absorption costing with no sales whatsoever! In contrast, under variable costing, the operating loss would be equal to the fixed manufacturing costs of $1,080,000.

TERMS TO LEARN

This chapter and the Glossary at the end of the text contain definitions of the following important terms:

absorption costing (**p. 323**)
direct costing (**p. 323**)
downward demand spiral (**p. 340**)
master-budget capacity utilization (**p. 337**)
normal capacity utilization (**p. 337**)
practical capacity (**p. 337**)
super-variable costing (**p. 334**)
theoretical capacity (**p. 337**)
throughput costing (**p. 334**)
variable costing (**p. 323**)

ASSIGNMENT MATERIAL

Questions

9-1 Differences in operating income between variable costing and absorption costing are due solely to accounting for fixed costs. Do you agree? Explain.

9-2 Why is the term *direct costing* a misnomer?

9-3 Do companies in either the service sector or the merchandising sector make choices about absorption costing versus variable costing?

9-4 Explain the main conceptual issue under variable costing and absorption costing regarding the timing for the release of fixed manufacturing overhead as expense.

9-5 "Companies that make no variable-cost/ fixed-cost distinctions must use absorption costing, and those that do make variable-cost/ fixed-cost distinctions must use variable costing." Do you agree? Explain.

9-6 The main trouble with variable costing is that it ignores the increasing importance of fixed costs in manufacturing companies. Do you agree? Why?

9-7 Give an example of how, under absorption costing, operating income could fall even though the unit sales level rises.

9-8 What are the factors that affect the breakeven point under (1) variable costing and (2) absorption costing?

9-9 Critics of absorption costing have increasingly emphasized its potential for leading to undesirable incentives for managers. Give an example.

9-10 What are two ways of reducing the negative aspects associated with using absorption costing to evaluate the performance of a plant manager?

9-11 What denominator-level capacity concepts emphasize the output a plant can supply? What denominator-level capacity concepts emphasize the output customers demand for products produced by a plant?

9-12 Describe the downward demand spiral and its implications for pricing decisions.

9-13 Will the financial statements of a company always differ when different choices at the start of the accounting period are made regarding the denominator-level capacity concept?

9-14 What is the IRS's requirement for tax reporting regarding the choice of a denominator-level capacity concept?

9-15 "The difference between practical capacity and master-budget capacity utilization is the best measure of management's ability to balance the costs of having too much capacity and having too little capacity." Do you agree? Explain.

Multiple-Choice Questions

9-16 In comparing the absorption and variable cost methods, each of the following statements is true except

a. Selling, general, and administrative (SG&A) fixed expenses are not included in inventory in either method.
b. Only the absorption costing method may be used for external financial reporting.
c. Variable costing charges fixed overhead costs to the period they are incurred.
d. When inventory increases over the period, variable net income will exceed absorption net income.

9-17 Queen Sales, Inc. has just completed its first year of operations. The company has not had any sales to date. Queen has incurred the following costs associated with its production as of December 31, Year 1:

Direct materials	$45,000
Production labor	35,000
Bookkeeper salary	28,000
Factory utilities	18,500
Office rent	12,000
Factory supervisor salary	9,600
Machine maintenance contract	7,500

Under absorption costing, what is the inventory amount shown on the balance sheet at December 31, Year 1?

a. $155,600 **c.** $98,500
b. $115,600 **d.** $80,000

9-18 King Tooling has produced and sold the following number of units of their only product during their first 2 years in business:

	Produced	Sold
Year ended December 31, Year 1	50,000	40,000
Year ended December 31, Year 2	50,000	55,000

Production costs per unit have not changed over the 2-year period. Under variable costing, what is the amount of cost of sales relative to the cost of sales shown on the GAAP income statement of the company?

Year 1	Year 2
a. Higher	Higher
b. Higher	Lower
c. Lower	Higher
d. Lower	Lower

9-19 The following information relates to Drexler Inc.'s Year 3 financials:

Direct labor	$420,000
Direct materials	210,000
Variable overhead	205,000
Fixed overhead	355,000
Variable SG&A expenses	150,000
Fixed SG&A expenses	195,000

Year 3 period costs for Drexler, under both the absorption and variable cost methods, will be

	Absorption Cost Method	Variable Cost Method
a.	$345,000	$700,000
b.	$345,000	$905,000
c.	$550,000	$700,000
d.	$550,000	$905,000

9-20 Which of the following statements is not true regarding the use of variable and absorption costing for performance measurement?

a. The net income reported under the absorption method is less reliable for use in performance evaluations because the cost of the product includes fixed costs, which means the level of inventory affects net income.
b. The net income reported under the contribution income statement is more reliable for use in performance evaluations because the product cost does not include fixed costs.
c. Variable costing isolates contribution margins to aid in decision making.
d. The IRS allows either absorption or variable costing as long as the method is not changed from year to year, while U.S. GAAP only allows absorption costing.

Exercises

9-21 Variable and absorption costing, explaining operating-income differences. Nascar Motors assembles and sells motor vehicles and uses standard costing. Actual data relating to April and May 2020 are as follows:

	A	B	C	D
1		**April**		**May**
2	Unit data:			
3	Beginning inventory	0		150
4	Production	500		400
5	Sales	350		520
6	Variable costs:			
7	Manufacturing cost per unit produced	$ 10,000		$ 10,000
8	Operating (marketing) cost per unit sold	3,000		3,000
9	Fixed costs:			
10	Manufacturing costs	$2,000,000		$2,000,000
11	Operating (marketing) costs	600,000		600,000

The selling price per vehicle is $24,000. The budgeted level of production used to calculate the budgeted fixed manufacturing cost per unit is 500 units. There are no price, efficiency, or spending variances. Any production-volume variance is written off to cost of goods sold in the month in which it occurs.

Required

1. Prepare April and May 2020 income statements for Nascar Motors under (a) variable costing and (b) absorption costing.
2. Prepare a numerical reconciliation and explanation of the difference between operating income for each month under variable costing and absorption costing.

9-22 Throughput costing (continuation of 9-21). The variable manufacturing costs per unit of Nascar Motors are as follows:

	A	B	C
1		**April**	**May**
12	Direct material cost per unit	$6,700	$6,700
13	Direct manufacturing labor cost per unit	1,500	1,500
14	Manufacturing overhead cost per unit	1,800	1,800

Required

1. Prepare income statements for Nascar Motors in April and May 2020 under throughput costing.
2. Contrast the results in requirement 1 with those in requirement 1 of Exercise 9-21.
3. Give one motivation for Nascar Motors to adopt throughput costing.

9-23 Variable and absorption costing, explaining operating-income differences. EntertainMe Corporation manufactures and sells 50-inch television sets and uses standard costing. Actual data relating to January, February, and March 2020 are as follows:

	January	*February*	*March*
Unit data:			
Beginning inventory	0	150	150
Production	1,500	1,400	1,520
Sales	1,350	1,400	1,530
Variable costs:			
Manufacturing cost per unit produced	$ 1,000	$ 1,000	$ 1,000
Operating (marketing) cost per unit sold	$ 800	$ 800	$ 800
Fixed costs:			
Manufacturing costs	$525,000	$525,000	$525,000
Operating (marketing) costs	$130,000	$130,000	$130,000

The selling price per unit is $3,300. The budgeted level of production used to calculate the budgeted fixed manufacturing cost per unit is 1,500 units. There are no price, efficiency, or spending variances. Any production-volume variance is written off to cost of goods sold in the month in which it occurs.

1. Prepare income statements for EntertainMe in January, February, and March 2020 under (a) variable costing and (b) absorption costing.
2. Explain the difference in operating income for January, February, and March under variable costing and absorption costing.

9-24 Throughput costing (continuation of 9-23). The variable manufacturing costs per unit of EntertainMe Corporation are as follows:

	January	*February*	*March*
Direct material cost per unit	$ 525	$ 525	$ 525
Direct manufacturing labor cost per unit	200	200	200
Manufacturing overhead cost per unit	275	275	275
	$1,000	$1,000	$1,000

Required

1. Prepare income statements for EntertainMe in January, February, and March 2020 under throughput costing.
2. Contrast the results in requirement 1 of this exercise with those in requirement 1 of Exercise 9-23.
3. Give one motivation for EntertainMe to adopt throughput costing.

9-25 Variable versus absorption costing. The Tomlinson Company manufactures trendy, high-quality, moderately priced watches. As Tomlinson's senior financial analyst, you are asked to recommend a method of inventory costing. The chief financial officer (CFO) will use your recommendation to prepare Tomlinson's 2020 income statement. The following data are for the year ended December 31, 2020:

Beginning inventory, January 1, 2020	90,000 units
Ending inventory, December 31, 2020	34,000 units
2020 sales	433,000 units
Selling price (to distributor)	$ 24.00 per unit
Variable manufacturing cost per unit, including direct materials	$ 5.40 per unit
Variable operating (marketing) cost per unit sold	$ 1.20 per unit sold
Fixed manufacturing costs	$1,852,200
Denominator-level machine-hours	6,300
Standard production rate	60 units per machine-hour
Fixed operating (marketing) costs	$1,130,000

Assume standard costs per unit are the same for units in beginning inventory and units produced during the year. Also, assume no price, spending, or efficiency variances. Any production-volume variance is written off to cost of goods sold.

Required

1. Prepare income statements under variable and absorption costing for the year ended December 31, 2020.
2. What is Tomlinson's operating income as percentage of revenues under each costing method?
3. Explain the difference in operating income between the two methods.
4. Which costing method would you recommend to the CFO? Why?

9-26 Absorption and variable costing. (CMA) Houston, Inc. planned and actually manufactured 220,000 units of its single product in 2020, its first year of operation. Variable manufacturing cost was $22 per unit produced. Variable operating (nonmanufacturing) cost was $9 per unit sold. Planned and actual fixed manufacturing costs were $660,000. Planned and actual fixed operating (nonmanufacturing) costs totaled $440,000. Houston sold 160,000 units of product at $44 per unit.

Required

1. Houston's 2020 operating income using absorption costing is (a) $1,160,000, (b) $980,000, (c) $1,420,000, (d) $1,600,000, or (e) none of these. Show supporting calculations.
2. Houston's 2020 operating income using variable costing is (a) $1,640,000, (b) $1,160,000, (c) $980,000, (d) $1,420,000, or (e) none of these. Show supporting calculations.

9-27 Absorption versus variable costing. Horace Company manufactures a professional-grade vacuum cleaner and began operations in 2020. For 2020, Horace budgeted to produce and sell 25,000 units. The company had no price, spending, or efficiency variances and writes off production-volume variance to cost of goods sold. Actual data for 2020 are as follows:

	A	B
1	Units produced	21,000
2	Units sold	18,500
3	Selling price	$ 432
4	Variable costs:	
5	Manufacturing cost per unit produced:	
6	Direct materials	$ 33
7	Direct manufacturing labor	23
8	Manufacturing overhead	62
9	Marketing cost per unit sold	46
10	Fixed costs:	
11	Manufacturing costs	$1,550,000
12	Administrative costs	906,300
13	Marketing costs	1,479,000

Required

1. Prepare a 2020 income statement for Horace Company using variable costing.
2. Prepare a 2020 income statement for Horace Company using absorption costing.
3. Explain the differences in operating incomes obtained in requirements 1 and 2.
4. Horace's management is considering implementing a bonus for its supervisors based on gross margin under absorption costing. What incentives will this bonus plan create for the supervisors? What modifications could Horace management make to improve such a plan? Explain briefly.

9-28 Variable and absorption costing, sales, and operating-income changes. Honeyland uses standard costing to produce a particularly popular type of candy. Honeyland's president, Tim Thorne, was unhappy after reviewing the income statements for the first 3 years of business. He said, "I was told by our accountants—and in fact, I have memorized—that our breakeven volume is 29,000 units. I was happy that we reached that sales goal in each of our first 2 years. But here's the strange thing: In our first year, we sold 29,000 units and indeed we broke even. Then in our second year we sold the same volume and had a significant, positive operating income. I didn't complain, of course... but here's the bad part. In our third year, we *sold 20% more* candy, but our *operating income dropped by nearly 90%* from what it was in the second year! We didn't change our selling price or cost structure over the past 3 years and have no price, efficiency, or spending variances... so what's going on?!"

	A	B	C	D
1	**Absorption Costing**			
2		**2019**	**2020**	**2021**
3	Sales (units)	29,000	29,000	34,800
4	Revenues	$2,233,000	$2,233,000	$2,679,600
5	Cost of goods sold:			
6	Beginning inventory	0	0	406,000
7	Production	2,030,000	2,436,000	2,030,000
8	Available for sale	2,030,000	2,436,000	2,436,000
9	Deduct ending inventory	0	(406,000)	0
10	Adjustment for production-volume variance	0	(324,800)	0
11	Cost of goods sold	2,030,000	1,705,200	2,436,000
12	Gross margin	203,000	527,800	243,600
13	Selling and administrative expenses (all fixed)	203,000	203,000	203,000
14	Operating income	$ 0	$ 324,800	$ 40,600
15				
16	Beginning inventory	0	0	5,800
17	Production (units)	29,000	34,800	29,000
18	Sales (units)	29,000	29,000	34,800
19	Ending inventory	0	5,800	0
20	Variable manufacturing cost per unit	$ 14	$ 14	$ 14
21	Fixed manufacturing overhead costs	$1,624,000	$1,624,000	$1,624,000
22	Fixed manuf. costs allocated per unit produced	$ 56	$ 56	$ 56

Required

1. What denominator level is Honeyland using to allocate fixed manufacturing costs to the candy? How is Honeyland treating any favorable or unfavorable production-volume variance at the end of the year? Explain your answer briefly.
2. How did Honeyland's accountants arrive at the breakeven volume of 29,000 units?
3. Prepare a variable costing-based income statement for each year. Explain the variation in variable costing operating income for each year based on contribution margin per unit and sales volume.
4. Reconcile the operating incomes under variable costing and absorption costing for each year, and use this information to explain to Tim Thorne the positive operating income in 2020 and the drop in operating income in 2021.

9-29 Capacity management, denominator-level capacity concepts. Match each of the following numbered descriptions with one or more of the denominator-level capacity concepts by putting the appropriate letter(s) by each item:

a. Theoretical capacity
b. Practical capacity
c. Normal capacity utilization
d. Master-budget capacity utilization

1. Measures the denominator level in terms of what a plant can supply
2. Is based on producing at full efficiency all the time
3. Represents the expected level of capacity utilization for the next budget period
4. Measures the denominator level in terms of demand for the output of the plant
5. Takes into account seasonal, cyclical, and trend factors
6. Should be used for performance evaluation in the current year
7. Represents an ideal benchmark
8. Highlights the cost of capacity acquired but not used
9. Should be used for long-term pricing purposes
10. Hides the cost of capacity acquired but not used
11. If used as the denominator-level concept, would avoid the restatement of unit costs when expected demand levels change

9-30 Denominator-level problem. Thunder Bolt, Inc., is a manufacturer of the very popular G36 motorcycles. The management at Thunder Bolt has recently adopted absorption costing and is debating which denominator-level concept to use. The G36 motorcycles sell for an average price of $8,200. Budgeted fixed manufacturing overhead costs for 2020 are estimated at $6,480,000. Thunder Bolt, Inc., uses subassembly operators that provide component parts. The following are the denominator-level options that management has been considering:

a. Theoretical capacity—based on three shifts, completion of five motorcycles per shift, and a 360-day year—$3 \times 5 \times 360 = 5{,}400$.
b. Practical capacity—theoretical capacity adjusted for unavoidable interruptions, breakdowns, and so forth—$3 \times 4 \times 320 = 3{,}840$.
c. Normal capacity utilization—estimated at 3,240 units.
d. Master-budget capacity utilization—the strengthening stock market and the growing popularity of motorcycles have prompted the marketing department to issue an estimate for 2020 of 3,600 units.

Required

1. Calculate the budgeted fixed manufacturing overhead cost rates under the four denominator-level concepts.
2. What are the benefits to Thunder Bolt, Inc., of using either theoretical capacity or practical capacity?
3. Under a cost-based pricing system, what are the negative aspects of a master-budget denominator level? What are the positive aspects?

9-31 Variable and absorption costing and breakeven points. Ardella, a leading firm in the sports industry, produces basketballs for the consumer market. For the year ended December 31, 2020, Ardella sold 177,700 basketballs at an average selling price of $37 per unit. The following information also relates to 2020 (assume constant unit costs and no variances of any kind):

Inventory, January 1, 2020:		32,800 basketballs
Inventory, December 31, 2020:		25,100 basketballs
Fixed manufacturing costs:	$1,020,000	
Fixed administrative costs:	$4,726,400	
Direct materials costs:	$	9 per basketball
Direct labor costs:	$	6 per basketball

Required

1. Calculate the breakeven point (in basketballs sold) in 2020 under:
   a. Variable costing
   b. Absorption costing
2. Suppose direct materials costs were $11 per basketball instead. Assuming all other data are the same, calculate the minimum number of basketballs Ardella must have sold in 2020 to attain a target operating income of $110,000 under
   a. Variable costing
   b. Absorption costing

9-32 Variable costing versus absorption costing. The Stenback Company uses an absorption-costing system based on standard costs. Variable manufacturing cost consists of direct material cost of $4 per unit and other variable manufacturing costs of $1.20 per unit. The standard production rate is 20 units per machine-hour. Total budgeted and actual fixed manufacturing overhead costs are $520,000. Fixed manufacturing overhead is allocated at $16 per machine-hour based on fixed manufacturing costs of $520,000 ÷ 32,500 machine-hours, which is the level Stenback uses as its denominator level.

The selling price is $13 per unit. Variable operating (nonmanufacturing) cost, which is driven by units sold, is $2 per unit. Fixed operating (nonmanufacturing) costs are $55,000. Beginning inventory in 2020 is 35,000 units; ending inventory is 45,000 units. Sales in 2020 are 575,000 units.

The same standard unit costs persisted throughout 2019 and 2020. For simplicity, assume that there are no price, spending, or efficiency variances.

Required

1. Prepare an income statement for 2020 assuming that the production-volume variance is written off at year-end as an adjustment to cost of goods sold.
2. The president has heard about variable costing. She asks you to recast the 2020 statement as it would appear under variable costing.
3. Explain the difference in operating income as calculated in requirements 1 and 2.

4. Graph how fixed manufacturing overhead is accounted for under absorption costing. That is, there will be two lines: one for the budgeted fixed manufacturing overhead (which is equal to the actual fixed manufacturing overhead in this case) and one for the fixed manufacturing overhead allocated. Show the production-volume variance in the graph.
5. Critics have claimed that a widely used accounting system has led to undesirable buildups of inventory levels. (a) Is variable costing or absorption costing more likely to lead to such buildups? Why? (b) What can managers do to counteract undesirable inventory buildups?

9-33 Throughput Costing (continuation of 9-32)

Required

1. Prepare an income statement under throughput costing for the year ended December 31, 2020 for Stenback Company.
2. Reconcile the difference between the contribution margin and the throughput margin for Stenback in 2020. Then reconcile the operating income between variable costing and throughput costing for Stenback in 2020.
3. Advocates of throughput costing say it provides managers less incentive to produce for inventory than either variable costing or, especially, absorption costing. Do you agree? Why or why not? Under what circumstances might you recommend that Stenback use throughput costing?

Problems

9-34 Variable costing and absorption costing, the Evergreen All-Fixed Corporation. (R. Marple, adapted) It is the end of 2020. Evergreen All-Fixed Corporation began operations in January 2019. The company is so named because it has no variable costs. All its costs are fixed; they do not vary with output.

Evergreen All-Fixed Corp. is located on the bank of a river and has its own hydroelectric plant to supply power, light, and heat. The company manufactures a synthetic fertilizer from air and river water and sells its product at a price that is not expected to change. It has a small staff of employees, all paid fixed annual salaries. The output of the plant can be increased or decreased by pressing a few buttons on a keyboard.

The following budgeted and actual data are for the operations of Evergreen All-Fixed. The company uses budgeted production as the denominator level and writes off any production-volume variance to cost of goods sold.

	2019	2020[a]
Sales	27,000 tons	27,000 tons
Production	54,000 tons	0 tons
Selling price	$ 125 per ton	$ 125 per ton
Costs (all fixed):		
Manufacturing	$2,700,000	$2,700,000
Operating (nonmanufacturing)	$ 103,000	$ 103,000

[a] Management adopted the policy, effective January 1, 2020, of producing only as much product as needed to fill sales orders. During 2020, sales were the same as for 2019 and were filled entirely from inventory at the start of 2020.

Required

1. Prepare income statements with one column for 2019, one column for 2020, and one column for the 2 years together using (a) variable costing and (b) absorption costing.
2. What is the breakeven point under (a) variable costing and (b) absorption costing?
3. What inventory costs would be carried in the balance sheet on December 31, 2019 and 2020 under each method?
4. Assume that the performance of the top manager of Evergreen All-Fixed is evaluated and rewarded largely on the basis of reported operating income. Which costing method would the manager prefer? Why?

9-35 Comparison of variable costing and absorption costing. Gammaro Company uses standard costing. Tim St. Germaine, the new president of Gammaro Company, is presented with the following data for 2020:

	A	B	C
1	**Gammaro Company**		
2	**Income Statements for the Year Ended December 31, 2020**		
3		**Variable**	**Absorption**
4		**Costing**	**Costing**
5	Revenues	$9,050,000	$9,050,000
6	Cost of goods sold (at standard costs)	4,665,000	5,875,000
7	Fixed manufacturing overhead (budgeted)	1,400,000	-
8	Fixed manufacturing overhead variances (all unfavorable):		
9	Spending	80,000	80,000
10	Production volume	-	350,000
11	Total marketing and administrative costs (all fixed)	1,560,000	1,560,000
12	Total costs	7,705,000	7,865,000
13	Operating income	$1,345,000	$1,185,000
14			
15	Inventories (at standard costs)		
16	December 31, 2019	$1,465,000	$1,745,000
17	December 31, 2020	75,000	195,000

Required

1. At what percentage of denominator level was the plant operating during 2020?
2. How much fixed manufacturing overhead was included in the 2019 and the 2020 ending inventory under absorption costing?
3. Reconcile and explain the difference in 2020 operating incomes under variable and absorption costing.
4. Tim St. Germaine is concerned: He notes that despite an increase in sales over 2019, 2020 operating income has actually declined under absorption costing. Explain how this occurred.

9-36 Effects of differing production levels on absorption costing income: Metrics to minimize inventory buildups. Northern Press produces textbooks for high school accounting courses. The company recently hired a new editor, Leslie Green, to handle production and sales of books for an introductory accounting course. Leslie's compensation depends on the gross margin associated with sales of this book. Leslie needs to decide how many copies of the book to produce. The following information is available for the fall semester of 2020:

Estimated sales	24,000 books
Beginning inventory	0 books
Average selling price	$ 84 per book
Variable production costs	$ 52 per book
Fixed production costs	$432,000 per semester

The fixed-cost allocation rate is based on expected sales and is therefore equal to $432,000/24,000 books = $18 per book.

Leslie has decided to produce either 24,000, 30,000, or 36,000 books.

Required

1. Calculate expected gross margin if Leslie produces 24,000, 30,000, or 36,000 books. (Make sure you include the production-volume variance as part of cost of goods sold.)
2. Calculate ending inventory in units and in dollars for each production level.
3. Managers who are paid a bonus that is a function of gross margin may be inspired to produce a product in excess of demand to maximize their own bonus. The chapter suggested metrics to discourage managers from producing products in excess of demand. Do you think the following metrics will accomplish this objective? Show your work.
   a. Incorporate a charge of 10% of the cost of the ending inventory as an expense for evaluating the manager.
   b. Include nonfinancial measures (such as the ones recommended on page 334) when evaluating management and rewarding performance.

9-37 Alternative denominator-level capacity concepts, effect on operating income. Zing Lager has just purchased the Chicago Brewery. The brewery is 2 years old and uses absorption costing. It will "sell" its product to Zing Lager at $44 per barrel. Peter Bryant, Zing Lager's controller, obtains the following information about Chicago Brewery's capacity and budgeted fixed manufacturing costs for 2020:

	A	B	C	D	E
1		Budgeted Fixed	Days of	Hours of	
2	Denominator-Level	Manufacturing	Production	Production	Barrels
3	Capacity Concept	Overhead per Period	per Period	per Day	per Hour
4	Theoretical capacity	$28,300,000	360	24	530
5	Practical capacity	$28,300,000	352	20	500
6	Normal capacity utilization	$28,300,000	352	20	395
7	Master-budget capacity utilization for each half year:				
8	(a) January–June 2020	$14,150,000	176	20	310
9	(b) July–December 2020	$14,150,000	176	20	480

Required

1. Compute the budgeted fixed manufacturing overhead rate per barrel for each of the denominator-level capacity concepts. Explain why they are different.
2. In 2020, the Chicago Brewery reported these production results:

	A	B
12	Beginning inventory in barrels, 1-1-2020	0
13	Production in barrels	2,640,000
14	Ending inventory in barrels, 12-31-2020	180,000
15	Actual variable manufacturing costs	$79,464,000
16	Actual fixed manufacturing overhead costs	$26,900,000

There are no variable cost variances. Fixed manufacturing overhead cost variances are written off to cost of goods sold in the period in which they occur. Compute the Chicago Brewery's operating income when the denominator-level capacity is (a) theoretical capacity, (b) practical capacity, and (c) normal capacity utilization.

9-38 Motivational considerations in denominator-level capacity selection (continuation of 9-37).

Required

1. If the plant manager of the Chicago Brewery gets a bonus based on operating income, which denominator-level capacity concept would he or she prefer to use? Explain.
2. What denominator-level capacity concept would Zing Lager prefer to use for U.S. income-tax reporting? Explain.
3. How might the IRS limit the flexibility of an absorption-costing company like Zing Lager attempting to minimize its taxable income?

9-39 Variable and absorption costing and breakeven points. Let It Snow, LLC (LIS) manufactures snowboards. LIS began 2020 with an inventory of 250 boards. During the year, it produced 1,200 boards and sold 1,400 for $300 each. Fixed production costs were $169,020, and variable production costs were $112 per unit. Fixed advertising, marketing, and other general and administrative expenses were $75,000, and variable shipping costs were $20 per board. Assume that the cost of each unit in beginning inventory is equal to 2020 inventory cost. LIS uses a denominator level of 1,200 units.

Required

1. Prepare an income statement assuming LIS uses variable costing.
2. Prepare an income statement assuming LIS uses absorption costing. Production-volume variances are written off to cost of goods sold.
3. Compute the breakeven point in units sold assuming LIS uses the following methods. Provide proof of your breakeven calculations.
   a. Variable costing
   b. Absorption costing

9-40 Downward demand spiral. No More Litter, Inc. (NML) recently patented its new electronic and remote-controlled litter box. Research indicates that the scooping of the litter is the task most abhorred by cat owners. NML's new product automatically "scoops" and fills the pan with fresh litter from the reservoir.

NML has budgeted 40,000 units for production and sales in the first year of operation. Practical capacity is 60,000 units.

Variable manufacturing costs per unit are as follows:

Materials	$15
Labor	$32
Overhead	$18

Fixed manufacturing overhead is $450,000 annually.

Required

1. Assume that NML uses absorption costing and uses master-budget utilization as the denominator level for calculating its fixed manufacturing overhead rate. Selling price is set at 150% of total manufacturing cost. Compute NML's selling price.

2. Due to a lagging economy, sales are not as robust as NML anticipated. Adding to the pressure on sales, Mr. Charles Buttons, President of NML, believes the stream of newcomers to the market are (1) using his patent-protected technology and (2) pricing their products at a loss. No change is made to the pricing model and budgeted sales and production for 2021 is 30,000 units. You are the CFO at NML. Explain to Mr. Buttons what effect this revised forecast will have in 2021.

3. Recompute the selling price using practical capacity as the denominator level of activity. How would this choice have affected NML's position in the marketplace? Generally, how would this choice affect the production-volume variance?

9-41 Absorption costing and production-volume variance—alternative capacity bases. Energy Glow Light (EGL), a producer of energy-efficient light bulbs, expects that demand will increase markedly over the next decade. Due to the high fixed costs involved in the business, EGL has decided to evaluate its financial performance using absorption costing income. The production-volume variance is written off to cost of goods sold. The variable cost of production is $2.70 per bulb. Fixed manufacturing costs are $1,020,000 per year. Variable and fixed selling and administrative expenses are $0.20 per bulb sold and $290,000, respectively. Because its light bulbs are currently popular with environmentally conscious customers, EGL can sell the bulbs for $9.60 each.

EGL is deciding among various concepts of capacity for calculating the cost of each unit produced. Its choices are as follows:

Theoretical capacity	850,000 bulbs
Practical capacity	425,000 bulbs
Normal capacity	272,000 bulbs (average expected output for the next 3 years)
Master-budget capacity	212,500 bulbs expected production this year

Required

1. Calculate the inventoriable cost per unit using each level of capacity to compute fixed manufacturing cost per unit.
2. Suppose EGL actually produces 250,000 bulbs. Calculate the production-volume variance using each level of capacity to compute the fixed manufacturing overhead allocation rate.
3. Assume EGL has no beginning inventory. If this year's actual sales are 212,500 bulbs (and production is 250,000 bulbs), calculate operating income for EGL using each type of capacity to compute fixed manufacturing cost per unit.

9-42 Operating income effects of denominator-level choice and adjustment for production-volume variance (continuation of 9-41).

Required

1. If EGL sells all 250,000 bulbs produced, what would be the effect on operating income of using each type of capacity as a basis for calculating manufacturing cost per unit?
2. Compare the results of operating income at different capacity levels when 212,500 bulbs are sold and when 250,000 bulbs are sold. What conclusion can you draw from the comparison?
3. Using the original data (that is, 250,000 units produced and 212,500 units sold) if EGL had used the proration approach to allocate the production-volume variance, what would operating income have been under each level of capacity? (Assume that there is no ending work in process.)

9-43 Variable and absorption costing, actual costing. The Iron City Company started business on January 1, 2020. Iron City manufactures a specialty honey beer, which it sells directly to state-owned distributors in Pennsylvania. Honey beer is produced and sold in six-packs, and in 2020, Iron City produced more six-packs than it was able to sell. In addition to variable and fixed manufacturing overhead, Iron City incurred direct materials costs of $880,000, direct manufacturing labor costs of $400,000, and fixed marketing and administrative costs of $295,000. For the year, Iron City sold a total of 180,000 six-packs for a sales revenue of $2,250,000.

Iron City's CFO is convinced that the firm should use an actual costing system but is debating whether to follow variable or absorption costing. The controller notes that Iron City's operating income for the year would be $438,000 under variable costing and $461,000 under absorption costing. Moreover, the ending finished-goods inventory would be valued at $7.15 under variable costing and $8.30 under absorption costing.

Iron City incurs no variable nonmanufacturing expenses.

Required

1. What is Iron City's total contribution margin for 2020?
2. Iron City incurs fixed manufacturing costs in addition to its fixed marketing and administrative costs. How much did Iron City incur in fixed manufacturing costs in 2020?
3. How many six-packs did Iron City produce in 2020?
4. How much in variable manufacturing overhead did Iron City incur in 2020?
5. For 2020, how much in total manufacturing overhead is expensed under variable costing, either through cost of goods sold or as a period expense?

9-44 Cost allocation, downward demand spiral. Cafe One operates a chain of 10 hospitals in the Los Angeles area. Its central food-catering facility, Cafeman, prepares and delivers meals to the hospitals. It has the capacity to deliver up to 1,025,000 meals a year. In 2020, based on estimates from each hospital controller, Cafeman budgeted for 925,000 meals that year. Budgeted fixed costs in 2020 were $1,517,000. Each hospital was charged $6.04 per meal—$4.40 variable costs plus $1.64 allocated budgeted fixed cost.

Recently, the hospitals have been complaining about the quality of Cafeman's meals and their rising costs. In mid-2020, Cafe One's president announces that all Cafe One hospitals and support facilities will be run as profit centers. Hospitals will be free to purchase quality-certified services from outside the system. Luke Hayward, Cafeman's controller, is preparing the 2021 budget. He hears that three hospitals have decided to use outside suppliers for their meals, which will reduce the 2021 estimated demand to 820,000 meals. No change in variable cost per meal or total fixed costs is expected in 2021.

Required

1. How did Hayward calculate the budgeted fixed cost per meal of $1.64 in 2020?
2. Using the same approach to calculating budgeted fixed cost per meal and pricing as in 2020, how much would hospitals be charged for each Cafeman meal in 2021? What would the reaction of the hospital controllers be to the price?
3. Suggest an alternative cost-based price per meal that Hayward might propose and that might be more acceptable to the hospitals. What can Cafeman and Hayward do to make this price profitable in the long run?

9-45 Cost allocation, responsibility accounting, ethics (continuation of 9-44). In 2021, only 740,000 Cafeman meals were produced and sold to the hospitals. Hayward suspects that hospital controllers had systematically inflated their 2021 meal estimates.

Required

1. Recall that Cafeman uses the master-budget capacity utilization to allocate fixed costs and to price meals. What was the effect of production-volume variance on Cafeman's operating income in 2021?
2. Why might hospital controllers deliberately overestimate their future meal counts?
3. What other evidence should Cafe One's president seek to investigate Hayward's concerns?
4. Suggest two specific steps that Hayward might take to reduce hospital controllers' incentives to inflate their estimated meal counts.

9-46 Costing methods and variances, comprehensive. Rob Kapito, the controller of Blackstar Paint Supply Company, has been exploring a variety of internal accounting systems. Rob hopes to get the input of Blackstar's board of directors in choosing one. To prepare for his presentation to the board, Rob applies four different cost accounting methods to the firm's operating data for 2020. The four methods are actual absorption costing, normal absorption costing, standard absorption costing, and standard variable costing.

With the help of a junior accountant, Rob prepares the following alternative income statements:

	A	B	C	D
Sales revenue	$900,000	$900,000	$900,000	$900,000
Cost of goods sold	$375,000	$250,000	$420,000	$395,000
(+) Variances:				
Direct materials	15,000	15,000	—	—
Direct labor	5,000	5,000	—	—
Manufacturing overhead	25,000	—	—	25,000
(+) Other costs (all fixed)	350,000	475,000	350,000	350,000
Total costs	$770,000	$745,000	$770,000	$770,000
Net income	$130,000	$155,000	$130,000	$130,000

Where applicable, Rob allocates both fixed and variable manufacturing overhead using direct labor hours as the driver. Blackstar carries no work-in-process inventory. Standard costs have been stable over time, and Rob writes off all variances to cost of goods sold. For 2020, there was no flexible budget variance for fixed overhead. In addition, the direct labor variance represents a price variance.

Required

1. Match each method below with the appropriate income statement (A, B, C, or D):

Actual absorption costing ________
Normal absorption costing ________
Standard absorption costing ________
Standard variable costing ________

2. During 2020, how did Blackstar's level of finished-goods inventory change? In other words, is it possible to know whether Blackstar's finished-goods inventory increased, decreased, or stayed constant during the year?
3. From the four income statements, can you determine how the actual volume of production during the year compared to the denominator (expected) volume level?
4. Did Blackstar have a favorable or unfavorable variable overhead spending variance during 2020?

9-47 Absorption, variable, and throughput costing. JetStar produces jet bridges for many domestic and international airports. Cost information for JetStar's jet bridges is as follows:

Variable costs per jet bridge:	
Materials	$ 5,400
Labor	$ 3,200
Manufacturing Overhead	$ 6,400
Selling	$ 1,400
General and administrative	$ 1,005
Fixed costs for the first 3 quarters of 2020:	
Manufacturing Overhead	$849,915 allocated based on budgeted production
Selling	$590,000
General and administrative	$895,000

Additional information for the first three quarters of 2020 for JetStar are shown below:

	1st Quarter	2nd Quarter	3rd Quarter
Budgeted production	60	65	62
Actual production	60	65	62
Sales	55	58	54
Sales price: $33,000 per jet bridge			
Fixed selling costs by quarter	200,000	200,000	190,000
Fixed G&A costs by quarter	395,000	250,000	250,000

JetStar's controller, Max, wishes to analyze the difference in the income statements between throughput costing, absorption costing, and variable costing for the first 3 quarters of 2020.

Assume no beginning inventory.

Required

1. Prepare an absorption costing income statement
2. Prepare a variable costing income statement
3. Prepare a throughput costing income statement
4. Explain the difference in the net income under each costing method.
5. Based on the information provided, which costing method do you believe JetStar is currently using to calculate the bonus for the production manager? Why?
6. If Q4 sales were 65 and Q4 actual and budgeted production was 50, what difference would you expect in Q4 income between absorption costing and variable costing? Why?

9-48 Absorption costing, undesirable incentives for managers to build up inventory. Rollalong Inc. produces wheelchairs that are sold primarily to hospitals. Rollalong's three plant managers' bonuses are based on operating income that is produced using absorption costing. The company suspects that the current buildup of inventory is a result of the managers' desire for higher bonuses. Senior management wishes to institute an inventory limit to eliminate this inventory buildup without changing or eliminating the bonus structure. The variable cost per wheelchair is $5,500 and the fixed costs for 2020 were $11,019,840. Fixed costs are allocated based on master-budget capacity utilization. Budgeted production was 12,480 chairs and actual sales were 12,000 units. Actual production in 2020 was 13,320. In 2019, inventory increased by 3,000 units and that was also the ending inventory in units.

Required

1. How much did inventory increase in 2020?
2. What amount of fixed costs was absorbed into inventory in 2020?
3. Why may it not be a good idea for senior management to institute an inventory limit?
4. Aside from instituting an inventory limit, how could senior management control the incentive of the plant managers to build up inventory in order to increase their bonuses?

10 Determining How Costs Behave

LEARNING OBJECTIVES

1. Describe linear cost functions and three common ways in which they behave
2. Explain the importance of causality in estimating cost functions
3. Understand various methods of cost estimation
4. Outline six steps in estimating a cost function using quantitative analysis
5. Describe three criteria used to evaluate and choose cost drivers
6. Explain nonlinear cost functions, in particular those arising from learning-curve effects
7. Be aware of data problems encountered in estimating cost functions

What is the value of looking at the past?

Perhaps it is to recall fond memories of family and friends or help you understand historical events. An organization looks at the past to analyze its performance and make the right decisions for improving its future performance. For example, managers gather information about costs and ascertain how they behave to predict what they will be "down the road." They also use past data to understand actions, such as preventive maintenance or inventory planning, that help reduce costs, and cost investments, such as brand building, advertising, and promotions, that help increase revenues and profits, Understanding the drivers of costs and revenues is a valuable technical skill whose importance has grown in recent years with the increased availability of new, massive datasets and cheap computing power to analyze them. The knowledge gained in this process can motivate an organization to reorganize its operations in innovative ways and tackle important challenges. We develop data analytic thinking skills in this chapter and the new chapter that follows.

SOUTHWEST USES "BIG DATA ANALYTICS" TO REDUCE FUEL CONSUMPTION AND COSTS[1]

Southwest Airlines operates a fleet of 700 aircraft, flying about 4,000 flights per day to over 100 national and international destinations. Southwest Airlines' second largest expense is fuel. Depending on market prices, the company spends between $4 billion and $6 billion on fuel every year. Any small percentage improvement in fuel costs represents huge savings.

Markus Mainka/Shutterstock

Southwest Airlines uses big data analytics to drill down on countless variables—such as fuel load and outside air humidity—on its more than one million flights annually to see how each variable altered fuel use and profitability. For example, if Southwest's analytics show that planes on a particular route consistently carry too much fuel, it will reduce fuel loads in the future to cut costs.

Thanks to available computing power, such complex analysis is done in minutes and yields significant cost savings for the company. In the first year itself, big data analytics helped Southwest save $105 million in fuel costs.

[1] *Sources:* Jessica Davis, "How Southwest Airlines Chooses Big Impact Analytics Projects," *Information Week*, April 9, 2018 (https://www.informationweek.com/big-data/software-platforms/how-southwest-airlines-chooses-big-impact-analytics-projects/d/d-id/1331469); Mark Egan, "How Big Data and the Industrial Internet Can Help Southwest Save $100 Million on Fuel," *GE Reports*, October 5, 2015 (https://www.ge.com/reports/big-data-industrial-internet-can-help-southwest-save-100-million-fuel/).

As the Southwest example illustrates, managers must understand how costs behave to make strategic and operating decisions that have a positive impact. This chapter will focus on how managers determine cost-behavior patterns—that is, how costs change in relation to changes in activity levels, in the quantity of products produced, and so on. We start with the most basic concepts and build to more modern data analytic models in Chapter 11.

Basic Assumptions and Examples of Cost Functions

LEARNING OBJECTIVE 1

Describe linear cost functions

. . . graph of cost function is a straight line

and three common ways in which they behave

. . . variable, fixed, and mixed

Managers understand cost behavior through cost functions, which are the basic building blocks for estimating costs. A **cost function** is a mathematical description of how a cost changes with changes in the level of an activity relating to that cost. Cost functions can be plotted on a graph by measuring the level of an activity, such as number of batches produced or number of machine-hours used, on the horizontal axis (called the *x*-axis). The amount of total costs corresponding to—or dependent on—the levels of that activity are measured on the vertical axis (called the *y*-axis).

Basic Assumptions

Managers often estimate cost functions based on two assumptions:

1. Variations in the level of a single activity (the cost driver) explain variations in the related total costs.
2. Cost behavior is approximated by a linear cost function within the relevant range. Recall from Chapter 2 that a *relevant range* is the range of the activity in which there is a relationship between total cost and the level of activity. For a **linear cost function**, total cost versus the level of a single activity related to that cost is a straight line within the relevant range.

We use these assumptions throughout most, but not all, of this chapter. Not all cost functions are linear and can be explained by a single activity. Later sections will discuss cost functions that do not rely on these assumptions.

Linear Cost Functions

To understand three basic types of linear cost functions and to see the role of cost functions in business decisions, consider the negotiations between StoreBox, a technology startup, and Forest Web Services (FWS), which provides StoreBox with enterprise-class cloud computing and data analytic services.

- **Alternative 1:** StoreBox pays $0.50 per CPU hour used. Total cost to StoreBox changes in proportion to the number of CPU hours used. The number of CPU hours used is the only factor whose change causes a change in total cost.

  Panel A in Exhibit 10-1 presents this *variable cost* for StoreBox. Under alternative 1, there is no fixed cost for cloud services. We write the cost function in Panel A of Exhibit 10-1 as

  $$y = \$0.50X$$

  where X measures the number of CPU hours used (on the x-axis) and y measures the total cost of the CPU hours used (on the y-axis), calculated using the cost function. Panel A illustrates the $0.50 **slope coefficient**, the amount by which total cost changes when a 1-hour change occurs in CPU usage. *Throughout the chapter, uppercase letters, such as X, refer to the actual observations, and lowercase letters, such as y, represent estimates or calculations made using a cost function.*
- **Alternative 2:** StoreBox pays a fixed amount of $1,000 per month. Total cost is fixed at $1,000 per month, regardless of the number of CPU hours used. (We use the same activity measure, number of CPU hours used, to compare cost-behavior patterns under the three alternatives.)

EXHIBIT 10-1 Examples of Linear Cost Functions

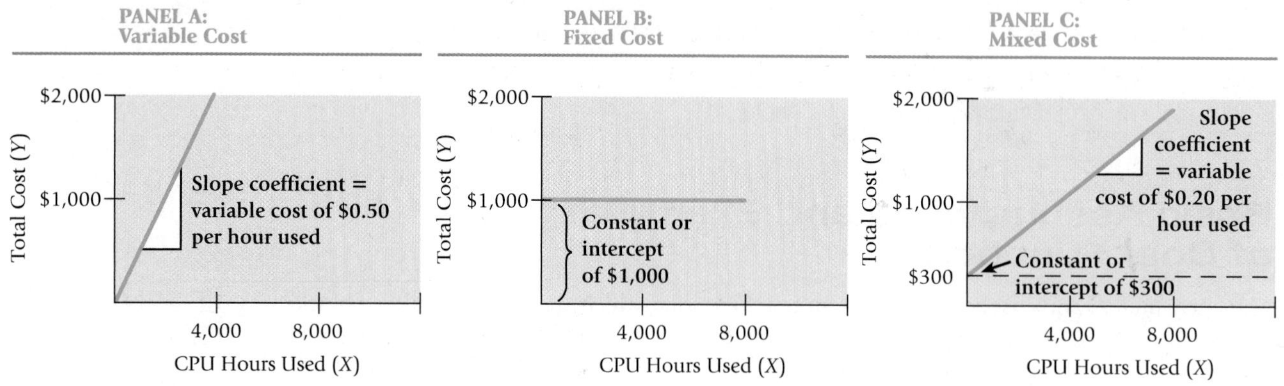

Panel B in Exhibit 10-1 shows the fixed-cost alternative for StoreBox. We write the cost function in Panel B as

$$y = \$1{,}000$$

The fixed cost of $1,000 is called a **constant**; it is the component of the total cost that does not vary with changes in the level of the activity. Graphically, the value of the constant is the point where it intersects the *y*-axis. Therefore, the *constant* is also called the **intercept.** In this example, the constant accounts for all the cost because there is no variable cost. Graphically, the slope coefficient of the cost function is zero.

- **Alternative 3:** StoreBox pays a fixed amount of $300 per month plus $0.20 per CPU hour used. This is an example of a mixed cost. A **mixed cost**—also called a **semivariable cost**—is a cost that has both fixed and variable elements.

  Panel C in Exhibit 10-1 plots the mixed-cost function for StoreBox. We write the cost function in Panel C of Exhibit 10-1 as

$$y = \$300 + \$0.20X$$

Unlike the graphs for alternatives 1 and 2, Panel C has both a constant value of $300 and a slope coefficient of $0.20. The total cost in the relevant range increases as the number of CPU hours used increases. However, the total cost does not vary strictly in proportion to the number of CPU hours used within the relevant range. For example, when 4,000 hours are used, the total cost equals $1,100 [$300 + (0.20 per hour × 4,000 hours)], and when 8,000 hours are used, the total cost equals $1,900 [$300 + ($0.20 per hour × 8,000 hours)]. Although the usage in terms of hours has doubled, the total cost has increased by only about 73% [($1,900 − $1,100) ÷ $1,100] because some of the costs are fixed costs, which do not increase with the number of CPU hours.

StoreBox's managers must understand the cost-behavior patterns in the three alternatives to choose the best deal. Suppose StoreBox expects to use *at least* 4,000 hours of CPU time each month. Its cost for 4,000 hours under the three alternatives are

- **Alternative 1:** $2,000 ($0.50 per hour × 4,000 hours)
- **Alternative 2:** $1,000
- **Alternative 3:** $1,100 [$300 + ($0.20 per hour × 4,000 hours)]

Alternative 2 is the least costly. Moreover, if StoreBox expects to use more than 4,000 hours, alternatives 1 and 3 would be even more costly. StoreBox's managers, therefore, should choose alternative 2.

Note that the graphs in Exhibit 10-1 are linear (straight lines). We simply need to know the constant, or intercept, amount (commonly designated *a*) and the slope coefficient (commonly designated *b*) to describe and graphically plot all values within the relevant range. The general form of this linear cost function is

$$y = a + bX$$

Under alternative 1, a = $0 and b = $0.50 per CPU hour used; under alternative 2, a = $1,000 and b = $0 per hour used; and under alternative 3, a = $300 and b = $0.20 per hour used.

10-1 TRY IT!

Write a linear cost function equation for each of the following conditions. Use y for estimated costs and X for activity of the cost driver.

a. Direct materials cost is $1.40 per pound.
b. Total cost is fixed at $7,000 per month regardless of the number of units produced.
c. Auto rental has a fixed fee of $70 per day plus $0.50 per mile driven.
d. Machine operating costs include $1,600 of maintenance per month and $17 of coolant usage costs for each day the machinery is in operation.

Review of Cost Classification

Before we discuss the issues related to estimating cost functions, we briefly review the three criteria laid out in Chapter 2 for classifying a cost into its variable and fixed components.

Choice of Cost Object

A particular cost item could be variable for one cost object and fixed for another cost object. Consider Super Shuttle, an airport transportation company. If the fleet of vans it owns is the cost object, then the annual van registration and license costs would be variable costs for the number of vans owned. But if a particular van is the cost object, then the registration and license costs for that van are fixed costs for the miles driven during a year.

Time Horizon

Whether a cost is variable or fixed for a particular activity depends on the time horizon managers are considering when making decisions. The longer the time horizon, all other things being equal, the more likely the cost will be variable. For example, inspection costs at Boeing Company are typically fixed in the short run because inspectors earn a fixed salary in a given year regardless of the number of inspection-hours of work done. But, in the long run, Boeing's total inspection costs will vary with the inspection-hours required. More inspectors will be hired if more inspection-hours are needed, and some inspectors will be reassigned to other tasks or laid off if fewer inspection-hours are needed.

Relevant Range

Variable and fixed cost-behavior patterns are valid for linear cost functions only within a given relevant range. Outside the relevant range, variable and fixed cost-behavior patterns change, causing costs to become nonlinear (nonlinear means the plot of the relationship on a graph is not a straight line). For example, Exhibit 10-2 plots the relationship (over several years) between total direct manufacturing labor costs and the number of snowboards produced each year by Winter Sports Authority at its Vermont plant. In this case, the nonlinearities outside the relevant range occur because of labor and other inefficiencies (first because workers are learning to produce snowboards and later because capacity limits are being stretched). Knowing the relevant range is essential to properly classify costs.

DECISION POINT

What is a linear cost function, and what types of cost behavior can it represent?

EXHIBIT 10-2

Linearity Within Relevant Range for Winter Sports Authority, Inc.

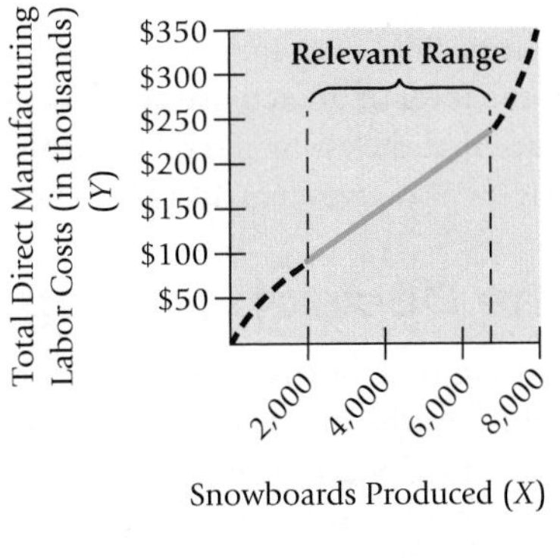

Identifying Cost Drivers

LEARNING OBJECTIVE 2

Explain the importance of causality in estimating cost functions

... only a cause-and-effect relationship establishes an economically plausible relationship between an activity and its costs

In the StoreBox example, we discussed variable-, fixed-, and mixed-cost functions using information about *future* cost structures StoreBox was considering. Often, however, managers use **cost estimation** to measure a relationship based on data from past costs and the related level of an activity. Managers are interested in estimating past cost functions primarily because they can help them make more accurate **cost predictions**, or forecasts, of future costs. For example, to choose the design features for its new TV models, LG's managers use past cost functions to evaluate the costs of alternative designs and compare it to what customers are willing to pay. Similarly, marketing managers at Audi identify cost drivers of customer-service costs (for example, the number of new car models introduced or the total number of cars sold) and the fixed and variable components of these costs. They use this information to prepare the customer-service budget.

The Cause-and-Effect Criterion

The most important factor in estimating a cost function is identifying the cost driver—a variable such as the level of activity that causally affects costs. Without a cause-and-effect relationship, managers are less confident about their ability to estimate, predict, or manage costs. We use the terms *level of activity* and *level of cost driver* interchangeably when estimating cost functions. The cause-and-effect relationship might arise as a result of the following:

- **A physical relationship between the level of activity and the costs.** Direct materials costs and production are an example. Producing more snowboards requires more plastic, which results in higher total direct materials costs.
- **A contractual arrangement.** Consider the contract between StoreBox and FWS. The contract specifies the number of CPU hours used as the level of activity that affects the cloud services costs. Consequently, there is a direct cause and effect between the two.
- **Knowledge of operations.** Based on their understanding of operations, managers might use number of parts as the cost driver of ordering costs. A Lenovo computer with many parts will incur higher ordering costs than a newer model with fewer parts.

Managers must be careful not to interpret a high correlation between two variables to mean that either variable causes the other. Consider Winston Furniture, which makes two types of (otherwise identical) tables, one with a granite surface and the other with a wooden surface. Granite tables have higher direct material costs but are available in precut blocks and so have lower direct manufacturing labor costs. Winston currently sells 10,000 granite tables and 30,000 wooden tables.

If Winston sells 20% more of each type of table (12,000 granite tables and 36,000 wooden tables), then total direct materials costs and total direct manufacturing labor costs will each increase by 20%. The two cost categories are highly correlated in this case, but neither is a cost driver of the other. Using one cost to predict the other is problematic.

To see why, suppose again that Winston sells 20% more tables (or a total of 48,000 tables), but now 18,000 are granite and 30,000 are wooden tables. Total direct manufacturing labor costs will increase by less than 20% because granite tables require less labor. Total direct materials costs will increase by more than 20% because granite is more expensive than wood. Total direct manufacturing labor costs would be a poor predictor of total direct materials costs. The best predictor of total direct materials costs are its cost drivers, the number of each type of table produced.

Only a cause-and-effect relationship—not merely correlation—establishes an economically plausible relationship between the level of an activity and its costs. Economic plausibility gives analysts and managers confidence that the estimated relationship will appear repeatedly in other sets of data. Identifying cost drivers also gives managers insights into ways to reduce costs.

Cost Drivers and the Decision-Making Process

Managers should always use a long time horizon to identify cost drivers. Why? Because costs may be fixed in the short run (during which time they have no cost driver), but they are usually variable and have a cost driver in the long run. Focusing on the short run may inadvertently cause a manager to believe that a cost has no cost driver.

Consider Elegant Rugs, which uses state-of-the-art automated weaving machines to produce carpets for homes and offices. Managers want to introduce new styles of carpets and manage costs. They follow the five-step decision-making process outlined in Chapter 1 to estimate costs and what styles of carpets they should introduce.

1. **Identify the problem and uncertainties.** Elegant Rugs' managers are confident about the direct materials and direct manufacturing labor costs of the new styles of carpets. They are less certain about the impact of different styles on indirect manufacturing labor costs such as supervision, maintenance, and quality control costs. Managers want to understand the drivers of indirect manufacturing labor costs and use this knowledge to determine the styles of carpets to produce as well as how best to manage costs.

2. **Obtain information.** Managers gather information about potential cost drivers of indirect manufacturing labor costs such as machine-hours or direct manufacturing labor-hours. They also begin to explore different techniques (discussed in the next section) for estimating the cost function. Their goal is to identify the best possible single cost driver.

3. **Make predictions about the future.** Managers use past data to estimate the relationship between the cost drivers and costs and use this relationship to predict future costs.

4. **Make decisions by choosing among alternatives.** As we will see (pages 378–381), managers chose machine-hours as the cost driver. Using regression analysis, they estimated indirect manufacturing labor costs per machine-hour both to manage costs and to choose alternative styles of carpets to maximize profits.

5. **Implement the decision, evaluate performance, and learn.** A year later managers evaluated the results of their decision. Comparing predicted to actual costs helped them determine how accurate the estimates were, set targets for continuous improvement, and seek ways to improve Elegant Rugs' efficiency and effectiveness.

DECISION POINT

What is the most important issue in estimating a cost function?

Cost Estimation Methods

LEARNING OBJECTIVE 3

Understand various methods of cost estimation

... for example, the regression analysis method determines the line that best fits past data

Four methods of cost estimation are (1) the industrial engineering method, (2) the conference method, (3) the account analysis method, and (4) the quantitative analysis method (which takes different forms). These methods differ in how expensive they are to implement, the assumptions they make, and information about the accuracy of the estimated cost function. The methods are not mutually exclusive, so many organizations use a combination of methods.

Industrial Engineering Method

Description of Method

The **industrial engineering method**, also called the **work-measurement method**, estimates cost functions by analyzing the relationship between inputs and outputs in physical terms. Elegant Rugs uses inputs of cotton, wool, dyes, direct manufacturing labor, machine time, and power. Production output is square yards of carpet. Time-and-motion studies analyze the time required to perform various operations. Suppose producing 10 square feet of carpet requires 1 hour of direct manufacturing labor. Standards and budgets transform these physical input measures into costs. The result is an estimated cost function relating direct manufacturing labor costs to the cost driver, square feet of carpet produced.

Advantages and Challenges

The industrial engineering method is a thorough and detailed way to estimate a cost function when there is a physical relationship between inputs and outputs. Some government contracts mandate its use. Many organizations, such as Bose and Nokia, use it to estimate direct manufacturing costs, but find it too costly or impractical to analyze their entire cost structure. For example, the physical relationships between inputs and outputs are difficult to specify for items such as indirect manufacturing costs, research and development costs, and advertising costs.

Conference Method

Description of Method

The **conference method** estimates cost functions on the basis of analysis and opinions about costs and their drivers gathered from various departments of a company (purchasing, process engineering, manufacturing, employee relations, and so on). Some banks, for example, develop cost functions for their retail banking products (such as checking accounts, credit cards, and mortgages) based on consensus estimates obtained from various departments. The costs of software development projects are often based on the collective judgment of experts. At Elegant Rugs, management accountants gather opinions from supervisors and production engineers about how indirect manufacturing labor costs vary with machine-hours and direct manufacturing labor-hours.

Advantages and Challenges

The conference method encourages interdepartmental cooperation. The pooling of expert knowledge from different business functions of the value chain gives the conference method credibility. Cost functions and cost estimates can be developed quickly because the conference method uses opinions and does not require detailed analysis of data. As a result, the accuracy of the cost estimates depends on the care and skill of the people providing inputs.

Account Analysis Method

Description of Method

The **account analysis method** estimates cost functions by classifying various cost accounts as variable, fixed, or mixed with regard to the identified level of activity. Typically, managers use qualitative rather than quantitative analysis to make these cost-classification decisions.

Consider the indirect manufacturing labor costs for a production area (or cell) at Elegant Rugs. These include the wages paid for supervision, maintenance, quality control, and setups. During the most recent 12-week period, Elegant Rugs ran the machines in the cell for a total of 862 hours and incurred total indirect manufacturing labor costs of \$12,501. Using qualitative analysis, the manager and the management accountant determine that indirect manufacturing labor costs are mixed costs with only one cost driver—machine-hours. As machine-hours vary, one component of the cost (such as supervision cost) is fixed, whereas another component (such as maintenance cost) is variable. To estimate a linear cost function for the cell's indirect manufacturing labor costs using number of machine-hours as the cost driver, they distinguish between variable and fixed cost components. Using experience and judgment, they divide total indirect manufacturing labor costs (\$12,501) into fixed costs (\$2,157) and variable costs (\$10,344) based on number of machine-hours used. The variable cost per machine-hour is \$10,344 ÷ 862 machine-hours = \$12 per machine-hour. Therefore, the linear cost equation, $y = a + bX$, is

$$\text{Indirect manufacturing labor costs} = \$2{,}157 + (\$12 \text{ per machine-hour} \times \text{Number of machine-hours})$$

Elegant Rugs' managers can use the cost function to estimate the indirect manufacturing labor costs of using, say, 1,000 machine-hours to produce a new style of carpet in the next 12-week period. The estimated costs equal \$2,157 + (1,000 machine-hours × \$12 per machine-hour) = \$14,157. Indirect manufacturing labor cost per machine-hour at 862 machine-hours is \$12,501 ÷ 862 machine-hours = \$14.50 per machine-hour. At 1,000 machine-hours, it decreases to \$14,157 ÷ 1,000 machine-hours = \$14.16 per machine-hour because fixed costs of \$2,157 are spread over a greater number of machine-hours.

Advantages and Challenges

The account analysis method is widely used because it is reasonably accurate, cost effective, and easy to use. To obtain reliable estimates of fixed and variable components of cost,

EXHIBIT 10-3

Weekly Indirect Manufacturing Labor Costs and Machine-Hours for Elegant Rugs

	A	B	C
1	**Week**	**Cost Driver: Machine-Hours**	**Indirect Manufacturing Labor Costs**
2		**(*X*)**	**(*Y*)**
3	1	68	$ 1,190
4	2	88	1,211
5	3	62	1,004
6	4	72	917
7	5	60	770
8	6	96	1,456
9	7	78	1,180
10	8	46	710
11	9	82	1,316
12	10	94	1,032
13	11	68	752
14	12	48	963
15	Total	862	$12,501
16			

organizations must ensure that individuals with thorough knowledge of the operations make the cost-classification decisions. Supplementing the account analysis method with the conference method improves credibility. The accuracy of the account analysis method depends on the accuracy of the qualitative judgments about which costs are fixed and which are variable.

Quantitative Analysis Method

Description of Method

Quantitative analysis uses a formal mathematical method to fit cost functions to past data observations. Columns B and C of Exhibit 10-3 show the breakdown of Elegant Rugs' total machine-hours (862) and total indirect manufacturing labor costs ($12,501) into weekly data for the most recent 12-week period. Note that the data are paired; for each week, there are data for the number of machine-hours and corresponding indirect manufacturing labor costs. For example, week 12 shows 48 machine-hours and indirect manufacturing labor costs of $963. The next section uses the data in Exhibit 10-3 to illustrate how to estimate a cost function using quantitative analysis. We examine two techniques: the relatively simple high-low method as well as the more common quantitative tool, regression analysis.

Advantages and Challenges

Quantitative analysis, in particular regression analysis, is a rigorous approach to estimate costs. Regression analysis requires detailed information about costs, cost drivers, and cost functions and is therefore more time consuming to implement. However, there are more data available today than ever before and with the declining costs of storage and analysis, it is far easier to do regression analysis and gain important insights than in the past. Newer data analytic techniques, requiring heavy computing power, continue to be developed. These techniques focus on prediction and introduce new ways of thinking about quantitative analysis. We develop these ideas and techniques later in this chapter and in the next chapter.

DECISION POINT

What are the different methods that can be used to estimate a cost function?

Estimating a Cost Function Using Quantitative Analysis

LEARNING OBJECTIVE 4

Outline six steps in estimating a cost function using quantitative analysis

... the end result (Step 6) is to evaluate the cost driver of the estimated cost function

There are six steps in estimating a cost function using quantitative analysis of past data. We illustrate the steps using the Elegant Rugs example.

Step 1: Choose the dependent variable. Which **dependent variable** (the cost to be predicted and managed) managers choose will depend on the specific cost function being estimated. In the Elegant Rugs example, the dependent variable is indirect manufacturing labor costs.

Step 2: Identify the independent variable, or cost driver. The **independent variable** (level of activity or *cost driver*) is the factor used to predict the dependent variable (costs). When the cost is an indirect cost, the independent variable is also called a cost-allocation base. Frequently, the management accountant, working with the management team, will cycle through the six steps several times, trying alternative economically plausible cost drivers to identify the one that best fits the data.

Recall that a cost driver should be measurable and have an *economically plausible* relationship with the dependent variable. Economic plausibility means that the relationship (describing how changes in the cost driver lead to changes in the costs being considered) is based on a physical relationship, a contract, or knowledge of operations and makes economic sense to the operating manager and the management accountant. As you learned in Chapter 5, all the individual items of costs included in the dependent variable should have the same cost driver; that is, the cost pool should be homogenous. When this is not the case, the management accountant should investigate the possibility of creating homogenous cost pools and estimating more than one cost function, one for each cost pool/cost driver pair.

As an example, consider several types of fringe benefits paid to employees and the cost drivers of the benefits:

Fringe Benefit	Cost Driver
Health benefits	Number of employees
Cafeteria meals	Number of employees
Pension benefits	Salaries of employees
Life insurance	Salaries of employees

The costs of health benefits and cafeteria meals can be combined into one homogenous cost pool because they have the same cost driver—the number of employees. Pension benefits and life insurance costs have a different cost driver—the salaries of employees—and, therefore, should not be combined with health benefits and cafeteria meals. Instead, they should be aggregated into a separate homogenous cost pool, which can be estimated using the salaries of employees receiving these benefits as the cost driver.

Step 3: Collect data on the dependent variable and the cost driver. This is usually the most difficult step in cost analysis. Management accountants obtain data from company documents, from interviews with managers, and through special studies. These data may be time-series data or cross-sectional data.

Time-series data pertain to the same entity (such as an organization, plant, or activity) over successive past periods. Weekly observations of Elegant Rugs' indirect manufacturing labor costs and number of machine-hours are examples of time-series data. The ideal time-series database would contain numerous observations for a company whose operations have not been affected by economic or technological change. A stable economy and stable technology ensure that data collected during the estimation period represent the same underlying relationship between the cost driver and the dependent variable.

Cross-sectional data pertain to different entities during the same period. For example, studies of loans processed and the related personnel costs at 50 individual, yet similar, branches of a bank during March 2020 would produce cross-sectional data for that month. The cross-sectional data should be drawn from entities that, within each entity, have a similar relationship between the cost driver and costs. Later in this chapter, we describe the problems that arise in data collection.

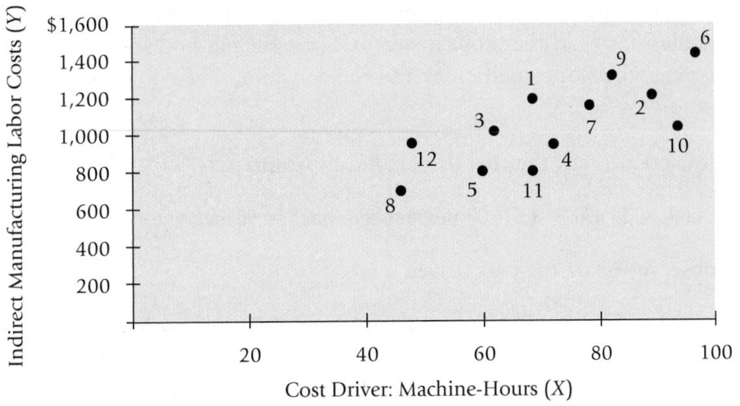

EXHIBIT 10-4

Plot of Weekly Indirect Manufacturing Labor Costs and Machine-Hours for Elegant Rugs

Step 4: Plot the data. The general relationship between the cost driver and costs can be readily seen by graphing a plot of the data. The plot provides insight into the relevant range of the cost function and reveals whether the relationship between the driver and costs is approximately linear. Moreover, the plot highlights extreme observations (observations outside the general pattern) that analysts should check. Was there an error in recording the data or an unusual event, such as a work stoppage, that makes these observations unrepresentative of the normal relationship between the cost driver and the costs?

Exhibit 10-4 is a plot of the weekly data from columns B and C in Exhibit 10-3. This graph provides strong visual evidence of a positive linear relationship between Elegant Rugs' number of machine-hours and indirect manufacturing labor costs (when machine-hours go up, so do indirect manufacturing labor costs). There are no extreme observations in Exhibit 10-4. The relevant range is from 46 to 96 machine-hours per week (weeks 8 and 6, respectively).

Step 5: Estimate the cost function. The two most common forms of quantitative analysis are the high-low method and regression analysis. We present these methods after Step 6.

Step 6: Evaluate the cost driver of the estimated cost function. In this step, managers and management accountants ask questions such as, is the cause-and effect relationship between the cost driver and cost plausible? How strong is the relationship? We next describe the high-low method.

High-Low Method

The simplest form of quantitative analysis to "fit" a line to data points is the **high-low method.** It uses only the highest and lowest observed values of the cost driver within the relevant range and their respective costs to estimate the slope coefficient and the constant of the cost function. It provides a quick first look at the relationship between a cost driver and costs. We illustrate the high-low method using data from Exhibit 10-3.

	Cost Driver: Machine-Hours (X)	Indirect Manufacturing Labor Costs (Y)
Highest observation of cost driver (week 6)	96	$1,456
Lowest observation of cost driver (week 8)	46	710
Difference	50	$ 746

The slope coefficient, b, is calculated as follows:

$$\text{Slope coefficient} = \frac{\text{Difference between costs associated with highest and lowest observations of the cost driver}}{\text{Difference between highest and lowest observations of the cost driver}}$$

$$= \$746 \div 50 \text{ machine-hours} = \$14.92 \text{ per machine-hour}$$

To compute the constant, we can use either the highest or the lowest observation of the cost driver. Both calculations yield the same answer because the method solves two linear equations with two unknowns, the slope coefficient and the constant. The equation of a line is given by $y = a + bX$, so $a = y - bX$.

At the highest observation of the cost driver, the constant, a, is

$$\text{Constant} = \$1{,}456 - (\$14.92 \text{ per machine-hour} \times 96 \text{ machine-hours}) = \$23.68$$

At the lowest observation of the cost driver, a is

$$\text{Constant} = \$710 - (\$14.92 \text{ per machine-hour} \times 46 \text{ machine-hours}) = \$23.68$$

Thus, the high-low estimate of the cost function, $y = a + bX$ is:

$$y = \$23.68 + (\$14.92 \text{ per machine hour} \times \text{Number of machine-hours})$$

The blue line in Exhibit 10-5 shows the estimated cost function using the high-low method, formed by joining the observations with the highest and lowest values of the cost driver (number of machine-hours). This simple high-low line falls "in between" the data points; there are three observations on the line, four above it and five below it. The intercept ($a = \$23.68$), the point where the dashed extension of the blue line meets the y-axis, is the constant component of the equation that provides the best linear approximation of how a cost behaves *within the relevant range* of 46–96 machine-hours. Managers should *not* interpret the intercept as an estimate of the fixed costs if no machines were run. Why? Because running no machines—that is, using zero machine-hours—is *outside the relevant range*.

Suppose Elegant Rugs' indirect manufacturing labor costs in week 6 were $1,280, instead of $1,456. In this case, the highest observation of the cost driver (96 machine-hours in week 6) will not coincide with the new highest observation of costs ($1,316 in week 9). How would this change affect our high-low calculation? Because the cause-and-effect relationship runs *from* the cost driver *to* costs, the high-low method still uses the highest and lowest observations of the cost driver and estimates the new cost function using data from weeks 6 (high) and 8 (low).

The high-low method is simple to compute and easy to understand. It gives Elegant Rugs' managers quick initial insight into how the cost driver—the number of machine-hours—affects the firm's indirect manufacturing labor costs. However, it is sometimes misleading for managers to rely on only two observations to estimate a cost function. Suppose a labor contract guarantees a minimum payment in week 8. Indirect manufacturing labor costs in week 8 are $1,000, instead of $710, when 46 machine-hours are used. The green line in Exhibit 10-5 shows the cost function estimated by the high-low method using this revised cost. Note that all of the data points lie on or below the line! In this case, choosing the highest and lowest observations for machine-hours results in an estimated cost function that poorly represents the underlying linear cost relationship between number of machine-hours and indirect manufacturing labor costs. In such a situation, managers modify the high-low method so that the two observations chosen to estimate the cost function are a *representative high* and a *representative low*.

EXHIBIT 10-5

High-Low Method for Weekly Indirect Manufacturing Labor Costs and Machine-Hours for Elegant Rugs

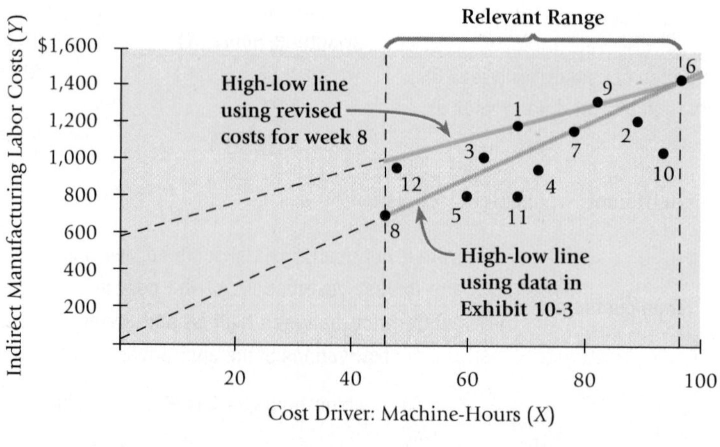

This adjustment avoids extreme observations arising from abnormal events influencing the estimate of the cost function. The modified cost function is more representative of the relationship between the cost driver and costs and, therefore, more useful for making decisions. Next, we describe the regression analysis method. Rather than just high and low values, it uses all available data to estimate the cost function.

10-2 TRY IT!

The Rexburg Company has assembled the following data pertaining to certain costs that cannot be easily identified as either fixed or variable. Rexburg has heard about a method of measuring cost functions called the high-low method and has decided to use it in this situation.

Month	Cost	Hours
January	$37,100	3,500
February	35,600	2,900
March	33,380	3,200
April	35,100	3,400
May	67,100	6,050
June	42,100	4,150

a. What is the slope coefficient?
b. What is the constant for the estimated cost equation?
c. What is the estimated cost function for the above data?
d. What is the estimated total cost at an operating level of 3,200 hours?

Regression Analysis Method

Regression analysis is a statistical method that measures the average amount of change in the dependent variable associated with a unit change in one or more independent variables. The method is widely used because it helps managers "get behind the numbers" so they understand why costs behave the way they do and what managers can do to influence them. For example, at Analog Devices, a maker of digital and analog integrated circuits, managers use regression analysis to evaluate how and why defect rates and product quality change over time. Managers who understand these relationships gain greater insights and make better decisions.

Simple regression analysis estimates the relationship between the dependent variable and *one* independent variable. In the Elegant Rugs example, the dependent variable is total indirect manufacturing labor costs; the single independent variable, or cost driver, is number of machine-hours. **Multiple regression** analysis estimates the relationship between the dependent variable and *two or more* independent variables. Multiple regression analysis for Elegant Rugs might use number of machine-hours and number of batches as independent variables. The chapter appendix explores simple regression and multiple regression in more detail.

Exhibit 10-6 shows the regression line that best fits the data in columns B and C of Exhibit 10-3. The cost function is

$$y = \$300.98 + \$10.31X$$

The regression line in Exhibit 10-6 is the line that minimizes the sum of the squared vertical distances from the data points (the various points in the graph) to the line. The vertical distance, called the **residual term**, measures the difference between actual cost and estimated cost for each observation of the cost driver. Exhibit 10-6 shows the residual term for week 1. The line from the observation to the regression line is drawn perpendicular to the horizontal axis, or x-axis. The smaller the residual terms, the better is the fit between the actual cost observations and estimated costs. *Goodness of fit* indicates the strength of the relationship between the cost driver and costs. The regression line in Exhibit 10-6 rises from left to right. The positive slope of this line and small residual terms indicate that, on average, indirect manufacturing labor costs increase as the number of machine-hours increases. The vertical dashed lines in Exhibit 10-6 indicate the relevant range, the range within which the cost function applies.

EXHIBIT 10-6

Regression Model for Weekly Indirect Manufacturing Labor Costs and Machine-Hours for Elegant Rugs

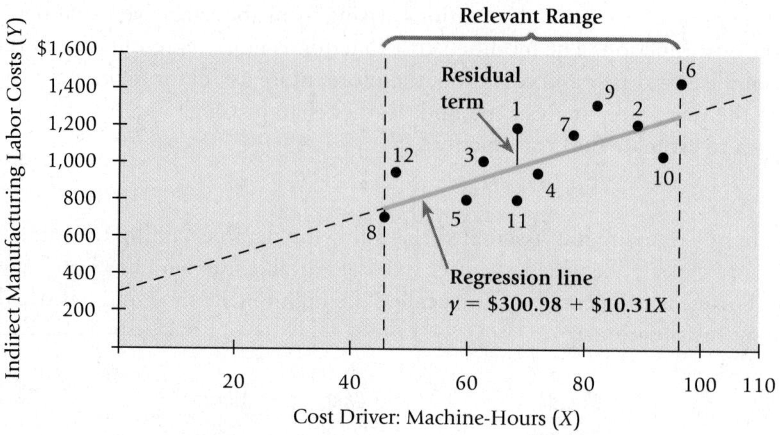

Instructors and students who want to explore the technical details of estimating the least-squares regression line can go to the appendix, pages 393–398, and return to this point without any loss of continuity.

The estimate of the slope coefficient, b, indicates that, on average, indirect manufacturing labor costs increase by \$10.31 for every machine-hour used within the relevant range. Managers can use the regression equation to set budgets. For example, if Elegant Rugs estimates it will use 90 machine-hours in the upcoming week, it will predict indirect manufacturing labor costs to be

$$y = \$300.98 + (\$10.31 \text{ per machine-hour} \times 90 \text{ machine-hours}) = \$1{,}228.88$$

The regression method is more accurate than the high-low method because it uses all observations to estimate the cost function while the high-low equation uses only two observations. The inaccuracies of the high-low method can mislead managers. Consider the high-low method equation in the previous section, y = \$23.68 + (\$14.92 per machine-hour × Number of machine-hours). For 90 machine-hours, the predicted weekly costs using the high-low method equation are \$23.68 + (\$14.92 per machine-hour × 90 machine-hours) = \$1,366.48. Suppose that over the next 12-week period, Elegant Rugs runs its machines for 90 hours each week. Assume the average indirect manufacturing labor costs for those 12 weeks are \$1,300. Based on the high-low method prediction of \$1,366.48, Elegant Rugs would conclude it has performed well because actual costs are lower than predicted costs. But comparing the \$1,300 performance with the more-accurate \$1,228.88 prediction of the regression model tells a different story and would prompt Elegant Rugs to search for ways to improve its cost performance.

Managers at Elegant Rugs are interested in evaluating whether changes in the production process (that resulted in the data in Exhibit 10-3) have reduced indirect manufacturing labor costs such as supervision, maintenance, and quality control costs. Using data on number of machine-hours used and indirect manufacturing labor costs of the previous process (not shown here), the manager estimates the prior regression equation to be

DECISION POINT

What are the steps to estimate a cost function using quantitative analysis?

$$y = \$546.26 + (\$15.86 \text{ per machine-hour} \times \text{Number of machine-hours})$$

The constant (\$300.98 versus \$545.26) and the slope coefficient (\$10.31 versus \$15.86) are both smaller for the new process relative to the old process indicating that indirect manufacturing labor costs have decreased.

Evaluating and Choosing Cost Drivers

Identifying cost drivers and estimating cost functions requires a good understanding of operations. Consider the costs to maintain and repair metal-cutting machines at Helix Corporation, a manufacturer of treadmills. Helix schedules repairs and maintenance during periods of low production to avoid having to take machines out of service when they are needed most. An analysis of the monthly data will then show high repair costs in months of low production and low repair costs in months of high production. Someone unfamiliar with operations might conclude that there is an inverse relationship between production and repair costs. The engineering link between units produced and repair costs, however, is usually clear-cut. Over time, there is a cause-and-effect relationship: the higher the level of production, the higher the repair costs. To estimate the relationship correctly, operating managers and analysts must recognize that repair costs tend to lag behind periods of high production and hence must use production of prior periods as the cost driver.

LEARNING OBJECTIVE 5

Describe three criteria used to evaluate and choose cost drivers

... economically plausible relationships, goodness of fit, and significant effect of the cost driver on costs

In other cases, choosing a cost driver is more subtle and difficult. Consider again indirect manufacturing labor costs at Elegant Rugs. Both number of machine-hours and number of direct manufacturing labor-hours are plausible cost drivers of indirect manufacturing labor costs. Managers are unsure which is the better cost driver. Exhibit 10-7 presents weekly data on indirect manufacturing labor costs and number of machine-hours for the most recent 12-week period from Exhibit 10-3, together with data on the number of direct manufacturing labor-hours for the same period.

What guidance do the different cost-estimation methods provide for choosing among cost drivers? The industrial engineering method relies on analyzing physical relationships between cost drivers and costs, which are difficult to specify in this case. The conference method and the account analysis method require managers to use their best subjective judgment to choose a cost driver and to estimate fixed and variable components of the cost function. Managers cannot use these methods to explore and test alternative cost drivers. The major advantage of quantitative methods, such as regression analysis, is that they are objective, so managers can use them to evaluate different cost drivers.

The cost analyst first estimates the following regression equation for the firm's indirect manufacturing labor costs using number of direct manufacturing labor-hours as the independent variable:

$$y = \$744.67 + \$7.72X$$

Exhibit 10-8 shows the plot of the data points for number of direct manufacturing labor-hours and indirect manufacturing labor costs and the regression line that best fits the data. Recall that Exhibit 10-6 shows the corresponding graph when number of machine-hours is the cost driver. To decide which of the two cost drivers Elegant Rugs should choose, the analyst compares the

EXHIBIT 10-7

Weekly Indirect Manufacturing Labor Costs, Machine-Hours, and Direct Manufacturing Labor-Hours for Elegant Rugs

Home | Insert | Page Layout | Formulas | Data | Review

	A	B	C	D
1	Week	Original Cost Driver: Machine-Hours	Alternate Cost Driver: Direct Manufacturing Labor-Hours (X)	Indirect Manufacturing Labor Costs (Y)
2	1	68	30	$ 1,190
3	2	88	35	1,211
4	3	62	36	1,004
5	4	72	20	917
6	5	60	47	770
7	6	96	45	1,456
8	7	78	44	1,180
9	8	46	38	710
10	9	82	70	1,316
11	10	94	30	1,032
12	11	68	29	752
13	12	48	38	963
14	Total	862	462	$12,501
15				

EXHIBIT 10-8

Regression Model for Weekly Indirect Manufacturing Labor Costs and Direct Manufacturing Labor-Hours for Elegant Rugs

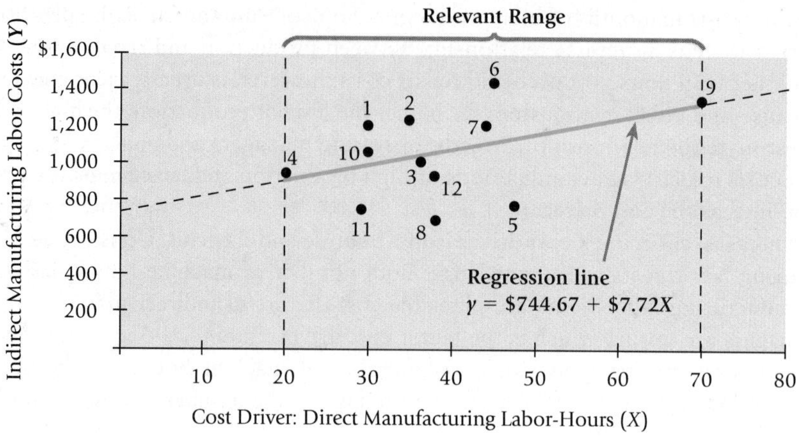

machine-hour regression equation and the direct manufacturing labor-hour regression equation and uses three criteria to make this evaluation.

1. **Economic plausibility.** Both cost drivers are economically plausible. However, in the state-of-the-art, highly automated production environment at Elegant Rugs, managers familiar with the operations believe that indirect manufacturing labor costs such as machine maintenance costs are likely to be more closely related to the number of machine-hours used than the number of direct manufacturing labor-hours used.
2. **Goodness of fit.** Compare Exhibits 10-6 and 10-8. The vertical differences between actual costs and predicted costs are much smaller for the machine-hours regression than for the direct manufacturing labor-hours regression. The number of machine-hours used has a stronger relationship—or goodness of fit—with indirect manufacturing labor costs.
3. **Significance of the independent variable.** Again compare Exhibits 10-6 and 10-8 (both of which have been drawn to roughly the same scale). The machine-hours regression line has a steep slope relative to the slope of the direct manufacturing labor-hours regression line. *For the same (or more) scatter of observations about the line (goodness of fit)*, a flat or slightly sloped regression line indicates a weak relationship between the cost driver and costs. In our example, changes in the direct manufacturing labor-hours appear to have a small effect on the indirect manufacturing labor costs.

Based on this evaluation, managers at Elegant Rugs select number of machine-hours as the cost driver and use the cost function y = $300.98 + ($10.31 per machine-hour × Number of machine-hours) to predict future indirect manufacturing labor costs.

Instructors and students who want to explore how regression analysis techniques can be used to choose among different cost drivers can go to the appendix, pages 398–402, and return to this point without any loss of continuity.

Why is choosing the correct cost driver to estimate indirect manufacturing labor costs important? Because identifying the wrong cost drivers or misestimating cost functions can lead to incorrect (and costly) decisions. Consider the following strategic decision at Elegant Rugs. The company is evaluating a new style of carpet that is similar to carpets it has manufactured in the past. It expects to sell 650 square feet of this carpet each week, requiring 72 machine-hours and 21 direct manufacturing labor-hours. Based on the machine-hour regression equation, Elegant Rugs would predict indirect manufacturing labor costs of y = $300.98 + ($10.31 per machine-hour × 72 machine-hours) = $1,043.30. Using direct manufacturing labor-hours as the cost driver, it would incorrectly predict costs of $744.67 + ($7.72 per labor-hour × 21 labor-hours) = $906.79. If other incorrect cost drivers also underestimated other indirect costs, managers would conclude that the costs of manufacturing the new style of carpet are low. But actual indirect costs driven by the number of machine-hours used and other correct cost drivers would be higher. Failing to identify the proper cost drivers leads managers to believe the new style of carpet is more profitable than it actually is. If managers had correctly estimated costs and profitability, they may have decided not to introduce it.

Incorrectly estimating the cost function also affects cost management and cost control. Suppose number of direct manufacturing labor-hours was used as the cost driver, and actual indirect manufacturing labor costs for the new carpet were \$990, higher than the predicted costs of \$906.79. Managers would then feel compelled to cut costs. In fact, based on the appropriate machine-hour cost driver, actual costs are lower than the \$1,043.30 predicted costs—a performance that management should seek to replicate, not change!

Cost Drivers and Activity-Based Costing

Activity-based costing (ABC) systems focus on individual activities, such as product design, machine setup, materials handling, distribution, and customer service, as the fundamental cost objects. Managers identify a cost driver for each activity. Consider materials-handling costs at Westronics, an electronic products manufacturer. Managers must decide whether number of loads moved or weight of loads moved is the cost driver of these costs. To do so, they apply methods described earlier in this chapter on data collected over a reasonably long period when any cause-and-effect relationship between the cost driver and costs is not masked by costs being fixed in the short run.

Managers apply all the methods described earlier to estimate cost relationships in ABC systems. The City of London police force uses input–output relationships (the industrial engineering method) to identify cost drivers and the cost of an activity. Using surveys of time required, officials determine costs associated with responding to house robberies, dealing with burglaries, and filling out police reports. The industrial engineering method is also used by U.S. government agencies, such as the U.S. Postal Service, to determine the cost of each post office transaction, and the U.S. Patent and Trademark Office, to identify the costs of each patent examination. Caterpillar uses the industrial engineering method to calculate the normalized cost of each activity in its manufacturing processes. Activity costs are then rolled up to the product level.

When choosing among methods to estimate cost functions, managers trade off level of detail, accuracy, feasibility, and costs. For example, to estimate the cost of opening a bank account or making a transfer payment, Bankinter in Spain uses work measurement methods, while Royal Bank of Canada uses advanced analytical techniques, including regression.

Increasingly, managers are using quantitative analysis to determine the cost drivers of activities. DHL Express, the international shipping company, recently switched from the conference method to performing in-depth quantitative analysis on its "big data" system. This system gives DHL the opportunity to do sophisticated analysis on large data sets at relatively low cost. A single, worldwide activity-based costing system shows the cost and profitability for every shipment in its network. Algorithms optimize the most profitable way to allocate shipments to its fleet of planes.

When estimating a cost function for a cost pool, managers must pay careful attention to the cost hierarchy. For example, if a cost is a batch-level cost such as setup cost, managers must only consider batch-level cost drivers like number of setup-hours. In some cases, the costs in a cost pool may have more than one cost driver from different levels of the cost hierarchy. The cost drivers for Elegant Rugs' indirect manufacturing labor costs could be machine-hours and the number of production batches of carpet manufactured. Furthermore, it may be difficult to subdivide the indirect manufacturing labor costs into two cost pools and to measure the costs associated with each cost driver. In cases like these, companies use multiple regression, as we discuss in the chapter appendix, to estimate costs based on more than one independent variable.

DECISION POINT

How should a company evaluate and choose cost drivers?

Nonlinear Cost Functions

LEARNING OBJECTIVE 6

Explain nonlinear cost functions

... graph of cost function is not a straight line, for example, because of quantity discounts or costs changing in steps

in particular, those arising from learning-curve effects

... either cumulative average-time learning, where cumulative average time per unit declines by a constant percentage, as units produced double

... or incremental unit-time learning, in which incremental time to produce the last unit declines by a constant percentage, as units produced double

Cost functions are not always linear. A **nonlinear cost function** is a cost function for which the graph of total costs (based on the level of a single activity) is not a straight line within the relevant range. To see what a nonlinear cost function looks like, return to Exhibit 10-2 (page 369). The relevant range is currently set at 2,000 to 6,500 snowboards. But if we extend the relevant range to cover the region from 0 to 8,000 snowboards produced, it is evident that the cost function over this expanded range is graphically not straight.

Consider another example. Economies of scale may enable an advertising agency to produce double the number of advertisements for less than double the costs. Even direct materials costs are not always linear. As Panel A of Exhibit 10-9 shows, total direct materials costs rise as the units of direct materials purchased increase. But, because of quantity discounts, these costs rise more slowly (as indicated by the changing slope coefficient) as the units of direct materials purchased increase. This cost function has a slope coefficient b = \$25 per unit for 1–1,000 units purchased, b = \$15 per unit for 1,001–2,000 units purchased, and b = \$10 per unit for 2,001–3,000 units purchased. The direct materials cost per unit falls with each price cut. The cost function is nonlinear over the relevant range from 1 to 3,000 units. Over a more narrow relevant range (for example, from 1 to 1,000 units), the cost function is linear.

Step cost functions are also nonlinear cost functions. A **step cost function** is a cost function in which the cost remains the same over various ranges of the level of activity but increases by discrete amounts—that is, increases in steps—as the level of activity increases from one range to the next. Panel B in Exhibit 10-9 shows a *step variable-cost function*, a step cost function in which cost remains the same over *narrow* ranges of the level of activity in each relevant range. Panel B shows the relationship between units of production and setup costs. The pattern is a step cost function because setup costs increase with each production batch started and then stay the same as each unit is produced. In the relevant range from 0 to 6,000 production units, the cost function is nonlinear. However, as shown by the green line in Panel B, managers often approximate step variable costs with a continuously variable cost function. This type of step cost pattern also occurs when production inputs such as materials-handling labor, supervision, and process engineering labor are acquired in discrete quantities but used in fractional quantities.

Panel C in Exhibit 10-9 shows a *step fixed-cost function* for Crofton Steel, a company that operates large heat-treatment furnaces to harden steel parts. Comparing Panels B and C, the main difference between a step variable-cost function and a step fixed-cost function is that in the latter the cost remains the same over *wide* ranges of the activity in each relevant range. The ranges indicate the number of furnaces being used (operating costs of each furnace are \$300,000). The cost increases from one range to the next higher range when another furnace is added. Within the relevant range of 7,500–15,000 hours of furnace time, the company expects to operate with two

EXHIBIT 10-9 Examples of Nonlinear Cost Functions

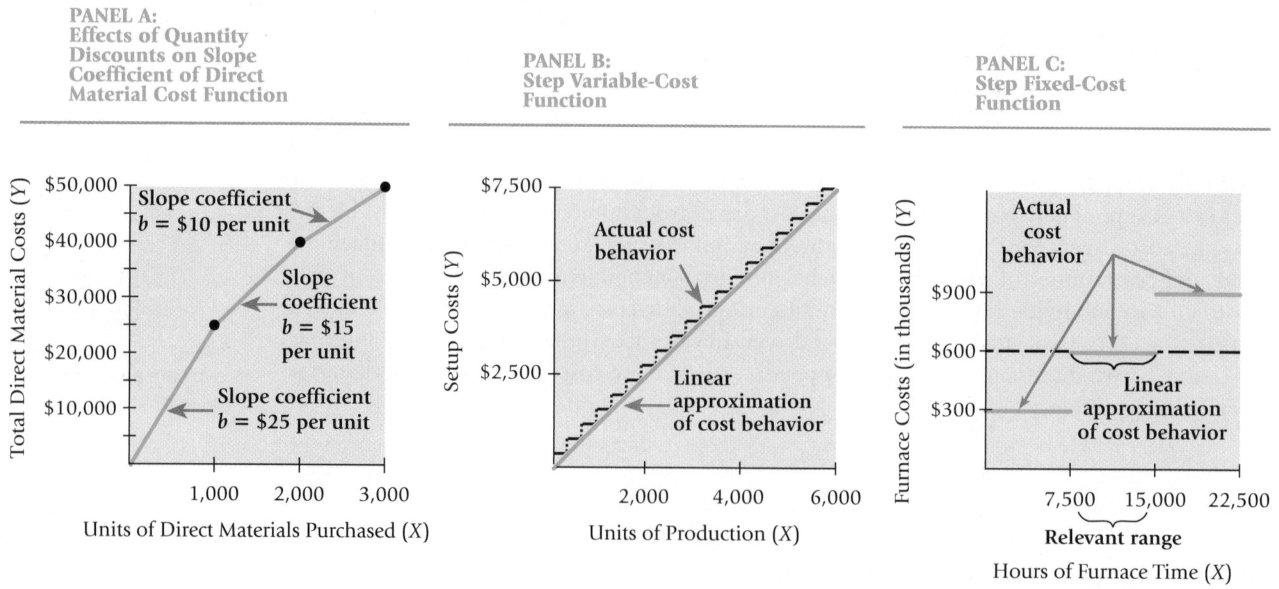

EXHIBIT 10-10

Linear and Logistic Regression

PANEL A:
FICO Credit Scores and Default Scores for Loans

Loan Number	1	2	3	4	5	6	7	8	9	10	11	12	13	14	15	16	17	18	19	20	21	22	23	24
FICO Credit Score	529	553	601	607	625	632	643	645	653	672	685	687	706	713	721	735	736	753	754	757	772	793	801	845
Default Score	1	1	1	1	0	1	1	1	0	1	1	0	0	1	0	1	0	1	0	0	0	0	0	0

PANEL B:
Plot and Graphs of Linear and Logistic Regression for FICO Credit Scores and Default Scores of Loans

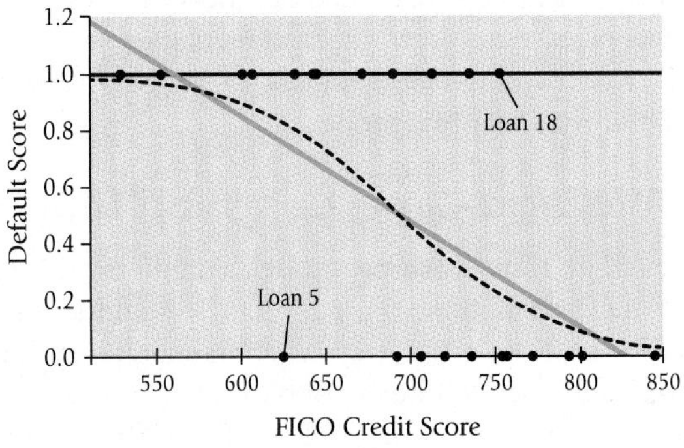

furnaces at a fixed cost of \$600,000. However, in the relevant range from 0 to 22,500 hours, the cost function is nonlinear: The graph in Panel C is not a single straight line; it is three broken lines.

Linear regression techniques can be adapted to estimate the non-linear relationships described in this section. For example, piece-wise linear regression could be used to estimate the different linear segments in Exhibit 10-9, Panel A. Different non-linear functional forms such as a quadratic relationship could be used to fit a curve to data. One of the most commonly used tools for building models in a world of "big data" is logistic regression. This technique is used when the dependent variable takes on a limited set of values, for example, a binary variable, such as whether or not a customer will leave a telecommunications company in the next 3 months or whether or not a borrower will default on a loan.

Consider a bank that is evaluating how it might use publicly available FICO sores that range from 300 to 850 based on an applicant's past credit history to evaluate the risk of default on a loan. Exhibit 10-10, Panel A, shows data on past loans where the dependent variable is coded as a 1 if an applicant defaulted on a loan and a 0 if the applicant did not. The independent variable is the applicant's FICO score. Exhibit 10-10, Panel B, shows a plot of the data. It also shows the regression line if a linear regression was fitted to the data. Although it is technically possible to fit a line to the data, the relationship between the independent variable (FICO score) and the independent variable (a 0 or a 1) is not linear. Fitting a linear regression to these data does not seem appropriate. Instead, as in Panel B, a logistic regression fits an S curve to the data using a technique called maximum likelihood estimation (MLE). Although the mathematical details are beyond the scope of this text, think of the MLE estimate (which ranges from 0 to 1) as a probability. The estimation technique fits an S curve with the objective of assigning a high probability (closer to 1) to defaulted loans and a low probability (closer to 0) to repaid loans. Of course, it cannot achieve this perfectly since there are loans (such as Loan 5) that have low FICO scores (similar to loans that usually default) but are in fact repaid and other loans (such as Loan 18) that have high FICO scores (similar to loans that usually repay) but are in fact in default. As we will see in the next chapter, the management accountant will work with management to determine a cutoff value trading off the interest the bank would earn from making the loan against the losses it would incur if the loan defaults. All borrowers with calculated values below the cutoff value (which correspond to relatively high FICO scores) will be given loans while all borrowers with calculated values above the cutoff value (which correspond to relatively low FICO scores) will not be given loans. We next turn our attention to another form of non-linear estimation—learning curves.

Learning Curves

Nonlinear cost functions also result from learning curves, a phenomenon first documented in aircraft assembly. A **learning curve** is a function that measures how labor-hours per unit decline as units of production increase because workers are learning and becoming better at their jobs. As workers become more familiar with their tasks, their efficiency improves. Managers learn how to more efficiently schedule work and operate the plant. Unit costs decrease as productivity increases, and the unit-cost function behaves nonlinearly. These nonlinearities must be considered when estimating and predicting unit costs.

The term *experience curve* describes a broader application of the learning curve—one that extends to other business functions in the value chain, such as marketing, distribution, and customer service. An **experience curve** measures the decline in the cost per unit of these various business functions as the amount of these activities increases. For companies such as Dell Computer, Walmart, and McDonald's, learning curves and experience curves are key elements of their strategies to reduce costs and increase customer satisfaction, market share, and profitability.

We now describe two learning-curve models: the cumulative average-time learning model and the incremental unit-time learning model.

Cumulative Average-Time Learning Model

In the **cumulative average-time learning model**, cumulative average time per unit declines by a constant percentage each time the cumulative quantity of units produced doubles. Consider Rayburn Corporation, a radar systems manufacturer. Rayburn has an 80% learning curve. This means that when Rayburn doubles the quantity of units produced, from X to 2X, the cumulative average time *per unit* for 2X units is 80% of the cumulative average time *per unit* for X units. In other words, the average time per unit drops by 20% (100% − 80%). Exhibit 10-11 shows the calculations for the cumulative average-time learning model for

EXHIBIT 10-11 Cumulative Average-Time Learning Model for Rayburn Corporation

Home Insert Page Layout Formulas Data Review View

	A	B	C	D	E	F	G
1	Cumulative Average-Time Learning Model for Rayburn Corporation						
2							
3		80% Learning Curve					
4							
5	Cumulative	Cumulative		Cumulative	Individual Unit		
6	Number	Average Time		Total Time:	Time for *X*th		
7	of Units (*X*)	per Unit (*y*)*: Labor-Hours		Labor-Hours	Unit: Labor-Hours		
8							
9				D = Col A × Col B			
10							E13 = D13 − D12
11	1	100.00		100.00	100.00		= 210.63 − 160.00
12	2	80.00	= (100 × 0.8)	160.00	60.00		
13	3	70.21		210.63	50.63		
14	4	64.00	= (80 × 0.8)	256.00	45.37		
15	5	59.56		297.82	41.82		
16	6	56.17		337.01	39.19		
17	7	53.45		374.14	37.13		
18	8	51.20	= (64 × 0.8)	409.60	35.46		
19	9	49.29		443.65	34.05		
20	10	47.65		476.51	32.86		
21	11	46.21		508.32	31.81		
22	12	44.93		539.22	30.89		
23	13	43.79		569.29	30.07		
24	14	42.76		598.63	29.34		
25	15	41.82		627.30	28.67		
26	16	40.96	= (51.2 × 0.8)	655.36	28.06		
27							

*The mathematical relationship underlying the cumulative average-time learning model is as follows:

$$y = aX^b$$

where y = Cumulative average time (labor-hours) per unit
X = Cumulative number of units produced
a = Time (labor-hours) required to produce the first unit
b = Factor used to calculate cumulative average time to produce units

The value of b is calculated as

$$\frac{\ln(\text{learning-curve \% in decimal form})}{\ln 2}$$

For an 80% learning curve, $b = \ln 0.8/\ln 2 = -0.2231/0.6931 = -0.3219$
For example, when $X = 3$, $a = 100$, $b = -0.3219$,

$$y = 100 \times 3^{-0.3219} = 70.21 \text{ labor-hours}$$

The cumulative total time when $X = 3$ is $70.21 \times 3 = 210.63$ labor-hours.
Numbers in table may not be exact because of rounding.

Rayburn Corporation. Note that as the number of units produced doubles from 1 to 2 in column A, the cumulative average time per unit declines from 100 hours to 80% of 100 hours (0.80×100 hours $= 80$ hours) in column B. As the number of units doubles from 2 to 4, the cumulative average time per unit declines to 80% of 80 hours $= 64$ hours, and so on. To obtain the cumulative total time in column D, multiply the cumulative average time per unit by the cumulative number of units produced. For example, to produce 4 cumulative units would require 256 labor-hours (4 units $\times$ 64 cumulative average labor-hours per unit).

Incremental Unit-Time Learning Model

In the **incremental unit-time learning model**, the incremental time needed to produce the last unit declines by a constant percentage each time the cumulative quantity of units produced doubles. Again, consider Rayburn Corporation and an 80% learning curve. With this model, the 80% means that when the quantity of units produced is doubled from X to 2X, the time needed to produce the unit corresponding to 2X is 80% of the time needed to produce the Xth unit. Exhibit 10-12 shows calculations for the incremental unit-time learning model. Note how when the units produced double from 2 to 4 in column A, the time to produce unit 4 (the last unit when 4 units are produced) is 64 hours in column B, which is 80% of the 80 hours needed to produce unit 2 (the last unit when 2 units are produced). We obtain the cumulative total time in column D by summing the individual unit times in column B. For example, to produce 4 cumulative units would require 314.21 labor-hours (100.00 + 80.00 + 70.21 + 64.00).

Exhibit 10-13 shows the cumulative average-time learning model (using data from Exhibit 10-11) and the incremental unit-time learning model (using data from Exhibit 10-12). Panel A plots the *cumulative average time per unit* as a function of cumulative units produced for

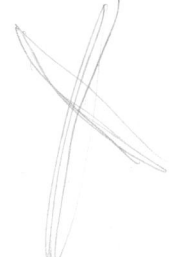

EXHIBIT 10-12 Incremental Unit-Time Learning Model for Rayburn Corporation

Incremental Unit-Time Learning Model for Rayburn Corporation

80% Learning Curve

Cumulative Number of Units (X)	Individual Unit Time for Xth Unit (y)*: Labor-Hours		Cumulative Total Time: Labor-Hours	Cumulative Average Time per Unit: Labor-Hours
				E = Col D ÷ Col A
1	100.00		100.00	100.00
2	80.00	=(100 × 0.8)	180.00	90.00
3	70.21		250.21	83.40
4	64.00	=(80 × 0.8)	314.21	78.55
5	59.56		373.77	74.75
6	56.17		429.94	71.66
7	53.45		483.39	69.06
8	51.20	=(64 × 0.8)	534.59	66.82
9	49.29		583.89	64.88
10	47.65		631.54	63.15
11	46.21		677.75	61.61
12	44.93		722.68	60.22
13	43.79		766.47	58.96
14	42.76		809.23	57.80
15	41.82		851.05	56.74
16	40.96	=(51.2 × 0.8)	892.01	55.75

D14 = D13 + B14
= 180.00 + 70.21

*The mathematical relationship underlying the incremental unit-time learning model is as follows:

$$y = aX^b$$

where y = Time (labor-hours) taken to produce the last single unit
X = Cumulative number of units produced
a = Time (labor-hours) required to produce the first unit
b = Factor used to calculate incremental unit time to produce units
$= \frac{\ln(\text{learning-curve \% in decimal form})}{\ln 2}$

For an 80% learning curve, $b = \ln 0.8 \div \ln 2 = -0.2231 \div 0.6931 = -0.3219$
For example, when $X = 3$, $a = 100$, $b = -0.3219$,
$y = 100 \times 3^{-0.3219} = 70.21$ labor-hours
The cumulative total time when $X = 3$ is $100 + 80 + 70.21 = 250.21$ labor-hours.
Numbers in the table may not be exact because of rounding.

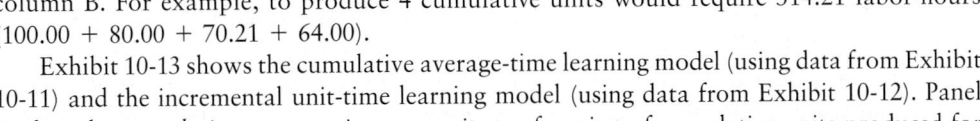

EXHIBIT 10-13 Plots for Cumulative Average-Time Learning Model and Incremental Unit-Time Learning Model for Rayburn Corporation

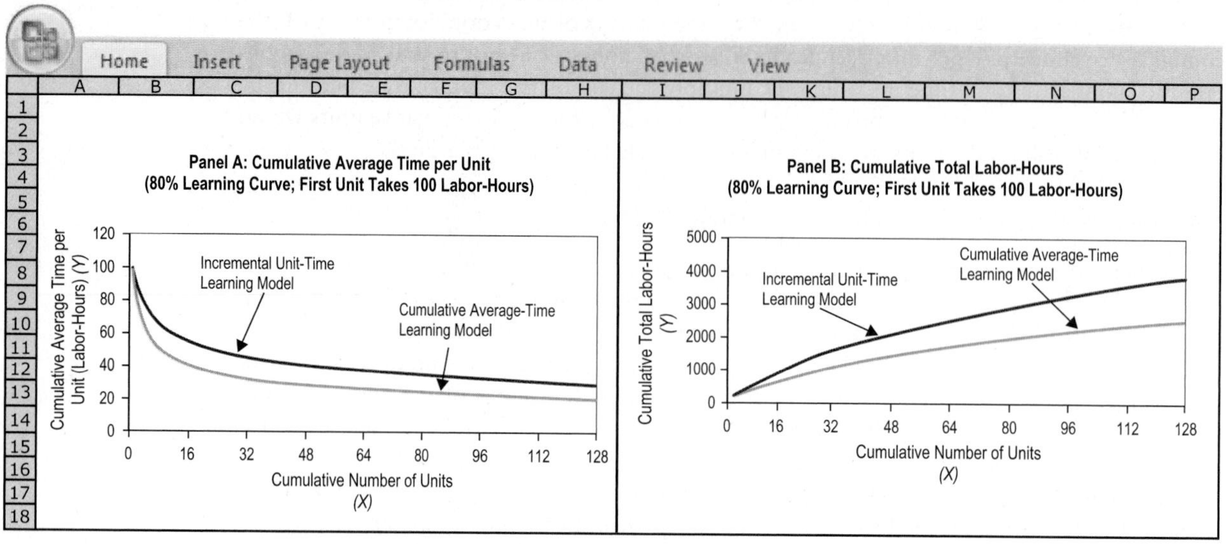

(1) the cumulative average-time learning model using data from Exhibit 10-11, column B, and (2) the incremental unit-time learning model using data from Exhibit 10-12, column E. Panel B plots the *cumulative total labor-hours* again as a function of cumulative units produced for (1) the cumulative average-time learning model using data from Exhibit 10-11, column D and (2) the incremental unit-time learning model using data from Exhibit 10-12, column D.

Assuming the learning rate is the same for both models, the cumulative average-time learning model represents a faster pace of learning. For example, in Exhibit 10-13, Panel B, the cumulative total labor-hours graph for the 80% incremental unit-time learning model lies above the graph for the 80% cumulative average-time learning model. To produce 4 cumulative units, the 80% incremental unit-time learning model predicts 314.21 labor-hours, whereas the 80% cumulative average-time learning model predicts 256.00 labor-hours. That's because under the cumulative average-time learning model the *average labor-hours needed to produce all 4 units* is 64 hours; the labor-hour amount needed to produce unit 4 is much less than 64 hours—it is 45.37 hours (see Exhibit 10-11). Under the incremental unit-time learning model, the labor-hour amount needed to produce unit 4 is 64 hours, and the labor-hours needed to produce each of the first 3 units is more than 64 hours, so the average time needed to produce all 4 units is more than 64 hours.

How do managers choose which model and what percent learning curve to use? They do so on a case-by-case basis. For example, they use the 80% learning-curve cumulative average-time learning model if the behavior of manufacturing labor-hour usage as production levels increase follows a pattern predicted by this model. Engineers, plant managers, and workers are good sources of information on the amount and type of learning actually occurring as production increases. Plotting this information and estimating the model that best fits the data are helpful when selecting the appropriate model.[2]

Incorporating Learning-Curve Effects Into Prices and Standards

How do companies use learning curves? Consider the data in Exhibit 10-11 for the cumulative average-time learning model at Rayburn Corporation. Suppose the variable costs subject to learning effects are direct manufacturing labor, at $20 per hour, and related overhead, at $30 per direct manufacturing labor-hour, for a total of $50 per direct manufacturing labor-hour. Managers should predict the costs shown in Exhibit 10-14.

[2] For details, see Charles Bailey, "Learning Curve Estimation of Production Costs and Labor-Hours Using a Free Excel Add-in," *Management Accounting Quarterly* (Summer 2000): 25–31. Free software for estimating learning curves is available at Dr. Bailey's Website, www.profbailey.com.

EXHIBIT 10-14

Predicting Costs Using Learning Curves at Rayburn Corporation

Home Insert Page Layout Formulas Data Review View

	A	B	C	D	E	F
1	Cumulative Number of Units	Cumulative Average Time per Unit: Labor-Hours[a]	Cumulative Total Time: Labor-Hours[a]	Cumulative Costs at $50 per Labor-Hour[b]	Additions to Cumulative Costs	Average Cost per Unit
2	1	100.00	100.00	$ 5,000	$ 5,000	$ 5,000
3	2	80.00	160.00	8,000	3,000	4,000
4	4	64.00	256.00	12,800	4,800	3,200
5	8	51.20	409.60	20,480	7,680	2,560
6	16	40.96	655.36	32,768	12,288	2,048
7						
8	[a]Based on the cumulative average-time learning model. See Exhibit 10-11 for the computations of these amounts					
9	[b]Cumulative Labor-Hours in Column C × $50 per Labor-Hour					

These data show that the effects of the learning curve could have a major impact on the decisions Rayburn Corporation's managers make. For example, the managers might price the firm's radar systems lower than the cost to produce the first few units to generate high demand. As production of the systems increases to meet the growing demand, the cost per unit drops (see column F), and Rayburn "rides the product down the learning curve" as it gains market share. Although it may have earned little operating income on its first unit sold—it may actually have lost money on that unit—Rayburn earns more operating income per unit as output increases.

Alternatively, depending on legal and other factors, Rayburn's managers might set a low price on just the final 8 units. The total labor and related overhead costs for these 8 units are predicted to be only $12,288 (see column E) and the $1,536 incremental cost per unit ($12,288 ÷ 8 units) is much lower than the $5,000 cost of the first unit produced.

Many companies, such as Pizza Hut and Home Depot, use learning curves to evaluate performance levels. The Nissan Motor Company sets assembly-labor efficiency standards and evaluates performance for new models of cars after taking into account the learning that will occur as more units are produced. The U.S. Department of Defense incorporates learning curves into its cost estimates for military weapons programs. Concepts in Action: Learning Curves and the Falling Prices of Renewable Energy shows how learning curves have helped reduce the price of renewable energy.

The learning-curve models examined in Exhibits 10-11 to 10-14 assume that learning is driven by a single variable (production output). Other models of learning have been developed (by companies such as Analog Devices and Hewlett-Packard) that focus on how quality—rather than manufacturing labor-hours—will change over time, regardless of whether more units are produced. Studies indicate that factors other than production output, such as job rotation and organizing workers into teams, contribute to learning that improves quality.

DECISION POINT

What is a nonlinear cost function, and in what ways do learning curves give rise to nonlinear costs?

10-3 TRY IT!

Maude Designs manufactures various picture frames. Each new employee takes 6 hours to make the first picture frame and 4.8 hours to make the second. The manufacturing overhead charge per hour is $25.

a. What is the learning-curve percentage, assuming the cumulative average method?
b. What is the time needed to build 8 picture frames by a new employee using the cumulative average-time method? You may use an index of −0.1520.
c. How much manufacturing overhead would be charged to the 8 picture frames under the cumulative average-time approach?
d. What is the learning-curve percentage, assuming the incremental unit-time method?
e. What is the time needed to produce the 16th frame by a new employee using the incremental unit-time method? You may use an index of −0.3219.

CONCEPTS IN ACTION

Learning Curves and the Falling Price of Renewable Energy[3]

Elena Elisseeva/Shutterstock

Over time, renewable energy providers have moved "up the learning curve" and reduced manufacturing and deployment costs. As the number of installations around the world increases, *learning by doing* has improved manufacturing and distribution operations, installation procedures, and sales and financing processes. Fixed costs have spread over a larger volume of production. Costs have also decreased with the adoption of newer technologies and spillover effects of innovation from other industries

The net effect is a dramatic drop in the price of renewable energy. From 2009 to 2017, the price of solar installations globally decreased 81%, while the cost to produce a kilowatt hour (kWh) of solar energy dropped 73% from \$0.36 to \$0.10. Similar price decreases have also occurred in the hydropower, offshore wind, and onshore wind markets.

It is anticipated that in the near future all renewable power-generation technologies that are now in commercial use will produce power at or below the kWh price for fossil fuels such as coal and oil. Thanks to learning curves, renewable energy is an increasingly competitive way to meet new energy generation needs around the world.

[3] *Sources:* Alan AtKisson, "The 'Big Push' Transforming the World's Energy Systems," *North Star* (blog), *GreenBiz*, January 23, 2018 (https://www.greenbiz.com/article/big-push-transforming-worlds-energy-systems); National Academies of Sciences, Engineering, and Medicine, *The Power of Change: Innovation for Development and Deployment of Increasingly Clean Electric Power Technologies*, Washington, DC: The National Academies Press, 2016 (https://www.nap.edu/catalog/21712/the-power-of-change-innovation-for-development-and-deployment-of); International Renewable Energy Agency, *Renewable Power Generation Costs in 2017*, Abu Dhabi: International Renewable Energy Agency, 2018 (https://www.irena.org/-/media/Files/IRENA/Agency/Publication/2018/Jan/IRENA_2017_Power_Costs_2018.pdf).

Data Collection and Adjustment Issues

LEARNING OBJECTIVE 7

Be aware of data problems encountered in estimating cost functions

... for example, unreliable data and poor recordkeeping, extreme observations, treating fixed costs as if they are variable, and a changing relationship between a cost driver and cost

The ideal database for estimating cost functions quantitatively has two characteristics:

1. **The database should contain numerous reliably measured observations of the cost driver (the independent variable) and the related costs (the dependent variable).** Errors in measuring the costs and the cost driver are serious. They result in inaccurate estimates of the effect of the cost driver on costs.
2. **The database should consider many values spanning a wide range for the cost driver.** Using only a few values of the cost driver that are grouped closely together cause managers to consider too small a segment of the relevant range and reduces the accuracy of the estimates obtained.

Unfortunately, management accountants typically do not work with a database having both characteristics. This section outlines some frequently encountered data problems and steps to overcome these problems. Managers should ask about these problems and assess how they have been resolved before they rely on cost estimates generated from the data.

- **The time period for measuring the dependent variable does not properly match the period for measuring the cost driver.** This problem often arises when a company does not keep accounting records on the accrual basis. Consider a cost function for a transportation company with engine-lubricant costs as the dependent variable and the number of truck-hours as the cost driver. Assume that the lubricant is purchased sporadically and stored for later use. Records maintained on the basis of lubricants purchased will indicate small lubricant costs in many months and large lubricant costs in a few months. These records present an inaccurate picture of the relationship between the cost driver and costs. The analyst should use accrual accounting to measure the cost of lubricants *consumed* to better match these costs with the truck-hours cost driver in this example.

- **Fixed costs are allocated as if they are variable.** For example, costs such as depreciation, insurance, or rent may be allocated to products to calculate the cost per unit of output. *The danger for managers is to regard these costs as variable rather than as fixed.* The costs appear to be variable because of the allocation methods used, not the actual behavior of costs. To avoid this problem, the analyst should carefully distinguish fixed costs from variable costs and not treat allocated fixed cost per unit as a variable cost.
- **Data are either not available for all observations or are not uniformly reliable.** Missing cost observations often arise because data have been entered manually rather than electronically and are not recorded or classified correctly. For example, a firm's marketing costs may be understated because the costs of sales visits to customers may be incorrectly recorded as customer-service costs. Errors also arise when data on cost drivers originate outside the internal accounting system. For example, the accounting department may obtain data on testing-hours for medical instruments from the company's manufacturing department and on number of items shipped from the distribution department. One or both of these departments might not be focused on keeping accurate records. To minimize these problems, the cost analyst should design data collection reports that regularly and routinely obtain the required data and follow up immediately whenever data are missing.
- **Extreme values of observations occur.** These values arise from (1) errors in recording costs (for example, a misplaced decimal point), (2) nonrepresentative periods (for example, from a period in which a major machine breakdown occurred), or (3) observations outside the relevant range. Analysts should adjust or eliminate unusual observations before estimating a cost relationship.
- **There is no homogeneous relationship between the cost driver and the individual cost items in the dependent variable-cost pool.** A homogeneous relationship exists when each activity whose costs are included in the dependent variable has the same cost driver. In this case, a single cost function can be estimated. As discussed in Step 2 for estimating a cost function using quantitative analysis (page 374), when the cost driver for each activity is different, separate cost functions (each with its own cost driver) should be estimated for each activity. Alternatively, as discussed on pages 399–401, the analyst should estimate the cost function with more than one independent variable using multiple regression.
- **The relationship between the cost driver and the cost is not stationary.** This occurs when the underlying process that generated the observations has not remained stable over time. For example, the relationship between number of machine-hours and manufacturing overhead costs is unlikely to be stationary when the data cover a period in which new technology was introduced. In this case, the analyst should split the sample into two parts and estimate separate cost relationships—one for the period before the technology was introduced and one for the period after the technology was introduced. If it turns out that the estimated coefficients for the two periods are similar, the analyst can pool the data to estimate a single cost relationship. When feasible, pooling data provides a larger dataset for the estimation, which increases confidence in the cost predictions being made.
- **Inflation has affected costs, the cost driver, or both.** For example, inflation may cause costs to change even when there is no change in the level of the cost driver. To study the underlying cause-and-effect relationship between the level of the cost driver and costs, the analyst should remove purely inflationary price effects from the data by dividing each cost by the price index on the date the cost was incurred.

In many cases, a cost analyst must expend considerable effort to reduce the effect of these problems before estimating a cost function on the basis of past data. Before making any decisions, a manager should carefully review any data that seem suspect and work closely with the company's analysts and accountants to obtain and process the correct and relevant information.

DECISION POINT

What are the common data problems a company must watch for when estimating costs?

PROBLEM FOR SELF-STUDY

The Helicopter Division of GLD, Inc., is examining helicopter assembly costs at its Indiana plant. It has received an initial order for eight of its new land-surveying helicopters. GLD can adopt the labor-intensive method or the machine-intensive method to assemble the helicopters as per the data shown in the following table:

	A	B	C	D	E
1		Labor-Intensive Assembly Method		Machine-Intensive Assembly Method	
2	Direct material cost per helicopter	$ 40,000		$36,000	
3	Direct-assembly labor time for first helicopter	2,000	labor-hours	800	labor-hours
4	Learning curve for assembly labor time per helicopter	85%	cumulative average-time*	90%	incremental unit-time**
5	Direct-assembly labor cost	$ 30	per hour	$ 30	per hour
6	Equipment-related indirect manufacturing cost	$ 12	per direct-assembly labor-hour	$ 45	per direct-assembly labor-hour
7	Material-handling-related indirect manufacturing cost	50%	of direct material cost	50%	of direct material cost
8					
9					
10	*Using the formula (page 384), for an 85% learning curve, $b = \frac{\ln 0.85}{\ln 2} = \frac{-0.162519}{0.693147} = -0.234465$				
11					
12					
13					
14					
15	**Using the formula (page 385), for a 90% learning curve, $b = \frac{\ln 0.90}{\ln 2} = \frac{-0.105361}{0.693147} = -0.152004$				
16					
17					

Required

1. How many direct-assembly labor-hours are required to assemble the first eight helicopters under (a) the labor-intensive method and (b) the machine-intensive method?
2. What is the total cost of assembling the first eight helicopters under (a) the labor-intensive method and (b) the machine-intensive method?

Solution

1. a. The following calculations show the labor-intensive assembly method based on an 85% cumulative average-time learning model:

	G	H	I	J	K
1	Cumulative	Cumulative		Cumulative	Individual
2	Number	Average Time		Total Time:	time for
3	of Units	per Unit (y):		Labor-Hours	Xth unit:
4	(X)	Labor-Hours			Labor-Hours
5				Col J = Col G × Col H	
6	1	2,000		2,000	2,000
7	2	1,700	(2,000 × 0.85)	3,400	1,400
8	3	1,546		4,637	1,237
9	4	1,445	(1,700 × 0.85)	5,780	1,143
10	5	1,371		6,857	1,077
11	6	1,314		7,884	1,027
12	7	1,267		8,871	987
13	8	1,228.25	(1,445 × 0.85)	9,826	955
14					

Cumulative average-time per unit for the Xth unit in column H is calculated as $y = aX^b$; see Exhibit 10-11 (page 384). For example, when $X = 3$, $y = 2{,}000 \times 3^{-0.234465} = 1{,}546$ labor-hours. It requires a total of 9,826 direct assembly labor-hours to assemble the first 8 helicopters.

b. The following calculations show the machine-intensive assembly method based on a 90% incremental unit-time learning model:

	G	H	I	J	K
1	Cumulative	Individual		Cumulative	Cumulative
2	Number	Unit Time		Total Time:	Average Time
3	of Units	for *X*th Unit (*y*):		Labor-Hours	Per Unit:
4	(*X*)	Labor-Hours			Labor-Hours
5					Col K = Col J ÷ Col G
6	1	800		800	800
7	2	720	(800 × 0.9)	1,520	760
8	3	677		2,197	732
9	4	648	(720 × 0.9)	2,845	711
10	5	626		3,471	694
11	6	609		4,081	680
12	7	595		4,676	668
13	8	583	(648 × 0.9)	5,258	657

Individual unit time for the Xth unit in column H is calculated as $y = aX^b$; see Exhibit 10-12 (page 385). For example, when $X = 3$, $y = 800 \times 3^{-0.152004} = 677$ labor-hours. It requires a total of 5,258 direct assembly labor-hours to assemble the first 8 helicopters.

2. Total costs of assembling the first eight helicopters are as follows:

	O	P	Q
1		Labor-Intensive	Machine-Intensive
2		Assembly Method	Assembly Method
3		(using data from part 1a)	(using data from part 1b)
4	Direct materials:		
5	8 helicopters × \$40,000; \$36,000 per helicopter	\$320,000	\$288,000
6	Direct-assembly labor:		
7	9,826 hrs.; 5,258 hrs. × \$30/hr.	294,780	157,740
8	Indirect manufacturing costs:		
9	Equipment related		
10	9,826 hrs. × \$12/hr.; 5,258 hrs. × \$45/hr.	117,912	236,610
11	Materials-handling related		
12	0.50 × \$320,000; \$288,000	160,000	144,000
13	Total assembly costs	\$892,692	\$826,350

The machine-intensive method's assembly costs are \$66,342 lower than the labor-intensive method (\$892,692 − \$826,350).

DECISION POINTS

The following question-and-answer format summarizes the chapter's learning objectives. Each decision presents a key question related to a learning objective. The guidelines are the answer to that question.

Decision	Guidelines
1. What is a linear cost function, and what types of cost behavior can it represent?	A linear cost function is a cost function in which, within the relevant range, the graph of total costs based on the level of a single activity is a straight line. Linear cost functions can be described by a constant, *a*, which represents the estimate of the total cost component that, within the relevant range, does not vary with changes in the level of the activity; and a slope coefficient, *b*, which represents the estimate of the amount by which total costs change for each unit change in the level of the activity within the relevant range. Three types of linear cost functions are variable, fixed, and mixed (or semivariable).
2. What is the most important issue in estimating a cost function?	The most important issue in estimating a cost function is determining whether a cause-and-effect relationship exists between the level of an activity and the costs related to it. Only a cause-and-effect relationship—not merely correlation—establishes an economically plausible relationship between the level of an activity and its costs.
3. What are the different methods that can be used to estimate a cost function?	Four methods for estimating cost functions are the industrial engineering method, the conference method, the account analysis method, and the quantitative analysis method (which includes the high-low method and the regression analysis method). If possible, the cost analyst should use more than one method. Each method is a check on the others.
4. What are the steps to estimate a cost function using quantitative analysis?	There are six steps to estimate a cost function using quantitative analysis: (a) Choose the dependent variable, (b) identify the cost driver, (c) collect data on the dependent variable and the cost driver, (d) plot the data, (e) estimate the cost function, and (f) evaluate the cost driver of the estimated cost function. In most situations, working closely with operations managers, the cost analyst will cycle through these steps several times before identifying an acceptable cost function.
5. How should a company evaluate and choose cost drivers?	Three criteria for evaluating and choosing cost drivers are (a) economic plausibility, (b) goodness of fit, and (c) the significance of the independent variable.
6. What is a nonlinear cost function, and in what ways do learning curves give rise to nonlinear costs?	A nonlinear cost function is one in which the graph of total costs based on the level of a single activity is not a straight line within the relevant range. Nonlinear costs can arise because of quantity discounts, step cost functions, the dependent variable taking on a limited set of values (for example, a binary variable), and learning-curve effects. When learning effects are present, labor-hours per unit decline as units of production increase. With the cumulative average-time learning model, the cumulative average-time per unit declines by a constant percentage each time the cumulative quantity of units produced doubles. With the incremental unit-time learning model, the time needed to produce the last unit declines by a constant percentage each time the cumulative quantity of units produced doubles.
7. What are the common data problems a company must watch for when estimating costs?	The most difficult task in cost estimation is collecting high-quality, reliably measured data on the costs and the cost driver. Common problems include missing data, extreme values of observations, changes in technology, and distortions resulting from inflation.

APPENDIX

Regression Analysis

This appendix describes estimation of the regression equation, several commonly used regression statistics, and how to choose among cost functions that have been estimated by regression analysis. We use the data for Elegant Rugs presented in Exhibit 10-3 (page 373) and displayed here again for easy reference.

Week	Cost Driver: Machine-Hours (*X*)	Indirect Manufacturing Labor Costs (*Y*)
1	68	$ 1,190
2	88	1,211
3	62	1,004
4	72	917
5	60	770
6	96	1,456
7	78	1,180
8	46	710
9	82	1,316
10	94	1,032
11	68	752
12	48	963
Total	862	$12,501

Estimating the Regression Line

The least-squares technique for estimating the regression line minimizes the sum of the squares of the vertical deviations from the data points to the estimated regression line (also called *residual term* in Exhibit 10-6, page 378). The objective is to find the values of a and b in the linear cost function $y = a + bX$, where y is the *predicted* cost value as distinguished from the *observed* cost value, which we denote by Y. We wish to find the numerical values of a and b that minimize $\Sigma(Y - y)^2$, the sum of the squares of the vertical deviations between Y and y. Generally, these computations are done using software packages such as R. For the data in our example,[4] $a = \$300.98$ and $b = \$10.31$, so that the equation of the regression line is $y = \$300.98 + \$10.31X$.

Goodness of Fit

Goodness of fit measures how well the predicted values, y, based on the cost driver, X, match actual cost observations, Y. The regression analysis method computes a measure of goodness of fit, called the **coefficient of determination (r^2)**. The coefficient of determination measures the percentage of variation in Y explained by X (the independent variable). It is more convenient

[4] The formulae for a and b are as follows:

$$a = \frac{(\Sigma Y)(\Sigma X^2) - (\Sigma X)(\Sigma XY)}{n(\Sigma X^2) - (\Sigma X)(\Sigma X)} \text{ and } b = \frac{n(\Sigma XY) - (\Sigma X)(\Sigma Y)}{n(\Sigma X^2) - (\Sigma X)(\Sigma X)}$$

where for the Elegant Rugs data in Exhibit 10-3,

n = number of data points = 12

ΣX = sum of the given X values = 68 + 88 + ⋯ + 48 = 862

ΣX^2 = sum of squares of the X values = $(68)^2 + (88)^2 + \cdots + (48)^2$ = 4,624 + 7,744 + ⋯ + 2,304 = 64,900

ΣY = sum of given Y values = 1,190 + 1,211 + ⋯ + 963 = 12,501

ΣXY = sum of the amounts obtained by multiplying each of the given X values by the associated observed Y value

= (68) (1,190) + (88) (1,211) + ⋯ + (48) (963)

= 80,920 + 106,568 + ⋯ + 46,224 = 928,716

$$a = \frac{(12{,}501)(64{,}900) - (862)(928{,}716)}{12(64{,}900) - (862)(862)} = \$300.98$$

$$b = \frac{12(928{,}716) - (862)(12{,}501)}{12(64{,}900) - (862)(862)} = \$10.31$$

to express the coefficient of determination as 1 minus the proportion of total variance that is *not* explained by the independent variable—that is, 1 minus the ratio of unexplained variation to total variation. The unexplained variance arises because of differences between the actual values, Y, and the predicted values, y. In the Elegant Rugs example, goodness of fit is given by[5]

$$r^2 = 1 - \frac{\text{Unexplained variation}}{\text{Total variation}} = 1 - \frac{\Sigma(Y - y)^2}{\Sigma(Y - \bar{Y})^2} = 1 - \frac{290{,}824}{607{,}699} = 0.52$$

The calculations indicate that r^2 increases as the predicted values, y, more closely approximate the actual observations, Y. The range of r^2 is from 0 (implying no explanatory power) to 1 (implying perfect explanatory power). Generally, an r^2 of 0.30 or higher passes the goodness-of-fit test. However, do not rely exclusively on goodness of fit. It can lead to the indiscriminate inclusion of independent variables that increase r^2 but have no economic plausibility as cost drivers. *Goodness of fit has meaning only if the relationship between the cost drivers and costs is economically plausible.*

An alternative and related way to evaluate goodness of fit is to calculate the *standard error of the regression*. The **standard error of the regression** is the standard deviation of the residuals. It is equal to

$$S = \sqrt{\frac{\Sigma(Y - y)^2}{\text{Degrees of freedom}}} = \sqrt{\frac{\Sigma(Y - y)^2}{n - 2}} = \sqrt{\frac{290{,}824}{12 - 2}} = \$170.54$$

Degrees of freedom equal the number of observations, 12, *minus* the number of coefficients estimated in the regression (in this case two, *a* and *b*). The standard error of \$170.54 is an estimate of the variation of the observed indirect manufacturing labor costs about the regression line. It is in the same unit of measurement (dollars) as indirect manufacturing labor costs, the dependent variable. For comparison, note that $\bar{Y}$, the average value of Y, is \$1,041.75. The smaller the standard error of the regression, the better the fit and the better the predictions for different values of X.

Significance of Independent Variables

Exhibit 10-15 shows a convenient format for summarizing the regression results for number of machine-hours and indirect manufacturing labor costs. Do changes in the economically plausible independent variable result in significant changes in the dependent variable? Or, alternatively stated, is the slope coefficient, $b = \$10.31$, of the regression line statistically significant (that is, different from \$0)? Recall that in the regression of number of machine-hours and indirect manufacturing labor costs in the Elegant Rugs' illustration, *b* is estimated from a sample of 12 weekly observations. The estimate, *b*, is subject to random factors, as are all sample statistics. That is, a different sample of 12 data points would give a different estimate of *b*. The **standard error of the estimated coefficient** indicates how much the estimated value, *b*, is likely to be affected by random factors.

The *t*-value of a coefficient measures how large the value of the estimated coefficient is relative to its standard error. The *t*-value (also called *t* Stat) for the slope coefficient *b* is the value of the estimated coefficient, \$10.31 ÷ the standard error of the estimated coefficient, \$3.12 = 3.30. This is compared to a critical or cutoff value to ensure that a relationship exists between the independent variable and the dependent variable that cannot be attributed to random chance alone. The cutoff *t*-value for making inferences is a function of the number of degrees of freedom and the significance level. It is typical to look for a 5% level of significance, which indicates that there is less than a 5% probability that random factors could have affected the coefficient *b*. The cutoff *t*-value at the 5% significance level and 10 degrees of freedom is 2.228.

---

[5] From footnote 4, $\Sigma Y = 12{,}501$ and $\bar{Y} = 12{,}501 \div 12 = 1{,}041.75$

$$\Sigma(Y - \bar{Y})^2 = (1{,}190 - 1{,}041.75)^2 + (1{,}211 - 1{,}041.75)^2 + \cdots + (963 - 1{,}041.75)^2 = 607{,}699$$

Each value of X generates a predicted value of y. For example, in week 1, $y = \$300.98 + (10.31 \times 68) = \$1002.06$; in week 2, $y = \$300.98 + (\$10.31 \times 88) = \$1{,}208.26$; and in week 12, $y = \$300.98 + (\$10.31 \times 48) = \$795.86$. Comparing the predicted and actual values,

$$\Sigma(Y - y)^2 = (1{,}190 - 1{,}002.06)^2 + (1{,}211 - 1208.26)^2 + \cdots + (963 - 795.86)^2 = 290{,}824.$$

EXHIBIT 10-15 Simple Regression Results With Indirect Manufacturing Labor Costs as Dependent Variable and Machine-Hours as Independent Variable (Cost Driver) for Elegant Rugs

	A	B	C	D
1		**Coefficients**	**Standard Error**	***t* Stat**
2		**(1)**	**(2)**	**(3) = (1) ÷ (2)**
3	Intercept	$300.98	$229.75	1.31
4	Independent Variable: Machine-Hours (*X*)	$ 10.31	$ 3.12	3.30
5				
6	**Regression Statistics**			
7	R Square	0.52		
8	Durbin-Watson Statistic	2.05		

Because the *t*-value for the slope coefficient *b* is 3.30, which exceeds 2.228, we can conclude that there is a statistically significant relationship between machine-hours and indirect manufacturing labor costs.[6]

An alternative way to test that the coefficient *b* is significantly different from zero is in terms of a *confidence interval*: There is less than a 5% chance that the true value of the machine-hours coefficient lies outside the range $10.31 ± (2.228 × $3.12), or $10.31 ± $6.95, or from $3.36 to $17.26. Because zero does not appear in the confidence interval, we can

10-4 TRY IT!

Yen's Palace restaurant has engaged in a series of promotional activities over recent months in an effort to generate customer interest. Jenny Chu, the restaurant's financial manager, wants to know whether these activities have had an impact on sales. She obtains the following data for the past 10 months:

Month	Promotional Costs	Sales Revenues
March	$12,000	$500,000
April	18,000	700,000
May	9,000	550,000
June	21,000	650,000
July	6,000	550,000
August	12,000	650,000
September	9,000	450,000
October	24,000	800,000
November	15,000	550,000
December	17,000	600,000

a. Plot the relationship between promotional costs and sales revenues.
b. Estimate the regression equation that captures the relationship between promotional costs and sales revenues.
c. Draw the regression line and evaluate it using the criteria of economic plausibility, goodness of fit, and slope of the regression line.
d. Within the relevant range, what is the increase in sales revenues for each $1,000 spent on promotion?

[6] If the estimated coefficient is negative, then a *t*-value lower than −2.228 would denote a statistically significant relationship. As one would expect, the absolute value of the cutoff is lower if the estimated relationship is based on a greater number of observations. For example, with 60 degrees of freedom, the cutoff *t*-value at the 5% significance level is 2.00.

conclude that changes in the number of machine-hours do affect indirect manufacturing labor costs. Similarly, using data from Exhibit 10-15, the *t*-value for the constant term *a* is \$300.98 ÷ \$229.75 = 1.31, which is less than 2.228. This *t*-value indicates that, within the relevant range, the constant term is *not* significantly different from zero. The Durbin-Watson statistic in Exhibit 10-15 will be discussed in the following section.

Specification Analysis of Estimation Assumptions

Specification analysis is the testing of the assumptions of regression analysis. If the assumptions of (1) linearity within the relevant range, (2) constant variance of residuals, (3) independence of residuals, and (4) normality of residuals all hold, then the simple regression procedures give reliable estimates of coefficient values. This section provides a brief overview of specification analysis. When these assumptions are not satisfied, more-complex regression procedures are necessary to obtain the best estimates.[7]

1. **Linearity within the relevant range.** A common assumption—and one that appears to be reasonable in many business applications—is that a linear relationship exists between the independent variable X and the dependent variable Y within the relevant range. If a linear relationship is assumed when the relationship is nonlinear, the coefficient estimates obtained will be inaccurate.[8]

   When there is only one independent variable, the easiest way to check for linearity is to study the data plotted in a scatter diagram, a step that often is unwisely skipped. Exhibit 10-6 (page 378) presents a scatter diagram for the indirect manufacturing labor costs and machine-hours variables of Elegant Rugs. The scatter diagram reveals that linearity appears to be a reasonable assumption for these data.

   The learning-curve models discussed in this chapter (pages 383–387) are examples of nonlinear cost functions. Costs increase when the level of production increases, but by lesser amounts than would occur with a linear cost function. In this case, the analyst should estimate a nonlinear cost function that incorporates learning effects.

2. **Constant variance of residuals.** The vertical deviation of the observed value Y from the regression line estimate *y* is called the *residual term, disturbance term*, or *error term*, $u = Y - y$. The assumption of constant variance implies that the residual terms are unaffected by the level of the cost driver. The assumption also implies that there is a uniform scatter, or dispersion, of the data points about the regression line as in Exhibit 10-16, Panel A. This assumption is likely to be violated, for example, in cross-sectional estimation of costs in operations of different sizes. For example, suppose Elegant Rugs has production areas of varying sizes. The company collects data from these different production areas to estimate the relationship between machine-hours and indirect manufacturing labor costs. It is possible that the residual terms in this regression will be larger for the larger production areas that have higher machine-hours and higher indirect manufacturing labor costs. There would not be a uniform scatter of data points about the regression line (see Exhibit 10-15, Panel B). Constant variance is also known as *homoscedasticity*. Violation of this assumption is called *heteroscedasticity*.

   Heteroscedasticity does not affect the accuracy of the regression estimates *a* and *b*. It does, however, reduce the reliability of the estimates of the standard errors and thus affects the precision with which inferences about the population parameters can be drawn from the regression estimates.

3. **Independence of residuals.** The assumption of independence of residuals is that the residual term for any one observation is not related to the residual term for any other observation.

[7] For details see, for example, William H. Greene, *Econometric Analysis*, 8th ed. (Upper Saddle River, NJ: Prentice Hall, 2017).

[8] Technically, linear regressions can be used to estimate non-linear relationships. For example, estimating the equation $y = a + bX^2$ can be done using a linear regression model because the coefficients *a* and *b* are linearly related. However, in most cost estimation models, the assumption is that the relationship between the estimated costs *y* and the cost driver *X* is linear (based on fixed costs and a variable cost per unit of the cost driver), that is, $y = a + bX$. We assume this linear cost relationship throughout the chapter.

EXHIBIT 10-16 Constant Variance of Residuals Assumption

PANEL A:
Constant Variance
(Uniform Scatter of Data Points Around Regression Line)

PANEL B:
Nonconstant Variance
(Higher Outputs Have Larger Residuals)

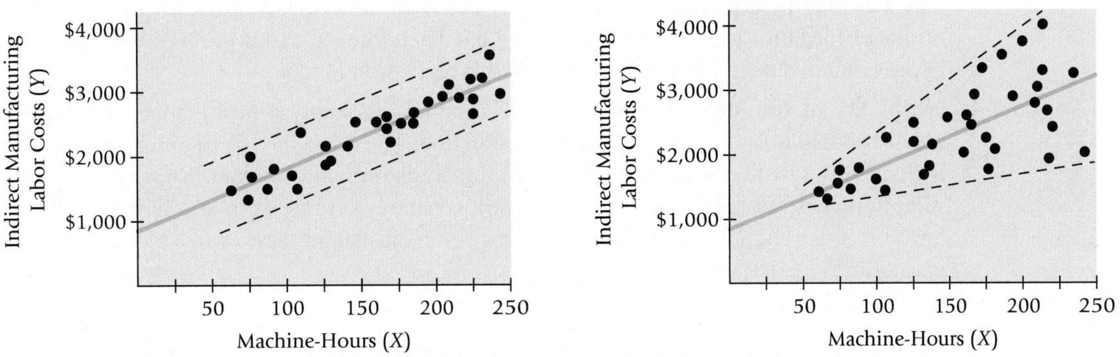

The problem of *serial correlation* (also called *autocorrelation*) in the residuals arises when there is a systematic pattern in the sequence of residuals such that the residual in observation n conveys information about the residuals in observations $n + 1$, $n + 2$, and so on. Consider another production cell at Elegant Rugs that has, over a 20-week period, seen an increase in production and hence machine-hours. Exhibit 10-17, Panel B, is a scatter diagram of machine-hours and indirect manufacturing labor costs. Observe the systematic pattern of the residuals in Panel B—positive residuals for extreme (high and low) quantities of machine-hours and negative residuals for moderate quantities of machine-hours. One reason for this observed pattern at low values of the cost driver is the "stickiness" of costs. When machine-hours are below 50 hours, indirect manufacturing labor costs do not decline. When machine-hours increase over time as production is ramped up, indirect manufacturing labor costs increase more as managers at Elegant Rugs struggle to manage the higher volume. How would the plot of residuals look if there were no auto-correlation? Like the plot in Exhibit 10-17, Panel A, that shows no pattern in the residuals.

EXHIBIT 10-17 Independence of Residuals Assumption

PANEL A:
Independence of Residuals
(No Pattern in Residuals)

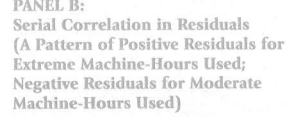

PANEL B:
Serial Correlation in Residuals
(A Pattern of Positive Residuals for Extreme Machine-Hours Used; Negative Residuals for Moderate Machine-Hours Used)

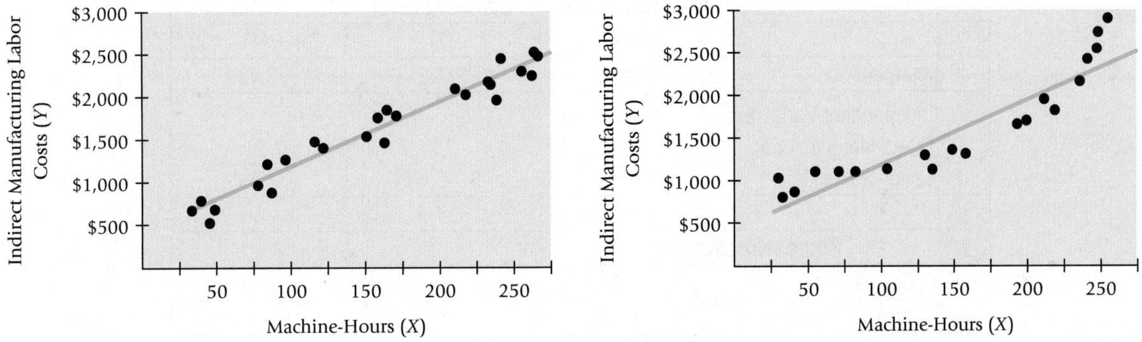

As with nonconstant variance of residuals, serial correlation does not affect the accuracy of the regression estimates *a* and *b*. It does, however, affect the standard errors of the coefficients and, therefore, the precision with which inferences about the population parameters can be drawn from the regression estimates.

The Durbin-Watson statistic is one measure of serial correlation in the estimated residuals. For samples of 10 to 20 observations, a Durbin-Watson statistic in the 1.10–2.90 range indicates that the residuals are independent. The Durbin-Watson statistic for the regression results of Elegant Rugs in Exhibit 10-15 is 2.05. Therefore, an assumption of independence in the estimated residuals is reasonable for this regression model.

4. **Normality of residuals.** The normality of residuals assumption means that the residuals are distributed normally around the regression line. The normality of residuals assumption is frequently satisfied when using regression analysis on real cost data. Even when the assumption does not hold, accountants can still generate accurate estimates based on the regression equation, but the resulting confidence interval around these estimates is likely to be inaccurate.

Using Regression Output to Choose Cost Drivers of Cost Functions

Consider the two choices of cost drivers we described earlier in this chapter for indirect manufacturing labor costs (*y*):

$$y = a + (b \times \text{Number of machine-hours})$$
$$y = a + (b \times \text{Number of direct manufacturing labor-hours})$$

Exhibits 10-6 and 10-8 show plots of the data for the two regressions. Exhibit 10-15 reports regression results for the cost function using number of machine-hours as the independent variable. Exhibit 10-18 presents comparable regression results for the cost function using number of direct manufacturing labor-hours as the independent variable.

On the basis of the material presented in this appendix, which regression is better? Exhibit 10-19 compares these two cost functions in a systematic way. On the basis of several criteria, the cost function based on machine-hours is preferable to the cost function based on direct manufacturing labor-hours. The economic plausibility criterion is especially important.

Do not assume that any one cost function will perfectly satisfy all the criteria in Exhibit 10-19. A cost analyst must often make a choice among "imperfect" cost functions, in the sense that

EXHIBIT 10-18 Simple Regression Results With Indirect Manufacturing Labor Costs as Dependent Variable and Direct Manufacturing Labor-Hours as Independent Variable (Cost Driver) for Elegant Rugs

Home Insert Page Layout Formulas Data Review View

	A	B	C	D
1		Coefficients	Standard Error	*t* Stat
2		(1)	(2)	(3) = (1) ÷ (2)
3	Intercept	$744.67	$217.61	3.42
4	Independent Variable: Direct Manufacturing Labor-Hours (*X*)	$ 7.72	$ 5.40	1.43
5				
6	Regression Statistics			
7	R Square	0.17		
8	Durbin-Watson Statistic	2.26		

EXHIBIT 10-19 Comparison of Alternative Cost Functions for Indirect Manufacturing Labor Costs Estimated With Simple Regression for Elegant Rugs

Criterion	Cost Function 1: Machine-Hours as Independent Variable	Cost Function 2: Direct Manufacturing Labor-Hours as Independent Variable
Economic plausibility	A positive relationship between indirect manufacturing labor costs (technical support labor) and machine-hours is economically plausible in Elegant Rugs' highly automated plant	A positive relationship between indirect manufacturing labor costs and direct manufacturing labor-hours is economically plausible, but less so than machine-hours in Elegant Rugs' highly automated plant on a week-to-week basis.
Goodness of fit	$r^2 = 0.52$; standard error of regression = \$170.54. Excellent goodness of fit.	$r^2 = 0.17$; standard error of regression = \$224.61. Poor goodness of fit.
Significance of independent variable(s)	The *t*-value of 3.30 is significant at the 0.05 level.	The *t*-value of 1.43 is not significant at the 0.05 level.
Specification analysis of estimation assumptions	Plot of the data indicates that assumptions of linearity, constant variance, independence of residuals (Durbin-Watson statistic = 2.05), and normality of residuals hold, but inferences drawn from only 12 observations are not reliable.	Plot of the data indicates that assumptions of linearity, constant variance, independence of residuals (Durbin-Watson statistic = 2.26), and normality of residuals hold, but inferences drawn from only 12 observations are not reliable.

the data of any particular cost function will not perfectly meet one or more of the assumptions underlying regression analysis. For example, both of the cost functions in Exhibit 10-18 are imperfect because inferences drawn from only 12 observations are generally not reliable.

Multiple Regression and Cost Hierarchies

In some cases, a satisfactory estimation of a cost function may be based on only one independent variable, such as number of machine-hours. In many cases, however, basing the estimation on more than one independent variable (that is, *multiple regression*) is more economically plausible and improves accuracy. The most widely used equations to express relationships between two or more independent variables and a dependent variable are linear in the form

$$y = a + b_1X_1 + b_2X_2 + \cdots + u$$

where,

y = Cost to be predicted

$X_1, X_2, \ldots$ = Independent variables on which the prediction is to be based

$a, b_1, b_2, \ldots$ = Estimated coefficients of the regression model

u = Residual term that includes the net effect of other factors not in the model as well as measurement errors in the dependent and independent variables

Example: Consider the Elegant Rugs data in Exhibit 10-20. The company's ABC analysis indicates that indirect manufacturing labor costs include large amounts incurred for setup and changeover costs when a new batch of carpets is started. Management believes that in addition to number of machine-hours (an output unit-level cost driver), indirect manufacturing labor costs are also affected by the number of batches of carpet produced during each

EXHIBIT 10-20

Weekly Indirect Manufacturing Labor Costs, Machine-Hours, Direct Manufacturing Labor-Hours, and Number of Production Batches for Elegant Rugs

	A	B	C	D	E
1	Week	Machine-Hours (X_1)	Number of Production Batches (X_2)	Direct Manufacturing Labor-Hours	Indirect Manufacturing Labor Costs (Y)
2	1	68	12	30	$ 1,190
3	2	88	15	35	1,211
4	3	62	13	36	1,004
5	4	72	11	20	917
6	5	60	10	47	770
7	6	96	12	45	1,456
8	7	78	17	44	1,180
9	8	46	7	38	710
10	9	82	14	70	1,316
11	10	94	12	30	1,032
12	11	68	7	29	752
13	12	48	14	38	963
14	Total	862	144	462	$12,501
15					

week (a batch-level driver). Elegant Rugs estimates the relationship between two independent variables—number of machine-hours and number of production batches of carpet manufactured during the week—and indirect manufacturing labor costs.

Exhibit 10-21 presents results for the following multiple regression model, using data in columns B, C, and E of Exhibit 10-20:

$$y = \$42.58 + \$7.60X_1 + \$37.77X_2$$

where X_1 is the number of machine-hours and X_2 is the number of production batches. It is economically plausible that both number of machine-hours and number of production batches would help explain variations in indirect manufacturing labor costs at Elegant Rugs. The r^2 of 0.52 for the simple regression using number of machine-hours (Exhibit 10-15) increases to 0.72

EXHIBIT 10-21 Multiple Regression Results With Indirect Manufacturing Labor Costs and Two Independent Variables of Cost Drivers (Machine-Hours and Production Batches) for Elegant Rugs

	A	B	C	D
1		Coefficients	Standard Error	*t* Stat
2		(1)	(2)	(3) = (1) ÷ (2)
3	Intercept	$42.58	$213.91	0.20
4	Independent Variable 1: Machine-Hours (X_1)	$ 7.60	$ 2.77	2.75
5	Independent Variable 2: Number of Production Batches (X_2)	$37.77	$ 15.25	2.48
6				
7	Regression Statistics			
8	R Square	0.72		
9	Durbin-Watson Statistic	2.49		

with the multiple regression in Exhibit 10-21. The t-values suggest that the independent variable coefficients of both number of machine-hours ($7.60) and number of production batches ($37.77) are significantly different from zero ($t = 2.74$ is the t-value for number of machine-hours, and $t = 2.48$ is the t-value for number of production batches, compared to the cutoff t-value of 2.26). The multiple regression model in Exhibit 10-21 satisfies both economic plausibility and statistical criteria, and explains much greater variation (that is, r^2 of 0.72 versus r^2 of 0.52) in indirect manufacturing labor costs than the simple regression model using only number of machine-hours as the independent variable.[9] The standard error of the regression equation that includes number of batches as an independent variable is

$$\sqrt{\frac{\Sigma(Y - y)^2}{n - 3}} = \sqrt{\frac{172{,}931}{9}} = \$138.62$$

which is lower than the standard error of the regression with only machine-hours as the independent variable, $170.54. That is, even though adding a variable reduces the degrees of freedom in the denominator, it substantially improves fit so that the numerator, $\Sigma\ (Y - y)^2$, decreases even more. Number of machine-hours and number of production batches are both important cost drivers of indirect manufacturing labor costs at Elegant Rugs.

In Exhibit 10-21, the slope coefficients—$7.60 for number of machine-hours and $37.77 for number of production batches—measure the change in indirect manufacturing labor costs associated with a unit change in an independent variable (assuming that the other independent variable is held constant). For example, indirect manufacturing labor costs increase by $37.77 when one more production batch is added, assuming that the number of machine-hours is held constant.

An alternative approach would create two separate cost pools for indirect manufacturing labor costs: one for costs related to number of machine-hours and another for costs related to number of production batches. Elegant Rugs would then estimate the relationship between the cost driver and the costs in each cost pool. The difficult task under this approach is to properly subdivide the indirect manufacturing labor costs into the two cost pools.

Multicollinearity

A major concern that arises with multiple regression is multicollinearity. **Multicollinearity** exists when two or more independent variables are highly correlated with each other. Generally, a *coefficient of correlation* between independent variables greater than 0.70 indicates multicollinearity. Multicollinearity increases the standard errors of the coefficients of the individual variables. That is, variables that are economically and statistically significant will appear not to be significantly different from zero.

The matrix of correlation coefficients of the different variables described in Exhibit 10-20 are as follows:

	Indirect Manufacturing Labor Costs	Machine-Hours	Number of Production Batches	Direct Manufacturing Labor-Hours
Indirect manufacturing labor costs	1			
Machine-hours	0.72	1		
Number of production batches	0.69	0.4	1	
Direct manufacturing labor-hours	0.41	0.12	0.31	1

9 Adding another variable always increases r^2. The question is whether adding another variable increases r^2 sufficiently. One way to get insight into this question is to calculate an adjusted r^2 as follows:

Adjusted $r^2 = 1 - (1 - r^2)\dfrac{n - 1}{n - p - 1}$, where n is the number of observations and p is the number of coefficients estimated, not including the constant term. In the model with only machine-hours as the independent variable, adjusted $r^2 = 1 - (1 - 0.52)\dfrac{12 - 1}{12 - 1 - 1} = 0.47$. In the model with both machine-hours and number of batches as independent variables, adjusted $r^2 = 1 - (1 - 0.72)\dfrac{12 - 1}{12 - 2 - 1} = 0.65$. Adjusted r^2 does not have the same interpretation as r^2, but the increase in adjusted r^2 when number of batches is added as an independent variable suggests that adding this variable significantly improves the fit of the model in a way that more than compensates for the degree of freedom lost by estimating another coefficient.

These results indicate that multiple regressions using any pair of the independent variables in Exhibit 10-20 are not likely to encounter multicollinearity problems.

When multicollinearity exists, try to obtain new data that do not suffer from multicollinearity problems. Do not drop an independent variable (cost driver) that should be included in a model because it is correlated with another independent variable. Omitting such a variable will cause the estimated coefficient of the independent variable included in the model to be biased away from its true value.

TERMS TO LEARN

This chapter and the Glossary at the end of this text contain definitions of the following important terms:

account analysis method (**p. 372**)
coefficient of determination (**p. 393**)
conference method (**p. 372**)
constant (**p. 368**)
cost estimation (**p. 370**)
cost function (**p. 367**)
cost predictions (**p. 370**)
cumulative average-time learning model (**p. 384**)
dependent variable (**p. 374**)
experience curve (**p. 384**)
high-low method (**p. 375**)
incremental unit-time learning model (**p. 385**)
independent variable (**p. 374**)
industrial engineering method (**p. 371**)
intercept (**p. 368**)
learning curve (**p. 384**)
linear cost function (**p. 367**)
mixed cost (**p. 368**)
multicollinearity (**p. 401**)
multiple regression (**p. 377**)
nonlinear cost function (**p. 382**)
regression analysis (**p. 377**)
residual term (**p. 377**)
semivariable cost (**p. 368**)
simple regression (**p. 377**)
slope coefficient (**p. 367**)
specification analysis (**p. 396**)
standard error of the estimated coefficient (**p. 394**)
standard error of the regression (**p. 394**)
step cost function (**p. 382**)
work-measurement method (**p. 371**)

ASSIGNMENT MATERIAL

Questions

10-1 What two assumptions are frequently made when estimating a cost function?

10-2 Describe three alternative linear cost functions.

10-3 What is the difference between a linear and a nonlinear cost function? Give an example of each type of cost function.

10-4 "High correlation between two variables means that one is the cause and the other is the effect." Do you agree? Explain.

10-5 Name four approaches to estimating a cost function.

10-6 Describe the conference method for estimating a cost function. What are two advantages of this method?

10-7 Describe the account analysis method for estimating a cost function.

10-8 List the six steps in estimating a cost function on the basis of an analysis of a past cost relationship. Which step is typically the most difficult for the cost analyst?

10-9 When using the high-low method, should you base the high and low observations on the dependent variable or on the cost driver?

10-10 Describe three criteria for evaluating cost functions and choosing cost drivers.

10-11 Define learning curve. Outline two models that can be used when incorporating learning into the estimation of cost functions.

10-12 Discuss four frequently encountered problems when collecting cost data on variables included in a cost function.

10-13 What are the four key assumptions examined in specification analysis in the case of simple regression?

10-14 All the independent variables in a cost function estimated with regression analysis are cost drivers." Do you agree? Explain.

10-15 Multicollinearity exists when the dependent variable and the independent variable are highly correlated." Do you agree? Explain.

Multiple-Choice Questions

In partnership with:
BECKER PROFESSIONAL EDUCATION®

10-16 HL Co. uses the high-low method to derive a total cost formula. Using a range of units produced from 1,500 to 7,500, and a range of total costs from $21,000 to $45,000, producing 2,000 units will cost HL:

a. $8,000 **b.** $12,000 **c.** $23,000 **d.** $29,000

10-17 A firm uses simple linear regression to forecast the costs for its main product line. If fixed costs are equal to $235,000 and variable costs are $10 per unit, how many units does it need to sell at $15 per unit to make a $300,000 profit?

a. 21,400 **b.** 47,000 **c.** 60,000 **d.** 107,000

10-18 In regression analysis, the coefficient of determination

a. Is used to determine the proportion of the total variation in the dependent variable (*Y*) explained by the independent variable (*X*).
b. Ranges between negative one and positive one.
c. Is used to determine the expected value of the net income based on the regression line.
d. Becomes smaller as the fit of the regression line improves.

10-19 A regression equation is set up, where the dependent variable is total costs and the independent variable is production. A correlation coefficient of 0.70 implies that

a. The coefficient of determination is negative.
b. The level of production explains 49% of the variation in total costs
c. There is a slightly inverse relationship between production and total costs.
d. A correlation coefficient of 1.30 would produce a regression line with better fit to the data.

10-20 What would be the approximate value of the coefficient of correlation between advertising and sales where a company advertises aggressively as an alternative to temporary worker layoffs and cuts off advertising when incoming jobs are on backorder?

a. 1.0 **b.** 0 **c.** −1.0 **d.** −100

Exercises

10-21 Estimating a cost function. The controller of the Blade Company is preparing the budget for 2021 and needs to estimate a cost function for delivery costs. Information regarding delivery costs incurred in the prior 2 months are

Month	Miles Driven	Delivery Costs
August	6,000	$4,000
September	10,000	$5,400

Required

1. Estimate the cost function for delivery.
2. Can the constant in the cost function be used as an estimate of fixed delivery cost per month? Explain.

10-22 Identifying variable-, fixed-, and mixed-cost functions. The Rolling Hills Corporation operates car rental agencies at more than 20 airports. Customers can choose from one of three contracts for car rentals of 1 day or less:

- Contract 1: $50 for the day
- Contract 2: $30 for the day plus $0.20 per mile traveled
- Contract 3: $1.00 per mile traveled

Required

1. Plot separate graphs for each of the three contracts, with costs on the vertical axis and miles traveled on the horizontal axis.
2. Express each contract as a linear cost function of the form $y = a + bX$.
3. Identify each contract as a variable-, fixed-, or mixed-cost function.

10-23 Various cost-behavior patterns. (CPA, adapted) The vertical axes of the graphs below represent total cost, and the horizontal axes represent units produced during a calendar year. In each case, the zero point of dollars and production is at the intersection of the two axes.

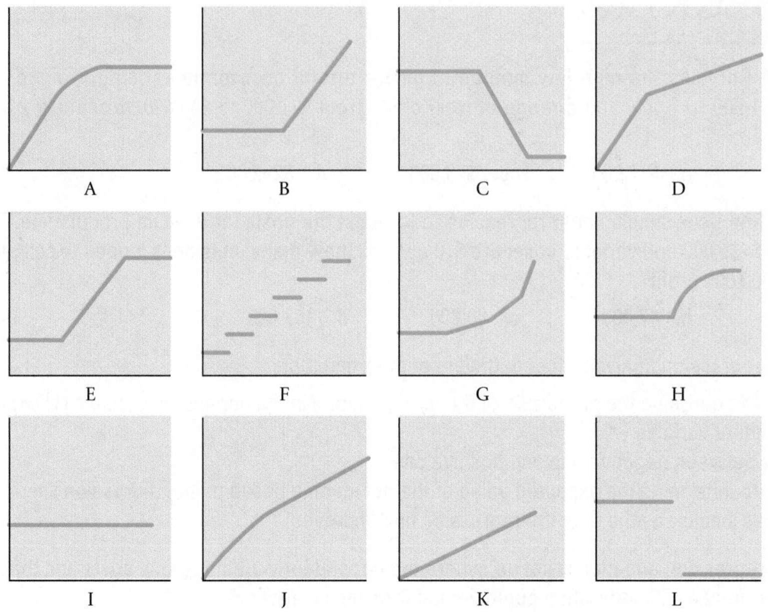

Required

Select the graph that matches the numbered manufacturing cost data (requirements 1–9). Indicate by letter which graph best fits the situation or item described. The graphs may be used more than once or not at all.

1. Annual depreciation of equipment, where the amount of depreciation charged is computed by the machine-hours method.
2. Electricity bill—a flat fixed charge, plus a variable cost after a certain number of kilowatt-hours are used, in which the quantity of kilowatt-hours used varies proportionately with quantity of units produced.
3. City water bill, which is computed as follows:

First 1,000,000 gallons or less	$1,000 flat fee
Next 10,000 gallons	$0.003 per gallon used
Next 10,000 gallons	$0.006 per gallon used
Next 10,000 gallons	$0.009 per gallon used
and so on	and so on

   The gallons of water used vary proportionately with the quantity of production output.
4. Cost of direct materials, where direct material cost per unit produced decreases with each pound of material used (for example, if 1 pound is used, the cost is $10; if 2 pounds are used, the cost is $19.98; if 3 pounds are used, the cost is $29.94), with a minimum cost per unit of $9.20.
5. Annual depreciation of equipment, where the amount is computed by the straight-line method. When the depreciation schedule was prepared, it was anticipated that the obsolescence factor would be greater than the wear-and-tear factor.
6. Rent on a manufacturing plant donated by the city, where the agreement calls for a fixed-fee payment unless 200,000 labor-hours are worked, in which case no rent is paid.
7. Salaries of repair personnel, where one person is needed for every 1,000 machine-hours or less (that is, 0 to 1,000 hours requires one person, 1,001 to 2,000 hours requires two people, and so on).
8. Cost of direct materials used (assume no quantity discounts).
9. Rent on a manufacturing plant donated by the county, where the agreement calls for rent of $100,000 to be reduced by $1 for each direct manufacturing labor-hour worked in excess of 200,000 hours, but a minimum rental fee of $20,000 must be paid.

10-24 Matching graphs with descriptions of cost and revenue behavior. (D. Green, adapted) Given here are a number of graphs.

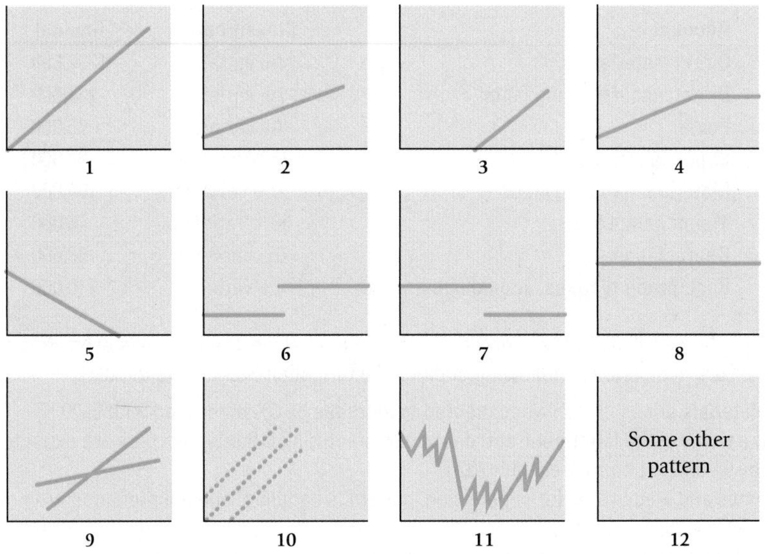

The horizontal axis of each graph represents the units produced over the year, and the vertical axis represents total cost or revenues.

Required

Indicate by number which graph best fits the situation or item described (a–h). Some graphs may be used more than once; some may not apply to any of the situations.

a. Direct material costs
b. Supervisors' salaries for one shift and two shifts
c. A cost–volume–profit graph
d. Mixed costs—for example, fixed charge plus a rate per unit produced
e. Depreciation of plant, computed on a straight-line basis
f. Data supporting the use of a variable-cost rate, such as manufacturing labor cost of $14 per unit produced
g. Incentive bonus plan that pays managers $0.10 for every unit produced above some level of production
h. Interest expense on $2 million borrowed at a fixed rate of interest

10-25 Account analysis, high-low. Smith Corporation wants to find an equation to estimate some of their monthly operating costs for the operating budget for 2021. The following cost and other data were gathered for 2020:

Month	Maintenance Costs	Machine Hours	Health Insurance	Number of Employees	Shipping Costs	Units Shipped
January	$4,510	170	$8,570	63	$28,240	7,060
February	$4,473	110	$8,570	73	$32,920	8,230
March	$4,660	239	$8,570	89	$31,600	7,900
April	$4,870	304	$8,570	102	$25,760	6,440
May	$5,120	459	$8,570	84	$23,760	5,940
June	$4,745	285	$8,570	85	$36,960	9,240
July	$4,927	338	$8,570	88	$34,800	8,700
August	$4,916	363	$8,570	80	$33,720	8,430
September	$5,055	429	$8,570	90	$26,960	6,740
October	$5,226	476	$8,570	101	$28,440	7,110
November	$5,370	500	$8,570	91	$22,000	5,500
December	$4,795	281	$8,570	101	$38,400	9,600

Required

1. Which of the preceding costs is variable? Fixed? Mixed? Explain.
2. Using the high-low method, determine the cost function for each cost.
3. Combine the preceding information to get a monthly operating cost function for the Smith Corporation.
4. Next month, Smith expects to use 350 machine hours, have 90 employees, and ship 8,600 units. Estimate the total operating cost for the month.

10-26 Account analysis method. Hamwey, Inc., a manufacturer of plastic products, reports the following manufacturing costs and account analysis classification for the year ended December 31, 2020.

Account	Classification	Amount
Direct materials	All variable	$337,500
Direct manufacturing labor	All variable	262,500
Power	All variable	75,000
Supervision labor	25% variable	60,000
Materials-handling labor	50% variable	105,000
Maintenance labor	50% variable	45,000
Depreciation	0% variable	88,000
Rent, property taxes, and administration	0% variable	110,000

Hamwey, Inc., produced 75,000 units of product in 2020. Hamwey's management is estimating costs for 2021 on the basis of 2020 numbers. The following additional information is available for 2021.

a. Direct materials prices in 2021 are expected to increase by 8% compared with 2020.
b. Under the terms of the labor contract, direct manufacturing labor wage rates are expected to increase by 8% in 2021 compared with 2020.
c. Power rates and wage rates for supervision, materials handling, and maintenance are not expected to change from 2020 to 2021.
d. Depreciation costs are expected to increase by 10%, and rent, property taxes, and administration costs are expected to increase by 9%.
e. Hamwey expects to manufacture and sell 82,500 units in 2021.

Required

1. Prepare a schedule of variable, fixed, and total manufacturing costs for each account category in 2021. Estimate total manufacturing costs for 2021.
2. Calculate Hamwey's total manufacturing cost per unit in 2020, and estimate total manufacturing cost per unit in 2021.
3. How can you obtain better estimates of fixed and variable costs? Why would these better estimates be useful to Hamwey?

10-27 Estimating a cost function, high-low method. Roy Travel offers helicopter service from suburban towns to John F. Kennedy International Airport in New York City. Each of its nine helicopters makes between 1,350 and 2,100 round-trips per year. The records indicate that a helicopter that has made 1,350 round-trips in the year incurs an average operating cost of $450 per round-trip, and one that has made 2,100 round-trips in the year incurs an average operating cost of $350 per round-trip.

Required

1. Using the high-low method, estimate the linear relationship $y = a + bX$, where y is the total annual operating cost of a helicopter and X is the number of round-trips it makes to JFK airport during the year.
2. Give examples of costs that would be included in a and in b.
3. If Roy Travel expects each helicopter to make, on average, 1,700 round-trips in the coming year, what should be its estimated operating budget for the helicopter fleet?

10-28 Estimating a cost function, high-low method. Lynsay Detz is examining customer-service costs in the southern region of Clancey Products. Clancey Products has more than 200 separate electrical products that are sold with a 6-month guarantee of full repair or replacement with a new product. When a product is returned by a customer, a service report is prepared. This service report includes details of the problem and the time and cost of resolving the problem. Weekly data for the most recent 8-week period are as follows:

Week	Customer-Service Department Costs	Number of Service Reports
1	$13,400	210
2	20,200	300
3	11,300	130
4	18,900	385
5	14,700	285
6	22,500	450
7	16,300	330
8	21,600	310

Required

1. Plot the relationship between customer-service costs and number of service reports. Is the relationship economically plausible?
2. Use the high-low method to compute the cost function relating customer-service costs to the number of service reports.
3. What variables, in addition to number of service reports, might be cost drivers of weekly customer-service costs of Clancey Products?

10-29 Linear cost approximation. Dr. Young, of Young and Associates, LLP, is examining how overhead costs behave as a function of monthly physician contact hours billed to patients. The historical data are as follows:

Total Overhead Costs	Physician Contact Hours Billed to Patients
$ 90,000	150
105,000	200
111,000	250
125,000	300
137,000	350
150,000	400

Required

1. Compute the linear cost function, relating total overhead costs to physician contact hours, using the representative observations of 200 and 300 hours. Plot the linear cost function. Does the constant component of the cost function represent the fixed overhead costs of Young and Associates? Why?
2. What would be the predicted total overhead costs for (a) 150 hours and (b) 400 hours using the cost function estimated in requirement 1? Plot the predicted costs and actual costs for 150 and 400 hours.
3. Dr. Young had a chance to do some school physicals that would have boosted physician contact hours billed to patients from 200 to 250 hours. Suppose Dr. Young, guided by the linear cost function, rejected this job because it would have brought a total increase in contribution margin of $9,000, before deducting the predicted increase in total overhead cost, $10,000. What is the total contribution margin actually forgone?

10-30 Cost–volume–profit and regression analysis. Grant Corporation manufactures a drink bottle, model CL24. During 2020, Grant produced 240,000 bottles at a total cost of $1,080,000. Wren Corporation has offered to supply as many bottles as Grant wants at a cost of $4.40 per bottle. Grant anticipates needing 255,000 bottles each year for the next few years.

Required

1. a. What is the average cost of manufacturing a drink bottle in 2020? How does it compare to Wren's offer?
   b. Can Grant use the answer in requirement 1a to determine the cost of manufacturing 255,000 drink bottles? Explain.
2. Grant's cost analyst uses annual data from past years to estimate the following regression equation with total manufacturing costs of the drink bottle as the dependent variable and drink bottles produced as the independent variable:

$$y = \$431{,}000 + \$3.00X$$

   During the years used to estimate the regression equation, the production of bottles varied from 229,000 to 265,000. Using this equation, estimate how much it would cost Grant to manufacture 255,000 drink bottles. How much more or less costly is it to manufacture the bottles than to acquire them from Wren?
3. What other information would you need to be confident that the equation in requirement 2 accurately predicts the cost of manufacturing drink bottles?

10-31 Regression analysis, service company. (CMA, adapted) Linda Olson owns a professional character business in a large metropolitan area. She hires local college students to play these characters at children's parties and other events. Linda provides balloons, cupcakes, and punch. For a standard party the cost on a per-person basis is as follows:

Balloons, cupcakes, and punch	$ 7
Labor (0.25 hour × $20 per hour)	5
Overhead (0.25 hour × $40 per hour)	10
Total cost per person	$22

Linda is quite certain about the estimates of the materials and labor costs but is not as comfortable with the overhead estimate. The overhead estimate was based on the actual data for the past 9 months, which are presented here. These data indicate that overhead costs vary with the direct labor-hours used. The $40 estimate was determined by dividing total overhead costs for the 9 months by total labor-hours.

Month	Labor-Hours	Overhead Costs
April	1,400	$ 65,000
May	1,800	71,000
June	2,100	73,000
July	2,200	76,000
August	1,650	67,000
September	1,725	68,000
October	1,500	66,500
November	1,200	60,000
December	1,900	72,500
Total	15,475	$619,000

Linda has recently become aware of regression analysis. She estimated the following regression equation with overhead costs as the dependent variable and labor-hours as the independent variable:

$$y = \$43,563 + \$14.66X$$

Required

1. Plot the relationship between overhead costs and labor-hours. Draw the regression line and evaluate it using the criteria of economic plausibility, goodness of fit, and slope of the regression line.
2. Using data from the regression analysis, what is the variable cost per person for a standard party?
3. Linda Olson has been asked to prepare a bid for a 20-child birthday party to be given next month. Determine the minimum bid price that Linda would be willing to submit to recoup variable costs.

10-32 High-low, regression. May Blackwell is the new manager of the materials storeroom for Clayton Manufacturing. May has been asked to estimate future monthly purchase costs for part #696, used in two of Clayton's products. May has purchase cost and quantity data for the past 9 months as follows:

Month	Cost of Purchase	Quantity Purchased
January	$12,675	2,710 parts
February	13,000	2,810
March	17,653	4,153
April	15,825	3,756
May	13,125	2,912
June	13,814	3,387
July	15,300	3,622
August	10,233	2,298
September	14,950	3,562

Estimated monthly purchases for this part based on expected demand of the two products for the rest of the year are as follows:

Month	Purchase Quantity Expected
October	3,340 parts
November	3,710
December	3,040

Required

1. The computer in May's office is down, and May has been asked to immediately provide an equation to estimate the future purchase cost for part #696. May grabs a calculator and uses the high-low method to estimate a cost equation. What equation does she get?
2. Using the equation from requirement 1, calculate the future expected purchase costs for each of the last 3 months of the year.
3. After a few hours, May's computer is fixed. May uses the first 9 months of data and regression analysis to estimate the relationship between the quantity purchased and purchase costs of part #696. The regression line May obtains is as follows:

$$y = \$2,582.6 + 3.54X$$

Evaluate the regression line using the criteria of economic plausibility, goodness of fit, and significance of the independent variable. Compare the regression equation to the equation based on the high-low method. Which is a better fit? Why?

4. Use the regression results to calculate the expected purchase costs for October, November, and December. Compare the expected purchase costs to the expected purchase costs calculated using the high-low method in requirement 2. Comment on your results.

10-33 Learning curve, cumulative average-time learning model. Global Defender manufactures radar systems. It has just completed the manufacture of its first newly designed system, RS-32. Manufacturing data for the RS-32 follow:

Direct materials cost	\$82,000 per unit of RS-32
Direct manufacturing labor time for first unit	3,600 direct manufacturing labor-hours
Learning curve for manufacturing labor time per radar system	85% cumulative average time[a]
Direct manufacturing labor costs	\$ 20 per direct manufacturing labor-hour
Variable manufacturing overhead costs	\$ 17 per direct manufacturing labor-hour

[a]Using the formula (page 384) for a 85% learning curve, $b = \frac{\ln 0.85}{\ln 2} = \frac{-0.162519}{0.693147} = -0.234465$

Calculate the total variable costs of producing 2, 4, and 8 units.

Required

10-34 Learning curve, incremental unit-time learning model. Assume the same information for Global Defender as in Exercise 10-33, except that Global Defender uses an 85% incremental unit-time learning model as a basis for predicting direct manufacturing labor-hours. (An 85% learning curve means $b = -0.234465$.)

Required

1. Calculate the total variable costs of producing 2, 3, and 4 units.
2. If you solved Exercise 10-33, compare your cost predictions in the two exercises for 2 and 4 units. Why are the predictions different? How should Global Defender decide which model it should use?

10-35 High-low method. Wayne Mueller, financial analyst at CELL Corporation, is examining the behavior of quarterly utility costs for budgeting purposes. Mueller collects the following data on machine-hours worked and utility costs for the past 8 quarters:

Quarter	Machine-Hours	Utility Costs
1	120,000	\$215,000
2	75,000	150,000
3	110,000	200,000
4	150,000	270,000
5	90,000	170,000
6	140,000	250,000
7	130,000	225,000
8	100,000	195,000

Required

1. Estimate the cost function for the quarterly data using the high-low method.
2. Plot and comment on the estimated cost function.
3. Mueller anticipates that CELL will operate machines for 125,000 hours in quarter 9. Calculate the predicted utility costs in quarter 9 using the cost function estimated in requirement 1.

Problems

10-36 High-low method and regression analysis. Market Thyme, a cooperative of organic family-owned farms, has recently started a fresh produce club to provide support to the group's member farms and to promote the benefits of eating organic, locally produced food. Families pay a seasonal membership fee of \$100 and place their orders a week in advance for a price of \$40 per order. In turn, Market Thyme delivers fresh-picked seasonal local produce to several neighborhood distribution points. Five hundred families joined the club for the first season, but the number of orders varied from week to week.

Tom Diehl has run the produce club for the first season. Tom is now a farmer but remembers a few things about cost analysis from college. In planning for next year, he wants to know how many orders will be needed each week for the club to break even, but first he must estimate the club's fixed and variable costs. He has collected the following data over the club's first season of operation:

Week	Number of Orders per Week	Weekly Total Costs
1	415	$26,900
2	435	27,200
3	285	24,700
4	325	25,200
5	450	27,995
6	360	25,900
7	420	27,000
8	460	28,315
9	380	26,425
10	350	25,750

Required

1. Plot the relationship between number of orders per week and weekly total costs.
2. Estimate the cost equation using the high-low method, and draw this line on your graph.
3. Tom uses his computer to calculate the following regression formula:

$$\text{Weekly total costs} = \$18{,}791 + (\$19.97 \times \text{Number of orders per week})$$

   Draw the regression line on your graph. Use your graph to evaluate the regression line using the criteria of economic plausibility, goodness of fit, and significance of the independent variable. Is the cost function estimated using the high-low method a close approximation of the cost function estimated using the regression method? Explain briefly.
4. Did Market Thyme break even this season? Remember that each of the families paid a seasonal membership fee of $100.
5. Assume that 500 families join the club next year and that prices and costs do not change. How many orders, on average, must Market Thyme receive each of 10 weeks next season to break even?

10-37 High-low method; regression analysis. (CIMA, adapted) Amy Mendenhall, sales manager of Fitzsimmons Arenas, is checking to see if there is any relationship between promotional costs and ticket revenues at the sports stadium. She obtains the following data for the past 9 months:

Month	Ticket Revenues	Promotional Costs
April	$220,000	$ 55,000
May	290,000	68,000
June	340,000	83,000
July	500,000	93,000
August	450,000	103,000
September	470,000	113,000
October	560,000	123,000
November	690,000	183,000
December	756,500	200,000

She estimates the following regression equation:

$$\text{Ticket revenues} = \$39{,}502 + (\$3.60 \times \text{Promotional costs})$$

Required

1. Plot the relationship between promotional costs and ticket revenues. Also draw the regression line and evaluate it using the criteria of economic plausibility, goodness of fit, and slope of the regression line.
2. Use the high-low method to compute the function relating promotional costs and revenues.
3. Using (a) the regression equation and (b) the high-low equation, what is the increase in revenues for each $10,000 spent on promotional costs within the relevant range? Which method should Amy use to predict the effect of promotional costs on ticket revenues? Explain briefly.

10-38 Regression, activity-based costing, choosing cost drivers. Sleep Late, a large hotel chain, has been using activity-based costing to determine the cost of a night's stay at their hotels. One of the activities, "Inspection," occurs to ensure the room is in good condition. Sleep Late has been using "number of rooms inspected" as the cost driver for inspection costs. A significant component of inspection costs is the cost of replacing cutlery, crockery, and furnishings as a result of an inspection.

Mary Adams, the chief inspector, is wondering whether inspection labor-hours might be a better cost driver for inspection costs. Adams gathers information for weekly inspection costs, rooms inspected, and inspection labor-hours as follows:

Week	Rooms Inspected	Inspection Labor-Hours	Inspection Costs
1	254	66	$1,740
2	322	110	2,500
3	335	82	2,250
4	431	123	2,800
5	198	48	1,400
6	239	62	1,690
7	252	108	1,720
8	325	127	2,200

Adams runs regressions on each of the possible cost drivers and estimates these cost functions:

$$\text{Inspection Costs} = \$193.19 + (\$6.26 \times \text{Number of rooms inspected})$$
$$\text{Inspection Costs} = \$944.66 + (\$12.04 \times \text{Inspection labor-hours})$$

Required

1. Explain why rooms inspected and inspection labor-hours are plausible cost drivers of inspection costs.
2. Plot the data and regression line for rooms inspected and inspection costs. Plot the data and regression line for inspection labor-hours and inspection costs. Which cost driver of inspection costs would you choose? Explain.
3. Adams expects inspectors to inspect 300 rooms and work for 105 hours next week. Using the cost driver you chose in requirement 2, what amount of inspection costs should Adams budget? Explain any implications of Adams choosing the cost driver you did not choose in requirement 2 to budget inspection costs.

10-39 Interpreting regression results. Spirit Freightways is a leader in transporting agricultural products in the western provinces of Canada. Reese Brown, a financial analyst at Spirit Freightways, is studying the behavior of transportation costs for budgeting purposes. Transportation costs at Spirit are of two types: (1) operating costs (such as labor and fuel) and (2) maintenance costs (primarily overhaul of vehicles).

Brown gathers monthly data on each type of cost, as well as the total freight miles traveled by Spirit vehicles in each month. The data collected are shown below (all in thousands):

Month	Operating Costs	Maintenance Costs	Freight Miles
January	$ 942	$ 974	1,710
February	1,008	776	2,655
March	1,218	686	2,705
April	1,380	694	4,220
May	1,484	588	4,660
June	1,548	422	4,455
July	1,568	352	4,435
August	1,972	420	4,990
September	1,190	564	2,990
October	1,302	788	2,610
November	962	762	2,240
December	772	1,028	1,490

Required

1. Conduct a regression using the monthly data of operating costs on freight miles. You should obtain the following result:

   Regression: Operating costs = $a + (b \times$ Number of freight miles)

Variable	Coefficient	Standard Error	*t*-Value
Constant	$445.76	$112.97	3.95
Independent variable: No. of freight miles	$ 0.26	$ 0.03	7.83

   $r^2 = 0.86$; Durbin-Watson statistic = 2.18

2. Plot the data and regression line for the above estimation. Evaluate the regression using the criteria of economic plausibility, goodness of fit, and slope of the regression line.
3. Brown expects Spirit to generate, on average, 3,600 freight miles each month next year. How much in operating costs should Brown budget for next year?

4. Name three variables, other than freight miles, that Brown might expect to be important cost drivers for Spirit's operating costs.
5. Brown next conducts a regression using the monthly data of maintenance costs on freight miles. Verify that she obtained the following result:

Regression: Maintenance costs = $a + (b \times$ Number of freight miles)

Variable	Coefficient	Standard Error	*t*-Value
Constant	$1,170.57	$91.07	12.85
Independent variable: No. of freight miles	$ −0.15	$ 0.03	−5.83

$r^2 = 0.77$; Durbin-Watson statistic = 1.94

6. Provide a reasoned explanation for the observed sign on the cost driver variable in the maintenance cost regression. What alternative data or alternative regression specifications would you like to use to better capture the above relationship?

10-40 Cost estimation, cumulative average-time learning curve. The WLJ Boat Company, which is under contract to the U.S. Navy, assembles troop deployment boats. As part of its research program, it completes the assembly of the first of a new model (PT109) of deployment boats. The Navy is impressed with the PT109. It requests that WLJ Boat submit a proposal on the cost of producing another six PT109s.

WLJ Boat reports the following cost information for the first PT109 assembled and uses a 90% cumulative average-time learning model as a basis for forecasting direct manufacturing labor-hours for the next six PT109s. (A 90% learning curve means b = −0.152004.)

Direct materials cost	$205,000 per PT109
Direct manufacturing labor time for first boat	15,200 direct manufacturing labor-hours
Learning curve for manufacturing labor time per boat	90% cumulative average time[a]
Direct manufacturing labor costs	$ 45 per direct manufacturing labor-hour
Variable manufacturing overhead costs	$ 21 per direct manufacturing labor-hour
Other manufacturing overhead	25% of direct manufacturing labor costs
Tooling costs[b]	$285,000

[a]Using the formula (page 384) for a 90% learning curve, $b = \frac{\ln 0.90}{\ln 2} = \frac{-0.105361}{0.693147} = -0.152004$

[b]Tooling can be reused at no extra cost because all of its cost has been assigned to the first deployment boat.

Required

1. Calculate predicted total costs of producing the six PT109s for the Navy. (WLJ Boat will keep the first deployment boat assembled, costed at $1,493,200, as a demonstration model for potential customers.)
2. What is the dollar amount of the difference between (a) the predicted total costs for producing the six PT109s in requirement 1 and (b) the predicted total costs for producing the six PT109s, assuming that there is no learning curve for direct manufacturing labor? That is, for (b) assume a linear function for units produced and direct manufacturing labor-hours.

10-41 Cost estimation, incremental unit-time learning model. Assume the same information for the WLJ Boat Company as in Problem 10-40 with one exception. This exception is that WLJ Boat uses a 90% incremental unit-time learning model as a basis for predicting direct manufacturing labor-hours in its assembling operations. (A 90% learning curve means $b = -0.152004$.)

Required

1. Prepare a prediction of the total costs for producing the six PT109s for the Navy.
2. If you solved requirement 1 of Problem 10-40, compare your cost prediction there with the one you made here. Why are the predictions different? How should WLJ Boat decide which model it should use?

10-42 Regression; choosing among models. Apollo Hospital specializes in outpatient surgeries for relatively minor procedures. Apollo is a nonprofit institution and places great emphasis on controlling costs in order to provide services to the community in an efficient manner.

Apollo's CFO, Julie Chen, has been concerned of late about the hospital's consumption of medical supplies. To better understand the behavior of this cost, Julie consults with Rhett Bratt, the person responsible for Apollo's cost system. After some discussion, Julie and Rhett conclude that there are two potential cost drivers for the hospital's medical supplies costs. The first driver is the total number of procedures performed. The second is the number of patient-hours generated by Apollo. Julie and Rhett view the latter as a potentially better cost driver because the hospital does perform a variety of procedures, some more complex than others.

Rhett provides the following data relating to the past year to Julie.

Month	Medical Supplies Costs	Number of Procedures	Number of Patient-Hours
January	$106,000	320	2,000
February	230,000	500	3,900
March	84,000	240	1,900
April	238,000	520	4,100
May	193,000	240	3,400
June	180,000	340	3,700
July	210,000	420	3,100
August	92,000	360	1,200
September	222,000	320	3,000
October	78,000	180	1,300
November	127,000	440	2,800
December	225,000	380	3,800

Required

1. Estimate the regression equation for (a) medical supplies costs and number of procedures and (b) medical supplies costs and number of patient-hours. You should obtain the following results:

Regression 1: Medical supplies costs = $a + (b \times$ Number of procedures)

Variable	Coefficient	Standard Error	*t*-Value
Constant	$36,939.77	$56,404.86	0.65
Independent variable: No. of procedures	$ 361.91	$ 152.93	2.37

$r^2 = 0.36$; Durbin-Watson statistic = 2.48

Regression 2: Medical supplies costs = $a + (b \times$ Number of patient-hours)

Variable	Coefficient	Standard Error	*t*-Value
Constant	$3,654.86	$23,569.51	0.16
Independent variable: No. of patient-hours	$ 56.76	$ 7.82	7.25

$r^2 = 0.84$; Durbin-Watson statistic = 1.91

2. On different graphs plot the data and the regression lines for each of the following cost functions:
   a. Medical supplies costs = $a + (b \times$ Number of procedures)
   b. Medical supplies costs = $a + (b \times$ Number of patient-hours)
3. Evaluate the regression models for "Number of procedures" and "Number of patient-hours" as the cost driver according to the format of Exhibit 10-19 (page 399).
4. Based on your analysis, which cost driver should Julie Chen adopt for Apollo Hospital? Explain.

10-43 Multiple regression (continuation of 10-42). After further discussion, Julie and Rhett wonder if they should view both the number of procedures and number of patient-hours as cost drivers in a multiple regression estimation in order to best understand Apollo's medical supplies costs.

Required

1. Conduct a multiple regression to estimate the regression equation for medical supplies costs using both number of procedures and number of patient-hours as independent variables. You should obtain the following result:

Regression 3: Medical supplies costs = $a + (b_1 \times$ No. of procedures) + $(b_2 \times$ No. of patient-hours)

Variable	Coefficient	Standard Error	*t*-Value
Constant	−$3,103.76	$30,406.54	−0.10
Independent variable 1: No. of procedures	$ 38.24	$ 100.76	0.38
Independent variable 2: No. of patient-hours	$ 54.37	$ 10.33	5.26

$r^2 = 0.84$; Durbin-Watson statistic = 1.96

2. Evaluate the multiple regression output using the criteria of economic plausibility goodness of fit, significance of independent variables, and specification of estimation assumptions.
3. What potential issues could arise in multiple regression analysis that are not present in simple regression models? Is there evidence of such difficulties in the multiple regression in this problem? Explain.
4. Which regression models from Problems 10-42 and 10-43 would you recommend Julie use? Explain.

10-44 Cost estimation. Hankuk Electronics started production on a sophisticated new smartphone running the Android operating system in January 2020. Given the razor-thin margins in the consumer electronics industry, Hankuk's success depends heavily on being able to produce the phone as economically as possible.

At the end of the first year of production, Hankuk's controller, Inbee Kim, gathered data on its monthly levels of output, as well as monthly consumption of direct labor-hours (DLH). Inbee views labor-hours as the key driver of Hankuk's direct and overhead costs. The information collected by Inbee is provided below:

Month	Output (Units)	Direct Labor-Hours
January	684	1,400
February	492	820
March	660	875
April	504	670
May	612	760
June	636	765
July	648	735
August	600	660
September	648	695
October	696	710
November	672	690
December	675	700

Required

1. Inbee is keen to examine the relationship between direct labor consumption and output levels. She decides to estimate this relationship using a simple linear regression based on the monthly data. Verify that the following is the result obtained by Inbee:

Regression 1: Direct labor-hours $= a + (b \times$ Output units)

Variable	Coefficient	Standard Error	*t*-Value
Constant	345.24	589.07	0.59
Independent variable: Output units	0.71	0.93	0.76
$r^2 = 0.054$; Durbin-Watson statistic $= 0.50$			

2. Plot the data and regression line for the above estimation. Evaluate the regression using the criteria of economic plausibility, goodness of fit, and slope of the regression line.
3. Inbee estimates that Hankuk has a variable cost of $17.50 per direct labor-hour. She expects that Hankuk will produce 650 units in the next month, January 2021. What should she budget as the expected variable cost? How confident is she of her estimate?

10-45 Cost estimation, learning curves (continuation of 10-44). Inbee is concerned that she still does not understand the relationship between output and labor consumption. She consults with Jim Park, the head of engineering, and shares the results of her regression estimation. Jim indicates that the production of new smartphone models exhibits significant learning effects—as Hankuk gains experience with production, it can produce additional units using less time. He suggests that it is more appropriate to specify the following relationship:

$$y = ax^b$$

where x is *cumulative production* in units, y is the *cumulative average* direct labor-hours per unit (i.e., cumulative DLH divided by cumulative production), and a and b are parameters of the learning effect.

To estimate this, Inbee and Jim use the original data to calculate the cumulative output and cumulative average labor-hours per unit for each month. They then take natural logarithms of these variables in order to be able to estimate a regression equation. Here is the transformed data:

Month	Cumulative Output (x)	Cumulative Direct Labor-Hours	Cumulative Average Direct Labor-Hours Per Unit (y)	Ln (y)	Ln (x)
January	684	1,400	2.047	0.716	6.528
February	1,176	2,220	1.888	0.635	7.070
March	1,836	3,095	1.686	0.522	7.515
April	2,340	3,765	1.609	0.476	7.758
May	2,952	4,525	1.533	0.427	7.990
June	3,588	5,290	1.474	0.388	8.185
July	4,236	6,025	1.422	0.352	8.351
August	4,836	6,685	1.382	0.324	8.484
September	5,484	7,380	1.346	0.297	8.610
October	6,180	8,090	1.309	0.269	8.729
November	6,852	8,780	1.281	0.248	8.832
December	7,527	9,480	1.259	0.231	8.926

Required

1. Estimate the relationship between the cumulative average direct labor-hours per unit and cumulative output (both in logarithms). Verify that the following is the result obtained by Inbee and Jim:

   Regression 1: Ln (Cumulative avg DLH per unit) $= a + [b \times$ Ln (Cumulative Output)]

Variable	Coefficient	Standard Error	*t*-Value
Constant	2.087	0.024	85.44
Independent variable: Ln (Cum Output)	−0.208	0.003	−69.046

$r^2 = 0.998$; Durbin-Watson statistic $= 2.66$

2. Plot the data and regression line for the above estimation. Evaluate the regression using the criteria of economic plausibility, goodness of fit, and slope of the regression line.
3. Verify that the estimated slope coefficient corresponds to an 86.6% cumulative average-time learning curve.
4. Based on this new estimation, how will Inbee revise her budget for Hankuk's variable cost for the expected output of 650 units in January 2021? How confident is she of this new cost estimate?

10-46 Interpreting regression results, matching time periods. Nandita Summers works at Modus, a store that caters to fashion for young adults. Nandita is responsible for the store's online advertising and promotion budget. For the past year, she has studied search engine optimization and has been purchasing keywords and display advertising on Google, Facebook, and Twitter. In order to analyze the effectiveness of her efforts and to decide whether to continue online advertising or move her advertising dollars back to traditional print media, Nandita collects the following data:

Month	Online Advertising Expense	Sales Revenue
September	$5,125	$44,875
October	5,472	42,480
November	3,942	53,106
December	1,440	64,560
January	4,919	34,517
February	4,142	59,438
March	1,290	51,840
April	5,722	36,720
May	5,730	62,564
June	2,214	59,568
July	1,716	35,450
August	1,875	36,211

Required

1. Nandita performs a regression analysis, comparing each month's online advertising expense with that month's revenue. Verify that she obtains the following result:

Sales revenue = \$51,999.64 − (0.98 × Online advertising expense)

Variable	Coefficient	Standard Error	*t*-Value
Constant	\$51,999.64	7,988.68	6.51
Independent variable: Online advertising expense	−0.98	1.99	−0.49

$r^2 = 0.02$; Durbin-Watson statistic = 2.14

2. Plot the preceding data on a graph and draw the regression line. What does the cost formula indicate about the relationship between monthly online advertising expense and monthly sales revenue? Is the relationship economically plausible?
3. After further thought, Nandita realizes there may have been a flaw in her approach. In particular, there may be a lag between the time customers click through to the Modus website and peruse its social media content (which is when the online ad expense is incurred) and the time they actually shop in the physical store. Nandita modifies her analysis by comparing each month's sales revenue to the advertising expense in the *prior* month. After discarding September sales revenue and August advertising expense, show that the modified regression yields the following:

Sales revenue = \$28,361.37 + (5.38 × Online advertising expense)

Variable	Coefficient	Standard Error	*t*-Value
Constant	\$28,361.37	5,428.69	5.22
Independent variable: Previous month's online advertising expense	5.38	1.31	4.12

$r^2 = 0.65$; Durbin-Watson statistic = 1.71

4. What does the revised formula indicate? Plot the revised data on a graph. Is this relationship economically plausible?
5. Can Nandita conclude that there is a cause-and-effect relationship between online advertising expense and sales revenue? Why or why not?

10-47 Purchasing department cost drivers, activity-based costing, simple regression analysis. Perfect Fit operates a chain of 10 retail department stores. Each department store makes its own purchasing decisions. Carl Hart, assistant to the president of Perfect Fit, is interested in better understanding the drivers of purchasing department costs. For many years, Perfect Fit has allocated purchasing department costs to products on the basis of the dollar value of merchandise purchased. A \$100 item is allocated 10 times as many overhead costs associated with the purchasing department as a \$10 item.

Hart recently attended a seminar titled "Cost Drivers in the Retail Industry." In a presentation at the seminar, Kaliko Fabrics, a leading competitor that has implemented activity-based costing, reported number of purchase orders and number of suppliers to be the two most important cost drivers of purchasing department costs. The dollar value of merchandise purchased in each purchase order was not found to be a significant cost driver. Hart interviewed several members of the purchasing department at the Perfect Fit store in Miami. They believed that Kaliko Fabrics' conclusions also applied to their purchasing department.

Hart collects the following data for the most recent year for Perfect Fit's 10 retail department stores:

	A	B	C	D	E
1	Department Store	Purchasing Department Costs (PDC)	Dollar Value of Merchandise Purchased (MP\$)	Number of Purchase Orders (No. of POs)	Number of Suppliers (No. of Ss)
2	Baltimore	\$1,522,000	\$ 68,307,000	4,345	125
3	Chicago	1,095,000	33,463,000	2,548	230
4	Los Angeles	542,000	121,800,000	1,420	8
5	Miami	2,053,000	119,450,000	5,935	188
6	New York	1,068,000	33,575,000	2,786	21
7	Phoenix	517,000	29,836,000	1,334	29
8	Seattle	1,544,000	102,840,000	7,581	101
9	St. Louis	1,761,000	38,725,000	3,623	127
10	Toronto	1,605,000	139,300,000	1,712	202
11	Vancouver	1,263,000	130,110,000	4,736	196

Hart decides to use simple regression analysis to examine whether one or more of three variables (the last three columns in the table) are cost drivers of purchasing department costs. Summary results for these regressions are as follows:

Regression 1: PDC = $a + (b \times$ MP$)

Variable	Coefficient	Standard Error	*t*-Value
Constant	$1,041,421	$346,709	3.00
Independent variable 1: MP$	0.0031	0.0038	0.83

$r^2 = 0.08$; Durbin-Watson statistic = 2.41

Regression 2: PDC = $a + (b \times$ No. of POs)

Variable	Coefficient	Standard Error	*t*-Value
Constant	$722,538	$265,835	2.72
Independent variable 1: No. of POs	$ 159.48	$ 64.84	2.46

$r^2 = 0.43$; Durbin-Watson statistic = 1.97

Regression 3: PDC = $a + (b \times$ No. of Ss)

Variable	Coefficient	Standard Error	*t*-Value
Constant	$828,814	$246,571	3.36
Independent variable 1: No. of Ss	$ 3,816	$ 1,698	2.25

$r^2 = 0.39$; Durbin-Watson statistic = 2.01

Required

1. Compare and evaluate the three simple regression models estimated by Hart. Graph each one. Also, use the format employed in Exhibit 10-19 (page 399) to evaluate the information.
2. Do the regression results support the Kaliko Fabrics' presentation about the purchasing department's cost drivers? Which of these cost drivers would you recommend in designing an ABC system?
3. How might Hart gain additional evidence on drivers of purchasing department costs at each of Perfect Fit's stores?

10-48 Purchasing department cost drivers, multiple regression analysis (continuation of 10-47). Carl Hart decides that the simple regression analysis used in Problem 10-47 could be extended to a multiple regression analysis. He finds the following results for two multiple regression analyses:

Regression 4: PDC = $a + (b_1 \times$ No. of POs) + $(b_2 \times$ No. of Ss)

Variable	Coefficient	Standard Error	*t*-Value
Constant	$484,522	$256,684	1.89
Independent variable 1: No. of POs	$ 126.66	$ 57.80	2.19
Independent variable 2: No. of Ss	$ 2,903	$ 1,459	1.99

$r^2 = 0.64$; Durbin-Watson statistic = 1.91

Regression 5: PDC = $a + (b_1 \times$ No. of POs) + $(b_2 \times$ No. of Ss) + $(b_3 \times$ MP$)

Variable	Coefficient	Standard Error	*t*-Value
Constant	$483,560	$312,554	1.55
Independent variable 1: No. of POs	$ 126.58	$ 63.75	1.99
Independent variable 2: No. of Ss	$ 2,901	$ 1,622	1.79
Independent variable 3: MP$	0.00002	0.0029	0.01

$r^2 = 0.64$; Durbin-Watson statistic = 1.91

The coefficients of correlation between combinations of pairs of the variables are as follows:

	PDC	MP$	No. of POs
MP$	0.28		
No. of POs	0.66	0.27	
No. of Ss	0.62	0.30	0.29

Required

1. Evaluate regression 4 using the criteria of economic plausibility, goodness of fit, significance of independent variables, and specification analysis. Compare regression 4 with regressions 2 and 3 in Problem 10-47. Which one of these models would you recommend that Hart use? Why?
2. Compare regression 5 with regression 4. Which model would you recommend that Hart use? Why?
3. Hart estimates the following data for the Baltimore store for next year: dollar value of merchandise purchased, $78,500,000; number of purchase orders, 4,100; number of suppliers, 110. How much should Hart budget for purchasing department costs for the Baltimore store for next year?
4. What difficulties do not arise in simple regression analysis that may arise in multiple regression analysis? Is there evidence of such difficulties in either of the multiple regressions presented in this problem? Explain.
5. Give two examples of decisions in which the regression results reported here (and in Problem 10-47) could be informative.

Data Analytic Thinking and Prediction

11

One of the most important roles of the management accountant is to help managers make decisions. In today's business environment, managers can access unprecedented amounts of data. Specifically, businesses generate vast amounts of data about customer preferences, supplier behavior, and marketing operations in the course of daily operations. Managers use data analytic techniques to make predictions based on these data. The business press refers to these trends as the age of big data, machine learning, and artificial intelligence. The management accountant helps companies derive value from big data by helping managers to use data-analytic techniques to transform the company and unlock significant cost-saving and revenue-generating opportunities, as the following vignette describes.

LEARNING OBJECTIVES

1. Explain how management accountants can work with data scientists to create value
2. Identify the questions management wants to ask and the relevant data
3. Explain the elements of a decision tree model
4. Describe how to refine a decision tree model to ensure the data represent the business context
5. Explain how to validate the predictions of full versus refined decision trees
6. Evaluate the predictions of different data science models to choose the best one for the business need and visualize and communicate model insights
7. Describe how to use and deploy data science models

PREDICTIVE ANALYTICS INSIDE: HOW INTEL DRIVES VALUE AND SPEEDS TIME TO MARKET[1]

For more than 50 years, Intel has been one of the world's leading semiconductor manufacturers. In recent years, the company's information technology (IT) department has turned to predictive analytics to help drive revenue and get its products to market more quickly.

In 2018, Intel's IT group delivered \$1.25 billion in business value through the use of predictive analytics across the company's sales, supply chain, and manufacturing operations. Applying analytics and artificial intelligence (AI) in its sales and marketing channels, Intel interprets marketplace data from around the world in real time to help customers configure their machines and increase customer satisfaction and revenues.

Additionally, using smart analytics, Intel improved the time to market for key company platforms and products by nearly 52 weeks. How? Intel created a machine learning platform to find potential bugs during the design phase of its products before they go into development. Testing and validation is now completed about 60 times more quickly and identifies 30% more bugs than the previous process, all before costly manufacturing begins.

jejim/Shutterstock

[1] *Sources:* Intel Corporation, *2018-2019 Intel IT Annual Performance Report* (Santa Clara, CA: Intel Corporation, 2019); Justine Brown, "Intel Is Saving \$656M per Year Using Predictive Analytics Across Departments," *CIO Dive*, June 1, 2017 (https://www.ciodive.com/news/intel-saving-predictive-analytics-across-department/443957/); Peter High, "Intel's CIO Leverages AI to Drive \$350 Million In Revenue Growth," *Forbes.com*, November 20, 2017. (https://www.forbes.com/sites/peterhigh/2017/11/20/intels-cio-leverages-ai-to-drive-350-million-in-revenue-growth/#54d43d9d6c1e).

Data Science Basics and Management Accounting

LEARNING OBJECTIVE 1

Explain how management accountants can work with data scientists to create value

... use data to predict outcomes and impact decision making

This chapter covers foundational concepts of data science for predictive modeling to aid decision making. **Data science** refers to the use of data analytics to draw conclusions from data. **Predictive modeling** is a data science technique used to make predictions based on past or current data.

Outcome Prediction

The increasing availability of inexpensive data storage and Web-based (cloud) computing power allows data scientists to use very large datasets to *train* sophisticated algorithmic models. These models learn from training data (thousands or millions of records) and can then *predict* a new record according to some feature of interest. For example, a feature of interest to a telecommunications provider is *churn*, that is, whether customers will switch providers in the next quarter. A cellular telecommunications operator, such as AT&T or T-Mobile, can use data, such as number of calls made, number of dropped calls, and number of family members who are on a family plan, to predict which customers are most likely to leave the company in the next 3 months. In this example, the feature churn takes two possible values (binary): likely to leave in 3 months (1), not likely to leave in 3 months (0). The management accountant can then work with marketing to determine the costs and benefits of keeping those customers or alternatively letting them leave. The ability to accurately predict outcomes can directly impact how an organization crafts its strategy.

As shown in Exhibit 11-1, data science sits at the intersection of (1) computer science and data skills, (2) math and statistics, and, critically, (3) substantive expertise in a particular area of interest or *domain* such as industry and management accounting knowledge. As the churn example in the telecommunications industry indicates, deep knowledge about the economics of a business and industry is important for formulating relevant questions for data science to address. Exhibit 11-1 also makes another point. Management accountants need to understand some of the computer science and statistics tools used in data science so that they can effectively interact with other members of the data science team. The circle representing the expertise needed by management accountants overlaps with computer science and statistical inference skills.

Value Creation

In Chapter 10, management accountants used linear regression and historic cost data to *estimate* costs and to *understand* cost drivers. Understanding how costs behaved helped managers make better decisions. In this chapter, the focus is on *predicting* future revenues and costs. The methods of prediction help managers and management accountants understand cost drivers, but this is not the primary goal.

EXHIBIT 11-1

Components of Data Science

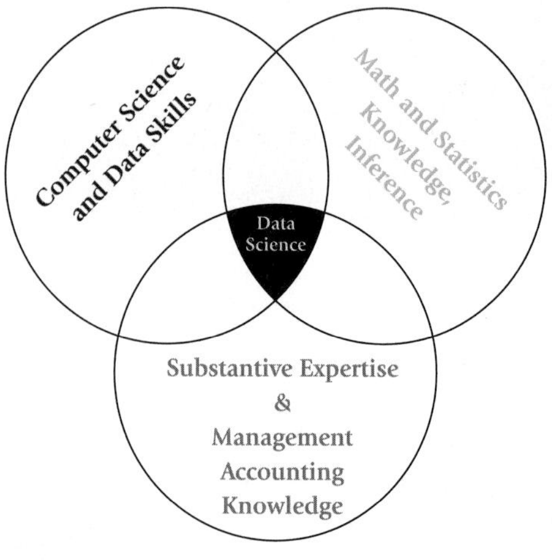

Management accountants work with data scientists to create value across all parts of the value chain. For example, they use data to identify what product design decisions and manufacturing parameters result in product defects. They then do a cost–benefit analysis to evaluate whether the company should spend additional resources to change designs or implement new manufacturing controls. Consider these specific examples:

- At Busbud, a travel site that sells bus tickets, management accountants work with data scientists to assess whether paying Google for advertising keywords helps drive more sales.
- At Kroger grocery stores, management accountants work with data scientists to help determine how much of each product to stock at each location and which location should be used to fulfill online orders based on demand predictions.
- At Visa, management accountants work with data scientists to determine how much to spend on detecting credit card fraud.
- At Whirlpool, management accountants work with data scientists to evaluate the costs and benefits of making a sale and extending credit to a customer based on predicted default risk.

- At Novartis, management accountants partner with data scientists to forecast sales and cash flow for prescription medicines based on internal and market information and also recommend how best to allocate marketing and sales resources.

Concepts in Action: Carnival Uses Big Data and Machine Learning to Sail Toward Greater Profitability describes the application of data science tools to manage revenues and costs in the cruise ship industry. As several of these examples illustrate, engaging with data science broadens the set of problems management accountants can engage with to create value. In particular, it helps management accountants to contribute to activities that increase revenues rather than focusing largely on managing costs.

Data Science Framework

Throughout this chapter we focus on Sierra Investments, a small wealth management firm. Sierra is evaluating whether it should invest in and buy certain loans. To make this decision, Sierra compares the interest revenue from the loans to the costs of acquiring loans, including costs of late payments, defaults, and collections activities. Paige Baumann, the management accountant at Sierra Investments, is interested in exploring how she might use data science to help managers make more effective investment decisions by identifying the payoffs and risks associated with different investment choices.[2]

CONCEPTS IN ACTION

Carnival Uses Big Data and Machine Learning to Sail Toward Greater Profitability[3]

rawpixel/123rf.com

Carnival, the largest cruise operator in the world, leverages big data, machine learning, and artificial intelligence (AI) to cut costs and drive revenue to create "smart cities at sea." Its goal: to operate more efficiently while increasing sustainability.

Carnival uses data from thousands of sensors on board its ships and machine learning to predict water consumption on cruise ships. This allows Carnival to optimize how much water it should carry for a specific route with a specific set of guests. By carrying less water, each ship saves as much as $200,000 each year in fuel costs while also reducing carbon emissions.

Carnival also uses data science to reduce waste. Cruise ships generate several types of waste while ferrying passengers: food waste, meal servicing waste, cardboard containers, cleaning waste, and engine waste. Big data analytics is helping Carnival to reduce and recycle waste and cut costs.

Beyond cost reduction, Carnival is also using big data and artificial intelligence (AI) for price optimization and personalization. The company's data science team regularly analyzes internal and external data from past consumers and vacationers to help match customers to the right cruise experience, whether that is a budget family cruise or a luxury voyage. Similarly, Carnival uses wearable devices and thousands of sensors to make personalized recommendations to customers for onboard activities. Delighting customers helps drive higher revenues.

[3] *Sources:* Rebecca Gibson, "Carnival Maritime Uses Machine Learning to Optimize Cruise Operations," *Cruise & Ferry*, February 2, 2017 (http://www.cruiseand-ferry.net/articles/carnival-maritime-uses-machine-learning-to-optimise-cruise-operations); Barbara Grady, "Trash 2.0? Nike, Carnival Cruises and Wading Through Waste Data," *GreenBiz*, October 8, 2015 (https://www.greenbiz.com/article/trash-20-nike-cruise-ships-and-wading-through-waste-data); Kim Nash, "Carnival Strategy Chief Bets That Big Data Will Optimize Prices," *The Wall Street Journal*, April 30, 2015 (https://blogs.wsj.com/cio/2015/04/30/carnival-strategy-chief-bets-that-big-data-will-optimize-prices/); Bernard Marr, "The Amazing Ways Carnival Cruises Is Using IoT and AI to Create Smart Cities at Sea," *Forbes.com*, March 22, 2019 (https://www.forbes.com/sites/bernardmarr/2019/03/22/the-amazing-ways-carnival-cruises-is-using-iot-and-ai-to-create-smart-cities-at-sea/#192d22ce5a64).

[2] The chapter is based on issues and challenges faced by companies in the peer-to-peer online lending industry. See, for example, the Harvard Business School LendingClub Case Series, Srikant Datar and Caitlin Bowler, "LendingClub (A): Data Analytic Thinking (Abridged)," HBS No. 119-020 (Boston: Harvard Business School Publishing, 2018); Srikant Datar and Caitlin Bowler, "LendingClub (B): Decision Trees & Random Forests," HBS No. 119-021 (Boston: Harvard Business School Publishing, 2018); and Srikant Datar and Caitlin Bowler, "LendingClub (C): Gradient Boosting & Payoff Matrix," HBS No. 119-022 (Boston: Harvard Business School Publishing, 2018). HBS cases are developed solely as the basis for classroom discussion, and they are not intended to serve as endorsements, sources of primary data, or illustrations of effective or ineffective management.

As she contemplates next steps, Paige goes through the data science framework, a seven-step decision-making process for applying machine learning techniques in business situations:

1. Gain a business understanding of the problem
2. Obtain and explore relevant data
3. Prepare the data
4. Build a model
5. Evaluate the model
6. Visualize and communicate insights
7. Deploy the model

We discuss each of these steps in subsequent sections. As you go through these steps, keep the "big picture" in mind. Data Science relies on backtesting and feedback to choose among models. To do this, data scientists subdivide their data into a training sample (used in Step 4 to build a model), a cross-validation sample (used in step 5 to evaluate and choose among models), and a holdout sample (used in step 5 to test how the model would perform on completely new data). Backtesting helps the data scientist to decide how detailed a model to build. Too simple a model may miss important features for making good predictions; too detailed a model may introduce irrelevant features that weaken predictions.

DECISION POINT

How can management accountants work with data scientists to create value?

Defining the Problem and the Relevant Data

LEARNING OBJECTIVE 2

Identify the questions management wants to ask and the relevant data

. . . why is the question important and what data should we use to address it

As the costs of gathering and storing data continue to decrease, organizations are saving large quantities of data. How these data should be used depends on the questions management would like to have answered. The management accountant plays an important role in helping management decide which questions and what data have the potential to create value for the organization. These are the first three steps in the decision-making process. We describe these steps and the management accountant's contribution in the context of the investment decision facing Sierra Investments.

Step 1: Gain a Business Understanding of the Problem

The first step in the decision-making process is gaining an understanding of the business problem. That is, what questions does the management accountant need to examine to advise the manager on a business decision. We illustrate the process by returning to Sierra Investments, which manages assets on behalf of clients. The firm is considering investing in loans offered by the peer-to-peer lending platform PeerLend Digital (PD), which connects individual borrowers to individual investor-lenders through an online platform. The platform allows all parties to bypass traditional banking infrastructure and their high operations costs. In exchange, borrowers get lower interest rates and investors get higher returns. The loans available on the PD platform range from $1,000 to $10,000. PD collects and keeps data on all loans that investors fund from the platform.

PD assigns a *grade* rating to each loan based on an estimate of the riskiness of a loan, that is, the probability of the borrower defaulting. To estimate risk, PD uses sophisticated models using historical loan data and features such as *credit score, annual income*, and *amount of loan*. PD assigns low risk loans a grade of A or B, moderate risk loans a grade of C or D, and high risk loans a grade of E or F.[4] PD assigns an interest rate to each grade that reflects the grade's level of risk. Exhibit 11-2 shows the default rate (number of default loans divided by the total number of loans), interest rate, and the adjusted net annualized return for a certain selection of PD loans. Note that the interest rate increases with default risk. The *adjusted net annualized return* is the return after considering PD service fees and losses from defaults. For example, investing in C-grade loans yields a net annualized return of 7.6% on an interest rate of 13.0% with a default rate of 19.6%. Note that when a borrower defaults, an investor does

[4] In practice, loans can be classified into many more finely defined categories.

EXHIBIT 11-2 Loan Grade Categories A Through F

Grade	A	B	C	D	E	F
Default rate	5.3%	11.4%	19.6%	26.0%	34.8%	40.8%
Interest rate	6.0%	9.3%	13.0%	17.4%	22.5%	31.1%
Adjusted net annualized return	5.2%	7.0%	7.6%	7.9%	7.4%	7.7%

not lose *all* of his or her investment. That is because a borrower often pays some interest and principal before the default.

How does PD earn money? PD charges the borrower a 3.5% origination fee on each loan and a 1% servicing fee to investors for collecting interest and principal. In the event of a default, PD charges investors collection fees to recover money from the borrower.[5]

Paige has two options:

1. Invest in a random sample of PD loans based on the level of risk she is willing to take. For example, invest in a random sample of C-grade loans and expect a return of 7.6%.
2. Do additional analyses to choose specific loans to invest in based on features about each loan available on the PD website.

The question is "Should Paige do further data analysis beyond what PD has already done to classify loans into different grades?" What might she learn from doing so?

Forming questions is a critical first step for the management accountant at the outset of any data science task. The widespread availability of data and access to computing resources allows the management accountant to run many different analyses. It is important, however, to pause and ask whether it is worthwhile to do so. In this case, Paige decides to run more analyses because the default rates and the cost of defaults are very high. If she can identify default loans more precisely, Sierra Investments can increase returns by avoiding those loans. Her next task is to identify data that would be most useful and relevant for the analysis.

Step 2: Obtain and Explore Relevant Data

An important role of the management accountant is to evaluate the data that managers use when making decisions. For example, how objective are the data? Are the data an estimate or carefully measured? What data and costs are relevant for the decision at hand?

The term *exploratory data analysis* refers to any activity that reveals deeper insight into a dataset. This activity may include *numeric analysis*, such as finding the mean, median, minimum, and maximum values for a feature like annual income.

Before the data science team builds a sophisticated model, Paige explores the PD dataset to understand its size and contents. There are 500,000 funded loans in the dataset from the years 2015 and 2016, of which 100,000 are defaults (loan status = 1) and 400,000 are repays (loan status = 0). The overall *default rate* is 20% (100,000 ÷ 500,000).

Each record in the PD dataset has a number of *features* that describe the characteristics of the loan and the borrower. The *target feature* is loan status. This is the feature the Sierra Investments team wants to predict (default or repay). The *independent* features of each record are the loan and borrower characteristics Paige plans to use to predict whether a loan will default or be repaid. Some independent features are from the past, such as *credit score, number of mortgages,* and *number of bankruptcies*. Other features are from the present, such as a borrower's *employment, annual income, amount of loan,* and the stated *purpose of the loan*. (See columns under "Phase 1" in Exhibit 11-3.) Examples of *purpose* are refinancing credit card debt or home renovation. PD has done a careful job of verifying information such as employment and annual income because its business model is based on being transparent and having high-quality data that lenders can trust when making their decisions.

[5] For example, consider a grade A borrower who applies for a $10,000 loan through PD. PD assigns the loan a grade of A and offers the borrower a 6.03% interest rate. PD charges the borrower a 3.5% origination fee ($350) and disburses $9,650 to the borrower. Each month the borrower pays the investor $304.36 (calculations not shown) and PD keeps $3.046 of that payment ($304.36 × 0.01) from the investor as a fee for servicing the loan. Of the $304.36, the first month's interest is $50.25 and the remaining $254.11 ($304.36 − $50.25) reduces the principal.

EXHIBIT 11-3 Features in the Unmodified PD Dataset

Phase 1 (Before)			Phase 2 (After)
Past Data	**Present Data**	**Decision to Invest**	**"Future" Data**
• Credit score • No. of mortgages • No. of bankruptcies	• Loan amount • Annual income • Debt-to-income • Purpose of loan • Grade • Homeownership • State	Yes or No	• Payments made • Payments missed • Number of late payments

Paige wonders whether the purpose of the loan is a feature she should include in her analysis. Should she have an *a priori* reason about why the purpose of the loan might help distinguish between default and repay loans? Or should she simply include this feature and let the analysis tell her whether it matters? Management accountants could include many independent features in the model because it is easy and inexpensive to handle large quantities of data. At the same time, it is important to understand why a particular feature might affect the target feature. Otherwise, as we discussed in Chapter 10, we might mistake correlation for causation. This type of critical thinking about what data should go into a model is a key role of the management accountant. However, as we shall see later in the chapter, there are data analytic methods that explicitly select those feature variables that best explain the target feature.

Step 3: Prepare the Data

In this step, the management accountant determines how to organize and process the data. What additional data might be needed? How should different variables be measured, and what variables should be excluded? For example, Paige must probe how PD measures "annual income." As the management accountant, she may draw different conclusions about the value of this measure depending on whether it refers to an average annual income over the past 5 years (indicating some stability of annual income) versus income from just the past year. To clarify this definition, she may have to refer to PD's *data dictionary* or find more detailed documentation of the collection process. This is an example of the importance of *substantive expertise* and *management accounting knowledge* in doing data science, as shown in Exhibit 11-1.

Dataset Features

Paige notices that the PD data contain "past" and "present" data as well as *loan performance data*. These features are shown in Exhibit 11-3 under the column "Phase 2." PD collects these data *after* the loan is funded and the borrower has begun to repay the loan. PD does not have these data at the time it approves a borrower and places the loan on the platform. Neither does Sierra Investments. From the point of view of the model, these data are *from the future*. The model Sierra Investments builds with these performance data will perform much better than a model it builds without it, because these data "from the future" add significant additional signals about loan performance. But these are data Sierra's managers must *not* use in building the model because the data are not available at the time of making the investment decision. If Sierra's managers did include future data, it would be an example of *target leakage*. Data scientists use the term **target leakage** to refer to data that are not available at the time of the analysis and that therefore should be excluded. Paige must use substantive expertise to determine which features might contribute to target leakage. In preparing the data, the management accountant must advise the data science team that these features cannot be used for training the predictive models.

To build a model to predict defaults, Sierra Investments downloads the dataset of 500,000 records for the period Q1 2015 to Q4 2016 from the PD website. All these loans are scheduled to come due between Q1 2018 and Q4 2019. Sierra Investments plans to use this model to predict which of the new loans PD offers in Q1 2020 it should avoid because these loans are likely to default. Paige wonders whether she should obtain data from even earlier periods such as from 2005 onward. If she did, she would have access to more data to estimate the model. The core of data science is using data from the past to predict the future. The judgment she must make is whether the older data are representative of the economic conditions in 2020. Paige is concerned that the older data come from a period spanning the global financial crisis. The circumstances of that time differ from what she expects in 2020. She is much more comfortable using the most recent data to make predictions. She also believes that 500,000 records are more than enough to run her models.

Data Privacy

Before releasing the historic loan data, PD scrubs the data of any information that would allow an investor to discover the individual identities of any borrowers. Knowledge of these identities *might* help the data science team make better-informed decisions. This would be particularly true if the team could integrate additional data about borrowers into its dataset. Such data might include preferences shared over social media, criminal records, driving records, etc. Any data that could indicate a leaning toward risky decision making and behavior might provide an additional "signal."

Paige might be tempted to seek out such data. However, personal data privacy has become a highly contested issue in the last several years and the legal landscape is rapidly changing. Before acting, she would have to research what activity for collecting data was legal. For example, data scientists could "scrape" data from websites, but they should only do so under the terms of the website. Some websites allow scraping of data; others limit this activity. In addition, she would need to think carefully about what activity was, and was not, ethical from the perspective of the firm. For example, if she could buy third-party data on the borrowers at PD, should she? Or could data on individual borrowers be discriminatory if information on race, religion, gender, age, or marital status is included?

DECISION POINT

Will solving the proposed problem create value, and are the relevant data available?

Data Algorithms and Models

LEARNING OBJECTIVE 3

Explain the elements of a decision tree model

. . . using rules to segment the target variable into different classes

In the last several years, data scientists have developed myriad models to analyze vast quantities of data. These range from simple regression techniques to sophisticated neural networks. The hallmark of most of these models is that they are extremely flexible in fitting to the data and rely heavily on computational power. This flexibility, however, comes with its own problems that the management accountant's skills can help address. In this section, we examine functional versus flexible relationships and introduce a specific model: the decision tree.

Step 4: Build a Model

In this step, the management accountant works with the data scientists to build models. They must decide what kinds of models to build and how to validate them.

Functional Relationship Model

Paige and the data science team recognize that the target (dependent variable) is binary: 1 if the loan defaults and 0 if the loan repays. As we saw in Chapter 10, the team could use logistic regression to estimate the relationship between independent feature variables (such as [annual] income, credit score, and amount of the loan) and the target variable. This approach assumes a particular functional form of the relationship between feature variables and the target variable to fit the curve shown in Exhibit 10-10 on p. 383. The data scientists on the team suggest that they could get better predictions of default if they fit more flexible models that do not assume a particular functional relationship between feature variables and the target variable. They propose to use a very popular data science technique called *decision trees.*

The Decision Tree: A Predictive Modeling Technique The **decision tree** is a technique for segmenting the target variable into different regions based on a set of rules. These rules make the model easier to interpret than some other models. Industry analyst Dean Abbot writes, "All trees can be read as a series of 'if-then-else' rules that ultimately generate a predicted value . . . [They are] much more accessible to decision makers than mathematical formulas." They are also easy to build and perform better with more data.

EXHIBIT 11-4 Default and Repay Loan Data for 24 Loans

Income (1)	Credit Score (2)	Loan Status (Default = 1) (3)	Income (4)	Credit Score (5)	Loan Status (Repay = 0) (6)
$50,000	530	1	$ 86,000	620	0
$62,000	552	1	$108,000	648	0
$57,000	594	1	$ 59,000	676	0
$45,000	604	1	$110,000	701	0
$64,000	627	1	$ 69,000	731	0
$84,000	637	1	$ 81,000	716	0
$49,000	638	1	$ 95,000	747	0
$66,000	667	1	$ 61,000	752	0
$33,000	674	1	$ 65,000	767	0
$75,000	708	1	$ 52,000	788	0
$43,000	730	1	$ 82,000	802	0
$53,000	748	1	$ 87,000	840	0

Paige is eager to learn why more flexible models yield better default predictions. She is also keen to understand the problems and challenges of the decision tree technique. This seems very difficult to do in the context of thousands of variables and hundreds of features. She asks the data science team whether it is possible to describe the approach in a simple visual way. She would then be able to use the output of the model to guide managers in their decision making.

To explain the technique, the team starts with a simple example that links directly to Sierra Investments' objective. They select a dataset of 24 loans containing 12 *default loans* (labeled as 1) and 12 *repay loans* (labeled as 0). Two features, *income* and *credit score*, describe each data point. Exhibit 11-4 presents the default loans in columns 1 through 3 and the repay loans in columns 4 through 6.

Exhibit 11-5 plots the data in Exhibit 11-4. The x-axis represents the income level. The y-axis represents credit score. Each default loan from Exhibit 11-4, column 3 is represented as a red dot. Each repay loan from Exhibit 11-4, column 6 is represented as a blue dot. For example, the red dot at an income level of $50,000 and credit score of 530 represents the first default loan (from columns 1, 2, and 3 in Exhibit 11-4). In this initial plot the 12 repay loans and 12 default loans sit within one rectangle. If Paige selects one dot at random from this pool, it is equally likely to be a blue dot as a red dot.

The Decision Tree Algorithm An algorithm is a set of instructions. The decision tree emerges from an *algorithmic* process of subdividing the data along the two possible features, *income* or *credit score*. The decision tree algorithm instructs Paige to divide the data with a *cut* or *line* parallel to the x-axis (income) or y-axis (credit score) such that each of the two smaller

EXHIBIT 11-5

Loan Data:
12 Default Loans and
12 Repay Loans

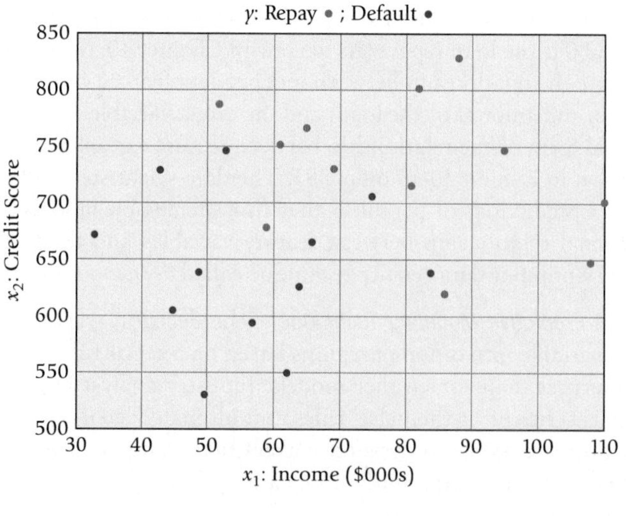

EXHIBIT 11-6 First Cut of Decision Tree (with income shown in $000s)

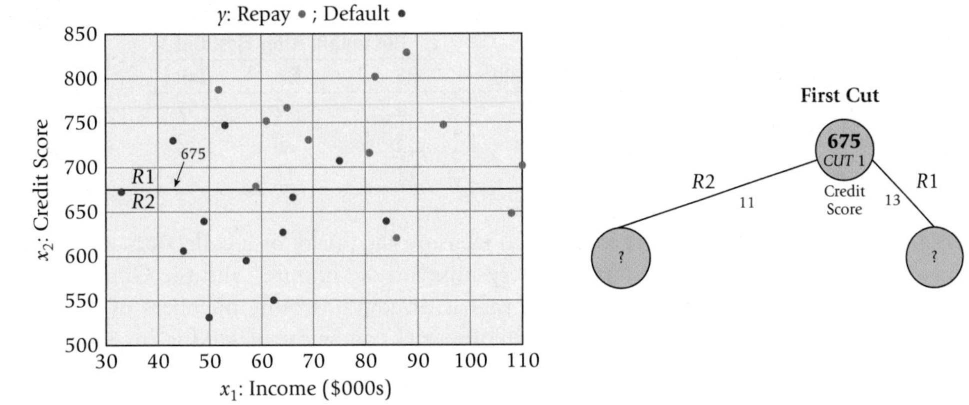

Loan Status	R1	R2	Total
Repay (blue)	10	2	12
Default (red)	3	9	12
Total	13	11	24

Note:

1. *Decision nodes:* These are indicated by circles. The label beneath is the feature on which the split was made. The number inside the circle indicates the value at which the rectangle was split.
2. *Connecting lines:* These lines connect nodes at various levels of the tree. The path to the right of the node represents observations greater than the cut-off value and the path to the left of the node represents observations less than the cut-off value. The number below indicates the number of observations that were directed down that path.
3. *Terminal nodes:* These are indicated by rectangles and they are groupings that are pure (no further classification can be done). They have no successors, hence the name "terminal." Because R1 and R2 are impure (they each contain repayers and defaulters), they end in decision nodes (circles) rather than terminal nodes.

rectangles contains a mix of dots that are *purer* than the original rectangle; that is, one rectangle contains more repay loans than default loans and the other rectangle contains more default loans than repay loans. For example, in the scatter plot on the left side of Exhibit 11-6, Paige places a cut at credit score of 675 (a horizontal line parallel to the *x*-axis).[6] This creates rectangle R1 above the line and rectangle R2 below the line. All borrowers in R1 have a credit score greater than 675 and there are more repay loans (10 blue dots) than default loans (3 red dots). All borrowers in R2 have credit scores less than 675 and there are fewer repay loans (2 blue dots) than default loans (9 red dots). Therefore, the mix of dots in rectangles R1 and R2 are each *purer* than the mix in the original rectangle, which had an equal number of red and blue dots. However, the mix in each is still impure: Rectangle R1 contains mostly repay loans, but also a few default loans, and rectangle R2 contains mostly default loans, but also a few repay loans. The table in Exhibit 11-6 shows the tally of default and repay loans across each of the two new rectangles.

At the top right of Exhibit 11-6 is a visualization of a decision tree as a series of *decision nodes* and *connecting lines*. In this example, the feature credit score with a value of 675 is the first decision node. The 13 borrowers with credit scores higher than 675 go to the right, to R1, while the 11 borrowers with credit scores less than 675 go to the left, to R2.

The process of subdividing the data into smaller subsets that get purer with each subdivision is the essence of the decision tree. The algorithm uses a measure of impurity, the focus of the following section, to calculate precisely how pure the resulting subsets will be at any specific cut.

[6] The cutoff boundary need not be at an actual credit score. For example, for a different sample, the decision tree algorithm might have placed the cutoff boundary at 675.5, which is not an actual credit score.

EXHIBIT 11-7 Distribution of Repay Loans and Default Loans Before and After Cut of 675

		Rectangle After First Cut		
Loan Status	**Original Rectangle**	**R1**	**R2**	**Total**
Repay	12	10	2	12
Default	12	3	9	12
Total	24	13	11	24

Measuring Impurity **Gini impurity** is a way to measure the purity of a collection of observations in a rectangle (set). If a rectangle is very mixed it is "impure" and the Gini impurity is high. As a rectangle becomes more pure, that is, it contains more members of one class than another, the Gini impurity decreases. Gini impurity can be calculated for any number of classes; in the Sierra Investments example, there are two classes: repay and default. The reduction in the Gini impurity from the level in the original rectangle to the levels in the new rectangles created by the cut (in our example R1 and R2) is called *information gain*. Information gain and Gini impurity are inversely related.

To place the first cut, as it did at credit score 675, the algorithm tests all possible values for vertical and horizontal cuts. It calculates the Gini impurity measure for each pair of rectangles that result from that cut and then compares the Gini impurity of the rectangles after the cut is made to the impurity of the rectangle(s) before the cut is made. The algorithm selects the value that *reduces* Gini impurity the most.

The equation for calculating Gini impurity for any point on the credit score or income axis is

$$\textit{probability of picking a repayer (blue)} \times (1 - \textit{probability of picking a repayer}) \\ + \textit{probability of picking a defaulter (red)} \times (1 - \textit{probability of picking a defaulter})$$

The process for calculating Gini impurity is shown below:

1. **Establish the baseline Gini impurity.** This calculation is based on the number of classes in the population. In this example there are two classes comprising 12 repay loans and 12 default loans. The initial calculation of the Gini impurity for the original rectangle is

$$\textit{probability of picking a repay loan [blue]} \times (1 - \textit{probability of picking a repay loan}) \\ + \textit{probability of picking a default loan [red]} \times (1 - \textit{probability of picking a default loan})$$

$$= \frac{12}{24} \times \left(1 - \frac{12}{24}\right) + \frac{12}{24} \times \left(1 - \frac{12}{24}\right) = \left(\frac{1}{2} \times \frac{1}{2}\right) + \left(\frac{1}{2} \times \frac{1}{2}\right) = \frac{1}{4} + \frac{1}{4} = \frac{1}{2}$$

The Gini impurity is ½, which in fact is the maximum value for the measure, given two classes.[7]

2. **Compare new Gini impurities for any possible cut.** With the baseline established, a software program then (a) tests each possible placement of a cut (at every value on either the credit score or income axis), (b) calculates the new Gini impurity values for each possible partition, R1 and R2, (c) calculates the difference between baseline and new values, and then (d) places the cut to maximize reduction in the Gini impurity. Note the very large number of calculations that need to be done to determine the optimal way to partition the data compared to the formulae used when doing multiple regressions in Chapter 10. These calculations would not be possible without access to cheap computing power. Note also the extreme flexibility of the techniques to separate default loans from repay loans. The partitions are based on the actual sample data without assuming any functional form (such as the linear relationship assumed in Chapter 10).

Exhibit 11-7 shows the distribution of classes (repay and default loans) in the original scatter plot and in the rectangles R1 and R2 that the first cut creates.

[7] If there were three classes of 12 each, you can verify that the Gini impurity would be 2/3.

For this cut at a credit score equal to 675, the Gini impurity calculations for R1 and R2 are as follows:

$$R1: \frac{10}{13} \times \left(1 - \frac{10}{13}\right) + \frac{3}{13} \times \left(1 - \frac{3}{13}\right) = \frac{10}{13} \times \frac{3}{13} + \frac{3}{13} \times \frac{10}{13} = \frac{60}{169} = 0.355$$

$$R2: \frac{2}{11} \times \left(1 - \frac{2}{11}\right) + \frac{9}{11} \times \left(1 - \frac{9}{11}\right) = \frac{2}{11} \times \frac{9}{11} + \frac{9}{11} \times \frac{2}{11} = \frac{36}{121} = 0.298$$

Weighted average Gini impurity for R1 and R2 =

proportion of observations in R1 × Gini impurity for R1

+ proportion of observations in R2 × Gini impurity for R2

$$= \frac{13}{24} \times 0.355 + \frac{11}{24} \times 0.298 = 0.329$$

By placing the first cut at credit score 675, the decision tree algorithm reduces the Gini impurity from 0.500 to 0.329.

Why did the algorithm choose to make the first cut at a credit score of 675? Return to Exhibit 11-6 and lay a ruler along this line, then pull it down so that it sits at a credit score of 600. Count and record the number of red and blue dots in the new R1 and the new R2. We can use these counts to calculate the reduction in Gini impurity if the algorithm had made the first cut at 600.

At credit score equals 600, the Gini impurity calculations for R1 and R2 are

$$R1: \frac{12}{21} \times \left(1 - \frac{12}{21}\right) + \frac{9}{21} \times \left(1 - \frac{9}{21}\right) = \frac{12}{21} \times \frac{9}{21} + \frac{9}{21} \times \frac{12}{21} = 0.490$$

$$R2: \frac{0}{3} \times \left(1 - \frac{0}{3}\right) + \frac{3}{3} \times \left(1 - \frac{3}{3}\right) = \frac{0}{3} \times \frac{3}{3} + \frac{3}{3} \times \frac{0}{3} = 0$$

Weighted average Gini impurity for R1 and R2 =

proportion of observations in R1 × Gini impurity for R1

+ proportion of observations in R2 × Gini impurity for R2

$$\frac{21}{24} \times 0.490 + \frac{0}{3} \times 0 = 0.429$$

By placing the first cut at credit score 600, the decision tree algorithm reduces the Gini impurity from 0.500 to 0.429. Exhibit 11-8 shows the counts and the Gini impurity values if the first cut had been made at several different values of credit score. It also shows counts and the Gini impurity values if the first cut had been made at several different values of income. A first cut at credit score 675 reduces the Gini impurity the most.

Continuing to Build the Tree The algorithm next evaluates all possible values for a horizontal cut on credit score or a vertical cut on income in any *one* rectangle. In the scatter plot in Exhibit 11-9, it places the second cut in rectangle R1 on the income feature of $56,000. This line cuts R1 into two smaller rectangles, R3 to the left and R4 to the right. The three loans in

EXHIBIT 11-8 Gini Impurity for Different Cuts Based on Credit Score and Income

		Credit Score					Income		
		600	650	675	700	800	$49,000	$74,000	$85,000
R1	Repay	12	10	10	9	2	12	5	7
	Default	9	5	3	3	0	8	10	12
	Total	21	15	13	12	2	20	15	19
R2	Repay	0	2	2	3	10	0	7	5
	Default	3	7	9	9	12	4	2	0
	Total	3	9	11	12	22	4	9	5
Gini Impurity		0.429	0.407	0.329	0.375	0.455	0.400	0.407	0.368

EXHIBIT 11-9 Second Cut of the Decision Tree (with income shown in $000s)

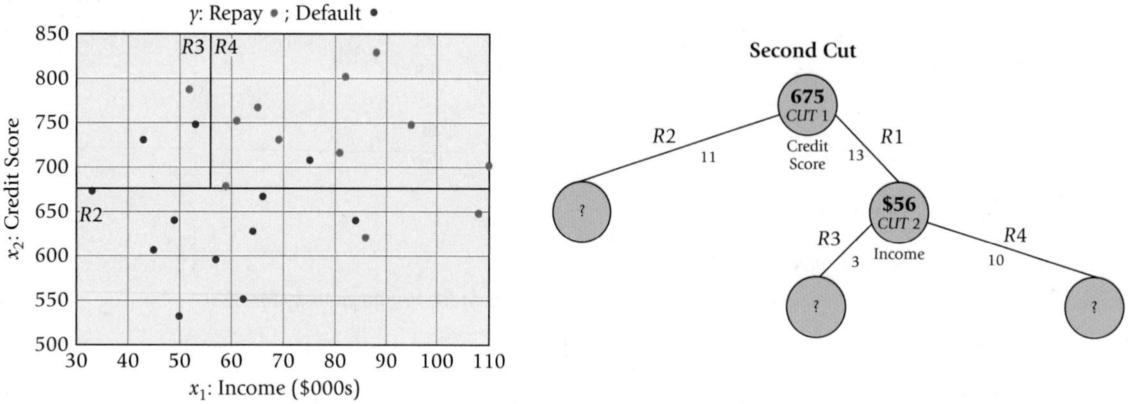

Loan Status	R1	R2	R3	R4	Total
Repay (blue)	n/a	2	1	9	12
Default (red)	n/a	9	2	1	12
Total	n/a	11	3	10	24

R3 have incomes less than $56,000, of which one is a repay loan and two are default loans. The 10 loans in R4 have incomes greater than $56,000, where nine are repay loans and one is a default loan. There are now three rectangles, R2, R3, and R4, and none is fully pure. In the Exhibit 11-9 decision tree, the node to the right of the first node now has an income value of $56,000. At the first node, the 13 borrowers whose credit score is greater than 675 go to the right; those 10 borrowers whose income is greater than $56,000 move again to the right, while the three borrowers whose income is less than $56,000 go to the left.

For the second cut at income equals $56,000, the Gini impurity calculations for R3 and R4 are

$$R3: \frac{1}{3} \times \left(1 - \frac{1}{3}\right) + \frac{2}{3} \times \left(1 - \frac{2}{3}\right) = \frac{1}{3} \times \frac{2}{3} + \frac{2}{3} \times \frac{1}{3} = \frac{4}{9} = 0.444$$

$$R4: \frac{9}{10} \times \left(1 - \frac{9}{10}\right) + \frac{1}{10} \times \left(1 - \frac{1}{10}\right) = \frac{9}{10} \times \frac{1}{10} + \frac{1}{10} \times \frac{9}{10} = \frac{18}{100} = 0.180$$

Weighted average Gini impurity for R2, R3, and R4 =

proportion of observations in R2 × Gini impurity for R2 + proportion of observations in R3 × Gini impurity for R3 + proportion of observations in R4 × Giniimpurity for R4

$$\frac{11}{24} \times 0.298 + \frac{3}{24} \times 0.444 + \frac{10}{24} \times 0.180 = 0.267$$

By placing the second cut at income $56,000, the decision tree algorithm reduces the Gini impurity from 0.329 to 0.267.

On its third iteration, the algorithm makes a cut on the income value of $85,000 in rectangle R2. In the scatter plot in Exhibit 11-10, it splits rectangle R2 into R5 to the left and R6 to the right. The nine borrowers in R5 have incomes less than $85,000 and zero are repay loans and nine are default loans. The two borrowers in R6 have incomes greater than $85,000; two are repay loans and zero are default loans. Both rectangles R5 and R6 are now pure. The purity of these nodes in the decision tree is indicated in Exhibit 11-10 by a rectangle around the name of the class. The third node has an income value of $85,000; the two borrowers with incomes higher than this move right. They both repay, so the terminal node is labeled "repay." The nine borrowers with incomes below $85,000 move to the left and, because they all default, this too is a terminal node and labeled "default."

EXHIBIT 11-10 Third Cut of the Decision Tree (with income shown in \$000s)

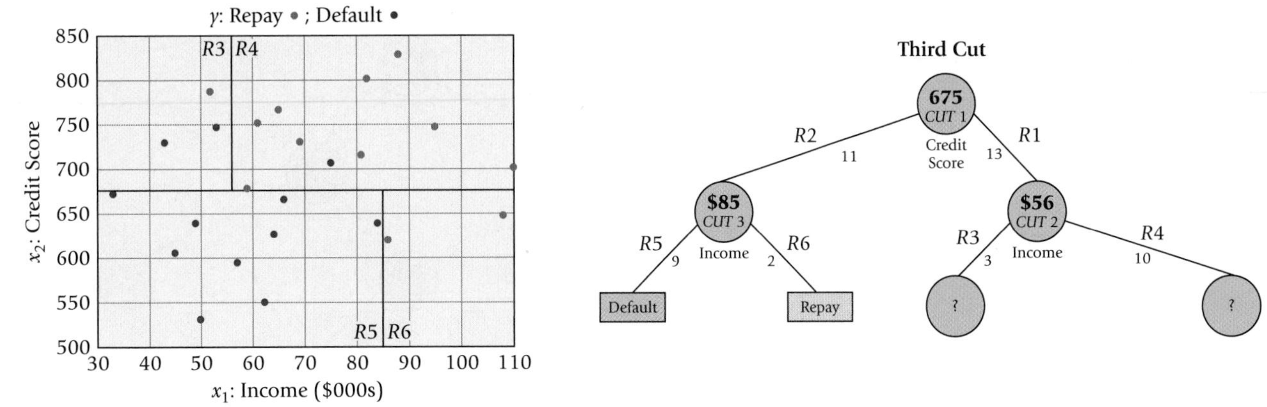

Loan Status	R1	R2	R3	R4	R5	R6	Total
Repay (blue)	n/a	n/a	1	9	0	2	12
Default (red)	n/a	n/a	2	1	9	0	12
Total	n/a	n/a	3	10	9	2	24

For the third cut in our example, at income equals \$85,000, the Gini impurity calculations for R5 and R6 are

$$R5: \frac{0}{9} \times \left(1 - \frac{0}{9}\right) + \frac{9}{9} \times \left(1 - \frac{9}{9}\right) = \frac{0}{9} \times \frac{9}{9} + \frac{9}{9} \times \frac{0}{9} = 0$$

$$R6: \frac{2}{2} \times \left(1 - \frac{2}{2}\right) + \frac{0}{2} \times \left(1 - \frac{0}{2}\right) = \frac{2}{2} \times \frac{0}{2} + \frac{0}{2} \times \frac{2}{2} = 0$$

Weighted average Gini impurity for R3, R4, R5, and R6 =

proportion of observations in R3 × Gini impurity for R3 + proportion of observations in R4 × Gini impurity for R4 + proportion of observations in R5 × Gini impurity for R5 + proportion of observations in R6 × Gini impurity for R6

$$\frac{3}{24} \times 0.444 + \frac{10}{24} \times 0.180 + \frac{9}{24} \times 0 + \frac{2}{24} \times 0 = 0.131$$

By placing the third cut at income of \$85,000, the decision tree algorithm reduces the Gini impurity from 0.267 to 0.131.

The algorithm continues this process over and over until all rectangles are pure. The technical term for this process is *recursive partitioning*. *Recursion* means to apply a procedure again and again. In this case, the algorithm is placing "cuts" to *partition* the space into smaller and smaller subsets. Exhibit 11-11 shows the full decision tree.

The full set of classification rules for defaults in the decision tree model in Exhibit 11-11 are as follows:

1. If credit score < 675 and income $<$ \$85,000, then $= 1$ (default), identified by red line (dashed). There are nine defaults identified by this rule.
2. If $675 <$ credit score < 768 and income $<$ \$56,000, then $= 1$ (default), identified by green line (solid). There are two defaults identified by this rule.
3. If $704.5 <$ credit score < 712 and income $>$ \$56,000, then $= 1$ (default), identified by blue line (dotted). There is one default identified by this rule.

If the borrower's features do not satisfy any of these conditions, then classify as $= 0$ (repay).

EXHIBIT 11-11 Fully Grown Decision Tree (with income shown in $000s)

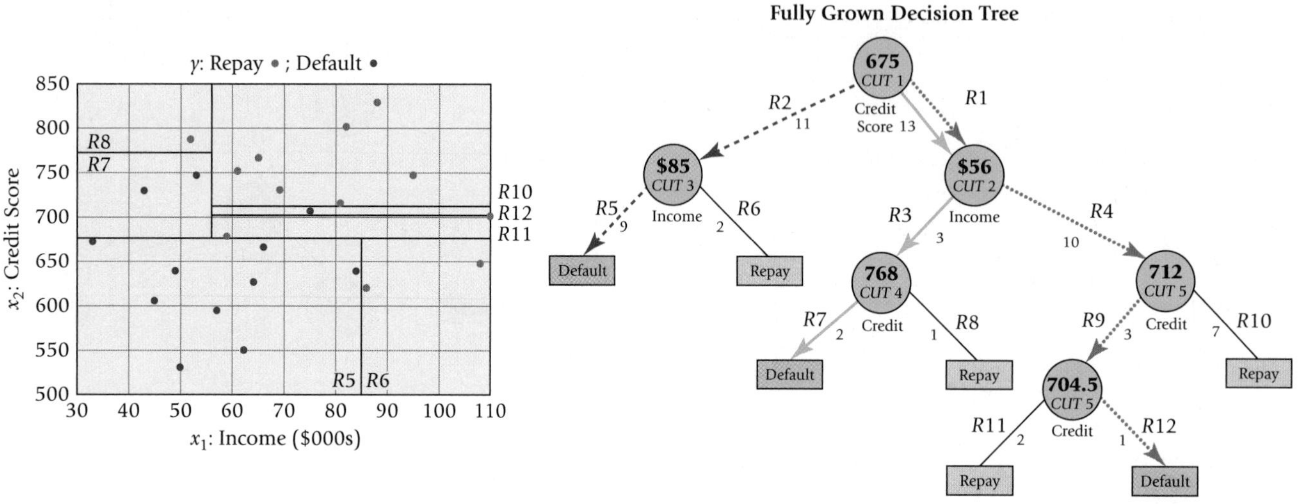

Paige is puzzled by this analysis. She observes that at the node labeled 704.5 the *default* terminal node is to the right of the *repay* terminal node. This suggests that for the same level of income (greater than $56,000), the decision tree will classify a borrower with a *higher* credit score (greater than 704.5) as a default, while classifying a borrower with a *lower* credit score (less than 704.5) as a *repay*. She wonders why this happened and whether it makes sense.

DECISION POINT

What are the strengths and weaknesses of a decision tree model?

TRY IT! 11-1

Rafael Alvarez, the management accountant at Wyatt Manufacturing, is reviewing defective products from the most recent batch of the plant's complex signature product, SB171. The product is produced across different machines in the factory and has a defect rate of 20%. Workers' experience (measured in years) and the level of machine automation (measured on an interval scale from 0 to 5) varies across these machines and Rafael hypothesizes that these two factors contribute to defects.

Wyatt produced 40 units of which 8 are defective ($40 \times 0.2 = 8$). Rafael selects the records of the eight defective units and eight randomly selected good units to build a training set of 16 observations. He then builds a decision tree using this dataset.

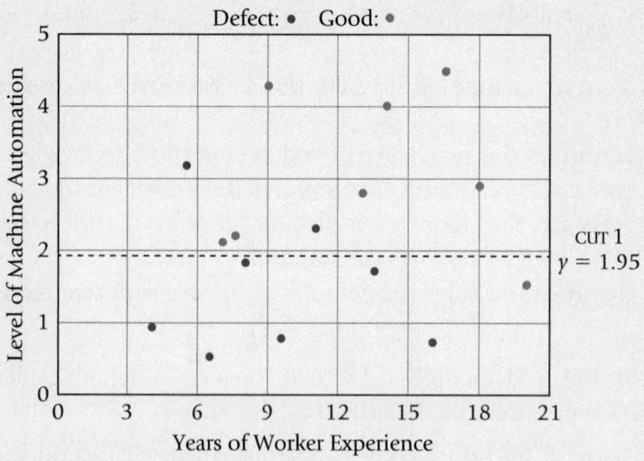

a. The figure shows a plot of the data and the first cut. Calculate the Gini impurity for this cut.
b. Using a ruler, consider other values on the *x*-axis (experience) or *y*-axis (level of automation) where you might make a cut. Confirm that there is no other first cut on the experience or automation dimension that has fewer than three misclassifications.

Refining the Decision Tree

LEARNING OBJECTIVE 4

Describe how to refine a decision tree model to ensure the data represent the business context

. . . pruning the decision tree to prevent overfitting and improving predictions

Management accountants have a unique ability to contribute to the development of decision models because they have a deep understanding of the economics of the business. We look at two specific areas that management accountants address when refining a decision tree to better match the economics of the business:

- Addressing *overfitting*, when a model matches the specific details of a dataset too closely, limiting its predictive powers
- *Pruning* the decision tree to sharpen the model's predictive powers

Developing effective decision models requires that management accountants and data scientists work together. It is this understanding that causes Paige to question the decision tree model.

Overfitting

Based on her understanding of the business, Paige concludes that the decision tree developed from the dataset of 24 borrowers accounted for 21 borrowers in a way that makes intuitive sense. However, the rules for the last two nodes, credit score 712 and credit score 704.5, are

If income > \$56,000 and 712 > credit score > 704.5 then = 1 (default)

If income > \$56,000 and credit score < 704.5 then = 0 (repay)

Consider two borrowers with identical incomes of \$65,000. Borrower 1 has a credit score of 700. Borrower 2 has a credit score of 710. These rules say that Borrower 1, with a credit score less than 704.5, lower than Borrower 2, will repay and that Borrower 2, with a credit score *greater* than 704.5 but *less* than 712 will default (= 1). This prediction contradicts the overall trend within the data—the *signal*—in which repayers have *higher* credit scores and incomes and defaulters have *lower* credit scores and incomes. This is an example of *overfitting*, which is a direct outcome of the flexibility and power of these models. **Overfitting** occurs when a model adheres too closely to the specific details of a dataset such that, in addition to signal, it captures *noise* from random chance, making it less effective at accurately classifying observations from a *new* dataset. Overfitting limits a model's ability to predict future outcomes.

Overfitting is an important concept for management accountants to recognize when using data analytic techniques. The decision tree algorithm, like many data analytic methods, is extremely flexible. It does not *a priori* assume a model for predicting defaults. Recall that in Chapter 10 we assumed a linear relation, $y = a + bX$ between machine hours (X) and indirect manufacturing labor costs (y) and then proceeded to estimate the coefficients a and b. In contrast, the decision tree algorithm simply partitions the data to separate repay loans from default loans (by reducing Gini impurity) and creates rules to predict new loan applications as either repay or default loans. Given the management accountant's training and skills, he or she will quickly realize that the decision tree method "fits" to observations even when:

1. Credit scores and income levels may have been recorded in error.
2. Other factors not considered by the model (for example, the amount of the loan; the model only considers income and credit score) may have affected whether a loan was repaid.
3. The borrower with the higher credit score defaulted because of some other chance or random event (for example, having to pay health care bills because of a freak accident to a family member).

Pruning

One solution to the problem of overfitting is *pruning*. **Pruning** is a technique in which the tree is not grown to its full size, but instead is only allowed to grow to a certain depth. Exhibit 11-12 shows the decision tree from the previous example grown to a depth of three layers.

EXHIBIT 11-12

Tree Pruned to Depth of Three (with income shown in $000s)

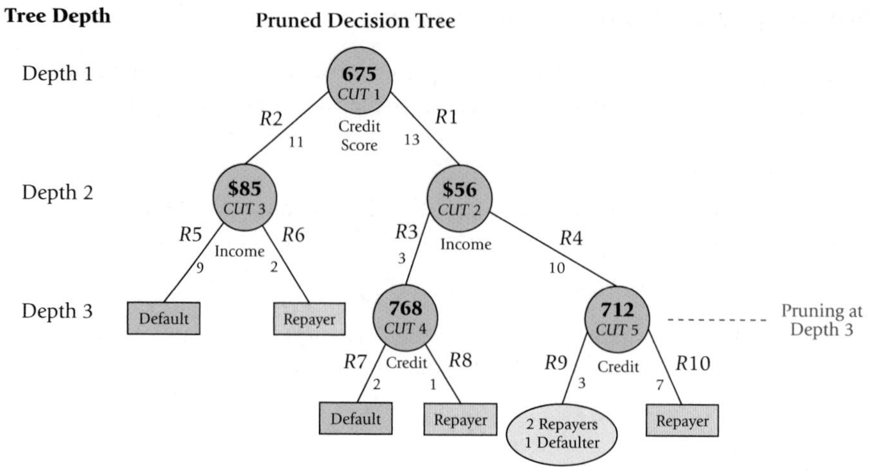

If we prune the tree to a depth of three layers, we get the following tree and rule for defaulters:

1. If credit score < 675 and income < $85,000, then = 1 (default).
2. If 675 < credit score < 768 and income < $56,000, then = 1 (default).
3. If 675 < credit score < 712 and income > $56,000, then default with probability 1/3.

If the borrower's features do not satisfy any of these conditions, then classify as = 0 (repay).

The first two rules for classifying defaulters in the pruned tree are identical to the rules for classifying defaulters in the fully grown tree (also called full tree). The third rule is different. Pruning creates one impure node in the lower right part of the tree, as shown in Exhibit 11-12. Of the three borrowers whose credit scores are less than 712, two borrowers at that node are repayers and one is a defaulter. Without purity in the node, the model classifies the three borrowers in *probabilistic* terms. When a borrower's credit score is less than 712 but greater than 675, and income is greater than $56,000, the pruned decision tree model indicates there is a 1/3 probability of a borrower defaulting (1 default loan out of 3 total loans).

TRY IT! 11-2

Rafael Alvarez, the management accountant at Wyatt Manufacturing, builds the following decision tree. He prunes the tree at a depth of 4. Write the rules for classifying defective products based on the pruned tree.

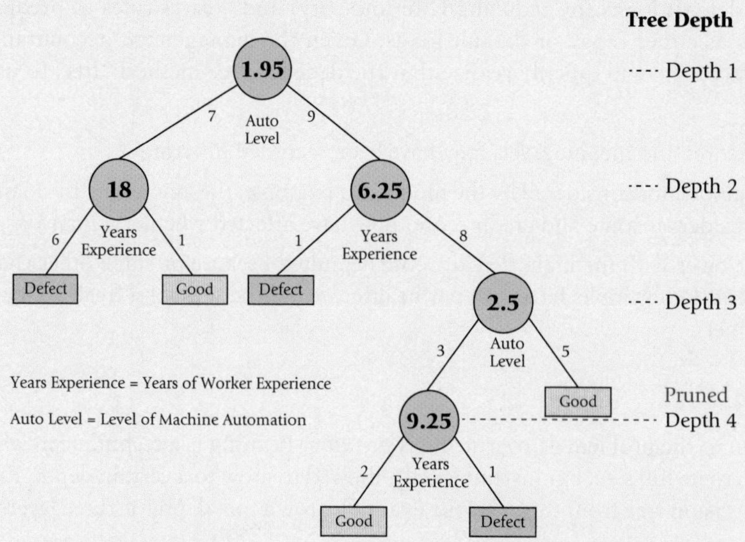

Building models by pruning trees raise two questions: (1) To what depth should the tree be pruned? For example, why not prune the tree up to depth 2 rather than depth 3? (2) How can a data scientist compare trees when there are thousands of data points and hundreds of features? In some contexts, as was the case in the prior example, the management accountant can use his or her understanding of the economics of a business to recognize overfitting, but in other, more complex models with many features, this may be more difficult. To choose among models and to decide where to prune, data scientists *cross-validate* the model. The management accountant uses his or her business knowledge to interpret and evaluate the selected model.

DECISION POINT

What is pruning, and why is it useful?

Validating and Choosing Models

LEARNING OBJECTIVE 5

Explain how to validate the predictions of full versus refined decision trees

. . . cross-validation using prediction accuracy and maximum likelihood and testing on holdout samples to balance the bias–variance tradeoff

Now that you understand full versus pruned decision trees and the related tradeoffs, we introduce three techniques: cross-validation using prediction accuracy, cross-validation using maximum likelihood, and testing on holdout samples that management accountants and data scientists use to choose among models such as the full and pruned decision tree.

Cross-Validation Using Prediction Accuracy to Choose Between Full and Pruned Decision Trees

Cross-validation is the process of comparing predictions of different models on a new set of data for which the actual outcomes (default or repay) are already known. Managers choose the model that predicts most accurately.

To determine whether the pruned tree performs better than the full tree, data scientists at Sierra test both models on 10 randomly selected new borrower records listed in Exhibit 11-13. For each new borrower listed in column 1, column 2 lists income, column 3 lists the credit score, and column 4 lists the actual outcome: default or repay. Of the 10 new observations, eight repaid and two defaulted; that is, the cross validation (also called validation) sample has the same 20% default rate as the population.

Exhibit 11-13 shows the predictions for each borrower made by the full tree (column 5) and the pruned tree (column 6).[8]

EXHIBIT 11-13 Choosing Among Models Based on Fewest Misclassifications

Observation	Income	Credit Score	Actual Outcome (*y*)	Full Tree Prediction	Pruned Tree Prediction
(1)	(2)	(3)	(4)	(5)	(6)
1	$60,000	690	Default	**Repay***	**Repay***(with probability 2/3)
2	$67,000	710	Repay	**Default***	Repay (with probability 2/3)
3	$55,000	772	Repay	Repay	Repay (with probability 1)
4	$61,000	702	Repay	Repay	Repay (with probability 2/3)
5	$58,000	715	Repay	Repay	Repay (with probability 1)
6	$54,000	725	Default	Default	Default (with probability 1)
7	$87,000	665	Repay	Repay	Repay (with probability 1)
8	$90,000	660	Repay	Repay	Repay (with probability 1)
9	$59,000	718	Repay	Repay	Repay (with probability 1)
10	$53,000	775	Repay	Repay	Repay (with probability 1)
		Correct Classification Rate		8/10	9/10

* Misclassified

[8] If a validation sample observation exactly equals the cutoff boundary, it is randomly assigned to either branch (rectangle). This has no effect on conclusions in large datasets.

Fully Grown Decision Tree

To compare how the fully grown tree and pruned tree classify each of the borrowers, consider record 2, with income of $67,000 and credit score of 710. Follow how the fully grown decision tree in Exhibit 11-11 classifies this record.

1. The cutoff at node 1 is credit score 675; with a credit score of 710, record 2 goes to the right.
2. The cutoff at node 2 is income of $56,000; with an income of $67,000, record 2 again goes to the right.
3. The cutoff at node 3 is credit score 712; with a credit score of 710, record 2 now goes left.
4. At the fourth and final node, which is at a depth of 4, the cutoff is credit score 704.5. With a credit score of 710, the tree sends record 2 to the right and classifies the record as default (column 5).

That default classification is wrong because the known actual outcome for record 2 in Exhibit 11-13 is repay.

Pruned Decision Tree

Now turn to the pruned tree in Exhibit 11-12 and follow how the pruned tree classifies record 2, noting that the path of the record for the first three nodes is the same as for the full tree:

1. The cutoff at node 1 is credit score 675; with a credit score of 710, record 2 goes to the right.
2. The cutoff at node 2 is income of $56,000; with an income of $67,000, record 2 again goes to the right.
3. The cutoff at node 3 is credit score 712; with a credit score of 710, record 2 goes to the left.
4. Record 2 now flows into a mixed pool that contains two repay loans and one default loan. The pruned tree cannot classify this record as *either* default or repay. It instead assigns a probability based on the contents of the pool. Only one of three observations in the pool is default, so there is a 1/3 probability that record 2 is default. In the simplest version of the model, any pool where the probability of default is less than 1/2 is classified as repay. Therefore, the pruned tree predicts record 2 as repay.

The actual outcome of record 2 in Exhibit 11-13 is also repay. The pruned tree correctly predicts the actual outcome.

Exhibit 11-13 shows the predictions of the fully grown decision tree and the pruned decision tree for the 10 new borrowers. The pruned tree more accurately classifies the validation set *overall* by correctly predicting 9 out of 10 loans (9/10), while the fully grown tree correctly predicts only 8 out of 10 loans (8/10). Data scientists at Sierra Investments recommend using the pruned tree model on new data because it performs better in predicting default and repay loans.

The data scientists also suggest a more sophisticated approach to comparing the full decision tree model to the pruned decision tree model.

Using Maximum Likelihood Values to Choose Between Fully Grown and Pruned Decision Trees

An alternative approach used by data scientists to compare the performance of the fully grown decision tree and the pruned decision tree is to calculate the *maximum likelihood value* of the predictions. Exhibit 11-14 describes the maximum likelihood computations for the fully grown decision tree and the pruned decision tree. In the description below, we focus on the pruned decision tree.

The first four columns are the cross-validation data from Exhibit 11-13 with the loan coded as 1 if it is a default and 0 if it is a repay. Now focus on column 7, which shows the probabilities of default for each of the cross-validation loans taken from Exhibit 11-13, column 6:

1. The pruned decision tree predicts observations 1, 2, and 4 will repay with a probability of 2/3 or, alternatively stated, will default with probability $1/3$ $(1 - 2/3)$. Exhibit 11-14, column 7 records the probability of default as 0.33 for observations 1, 2, and 4.

2. The pruned decision tree predicts observations 3, 5, 7, 8, 9, and 10 in Exhibit 11-13, column 6, will repay with probability 1 (or alternatively stated, default with probability 0). Exhibit 11-14, column 7 records the probability of default as 0.01.[9]
3. Finally, the pruned tree predicts observation 6 in Exhibit 11-13, column 6 will default with probability 1.00 so Exhibit 11-14, column 7 records the probability of default as 0.99.[10]

For each observation in the validation sample, Exhibit 11-14, column 8 calculates the likelihood value $L = p^y \times (1 - p)^{1-y}$, based on the pruned decision tree model, where p is the predicted probability of default and y equals 1 if the loan defaults and 0 otherwise. What does the likelihood value do? It ranges between 0 and 1 with a value near 0 when the predicted probability is very far from the actual value and a value close to 1 when the predicted probability is close to the actual value.

Consider a loan that defaults so $y = 1$. If the prediction model predicts a high probability of default, say $p = 0.99$, the likelihood value $L = 0.99^1 \times (1 - 0.99)^{1-1} = 0.99$. If, however, the prediction model predicts a low probability of default, $p = 0.01$, the likelihood value $L = 0.01^1 \times (1 - 0.01)^{1-1} = 0.01$. When $y = 1$, the likelihood value is maximized when p is close to 1.

Now consider a loan that repays so $y = 0$. If the prediction model predicts a low probability of default, say $p = 0.01$, the likelihood value $L = 0.01^0 \times (1 - 0.01)^{1-0} = 0.99$. If, however, the prediction model predicts a high probability of default in this case, $p = 0.99$, the likelihood value $L = 0.99^0 \times (1 - 0.99)^{1-0} = 0.01$. When $y = 0$, the likelihood value is maximized when p is close to 0.

Consider the likelihood calculation for observation 1 in column 8 for the pruned tree. The actual outcome is a default $(y = 1)$ while the predicted probability of default is 0.33. The likelihood value $L = (0.33)^1 \times (1 - 0.33)^{1-1} = 0.33 \times 1 = 0.33$, indicating that for this observation the model did not do a good job of assessing default. Exhibit 11-14, column 8 shows the likelihood value calculations for all 10 observations in the cross-validation sample. The likelihood values range from a low of 0.33 to a high of 0.99 for these observations.

EXHIBIT 11-14 Choosing Between Fully Grown and Pruned Decision Tree Models Using Maximum Likelihood Estimates

				For Fully Grown Tree		For Pruned Tree	
Observation	Income	Credit Score	Actual Outcome (y)	Probability of Default (p)	Likelihood Value $p^y \times (1-p)^{1-y}$	Probability of Default (p)	Likelihood Value $p^y \times (1-p)^{1-y}$
(1)	(2)	(3)	(4)	(5)	(6)	(7)	(8)
1	$60,000	690	1 (Default)	0.01	0.01[a]	0.33	0.33[e]
2	$67,000	710	0 (Repay)	0.99	0.01	0.33	0.67[f]
3	$55,000	772	0 (Repay)	0.01	0.99[b]	0.01	0.99
4	$61,000	702	0 (Repay)	0.01	0.99	0.33	0.67[g]
5	$58,000	715	0 (Repay)	0.01	0.99	0.01	0.99
6	$54,000	725	1 (Default)	0.99	0.99[c]	0.99	0.99
7	$87,000	665	0 (Repay)	0.01	0.99	0.01	0.99
8	$90,000	660	0 (Repay)	0.01	0.99	0.01	0.99
9	$59,000	718	0 (Repay)	0.01	0.99	0.01	0.99
10	$53,000	775	0 (Repay)	0.01	0.99	0.01	0.99
					$L_f = 0.000092$[d]		$L_p = 0.13807$[h]

[a] $(0.01)^1 \times (1 - 0.01)^{1-1} = 0.01 \times 1 = 0.01$; [b] $(0.01)^0 \times (1 - 0.01)^{1-0} = 1 \times 0.99 = 0.99$; [c] $(0.99)^1 \times (1 - 0.99)^{1-1} = 0.99 \times 1 = 0.99$

[d] $0.01 \times 0.01 \times 0.99 \times 0.99 \times 0.99 \times 0.99 \times 0.99 \times 0.99 \times 0.99 \times 0.99 = 0.000092$

[e] $(0.33)^1 \times (1 - 0.33)^{1-1} = 0.33 \times 1 = 0.33$; [f] $(0.33)^0 \times (1 - 0.33)^{1-0} = 1 \times 0.67 = 0.67$; [g] $(0.33)^0 \times (1 - 0.33)^{1-0} = 1 \times 0.67 = 0.67$

[h] $0.33 \times 0.67 \times 0.99 \times 0.67 \times 0.99 \times 0.99 \times 0.99 \times 0.99 \times 0.99 \times 0.99 = 0.13807$

[9] Because (likelihood) values will be later multiplied together, data scientists do not record the probability of default as 0 but as some very small number; for example, they could write it as 0.000001, but 0.01 keeps the math simpler.

[10] Recording the probability as a number very close to 1 rather than 1 avoids mathematical complexity such as the value of 0 raised to the power of 0.

How well does the model do in predicting defaults across all observations taken together? To measure this performance, data scientists multiply the likelihood values calculated for the individual observations.[11] Exhibit 11-14, column 8 shows the overall likelihood value for the pruned decision tree model, $L_p = 0.13807$. Exhibit 11-14, column 7 shows the overall likelihood value for the full decision tree model, $L_f = 0.000092$. In this example, the overall likelihood is maximized for the pruned decision tree model because it has a higher overall likelihood value than the fully grown decision tree model. This means that, when measured across all observations, the predictions of the pruned decision tree model are closer to actual values. Sierra Investments prefers the pruned decision tree model to the fully grown decision tree model for predicting defaults. In other contexts, the fully grown decision tree model might have a higher likelihood value than the pruned decision tree model.

Paige still has some doubts about this approach. Choosing a model based on feedback from the validation sample means that the data scientist is, in effect, using the validation sample to make decisions about which model performs better. The real test is how well the pruned decision tree model performs against data it has not seen. Paige proposes testing the pruned decision tree model on a completely new dataset called a *holdout* sample (sometimes also called a *test* sample). She would be more confident of the model's ability to predict defaults if the overall likelihood value is similar to the overall likelihood value in the cross-validation set.

Testing the Pruned Decision-Tree Model on the Holdout Sample

Managers randomly select ten new borrower records listed in Exhibit 11-15. For each new borrower listed in column 1, column 2 lists the income, column 3 lists the credit score, and column 4 lists the actual outcome: default or repay. Of the 10 new observations, eight repaid and two defaulted. Based on the pruned decision tree model, the table shows the predicted probability of default for each borrower (column 5) and the likelihood value calculation (column 6). The overall likelihood value is 0.18972, very similar to the overall likelihood value in the validation

EXHIBIT 11-15 Likelihood Value of Predictions for Pruned Decision Tree in Holdout Sample

Observation	Income	Credit Score	Actual Outcome (y)	Probability of Default (p)	Likelihood Value $p^y \times (1-p)^{1-y}$
(1)	(2)	(3)	(4)	(5)	(6)
1	$87,000	650	0 (Repay)	0.01	0.99[a]
2	$79,000	670	1 (Default)	0.99	0.99[b]
3	$70,000	708	0 (Repay)	0.33	0.67[c]
4	$51,000	695	1 (Default)	0.99	0.99[b]
5	$64,000	700	0 (Repay)	0.33	0.67[c]
6	$68,000	710	0 (Repay)	0.33	0.67[c]
7	$59,000	690	0 (Repay)	0.33	0.67[c]
8	$92,000	670	0 (Repay)	0.01	0.99[a]
9	$52,000	778	0 (Repay)	0.01	0.99[a]
10	$65,000	720	0 (Repay)	0.01	0.99[a]
			Overall likelihood value		$L_f = 0.18972$[d]

[a] $(0.01)^0 \times (1 - 0.01)^{1-0} = 1 \times 0.99 = 0.99$; [b] $(0.99)^1 \times (1 - 0.99)^{1-1} = 0.99 \times 1 = 0.99$;
[c] $(0.33)^0 \times (1 - 0.33)^{1-0} = 1 \times 0.67 = 0.67$
[d] $0.99 \times 0.99 \times 0.67 \times 0.99 \times 0.67 \times 0.67 \times 0.67 \times 0.99 \times 0.99 \times 0.99 = 0.18972$

[11] For very large numbers of observations in the validation sample, multiplying a series of numbers less than 1 makes the product very, very small, running into several thousand decimal places. Instead, data scientists calculate the natural logarithm of the likelihood values. The logarithm of a product of numbers is the sum of the logarithms so instead of multiplying the likelihood values, computer models add the natural logarithms of the likelihood values. The natural logarithms of numbers less than 1 is negative, which means maximizing a negative number. Data scientists often flip the sign of the logarithm likelihood value and minimize the negative of the logarithm likelihood, that is, minimize the log loss.

sample. Paige is now more confident using the pruned decision tree to predict probability of defaults. If the holdout sample had given results very different from the validation sample, Sierra's data science team would have needed to go back and rework the model.

Criteria for the Model Choice

Two important principles guide the choice of models:

1. ***Feedback* loops are fundamental to data science.** Data scientists use a training dataset to train models. They choose among competing models based on how well the models perform in making classifications or predictions on a separate randomly selected cross-validation set. Data scientists do not rely on statistical measures like R^2, *t*-values, and *F*-values to choose among models. Instead, the feedback loop from the cross-validation set becomes the basis for choosing among competing models.
2. **The choice of model is based on performance on the cross-validation data, not the training data.** In the Sierra Investments example, the fully grown tree does better than the pruned tree in identifying default loans and repay loans in the training data by fitting the model to the peculiarities and specifics of the training data. As a result, it overfits the model to the training data and so performs poorly on the validation data. The pruned tree predicts default probabilities more accurately compared to the fully grown tree in the validation sample. This raises the question of whether further pruning would yield more accurate predictions.

The Bias–Variance Tradeoff

What are the tradeoffs of further pruning? As we have already discussed, the benefit of pruning is that it avoids overfitting the model to *noise*, so a different training dataset would have yielded a fairly similar model. The risk of further pruning is that it might weaken the *signals* in the feature variables that help more accurately assess the probability of default. The model would be underutilizing information signals in the data. Pruning the tree too much would "underfit" the data, *biasing* the model from fully understanding features that help distinguish between default loans and repay loans.

In contrast, building out the tree allows features to be more fully used to separate default loans from repay loans. A fully grown tree captures more richness of the data and so more accurately reflects the underlying reality. But, as mentioned, it also risks overfitting the model to the noise and randomness in the training data. Slightly different datasets would lead to very different models. Building fully grown trees would increase the *variance* of the model, making it less reliable in predicting default probabilities in a new sample of loans. In general, the *more* complex the model, the *lower* the bias and the *higher* the variance. Inversely, the *less* complex the model, the *higher* the bias and the *lower* the variance.

Data scientists try to balance the *bias–variance* tradeoff by, for example, pruning trees to various depths. The greater the depth, the lower the bias and the higher the variance of the model. But at what point is the tradeoff optimal? There is nothing that Sierra Investments can do *a priori* to determine whether pruning the tree to a depth of 2 or a depth of 3 is better. It must simply try both models and see which model has a higher overall likelihood value. This is the model that optimizes the bias–variance tradeoff. In the context of decision trees, the depth to which to prune is called a *hyperparameter*. A **hyperparameter** is a parameter that cannot be learned by running the model. It must be chosen prior to doing the analysis.[12]

Pruning Guidelines

In large datasets, it would be difficult to detect the anomalies that result from fully growing the tree and then pruning, as we did in our example. Data scientists use some rules of thumb to guide their pruning.

1. **Stop growing the tree after a certain depth.** In the example, the data scientist grows the tree to a maximum depth of 3. Therefore, no further cuts are made even though rectangle 9 (R9) is impure with two repay loans and one default loan.

[12] In addition to pruning, more sophisticated data science models such as random forests, gradient boosting, and neural networks can be used to obtain more accurate probabilities of default in the PeerLend Digital (PD) setting to optimize the bias–variance tradeoff. These techniques are beyond the scope of this text.

2. **Stop growing the tree if a node contains fewer than a certain number of data points.** In the example, the data scientist might choose to stop growing the tree if it has fewer than four data points. If this rule were applied, the cut at a credit score of 768 of rectangle 3 (R3) into rectangles 7 and 8 (R7 and R8) would not be made. Why? Because there are only three data points for income levels less than \$56,000. The decision tree would classify loans with a credit score greater than 675 and income less than \$56,000 as an impure node—a default loan with probability 2/3.

Management Accounting Insights

Management accountants provide important insights into the models that data scientists evaluate. For example if the tree were pruned to a depth of 2, then it follows from Exhibit 11-10 (p. 431) that the rule for defaults would be

If credit score < 675 and income < \$85,000, then = 1 (default)

If the borrower's features do not satisfy this condition, then classify as 0 (repay) because for a decision tree pruned to depth 2, the probability of repayment at all other nodes would be greater than 0.5.

Even if cross-validation using prediction accuracy or maximum likelihood was slightly better for the model pruned to a depth of 2 than for a model pruned to a depth of 3, the management accountant might suggest that the model provides only weak signals about the probability of default.

1. It signals default when both the credit score and income levels are below certain thresholds. Based on business knowledge, the management accountant might suggest that the model is largely being driven by the credit score since many borrowers have incomes below \$85,000.
2. From a business standpoint, the management accountant might ask whether the model could be strengthened to identify defaults when income is low but credit score is high.

Balanced Versus Unbalanced Samples

Paige is curious about one more point. Although the number of default loans in the dataset is close to 20%, the training sample consists of an equal number of default and repay loans, while the validation and holdout samples have 20% default loans. She wonders whether the number of default and repay loans in the training data should also be representative of the population (20% default loans and 80% repay loans) or should the training data comprise 50% default loans and 50% repay loans. To her the tradeoffs seem clear: If the decision tree models are built using the population distribution of default loans and repay loans, the models would be driven by repay loans since they are greater in number. But, just as in the case of detecting credit card fraud, the main goal of the "ask" is to identify default loans. Choosing more default loans in the training data than appear in the population will emphasize default loans and give the model more default data to use to help identify the characteristics of default loans.

TRY IT! 11-3

Rafael Alvarez, the management accountant at Wyatt Manufacturing, obtains the validation sample for product SB171, shown below. The sample contains data on workers' experience (measured in years), the level of machine automation (measured on an interval scale from 0 to 5), and the actual outcome (defective = 1 and good = 0).

Use the format of Exhibit 11-14 to calculate (a) the probability of defect for each observation using the pruned tree shown in Try It 11-2. (If the observation is predicted to be a defective unit at a pure (terminal) node, write the probability as 0.99; if the observation is predicted to be a good unit at a pure (terminal) node, write the probability as 0.01; if the observation is predicted to be in a mixed node, write the probability of a defective unit for that node as defined by the decision tree rules you wrote.) (b) Calculate the likelihood value for each observation in the cross validation set using the equation, $L = p^y \times (1 - p)^{1-y}$. Remember: $x^1 = x$ and $x^0 = 1$. (c) Calculate the overall likelihood value for the cross validation set.

Observation #	1	2	3	4	5	6	7	8	9	10
Automation Level	3.5	1.5	2.25	2.1	2.6	1.7	2.3	3.4	3.2	2.3
Years' Experience	9	15	10	11	12	19	8.5	11	10	11.5
Actual Outcome	0	1	0	1	0	0	0	0	0	0

The downside is that the decision tree models are being built on data that are not representative of the population (20% default loans, not 50%). Of course, the cross validation and holdout samples are representative of the population (they each contain 20% of default loans) and so the models are being selected and tested using the proportion of default loans the model will be encountering in practice. There is no clear answer, but in many circumstances choosing a "balanced" sample of default and repay loans (50% of each) in the training sample often performs better than an "unbalanced" sample (20% default loans and 80% repay loans). The data scientist will often run different training models using both "balanced" and "unbalanced" data and see which approach has a higher overall likelihood value and gives better predictions in the cross validation and holdout samples.

DECISION POINT

How do managers choose among different data science models?

Evaluating Data Science Models

LEARNING OBJECTIVE 6

Evaluate the predictions of different data science models to choose the best one for the business need and visualize and communicate model insights

. . . use likelihood values, feature variables, receiver operating characteristic curve, confusion matrix, payoff matrix

Management accountants play a pivotal role in helping managers evaluate and use data science models. Does the model make economic sense? Does it reflect underlying reality? In the Sierra Investments context, can the pruned decision tree model classify loans as repay or default well enough to inform investment decisions? We will present Step 5 in our data science framework by examining five methods for evaluating a model and then conclude with Step 6, in which the management accountant visualizes and communicates insights.

Step 5: Evaluate the Model

Having selected a model, in Step 5 of the decision-making process, Paige helps to evaluate the model and answer important questions. There are several ways to evaluate the model and Paige considers each of them in turn: (1) the magnitude of the likelihood values, (2) evaluation of feature variables, (3) receiver operating characteristic (ROC) curve, (4) confusion matrix classifications, and (5) quantifying predictions using the payoff matrix.

Magnitude of the Likelihood Values

Models with high likelihood values give better predictions. Sometimes even the most sophisticated data science models do not do a good job of prediction because the problem itself is complex, important variables are missing, or the data has errors or is incomplete. It appears from Exhibits 11-14 and 11-15 that the model does very well in predicting the probability of default in both the validation and holdout samples. The average of the likelihood values is about 0.86.[13] Average values above 0.65 indicate that the model's predictions are good. A likelihood value of 0.5 would indicate that it is just a random chance that the model would distinguish default loans from repay loans.

Evaluation of Feature Variables

Management accountants use their knowledge of the business to judge whether the feature variables used to make predictions about the target variable make economic sense. In the Sierra Investments example, Paige is comfortable with the model features used to separate default loans from repay loans. Income levels indicate an ability to repay, and credit scores indicate how borrowers have managed debt in the past. The decision tree partitions identify borrowers with low income levels and low credit scores to be more likely to default and those with high income levels and high credit scores as more likely to repay. These results make intuitive sense and reflect what she believes to be the underlying economic reality. She cannot judge the exact cutoff values derived from the model, but the broad insights are consistent with her business experience.

Identifying Misclassifications

Data science models are not perfect and misclassify predictions. In the Sierra Investments case, the model (1) correctly classifies some default loans but misclassifies other default loans as

[13] From Exhibit 11-14, column 8, average likelihood value = (0.33 + 0.67 + 0.99 + 0.67 + 0.99 + 0.99 + 0.99 + 0.99 + 0.99 + 0.99) ÷ 10 = 0.86

repay loans and (2) correctly classifies some repay loans but misclassifies other repay loans as default loans. Classifying a default loan as a repay loan and a repay loan as a default loan creates risk.

To identify misclassifications, Paige constructs Exhibit 11-16 using information from the pruned decision tree validation sample in Exhibit 11-14, column 7. Columns 1 and 2 in Exhibit 11-16 order the information in Exhibit 11-14, column 7 from the highest to the lowest predicted probabilities of default. Observation 6 has the highest predicted probability of default of 0.99. She records this as the first observation in Exhibit 11-16, columns 1 and 2. Observations 1, 2, and 4 each have a predicted default probability of 0.33. She records these as the next three observations in Exhibit 11-16, columns 1 and 2. Finally, observations 3, 5, 7, 8, 9, and 10 each have a predicted default probability of 0.01. She records these as the final six observations in Exhibit 11-16, columns 1 and 2. Column 3 records the actual outcome for each observation.

Columns 4 and 5 record the cumulative number of zeroes (repay loans) and ones (default loans) based on the information in column 3. For example, the first observation in column 3 is a 1 (default) so the cumulative number of zeroes after the first observation is 0 and the cumulative number of ones is 1. The second, third, and fourth observations have the *same* probability of default and are all part of a group. The actual values are 1, 0, and 0. The cumulative number of zeroes after this group of observations is 2 and the cumulative number of ones is also 2.[14] After the fifth, sixth, seventh, eighth, ninth, and tenth observations, all of which are zeroes, the cumulative number of zeroes is 8 and the cumulative number of ones is 2.

Columns 6 and 7 in Exhibit 11-16 calculate the false positive rate and the true positive rate. At Sierra Investments, the target (positive) feature variable is defaults. The **false positive rate** in a classification problem is the fraction of negatives (repay loans) incorrectly identified as positives (default loans) at a given threshold value. The **true positive rate** in a classification problem is the fraction of positives (default loans) correctly identified as positive (default loans) at a given threshold value. Exhibit 11-16, column 6 calculates the *false positive rate* equal to the cumulative number of repay loans divided by the total number of repay loans (column (4) ÷ 8). Exhibit 11-16, column 7 calculates the *true positive rate* equal to the cumulative number of default loans divided by the total number of default loans (column (5) ÷ 2).

There are two primary ways that Paige can use Exhibit 11-16. First, she can plot the *receiver operating characteristic curve*, and, second, she can construct the *confusion matrix*.

EXHIBIT 11-16 Actual Outcomes and Prediction Probabilities of Default From the Validation Sample of the Pruned Decision Tree

Observation Number (from Exhibit 11-14) (1)	Predicted Probability of Default Ranked from Highest to Lowest (from Exhibit 11-14) (2)	Actual Outcome (from Exhibit 11-14) (3)	Cumulative Number of 0s (4)	Cumulative Number of 1s (5)	False Positive Rate (*x*-axis) (6) = (4) ÷ 8	True Positive Rate (*y*-axis) (7) = (5) ÷ 2
6	0.99	1	0	1	0	0.5
1	0.33	1				
2	0.33	0				
4	0.33	0	2	2	0.25	1.0
3	0.01	0				
5	0.01	0				
7	0.01	0				
8	0.01	0				
9	0.01	0				
10	0.01	0	8	2	1.0	1.0

[14] We cannot calculate the cumulative number of 0s and 1s after each observation since at the probability of 0.33 all three outcomes occur simultaneously. The three horizontal lines in the table indicate these groupings.

Receiver Operating Characteristic (ROC) Curve

A useful and commonly used tool to evaluate a model is the **receiver operating characteristic (ROC) curve** that plots the *false positive rate* (FP) on the x-axis and the *true positive rate* (TP) on the y-axis. Comparing these two rates provides insight into how well a model correctly classifies borrowers at any threshold value. Exhibit 11-17 presents the ROC curve based on the false positive rate (column 6) and the true positive rate (column 7) in Exhibit 11-16. Point A on the ROC curve indicates that the default prediction model can choose a cutoff to get 50% of the true positives (value on the y-axis) without attracting any false positives. This is the case when the cutoff value is set at a default probability above 0.33, say 0.50. At this cutoff default probability, the model correctly predicts loan 6—with a predicted probability of default of 0.99, which is greater than 0.50—to be a default (true positive for one of the two defaulting loans). The model does not predict any repaying loan as a default (zero false positives) because all repaying loans have a predicted probability of default less than 0.50. If, however, Paige wants to avoid lending to both actual defaulters (100% of true positives), she must move to point B on the ROC curve (and choose a default probability below 0.33, say 0.30). At this point, however, Sierra must accept 25% false positives. That is, although this cutoff probability correctly predicts both default loans, it also misidentifies two of eight repay loans as default loans (25%). Increasing the true positive rate also increases the false positive rate.

EXHIBIT 11-17

Receiver Operating Characteristic (ROC) Curve for the Validation Sample of the Pruned Decision Tree

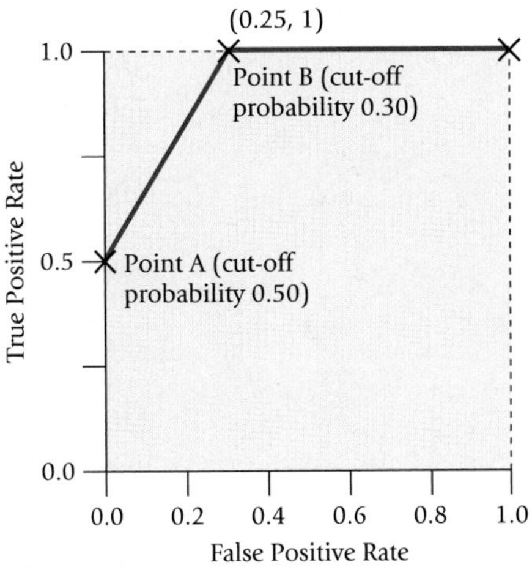

The more accurately a model predicts defaults as defaults and repays as repays, the closer the ROC curve will go up along the y-axis on the left and then move horizontally across the top. Exhibit 11-18, Panel A shows such an ROC curve. In the context of Sierra Investments, such an ROC curve would mean there is a cutoff probability such that all defaulting loans have a probability of default above the cutoff (100% true positives) without classifying any repayer loans as defaults (0% false positives). In other words, the model has a very good hit rate without any false alarms! The closer an ROC curve follows the diagonal line from the origin (0, 0) to the upper-right corner (1, 1) as in Exhibit 11-18, Panel B, the less effective the model is at correctly predicting a new loan (increasing the true positives increases the false positives at the same rate). Exhibit 11-18, Panel C shows a reasonably good ROC curve, much like the ROC curve in Exhibit 11-17. If the actual ROC curve for the full dataset is like this ROC curve, Paige will be more confident that the model predictions will be useful for predicting defaults without the risk of too many false positives.

Data scientists cannot make perfect predictions. As we have seen, they may predict a loan to default that ultimately is repaid. They may also predict a loan to be repaid that eventually defaults. Based only on the ROC curves, the data scientist favors a point corresponding to a default probability cutoff where the ROC curve starts to flatten out resulting in a high true positive rate without a correspondingly high false positive rate. Paige points out that a far better way to choose a default probability cutoff is to estimate the payoffs—the rewards and costs of each of the four quadrants of the confusion matrix.

EXHIBIT 11-18 ROC Curves

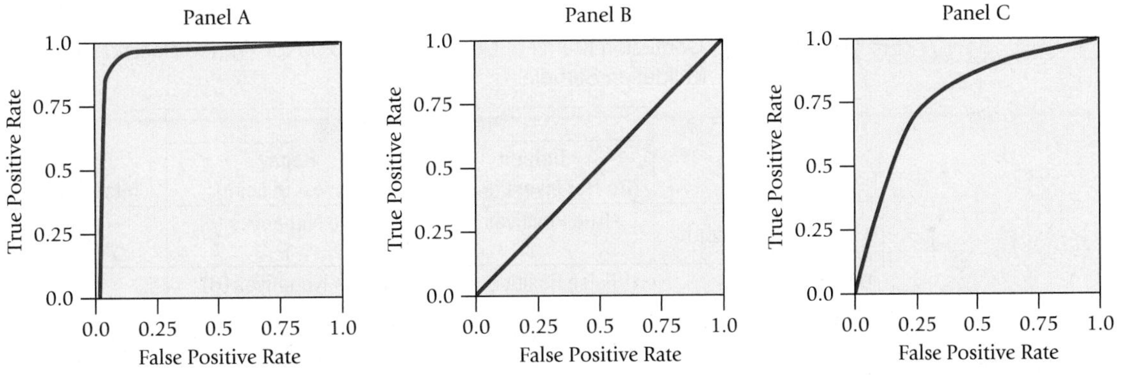

Confusion Matrix

A **confusion matrix** is a matrix that shows the predicted and actual classifications at a given threshold value. In the Sierra Investments example, this threshold value is the cutoff value for the default probability above which the model would indicate not to invest in the loan and below which the model would suggest investing in the loan. *We will label the decision not to invest in the loan as the model predicting default (or, more accurately, high risk of losses because of default risk) and the decision to invest in the loan as the model predicting repay (or, more accurately, high returns because of the likelihood of repayment).*

Just as we did in Exhibit 11-13, the most intuitive cutoff value is a default probability of 0.50. That is, for all values greater than 0.50, the model would predict not to invest (default) and for all values less than 0.50, the model would predict invest (repay). Exhibit 11-19 shows the confusion matrix for the validation sample using the pruned decision tree and a cutoff probability of 0.50.

To see how to build the confusion matrix at a cutoff value of 0.50, consider the line drawn at a value of 0.50 in Exhibit 11-16 between the probability values of 0.33 and 0.99. The cutoff probability of 0.50 means that Sierra Investments will reject all loans for which the predicted default probability is greater than or equal to 0.50 (that is, all loans above the line) and invest in all loans for which the predicted default probability is less than 0.50 (that is, all loans below the line). Ideally, Sierra would like (1) all loans above the line to be default loans (coded as 1) with no repay loans (coded as 0) and (2) all loans below the line to be repay loans (coded as 0) with no default loans (coded as 1).

From Exhibit 11-16, Sierra Investments will predict loan 6 as default and will not invest in this loan (which has a predicted probability of default of 0.99). It will predict all other loans as repays and invest in these loans (which have a predicted probability of default of 0.33 or 0.01). The cutoff probability of 0.50 correctly predicts that loan 6 will actually default, but it predicts that Sierra should invest in loan 1 when it actually defaults. It correctly predicts the other eight loans below the cutoff as repays. Using the cutoff probability of 0.50 results in only one misclassification.

This leads to the confusion matrix in Exhibit 11-19. The first column shows the only predicted default, loan 6, which actually defaults and appears in the box labeled (A) as **true positives** (TP)—positives correctly predicted as positives, that is, default loans correctly predicted as defaults. Sierra Investments does not invest in loans predicted as default and avoids those losses. Loans that are actually repays but are falsely predicted as defaults appear in the box labeled (Y) as **false positives** (FP)—negatives incorrectly predicted as positives. These are good loans that Sierra would like to invest in and earn interest on but will not because the model wrongly predicts them as default loans. At a cutoff probability of 0.50 there are no such loans, so the box labeled Y has a value of 0.

The second column in Exhibit 11-19 shows the predicted repay loans – 1, 2, 3, 4, 5, 7, 8, 9, and 10. Of these nine loans, eight actually repay and appear in the box labeled (B) as **true negatives** (TN)—negatives correctly predicted as negatives, that is, repay loans correctly predicted as repays. Sierra invests in the loans classified as repay and gets the benefit of interest payments on these fully paid loans. There is one loan (loan 1) in the box labeled (Z) or **false negatives** (FN)—positives incorrectly predicted as negatives, that is loans predicted to repay, leading Sierra to invest, but which actually default. Sierra would like to avoid loans in box Z because they lead to loss of principal as a result of a default.

EXHIBIT 11-19 Confusion Matrix at Cutoff Value of 0.50 for Pruned Decision Tree Validation Sample

		Predicted Outcomes		
		Default (Do Not Invest in Loan)	**Repay (Invest in Loan)**	**Total**
Actual Outcomes	**Default**	True Positives (A) 1	False Negatives (Z) 1	2
	Repay	False Positives (Y) 0	True Negatives (B) 8	8
	Total	1	9	10

So, what is the consequence of setting the cutoff probability at 0.50? The good news is that Sierra invests in all loans that repay. The downside is that Sierra invests in one loan, loan 1, which the model misclassifies as repay but which actually defaults (false negative).

As the management accountant, Paige has insight into this problem that data scientists do not have. She understands that it is very costly for Sierra to invest in loans that default. Even though a cutoff probability of default of 0.50 may sound very appealing for separating default loans from repay loans, Sierra may want to be conservative and minimize investing in loans that default even if it means not investing in some loans that repay. One way for Sierra to invest in fewer default loans is to set the cutoff probability lower at, say, 0.30. At this cutoff, Sierra will only invest in loans when the predicted default probability is less than 0.30 and not invest in loans when the predicted default probability is greater than 0.30.[15]

The lower cutoff probability means lowering the line in Exhibit 11-16 below loans 1, 2, and 4, which have a predicted probability of default of 0.33. This means loans 6, 1, 2, and 4 with a predicted default probability of 0.99 and 0.33 are above the cutoff line. Sierra will not invest in these loans because they are above the cutoff probability. It will invest in loans 3, 5, 7, 8, 9, and 10 that are below the cutoff line (with a predicted default probability of 0.01). This leads to the confusion matrix in Exhibit 11-20. The first column shows the loans Sierra will not invest in (called predicted defaults)—loans 6, 1, 2, and 4. Of these loans two loans, 6 and 1, actually default and appear in the box labeled (A) as true positives (TP). Sierra does not invest in these loans and avoids these losses. Two loans, 2 and 4, actually repay but are above the cutoff probability and appear in the box labeled (Y) as false positives (FP). These are repay loans that Sierra would have liked to invest in and earn interest on but will not because the predicted default probability is above the cutoff probability.

The second column in Exhibit 11-20 shows the loans Sierra will invest in (called predicted repay)—3, 5, 7, 8, 9, and 10. All six of these loans actually repay and appear in the box labeled (B) as true negatives (TN). There are no loans in the box labeled (Z) as false negatives (FN). At the 0.30 cutoff, Sierra avoids investing in loans that are predicted to repay but actually default.

The two confusion matrices indicate the nature of the tradeoff in choosing the cutoff default probability. If the cutoff probability is set low (0.30), Sierra would only invest in loans that have a default probability of less than 0.30. It would avoid investing in loans that default (false negatives) but would also miss out on investing in loans that repay (true negatives). By raising the cutoff default probability to 0.50, Sierra would be more aggressive and invest in loans with a default probability less than 0.50. It would then invest in more loans that repay (true negatives) but would also be stuck with some loans that default (false negatives). In summary, raising the cutoff decreases true positives and false positives and increases true negatives and false negatives.

So which cutoff should Sierra choose? At first glance, the cutoff probability of 0.50 appears more appealing—it is intuitive in that loans with default probabilities above 0.50 are rejected while those with default probabilities below 0.50 are accepted. The confusion matrix in Exhibit 11-19 at a cutoff probability of 0.50 also misclassifies only one loan (loan 1 as a false negative). In contrast, the confusion matrix in Exhibit 11-20 at a cutoff probability of 0.30 misclassifies two loans (loans 2 and 4 as false positives). But choosing cutoffs is seldom obvious. It depends on the payoffs for each quadrant of the confusion matrix.

EXHIBIT 11-20 Confusion Matrix at Cutoff Value of 0.30 for Pruned Decision Tree Validation Sample

		Predicted Outcomes		
		Default (Do Not Invest in Loan)	**Repay (Invest in Loan)**	**Total**
Actual Outcomes	**Default**	True Positives (A) 2	False Negatives (Z) 0	2
	Repay	False Positives (Y) 2	True Negatives (B) 6	8
	Total	4	6	10

[15] In many data science applications, the cutoff default probability is set below 0.50 because of data quality issues even absent payoff or risk considerations.

Quantifying Predictions Using the Payoff Matrix

Management accountants use their insights and knowledge of the business to estimate the payoffs. In the Sierra Investments example, Paige must choose between the 0.30 default probability cutoff of Exhibit 11-19 or the 0.50 default probability cutoff of Exhibit 11-20. Paige estimates the payoffs to Sierra for each of the four quadrants of the confusion matrix over the 3-year period of the loans. For simplicity, she ignores the time value of money. She prepares the payoffs assuming she invests $100 in a loan.

1. The payoff for the true negatives in quadrant B—loans that Sierra invests in that actually repay—is relatively easy. If Sierra invests $100 in each loan, Sierra will receive a payoff of 15% per year or $45 over 3 years, in addition to getting back the $100 the firm invested for a net payoff of $45.
2. The computations for the false negatives in quadrant Z—loans Sierra invests in but which actually default—is not so straightforward. Sierra would not lose all the $100 invested in these loans. That's because defaulting loans start defaulting sometime along the way during the next 3 years. Paige does a detailed analysis of how much borrowers repay before they default. She estimates that Sierra will, on average, receive $30 as interest and principal repayments on the loan before the loan defaults. She therefore concludes that the payoff for false negatives in quadrant Z is −$70.
3. Next, she considers the payoffs for all outcomes where Sierra does not invest in the PD loan because the model predicts a high default risk. These are the true positives in quadrant A—loans that are predicted to have high default risk and actually default and the false positives in quadrant Y—loans that are predicted to have high default risk but actually repay. In either case, once the model predicts these loans as having high default risk, Sierra will not invest in these loans even though in the false positive case, it would have been beneficial for Sierra to invest. The key question is the payoff Sierra would get elsewhere from the money not invested in PeerLend Digital.

Case A: Paige learns that Sierra would invest $100 not invested in PeerLend Digital in a bond fund that is expected to earn 4% per year or $12 over 3 years. She uses a payoff of $12 for both quadrant A and quadrant Y. Exhibit 11-21 presents the payoff matrix.

If Paige chooses a default probability cutoff of 0.30, her payoff for that strategy equals the number of loans in each quadrant in Exhibit 11-20 multiplied by the payoff for the corresponding quadrant in Exhibit 11-21:

$$\$12 \times 2\ (\text{quadrant A}) + \$12 \times 2\ (\text{quadrant Y}) + \$(-\$70) \times 0\ (\text{quadrant Z}) + \$45 \times 6\ (\text{quadrant B})$$
$$= \$24 + \$24 + \$0 + \$270 = \$318$$

The total investment for all 10 loans is $100 × 10 = $1,000 so a $318 net payoff would equal a return of 31.8% ($318 ÷ $1,000) over 3 years or an average of 10.6% per year (31.8% ÷ 3).

If Paige chooses a default probability cutoff of 0.50, her payoff for that strategy equals the number of loans in each quadrant in Exhibit 11-19 multiplied by the payoff for the corresponding quadrant in Exhibit 11-21:

$$\$12 \times 1\ (\text{quadrant A}) + \$12 \times 0\ (\text{quadrant Y}) + (-\$70) \times 1\ (\text{quadrant Z}) + \$45 \times 8\ (\text{quadrant B})$$
$$= \$12 + \$0 - \$70 + \$360 = \$302$$

EXHIBIT 11-21 Payoff Matrix

		Predicted Outcomes	
		Default (Do Not Invest in Loan)	**Repay (Invest in Loan)**
Actual Outcomes	**Default**	True Positives (A) $12	False Negatives (Z) –$70
	Repay	False Positives (Y) $12	True Negatives (B) $45

What if Paige had chosen not to develop the decision tree model to predict defaults and had done no analysis? She could then simply invest in all 10 loans in the validation sample. In this case, Sierra's expected payoff would be \$45 for the eight repay loans and −\$70 for the two default loans or $(\$45 \times 8) + (-\$70 \times 2) = \$220$, or a return of 22% $(\$220 \div \$1{,}000)$ over 3 years or 7.33% $(22\% \div 3)$ per year.

On the basis of these assumptions, Paige will recommend to her managers that Sierra should be conservative and use a default probability cutoff of 0.30 to invest in the loans. That is, only invest in loans for which the predicted probability of default is less than 0.30. This means that Sierra will only invest in 6 of the 10 loans so as to avoid the losses that come from defaulting loans. Using the decision tree model to invest in loan decisions increases Sierra's profitability from 7.33% to 10.6%.

Case B: If the outside investment opportunities yield a payoff of only 2% per year, or \$6 over 3 years, the expected payoffs are as follows:

$$\text{Cutoff of 0.30: } \$6 \times 2\,(A) + \$6 \times 2\,(Y) + (-\$70) \times 0\,(Z) + \$45 \times 6\,(B) = \$12 + \$12 + \$0 + \$270 = \$294$$

$$\text{Cutoff of 0.50: } \$6 \times 1\,(A) + \$6 \times 0\,(Y) + (-\$70) \times 1\,(Z) + \$45 \times 8\,(B) = \$6 + \$0 - \$70 + \$360 = \$296$$

In this scenario, the outside investment opportunities are sufficiently unattractive that Sierra is willing to be more aggressive (invest in loans with a default probability less than 0.50). Sierra will invest in many more repaying PeerLend Digital loans (true negatives) even though this means accepting some false negatives (default loans) as well.

Depending on the outside investment opportunities (Case A or Case B), the decision tree model helps Sierra increase the payoff to approximately \$300 or 30% $(\$300 \div \$1{,}000)$ over 3 years, or 10% $(30\% \div 3)$ per year. Paige can now clearly visualize what the model is doing and is eager communicate her takeaways to managers.

Step 6: Visualize and Communicate Insights

Visualizing and communicating the insights of data science models is an important task for the management accountant because it helps managers understand the value and tradeoffs from using these models. We have already seen ways of visualizing how models work (for example, using a decision tree diagram to explain how different values of the feature variables separate different classes of the target variable). The ROC curve and the confusion matrix help managers visualize the performance of a model by identifying the tradeoff between false positives and true positives (and the corresponding false negatives and true negatives). The visual shape of the ROC curve communicates how accurately a model can classify the target value of interest (default loans in Exhibit 11-18).

Communicating the output of a model can help managers grasp the choices they face and the judgments they must make. For example, Paige should try to communicate and explain intuitively why the decision tree model helps to generate higher returns. Suppose the outside investment opportunities are as described in Case B. At a default probability cutoff of 0.50, the decision tree model identifies one of the two defaulting loans without classifying any of the repaying loans as defaults. As a result, Sierra will invest in nine PD loans, of which one loan is a default. In the absence of the model, Sierra would have invested in 10 PD loans, of which two would be defaults. Correctly identifying one default loan and not investing in it increases Sierra's payoff by \$70 from \$220 to \$290 (\$220 + \$70). In addition, Sierra earns \$6 by investing in a loan outside PeerLend Digital, resulting in a total payoff of \$296.

What if the manager chooses the lower default probability cutoff of 0.30? Paige explains that at this cutoff, Sierra would avoid investing in both default loans but will misclassify two repay loans as defaults and so not invest in those repay loans. Correctly identifying two default loans and not investing in them increases Sierra's payoff by \$140 $(\$70 \times 2)$. But not investing in two of the repay loans lowers Sierra's payoff by \$90 $(\$45 \times 2)$. The result is an increase in the payoff by \$50 $(\$140 - \$90)$ from \$220 to \$270. In addition, Sierra earns \$24 by investing in four loans outside PeerLend Digital at \$6 per loan, resulting a total payoff at the 0.30 cutoff of \$294 $(\$270 + \$24)$.

Paige should also communicate to her manager when the model would not be effective in increasing returns. Suppose that at the default probability cutoff of 0.30, the model correctly

TRY IT! 11-4

Rafael Alvarez, the management accountant at Wyatt Manufacturing, estimates that the company earns $200 for each good product it sells. It loses $300 on each defective product produced. Rafael believes that if he can predict defects using a model based on workers' experience and level of machine automation, he can re-purpose the manufacturing capacity to produce a simpler product that less-skilled workers can successfully produce on less-automated machines. The company will earn $40 on each unit of this alternate product.

a. Refer to the validation sample table in Try It question 3. Construct a confusion matrix for the cutoff points 0.30 and 0.50.
b. Construct the payoff matrix.
c. What cutoff point should Rafael choose? Explain your answer briefly.

identified only one of the two defaulting loans (true positives), but in the process also classified two repaying loans as defaults (false positives). Once again, correctly identifying and not investing in the default loan will increase Sierra's payoff by $70 but now Sierra will also not invest in two of the repay loans, resulting in the payoff decreasing by $90 ($45 $\times$ 2). Sierra would be worse off by $20. By investing in three outside loans, Sierra will gain $18 ($6 $\times$ 3), but is still worse off by using the model. The model only has value if it can identify true positives (default loans) without classifying too many repay loans as defaults (false positives).

Working With PeerLend Digital Data

Having understood the tools and methods data scientists use and their strengths and weaknesses, Paige is ready to train a model from the full PD dataset and construct a payoff matrix to quantify the value of its predictions on the new loans PD offers in Q1 2020. Paige's team returns to the PD dataset described in **Step 2: Obtain and Explore Relevant Data.** There are 500,000 funded loans in the dataset, of which 100,000 are loans that default (loan status = 1) and 400,000 are loans that repay (loan status = 0). The overall *default rate* is 20% (100,000 ÷ 500,000).

Per **Step 3: Prepare the Data**, the team cleans the data to eliminate any features that would contribute to target leakage. It then separates the dataset into a training, validation, and holdout samples. The holdout sample is 20% of the total set (500,000 $\times$ 0.20 = 100,000), the training set is 60% of the total set (500,000 $\times$ 0.60 = 300,000), and the cross-validation set is 20% of the total set (500,000 $\times$ 0.20 = 100,000).

In **Step 4: Build a Model**, the team trains its models on the sample of 300,000 loans and cross-validates them with a sample of 100,000. It chooses the pruned decision tree that maximizes the likelihood value in the validation sample.[16] The team then runs the model on the holdout sample and obtains a similar likelihood value.

Per **Step 5: Evaluate the Model**, Paige and the team consider some important metrics to understand how much they can rely on the model to give accurate predictions on a set of new loan data. The first metric, the model's likelihood value computed on the validation set, is very good: it is 0.85.[17] The model will provide reasonably accurate predictions. The second set of metrics is feature impact. Exhibit 11-22 presents the feature impacts. The feature impact is a value (0 to 100) assigned to each feature variable in the training set that indicates how important it is in partitioning the data to minimize Gini impurity, that is, how frequently a feature is used in making cuts at various nodes of the decision-tree model. The variable that is used most often (grade) is normalized to a value of 100. The next most important variable in making cuts is credit score with a value of 18, indicating that it is used 18% as frequently as grade is to make a cut.

Not surprisingly, the grade assigned to the loan by PeerLend Digital was by far the most important feature for distinguishing default loans from repay loans. Grades A and B had a high number of repay loans, while Grades E and F had many more default loans. It suggested, as Paige had expected, that PeerLend Digital was doing a good job of identifying default risk. Interestingly,

[16] After separating the full dataset into a holdout set and a training set, data scientists often partition the training set into several smaller subsets equal in size instead of just two as described in this chapter. For example, they might separate the training set into four folds, so that folds 1–3 can train the model and fold 4 serves as validation. They can then recombine the folds, use sets 2–4, say, to train the model and use fold 1 to serve as validation. By systematically mixing smaller slices of data, they can artificially create an even larger dataset. This can be helpful when too little data are available.

[17] It is similarly high on the holdout set.

however, credit score, debt-to-income, annual income, and loan amount were also relevant features (though much less important than grade) for separating repay loans from default loans in the decision-tree model. This meant that there was incremental information content in these variables for identifying default loans over and above what was available in the grade feature. These variables might help to identify more of the default loans (true positives) without classifying too many repay loans as default loans (false positives). If they could do so, Sierra would not invest in loans predicted to default and earn a return greater than what it would have earned by investing in all PD loans.

Paige is surprised by some features not being relevant to identifying default loans. For example, she had anticipated that homeownership would have a higher impact; she hypothesized that loan applicants who owned homes tended to have more stable incomes, savings, and lives, which were all characteristics that would make them more likely to repay a small loan. Instead, the model showed this feature had no discernable impact. Nevertheless, Paige is comfortable with the features used by the model to identify default loans. They make intuitive sense. She is ready to evaluate how well the model performs in classifying default and repay loans.

Paige turns to the ROC curve. Exhibit 11-23 presents the ROC curve. It moves nicely up along the *y*-axis far away from the diagonal line joining the origin (0, 0) to the upper-right corner (1, 1), indicating that the model does well in partitioning defaults from repays. The shape of the curve suggests that the model predictions will be useful for predicting defaults without the risk of too many false positives and false negatives.

Paige explores several confusion matrixes using different default probability cutoffs. Exhibit 11-24 presents the contents of the confusion matrixes vertically for easy comparison of the distribution of predictions across six selected default probability cutoffs for the validation sample of 100,000 loans. Sierra plans to invest $100 in each of the 100,000 loans; if Sierra does not invest in a PeerDigital loan, Sierra will invest the $100 earmarked for that loan in the alternate investment. Recall that Paige rejects all loans above the default probability cutoff (classified as positive with a high predicted probability of default) and accepts all loans below the default probability cutoff (classified as negative with a low predicted probability of default). For example, at the 0.35 cutoff, Sierra rejects all loans with a predicted default probability greater than 0.35—the true positives of 3,942 and the false positives of 5,072 for a total of 9,014 (3,942 + 5,072) loans—and invests in all loans with a predicted default probability below 0.35—the true negatives of 76,959 and the false negatives of 14,027 for a total of 90,986 (76,959 + 14,027) loans.

Consistent with the simple example, a higher default probability cutoff means that Sierra is rejecting fewer loans and accepting more loans. Therefore, as the default probability cutoff

EXHIBIT 11-22

Feature Impact Scores for PeerLend Digital

Feature	Impact Score
Grade	100
Credit score	18
Debt-to-income	17
Annual income	15
Loan amount	11
Purpose of loan	1
Homeownership	1

EXHIBIT 11-23

Receiver Operating Characteristic (ROC) Curve for PeerLend Digital

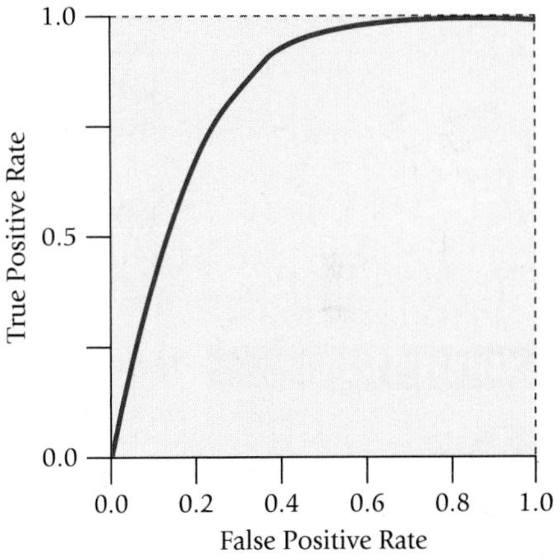

EXHIBIT 11-24 Classification of Loans in Validation Sample for PeerLend Digital

	A	B	C	D	E	F	G
1	**Number of Loans in Each Quadrant of the Confusion Matrix**						
2	**Model Classification**	**0.20**	**0.25**	**0.30**	**0.35**	**0.37**	**0.40**
3	True positive	10,840	8,082	5,590	3,942	3,183	2,369
4	True negative	57,702	67,035	73,586	76,959	78,201	79,392
5	False positive	24,328	14,994	8,444	5,072	3,828	2,637
6	False negative	7,130	9,889	12,380	14,027	14,788	15,602
7	Total Number of Loans	100,000	100,000	100,000	100,000	100,000	100,000
8	Dollar investment	$ 10,000,000	$ 10,000,000	$ 10,000,000	$ 10,000,000	$ 10,000,000	$ 10,000,000

increases, Sierra rejects fewer default loans (true positives) and also has fewer repay loans misclassified as defaults (false positives). At a higher default probability cutoff, Sierra accepts more loans that repay (true negatives) but also has more default loans misclassified as repay (false negatives).

Paige uses values from her payoff matrix to determine which default probability cutoff is the most profitable investment. Recall that Paige assigns \$45 to each true negative (repay loans) and −\$70 to a false negative (default loan). She uses two values for the alternative investment opportunities, \$6 over 3 years and \$12 over 3 years, to model a more-conservative and a less-conservative payoff scenario. Exhibit 11-25 presents these two payoff scenarios and the cumulative and annual return on investment (ROI) on the \$10,000,000 investment. Consider the payoff column for the 0.35 default probability cutoff and the alternate investment payoff of \$6 over 3 years.

On the 76,959 true negative loans, Sierra earns \$3,463,155 (76,959 loans × \$45). On the 14,027 false negative loans, Sierra loses \$981,890 (14,027 × (−\$70)). Sierra does not invest in the 3,942 loans it classifies as true positives. Instead it invests the available funds \$394,200 (3,942 loans × \$100 per loan) in the safe bond to earn 6% over 3 years equal to \$23,652 (6% × \$394,200). Sierra also does not invest in the 5,072 loans it classifies as false positives and instead invests \$507,200 in the safe bond to earn \$30,432 (6% × \$507,200). The 0.35 default probability cutoff yields the highest ROI of \$2,535,349 ÷ \$10,000,000 = 25.35% over 3 years or 8.45% (25.35% ÷ 3) per year.[18]

From a technical perspective, Paige is pleased with the analysis. In the \$6 alternative-payout scenario, the optimal default probability cutoff of 0.35 yields an annual return of 8.45%, which is 1% greater than what Sierra would have earned by investing in all

EXHIBIT 11-25 Two Payoff Scenarios for PeerLend Digital

	A	B	C	D	E	F	G	H
1	Alternate Investment Payout (3yr): \$6							
2	Model Classification	Payoffs	0.20	0.25	0.30	0.35	0.37	0.40
3	True positive	\$ 6.00	\$ 65,040	\$ 48,492	\$ 33,540	\$ 23,652	\$ 19,098	\$ 14,214
4	True negative	\$ 45.00	\$ 2,596,590	\$ 3,016,575	\$ 3,311,370	\$ 3,463,155	\$ 3,519,045	\$ 3,572,640
5	False positive	\$ 6.00	\$ 145,968	\$ 89,964	\$ 50,664	\$ 30,432	\$ 22,968	\$ 15,822
6	False negative	\$ (70.00)	\$ (499,100)	\$ (692,230)	\$ (866,600)	\$ (981,890)	\$ (1,035,160)	\$ (1,092,140)
7	Total		\$ 2,308,498.00	\$ 2,462,801.00	\$ 2,528,974.00	\$ 2,535,349.00	\$ 2,525,951.00	\$ 2,510,536.00
8	ROI % (3 years)		23.08%	24.63%	25.29%	25.35%	25.26%	25.11%
9	ROI % (1 year)		7.69%	8.21%	8.43%	8.45%	8.42%	8.37%
10								
11	Alternate Investment Payout (3yr): \$12							
12	Model Classification	Payoffs	0.20	0.25	0.30	0.35	0.37	0.40
13	True positive	\$ 12.00	\$ 130,080	\$ 96,984	\$ 67,080	\$ 47,304	\$ 38,196	\$ 28,428
14	True negative	\$ 45.00	\$ 2,596,590	\$ 3,016,575	\$ 3,311,370	\$ 3,463,155	\$ 3,519,045	\$ 3,572,640
15	False positive	\$ 12.00	\$ 291,936	\$ 179,928	\$ 101,328	\$ 60,864	\$ 45,936	\$ 31,644
16	False negative	\$ (70.00)	\$ (499,100)	\$ (692,230)	\$ (866,600)	\$ (981,890)	\$ (1,035,160)	\$ (1,092,140)
17	Total		\$ 2,519,506	\$ 2,601,257	\$ 2,613,178	\$ 2,589,433	\$ 2,568,017	\$ 2,540,572
18	ROI % (3 years)		25.20%	26.01%	26.13%	25.89%	25.68%	25.41%
19	ROI % (1 year)		8.40%	8.67%	8.71%	8.63%	8.56%	8.47%

[18] The payoffs could be further refined based on how many of the different classes of loans (A, B, C, D, E, and F) Sierra continues to invest in at each cutoff value. For example, if at the cutoff of 0.35 Sierra invests in fewer E and F class loans that offer higher interest rates, the average return from the true positives will be less than \$15 (which is the average interest rate across all 100,000 loans in the validation sample). Similarly, if loans in classes A, B, C, and D repay for longer periods (25 months, say) before defaulting, the losses from false negatives will be smaller than \$70, which is the average loss based on repayment patterns across all six classes of loans in the validation sample. These are additional ways in which the management accountant can add value.

100,000 PD loans. Twenty percent of the loans would have defaulted and 80% would have repaid, for a payout of $20{,}000 \times \$(-70) + 80{,}000 \times \$45 = -\$1{,}400{,}000 + \$3{,}600{,}000 = \$2{,}200{,}000$. The return over 3 years, based on the \$10,000,000 investment, would be $\$2{,}200{,}000 \div \$10{,}000{,}000 = 22\%$ or $22\% \div 3 = 7.33\%$ per year. Data science allows her to make better investments on behalf of clients to increase their returns and increase the firm's profit.

DECISION POINT

How do management accountants help managers evaluate data science models?

Using Data Science Models

LEARNING OBJECTIVE 7

Describe how to use and deploy data science models

. . . understand critical inputs to exercise judgment to reach conclusions

Management accountants work with managers to operationalize the data science model to make decisions. In doing so, they evaluate what elements need to be modified in light of the model inputs and how best to balance quantitative and qualitative assessments. We use the Sierra Investments context to describe these general insights.

Step 7: Deploy the Model

As the manager prepares to implement the model, the management accountant must underscore critical model inputs and areas of significant judgment. These normally pertain to data and cutoff values.

Data

Data issues can be tricky and require judgment. Are the data adequate for the intended purpose? How accurate are the data? How representative are the past data for predicting the future? Are past conditions different from what might be encountered in the future? Paige knows from her understanding of data science models and the bias–variance tradeoff that the models are powerful enough to deal with spotty data. But if she judges the data to be more suspect, it is a problem that data scientists cannot overcome.

For example, Paige trusts that PD is providing relevant and accurate data. That's because creating and maintaining the integrity of pertinent and appropriate data is one of PD's major value propositions to lender-investors. It is an issue PD takes very seriously. However, it is very costly for PD to verify all lender information. Paige reviews the data that individual applicants provide to PD to secure a loan and uses qualitative judgment to evaluate whether the data are accurate enough to use in the models.

Paige is also aware that the model reflects PD loan activity up to a specific moment in time. These are the data she uses to build a model to predict the future. The model only works if historical data are representative of the future. Market conditions change all the time. Paige will have to use qualitative judgment to assess whether the model is still useful 2 years from now or whether she needs to obtain newer data from PD to train new models. These are important judgments that she will have to make. She thinks back to the recession that began in October 2008. Wall Street's most sophisticated models failed to predict the calamitous stock market crash and resulting recession caused by a particular mix of conditions and dynamics that had never happened before. Paige will make the manager aware of these issues. But in her own judgment, she concludes that the data are rich, accurate, and representative enough to use to predict defaulting loans in the future.

Cutoff Values

The choice of the cutoff depends heavily on the payoff matrix, so it is important to get good estimates of the payoffs. The management accountant best understands the economic consequences of different decisions and how certain he or she is about the different payoff values. Where there is uncertainty, the management accountant evaluates the sensitivity of different payoffs on the cutoff decision.

Paige has a strong understanding of the effect of alternate investment strategies on the PeerLend Digital investment decision. She is fairly confident about the payoffs if the loans repay since these are contracted amounts and the returns from alternative investments if Sierra does not invest in PD loans. She is less sure about the value she should assign to false negatives. She varies the loss from \$60 to \$80 on a \$100 loan. The cutoff values change but, as in Exhibit 11-25, the overall payoffs are reasonably close to each other and well above the payoffs from investing in all 500,000 PD loans. She plans to share these analyses with the manager to support her recommendation to use the model to invest in PD loans.

DECISION POINT

How can management accountants help managers to operationalize data science models?

Advances in data science create many exciting opportunities for organizations. Although the algorithms vary, the basic approach to data science follows the methods described in this chapter—avoiding overfitting, balancing the bias–variance tradeoff, identifying false positives and false negatives, evaluating models, and measuring economic impact. Management accountants bring deep insights about the economic consequences of decisions. By understanding the statistical and computer science tools that data scientists use, management accountants can take advantage of these tools to build models that create value.

PROBLEM FOR SELF-STUDY

It is June, and the manager of the retail chain PriceTrimmer wants to increase revenues during the back-to-school period. He plans to identify parents in early August whose children are entering school for the first time in September. His question for the management accountant and the data science team is how to identify and target these households whose children will need to purchase school supplies.

PriceTrimmer's data science team extracts prior-year data on 10,000 households from its customer database and trains a new model. The team partitions the sample into three subsamples: a training sample of 6,000 observations, a validation sample of 2,000 observations, and a holdout sample of 2,000 observations. The rate of households with a child entering school for the first time in each subsample is 18%.

Required

1. Is this an interesting problem for PriceTrimmer to solve? Why?
2. What data might be available to help solve this problem?
3. Complete the confusion matrices below for the validation sample.

A Confusion Matrix (Cutoff 0.5)

		Predicted Outcomes		
		First-Time Kids	No First-Time Kids	Total
Actual Outcomes	First-Time Kids	(TP) 100	(FN) ?	360
	No First-Time Kids	(FP) ?	(TN) 1,440	1,640
	Total	300	1,700	2,000

B Confusion Matrix (Cutoff 0.3)

		Predicted Outcomes		
		First-Time Kids	No First-Time Kids	Total
Actual Outcomes	First-Time Kids	(TP) ?	(FN) ?	360
	No First-Time Kids	(FP) 900	(TN) ?	1,640
	Total	1,210	?	2,000

4. As the management accountant you have determined the following. Without doing any promotion, PriceTrimmer earns an average of $20 from every family sending a child to school for the first time. If it decides to promote the program, it will cost PriceTrimmer $10 per child in the form of mailers and promotions sent to households that are predicted to have a child entering school. This money would yield no return if the family was not sending a child to school for the first time. If, however, the family was sending a child to school for the first time, PriceTrimmer would earn $50 (net of the cost of the promotion) instead of $20. Develop a payoff matrix for this situation.
5. Which cutoff probability of first-time kids would you select: (a) 0.3 or (b) 0.5? Comment briefly on the results.

Solution

1. This is an interesting problem for PriceTrimmer to solve because households with children who are going to school for the first time are more likely to purchase many more school supplies than households with children who have already been to school and have many of the necessary supplies. The first-time households are looking for a store that can help

them with all that they need both now and later in the year. If PriceTrimmer can accurately identify these households and their needs and promote their products to the households just at the time they are looking for these materials, it is a good opportunity to increase revenues.

2. PriceTrimmer may already have these data for households with loyalty cards. Some loyalty programs ask for data on all household members. For those who have not provided such explicit data, PriceTrimmer may be able to identify these households based on their past purchasing behavior. For example, there may be a progression of items a household buys for a child who grows from age 3, to 4, and then 5 when he or she enters kindergarten and needs a backpack, pencil case, and lunchbox. If PriceTrimmer can identify this pattern for past customers, it could build a model to predict those households that will behave similarly in the future.
3. The rate of households with children attending school for the first time is 18%, so the number of instances of this target feature in the validation set is 360 (2,000 × 0.18 = 360).

A Confusion Matrix (Cutoff 0.5)

		Predicted Outcomes		
		First-Time Kids	No First-Time Kids	Total
Actual Outcomes	First-Time Kids	(TP) 100	(FN) 260	360
	No First-Time Kids	(FP) 200	(TN) 1,440	1,640
	Total	300	1,700	2,000

B Confusion Matrix (Cutoff 0.3)

		Predicted Outcomes		
		First-Time Kids	No First-Time Kids	Total
Actual Outcomes	First-Time Kids	(TP) 310	(FN) 50	360
	No First-Time Kids	(FP) 900	(TN) 740	1,640
	Total	1,210	790	2,000

4. The payoff matrix follows.

Payoff Matrix

		Predicted Outcomes	
		First-Time Kids	No First-Time Kids
Actual Outcomes	First-Time Kids	(TP) \$50	(FN) \$20
	No First-Time Kids	(FP) −\$10	(TN) \$0

Predicted First-Time Kids

- *True positives (TP):* These are households PriceTrimmer correctly predicts have a child going to school for the first time (true positives). The store sends them a promotion believing they are likely to buy many supplies, which on average will yield \$50.
- *False positives (FP):* These are households PriceTrimmer predicts to have a child going to school for the first time, but actually, they do not. The −\$10 represents the marketing cost of reaching out to these customers with no benefit.

Predicted No First-Time Kids

- *True negatives (TN):* These are households the model correctly predicts do not have a child going to school for the first time. PriceTrimmer does not target them and they generate \$0 incremental cash since these customers are not in the market for first-time supplies.
- *False negatives (FN):* These are households PriceTrimmer predicts to *not* have a child going to school for the first time, but actually they do. The \$20 represents the additional revenue these households spend at PriceTrimmer based on what they would buy without any targeted promotion. It is much less than the payoff from households PriceTrimmer correctly predicts had a child going to school for the first time because they do not receive a promotion and shop at competitor stores for some of the other items.

5. To calculate the payoff for the model at a particular cutoff probability of first-time kids, multiply the payoff matrix by the confusion matrix and add the products from each quadrant together.

At the 0.3 cutoff,

$$\text{Payoff} = (\$50 \times 310) + (\$20 \times 50) + (-\$10 \times 900) + (\$0 \times 740)$$
$$= \$15{,}500 + \$1{,}000 - \$9{,}000 + 0 = \$7{,}500$$

At the 0.5 cutoff,

$$\text{Payoff} = (\$50 \times 100) + (\$20 \times 260) + (-\$10 \times 200) + (\$0 \times 1{,}440)$$
$$= \$5{,}000 + \$5{,}200 - \$2{,}000 + 0 = \$8{,}200$$

The management accountant will select the cutoff of 0.5 because the payoff of $8,200 is higher than the payoff for the cutoff at 0.3, which is $7,500.

The key insight is that by lowering the cutoff probability of first-time kids to 0.3, PriceTrimmer would market its products to many more customers—from 300 to 1,210. Of these, 310 are true first-time households, an increase of 210 from the 100 PriceTrimmer reached by setting the cutoff probability of first-time kids at 0.5. These 210 kids increase PriceTrimmer's cash flow by $6,300 (210 × ($50 − $20)) but the false positives increase by 700, from 200 to 900, resulting in additional marketing expenses with no benefit of $7,000. The net effect is a decrease in cash flow of $700 ($6,300 − $7,000). Lowering the cutoff probability of first-time kids would be better only if the cost of marketing and promotion were significantly lower or if the benefits from targeting were significantly higher.

DECISION POINTS

The following question-and-answer format summarizes the chapter's learning objectives. Each decision presents a key question related to a learning objective. The guidelines are the answer to that question.

Decision	Guidelines
1. How can management accountants work with data scientists to create value?	Management accountants can contribute in each step of the seven-step decision-making process for applying machine learning techniques in business situations: (1) Gain a business understanding of the problem, (2) Obtain and explore relevant data, (3) Prepare the data, (4) Build a model, (5) Evaluate the model, (6) Visualize and communicate insights, and (7) Deploy the model.
2. Will solving the proposed problem create value, and are the relevant data available?	The management accountant must work with data scientists to judge whether addressing the problem will create value. The management accountant must avoid target leakage and ensure that the data are objective, correctly measured, and relevant for predicting the target feature.
3. What are the strengths and weaknesses of a decision tree model?	A decision tree model is an algorithmic predictive modeling technique that subdivides data along features to reduce Gini impurity so that each partition is purer (contains more members of one class than another). Its strength is that it is very flexible to fit the dataset on which it is trained. Its weakness is that it will fit to noise, not just the signal, and so will not perform well on a brand-new dataset.
4. What is pruning, and why is it useful?	Pruning is a technique by which the tree is not grown to its full size, but instead only allowed to grow to a certain depth. The benefit of pruning is that it helps to avoid overfitting that occurs when a model adheres too closely to the specific details of a dataset such that, in addition to signal, it captures *noise* from random chance.

Decision	Guidelines
5. How do managers choose among different data science models?	Managers ask data scientists to cross-validate the model by comparing predictions of different models on a new set of data for which the actual outcomes (for example, default or repay) are already known. Managers choose the model that predicts most accurately based on the overall number of correct predictions or a higher overall likelihood value. The selected model best balances the bias–variance tradeoff. In the context of decision trees, the greater the depth, the lower the bias and the higher the variance of the model. Data scientists also verify that the overall likelihood value of the validation sample used to choose the model is similar to the overall likelihood value of a brand-new and yet-unseen (by the model) hold-out sample.
6. How do management accountants help managers evaluate data science models?	Management accountants help managers answer the following questions when evaluating models: (1) Are the likelihood values big enough? (2) Are the confusion matrix and receiver operating characteristic (ROC) curve useful to inform decisions? (3) Do the model and feature variables make economic sense? (4) Does the model reflect underlying reality? (5) Is there confidence in the payoff matrix to guide decisions? To help managers evaluate models, management accountants visualize and communicate insights from the model.
7. How can management accountants help managers to operationalize data science models?	Management accountants help managers understand the critical inputs to be monitored and evaluated to implement models. They combine quantitative and qualitative judgment about how the data and the model should be used to reach conclusions.

TERMS TO LEARN

This chapter and the Glossary at the end of the text contain definitions of the following important terms:

confusion matrix (**p. 444**)
cross-validation (**p. 435**)
data science (**p. 420**)
decision tree (**p. 425**)
false negatives (FN) (**p. 444**)
false positive rate (**p. 442**)
false positives (FP) (**p. 444**)
Gini impurity (**p. 428**)
hyperparameter (**p. 439**)
overfitting (**p. 433**)
predictive modeling (**p. 420**)
pruning (**p. 433**)
receiver operating characteristic (ROC) curve (**p. 443**)
target leakage (**p. 424**)
true positive rate (**p. 442**)
true positives (TP) (**p. 444**)
true negatives (TN) (**p. 444**)

ASSIGNMENT MATERIAL

Questions

11-1 How do management accountants work with data scientists to create value for an organization?
11-2 What is the seven-step decision-making process for applying machine-learning techniques in business situations?
11-3 Define target leakage.
11-4 Describe the decision tree technique of predictive modeling.
11-5 What is Gini impurity?

11-6 Why does overfitting occur?
11-7 What is pruning? Why is it helpful?
11-8 How do data scientists use cross-validation and holdout samples?
11-9 What is the likelihood value? Why do prediction models attempt to maximize it?
11-10 Explain the bias–variance tradeoff.
11-11 What is the receiver operating characteristic (ROC) curve?
11-12 What is the confusion matrix?
11-13 Explain false positives (FP) and false negatives (FN).
11-14 How does the management accountant use the payoff matrix to make decisions using data science models?
11-15 How do management accountants help managers to operationalize data science models?

Multiple-Choice Questions

In partnership with: BECKER PROFESSIONAL EDUCATION®

11-16 Which of the following is not a primary component of business applications of data science?

a. Computer science and data skills
b. Substantive expertise in natural sciences
c. Math and statistics
d. Substantive expertise in an applicable business

11-17 Which of the following statements describes cross-validation?

a. Cross-validation is close and intense monitoring of all the manufacturing steps and critical points in at least the first three production-scale batches.
b. Cross-validation is an automatic computer check to ensure that the data entered is sensible and reasonable and conforms to general data-type expectations. It does not check the accuracy of data.
c. Cross-validation is using historical data to provide documentary evidence that practices, policies and/or products exist in the state in accordance with their design specifications
d. Cross-validation is the process of comparing predictions of different models on a new set of data for which the actual outcomes are already known.

11-18 What is the proper order of the steps in the data science framework?

a. Visualize and communicate insights, build a model, obtain and explore relevant data, prepare data, deploy the model, evaluate the model, gain a business understanding of the model.
b. Build a model, obtain and explore relevant data, prepare data, deploy the model, evaluate the model, gain a business understanding of the problem, visualize and communicate insights.
c. Gain a business understanding of the problem, obtain and explore relevant data, prepare data, build a model, evaluate the model, visualize and communicate insights, deploy the model.
d. Build a model, evaluate the model, deploy the model, obtain and explore relevant data, prepare data, visualize and communicate insights, gain a business understanding of the problem.

11-19 Which of the following statements about decision trees is true?

a. Evaluate and choose among candidate decision trees based on their performance on the cross-validation data, not the training data they were built from.
b. The more branches a tree has, the more precisely and correctly it will make predictions.
c. Decision trees should take into account all available data on a topic, even data which is unavailable at the time a choice is to be made.
d. To make accurate predictions, decision trees need to be fully built out so that all nodes are pure.

11-20 At what point does an analyst stop the building and/or pruning process of a decision tree model?

a. Several models with different amounts of pruning are evaluated against the validation sample to find the best model.
b. Several models with different amounts of pruning are evaluated against the training sample to find the best model.
c. Decision trees continue adding branches until all resulting rectangles are pure. This is therefore the perfect model and should be deployed.
d. Decision trees continue adding branches until the Gini impurity reaches a threshold set by the analyst.

Exercises

11-21 Gini impurity. Kevin Brown is the management accountant at Boehm and Sons Bank. Some of his colleagues attended a conference recently where they learned that machine learning can be used to accurately predict loan performance. Excited by the possibilities, they asked Kevin to work with the data science team to develop a machine learning model that predicts whether a loan will repay or default. Kevin knows that defaulting loans have significantly hurt Boehm and Sons' profitability.

Kevin tells the data science team that his colleagues will appreciate a model that is interpretable and easy to understand, so they decide to use a decision tree. The team selects a random sample of eight loans (three loans that defaulted and five loans that repaid) from Boehm and Sons' internal loan database and begins the analysis.

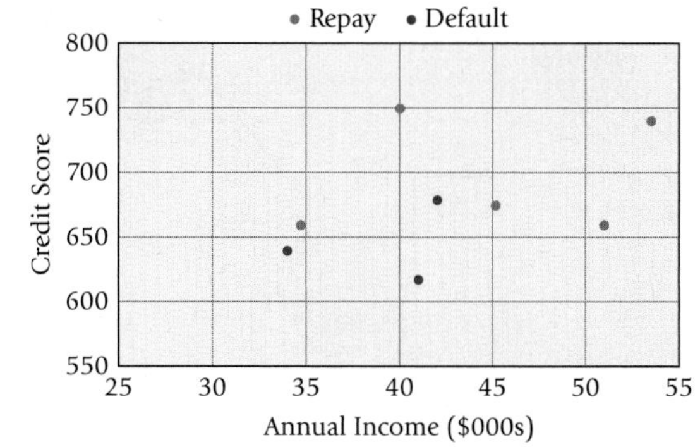

Required

1. Use your ruler to identify two possible places to make the first cut. Visually, is one of these cuts better than the other at separating the data?
2. For each potential cut, calculate the Gini impurity and the information gain. Based on these calculations, which cut should be used to form the first node of the decision tree? Is this consistent with your visual intuition from requirement 1?
3. How could Kevin use the decision tree analysis to help senior managers at Boehm and Sons improve profitability?

11-22 Gini impurity. Laurie Rech is a management accountant at Donnelly Bank, which has recently suffered significant loan losses. Rech and her team are worried that they do not fully understand the risk profile of their loans, so they would like some way of identifying loans that are likely to default. One team member suggests developing a decision tree so that loans can be quickly and easily classified as "likely to default" or "likely to repay."

After plotting and inspecting a sample of seven loans (three loans that defaulted and four loans that repaid), Rech and her team notice there are two different cuts that result in only one misplaced observation: Credit Score = 650 and Income = $70,000. Based on this, they conclude that either would be fine to use as the first node for their decision tree.

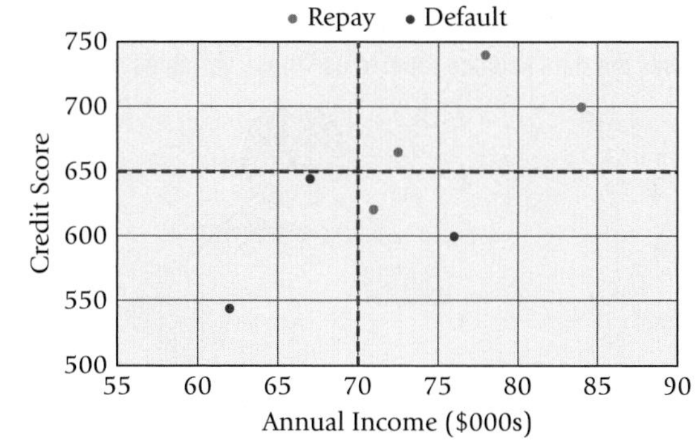

Required

1. Are Rech and her team correct that the two cuts are equivalent? Which one would you choose to be the first node of the decision tree?
2. Why might Rech care about Gini impurities when making decisions?

11-23 Decision trees. The data science team at Swift Investments uses a sample of 16 loans to build a decision tree that predicts whether a loan will repay or default. Although the data science team is very familiar with decision trees and other machine learning models, they do not have much experience in the finance or lending industries.

The team shows the decision tree to Royce Brown, the management accountant at Swift, who indicates that some of the decisions made by the model seem incorrect. To understand how the decision tree partitions the data, the team writes out the rules and thinks through some examples.

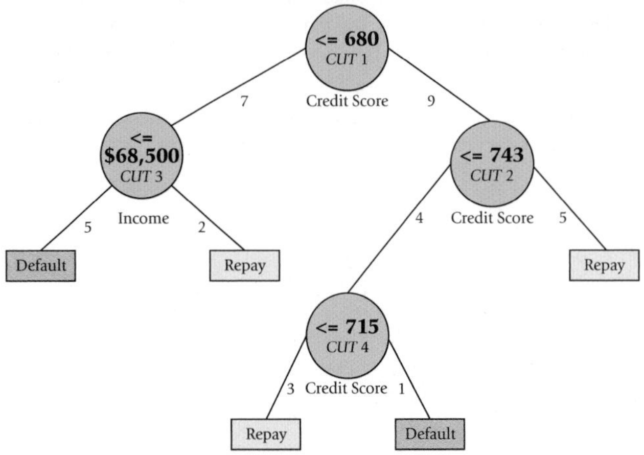

Required

1. Write out the rules dictated by this decision tree.
2. How would the decision tree classify the following loans?
   a. Borrower has a credit score of 650 and income of $62,000
   b. Borrower has a credit score of 670 and income of $75,500
   c. Borrower has a credit score of 690 and income of $58,000
   d. Borrower has a credit score of 725 and income of $62,000
3. Is Brown correct that something is wrong with the model? If so, what might explain this? Why is understanding the model important to Brown in his role as a management accountant?

11-24 Decision trees. TelMark Mobile Services provides mobile phone services to millions of customers in the U.S. TelMark's customer base is constantly changing as old customers leave the service and new customers join. This is called *churn* and it is a very important dynamic for the company to manage effectively because it has significant profit implications. Churn has increased recently, so managers at TelMark have started a program to offer targeted promotions to customers who are likely to abandon the service. They would like to develop a machine learning model to help identify these customers. Sylvia Restler is the management accountant assigned to work on the project with the data science team.

Sylvia speaks with a few members of the customer service team to better understand why customers leave their platform. The team tells her that two variables are highly related to customer churn: *number of lines per customer family plan* and *number of months the customer has been with the company.* According to their data, customers who have already been with the company for a long time tend to stay, as do customers with many lines on their family plan. Sylvia asks the data science team to use these variables to create a decision tree.

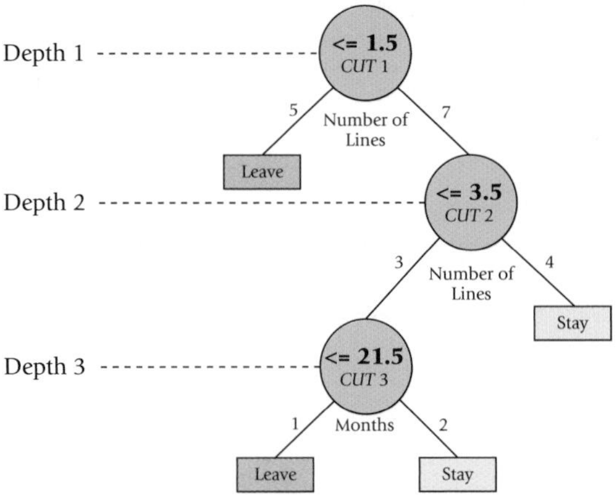

The team uses the following as a validation set:

Observation	Number of Lines	Number of Months	Actual Outcome
(1)	(2)	(3)	(4)
1	2	13	Leave
2	2	23	Stay
3	1	20	Stay
4	4	21	Stay
5	3	27	Stay
6	3	19	Leave
7	5	25	Stay
8	1	21	Stay
9	3	23	Stay

Required

1. Write out the rules for this decision tree.
2. Using the full decision tree, classify each customer in the validation sample as leave or stay. Calculate the proportion of customers correctly classified as in Exhibit 11-13, column 5.

11-25 Decision trees and pruning (continuation of 11-24). Assume the same information for TelMark as in Exercise 11-24. A member of the data science team points out that overfitting is often an issue with decision trees. To avoid this issue, he suggests pruning the tree at depth 3 so that the third cut is not made.

Required

1. Using the pruned tree, classify each customer in the validation sample as leave or stay (if the probability of leave is greater than 0.5, classify the customer as leave). Calculate the proportion of customers correctly classified as in Exhibit 11-13, column 6.
2. Based on your answer to requirement 1 of this problem and Exercise 11-24, requirement 2, which tree should Sylvia use to identify customers who are likely to leave?
3. As the management accountant, what business recommendations could Sylvia make to management based on the decision tree model?

11-26 Maximum Likelihood. Margo London is the management accountant at Norse Credit. Norse Credit spends a lot of time and resources trying to detect fraudulent activity within customers' accounts. For most customers this is a low probability event. However, if it happens and Norse Credit does not detect it, it is very costly for the company.

London is working with the data science team to improve models for predicting fraudulent activity in customers' accounts. The table below lists six observations in a model's validation sample and the probability of default predicted by the (pruned) decision tree.

Observation	Actual Outcome (y)	Probability of Fraud Predicted by the Pruned Decision Tree (p)
(1)	(2)	(3)
1	1 (fraud)	0.45
2	0 (clean)	0.30
3	0 (clean)	0.01
4	0 (clean)	0.99
5	0 (clean)	0.70
6	0 (clean)	0.01

Required

1. Calculate the likelihood value for each observation in the validation set as in Exhibit 11-14, column 8 using the following equation $L = p^y \times (1 - p)^{1-y}$ (remember $x^1 = x$ and $x^0 = 1$).
2. Calculate the overall likelihood value for this set of predictions by multiplying the likelihood values for each observation together.
3. As the management accountant, would you use this model for decision making? Explain.
4. After becoming more familiar with the data, London's team returns with a second model. The table below lists the six observations in the model's validation sample and the probability of fraud predicted by the (pruned) decision tree. How does this model compare to the previous one? Should London be satisfied with the accuracy of the new model? Explain.

Observation	Actual Outcome (y)	Probability of Fraud Predicted by the Pruned Decision Tree (p)
(1)	(2)	(3)
1	1 (fraud)	0.99
2	0 (clean)	0.20
3	0 (clean)	0.33
4	0 (clean)	0.01
5	0 (clean)	0.01
6	0 (clean)	0.01

11-27 Receiver operating characteristic (ROC) curve. An ROC curve plots the false positive rate (*x*-axis) against the true positive rate (*y*-axis) for different model thresholds. The graph below shows three different ROC curves labeled 1, 2, and 3.

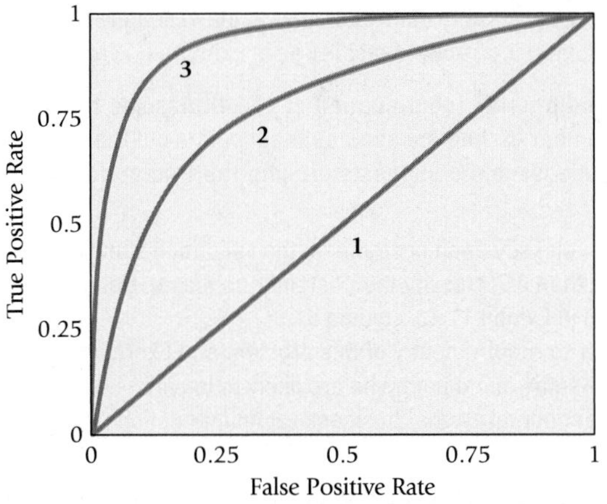

Required

1. Compare the curves labeled 1, 2, and 3 in the chart above. Which curve represents the model that would be most useful for a management accountant? Explain.
2. Explain what a "straight line" ROC curve actually represents.

11-28 Confusion matrices, payoff matrix, and choosing cutoff values. Sun TV sells TV sets. It does not sell smart TVs so customers do not come to Sun TV if they want to purchase smart TVs. Sun TV wants to start selling smart TVs and will only sell smart TVs to customers to whom they advertise. Managers use customer information (income level, previous purchase history) to decide which customers they should target.

The team needs to decide how sure it must be in predicting customer interest in a smart TV. If it is too cautious, it will choose a very high cutoff probability and only market to customers who it believes are very likely to be in the market for a smart TV. This may cause them to miss out on many customers. If they are too aggressive and choose a low cutoff probability, they may identify more individuals interested in buying smart TVs but also end up wasting marketing dollars on customers who are not interested in purchasing smart TVs.

To choose a cutoff probability, the team develops the confusion matrices below for two cutoff probabilities on a validation sample of 1,000 households comprising 100 buyers and 900 non-buyers of smart TVs.

Confusion Matrix (0.70)

		Predicted Outcomes		
		Buyers	Non-Buyers	Total
Actual Outcomes	Buyers	20		100
	Non-Buyers			900
	Total	120		1,000

Confusion Matrix (0.30)

		Predicted Outcomes		
		Buyers	Non-Buyers	Total
Actual Outcomes	Buyers	90		100
	Non-Buyers			900
	Total	750		1,000

Required

1. Complete the confusion matrices for the validation set as in Exhibits 11-19 and 11-20.
2. A team of management accountants at SunTV estimates the payoffs from their actions. For every customer it targets, SunTV will spend $20 to market to that customer. For every smart TV it sells, SunTV makes a profit of $200 after taking into account the $20 it spends on that customer. Construct the payoff matrix as in Exhibit 11-21 and determine which cut off value SunTV should use.
3. Are there any other factors SunTV should consider before building such a model?

11-29 Model thresholds and payoff matrices. Blanda Brothers is a produce processing company that specializes in fruits, with apple sales representing the majority of their revenue. Their main facility receives a daily shipment of apples, which are then sorted and shipped to grocery stores and to producers of apple jelly and juice, depending on the apple quality (sweetness, taste, color, etc.). The acceptable-quality apples are sold to grocery stores and low-quality apples are sold to apple processors. If a low-quality apple is sold to a grocery store, the apples are returned and Blanda must pay the stores a fee to compensate the store for lost sales and for the extra work of shipping the apples back. Blanda's reputation also suffers, affecting future business. Blanda has an algorithm to determine apple quality, but the algorithm is not perfect and misclassifies apples.

The data science team presents their work to Cindy Hansen, the management accountant at Blanda, to help them choose between two cutoff prediction probabilities for low-quality apples of 0.50 and 0.30. Apples with a predicted probability above the cut-off probability are classified as low quality, and apples below the cut-off probability are classified as acceptable quality apples. The following confusion matrices are based on the validation sample.

Confusion Matrix (0.30)

		Predicted Outcomes	
		Low Quality	Acceptable Quality
Actual Outcomes	Low Quality	130	20
	Acceptable Quality	230	620

Confusion Matrix (0.50)

		Predicted Outcomes	
		Low Quality	Acceptable Quality
Actual Outcomes	Low Quality	100	50
	Acceptable Quality	120	730

Required

1. Cindy estimates that apples of acceptable quality result in a profit of $0.30 per apple. She also knows that low-quality apples can be sold to juice companies at a profit of $0.04. Finally, she estimates that the cost to Blanda of selling a low-quality apple to the grocery store as an acceptable-quality apple is $1.05 for each low-quality apple. Use this information to construct a payoff matrix as in Exhibit 11-21.
2. Using Cindy's knowledge about the payoff of each outcome, which threshold should the team choose?

11-30 Model thresholds and payoff matrices (continuation of 11-29). Assume the same information for Blanda Brothers as in Problem 11-29. Due to increased competition among grocery stores, the cost to Blanda of selling a low-quality apple to the grocery store as an acceptable-quality apple is now $0.75 instead of $1.05 for each low-quality apple.

Required

1. Cindy realizes that the change in the cost of selling a low-quality apple to the grocery store as an acceptable-quality apple may change the optimal model cutoff. Re-evaluate the two cutoffs based on the new payoff matrix. How does this compare to the decision in Problem 11-29, requirement 2?
2. Why is it important for Cindy as the management accountant and the data science team to partner with each other?

Problems

11-31 Thinking through the data. James Silva is a management accountant at Keebler-Olson, where he is in charge of their investment portfolio. In 2015, James worked with a data scientist to develop a model that predicts how a given loan will perform in the future based on the characteristics of the borrower available on the peer-to-peer lending platform Mandel Credit. On April 1, 2016, he purchased $100,000 worth of loans with 36-month terms (3 years). His investments had performed well. James planned to invest another $100,000 on January 1, 2020. Looking ahead, he considers some strategic questions around the model.

Required

1. James wonders whether he should use new data to train a new model in December 2019, just prior to his planned investment on January 1, 2020. What should he do with the older data?
2. How much of the actual performance of the loans (such as repayments, loan restructuring, delayed repayments, hardship plans, etc.) should James use in classifying loans as default or repay when building his prediction model?

11-32 Decision trees. Assume the same information for Keebler-Olson as in Problem 11-31. James Silva and the data scientist on his team work together to develop the following decision tree:

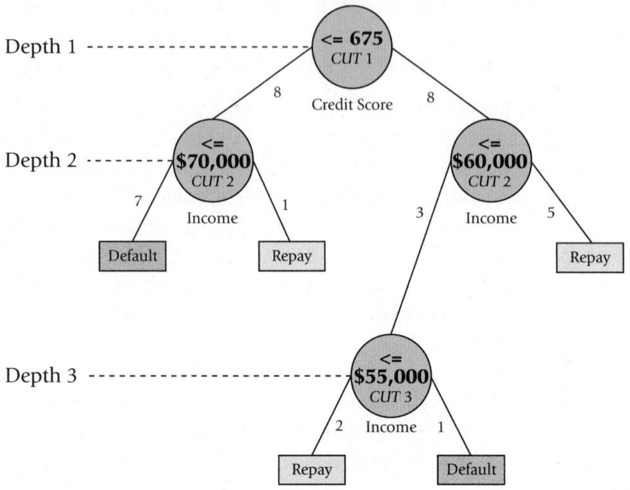

The data science team tests the model on the following validation set:

Observation	Income	Credit Score	Actual Outcome
(1)	(2)	(3)	(4)
1	$85,000	710	(0) Repay
2	$62,000	650	(1) Default
3	$72,000	660	(0) Repay
4	$75,000	640	(0) Repay
5	$71,000	680	(0) Repay
6	$59,000	705	(0) Repay
7	$48,000	690	(1) Default
8	$57,000	685	(0) Repay

Required

1. Write out the rules for this full decision tree.
2. Classify each loan in the validation sample as repay or default. Calculate the proportion of loans correctly classified as in Exhibit 11-13, column 5.
3. Based on his experience in management accounting, James reviews the model and notes that something appears to be wrong with the tree at a depth of 3. What problem did James observe? What should James propose?

11-33 Decision trees and pruning (continuation of 11-32). Assume the same information for Keebler-Olson as in Problems 11-31 and 11-32.

Required

1. Prune the tree at depth 3. Using the pruned tree, classify each loan in the validation sample as repay or default (if the probability of default is greater than 0.5 classify the loan as default). Calculate the proportion of loans correctly classified as in Exhibit 11-13, column 6.
2. Based on your answer to requirement 1 of this problem and Problem 11-32, requirement 2, which decision tree should James use to identify default and repay loans?
3. James has to present both models and the conclusions to the president of Keebler-Olson. He knows that in the past the president has preferred using models based on full decision trees because they seem to fit the training data more closely. How should James explain the pruned decision tree model?

11-34 Calculate likelihood values (continuation of 11-32 and 11-33). Assume the same information for Keebler-Olson as in Problems 11-31, 11-32, and 11-33. While James is presenting his work to the president and his team, someone asks whether he had calculated the overall likelihood value for the trees. Wanting to make sure that he had fully evaluated the model, James agrees that this is a good idea.

Required

1. For the full and pruned trees, calculate likelihood values for the validation set in Problem 11-32 as in Exhibit 11-14, columns 6 and 8.
2. Calculate the overall likelihood value for the full and pruned trees.
3. As the management accountant, which model would you use for decision making based on the likelihood values? Does this differ from your answer to Problem 11-33, requirement 2? Explain.

11-35 Payoff matrix and choosing cutoff values (continuation of 11-32, 11-33, and 11-34). Assume the same information for Keebler-Olson as in Problems 11-31, 11-32, 11-33, and 11-34. James plans to invest $100 in each of the 1,000 loans he is examining. If he decides not to invest in a loan, he will invest the $100 in an alternative investment. As James and the data scientist work to improve their model, James mentions that different model predictions are associated with different payoffs for Keebler-Olson. Based on his management accounting experience, James estimates that the average payout for a repay loan of 3 years is $48 dollars. James also estimates that Keebler-Olson loses $60 over 3 years if it purchases a default loan. If Keebler-Olson does not invest in a loan, it places the money in an alternative investment with a payout of $14 over 3 years. James uses the pruned tree to evaluate the total payoff at a cutoff value of 0.25 and a cutoff value of 0.50.

Required

1. Fill in the payoff matrix below as in Exhibit 11-21.

Payoff Matrix

		Predicted Outcomes	
		Default (Do Not Invest in Loan)	Repay (Invest in Loan)
Actual Outcomes	Default		
	Repay		

2. James is deciding whether to use a cutoff of 0.25 or 0.5. Complete the confusion matrices below using the pruned tree for each cutoff as in Exhibits 11-19 and 11-20.

Confusion Matrix (0.50)

		Predicted Outcomes	
		Default (Do Not Invest in Loan)	Repay (Invest in Loan)
Actual Outcomes	Default		
	Repay		

Confusion Matrix (0.25)

		Predicted Outcomes	
		Default (Do Not Invest in Loan)	Repay (Invest in Loan)
Actual Outcomes	Default		
	Repay		

3. What cutoff value should James use? Explain.

11-36 Maximum likelihood. Sarah Letourneau is the management accountant at Turcotte Manufacturing, an auto supplier that produces brake pads. Turcotte's customers have high safety standards, and managers at Turcotte believe they can gain a competitive advantage by reducing the number of defective brake pads they produce. Sarah works with an external data science consulting company to develop a prediction model that identifies defective brake pads ($y = 1$) before they are shipped to Turcotte's clients. After building the model on a training dataset, Sarah tests its accuracy on the validation set below.

Observation number	1	2	3	4	5	6	7
Model probability (p)	0.99	0.01	0.33	0.20	0.01	0.33	0.33
Actual outcome (y)	1	0	1	0	0	0	0

Required

1. Calculate the likelihood value for each observation in the validation set using the following equation: $L = p^y \times (1 - p)^{1-y}$ (remember $x^1 = x$ and $x^0 = 1$)
2. Calculate the overall likelihood value for the validation set.
3. As the management accountant, what should Sarah do with this information?

11-37 Payoff matrix and choosing cutoff values (continuation of 11-36). Assume the same information for Turcotte as in Problem 11-36. Working brake pads yield a profit of $25. If defective brake pads are identified before they are shipped, they can be fixed and sold as working brake pads. However, the process of inspecting and repairing brake pads that are predicted to be defective incurs costs. If a brake pad is predicted to be defective, it costs $8 to re-inspect it and, if found to be actually defective, it costs an additional $12 to repair. Turcotte incurs a net loss of $50 for defective brake pads shipped to customers because of additional costs (including reputation costs).

Required

1. Fill in the payoff matrix below as in Exhibit 11-21.

Payoff Matrix

		Predicted Outcomes	
		Defective	Working
Actual Outcomes	Defective		
	Working		

2. Sarah is debating two different model cutoffs of 0.50 and 0.30. Using the table below, fill in the confusion matrices as in Exhibits 11-19 and 11-20 based on the validation set presented in Problem 11-36.

Confusion Matrix (0.50)

		Predicted Outcomes	
		Defective	Working
Actual Outcomes	Defective		
	Working		

Confusion Matrix (0.30)

		Predicted Outcomes	
		Defective	Working
Actual Outcomes	Defective		
	Working		

3. What cutoff value should Sarah choose? Explain.
4. Sarah is uncertain about the $50 net loss if a defective brake pad is shipped to customers. At what loss would Sarah prefer to use the other cutoff value (i.e., the cutoff value Sarah did not choose in requirement 3)?

11-38 Receiver operating characteristic (ROC) curve. It is June, and the manager of the retail chain Stapleton wants to increase revenues during the back-to-school period. To do that, he plans to attract more customers in August whose children are entering school for the first time. By marketing to households who have kids entering school for the first time, Stapleton expects these households will purchase more products from Stapleton throughout the year. His question for the data science team is how to identify and target those households.

Caitlin Finch is the management accountant assigned to the project. The data science team has built a predictive model. The nodes of the decision tree result in four possible prediction probabilities (0.99, 0.55, 0.33, and 0.01). The validation sample of 1,000 records comprises 100 households with a child going to school for the first time and 900 households with no children going to school for the first time. The team prepares the following table, like the one in Exhibit 11-16. The table orders the predicted probabilities of households having kids entering school for the first time ranked from highest to lowest (as in Exhibit 11-16, column 2) based on the model, the cumulative number of households with no kids entering school for the first time (as in Exhibit 11-16, column 4), and the cumulative number of households with kids entering school for the first time (as in Exhibit 11-16, column 5). To ease exposition, we refer to households with kids entering school for the first time as "Households With Kids" or simply as "Kids" and households with no kids entering school for the first time as "Households With No Kids" or simply as "No Kids." This means, for example, that at a cutoff probability of 0.50, the model would correctly predict 50 households with kids entering school for the first time but also incorrectly predict 135 households with kids entering school for the first time when those households do not have kids entering school for the first time.

Predicted Probability of Household With Kids Ranked From Highest to Lowest (1)	Cumulative Number of Households With No Kids (0s) (2)	Cumulative Number of Households With Kids (1s) (3)
0.95	0	30
0.55	135	50
0.33	585	90
0.01	900	100

Required

1. Calculate the false positive rate and true positive rate for the above table as in Exhibit 11-16, columns 6 and 7.
2. Draw the ROC curve. Would you recommend using this ROC curve to make predictions about households with kids entering school for the first time?
3. Use the preceding table to determine how many true positives and false positives the model identifies at a cutoff of 0.25 and 0.50. Fill in the confusion matrices below as in Exhibits 11-19 and 11-20.

Confusion Matrix (0.5)

		Predicted Outcomes	
		Kids	No Kids
Actual Outcomes	Kids		
	No Kids		

Confusion Matrix (0.25)

		Predicted Outcomes	
		Kids	No Kids
Actual Outcomes	Kids		
	No Kids		

4. For those households predicted to have kids going to school for the first time, Stapleton will spend $2 promoting products to each household. Stapleton expects to make $25 (after taking into account the $2 spent on promotion) from those households that it correctly identifies as having kids. Without doing promotion, Stapleton will earn an average of $10 from every household with a kid entering school for the first time. Using this information, create a payoff matrix as in Exhibit 11-21 and determine whether Caitlin should use a cutoff probability of 0.5 or 0.25.
5. When might a large increase in false positives be acceptable to Stapleton if the number of true positives also increases?

11-39 Model thresholds and payoff matrices. David Porter is the management accountant at Spruce Bank, where the data science department is leading an initiative to predict whether loans will default or repay. The default rate in the training set is 15%. After building a model on the training set that predicts whether a loan will default or repay, the data scientist applies it to the validation set of 400 observations to evaluate its performance.

Required

1. Help the data scientist complete the confusion matrixes below for different model thresholds as in Exhibits 11-19 and 11-20.

Confusion Matrix (0.40)

		Predicted Outcomes		
		Default	Repay	Total
Actual Outcomes	Default			
	Repay	200	140	340
	Total	250		400

Confusion Matrix (0.55)

		Predicted Outcomes		
		Default	Repay	Total
Actual Outcomes	Default	40		60
	Repay			340
	Total		240	

2. Assume that Spruce Bank has $1,000 to invest in each loan of the validation sample. If Spruce Bank does not invest in a loan, it keeps the money in a risk-free investment at 3% a year for 3 years (ignore the time value of money). If Spruce invests in a loan that eventually repays, it receives 10% a year for 3 years. If Spruce invests in a loan that eventually defaults, Spruce loses 65% of the amount of the loan. Fill in the payoff matrix below as in Exhibit 11-21. Which model threshold should David and the data scientist use?

Payoff Matrix

		Predicted Outcomes	
		Default (Do Not Invest in Loan)	Repay (Invest in Loan)
Actual Outcomes	Default		
	Repay		

11-40 Model thresholds and payoff matrices, sensitivity analysis (continuation of 11-39). Assume the same information for Spruce Bank as in Problem 11-39. David believes that within the pool of borrowers he invests in, the timing of when borrowers ultimately default could be different from what he has assumed. That means he might lose more or less than the 65% he has assumed in the payoff matrix. He decides to model "worst case" and "best case" scenarios of losing 75% and 55%, respectively, of the amount of the loan in the event of a default.

Required

1. Calculate the model payoffs for both the worst- and best-case scenarios for each cutoff.
2. If you were David, how would this analysis impact your decision making?

12 Decision Making and Relevant Information

LEARNING OBJECTIVES

1. Use the five-step decision-making process
2. Distinguish relevant from irrelevant information in decision situations
3. Explain the concept of opportunity cost and why managers should consider it when making insourcing-versus-outsourcing decisions
4. Know how to choose which products to produce when there are capacity constraints
5. Explain how to manage bottlenecks
6. Discuss the factors managers must consider when adding or dropping customers or business units
7. Explain why book value of equipment is irrelevant to managers making equipment-replacement decisions
8. Explain how conflicts can arise between the decision model a manager uses and the performance-evaluation model top management uses to evaluate managers

How many decisions have you made today?

Maybe you made a big decision, such as investing in a mutual fund. Or a simple one such as buying a coffee maker or choosing a restaurant for dinner. Regardless of the decision, the decision process often includes evaluating the costs and benefits of each choice. For decisions that involve costs, some costs are irrelevant. For example, once you purchase a coffee maker, its cost is irrelevant when calculating how much money you save each time you brew coffee at home versus buy it at Starbucks. You incurred the cost of the coffee maker in the past, and you can't recoup that cost. This chapter will explain which costs and benefits are relevant and which are not—and how you should think of them when choosing among alternatives.

RELEVANT COSTS AND BROADWAY SHOWS[1]

The incremental cost to a Broadway producer for an additional customer to attend a show like "Hamilton" is incredibly small. Most costs (actor fees, performance sets, theater rental, and publicity and marketing) are fixed weeks and months in advance of the performance. An orchestra ticket for "Hamilton" sells for $200. But because incremental costs are so small, should the show's producer sell tickets considerably below this price to fill empty seats?

If demand is high and the show is sold out, the producer would not sell tickets for anything less than $200 because there are theatergoers willing to pay full price to see the show. But if on the day before the show the venue will not be full, the producer may be willing to lower ticket prices significantly to attract more theatergoers and earn a profit on the unfilled seats.

Enter TKTS. The famous discount ticket booth in Times Square sells same-day tickets to Broadway musicals, plays, and dance productions for up to 50% of face value. Theatergoers can browse real-time listings on the TKTS mobile app to check availability.

Just like on Broadway, managers at corporations around the world use their deep understanding of costs to make decisions. JPMorgan Chase managers gather information about financial markets, consumer preferences, economic trends, and costs before determining whether to offer a new service to customers. Managers at Macy's obtain information about customer demand and costs of buying products when pricing merchandise at its retail stores. Managers at Porsche gather cost information to decide whether to manufacture a

Francis Vachon/Alamy Stock Photo

[1] *Sources:* Musical Workshop, "Production Costs and ROI of Theatrical Shows—From Broadway to West End" (http://www.musicalworkshop.org/workshop/production-costs-and-roi-of-theatrical-shows-from-broadway-to-west-end/), accessed June 2019; Theatre Development Fund, "TKTS Ticket Booths" (https://www.tdf.org/nyc/7/TKTS-Overview), accessed June 2019.

component part or purchase it from a supplier. The decision process may not always be easy, but as Peter Drucker said, "Wherever you see a successful business, someone once made a courageous decision."

Information and the Decision Process

Managers usually follow a *decision model* for choosing among different courses of action. A **decision model** is a formal method of making a choice that often involves both quantitative and qualitative analyses. Management accountants analyze and present relevant data to guide managers' decisions.

Consider a strategic decision facing managers at Precision Sporting Goods, a manufacturer of golf clubs: Should they (1) reorganize or (2) not reorganize manufacturing operations to reduce manufacturing costs?.

Reorganization will eliminate all manual handling of materials. Current manufacturing labor consists of 15 workers who operate machines and 5 who handle materials. The five materials-handling workers are on contracts that permit layoffs without additional payments. Each worker works 2,000 hours annually. Reorganization is predicted to cost $90,000 per year (mostly for new equipment leases). The reorganization will not affect the production output of 25,000 units, the selling price of $250, the direct material cost per unit of $50, manufacturing overhead of $750,000, or marketing costs of $2,000,000.

Managers use the five-step decision-making process presented in Exhibit 12-1 and first introduced in Chapter 1 to make this decision. Study the sequence of steps in this exhibit. Note how managers do not consider information about production volumes, selling price, and costs unaffected by the decision. Step 5 evaluates performance to provide feedback about actions taken in previous steps. This feedback might affect future predictions, the prediction methods used, the way choices are made, or the implementation of the decision.

LEARNING OBJECTIVE 1

Use the five-step decision-making process

... the five steps are identify the problem and uncertainties; obtain information; make predictions about the future; make decisions by choosing among alternatives; and implement the decision, evaluate performance, and learn

DECISION POINT

What is the five-step process that managers can use to make decisions?

The Concept of Relevance

Much of this chapter focuses on Step 4 in Exhibit 12-1 and on the concepts of relevant costs and relevant revenues when choosing among alternatives.

Relevant Costs and Relevant Revenues

Relevant costs are *expected future costs*, and **relevant revenues** are *expected future revenues* that differ among the alternative courses of action being considered. Costs and revenues that are *not relevant* are called *irrelevant*. Relevant costs and relevant revenues *must*

- **Occur in the future**—every decision deals with a manager selecting a course of action based on its expected future results.
- **Differ among the alternative courses of action**—future costs and revenues that do not differ will not matter and, therefore, will have no bearing on the decision being made.

The question is always "What difference will a particular action make?"

Exhibit 12-2 presents the financial data underlying the choice between the do-not-reorganize and reorganize alternatives for Precision Sporting Goods. Managers can analyze the data in two ways: by considering "all costs and revenues" or considering only "relevant costs and revenues."

The first two columns describe the first way and present *all data*. The last two columns describe the second way and present *only relevant costs*: the $640,000 and $480,000 expected future manufacturing labor costs and the $90,000 expected future reorganization costs that differ between the two alternatives. Managers can ignore the revenues, direct materials, manufacturing overhead, and marketing items because these costs will remain the same whether or

LEARNING OBJECTIVE 2

Distinguish relevant from irrelevant information in decision situations

... only costs and revenues that are expected to occur in the future and differ among alternative courses of action are relevant

EXHIBIT 12-1

Five-Step Decision-Making Process for Precision Sporting Goods

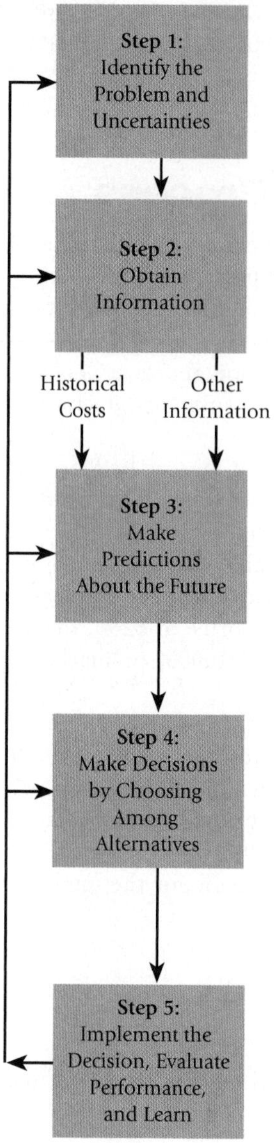

Should Precision Sporting Goods reorganize its manufacturing operations to reduce manufacturing costs? An important uncertainty is how the reorganization will affect employee morale.

Historical hourly wage rates are $14 per hour. However, a recently negotiated increase in employee benefits of $2 per hour will increase wages to $16 per hour. The reorganization of manufacturing operations is expected to reduce the number of workers from 20 to 15 by eliminating all 5 workers who handle materials. The reorganization is likely to have negative effects on employee morale.

Managers use information from Step 2 as a basis for predicting future manufacturing labor costs. Under the existing do-not-reorganize alternative, costs are predicted to be $640,000 (20 workers × 2,000 hours per worker per year × $16 per hour), and under the reorganize alternative, costs are predicted to be $480,000 (15 workers × 2,000 hours per worker per year × $16 per hour). Recall, the reorganization is predicted to cost $90,000 per year.

Managers compare the predicted benefits calculated in Step 3 ($640,000 − $480,000 = $160,000—that is, savings from eliminating materials-handling labor costs, 5 workers × 2,000 hours per worker per year × $16 per hour = $160,000) against the cost of the reorganization ($90,000) along with other considerations (such as likely negative effects on employee morale). Management chooses the reorganize alternative because the financial benefits are significant and the effects on employee morale are expected to be temporary and relatively small.

Evaluating performance after the decision is implemented provides critical feedback for managers, and the five-step sequence is then repeated in whole or in part. Managers learn from actual results that the new manufacturing labor costs are $540,000, rather than the predicted $480,000, because of lower-than-expected manufacturing labor productivity. They also learn about the effects on employee morale. This (now) historical information can help managers make better subsequent predictions. Managers will also try to improve implementation via employee training, increased employee engagement, and better supervision.

not Precision Sporting Goods reorganizes. These costs do not differ between the alternatives and, therefore, are irrelevant.

Notice that the past (historical) manufacturing hourly wage rate of $14 and total past (historical) manufacturing labor costs of $560,000 (20 workers × 2,000 hours per worker per year × $14 per hour) do not appear in Exhibit 12-2. *Although they may be a useful basis for making informed predictions of the expected future manufacturing labor costs of $640,000 and $480,000, historical costs themselves are past costs that, therefore, are irrelevant to decision making.* Past costs are also called **sunk costs** because they are unavoidable and cannot be changed no matter what action is taken.

The analysis in Exhibit 12-2 indicates that reorganizing the manufacturing operations will increase predicted operating income by $70,000 each year. Note that the managers at Precision Sporting Goods reach the same conclusion whether they use all data or include only relevant data in the analysis. By confining the analysis to only relevant data, managers can clear away the clutter of potentially confusing irrelevant data. Focusing on relevant data is especially helpful when all the information needed to prepare a detailed income statement is unavailable.

EXHIBIT 12-2 Determining Relevant Revenues and Relevant Costs for Precision Sporting Goods

	All Revenues and Costs		Relevant Revenues and Costs	
	Alternative 1: Do Not Reorganize	Alternative 2: Reorganize	Alternative 1: Do Not Reorganize	Alternative 2: Reorganize
Revenues[a]	$6,250,000	$6,250,000	—	—
Costs:				
Direct materials[b]	1,250,000	1,250,000	—	—
Manufacturing labor	640,000[c]	480,000[d]	$ 640,000[c]	$ 480,000[d]
Manufacturing overhead	750,000	750,000	—	—
Marketing	2,000,000	2,000,000	—	—
Reorganization costs	—	90,000	—	90,000
Total costs	4,640,000	4,570,000	640,000	570,000
Operating income	$1,610,000	$1,680,000	$(640,000)	$(570,000)
	$70,000 Difference		$70,000 Difference	

[a]25,000 units × $250 per unit = $6,250,000
[b]25,000 units × $50 per unit = $1,250,000
[c]20 workers × 2,000 hours per worker × $16 per hour = $640,000
[d]15 workers × 2,000 hours per worker × $16 per hour = $480,000

Understanding which costs are relevant and which are irrelevant helps the decision maker concentrate on obtaining only the pertinent data.

Qualitative and Quantitative Relevant Information

Managers divide the outcomes of decisions into two broad categories: *quantitative* and *qualitative*. **Quantitative factors** are outcomes that are measured in numerical terms. Some quantitative factors are financial; they can be expressed in monetary terms. Examples include the cost of direct materials, direct manufacturing labor, and marketing. Other quantitative factors are nonfinancial; they can be measured numerically, but they are not expressed in monetary terms. Examples include reduction in new product-development time for companies such as Microsoft and the percentage of on-time flight arrivals for companies such as JetBlue. **Qualitative factors** are outcomes that are difficult to measure accurately in numerical terms. Employee morale is an example.

Relevant-cost analysis generally emphasizes quantitative factors that can be expressed in financial terms. *Although quantitative nonfinancial factors and qualitative factors are difficult to measure in financial terms, they are important for managers to consider.* In the Precision Sporting Goods example, managers carefully considered the negative effect on employee morale of laying off materials-handling workers, a qualitative factor, before choosing the reorganize alternative. It is often difficult for managers to consider and trade off nonfinancial and financial considerations. For example, the benefits of decisions to reduce environmental impacts include the reputation benefits of these actions with consumers, employees, and investors. These benefits are not easy to measure but are relevant and important for managers to evaluate and weigh against the costs of reducing harmful environmental effluents. Managers must consider all the consequences of their decisions and not focus on financial factors alone.

Exhibit 12-3 summarizes the key features of relevant information that apply to all decision situations. We present some of these decision situations in this chapter. Later chapters describe other decision situations that require managers to apply the relevance concept, such as joint costs (Chapter 17), quality and timeliness (Chapter 20), inventory management and supplier evaluation (Chapter 21), capital investment (Chapter 22), and transfer pricing (Chapter 23). We start our discussion on relevance by considering a decision that affects output levels, such as whether to introduce a new product or to try to sell more units of an existing product.

EXHIBIT 12-3 Key Features of Relevant Information

- Past (historical) costs may be helpful as a basis for making *predictions*. However, past costs themselves are always irrelevant when making *decisions*.
- Different alternatives can be compared by examining differences in expected total future revenues and expected total future costs.
- Not all expected future revenues and expected future costs are relevant. Expected future revenues and expected future costs that do not differ among alternatives are irrelevant and, therefore, can be eliminated from the analysis. The key question is always "What difference will an action make?"
- Appropriate weight must be given to qualitative factors and quantitative nonfinancial factors.

One-Time-Only Special Orders

One type of decision that affects output levels involves accepting or rejecting special orders when there is idle capacity and the special orders have no long-run implications. We use the term **one-time-only special order** to describe these conditions.

> **Example 1:** Surf Gear manufactures quality beach towels at its highly automated Burlington, North Carolina, plant. The plant has a production capacity of 45,000 towels each month. Current monthly production is 30,000 towels. Retail department stores account for all existing sales. Exhibit 12-4 shows the expected results for the coming month (August). (These amounts are predictions based on past costs.) We assume that in the short run all costs can be classified as either fixed or variable for a single cost driver (units of output).
>
> Azelia is a luxury hotel chain that purchases towels from Mugar Corporation. The workers at Mugar are on strike, so Azelia must find a new supplier. In August, Azelia contacts Surf Gear and offers to buy 5,000 towels from them at $11 per towel. Based on the following facts, should Surf Gear's managers accept Azelia's offer?

The management accountant gathers the following additional information.

- No subsequent sales to Azelia are anticipated.
- Fixed manufacturing costs are based on the 45,000-towel production capacity. That is, fixed manufacturing costs relate to the production capacity available and not the actual capacity used. If Surf Gear accepts the special order, it will use existing idle capacity to produce the 5,000 towels and fixed manufacturing costs will not change.
- No marketing costs will be necessary for the 5,000-unit one-time-only special order.
- Accepting this special order is not expected to affect the selling price or the quantity of towels sold to regular customers.

The management accountant prepares the data shown in Exhibit 12-4 on an absorption-costing basis (that is, as required by Generally Accepted Accounting Principles, both variable and fixed manufacturing costs are included in inventoriable costs and cost of goods sold). In this exhibit, therefore, the manufacturing cost of $12 per unit and the marketing cost of $7 per unit include both variable and fixed costs. The sum of all costs (variable and fixed) in a particular business function of the value chain, such as manufacturing costs or marketing costs, are called **business function costs**. **Full costs of the product**, in this case $19 per unit, are the sum of all variable and fixed costs in all business functions of the value chain (research and development [R&D], design, production, marketing, distribution, and customer service). For Surf Gear, full costs of the product consist of costs in manufacturing and marketing because

EXHIBIT 12-4

Budgeted Income Statement for August, Absorption-Costing Format for Surf Gear

	A	B	C	D
1		**Total**	**Per Unit**	
2	Units sold	30,000		
3				
4	Revenues	$600,000	$20.00	
5	Cost of goods sold (manufacturing costs)			
6	Variable manufacturing costs	225,000	7.50[b]	
7	Fixed manufacturing costs	135,000	4.50[c]	
8	Total cost of goods sold	360,000	12.00	
9	Marketing costs[a]			
10	Variable marketing costs	150,000	5.00	
11	Fixed marketing costs	60,000	2.00	
12	Total marketing costs	210,000	7.00	
13	Full costs of the product	570,000	19.00	
14	Operating income	$ 30,000	$ 1.00	
15				
16	[a]Surf Gear incurs no R&D, product-design, distribution, or customer-service costs			
17	[b]Variable manufacturing	= Direct material	+ Variable direct manufacturing	+ Variable manufacturing
18	cost per unit	cost per unit	labor cost per unit	overhead cost per unit
19		= $6.00 + $0.50 + $1.00 = $7.50		
20	[c]Fixed manufacturing	= Fixed direct manufacturing	+ Fixed manufacturing	
21	cost per unit	labor cost per unit	overhead cost per unit	
22		= $1.50 + $3.00 = $4.50		

these are the only business functions. Because no marketing costs are necessary for the special order, the manager of Surf Gear will focus only on manufacturing costs. Based on the manufacturing cost per unit of $12, which is greater than the $11-per-unit price Azelia offered, the manager might decide to reject the offer.

In Exhibit 12-5, the management accountant separates manufacturing and marketing costs into their variable- and fixed-cost components and presents data in the format of a contribution income statement. The relevant revenues and costs are the expected future revenues and costs that differ as a result of Surf Gear accepting the special offer: revenues of $55,000 ($11 per unit × 5,000 units) and variable manufacturing costs of $37,500 ($7.50 per unit × 5,000 units). The fixed manufacturing costs and all marketing costs (*including variable marketing costs*) are irrelevant in this case because these costs will not change in total whether the special order is accepted or rejected. Surf Gear would gain an additional $17,500 (relevant revenues, $55,000 − relevant costs, $37,500) in operating income by accepting the special order. In this example, by comparing total amounts for 30,000 units versus 35,000 units or focusing only on the relevant amounts in the difference column in Exhibit 12-5, the manager avoids a misleading implication: to reject the special order because the $11-per-unit selling price is lower than the manufacturing cost per unit of $12 (Exhibit 12-4), which includes both variable and fixed manufacturing costs.

The assumption of no long-run or strategic implications is crucial to a manager's analysis of the one-time-only special-order decision. Suppose the manager concludes that the retail department stores (Surf Gear's regular customers) will demand a lower price if Surf Gear sells towels at $11 apiece to Azelia. In this case, revenues from regular customers will be relevant. Why? Because the future revenues from regular customers will differ depending on whether Surf Gear accepts the special order. The Surf Gear manager would need to modify the relevant-revenue and relevant-cost analysis of the Azelia order to consider both the short-run benefits from accepting the order and the long-run consequences on profitability if Surf Gear lowered prices to all regular customers.

EXHIBIT 12-5

One-Time-Only Special-Order Decision for Surf Gear: Comparative Contribution Income Statements

Home | Insert | Page Layout | Formulas | Data | Review | View

	A	B	D	F	H
1		Without the Special Order		With the Special Order	Difference: Relevant Amounts
2		30,000		35,000	for the
3		Units to Be Sold		Units to Be Sold	5,000
4		Per Unit	Total	Total	Units Special Order
5		(1)	(2) = (1) × 30,000	(3)	(4) = (3) − (2)
6	Revenues	$20.00	$600,000	$655,000	$55,000[a]
7	Variable costs:				
8	Manufacturing	7.50	225,000	262,500	37,500[b]
9	Marketing	5.00	150,000	150,000	0[c]
10	Total variable costs	12.50	375,000	412,500	37,500
11	Contribution margin	7.50	225,000	242,500	17,500
12	Fixed costs:				
13	Manufacturing	4.50	135,000	135,000	0[d]
14	Marketing	2.00	60,000	60,000	0[d]
15	Total fixed costs	6.50	195,000	195,000	0
16	Operating income	$ 1.00	$ 30,000	$ 47,500	$17,500
17					
18	[a]5,000 units × $11.00 per unit = $55,000.				
19	[b]5,000 units × $7.50 per unit = $37,500.				
20	[c]No variable marketing costs would be incurred for the 5,000-unit one-time-only special order.				
21	[d]Fixed manufacturing costs and fixed marketing costs would be unaffected by the special order.				

TRY IT! 12-1

The Gannett Company provides landscaping services to corporations and businesses. All its landscaping work requires Gannett to use landscaping equipment. Its landscaping equipment has the capacity to do 14,000 hours of landscaping work. It is currently utilizing 13,200 hours of equipment time. Gannett charges $115 per hour for landscaping work. Cost information for the current activity level is as follows:

Revenues ($115 × 13,200 hours)	$1,518,000
Variable landscaping costs (largely labor), which vary with the number of hours worked ($60 per hour × 13,200 hours)	792,000
Fixed landscaping costs	110,000
Variable marketing costs (5% of revenues)	75,900
Fixed marketing costs	74,000
Total costs	1,051,900
Operating income	$ 466,100

Gannett has just received a one-time only special order for landscaping work from Flora Corporation at $65 per hour that would require 800 hours of equipment time. No marketing costs will be necessary for the one-time only special order. Should Gannett accept the offer even though revenue per hour is less than Gannett's landscaping cost of $68.33 per hour [($792,000 + $110,000) ÷ 13,200 hours)]?

Potential Problems in Relevant-Cost Analysis

Managers should avoid two potential problems in relevant-cost analysis. First, they must watch for incorrect general assumptions, such as all variable costs are relevant and all fixed costs are irrelevant. In the Surf Gear example, the variable marketing cost of $5 per unit is irrelevant because Surf Gear will incur no extra marketing costs by accepting the special order. But fixed manufacturing costs could be relevant. The extra production of 5,000 towels per month from 30,000 towels to 35,000 towels does not affect fixed manufacturing costs because we assumed that the existing level of fixed manufacturing cost can support any level of production in the relevant range from 30,000 to 45,000 towels per month. In some cases, however, producing the extra 5,000 towels might increase fixed manufacturing costs (and also increase variable manufacturing cost per unit). Suppose Surf Gear would need to run three shifts of 15,000 towels per shift to achieve full capacity of 45,000 towels per month. Increasing monthly production from 30,000 to 35,000 would require a partial third shift (or overtime payments) because two shifts could produce only 30,000 towels. The partial shift would increase fixed manufacturing costs, thereby making these additional fixed manufacturing costs relevant for this decision.

Second, unit-fixed-cost data can potentially mislead managers in two ways:

1. **When irrelevant costs are included.** Consider the \$4.50 of fixed manufacturing cost per unit (direct manufacturing labor, \$1.50 per unit, plus manufacturing overhead, \$3.00 per unit) included in the \$12-per-unit manufacturing cost in the one-time-only special-order decision (see Exhibits 12-4 and 12-5). This \$4.50-per-unit cost is irrelevant because this cost will not change if the one-time-only special order is accepted, and so managers should not consider it.
2. **When the same unit fixed costs are used at different output levels.** Generally, managers should use total fixed costs rather than unit fixed costs because total fixed costs are easier to work with and reduce the chance for erroneous conclusions. Then, if desired, the total fixed costs can be unitized. In the Surf Gear example, total fixed manufacturing costs remain at \$135,000 even if the company accepts the special order and produces 35,000 towels. Including the fixed manufacturing cost per unit of \$4.50 as a cost of the special order would lead managers to the erroneous conclusion that total fixed manufacturing costs would increase to \$157,500 (\$4.50 per towel × 35,000 towels).

The best way for managers to avoid these two potential problems is to keep focusing on (1) total fixed costs (rather than unit fixed cost) and (2) the relevance concept. Managers should always require all items included in an analysis to be expected total future revenues and expected total future costs that differ among the alternatives.

Short-Run Pricing Decisions

In the one-time-only special-order decision in the previous section, Surf Gear's managers had to decide whether to accept or reject Azelia's offer to supply towels at \$11 each. Sometimes managers must decide on the price to bid on a one-time-only special order. This is an example of a short-run pricing decision—decisions that have a time horizon of only a few months.

Consider a short-run pricing decision facing managers at Surf Gear. Cranston Corporation has asked Surf Gear to bid on supplying 5,000 towels in September after Surf Gear has fulfilled its obligation to Azelia in August. Cranston is unlikely to place any future orders with Surf Gear. Cranston will sell Surf Gear's towels under its own brand name in regions and markets where Surf Gear does not sell its towels. Whether Surf Gear accepts or rejects this order will not affect Surf Gear's revenues—neither the units sold nor the selling price—from existing sales channels.

Relevant Costs for Short-Run Pricing Decisions

As before, Surf Gear's managers estimate how much it will cost to supply the 5,000 towels. There are no incremental marketing costs, so the relevant costs are the variable manufacturing costs of \$7.50 calculated in the previous section. As before, the extra production of 5,000 towels in September from 30,000 to 35,000 towels does not affect fixed manufacturing costs because the relevant range is from 30,000 to 45,000 towels per month. Any selling price above \$7.50 will improve Surf Gear's profitability in the short run. What price should Surf Gear's managers bid for the order of 5,000 towels?

Strategic and Other Factors in Short-Run Pricing

Based on market intelligence, Surf Gear's managers believe that competing bids will be between \$10 and \$11 per towel, so they decide to bid \$10 per towel. If Surf Gear wins this bid, operating income will increase by \$12,500 (relevant revenues, $\$10 \times 5{,}000 = \$50{,}000$ − relevant costs, $\$7.50 \times 5{,}000 = \$37{,}500$). In light of the extra capacity and strong competition, management's strategy is to bid as high above \$7.50 as possible while remaining lower than competitors' bids. Note how Surf Gear chooses the price after looking at the problem through the eyes of its competitors, not based on just its own costs.

What if Surf Gear was the only supplier and Cranston could undercut Surf Gear's selling price in Surf Gear's current markets? The relevant cost of the bidding decision would then include the contribution margin lost on sales to existing customers. What if there were many parties eager to bid and win the Cranston contract? In this case, the contribution margin lost on sales to Surf Gear's existing customers would be irrelevant to the decision because Cranston would undercut the existing business regardless of whether Surf Gear supplied towels to Cranston.

In contrast to the Surf Gear case, in some short-run situations, a company may experience strong demand for its products or have limited capacity. In these circumstances, managers will strategically increase prices in the short run to as much as the market will bear. We observe high short-run prices in the case of new products or new models of older products, such as microprocessors, computer chips, cell phones, and software.

DECISION POINT

When is a revenue or cost item relevant for a particular decision, and what potential problems should managers avoid in relevant-cost analysis?

Insourcing-Versus-Outsourcing and Make-or-Buy Decisions

LEARNING OBJECTIVE 3

Explain the concept of opportunity cost and why managers should consider it when making insourcing-versus-outsourcing decisions

... in all decisions, it is important to consider the contribution to income forgone by choosing a particular alternative and rejecting others

We now apply the concept of relevance to another strategic decision: whether a company should make a component part or buy it from a supplier. We again assume idle capacity.

Outsourcing and Idle Facilities

Outsourcing is purchasing goods and services from outside vendors rather than **insourcing**, producing the same goods or providing the same services within an organization. For example, Novartis prefers to manufacture its own medicines (insourcing), but has HCL Technologies manage some of its information technology infrastructure (outsourcing). Honda relies on outside vendors to supply some component parts (outsourcing) but chooses to manufacture other parts internally (insourcing).

Decisions about whether a producer of goods or services will insource or outsource are called **make-or-buy decisions**. Surveys of companies indicate that managers consider quality, dependability of suppliers to deliver according to a schedule, and costs as the most important factors in the make-or-buy decision. Sometimes, however, qualitative factors dominate management's make-or-buy decision. For example, Dell Computer buys the Intel Core i9 processor for its computers from Intel because Dell does not have the know-how and technology to make the processor itself. In contrast, to maintain the secrecy of its formula, Coca-Cola does not outsource the manufacture of its concentrate.

Example 2: The Soho Company manufactures a 2-in-1 system consisting of a DVD player and a digital media receiver (that downloads music and video from Internet sites). Columns 1 and 2 of the following table show the expected total and per-unit costs for manufacturing the DVD player. Soho plans to manufacture the 250,000 units in 2,000 batches of 125 units each. Variable batch-level costs of \$625 per batch vary with the number of batches, not the total number of units produced.

Broadfield, Inc., a manufacturer of DVD players, offers to sell Soho 250,000 DVD players next year for \$64 per unit on Soho's preferred delivery schedule. Assume that financial factors will be the basis of this make-or-buy decision. Should Soho's managers make or buy the DVD player?

	Expected Total Costs of Producing 250,000 Units in 2,000 Batches Next Year (1)	Expected Cost per Unit (2) = (1) ÷ 250,000
Direct materials ($36 per unit × 250,000 units)	$ 9,000,000	$36.00
Variable direct manufacturing labor ($10 per unit × 250,000 units)	2,500,000	10.00
Variable manufacturing overhead costs of power and utilities ($6 per unit × 250,000 units)	1,500,000	6.00
Mixed (variable and fixed) batch-level manufacturing overhead costs of materials handling and setup [$750,000 + ($625 per batch × 2,000 batches)]	2,000,000	8.00
Fixed manufacturing overhead costs of plant lease, insurance, and administration	3,000,000	12.00
Total manufacturing cost	$18,000,000	$72.00

Columns 1 and 2 of the preceding table indicate the expected total costs and expected cost per unit of producing 250,000 DVD players next year. The expected manufacturing cost per unit for next year is $72. At first glance, it appears that Soho's managers should buy DVD players because the expected $72-per-unit cost of making the DVD player is more than the $64 per unit to buy it. But a make-or-buy decision is rarely obvious. To make a decision, managers need to consider the question "What is the difference in relevant costs between the alternatives?"

For the moment, suppose (1) the capacity now used to make the DVD players will become idle next year if the DVD players are purchased; (2) the $3,000,000 of fixed manufacturing overhead will continue to be incurred next year regardless of the decision made; and (3) the $750,000 in fixed salaries to support materials handling and setup will not be incurred if the manufacture of DVD players is completely shut down.

Exhibit 12-6 presents the relevant-cost computations, which show that Soho will *save* $1,000,000 by making the DVD players rather than buying them from Broadfield. Based on this analysis, Soho's managers decide to make the DVD players.

EXHIBIT 12-6 Relevant (Incremental) Items for Make-or-Buy Decision for DVD Players at Soho Company

	Total Relevant Costs		Relevant Cost per Unit	
Relevant Items	**Make**	**Buy**	**Make**	**Buy**
Outside purchase of parts ($64 × 250,000 units)		$16,000,000		$64
Direct materials	$ 9,000,000		$36	
Direct manufacturing labor	2,500,000		10	
Variable manufacturing overhead	1,500,000		6	
Mixed (variable and fixed) materials-handling and setup overhead	2,000,000		8	
Total relevant costs[a]	$15,000,000	$16,000,000	$60	$64
Difference in favor of making DVD players	$1,000,000		$4	

[a]The $3,000,000 of plant-lease, plant-insurance, and plant-administration costs could be included under both alternatives. Conceptually, they do not belong in a listing of relevant costs because these costs are irrelevant to the decision. Practically, some managers may want to include them in order to list all costs that will be incurred under each alternative.

Note how the key concepts of relevance presented in Exhibit 12-3 apply here:

- Exhibit 12-6 compares differences in expected total future revenues and expected total future costs. Past costs are always irrelevant when making decisions.
- Exhibit 12-6 shows \$2,000,000 of future materials-handling and setup costs under the make alternative but not under the buy alternative. Why? Because Soho will incur these future variable costs per batch and avoidable fixed costs only if it manufactures DVD players and not if it buys them. The \$2,000,000 represents future costs that differ between the alternatives and so are relevant to the make-or-buy decision.
- Exhibit 12-6 excludes the \$3,000,000 of plant-lease, plant-insurance, and plant-administration costs under both alternatives. Why? Because these future costs will not differ between the alternatives, so they are irrelevant.

A common term in decision making is *incremental cost*. An **incremental cost** is the additional total cost incurred for an activity. In Exhibit 12-6, the incremental cost of making DVD players is the additional total cost of \$15,000,000 that Soho will incur if it decides to make DVD players. The \$3,000,000 of fixed manufacturing overhead is not an incremental cost because Soho will incur these costs whether or not it makes DVD players. Similarly, the incremental cost of buying DVD players from Broadfield is the additional total cost of \$16,000,000 that Soho will incur if it decides to buy DVD players. A **differential cost** is the difference in total (relevant) cost between two alternatives. In Exhibit 12-6, the differential cost between the make-DVD-players and buy-DVD-players alternatives is \$1,000,000 (\$16,000,000 − \$15,000,000). Note that *incremental cost* and *differential cost* are sometimes used interchangeably in practice. When faced with these terms, always be sure to clarify what they mean.

We define *incremental revenue* and *differential revenue* similarly to incremental cost and differential cost. **Incremental revenue** is the additional total revenue from an activity. **Differential revenue** is the difference in total revenue between two alternatives.

Strategic and Qualitative Factors

Strategic and qualitative factors affect outsourcing decisions. For example, Soho's managers may prefer to manufacture DVD players in-house to retain control over design, quality, reliability, and delivery schedules. Conversely, despite the cost advantages documented in Exhibit 12-6, Soho's managers may prefer to outsource DVD players and focus on developing its expertise in digital media receivers. This is true in other industries such as advertising. For example, Wunderman Thompson focuses on the creative and planning aspects of advertising (their core competencies) and outsources production activities such as film and photographs.

Outsourcing is risky. As a company's dependence on its suppliers increases, suppliers could increase prices and let quality and delivery performance slip. To minimize these risks, managers generally enter into long-run contracts specifying costs, quality, and delivery schedules with their suppliers. Wise managers go further and build close partnerships with suppliers. Toyota engineers, for example, help suppliers improve their processes. Companies such as Ford, Hyundai, Panasonic, and Sony partner with their suppliers to develop innovative products that they themselves could not have developed. Almost always, strategic and qualitative factors become important judgments in the outsourcing decision.

International Outsourcing

What additional factors would Soho's managers have to consider if the DVD-player supplier was based in Mexico? One important factor would be exchange-rate risk. Suppose the Mexican supplier offers to sell Soho 250,000 DVD players for 320,000,000 pesos. Should Soho make or buy? The answer depends on the exchange rate that Soho's managers expect next year. If they forecast an exchange rate of 20 pesos per \$1, Soho's expected purchase cost equals \$16,000,000 (320,000,000 pesos ÷ 20 pesos per \$), greater than the \$15,000,000 relevant costs for making the DVD players in Exhibit 12-6, so Soho's managers would prefer to make DVD players rather than buy them. If, however, Soho's managers anticipate an exchange rate of 22 pesos per \$1, Soho's expected purchase cost equals \$14,545,454 (320,000,000 pesos ÷ 22 pesos per \$), which is less than the \$15,000,000 relevant costs for making the DVD players, so Soho's managers would prefer to buy rather than make the DVD players.

Soho's managers have yet another option. Soho could enter into a forward contract to purchase 320,000,000 pesos. A forward contract allows Soho to contract today to purchase pesos next year at a predetermined, fixed cost, thereby protecting itself against exchange-rate risk. If Soho's managers choose this route, they would make (buy) DVD players if the cost of the contract is greater (less) than \$15,000,000.

International outsourcing requires managers to evaluate manufacturing and transportation costs, exchange-rate risks, and the other strategic and qualitative factors such as quality, reliability, and efficiency of the supply chain. Concepts in Action: "Starbucks Brews Up Domestic Production" describes how Starbucks brought back production to the United States.

The Total Alternatives Approach

In the simple make-or-buy decision in Exhibit 12-6, we assumed that the capacity currently used to make DVD players will remain idle if Soho purchases DVDs from Broadfield. Often, however, the released capacity can be used for other, profitable purposes. In this case, Soho's managers must choose whether to make or buy based on how best to use available production capacity.

CONCEPTS IN ACTION

Starbucks Brews Up Domestic Production[2]

Andrew Winning/Reuters/Alamy Stock Photo

After years of outsourcing production to lower-cost countries around the world, many American-based companies are relocating their manufacturing activities within the United States. Starbucks, the world's largest coffee chain, is a leader in the domestic outsourcing movement. In 2012, the company began sourcing its coffee mugs from American Mug and Stein, a reopened ceramics factory in northeastern Ohio. Starbucks also built a \$172 million facility in Georgia to produce its ready-brew VIA coffee and the coffee base for its Frappuccino blended beverages.

While labor costs at the Ohio and Georgia plants are higher than in many offshore locations, there are several cost-savings benefits from domestic production. These include

- Access to highly skilled labor, which helps with production efficiency;
- Reduced transportation and warehousing costs, since more than 50% of Starbucks' retail stores are in the United States;
- Greater speed to market, which cuts lead time and inventory carrying costs.

While many companies continue to benefit from the global supply chain, Starbucks is among many United States-based companies, including American Apparel and Ralph Lauren, that have benefited from having domestic manufacturing and outsourcing as part of their production mix.

[2] *Sources:* Zachary Hines, "Case Study: Starbucks' New Manufacturing in the USA," University of San Diego Reshoring Institute (San Diego: University of San Diego, 2015) (http://www.reshoringinstitute.org/wp-content/uploads/2015/05/Starbucks-Casestudy.pdf) accessed June 2019; Shan Li, Tiffany Hsu, and Andrea Chang, "American Apparel, Others Try to Profit From Domestic Production," *Los Angeles Times*, August 10, 2014 (http://www.latimes.com/business/la-fi-american-apparel-made-in-usa-20140810-story.html); Adrienne Selko, "Starbucks Chooses Domestic Production," *Industry Week*, July 13, 2012 (http://www.industryweek.com/expansion-management/starbucks-chooses-domestic-production).

Example 3: If Soho decides to buy DVD players for its 2-in-1 systems from Broadfield, Soho's best use of the capacity that becomes available is to produce 100,000 Digiteks, a portable, stand-alone DVD player. From a manufacturing standpoint, Digiteks are similar to the DVD players Soho currently makes for its 2-in-1 system. Soho's management accountant estimates the following future revenues and costs if Soho decides to manufacture and sell Digiteks:

Incremental future revenues		$8,000,000
Incremental future costs		
Direct materials	$3,400,000	
Variable direct manufacturing labor	1,000,000	
Variable overhead (such as power, utilities)	600,000	
Materials-handling and setup overheads	500,000	
Total incremental future costs		5,500,000
Incremental future operating income		$2,500,000

Because of capacity constraints, Soho can make either DVD players for its 2-in-1 system unit or Digiteks, but not both. Which of the two alternatives should Soho's managers choose: (1) make DVD players for its 2-in-1 system and do not make Digiteks or (2) buy DVD players for its 2-in-1 system and make Digiteks?

Exhibit 12-7, Panel A, summarizes the "total-alternatives" approach, the future costs and revenues for *all* products. Soho's managers will choose alternative 2, buy DVD players for its 2-in-1 system and use the available capacity to make and sell Digiteks. The future incremental costs of buying DVD players for its 2-in-1 system from an outside supplier ($16,000,000) exceed the future incremental costs of making 2-in-1 system DVD players in-house ($15,000,000). But Soho can use the capacity freed up by buying DVD players for its 2-in-1 system to gain $2,500,000 in operating income (incremental future revenues of $8,000,000 minus total incremental future costs of $5,500,000) by making and selling Digiteks. The *net relevant* costs of buying 2-in-1 system DVD players and making and selling Digiteks are $16,000,000 − $2,500,000 = $13,500,000.

The Opportunity-Cost Approach

Deciding to use a resource one way means a manager must forgo the opportunity to use the resource in any other way. This lost opportunity is a cost that the manager must consider when making a decision. **Opportunity cost** is the contribution to operating income that is forgone by not using a limited resource in its next-best alternative use. For example, the (relevant) cost of going to school for a bachelor's degree in accounting is not only the cost of tuition, books, lodging, and food, but also the income sacrificed (opportunity cost) by not working. Presumably, however, the estimated future benefits of obtaining an accounting degree (such as a higher-paying career) will exceed these out-of-pocket and opportunity costs.

Exhibit 12-7, Panel B, displays the opportunity-cost approach for analyzing the alternatives Soho faces. *Note that the alternatives are defined differently under the two approaches*:

In the total alternatives approach:
1. Make DVD players for its 2-in-1 system and do not make Digiteks
2. Buy DVD players for its 2-in-1 system and make Digiteks

In the opportunity cost approach:
1. Make DVD players for its 2-in-1 system
2. Buy DVD players for its 2-in-1 system

EXHIBIT 12-7 Total-Alternatives Approach and Opportunity-Cost Approach to Make-or-Buy Decisions for Soho Company

	Alternatives for Soho	
Relevant Items	**1. Make 2-in-1 System DVD Players and Do Not Make Digiteks**	**2. Buy 2-in-1 System DVD Players and Make Digiteks**
PANEL A Total-Alternatives Approach to Make-or-Buy Decisions		
Total incremental future costs of making/buying 2-in-1 system DVD players (from Exhibit 12-6)	$15,000,000	$16,000,000
Deduct excess of future revenues over future costs from Digiteks	0	(2,500,000)
Total relevant costs under total-alternatives approach	$15,000,000	$13,500,000
	1. Make 2-in-1 System DVD Players	**2. Buy 2-in-1 System DVD Players**
PANEL B Opportunity-Cost Approach to Make-or-Buy Decisions		
Total incremental future costs of making/buying 2-in-1 system DVD players (from Exhibit 12-6)	$15,000,000	$16,000,000
Opportunity cost: Profit contribution forgone because capacity will not be used to make Digiteks, the next-best alternative	2,500,000	0
Total relevant costs under opportunity-cost approach	$17,500,000	$16,000,000

Note that the differences in costs across the columns in Panels A and B are the same: The cost of alternative 2 is $1,500,000 less than the cost of alternative 1.

The opportunity-cost approach does not reference Digiteks. Under the opportunity-cost approach, the cost of each alternative includes (1) the incremental costs and (2) the opportunity cost, the profit forgone from not making Digiteks. This opportunity cost arises because Digiteks is excluded from formal consideration in the alternatives.

Consider alternative 1, making DVD players for its 2-in-1 system. What are all the costs of making DVD players for its 2-in-1 system? Certainly Soho will incur $15,000,000 of incremental costs to make DVD players for its 2-in-1 system, but is this the entire cost? No, because by deciding to use limited manufacturing resources to make DVD players for its 2-in-1 system, Soho will give up the opportunity to earn $2,500,000 by not using these resources to make Digiteks. Therefore, the relevant costs of making DVD players for its 2-in-1 system are the incremental costs of $15,000,000 plus the opportunity cost of $2,500,000.

Next, consider alternative 2, buying DVD players for its 2-in-1 system. The incremental cost of buying DVD players for its 2-in-1 system is $16,000,000. The opportunity cost is zero. Why? Because by choosing this alternative, Soho will not forgo the profit it can earn from making and selling Digiteks.

Panel B leads managers to the same conclusion as Panel A: buying DVD players for its 2-in-1 system and making Digiteks is the preferred alternative.

Panels A and B in Exhibit 12-7 describe two consistent approaches to decision making with capacity constraints. The total-alternatives approach in Panel A includes all future incremental costs and revenues. For example, under alternative 2, the additional future operating income from *using capacity to make and sell Digiteks* ($2,500,000) is subtracted from the future incremental cost of buying DVD players for its 2-in-1 system ($16,000,000). The opportunity-cost analysis in Panel B takes the opposite approach. It focuses only on DVD players for its 2-in-1 system. Whenever capacity is not going to be used to make and sell Digiteks, the future forgone operating income is added as an opportunity cost of making DVD players for its 2-in-1 system, as in alternative 1. (Note that when Digiteks are made, as in alternative 2, there is no "opportunity cost of not making Digiteks.") Therefore, whereas Panel A *subtracts* $2,500,000 under alternative 2, Panel B *adds* $2,500,000 under alternative 1. *Panel B highlights the idea that when capacity is constrained, the relevant revenues and costs of any alternative equal (1) the incremental future revenues and costs plus (2) the opportunity cost.* However, when managers are considering more than two alternatives simultaneously, it is generally easier to use the total-alternatives approach.

Opportunity costs are not recorded in financial accounting systems. Why? Because historical recordkeeping is limited to transactions involving alternatives that managers *actually select* rather than alternatives that they reject. Rejected alternatives do not produce transactions and are not recorded. If Soho makes DVD players for its 2-in-1 system, it will not make Digiteks, and it will not record any accounting entries for Digiteks. Yet the opportunity cost of making DVD players for its 2-in-1 system, which equals the operating income that Soho forgoes by not making Digiteks, is a crucial input into the make-or-buy decision. Consider again Exhibit 12-7, Panel B. On the basis of only the incremental costs that are systematically recorded in accounting systems, it is less costly for Soho to make rather than buy DVD players for its 2-in-1 system. Recognizing the unrecorded opportunity cost of $2,500,000 leads to a different conclusion: buying DVD players for its 2-in-1 system is preferable to making them.

Suppose Soho has sufficient capacity to make Digiteks even if it makes DVD players for its 2-in-1 system. In this case, the opportunity cost of making DVD players for its 2-in-1 system is $0 because Soho does not give up the $2,500,000 operating income from making and selling Digiteks even if it chooses to make DVD players for its 2-in-1 system. The relevant costs are $15,000,000 (incremental costs of $15,000,000 plus opportunity cost of $0). Under these conditions, Soho's managers would prefer to make DVD players for its 2-in-1 system, rather than buy them, and also make Digiteks.

Besides quantitative considerations, managers also consider strategic and qualitative factors in make-or-buy decisions. In deciding to buy DVD players for its 2-in-1 system from an outside supplier, Soho's managers consider factors such as the supplier's reputation for quality and timely delivery. They also consider the strategic consequences of selling Digiteks. For example, will selling Digiteks take Soho's focus away from its 2-in-1 system?

TRY IT! 12-2

The Gannett Company provides landscaping services to corporations and businesses. All its landscaping work requires Gannett to use landscaping equipment. Its landscaping equipment has the capacity to do 14,000 hours of landscaping work. It currently anticipates getting orders that would utilize 13,200 hours of equipment time from existing customers. Gannett charges $115 per hour for landscaping work. Cost information for the current expected activity level is as follows:

Revenues ($115 × 13,200 hours)	$1,518,000
Variable landscaping costs (largely labor), which vary with the number of hours worked ($60 per hour × 13,200 hours)	792,000
Fixed landscaping costs	110,000
Variable marketing costs (5% of revenue)	75,900
Fixed marketing costs	74,000
Total costs	1,051,900
Operating income	$ 466,100

Gannett has received an order for landscaping work from Gerald Corporation at $80 per hour that would require 4,600 hours of equipment time. Variable landscaping costs for the Gerald Corporation order are $60 per hour and variable marketing costs are 5% of revenues. Gannett can either accept the Gerald offer in whole or reject it. Should Gannett accept the offer?

Carrying Costs of Inventory

To see another example of an opportunity cost, consider the following data for Soho's DVD player purchasing decision:

Estimated DVD player requirements for its 2-in-1 system for next year	250,000 units
Cost per unit when each purchase is equal to 2,500 units	$ 64.00
Cost per unit when each purchase is equal to or greater than 30,000 units ($64 − 0.5% discount)	$ 63.68
Cost of a purchase order	$ 150.00
Soho's managers are evaluating the following alternatives:	
A. Make 100 purchases (twice a week) of 2,500 units each during next year	
B. Make 8 purchases (twice a quarter) of 31,250 units during the year	
Average investment in inventory:	
A. (2,500 units × $64.00 per unit) ÷ 2[a]	$ 80,000
B. (31,250 units × $63.68 per unit) ÷ 2[a]	$995,000
Annual rate of return if cash is invested elsewhere (for example, bonds or stocks) at the same level of risk as investment in inventory	12%

[a] The example assumes that DVD-player purchases for its 2-in-1 system will be used uniformly throughout the year. The average investment in inventory during the year is the cost of the inventory when a purchase is received plus the cost of inventory just before the next purchase is delivered (in our example, zero) divided by 2.

Soho will pay cash for the DVD players it buys for its 2-in-1 system. Which purchasing alternative is more economical for Soho?

The management accountant presents the following analysis to the company's managers using the total alternatives approach, recognizing that Soho has, on average, $995,000 of cash available to invest. If Soho invests only $80,000 in inventory as in alternative A, it will have $915,000 ($995,000 − $80,000) of cash available to invest elsewhere, which at a 12% rate of return will yield a total return of $109,800. This income is subtracted from the ordering and purchasing costs incurred under alternative A. If Soho invests all $995,000 in inventory as in alternative B, it will have $0 ($995,000 − $995,000) available to invest elsewhere and will earn no return on the cash.

	Alternative A: Make 100 Purchases of 2,500 Units Each During the Year and Invest Any Excess Cash (1)	Alternative B: Make 8 Purchases of 31,250 Units Each During the Year and Invest Any Excess Cash (2)	Difference (3) = (1) − (2)
Annual purchase-order costs (100 purch. orders × $150/purch. order; 8 purch. orders × $150/purch. order)	$ 15,000	$ 1,200	$ 13,800
Annual purchase costs (250,000 units × $64.00/unit; 250,000 units × $63.68/unit)	16,000,000	15,920,000	80,000
Deduct annual rate of return earned by investing cash not tied up in inventory elsewhere at the same level of risk [0.12 × ($995,000 − $80,000); 0.12 × ($995,000 − $995,000)]	(109,800)	0	(109,800)
Relevant costs	$15,905,200	$15,921,200	$ (16,000)

Consistent with the trends toward holding smaller inventories, it is more economical (by $16,000) for Soho's managers to purchase smaller quantities of 2,500 units 100 times a year than to purchase 31,250 units 8 times a year even though the purchase and purchase-order costs are higher when purchasing smaller quantities.

The following table presents the management accountant's analysis of the two alternatives using the opportunity-cost approach. Each alternative is defined only in terms of the two purchasing choices with no explicit reference to investing the excess cash.

	Alternative A: Make 100 Purchases of 2,500 Units Each During the Year (1)	Alternative B: Make 8 Purchases of 31,250 Units Each During the Year (2)	Difference (3) = (1) − (2)
Annual purchase-order costs (100 purch. orders × $150/purch. order; 8 purch. orders × $150/purch. order)	$ 15,000	$ 1,200	$ 13,800
Annual purchase costs (250,000 units × $64.00/unit; 250,000 units × $63.68/unit)	16,000,000	15,920,000	80,000
Opportunity cost: Annual rate of return that could be earned if investment in inventory were invested elsewhere at the same level of risk (0.12 × $80,000; 0.12 × $995,000)	9,600	119,400	(109,800)
Relevant costs	$16,024,600	$16,040,600	$ (16,000)

Recall that under the opportunity-cost approach, the relevant cost of any alternative is (1) the incremental cost of the alternative plus (2) the opportunity cost of the profit forgone from choosing that alternative. The opportunity cost of holding inventory is the income forgone by tying up money in inventory and not investing it elsewhere. The opportunity cost would not be recorded in the accounting system because, once the money is invested in inventory, there is no money available to invest elsewhere and so no return related to this investment to record. On the basis of the costs recorded in the accounting system (purchase-order costs and purchase costs), Soho's managers would erroneously conclude that making eight purchases of 31,250 units each is the less costly alternative. Column 3, however, indicates that, as in the total-alternatives approach, purchasing smaller quantities of 2,500 units 100 times a year is more economical than purchasing 31,250 units eight times during the year by $16,000. Why? Because the lower opportunity cost of holding smaller inventory exceeds the higher purchase and ordering costs. If the opportunity cost of money tied up in inventory were greater than 12% per year, or if other incremental benefits of holding lower inventory were considered, such as lower insurance, materials-handling, storage, obsolescence, and breakage cost, making 100 purchases would be even more economical.

DECISION POINT

What is an opportunity cost, and why should managers consider it when making insourcing-versus-outsourcing decisions?

Product-Mix Decisions With Capacity Constraints

LEARNING OBJECTIVE 4

Know how to choose which products to produce when there are capacity constraints

... select the product with the highest contribution margin per unit of the limiting resource

We now examine how the concept of relevance applies to **product-mix decisions**, the decisions managers make about which products to sell and in what quantities. These decisions usually have only a short-run focus because they typically arise in the context of capacity constraints that can be relaxed in the long run. In the short run, for example, BMW, the German car manufacturer, continually adapts the mix of its different models of cars (for example, 328i, 528i, and 750i) to fluctuations in selling prices and demand.

To determine product mix, managers maximize operating income, subject to constraints such as capacity and demand. Throughout this section, we assume that as short-run changes in product mix occur, the only costs that change are costs that are variable with the number of units produced (and sold). Under this assumption, the analysis of individual product contribution margins provides insight into the product mix that maximizes operating income. The same basic concepts apply in the more general cases except that we then need to consider contribution margins based on variable costs at different levels of the cost hierarchy.

Example 4: Power Recreation assembles two engines, a snowmobile engine and a boat engine, at its Lexington, Kentucky, plant. The following table shows the selling prices, costs, and contribution margins of these two engines:

	Snowmobile Engine	Boat Engine
Selling price	$800	$1,000
Variable cost per unit	560	625
Contribution margin per unit	$240	$ 375
Contribution-margin percentage ($240 ÷ $800; $375 ÷ $1,000)	30%	37.5%

Only 600 machine-hours are available daily for assembling engines. Additional capacity cannot be obtained in the short run. Power Recreation can sell as many engines as it produces. The constraining resource, then, is machine-hours. It takes 2 machine-hours to assemble one snowmobile engine and 5 machine-hours to assemble one boat engine. What product mix should Power Recreation's managers choose to maximize operating income?

In terms of contribution margin per unit and contribution-margin percentage, the data in Example 4 shows that boat engines are more profitable than snowmobile engines. Should Power Recreation produce and sell boat engines? Not necessarily. The following table shows that managers should choose the product with *the highest contribution margin per unit of the constraining resource (factor)*. That's the resource that restricts or limits the production or sale of products.

	Snowmobile Engine	Boat Engine
Contribution margin per unit	$240	$375
Machine-hours required to assemble one unit	2 machine-hours	5 machine-hours
Contribution margin per machine-hour		
$240 per unit ÷ 2 machine-hours/unit	$120/machine-hour	
$375 per unit ÷ 5 machine-hours/unit		$75/machine-hour
Total contribution margin for 600 machine-hours		
$120/machine-hour × 600 machine-hours	$72,000	
$75/machine-hour × 600 machine-hours		$45,000

The number of machine-hours is the constraining resource in this example, and snowmobile engines earn more contribution margin per machine-hour ($120/machine-hour) compared with boat engines ($75/machine-hour). Therefore, choosing to produce and sell snowmobile engines maximizes *total* contribution margin ($72,000 vs. $45,000 from producing and selling boat engines) and operating income. Other constraints in manufacturing settings can be the availability of direct materials, components, or skilled labor, as well as financial and sales factors. In a retail department store, the constraining resource may be linear feet of display space. Regardless of the specific constraining resource, managers will maximize *total* contribution margin by choosing products with the highest contribution margin per unit of the constraining resource.

In many cases, a manufacturer or retailer has the challenge of trying to maximize total operating income for a variety of products, each with more than one constraining resource. Some constraints may require a manufacturer or retailer to stock minimum quantities of products even if these products are not very profitable. For example, supermarkets must stock less-profitable products, such as paper towels and toilet paper, because customers will only shop at supermarkets that carry a wide range of products. To determine the most profitable product mix, the manufacturer or retailer must maximize total contribution margin in the face of many constraints. Optimization techniques, such as linear programming, discussed in the appendix to this chapter, help solve these more complex problems.

At the same time, managers work to relieve the bottleneck constraint to increase output and contribution margin. Can the available machine-hours for assembling engines be

DECISION POINT

When a resource is constrained, how should managers choose which of multiple products to produce and sell?

increased beyond 600, for example, by reducing idle time? Can the time needed to assemble each snowmobile engine (2 machine-hours) or each boat engine (5 machine-hours) be reduced, for example, by reducing setup time and processing time of assembly? Can some of the assembly operations be outsourced to allow more engines to be built? We address these questions in the following section.

TRY IT! 12-3

The Gannett Company provides landscaping services to corporations and businesses. All its landscaping work requires Gannett to use landscaping equipment. Its landscaping equipment has the capacity to do 14,000 hours of landscaping work. It currently anticipates getting orders that would utilize 13,200 hours of equipment time. Gannett charges $115 per hour for landscaping work. Cost information for the current expected activity level is as follows:

Revenues ($115 × 13,200 hours)	$1,518,000
Variable landscaping costs (largely labor), which vary with the number of hours worked ($60 per hour × 13,200 hours)	792,000
Fixed landscaping costs	110,000
Variable marketing costs (5% of revenue)	75,900
Fixed marketing costs	74,000
Total costs	1,051,900
Operating income	$ 466,100

In order to fill its available capacity, Gannett's salespersons are trying to find new business. Russell Corporation wants Gannett to do 4,600 hours of landscaping work for $100 per hour. Variable landscaping costs for the Russell Corporation order are $50 per hour and variable marketing costs are 5% of revenues. Gannett can accept as much or as little of the 4,600 hours of Russell's landscaping work. What should Gannett Corporation do?

Bottlenecks, Theory of Constraints, and Throughput-Margin Analysis

LEARNING OBJECTIVE 5

Explain how to manage bottlenecks

... keep bottlenecks busy and increase their efficiency and capacity by increasing throughput (contribution) margin

Suppose Power Recreation's snowmobile engine must go through a forging operation before it goes to the assembly operation. The company has 1,200 hours of daily forging capacity dedicated to manufacturing snowmobile engines. It takes 3 hours to forge each snowmobile engine, so Power Recreation can forge 400 snowmobile engines per day (1,200 hours ÷ 3 hours per snowmobile engine). Recall that it can assemble only 300 snowmobile engines per day (600 machine-hours ÷ 2 machine-hours per snowmobile engine). The production of snowmobile engines is constrained by the assembly operation, not the forging operation.

The **theory of constraints (TOC)** describes methods to maximize operating income when faced with some bottleneck and some nonbottleneck operations.[3] To implement TOC, we define and use three measures:

1. **Throughput margin** equals revenues minus the direct material costs of the goods sold.
2. *Investments* equal the sum of (a) material costs in direct materials, work-in-process, and finished-goods inventories; (b) R&D costs; and (c) capital costs of equipment and buildings.
3. *Operating costs* equal all costs of operations (other than direct materials) incurred to earn throughput margin. Operating costs include costs such as salaries and wages, rent, utilities, and depreciation.

[3] See Eliyahu M. Goldratt and Jeff Cox, *The Goal* (New York: North River Press, 1986); Eliyahu M. Goldratt, *The Theory of Constraints* (New York: North River Press, 1990); Umesh Nagarkatte and Nancy Oley, *The Theory of Constraints: Creative Problem Solving* (Florida: Productivity Press, 2018).

The objective of the TOC is to increase throughput margin while decreasing investments and operating costs. *The TOC considers a short-run time horizon of a few months and assumes operating costs are fixed and direct material costs are the only variable costs. In a situation where some of the operating costs are also variable in the short run, throughput margin is replaced by contribution margin—revenues minus direct material costs minus other variable operating costs.* In the Power Recreation example, each snowmobile engine sells for $800. We assume that the variable costs of $560 consist only of direct material costs (incurred in the forging department), so throughput margin equals contribution margin. For ease of exposition and consistency with the previous section, we use the term *contribution margin* instead of *throughput margin* throughout this section.

TOC focuses on managing bottleneck operations, as explained in the following steps:

Step 1: Recognize that the bottleneck operation determines the contribution margin of the entire system. In the Power Recreation example, output in the assembly operation determines the output of snowmobile engines.

Step 2: Identify the bottleneck operation by identifying operations with large quantities of inventory waiting to be worked on. If snowmobile engines are produced to capacity at the forging operation, inventories will build up at the assembly operation because daily assembly capacity of 300 snowmobile engines is less than the daily forging capacity of 400 snowmobile engines.

Step 3: Keep the bottleneck operation busy and subordinate all nonbottleneck operations to the bottleneck operation. To maximize contribution margin of the constrained or bottleneck resource, the bottleneck assembly operation is always kept running; workers are never waiting to assemble engines. How? By maintaining a small buffer inventory of snowmobile engines that have gone through the forging operation and are waiting to be assembled. The assembly operation operates at capacity based on a detailed production schedule at the forging operation that ensures the assembly operation is not waiting for work. The bottleneck assembly operation sets the pace for the nonbottleneck forging operations to avoid forging snowmobile engines that cannot be assembled. Doing so does not increase output or contribution margin; it only creates excess inventory of unassembled snowmobile engines.

Step 4: Take actions to increase the efficiency and capacity of the bottleneck operation as long as the incremental contribution margin exceeds the incremental costs of increasing efficiency and capacity.

We illustrate Step 4 using data from the forging and assembly operations.

	Forging	Assembly
Capacity per day	400 units	300 units
Daily production and sales	300 units	300 units
Other fixed operating costs per day (excluding direct materials)	$24,000	$18,000
Other fixed operating costs per unit produced ($24,000 ÷ 300 units; $ 18,000 ÷ 300 units)	$ 80 per unit	$ 60 per unit

Power Recreation's output is constrained by the capacity of 300 units in the assembly operation. What can Power Recreation's managers do to relieve the bottleneck constraint of the assembly operation?

Desirable actions include the following:

1. **Eliminate idle time at the bottleneck operation (time when the assembly machine is neither being set up to assemble nor actually assembling snowmobile engines).** Power Recreation's manager is evaluating permanently positioning two workers at the assembly operation to unload snowmobile engines as soon as they are assembled and to set up the machine to begin assembling the next batch of snowmobile engines. This action will cost $320 per day and increase bottleneck output by three snowmobile engines per day. Should Power Recreation's managers incur the additional costs? Yes, because Power Recreation's contribution margin will increase by $720 per day

($240 per snowmobile engine × 3 snowmobile engines), which is greater than the incremental cost of $320 per day. All other costs are irrelevant.

2. **Shift products that do not have to be made on the bottleneck machine to nonbottleneck machines or to outside processing facilities.** Suppose Spartan Corporation, an outside contractor, offers to assemble five snowmobile engines each day at $75 per snowmobile engine from engines that have gone through the forging operation. Spartan's quoted price is greater than Power Recreation's own operating costs in the assembly department of $60 per snowmobile engine. Should Power Recreation's managers accept the offer? Yes, because assembly is the bottleneck operation. Getting Spartan to assemble additional snowmobile engines will increase contribution margin by $1,200 per day ($240 per snowmobile engine × 5 snowmobile engines), while the relevant cost of increasing capacity will be $375 per day ($75 per snowmobile engine × 5 snowmobile engines). The fact that Power Recreation's unit cost is less than Spartan's quoted price is irrelevant.

   Suppose Gemini Industries, another outside contractor, offers to do the forging operation for eight snowmobile engines per day for $65 per snowmobile engine from direct materials supplied by Power Recreation. Gemini's price is lower than Power Recreation's operating cost of $80 per snowmobile engine in the forging department. Should Power Recreation's managers accept Gemini's offer? No, because other operating costs are fixed costs. Power Recreation will not save any costs by subcontracting the forging operations. Instead, its costs will increase by $520 per day ($65 per snowmobile engine × 8 snowmobile engines) with no increase in contribution margin, which is constrained by assembly capacity.

3. **Reduce setup time and processing time at bottleneck operations (for example, by simplifying the design or reducing the number of parts in the product).** Suppose Power Recreation can assemble 10 more snowmobile engines each day at a cost of $1,000 per day by reducing setup time at the assembly operation. Should Power Recreation's managers incur this cost? Yes, because the contribution margin will increase by $2,400 per day ($240 per snowmobile engine × 10 snowmobile engines), which is greater than the incremental costs of $1,000 per day.

   Will Power Recreation's managers find it worthwhile to incur costs to reduce machining time at the nonbottleneck forging operation? No. Other operating costs will increase, while the contribution margin will remain unchanged, constrained by bottleneck capacity at the assembly operation, which has not increased.

4. **Improve the quality of parts or products manufactured at the bottleneck operation.** Poor quality is more costly at a bottleneck operation than at a nonbottleneck operation. The cost of poor quality at a nonbottleneck operation is the cost of materials wasted. If Power Recreation produces five defective snowmobile engines at the forging operation, the cost of poor quality is $2,800 (direct material cost per snowmobile engine, $560 × 5 snowmobile engines). No contribution margin is forgone because forging has unused capacity. Despite the defective production, forging can produce and transfer 300 good-quality snowmobile engines to the assembly operation. At a bottleneck operation, the cost of poor quality is the cost of materials wasted *plus* the opportunity cost of lost contribution margin. Bottleneck capacity not wasted in producing defective snowmobile engines could be used to generate additional contribution margin. If Power Recreation produces five defective units at the assembly operation, the cost of poor quality is the lost revenue of $4,000 ($800 per snowmobile engine × 5 snowmobile engines) or, alternatively stated, direct material costs of $2,800 (direct material cost per snowmobile engine, $560 × 5 snowmobile engines) plus the forgone contribution margin of $1,200 ($240 per snowmobile engine × 5 snowmobile engines).

   The high cost of poor quality at the bottleneck operation means that bottleneck time should not be wasted processing units that are defective. That is, engines should be inspected before the bottleneck operation to ensure that only good-quality parts are processed at the bottleneck operation. Furthermore, quality-improvement programs should place special emphasis on minimizing defects at bottleneck machines.

If successful, the actions in Step 4 will increase the capacity of the assembly operation until it eventually exceeds the capacity of the forging operation. The bottleneck will then shift to the forging operation. Power Recreation would then focus continuous-improvement actions on increasing forging operation efficiency and capacity. For example, the contract with Gemini Industries to forge eight snowmobile engines per day at $65 per snowmobile engine from direct material supplied by Power Recreation will become attractive because the contribution margin will increase by $1,920 per day ($240 per snowmobile engine × 8 snowmobile engines), which is greater than the incremental costs of $520 ($65 per snowmobile engine × 8 snowmobile engines).

The experience of the Apple Watch illustrates many of the issues discussed in this section. During final testing, the company found that the "taptic engine" motor (designed by Apple to produce the sensation of being tapped on the wrist) made by one of its two suppliers started to break down. As a result, Apple had to scrap some completed watches and move the production of this component to a second supplier. While the second supplier's part did not experience the same problems, it took time for that supplier to increase production. Consequently, Apple asked other component suppliers to align their production to the output of the taptic engine bottleneck.

The theory of constraints emphasizes management of bottleneck operations as the key to improving performance of production operations as a whole. It focuses on short-run maximization of contribution margin. Because TOC regards operating costs as difficult to change in the short run, it does not identify individual activities and drivers of costs. Therefore, TOC is less useful for the long-run management of costs. In contrast, activity-based costing (ABC) systems take a long-run perspective and focus on improving processes by eliminating non-value-added activities and reducing the costs of performing value-added activities. ABC systems are therefore more useful than TOC for long-run pricing, cost control, and capacity management. The short-run TOC emphasis on maximizing contribution margin by managing bottlenecks complements the long-run strategic-cost-management focus of ABC.[4]

DECISION POINT

What steps can managers take to manage bottlenecks?

Customer Profitability and Relevant Costs

LEARNING OBJECTIVE 6

Discuss the factors managers must consider when adding or dropping customers or business units

... managers should focus on how total revenues and costs differ among alternatives and ignore allocated overhead costs

Managers must often make decisions about adding or dropping a product line or a business segment. Similarly, if the cost object is a customer, managers must decide about adding or dropping customers (analogous to a product line) or a branch office (analogous to a business segment or division). We illustrate relevant-revenue and relevant-cost analysis for these decisions using customers rather than products as the cost object.

Example 5: Allied West, the West Coast sales office of Allied Furniture, a wholesaler of specialized furniture, supplies furniture to three local retailers: Vogel, Brenner, and Wisk. Exhibit 12-8 presents expected revenues and costs of Allied West by customer for the upcoming year using its activity-based costing system. Allied West's management accountant assigns costs to customers based on the activities needed to support each customer. Information on Allied West's costs for different activities at various levels of the cost hierarchy are as follows:

- Furniture-handling labor costs vary with the number of units of furniture shipped to customers.
- Allied West reserves different areas of the warehouse for different customers. For simplicity, we assume that furniture-handling equipment in an area and depreciation costs on the equipment that Allied West has already acquired are identified with individual customers (customer-level costs). Any unused equipment remains idle. The equipment has a 1-year useful life and zero disposal value.

[4] For an excellent evaluation of TOC, operations management, cost accounting, and the relationship between TOC and activity-based costing, see Anthony Atkinson, *Cost Accounting, the Theory of Constraints, and Costing* (Issue Paper, CMA Canada, December 2000).

EXHIBIT 12-8 Customer Profitability Analysis for Allied West

	Customer			
	Vogel	**Brenner**	**Wisk**	**Total**
Revenues	$500,000	$300,000	$400,000	$1,200,000
Cost of goods sold	370,000	220,000	330,000	920,000
Furniture-handling labor	41,000	18,000	33,000	92,000
Furniture-handling equipment cost written off as depreciation	12,000	4,000	9,000	25,000
Rent	14,000	8,000	14,000	36,000
Marketing support	11,000	9,000	10,000	30,000
Sales order and delivery processing	13,000	7,000	12,000	32,000
General administration	20,000	12,000	16,000	48,000
Allocated corporate-office costs	10,000	6,000	8,000	24,000
Total costs	491,000	284,000	432,000	1,207,000
Operating income	$ 9,000	$ 16,000	$ (32,000)	$ (7,000)

- Allied West allocates its fixed rent costs to each customer on the basis of the amount of warehouse space reserved for that customer.
- Marketing support costs vary with the number of sales visits made to customers.
- Sales-order costs are batch-level costs that vary with the number of sales orders received from customers. Delivery-processing costs are batch-level costs that vary with the number of shipments made.
- Allied West allocates fixed general-administration costs (facility-level costs) to customers on the basis of customer revenues.
- Allied Furniture allocates its fixed corporate-office costs to sales offices on the basis of the budgeted costs of each sales office. Allied West then allocates these costs to customers on the basis of customer revenues.

In the following sections, we consider several decisions that Allied West's managers face: Should Allied West drop the Wisk account? Should it add a fourth customer, Loral? Should Allied Furniture close down Allied West? Should it open another sales office, Allied South, whose revenues and costs are identical to those of Allied West?

Relevant-Revenue and Relevant-Cost Analysis of Dropping a Customer

Exhibit 12-8 indicates a loss of $32,000 on the Wisk account because Wisk places low-margin orders with Allied and has relatively high sales-order, delivery-processing, furniture-handling, and marketing costs. Allied West's managers are considering several possible actions for the Wisk account: reducing the costs of supporting Wisk by becoming more efficient; cutting back on some of the services Allied West offers Wisk; asking Wisk to place larger, less frequent orders; charging Wisk higher prices; or dropping the Wisk account. The following analysis focuses on the annual operating-income effect of dropping the Wisk account.

Allied West's managers and management accountants first focus on relevant revenues and relevant costs. Dropping the Wisk account will

- Save cost of goods sold, furniture-handling labor, marketing support, sales-order and delivery-processing costs incurred on the account;

EXHIBIT 12-9 Relevant-Revenue and Relevant-Cost Analysis for Dropping the Wisk Account and Adding the Loral Account

	(Incremental Loss in Revenues) and Incremental Savings in Costs from Dropping Wisk Account (1)	Incremental Revenues and (Incremental Costs) from Adding Loral Account (2)
Revenues	$(400,000)	$400,000
Cost of goods sold	330,000	(330,000)
Furniture-handling labor	33,000	(33,000)
Furniture-handling equipment cost written off as depreciation	0	(9,000)
Rent	0	0
Marketing support	10,000	(10,000)
Sales order and delivery processing	12,000	(12,000)
General administration	0	0
Corporate-office costs	0	0
Total costs	385,000	(394,000)
Effect on operating income (loss)	$ (15,000)	$ 6,000

- Leave idle the warehouse space and furniture-handling equipment currently used to supply products to Wisk;
- Not affect the fixed rent costs, general administration costs, or corporate-office costs.

Exhibit 12-9, column 1, presents the relevant-revenue and relevant-cost analysis using data from the Wisk column in Exhibit 12-8. The $385,000 cost savings from dropping the Wisk account will not be enough to offset the $400,000 loss in revenues. Because Allied West's operating income will be $15,000 lower if it drops the Wisk account, Allied West's managers decide to keep the Wisk account. They will, of course, continue to find ways to become more efficient, change Wisk's ordering patterns, or charge higher prices.

Depreciation on equipment that Allied West has already acquired is a past cost and therefore irrelevant. Rent, general administration, and corporate-office costs are future costs that will not change if Allied West drops the Wisk account and are also irrelevant.

Corporate-office costs allocated to the sales office and individual customers are always irrelevant. The only question is, will expected total corporate office costs decrease as a result of dropping the Wisk account? In our example, they will not, so these costs are irrelevant. *If expected total corporate-office costs* were to decrease by dropping the Wisk account, those savings would be relevant even if *the amount allocated to Wisk did not change.*

Note that there is no opportunity cost of using warehouse space and equipment for Wisk because there is no alternative use for them. That is, the space and equipment will remain idle if managers drop the Wisk account. But suppose Allied West could lease the available extra space and equipment to Sanchez Corporation for $20,000 per year. Then $20,000 would be Allied West's opportunity cost of continuing to use the warehouse to service Wisk. Allied West would gain $5,000 by dropping the Wisk account ($20,000 from lease revenue minus lost operating income of $15,000). Under the total alternatives approach, the revenue loss from dropping the Wisk account would be $380,000 ($400,000 − $20,000) versus the savings in costs of $385,000 (Exhibit 12-9, column 1). Before reaching a decision, Allied West's managers must examine whether Wisk can be made more profitable so that supplying products to Wisk earns more than the $20,000 from leasing to Sanchez. The managers must also consider strategic factors such as the effect of dropping the Wisk account on Allied West's reputation for developing stable, long-run business relationships with its customers.

Relevant-Revenue and Relevant-Cost Analysis of Adding a Customer

Suppose that Allied West's managers are evaluating the profitability of adding another customer, Loral, to its existing customer base of Vogel, Brenner, and Wisk. There is no other alternative use of the Allied West facility. Loral has a customer profile much like Wisk's, so managers predict revenues and costs of doing business with Loral to be the same as the revenues and costs described under the Wisk column in Exhibit 12-8. In particular, Allied West would have to acquire furniture-handling equipment for the Loral account costing $9,000, with a 1-year useful life and zero disposal value. If Loral is added as a customer, warehouse rent costs ($36,000), general administration costs ($48,000), and *actual total* corporate-office costs will not change. Should Allied West's managers add Loral as a customer?

Exhibit 12-9, column 2, shows relevant revenues exceed relevant costs by $6,000. The opportunity cost of adding Loral is $0 because there is no alternative use of the Allied West facility. On the basis of this analysis, Allied West's managers recommend adding Loral as a customer. Rent, general administration, and corporate-office costs are irrelevant because these costs will not change if Loral is added as a customer. However, the cost of new equipment to support the Loral order (written off as depreciation of $9,000 in Exhibit 12-9, column 2) is relevant. That's because this cost can be avoided if Allied West decides not to add Loral as a customer. Note the critical distinction here: *Depreciation cost is irrelevant in deciding whether to drop Wisk as a customer because depreciation on equipment that has already been purchased is a past cost, but the cost of purchasing new equipment in the future that will then be written off as depreciation is relevant in deciding whether to add Loral as a customer.*

Relevant-Revenue and Relevant-Cost Analysis of Closing or Adding Branch Offices or Business Divisions

Companies periodically confront decisions about closing or adding branch offices or business divisions. For example, given Allied West's expected annual loss of $7,000 (see Exhibit 12-8), should Allied Furniture close Allied West? Closing Allied West will save all Allied West's costs, but there is no disposal value for Allied West's equipment and no alternative use for its space. Closing Allied West will have no effect on total corporate-office costs.

Exhibit 12-10, column 1, presents the relevant-revenue and relevant-cost analysis using data from the "Total" column in Exhibit 12-8. The revenue losses of $1,200,000 will exceed the cost savings of $1,158,000, and decrease operating income by $42,000. Allied West should not be closed. The key reasons are that closing Allied West will not save depreciation cost or actual total corporate-office costs. Depreciation cost is past or sunk because it represents the cost of equipment that Allied West has already purchased. The $24,000 of corporate-office costs no longer allocated to Allied West will be allocated to other sales offices, *but the total amount of these costs will not decline* and so are irrelevant.

DECISION POINT

In deciding to add or drop customers or to add or discontinue branch offices or business divisions, what should managers focus on, and how should they take into account allocated overhead costs?

Finally suppose Allied Furniture has the opportunity to open another sales office, Allied South, whose revenues and costs are identical to Allied West's costs, including a cost of $25,000 to acquire furniture-handling equipment with a 1-year useful life and zero disposal value. Opening this office will have no effect on total corporate-office costs. Should Allied Furniture's managers open Allied South? Exhibit 12-10, column 2, indicates that they should because opening Allied South will increase operating income by $17,000. As before, the cost of new equipment to be purchased in the future (and written off as depreciation) is relevant and *allocated* corporate-office costs are irrelevant because total corporate-office costs will not change if Allied South is opened.

EXHIBIT 12-10 Relevant-Revenue and Relevant-Cost Analysis for Closing Allied West and Opening Allied South

	(Incremental Loss in Revenues) and Incremental Savings in Costs from Closing Allied West (1)	Incremental Revenues and (Incremental Costs) from Opening Allied South (2)
Revenues	$(1,200,000)	$1,200,000
Cost of goods sold	920,000	(920,000)
Furniture-handling labor	92,000	(92,000)
Furniture-handling equipment cost written off as depreciation	0	(25,000)
Rent	36,000	(36,000)
Marketing support	30,000	(30,000)
Sales order and delivery processing	32,000	(32,000)
General administration	48,000	(48,000)
Corporate-office costs	0	0
Total costs	1,158,000	(1,183,000)
Effect on operating income (loss)	$ (42,000)	$ 17,000

12-4 TRY IT!

Sloan Corporation runs two stores, one in Medfield and one in Oakland. Operating income for each store in 2020 is as follows:

	Medfield Store	Oakland Store
Revenues	$2,200,000	$1,600,000
Operating costs		
Cost of goods sold	1,400,000	1,230,000
Variable operating costs (labor, utilities)	210,000	120,000
Lease rent (renewable each year)	152,000	165,000
Depreciation of equipment	47,000	42,000
Allocated corporate overhead	89,000	80,000
Total operating costs	1,898,000	1,637,000
Operating income (loss)	$ 302,000	$ (37,000)

The equipment has zero disposal value.

1. By closing down the Oakland store, Sloan can reduce overall corporate overhead costs by $90,000. Should Sloan Corporation close down the Oakland store?
2. Instead of closing down the Oakland store, Sloan Corporation is thinking of opening another store with revenues and costs identical to the Oakland store (including a cost of $42,000 to acquire equipment with a 1-year useful life and zero disposal value). Opening this store will increase corporate overhead costs by $9,000. Should Sloan Corporation open another store like the Oakland store? Explain.

Irrelevance of Past Costs and Equipment-Replacement Decisions

LEARNING OBJECTIVE 7

Explain why book value of equipment is irrelevant to managers making equipment-replacement decisions

... it is a past cost

At several points in this chapter, we reasoned that past (historical or sunk) costs are irrelevant because a decision cannot change something that has already happened. We now apply this concept to decisions about replacing equipment. We stress the idea that **book value**—original cost minus accumulated depreciation—of existing equipment is a past cost that is irrelevant.

Example 6: Toledo Company, a manufacturer of aircraft components, is considering replacing a metal-cutting machine with a newer model. The new machine is more efficient than the old machine, but has a shorter life. Revenues from aircraft parts ($1.1 million per year) will be unaffected by the replacement decision. The management accountant prepares the following data for the existing (old) machine and the replacement (new) machine:

	Old Machine	New Machine
Original cost	$1,000,000	$600,000
Useful life	5 years	2 years
Current age	3 years	0 years
Remaining useful life	2 years	2 years
Accumulated depreciation	$ 600,000	Not acquired yet
Book value	$ 400,000	Not acquired yet
Current disposal value (in cash)	$ 40,000	Not acquired yet
Terminal disposal value (in cash 2 years from now)	$ 0	$ 0
Annual operating costs (maintenance, energy, repairs, coolants, and so on)	$ 800,000	$460,000

Toledo Corporation uses straight-line depreciation. To focus on relevance, we ignore the time value of money and income taxes.[5] Should Toledo's managers replace its old machine?

Exhibit 12-11 presents a cost comparison of the two machines. Consider why each of the following four items in Toledo's equipment-replacement decision are relevant or irrelevant:

1. **Book value of old machine, $400,000.** Irrelevant, because it is a past or sunk cost. All past costs are "down the drain." Nothing can change what the company has already spent or what has already happened.
2. **Current disposal value of old machine, $40,000.** Relevant, because it is an expected future benefit that will only occur if the company replaces the machine.

EXHIBIT 12-11 Operating Income Comparison: Replacement of Machine, Relevant, and Irrelevant Items for Toledo Company

	Two Years Together		
	Keep (1)	Replace (2)	Difference (3) = (1) – (2)
Revenues	$2,200,000	$2,200,000	—
Operating costs			
Cash operating costs ($800,000/yr. × 2 years; $460,000/yr. × 2 years)	1,600,000	920,000	$ 680,000
Book value of old machine			
Periodic write-off as depreciation or	400,000	—	—
Lump-sum write-off	—	400,000[a]	
Current disposal value of old machine	—	(40,000)[a]	40,000
New machine cost, written off periodically as depreciation	—	600,000	(600,000)
Total operating costs	2,000,000	1,880,000	120,000
Operating income	$ 200,000	$ 320,000	$(120,000)

[a]In a formal income statement, these two items would be combined as "loss on disposal of machine" of $360,000.

[5] See Chapter 22 for a discussion of time-value-of-money and income-tax considerations in capital investment decisions.

EXHIBIT 12-12 Cost Comparison: Replacement of Machine, Relevant Items Only, for Toledo Company

	Two Years Together		
	Keep (1)	Replace (2)	Difference (3) = (1) − (2)
Cash operating costs	$1,600,000	$ 920,000	$680,000
Current disposal value of old machine	—	(40,000)	40,000
New machine, written off periodically as depreciation	—	600,000	(600,000)
Total relevant costs	$1,600,000	$1,480,000	$120,000

3. **Loss on disposal, $360,000.** This is the difference between amounts in items 1 and 2. This amount is a meaningless combination blurring the distinction between the irrelevant book value and the relevant disposal value. Managers should consider each value separately, as was done in items 1 and 2.
4. **Cost of new machine, $600,000.** Relevant, because it is an expected future cost that will only occur if the company purchases the machine.

Exhibit 12-11 clarifies these assertions. Column 3 in Exhibit 12-11 shows that the book value of the old machine does not differ between the alternatives and could be ignored for decision-making purposes. No matter what the timing of the write-off—whether a lump-sum charge in the current year or depreciation charges over the next 2 years—the total amount is still $400,000 because it is a past (historical) cost. In contrast, the $600,000 cost of the new machine and the current disposal value of $40,000 for the old machine are relevant because they would not arise if Toledo's managers decided not to replace the machine. Considering the cost of replacing the machine and savings in cash operating costs, Toledo's managers should replace the machine because the operating income from replacing it is $120,000 higher for the 2 years together.

Exhibit 12-12 concentrates only on relevant items and leads to the same answer—-replacing the machine leads to lower costs and higher operating income of $120,000—even though book value is omitted from the calculations. The only relevant items are the cash operating costs, the disposal value of the old machine, and the cost of the new machine, which is represented as depreciation in Exhibit 12-12.

DECISION POINT

Is book value of existing equipment relevant in equipment-replacement decisions?

Decisions and Performance Evaluation

Consider our equipment-replacement example in light of the five-step sequence in Exhibit 12-1 (page 468):

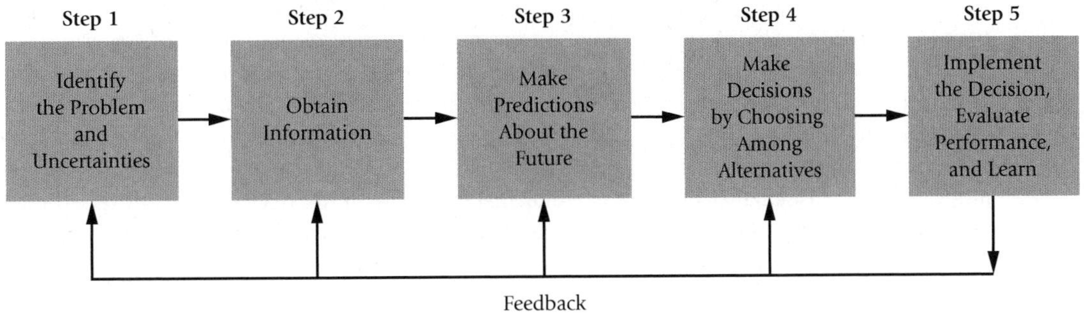

The decision model (Step 4), which is presented in Exhibits 12-11 and 12-12, dictates replacing the machine rather than keeping it. In the real world, however, would the manager

LEARNING OBJECTIVE 8

Explain how conflicts can arise between the decision model a manager uses and the performance-evaluation model top management uses to evaluate managers

... tell managers to take a multiple-year view in decision making but judge their performance only on the basis of the current year's operating income

replace the machine? An important factor is the manager's perception of whether the decision model is consistent with how the company will judge his or her performance after the decision is implemented (the performance-evaluation model in Step 5).

From the perspective of their own careers, managers tend to favor the alternative that makes their performance look better. In our earlier examples, the decision model and the performance-evaluation model were consistent. If, however, the performance-evaluation model conflicts with the decision model, the performance-evaluation model often prevails in influencing managers' decisions. The following table compares Toledo's accrual accounting income for the first year and the second year when the manager decides to keep the machine versus when the manager decides to replace the machine.

	Accrual Accounting First-Year Results		Accrual Accounting Second-Year Results	
	Keep	Replace	Keep	Replace
Revenues	$1,100,000	$1,100,000	$1,100,000	$1,100,000
Operating costs				
Cash-operating costs	800,000	460,000	800,000	460,000
Depreciation	200,000	300,000	200,000	300,000
Loss on disposal	—	360,000	—	—
Total operating costs	1,000,000	1,120,000	1,000,000	760,000
Operating income (loss)	$ 100,000	$ (20,000)	$ 100,000	$ 340,000

Total accrual accounting income for the 2 years together is $120,000 higher if the machine is replaced, as in Exhibit 12-11. But if the promotion or bonus of the manager at Toledo hinges on his or her first year's operating-income performance under accrual accounting, the manager would be very tempted to keep the old machine. Why? Because the accrual accounting model for measuring performance will show a first-year operating income of $100,000 if the old machine is kept versus an operating loss of $20,000 if the machine is replaced. Even though top management's goals encompass the 2-year period (consistent with the decision model), the manager will focus on first-year results if top management evaluates his or her performance on the basis of short-run measures such as the first-year's operating income.

It is often difficult to resolve the conflict between the decision model and the performance-evaluation model. In theory, resolving the difficulty seems obvious: Senior managers should design models that are consistent. Consider our replacement example. Year-by-year effects on operating income of replacement can be budgeted for the 2-year planning horizon. The lower-level manager then would be evaluated on the expectation that the first year would be poor and the next year would be much better. Doing this for every decision, however, makes the performance-evaluation model very cumbersome. As a result of these practical difficulties, accounting systems rarely track each decision separately. Performance evaluation focuses on responsibility centers for a specific period, not on projects or individual items of equipment over their useful lives. Thus, the effects of many different decisions are combined in a single performance report and evaluation measure, say operating income. Lower-level managers make decisions to maximize operating income, and top management—through the reporting system—is rarely aware of particular desirable alternatives that lower-level managers did *not* choose because of conflicts between the decision and performance-evaluation models.

DECISION POINT

How can conflicts arise between the decision model a manager uses and the performance-evaluation model top management uses to evaluate that manager?

Consider another conflict between the decision model and the performance-evaluation model. Suppose a manager buys a particular machine only to discover shortly afterward that he or she could have purchased a better machine instead. The decision model may suggest replacing the machine that was just bought with the better machine, but will the manager do so? Probably not. Why? Because replacing the machine so soon after its purchase will reflect badly on the manager's capabilities and performance. If the manager's bosses have no knowledge of the better machine, the manager may prefer to keep the recently purchased machine rather than alert them to the better machine.

Many managers consider it unethical to take actions that make their own performance look good when these actions are not in the best interests of the firm. But critics believe that it was precisely these kinds of behaviors that contributed to the global financial crisis in 2008. To discourage such behaviors, managers develop codes of conduct, emphasize values, and build cultures that focus on doing the right things. Chapter 24 discusses performance-evaluation models, ethics, and ways to reduce conflict between the decision model and the performance-evaluation model in more detail.

PROBLEM FOR SELF-STUDY

Wally Lewis is manager of the engineering development division of Goldcoast Products. Lewis has just received a proposal signed by his engineers to replace workstations with networked personal computers (networked PCs). Lewis is not enthusiastic about the proposal.

Data on workstations and networked PCs are as follows:

	Workstations	Networked PCs
Original cost	$ 300,000	$ 135,000
Useful life	5 years	3 years
Current age	2 years	0 years
Remaining useful life	3 years	3 years
Accumulated depreciation	$ 120,000	Not acquired yet
Current book value	$ 180,000	Not acquired yet
Current disposal value (in cash)	$ 95,000	Not acquired yet
Terminal disposal value (in cash 3 years from now)	$ 0	$ 0
Annual computer-related cash operating costs	$ 40,000	$ 10,000
Annual revenues	$1,000,000	$1,000,000
Annual non-computer-related cash operating costs	$ 880,000	$ 880,000

Lewis's annual bonus includes a component based on division operating income. He has a promotion possibility next year to become a group vice president of Goldcoast Products.

Required

1. Compare the costs of workstations and networked PCs. Consider the cumulative results for the 3 years together, ignoring the time value of money and income taxes.
2. Why might Lewis be reluctant to purchase the networked PCs?

Solution

1. The table on the following page considers all cost items when comparing future costs of workstations and networked PCs:

All Items	Three Years Together Workstations (1)	 Networked PCs (2)	 Difference (3) = (1) − (2)
Revenues	$3,000,000	$3,000,000	—
Operating costs			
Non-computer-related cash operating costs ($880,000 per year × 3 years)	2,640,000	2,640,000	—
Computer-related cash operating costs ($40,000 per year; $10,000 per year × 3 years)	120,000	30,000	$ 90,000
Workstations' book value			
Periodic write-off as depreciation or	180,000	—	—
Lump-sum write-off	—	180,000	
Current disposal value of workstations	—	(95,000)	95,000
Networked PCs, written off periodically as depreciation	—	135,000	(135,000)
Total operating costs	2,940,000	2,890,000	50,000
Operating income	$ 60,000	$ 110,000	$ (50,000)

Alternatively, the analysis could focus on only those items in the preceding table that differ between the alternatives.

Relevant Items	Three Years Together Workstations	 Networked PCs	 Difference
Computer-related cash operating costs ($40,000 per year × 3 years; $10,000 per year × 3 years)	$120,000	$ 30,000	$ 90,000
Current disposal value of workstations	—	(95,000)	95,000
Networked PCs, written off periodically as depreciation	—	135,000	(135,000)
Total relevant costs	$120,000	$ 70,000	$ 50,000

The analysis suggests that it is cheaper to replace the workstations with the networked PCs.

2. The accrual-accounting operating incomes *for the first year* under the alternatives of "keep workstations" versus the "buy networked PCs" are as follows:

	Keep Workstations		Buy Networked PCs	
Revenues		$1,000,000		$1,000,000
Operating costs				
Non-computer-related operating costs	$880,000		$880,000	
Computer-related cash operating costs	40,000		10,000	
Depreciation	60,000		45,000	
Loss on disposal of workstations	—		85,000[a]	
Total operating costs		980,000		1,020,000
Operating income (loss)		$ 20,000		$ (20,000)

[a] $85,000 = Book value of workstations, $180,000 − Current disposal value, $95,000.

Lewis would prefer to show an operating income of $20,000 if the workstations are kept than the operating loss of $20,000 if the networked PCs are purchased. Buying the networked PCs would eliminate the component of his bonus based on operating income. He might also perceive the $20,000 operating loss as reducing his chances of being promoted to group vice president.

DECISION POINTS

The following question-and-answer format summarizes the chapter's learning objectives. Each decision presents a key question related to a learning objective. The guidelines are the answer to that question.

Decision	Guidelines
1. What is the five-step process that managers can use to make decisions?	The five-step decision-making process is (a) identify the problem and uncertainties; (b) obtain information; (c) make predictions about the future; (d) make decisions by choosing among alternatives; and (e) implement the decision, evaluate performance, and learn.
2. When is a revenue or cost item relevant for a particular decision, and what potential problems should managers avoid in relevant-cost analysis?	To be relevant for a particular decision, a revenue or cost item must (a) be an expected future revenue or expected future cost and (b) differ among alternative courses of action. Relevant-revenue and relevant-cost analysis only consider quantitative outcomes that can be expressed in financial terms. But managers must also consider nonfinancial quantitative factors and qualitative factors, such as employee morale, when making decisions. Two potential problems to avoid in relevant-cost analysis are (a) making incorrect general assumptions—such as all variable costs are relevant and all fixed costs are irrelevant—and (b) losing sight of total fixed costs and focusing instead on unit fixed costs.
3. What is an opportunity cost, and why should managers consider it when making insourcing-versus-outsourcing decisions?	Opportunity cost is the contribution to income that is forgone by not using a limited resource in its next-best alternative use. Opportunity cost is included in decision making because the relevant cost of any decision is (a) the incremental cost of the decision plus (b) the opportunity cost of the profit forgone from making that decision. When capacity is constrained, managers must consider the opportunity cost of using the capacity when deciding whether to produce a product in-house versus outsourcing it.
4. When a resource is constrained, how should managers choose which of multiple products to produce and sell?	When a resource is constrained, managers should select the product that yields the highest contribution margin per unit of the constraining or limiting resource (factor). This will maximize total contribution margin.
5. What steps can managers take to manage bottlenecks?	Managers can take four steps to manage bottlenecks: (a) recognize that the bottleneck operation determines throughput (contribution) margin, (b) identify the bottleneck, (c) keep the bottleneck busy and subordinate all nonbottleneck operations to the bottleneck operation, and (d) increase bottleneck efficiency and capacity.
6. In deciding to add or drop customers or to add or discontinue branch offices or business divisions, what should managers focus on, and how should they take into account allocated overhead costs?	When making decisions about adding or dropping customers or adding or discontinuing branch offices and business divisions, managers should focus on only those costs that will change and any opportunity costs. Managers should ignore allocated overhead costs.
7. Is book value of existing equipment relevant in equipment-replacement decisions?	Book value of existing equipment is a past (historical or sunk) cost and, therefore, is irrelevant in equipment-replacement decisions.
8. How can conflicts arise between the decision model a manager uses and the performance-evaluation model top management uses to evaluate that manager?	Top management faces a persistent challenge: making sure that the performance-evaluation model of lower-level managers is consistent with the decision model. A common inconsistency is to tell these managers to take a multiple-year view in their decision making but then to judge their performance only on the basis of the current year's operating income.

APPENDIX

Linear Programming

In this chapter's Power Recreation example (pages 482–484), suppose both the snowmobile and boat engines must be tested on a very expensive machine before they are shipped to customers. The available machine-hours for testing are limited. Production data are as follows:

		Use of Capacity in Hours per Unit of Product		Daily Maximum Production in Units	
Department	Available Daily Capacity in Hours	Snowmobile Engine	Boat Engine	Snowmobile Engine	Boat Engine
Assembly	600 machine-hours	2.0 machine-hours	5.0 machine-hours	300[a] snowmobile engines	120 boat engines
Testing	120 testing-hours	1.0 machine-hour	0.5 machine-hour	120 snowmobile engines	240 boat engines

[a] For example, 600 machine-hours ÷ 2.0 machine-hours per snowmobile engine = 300, the maximum number of snowmobile engines that the assembly department can make if it works exclusively on snowmobile engines.

Exhibit 12-13 summarizes these and other relevant data. In addition, as a result of material shortages for boat engines, Power Recreation cannot produce more than 110 boat engines per day. How many engines of each type should Power Recreation's managers produce and sell daily to maximize operating income?

Because there are multiple constraints, managers can use a technique called *linear programming* (*LP*) to determine the number of each type of engine to produce. LP models typically assume that all costs are either variable or fixed for a single cost driver (units of output). We will see that LP models also require certain other linear assumptions to hold. When these assumptions fail, managers should consider other decision models.[6]

Steps in Solving an LP Problem

We use the data in Exhibit 12-13 to illustrate the three steps in solving an LP problem. Throughout this discussion, S equals the number of snowmobile engines produced and sold, and B equals the number of boat engines produced and sold.

Step 1: Determine the Objective Function. The **objective function** of a linear program expresses the objective or goal to be maximized (say, operating income) or minimized (say, operating costs). In our example, the objective is to find the combination of snowmobile engines and boat engines that maximizes total contribution margin. Fixed costs remain the same regardless of the product-mix decision and are irrelevant. The linear function expressing the objective for the total contribution margin (TCM) is

$$TCM = \$240S + \$375B$$

EXHIBIT 12-13 Operating Data for Power Recreation

	Department Capacity (per Day) in Product Units				
	Assembly	Testing	Selling Price	Variable Cost per Unit	Contribution Margin per Unit
Only snowmobile engines	300	120	\$ 800	\$560	\$240
Only boat engines	120	240	\$1,000	\$625	\$375

[6] Other decision models are described in Barry Render, Ralph M. Stair, and Michael E. Hanna, *Quantitative Analysis for Management*, 13th ed. (Upper Saddle River, NJ: Prentice Hall, 2017); and Steven Nahmias, *Production and Operations Analysis*, 7th ed. (New York: McGraw-Hill/Irwin, 2015).

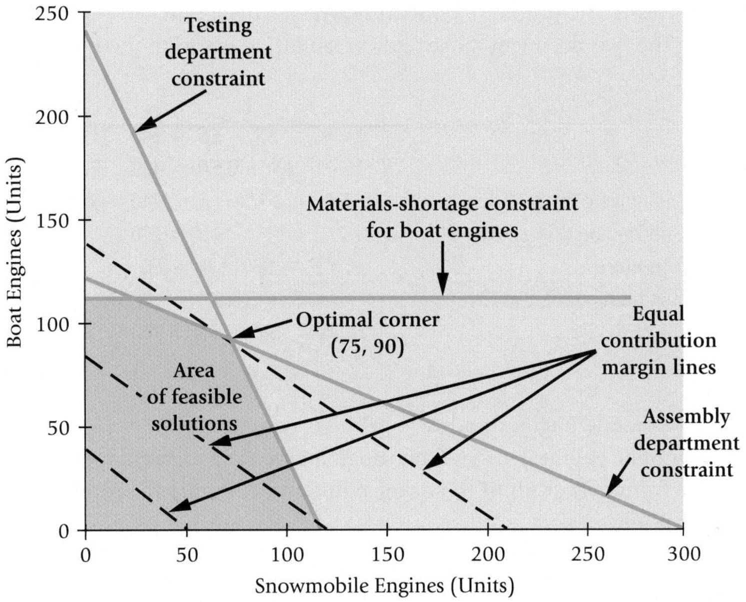

EXHIBIT 12-14

Linear Programming: Graphic Solution for Power Recreation

Step 2: Specify the Constraints. A **constraint** is a mathematical inequality or equality that must be satisfied by the variables in a mathematical model. The following linear inequalities express the relationships in our example:

Assembly department constraint	$2S + 5B \leq 600$
Testing department constraint	$1S + 0.5B \leq 120$
Materials-shortage constraint for boat engines	$B \leq 110$
Negative production is impossible	$S \geq 0$ and $B \geq 0$

The three solid lines on the graph in Exhibit 12-14 show the existing constraints for assembly and testing and the materials-shortage constraint.[7] The feasible or technically possible alternatives are those combinations of quantities of snowmobile engines and boat engines that satisfy all the constraining resources or factors. The shaded "area of feasible solutions" in Exhibit 12-14 shows the boundaries of those product combinations that are feasible.

Step 3: Compute the Optimal Solution. **Linear programming (LP)** is an optimization technique used to maximize the *objective function* when there are multiple *constraints*. We present two approaches for finding the optimal solution using LP: trial-and-error approach and graphic approach. These approaches are easy to use in our example because there are only two variables in the objective function and a small number of constraints. Understanding these approaches provides insight into LP. In most real-world LP applications, managers use computer software packages to calculate the optimal solution.[8]

Trial-and-Error Approach

Managers can find the optimal solution by trial and error, by working with coordinates of the corners of the area of feasible solutions. As we will see, the optimal solution always lies at an extreme point of the feasible region.

First, select any set of corner points and compute the total contribution margin. Five corner points appear in Exhibit 12-14. It is helpful to use simultaneous equations to obtain

[7] As an example of how the lines are plotted in Exhibit 12-14, use equal signs instead of inequality signs and assume for the assembly department that $B = 0$; then $S = 300$ (600 machine-hours $\div$ 2 machine-hours per snowmobile engine). Assume that $S = 0$; then $B = 120$ (600 machine-hours $\div$ 5 machine-hours per boat engine). Connect those two points with a straight line.

[8] Standard computer software packages rely on the *simplex method*, which is an iterative step-by-step procedure for determining the optimal solution to an LP problem. This method starts with a specific feasible solution and then tests it by substitution to see whether the result can be improved. These substitutions continue until no further improvement is possible and the optimal solution is obtained.

the exact coordinates in the graph. To illustrate, the corner point $(S = 75, B = 90)$ can be derived by solving the two pertinent constraint inequalities as simultaneous equations:

	$2S + 5B = 600$	(1)
	$1S + 0.5B = 120$	(2)
Multiplying (2) by 2:	$2S + B = 240$	(3)
Subtracting (3) from (1):	$4B = 360$	
Therefore,	$B = 360 \div 4 = 90$	
Substituting for B in (2):	$1S + 0.5(90) = 120$	
	$S = 120 - 45 = 75$	

Given $S = 75$ snowmobile engines and $B = 90$ boat engines, TCM = (\$240 per snowmobile engine × 75 snowmobile engines) + (\$375 per boat engine × 90 boat engines) = \$51,750.

Second, move from corner point to corner point and compute the total contribution margin at each corner point.

Trial	Corner Point (*S, B*)	Snowmobile Engines (*S*)	Boat Engines (*B*)	Total Contribution Margin
1	(0, 0)	0	0	\$240(0) + \$375(0) = \$0
2	(0, 110)	0	110	\$240(0) + \$375(110) = \$41,250
3	(25,110)	25	110	\$240(25) + \$375(110) = \$47,250
4	(75, 90)	75	90	\$240(75) + \$375(90) = \$51,750[a]
5	(120, 0)	120	0	\$240(120) + \$375(0) = \$28,800

[a] The optimal solution.

The optimal product mix is the mix that yields the highest total contribution: 75 snowmobile engines and 90 boat engines. To understand the solution, consider what happens when moving from the point (25, 110) to (75, 90). Power Recreation gives up \$7,500 $[\$375 \times (110 - 90)]$ in contribution margin from boat engines while gaining \$12,000 $[\$240 \times (75 - 25)]$ in contribution margin from snowmobile engines. This results in a net increase in contribution margin of \$4,500 $(\$12,000 - \$7,500)$, from \$47,250 to \$51,750.

Graphic Approach

Consider all possible combinations that will produce the same total contribution margin of, say, \$12,000. That is,

$$\$240S + \$375B = \$12,000$$

This set of \$12,000 contribution margins is a straight dashed line through $[S = 50$ $(\$12,000 \div \$240); B = 0]$ and $[S = 0; B = 32\ (\$12,000 \div \$375)]$ in Exhibit 12-14. Other equal total contribution margins can be represented by lines parallel to this one. In Exhibit 12-14, we show three dashed lines. Lines drawn farther from the origin represent more sales of both products and higher amounts of equal contribution margins.

The optimal line is the one farthest from the origin but still passing through a point in the area of feasible solutions. This line represents the highest total contribution margin. The optimal solution—the number of snowmobile engines and boat engines that will maximize the objective function, total contribution margin—is the corner point $(S = 75, B = 90)$. This solution will become apparent if you put a straight-edge ruler on the graph and move it outward from the origin and parallel with the \$12,000 contribution margin line. Move the ruler as far away from the origin as possible—that is, increase the total contribution margin—without leaving the area of feasible solutions. In general, the optimal solution in a maximization problem lies at the corner where the dashed line intersects an extreme point of the area of feasible solutions. Moving the ruler out any farther puts it outside the area of feasible solutions.

Sensitivity Analysis

What are the implications of uncertainty about the accounting or technical coefficients used in the objective function (such as the contribution margin per unit of snowmobile engines or boat engines) or the constraints (such as the number of machine-hours it takes to make a snowmobile engine or a boat engine)? Consider how a change in the contribution margin of snowmobile engines from \$240 per unit to \$300 per unit would affect the optimal solution. Assume the contribution margin for boat engines remains unchanged at \$375 per unit. The revised objective function will be

$$TCM = \$300S + \$375B$$

Using the trial-and-error approach to calculate the total contribution margin for each of the five corner points described in the previous table, the optimal solution is still $(S = 75, B = 90)$. What if the contribution margin of snowmobile engines falls to \$160 per unit? The optimal solution remains the same $(S = 75, B = 90)$. Thus, big changes in the contribution margin per unit of snowmobile engines have no effect on the optimal solution in this case. That's because, although the slopes of the equal contribution margin lines in Exhibit 12-14 change as the contribution margin of snowmobile engines changes from \$240 to \$300 to \$160 per unit, the farthest point at which the equal contribution margin lines intersect the area of feasible solutions is still $(S = 75, B = 90)$.

TERMS TO LEARN

This chapter and the Glossary at the end of the text contain definitions of the following important terms:

book value (**p. 491**)
business function costs (**p. 470**)
constraint (**p. 499**)
decision model (**p. 467**)
differential cost (**p. 476**)
differential revenue (**p. 476**)
full costs of the product (**p. 470**)
incremental cost (**p. 476**)
incremental revenue (**p. 476**)
insourcing (**p. 474**)
linear programming (LP) (**p. 499**)
make-or-buy decisions (**p. 474**)
objective function (**p. 498**)
one-time-only special order (**p. 470**)
opportunity cost (**p. 478**)
outsourcing (**p. 474**)
product-mix decisions (**p. 482**)
qualitative factors (**p. 469**)
quantitative factors (**p. 469**)
relevant costs (**p. 467**)
relevant revenues (**p. 467**)
sunk costs (**p. 468**)
theory of constraints (TOC) (**p. 484**)
throughput margin (**p. 484**)

ASSIGNMENT MATERIAL

Questions

12-1 Outline the five-step sequence in a decision process.
12-2 Define relevant costs. Why are historical costs irrelevant?
12-3 "All future costs are relevant." Do you agree? Why?
12-4 Distinguish between quantitative and qualitative factors in decision making.
12-5 Describe two potential problems that should be avoided in relevant-cost analysis.
12-6 "Variable costs are always relevant, and fixed costs are always irrelevant." Do you agree? Why?
12-7 "A component part should be purchased whenever the purchase price is less than its total manufacturing cost per unit." Do you agree? Why?
12-8 Define opportunity cost.
12-9 "Managers should always buy inventory in quantities that result in the lowest purchase cost per unit." Do you agree? Why?
12-10 "Management should always maximize sales of the product with the highest contribution margin per unit." Do you agree? Why?
12-11 "A branch office or business segment that shows negative operating income should be shut down." Do you agree? Explain briefly.
12-12 "Cost written off as depreciation on equipment already purchased is always irrelevant." Do you agree? Why?

12-13 "Managers will always choose the alternative that maximizes operating income or minimizes costs in the decision model." Do you agree? Why?

12-14 Describe the three steps in solving a linear programming problem.

12-15 How might the optimal solution of a linear programming problem be determined?

Multiple-Choice Questions

In partnership with: BECKER PROFESSIONAL EDUCATION®

12-16 Qualitative and quantitative factors. Which of the following is not a qualitative factor that Atlas Manufacturing should consider when deciding whether to buy or make a part used in manufacturing their product?

a. Quality of the outside producer's product.
b. Potential loss of trade secrets.
c. Manufacturing deadlines and special orders.
d. Variable cost per unit of the product.

12-17 Special order, opportunity cost. Chade Corp. is considering a special order brought to it by a new client. If Chade determines the variable cost to be $9 per unit, and the contribution margin of the next best alternative of the facility to be $5 per unit, then if Chade has

a. Full capacity, the company will be profitable at $4 per unit.
b. Excess capacity, the company will be profitable at $6 per unit.
c. Full capacity, the selling price must be greater than $5 per unit.
d. Excess capacity, the selling price must be greater than $9 per unit.

12-18 Special order, opportunity cost. In order to determine whether a special order should be accepted at full capacity, the sales price of the special order must be compared to the per unit

a. Contribution margin of the special order.
b. Variable cost and contribution margin of the special order.
c. Variable cost and contribution margin of the next best alternative.
d. Variable cost of current production and the contribution margin of the next best alternative.

12-19 Keep or drop a business segment. Lees Corp. is deciding whether to keep or drop a small segment of its business. Key information regarding the segment include:

Contribution margin: 35,000
Avoidable fixed costs: 30,000
Unavoidable fixed costs: 25,000

Given the information above, Lees should

a. Drop the segment because the contribution margin is less than total fixed costs.
b. Drop the segment because avoidable fixed costs exceed unavoidable fixed costs.
c. Keep the segment because the contribution margin exceeds avoidable fixed costs.
d. Keep the segment because the contribution margin exceeds unavoidable fixed costs.

12-20 Relevant costs. Ace Cleaning Service is considering expanding into one or more new market areas. Which costs are relevant to Ace's decision on whether to expand?

	Sunk Costs	Variable Costs	Opportunity Costs
a.	No	Yes	Yes
b.	Yes	Yes	Yes
c.	No	Yes	No
d.	Yes	No	Yes

Exercises

12-21 Disposal of assets. Answer the following questions.

1. A company has an inventory of 1,250 assorted parts for a line of missiles that has been discontinued. The inventory cost is $72,000. The parts can be either (a) remachined at total additional costs of $28,000 and then sold for $33,500 or (b) sold as scrap for $3,500. Which action is more profitable? Show your calculations.
2. A truck, costing $103,500 and uninsured, is wrecked its first day in use. It can be either (a) disposed of for $16,500 cash and replaced with a similar truck costing $102,000 or (b) rebuilt for $84,000 and thus be brand-new as far as operating characteristics and looks are concerned. Which action is less costly? Show your calculations.

12-22 Relevant and irrelevant costs. Answer the following questions.

1. Davanit Computers makes 5,600 units of a circuit board, CB76, at a cost of $200 each. Variable cost per unit is $160 and fixed cost per unit is $40. Peach Electronics offers to supply 5,600 units of CB76 for $180. If Davanit buys from Peach, it will be able to save $15 per unit in fixed costs but continue to incur the remaining $25 per unit. Should Davanit accept Peach's offer? Explain.
2. LF Manufacturing is deciding whether to keep or replace an old machine. It obtains the following information:

	Old Machine	New Machine
Original cost	$10,900	$ 8,200
Useful life	10 years	3 years
Current age	7 years	0 years
Remaining useful life	3 years	3 years
Accumulated depreciation	$ 7,630	Not acquired yet
Book value	$ 3,270	Not acquired yet
Current disposal value (in cash)	$ 2,700	Not acquired yet
Terminal disposal value (3 years from now)	$ 0	$ 0
Annual cash operating costs	$17,500	$14,500

LF Manufacturing uses straight-line depreciation. Ignore the time value of money and income taxes. Should LF Manufacturing replace the old machine? Explain.

12-23 Multiple choice. (CPA) Choose the best answer.

1. The Fresno Company manufactures slippers and sells them at $13 a pair. Variable manufacturing cost is $6.50 a pair, and allocated fixed manufacturing cost is $2.00 a pair. It has enough idle capacity available to accept a one-time-only special order of 5,000 pairs of slippers at $8.50 a pair. Fresno will not incur any marketing costs as a result of the special order. What would the effect on operating income be if the special order could be accepted without affecting normal sales: (a) $0, (b) $10,000 increase, (c) $32,500 increase, or (d) $42,500 increase? Show your calculations.
2. The Portland Company manufactures Part No. 498 for use in its production line. The manufacturing cost per unit for 20,000 units of Part No. 498 is as follows:

Direct materials	$ 4
Variable direct manufacturing labor	22
Variable manufacturing overhead	17
Fixed manufacturing overhead allocated	20
Total manufacturing cost per unit	$63

The Counter Company has offered to sell 20,000 units of Part No. 498 to Portland for $58 per unit. Portland will make the decision to buy the part from Counter if there is an overall savings of at least $20,000 for Portland. If Portland accepts Counter's offer, $5 per unit of the fixed manufacturing overhead allocated would be eliminated. Furthermore, Portland has determined that the released facilities could be used to save relevant costs in the manufacture of Part No. 575. For Portland to achieve an overall savings of $20,000, the amount of relevant costs that would have to be saved by using the released facilities in the manufacture of Part No. 575 would be which of the following: (a) $100,000, (b) $220,000, (c) $20,000, or (d) $300,000? Show your calculations. What other factors might Portland consider before outsourcing to Counter?

12-24 Special order, activity-based costing. (CMA, adapted) The Reward One Company manufactures windows. Its manufacturing plant has the capacity to produce 12,000 windows each month. Current production and sales are 10,000 windows per month. The company normally charges $250 per window. Cost information for the current activity level is as follows:

Variable costs that vary with number of units produced	
Direct materials	$ 600,000
Direct manufacturing labor	700,000
Variable costs (for setups, materials handling, quality control, and so on) that vary with number of batches, 100 batches × $1,500 per batch	150,000
Fixed manufacturing costs	250,000
Fixed marketing costs	400,000
Total costs	$2,100,000

Reward One has just received a special one-time-only order for 2,000 windows at $225 per window. Accepting the special order would not affect the company's regular business or its fixed costs. Reward One makes windows for its existing customers in batch sizes of 100 windows (100 batches × 100 windows per batch = 10,000 windows). The special order requires Reward One to make the windows in 25 batches of 80 windows.

Required

1. Should Reward One accept this special order? Show your calculations.
2. Suppose plant capacity were only 11,000 windows instead of 12,000 windows each month. The special order must either be taken in full or be rejected completely. Should Reward One accept the special order? Show your calculations.
3. As in requirement 1, assume that monthly capacity is 12,000 windows. Reward One is concerned that if it accepts the special order, its existing customers will immediately demand a price discount of $20 in the month in which the special order is being filled. They would argue that Reward One's capacity costs are now being spread over more units and that existing customers should get the benefit of these lower costs. Should Reward One accept the special order under these conditions? Show your calculations.

12-25 Make versus buy, activity-based costing. The Svenson Corporation manufactures cellular modems. It manufactures its own cellular modem circuit boards (CMCB), an important part of the cellular modem. It reports the following cost information about the costs of making CMCBs in 2020 and the expected costs in 2021:

	Current Costs in 2020	Expected Costs in 2021
Variable manufacturing costs		
Direct material cost per CMCB	$ 180	$ 170
Direct manufacturing labor cost per CMCB	50	45
Variable manufacturing cost per batch for setups, materials handling, and quality control	1,600	1,500
Fixed manufacturing cost		
Fixed manufacturing overhead costs that can be avoided if CMCBs are not made	320,000	320,000
Fixed manufacturing overhead costs of plant depreciation, insurance, and administration that cannot be avoided even if CMCBs are not made	800,000	800,000

Svenson manufactured 8,000 CMCBs in 2020 in 40 batches of 200 each. In 2021, Svenson anticipates needing 10,000 CMCBs. The CMCBs would be produced in 80 batches of 125 each.

The Minton Corporation has approached Svenson about supplying CMCBs to Svenson in 2021 at $300 per CMCB on whatever delivery schedule Svenson wants.

Required

1. Calculate the total expected manufacturing cost per unit of making CMCBs in 2021.
2. Suppose the capacity currently used to make CMCBs will become idle if Svenson purchases CMCBs from Minton. On the basis of financial considerations alone, should Svenson make CMCBs or buy them from Minton? Show your calculations.

3. Now suppose that if Svenson purchases CMCBs from Minton, its best alternative use of the capacity currently used for CMCBs is to make and sell special circuit boards (CB3s) to the Essex Corporation. Svenson estimates the following incremental revenues and costs from CB3s:

Total expected incremental future revenues	$2,000,000
Total expected incremental future costs	$2,150,000

On the basis of financial considerations alone, should Svenson make CMCBs or buy them from Minton? Show your calculations.

12-26 Inventory decision, opportunity costs. Ever Lawn, a manufacturer of lawn mowers, predicts that it will purchase 228,000 spark plugs next year. Ever Lawn estimates that 19,000 spark plugs will be required each month. A supplier quotes a price of $7 per spark plug. The supplier also offers a special discount option: If all 228,000 spark plugs are purchased at the start of the year, a discount of 4% off the $7 price will be given. Ever Lawn can invest its cash at 10% per year. It costs Ever Lawn $210 to place each purchase order.

Required

1. What is the opportunity cost of interest forgone from purchasing all 228,000 units at the start of the year instead of in 12 monthly purchases of 19,000 units per order?
2. Would this opportunity cost be recorded in the accounting system? Why?
3. Should Ever Lawn purchase 228,000 units at the start of the year or 19,000 units each month? Show your calculations.
4. What other factors should Ever Lawn consider when making its decision?

12-27 Relevant costs, contribution margin, product emphasis. The Seashore Stand is a take-out food store at a popular beach resort. Cindy Smith, owner of the Seashore Stand, is deciding how much refrigerator space to devote to four different drinks. Pertinent data on these four drinks are as follows:

	Cola	Lemonade	Punch	Natural Orange Juice
Selling price per case	$19.25	$20.60	$27.70	$38.80
Variable cost per case	$13.80	$16.90	$20.90	$30.30
Cases sold per foot of shelf space per day	7	20	22	4

Smith has a maximum front shelf space of 12 feet to devote to the four drinks. She wants a minimum of 1 foot and a maximum of 6 feet of front shelf space for each drink.

Required

1. Calculate the contribution margin per case of each type of drink.
2. A coworker of Smith's recommends that she maximize the shelf space devoted to those drinks with the highest contribution margin per case. Do you agree with this recommendation? Explain briefly.
3. What shelf-space allocation for the four drinks would you recommend for the Seashore Stand? Show your calculations.

12-28 Selection of most profitable product. Planet Fit, Inc., produces two basic types of weight-lifting equipment, Model 9 and Model 14. Pertinent data are as follows:

	Per Unit	
	Model 9	Model 14
Selling price	$125.00	$65.00
Costs		
Direct material	22.00	20.00
Variable direct manufacturing labor	12.00	10.00
Variable manufacturing overhead	21.00	10.50
Fixed manufacturing overhead*	8.00	4.00
Marketing (all variable)	11.00	7.00
Total costs	74.00	51.50
Operating income	$ 51.00	$13.50

*Allocated on the basis of machine-hours

The weight-lifting craze suggests that Planet Fit can sell enough of either Model 9 or Model 14 to keep the plant operating at full capacity. Both products are processed through the same production departments. Which product should the company produce? Briefly explain your answer.

Required

12-29 Theory of constraints, throughput margin, relevant costs. The Phoenix Corporation manufactures filing cabinets in two operations: machining and finishing. It provides the following information:

	Machining	Finishing
Annual capacity	160,000 units	135,000 units
Annual production	135,000 units	135,000 units
Fixed operating costs (excluding direct materials)	$1,620,000	$1,350,000
Fixed operating costs per unit produced ($1,620,000 ÷ 135,000; $1,350,000 ÷ 135,000)	$ 12 per unit	$ 10 per unit

Each cabinet sells for $100 and has direct material costs of $70 incurred at the start of the machining operation. Phoenix has no other variable costs. Phoenix can sell whatever output it produces. The following requirements refer only to the preceding data. There is no connection between the requirements.

Required

1. Phoenix is considering using some modern jigs and tools in the finishing operation that would increase annual finishing output by 1,400 units. The annual cost of these jigs and tools is $40,000. Should Phoenix acquire these tools? Show your calculations.
2. The production manager of the machining department has submitted a proposal to do faster setups that would increase the annual capacity of the machining department by 14,000 units and would cost $22,000 per year. Should Phoenix implement the change? Show your calculations.
3. An outside contractor offers to do the finishing operation for 18,000 units at $20 per unit, double the $10 per unit that it costs Phoenix to do the finishing in-house. Should Phoenix accept the subcontractor's offer? Show your calculations.
4. The Henry Corporation offers to machine 5,600 units at $6 per unit, half the $12 per unit that it costs Phoenix to do the machining in-house. Should Phoenix accept Henry's offer? Show your calculations.
5. Phoenix produces 1,800 defective units at the machining operation. What is the cost to Phoenix of the defective items produced? Explain your answer briefly.
6. Phoenix produces 1,800 defective units at the finishing operation. What is the cost to Phoenix of the defective items produced? Explain your answer briefly.

12-30 Closing and opening stores. Rivera Corporation runs two convenience stores, one in Connecticut and one in Rhode Island. Operating income for each store in 2020 is as follows:

	Connecticut Store	Rhode Island Store
Revenues	$1,110,000	$ 830,000
Operating costs		
Cost of goods sold	790,000	620,000
Lease rent (renewable each year)	94,000	79,000
Labor costs (paid on an hourly basis)	49,000	37,000
Depreciation of equipment	24,000	23,000
Utilities (electricity, heating)	46,000	50,000
Allocated corporate overhead	47,000	39,000
Total operating costs	1,050,000	848,000
Operating income (loss)	$ 60,000	$ (18,000)

The equipment has a zero disposal value. In a senior management meeting, Maria Lopez, the management accountant at Rivera Corporation, makes the following comment: "Rivera can increase its profitability by closing down the Rhode Island store or by adding another store like it."

Required

1. By closing down the Rhode Island store, Rivera can reduce overall corporate overhead costs by $46,000. Calculate Rivera's operating income if it closes the Rhode Island store. Is Maria Lopez's statement about the effect of closing the Rhode Island store correct? Explain.
2. Calculate Rivera's operating income if it keeps the Rhode Island store open and opens another store with revenues and costs identical to the Rhode Island store (including a cost of $23,000 to acquire equipment with a 1-year useful life and zero disposal value). Opening this store will increase corporate overhead costs by $5,000. Is Maria Lopez's statement about the effect of adding another store like the Rhode Island store correct? Explain.

12-31 Choosing customers. Central Printers operates a printing press with a monthly capacity of 4,000 machine-hours. Central has two main customers: Trent Corporation and Jessica Corporation. Data on each customer for January are:

	Trent Corporation	Jessica Corporation	Total
Revenues	$270,000	$180,000	$450,000
Variable costs	150,000	125,000	275,000
Contribution margin	120,000	55,000	175,000
Fixed costs (allocated)	96,000	64,000	160,000
Operating income	$ 24,000	$ (9,000)	$ 15,000
Machine-hours required	3,000 hours	1,000 hours	4,000 hours

Jessica Corporation indicates that it wants Central to do an *additional* $180,000 worth of printing jobs during February. These jobs are identical to the existing business Central did for Jessica in January in terms of variable costs and machine-hours required. Central anticipates that the business from Trent Corporation in February will be the same as that in January. Central can choose to accept as much of the Trent and Jessica business for February as its capacity allows. Assume that total machine-hours and fixed costs for February will be the same as in January.

Required

What action should Central take to maximize its operating income? Show your calculations. What other factors should Central consider before making a decision?

12-32 Relevance of equipment costs. Janet's Bakery is thinking about replacing the convection oven with a new, more energy-efficient model. Information related to the old and new ovens follows:

	Old Oven	New Oven
Original cost	$21,000	$40,000
Accumulated depreciation	$ 6,000	Not acquired yet
Book value	$15,000	Not acquired yet
Current disposal value	$10,000	Not acquired yet
Installation cost	Not applicable	$2,000
Annual operating cost	$12,000	$5,000
Useful life	7 years	5 years
Current age	2 years	0 years
Remaining useful life	5 years	5 years
Terminal disposal value (in 5 years)	$ 0	$ 0

Ignore the effect of income taxes and the time value of money.

Required

1. Which of the costs and benefits above are relevant to the decision to replace the oven?
2. What information is irrelevant? Why is it irrelevant?
3. Should Janet's Bakery purchase the new oven? Provide support for your answer.
4. Is there any conflict between the decision model and the incentives of the manager who has purchased the "old" oven and is considering replacing it only 2 years later?
5. At what purchase price would Janet's Bakery be indifferent between purchasing the new oven and continuing to use the old oven?

12-33 Equipment upgrade versus replacement. (A. Spero, adapted) The TechGuide Company produces and sells 7,500 modular computer desks per year at a selling price of $750 each. Its current production equipment, purchased for $1,800,000 and with a 5-year useful life, is only 2 years old. It has a terminal disposal value of $0 and is depreciated on a straight-line basis. The equipment has a current disposal price of $450,000. However, the emergence of a new molding technology has led TechGuide to consider either upgrading or replacing the production equipment. The following table presents data for the two alternatives:

	A	B	C
1		Upgrade	Replace
2	One-time equipment costs	$3,000,000	$4,800,000
3	Variable manufacturing cost per desk	$ 150	$ 75
4	Remaining useful life of equipment (in years)	3	3
5	Terminal disposal value of equipment	$ 0	$ 0

All equipment costs will continue to be depreciated on a straight-line basis. For simplicity, ignore income taxes and the time value of money.

Required

1. Should TechGuide upgrade its production line or replace it? Show your calculations.
2. Now suppose the one-time equipment cost to replace the production equipment is somewhat negotiable. All other data are as given previously. What is the maximum one-time equipment cost that TechGuide would be willing to pay to replace rather than upgrade the old equipment?
3. Assume that the capital expenditures to replace and upgrade the production equipment are as given in the original exercise, but that the production and sales quantity is not known. For what production and sales quantity would TechGuide (a) upgrade the equipment or (b) replace the equipment?
4. Assume that all data are as given in the original exercise. Dan Doria is TechGuide's manager, and his bonus is based on operating income. Because he is likely to relocate after about a year, his current bonus is his primary concern. Which alternative would Doria choose? Explain.

Problems

12-34 Special order, short-run pricing. Diamond Corporation produces baseball bats for kids that it sells for $37 each. At capacity, the company can produce 54,000 bats a year. The costs of producing and selling 54,000 bats are as follows:

	Cost per Bat	Total Costs
Direct materials	$14	$ 756,000
Variable direct manufacturing labor	4	216,000
Variable manufacturing overhead	2	108,000
Fixed manufacturing overhead	5	270,000
Variable selling expenses	2	108,000
Fixed selling expenses	3	162,000
Total costs	$30	$1,620,000

Required

1. Suppose Diamond is currently producing and selling 44,000 bats. At this level of production and sales, its fixed costs are the same as given in the preceding table. Home Run Corporation wants to place a one-time special order for 10,000 bats at $21 each. Diamond will incur no variable selling costs for this special order. Should Diamond accept this one-time special order? Show your calculations.
2. Now suppose Diamond is currently producing and selling 54,000 bats. If Diamond accepts Home Run's offer, it will have to sell 10,000 fewer bats to its regular customers. (a) On financial considerations alone, should Diamond accept this one-time special order? Show your calculations. (b) On financial considerations alone, at what price would Diamond be indifferent between accepting the special order and continuing to sell to its regular customers at $37 per bat. (c) What other factors should Diamond consider in deciding whether to accept the one-time special order?

12-35 Short-run pricing, capacity constraints. Jersey Acres Dairy, maker of specialty cheeses, produces a soft cheese from the milk of Friesian cows raised on a special corn-based diet. One kilogram of soft cheese, which has a contribution margin of $8, requires 4 liters of milk. A well-known gourmet restaurant has asked Jersey Acres to produce 2,000 kilograms of a hard cheese from the same milk of Friesian cows. Knowing that the dairy has sufficient unused capacity, Ellen Pavotti, owner of Jersey Acres, calculates the costs of making one kilogram of the desired hard cheese:

Milk (10 liters × $1.50 per liter)	$15
Variable direct manufacturing labor	4
Variable manufacturing overhead	2
Fixed manufacturing cost allocated	5
Total manufacturing cost	$26

Required

1. Suppose Jersey Acres can acquire all the Friesian milk that it needs. What is the minimum price per kilogram the company should charge for the hard cheese?
2. Now suppose that the Friesian milk is in short supply. Every kilogram of hard cheese Jersey Acres produces will reduce the quantity of soft cheese that it can make and sell. What is the minimum price per kilogram the company should charge to produce the hard cheese?

12-36 International outsourcing. Riverside Clippers Corp manufactures garden tools in a factory in Taneytown, Maryland. Recently, the company designed a collection of tools for professional use rather than consumer use. Management needs to make a good decision about whether to produce this line in their existing space in Maryland, where space is available or to accept an offer from a manufacturer in Taiwan. Data concerning the decision are as follows:

Expected annual sales of tools (in units)	800,000
Average selling price of tools	$12
Price quoted by Taiwanese company, in New Taiwanese Dollars (NTD)	175
Current exchange rate	35NTD = $1
Variable manufacturing costs	$4.75 per unit
Incremental annual fixed manufacturing costs associated with the new product line	$400,000
Variable selling and distribution costs[a]	$1 per unit
Annual fixed selling and distribution costs[a]	$220,000

[a] Selling and distribution costs are the same regardless of whether the tools are manufactured in Maryland or imported.

Required

1. Should Riverside Clippers Corp manufacture the 800,000 garden tools in the Maryland facility or purchase them from the supplier in Taiwan? Explain.
2. Riverside Clippers Corp believes that the U.S. dollar may weaken in the coming months against the New Taiwanese Dollar and does not want to face any currency risk. Assume that Riverside Clippers Corp can enter into a forward contract today to purchase 175 NTD for $5.35. Should Riverside Clippers Corp manufacture the 800,000 garden tools in the Maryland facility or purchase them from the Taiwan supplier? Explain.
3. What are some of the qualitative factors that Riverside Clippers Corp should consider when deciding whether to outsource the garden tools manufacturing to Taiwan?

12-37 Relevant costs, opportunity costs. Mitch McCalister, the general manager of Time Sprint, must decide when to release the new version of Time Sprint's fitness watch, TS-12. Development of TS-12 is complete, but the product has not yet been produced. The product can be shipped starting July 1, 2020.

The major problem is that Time Sprint has overstocked the previous version of its fitness watch, TS-11. McCalister knows that once TS-12 is introduced, Time Sprint will not be able to sell any more units of TS-11. Rather than just throwing away the inventory of TS-11, McCalister is wondering whether it might be better to continue to sell TS-11 for the next 3 months and introduce TS-12 on October 1, 2020, when the inventory of TS-11 will be sold out.

The following information is available:

	TS-11	TS-12
Selling price	$170	$220
Variable cost per unit	29	43
Development cost per unit	60	95
Marketing and administrative cost per unit	31	41
Total cost per unit	120	179
Operating income per unit	$ 50	$ 41

Development cost per unit for each product equals the total costs of developing the watch divided by the anticipated unit sales over the life of the product. Marketing and administrative costs are fixed costs in 2020, incurred to support all marketing and administrative activities of Time Sprint and are allocated to products on the basis of the budgeted revenues of each product. The preceding unit costs assume TS-12 will be introduced on October 1, 2020.

Required

1. On the basis of financial considerations alone, should McCalister introduce TS-12 on July 1, 2020, or wait until October 1, 2020? Show your calculations, clearly identifying relevant and irrelevant revenues and costs.
2. What other factors might McCalister consider in making a decision?

12-38 Opportunity costs and relevant costs. Sandy's Paint Shop paints exterior surfaces for commercial and residential customers. It charges $175 per hour for a crew of painters. For March 2020, Sandy expects the crew to operate at 80% of capacity, 160 hours of the 200 hours available that month.

Operating income for March 2020 is anticipated to be as follows:

Revenues ($175 × 160)	$28,000
Variable cost, including paint and labor ($100 × 160)	16,000
Fixed painting costs	2,500
Fixed marketing costs	3,000
Fixed administrative costs	3,500
Total costs	25,000
Operating income	$ 3,000

Jenny's Pizza has approached Sandy to paint its storefronts for $150 per hour. The job needs to be done in March 2020 and is expected to take 60 hours of the crew time. It is not expected to change fixed painting costs. There are no marketing or additional administrative costs associated with the Jenny job. Sandy must either take the entire job or none of it.

Required

1. Should Sandy's Paint Shop accept the special order? Show your calculations.
2. Perry's Paint Shop has offered to provide paint and a crew to Sandy for $125 per hour if she needs help in March 2020. Should Sandy (a) accept the special order and reject Perry's offer, (b) accept the special order and accept Perry's offer or (c) reject the special order. Show your calculations.
3. What other factors should Sandy consider in choosing among the three alternatives in requirement 2?

12-39 Opportunity costs. (H. Schaefer, adapted) The Wild Orchid Corporation is working at full production capacity producing 13,000 units of a unique product, Everlast. Manufacturing cost per unit for Everlast is as follows:

Direct materials	$10
Variable direct manufacturing labor	2
Manufacturing overhead	14
Total manufacturing cost	$26

Manufacturing overhead cost per unit is based on variable cost per unit of $8 and fixed costs of $78,000 (at full capacity of 13,000 units). Marketing cost per unit, all variable, is $4, and the selling price is $52.

A customer, the Apex Company, has asked Wild Orchid to produce 3,500 units of Stronglast, a modification of Everlast. Stronglast would require the same manufacturing processes as Everlast. Apex has offered to pay Wild Orchid $40 for a unit of Stronglast and share half of the marketing cost per unit.

Required

1. What is the opportunity cost to Wild Orchid of producing the 3,500 units of Stronglast? (Assume that no overtime is worked.)
2. The Chesapeake Corporation has offered to produce 3,500 units of Everlast for Wild Orchid so that Wild Orchid may accept the Apex offer. That is, if Wild Orchid accepts the Chesapeake offer, Wild Orchid would manufacture 9,500 units of Everlast and 3,500 units of Stronglast and purchase 3,500 units of Everlast from Chesapeake. Chesapeake would charge Wild Orchid $36 per unit to manufacture Everlast. On the basis of financial considerations alone, should Wild Orchid accept the Chesapeake offer? Show your calculations.
3. Suppose Wild Orchid had been working at less than full capacity, producing 9,500 units of Everlast, at the time the Apex offer was made. Calculate the minimum price Wild Orchid should accept for Stronglast under these conditions. (Ignore the previous $40 selling price.)

12-40 Make or buy, unknown level of volume. (A. Atkinson, adapted) Denver Engineering manufactures small engines that it sells to manufacturers who install them in products such as lawn mowers. The company currently manufactures all the parts used in these engines but is considering a proposal from an external supplier who wishes to supply the starter assemblies used in these engines.

The starter assemblies are currently manufactured in Division 3 of Denver Engineering. The costs relating to the starter assemblies for the past 12 months were as follows:

Direct materials	$ 400,000
Variable direct manufacturing labor	300,000
Manufacturing overhead	800,000
Total	$1,500,000

Over the past year, Division 3 manufactured 150,000 starter assemblies. The average cost for each starter assembly is $10 ($1,500,000 ÷ 150,000).

Further analysis of manufacturing overhead revealed the following information. Of the total manufacturing overhead, only 25% is considered variable. Of the fixed portion, $300,000 is an allocation of general overhead that will remain unchanged for the company as a whole if production of the starter assemblies is discontinued. A further $200,000 of the fixed overhead is avoidable if production of the starter assemblies is discontinued. The balance of the current fixed overhead, $100,000, is the division manager's salary. If Denver Engineering discontinues production of the starter assemblies, the manager of Division 3 will be transferred to Division 2 at the same salary. This move will allow the company to save the $80,000 salary that would otherwise be paid to attract an outsider to this position.

Required

1. Tutwiler Electronics, a reliable supplier, has offered to supply starter-assembly units at $8 per unit. Because this price is less than the current average cost of $10 per unit, the vice president of manufacturing is eager to accept this offer. On the basis of financial considerations alone, should Denver Engineering accept the outside offer? Show your calculations. (*Hint:* Production output in the coming year may be different from production output in the past year.)
2. How, if at all, would your response to requirement 1 change if the company could use the vacated plant space for storage and, in so doing, avoid $100,000 of outside storage charges currently incurred? Why is this information relevant or irrelevant?

12-41 Make versus buy, activity-based costing, opportunity costs. The Allen Company produces chairs. This year's expected production is 30,000 units. Currently, Allen makes the upholstery for the chairs in its factory. Allen's management accountant reports the following costs for the upholstery for the 30,000 chairs:

	Cost per Unit	Costs for 30,000 Units
Direct materials	$10.00	$300,000
Variable direct manufacturing labor	5.00	150,000
Variable manufacturing overhead	3.00	90,000
Variable inspection, setup, materials handling		120,000
Allocated fixed costs of plant administration, taxes, and insurance		105,000
Total costs		$765,000

Allen has received an offer from an outside vendor to supply the upholstery for the chairs Allen requires at $23 per chair.

Required

1. Assume that if the outside vendor supplies the upholstery, the facility where the upholstery is currently made will remain idle. On the basis of financial considerations alone, should Allen accept the outside vendor's offer at the anticipated volume of 30,000 chairs? Show your calculations.
2. For this question, assume that if the upholstery is purchased outside, the available unused facilities will be used to make pillows to match the chairs. Each pillow sells for $25 with a variable cost of $15. No other costs would change and the company expects to sell 10,000 pillows. On the basis of financial considerations alone, should Allen make or buy the upholstery for their chairs, assuming that 30,000 chairs are produced (and sold)? Show your calculations.
3. The sales manager at Allen is concerned that the estimate of 30,000 chairs may be high and believes that only 24,000 chairs will be sold. Production will be cut back, freeing up work space. This space can be used to make 10,000 pillows whether Allen buys the upholstery or makes it in-house. On the basis of financial considerations alone, should Allen purchase the upholstery from the outside vendor? Show your calculations.

12-42 Product mix, constrained resource. Wechsler Company produces three products: A130, B324, and C587. All three products use the same direct material, Brac. Unit data for the three products are as follows:

	Product		
	A130	B324	C587
Selling price	$252	$168	$210
Variable costs			
Direct materials	$ 72	$ 45	$ 27
Labor and other costs	$ 84	$ 81	$120
Quantity of Brac per unit	8 lb.	5 lb.	3 lb.

The demand for the products far exceeds the direct materials available to produce the products. Brac costs $9 per pound, and a maximum of 5,000 pounds is available each month. Wechsler must produce a minimum of 200 units of each product.

Required

1. How many units of product A130, B324, and C587 should Wechsler produce?
2. What is the maximum amount Wechsler would be willing to pay for another 1,200 pounds of Brac?

12-43 Product mix, special order. (N. Melumad, adapted) Gormley Precision Tools makes cutting tools for metalworking operations. It makes two types of tools: A6, a regular cutting tool, and EX4, a high-precision cutting tool. A6 is manufactured on a regular machine, but EX4 must be manufactured on both the regular machine and a high-precision machine. The following information is available:

	A6	EX4
Selling price	$ 180	$ 280
Variable manufacturing cost per unit	$ 110	$ 190
Variable marketing cost per unit	$ 20	$ 60
Budgeted total fixed overhead costs	$700,000	$1,100,000
Hours required to produce one unit on the regular machine	1.0	0.5

Additional information includes the following:

a. Gormley faces a capacity constraint on the regular machine of 50,000 hours per year.
b. The capacity of the high-precision machine is not a constraint.
c. Of the $1,100,000 budgeted fixed overhead costs of EX4, $600,000 are lease payments for the high-precision machine. This cost is charged entirely to EX4 because Gormley uses the machine exclusively to produce EX4. The company can cancel the lease agreement for the high-precision machine at any time without penalties.
d. All other overhead costs are fixed and cannot be changed.

Required

1. What product mix—that is, how many units of A6 and EX4—will maximize Gormley's operating income? Show your calculations.
2. Suppose Gormley can increase the annual capacity of its regular machines by 15,000 machine-hours at a cost of $300,000. Should Gormley increase the capacity of the regular machines by 15,000 machine-hours? By how much will Gormley's operating income increase or decrease? Show your calculations.
3. Suppose that the capacity of the regular machines has been increased to 65,000 hours. Gormley has been approached by Clark Corporation to supply 20,000 units of another cutting tool, V2, for $240 per unit. Gormley must either accept the order for all 20,000 units or reject it totally. V2 is exactly like A6 except that its variable manufacturing cost is $130 per unit. (It takes 1 hour to produce one unit of V2 on the regular machine, and variable marketing cost equals $20 per unit.) What product mix should Gormley choose to maximize operating income? Show your calculations.

12-44 Theory of constraints, throughput margin, and relevant costs. Washington Industries manufactures electronic testing equipment. Washington also installs the equipment at customers' sites and ensures that it functions smoothly. Additional information on the manufacturing and installation departments is as follows (capacities are expressed in terms of the number of units of electronic testing equipment):

	Equipment Manufactured	Equipment Installed
Annual capacity	285 units per year	250 units per year
Equipment manufactured and installed	250 units per year	250 units per year

Washington manufactures only 250 units per year because the installation department has only enough capacity to install 250 units. The equipment sells for $55,000 per unit (installed) and has direct material costs of $30,000. All costs other than direct material costs are fixed. The following requirements refer only to the preceding data. There is no connection between the requirements.

Required

1. Washington's engineers have found a way to reduce equipment manufacturing time. The new method would cost an additional $500 per unit and would allow Washington to manufacture 30 additional units a year. Should Washington implement the new method? Show your calculations.
2. Washington's designers have proposed a change in direct materials that would increase direct material costs by $2,000 per unit. This change would enable Washington to install 285 units of equipment each year. If Washington makes the change, it will implement the new design on all equipment sold. Should Washington use the new design? Show your calculations.
3. A new installation technique has been developed that will enable Washington's engineers to install seven additional units of equipment a year. The new method will increase installation costs by $145,000 each year. Should Washington implement the new technique? Show your calculations.
4. Washington is considering how to motivate workers to improve their productivity (output per hour). One proposal is to evaluate and compensate workers in the manufacturing and installation departments on the basis of their productivities. Do you think the new proposal is a good idea? Explain briefly.

12-45 Theory of constraints, contribution margin, sensitivity analysis. Mpharm Industries manufactures pharmaceutical products in two departments: mixing and tablet-making. Additional monthly information on the two departments follows. Each tablet contains 0.5 gram of direct materials.

	Mixing	Tablet Making
Capacity per hour	150 grams	200 tablets
Monthly capacity (2,000 hours available in each department)	300,000 grams	400,000 tablets
Monthly production	200,000 grams	390,000 tablets
Fixed operating costs (excluding direct materials)	$ 16,000	$ 39,000
Fixed operating cost per tablet ($16,000 ÷ 200,000 grams; $39,000 ÷ 390,000 tablets)	$ 0.08 per gram	$ 0.10 per tablet

The mixing department makes 200,000 grams of direct materials mixture (enough to make 400,000 tablets) because the tablet-making department has only enough capacity to process 400,000 tablets. All direct material costs of $156,000 are incurred in the mixing department. The tablet-making department manufactures only 390,000 tablets from the 200,000 grams of mixture processed; 2.5% of the direct materials mixture is lost in the tablet-making process. Each tablet sells for $1. All costs other than direct material costs are fixed costs. The following requirements refer only to the preceding data. There is no connection between the requirements.

Required

1. An outside contractor makes the following offer: If Mpharm will supply the contractor with 10,000 grams of mixture, the contractor will manufacture 19,500 tablets for Mpharm (allowing for the normal 2.5% loss of the mixture during the tablet-making process) at $0.12 per tablet. Should Mpharm accept the contractor's offer? Show your calculations.
2. Another company offers to prepare 20,000 grams of mixture a month from direct materials Mpharm supplies. The company will charge $0.07 per gram of mixture. Should Mpharm accept the company's offer? Show your calculations.
3. Mpharm's engineers have devised a method that would improve quality in the tablet-making department. They estimate that the 10,000 tablets currently being lost would be saved. The modification would cost $7,000 a month. Should Mpharm implement the new method? Show your calculations.
4. Suppose that Mpharm also loses 10,000 grams of mixture in its mixing department. These losses can be reduced to zero if the company is willing to spend $9,000 per month in quality-improvement methods. Should Mpharm adopt the quality-improvement method? Show your calculations.
5. What are the benefits of improving quality in the mixing department compared with improving quality in the tablet-making department?

12-46 Closing down divisions. Ainsley Corporation has four operating divisions. The budgeted revenues and expenses for each division for 2020 follow:

	Division			
	A	B	C	D
Sales	$504,000	$ 948,000	$960,000	$1,240,000
Cost of goods sold	440,000	930,000	765,000	925,000
Selling, general, and administrative expenses	96,000	202,500	144,000	210,000
Operating income/loss	$ (32,000)	$(184,500)	$ 51,000	$ 105,000

Further analysis of costs reveals the following percentages of variable costs in each division:

Cost of goods sold	90%	80%	90%	85%
Selling, general, and administrative expenses	50%	50%	60%	60%

Closing down any division would result in savings of 40% of the fixed costs of that division.

Top management is very concerned about the unprofitable divisions (A and B) and is considering closing them for the year.

Required

1. Calculate the increase or decrease in operating income if Ainsley closes division A.
2. Calculate the increase or decrease in operating income if Ainsley closes division B.
3. What other factors should the top management of Ainsley consider before making a decision?

12-47 Dropping a product line, selling more tours. Norman City Tour, offers two types of guided tours, basic and deluxe. Operating income for each tour type in 2020 follows:

	Basic	Deluxe
Revenues (500 × $900; 400 × $1,650)	$450,000	$660,000
Operating costs		
Administrative salaries	120,000	100,000
Guide wages	130,000	380,000
Supplies	50,000	100,000
Depreciation of equipment	25,000	60,000
Vehicle fuel	30,000	24,000
Allocated corporate overhead	45,000	66,000
Total operating costs	400,000	730,000
Operating income (loss)	$ 50,000	$ (70,000)

The equipment has a zero disposal value. Guide wages, supplies, and vehicle fuel are variable costs with respect to the number of tours. Administrative salaries are fixed costs with respect to the number of tours. Brad Barrett, Norman City Tour's president, is concerned about the losses incurred on the deluxe tours. He is considering dropping the deluxe tour and offering only the basic tour.

Required

1. If the deluxe tours are discontinued, one administrative position could be eliminated, saving the company $50,000. Assuming no change in the sales of basic tours, what effect would dropping the deluxe tour have on the company's operating income?
2. Refer back to the original data. If Norman City Tour drops the deluxe tours, Barrett estimates that sales of basic tours would increase by 50%. He believes that he could still eliminate the $50,000 administrative position. Equipment currently used for the deluxe tours would be used by the additional basic tours. Should Barrett drop the deluxe tour? Explain.
3. What additional factors should Barrett consider before dropping the deluxe tours?

12-48 Optimal product mix. (CMA adapted) Della Simpson, Inc., sells two popular brands of cookies: Della's Delight and Bonny's Bourbon. Della's Delight goes through the mixing and baking departments, and Bonny's Bourbon, a filled cookie, goes through the mixing, filling, and baking departments.

Michael Shirra, vice president for sales, believes that at the current price, Della Simpson can sell all of its daily production of Della's Delight and Bonny's Bourbon. Both cookies are made in batches of 3,000. In each department, the time required per batch and the total time available each day are as follows:

	A	B	C	D
1		Department Minutes		
2		Mixing	Filling	Baking
3	Della's Delight	30	0	10
4	Bonny's Bourbon	15	15	15
5	Total available per day	660	270	300

Revenue and cost data for each type of cookie are as follows:

	A	B	C
7		Della's	Bonny's
8		Delight	Bourbon
9	Revenue per batch	$ 475	$ 375
10	Variable cost per batch	175	125
11	Contribution margin per batch	$ 300	$ 250
12	Monthly fixed costs		
13	(allocated to each product)	$18,650	$22,350

Required

1. Using *D* to represent the batches of Della's Delight and *B* to represent the batches of Bonny's Bourbon made and sold each day, formulate Shirra's decision as an LP model.
2. Compute the optimal number of batches of each type of cookie that Della Simpson, Inc., should make and sell each day to maximize operating income.

12-49 Dropping a customer, activity-based costing, ethics. Justin Anders is the management accountant for Carey Restaurant Supply (CRS). Sara Brinkley, the CRS sales manager, and Justin are meeting to discuss the profitability of one of the customers, Donnelly's Pizza. Justin hands Sara the following analysis of Donnelly's activity during the last quarter, taken from CRS's activity-based costing system:

Sales	$43,680
Cost of goods sold (all variable)	26,180
Order processing (50 orders processed at $280 per order)	14,000
Delivery (5,000 miles driven at $0.70 per mile)	3,500
Rush orders (6 rush orders at $154 per rush order)	924
Customer sales visits (6 sales calls at $140 per call)	840
Total costs	45,444
Operating income	$ (1,764)

Sara looks at the report and remarks, "I'm glad to see all my hard work is paying off with Donnelly's. Sales have gone up 10% over the previous quarter!"

Justin replies, "Increased sales are great, but I'm worried about Donnelly's margin, Sara. We were showing a profit with Donnelly's at the lower sales level, but now we're showing a loss. Gross margin percentage this quarter was 40%, down five percentage points from the prior quarter. I'm afraid that corporate will push hard to drop them as a customer if things don't turn around."

"That's crazy," Sara responds. "A lot of that overhead for things like order processing, deliveries, and sales calls would just be allocated to other customers if we dropped Donnelly's. This report makes it look like we're losing money on Donnelly's when we're not. In any case, I am sure you can do something to make its profitability look closer to what we think it is. No one doubts that Donnelly's is a very good customer."

Required

1. Assume that Sara is partly correct in her assessment of the report. Upon further investigation, it is determined that 10% of the order processing costs and 20% of the delivery costs would not be avoidable if CRS were to drop Donnelly's. Would CRS benefit from dropping Donnelly's? Show your calculations.
2. Sara's bonus is based on meeting sales targets. Based on the preceding information regarding gross margin percentage, what might Sara have done last quarter to meet her target and receive her bonus? How might CRS revise its bonus system to address this?
3. Should Justin rework the numbers? How should he respond to Sara's comments about making Donnelly's look more profitable?

12-50 Equipment replacement decisions and performance evaluation. Susan Smith manages the Wexford plant of Sanchez Manufacturing. A representative of Darnell Engineering approaches Smith about replacing a large piece of manufacturing equipment that Sanchez uses in its process with a more efficient model. While the representative made some compelling arguments in favor of replacing the 3-year-old equipment, Smith is hesitant. Smith is hoping to be promoted next year to manager of the larger Detroit plant, and she knows that the accrual-basis net operating income of the Wexford plant will be evaluated closely as part of the promotion decision. The following information is available concerning the equipment-replacement decision:

	Old Machine	New Machine
Original cost	$900,000	$540,000
Useful life	5 years	2 years
Current age	3 years	0 years
Remaining useful life	2 years	2 years
Accumulated depreciation	$540,000	Not acquired yet
Book value	$360,000	Not acquired yet
Current disposal value (in cash)	$216,000	Not acquired yet
Terminal disposal value (in cash 2 years from now)	$0	$0
Annual operating costs (maintenance, energy, repairs, coolants, and so on)	$995,000	$800,000

Sanchez uses straight-line depreciation on all equipment. Annual depreciation expense for the old machine is $180,000 and will be $270,000 on the new machine if it is acquired. For simplicity, ignore income taxes and the time value of money.

Required

1. Assume that Smith's priority is to receive the promotion and she makes the equipment-replacement decision based on the next 1-year's accrual-based operating income. Which alternative would she choose? Show your calculations.
2. What are the relevant factors in the decision? Which alternative is in the best interest of the company over the next 2 years? Show your calculations.
3. At what cost would Smith be willing to purchase the new equipment? Explain.

Strategy, Balanced Scorecard, and Strategic Profitability Analysis

13

Olive Garden wants to know.

So do Target and PepsiCo. Even your local car dealer and transit authority are curious. They all want to know whether they are meeting their goals. Many companies, like Barclays PLC in the United Kingdom, have successfully used the balanced scorecard approach to measure their progress.

LEARNING OBJECTIVES

1. Recognize which of two generic strategies a company is using
2. Understand the four perspectives of the balanced scorecard
3. Analyze changes in operating income to evaluate strategy
4. Identify unused capacity and learn how to manage it

BARCLAYS TURNS TO THE BALANCED SCORECARD[1]

A series of scandals from 2008 to 2012 tarnished the reputation of Barclays, the British multinational bank. From fraudulently selling mortgage-backed securities in the run-up to the financial crisis to rigging a key interest rate called LIBOR, a benchmark rate that helps set global borrowing costs, Barclays' image and financial performance took a beating. When new leadership was tasked with turning Barclays around, the company turned to the balanced scorecard to change the company's performance goals and incentive structure.

Introduced in 2014, Barclays' balanced scorecard set out specific goals and metrics across each of the company's "5Cs": customer and client, colleague, citizenship, conduct, and company. With the goal of becoming the world's "go to" bank, the balanced scorecard became the instrument to ensuring Barclays was "helping people achieve their ambitions—in the right way" and balancing "stakeholders' needs across the short and long term."

Rather than focusing solely on short-term financial results, Barclays' balanced scorecard aligned the company's 5Cs with the broader perspectives of the balanced scorecard. Most notably, the learning and growth perspective incorporated Barclays' conduct and citizenship goals, which included new purpose and value

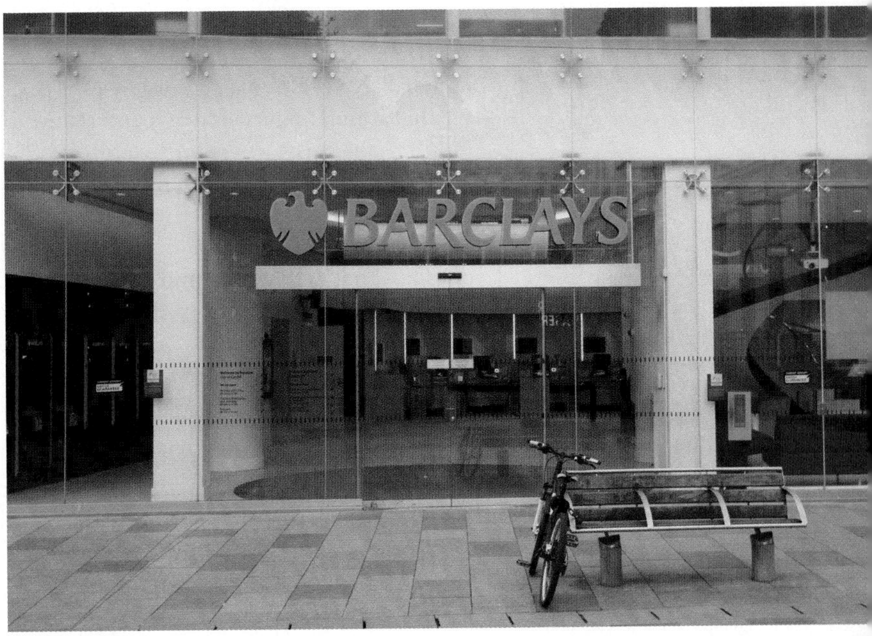

Matthew Horwood/Alamy Stock Photo

[1] *Sources:* Jed Horowitz, "New Barclays Chief Ties Executive Compensation to Societal Goals," *Reuters,* September 24, 2012 (http://www.reuters.com/article/us-barclays-jenkins-idUSBRE88N0YY20120924); Alex Brownsell, "Barclays Reveals '5Cs' Values Scorecard in Drive for Brand Transformation," *Marketing,* November 2, 2014 (http://www.marketingmagazine.co.uk/article/1230626/barclays-reveals-5cs-values-scorecard-drive-brand-transformation); Kadhim Shubber, "Barclays to Pay $2Bn to Settle US Mortgage Mis-Selling Probe," *Financial Times,* March 29, 2018 (https://www.ft.com/content/9ff69988-3352-11e8-ac48-10c6fdc22f03); Barclays PLC, "Barclays' Balanced Scorecard" (https://www.home.barclays/about-barclays/balanced-scorecard.html), accessed December 2018; Barclays PLC, 2017 Annual Report (London: Barclays PLC, 2018).

statements for the company. The company even took the extraordinary step of tying the performance bonuses of managers to Barclays' corporate ethics and citizenship goals, rather than just quarterly profits and stock price gains.

The company evolved its balanced scorecard performance measurement in 2016 to identify new key performance indicators (KPIs) that continued to prioritize customer and client, colleague, and citizenship metrics, underpinned by conduct and culture (renamed from company) firmwide. By 2018, Barclays was making significant progress toward its new KPIs. The company's recent annual report noted, "By incorporating a broad range of financial and non-financial measures, our framework is focused on achieving positive and sustainable outcomes for our diverse group of stakeholders, and influences incentive outcomes for Barclays' employees."

This chapter focuses on how management accounting information helps companies such as Cigna, Disney, Pfizer, and Siemens implement and evaluate their strategies. Strategy drives the operations of a company and guides managers' short- and long-run decisions. We describe the balanced scorecard approach to implementing strategy and methods to analyze operating income to evaluate the success of a strategy.

What Is Strategy?

LEARNING OBJECTIVE 1

Recognize which of two generic strategies a company is using

. . . product differentiation or cost leadership

Strategy specifies how an organization matches its own capabilities with the opportunities in the marketplace to accomplish its objectives. In other words, strategy describes how an organization can create value for its customers while differentiating itself from its competitors. For example, Walmart, the retail giant, creates value for its customers by locating stores in suburban and rural areas and by offering low prices, a wide range of product categories, and few choices within each product category. Consistent with this strategy, Walmart has developed the capability to keep costs down by aggressively negotiating low prices with its suppliers in exchange for high volumes and by maintaining a no-frills, cost-conscious environment with minimal sales staff.

In formulating its strategy, an organization must first thoroughly understand its industry. Industry analysis focuses on five forces: (1) competitors, (2) potential entrants into the market, (3) equivalent products, (4) bargaining power of customers, and (5) bargaining power of input suppliers.[2] The collective effect of these forces shapes an organization's profit potential. In general, profit potential decreases with greater competition, stronger potential entrants, products that are similar, and more demanding customers and suppliers. Below we illustrate these five forces for Chipset, Inc., a maker of linear integrated circuit devices (LICDs) used in amplifiers, modems, and communication networks. Chipset produces a single specialized product, CX1, a standard, high-performance microchip that can be used in multiple applications. Chipset designed CX1 after extensive market research and input from its customer base.

1. **Competitors.** The CX1 model faces severe competition based on price, timely delivery, and quality. Companies in the industry have high fixed costs and persistent pressures to reduce selling prices and utilize capacity fully. Price reductions spur growth because it makes LICDs a cost-effective option in applications such as digital subscriber lines (DSLs).
2. **Potential entrants into the market.** The small profit margins and high capital costs discourage new entrants. Moreover, incumbent companies such as Chipset have experience lowering costs and building close relationships with customers and suppliers.
3. **Equivalent products.** Chipset tailors CX1 to customer needs and lowers prices by continuously improving CX1's design and processes to reduce production costs. This reduces the risk of equivalent products or new technologies replacing CX1.
4. **Bargaining power of customers.** Customers, such as EarthLink and Verizon, negotiate aggressively with Chipset and its competitors to keep prices down because they buy large quantities of product.

[2] Michael Porter, *Competitive Strategy* (New York: Free Press, 1998); Michael Porter, *Competitive Advantage* (New York: Free Press, 1998); Michael Porter, "What Is Strategy?" *Harvard Business Review* (November–December 1996): 61–78.

5. **Bargaining power of input suppliers.** To produce CX1, Chipset requires high-quality materials (such as silicon wafers, pins for connectivity, and plastic or ceramic packaging) and skilled engineers, technicians, and manufacturing labor. The high level of skills required of suppliers and employees gives them bargaining power to demand higher prices and wages.

In summary, strong competition and the bargaining powers of customers and suppliers put significant pressure on Chipset's selling prices. To respond to these challenges, Chipset must choose between two basic strategies: *differentiating its product* or *achieving cost leadership*.

Product differentiation is an organization's ability to offer products or services its customers perceive to be superior and unique relative to the products or services of its competitors. Apple Inc. has successfully differentiated its products in the consumer electronics industry, as have Johnson & Johnson in the pharmaceutical industry and Coca-Cola in the soft drink industry. These companies have achieved differentiation through innovative product research and development (R&D), careful development and promotion of their brands, and the rapid push of products to market. Managers use differentiation to increase brand loyalty and charge higher prices.

Cost leadership is an organization's ability to achieve lower costs relative to competitors through productivity and efficiency improvements, elimination of waste, and tight cost control. Cost leaders in their respective industries include McDonald's and Walmart (consumer products), Home Depot and Lowe's (home improvement products), Best Buy (consumer electronics), and Emerson Electric (electric motors). These companies provide products and services that are similar to—not differentiated from—their competitors, but at a lower cost to the customer. Lower selling prices, rather than unique products or services, provide a competitive advantage for these cost leaders.

To evaluate the success of its strategy, a company must be able to trace the sources of its profitability to its strategy of product differentiation or cost leadership. For example, Porsche's source of profitability is closely tied to successfully differentiating its cars from those of its competitors. Product differentiation enables Porsche to increase its profit margins and grow sales. Changes in Home Depot's profitability are due to successful implementation of its cost-leadership strategy through productivity and quality improvements.

What strategy should Chipset follow? In order to make this decision, Chipset managers develop the customer preference map shown in Exhibit 13-1. The y-axis describes various attributes of the product desired by customers. The x-axis describes how well Chipset and its competitor, Visilog, which follows a product-differentiation strategy, score along various attributes desired by customers from 1 (poor) to 5 (very good). The map highlights the tradeoffs in any strategy. It shows that CX1 enjoys advantages in terms of price, scalability,[3] and customer service while Visilog's chips are faster and more powerful and customized to different types of modems and communication networks.

CX1 is already somewhat differentiated from competing products. Differentiating CX1 further would be costly, but Chipset may be able to charge a higher price. Conversely, reducing the cost of manufacturing CX1 would allow Chipset to lower prices, spur growth, and

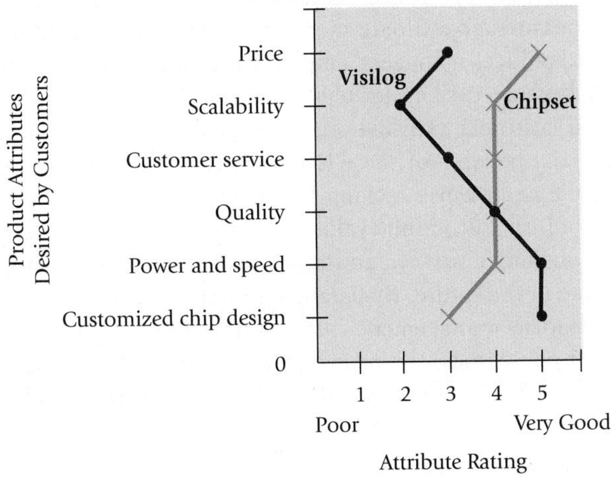

EXHIBIT 13-1

Customer Preference Map for LICDs

[3] The ability to achieve different performance levels by altering the number of CX1 units in a product.

increase market share. The scalability of CX1 makes it an effective solution for meeting varying customer needs. Chipset has, over the years, recruited an engineering staff that is more skilled at making product and process improvements than at creatively designing new products and technologies. The market benefit from lowering prices by improving manufacturing efficiency through process improvements coupled with its own internal capabilities leads Chipset to choose a cost-leadership strategy.

To achieve its cost-leadership strategy, Chipset has deemed it critical to improve its manufacturing quality and efficiency. This can be achieved by actions such as eliminating excess capacity, reducing defect rates, and training workers in quality-management techniques to identify the root causes of defects and take actions to improve manufacturing quality. At the same time, Chipset's management team does not want to make cuts in personnel that would hurt company morale and hinder future growth. In addition to improving manufacturing quality and efficiency, Chipset has identified reducing the delivery time to customers—the time between when customers order a product and when they receive it—as a critical component for achieving its cost-leadership strategy (some customers have complained about long waiting periods). We explore these different strategic components in the next section, where we look at how Chipset can effectively implement its strategy.

DECISION POINT

What are the two generic strategies a company can use?

Strategy Implementation and the Balanced Scorecard

LEARNING OBJECTIVE 2

Understand the four perspectives of the balanced scorecard

. . . financial, customer, internal business process, and learning and growth

Many organizations, such as Allstate Insurance, Bank of Montreal, British Petroleum, Dow Chemical, and Duke University Hospital, have introduced a *balanced scorecard* approach to track progress and manage the implementation of their strategies.

The Balanced Scorecard

The **balanced scorecard** translates an organization's mission and strategy into a set of performance measures that serves as the framework for implementing the organization's strategy.[4] Not only does the balanced scorecard focus on achieving financial objectives, it also highlights the nonfinancial objectives that an organization must achieve to meet and sustain its financial objectives. The scorecard measures an organization's performance from four perspectives:

1. Financial: the profits and value created for shareholders
2. Customer: the success of the company in its target market
3. Internal business processes: the internal operations that create value for customers
4. Learning and growth: the people and system capabilities that support the internal operations

The measures that a company uses to track performance depend on its strategy. This set of measures is called a "balanced scorecard" because it balances the use of financial and nonfinancial performance measures to evaluate short- and long-run performance in a single report. The balanced scorecard reduces managers' emphasis on short-run financial performance, such as quarterly earnings, because the key strategic nonfinancial and operational indicators, such as product quality and customer satisfaction, measure a company's long-run investments in those areas. The financial benefits of these long-run investments may not show up immediately in short-run earnings; however, strong improvement in nonfinancial measures usually indicates the creation of future economic value. For example, an increase in customer satisfaction, as measured by customer surveys and repeat purchases, signals a strong likelihood of higher sales and income in the future. By balancing financial with nonfinancial measures, the balanced scorecard broadens management's attention to short-run *and* long-run performance.

In many for-profit companies, the primary goal of the balanced scorecard is to sustain long-run financial performance. Nonfinancial measures simply serve as leading indicators for

[4] See Robert S. Kaplan and David P. Norton, *The Balanced Scorecard* (Boston: Harvard Business School Press, 1996); Robert S. Kaplan and David P. Norton, *Strategy Maps: Converting Intangible Assets into Tangible Outcomes* (Boston: Harvard Business School Press, 2004); Robert S. Kaplan and David P. Norton, *Alignment: Using the Balanced Scorecard to Create Corporate Synergies* (Boston: Harvard Business School Press, 2006); and Sanjiv Anand, *Execution Excellence* (New Jersey: Wiley, 2016).

the hard-to-measure long-run financial performance. Some companies explicitly set social and environmental goals. Some of these companies view meeting social and environmental goals as a means to achieving long-run financial goals because good performance on social and environmental factors attracts customers, employees, and investors to the company. Other companies focus on social and environmental goals because they take the view that a company has obligations to multiple stakeholders, not just financial investors.

Strategy Maps and the Balanced Scorecard

In this section, we use the Chipset example to develop strategy maps and the four perspectives of the balanced scorecard. The objectives and measures Chipset's managers choose for each perspective relate to the action plans for furthering Chipset's cost-leadership strategy: *improving manufacturing quality and efficiency.*

Strategy Maps

A useful first step in designing a balanced scorecard is a *strategy map.* A **strategy map** is a diagram that describes how an organization intends to create value by connecting strategic objectives in the financial, customer, internal-business-process, and learning-and-growth perspectives in explicit cause-and-effect relationships. Exhibit 13-2 presents Chipset's strategy map. Follow the arrows to see how a strategic objective affects other strategic objectives in the same or in a different perspective. For example, empowering the workforce helps align employee and organization goals and improves manufacturing and business processes, which, in

EXHIBIT 13-2 Strategy Map for Chipset, Inc., for 2020

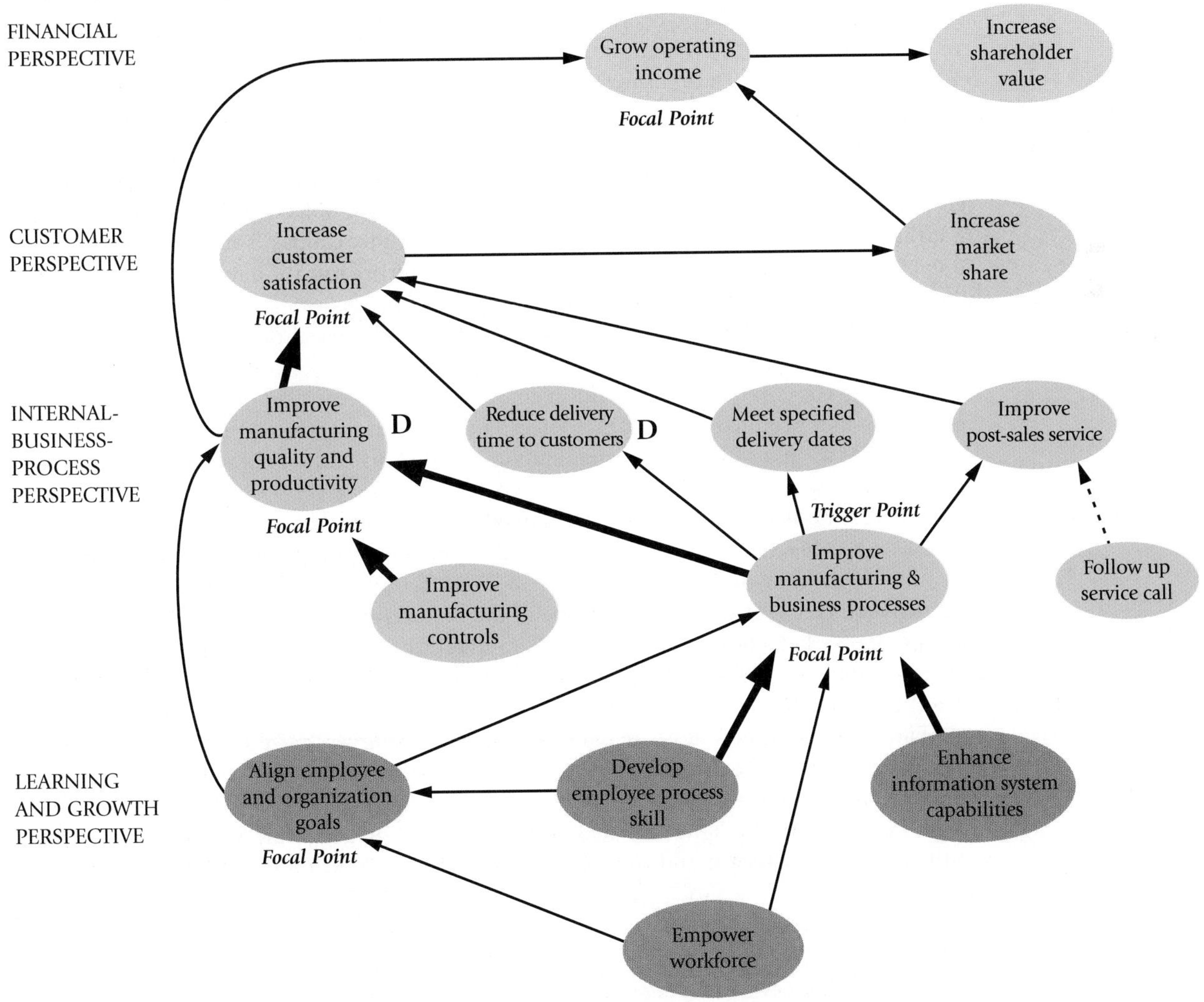

turn, improves manufacturing quality and productivity, reduces customer delivery time, helps to meet delivery dates, and improves post-sales service, all of which lead to an increase in customer satisfaction. Improving manufacturing quality and productivity grows operating income directly; it also increases customer satisfaction that, in turn, increases market share, which then leads to growth in operating income and shareholder value.

Chipset could include many other cause-and-effect relationships in the strategy map in Exhibit 13-2. But Chipset, like many other companies implementing the balanced scorecard, focuses on only those relationships that it believes to be the most significant so that the scorecard does not become unwieldy and difficult to understand.

Structural Analysis of Strategy Maps

Chipset's managers step back to assess and refine the strategy map before developing the balanced scorecard. They use structural analysis to think carefully about the causal links in the strategy map. The analysis helps Chipset's managers to "read" and gain insights into the strategy map.

There are five types of items to consider in a structural analysis: strength of ties (causal links), orphan objectives, focal points, trigger points, and distinctive objectives.[5] We define these items below and refer to the strategy map we developed in Exhibit 13-2 to illustrate them. In the discussion, we refer to the learning and growth perspective as the bottom of the map and the financial perspective as the top.

Strength of Ties *Ties* are the causal links between strategic objectives and can be qualified as strong, moderate, or weak. *Strong ties* are those causal links where the impact of one strategic objective on another is high, relative to other ties in the map. Similarly, *moderate ties* (alternatively, *weak ties*) are those causal links where the impact of one strategic objective on another is average (alternatively, low), relative to other ties in the map. Managers and management accountants, who have a deep understanding of the business, determine whether a tie is strong, moderate, or weak, based on historical data, logic, and judgment. In Exhibit 13-2, strong ties are indicated with dark, thick arrows; moderate ties are indicated with thin arrows; and weak ties are indicated with dotted arrows.

A strong tie indicates that if managers successfully implement a particular strategic objective, it will have a strong causal impact on the strategic objective that is affected. Note that there are five strong ties in Exhibit 13-2. For example, Chipset's managers believe that to improve manufacturing quality and productivity, the organization must improve its manufacturing controls and manufacturing and business processes. To achieve the latter, the organization must in turn enhance its information system capabilities and develop employee process skill.

Aligning employee and organization goals is also important for improving manufacturing quality and productivity, but this effect is deemed moderate and thus is not as strong or important as that of improving manufacturing controls and manufacturing and business processes.

Where a tie is moderate or weak, managers anticipate that implementing the respective strategic objective will not have a strong impact on accomplishing the strategic objectives linked to it. A tie may be moderate because factors outside the organization's and the manager's control affect the outcome of the linked strategic objective. For example, an increase in market share might have only a moderate effect on operating income because other factors, such as bargaining by customers or price pressure from competitors, affect operating income.

Tie strength affects how managers allocate resources across strategic objectives. Because managers believe that a strategic objective with a strong tie will heavily impact the objective linked to it, they may be willing to invest more resources in these objectives. As we will see later, tie strength may also influence how managers craft initiatives and metrics in the balanced scorecard and the weights that managers put on different elements of the scorecard.

---

[5] For a more detailed discussion, see Jacob Goldenberg, Amnon Levav, David Mazursky, and Sorin Solomon, *Cracking the Ad Code* (New York: Cambridge University Press, 2009).

There are many moderate ties and one weak tie in the map depicted in Exhibit 13-2. Chipset's managers closely examine weak ties. Consider the strategic objective of a *follow-up service call*. Chipset's managers believe that even if they were to achieve this objective, it will only have a weak effect on improving post-sales service. That's because in the technology-heavy context of linear integrated circuit devices (LICDs), customers are not interested in post-sales follow-up calls. What customers really want is for Chipset to respond quickly and to solve aggressively any problems they might have when these problems arise. It is Chipset's responsiveness to specific problems rather than routine follow-up calls that customers value.

Orphan objectives Consider again Exhibit 13-2. We refer to the strategic objective of *follow-up service call* as an orphan. An *orphan objective* is a strategic objective with only weak ties (if any) leading out of it to other strategic objectives. Orphan status usually indicates that the strategic objective does not contribute to the larger strategy in a way that warrants allocation of resources. At the very least, management should analyze the value that each orphan objective brings to the organization's overall strategy. In Chipset's case managers decide to not conduct any more *follow-up service calls* and to remove the item from its strategy map because this strategic objective has at best a weak effect on *improving post-sales service*.

Focal points Some strategic objectives have a hub-and-spoke quality and have multiple ties flowing into and/or out of them. A *focal point* is a strategic objective that has multiple links from other objectives funneling *into* it (see Exhibit 13-2). A focal point indicates strategic complexity; multiple strategic objectives need to be coordinated to fully achieve the focal objective. For example, *improve manufacturing quality and productivity* (in the internal business process perspective) is a focal point because three other strategic objectives—*improve manufacturing and business processes, improve manufacturing controls*, and *align employee and organization goals*—must be met for Chipset to fully see an *improvement in manufacturing quality and productivity*. Even though it is complex to fully deliver on focal point strategic objectives, it is important for Chipset to achieve it. That's because, without it, Chipset may not be able to meet its overarching strategic objectives to *grow operating income* and to *increase shareholder value*. If, however, the focal point has only weak ties emanating from it, the strategy map analysis would suggest that the company not invest resources in the focal point objective. That's because it is complex to fully achieve the strategic objective, and the objective only has questionable benefits, even if it is successfully achieved.

Trigger points A *trigger point* is a strategic objective that has multiple ties to other objectives spurring *out* from it. Trigger points are exciting because if an organization can fully achieve the trigger point strategic objectives, they enable the achievement of multiple other strategic objectives. In Exhibit 13-2, *improve manufacturing and business processes* (internal-business-process perspective) is a trigger point because it supports and helps achieve four other strategic objectives (*improve manufacturing quality and productivity, reduce delivery time to customers, meet specified delivery dates*, and *improve post-sales service*). Because of their centrality to many other strategic objectives across the strategy map, trigger points require special attention from managers. Trigger points are interesting even if one of the links emanating from it is weak, as long as the other ties are strong or moderate.

Distinctive objectives Strategic objectives that distinguish an organization from its competitors and that are viewed as critical for achieving the organization's strategy are *distinctive objectives*. They are frequently located within the learning and growth and internal-business-process perspectives, because they define important activities undertaken by a company to satisfy customers and achieve financial performance. In the map, these strategic objectives are labeled with a "D."

Recall that based on its competitive analysis, Chipset's management chooses to pursue a cost-leadership strategy—lowering costs and reducing prices instead of developing more advanced chips and charging a higher price. The key steps to achieving cost leadership require Chipset to enhance manufacturing quality and efficiency by, for example, eliminating excess capacity, and to reduce delivery time to customers. As a result, Chipset's managers and management accountants identify *improving manufacturing quality and productivity* and *reducing delivery time to customers* as *distinctive objectives* that allow Chipset to differentiate itself from its competitors. Chipset's managers debate whether they should choose "lower level" strategic objectives such as *improve manufacturing controls* or *improve manufacturing and business processes* as distinctive objectives rather than the ones they have chosen. They do not because Chipset's managers, like managers at many companies, prefer to choose as distinctive objectives those objectives that customers experience. It is higher manufacturing quality and productivity and lower delivery times that give Chipset a distinctive competitive advantage, while improving manufacturing controls and manufacturing and business processes are important steps in achieving those objectives.

Thinking about distinctiveness within the internal-business-process perspective has two other benefits. First, the objectives in the internal-business-process perspective describe the development of core capabilities. As a result, these strategic objectives produce long-term benefits in addition to short-term ones, creating sustainable competitive advantage. Second, the objectives in the internal-business-process perspective force senior managers to develop nonfinancial metrics to measure important, but difficult-to-quantify activities, within which competitive advantage resides.

If no strategic objective is truly distinctive, managers need to revisit the strategic objectives and think about how to modify or replace them to achieve a strategy that distinguishes the company from its competitors while creating value for its customers. In this way, a structural analysis, that is, "reading" a strategy map helps companies both implement and refine their strategies.

Insights into strategy maps Let us summarize the insights that Chipset's managers gain from using the five tools of structural analysis—strength of ties, orphan objectives, focal points, trigger points, and distinctive objectives. To achieve its financial goals, Chipset needs to delight its customers by *improving manufacturing quality and productivity* and *reducing delivery time to customers*, which are the two distinctive objectives that distinguish Chipset from its competitors. The multitude of focal points leading up to these distinctive objectives suggests that it will be difficult for a competitor to successfully compete with Chipset. A number of strong ties lead into *improving manufacturing quality and productivity*. Chipset's managers believe that *developing employee process skills, enhancing information system capabilities, improving manufacturing controls*, and *improving manufacturing and business processes* will have a strong impact on *manufacturing quality and productivity*. The links into *reducing delivery time to customers* are not as strong. Chipset's managers will have to continue to monitor how well its new order-delivery process is working. On the positive side, it appears that customers care more about quality and cost (strong tie) than they do about delivery time (moderate tie).

Chipset's managers will use the insights from structural analysis to carefully allocate resources across the different strategic objectives (for example, allocating more resources to improving manufacturing quality and productivity than to reducing delivery time). They do not allocate any resources to orphan objectives and drop *follow-up service calls* from the strategy map and the balanced scorecard.

Chipset uses the strategy map from Exhibit 13-2 to build the balanced scorecard presented in Exhibit 13-3. The scorecard highlights the four perspectives of performance: financial, customer, internal business process, and learning and growth. The first column presents the strategic objectives from the strategy map in Exhibit 13-2. At the beginning of 2020, the company's managers specify the strategic objectives, measures, initiatives (the actions necessary to achieve the objectives), and target performance (the first four columns of Exhibit 13-3).

Chipset wants to use the balanced scorecard targets to drive the organization to higher levels of performance. Managers therefore set targets at a level of performance that is achievable yet distinctly better than competitors'. Chipset's managers complete the fifth column, reporting actual performance at the end of 2020, which allows for a comparison to target performance.

EXHIBIT 13-3 The Balanced Scorecard for Chipset, Inc., for 2020

Strategic Objectives	Measures	Initiatives	Target Performance	Actual Performance
Financial Perspective				
Grow operating income	Operating income from productivity gain	Manage costs and unused capacity	\$1,850,000	\$1,912,500
Increase shareholder value	Operating income from growth	Build strong customer relationships	\$2,500,000	\$2,820,000
	Revenue growth		9%	10%[a]
Customer Perspective				
Increase market share	Market share in communication-networks segment	Identify future needs of customers	6%	7%
Increase customer satisfaction	Number of new customers	Identify new target-customer segments	1	1[b]
	Customer-satisfaction ratings	Increase customer focus of sales organization	90% of customers give top two ratings	87% of customers give top two ratings
Internal-Business-Process Perspective				
Improve postsales service	Service response time	Improve customer-service process	Within 4 hours	Within 3 hours
Improve manufacturing quality and productivity	Yield	Identify root causes of problems and improve quality	91%	92.3%
Reduce delivery time to customers	Order-delivery time	Reengineer order-delivery process	30 days	30 days
Meet specified delivery dates	On-time delivery	Reengineer order-delivery process	97%	95%
Improve manufacturing and business processes	Number of major improvements in manufacturing and business processes	Organize teams from manufacturing and sales to modify processes to specified target levels	5	5
Improve manufacturing controls	Percentage of processes with advanced controls	Organize R&D/manufacturing teams to implement advanced controls	90%	90%
Learning-and-Growth Perspective				
Align employee and organization goals	Employee-satisfaction ratings	Employee participation and suggestions program to build teamwork	80% of employees give top two ratings	88% of employees give top two ratings
Empower workforce	Percentage of line workers empowered to manage processes	Have supervisors act as coaches rather than decision makers	92%	94%
Develop employee process skill	Percentage of employees trained in process and quality management	Employee training programs	94%	96%
Enhance information-system capabilities	Percentage of manufacturing processes with real-time feedback	Improve online and offline data gathering	93%	93%

[a] (Revenues in 2020 − Revenues in 2019) ÷ Revenues in 2019 = (\$25,300,000 − \$23,000,000) ÷ \$23,000,000 = 10%.

[b] Number of customers increased from seven to eight in 2020.

Four Perspectives of the Balanced Scorecard

We next describe the four perspectives and illustrate each one using the measures Chipset's managers chose to achieve the individual strategic objectives and to implement its overall strategy. When analyzing the scorecard we discuss measures at the bottom of each perspective (the cause) and work our way upward to the top (the effect).

1. **Financial perspective.** This perspective evaluates the profitability of the strategy and the creation of shareholder value. Because Chipset's key strategic initiatives are cost reduction relative to competitors' costs and sales growth, the financial perspective focuses on revenue growth and how much operating income results from reducing costs and selling more units of CX1.
2. **Customer perspective.** This perspective identifies targeted customer and market segments and measures the company's success in these segments. To monitor its customer objectives, Chipset's managers use (a) market research, such as surveys and interviews, to determine market share in the communication-networks segment, and (b) information about the number of new customers and customer-satisfaction ratings from its customer management systems.
3. **Internal-business-process perspective.** This perspective focuses on internal operations that create value for customers that, in turn, help achieve financial performance. Managers at Chipset determine internal-business-process improvement targets after benchmarking against its main competitors. Benchmarking involves getting information about competitors from published financial statements, prevailing prices, customers, suppliers, former employees, industry experts, and financial analysts. The internal-business-process perspective is composed of three subprocesses:
   - **Post-sales-service process:** Providing service and support to the customer after the sale of a product or service. Chipset monitors how quickly and accurately it is responding to customer-service requests.
   - **Operations process:** Producing and delivering existing products and services that will meet the needs of customers. Chipset's strategic objectives are (a) improving manufacturing quality and productivity, (b) reducing delivery time to customers, and (c) meeting specified delivery dates, so it measures yield, order-delivery time, and on-time delivery.
   - **Innovation process:** Creating products, services, and processes that will meet the needs of customers. This is an important process for companies that follow a product-differentiation strategy and must constantly design and develop innovative new products to remain competitive in the marketplace. Chipset's innovation focuses on improving its manufacturing capability and process controls to lower costs and improve manufacturing quality. Chipset measures innovation by the number of improvements in manufacturing processes and percentage of processes with advanced controls.
4. **Learning-and-growth perspective.** This perspective identifies the people and information capabilities necessary for an organization to learn, improve, and grow. These capabilities help achieve superior internal processes that in turn create value for customers and shareholders. Chipset's learning-and-growth perspective emphasizes three capabilities:
   - Motivation of employees to achieve organizational goals, measured by employee satisfaction, and the level of empowerment, measured by the percentage of manufacturing and sales employees (also called line workers) empowered to manage processes
   - Employee process capabilities, measured by the percentage of employees trained in process and quality management
   - Information-system capabilities, measured by the percentage of manufacturing processes with real-time feedback

The arrows in Exhibit 13-3 indicate the *broad* cause-and-effect linkages: how gains in the learning-and-growth perspective lead to improvements in internal business processes, which lead to higher customer satisfaction and market share, and finally lead to superior financial performance. The detailed causal linkages within each perspective are described in the strategy map in Exhibit 13-2. Note how the scorecard describes elements of Chipset's strategy implementation. Worker training and empowerment improve employee satisfaction and lead to manufacturing and business-process improvements that improve quality and reduce delivery time, which, in turn, results in increased customer satisfaction and higher market share. The last column in Exhibit 13-3 indicates that Chipset's actions have been successful from a financial perspective. Chipset has earned significant operating income from executing its cost-leadership strategy, and that strategy has also led to growth.

To sustain long-run financial performance, a company must strengthen all links across its different balanced scorecard perspectives. For example, Southwest Airlines' high employee satisfaction levels and low employee turnover (learning-and-growth perspective) lead to greater efficiency and customer-friendly service (internal-business-process perspective) that enhances customer satisfaction (customer perspective) and boosts profits and return on investment (financial perspective).

A major benefit of the balanced scorecard is that it promotes causal thinking as described in the previous paragraph—where improvement in one area causes an improvement in another. Think of the balanced scorecard as a *linked scorecard* or a *causal scorecard*. Managers must search for empirical evidence (rather than rely on intuition alone) to test the validity and strength of the various connections. A causal scorecard enables a company to focus on the key drivers that steer the implementation of its strategy. Without convincing links, the scorecard loses much of its value.

Implementing a Balanced Scorecard

To successfully implement a balanced scorecard, division leaders and subordinate managers require commitment and leadership from top management. At Chipset, the vice president of strategic planning headed the team building the balanced scorecard. The team conducted interviews with senior managers; asked executives about customers, competitors, and technological developments; and sought proposals for balanced scorecard objectives across the four perspectives. The team then met to discuss the responses and build a prioritized list of objectives.

In a meeting with all senior managers, the team sought to achieve consensus on the scorecard objectives. The vice president of strategic planning then divided senior management into four groups, with each group responsible for one of the perspectives. In addition, each group broadened the base of inputs by including representatives from the next-lower levels of management and key functional managers. The groups identified measures for each objective and the sources of information for each measure. The groups then met to finalize scorecard strategic objectives, measures, targets, and the initiatives to achieve the targets. Management accountants played an important role in the design and implementation of the balanced scorecard, particularly in determining measures that represent the realities of the business. This required management accountants to understand the economic environment of the industry, Chipset's customers and competitors, and internal business issues such as human resources, operations, and distribution.

Managers at Chipset made sure that employees understood the scorecard and the scorecard process. The final balanced scorecard was communicated to all employees. Sharing the scorecard allowed engineers and operating personnel, for example, to understand the reasons for customer satisfaction and dissatisfaction and to make suggestions for improving internal processes directly aimed at satisfying customers and implementing Chipset's strategy. Too often, only a select group of managers see scorecards. By limiting the scorecard's exposure, Chipset would lose the opportunity for widespread organization engagement and alignment. Companies such as Citibank, Exxon Mobil, and Novartis share their scorecards widely across their divisions and departments.

Chipset also encourages each department to develop its own scorecard that ties into Chipset's overall scorecard described in Exhibit 13-3. For example, the quality control department's scorecard has measures that its department managers use to improve yield—number of quality circles, statistical process control charts, Pareto diagrams, and root-cause analyses (see Chapter 20, pages 784–787, for more details). Department scorecards help align the actions of each department to implement Chipset's overall strategy.

Companies frequently use balanced scorecards to evaluate and reward managerial performance and to influence managerial behavior. Using the balanced scorecard for performance evaluation widens the performance management lens and motivates managers to give greater attention to nonfinancial drivers of performance. Surveys indicate, however, that companies continue to assign more weight to the financial perspective (45–55%) than to the other perspectives—customer (15–25%), internal business process (10–20%), and learning and growth (10–20%). Companies cite several reasons for the relatively smaller weight on nonfinancial measures, including difficulty evaluating the relative importance of nonfinancial measures; challenges in measuring and quantifying qualitative, nonfinancial data; and difficulty in compensating managers despite poor financial performance (see Chapter 24 for a more detailed discussion of performance evaluation). Companies put more weight on nonfinancial measures that represent distinctive objectives, have strong ties to financial results, and can be measured reasonably well. For example, in evaluating its senior managers, Chipset places greater weight on the percentage of employees trained in process and quality management (a measure of employee process skills) and yield (a measure of improvements in manufacturing quality and productivity). That's because Chipset believes that these measures create distinctive competitive advantage with strong ties to customer satisfaction and operating income.

A growing number of companies in the manufacturing, merchandising, and service sectors are giving greater weight to nonfinancial measures when promoting employees because they believe that nonfinancial measures—such as customer satisfaction, process improvements, and employee motivation—better assess a manager's potential to succeed at senior levels of management. As this trend continues, operating managers will put more weight on nonfinancial factors when making decisions even though these factors carry smaller weights when determining their annual compensation. For the balanced scorecard to be effective, however, managers must view it as a fair way to assess and reward all important aspects of a manager's performance and promotion prospects.

Different Strategies Lead to Different Scorecards

Recall that while Chipset follows a cost-leadership strategy, its competitor, Visilog, follows a product-differentiation strategy by designing custom chips for modems and communication networks. Visilog designs its balanced scorecard to fit its product-differentiation strategy. For example, in the financial perspective, Visilog evaluates how much of its operating income comes from charging premium prices for its products. In the customer perspective, Visilog measures the percentage of its revenues from new products and new customers. In the internal-business-process perspective, Visilog measures the number of new products introduced and new product development time. In the learning-and-growth perspective, Visilog measures the development of advanced manufacturing capabilities to produce custom chips.

Visilog also uses some of the measures described in Chipset's balanced scorecard in Exhibit 13-3. For example, revenue growth, customer satisfaction ratings, order-delivery time, on-time delivery, percentage of frontline workers empowered to manage processes, and employee-satisfaction ratings are also important measures under the product-differentiation strategy.[6] Exhibit 13-4 presents some common measures found in company scorecards in the service, retail, and manufacturing sectors.

Environmental and Social Performance and the Balanced Scorecard

The Brundtland Commission[7] defined a sustainable society as one where "the current generation meets its needs without jeopardizing the ability of future generations to meet their needs." Given the accelerating progression of climate change in recent years, working toward sustainability is increasingly becoming a priority for many countries around the world. There are different views on the role that companies and managers should take in trying to achieve sustainability goals.

---

[6] For simplicity, we have presented the balanced scorecard in the context of companies that follow either a cost-leadership or a product-differentiation strategy. Of course, a company may have some divisions for which cost leadership is critical and other divisions for which product differentiation is important. The company will then develop separate scorecards to implement the different strategies. In still other contexts, product differentiation may be of primary importance, but some cost leadership must also be achieved. The balanced scorecard measures would then be linked in a cause-and-effect way to this strategy.

[7] The Brundtland Commission was set up by the United Nations as the World Commission on Environment and Development. It issued its report, *Our Common Future*, in 1987.

EXHIBIT 13-4 Frequently Cited Balanced Scorecard Measures

Financial Perspective
Income measures: Operating income, gross margin percentage
Revenue and cost measures: Revenue growth, revenues from new products, cost reductions in key areas
Income and investment measures: Economic value added[a] (EVA®), return on investment
Customer Perspective
Market share, customer satisfaction, customer-retention percentage, time taken to fulfill customers' requests, number of customer complaints
Internal-Business-Process Perspective
Innovation process: Percentage of processes with advanced controls, number of new products or services, new-product development times, and number of new patents
Operations process: Yield, defect rates, percentage of on-time deliveries, average time taken to respond to orders, setup time, manufacturing downtime
Post-sales service process: Time taken to replace or repair defective products, hours of customer training for using the product
Learning-and-Growth Perspective
Employee measures: Employee education and skill levels, employee-satisfaction ratings, employee turnover rates, percentage of employee suggestions implemented, percentage of compensation based on individual and team incentives
Technology measures: Information system availability, percentage of processes with real-time feedback

[a]This measure is described in Chapter 24.

In order to raise awareness on the part of companies and shareholders about the importance of a sustainable future for companies' business models, governments are increasingly pushing companies to report on the risks that environmental and social challenges put on their ability to deliver future value. For example, the Securities and Exchange Commission passed a rule in 2010 that requires companies to include the business risks related to climate change and its consequences in their annual reports to shareholders. Similarly, the European Union introduced the Non-Financial Reporting Directive ("NFR Directive," Directive 2014/95/EU) in 2014. The Directive requires that, starting in 2018, large public companies operating in Europe disclose in their annual reports to shareholders information on environmental, social, human rights and anti-corruption matters that is important in understanding the company's development, performance, position, and impact.

There are two fundamental schools of thought on whether companies should promote sustainability. The first view is that managers should focus only on long-run financial performance, and not be distracted by pursuing social and environmental goals beyond the minimum levels required by law. According to this view, companies' responsibilities in society are adequately captured by the sole goal of long-run financial performance. However, even companies and managers that subscribe to this point of view are recognizing that environmental and social objectives are increasingly important for their organizations in order to maximize long-run financial performance. In these companies, sustainability objectives are part of the implementation of a strategy to maximize long-run financial performance. For example, managers have recognized that promotion of environmental and social goals helps to attract and inspire outstanding employees, improve employee safety and health, increase productivity, and lower operating costs, all contributing to long-run financial performance. Promoting environmental and social performance and being a good corporate citizen may also be in a company's best interest from a risk-minimization perspective. For example, reducing greenhouse gases might ward off fines or more stringent carbon emission caps from the U.S. Environmental Protection Agency and decrease the risk of lawsuits and negative media attention and stakeholder activism that can damage a company's reputation.

The second perspective is that companies and managers must pursue environmental and social objectives beyond what is legally required, and in addition to long-run financial goals—often called the *triple bottom line*—as part of a company's societal responsibility. According to this view, environmental and social objectives are overall goals next to long-run financial performance, not just a means to an end. While pursuing sustainability objectives, such as reducing greenhouse gas emissions and non-recycled waste, and minimizing corruption may come at the expense of financial objectives—especially in the short run—it may also generate opportunities for the company that lead to strategic advantages and financial performance in the long-term. In fact, a distinguishing organizational characteristic of companies that emphasize environmental and social performance is their long-term orientation. For example, companies aiming for the triple bottom line may successfully benefit from innovating in technologies, processes, products, and business models that reduce the tradeoffs between financial and sustainability goals. These companies may also build transformational and transitional leadership and change capabilities needed to implement the strategies to achieve the multiple goals. Pursuing sustainability objectives may also enhance a company's reputation with socially conscious employees, customers, and investors and boost its image and relationships with governments and citizens.

Managers interested in measuring environmental and social performance incorporate these factors into their balanced scorecards to set priorities for initiatives, guide decisions and actions, and fuel discussions around strategies and business models to improve performance. Suppose Chipset decides to emphasize environmental and social goals in its balanced scorecard. What measures might it add to the balanced scorecard presented in Exhibit 13-3? Exhibit 13-5 presents these additional environmental and social measures. In practice, Chipset, like most companies that emphasize environmental and social goals, integrates sustainability goals and measures presented in Exhibit 13-5 with business goals and measures presented in Exhibit 13-3 into a single combined scorecard.

One of the main benefits that Chipset gains from measuring environmental and social performance is that it improves competitiveness and provides strategic advantages to the business. For example, reducing greenhouse gas emissions motivates Chipset to redesign its product and processes to reduce energy consumption. Measuring non-recycled hazardous and nonhazardous waste prompts Chipset to work with its suppliers to redesign and reduce packaging and toxic substances in its materials and components. Measuring worker-related injuries and illnesses motivates Chipset to redesign processes to lessen the number of such incidents. In each of these initiatives, Chipset achieves environmental and social goals as well as gains competitive advantage by reducing costs and pushing itself to innovate and build a social and environmental value proposition into its business strategy.

If Chipset can measure growth in revenue or operating income from customers attracted to Chipset's environmental and social actions with reasonable accuracy, the company might add that measure in its financial perspective. The scorecard shows that Chipset has achieved all its environmental and social goals, indicating that its environmental and social actions are translating into financial gains. These results would encourage Chipset to continue its environmental and social efforts.

Companies use a variety of measures for environmental and social performance in addition to the ones described in the Chipset example:

1. **Financial perspective.** Carbon taxes or fees (in countries that levy a carbon tax for emissions), cost of preventing and remediating environmental damage (training, cleanup, legal costs, and costs of consumer boycotts), cost of recycled materials to total cost of materials
2. **Customer perspective.** Brand image (percentage of survey respondents who rate the company high on trust)
3. **Internal-business perspective.** Energy consumption (joules per $1,000 of sales), water use (millions of cubic meters); wastewater discharge (thousands of cubic meters); individual quantities of different greenhouse gases, for example, carbon dioxide, nitrous oxide, or sulphur dioxide (grams per $1 million in sales); number of environmental incidents (such as unexpected discharge of air, water, or solid waste); codes of conduct violations (percentage of total employees); contributions to community-based nonprofit organizations; number of joint ventures and partnerships between the company and community organizations
4. **Learning-and-growth perspective.** Implementation of International Organization for Standardization (ISO) 14000 environmental management standards (subjective score); employees trained and certified in codes of conduct (percentage of total employees); employees trained in United Nations global compact, for example, human rights, fair wage, no child labor, corruption and bribery prevention (percentage of total employees)

EXHIBIT 13-5 Environmental and Social Balanced Scorecard Measures for Chipset, Inc., for 2020

Strategic Objectives	Measures	Initiatives	Target Performance	Actual Performance
Financial Perspective				
Reduce waste	Cost savings from reducing energy use and waste	Quality improvement programs	$400,000	$415,000
Reduce cost of time lost from work injuries and illness	Cost savings from fewer work injuries and illness	Train workers in safety methods and hygiene	$50,000	$55,000
Customer Perspective				
Enhance reputation for sustainability with customers	Percentage of customers giving top two ratings for environmental and social performance	Communicate environmental and social goals and performance	90%	92%
Internal-Business-Process Perspective				
Reduce greenhouse gas emissions	Greenhouse gas emissions per million dollars of sales	Increase energy efficiency and reduce carbon footprint by planting trees	27 grams/$1 million of sales	25.6 grams/$1 million of sales
Reduce operational waste not recycled	Hazardous and non-hazardous waste not recycled per million dollars of sales	Increase recycling programs and redesign products	130 grams/$1 million of sales	126 grams/$1 million of sales
Reduce work-related injuries and illnesses	Days of lost time per worker per year due to injury or illness	Redesign processes to improve worker safety and hygiene	0.20 days per worker per year	0.18 days per worker per year
Learning-and-Growth Perspective				
Inspiring employees through environmental and social goals	Percentage of employees giving top two ratings for environmental and social performance	Training employees about environmental and social benefits	87%	90%
Diversity of employees	Percentage of women and minorities in managerial positions	Develop human resource practices to support mentoring and coaching for women and minorities	40%	42%

Features of a Good Balanced Scorecard

A well-designed balanced scorecard has several features:

1. **It tells the story of a company's strategy, articulating a sequence of cause-and-effect relationships—the links between the various strategic objectives that outline the implementation of the organization's strategy.** In for-profit companies, each measure in the scorecard is part of a cause-and-effect chain leading to financial outcomes. Not-for-profit organizations, such as the World Bank and Teach for America, design the cause-and-effect chain to achieve their strategic service objectives—for example, reducing the number of people in poverty or raising high school graduation rates.

2. **It helps to communicate the strategy to all members of the organization by translating the strategy into a coherent and linked set of understandable and measurable operational targets.** Guided by the scorecard, managers and employees take actions and make decisions to achieve the company's strategy. Companies that have distinct strategic business units (SBUs)—such as consumer products and pharmaceuticals at Johnson & Johnson—develop their balanced scorecards at the SBU level. Each SBU has its own unique strategy and implementation goals, so building separate scorecards allows managers of each SBU to choose measures that help implement its distinctive strategy.
3. **In for-profit companies, the balanced scorecard motivates managers to take actions that eventually result in improvements in financial performance.** Managers sometimes tend to focus too much on quality and customer satisfaction as ends in themselves. For example, Xerox discovered that higher customer satisfaction, through service guarantees, did not increase customer loyalty and financial returns because customers also wanted product innovations, such as high-speed color printing, that met their needs. Some companies use statistical methods, such as regression analysis, to test the anticipated cause-and-effect relationships among nonfinancial measures and financial performance. The data for this analysis can come from either time-series data (collected over time) or cross-sectional data (collected, for example, across multiple stores of a retail chain). In the Chipset example, improvements in nonfinancial factors have, in fact, already led to improvements in financial factors.
4. **It focuses attention on only the most critical measures.** Chipset's scorecard, for example, has 16 measures, between three and six measures for each perspective. Limiting the number of measures focuses managers' attention on those that most affect strategy implementation. Using too many measures makes it difficult for managers to process relevant information.
5. **It highlights less-than-optimal tradeoffs that managers may make when they fail to consider operational and financial measures together.** Consider, for example, a company that follows an innovation and product differentiation strategy and so invests in R&D. The company could achieve superior short-run financial performance by reducing R&D spending. A good balanced scorecard would signal that the short-run financial performance has been achieved by taking actions that hurt future financial performance because a leading indicator of future performance, R&D spending and R&D output, has declined.

Pitfalls in Implementing a Balanced Scorecard

Pitfalls to avoid in implementing a balanced scorecard include the following:

1. **Managers should not assume the cause-and-effect linkages are precise.** The linkages are merely hypotheses. Over time, a company must gather evidence of the strength and timing of the linkages between the different measures, and use this feedback to inform future strategies and implementation plans. With experience, organizations should alter their scorecards to include those nonfinancial strategic objectives and measures that are the best leading indicators (the causes) of financial performance (a lagging indicator or the effect). Understanding that the scorecard will evolve over time helps managers avoid wasting time and money trying to design the "perfect" scorecard at the outset. Moreover, as the business environment and strategy change over time, the measures in the scorecard also need to be updated. For example, when the Novartis division Sandoz, a manufacturer of generic pharmaceutical chemicals, shifted its strategy to also produce biologic medicines that required significant investment in new technologies and patient trials, its balanced scorecard was updated from only emphasizing productivity and cost efficiency to including measures of innovation.
2. **Managers should not seek improvements across all of the measures all of the time.** Managers should strive for quality and on-time performance but not beyond the point at which further improvement in these objectives is so costly that it is inconsistent with long-run profit maximization. Cost–benefit considerations should always be central when designing a balanced scorecard.

3. **Managers should not use only objective measures in the balanced scorecard.** Chipset's balanced scorecard includes both objective measures (such as operating income from cost leadership, market share, and manufacturing yield) and subjective measures (such as customer- and employee-satisfaction ratings). When using subjective measures, however, managers must be careful that the benefits of this potentially rich information are not lost by using measures that are inaccurate or that can be easily manipulated.
4. **Despite challenges of measurement, top management should not ignore nonfinancial measures when evaluating managers and other employees.** Managers tend to focus on the measures that are used to reward their performance. Excluding nonfinancial measures (such as customer satisfaction or product quality) when evaluating the performance of managers will reduce their significance and importance to managers.

DECISION POINT

How can an organization translate its strategy into a set of performance measures?

Evaluating the Success of Strategy and Implementation

To evaluate how successful Chipset's strategy and its implementation have been, its management compares the target- and actual-performance columns in the balanced scorecard (Exhibit 13-3). Chipset met most targets set on the basis of competitor benchmarks in 2020 as improvements in Chipset's learning-and-growth perspective quickly rippled through to the financial perspective. While Chipset will continue to make improvements to achieve the targets it did not meet, managers are satisfied that the strategic initiatives that Chipset identified and measured for learning and growth resulted in improvements in internal business processes, customer measures, and financial performance.

If Chipset did not meet all its balanced scorecard goals, how could it tell if the failure to meet its objectives was because of problems in strategy implementation or because of problems with its strategy? Consider first, the situation where Chipset did not meet its goals on the two internally focused perspectives: learning and growth and internal business processes. In this case, Chipset would conclude that it did not implement its strategy because it did not implement the activities that would give it competitive advantage. But what if Chipset performed well on learning and growth and internal business processes, but customer measures and financial performance in this year and the next year still did not improve? Chipset's managers would then conclude that Chipset did a good job of implementation, as the various internal nonfinancial measures it targeted improved, but that its strategy was faulty because there was no effect on customers or on long-run financial performance and value creation. In this case, management failed to identify the correct causal links but did a good job implementing the wrong strategy! Management would then reevaluate the strategy and the factors that drive it.

13-1 TRY IT!

Strategy Map—Retail Company

Nile is an online, mail-order company that provides customers with a wide variety of products.

The managers of Nile have identified their financial objectives: grow operating income and increase shareholder value. To accomplish the company's financial goals, the managers have determined the company needs to increase customer satisfaction and market share. To increase customer satisfaction and market share, Nile needs to reduce delivery time, increase product offerings, and improve customer service. To meet these objectives, Nile will need to attract and retain quality employees and continually improve the quality of employee training. The information technology systems to support the online orders are on par with Nile's competitors.

1. Draw a strategy map as in Exhibit 13-2 describing the cause-and-effect relationships among the strategic objectives you would expect to see. Present at least two strategic objectives you would expect to see under each balanced scorecard perspective. Identify what you believe are any (a) strong ties, (b) focal points, (c) trigger points, and (d) distinctive objectives. Comment on your structural analysis of the strategy map.
2. For each strategic objective, suggest a measure you would recommend in Nile's balanced scorecard.

Strategic Analysis of Operating Income

LEARNING OBJECTIVE 3

Analyze changes in operating income to evaluate strategy

. . . growth, price recovery, and productivity

As we have discussed, Chipset performed well on its various nonfinancial measures, and operating income also increased. As a result, Chipset's managers might be tempted to declare the cost-leadership strategy a success. However, more analysis is needed before managers can conclude that Chipset successfully formulated and implemented its intended strategy. Operating income could have increased simply because prices of inputs decreased or the entire market expanded. Alternatively, a company that has chosen a cost-leadership strategy, like Chipset, may find that its operating-income increase actually resulted from some degree of product differentiation. *To evaluate the success of a strategy, managers and management accountants need to link strategy to the sources of operating-income increases.* These are the kinds of analyses that top management and boards of directors routinely discuss in their meetings when evaluating performance. Managers who have mastered the strategic analysis of operating income changes gain an understanding of the levers of strategy and strategy implementation that help them deliver sustained operating performance.

Can Chipset's managers conclude they were successful in implementing their strategy? They can only do so if improvements in the company's financial performance and operating income over time can be attributed to achieving targeted cost savings and growth in market share. The top two rows of Chipset's balanced scorecard in Exhibit 13-3 show that operating-income gains from productivity ($1,912,500) and growth ($2,820,000) exceeded targets. (The next section of this chapter describes how these numbers were calculated.) This means that Chipset's strategy formulation and implementation, not other factors, led to increases in operating income. The success of its strategy means that Chipset's management can be more confident that the gains will be sustained in subsequent years.

We next discuss how Chipset's management accountants subdivide changes in operating income into components that can be identified with product differentiation, cost leadership, and growth. Subdividing the change in operating income to evaluate the success of a strategy is conceptually similar to the variance analysis discussed in Chapters 7 and 8. One difference, however, is that in strategic analysis of operating income, management accountants compare actual operating performance over *two different periods*, not actual to budgeted numbers in the *same time period* as in variance analysis.[8] A second difference is that the analysis in this section breaks down changes in operating income rather than focus on differences in individual cost categories (direct materials, direct manufacturing labor, and overhead) as we did in Chapters 7 and 8.

We next explain how the change in operating income between *any* two periods can be subdivided into product differentiation, cost leadership, and growth components.[9] We illustrate the analysis using data from 2019 and 2020 because Chipset implemented key elements of its strategy in late 2019 and early 2020 and expects the financial consequences of these strategies to occur in 2020. Suppose the financial consequences of these strategies had been expected to affect operating income in only 2021. Then we could just as easily have compared 2019 to 2021. If necessary, we could also have compared 2019 to 2020 and 2021 taken together.

Chipset's data for 2019 and 2020 follow:

	2019	2020
1. Units of CX1 produced and sold	1,000,000	1,150,000
2. Selling price	$23	$22
3. Direct materials (square centimeters of silicon wafers)	3,000,000	2,900,000
4. Direct material cost per square centimeter	$1.40	$1.50
5. Manufacturing processing capacity (in square centimeters of silicon wafer)	3,750,000	3,500,000
6. Conversion costs (all manufacturing costs other than direct material costs)	$16,050,000	$15,225,000
7. Conversion cost per unit of capacity (row 6 ÷ row 5)	$4.28	$4.35

[8] Other examples of focusing on actual performance over two periods rather than comparisons of actuals to budgets can be found in Jeremy Hope and Robin Fraser, *Beyond Budgeting* (Boston, MA: Harvard Business School Press, 2003).

[9] For further details, see Rajiv D. Banker, Srikant M. Datar, and Robert S. Kaplan, "Productivity Measurement and Management Accounting," *Journal of Accounting, Auditing and Finance* (1989): 528–554; and Anthony J. Hayzens, and James M. Reeve, "Examining the Relationships in Productivity Accounting," *Management Accounting Quarterly* (2000): 32–39.

Chipset managers obtain the following additional information:

1. Conversion costs (labor and overhead costs) for each year depend on the production processing capacity defined in terms of the quantity of square centimeters of silicon wafers that Chipset can process. These costs do not vary with the actual quantity of silicon wafers processed.
2. Chipset incurs no R&D costs. Its marketing, sales, and customer-service costs are small relative to the other costs. Chipset has eight customers in 2020, each purchasing roughly the same quantities of CX1. Because of the highly technical nature of the product, Chipset uses a cross-functional team for its marketing, sales, and customer-service activities. This cross-functional approach ensures that, although marketing, sales, and customer-service costs are small, the entire Chipset organization, including manufacturing engineers, remains focused on increasing customer satisfaction and market share. (The Problem for Self-Study at the end of this chapter describes a situation in which marketing, sales, and customer-service costs are significant.)
3. Chipset's asset structure is very similar in 2019 and 2020.
4. Operating income for each year is as follows:

	2019	2020
Revenues		
($23 per unit × 1,000,000 units; $22 per unit × 1,150,000 units)	$23,000,000	$25,300,000
Costs		
Direct material costs		
(1.40/sq. cm. × 3,000,000 sq. cm.; $1.50/sq. cm. × 2,900,000 sq. cm.)	4,200,000	4,350,000
Conversion costs		
($4.28/sq. cm. × 3,750,000 sq. cm.; $4.35/sq. cm. × 3,500,000 sq. cm.)	16,050,000	15,225,000
Total costs	20,250,000	19,575,000
Operating income	$ 2,750,000	$ 5,725,000
Change in operating income	$2,975,000 F	

The goal of Chipset's managers is to evaluate how much of the $2,975,000 increase in operating income was caused by the successful implementation of the company's cost-leadership strategy. To do this evaluation, management accountants start by analyzing three main factors: (1) growth, (2) price recovery, and (3) productivity.

The **growth component** measures the change in operating income attributable solely to the change in the quantity of output sold between 2019 and 2020. It evaluates how revenues and costs change as a company sells more products and services. The **price-recovery component** measures the change in operating income attributable solely to changes in Chipset's prices of inputs and outputs between 2019 and 2020. The price-recovery component measures the change in revenues as a result of a change in output price compared with the change in costs as a result of changes in input prices. A company that has successfully implemented a strategy of product differentiation will be able to increase its output price faster than its input prices increase, boosting profit margins and operating income; these companies will show a large positive price-recovery component.

The **productivity component** measures the change in costs attributable to a change in the quantity of inputs used in 2020 relative to the quantity of inputs that would have been used in 2019 to produce the 2020 output. The productivity component measures the amount by which operating income increased as a result of using inputs efficiently and thereby lowering costs. In the case of fixed costs, productivity improvement takes the form of reducing the costs of unused capacity. A company that has successfully pursued a strategy of cost leadership will be able to produce a given quantity of output with a lower cost of inputs and will show a large positive productivity component. Given Chipset's strategy of cost leadership, managers expect the increase in operating income to be attributable to the productivity and growth components, not to price recovery. We now examine these three components in detail.

Growth Component of Change in Operating Income

The growth component of the change in operating income measures the increase in revenues minus the increase in costs from selling more units of CX1 in 2020 (1,150,000 units) than in 2019 (1,000,000 units), *assuming nothing else has changed.*

Revenue Effect of Growth

$$\text{Revenue effect of growth} = \left(\begin{array}{c}\text{Actual units of}\\ \text{output sold}\\ \text{in 2020}\end{array} - \begin{array}{c}\text{Actual units of}\\ \text{output sold}\\ \text{in 2019}\end{array}\right) \times \begin{array}{c}\text{Selling}\\ \text{price}\\ \text{in 2019}\end{array}$$

$$= (1{,}150{,}000 \text{ units} - 1{,}000{,}000 \text{ units}) \times \$23 \text{ per unit}$$

$$= \$3{,}450{,}000 \text{ F}$$

This growth component is favorable (F) because the increase in output sold in 2020 compared to 2019 increases operating income, assuming nothing else has changed. Components that decrease operating income are unfavorable (U).

Note that Chipset uses the 2019 price of CX1 and focuses only on the increase in units sold between 2019 and 2020 because the revenue effect of the growth component measures how much revenues would have changed in 2019 if Chipset had sold 1,150,000 units instead of 1,000,000 units.

Cost Effect of Growth

If Chipset had produced more units in 2019, it would also have incurred more costs to produce those units. These additional costs would have to be offset against the higher revenues from producing and selling the additional units to determine how much operating income would change as a result of growth. The cost effect of growth measures how much costs would have changed in 2019 if Chipset had produced 1,150,000 units of CX1 instead of 1,000,000 units. To measure the cost effect of growth, Chipset's management accountants distinguish variable costs (only direct material costs) and fixed costs (conversion costs) because as units produced (and sold) increase, variable costs increase proportionately but fixed costs, generally, do not change.

$$\begin{array}{c}\text{Cost effect of}\\ \text{growth for}\\ \text{variable costs}\end{array} = \left(\begin{array}{c}\text{Units of input}\\ \text{required to}\\ \text{produce 2020}\\ \text{output in 2019}\end{array} - \begin{array}{c}\text{Actual units of}\\ \text{input used}\\ \text{to produce}\\ \text{2019 output}\end{array}\right) \times \begin{array}{c}\text{Input}\\ \text{price}\\ \text{in 2019}\end{array}$$

$$\begin{array}{c}\text{Cost effect of}\\ \text{growth for}\\ \text{direct materials}\end{array} = \left(3{,}000{,}000 \text{ sq. cm} \times \frac{1{,}150{,}000 \text{ units}}{1{,}000{,}000 \text{ units}} - 3{,}000{,}000 \text{ sq. cm.}\right) \times \$1.40 \text{ per sq. cm.}$$

$$= (3{,}450{,}000 \text{ sq. cm.} - 3{,}000{,}000 \text{ sq. cm.}) \times \$1.40 \text{ per sq. cm.} = \$630{,}000 \text{ U}$$

The units of input required to produce 2020 output in 2019 can also be calculated as follows:

$$\text{Units of input per unit of output in 2019} = \frac{3{,}000{,}000 \text{ sq. cm}}{1{,}000{,}000 \text{ units}} = 3 \text{ sq. cm./unit}$$

Units of input required to produce 2020 output of 1,150,000 units in 2019 = 3 sq. cm. per unit × 1,150,000 units = 3,450,000 sq. cm.

$$\begin{array}{c}\text{Cost effect of}\\ \text{growth for}\\ \text{fixed costs}\end{array} = \left(\begin{array}{c}\text{Actual units of capacity in}\\ \text{2019 because adequate capacity}\\ \text{exists to produce 2020 output in 2019}\end{array} - \begin{array}{c}\text{Actual units}\\ \text{of capacity}\\ \text{in 2019}\end{array}\right) \times \begin{array}{c}\text{Price per}\\ \text{unit of}\\ \text{capacity}\\ \text{in 2019}\end{array}$$

$$\begin{array}{c}\text{Cost effect of}\\ \text{growth for}\\ \text{conversion costs}\end{array} = (3{,}750{,}000 \text{ sq. cm} - 3{,}750{,}000 \text{ sq. cm.}) \times \$4.28 \text{ per sq. cm.} = \$0$$

Conversion costs are fixed costs at a given level of capacity. Chipset has manufacturing capacity to process 3,750,000 square centimeters of silicon wafers in 2019 at a cost of $4.28 per square centimeter (rows 5 and 7 of data on page 534). To produce 1,150,000 units of output in 2019, Chipset needs to process 3,450,000 square centimeters of direct materials, which is less than the available capacity of 3,750,000 sq. cm. Throughout this chapter, we assume adequate capacity exists in 2019 to produce 2020 output. Under this assumption, the cost effect of growth for capacity-related fixed costs is, by definition, $0. Had 2019 capacity been inadequate to produce 2020 output in 2019, we would need to calculate the costs of the additional capacity required to produce 2020 output in 2019. These calculations are beyond the scope of this text.

In summary, the net increase in operating income attributable to growth equals the following:

Revenue effect of growth		$3,450,000 F
Cost effect of growth		
Direct material costs	$630,000 U	
Conversion costs	0	630,000 U
Change in operating income due to growth		$2,820,000 F

Price-Recovery Component of Change in Operating Income

Assuming that the 2019 relationship between inputs and outputs continued in 2020, the price-recovery component of the change in operating income measures solely the effect of changes in selling price on revenues *minus* the effect of changes in input prices on costs to produce and sell the 1,150,000 units of CX1 in 2020.

Revenue Effect of Price Recovery

$$\text{Revenue effect of price recovery} = \left(\text{Selling price in 2020} - \text{Selling price in 2019}\right) \times \text{Actual units of output sold in 2020}$$

$$= (\$22 \text{ per unit} - \$23 \text{ per unit}) \times 1{,}150{,}000 \text{ units}$$

$$= \$1{,}150{,}000 \text{ U}$$

Note that the calculation focuses on revenue changes caused by the decrease in the selling price of CX1 between 2019 ($23) and 2020 ($22).

Cost Effect of Price Recovery

Chipset's management accountants calculate the cost effects of price recovery separately for variable costs and for fixed costs, just as they did when calculating the cost effect of growth.

$$\text{Cost effect of price recovery for variable costs} = \left(\text{Input price in 2020} - \text{Input price in 2019}\right) \times \text{Units of input required to produce 2020 output in 2019}$$

$$\text{Cost effect of price recovery for direct materials} = (\$1.50 \text{ per sq. cm.} - \$1.40 \text{ sq. cm.}) \times 3{,}450{,}000 \text{ sq. cm.} = \$345{,}000 \text{ U}$$

Recall that the direct materials of 3,450,000 square centimeters required to produce 2020 output in 2019 had already been calculated when computing the cost effect of growth (page 536).

$$\text{Cost effect of price recovery for fixed costs} = \left(\text{Price per unit of capacity in 2020} - \text{Price per unit of capacity in 2019}\right) \times \text{Actual units of capacity in 2019 (because adequate capacity exists to produce 2020 output in 2019)}$$

Cost effect of price recovery for fixed costs is as follows:

$$\text{Conversion costs: } (\$4.35 \text{ per sq. cm.} - \$4.28 \text{ per sq. cm.}) \times 3{,}750{,}000 \text{ sq. cm.} = \$262{,}500 \text{ U}$$

Recall that the detailed analyses of capacities were presented when computing the cost effect of growth (pages 536–537).

In summary, the net decrease in operating income attributable to price recovery equals the following:

Revenue effect of price recovery		\$1,150,000 U
Cost effect of price recovery		
Direct material costs	\$345,000 U	
Conversion costs	262,500 U	607,500 U
Change in operating income due to price recovery		\$1,757,500 U

The price-recovery analysis indicates that, even as the prices of its inputs increased, the selling prices of CX1 decreased and Chipset did not pass on input-price increases to its customers.

Productivity Component of Change in Operating Income

The productivity component of the change in operating income uses 2020 input prices to measure how costs have decreased as a result of using fewer inputs, a better mix of inputs, and/or less capacity to produce 2020 output, compared with the inputs and capacity that would have been used to produce this output in 2019.

The productivity-component calculations use 2020 prices and output because the productivity component isolates the change in costs between 2019 and 2020 caused solely by the change in the quantities, mix, and/or capacities of inputs.[10]

$$\begin{array}{c}\text{Cost effect of}\\ \text{productivity for}\\ \text{variable costs}\end{array} = \left(\begin{array}{c}\text{Actual units of}\\ \text{input used}\\ \text{to produce}\\ \text{2020 output}\end{array} - \begin{array}{c}\text{Units of input}\\ \text{required to}\\ \text{produce 2020}\\ \text{output in 2019}\end{array}\right) \times \begin{array}{c}\text{Input}\\ \text{price}\\ \text{in 2020}\end{array}$$

Using the 2020 data given on page 534 and the calculation of units of input required to produce 2020 output in 2019 derived when discussing the cost effects of growth (page 536),

$$\begin{aligned}\begin{array}{c}\text{Cost effect of}\\ \text{productivity for}\\ \text{direct materials}\end{array} &= (2{,}900{,}000 \text{ sq. cm.} - 3{,}450{,}000 \text{ sq. cm.}) \times \$1.50 \text{ per sq. cm.}\\ &= 550{,}000 \text{ sq. cm.} \times \$1.50 \text{ per sq. cm.} = \$825{,}000 \text{ F}\end{aligned}$$

Chipset's quality and yield improvements reduced the quantity of direct materials needed to produce output in 2020 relative to 2019.

$$\begin{array}{c}\text{Cost effect of}\\ \text{productivity for}\\ \text{fixed costs}\end{array} = \left(\begin{array}{c}\text{Actual units of}\\ \text{capacity}\\ \text{in 2020}\end{array} - \begin{array}{c}\text{Actual units of capacity in}\\ \text{2019 because adequate}\\ \text{capacity exists to produce}\\ \text{2020 output in 2019}\end{array}\right) \times \begin{array}{c}\text{Price per}\\ \text{unit of}\\ \text{capacity}\\ \text{in 2020}\end{array}$$

To calculate the cost effect of productivity for fixed costs, we use the 2020 price data (page 534) and the analyses of capacity required to produce 2020 output in 2019 conducted when discussing the cost effect of growth (pages 536–537).

Cost effects of productivity for fixed costs are

$$\text{Conversion costs: } (3{,}500{,}000 \text{ sq. cm} - 3{,}750{,}000 \text{ sq. cm.}) \times \$4.35 \text{ per sq. cm.} = \$1{,}087{,}500 \text{ F}$$

[10] Note that the productivity-component calculation uses actual 2020 input prices, whereas its counterpart, the efficiency variance in Chapters 7 and 8, uses budgeted prices. (In effect, the budgeted prices correspond to 2019 prices.) Year 2020 prices are used in the productivity calculation because Chipset wants its managers to choose input quantities to minimize costs in 2020 based on currently prevailing prices. If 2019 prices had been used in the productivity calculation, managers would choose input quantities based on irrelevant input prices that prevailed a year ago! Why does using budgeted prices in Chapters 7 and 8 not pose a similar problem? Because, unlike 2019 prices that describe what happened a year ago, budgeted prices represent prices that are expected to prevail in the current period. Moreover, budgeted prices can be changed, if necessary, to bring them in line with actual current-period prices.

EXHIBIT 13-6 Strategic Analysis of Profitability

	Income Statement Amounts in 2019 (1)	Revenue and Cost Effects of Growth Component in 2020 (2)	Revenue and Cost Effects of Price-Recovery Component in 2020 (3)	Cost Effect of Productivity Component in 2020 (4)	Income Statement Amounts in 2020 (5) = (1) + (2) + (3) + (4)
Revenues	$23,000,000	$3,450,000 F	$1,150,000 U	—	$25,300,000
Costs	20,250,000	630,000 U	607,500 U	$1,912,500 F	19,575,000
Operating income	$ 2,750,000	$2,820,000 F	$1,757,500 U	$1,912,500 F	$ 5,725,000

$2,975,000 F

Change in operating income

Chipset's managers decreased manufacturing capacity in 2020 to 3,500,000 square centimeters by selling off old equipment and reducing the workforce using a combination of retirements and layoffs.

In summary, the net increase in operating income attributable to productivity improvements equals:

Cost effect of productivity:	
Direct material costs	$ 825,000 F
Conversion costs	1,087,500 F
Change in operating income due to productivity	$1,912,500 F

The productivity component indicates that Chipset was able to increase operating income by improving manufacturing quality and productivity and by eliminating capacity, all of which lead to reductions in costs. The appendix to this chapter examines partial and total factor productivity changes between 2019 and 2020 and describes how management accountants can obtain a deeper understanding of Chipset's cost-leadership strategy. Note that the productivity component focuses exclusively on costs, so there is no revenue effect for this component.

Exhibit 13-6 summarizes the growth, price-recovery, and productivity components of the changes in operating income. Generally, companies that have been successful at cost leadership will show favorable productivity and growth components. Companies that have successfully differentiated their products will show favorable price-recovery and growth components. In Chipset's case, consistent with the organization's strategy and its implementation, productivity contributed $1,912,500 to the increase in operating income and growth contributed $2,820,000. Price recovery decreased operating income by $1,757,500 because even as input prices increased, the selling price of CX1 decreased. Had Chipset been able to differentiate its product and charge a higher price, the price-recovery effects might have been less unfavorable or perhaps even favorable. As a result, Chipset's managers plan to evaluate some modest changes in product features that might help differentiate CX1 somewhat more from competing products.

Further Analysis of Growth, Price-Recovery, and Productivity Components

As in all variance and profit analysis, Chipset's managers may want to further analyze the change in operating income. For example, Chipset's growth might have been helped by an increase in industry market size. Therefore, at least part of the increase in operating income may be attributable to favorable economic conditions in the industry rather than to any successful implementation of strategy. Some of the growth might relate to the management decision to decrease selling price, made possible by the productivity gains. In this case, the increase in operating income from cost leadership must include operating income from productivity-related growth in market share in addition to the productivity gain.

TRY IT! 13-2

Strategic Analysis of Operating Income

Costa Associates is a construction engineering firm that prepares detailed construction drawings for single-family homes. The market for this service is very competitive. To compete successfully Costa must deliver quality service at low cost. Costa presents the following data for 2019 and 2020.

	2019	2020
1. Number of jobs billed	450	650
2. Selling price per job	$ 3,500	$ 3,300
3. Engineering labor-hours	27,000	32,000
4. Cost per engineering labor-hour	$ 39	$ 40
5. Engineering support capacity (number of jobs the firm can do)	850	850
6. Total cost of engineering support (space rent, equipment, etc.)	$263,500	$306,000
7. Engineering support-capacity cost per job	$ 310	$ 360

Engineering labor-hour costs are variable costs. Engineering support costs for each year depend on the engineering support capacity that Costa chooses to maintain each year (that is, the number of jobs it can do each year). Engineering support costs do not vary with the actual number of jobs done in a year.

1. Calculate the operating income of Costa Associates in 2019 and 2020.
2. Calculate the growth, price-recovery, and productivity components that explain the change in operating income from 2019 to 2020.
3. Comment on your answer in requirement 2. What do these components indicate?

We illustrate these ideas, using the Chipset example and the following additional information. *Instructors who do not wish to cover these detailed calculations can go to the next section without any loss of continuity.*

- The market growth rate in the industry is 8% in 2020. Of the 150,000 (1,150,000 − 1,000,000) units of increased sales of CX1 between 2019 and 2020, 80,000 (0.08 × 1,000,000) units are due to an increase in industry market size (which Chipset should have benefited from regardless of its productivity gains), and the remaining 70,000 units are due to an increase in market share.
- During 2020, Chipset could have maintained the price of CX1 at the 2019 price of $23 per unit. But management decided to take advantage of the productivity gains to reduce the price of CX1 by $1 to grow market share leading to the 70,000-unit increase in sales.

The effect of the industry-market-size factor on operating income (not any specific strategic action) is as follows:

Change in operating income due to growth in industry market size

$$\$2{,}820{,}000 \text{ (Exhibit 13-6, column 2)} \times \frac{80{,}000 \text{ units}}{150{,}000 \text{ units}} = \underline{\underline{\$1{,}504{,}000 \text{ F}}}$$

Even while lacking a differentiated product, Chipset could have maintained the price of CX1 at $23 per unit. Under this assumption the revenue effect of price recovery of $1,150,000 (Exhibit 13-6, column 3) cannot be attributed to a lack of product differentiation. The lack of product differentiation affects operating income only as a result of higher input prices.

The effect of product differentiation on operating income is as follows:

Change in prices of inputs (cost effect of price recovery)	$607,500 U
Change in operating income due to product differentiation	$607,500 U

To exercise cost and price leadership and to achieve faster growth, Chipset made the strategic decision to cut the selling price of CX1 by $1. This decision resulted in an increase in market share and 70,000 units of additional sales.

The effect of cost leadership on operating income is as follows:

Productivity component	$1,912,500 F
Effect of strategic decision to reduce price ($1/unit × 1,150,000 units)	1,150,000 U
Growth in market share due to productivity improvement and strategic decision to reduce prices	
$\$2{,}820{,}000 \text{ (Exhibit 13-6, column 2)} \times \dfrac{70{,}000 \text{ units}}{150{,}000 \text{ units}}$	1,316,000 F
Change in operating income due to cost leadership	$2,078,500 F

A summary of the change in operating income between 2019 and 2020 follows.

Change due to industry market size	$1,504,000 F
Change due to product differentiation	607,500 U
Change due to cost leadership	2,078,500 F
Change in operating income	$2,975,000 F

Consistent with its cost-leadership strategy, the productivity gains of $1,912,500 in 2020 were a big part of the increase in operating income from 2019 to 2020. Chipset took advantage of these productivity gains to decrease price by $1 per unit at a cost of $1,150,000 to gain $1,316,000 in operating income by selling 70,000 additional units. *Under different assumptions about the change in selling price of CX1, the analysis will attribute different amounts of the change in operating income to the different strategies.*

The Problem for Self-Study on pages 543–546 describes the analysis of the growth, price-recovery, and productivity components for a company following a product-differentiation strategy. The Concepts in Action: Operating Income Analysis and the Decline of Casual Dining Restaurants describes how analysis of operating income revealed strategic challenges at chain restaurants like Buffalo Wild Wings.

DECISION POINT

How can a company analyze changes in operating income to evaluate the success of its strategy?

CONCEPTS IN ACTION

Operating Income Analysis and the Decline of Casual Dining Restaurants[11]

George Sheldon/Shutterstock

For decades, chain restaurants like Olive Garden and TGI Fridays dominated the dining landscape. With thousands of locations to grab a booth and order off the menu in shopping and strip malls across America, the casual dining industry was very robust and profitable.

By the mid-2010s, however, analyzing the operating income of these chains revealed strategic challenges. At Buffalo Wild Wings, for example, though revenue increased 31% from 2014 to 2016, operating income fell 23% over the same period. Meanwhile, same store sales were declining and the costs of sales, labor, and operating expenses were rising. The reason: Younger diners were fleeing Buffalo Wild Wings and other restaurant chains in favor of trendier, tech-savvy, and more health-conscious options. According to former Buffalo Wild Wings CEO Sally Smith, "Millennial consumers are more attracted than their elders to cooking at home, ordering delivery from restaurants, and eating quickly, in fast-casual or quick-serve restaurants."

To turn things around, chains from Chili's to Outback Steakhouse are moving quickly to reshape their menus and renovate their restaurants to attract younger consumers—including creating Instagrammable atmospheres with picturesque, healthier menu items and introducing new to-go and mobile ordering services. It may be too late for some chains, however. In 2018, Applebee's announced plans to close 80 locations and IHOP shuttered 40 locations as well. As for Buffalo Wild Wings, unable to quickly attract a younger clientele, it was acquired by Roark Capital Group, the parent company of Arby's, for $2.9 billion in 2018.

[11] *Sources:* Katie Richards, "Younger Consumers Are Abandoning Casual Chains. Here's What Restaurants Are Doing to Fix It," *AdWeek*, April 8, 2018 (https://www.adweek.com/brand-marketing/younger-consumers-are-still-abandoning-casual-chains-heres-what-theyre-doing-to-fix-it/); Kate Taylor, "Buffalo Wild Wings Was Sucked Into a Downward Spiral as Millennials Ditched the Chain — But the New CEO Has a Plan for a Comeback," *Business Insider*, February 11, 2018 (https://www.businessinsider.com/buffalo-wild-wings-comeback-plan-2018-2); "Buffalo Wild Wings President and CEO Sends Letter to Shareholders," Buffalo Wild Wings, Inc. press release, Minneapolis, May 30, 2017 (https://www.businesswire.com/news/home/20170530005597/en/Buffalo-Wild-Wings-President-CEO-Sends-Letter); Buffalo Wild Wings, Inc., 2016 Annual Report (Minneapolis: Buffalo Wild Wings, Inc., 2017).

TRY IT! 13-3

Analysis of Growth, Price-Recovery, and Productivity Components

Refer to the information on Costa Associates in Try It! 13-2. Suppose that during 2020, the market for construction drawing jobs increases by 14%. Assume that any increase in market share more than 14% and any decrease in selling price are the result of strategic choices by Costa's management to implement its strategy.

Calculate how much of the change in operating income from 2019 to 2020 is due to the industry-market-size factor, product differentiation, and cost leadership. How successful has Costa been in implementing its strategy? Explain.

Downsizing and the Management of Capacity

LEARNING OBJECTIVE 4

Identify unused capacity

. . . capacity available minus capacity used

and learn how to manage it

. . . downsize to reduce capacity

As we saw in our discussion of the productivity component (page 538), fixed costs are tied to capacity. Unlike variable costs, fixed costs do not change automatically with changes in activity levels (for example, fixed conversion costs do not change with changes in the quantity of silicon wafers started into production). How then can managers reduce capacity-based fixed costs? By measuring and managing **unused capacity**, which is the amount of productive capacity available over and above the productive capacity employed to meet customer demand in the current period.

Cost-leadership strategies require managers to pay special attention to capacity costs. Companies such as United Airlines have struggled to achieve profitability because of the difficulties they have had in managing capacity-related fixed costs. For a given number of flights, most of United's costs, such as the cost of airplane leases, fuel, and wages, are fixed. United must anticipate future revenues and decide on a level of capacity and the related costs. If revenues fall short, it is difficult for United Airlines to reduce its costs quickly.

Identifying Unused Capacity Costs

Consider conversion costs. At the start of 2019, Chipset committed to capacity to process 3,750,000 square centimeters of silicon wafers for the year. Chipset ended up producing 1,000,000 units of CX1 by processing 3,000,000 square centimeters of silicon wafers in 2019. Unused manufacturing capacity for 2019 is 750,000 (3,750,000 − 3,000,000) square centimeters of silicon-wafer processing capacity. At the 2019 conversion cost of $4.28 per square centimeter,

$$\text{Cost of unused capacity} = \text{Cost of capacity committed to at the beginning of the year} - \text{Manufacturing resources used during the year}$$

$$= (3{,}750{,}000 \text{ sq. cm.} \times \$4.28 \text{ per sq. cm.}) - (3{,}000{,}000 \text{ sq. cm.} \times \$4.28 \text{ per sq. cm.})$$

$$= \$16{,}050{,}000 - \$12{,}840{,}000 = \$3{,}210{,}000$$

Managing Unused Capacity

What actions can Chipset's management take when it identifies unused capacity? In general, it has two alternatives: eliminate unused capacity or grow output to utilize the unused capacity.

In recent years, many companies have *downsized* in an attempt to eliminate unused capacity. **Downsizing** (also called **rightsizing**) is an integrated approach of configuring processes, products, and people to match costs to the activities that need to be performed to operate effectively and efficiently in the present and future. Companies such as AT&T, Delta Airlines, Ford Motor Company, and IBM have downsized to focus on their core businesses and have instituted organization changes to increase efficiency, reduce costs, and improve quality. However, downsizing often means eliminating jobs, which can adversely affect employee morale and the culture of a company.

Consider Chipset's alternatives for dealing with unused manufacturing capacity. Because it needs to process 2,900,000 square centimeters of silicon wafers in 2020, the company could reduce capacity from 3,750,000 to 3,000,000 square centimeters at the beginning of 2020

(Chipset can add or reduce manufacturing capacity in increments of 250,000 sq. cm.), resulting in cost savings of \$3,262,500 [(3,750,000 sq. cm. − 3,000,000 sq. cm.) × \$4.35 per sq. cm.]. Chipset's strategy, however, is not just to reduce costs but also to grow its business. So in early 2020, Chipset reduces its manufacturing capacity by only 250,000 square centimeters—from 3,750,000 square centimeters to 3,500,000 square centimeters—saving \$1,087,500 (\$4.35 per sq. cm. × 250,000 sq. cm.). It retains some extra capacity for future growth. By avoiding greater reductions in capacity, it also maintains the morale of its skilled and capable workforce. The success of this strategy will depend on Chipset achieving the future growth it has projected.

DECISION POINT

How can a company identify and manage unused capacity?

Identifying and Managing Unused Capacity

Refer to the information on Costa Associates in Try It! 13-2.

13-4 TRY IT!

1. Calculate the amount and cost of unused engineering support capacity at the beginning of 2020, based on the number of jobs actually done in 2020.
2. Suppose Costa can add or reduce its engineering support capacity in increments of 50 jobs. What is the maximum amount of costs that Costa could save in 2020 by downsizing engineering support capacity?
3. Costa, in fact, does not eliminate any of its unused engineering support capacity. Why might Costa not downsize?

PROBLEM FOR SELF-STUDY

Following a strategy of product differentiation, Westwood Corporation makes a high-end kitchen range hood, KE8. Westwood's data for 2019 and 2020 are shown below:

	2019	2020
1. Units of KE8 produced and sold	40,000	42,000
2. Selling price	\$100	\$110
3. Direct materials (square feet)	120,000	123,000
4. Direct material cost per square foot	\$10	\$11
5. Manufacturing capacity for KE8	50,000 units	50,000 units
6. Conversion costs	\$1,000,000	\$1,100,000
7. Conversion cost per unit of capacity (row 6 ÷ row 5)	\$20	\$22
8. Selling and customer-service capacity	30 customers	29 customers
9. Selling and customer-service costs	\$720,000	\$725,000
10. Cost per customer of selling and customer-service capacity (row 9 ÷ row 8)	\$24,000	\$25,000

In 2020, Westwood reduced direct material usage per unit of KE8. Conversion costs in each year are tied to manufacturing capacity. Selling and customer-service costs are related to the number of customers that the selling and customer-service functions are designed to support. Westwood had 23 customers (wholesalers) in 2019 and 25 customers in 2020.

Required

1. Describe briefly the key elements you would include in Westwood's balanced scorecard.
2. Calculate the growth, price-recovery, and productivity components that explain the change in operating income from 2019 to 2020.
3. Suppose during 2020, the market size for high-end kitchen range hoods grew 3% in terms of number of units and all increases in market share (that is, increases in the number of units sold greater than 3%) are due to Westwood's product-differentiation strategy. Calculate how much of the change in operating income from 2019 to 2020 is due to the industry-market-size factor, cost leadership, and product differentiation.
4. How successful has Westwood been in implementing its strategy? Explain.

Solution

1. The balanced scorecard should describe Westwood's product-differentiation strategy. Key elements that should be included in its balanced scorecard are as follows:
   - **Financial perspective.** Increase in operating income from higher margins on KE8 and from growth
   - **Customer perspective.** Customer satisfaction ratings and market share in the high-end market
   - **Internal-business-process perspective.** Number of major new product features, development time for new products, number of advanced controls in manufacturing processes, number of reworked products, order-delivery time, and on-time delivery
   - **Learning-and-growth perspective.** Number of employees in product development, percentage of employees trained in process and quality management, and employee satisfaction ratings
2. Operating income for each year is as follows:

	2019	2020
Revenues		
($100 per unit × 40,000 units; $110 per unit × 42,000 units)	$4,000,000	$4,620,000
Costs		
Direct material costs		
($10 per sq. ft. × 120,000 sq. ft.; $11 per sq. ft. × 123,000 sq. ft.)	1,200,000	1,353,000
Conversion costs		
($20 per unit × 50,000 units; $22 per unit × 50,000 units)	1,000,000	1,100,000
Selling and customer-service cost		
($24,000 per customer × 30 customers; $25,000 per customer × 29 customers)	720,000	725,000
Total costs	2,920,000	3,178,000
Operating income	$1,080,000	$1,442,000
Change in operating income	$362,000 F	

Growth Component of Change in Operating Income

$$\text{Revenue effect of growth} = \left(\begin{array}{c}\text{Actual units of}\\ \text{output sold}\\ \text{in 2020}\end{array} - \begin{array}{c}\text{Actual units of}\\ \text{output sold}\\ \text{in 2019}\end{array}\right) \times \begin{array}{c}\text{Selling}\\ \text{price}\\ \text{in 2019}\end{array}$$

$$= (42{,}000 \text{ units} - 40{,}000 \text{ units}) \times \$100 \text{ per unit} = \$200{,}000\ \text{F}$$

$$\begin{array}{c}\text{Cost effect of}\\ \text{growth for}\\ \text{variable costs}\end{array} = \left(\begin{array}{c}\text{Units of input}\\ \text{required to}\\ \text{produce 2020}\\ \text{output in 2019}\end{array} - \begin{array}{c}\text{Actual units of}\\ \text{input used}\\ \text{to produce}\\ \text{2019 output}\end{array}\right) \times \begin{array}{c}\text{Input}\\ \text{price}\\ \text{in 2019}\end{array}$$

$$\begin{array}{c}\text{Cost effect}\\ \text{of growth for}\\ \text{direct materials}\end{array} = \left(120{,}000 \text{ sq. ft.} \times \frac{42{,}000 \text{ units}}{40{,}000 \text{ units}} - 120{,}000 \text{ sq. ft.}\right) \times \$10 \text{ per sq. ft.}$$

$$= (126{,}000 \text{ sq. ft.} - 120{,}000 \text{ sq. ft.}) \times \$10 \text{ per sq. ft.} = \$60{,}000\ \text{U}$$

$$\begin{array}{c}\text{Cost effect}\\ \text{of growth for}\\ \text{fixed costs}\end{array} = \left(\begin{array}{c}\text{Actual units of capacity in}\\ \text{2019 because adequate capacity}\\ \text{exists to produce 2020 output in 2019}\end{array} - \begin{array}{c}\text{Actual units}\\ \text{of capacity}\\ \text{in 2019}\end{array}\right) \times \begin{array}{c}\text{Price per}\\ \text{unit of}\\ \text{capacity}\\ \text{in 2019}\end{array}$$

$$\begin{array}{c}\text{Cost effect of}\\ \text{growth for}\\ \text{fixed conversion costs}\end{array} = (50{,}000 \text{ units} - 50{,}000 \text{ units}) \times \$20 \text{ per unit} = \$0$$

$$\text{Cost effect of growth for fixed selling and customer-service costs} = (30 \text{ customers} - 30 \text{ customers}) \times \$24{,}000 \text{ per customer} = \$0$$

In summary, the net increase in operating income attributable to growth equals

Revenue effect of growth		$200,000 F
Cost effect of growth		
Direct material costs	$60,000 U	
Conversion costs	0	
Selling and customer-service costs	0	60,000 U
Change in operating income due to growth		$140,000 F

Price-Recovery Component of Change in Operating Income

$$\text{Revenue effect of price recovery} = \left(\text{Selling price in 2020} - \text{Selling price in 2019}\right) \times \text{Actual units of output sold in 2020}$$

$$= (\$110 \text{ per unit} - \$100 \text{ per unit}) \times 42{,}000 \text{ units} = \$420{,}000 \text{ F}$$

$$\text{Cost effect of price recovery for variable costs} = \left(\text{Input price in 2020} - \text{Input price in 2019}\right) \times \text{Units of input required to produce 2020 output in 2019}$$

$$\text{Direct material costs: } (\$11 \text{ per sq. ft.} - \$10 \text{ per sq. ft.}) \times 126{,}000 \text{ sq. ft.} = \$126{,}000 \text{ U}$$

$$\text{Cost effect of price recovery for fixed costs} = \left(\text{Price per unit of capacity in 2020} - \text{Price per unit of capacity in 2019}\right) \times \text{Actual units of capacity in 2019 because adequate capacity exists to produce 2020 output in 2019}$$

Cost effects of price recovery for fixed costs are

$$\text{Conversion costs: } (\$22 \text{ per unit} - 20 \text{ per unit}) \times 50{,}000 \text{ units} = \$100{,}000 \text{ U}$$

$$\text{Selling and cust.-service costs: } (\$25{,}000 \text{ per cust.} - \$24{,}000 \text{ per cust.}) \times 30 \text{ customers} = \$30{,}000 \text{ U}$$

In summary, the net increase in operating income attributable to price recovery equals

Revenue effect of price recovery		$420,000 F
Cost effect of price recovery:		
Direct material costs	$126,000 U	
Conversion costs	100,000 U	
Selling and customer-service costs	30,000 U	256,000 U
Change in operating income due to price recovery		$164,000 F

Productivity Component of Change in Operating Income

$$\text{Cost effect of productivity for variable costs} = \left(\text{Actual units of input used to produce 2020 output} - \text{Units of input required to produce 2020 output in 2019}\right) \times \text{Input price in 2020}$$

$$\text{Cost effect of productivity for direct materials} = (123{,}000 \text{ sq. ft.} - 126{,}000 \text{ sq. ft.}) \times \$11 \text{ per sq. ft.} = \$33{,}000 \text{ F}$$

$$\text{Cost effect of productivity for fixed costs} = \left(\text{Actual units of capacity in 2020} - \text{Actual units of capacity in 2019 because adequate capacity exists to produce 2020 output in 2019}\right) \times \text{Price per unit of capacity in 2020}$$

Cost effects of productivity for fixed costs are

Conversion costs: (50,000 units − 50,000 units) × $22 per unit = $0

Selling and customer-service costs: (29 customers − 30 customers) × $25,000/customer = $25,000 F

In summary, the net increase in operating income attributable to productivity equals

Cost effect of productivity:	
Direct material costs	$33,000 F
Conversion costs	0
Selling and customer-service costs	25,000 F
Change in operating income due to productivity	$58,000 F

A summary of the change in operating income between 2019 and 2020 follows.

	Income Statement Amounts in 2019 (1)	Revenue and Cost Effects of Growth Component in 2020 (2)	Revenue and Cost Effects of Price-Recovery Component in 2020 (3)	Cost Effect of Productivity Component in 2020 (4)	Income Statement Amounts in 2020 (5) = (1) + (2) + (3) + (4)
Revenue	$4,000,000	$200,000 F	$420,000 F	—	$4,620,000
Costs	2,920,000	60,000 U	256,000 U	$58,000 F	3,178,000
Operating income	$1,080,000	$140,000 F	$164,000 F	$58,000 F	$1,442,000

$362,000 F

Change in operating income

3. **Effect of the Industry-Market-Size Factor on Operating Income**
Of the increase in sales from 40,000 to 42,000 units, 3%, or 1,200 units (0.03 × 40,000), are due to growth in market size, and 800 units (2,000 − 1,200) are due to an increase in market share. The change in Westwood's operating income from the industry-market-size factor rather than specific strategic actions is:

$$\$140{,}000\ (\text{column 2 of preceding table}) \times \frac{1{,}200\ \text{units}}{2{,}000\ \text{units}} \qquad \$\ 84{,}000\ \text{F}$$

Effect of Product Differentiation on Operating Income

Increase in the selling price of KE8 (revenue effect of the price-recovery component)	$ 420,000 F
Increase in prices of inputs (cost effect of the price-recovery component)	256,000 U
Growth in market share due to product differentiation	
$140,000 (column 2 of preceding table) × $\frac{800\ \text{units}}{2{,}000\ \text{units}}$	56,000 F
Change in operating income due to product differentiation	$ 220,000 F

Effect of Cost Leadership on Operating Income

Productivity component	$ 58,000 F

A summary of the net increase in operating income from 2019 to 2020 follows:

Change due to the industry-market-size factor	$ 84,000 F
Change due to product differentiation	220,000 F
Change due to cost leadership	58,000 F
Change in operating income	$362,000 F

4. The analysis of operating income indicates that a significant amount of the increase in operating income resulted from Westwood's successful implementation of its product-differentiation strategy (operating income attributable to product differentiation, $220,000 F). The company was able to continue to charge a premium price for KE8 while increasing market share. Westwood was also able to earn additional operating income from improving its cost leadership through productivity improvement (operating income attributable to cost leadership, $58,000 F).

DECISION POINTS

The following question-and-answer format summarizes the chapter's learning objectives. Each decision presents a key question related to a learning objective. The guidelines are the answer to that question.

Decision	Guidelines
1. What are the two generic strategies a company can use?	The two generic strategies are product differentiation and cost leadership. Product differentiation is offering products and services that customers perceive as superior and unique. Cost leadership is achieving lower costs and prices relative to competitors. A company chooses its strategy based on an understanding of customer preferences and its own internal capabilities to differentiate itself from its competitors.
2. How can an organization translate its strategy into a set of performance measures?	An organization can develop a balanced scorecard that provides the framework for a strategic measurement and management system. The balanced scorecard measures performance from four perspectives: (a) financial, (b) customer, (c) internal business processes, and (d) learning and growth. To build their balanced scorecards, organizations often create strategy maps to represent the cause-and-effect relationships across various strategic objectives.
3. How can a company analyze changes in operating income to evaluate the success of its strategy?	To evaluate the success of its strategy, a company can subdivide the change in operating income into growth, price-recovery, and productivity components. The growth component measures the change in revenues and costs from selling more or less units, assuming nothing else has changed. The price-recovery component measures changes in revenues and costs solely as a result of changes in the prices of outputs and inputs. The productivity component measures the decrease in costs from using fewer inputs, using a better mix of inputs, and reducing capacity. If a company is successful in implementing its strategy, changes in components of operating income align closely with strategy.
4. How can a company identify and manage unused capacity?	Unused capacity costs are the portion of capacity costs that were committed to at the beginning of the period that are not used productively during the period. Downsizing is an approach to managing unused capacity that matches costs to the activities that need to be performed to operate effectively.

APPENDIX

Productivity Measurement

Productivity measures the relationship between actual inputs used (both quantities and costs) and actual outputs produced. The lower the inputs for a given quantity of outputs or the higher the outputs for a given quantity of inputs, the higher the productivity. Measuring productivity improvements over time highlights the specific input–output relationships that contribute to cost leadership. The productivity measures discussed in this appendix relate closely to the productivity component introduced in this chapter.

Partial Productivity Measures

Partial productivity, the most frequently used productivity measure, compares the quantity of output produced with the quantity of an individual input used. In its most common form, partial productivity is expressed as a ratio:

$$\text{Partial productivity} = \frac{\text{Quantity of output produced}}{\text{Quantity of input used}}$$

The higher the ratio, the greater the productivity.

Consider direct materials productivity at Chipset in 2020.

$$\begin{aligned}\text{Direct materials partial productivity} &= \frac{\text{Quantity of CX1 units produced during 2020}}{\text{Quantity of direct materials used to produce CX1 in 2020}}\\ &= \frac{\text{1,150,000 units of CX1}}{\text{2,900,000 sq. cm. of silicon wafers}}\\ &= \text{0.397 units of CX1 per sq. cm. of silicon wafers}\end{aligned}$$

Note that direct materials partial productivity ignores Chipset's other input, manufacturing conversion capacity. Partial-productivity measures become more meaningful when comparisons are made that examine productivity changes over time, either across different facilities or relative to a benchmark. Exhibit 13-7 presents partial-productivity measures for Chipset's inputs for 2020 and the comparable 2019 inputs that would have been used to produce 2020 output, using information from the productivity-component calculations on pages 538–539. These measures compare actual inputs used in 2020 to produce 1,150,000 units of CX1 with inputs that would have been used in 2020 had the input–output relationship from 2019 carried over to 2020.

Evaluating Changes in Partial Productivities

Note how the partial-productivity measures differ for variable-cost and fixed-cost components. For variable-cost elements, such as direct materials, productivity improvements measure the reduction in input resources used to produce output (3,450,000 square centimeters of silicon wafers to 2,900,000 square centimeters). For fixed-cost elements such as manufacturing conversion capacity, partial productivity measures the reduction in overall capacity from 2019 to 2020 (3,750,000 square centimeters of silicon wafers to 3,500,000 square centimeters) regardless of the amount of capacity actually used in each period.

An advantage of partial-productivity measures is that they focus on a single input. As a result, they are simple to calculate and easy for operations personnel to understand. Managers and operators examine these numbers and try to understand the reasons for the productivity changes—such as better training of workers, lower labor turnover, better incentives, improved methods, or substitution of materials for labor. Isolating the relevant factors helps Chipset implement and sustain these practices in the future.

EXHIBIT 13-7 Comparing Chipset's Partial Productivities in 2019 and 2020

Input (1)	Partial Productivity in 2020 (2)	Comparable Partial Productivity Based on 2019 Input–Output Relationships (3)	Percentage Change from 2019 to 2020 (4)
Direct materials	$\frac{1{,}150{,}000}{2{,}900{,}000} = 0.397$	$\frac{1{,}150{,}000}{3{,}450{,}000} = 0.333$	$\frac{0.397 - 0.333}{0.333} = 19.2\%$
Manufacturing conversion capacity	$\frac{1{,}150{,}000}{3{,}500{,}000} = 0.329$	$\frac{1{,}150{,}000}{3{,}750{,}000} = 0.307$	$\frac{0.329 - 0.307}{0.307} = 7.2\%$

For all their advantages, partial-productivity measures also have serious drawbacks. Because partial productivity focuses on only one input at a time rather than on all inputs simultaneously, managers cannot evaluate the effect on overall productivity, if (say) manufacturing-conversion-capacity partial productivity increases while direct materials partial productivity decreases. Total factor productivity (TFP), or total productivity, is a measure of productivity that considers all inputs simultaneously.

Total Factor Productivity

Total factor productivity (TFP) is the ratio of the quantity of output produced to the costs of all inputs used based on current-period prices.

$$\text{Total factor productivity} = \frac{\text{Quantity of output produced}}{\text{Costs of all inputs used}}$$

TFP considers all inputs simultaneously and the tradeoffs across inputs based on current input prices. Do not think of all productivity measures as physical measures lacking financial content—how many units of output are produced per unit of input. TFP is intricately tied to minimizing total cost—a financial objective.

Calculating and Comparing Total Factor Productivity

We first calculate Chipset's TFP in 2020, using 2020 prices and 1,150,000 units of output produced (based on information from the first part of the productivity-component calculations on pages 538–539).

$$\begin{aligned}\begin{array}{c}\text{Total factor productivity}\\ \text{for 2020 using 2020 prices}\end{array} &= \frac{\text{Quantity of output produced in 2020}}{\text{Costs of inputs used in 2020 based on 2020 prices}}\\ &= \frac{1{,}150{,}000}{(2{,}900{,}000 \times \$1.50) + (3{,}500{,}000 \times \$4.35)}\\ &= \frac{1{,}150{,}000}{\$19{,}575{,}000}\\ &= 0.058748 \text{ units of output per dollar of input cost}\end{aligned}$$

By itself, the 2020 TFP of 0.058748 units of CX1 per dollar of input costs is not particularly helpful. We need something to compare the 2020 TFP against. One alternative is to compare TFPs of other similar companies in 2020. However, finding similar companies and obtaining accurate comparable data are often difficult. Companies, therefore, usually compare their own TFPs over time. In the Chipset example, we use as a benchmark TFP calculated using the inputs that Chipset would have used in 2019 to produce 1,150,000 units of CX1 at 2020 prices (that is, we use the costs calculated from the second part of the productivity-component calculations on pages 538–539). Why do we use 2020 prices? Because using the current year's prices in both calculations controls for input-price differences and focuses the analysis on adjustments the manager made in quantities of inputs in response to changes in prices.

$$\begin{aligned}\begin{array}{c}\text{Benchmark}\\ \text{TFP}\end{array} &= \frac{\text{Quantity of output produced in 2020}}{\text{Costs of inputs at 2020 prices that would have been used in 2019}}\\ &= \frac{1{,}150{,}000}{(3{,}450{,}000 \times \$1.50) + (3{,}750{,}000 \times \$4.35)}\\ &= \frac{1{,}150{,}000}{\$21{,}487{,}500}\\ &= 0.053519 \text{ units of output per dollar of input cost}\end{aligned}$$

Using 2020 prices, TFP increased 9.8% [(0.058748 − 0.053519) ÷ 0.053519 = 0.098, or 9.8%] from 2019 to 2020. Note that the 9.8% increase in TFP also equals the $1,912,500 gain (Exhibit 13-6, column 4) divided by the $19,575,000 of actual costs incurred in 2020 (Exhibit 13-6, column 5). Total factor productivity increased because Chipset produced more output per dollar of input cost in 2020 relative to 2019, measured in both years using 2020 prices. The gain in TFP occurs because Chipset increases the partial productivities of individual inputs and, consistent with its strategy, combines inputs to lower costs. Note that increases in TFP cannot be due to differences in input prices because we used 2020 prices to evaluate both the inputs that Chipset would have used in 2019 to produce 1,150,000 units of CX1 and the inputs actually used in 2020.

Using Partial and Total Factor Productivity Measures

A major advantage of TFP is that it measures the combined productivity of all inputs used to produce output and explicitly considers gains from using fewer physical inputs as well as substitution among inputs. Managers can analyze these numbers to understand the reasons for changes in TFP—for example, better human resource management practices, higher quality of materials, or improved manufacturing methods.

Although TFP measures are comprehensive, operations personnel find financial TFP measures more difficult to understand and less useful than physical partial-productivity measures. For example, companies that are more labor intensive than Chipset use manufacturing-labor partial-productivity measures. However, if productivity-based bonuses depend on gains in manufacturing-labor partial productivity alone, workers have incentives to substitute materials (and capital) for labor. This substitution improves their own productivity measure, while possibly decreasing the overall productivity of the company as measured by TFP. To overcome these incentive problems, companies—for example, Eaton and Whirlpool—explicitly adjust bonuses based on manufacturing-labor partial productivity for the effects of other factors such as investments in new equipment and higher levels of scrap. That is, they combine partial productivity with TFP-like measures.

Many companies such as Behlen Manufacturing, a steel fabricator, and Dell Computers use both partial productivity and total factor productivity to evaluate performance. *Partial productivity and TFP measures work best together because the strengths of one offset the weaknesses of the other.*

TERMS TO LEARN

This chapter and the Glossary at the end of the text contain definitions of the following important terms:

balanced scorecard (**p. 520**)
cost leadership (**p. 519**)
downsizing (**p. 542**)
growth component (**p. 535**)
partial productivity (**p. 548**)
price-recovery component (**p. 535**)
product differentiation (**p. 519**)
productivity (**p. 547**)
productivity component (**p. 535**)
rightsizing (**p. 542**)
strategy map (**p. 521**)
total factor productivity (TFP) (**p. 549**)
unused capacity (**p. 542**)

ASSIGNMENT MATERIAL

Questions

13-1 Define strategy.
13-2 Describe the five key forces to consider when analyzing an industry.
13-3 Describe the two generic strategies.
13-4 What is a customer preference map, and why is it useful?
13-5 What are ways that a company can achieve cost leadership?
13-6 What are the four key perspectives in the balanced scorecard?

13-7 What are the five types of items to consider when evaluating a strategy map?
13-8 Describe three features of a good balanced scorecard.
13-9 What are three important pitfalls to avoid when implementing a balanced scorecard?
13-10 Describe three key components in doing a strategic analysis of operating income.
13-11 Why might an analyst incorporate the industry-market-size factor and the interrelationships among the growth, price-recovery, and productivity components into a strategic analysis of operating income?
13-12 What are unused capacity costs?
13-13 What is downsizing?
13-14 What is a partial-productivity measure?
13-15 "We are already measuring total factor productivity. Measuring partial productivities would be of no value." Do you agree? Explain briefly.

Multiple-Choice Questions

In partnership with:
BECKER PROFESSIONAL EDUCATION®

13-16 Jacobs Inc. is a relatively new company that has established a position in the highly competitive biotechnology industry. Which of the following statements is correct regarding Jacobs' profitability?

a. Profits will increase when buyers have lower switching costs.
b. Significant up-front capital requirements for new entrants will help Jacobs' profit margins.
c. Profitability is diminished when there are many suppliers.
d. Rival firms willing to spend a lot of money on advertising will increase Jacobs' profits

13-17 The balanced scorecard describes all of the following except which one?

a. The initiatives critical for the organization's performance.
b. The strategic goals.
c. The related measures associated with strategic and tactical goals.
d. The definition of strategic business

13-18 Canarsie Corporation uses a balanced scorecard to evaluate its digital camera manufacturing operation. Which of the following statements with respect to balanced scorecards is/are correct?

I. A balanced scorecard reports management information regarding organizational performance in achieving goals classified by critical success factors to demonstrate that no single dimension of organizational performance can be relied upon to evaluate success.
II. Performance measures used in a balanced scorecard tend to be divided into financial, customer, internal business process, and learning and growth.
III. In a balanced scorecard, internal business processes are what the company does in its attempts to satisfy customers.

1. I and II only are correct.
2. II and III only are correct.
3. III only is correct.
4. I, II, and III are correct

Exercises

13-19 Balanced scorecard. Pineway Electric manufactures electric motors. It competes and plans to grow by selling high-quality motors at a low price and by delivering them to customers in a reasonable time after receiving customers' orders. There are many other manufacturers who produce similar motors. Pineway believes that continuously improving its manufacturing processes and having satisfied employees are critical to implementing its strategy in 2020.

Required

1. Is Pineway's 2020 strategy one of product differentiation or cost leadership? Explain briefly.
2. Ramsey Corporation, a competitor of Pineway, manufactures electric motors with more sizes and features than Pineway at a higher price. Ramsey's motors are of high quality but require more time to produce and so have longer delivery times. Draw a simple customer preference map as in Exhibit 13-1 for Pineway and Ramsey using the attributes of price, delivery time, quality, and design features.
3. Draw a strategy map as in Exhibit 13-2 with at least two strategic objectives you would expect to see under each balanced scorecard perspective. Identify what you believe are any (a) strong ties, (b) focal points, (c) trigger points, and (d) distinctive objectives. Comment on the structural analysis of your strategy map.
4. For each strategic objective, indicate a measure you would expect to see in Pineway's balanced scorecard for 2020.

13-20 Analysis of growth, price-recovery, and productivity components (continuation of 13-19). An analysis of Pineway's operating-income changes between 2019 and 2020 shows the following:

Operating income for 2019	$1,500,000
Add growth component	91,000
Deduct price-recovery component	(82,000)
Add productivity component	145,000
Operating income for 2020	$1,654,000

The industry market size for electric motors did not grow in 2020, input prices did not change, and Pineway reduced the prices of its motors.

Required

1. Was Pineway's gain in operating income in 2020 consistent with the strategy you identified in requirement 1 of Exercise 13-19?
2. Explain the productivity component. In general, does it represent savings in only variable costs, only fixed costs, or both variable and fixed costs?

13-21 Strategy, balanced scorecard, merchandising operation. Gianni & Sons buys T-shirts in bulk, applies its own trendsetting silk-screen designs, and then sells the T-shirts to a number of retailers. Gianni wants to be known for its trendsetting designs, and it wants every teenager to be seen in a distinctive Gianni T-shirt. Gianni presents the following data for its first 2 years of operations, 2019 and 2020.

	2019	2020
1. Number of T-shirts purchased	215,000	245,000
2. Number of T-shirts discarded	15,000	20,000
3. Number of T-shirts sold	200,000	225,000
4. Average selling price	$ 30	$ 31
5. Average cost per T-shirt	$ 15	$ 13
6. Administrative capacity (number of customers)	4,500	4,250
7. Administrative costs	$1,633,500	$1,593,750
8. Administrative cost per customer	$ 363	$ 375

Administrative costs depend on the number of customers Gianni has created capacity to support, not on the actual number of customers served. Gianni had 3,600 customers in 2019 and 3,500 customers in 2020.

Required

1. Is Gianni's strategy one of product differentiation or cost leadership? Explain briefly.
2. Describe briefly the key measures Gianni should include in its balanced scorecard and the reasons for doing so.

13-22 Strategic analysis of operating income (continuation of 13-21). Refer to Exercise 13-21.

Required

1. Calculate Gianni's operating income in both 2019 and 2020.
2. Calculate the growth, price-recovery, and productivity components that explain the change in operating income from 2019 to 2020.
3. Comment on your answers in requirement 2. What does each of these components indicate?

13-23 Analysis of growth, price-recovery, and productivity components (continuation of 13-21 and 13-22). Refer to Exercise 13-21. Suppose that the market for silk-screened T-shirts grew by 10% during 2020. All increases in sales greater than 10% are the result of Gianni's strategic actions.

Required

Calculate the change in operating income from 2019 to 2020 due to growth in market size, product differentiation, and cost leadership. How successful has Gianni been in implementing its strategy? Explain.

13-24 Identifying and managing unused capacity (continuation of 13-21). Refer to Exercise 13-21.

Required

1. Calculate the amount and cost of unused administrative capacity at the beginning of 2020, based on the actual number of customers Gianni served in 2020.
2. Suppose Gianni can only add or reduce administrative capacity in increments of 250 customers. What is the maximum amount of costs that Gianni can save in 2020 by downsizing administrative capacity?
3. What factors, other than cost, should Gianni consider before it downsizes administrative capacity?

13-25 Strategy, balanced scorecard. Methuen Corporation makes a special-purpose machine, D4H, used in the textile industry. Methuen has designed the D4H machine for 2020 to be distinct from its competitors. It has been generally regarded as a superior machine. Methuen presents the following data for 2019 and 2020.

	2019	2020
1. Units of D4H produced and sold	200	210
2. Selling price	$43,000	$45,000
3. Direct materials (kilograms)	310,000	317,500
4. Direct material cost per kilogram	$7.25	$8.00
5. Manufacturing capacity in units of D4H	275	275
6. Total conversion costs	$2,145,000	$2,172,500
7. Conversion cost per unit of capacity	$7,800	$7,900
8. Selling and customer-service capacity	95 customers	90 customers
9. Total selling and customer-service costs	$1,045,000	$900,000
10. Selling and customer-service capacity cost per customer	$11,000	$10,000

Methuen produces no defective machines, but it wants to reduce direct materials usage per D4H machine in 2020. Conversion costs in each year depend on production capacity defined in terms of D4H units that can be produced, not the actual units produced. Selling and customer-service costs depend on the number of customers that Methuen can support, not the actual number of customers it serves. Methuen has 79 customers in 2019 and 84 customers in 2020.

Required

1. Is Methuen's strategy one of product differentiation or cost leadership? Explain briefly.
2. Describe briefly key measures that you would include in Methuen's balanced scorecard and the reasons for doing so.

13-26 Strategic analysis of operating income (continuation of 13-25). Refer to Exercise 13-25.

Required

1. Calculate the operating income of Methuen Corporation in 2019 and 2020.
2. Calculate the growth, price-recovery, and productivity components that explain the change in operating income from 2019 to 2020.
3. Comment on your answer in requirement 2. What do these components indicate?

13-27 Analysis of growth, price-recovery, and productivity components (continuation of 13-25 and 13-26). Suppose that during 2020, the market for Methuen's special-purpose machines grew by 3%. All increases in market share (that is, sales increases greater than 3%) are the result of Methuen's strategic actions.

Required

Calculate how much of the change in operating income from 2019 to 2020 is due to the industry-market-size factor, product differentiation, and cost leadership. How successful has Methuen been in implementing its strategy? Explain.

13-28 Identifying and managing unused capacity (continuation of 13-25). Refer to Exercise 13-25.

Required

1. Calculate the amount and cost of (a) unused manufacturing capacity and (b) unused selling and customer-service capacity at the beginning of 2020 based on actual production and actual number of customers served in 2020.
2. Suppose Methuen can add or reduce its manufacturing capacity in increments of 40 units. What is the maximum amount of costs that Methuen could save in 2020 by downsizing manufacturing capacity?
3. Methuen, in fact, does not eliminate any of its unused manufacturing capacity. Why might Methuen not downsize?

13-29 Strategy, balanced scorecard, service company. Krater Associates is an architectural firm that has been in practice only a few years. Because it is a relatively new firm, the market for the firm's services is very competitive. To compete successfully, Krater must deliver quality services at a low cost. Krater presents the following data for 2019 and 2020.

	2019	2020
1. Number of jobs billed	44	46
2. Selling price per job	$36,000	$35,000
3. Architect labor-hours	19,000	30,000
4. Cost per architect labor-hour	$38	$39
5. Architect support capacity (number of jobs the firm can do)	61	61
6. Total cost of software-implementation support	$164,700	$176,900
7. Software-implementation support-capacity cost per job	$2,700	$2,900

Architect labor-hour costs are variable costs. Architect support costs for each year depend on the architect support capacity that Krater chooses to maintain each year (that is, the number of jobs it can do each year). Architect support costs do not vary with the actual number of jobs done that year.

Required

1. Is Krater Associate's strategy one of product differentiation or cost leadership? Explain briefly.
2. Describe key measures you would include in Krater's balanced scorecard and your reasons for doing so.

13-30 Strategic analysis of operating income (continuation of 13-29). Refer to Exercise 13-29.

Required

1. Calculate the operating income of Krater Associates in 2019 and 2020.
2. Calculate the growth, price-recovery, and productivity components that explain the change in operating income from 2019 to 2020.
3. Comment on your answer in requirement 2. What do these components indicate?

13-31 Analysis of growth, price-recovery, and productivity components (continuation of 13-29 and 13-30). Suppose that during 2020, the market for architectural jobs increases by 10%. Assume that any increase in market share more than 10% and any decrease in selling price are the result of strategic choices by Krater's management to implement its strategy.

Required

Calculate how much of the change in operating income from 2019 to 2020 is due to the industry-market-size factor, product differentiation, and cost leadership. How successful has Krater been in implementing its strategy? Explain.

13-32 Identifying and managing unused capacity (continuation of 13-29). Refer to Exercise 13-29.

Required

1. Calculate the amount and cost of unused architectural support capacity at the beginning of 2020, based on the number of jobs actually done in 2020.
2. Suppose Krater can add or reduce its architectural support capacity in increments of 15 units. What is the maximum amount of costs that Krater could save in 2020 by downsizing architectural support capacity?
3. Krater, in fact, does not eliminate any of its unused architectural support capacity. Why might Krater not downsize?

Problems

13-33 Balanced scorecard and strategy. The R and J Company manufactures a robotic vacuum called the Baxter. The company sells the vacuum to discount stores throughout the country. The Baxter is a basic robotic vacuum with a remote and is significantly less expensive than the robotic vacuum that requires a smartphone and app offered by competitor Stone Manufacturing. Furthermore, the Baxter has experienced production problems that have resulted in significant rework costs. Stone's model has an excellent reputation for quality.

Required

1. Is R and J's current strategy that of product differentiation or cost leadership? What about the strategy of Stone Manufacturing?
2. R and J would like to improve quality and decrease costs by improving processes and training workers to reduce rework. R and J's managers believe the increased quality will increase sales. Sketch a strategy map for R and J.
3. For each of the four perspectives, suggest a measure you would include in a balanced scorecard for R and J.

13-34 Strategic analysis of operating income. XBlast manufactures an entry-level hoverboard, HOV-X. Pursuing a cost-leadership strategy, the company has tried to improve quality and reduce costs. As a result of the actions taken over the last year, quality has significantly improved in 2020 while rework and unit costs of the HOV-X have decreased. XBlast has reduced manufacturing capacity because capacity is no longer needed to support rework. XBlast has also lowered HOV-X's selling price to gain market share and unit sales have increased. Information about the current period (2020) and last period (2019) follows:

	2019	2020
1. Units of HOV-X produced and sold	15,000	25,000
2. Selling price	$125	$100
3. Direct materials used (kits[a])	18,000	27,000
4. Direct material cost per kit[a]	$30	$30
5. Manufacturing capacity in kits processed	30,000	28,000
6. Total conversion costs	$660,000	$616,000
7. Conversion cost per unit of capacity (row6 ÷ row5)	$22	$22
8. Selling and customer-service capacity	200 customers	200 customers
9. Total selling and customer-service costs	$35,000	$38,000
10. Selling and customer-service capacity cost per customer (row9 ÷ row8)	$175	$190

[a] A kit is composed of all the major components needed to produce a hoverboard.

Conversion costs in each year depend on production capacity defined in terms of kits that can be processed, not the actual kits started. Selling and customer-service costs depend on the number of customers that XBlast can support, not the actual number of customers it serves. XBlast has 125 customers in 2019 and 150 customers in 2020.

Required

1. Calculate operating income of XBlast for 2019 and 2020.
2. Calculate the growth, price-recovery, and productivity components that explain the change in operating income from 2019 to 2020.
3. Comment on your answer in requirement 2. What do these components indicate?

13-35 Analysis of growth, price-recovery, and productivity components (continuation of 13-34). Suppose that during 2020, the market for hoverboards increased by 25%. All increases in market share (that is, sales increases greater than 25%) and decreases in the selling price of HOV-X are the result of XBlast's strategic actions.

Required

Calculate how much of the change in operating income from 2019 to 2020 is due to the industry-market-size factor, product differentiation, and cost leadership. How does this relate to XBlast's strategy and its success in implementation? Explain.

13-36 Identifying and managing unused capacity (continuation of 13-34). Refer to the information for XBlast in Problem 13-34.

Required

1. Calculate the amount and cost of (a) unused manufacturing capacity and (b) unused selling and customer-service capacity at the beginning of 2020 based on actual production and actual number of customers served in 2020.
2. Suppose XBlast can add or reduce its selling and customer-service capacity in increments of 10 customers. What is the maximum amount of costs that XBlast could save in 2020 by downsizing selling and customer-service capacity?
3. XBlast, in fact, does not eliminate any of its unused selling and customer-service capacity. Why might XBlast not downsize?

13-37 Balanced scorecard. Following is a random-order listing of perspectives, strategic objectives, and performance measures for the balanced scorecard.

Perspectives	Performance Measures
Internal business process	Percentage of defective-product units
Customer	Return on assets
Learning and growth	Number of patents
Financial	Employee turnover rate
	Net income
Strategic Objectives	Customer profitability
Acquire new customers	Percentage of processes with real-time feedback
Increase shareholder value	Return on sales
Retain customers	Average job-related training-hours per employee
Improve manufacturing quality	Return on equity
Develop profitable customers	Percentage of on-time deliveries by suppliers
Increase proprietary products	Product cost per unit
Increase information-system capabilities	Profit per salesperson
Enhance employee skills	Percentage of error-free invoices
On-time delivery by suppliers	Customer cost per unit
Increase profit generated by each salesperson	Earnings per share
Introduce new products	Number of new customers
Minimize invoice-error rate	Percentage of customers retained

Required

For each perspective, select those strategic objectives from the list that best relate to it. For each strategic objective, select the most appropriate performance measure(s) from the list.

13-38 Balanced scorecard. (R. Kaplan, adapted) Petrocal, Inc., refines gasoline and sells it through its own Petrocal gas stations. On the basis of market research, Petrocal determines that 60% of the overall gasoline market consists of "service-oriented customers," medium- to high-income individuals who are willing to pay a higher price for gas if the gas stations can provide excellent customer service such as a clean facility, a convenience store, friendly employees, a quick turnaround, the ability to pay by credit card, and high-octane premium gasoline. The remaining 40% of the overall market are "price shoppers" who look to buy the cheapest gasoline available. Petrocal's strategy is to focus on the 60% of service-oriented customers. Petrocal's balanced scorecard for 2020 follows. For brevity, the initiatives taken under each objective are omitted.

Objectives	Measures	Target Performance	Actual Performance
Financial Perspective			
Increase shareholder value	Operating-income changes from price recovery	$80,000,000	$85,000,000
	Operating-income changes from growth	$60,000,000	$62,000,000
Customer Perspective			
Increase market share	Market share of overall gasoline market	4%	3.8%
Internal-Business-Process Perspective			
Improve gasoline quality	Quality index	92 points	93 points
Improve refinery performance	Refinery-reliability index (%)	91%	91%
Ensure gasoline availability	Product-availability index (%)	99%	99.5%
Learning-and-Growth Perspective			
Increase refinery process capability	Percentage of refinery processes with advanced controls	94%	95%

Required

1. Was Petrocal successful in implementing its strategy in 2020? Explain your answer.
2. Would you have included some measure of employee satisfaction and employee training in the learning-and-growth perspective? Are these objectives critical to Petrocal for implementing its strategy? Why or why not? Explain briefly.

3. Explain how Petrocal did not achieve its target market share in the total gasoline market but still exceeded its financial targets. Is "market share of overall gasoline market" the correct measure of market share? Explain briefly.
4. Is there a cause-and-effect linkage between improvements in the measures in the internal-business-process perspective and the measure in the customer perspective? That is, would you add other measures to the internal-business-process perspective or the customer perspective? Why or why not? Explain briefly.
5. Do you agree with Petrocal's decision not to include measures of changes in operating income from productivity improvements under the financial perspective of the balanced scorecard? Explain briefly.

13-39 Balanced scorecard. Vic Corporation manufactures various types of color laser printers in a highly automated facility with high fixed costs. The market for laser printers is competitive. The various color laser printers on the market are comparable in terms of features and price. Vic believes that satisfying customers with products of high quality at low costs is important to achieving its target profitability. For 2020, Vic plans to achieve higher quality and lower costs by improving yields and reducing defects in its manufacturing operations. Vic will train workers and encourage and empower them to take the necessary actions. Currently, a significant amount of Vic's capacity is used to produce products that are defective and cannot be sold. Vic expects that higher yields will reduce the capacity that Vic needs to manufacture products. Vic does not anticipate that improving manufacturing will automatically lead to lower costs because many costs are fixed costs. To reduce fixed costs per unit, Vic could lay off employees and sell equipment, or it could use the capacity to produce and sell more of its current products or improved models of its current products.

Vic's balanced scorecard (initiatives omitted) for the just-completed fiscal year 2020 follows.

Objectives	Measures	Target Performance	Actual Performance
Financial Perspective			
Increase shareholder value	Operating-income changes from productivity improvements	\$2,000,000	\$1,200,000
	Operating-income changes from growth	\$2,500,000	\$1,100,000
Customer Perspective			
Increase market share	Market share in color laser printers	4%	3.6%
Internal-Business-Process Perspective			
Improve manufacturing quality	Yield	88%	90%
Reduce delivery time to customers	Order-delivery time	23 days	20 days
Learning-and-Growth Perspective			
Develop process skills	Percentage of employees trained in process and quality management	92%	93%
Enhance information-system capabilities	Percentage of manufacturing processes with real-time feedback	90%	92%

Required

1. Was Vic successful in implementing its strategy in 2020? Explain.
2. Is Vic's balanced scorecard useful in helping the company understand why it did not reach its target market share in 2020? If it is, explain why. If it is not, explain what other measures you might want to add under the customer perspective and why.
3. Would you have included some measure of employee satisfaction in the learning-and-growth perspective and new-product development in the internal-business-process perspective? That is, do you think employee satisfaction and development of new products are critical for Vic to implement its strategy? Why or why not? Explain briefly.
4. What problems, if any, do you see in Vic improving quality and significantly downsizing to eliminate unused capacity?

13-40 Balanced scorecard, environmental, and social performance. Gardini Chocolates makes custom-labeled, high-quality, specialty candy bars for special events and advertising purposes. The company employs several chocolatiers who were trained in Germany. The company offers many varieties of chocolate, including milk, semi-sweet, white, and dark chocolate. It also offers a variety of ingredients such as coffee, berries, and fresh mint. The real appeal for the company's product, however, is its custom labeling. Customers can order labels for special occasions (for example, wedding invitation labels) or business purposes (for example, business card labels). The company's balanced scorecard for 2020 follows. For brevity, the initiatives taken under each objective are omitted.

Objectives	Measures	Target Performance	Actual Performance
Financial Perspective			
Increase shareholder value	Operating-income changes from price recovery	$1,000,000	$1,500,000
	Operating-income changes from growth	$200,000	$250,000
	Cost savings due to reduced packaging size	$40,000	$50,000
Customer Perspective			
Increase market share	Market share of overall candy bar market	8%	7.8%
Increase the number of new product offerings	Number of new product offerings	5	7
Increase customer acquisitions due to sustainability efforts	Percentage of new customers surveyed who required recycled paper options	35%	40%
Internal-Business-Process Perspective			
Reduce time to customer	Average design time	3 days	3 days
Increase quality	Internal quality rating (10-point scale)	7 points	8 points
Increase use of recycled materials	Recycled materials used as a percentage of total materials used	30%	32%
Learning-and-Growth Perspective			
Increase number of professional chocolatiers	Number of chocolatiers	5	6
Increase number of women and minorities in the workforce	Percentage of women and minorities in the workforce	40%	38%

Required

1. Was Gardini successful in implementing its strategy in 2020? Explain your answer.
2. Would you have included some measure of customer satisfaction in the customer perspective? Are these objectives critical to Gardini for implementing its strategy? Why or why not? Explain briefly.
3. Explain why Gardini did not achieve its target market share in the candy bar market but still exceeded its financial targets. Is "market share of overall candy bar market" a good measure of market share for Gardini? Explain briefly.
4. Do you agree with Gardini's decision not to include measures of changes in operating income from productivity improvements under the financial perspective of the balanced scorecard? Explain briefly.
5. Why did Gardini include balanced scorecard standards relating to environmental and social performance? Is the company meeting its performance objectives in these areas?

13-41 Balanced scorecard, social performance. Comtex Company provides cable and internet services in the greater Boston area. There are many competitors that provide similar services. Comtex believes that the key to financial success is to offer a quality service at the lowest cost. Comtex currently spends a significant number of hours on installation and post-installation support. This is one area that the company has targeted for cost reduction. Comtex's balanced scorecard for 2020 follows.

Objectives	Measures	Target Performance	Actual Performance
Financial Perspective			
Increase shareholder value	Operating-income changes from productivity	$2,400,000	$800,000
	Operating-income changes from growth	$520,000	$250,000
	Increase in revenue from new customer acquisition	$50,000	$24,000
Customer Perspective			
Increase customer satisfaction	Positive customer survey responses	70%	65%
Increase customer acquisition	New customers acquired through company sponsored community events	475	350
Internal-Business-Process Perspective			
Develop innovative services	Research and development costs as a percentage of revenue	5%	6%
Increase installation efficiency	Installation time per customer	5 hours	4.5 hours
Increase community involvement	Number of new programs with community organizations	12	15
Decrease workplace injuries	Number of employees injured in the workplace	<3	7
Learning-and-Growth Perspective			
Increase employee competence	Number of annual training-hours per employee	10	11
Increase leadership skills	Number of leadership workshops offered	2	1
Increase employee safety awareness	Percent of employees who have completed safety certification training	100%	95%

Required

1. Was Comtex successful in implementing its strategy in 2020? Explain.
2. Do you agree with Comtex's decision to include measures of developing innovative services (R&D costs) in the internal-business-process perspective of the balanced scorecard? Explain briefly.
3. Is there a cause-and-effect linkage between the measures in the internal-business-process perspective and the customer perspective? That is, would you add other measures to the internal-business-process perspective or the customer perspective? Why or why not?
4. Why do you think Comtex included balanced scorecard measures relating to employee safety and community engagement? How well is the company doing on these measures?

13-42 Balanced scorecard, environmental, and social performance. WrightAir is a no-frills airline that services the Midwest. Its mission is to be the only short-haul, low-fare, high-frequency, point-to-point carrier in the Midwest. However, there are several large commercial carriers offering air transportation, and WrightAir knows that it cannot compete with them based on the services those carriers provide. WrightAir has chosen to reduce costs by not offering many inflight services such as food and entertainment options. Instead, the company is dedicated to providing the highest quality transportation at the lowest fare. WrightAir's balanced scorecard measures (and actual results) for 2020 follow:

Objectives	Measures	Target Performance	Actual Performance
Financial Perspective			
Increase shareholder value	Operating-income changes from productivity	$7,200,000	$8,400,000
	Operating-income changes from price recovery	$2,700,000	$3,600,000
	Operating-income changes from growth	$3,000,000	$3,960,000
	Cost savings due to reduction in jet fuel consumption	$900,000	$1,080,000
Customer Perspective			
Increase the number of on-time arrivals	FAA on-time arrival ranking	1st in industry	2nd in industry
Improve brand image	Percentage of customer survey respondents with greater than 90% approval rating on company's sustainability efforts	100%	96%
Internal-Business-Process Perspective			
Reduce turnaround time	On-ground time	$<$25 minutes	30 minutes
Reduce CO_2 emissions	Number of engineering changes that decreased CO_2 emissions	10	9
Learning-and-Growth Perspective			
Align ground crews	% of ground crew stockholders	70%	68%
Acquire new energy management tool and technology	Achieve ISO 50001 certification in energy management	Acquire certification by Dec. 31	Acquired certification by Dec. 31

Required

1. What is WrightAir's strategy? Was WrightAir successful in implementing its strategy in 2020? Explain your answer.
2. Draw a strategy map as in Exhibit 13-2 for WrightAir describing the cause-and-effect relationships among the strategic objectives described in the balanced scorecard. Identify what you believe are any (a) strong ties, (b) focal points, (c) trigger points, and (d) distinctive objectives. Comment on your structural analysis of the strategy map.
3. Based on the strategy identified in requirement 1 above, what role does the price-recovery component play in explaining the success of WrightAir?
4. Would you have included customer-service measures in the customer perspective? Why or why not?
5. Would you have included some measure of employee satisfaction and employee training in the learning-and-growth perspective? Would you consider this objective critical to WrightAir for implementing its strategy? Why or why not?
6. Why do you think WrightAir has introduced environmental measures in its balanced scorecard? Is the company meeting its performance objectives in this area?

13-43 Partial-productivity measurement. Goldstein Company manufactures wallets from fabric. In 2019, Goldstein made 2,700,000 wallets using 1,875,000 yards of fabric. In 2019, Goldstein has capacity to make 3,600,000 wallets and incurs a cost of $10,800,000 for this capacity. In 2020, Goldstein plans to make 3,348,000 wallets, make fabric use more efficient, and reduce capacity.

Suppose that in 2020 Goldstein makes 3,348,000 wallets, uses 2,160,000 yards of fabric, and reduces capacity to 3,100,000 wallets at a cost of $10,540,000.

Required

1. Calculate the partial-productivity ratios for materials and conversion (capacity costs) for 2020, and compare them to a benchmark for 2019 calculated based on 2020 output.
2. How can Goldstein Company use the information from the partial-productivity calculations?

13-44 Total factor productivity (continuation of 13-43). Refer to the data for Problem 13-43. Assume the fabric costs $4.40 per yard in 2020 and $4.55 per yard in 2019.

Required

1. Compute Goldstein Company's total factor productivity (TFP) for 2020.
2. Compare TFP for 2020 with a benchmark TFP for 2019 inputs based on 2020 prices and output.
3. What additional information does TFP provide that partial-productivity measures do not?

14 Pricing Decisions and Cost Management

LEARNING OBJECTIVES

1. Discuss the three major factors that affect pricing decisions
2. Understand how companies make long-run pricing decisions
3. Price products using the target-costing approach
4. Apply the concepts of cost incurrence and locked-in costs
5. Price products using the cost-plus approach
6. Use life-cycle budgeting and costing when making pricing decisions
7. Explain the effects of legal restrictions on pricing and the broader notion of price discrimination

Most companies carefully analyze their input costs and the prices of their products.

They know if the price is too high, customers will go to competitors; if the price is too low, the company won't be able to cover the cost of making the product. A company must also know how its customers will react to particular pricing strategies. Understanding these factors has been a key factor in IKEA's success.

EXTREME PRICING AND COST MANAGEMENT AT IKEA[1]

IKEA is a global furniture retailing industry phenomenon. Known for products named after Swedish towns, modern design, flat packaging, and do-it-yourself instructions, IKEA has grown into the world's largest furniture retailer with 355 stores in 29 countries. How did this happen? Through aggressive pricing, coupled with relentless cost management.

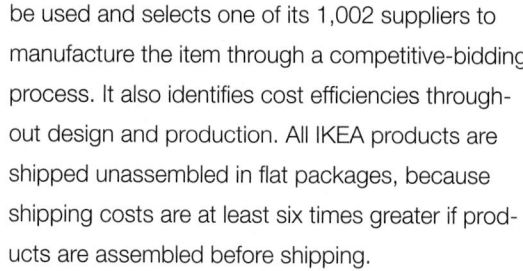

When IKEA decides to create a new product, product developers survey competitors to determine how much they charge for similar items and then select a target price that is 30% to 50% lower than competitors' prices. IKEA calls these "breathtaking items." With a product and price established, IKEA determines the materials to be used and selects one of its 1,002 suppliers to manufacture the item through a competitive-bidding process. It also identifies cost efficiencies throughout design and production. All IKEA products are shipped unassembled in flat packages, because shipping costs are at least six times greater if products are assembled before shipping.

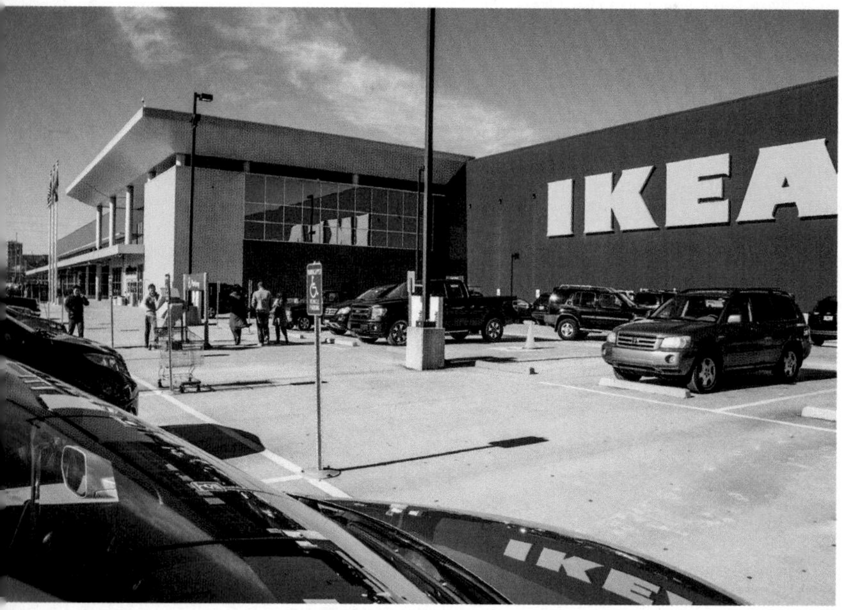

Steve Allen/Allen Creative/Alamy Stock Photo

IKEA applies the same cost management techniques to existing products. For example, one of IKEA's best-selling products, the Lack bedside table, has retailed for the same low price since 1981 despite increases in raw material prices and wage rates. Since hitting store shelves, more than 100 technical development projects have been performed on the Lack table to reduce product and distribution costs and maintain profitability.

[1] *Sources:* Lisa Margonelli, "How IKEA Designs Its Sexy Price Tags," Business 2.0, October 2002; Enrico Baraldi and Torkel Strömsten, "Managing Product Development the IKEA Way - The Role of Accounting and Control in Networks," in Proceedings of the 25th IMP conference, Marseille, France, September 3-5, 2009; Beth Kowitt, "It's IKEA's World, We Just Live in It," *Fortune,* March 10, 2015 (http://fortune.com/ikea-world-domination/); Richard Milne, "Ikea Vows 'Transformation' as It Reshapes Business Model," *Financial Times,* April 10, 2018 (https://www.ft.com/content/1a66c838-3cc1-11e8-b7e0-52972418fec4).

In response to changing shopping habits and a shift to online sales, IKEA is now turning its focus to new digital commerce solutions, including virtual reality, and providing delivery and assembly services for customers at an affordable price. Doing so while aggressively managing costs is consistent with the way IKEA has operated for more than 75 years. As founder Ingvar Kamprad once summarized, "Waste of resources is a mortal sin at IKEA. Expensive solutions are a sign of mediocrity, and an idea without a price tag is never acceptable."

Like IKEA, managers at many companies, such as Amazon, Unilever, and Walmart, are strategic in their pricing decisions. This chapter describes how managers evaluate demand at different prices and manage customers and costs across the value chain and over a product's life cycle to achieve profitability.

Major Factors That Affect Pricing Decisions

LEARNING OBJECTIVE 1

Discuss the three major factors that affect pricing decisions

. . . customers, competitors, and costs

Consider for a moment how managers at Adidas might price their newest line of sneakers or how decision makers at Comcast would determine how much to charge for a monthly subscription for Internet service. How managers price a product or a service ultimately depends on demand and supply. Three influences on demand and supply are customers, competitors, and costs.

Customers

Customers influence price through their effect on the demand for a product or service. The demand is affected by factors such as the features of a product and its quality. Managers always examine pricing decisions through the eyes of their customers and then manage costs to earn a profit.

Competitors

No business operates in a vacuum. Managers must always be aware of the actions of their competitors. At one extreme, for companies such as Home Depot or Texas Instruments, alternative or substitute products of competitors hurt demand and cause them to lower prices. At the other extreme, companies such as Apple, Miele, and Porsche have distinctive products and limited competition and are free to set higher prices. When there are competitors, managers try to learn about competitors' technologies, plant capacities, and operating strategies to estimate competitors' costs—valuable information when setting prices because it helps managers understand how low competitors are willing to go on price without incurring a loss.

Because competition spans international borders, tariffs and fluctuations in exchange rates between different countries' currencies affect costs and pricing decisions. For example, if the U.S. government imposes 25% import tariffs on certain products from Mexico, Mexican producers have to pass the additional costs on to U.S. consumers in the form of higher prices if they want to maintain their profits, making the products less competitive in U.S. markets. In contrast, if the peso weakens against the U.S. dollar, Mexican producers receive more pesos for each dollar of sales. These producers can lower prices and still make a profit; Mexican products become cheaper for American consumers and, consequently, more competitive in U.S. markets.

Costs

Costs influence prices because they affect supply. The lower the cost of producing a product, such as a Toyota Prius or a Nokia cell phone, the greater the quantity of product the company is willing to supply. Companies supply products as long as the revenue from selling additional units exceeds the cost of producing them. Managers who understand the cost of producing products set prices that make the products attractive to customers while maximizing operating income.

Weighing Customers, Competitors, and Costs

Surveys indicate that managers at different companies weigh customers, competitors, and costs differently when making pricing decisions. At one extreme, companies operating in a perfectly competitive market sell very similar commodity products, such as wheat, rice, steel, and aluminum. The managers at these companies have no control over setting prices and must accept the price determined by a market consisting of many participants. Cost information helps managers decide the quantity of output to produce that will maximize operating income.

In less competitive markets, such as those for smartphones, laptops, and televisions, products are differentiated, and all three factors affect prices: The value customers place on a product and the prices charged for competing products affect demand, and the costs of producing and delivering the product affect supply. As competition lessens in a market, such as in microprocessors and operating software, the key factor affecting pricing decisions is the customer's willingness to pay based on the value that customers place on the product or service, not costs or competitors. In the extreme, there are monopolies. A monopolist has no competitors and has much more leeway to set high prices. Nevertheless, there are limits. The higher the price a monopolist sets, the lower the demand for the monopolist's product because customers will either seek substitute products or forgo buying the product.

DECISION POINT

What are the three major factors affecting pricing decisions?

Costing and Pricing for the Long Run

LEARNING OBJECTIVE 2

Understand how companies make long-run pricing decisions

. . . consider all future variable and fixed costs and earn a target return on investment

Long-run pricing is a strategic decision designed to build long-run relationships with customers based on stable and predictable prices. Managers prefer a stable price because it reduces the need for continuous monitoring of prices, improves planning, and builds long-run buyer–seller relationships. McDonald's maintains a stable price with its Dollar Menu of fast-food items. Nespresso's price of $0.70 per coffee pod has also remained stable over an extended period of time. But to charge a stable price and earn the target long-run return, managers must know and manage long-run costs of supplying products to customers, which includes *all* future direct and indirect costs. Recall that *indirect costs* of a particular cost object are costs that are related to that cost object, but that cannot easily and unambiguously be traced to it. These costs often comprise a large percentage of the overall costs assigned to products.

Consider cost-allocation issues at Astel Computers. Astel manufactures two products: a high-end computer called Deskpoint and an Intel Core i9 chip–based laptop computer called Provalue. The following figure illustrates six business functions in Astel's value chain.

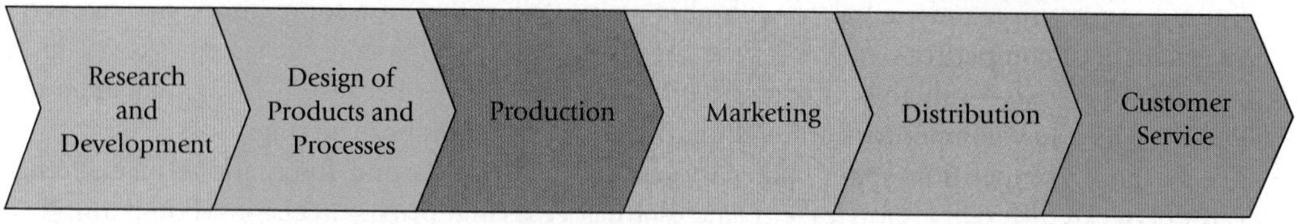

Exhibit 14-1 illustrates four purposes of cost allocation. Different sets of costs are appropriate for different purposes described in the exhibit. When making pricing decisions for Deskpoint and Provalue, Astel's managers allocate indirect costs from all six business functions. Why? Because in the long run, it is only worthwhile to sell a product if the price customers are willing to pay for the product exceeds all costs incurred to produce and sell it while earning a reasonable return on invested capital.

Cost allocations and product profitability analyses affect the products promoted by a company. To increase profits, managers focus on high-margin products. They compensate salespersons based on product profitability, in addition to revenues, to motivate the sales staff to sell products that increase operating income and not just revenues. Cost allocations also influence managers' cost management decisions. For example, identifying all costs of purchasing and ordering prompts Astel's managers to design Provalue with fewer components to reduce these costs.

Cost allocations are sometimes used for cost reimbursements. Astel's contract to supply computers to the U.S. government is based on costs plus a profit margin. The cost

EXHIBIT 14-1

Purposes of Cost Allocation

Purpose	Examples
1. To provide information for economic decisions	To decide on the selling price for a product or service To decide whether to add a new product feature
2. To motivate managers and other employees	To encourage the design of products that are simpler to manufacture or less costly to service To encourage sales representatives to emphasize high-margin products or services
3. To justify costs or compute reimbursement amounts	To cost products at a "fair" price, often required by law and government contracts To compute reimbursement for a consulting firm based on a percentage of the cost savings resulting from the implementation of its recommendations
4. To measure income and assets	To cost inventories for reporting to external parties To cost inventories for reporting to tax authorities

reimbursement rules for the U.S. government allow fully allocated manufacturing and design costs, but explicitly exclude marketing costs.

Inventory valuation for income and asset measurement on the income statement and balance sheet requires costs to be allocated to calculate the cost of manufacturing inventory. For this purpose, Astel allocates only manufacturing costs to products and no costs from other parts of the value chain such as research and development (R&D), marketing, or distribution.

Cost allocation is another example of the different costs for different purposes theme of the text. We will discuss cost allocation in the next several chapters. In this chapter, we focus on the role of cost allocation when making long-run pricing decisions based on costs incurred throughout the value chain.

Calculating Product Costs for Long-Run Pricing Decisions

Astel's market research indicates that the market for Provalue is becoming increasingly competitive. Astel's managers face an important decision about the price to charge for Provalue.

Managers first review data for the year just ended—2019. Astel has no beginning or ending inventory of Provalue and manufactures and sells 150,000 units during the year. Astel uses activity-based costing (ABC) to allocate costs and calculate the manufacturing cost of Provalue. Astel's ABC system has the following features:

- Three direct manufacturing costs: direct materials, direct manufacturing labor, and direct machining costs.
- Three manufacturing overhead cost pools: ordering and receiving components, testing and inspection of final products, and rework (correcting and fixing errors and defects).

Astel considers machining costs as a direct cost of Provalue because these machines are dedicated to manufacturing Provalue.[2]

Astel uses a long-run time horizon (1 year) to price Provalue. Over this horizon, Astel's managers observe the following:

- Direct material costs vary with the number of units of Provalue produced.
- Direct manufacturing labor costs vary with the number of direct manufacturing labor-hours used.

[2] Recall that Astel makes a high-end computer, Deskpoint, and a laptop computer, Provalue. If Deskpoint and Provalue were manufactured using the same machines, machining costs would be indirect, and Astel would have allocated the costs on the basis of the budgeted machine-hours used to manufacture the two products.

- Direct machining costs are fixed costs of leasing 300,000 machine-hours of capacity each year for multiple years. These costs do not vary with the number of machine-hours used each year. Each unit of Provalue requires 2 machine-hours. In 2019, Astel uses the entire machining capacity to manufacture Provalue (2 machine-hours per unit × 150,000 units = 300,000 machine-hours).
- Ordering and receiving, testing and inspection, and rework costs vary with the quantity of their respective cost drivers. For example, ordering and receiving costs vary with the number of orders. In the long run, staff members responsible for placing orders can be reassigned or laid off if fewer orders need to be placed or increased if more orders need to be processed.

The following Excel spreadsheet summarizes manufacturing cost information to produce 150,000 units of Provalue in 2019. As described in Chapter 5, management accountants calculate the indirect cost per unit of the cost driver in column (6) by dividing Astel's total costs in each cost pool by the total quantity of the cost driver for that cost pool. (Calculations not shown.)

	A	B	C	D	E	F	G	H
1		Manufacturing Cost Information						
2		to Produce 150,000 Units of Provalue						
3	Cost Category	Cost Driver	Details of Cost Driver Quantities				Total Quantity of Cost Driver	Cost per Unit of Cost Driver
4	(1)	(2)	(3)		(4)		(5) = (3) × (4)	(6)
5	**Direct Manufacturing Costs**							
6	Direct materials	No. of kits	1	kit per unit	150,000	units	150,000	$460
7	Direct manufacturing labor (DML)	DML-hours	3.2	DML-hours per unit	150,000	units	480,000	$ 20
8	Direct machining (fixed)	Machine-hours					300,000	$ 38
9	**Manufacturing Overhead Costs**							
10	Ordering and receiving	No. of orders	50	orders per component	450	components	22,500	$ 80
11	Testing and inspection	Testing-hours	30	testing-hours per unit	150,000	units	4,500,000	$ 2
12	Rework				8%	defect rate		
13		Rework-hours	2.5	rework-hours per defective unit	12,000[a]	defective units	30,000	$ 40
14								
15	[a]8% defect rate × 150,000 units = 12,000 defective units							

Exhibit 14-2 shows the total cost of manufacturing Provalue in 2019 of $102 million by various categories of direct costs and indirect costs. The manufacturing cost per unit in Exhibit 14-2 is $680. Manufacturing, however, is just one business function in the value chain. To set long-run prices, Astel's managers must calculate the *full cost* of producing and selling Provalue by allocating costs in all functions of the value chain.

Exhibit 14-3 shows the full cost for Provalue. For each nonmanufacturing business function, Astel's managers trace direct costs to products and allocate indirect costs using cost

EXHIBIT 14-2

Manufacturing Costs of Provalue for 2019 Using Activity-Based Costing

	A	B	C
1		Total Manufacturing	
2		Costs for	Manufacturing
3		150,000 Units	Cost per Unit
4		(1)	(2) = (1) ÷ 150,000
5	Direct manufacturing costs		
6	Direct material costs		
7	(150,000 kits × $460 per kit)	$ 69,000,000	$460
8	Direct manufacturing labor costs		
9	(480,000 DML-hours × $20 per hour)	9,600,000	64
10	Direct machining costs		
11	(300,000 machine-hours × $38 per machine-hour)	11,400,000	76
12	Direct manufacturing costs	90,000,000	600
13			
14	Manufacturing overhead costs		
15	Ordering and receiving costs		
16	(22,500 orders × $80 per order)	1,800,000	12
17	Testing and inspection costs		
18	(4,500,000 testing-hours × $2 per hour)	9,000,000	60
19	Rework costs		
20	(30,000 rework-hours × $40 per hour)	1,200,000	8
21	Manufacturing overhead cost	12,000,000	80
22	Total manufacturing costs	$102,000,000	$680

EXHIBIT 14-3

Profitability of Provalue Division for 2019 Using Value-Chain Activity-Based Costing

	A	B	C
1		Total Amounts	
2		for 150,000 Units	Per Unit
3		(1)	(2) = (1) ÷ 150,000
4	Revenues	$150,000,000	$1,000
5	Costs of goods sold[a] (from Exhibit 14-2)	102,000,000	680
6	Operating costs[b]		
7	R&D costs	2,400,000	16
8	Design costs of product and process	3,000,000	20
9	Marketing and administration costs	15,000,000	100
10	Distribution costs	9,000,000	60
11	Customer-service costs	3,600,000	24
12	Operating costs	33,000,000	220
13	Full cost of the product	135,000,000	900
14	Operating income	$ 15,000,000	$ 100
15			
16	[a]Cost of goods sold = Total manufacturing costs because there is no beginning or ending inventory		
17	of Provalue in 2019		
18	[b]Numbers for operating cost line-items are assumed without supporting calculations		

pools and cost drivers that measure cause-and-effect relationships (supporting calculations not shown). The exhibit summarizes Provalue's 2019 operating income and shows that Astel earned $15 million from Provalue, or $100 per unit sold in 2019.

Alternative Long-Run Pricing Approaches

How should managers at Astel use product cost information to price Provalue in 2020? Two different approaches for pricing decisions are

1. Market-based
2. Cost-based, which is also called cost-plus

The market-based approach to pricing starts by asking, "Given what our customers want and how our competitors will react to what we do, what price should we charge?" Based on this price, managers control costs to earn a target return on investment. The cost-based approach to pricing starts by asking, "Given what it costs us to make this product, what price should we charge that will recoup our costs and achieve a target return on investment?"

Companies operating in *competitive* markets (for example, commodities such as steel, oil, and natural gas) have to use the market-based approach. The products produced or services provided by one company are highly substitutable with products produced or services provided by others. Companies in these markets must accept the prices set by the market.

TRY IT! 14-1

Guppy Inc. is a small distributor of mechanical pencils. Guppy identifies its three major activities and cost pools as ordering, receiving and storage, and shipping, and it reports the following details for 2019:

Activity	Cost Driver	Quantity of Cost Driver	Cost per Unit of Cost Driver
1. Placing and paying for orders of pencil packs	Number of orders	800	$100 per order
2. Receiving and storage	Loads moved	4,500	$ 60 per load
3. Shipping of pencil packs to retailers	Number of shipments	1,500	$ 70 per shipment

For 2019, Guppy buys 250,000 pencil packs at an average cost of $3 per pack and sells them to retailers at an average price of $7 per pack. Assume Guppy has no fixed costs and no inventories.

Calculate Guppy's operating income for 2019.

Companies operating in *less competitive* markets offer products or services that differ from each other (for example, automobiles, computers, management consulting, and legal services) and can use either the market-based or cost-based approach as the starting point for pricing decisions. Some companies use the cost-based approach: They first look at costs because cost information is more easily available and then consider customers and competitors. Other companies use the market-based approach: They first look at customers and competitors and then look at costs. Both approaches consider customers, competitors, and costs. Only their starting points differ. Managers must always keep in mind market forces, regardless of which pricing approach they use. For example, building contractors often start bidding on a cost-plus basis but then reduce their prices during negotiations to respond to other lower-cost bids.

DECISION POINT

How do companies make long-run pricing decisions?

Companies operating in markets that are *not competitive* (for example electric utilities) follow cost-based approaches. That's because these companies do not need to respond or react to competitors' prices. The margin they add to costs to determine price depends on the ability and willingness of customers to pay for the product or service. In many of these noncompetitive markets, though, regulators intervene to set prices to limit the profits that companies can earn.

We consider first the market-based approach.

Market-Based Approach: Target Costing for Target Pricing

LEARNING OBJECTIVE 3

Price products using the target-costing approach

. . . target costing identifies an estimated price customers are willing to pay and then computes a target cost to earn the desired profit

Market-based pricing starts with a **target price**, which is the estimated price for a product or service that potential customers are willing to pay. Managers base this estimate on an understanding of customers' perceived value for a product or service and how competitors will price competing products or services.

Understanding Customers' Perceived Value

A company's sales and marketing organization, through close contact and interaction with customers, identifies customer needs and perceptions of product value. Companies also conduct market research on what customers want and the prices they are willing to pay.

Competitor Analysis

To gauge how competitors might react to a prospective price, a manager must understand competitors' technologies, products or services, costs, and financial conditions. In general, the more distinctive a product or service, the higher the price a company can charge. Where do companies obtain information about their competitors? Usually from former customers, suppliers, and employees of competitors. Some companies *reverse-engineer*—disassemble and analyze competitors' products to determine product designs and materials and understand their technologies. At no time should a manager resort to illegal or unethical means to obtain information about competitors. For example, a manager should never bribe current employees or pose as a supplier or customer to obtain competitor information.

Implementing Target Pricing and Target Costing

We use the Provalue example to illustrate the four steps in developing target prices and target costs.

Step 1: Develop a Product That Satisfies the Needs of Potential Customers. Astel's managers use customer feedback and information about competitors' products to change product features and designs of Provalue in 2020. Their market research indicates that customers do not value Provalue's extra features, such as special audio elements and designs that make the PC run faster. Instead, customers want Astel to redesign Provalue into a basic, reliable and low-priced PC.

Step 2: Choose a Target Price. Competitors are expected to lower the prices of PCs to \$850. Astel's managers want to respond aggressively by reducing the price of Provalue by 20%, from \$1,000 to \$800 per unit. At this lower price, the marketing manager forecasts an increase in annual sales from 150,000 to 200,000 units.

Step 3: Derive a Target Cost per Unit by Subtracting Target Operating Income per Unit From the Target Price. **Target operating income per unit** is the operating income that a company aims to earn per unit of a product or service sold. **Target cost per unit** is the estimated long-run cost per unit of a product or service that enables the company to achieve its target operating income per unit when selling at the target price.[3] *Target cost per unit* is the target price minus *target operating income per unit*. It is often lower than the existing *full cost of the product*. Target cost per unit is really just that—a target—something the company must strive to achieve.

To earn the target return on capital, Astel needs to earn 10% target operating income per unit on the 200,000 units of Provalue it plans to sell.

[3] For a more detailed discussion of target costing, see Shahid L. Ansari, Jan E. Bell, and the CAM-I Target Cost Core Group, *Target Costing: The Next Frontier in Strategic Cost Management* (Martinsville, IN: Mountain Valley Publishing, 2009). For implementation information, see Shahid L. Ansari, Dan Swenson, and Jan E. Bell, "A Template for Implementing Target Costing," *Cost Management* (September–October 2006): 20–27.

Total target revenue	$= \$800$ per unit $\times$ 200,000 units $= \$160,000,000$
Total target operating income	$= 10\% \times \$160,000,000 = \$16,000,000$
Target operating income per unit	$= \$16,000,000 \div 200,000$ units $= \$80$ per unit
Target cost per unit	= Target price − Target operating income per unit
	$= \$800$ per unit $- \$80$ per unit $= \$720$ per unit
Total current full costs of Provalue	= \$135,000,000 (from Exhibit 14-3)
Current full cost per unit of Provalue	$= \$135,000,000 \div 150,000$ units $= \$900$ per unit

Provalue's \$720 target cost per unit is \$180 below its current unit cost of \$900. To achieve the target cost, Astel must attempt to reduce costs in all parts of the value chain, from R&D to customer service.

Target costs include *all* future costs, variable costs as well as costs that are fixed in the short run, because in the long run a company's prices and revenues must exceed its total costs if it is to remain in business. In contrast, for short-run pricing or one-time-only special-order decisions, managers only consider costs that vary in the short run.

CONCEPTS IN ACTION

Zara Uses Target Pricing to Become the World's Largest Fashion Retailer[4]

BCFC/Shutterstock

In recent years, fast fashion has taken the apparel world by storm. Quickly designed and manufactured to respond to the latest fashion trends, fast fashion retailers work to ensure their store shelves are always stocked with the trendiest clothes at affordable prices. At Zara, many of the items you see in stores today will have been designed as little as 2 weeks before. This has allowed Zara's parent company, Inditex SA, to become the world's largest fashion retailer by sales. In 2017, Zara sold nearly \$20 billion worth of the 18,000 fast-fashion designs on its racks in 2,251 stores in 50 countries. How did this happen? Aggressive target pricing, coupled with a unique business model focused on speed to market and reducing unnecessary costs.

Every day, more than 200 designers located at Zara headquarters in Spain collect information about the decisions made by customers in each of the chain's stores. When Zara decides to produce an item, an in-house team of designers, production managers, and logisticians establish its price and how many will be made. Unlike most fashion retailers who focus only on their spring and fall collections, Zara changes its inventory every 15 days or so. They produce items in small batches, which allows more than 60% of its garments to be manufactured in Spain and nearby countries in a matter of days. This is critical for Zara, because all garments are shipped directly to stores from its headquarters, meaning it does not use warehouses to store excess inventory. This means that Zara has much lower inventories than its rivals, and therefore lower inventory costs and less need to discount unsold goods. On average, only 15–20% of Zara items are marked down, compared to 45% for competitor H&M. When a Zara store needs more inventory of a particular item, it notifies managers at headquarters and the process begins anew.

This model inspires customers to spend their money differently. In Zara, every purchase is an impulse buy; that trendy leather jacket in the window is likely to be gone in a matter of days. As a result, Zara customers typically visit stores four or five times more often than customers of more traditional fashion retailers.

[4] *Sources:* Intedex SA, *2017 Annual Report* (Arteixo, Spain: Intedex SA, 2018); Karan Girotra and Serguei Netessine, "Business Model Innovation is the Gift That Keeps on Giving," HBR.org, December 5, 2012 (https://hbr.org/2012/12/the-gift-that-keeps-giving-bus); Tobias Buck, "Fashion: A Better Business Model," *Financial Times,* June 18, 2014 (https://www.ft.com/content/a7008958-f2f3-11e3-a3f8-00144feabdc0); Jose Colon, "A Model for Fast Fashion," *The Wall Street Journal,* December 7, 2016 (https://www.wsj.com/articles/fast-fashion-how-a-zara-coat-went-from-design-to-fifth-avenue-in-25-days-1481020203); Suzy Hansen, "How Zara Grew Into the World's Largest Fashion Retailer," *The New York Times Magazine,* November 9, 2012 (https://www.nytimes.com/2012/11/11/magazine/how-zara-grew-into-the-worlds-largest-fashion-retailer.html).

Step 4: Perform Value Engineering to Achieve Target Cost. **Value engineering** is a systematic evaluation of all aspects of the value chain, with the objective of reducing costs and achieving a quality level that satisfies customers. Value engineering entails improvements in product designs, changes in materials specifications, and modifications in process methods. The Concepts in Action: Zara Uses Target Pricing to Become the World's Largest Fashion Retailer describes Zara's approach to target pricing and target costing.

DECISION POINT

How do companies determine target costs?

14-2 TRY IT!

Assume the same information for 2019 for Guppy Inc. as given in Try It! 14-1. For 2020, retailers are demanding a 6% discount off the 2019 price. Guppy's suppliers are only willing to give a 5% discount. Guppy expects to sell the same quantity of pencil packs in 2020 as it did in 2019.

If all other costs and cost-driver information remain the same, by how much must Guppy reduce its total cost and cost per unit if it is to earn the same target operating income in 2020 as it earned in 2019 (and thereby earn its required rate of return on investment)?

Value Engineering, Cost Incurrence, and Locked-In Costs

LEARNING OBJECTIVE 4

Apply the concepts of cost incurrence

. . . when resources are consumed

and locked-in costs

. . . when resources are committed to be incurred in the future

To implement value engineering, managers distinguish value-added activities and costs from non-value-added activities and costs. A **value-added cost** is a cost that, if eliminated, would reduce the actual or perceived value or utility (usefulness) customers experience from using the product or service. In the Provalue example, value-added costs are specific product features and attributes desired by customers, such as reliability, adequate memory, preloaded software, and prompt customer service.

A **non-value-added cost** is a cost that, if eliminated, would not reduce the actual or perceived value or utility (usefulness) customers gain from using the product or service. Examples of non-value-added costs are the costs of defective products and machine breakdowns. Companies seek to minimize non-value-added costs because they do not provide benefits to customers.

Activities and costs do not always fall neatly into value-added or non-value-added categories, so managers often have to apply judgment to classify costs. Several costs, such as supervision and production control, have both value-added and non-value-added components. When in doubt, some managers prefer to classify costs as non-value-added to focus organizational attention on cost reduction. The risk with this approach is that an organization may cut some costs that are value-adding, leading to poor product quality and customer experiences.

Despite these difficult gray areas, managers find it useful to distinguish value-added from non-value-added costs for value engineering. In the Provalue example, direct materials, direct manufacturing labor, and direct machining costs are value-added costs; ordering, receiving, testing, and inspection costs have both value-added and non-value-added components; and rework costs are non-value-added costs.

Astel's managers next distinguish cost incurrence from locked-in costs. **Cost incurrence** describes when a resource is consumed (or a benefit is forgone) to meet a specific objective. Costing systems measure cost incurrence. For example, Astel recognizes direct material costs of Provalue only when Provalue is assembled and sold. But Provalue's direct material cost per unit is *locked in*, or *designed in*, much earlier, when product designers choose the specific components in Provalue. **Locked-in costs**, or **designed-in costs**, are costs that have not yet been incurred, but will be incurred in the future based on decisions that have already been made.

The best opportunity to manage costs is before they are locked in. Astel's managers model the effect of different product design choices on non-value-added costs such as scrap and rework that will only be incurred later during manufacturing and try to minimize these costs by making wise design choices.

Exhibit 14-4 illustrates the locked-in cost curve and the cost-incurrence curve for Provalue. The bottom curve uses information from Exhibit 14-3 to plot the cumulative cost

EXHIBIT 14-4

Pattern of Cost Incurrence and Locked-In Costs for Provalue

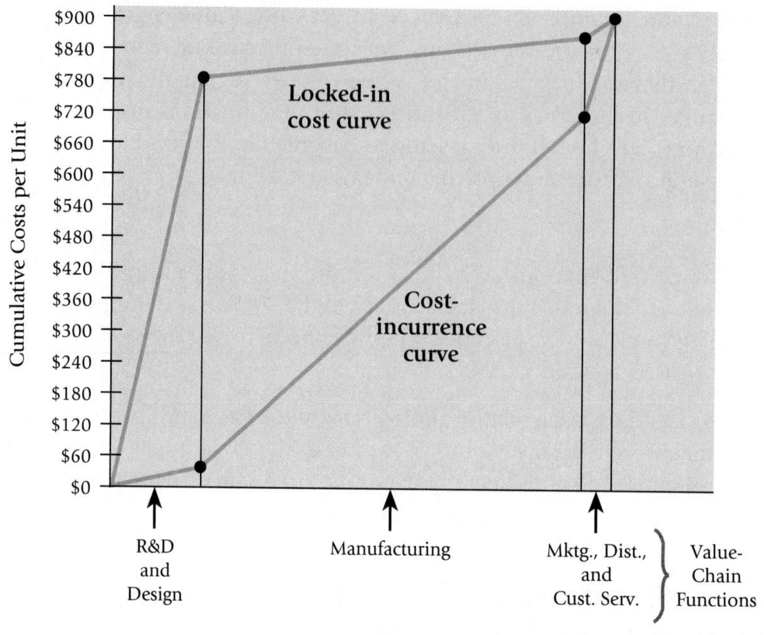

per unit incurred in different business functions of the value chain. The top curve plots cumulative locked-in costs. (The specific numbers underlying this curve are not presented.) Total cumulative cost per unit for both curves is $900, but there is *wide divergence between locked-in costs and costs incurred.* For example, product design decisions lock in more than 86% ($780 ÷ $900) of the unit cost of Provalue (including costs of direct materials, ordering, testing, rework, distribution, and customer service), whereas they only account for about 4% ($36 ÷ 900) of the unit cost incurred!

Value-Chain Analysis and Cross-Functional Teams

A cross-functional value-engineering team consisting of marketing managers, product designers, manufacturing engineers, purchasing managers, suppliers, dealers, and management accountants redesign Provalue—called Provalue II—to reduce costs while retaining features that customers value. Some of the team's ideas are listed below:

- Use a simpler, more reliable motherboard without complex features to reduce manufacturing and repair costs.
- Snap-fit rather than solder parts together to decrease direct manufacturing labor-hours and related costs.
- Use fewer components to decrease ordering, receiving, testing, and inspection costs.
- Make Provalue lighter and smaller to reduce distribution and packaging costs.

Management accountants use their understanding of the value chain to estimate cost savings.

The team focuses on design decisions to reduce costs before costs get locked in. However, not all costs are locked in at the design stage. Managers also use *kaizen*, or *continuous improvement* techniques, to reduce the time it takes to complete a task, eliminate waste, and improve operating efficiency and productivity. To summarize, the key steps in value-engineering are as follows:

1. Understanding customer requirements and value-added and non-value-added costs.
2. Anticipating how costs are locked in before they are incurred.
3. Using cross-functional teams to redesign products and processes to reduce costs while meeting customer needs.

Achieving the Target Cost per Unit for Provalue

Exhibit 14-5 uses an activity-based approach to compare cost-driver quantities and rates for the 150,000 units of Provalue manufactured and sold in 2019 and the 200,000 units of Provalue II budgeted for 2020. Value engineering decreases both value-added costs (by designing Provalue II to reduce direct materials costs, direct manufacturing labor-hours, the number of components and testing-hours) and non-value-added costs (by simplifying Provalue II's design to reduce rework). Value engineering also reduces the machine-hours required to manufacture Provalue II to 1.5 hours per unit. Astel can now use the 300,000 machine-hours of capacity to make 200,000 units of Provalue II (vs. 150,000 units for Provalue), reducing machining cost per unit. For simplicity, we assume that value engineering will not reduce the $20 cost per direct manufacturing labor-hour, the $80 cost per order, the $2 cost per testing-hour, or the $40 cost

EXHIBIT 14-5 Cost-Driver Quantities and Rates for Provalue in 2019 and Provalue II for 2020 Using Activity-Based Costing

	A	B	C	D	E	F	G	H	I	J	K	L	M	N
1–2				Manufacturing Cost Information for 150,000 Units of Provalue in 2019					Manufacturing Cost Information for 200,000 Units of Provalue II for 2020					
3	Cost Category	Cost Driver	Details of Actual Cost Driver Quantities				Actual Total Quantity of Cost Driver	Actual Cost per Unit of Cost Driver (p. 566)	Details of Budgeted Cost Driver Quantities				Budgeted Total Quantity of Cost Driver	Budgeted Cost per Unit of Cost Driver (Given)
4	(1)	(2)	(3)		(4)		(5)=(3)×(4)	(6)	(7)		(8)		(9)=(7)×(8)	(10)
5	**Direct Manufacturing Costs**													
6	Direct materials	No. of kits	1	kit per unit	150,000	units	150,000	$460	1	kit per unit	200,000	units	200,000	$385
7	Direct manuf. labor (DML)	DML hours	3.2	DML hours per unit	150,000	units	480,000	$ 20	2.65	DML hours per unit	200,000	units	530,000	$ 20
8	Direct machining (fixed)	Machine-hours					300,000	$ 38					300,000	$ 38
9	**Manufacturing Overhead Costs**													
10	Ordering and receiving	No. of orders	50	orders per component	450	components	22,500	$ 80	50	orders per component	425	components	21,250	$ 80
11	Testing and inspection	Testing-hours	30	testing-hours per unit	150,000	units	4,500,000	$ 2	15	testing hours per unit	200,000	units	3,000,000	$ 2
12	Rework				8%	defect rate					6.5%	defect rate		
13		Rework-hours	2.5	rework-hours per defective unit	12,000[a]	defective units	30,000	$ 40	2.5	rework-hours per defective unit	13,000[b]	defective units	32,500	$ 40
14														
15	[a]8% defect rate × 150,000 units = 12,000 defective units													
16	[b]6.5% defect rate × 200,000 units = 13,000 defective units													

per rework-hour. (The Problem for Self-Study, pages 582–584, explores how value engineering can also reduce these cost-driver rates.)

Exhibit 14-6 presents the target manufacturing costs of Provalue II, using cost driver and cost-driver rate data from Exhibit 14-5. For comparison, Exhibit 14-6 also shows the actual 2019 manufacturing cost per unit of Provalue from Exhibit 14-2. Astel's managers expect the new design to reduce total manufacturing cost per unit by $140 (from $680 to $540) and cost per unit in other business functions from $220 (Exhibit 14-3) to $180 (calculations not shown) at the budgeted sales quantity of 200,000 units. The budgeted full unit cost of Provalue II is $720 ($540 + $180), which is the target cost per unit. At the end of 2020, Astel's managers will compare actual costs and target costs to understand improvements they can make in subsequent target-costing efforts.

Unless managed properly, value engineering and target costing can have undesirable effects:

- Employees may feel frustrated if they fail to attain target costs.
- The cross-functional team may add too many features just to accommodate the different wishes of team members.
- A product may be in development for a long time as the team repeatedly evaluates alternative designs.
- Organizational conflicts may develop as the burden of cutting costs falls unequally on different business functions in the company's value chain, for example, more on manufacturing than on marketing.

To avoid these pitfalls, target-costing efforts should always (1) encourage employee participation and celebrate small improvements toward achieving the target cost, (2) focus on the customer, (3) pay attention to schedules, and (4) set cost-cutting targets for all value-chain functions to encourage a culture of teamwork and cooperation.

EXHIBIT 14-6 Target Manufacturing Costs of Provalue II for 2020

	A	B	C	D	E	F
1		PROVALUE II				PROVALUE
2		Budgeted		Budgeted		Actual Manufacturing
3		Manufacturing Costs		Manufacturing		Cost per Unit
4		for 200,000 Units		Cost per Unit		(Exhibit 14-2)
5		(1)		(2) = (1) ÷ 200,000		(3)
6	Direct manufacturing costs					
7	Direct material costs					
8	(200,000 kits × $385 per kit)	$ 77,000,000		$385.00		$460.00
9	Direct manufacturing labor costs					
10	(530,000 DML-hours × $20 per hour)	10,600,000		53.00		64.00
11	Direct machining costs					
12	(300,000 machine-hours × $38 per machine-hour)	11,400,000		57.00		76.00
13	Direct manufacturing costs	99,000,000		495.00		600.00
14	Manufacturing overhead costs					
15	Ordering and receiving costs					
16	(21,250 orders × $80 per order)	1,700,000		8.50		12.00
17	Testing and inspection costs					
18	(3,000,000 testing-hours × $2 per hour)	6,000,000		30.00		60.00
19	Rework costs					
20	(32,500 rework-hours × $40 per hour)	1,300,000		6.50		8.00
21	Manufacturing overhead costs	9,000,000		45.00		80.00
22	Total manufacturing costs	$108,000,000		$540.00		$680.00

The target-pricing approach is another illustration of the five-step decision-making process introduced in Chapter 1.

1. **Identify the problem and uncertainties.** The problem is the price to charge for Provalue in 2020. The uncertainties are identifying what customers want, how competitors will respond, and how to manage costs.
2. **Obtain information.** Astel's managers do market research to identify customer needs, the prices that competitors are likely to charge, and the opportunities to reduce costs.
3. **Make predictions about the future.** Managers make predictions about the effect of different prices on sales volumes and how much they can reduce costs through value engineering and product redesign.
4. **Make decisions by choosing among alternatives.** Managers decide to reduce Provalue's price from $1,000 to $800, anticipating sales to increase from 150,000 units to 200,000 units in 2020.
5. **Implement the decision, evaluate performance, and learn.** Cross-functional value-engineering teams redesign Provalue to achieve a target cost of $720 per unit, considerably lower than the current cost of $900. At the end of 2020, managers will compare actual and target costs to evaluate performance and to identify ways to reduce costs even further.

DECISION POINT

Why is it important for managers to distinguish cost incurrence from locked-in costs?

14-3 TRY IT!

Assume the same information for 2019 and 2020 for Guppy Inc. as given in Try It! Problems 14-1 and 14-2.

Using value engineering, Guppy decides to make changes to its ordering and receiving-and-storing practices. By placing long-run orders with its key suppliers, Guppy expects to reduce the number of orders to 700 and the cost per order to $75. By redesigning the layout of the warehouse and reconfiguring the crates in which the pencil packs are moved, Guppy expects to reduce the number of loads moved to 4,000 and the cost per load moved to $50.

Will Guppy achieve its target operating income of $545,000 and its target operating income per unit of $2.18 per pencil pack in 2020? Show your calculations.

Cost-Plus Pricing

LEARNING OBJECTIVE 5

Price products using the cost-plus approach

. . . cost-plus pricing is based on some measure of cost plus a markup

While managers use market-based approaches for long-run pricing decisions in competitive markets, they sometimes use a cost-based approach when pricing distinct products or services. The general formula for setting a cost-based selling price is to add a markup component to the cost base. Because a markup is added, cost-based pricing is often called cost-plus pricing, where the plus refers to the markup component. When using the cost-plus pricing formula, managers use the cost base as a starting point. The markup component is usually flexible, depending on the behavior of customers and competitors. In other words, market conditions ultimately determine the size of the markup component.[5] Consider, for example, Costco, the large warehouse store. Costco uses cost-plus pricing when setting product prices. Costco's managers, however, will reduce prices if competitors such as Sam's Club offer similar products at lower prices.

Cost-Plus Target Rate of Return on Investment

Suppose Astel uses a 12% markup on the full unit cost of Provalue II to compute the selling price. The cost-plus price is as follows:

Cost base (full unit cost of Provalue II)	$720.00
Markup component of 12% (0.12 × $720)	86.40
Prospective selling price	$806.40

[5] Exceptions are pricing of electricity and natural gas in many countries, where prices are set by the government on the basis of costs plus a fixed return on invested capital. In these situations, products are not subject to competitive forces and cost accounting techniques substitute for markets as the basis for setting prices.

How do managers determine the markup percentage of 12% of full unit costs? One way is to choose the markup based on a **target rate of return on investment**, which is the target annual operating income divided by invested capital. Invested capital can be defined in many ways. In this chapter, we define it as total assets—that is, long-term assets plus current assets. Suppose Astel's (pretax) target rate of return on investment is 15%, and Provalue II's capital investment (total assets) is $115.2 million. The target annual operating income for Provalue II is:

Invested capital	$115,200,000
Target rate of return on investment	15%
Target annual operating income (0.15 × $115,200,000)	$ 17,280,000
Target operating income per unit of Provalue II ($17,280,000 ÷ 200,000 units)	$ 86.40

This calculation indicates that Astel needs to earn a target operating income of $86.40 on each unit of Provalue II. The markup ($86.40) expressed as a percentage of the full unit cost of the product ($720) equals 12% ($86.40 ÷ $720).

Do not confuse the 15% target rate of return on investment with the 12% markup percentage.

- The 15% target rate of return on investment expresses Astel's target annual operating income as a percentage of investment.
- The 12% markup expresses operating income per unit as a percentage of the full product cost per unit.

Astel uses the target rate of return on investment to calculate the markup percentage.

Alternative Cost-Plus Methods

Computing the specific amount of capital invested in a product is challenging because it requires difficult and sometimes arbitrary allocations of investments in equipment and buildings to individual products. The following table uses alternative cost bases (without supporting calculations) and assumed markup percentages to set prospective selling prices for Provalue II without explicitly calculating invested capital to set prices.

Cost Base	Estimated Cost per Unit (1)	Markup Percentage (2)	Markup Component (3) = (1) × (2)	Prospective Selling Price (4) = (1) + (3)
Variable manufacturing cost	$475	65%	$308.75	$783.75
Variable cost of the product	547	45	246.15	793.15
Manufacturing cost	540	50	270.00	810.00
Full cost of the product	720	12	86.40	806.40

The different cost bases and markup percentages give four prospective selling prices that are close to each other. The markup percentages in the preceding table vary a great deal, from a high of 65% on variable manufacturing cost to a low of 12% on full cost of the product. Why the wide variation? When determining a prospective selling price, a cost base such as variable manufacturing cost that includes fewer costs requires a higher markup percentage because the price needs to be set to earn a profit margin *and* to recover the costs (fixed manufacturing costs and all nonmanufacturing costs) that have been excluded from the cost base.

Surveys indicate that many managers use the full cost of the product for cost-based pricing decisions—that is, they include variable costs and costs that are fixed in the short run when calculating the cost per unit. Managers include the fixed cost per unit in the cost base for several reasons:

1. **Full recovery of all costs of the product.** In the long run, the price of a product must exceed the full cost of the product if a company is to remain in business. Using just the variable cost as the base may tempt managers to cut prices as long as prices are above variable cost and generate a positive contribution margin. As the experience in the airline industry has shown, price wars, when airline companies cut prices as long as they exceed variable

costs, have caused airlines to lose money because revenues are too low to recover the full cost of the product. Using the full cost of the product as the basis for pricing reduces the temptation to cut prices below full costs.

2. **Price stability.** Using the full cost of a product as the basis for pricing decisions limits the ability and temptation of salespeople to cut prices, which also promotes price stability. Stable prices facilitate more accurate forecasting and planning for both sellers and buyers.
3. **Simplicity.** A full-cost formula for pricing does not require the management accountant to perform a detailed analysis of cost-behavior patterns to separate product costs into variable and fixed components. Variable and fixed cost components are difficult to identify for many costs such as testing, inspection, and setups, and in many service businesses such as accounting and management consulting.

Including fixed cost per unit in the cost base for pricing decisions can be challenging. Allocating fixed costs to products can be arbitrary. Also, calculating fixed cost per unit requires a denominator level that is based on an estimate of capacity or expected units of future sales. Errors in these estimates will cause actual full cost per unit of the product to differ from the estimated amount. Despite these challenges, managers generally include fixed costs when making cost-based pricing decisions.

14-4 TRY IT!

Dory Inc. competes with Guppy Inc. in the distribution of mechanical pencils. Dory also identifies its primary activities and cost pools as ordering, receiving and storage, and shipping. It reports the following details for 2020:

Activity	Cost Driver	Quantity of Cost Driver	Cost per Unit of Cost Driver
1. Placing and paying for orders of pencil packs	Number of orders	300	$75 per order
2. Receiving and storage	Loads moved	3,600	$50 per load
3. Shipping of pencil packs to retailers	Number of shipments	1,500	$90 per shipment

For 2020, Dory buys 250,000 pencil packs at an average cost of $4.75 per pack. Dory plans to use cost-plus pricing.

Calculate the prospective selling price (1) if Dory marks up the purchase costs of the pencil packs by 20% and (2) if Dory marks up the full cost of the pencil packs by 6%.

Cost-Plus Pricing and Target Pricing

The selling prices computed under cost-plus pricing are *prospective* prices. Suppose Astel's initial product design results in a $750 full cost estimate for Provalue II. Assuming a 12% markup, Astel sets a prospective price of $840 [$750 + (0.12 × $750)]. In the competitive personal computer market, customer and competitor reactions to this price may force Astel to reduce the markup percentage and lower the price to, say, $800. Astel may then want to redesign Provalue II to reduce the full cost to $720 per unit, as in our example, and achieve a markup close to 12% at the price of $800. The eventual design and cost-plus price must balance cost, markup, and customer reactions.

The target-pricing approach reduces the need to go back and forth among prospective cost-plus prices, customer reactions, and design modifications. In contrast to cost-plus pricing, the target pricing approach first determines product characteristics and a target price on the basis of customer preferences and expected competitor responses and then computes a target cost.

Companies that provide many distinctive products and services to their customers, such as accountants, management consultants, and lawyers, usually use cost-plus pricing. Each job that professional service firms do for their clients is unique. They set prices based on hourly cost-plus billing rates of partners, managers, and associates. These prices are, however, lowered in competitive situations. Professional service firms also take a multiple-year client perspective when deciding prices because clients prefer to work with the same firm over multiple periods. Certified public accountants, for example, sometimes charge a client a low price initially to get the account and then recover the lower profits or losses in the initial years by charging higher prices in later years.

Service companies such as home repair services, automobile repair services, and architectural firms use a cost-plus pricing method called the *time-and-materials method*. Individual jobs are priced based on materials and labor time. The price charged for materials equals the cost of materials plus a markup. The price charged for labor represents the cost of labor plus a markup. That is, the price charged for each direct cost item includes its own markup. Companies choose the markups to recover overhead costs and to earn a profit.

DECISION POINT

How do companies price products using the cost-plus approach?

Life-Cycle Product Budgeting and Costing

LEARNING OBJECTIVE 6

Use life-cycle budgeting and costing when making pricing decisions

. . . accumulate all costs of a product from initial R&D to final customer service for each year of the product's life

Managers sometimes need to consider target prices and target costs over a multiple-year product life cycle. The **product life cycle** spans the time from initial R&D on a product to when customer service and support is no longer offered for that product. For automobile companies such as BMW, Ford, and Nissan, the typical product life cycle of a car model is 12 to 15 years from design to product introduction and sale, and, eventually, service. For pharmaceutical companies such as Pfizer, Merck, and Roche, the life cycle of a successful new medication may be 15 to 20 years. For banks such as Bank of America and Chase, a product such as a newly designed savings account with specific privileges can have a life cycle of 10 to 20 years. Personal computers have a shorter life cycle of 2 to 3 years because rapid innovations in the computing power and the speed of microprocessors that run the computers make older models obsolete fairly quickly.

In **life-cycle budgeting**, managers estimate the revenues and business function costs across the entire value chain from a product's initial R&D to its final customer service and support. **Life-cycle costing** tracks and accumulates business function costs across the entire value chain from a product's initial R&D to its final customer service and support. Life-cycle budgeting and life-cycle costing span several years.

Life-Cycle Budgeting and Pricing Decisions

Budgeted life-cycle costs provide useful information for strategically evaluating pricing decisions. Consider Insight, Inc., a computer software company, which is developing a new business accounting package, "General Ledger." Assume the following budgeted amounts for General Ledger over a 6-year product life cycle:

Years 1 and 2

	Total Fixed Costs
R&D costs	$240,000
Design costs	160,000

Years 3 to 6

	Total Fixed Costs	Variable Cost per Package
Production costs	$100,000	$25
Marketing costs	70,000	24
Distribution costs	50,000	16
Customer-service costs	80,000	30

Exhibit 14-7 presents the 6-year life-cycle budget for "General Ledger" for three alternative-selling-price/sales-quantity combinations.

EXHIBIT 14-7

Budgeting Life-Cycle Revenues and Costs for the "General Ledger" Software Package of Insight, Inc.[a]

	Alternative-Selling-Price/Sales-Quantity Combinations		
	A	B	C
Selling price per package	$400	$480	$600
Sales quantity in units	5,000	4,000	2,500
Life-cycle revenues			
($400 × 5,000; $480 × 4,000; $600 × 2,500)	$2,000,000	$1,920,000	$1,500,000
Life-cycle costs			
R&D costs	240,000	240,000	240,000
Design costs of product/process	160,000	160,000	160,000
Production costs			
$100,000 + ($25 × 5,000); $100,000 + ($25 × 4,000); $100,000 + ($25 × 2,500)	225,000	200,000	162,500
Marketing costs			
$70,000 + ($24 × 5,000); $70,000 + ($24 × 4,000); $70,000 + ($24 × 2,500)	190,000	166,000	130,000
Distribution costs			
$50,000 + ($16 × 5,000); $50,000 + ($16 × 4,000); $50,000 + ($16 × 2,500)	130,000	114,000	90,000
Customer-service costs			
$80,000 + ($30 × 5,000); $80,000 + ($30 × 4,000); $80,000 + ($30 × 2,500)	230,000	200,000	155,000
Total life-cycle costs	1,175,000	1,080,000	937,500
Life-cycle operating income	$ 825,000	$ 840,000	$ 562,500

[a]This exhibit does not take into consideration the time value of money when computing life-cycle revenues or life-cycle costs. Chapter 22 outlines how this important factor can be incorporated into such calculations.

Life-cycle budgeting is particularly important in certain situations, such as the following:

1. **The development period for R&D and design is long and costly.** When a company incurs a large percentage of total life-cycle costs before any production begins and any revenues are received, as in the "General Ledger" example, managers need to evaluate revenues and costs over the life cycle of the product in order to decide whether to begin the costly R&D and design activities.
2. **Many costs are locked in at the R&D and design stages, even if R&D and design costs themselves are small.** In our "General Ledger" example, design and quality decisions about the accounting software package will affect marketing, distribution, and customer-service costs in several subsequent years. A life-cycle revenue-and-cost budget prevents Insight's managers from overlooking these multiple-year relationships among business-function costs. Life-cycle budgeting highlights costs throughout the product's life cycle and, in doing so, facilitates target pricing, target costing, and value engineering at the design stage before costs are locked in. The amounts presented in Exhibit 14-7 are the outcome of value engineering.

Insight's managers decide to sell the "General Ledger" package for $480 per package because this price maximizes life-cycle operating income. They then compare actual costs to life-cycle budgets to obtain feedback and to learn about how to better estimate costs for subsequent products. Exhibit 14-7 assumes that the selling price per package is the same over the entire life cycle. For strategic reasons, however, Insight's managers may decide to *skim the market* by charging higher prices to eager customers when "General Ledger" is first introduced and lowering prices later as the product matures. Managers may also decide to add new features in later years to differentiate the product to achieve higher prices and sales. The life-cycle budget will then incorporate the revenues and costs of these strategic decisions.

Managing Environmental and Sustainability Costs

Managing environmental costs is a critical area where managers apply life-cycle costing and value engineering. Environmental laws like the U.S. Clean Air Act and the U.S. Superfund Amendment and Reauthorization Act have introduced tougher environmental standards, imposed stringent cleanup requirements, and introduced severe penalties for polluting the air and contaminating subsurface soil and groundwater. In some countries, such as Sweden, the government levies a carbon tax, a fee or surcharge on carbon-based fuels and other sources of pollution. A carbon tax puts a monetary price on greenhouse gas emissions. Other regions such as the European Union use a cap-and-trade system, where the government puts a limit or cap on the overall level of carbon pollution and conducts a market auction for pollution quotas. Companies pay for the right to pollute and can then either sell (or buy) these rights to (or from) other companies if they pollute less (or more) than their quotas.

Environmental costs that are incurred over several years of the product's life cycle are often locked in at the product- and process-design stage. To avoid environmental liabilities, reduce carbon taxes, or the cost of buying pollution quotas, managers in industries such as oil refining, chemical processing, and automobile manufacturing value engineer and design products and processes to prevent and reduce pollution over the product's life cycle. In the computer industry, laptop manufacturers like Hewlett-Packard and Apple have introduced recycling programs to ensure that chemicals from nickel-cadmium batteries do not leak hazardous chemicals into the soil. The carbon tax has spurred innovation in the design of energy-efficient products and clean energy solutions, such as solar and wind power.[6]

What is the effect of sustainability investments on overall financial performance in subsequent periods? A new organization, the Sustainability Accounting Standards Board has begun defining standards for environmental, social, and governance (ESG) performance for different industries. The relevant (or material) ESG standards vary across industries based on financial impact and interest of user groups. For example, the relevant ESG standards in the oil and gas industry include greenhouse gas emissions and water and wastewater management, while the relevant ESG standards in the technology and communications industry include life-cycle impacts of products and services and energy management. When measured over multiple periods, companies that have higher relevant ESG ratings have higher future profitability and financial performance, perhaps because of customer loyalty and satisfaction, employee engagement, or brand and reputation.[7]

Customer Life-Cycle Costing

In the previous section, we considered life-cycle costs from the perspective of a product or service. **Customer life-cycle costs** focus on the total costs incurred by a customer to acquire, use, maintain, and dispose of a product or service.

Customer life-cycle costs influence the prices a company can charge for its products. For example, Ford can charge a higher price and/or gain market share if its cars require minimal maintenance for 100,000 miles. Similarly, Maytag charges higher prices for appliances that save electricity and have low maintenance costs. Boeing Corporation justifies a higher price for the Boeing 777 because the plane's design allows mechanics easier access to different areas of the plane to perform routine maintenance, reduces the time and cost of maintenance, and significantly decreases the life-cycle cost of owning the plane.

DECISION POINT

Describe life-cycle budgeting and life-cycle costing. When should companies use these techniques?

Noncost Factors in Pricing Decisions

We have seen so far that cost is a major factor in setting prices. We now explore how legal, political, and economic considerations influence firms' ability to set prices in relation to their cost of producing and delivering products and services.

6 Although Sweden has one of the highest carbon taxes at $140 per ton of carbon pollution, its economy has continued to grow strongly since the tax was introduced in 1991.

7 M. Khan, G. Serafeim, and A. Yoon, "Corporate Sustainability: First Evidence on Materiality," *The Accounting Review* (September 2016).

Predatory Pricing

In the United States, antitrust laws, such as the Sherman Act, the Clayton Act, the Federal Trade Commission Act, and the Robinson-Patman Act, mandate that prices must not be predatory. A company engages in **predatory pricing** when it deliberately prices below its costs in an effort to drive competitors out of the market to restrict supply and then recoups its losses by raising prices or enlarging demand.[8]

The U.S. Supreme Court established the following conditions to prove that predatory pricing has occurred:

- The predator company charges a price below an appropriate measure of its costs, generally taken to be short-run marginal or average variable costs.
- The predator company has a reasonable prospect of recovering in the future, through larger market share or higher prices, the money it lost by pricing below cost.

The need to demonstrate both of these conditions has generally made it very difficult to prove that companies have engaged in predatory pricing.[9]

LEARNING OBJECTIVE 7

Explain the effects of legal restrictions on pricing

. . . limit the ability to price below costs (predatory pricing) or in coordination with competitors (collusive pricing) or to charge higher prices in the United States than in a home country (dumping)

and the broader notion of price discrimination

. . . charging different customers different prices for the same product—for example, when orders arrive as demand approaches capacity limits (peak-load pricing)

Collusive Pricing

While predatory pricing laws prevent firms from charging prices that are too low, other violations of antitrust law occur when prices are too high. **Collusive pricing** occurs when companies in an industry conspire in their pricing and production decisions to achieve a price above the competitive price and so restrain trade. In 2015, for example, an appeals court upheld a 2013 ruling that Apple had illegally conspired with five large book publishers on the pricing of ebooks. The goal was to promote Apple's new iPad and to prevent Amazon from undercutting its title prices of ebooks. The case resulted in a $450 million settlement in which Apple paid purchasers twice their losses.

Price Discrimination

Consider the prices airlines charge for a round-trip flight from New York to London. A coach-class ticket for a flight with a 7-day advance purchase is $1,100 if the passenger stays in London over a Saturday night. The ticket is $2,000 if the passenger returns without staying over a Saturday night. Can this price difference be explained by the difference in the cost to the airline of these round-trip flights? No, because it costs the airline the same amount to transport the passenger from New York to London and back, regardless of whether the passenger stays in London over a Saturday night. This difference in price is due to *price discrimination.*

Price discrimination is the practice of charging different customers different prices for the same product or service. How does price discrimination work in the airline example? The demand for airline tickets comes from two main sources: business travelers and pleasure travelers. Business travelers must travel to conduct business for their organizations, so their demand for air travel is relatively insensitive to price. Airlines can earn higher operating incomes by charging business travelers higher prices. Insensitivity of demand to price changes is called *demand inelasticity*. Also, business travelers generally go to their destinations, complete their work, and return home without staying over a Saturday night. Pleasure travelers, in contrast, usually don't need to return home during the week and prefer to spend weekends at their destinations. Because they pay for their tickets themselves, pleasure travelers' demand is price-elastic; lower prices stimulate demand while higher prices restrict demand. Airlines can earn higher operating incomes by charging pleasure travelers lower prices.

How can airlines keep fares high for business travelers while keeping fares low for pleasure travelers? Requiring a Saturday night stay discriminates between the two customer segments by taking advantage of their differential travel habits.

---

[8] For more details, see W. Kip Viscusi, Joseph E. Harrington, and David E. M. Sappington, *Economics of Regulation and Antitrust*, 5th ed. (Cambridge, MA: MIT Press, 2018).

[9] A celebrated example that illustrates the hurdle is the 1993 case of Brooke Group Ltd. v. Brown & Williamson Tobacco Corp (BWT). The U.S. Supreme Court held that BWT priced below cost but was not guilty of predatory pricing. Justice Kennedy noted that at its market share of 12%, BWT would have to make nine dollars in future profits for every dollar spent in under-cutting prices, and therefore its likelihood of recouping its losses was practically nil.

From a legal standpoint, the Robinson-Patman Act of 1936 and related laws specify that

1. Price discrimination is permissible if differences in prices can be justified by differences in costs.
2. Price discrimination is illegal only if the intent is to lessen or prevent competition.

In the airline situation, there is clearly no difference in cost in serving the two customer segments; however, the price discrimination is legal because the practice does not hinder competition.

International Pricing

When the same product is sold in different countries, many economic and regulatory factors come into play. Consider software or electronic products produced in one country and sold globally. The prices charged in each country may vary much more than the costs of delivering the product to each country because of differences in purchasing power of consumers in different countries (a form of price discrimination). Government restrictions may also limit the prices that overseas companies can charge, as in the case of some life-saving medications.

On the other hand, **dumping** occurs when a foreign company sells a product in the United States at a price below the market price in the country where it is produced, and this lower price materially injures (or threatens to injure) an industry in the United States. If dumping is proven, an antidumping duty, equal to the price differential, can be imposed under United States tariff laws. The current prolonged global trade war has led to the United States announcing antidumping duties of up to 80% on Chinese-made stainless steel beer kegs and of 1,731% on Chinese-made mattresses, while China has set antidumping taxes of between 58% and 148% on alloy-steel seamless tubes and pipes made in the United States and the European Union.

Peak-Load Pricing

In addition to the factors described above, capacity constraints affect pricing decisions. **Peak-load pricing** is the practice of charging a higher price for the same product or service when demand approaches the physical limit of the capacity to produce that product or service. When demand is high and production capacity and therefore supply are limited, customers are willing to pay more to get the product or service. In contrast, slack or excess capacity leads companies to lower prices in order to stimulate demand and utilize capacity. Peak-load pricing occurs in the telephone, telecommunications, hotel, car rental, and electric-utility industries. For example, Uber Technologies Inc. uses surge pricing during high-demand times such as on Saturday nights. Another example is the 2016 Summer Olympics in Rio de Janeiro when hotels charged high rates and required multiple-night stays. Airlines charged high fares for flights into and out of many cities in the region for roughly a month around the time of the Games. Demand far exceeded capacity and the hospitality industry and airlines employed peak-load pricing to increase their profits.

DECISION POINT

What non-cost considerations influence firms' ability to set prices in relation to their cost of producing and delivering products and services?

PROBLEM FOR SELF-STUDY

Reconsider the Astel Computer example (pages 565–568). Astel's marketing manager realizes that a further reduction in price is necessary to sell 200,000 units of Provalue II. To maintain a target profitability of $16 million, or $80 per unit, Astel will need to reduce costs of Provalue II by $6 million, or $30 per unit. Astel targets a reduction of $4 million, or $20 per unit, in manufacturing costs, and $2 million, or $10 per unit, in marketing, distribution, and customer-service costs. The cross-functional team assigned to this task proposes the following changes to manufacture a different version of Provalue, called Provalue III:

1. Reduce direct materials and ordering costs by purchasing subassembled components rather than individual components.

2. Reengineer ordering and receiving to reduce ordering and receiving costs per order.
3. Reduce testing time and the labor and power required per hour of testing.
4. Develop new rework procedures to reduce rework costs per hour.

No changes are proposed in direct manufacturing labor cost per unit and in total machining costs.

The following table summarizes the cost-driver quantities and the cost per unit of each cost driver for Provalue III compared with Provalue II.

Home | Insert | Page Layout | Formulas | Data | Review | View

	A	B	C	D	E	F	G	H	I	J	K	L	M	N
1			Manufacturing Cost Information						Manufacturing Cost Information					
2			for 200,000 Units of Provalue II for 2020						for 200,000 Units of Provalue III for 2020					
3	Cost Category	Cost Driver	Details of Budgeted Cost Driver Quantities				Budgeted Total Quantity of Cost Driver	Budgeted Cost per Unit of Cost Driver	Details of Budgeted Cost Driver Quantities				Budgeted Total Quantity of Cost Driver	Budgeted Cost per Unit of Cost Driver
4	(1)	(2)	(3)		(4)		(5)=(3)×(4)	(6)	(7)		(8)		(9)=(7)×(8)	(10)
5	Direct materials	No. of kits	1	kit per unit	200,000	units	200,000	$385	1	kit per unit	200,000	units	200,000	$ 375
6	Direct manuf. labor (DML)	DML hours	2.65	DML hours per unit	200,000	units	530,000	$ 20	2.65	DML hours per unit	200,000	units	530,000	$ 20
7	Direct machining (fixed)	Machine-hours					300,000	$ 38					300,000	$ 38
8	Ordering and receiving	No. of orders	50	orders per component	425	components	21,250	$ 80	50	orders per component	400	components	20,000	$ 60
9	Test and inspection	Testing-hours	15	testing-hours per unit	200,000	units	3,000,000	$ 2	14	testing-hours per unit	200,000	units	2,800,000	$1.70
10	Rework				6.5%	defect rate					6.5%	defect rate		
11		Rework-hours	2.5	rework-hours per defective unit	13,000[a]	defective units	32,500	$ 40	2.5	rework-hours per defective unit	13,000[a]	defective units	32,500	$ 32
12														
13	[a]6.5% defect rate × 200,000 units = 13,000 defective units													

Required

Will the proposed changes achieve Astel's targeted reduction of $4 million, or $20 per unit, in manufacturing costs for Provalue III? Show your computations.

Solution

Exhibit 14-8 presents the manufacturing costs for Provalue III based on the proposed changes. Manufacturing costs will decline from $108 million, or $540 per unit (Exhibit 14-6), to $104 million, or $520 per unit (Exhibit 14-8), and will achieve the target reduction of $4 million, or $20 per unit.

EXHIBIT 14-8 Target Manufacturing Costs of Provalue III for 2020 Based on Proposed Changes

	A	B	C	D
1		**Budgeted**		**Budgeted**
2		**Manufacturing Costs**		**Manufacturing**
3		**for 200,000 Units**		**Cost per Unit**
4		**(1)**		**(2) = (1) ÷ 200,000**
5	Direct manufacturing costs			
6	Direct material costs			
7	(200,000 kits × $375 per kit)	$ 75,000,000		$375.00
8	Direct manufacturing labor costs			
9	(530,000 DML-hours × $20 per hour)	10,600,000		53.00
10	Direct machining costs			
11	(300,000 machine-hours × $38 per machine-hour)	11,400,000		57.00
12	Direct manufacturing costs	97,000,000		485.00
13				
14	Manufacturing overhead costs			
15	Ordering and receiving costs			
16	(20,000 orders × $60 per order)	1,200,000		6.00
17	Testing and inspection costs			
18	(2,800,000 testing-hours × $1.70 per hour)	4,760,000		23.80
19	Rework costs			
20	(32,500 rework-hours × $32 per hour)	1,040,000		5.20
21	Manufacturing overhead costs	7,000,000		35.00
22	Total manufacturing costs	$104,000,000		$520.00

DECISION **POINTS**

The following question-and-answer format summarizes the chapter's learning objectives. Each decision presents a key question related to a learning objective. The guidelines are the answers to that question.

Decision	**Guidelines**
1. What are the three major factors affecting pricing decisions?	Customers, competitors, and costs influence prices through their effects on demand and supply; customers and competitors affect demand; and costs affect supply.
2. How do companies make long-run pricing decisions?	Companies consider all future costs (whether variable or fixed in the short run) and use a market-based or a cost-based pricing approach to earn a target return on investment.
3. How do companies determine target costs?	One approach to long-run pricing is to determine a target price. A target price is the estimated price that potential customers are willing to pay for a product or service. The target cost per unit equals the target price minus the target operating income per unit. The target cost per unit is the estimated long-run cost of a product or service that, when sold, enables the company to achieve the target operating income per unit. Value-engineering methods help a company make the cost improvements necessary to achieve a target cost.

Decision	Guidelines
4. Why is it important for managers to distinguish cost incurrence from locked-in costs?	Cost incurrence describes when a resource is sacrificed. Locked-in costs are costs that have not yet been incurred but, based on decisions that have already been made, will be incurred in the future. Value engineering techniques are most effective for reducing costs *before* costs are locked in.
5. How do companies price products using the cost-plus approach?	The cost-plus approach to pricing adds a markup component to a cost base as the starting point for pricing decisions. Many different costs, such as full cost of the product or manufacturing cost, can serve as the cost base for applying the cost-plus formula. Prices are then modified on the basis of customers' reactions and competitors' responses, that is, the size of the "plus" is determined by the marketplace.
6. Describe life-cycle budgeting and life-cycle costing. When should companies use these techniques?	Life-cycle budgeting estimates and life-cycle costing tracks and accumulates the costs (and revenues) attributable to a product from its initial R&D to its final customer service and support. These life-cycle techniques are particularly important when (a) a high percentage of total life-cycle costs are incurred before production begins while revenues are earned over several years or (b) a high fraction of life-cycle costs are locked in at the R&D and design stages.
7. What non-cost considerations influence firms' ability to set prices in relation to their cost of producing and delivering products and services?	Pricing below costs in an effort to drive competitors out of the market (predatory pricing) is illegal, as is colluding with other companies in the same industry to charge excessively high prices. Price discrimination refers to charging differential prices to customers for the same product or service. This may result from charging higher prices when demand approaches physical-capacity limits (peak-load pricing), or to reflect cross-country differences in regulations or the purchasing power of consumers.

TERMS TO LEARN

The chapter and the Glossary at the end of the text contain definitions of the following important terms:

collusive pricing (**p. 581**)
cost incurrence (**p. 571**)
customer life-cycle costs (**p. 580**)
designed-in costs (**p. 571**)
dumping (**p. 582**)
life-cycle budgeting (**p. 578**)
life-cycle costing (**p. 578**)
locked-in costs (**p. 571**)
non-value-added cost (**p. 571**)
peak-load pricing (**p. 582**)
predatory pricing (**p. 581**)
price discrimination (**p. 581**)
product life cycle (**p. 578**)
target cost per unit (**p. 569**)
target operating income per unit (**p. 569**)
target price (**p. 569**)
target rate of return on investment (**p. 576**)
value-added cost (**p. 571**)
value engineering (**p. 571**)

ASSIGNMENT MATERIAL

Questions

14-1 What are the three major influences on pricing decisions?
14-2 "Relevant costs for pricing decisions are full costs of the product." Do you agree? Explain.
14-3 Describe four purposes of cost allocation.
14-4 How is activity-based costing useful for pricing decisions?
14-5 Describe two alternative approaches to long-run pricing decisions.
14-6 What is a target cost per unit?
14-7 Describe value engineering and its role in target costing.
14-8 Give two examples of a value-added cost and two examples of a non-value-added cost.
14-9 "It is not important for a company to distinguish between cost incurrence and locked-in costs." Do you agree? Explain.
14-10 What is cost-plus pricing?
14-11 Describe three alternative cost-plus pricing methods.
14-12 What is life-cycle budgeting?
14-13 What are three benefits of using a product life-cycle reporting format?
14-14 Define price discrimination and give an example.
14-15 Describe peak-load pricing and give an example.

Multiple-Choice Questions

In partnership with:

BECKER PROFESSIONAL EDUCATION®

14-16 Which of the following statements regarding price elasticity is incorrect?

a. A product with a perfectly inelastic demand would have the same demand even as prices change.
b. A product with a perfectly inelastic demand would see demand change as prices change.
c. When demand is price elastic, lower prices stimulate demand.
d. When demand is price elastic, higher prices reduce demand.

Exercises

14-17 Value-added, non-value-added costs. The Magill Repair Shop repairs and services machine tools. A summary of its costs (by activity) for 2020 is as follows:

a. Materials and labor for servicing machine tools	$1,100,000
b. Rework costs	90,000
c. Expediting costs caused by work delays	65,000
d. Materials-handling costs	80,000
e. Materials-procurement and inspection costs	45,000
f. Preventive maintenance of equipment	55,000
g. Breakdown maintenance of equipment	75,000

Required

1. Classify each cost as value-added, non-value-added, or in the gray area between.
2. For any cost classified in the gray area, assume 60% is value-added and 40% is non-value-added. How much of the total of all seven costs is value-added and how much is non-value-added?

3. Magill is considering the following changes: (a) introducing quality-improvement programs whose net effect will be to reduce rework and expediting costs by 40% and materials and labor costs for servicing machine tools by 5%, (b) working with suppliers to reduce materials-procurement and inspection costs by 20% and materials-handling costs by 30%, and (c) increasing preventive-maintenance costs by 70% to reduce breakdown-maintenance costs by 50%. Calculate the effect of programs (a), (b), and (c) on value-added costs, non-value-added costs, and total costs. Comment briefly.

14-18 Target operating income, value-added costs, service company. Calvert Associates prepares architectural drawings to conform to local structural-safety codes. Its income statement for 2020 is as follows:

Revenues	$701,250
Salaries of professional staff	390,000
Travel	15,000
Administrative and support costs	171,600
Total costs	576,600
Operating income	$124,650

The percentage of time spent by professional staff on various activities follows:

Making calculations and preparing drawings for clients	77%
Checking calculations and drawings	3
Correcting errors found in drawings (not billed to clients)	8
Making changes in response to client requests (billed to clients)	5
Correcting own errors regarding building codes (not billed to clients)	7
Total	100%

Assume administrative and support costs vary with professional-labor costs. Consider each requirement independently.

Required

1. How much of the total costs in 2020 are value-added, non-value-added, or in the gray area between? Explain your answers briefly. What actions can Calvert take to reduce its costs?
2. What are the consequences of misclassifying a non-value-added cost as a value-added cost? When in doubt, would you classify a cost as a value-added or non-value-added cost? Explain briefly.
3. Suppose Calvert could eliminate all errors so that it did not need to spend any time making corrections and, as a result, could proportionately reduce professional-labor costs. Calculate Calvert's operating income for 2020.
4. Now suppose Calvert could take on as much business as it could complete, but it could not add more professional staff. Assume Calvert could eliminate all errors so that it does not need to spend any time correcting errors. Assume Calvert could use the time saved to increase revenues proportionately. Assume travel costs will remain at $15,000. Calculate Calvert's operating income for 2020.

14-19 Target prices, target costs, activity-based costing. Snappy Tiles is a small distributor of marble tiles. Snappy identifies its three major activities and cost pools as ordering, receiving and storage, and shipping, and it reports the following details for 2019:

Activity	Cost Driver	Quantity of Cost Driver	Cost per Unit of Cost Driver
1. Placing and paying for orders of marble tiles	Number of orders	500	$50 per order
2. Receiving and storage	Loads moved	4,000	$30 per load
3. Shipping of marble tiles to retailers	Number of shipments	1,500	$40 per shipment

For 2019, Snappy buys 250,000 marble tiles at an average cost of $3 per tile and sells them to retailers at an average price of $4 per tile. Assume Snappy has no fixed costs and no inventories.

Required

1. Calculate Snappy's operating income for 2019.
2. For 2020, retailers are demanding a 5% discount off the 2019 price. Snappy's suppliers are only willing to give a 4% discount. Snappy expects to sell the same quantity of marble tiles in 2020 as in 2019. If all other costs and cost-driver information remain the same, calculate Snappy's operating income for 2020.
3. Suppose further that Snappy decides to make changes in its ordering and receiving-and-storing practices. By placing long-run orders with its key suppliers, Snappy expects to reduce the number of orders to 200 and the cost per order to $25 per order. By redesigning the layout of the warehouse and

reconfiguring the crates in which the marble tiles are moved, Snappy expects to reduce the number of loads moved to 3,125 and the cost per load moved to $28. Will Snappy achieve its target operating income of $0.30 per tile in 2020? Show your calculations.

14-20 Target costs, effect of product-design changes on product costs. Neuro Instruments uses a manufacturing costing system with one direct-cost category (direct materials) and three indirect-cost categories:

a. Setup, production-order, and materials-handling costs that vary with the number of batches
b. Manufacturing-operations costs that vary with machine-hours
c. Costs of engineering changes that vary with the number of engineering changes made

In response to competitive pressures at the end of 2019, Neuro Instruments used value-engineering techniques to reduce manufacturing costs. Actual information for 2019 and 2020 is as follows:

	2019	2020
Setup, production-order, and materials-handling costs per batch	$ 8,900	$8,000
Total manufacturing-operations cost per machine-hour	$ 64	$ 48
Cost per engineering change	$16,000	$8,000

The management of Neuro Instruments wants to evaluate whether value engineering has succeeded in reducing the target manufacturing cost per unit of one of its products, HJ6, by 5%.

Actual results for 2019 and 2020 for HJ6 are as follows:

	Actual Results for 2019	Actual Results for 2020
Units of HJ6 produced	2,700	4,600
Direct material cost per unit of HJ6	$ 1,400	$ 1,300
Total number of batches required to produce HJ6	60	70
Total machine-hours required to produce HJ6	20,000	30,000
Number of engineering changes made	24	7

Required

1. Calculate the manufacturing cost per unit of HJ6 in 2019.
2. Calculate the manufacturing cost per unit of HJ6 in 2020.
3. Did Neuro Instruments achieve the target manufacturing cost per unit for HJ6 in 2020? Explain.
4. Explain how Neuro Instruments reduced the manufacturing cost per unit of HJ6 in 2020.
5. What challenges might managers at Neuro Instruments encounter in achieving the target cost? How might they overcome these challenges?

14-21 Target costs, effect of process-design changes on service costs. Sunlight Energy Systems (SES) sells solar heating systems in residential areas of eastern Pennsylvania. A successful sale results in the homeowner purchasing a solar heating system and obtaining rebates, tax credits, and financing for which SES completes all the paperwork. The company has identified three major activities that drive the cost of selling heating systems: identifying new contacts (varies with the number of new contacts); traveling to and between appointments (varies with the number of miles driven); and preparing and filing rebates and tax forms (varies with the number of solar systems sold). Actual costs for each of these activities in 2019 and 2020 are shown below:

	2019	2020
Average cost per new contact	$ 12.00	$ 10.00
Travel cost per mile	0.55	0.80
Preparing and filing cost per new system	260.00	250.00

After experiencing high costs in 2019, SES used value engineering to reduce the cost of selling solar heating systems. Managers at SES want to evaluate whether value engineering has succeeded in reducing the selling cost per sale by the targeted 5% in 2020.

Actual results for 2019 and 2020 for SES are as follows:

	Actual Results for 2019	Actual Results for 2020
Sales of heating systems	180	200
Number of new contacts	220	230
Miles driven	1,600	1,400

Required

1. Calculate the cost per sale in 2019.
2. Calculate the cost per sale in 2020.
3. Did SES achieve the target cost per sale in 2020? Explain.
4. What challenges might managers at SES encounter in achieving the target cost and how might they overcome these challenges?

14-22 Cost-plus target return on investment pricing. Jason Brady is the managing partner of a business that has just finished building a 60-room motel. Brady anticipates that he will rent these rooms for 15,000 nights next year (or 15,000 room-nights). All rooms are similar and will rent for the same price. Brady estimates the following operating costs for next year:

Variable operating costs	$3 per room-night
Fixed costs	
Salaries and wages	$177,000
Maintenance of building and pool	38,000
Other operating and administration costs	190,000
Total fixed costs	$405,000

The capital invested in the motel is $1,500,000. The partnership's target return on investment is 20%. Brady expects demand for rooms to be uniform throughout the year. He plans to price the rooms at full cost plus a markup on full cost to earn the target return on investment.

Required

1. What price should Brady charge for a room-night? What is the markup as a percentage of the full cost of a room-night?
2. Brady's market research indicates that if the price of a room-night determined in requirement 1 is reduced by 10%, the expected number of room-nights Brady could rent would increase by 10%. Should Brady reduce prices by 10%? Show your calculations.

14-23 Cost-plus, target pricing, working backward. KidsPlay, Inc., manufactures and sells table sets. In 2019, it reported the following:

Units produced and sold	3,000
Investment	$3,000,000
Markup percentage on full cost	10%
Rate of return on investment	15%
Variable cost per unit	$ 600

Required

1. What was KidsPlay's operating income in 2019? What was the full cost per unit? What was the selling price? What was the percentage markup on variable cost to achieve the selling price? What are the total fixed costs?
2. KidsPlay is considering increasing the annual spending on advertising by $200,000. The managers believe that the investment will translate into a 10% increase in unit sales. Should the company make the investment? Show your calculations.
3. Refer back to the original data. In 2020, KidsPlay believes that it will be able to sell only 2,700 units at the price calculated in requirement 1. Management has identified $185,000 in fixed cost that can be eliminated. If KidsPlay wants to maintain a 10% markup on full cost, what is the target variable cost per unit?

14-24 Life-cycle budgeting and costing. Teletronics is going to introduce a combination phone/tablet product.

Design and testing will take 8 months. Teletronics expects to sell 24,000 units during the first 6 months of sales. Sales over the next 12 months are expected to be less robust at 20,000. And, sales in the final 6 months of the expected life cycle are expected to be 9,000.

Teletronics is budgeting for this product as follows:

Months	Type of Cost	Total Fixed Cost for the Period	Variable cost per Unit
Months 0–8	Design costs	$ 800,200	
Months 9–14	Production	$ 998,400	$65 per unit
	Marketing	$ 840,000	
	Distribution	$ 432,000	$ 5 per unit
Months 15–26	Production	$ 760,000	$60 per unit
	Marketing	$1,350,000	
	Distribution	$ 360,000	$ 5 per unit
Months 27–32	Production	$ 351,000	$58 per unit
	Marketing	$ 480,000	
	Distribution	$ 162,000	$ 5 per unit

Ignore the time value of money.

Required

1. If Teletronics prices the phone/tablets at $280 each, how much operating income will the company make over the product's life cycle? What is the operating income per unit?
2. Excluding the initial product design costs, what is the operating income in each of the three sales phases of the product's life cycle, assuming the price stays at $280?
3. How would you explain the change in budgeted operating income over the product's life cycle? What other factors does the company need to consider before developing the new combination phone/tablet product?
4. Teletronics is concerned about the number of units it expects to sell in the first sales phase. The company is considering pricing the phone/tablet at $220 for the first 6 months and then increasing the price to $280 thereafter. With this pricing strategy, Teletronics expects to sell 27,000 units instead of the originally forecast 24,000 units in the first sales phase, and the same number of units for the remaining life cycle. Assuming the same cost structure as given in the problem, which pricing strategy would you recommend? Explain.

14-25 Considerations other than cost in pricing decisions. Happy Times Hotel operates a 100-room hotel near a busy amusement park. During June, a 30-day month, Happy Times Hotel experiences a 70% occupancy rate from Monday evening through Thursday evening (weeknights). On Friday through Sunday evenings (weekend nights), however, occupancy increases to 90%. (There were 18 weeknights and 12 weekend nights in June.) Happy Times Hotel charges $80 per night for a suite. The company recently hired Gina Davis to manage the hotel to increase the hotel's profitability. The following information relates to Happy Times Hotel's costs:

	Fixed Cost	Variable Cost
Depreciation	$25,000 per month	
Administrative costs	$40,000 per month	
Housekeeping and supplies	$25,000 per month	$15 per room-night
Breakfast	$12,000 per month	$ 8 per breakfast served

Happy Times Hotel offers free breakfast to guests. In June, there are an average of two breakfasts served per room-night on weeknights and four breakfasts served per room-night on weekend nights.

Required

1. What was Happy Times Hotel's operating income or loss for the month?
2. Gina Davis estimates that if Happy Times Hotel decreases the nightly rates to $70, weeknight occupancy will increase to 80%. She also estimates that if the hotel increases the nightly rate on weekend nights to $100, occupancy on those nights will remain at 90%. Would this be a good move for Happy Times Hotel? Show your calculations.
3. Why would Happy Times Hotel have a $30 price difference between weeknights and weekend nights?
4. A discount travel clearinghouse has approached Happy Times Hotel with a proposal to offer last-minute deals on empty rooms on both weeknights and weekend nights. Assuming that there will be an average of three breakfasts served per night per room, what is the minimum price that Happy Times Hotel could accept on the last-minute rooms?

Problems

14-26 Cost-plus, target pricing, working backward. The new chief executive officer (CEO) of Richard Manufacturing has asked for a variety of information about the operations of the firm from last year. The CEO is given the following information, but with some data missing:

Total sales revenue	?
Number of units produced and sold	500,000 units
Selling price	?
Operating income	$210,000
Total investment in assets	$2,500,000
Variable cost per unit	$2.25
Fixed costs for the year	$3,250,000

Required

1. Find (a) total sales revenue, (b) selling price, (c) rate of return on investment, and (d) markup percentage on full cost for this product.
2. The new CEO has a plan to reduce fixed costs by $250,000 and variable costs by $0.75 per unit while continuing to produce and sell 500,000 units. Using the same markup percentage as in requirement 1, calculate the new selling price.
3. Assume the CEO institutes the changes in requirement 2 including the new selling price. However, the reduction in variable cost has resulted in lower product quality, resulting in 15% fewer units being sold compared to before the change. Calculate operating income (loss).
4. What concerns, if any, other than the quality problem described in requirement 3, do you see in implementing the CEO's plan? Explain briefly.

14-27 Value engineering, target pricing, and target costs. Westerly Cosmetics manufactures and sells a variety of makeup and beauty products. The company has developed its own patented formula for a new anti-aging cream. The company president wants to make sure the product is priced competitively because its purchase will also likely increase sales of other products. The company anticipates that it will sell 400,000 units of the product in the first year with the following estimated costs:

Product design and licensing	$1,700,000
Direct materials	4,000,000
Direct manufacturing labor	1,600,000
Variable manufacturing overhead	400,000
Fixed manufacturing overhead	2,500,000
Fixed marketing	3,000,000

Required

1. The company believes that it can successfully sell the product for $45 a bottle. The company's target operating income is 30% of revenue. Calculate the target full cost of producing the 400,000 units. Does the cost estimate meet the company's requirements? Is value engineering needed?
2. A component of the direct materials cost requires the nectar of a specific plant in South America. If the company could eliminate this special ingredient, the materials cost would decrease by 25%. However, this would require design changes of $300,000 to engineer a chemical equivalent of the ingredient. Will this design change allow the product to meet its target cost?
3. The company president does not believe that the formula should be altered for fear it will tarnish the company's brand. She prefers that the company become more efficient in manufacturing the product. If fixed manufacturing costs can be reduced by $250,000 and variable direct manufacturing labor costs are reduced by $1 per unit, will Westerly achieve its target cost?
4. Would you recommend the company follow the proposed solution in requirement 2 or requirement 3?

14-28 Target service costs, value engineering, activity-based costing. Lagoon is an amusement park that offers family-friendly entertainment and attractions. The park boasts more than 25 acres of fun. The admission price to enter the park, which includes access to all attractions, is $35. To earn the required rate of return on investment, Lagoon's target operating income is 35% of total revenues. Lagoon's managers have identified the major activities that drive the cost of operating the park. The activity cost pools, the cost driver for each activity, and the cost per unit of the cost driver for each pool are shown on the next page:

Activity	Description of Activity	Cost Driver	Cost per Unit of Cost Driver
1. Ticket sales and verification	Selling and verifying tickets for entry into the park	Number of tickets sold	$3.35 per ticket sold
2. Operating attractions	Loading, monitoring, off-loading patrons on attractions	Number of runs	$90 per run
3. Litter patrol	Roaming the park and cleaning up waste as necessary	Number of litter patrol hours	$20 per hour

The following information describes the existing operations:

a. The average number of patrons per week is 55,000.
b. The total number of runs across all attractions is 11,340 runs each week.
c. It requires 1,750 hours of litter patrol hours to keep the park clean.

In response to competitive pressures and to continue to attract 55,000 patrons per week, Lagoon has decided to lower ticket prices to $33 per patron. To maintain the same level of profits as before, Lagoon is looking to make the following changes to reduce operating costs:

a. Reduce the cost of selling and verifying tickets by $0.35 per ticket sold.
b. Reduce the total number of runs across all attractions by 1,000 runs by reducing the operating hours of some of the attractions that are not very popular.
c. Increase the number of refuse containers in the park at an additional cost of $250 per week. This will decrease the litter patrol hours by 20%.

The cost per unit of cost driver for all other activities will remain the same.

Required

1. Will Lagoon achieve its target operating income of 35% of revenues at ticket prices of $35 per ticket before any operating changes?
2. After Lagoon reduces ticket prices and makes the changes and improvements described above, will Lagoon achieve its target operating income in dollars calculated in requirement 1? Show your calculations.
3. What challenges might managers at Lagoon encounter in achieving the target cost? How might they overcome these challenges?
4. A new carbon tax of $3 per run is proposed to be levied on the energy consumed to operate the attractions. Will Lagoon achieve its target operating income calculated in requirement 1? If not, by how much will Lagoon have to reduce its costs through value engineering to achieve the target operating income calculated in requirement 1?

14-29 Cost-plus, target return on investment pricing. ChocAttack makes candy bars for vending machines and sells them to vendors in cases of 30 bars. Although ChocAttack makes a variety of candies, the cost differences are insignificant, and the cases all sell for the same price.

ChocAttack has a total capital investment of $12,000,000. It expects to produce and sell 450,000 cases of candy next year. ChocAttack requires a 12% target return on investment.

Expected costs for next year are shown below:

Variable production costs	$4.00 per case
Variable marketing and distribution costs	$1.50 per case
Fixed production costs	$435,000
Fixed marketing and distribution costs	$800,000
Other fixed costs	$250,000

ChocAttack prices the cases of candy at full cost plus markup to generate profits equal to the target return on capital.

Required

1. What is the target operating income?
2. What is the selling price ChocAttack needs to charge to earn the target operating income? Calculate the markup percentage on full cost.
3. ChocAttack is considering increasing its selling price to $13 per case. Assuming production and sales decrease by 6%, calculate ChocAttack's return on investment. Is increasing the selling price a good idea?

14-30 Cost-plus, time and materials, ethics. V & S Mechanical sells and services plumbing, heating, and air-conditioning systems. V & S's cost accounting system tracks two cost categories: direct labor and direct materials. V & S uses a time-and-materials pricing system, with direct labor marked up 100% and direct materials marked up 50% to recover indirect costs of support staff, support materials, and shared equipment and tools, and to earn a profit.

During a hot summer day, the central air-conditioning in Linda Lowry's home stops working. V & S technician Tom Dryden arrives at Lowry's home and inspects the air conditioner. He considers two options: replace the compressor or repair it. The cost information available to Dryden follows:

	Labor	Materials
Repair option	5 hrs.	$160
Replace option	1 hr.	$220
Labor rate	$40 per hr.	

Required

1. If Dryden presents Lowry with the replace or repair options, what price would he quote for each?
2. If the two options were equally effective for the 3 years that Lowry intends to live in the home, which option would she choose?
3. If Dryden's objective is to maximize profits, which option would he recommend to Lowry? What would be the ethical course of action?

14-31 Cost-plus and market-based pricing. Florida Temps, a large labor contractor, supplies contract labor to construction companies. For 2020, Florida Temps has budgeted to supply 82,000 hours of contract labor. Its variable costs are $11 per hour, and its fixed costs are $328,000. Roger Mason, the general manager, has proposed a cost-plus approach for pricing labor at full cost plus 15%.

Required

1. Calculate the price per hour that Florida Temps should charge based on Mason's proposal.
2. The marketing manager supplies the following information on demand levels at different prices:

Price per Hour	Demand (Hours)
$16	123,000
18	101,000
19	82,000
20	71,000
22	66,000

   Florida Temps can meet any of these demand levels. Fixed costs will remain unchanged for all the demand levels. On the basis of this additional information, calculate the price per hour that Florida Temps should charge to maximize operating income.
3. Comment on your answers to requirements 1 and 2. Why are they the same or different?

14-32 Cost-plus and market-based pricing. (CMA, adapted) Accurate Laboratories evaluates the reaction of materials to extreme increases in temperature. Much of the company's early growth was attributable to government contracts, but recent growth has come from expansion into commercial markets. Two types of testing at Accurate are heat testing (HTT) and Arctic-condition testing (ACT). Currently, all of the budgeted operating costs are collected in a single overhead pool. All of the estimated testing-hours are also collected in a single pool. One rate per test-hour is used for both types of testing. This hourly rate is marked up by 35% to recover administrative costs and taxes and to earn a profit.

Ethan Poole, Accurate's controller, believes that there is enough variation in the test procedures and cost structure to establish separate costing rates and billing rates at a 35% markup. He also believes that the inflexible rate structure the company is currently using is inadequate in today's competitive environment. After analyzing the company data, he has divided operating costs into the following three cost pools:

Labor and supervision	$ 452,400
Setup and facility costs	343,140
Utilities	286,400
Total budgeted costs for the period	$1,081,940

Ethan budgets 116,000 total test-hours for the coming period. Test-hours is also the cost driver for labor and supervision. The budgeted quantity of cost driver for setup and facility costs is 700 setup hours. The budgeted quantity of cost driver for utilities is 8,000 machine-hours.

Ethan has estimated that HTT uses 70% of the test-hours, 30% of the setup-hours, and half the machine-hours.

Required

1. Find the single rate for operating costs based on test-hours, and the hourly billing rate for HTT and ACT.
2. Find the three activity-based rates for operating costs.
3. What will the billing rate for HTT and ACT be based on the activity-based costing structure? State the rates in terms of test-hours. Referring to both requirements 1 and 2, which rates make more sense for Accurate?
4. If Accurate's competition all charge $18 per hour for ACT, what can Accurate do to stay competitive?

14-33 Life-cycle costing. Life Cycle Metal Recycling and Salvage receives the opportunity to salvage scrap metal and other materials from an old industrial site. The current owners of the site will sign over the site to Life Cycle at no cost. Life Cycle intends to extract scrap metal at the site for 24 months and then will clean up the site, return the land to useable condition, and sell it to a developer. Projected costs associated with the project follow:

		Fixed	Variable
Months 1–24	Metal extraction and processing	$5,500 per month	$50 per ton
Months 1–27	Rent on temporary buildings	$4,500 per month	—
	Administration	$2,000 per month	—
Months 25–27	Clean-up	$33,000 per month	—
	Land restoration	$223,500 total	—
	Cost of selling land	$120,000 total	—

Ignore the time value of money.

Required

1. Assuming that Life Cycle expects to salvage 30,000 tons of metal from the site, what is the total project life-cycle cost?
2. Suppose Life Cycle can sell the metal for $80 per ton and wants to earn a profit (before taxes) of $30 per ton. At what price must Life Cycle sell the land at the end of the project to achieve its target profit per ton?
3. Now suppose Life Cycle can only sell the metal for $70 per ton and the land at $141,000 less than what you calculated in requirement 2. If Life Cycle wanted to maintain the same markup percentage on total project life-cycle cost as in requirement 2, by how much would the company have to reduce its total project life-cycle cost?

14-34 Airline pricing, considerations other than cost in pricing. Air Americo is about to introduce a daily round-trip flight from New York to Los Angeles and is determining how to price its round-trip tickets.

The market research group at Air Americo segments the market into business and pleasure travelers. It provides the following information on the effects of two different prices on the number of seats expected to be sold and the variable cost per ticket, including the commission paid to travel agents:

		Number of Seats Expected to Be Sold	
Price Charged	**Variable Cost per Ticket**	**Business**	**Pleasure**
$ 800	$ 75	300	150
2,100	185	285	30

Pleasure travelers start their travel during one week, spend at least 1 weekend at their destination, and return the following week or thereafter. Business travelers usually start and complete their travel within the same work week. They do not stay over weekends.

Assume that round-trip fuel costs are fixed costs of $24,500 and that fixed costs allocated to the round-trip flight for airplane-lease costs, ground services, and flight-crew salaries total $188,000.

Required

1. If you could charge different prices to business travelers and pleasure travelers, would you? Show your computations.
2. Explain the key factor (or factors) for your answer in requirement 1.
3. How might Air Americo implement price discrimination? That is, what plan could the airline formulate so that business travelers and pleasure travelers each pay the price the airline desires?

14-35 Pricing products using the target-costing approach. ProDry is entering the professional hair dryer market. Research shows that their customers wish to pay $310 or less for each dryer. Cost accountants at the manufacturer have collected the following information:

Direct material/unit	$ 50
Direct labor/unit	$ 30
Variable overhead	$ 30
Fixed costs (annually)	$206,250
Estimated production for year one	3,750

Required

1. What is the estimated cost per unit for ProDry?
2. What is the range of prices that ProDry could charge to make a profit?
3. Assume that ProDry's target operating income per unit is $165. What is the target cost for the dryer?
4. What can the company do to achieve its target cost calculated in requirement 3?
5. Should the target cost calculated in requirement 3 include all costs (direct, and variable and fixed overhead)? Why or why not?

14-36 Pricing products using the cost-plus approach (continued from 14-35)
The management of ProDry is considering use of the cost-plus approach rather than the target-cost approach used in 14-35. Refer to the information in 14-35.

Required

1. Do you think that it's a good idea for ProDry to use the cost-plus approach to price the hair dryer?
2. What strategies could ProDry's management use to make a profit if the company insisted on using the cost-plus approach to price the hair dryer?

14-37 Value engineering, target pricing, and locked-in costs. Sylvan Creations designs, manufactures, and sells modern wood sculptures. Sandra Johnson is an artist for the company. Johnson has spent much of the past month working on the design of an intricate abstract piece. Jim Chase, product development manager, likes the design. However, he wants to make sure that the sculpture can be priced competitively. Ellen Cooper, Sylvan's cost accountant, presents Chase with the following cost data for the expected production of 75 sculptures:

Design cost	$10,000
Direct materials	80,000
Direct manufacturing labor	27,500
Variable manufacturing overhead	10,000
Fixed manufacturing overhead	42,500
Fixed marketing costs	17,500

Required

1. Chase thinks that Sylvan Creations can successfully market each piece for $3,000. To earn the required return on capital, the company's target operating income per unit is 20% of target price. Calculate the target full cost per unit of producing the 75 sculptures. Does the cost estimate Cooper developed meet Sylvan's requirements? Is value engineering needed? What is the total target operating income for the 75 sculptures?
2. Chase believes that competition will require Sylvan to reduce the price of the sculpture to $2,800. Rather than using the highest-grade wood available, Sylvan could use standard grade wood and lower the cost of direct materials by 25%. This redesign will require an additional $1,500 of design cost. Will this design change allow Sylvan to earn its total target operating income on the 75 sculptures? Is the cost of wood a locked-in cost?
3. If the price of the sculpture is $2,800, what is the total amount Sylvan can spend on direct materials for the 75 sculptures to earn the total target operating income calculated in requirement 1? What is the target cost per sculpture?
4. What challenges might managers at Sylvan Creations encounter in achieving the target cost and how might they overcome these challenges?

15 Cost Allocation, Customer-Profitability Analysis, and Sales-Variance Analysis

LEARNING OBJECTIVES

1. Discuss why a company's revenues and costs differ across customers
2. Identify the importance of customer-profitability profiles
3. Understand the cost-hierarchy-based operating income statement
4. Understand criteria to guide cost-allocation decisions
5. Discuss decisions faced when collecting and allocating indirect costs to customers
6. Subdivide the sales-volume variance into the sales-mix variance and the sales-quantity variance and the sales-quantity variance into the market-share variance and the market-size variance

Companies desperately want to make their customers happy.

But how far should they go to please them, and at what price? Should a company differentiate among its customers and not treat all customers the same? The following article explains that companies go out of their way to please their most profitable customers.

STARBUCKS REWARDS STARTS REWARDING BIG SPENDERS[1]

In 2016, Starbucks introduced its revamped Starbucks Rewards program to its then-11 million members. Why? Starbucks wanted to better align its rewards program with customer spending. The old Starbucks Rewards program gave customers a "star" for each visit, regardless of how much they spent. After collecting 12 stars, customers received a free beverage. This resulted in big rewards for low spenders. Customers asked baristas to ring up one item at a time to collect more stars for each transaction. This created delays at the cash register and increased costs for the company by extending the staff time required for purchases.

Under the overhauled Starbucks Rewards program, customers receive two stars for every dollar spent on beverages, food, and other items at Starbucks. Gold members (customers who earn at least 300 stars in 1 year) now earn free beverages and receive special benefits like free coffee refills and the ability to pre-order and pay using the Starbucks mobile app.

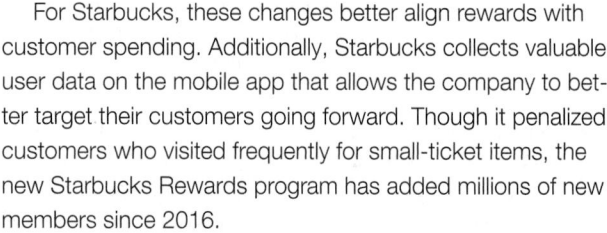

For Starbucks, these changes better align rewards with customer spending. Additionally, Starbucks collects valuable user data on the mobile app that allows the company to better target their customers going forward. Though it penalized customers who visited frequently for small-ticket items, the new Starbucks Rewards program has added millions of new members since 2016.

Nor Gal/Shutterstock

To determine which product, customer, program, or department is profitable, organizations need to allocate costs. In this chapter and the next, we build on the activity-based costing (ABC) ideas introduced in Chapter 5 and provide insight into cost allocation. This chapter emphasizes macro issues in cost allocation: allocation of costs to divisions and customers. Chapter 16 describes micro issues in cost allocation—allocating support-department costs to operating departments and allocating costs to different users and activities—as well as revenue allocations.

[1] *Sources:* Phil Wahba, "Why Starbucks Is Overhauling Its Loyalty Rewards Program," *Fortune,* February 22, 2016 (http://fortune.com/2016/02/22/starbucks-loyalty/); Samir Palnitkar, "Loyalty Rewards Case Study – New Starbucks Rewards Program," *Zinrelo,* April 12, 2017 (https://zinrelo.com/loyalty-rewards-case-study-new-starbucks-rewards-program.html); Erica Sweeney, "Starbucks Eyes Expanded Loyalty Offerings as Digital Push Delivers," *Marketing Dive,* July 30, 2018 (https://www.marketingdive.com/news/starbucks-eyes-expanded-loyalty-offerings-as-digital-push-delivers/528847/).

Customer-Profitability Analysis

LEARNING OBJECTIVE 1

Discuss why a company's revenues and costs differ across customers

... revenues differ because of differences in quantities purchased and price discounts, while costs differ because of different demands placed by customers on a company's resources

Customer-profitability analysis is the reporting and assessment of revenues earned from customers and the costs incurred to earn those revenues. An analysis of customer differences in revenues and costs reveals why differences exist in the operating income earned from different customers. Managers use this information to ensure that customers making large contributions to the operating income of a company receive a high level of attention from the company and that loss-making customers do not use more resources than the revenues they provide. As described at the start of this chapter, at Starbucks, managers use customer-profitability analysis to reward profitable customers who spend more with many perks.

Consider again Astel Computers from Chapter 14. Recall that Astel has two divisions: the Deskpoint Division manufactures and sells high-end computers, and the Provalue Division manufactures and sells Intel Core i9 chip-based laptop computers. Exhibit 15-1, which is the same as Exhibit 14-3, presents data for the Provalue Division of Astel Computers for the year ended 2019. Astel sells and distributes Provalue through two channels: (1) wholesalers who sell Provalue to retail outlets and (2) direct sales to business customers. Astel sells the same Provalue computer to wholesalers and to business customers, so the full manufacturing cost of Provalue of $680 is the same regardless of where it is sold. Provalue's listed selling price in 2019 was $1,100, but price discounts reduced the average selling price to $1,000. We focus on customer profitability for the Provalue Division's 10 wholesale distributors.

Customer-Revenue Analysis

Consider revenues from four of Provalue's 10 wholesale customers in 2019:

	A	B	C	D	E
1			CUSTOMER		
2		A	B	G	J
3	Units of Provalue sold	30,000	25,000	5,000	4,000
4	List selling price	$ 1,100	$ 1,100	$ 1,100	$ 1,100
5	Price discount	$ 100	$ 50	$ 150	—
6	Invoice price	$ 1,000	$ 1,050	$ 950	$ 1,100
7	Revenues (Row 3 × Row 6)	$30,000,000	$26,250,000	$4,750,000	$4,400,000

Two variables explain revenue differences across these four wholesale customers: (1) the number of computers they purchased and (2) the magnitude of price discounting. A **price discount** is the reduction in selling price below list selling price to encourage customers to purchase more quantities. Companies that record only the final invoice price in their information system cannot readily track the magnitude of their price discounting.[2]

Price discounts are a function of multiple factors, including the volume of product purchased (higher-volume customers receive higher discounts) and the desire to sell to a customer who might help promote sales to other customers. In some cases, discounts result from poor negotiating by a salesperson or the unwanted effect of a company's incentive plan based only on revenues. At no time, however, should price discounts stem from illegal activities such as price discrimination, predatory pricing, or collusive pricing (pages 580–582).

Tracking price discounts by customer and by salesperson helps improve customer profitability. For example, the Provalue Division managers could decide to strictly enforce its volume-based price discounting policy. The company could also require its salespeople to give only a limited number of discounts to customers who do not normally qualify for

[2] Further analysis of customer revenues could distinguish gross revenues from net revenues. This approach highlights differences across customers in sales returns. Additional discussion of ways to analyze revenue differences across customers is in Robert S. Kaplan and Robin Cooper, *Cost and Effect: Using Integrated Cost Systems to Drive Profitability and Performance* (Boston: Harvard Business School Press, 1998), Chapter 10; and Gary Cokins, *Activity-Based Cost Management: An Executive's Guide* (New York: Wiley, 2001), Chapter 3.

EXHIBIT 15-1

Profitability of Provalue Division for 2019 Using Value-Chain Activity-Based Costing

	A	B	C
1		Total Amounts	
2		for 150,000 Units	Per Unit
3		(1)	(2) = (1) ÷ 150,000
4	Revenues	$150,000,000	$1,000
5	Costs of goods sold[a] (from Exhibit 14-2)	102,000,000	680
6	Operating costs[b]		
7	R&D costs	2,400,000	16
8	Design costs of product and process	3,000,000	20
9	Marketing and administration costs	15,000,000	100
10	Distribution costs	9,000,000	60
11	Customer-service costs	3,600,000	24
12	Operating costs	33,000,000	220
13	Full cost of the product	135,000,000	900
14	Operating income	$ 15,000,000	$ 100
15			
16	[a]Cost of goods sold = Total manufacturing costs because there is no beginning or ending inventory		
17	of Provalue in 2019		
18	[b]Numbers for operating cost line-items are provided without supporting calculations		

them. In addition, the company could track future sales to customers, such as Customer G, who have received sizable price discounts on the basis of their "high growth potential."

Customer revenues are one element of customer profitability. The other, equally important element is the cost of acquiring, serving, and retaining customers.

Customer-Cost Analysis

We apply to customers the cost hierarchy discussed in Chapter 5 (pages 159–160). A **customer-cost hierarchy** categorizes costs related to customers into different cost pools on the basis of different types of cost drivers, or cost-allocation bases, or different degrees of difficulty in determining cause-and-effect or benefits-received relationships. The Provalue Division customer costs are composed of (1) marketing and administration costs, $15,000,000; (2) distribution costs, $9,000,000; and (3) customer-service costs, $3,600,000 (see Exhibit 15-1). Managers identify five categories of indirect costs in its customer-cost hierarchy:

1. **Customer output unit-level costs**—costs of activities to sell each unit (computer) to a customer. An example is product-handling costs of each computer sold.
2. **Customer batch-level costs**—costs of activities related to a group of units (computers) sold to a customer. Examples are costs incurred to process orders or to make deliveries.
3. **Customer-sustaining costs**—costs of activities to support individual customers, regardless of the number of units or batches of product delivered to the customer. Examples are costs of visits to customers or costs of displays at customer sites.
4. **Distribution-channel costs**—costs of activities related to a particular distribution channel rather than to each unit of product, each batch of product, or specific customers. An example is the salary of the manager of the Provalue Division's wholesale distribution channel.
5. **Division-sustaining costs**—costs of division activities that cannot be traced to individual customers or distribution channels. An example is the salary of the Provalue Division manager.

Note from these descriptions that four of the five levels of Provalue Division's cost hierarchy closely parallel the cost hierarchy described in Chapter 5 except that the

Provalue Division focuses on *customers* whereas the cost hierarchy in Chapter 5 focused on *products*. The Provalue Division has one additional cost-hierarchy category, distribution-channel costs, for the costs it incurs to support its wholesale and business-sales channels.

Customer-Level Costs

Exhibit 15-2 summarizes details of the costs incurred in marketing and administration, distribution, and customer service by activity. The exhibit also identifies the cost driver (where appropriate), the total costs incurred for the activity, the total quantity of the cost driver, the cost per unit of the cost driver, and the customer cost-hierarchy category for each activity.

For example, here is a breakdown of Provalue Division's $15,000,000 of marketing and administration costs:

- $6,750,000 of sales-order costs, which include negotiating, finalizing, issuing, and collecting on 6,000 sales orders at a cost of $1,125 ($6,750,000 ÷ 6,000) per sales order. Recall that sales-order costs are customer batch-level costs because these costs vary with the number of sales orders issued and not with the number of Provalue computers in a sales order.
- $4,200,000 for customer visits, which are customer-sustaining costs. The amount per customer varies with the number of visits to that customer rather than the number of units or batches of Provalue delivered to that customer.
- $800,000 on managing the wholesale channel, which are distribution-channel costs.
- $1,350,000 on managing the business-sales channel, which are distribution-channel costs.
- $1,900,000 on general administration of the Provalue Division, which are division-sustaining costs.

The Provalue Division managers are particularly interested in analyzing *customer-level indirect costs*—costs incurred in the first three categories of the customer-cost hierarchy: customer output unit–level costs, customer batch-level costs, and customer-sustaining costs.

EXHIBIT 15-2 Marketing, Administration, Distribution, and Customer Service Activities, Costs, and Cost Driver Information for Provalue Division in 2019

	A	B	C	D	E	F	G	H
1	Marketing, Administration, Distribution, and Customer Service Costs for 150,000 Units of Provalue in 2019							
2								
3	Activity Area	Cost Driver	Total Cost of Activity	Total Quantity of Cost Driver		Cost per Unit of Cost Driver		Cost Hierarchy Category
4	(1)	(2)	(3)	(4)		(5) = (3) ÷ (4)		(6)
5	**Marketing and Administration**							
6	Sales orders	Number of sales orders	$ 6,750,000	6,000	sales orders	$1,125	per sales order	Customer batch-level costs
7	Customer visits	Number of customer visits	4,200,000	750	customer visits	$5,600	per customer visit	Customer-sustaining costs
8	Wholesale channel marketing		800,000					Distribution-channel costs
9	Business-sales channel marketing		1,350,000					Distribution-channel costs
10	Provalue division administration		1,900,000					Division-sustaining costs
11	Total marketing & administration costs		$15,000,000					
12								
13	**Distribution**							
14	Product handling	Number of cubic feet moved	$ 4,500,000	300,000	cubic feet	$ 15	per cubic foot	Customer output unit-level costs
15	Regular shipments	Number of regular shipments	3,750,000	3,000	regular shipments	$1,250	per regular shipment	Customer batch-level costs
16	Rush shipments	Number of rush shipments	750,000	150	rush shipments	$5,000	per rush shipment	Customer batch-level costs
17	Total distribution costs		$ 9,000,000					
18								
19	**Customer Service**							
20	Customer service	Number of units shipped	$ 3,600,000	150,000	units shipped	$ 24	per unit shipped	Customer output unit-level costs

Managers believe they can work with customers to influence customer actions to reduce these costs. Information on the quantity of cost drivers used by each of four representative wholesale customers follows:

	A	B	C	D	E	F
1			CUSTOMER			
2	**Activity**	**Quantity of Cost Driver**	**A**	**B**	**G**	**J**
3	**Marketing**					
4	Sales orders	Number of sales orders	1,200	1,000	600	300
5	Customer visits	Number of customer visits	150	100	50	25
6	**Distribution**					
7	Product handling	Number of cubic feet moved	60,000	50,000	10,000	8,000
8	Regular shipments	Number of regular shipments	600	400	300	120
9	Rush shipments	Number of rush shipments	25	5	20	3
10	**Customer Service**					
11	Customer service	Number of units shipped	30,000	25,000	5,000	4,000

Exhibit 15-3 shows customer-level operating income for the four wholesale customers using information on customer revenues previously presented (page 597) and customer-level indirect costs, obtained by multiplying the rate per unit of cost driver (from Exhibit 15-2) by the quantities of the cost driver used by each customer (in the preceding table). Exhibit 15-3 shows that the Provalue Division makes losses on Customer G (the cost of resources used exceeds revenues) while Customer J is profitable on smaller revenues. In a similar vein, the Provalue Division has higher operating income from Customer B than Customer A even though it sells fewer computers to Customer B compared to Customer A.

The Provalue Division's managers can use the information in Exhibit 15-3 to work with customers to reduce the quantity of activities needed to support them. Consider, for example, Customer G and Customer J. Customer G purchases 25% more computers than Customer J (5,000 versus 4,000) but the company offers Customer G significant price discounts to achieve these sales. Compared with Customer J, Customer G places twice as many sales orders, requires twice as many customer visits, and generates two-and-a-half times as many regular shipments and almost seven times as many rush shipments. Selling smaller quantities of Provalue is profitable so long as price discounting is limited and customers do not use large amounts of division resources. For example, charging customers for marketing (sales orders and customer visits) and distribution services (regular and rush shipments) might motivate Customer G to place fewer but larger sales orders and require fewer customer visits, regular shipments, and rush shipments. A similar analysis might help managers understand the reasons for the lower profitability of Customer A relative to Customer B and actions they might take to improve Customer A's profitability.

Owens and Minor, a distributor of medical supplies to hospitals, separately prices each of its services such as a rush delivery or special packaging. How have its customers reacted? Hospitals that value these services continue to demand and pay for them, while hospitals that do not value these services stop asking for them, saving Owens and Minor some costs. This pricing strategy influences customer behavior in a way that increases Owens and Minor's revenues or decreases its costs.

The ABC system also highlights a second opportunity for cost reduction. Provalue Division managers can reduce the costs of activities by applying a value-engineering process to nonmanufacturing costs: (1) understand customer requirements and value-added and non-value-added costs, (2) anticipate how costs are locked in before they are incurred, and (3) use cross-functional teams to redesign products and processes to reduce costs while

EXHIBIT 15-3 Customer-Profitability Analysis for Provalue Division's Four Wholesale-Channel Customers for 2019

	A	B	C	D	E
1		**Customer A**	**Customer B**	**Customer G**	**Customer J**
2	Revenues at list price	$33,000,000	$27,500,000	$5,500,000	$4,400,000
3	Price discount	3,000,000	1,250,000	750,000	-
4	Revenues	30,000,000	26,250,000	4,750,000	4,400,000
5					
6	Cost of goods sold[a]	20,400,000	17,000,000	3,400,000	2,720,000
7					
8	Gross margin	9,600,000	9,250,000	1,350,000	1,680,000
9					
10	Customer-level costs				
11	Marketing costs				
12	Sales orders[b]	1,350,000	1,125,000	675,000	337,500
13	Customer visits[c]	840,000	560,000	280,000	140,000
14	Distribution costs				
15	Product handling[d]	900,000	750,000	150,000	120,000
16	Regular shipments[e]	750,000	500,000	375,000	150,000
17	Rush shipments[f]	125,000	25,000	100,000	15,000
18	Customer service costs				
19	Customer service[g]	720,000	600,000	120,000	96,000
20					
21	Total customer-level costs	4,685,000	3,560,000	1,700,000	858,500
22					
23	Customer-level operating income	$ 4,915,000	$ 5,690,000	$ (350,000)	$ 821,500
24	[a]\$680 × 30,000; 25,000; 5,000; 4,000 [b]\$1,125 × 1,200; 1,000; 600; 300 [c]\$5,600 × 150; 100; 50; 25 [d]\$15 × 60,000; 50,000; 10,000;				
25	8,000 [e]\$1,250 × 600; 400; 300; 120 [f]\$5,000 × 25; 5; 20; 3 [g]\$24 × 30,000; 25,000; 5,000; 4,000				

15-1 TRY IT!

Mason Inc. has only two retail and two wholesale customers. Information relating to each customer for 2020 follows:

	Wholesale Customers		Retail Customers	
	West Region Wholesaler	**East Region Wholesaler**	**Sloan Inc.**	**Snyder Corp**
Revenues at list prices	$745,000	$1,200,000	$330,000	$320,000
Discounts from list prices	52,300	78,500	20,200	6,130
Cost of goods sold	610,000	1,010,000	302,000	170,000
Delivery costs	28,100	23,470	16,530	14,300
Order processing costs	12,680	16,890	9,420	7,230
Costs of sales visits	12,700	10,300	9,310	8,160

Calculate customer-level operating income using the format in Exhibit 15-3.

meeting customer needs. For example, improving the efficiency of the ordering process (through electronic ordering) reduces sales-order costs even if customers place the same number of orders.

Simplifying the design and reducing the weight of the newly designed Provalue II for 2020 reduces the cost per cubic foot of handling Provalue and total product-handling costs. By influencing customer behavior and improving marketing, distribution, and customer-service operations, managers aim to reduce the nonmanufacturing cost of Provalue II to $180 per computer and achieve the target cost of $720 for Provalue II.

DECISION POINT

How can a company's revenues and costs differ across customers?

Customer-Profitability Profiles

LEARNING OBJECTIVE 2

Identify the importance of customer-profitability profiles

... expand relationships with profitable customers, change behavior patterns of unprofitable customers, and highlight that a small percentage of customers contributes a large percentage of operating income

Customer-profitability profiles are a useful tool for managers. Exhibit 15-4 ranks the Provalue Division's 10 wholesale customers based on customer-level operating income. (We analyzed four of these customers in Exhibit 15-3.)

Column 4, computed by adding the individual amounts in column 1, shows the cumulative customer-level operating income. For example, Customer C shows a cumulative income of $13,260,000 in column 4. This $13,260,000 is the sum of $5,690,000 for Customer B, $4,915,000 for Customer A, and $2,655,000 for Customer C.

Column 5 shows what percentage the $13,260,000 *cumulative* total for customers B, A, and C is of the total customer-level operating income of $15,027,500 earned in the wholesale distribution channel from all 10 customers. The three most profitable customers contribute 88% of total customer-level operating income. These customers deserve the highest service and priority. It is common for a small number of customers to contribute a high percentage of operating income. Microsoft uses the phrase "not all revenue dollars are endowed equally in profitability" to stress this point. Companies keep their best customers happy in a number of ways, including special phone numbers and upgrade privileges for elite-level frequent flyers and free usage of luxury hotel suites and big credit limits for high rollers at casinos. Concepts in Action: Amazon Prime and Customer Profitability (page 603) describes how Amazon introduced Amazon Prime to support its most profitable customers.

EXHIBIT 15-4 Cumulative Customer-Profitability Analysis for Provalue Division's Wholesale-Channel Customers: Astel Computers, 2019

	A	B	C	D	E	F
1	Retail Customer Code	Customer-Level Operating Income	Customer Revenue	Customer-Level Operating Income Divided by Revenue	Cumulative Customer-Level Operating Income	Cumulative Customer-Level Operating Income as a % of Total Customer-Level Operating Income
2		(1)	(2)	(3) = (1) ÷ (2)	(4)	(5) = (4) ÷ $15,027,500
3	B	$ 5,690,000	$26,250,000	21.7%	$ 5,690,000	38%
4	A	4,915,000	30,000,000	16.4%	10,605,000	71%
5	C	2,655,000	13,000,000	20.4%	13,260,000	88%
6	D	1,445,000	7,250,000	19.9%	14,705,000	98%
7	F	986,000	5,100,000	19.3%	15,691,000	104%
8	J	821,500	4,400,000	18.7%	16,512,500	110%
9	E	100,000	1,800,000	5.6%	16,612,500	111%
10	G	(350,000)	4,750,000	−7.4%	16,262,500	108%
11	H	(535,000)	2,400,000	−22.3%	15,727,500	105%
12	I	(700,000)	2,600,000	−26.9%	15,027,500	100%
13	Total	$15,027,500	$97,550,000			

CONCEPTS IN ACTION

Amazon Prime and Customer Profitability[3]

B Christopher/Alamy Stock Photo

Amazon Prime is a subscription program where, for an annual fee, customers receive free 2-day shipping on all orders on Amazon. Since its introduction, Amazon Prime has transformed subscribers' e-commerce expectations, while expanding into an all-inclusive package of streaming video, e-book lending, and exclusive access to a growing stable of Amazon-branded products.

By 2019, an estimated 100 million subscribers paid $119 annually for Amazon Prime. With the high costs of the program, many industry observers concluded that the company lost money on each Amazon Prime subscription. In fact, Amazon Prime subscribers are actually the company's most profitable customers!

While the Prime program has high costs, Amazon Prime subscribers spend nearly twice as much with Amazon compared to nonsubscribers ($2,486 versus $600). Many of these subscribers order more often from Amazon and purchase items from Amazon that they would not have previously. New perks, such as discounts at Whole Foods and 2-hour delivery in major cities, ensure that the most profitable customers make Amazon their first-choice retail provider every day.

[3] *Sources:* Heather Haddon and Laura Stevens, "It's Amazon Prime Time at Whole Foods," *The Wall Street Journal*, June 18, 2018 (https://www.wsj.com/articles/attention-amazon-prime-members-who-shop-at-whole-foods-youre-in-luck-1529154000); Jonathan Varian, "Amazon Has Over 100 Million Prime Members," *Fortune*, April 28, 2018 (http://fortune.com/2018/04/18/amazon-prime-members-millions/).; Rafi Mohammed, "The Logic Behind Amazon's Prime Day," *HBR.org*, July 13, 2015 (https://hbr.org/2015/07/the-logic-behind-amazons-prime-day).

Column 3 shows the profitability per dollar of revenue by customer. This measure of customer profitability indicates that, although Customer A contributes the second-highest operating income, the profitability per dollar of revenue is lowest among the top six customers because of high price discounts and higher customer-level costs (see pages 597 and 600). To increase operating income margins for Customer A, managers would need to decrease price discounts or save customer-level costs while maintaining or increasing sales. Customers D, F, and J have high operating income margins but low total sales. For these customers, managers would like to increase sales while maintaining margins. With Customers E, G, H, and I, managers have the dual challenge of boosting sales and operating income.

Presenting Profitability Analysis

Exhibit 15-5 illustrates two common ways of displaying the results of customer-profitability analysis. The bar chart presentation in Panel A (based on Exhibit 15-4, column 1) is an intuitive way to visualize customer profitability because (1) the highly profitable customers clearly stand out and (2) the number of "unprofitable" customers and the magnitude of their losses are apparent. Panel B of Exhibit 15-5 is a popular alternative way to express customer profitability. It plots the contents of Exhibit 15-4, column 5. This chart is called the **whale curve** because it is backward-bending at the point where customers start to become unprofitable (cumulative customer-level operating income goes from 111% after accounting for Customer E to 100% after accounting for Customer I) and thus resembles a humpback whale.[4]

Exhibits 15-2 to 15-5 emphasize *annual* customer profitability. Managers should also consider other factors when prioritizing customers, including the following:

- **Likelihood of customer retention.** The more likely a customer will continue to do business with a company, the more valuable the customer, for example, wholesalers who have sold Provalue each year over the last several years. Customers differ in their loyalty and their willingness to frequently "shop their business."

[4] In practice, the curve of the chart can be quite steep. The whale curve for cumulative profitability usually reveals that the most profitable 20% of customers generate between 150% and 300% of total profits, the middle 70% of customers break even, and the least profitable 10% of customers lose from 50% to 200% of total profits [see Robert S. Kaplan and V. G. Narayanan, "Measuring and Managing Customer Profitability," *Journal of Cost Management* (September/October 2001): 1–11].

EXHIBIT 15-5

Panel A: Bar Chart of Customer-Level Operating Income for Provalue Division's Wholesale-Channel Customers in 2019

Panel B: The Whale Curve of Cumulative Profitability for Provalue Division's Wholesale-Channel Customers in 2019

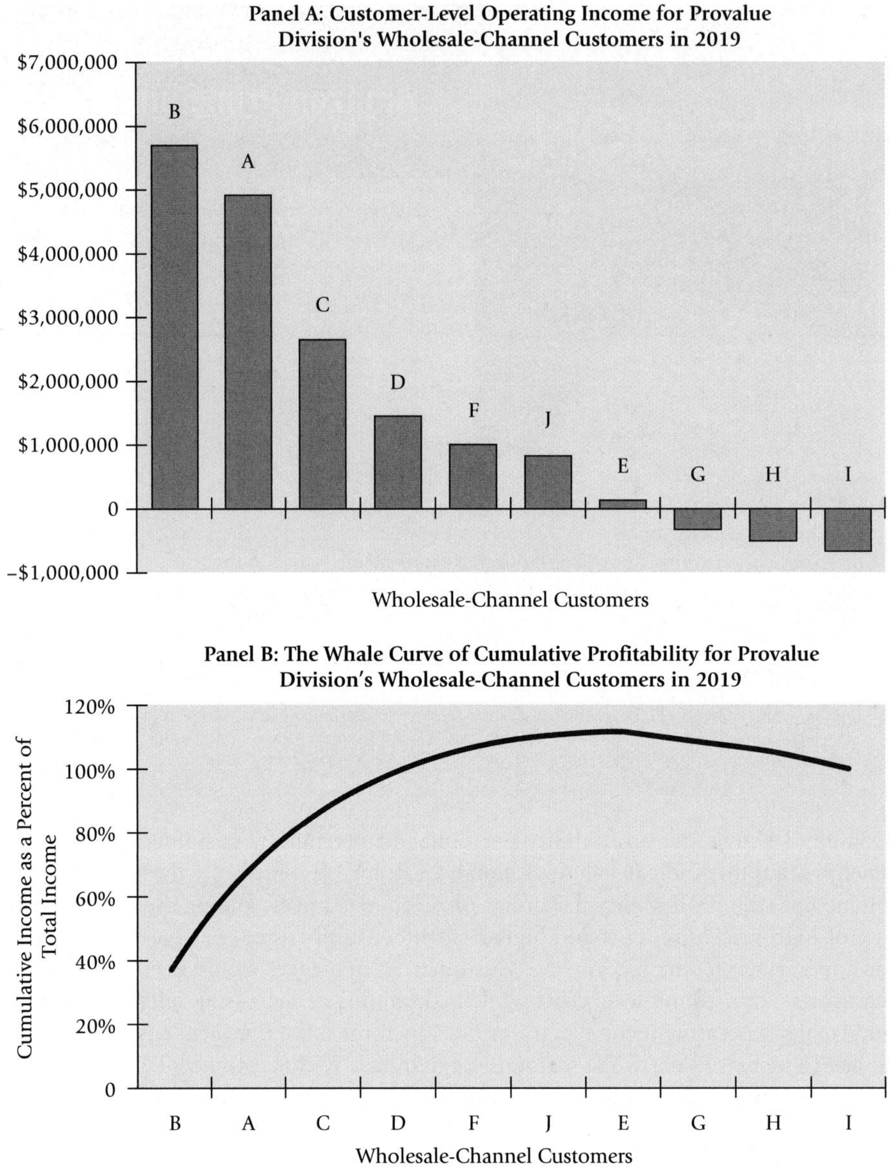

- **Potential for sales growth.** The higher the likely future sales to a customer, the more valuable the customer. Customers to whom a company can cross-sell other products profitably are even more desirable, for example, wholesalers also willing to distribute Astel's Deskpoint brands. If wholesalers sell both Provalue and Deskpoint, managers need to assess customer profitability based on sales of both Provalue and Deskpoint.
- **Long-run customer profitability.** This factor is influenced by the first two factors—likelihood of customer retention and potential sales growth—and the cost of customer-support staff and special services required to support the customer.
- **Increases in overall demand from having reference customers.** Customers with established reputations, also called reference customers, help generate sales from other customers through product endorsements.
- **Ability to learn from customers.** Customers who provide ideas about new products or ways to improve existing products are especially valuable, for example, wholesalers who give Astel feedback about key features such as size of memory or video displays.

Managers should be cautious about discontinuing customers. In Exhibit 15-4, the current unprofitability of Customer G, for example, may not be indicative of Customer G's profitability in the long run, for example, because of higher anticipated sales. Moreover, as in any ABC-based system, the costs assigned to Customer G are not all variable. In the short run, it may be efficient for the Provalue Division managers to use spare capacity to serve Customer G on a contribution-margin basis. Discontinuing Customer G will not eliminate all costs assigned to Customer G and may result in losing more revenues relative to costs saved.

Of course, particular customers might be chronically unprofitable and hold limited future prospects. Or they might fall outside a company's target market or require unsustainably high levels of service relative to the company's strategies and capabilities. In such cases, organizations sever customer relationships. For example, Capital One 360, one of the largest direct lenders and fast-growing financial services organizations in the United States, asks 10,000 "high maintenance" customers (for example, those who maintain low balances and make frequent deposits and withdrawals) to close their accounts each month.[5]

Using the Five-Step Decision-Making Process to Manage Customer Profitability

In this section, we apply the five-step decision-making process (introduced in Chapter 1) to help understand how managers use customer analyses to allocate resources across customers.

1. **Identify the problem and uncertainties.** The problem is how to manage and allocate resources across customers. Managers are uncertain how their actions will affect future customer profitability.
2. **Obtain information.** Managers identify past revenues generated by each customer and customer-level costs incurred in the past to support each customer.
3. **Make predictions about the future.** Managers estimate the revenues they expect from each customer and the customer-level costs they will incur in the future. In making these predictions, managers consider the effects that future price discounts will have on revenues, the effect that pricing for different services (such as rush deliveries) will have on customer demand for these services, and ways to reduce the cost of providing services. For example, Deluxe Corporation, a leading check printer, reduced the cost to serve customers by opening an electronic channel to shift customers from paper to automated ordering.
4. **Make decisions by choosing among alternatives.** Managers use customer-profitability profiles to identify the small set of customers who deserve the highest service and priority and also to find ways to make less-profitable customers (such as Astel's Customer G) more profitable. Banks, for example, impose minimum balance requirements on customers. Distribution firms require minimum order quantities or levy a surcharge for smaller or customized orders. In making resource-allocation decisions, managers also consider long-term effects, such as the potential for future sales growth and the opportunity to leverage a particular customer account to make sales to other customers.
5. **Implement the decision, evaluate performance, and learn.** After the decision is implemented, managers compare actual results to predicted outcomes to evaluate the decision they made, its implementation, and ways to improve profitability.

DECISION POINT

How do customer-profitability profiles help managers?

Cost-Hierarchy-Based Operating Income Statement

LEARNING OBJECTIVE 3

Understand the cost-hierarchy-based operating income statement

... allocate only those costs that will be affected by actions at a particular hierarchical level

Our analysis so far has focused on customer-level costs—costs of activities that managers can work with customers to influence such as sales orders, customer visits, and shipments. We now consider other costs of the Provalue Division (such as research and development [R&D] and design costs, costs to manage different distribution channels, and costs of division administration) and corporate costs incurred by Astel Computers (such as corporate brand advertising and general administration costs). Customer actions do not influence these costs, which raises two important questions: (1) Should these costs be allocated to customers when calculating customer profitability, and (2) if they are allocated, on what basis should they be allocated given the weak cause-and-effect relationship between these costs and customer actions? We start by considering the first question and introduce the cost-hierarchy-based operating income statement, which does not allocate noncustomer-level costs.

[5] See, for example, "The New Math of Customer Relationships" at http://hbswk.hbs.edu/item/5884.html.

EXHIBIT 15-6 Operating Income Statement of Provalue Division for 2019 Using the Cost Hierarchy

	A	B	C	D	E	F	G	H	K	L	M	N	O
1				CUSTOMER DISTRIBUTION CHANNELS									
2				Wholesale Customers					Business-Sales Customers				
3		Total	Total	A**		B**	C		Total	BA	BB	BC	
4		(1) = (2) + (7)	(2)	(3)		(4)	(5)	(6)	(7)	(8)	(9)	(10)	(11)
5	Revenues (at actual prices)	$150,000,000	$97,550,000	$30,000,000		$26,250,000	-	-	$52,450,000	$7,000,000	$6,250,000	-	-
6	Cost of goods sold plus customer-level costs	125,550,000*	82,522,500	25,085,000	a	20,560,000	-	-	43,027,500	5,385,000	4,760,000	-	-
7	Customer-level operating income	24,450,000	15,027,500	$ 4,915,000		$ 5,690,000	-	-	9,422,500	$1,615,000	$1,490,000	-	-
8	Distribution-channel costs	2,150,000	800,000						1,350,000				
9	Distribution-channel-level operating income	22,300,000	$14,227,500						$ 8,072,500				
10	Division-sustaining costs:												
11	Administration costs	1,900,000											
12	R&D Costs	2,400,000											
13	Design Costs	3,000,000											
14	Total division-sustaining costs	7,300,000											
15	Division operating income	$ 15,000,000											
16	*Cost of goods sold, $102,000,000 (Exhibit 15-1) + Sales order costs, $6,750,000 + Customer visit costs, $4,200,000 + Product handling costs, $4,500,000 + Regular shipment costs, $3,750,000 + Rush shipment costs, $750,000 + Customer service costs, $3,600,000 (all from Exhibit 15-2)												
17	**Full details are presented in Exhibit 15-3												
18	[a]Cost of goods sold + total customer-level costs from Exhibit 15-3 for Customer A = $20,400,000 + $4,685,000 = $25,085,000.												

Exhibit 15-6 shows an operating income statement for the Provalue Division for 2019. The customer-level operating incomes of Customers A and B in Exhibit 15-3 are shown in columns 3 and 4 in Exhibit 15-6. The format of Exhibit 15-6 is based on the Provalue Division's cost hierarchy. As described in Exhibit 15-2, some costs of serving customers, such as the salary of the wholesale distribution-channel manager, are not customer-level costs and are therefore not allocated to customers in Exhibit 15-6. Managers identify these costs as distribution-channel costs because changes in customer behavior will have no effect on these costs. Only decisions pertaining to the channel, such as a decision to discontinue wholesale distribution, will influence these costs. Many managers also believe that salespeople responsible for managing individual customer accounts would lose motivation if sales bonuses were adversely affected as a result of allocating to customers distribution-channel costs over which they have minimal influence. As Exhibit 15-6 shows, Astel subtracts wholesale distribution-channel costs from the total customer-level operating income of the wholesale channel without allocating these costs to individual wholesale customers.

Next, consider division-sustaining costs such as R&D, design, and administration costs of the Provalue Division. Managers believe there is no direct cause-and-effect relationship between these costs and customer or sales manager's actions. Under this view, allocating division-sustaining costs serves no useful purpose in decision making, performance evaluation, or motivation. Suppose, for example, that the Provalue Division allocates the $7,300,000 of division-sustaining costs to its distribution channels and that in some subsequent period this allocation results in a business-sales channel showing a loss. Should the Provalue Division shut down that business-sales distribution channel? Not if (as we discussed in Chapter 12) division-sustaining costs are unaffected by shutting down the business-sales distribution channel. Allocating division-sustaining costs to distribution channels gives the misleading impression that potential cost savings from discontinuing a distribution channel are greater than they are. The cost-hierarchy-based income statement in Exhibit 15-6 therefore subtracts division-sustaining costs of the Provalue Division from the total operating income at the distribution-channel level without allocating division-sustaining costs either to the distribution channel or to individual customers.

In a cost-hierarchy-based income statement, how should we treat the corporate costs for brand advertising, $1,050,000, and administration, $4,400,000, incurred by Astel Computers to support the Provalue and Deskpoint divisions? The Deskpoint Division has revenues of $200,000,000 and operating costs of $170,000,000. Exhibit 15-7 presents the

EXHIBIT 15-7

Income Statement of Astel Computers for 2019 Using the Cost Hierarchy

	A	B	C	D
1	**Income Statement of Astel Computers for 2019 Using the Cost Hierarchy**			
2				
3		**Total**	**Provalue Division**	**Deskpoint Division**
4				
5	Revenues	$350,000,000	$150,000,000	$200,000,000
6	Division operating costs	(305,000,000)	(135,000,000)*	(170,000,000)
7	Division operating income before corporate costs	45,000,000	$ 15,000,000	$ 30,000,000
8	Corporate advertising	(1,050,000)		
9	Corporate administration	(4,400,000)		
10	Operating income	$ 39,550,000		
11	*135,000,000 = $125,550,000 + $2,150,000 + $7,300,000, all from Exhibit 15-6, Column 1			

cost-hierarchy-based income statement for Astel Computers as a whole. Corporate-sustaining costs are not allocated either to divisions or to channels or to customers. That's because, as discussed earlier in the context of division-sustaining costs, there is no direct cause-and-effect relationship between these costs and the profitability of different customers or divisions. These costs are unaffected by the actions of division managers or customers, so corporate-sustaining costs are subtracted as a lump-sum amount after aggregating operating incomes of the divisions.

Some managers and management accountants advocate fully allocating all costs to distribution channels and to customers because all costs are incurred to support the sales of products to customers. Allocating all corporate costs motivates division managers to examine how corporate costs are planned and controlled. Similarly, allocating division costs to distribution channels motivates the managers of the distribution channels to monitor costs incurred in the division. Managers who want to calculate the full costs of serving customers must allocate all corporate, division, and distribution-channel costs to customers. These managers and management accountants argue that, in the long run, customers and products must eventually be profitable on a full-cost basis. As we discussed in Chapter 14, for some decisions such as pricing, allocating all costs ensures that long-run prices are set at a level to cover the cost of all resources used to produce and sell products. In this case, the sum of operating incomes of all customers equals companywide operating income.

Still other companies allocate only those corporate costs, division costs, or channel costs to customers that are widely perceived as causally influencing customer actions or that provide explicit benefits to customer profitability. Corporate advertising is an example of such a cost. These companies exclude other costs such as corporate administration or donations to charitable foundations because the benefits to the customers are less evident or too remote. If a company decides not to allocate some or all corporate, division, or channel costs, it results in total company profitability being less than the sum of individual customer profitabilities.

For some decision purposes, allocating some but not all indirect costs may be the preferred alternative. Consider the performance evaluation of the wholesale-channel manager of the Provalue Division. The controllability notion (see page 215) is frequently used to justify excluding corporate costs such as salaries of the top management at corporate headquarters from responsibility accounting reports of the wholesale-channel manager. Although the wholesale-channel manager tends to benefit from these corporate costs, he or she has no say in ("is not responsible for") how much of these corporate resources to use or how much they cost.

The value of the hierarchical format in Exhibits 15-6 and 15-7 is to distinguish among various degrees of objectivity when allocating costs so that it dovetails with the different levels at which managers make decisions and evaluate performance. The issue of when and what costs to allocate is another example of the "different costs for different purposes" theme emphasized throughout this text.

In the next section, we calculate customer profitability if Astel's managers decide to allocate distribution-channel costs (such as costs of the wholesale channel), division-sustaining costs (such as costs of R&D and design), and corporate-sustaining costs (such as corporate administration costs of Astel Computers) to individual customers.

DECISION POINT

Why do managers prepare cost-hierarchy-based operating income statements?

TRY IT! 15-2

Mason Inc. has only two retail and two wholesale customers. Information relating to each customer for 2020 follows:

	Wholesale Customers		Retail Customers	
	West Region Wholesaler	East Region Wholesaler	Sloan Inc.	Snyder Corp
Revenues at list prices	$745,000	$1,200,000	$330,000	$320,000
Discounts from list prices	52,300	78,500	20,200	6,130
Cost of goods sold	610,000	1,010,000	302,000	170,000
Delivery costs	28,100	23,470	16,530	14,300
Order processing costs	12,680	16,890	9,420	7,230
Costs of sales visits	12,700	10,300	9,310	8,160

Mason's annual distribution-channel costs are $35,000 for wholesale customers and $16,000 for retail customers. Changes in customer behavior do not affect distribution-channel costs. The company's annual corporate costs are $46,000. There is no cause-and-effect or benefits-received relationship between any cost-allocation base and corporate-sustaining costs. That is, Mason could save corporate-sustaining costs only if the company completely shuts down.

Prepare a customer-cost hierarchy report, using the format in Exhibit 15-6.

Criteria to Guide Cost Allocations

LEARNING OBJECTIVE 4

Understand criteria to guide cost-allocation decisions

... such as identifying factors that cause resources to be consumed

Exhibit 15-8 presents four criteria managers use to guide cost-allocation decisions. These decisions affect both the number of indirect-cost pools and the cost-allocation base for each indirect-cost pool. As we have indicated in previous chapters, we emphasize the superiority of the cause-and-effect and the benefits-received criteria, especially when the purpose of cost allocation is to provide information for economic decisions or to motivate managers and employees. Cause and effect is the primary criterion used in activity-based costing (ABC) systems. ABC systems use the cost hierarchy to identify the cost driver that best represents the cause-and-effect relationship between an activity and the costs in the related cost pool. The cost

EXHIBIT 15-8 Criteria for Cost-Allocation Decisions

1. **Cause and Effect.** Using this criterion, managers identify the variables that cause resources to be consumed. For example, managers may use number of sales orders as the variable when allocating the costs of order taking to products and customers. Cost allocations based on the cause-and-effect criterion are likely to be the most credible to operating personnel.
2. **Benefits Received.** Using this criterion, managers identify the beneficiaries of the outputs of the cost object. The costs of the cost object are allocated among the beneficiaries in proportion to the benefits each receives. Consider the decision of how to allocate corporatewide advertising costs to divisions when these costs promote the general image of the corporation rather than specific products of the divisions. The costs of this program may be allocated to divisions on the basis of division revenues; the higher the revenues, the higher the division's allocated cost of the advertising program The rationale behind this allocation is that divisions with higher revenues presumably benefited more from the advertising than divisions with lower revenues and, therefore, ought to be allocated more of the advertising costs
3. **Fairness or Equity.** This criterion is often cited in government contracts when cost allocations are the basis for establishing a price satisfactory to the government and its suppliers. Cost allocation here is viewed as a "reasonable" or "fair" means of establishing a selling price in the minds of the contracting parties. For most allocation decisions, fairness is a matter of judgment rather than an operational criterion.
4. **Ability to Bear.** This criterion advocates allocating costs in proportion to the cost object's ability to bear costs allocated to it. An example is the allocation of corporate administration costs on the basis of division operating income. The presumption is that the more-profitable divisions have a greater ability to absorb corporate administration costs.

drivers are then chosen as cost-allocation bases. Cause and effect is often difficult to determine in the case of division-sustaining and corporate-sustaining costs. In these situations, managers and management accountants interested in allocating costs use other methods, such as benefits received, fairness (or equity), or ability to bear, summarized in Exhibit 15-8.[6]

The best way to allocate costs if cause and effect cannot be established is to use the benefits-received criterion by identifying the beneficiaries of the output of the cost object. Consider, for example, the cost of managing the wholesale channel for Provalue, such as the salary of the manager of the wholesale channel. There is no cause-and-effect relationship between these costs and sales made by wholesalers. But it is plausible to assume that customers with higher revenues benefited more from the wholesale-channel support than customers with lower revenues. The benefits-received criterion justifies allocating the costs of managing the wholesale channel of $800,000 to customers based on customer revenues.

Fairness and ability to bear are less frequently used and more problematic criteria than cause and effect or benefits received. It's difficult for two parties to agree on criteria for fairness. What one party views as fair another party may view as unfair.[7] For example, a university may view allocating a share of general administrative costs to government contracts for scientific and medical research as fair because general administrative costs are incurred to support all activities of the university. The government may view the allocation of such costs as unfair because the general administrative costs would have been incurred by the university regardless of whether the government contract existed. Perhaps the fairest way to resolve this issue is to understand, as well as possible, the cause-and-effect relationship between the government contract activity and general administrative costs. This is difficult. In other words, fairness is more a matter of judgment than an easily implementable choice criterion.

To get a sense of the issues that arise when using the ability-to-bear criterion, consider Customer G where customer-level costs exceed revenues before allocating any division-sustaining or corporate-sustaining costs. This customer has no ability to bear any division- or corporate-sustaining costs, so under the ability-to-bear criterion none of these costs will be allocated to Customer G. The logic for not allocating these costs to Customer G is that Provalue Division managers will reduce Customer G's demands on division- and corporate-sustaining costs (such as administration costs) to restore Customer G's profitability. However, if division- and corporate-sustaining costs are not reduced but simply allocated to other customers, these customers would subsidize Customer G. The ability-to-bear criterion would then result in artificially lower customer profitability for profitable customers and the potential for incorrect actions, such as increasing prices to restore profitability, which might invite competition.

Most importantly, companies must weigh the costs and benefits when designing and implementing their cost allocations. Companies incur costs not only in collecting data but also in taking the time to educate managers about cost allocations. In general, the more complex the cost allocations, the higher these education costs.

The costs of designing and implementing complex cost allocations are highly visible. Unfortunately, the benefits from using well-designed cost allocations, such as enabling managers to make better-informed sourcing, pricing, and cost-control decisions, are difficult to measure. Nevertheless, when making cost allocations, managers should always consider the costs as well as the benefits. As the costs of collecting and processing information decrease, more detailed cost allocations will be better able to pass the cost–benefit test.

DECISION POINT

What criteria should managers use to guide cost-allocation decisions?

Fully Allocated Customer Profitability

LEARNING OBJECTIVE 5

Discuss decisions faced when collecting and allocating indirect costs to customers

... determining the number of cost pools and the costs to be included in each cost pool

In this section, we focus on the first purpose of cost allocation (see Exhibit 14-1): to provide information for economic decisions, such as pricing, by measuring the full costs of delivering products to different customers based on an ABC system.

[6] The Federal Accounting Standards Advisory Board (which sets standards for management accounting for U.S. government departments and agencies) recommends the following: "The cost assignments should be performed using the following methods listed in order of preference: (a) directly tracing costs whenever feasible and economically practicable, (b) assigning costs on a cause-and-effect basis, and (c) allocating costs on a reasonable and consistent basis" (*FASAB*, Handbook, Version 17, June 2018).

[7] Kaplow and Shavell, in a review of the legal literature, note that "notions of fairness are many and varied. They are analyzed and rationalized by different writers in different ways, and they also typically depend upon the circumstances under consideration. Accordingly, it is not possible to identify a consensus view on these notions." See Louis Kaplow and Steven Shavell, "Fairness Versus Welfare," *Harvard Law Review* (February 2001); and Louis Kaplow and Steven Shavell, *Fairness Versus Welfare* (Boston: Harvard University Press, 2002).

We continue with the Astel Computers example introduced earlier in this chapter and focus on the fully allocated customer-profitability calculations for the 10 wholesale customers in the Provalue Division. The Provalue Division also uses a direct sales channel to sell Provalue computers directly to business customers. Recall that Astel has another division, the Deskpoint Division, which sells high-end computers. We illustrate how costs incurred in different parts of a company can be assigned, and then reassigned, to calculate customer profitability.

We summarize the cost categories as follows:

- **Corporate costs**—There are two major categories of corporate costs:
  1. **Corporate advertising costs**—advertising and promotion costs to promote the Astel brand, \$1,050,000.
  2. **Corporate administration costs**—executive salaries, rent, and general administration costs, \$4,400,000.
- **Division costs**—The Provalue Division, which is the focus of our analysis, has three indirect-cost pools—one cost pool for each of the different cost drivers for allocating division costs to distribution channels: (1) cost pool 1, which comprises all division costs allocated to the wholesale and business-sales channels based on revenues of each channel (benefits received by each channel); (2) cost pool 2, which comprises R&D and design costs allocated to the distribution channels on some fair and equitable basis; and (3) cost pool 3, which consists of all division costs allocated to the wholesale and business-sales channels based on the operating incomes of each channel before such allocations, if positive (each channel's ability to bear). The cost pools are *homogeneous*, that is, all costs in a cost pool have the same or similar cause-and-effect, benefits-received, fair-and-equitable, or ability-to-bear relationship with the cost-allocation base. Different cost pools need different cost-allocation bases to allocate the costs in the cost pools to distribution channels.
- **Channel costs**—Each distribution channel in the Provalue Division has two indirect-cost pools: (1) a cost pool that comprises all channel costs allocated to customers based on customer revenues (benefits received by each customer) and (2) a cost pool that consist of all channel costs allocated to customers based on operating incomes of customers before such allocations, if positive (each customer's ability to bear).

Exhibit 15-9 presents an overview diagram of the allocation of corporate, division, and distribution-channel indirect costs to wholesale customers of the Provalue Division. Note that the Deskpoint Division has its own indirect-cost pools used to allocate costs to its customers. These cost pools and cost-allocation bases parallel the indirect-cost pools and allocation bases for the Provalue Division.

Implementing Corporate and Division Cost Allocations

Exhibit 15-10 allocates all overhead costs to customers based on the overview diagram in Exhibit 15-9. We describe some of the allocation choices based on the criteria for allocating costs explained in Exhibit 15-8.

1. Start at the top of Exhibit 15-9 with the allocation of corporate advertising and corporate administration costs based on the demands that the Provalue Division and Deskpoint Division customers place on corporate resources. The first two columns in Exhibit 15-10 present the allocation of corporate advertising and corporate administration costs to the Provalue division.

   a. Astel allocates a total of \$1,050,000 of corporate advertising costs to the two divisions on the basis of the revenues of each division (benefits received). It is plausible to assume that customers with higher revenues benefited more from corporate advertising costs than customers with lower revenues (see Exhibit 15-7 for information on revenues of each division):

$$\text{Provalue Division: } \$1{,}050{,}000 \times \frac{\$150{,}000{,}000}{\$150{,}000{,}000 + \$200{,}000{,}000} = \$450{,}000$$

$$\text{Deskpoint Division: } \$1{,}050{,}000 \times \frac{\$200{,}000{,}000}{\$150{,}000{,}000 + \$200{,}000{,}000} = \$600{,}000$$

EXHIBIT 15-9 Overview Diagram for Allocating Corporate, Division, and Channel Indirect Costs to Wholesale Customers of Provalue Division

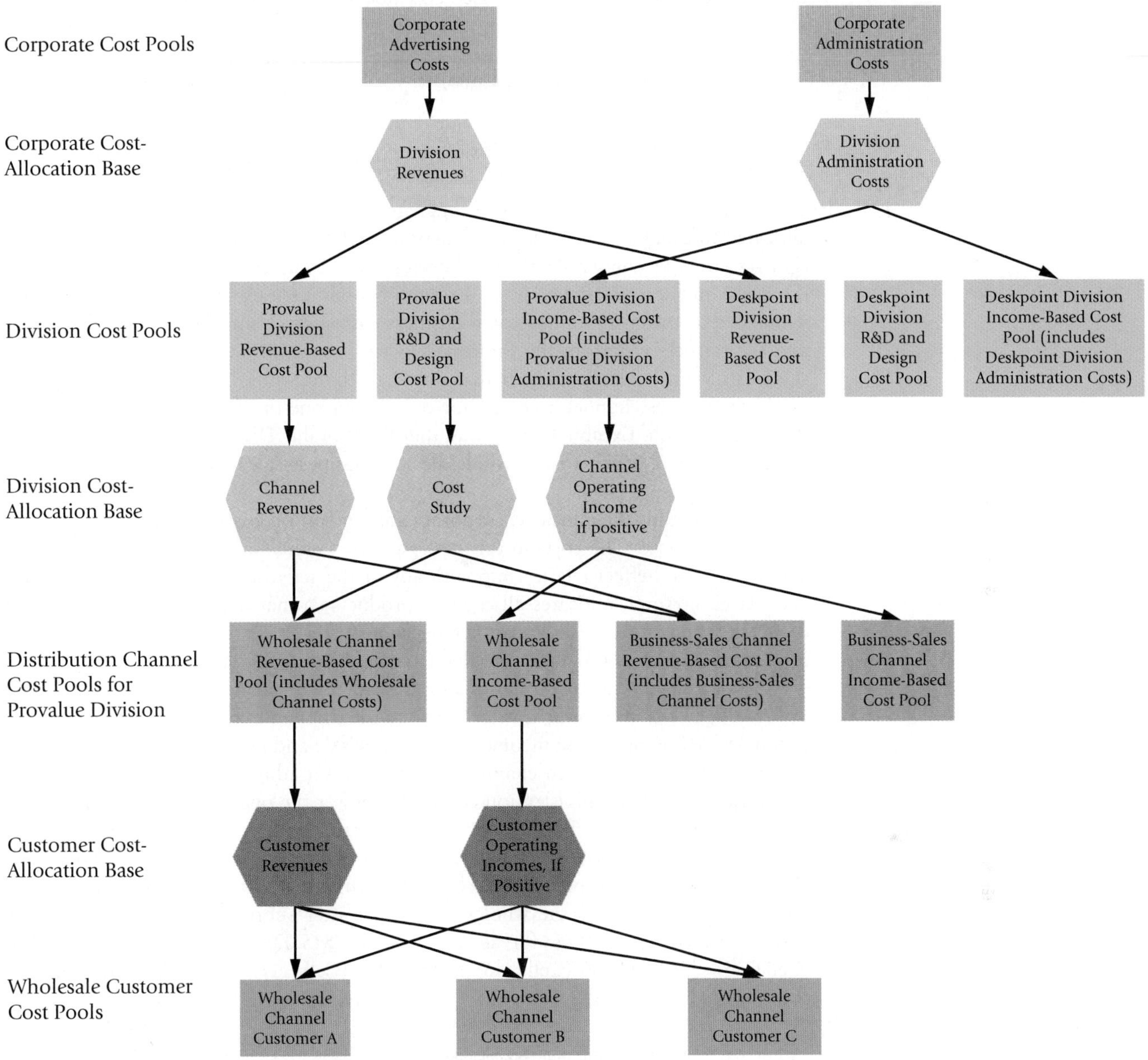

b. Using the benefits-received criterion, Astel allocates corporate administration costs of \$4,400,000 to each division on the basis of division administration costs because corporate administration's main role is to support division administration. Exhibit 15-6 shows division administration costs for Provalue Division of \$1,900,000. Division administration costs for Deskpoint Division are \$2,100,000. The allocations are as follows:

$$\text{Provalue Division: } \$4{,}400{,}000 \times \frac{\$1{,}900{,}000}{\$1{,}900{,}000 + \$2{,}100{,}000} = \$2{,}090{,}000$$

$$\text{Deskpoint Division: } \$4{,}400{,}000 \times \frac{\$2{,}100{,}000}{\$1{,}900{,}000 + \$2{,}100{,}000} = \$2{,}310{,}000$$

2. Next, drop down one level in Exhibit 15-9 and focus on the allocation of costs from the division cost pools to the distribution-channel cost pools for the Provalue Division. The three columns labeled "Provalue Division Cost Pools" in Exhibit 15-10 show the allocations of the Provalue Division costs to the wholesale channel and the business-sales channel.

a. Using the benefits-received criterion, the corporate advertising cost of $450,000 that had been allocated to the Provalue Division is now reallocated to the wholesale and business-sales channels' revenue-based cost pools on the basis of the revenues of each channel (see Exhibit 15-6).

$$\text{Wholesale Channel: } \$450{,}000 \times \frac{\$97{,}550{,}000}{\$97{,}550{,}000 + \$52{,}450{,}000} = \$292{,}650$$

$$\text{Business-Sales Channel: } \$450{,}000 \times \frac{\$52{,}450{,}000}{\$52{,}450{,}000 + \$97{,}550{,}000} = \$157{,}350$$

b. The R&D costs and design costs are aggregated into one homogeneous cost pool and allocated to channels on the basis of a study analyzing the demand for R&D and design resources by the wholesale and business-sales channels. A significant amount of the R&D and design costs arises as a result of modifications to the Provalue computer demanded by the more sophisticated business customers. Using the results of the study and the fairness criterion, the Provalue Division allocates half of the R&D and design costs to the business-sales channel (and half to the wholesale channel) even though the business-sales channel accounts for only about one-third of the total sales of the Provalue Division. Exhibit 15-10 shows that the Provalue Division allocates $2,700,000 ($5,400,000 ÷ 2) each to the wholesale and business-sales channels' revenue-based cost pools.

c. Each division adds the allocated corporate administration costs to the division administration cost pool. The costs in this cost pool are facility-sustaining costs and do not have a cause-and-effect relationship with any of the activities in the distribution channels. Astel, however, allocates all costs to products so that managers are aware of all costs when making pricing and other decisions. The Provalue Division allocates the total costs of $3,990,000 in the Provalue Division Administration cost pool ($2,090,000 of Corporate Administration Costs allocated to the Provalue Division + $1,900,000 of Provalue Division Administration Costs) to the wholesale channel and business-sales channel based on operating incomes of the wholesale and business-sales channels, representing the ability of each channel to bear division administration costs (including allocated corporate administration costs). The lower the operating income of a channel, the lower the division costs allocated to it. As described earlier in the chapter, the rationale for the ability-to-bear criterion is that the Provalue Division will work hard to reduce the support it provides to channels with lower incomes. From Exhibit 15-10, the operating income of the wholesale channel after subtracting all costs that have been allocated to it thus far is $11,234,850 ($15,027,500 (Cell R7) − $292,650 (Cell G15) − $2,700,000 (Cell G16) − $800,000 (Cell G17) while the operating income of the business-sales channel is $5,215,150 (calculations not shown).

$$\text{Wholesale Channel: } \$3{,}990{,}000 \times \frac{\$11{,}234{,}850}{\$11{,}234{,}850 + \$5{,}215{,}150} = \$2{,}725{,}049$$

$$\text{Business-Sales Channel: } \$3{,}990{,}000 \times \frac{\$5{,}215{,}150}{\$11{,}234{,}850 + \$5{,}215{,}150} = \$1{,}264{,}951$$

3. Finally, focus on the bottom rows in Exhibit 15-9 and the allocation of costs from the wholesale distribution-channel cost pools of the Provalue Division to individual wholesale-channel customers. The four columns labeled "Provalue Division Distribution Channel Cost Pools" in Exhibit 15-10 show costs accumulated in the wholesale channel and the business-sales channel. Exhibit 15-10 only presents the allocation of wholesale-channel costs to wholesale customers.

a. The wholesale-channel revenue-based cost pool is allocated to individual wholesale customers on the basis of revenues because revenues are a good measure of how individual customers benefit from these costs. The costs in this cost pool total $3,792,650 and are composed of three costs: (1) $292,650 of corporate advertising costs allocated to the wholesale channel revenue-based cost pool in Step 2a, (2) $2,700,000 of R&D and design costs allocated to the wholesale channel revenue-based cost pool in Step 2b,

EXHIBIT 15-10 Profitability of Wholesale Customers of Provalue Division After Fully Allocating Corporate, Division, and Channel Indirect Costs (in thousands, rounded)

	A	B	C	D	E	F	G			
1							Provalue Division			
2		Astel Corporation Cost Pools		Provalue Division Cost Pools			Distribution Channel Cost Pools			
3		Costs Allocated Based on Division Revenues	Costs Allocated Based on Division Administration Costs	Costs Allocated Based on Channel Revenues	R&D and Design Cost Allocation Pool	Costs Allocated Based on Channel Operating Incomes	Wholesale Channel Costs Allocated Based on Customer Revenues	Wholesale Channel Costs Allocated Based on Customer Operating Incomes	Business-Sales Channel Costs Allocated Based on Customer Revenues	Business-Sales Channel Costs Allocated Based on Customer Operating Incomes
4										
5	Revenues (Exhibit 15-4)									
6	Customer-level costs (Exh. 15-4, Col. 2-Col.1)									
7	Customer-level operating income (Exh. 15-4)									
8	Astel corporate advertising costs	$(1,050)								
9	Astel corporate administration costs		$(4,400)							
10	Allocate corporate advertising costs to divisions based on division revenues[1]	1,050		$(450)						
11	Allocate corporate administration costs to divisions based on division administration costs[2]		4,400			$(2,090)				
12	R&D costs				$(2,400)					
13	Design costs				(3,000)					
14	Division administration costs					(1,900)				
15	Allocate corporate advertising costs from Provalue Division to channels based on channel revenues[3]			450			$ (293)		$ (157)	
16	Allocate R&D and Design costs to channels based on fairness[4]				5,400		(2,700)		(2,700)	
17	Distribution channel costs						(800)		(1,350)	
18	Allocate division administration costs from Provalue division to channels based on channel operating incomes[5]					3,990		$(2,725)		$(1,265)
19	Allocate wholesale channel costs to customers based on customer revenues						3,793			
20	Operating income before allocation of wholesale channel administration costs									
21	Allocate wholesale channel costs to customers based on customer operating income, if positive (ability to bear)							2,725		
22	Fully allocated customer profitability									
23										
24	[1]$1,050 × $150,000 / ($150,000 + $200,000) = $450									
25	[2]$4,400 × $1,900 / ($1,900 + $2,100) = $2,090									
26	[3]$450 × $97,550 / $150,000 = $293; $450 × $52,450 / $150,000 = $157									
27	[4]$5,400 / 2 = $2,700									
28	[5]$3,990 × $11,235 / $16,450 = $2,725; $3,990 × $5,215 / $16,450 = $1,265									

	A	H	I	J	K	L	M	N	O	P	Q	R
3		Wholesale Channel Customers										
4		A	B	C	D	E	F	G	H	I	J	Total
5	Revenues (Exhibit 15-4)	$30,000	$26,250	$13,000	$7,250	$1,800	$5,100	$4,750	$2,400	$2,600	$4,400	$97,550
6	Customer-level costs (Exh. 15-4, Col. 2-Col.1)	(25,085)	(20,560)	(10,345)	(5,805)	(1,700)	(4,114)	(5,100)	(2,935)	(3,300)	(3,578)	(82,522)
7	Customer-level operating income (Exh. 15-4)	4,915	5,690	2,655	1,445	100	986	(350)	(535)	(700)	822	15,028
19	Allocate wholesale channel costs to customers based on customer revenues	(1,166)	(1,021)	(505)	(282)	(70)	(198)	(185)	(93)	(101)	(172)	(3,793)
20	Operating income before allocation of wholesale channel administration costs	3,749	4,669	2,150	1,163	30	788	(535)	(628)	(801)	650	11,235
21	Allocate wholesale channel costs to customers based on customer operating income, if positive (ability to bear)	(774)	(964)	(444)	(240)	(6)	(163)				(134)	(2,725)
22	Fully allocated customer profitability	$ 2,975	$ 3,705	$ 1,706	$ 923	$ 24	$ 625	$ (535)	$ (628)	$ (801)	$ 516	$ 8,510

and (3) \$800,000 of costs of the wholesale-distribution channel itself (Exhibit 15-6). In Exhibit 15-10, the costs allocated to Customer A and Customer B, for example, are shown below:

$$\text{Customer A: } \$3{,}792{,}650 \times \frac{\$30{,}000{,}000}{\$97{,}550{,}000} = \$1{,}166{,}371$$

$$\text{Customer B: } \$3{,}792{,}650 \times \frac{\$26{,}250{,}000}{\$97{,}550{,}000} = \$1{,}020{,}574$$

b. The second wholesale-channel cost pool is composed of \$2,725,049 of the division-administrative costs allocated to the wholesale channel operating-income-based cost pool in Step 2c. These costs are allocated to individual wholesale customers in Exhibit 15-10, row 21, on the basis of operating incomes (if positive) (see Exhibit 15-10, row 20) because operating incomes represent the ability of customers to bear these costs. In Exhibit 15-10, the sum of all the positive amounts in row 20 equals \$13,195,922. The costs allocated to Customer A and Customer B, for example, are as follows:

$$\text{Customer A: } \$2{,}725{,}049 \times \frac{\$3{,}748{,}629}{\$13{,}195{,}922} = \$774{,}117$$

$$\text{Customer B: } \$2{,}725{,}049 \times \frac{\$4{,}669{,}426}{\$13{,}195{,}922} = \$964{,}269$$

Issues in Allocating Corporate Costs to Divisions and Customers

Astel's management team makes several choices when accumulating and allocating corporate costs to divisions. We present two such issues next.

1. When allocating corporate costs to divisions, should Astel allocate only corporate costs that vary with division activity or assign fixed costs as well? Astel's managers allocate both variable and fixed costs to divisions and then to customers because the resulting costs are useful for making long-run strategic decisions, such as which customers to emphasize and what prices to offer. To make good long-run decisions, managers need to know the cost of all resources (whether variable or fixed in the short run) required to sell products to customers. Why? Because in the long run, firms can manage the levels of virtually all of their costs; very few costs are truly fixed. Moreover, to survive and prosper in the long run, firms must ensure that the revenues received from a customer exceed the total resources consumed to support the customer, regardless of whether these costs are variable or fixed in the short run.

   At the same time, companies that allocate corporate costs to divisions must carefully identify relevant costs for specific decisions. Suppose a division is profitable before any corporate costs are allocated but "unprofitable" after allocation of corporate costs. Should the division be closed down in the short run? The relevant corporate costs in this case are not the allocated corporate costs but only those corporate costs that will be saved if the division is closed down. If division profits exceed the relevant corporate costs, the division should not be closed.

2. When allocating costs to divisions, channels, and customers, how many cost pools should Astel use? One extreme is to aggregate all costs into a single cost pool. The other extreme is to have numerous individual cost pools. As discussed in Chapter 5, a major consideration is to construct **homogeneous cost pools** so that all costs in a cost pool have the same or similar cause-and-effect or benefits-received relationship with the cost-allocation base.

   For example, when allocating corporate costs to divisions, Astel can combine corporate advertising costs and corporate administration costs into a single cost pool if both cost categories have the same or similar cause-and-effect relationship with the same cost-allocation base. If, however, as is the case here, each cost category has a cause-and-effect or benefits-received relationship with a different cost-allocation base (for example, revenues of each division benefit from corporate advertising costs whereas corporate administration costs support the administration costs of each division), the company should maintain separate cost pools for each of these costs. Determining homogeneous cost pools requires judgment and should be revisited on a regular basis.

Managers must balance the benefit of using a multiple cost-pool system against the costs of implementing it. Advances in information-gathering technology make it more likely that multiple cost-pool systems will pass the cost–benefit test.

Using Fully Allocated Costs for Decision Making

How might Astel's managers use the fully allocated customer-profitability analysis in Exhibit 15-10? As we discussed in Chapter 14 when discussing product pricing, managers frequently favor using the full cost of a product when making pricing decisions. There are similar benefits to calculating fully allocated customer costs.

Consider, for example, Customer E, who shows a profitability of $24,000 in Exhibit 15-10. If this customer demanded a price reduction of $50,000, how should the Provalue Division respond? Based on the analysis in Exhibit 15-4, Customer E shows a profitability of $100,000 and it would appear that even a $50,000 reduction in price would still leave Customer E as a profitable customer. But in the long run, Customer E must generate sufficient profits to recover all the division-support costs of the Provalue Division and the corporate costs of Astel. A $50,000 reduction in price may not be sustainable in the long run. As the Provalue Division begins making plans for Provalue II in 2020 (see Chapter 14), it simultaneously must consider what it can do to better manage its customers to improve profitability.

Another advantage of allocating costs to customers is that it highlights opportunities to manage costs. For example, the manager of the wholesale channel might want to probe whether the amounts spent on corporate advertising or on R&D and design help in promoting sales to wholesale customers. These discussions might prompt a reevaluation of the amount and type of advertising, R&D, and design activity.

DECISION POINT

What are two key decisions managers must make when collecting and allocating costs in indirect-cost pools?

15-3 TRY IT!

Mason Inc. has only two retail and two wholesale customers. Information relating to each customer for 2020 follows:

	Wholesale Customers		Retail Customers	
	West Region Wholesaler	East Region Wholesaler	Sloan Inc.	Snyder Corp
Revenues at list prices	$745,000	$1,200,000	$330,000	$320,000
Discounts from list prices	52,300	78,500	20,200	6,130
Cost of goods sold	610,000	1,010,000	302,000	170,000
Delivery costs	28,100	23,470	16,530	14,300
Order processing costs	12,680	16,890	9,420	7,230
Costs of sales visits	12,700	10,300	9,310	8,160

Mason's annual distribution-channel costs are $35,000 for wholesale customers and $16,000 for retail customers. The company's annual corporate-sustaining costs are $46,000.

The company allocates distribution channel cost to customers in each channel on the basis of revenues (at actual prices). It allocates corporate overhead costs (1) to distribution channels based on channel operating incomes, if positive and (2) from channels to customers based on customer operating income, if positive.

Prepare a customer profitability report based on fully allocated costs as in Exhibit 15-10.

Sales Variances

The customer-profitability analysis in the previous section focused on the actual profitability of individual customers within a distribution channel (wholesale, for example) and their effect on the Provalue Division's profitability for 2019. At a more strategic level, however, recall that Provalue Division sells Provalue in two different markets: wholesale and directly to businesses. The operating margins in the business-sales market are higher than the operating margins in the wholesale market. In 2019, the Provalue Division had budgeted to sell 60% of Provalue through wholesalers and 40% directly to businesses. It sold fewer Provalue computers

LEARNING OBJECTIVE 6

Subdivide the sales-volume variance into the sales-mix variance

... this variance arises because actual sales mix differs from budgeted sales mix

and the sales-quantity variance

... this variance arises because actual total unit sales differ from budgeted total unit sales

and the sales-quantity variance into the market-share variance

... this variance arises because actual market share differs from budgeted market share

and the market-size variance

... this variance arises because actual market size differs from budgeted market size

in total than it had budgeted, and its actual sales mix (in computers) was 66.67% to wholesalers and 33.33% directly to businesses. Regardless of the profitability of sales to individual customers within each of the wholesale and business-sales channels, the Provalue Division's actual operating income, relative to the master budget, is likely to be negatively affected by the lower number of Provalue computers sold and the shift in mix toward the less profitable wholesale customers. Sales-quantity and sales-mix variances can identify the effect of each of these factors on the Provalue Division's profitability. Companies such as Cisco, GE, and Hewlett-Packard perform similar analyses because they sell products through multiple distribution channels like the Internet, the telephone, and retail stores.

The Provalue Division classifies all customer-level costs, other than fixed machining costs of $11,400,000, as variable costs and all distribution-channel, division-sustaining, and corporate-sustaining costs as fixed costs. To simplify the sales-variance analysis and calculations, we assume that variable costs vary with the number of Provalue computers sold. (This means that average batch sizes remain the same as the total number of Provalue computers produced and sold change.) Without this assumption, the analysis becomes more complex and needs to be done using the ABC-variance analysis approach described in Chapter 8, pages 300–304. The basic insights, however, do not change.

Budgeted and actual operating data for 2019 are as follows:

Budget Data for 2019

	Selling Price (1)	Variable Cost per Unit (2)	Contribution Margin per Unit (3) = (1) − (2)	Sales Volume in Units (4)	Sales Mix (Based on Units) (5)	Contribution Margin (6) = (3) × (4)
Wholesale channel	$ 980	$755	$225	93,000	60%[a]	$20,925,000
Business-sales channel	1,050	775	275	62,000	40%	17,050,000
Total				155,000	100%	$37,975,000

[a]Percentage of total unit sales in wholesale channel = 93,000 units ÷ 155,000 total units = 60%.

Actual Results for 2019

	Selling Price (1)	Variable Cost per Unit (2)	Contribution Margin per Unit (3) = (1) − (2)	Sales Volume in Units (4)	Sales Mix (Based on Units) (5)	Contribution Margin (6) = (3) × (4)
Wholesale channel	$ 975.50	$749.225	$226.275	100,000	66.67%[a]	$22,627,500
Business-sales channel	1,049.00	784.55	264.45	50,000	33.33%	13,222,500
Total				150,000	100.00%	$35,850,000

[a]Percentage of total unit sales in wholesale channel = 100,000 units ÷ 150,000 total units = 66.67%.

The budgeted and actual fixed distribution-channel costs, division costs, and corporate-level costs are the same (see Exhibit 15-6, page 606, and Exhibit 15-7, page 607).

Recall that the levels of detail introduced in Chapter 7 (pages 246–252) included the static-budget variance (level 1), the flexible-budget variance (level 2), and the sales-volume variance (level 2). The sales-quantity and sales-mix variances discussed in this chapter are level 3 variances that subdivide the sales-volume variance.[8]

Static-Budget Variance

The *static-budget variance* is the difference between an actual result and the corresponding budgeted amount in the static budget. Our analysis focuses on the difference between actual and budgeted contribution margins (column 6 in the preceding tables). The total static-budget variance is $2,125,000 unfavorable variance (U) (actual contribution margin

[8] The presentation of the variances in this chapter draws on teaching notes prepared by J. K. Harris.

EXHIBIT 15-11 Flexible-Budget and Sales-Volume Variance Analysis of Provalue Division for 2019

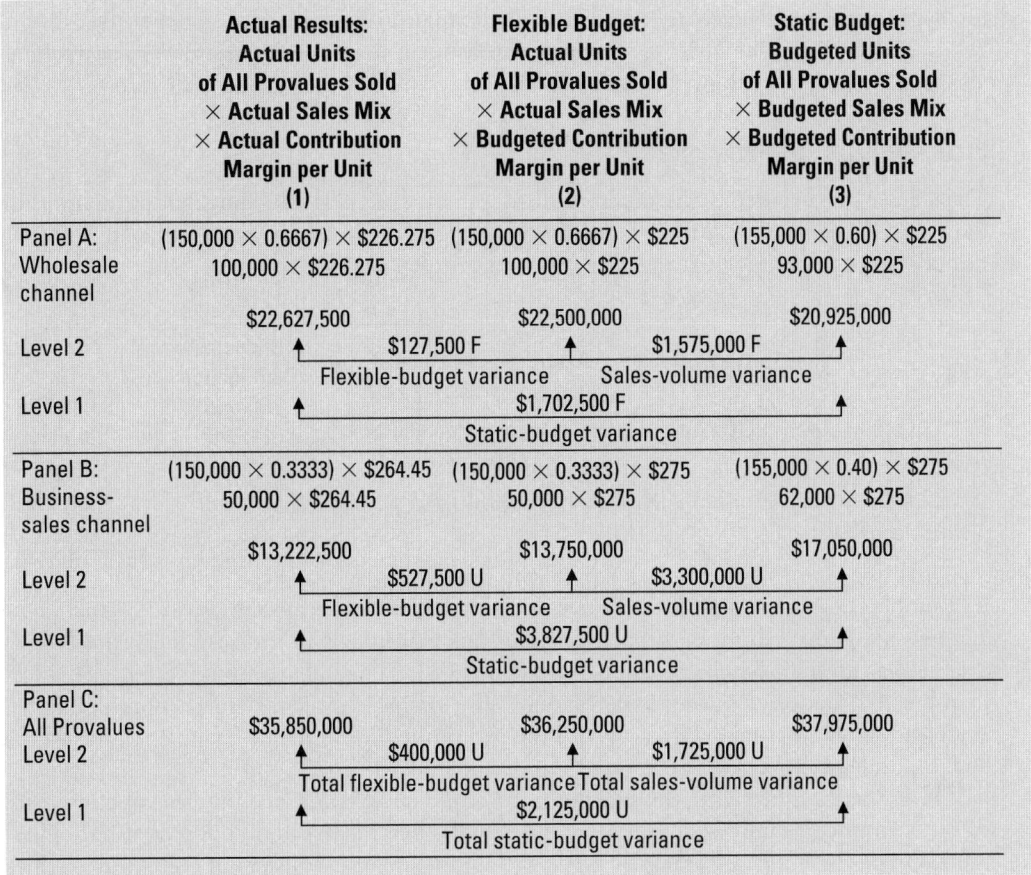

	Actual Results: Actual Units of All Provalues Sold × Actual Sales Mix × Actual Contribution Margin per Unit (1)	Flexible Budget: Actual Units of All Provalues Sold × Actual Sales Mix × Budgeted Contribution Margin per Unit (2)	Static Budget: Budgeted Units of All Provalues Sold × Budgeted Sales Mix × Budgeted Contribution Margin per Unit (3)
Panel A: Wholesale channel	(150,000 × 0.6667) × \$226.275 100,000 × \$226.275	(150,000 × 0.6667) × \$225 100,000 × \$225	(155,000 × 0.60) × \$225 93,000 × \$225
	\$22,627,500	\$22,500,000	\$20,925,000
Panel B: Business-sales channel	(150,000 × 0.3333) × \$264.45 50,000 × \$264.45	(150,000 × 0.3333) × \$275 50,000 × \$275	(155,000 × 0.40) × \$275 62,000 × \$275
	\$13,222,500	\$13,750,000	\$17,050,000
Panel C: All Provalues	\$35,850,000	\$36,250,000	\$37,975,000

	Level 2: (1) − (2)	Level 2: (2) − (3)	Level 1: (1) − (3)
Panel A: Wholesale channel	\$127,500 F Flexible-budget variance	\$1,575,000 F Sales-volume variance	\$1,702,500 F Static-budget variance
Panel B: Business-sales channel	\$527,500 U Flexible-budget variance	\$3,300,000 U Sales-volume variance	\$3,827,500 U Static-budget variance
Panel C: All Provalues	\$400,000 U Total flexible-budget variance	\$1,725,000 U Total sales-volume variance	\$2,125,000 U Total static-budget variance

of \$35,850,000 − budgeted contribution margin of \$37,975,000). Exhibit 15-11 (columns 1 and 3) uses the columnar format introduced in Chapter 7 to show detailed calculations of the static-budget variance. Managers can gain more insight about the static-budget variance by subdividing it into the flexible-budget variance and the sales-volume variance.

Flexible-Budget Variance and Sales-Volume Variance

The *flexible-budget variance* is the difference between an actual result and the corresponding flexible-budget amount based on actual output level in the budget period. The flexible-budget contribution margin is equal to budgeted contribution margin per unit times actual units sold of each product. Exhibit 15-11, column 2, shows the flexible-budget calculations. The flexible budget measures the contribution margin that the Provalue Division would have budgeted for the actual quantities of cases sold. The flexible-budget variance is the difference between columns 1 and 2 in Exhibit 15-11. The only difference between columns 1 and 2 is that actual units sold of each product is multiplied by actual contribution margin per unit in column 1 and budgeted contribution margin per unit in column 2. The \$400,000 U total flexible-budget variance arises because actual contribution margin on business sales of \$264.45 per Provalue is lower than the budgeted amount of \$275 per Provalue and offsets the slightly higher actual contribution margin of \$226.275 versus the budgeted contribution margin of \$225 on wholesale-channel sales. The Provalue Division managers are aware that the lower contribution margin of \$10.55 (\$275 − \$264.45) per computer on business sales resulted from higher variable ordering and testing costs and have put in place action plans to reduce these costs in the future.

The *sales-volume variance* is the difference between a flexible-budget amount and the corresponding static-budget amount. In Exhibit 15-11, the sales-volume variance shows the effect on the budgeted contribution margin of the difference between the actual quantity of units sold and the budgeted quantity of units sold. The sales-volume variance of $1,725,000 U is the difference between columns 2 and 3 in Exhibit 15-11. In this case, it is unfavorable overall because while unit sales of Provalue in the wholesale-channel were higher than budgeted, unit sales in the business-channel, which are expected to be more profitable on a per computer basis, were below budget. Provalue Division managers can gain substantial insight into the sales-volume variance by subdividing it into the sales-mix variance and the sales-quantity variance.

Sales-Mix Variance

The **sales-mix variance** is the difference between (1) the budgeted contribution margin for the *actual sales mix* and (2) the budgeted contribution margin for the *budgeted sales mix*. The formula and computations (using data from page 616) are as follows:

	Actual Units of All Provalues Sold	×	(Actual Sales-Mix Percentage − Budgeted Sales-Mix Percentage)	×	Budgeted Contribution Margin per Unit	=	Sales-Mix Variance
Wholesale	150,000 units	×	(0.66667 − 0.60)	×	$225 per unit	=	$2,250,000 F
Business-Sales	150,000 units	×	(0.33333 − 0.40)	×	$275 per unit	=	2,750,000 U
Total sales-mix variance							$ 500,000 U

A favorable sales-mix variance arises for the wholesale channel because the 66.67% actual sales-mix percentage exceeds the 60% budgeted sales-mix percentage. In contrast, the business-sales channel has an unfavorable variance because the 33.33% actual sales-mix percentage is less than the 40% budgeted sales-mix percentage. The total sales-mix variance is unfavorable because the actual sales mix shifted toward the less profitable wholesale channel relative to the budgeted sales mix.

The concept underlying the sales-mix variance is best explained in terms of composite units. A **composite unit** is a hypothetical unit with weights based on the mix of individual units. Given the budgeted sales for 2019, the composite unit consists of 0.60 units of sales to the wholesale channel and 0.40 units of sales to the business-sales channel. Therefore, the budgeted contribution margin per composite unit for the budgeted sales mix is as follows:

$$0.60 \times \$225 + 0.40 \times \$275 = \$245$$ [9]

Similarly, for the actual sales mix, the composite unit consists of 0.66667 units of sales to the wholesale channel and 0.33333 units of sales to the business-sales channel. The budgeted contribution margin per composite unit for the actual sales mix is therefore

$$0.66667 \times \$225 + 0.33333 \times \$275 = \$241.6667$$

The impact of the shift in sales mix is now evident. The Provalue Division obtains a lower budgeted contribution margin per composite unit of $3.3333 ($245 − $241.6667). For the 150,000 units actually sold, this decrease translates to a $500,000 U sales-mix variance ($3.3333 per unit × 150,000 units).

Managers should probe why the $500,000 U sales-mix variance occurred in 2019. Is the shift in sales mix because profitable business customers proved to be more difficult to find? Is it because of a competitor in the business-sales channel providing better service at a lower price? Or is it because the initial sales-volume estimates were made without adequate analysis of the potential market?

Exhibit 15-12 uses the columnar format to calculate the sales-mix variance and the sales-quantity variances.

[9] Budgeted contribution margin per composite unit can be computed in another way by dividing total budgeted contribution margin of $37,975,000 by total budgeted units of 155,000 (page 616): $37,975,000/155,000 units = $245 per unit.

EXHIBIT 15-12 Sales-Mix and Sales-Quantity Variance Analysis of Provalue Division for 2019

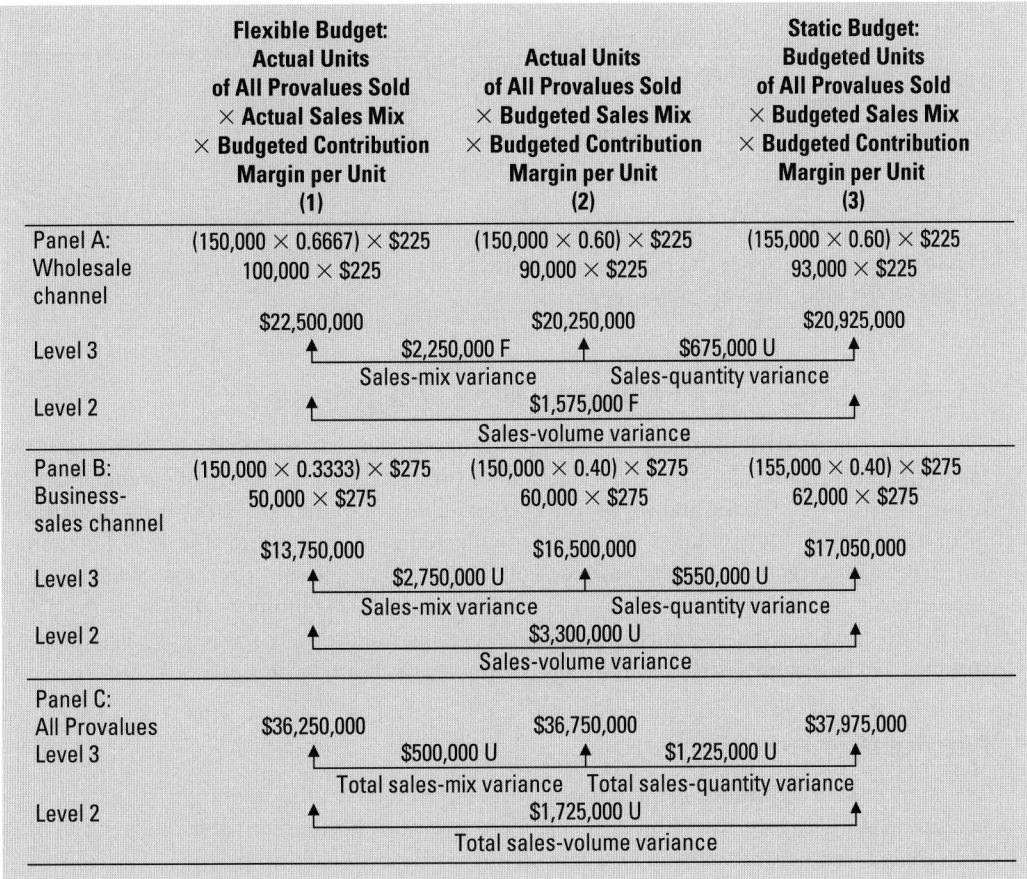

	Flexible Budget: Actual Units of All Provalues Sold × Actual Sales Mix × Budgeted Contribution Margin per Unit (1)		Actual Units of All Provalues Sold × Budgeted Sales Mix × Budgeted Contribution Margin per Unit (2)		Static Budget: Budgeted Units of All Provalues Sold × Budgeted Sales Mix × Budgeted Contribution Margin per Unit (3)
Panel A: Wholesale channel	(150,000 × 0.6667) × $225 100,000 × $225		(150,000 × 0.60) × $225 90,000 × $225		(155,000 × 0.60) × $225 93,000 × $225
	$22,500,000		$20,250,000		$20,925,000
Level 3		$2,250,000 F Sales-mix variance		$675,000 U Sales-quantity variance	
Level 2			$1,575,000 F Sales-volume variance		
Panel B: Business-sales channel	(150,000 × 0.3333) × $275 50,000 × $275		(150,000 × 0.40) × $275 60,000 × $275		(155,000 × 0.40) × $275 62,000 × $275
	$13,750,000		$16,500,000		$17,050,000
Level 3		$2,750,000 U Sales-mix variance		$550,000 U Sales-quantity variance	
Level 2			$3,300,000 U Sales-volume variance		
Panel C: All Provalues	$36,250,000		$36,750,000		$37,975,000
Level 3		$500,000 U Total sales-mix variance		$1,225,000 U Total sales-quantity variance	
Level 2			$1,725,000 U Total sales-volume variance		

Sales-Quantity Variance

The **sales-quantity variance** is the difference between (1) budgeted contribution margin based on *actual units sold of all products* at the budgeted mix and (2) contribution margin in the static budget (which is based on *budgeted units of all products to be sold* at budgeted mix). The formula and computations (using data from page 616) are as follows:

	Actual Total Provalues Sold-Budgeted Total Provalues Sold	×	Budgeted Sales-Mix Percentages	×	Budgeted Contribution Margin per Unit	=	Sales-Quantity Variance
Wholesale	(150,000 units − 155,000 units)	×	0.60	×	$225 per unit	=	$ 675,000 U
Business sales	(150,000 units − 155,000 units)	×	0.40	×	$275 per unit	=	550,000 U
Total sales-quantity variance							$1,225,000 U

This variance is unfavorable when actual units of all products sold are less than the budgeted units of all products sold. The Provalue Division sold 5,000 fewer Provalues than were budgeted, resulting in a $1,225,000 sales-quantity variance (also equal to budgeted contribution margin per composite unit for the budgeted sales mix times fewer units sold, $245 × 5,000). Managers would want to probe the reasons for the decrease in sales. Did lower sales come as a result of a competitor's aggressive marketing? Poorer customer service? Or decline in the overall market? Managers can gain additional insight into the causes of the sales-quantity variance by analyzing changes in Provalue Division's share of the total industry market and in the size of that market. The sales-quantity variance can be decomposed into market-share and market-size variances, as we describe in the next section.

TRY IT! 15-4

Forever Corp. buys and sells two types of sunglasses in New York: Duma and Kool. Budgeted and actual results for 2020 are as follows:

	Budget for 2020			Actual for 2020		
Product	Selling Price	Variable Cost per Unit	Units Sold	Selling Price	Variable Cost per Unit	Units Sold
Duma	$23	$19	88,000	$21	$18	90,000
Kool	$29	$24	132,000	$31	$25	110,000

Compute the total sales-volume variance, the total sales-mix variance, and the total sales-quantity variance. (Calculate all variances in terms of contribution margin.) Show results for each product in your computations.

Market-Share and Market-Size Variances

The total quantity of Provalues sold depends on overall demand for similar computers in the market, as well as Provalue Division's share of the market. Assume that the Provalue Division derived its total unit sales budget of 155,000 Provalue computers for 2019 from a management estimate of a 20% market share and a budgeted industry market size of 775,000 units $(0.20 \times 775{,}000 \text{ units} = 155{,}000 \text{ units})$. For 2019, actual market size was 800,000 units and actual market share was 18.75% $(150{,}000 \text{ units} \div 800{,}000 \text{ units} = 0.1875 \text{ or } 18.75\%)$. Exhibit 15-13 shows the columnar presentation of how the Provalue Division's sales-quantity variance can be decomposed into market-share and market-size variances.

Market-Share Variance

The **market-share variance** is the difference in budgeted contribution margin for actual market size in units caused solely by *actual market share* being different from *budgeted market share*. The formula for computing the market-share variance is shown below:

$$\text{Market-share variance} = \begin{array}{c}\text{Actual}\\ \text{market size}\\ \text{in units}\end{array} \times \left(\begin{array}{c}\text{Actual}\\ \text{market}\\ \text{share}\end{array} - \begin{array}{c}\text{Budgeted}\\ \text{market}\\ \text{share}\end{array}\right) \times \begin{array}{c}\text{Budgeted contribution}\\ \text{margin per composite unit}\\ \text{for budgeted mix}\end{array}$$

$$= 800{,}000 \text{ units} \times (0.1875 - 0.20) \times \$245 \text{ per unit}$$
$$= \$2{,}450{,}000 \text{ U}$$

The Provalue Division lost 1.25 market-share percentage points—from the 20% budgeted share to the actual share of 18.75%. The $2,450,000 U market-share variance is the decline in contribution margin as a result of those lost sales.

Market-Size Variance

The **market-size variance** is the difference in budgeted contribution margin at budgeted market share caused solely by *actual market size in units* being different from *budgeted market size in units*. The formula for computing the market-size variance is as follows:

$$\text{Market-size variance} = \left(\begin{array}{c}\text{Actual}\\ \text{market}\\ \text{size}\end{array} - \begin{array}{c}\text{Budgeted}\\ \text{market}\\ \text{size}\end{array}\right) \times \begin{array}{c}\text{Budgeted}\\ \text{market}\\ \text{share}\end{array} \times \begin{array}{c}\text{Budgeted contribution}\\ \text{margin per composite unit}\\ \text{for budgeted mix}\end{array}$$

$$= (800{,}000 \text{ units} - 775{,}000 \text{ units}) \times 0.20 \times \$245 \text{ per unit}$$
$$= \$1{,}225{,}000 \text{ F}$$

EXHIBIT 15-13 Market-Share and Market-Size Variance Analysis of Provalue Division of Astel Computers for 2019[a]

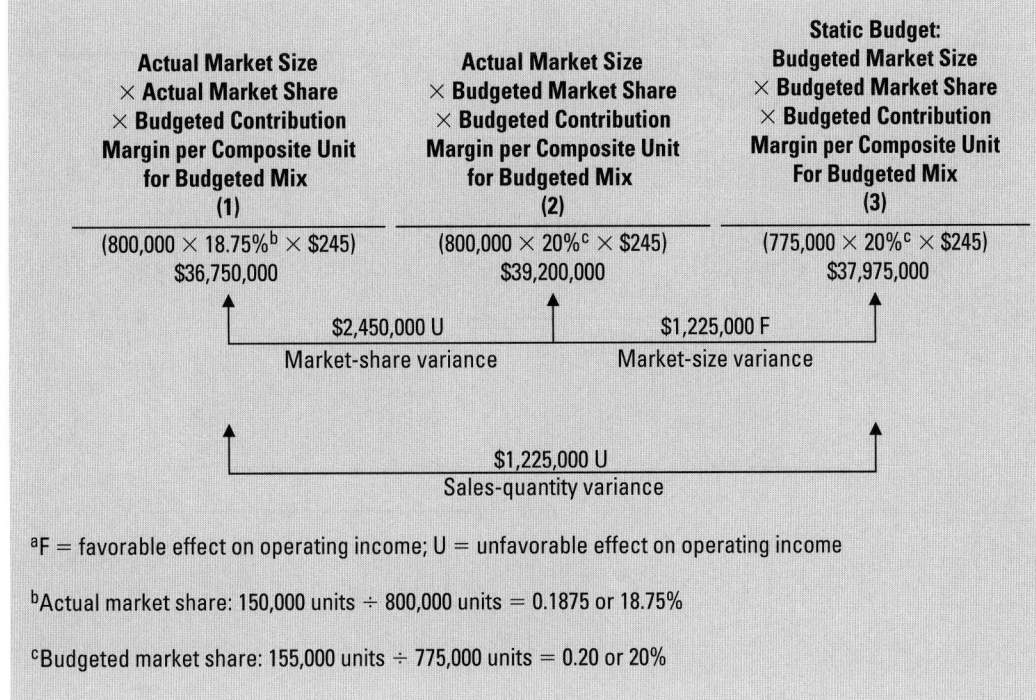

Actual Market Size × Actual Market Share × Budgeted Contribution Margin per Composite Unit for Budgeted Mix (1)	Actual Market Size × Budgeted Market Share × Budgeted Contribution Margin per Composite Unit for Budgeted Mix (2)	Static Budget: Budgeted Market Size × Budgeted Market Share × Budgeted Contribution Margin per Composite Unit For Budgeted Mix (3)
(800,000 × 18.75%[b] × \$245)	(800,000 × 20%[c] × \$245)	(775,000 × 20%[c] × \$245)
\$36,750,000	\$39,200,000	\$37,975,000

Between (1) and (2): \$2,450,000 U — Market-share variance

Between (2) and (3): \$1,225,000 F — Market-size variance

Between (1) and (3): \$1,225,000 U — Sales-quantity variance

[a]F = favorable effect on operating income; U = unfavorable effect on operating income

[b]Actual market share: 150,000 units ÷ 800,000 units = 0.1875 or 18.75%

[c]Budgeted market share: 155,000 units ÷ 775,000 units = 0.20 or 20%

The market-size variance is favorable (F) because actual market size increased 3.23% [(800,000 − 775,000) ÷ 775,000 = 0.0323, or 3.23%] compared to budgeted market size.

Managers should probe the reasons for the market-size and market-share variances for 2019. Is the \$1,225,000 F market-size variance because of an increase in market size that can be expected to continue in the future? If yes, the Provalue Division has much to gain by attaining or exceeding its budgeted 20% market share. Was the \$2,450,000 unfavorable market-share variance because of competitors providing better offerings or greater value to customers? Did competitors aggressively cut prices to stimulate market demand? Although Provalue Division managers reduced prices a little relative to the budget, should they have reduced prices even more, particularly for business-sales customers where Provalue sales were considerably below budget and selling prices significantly higher than the prices charged to wholesalers? Was the quality and reliability of Provalue computers as good as the quality and reliability of competitors?

Some companies place more emphasis on the market-share variance than the market-size variance when evaluating their managers. That's because they believe the market-size variance is influenced by economy-wide factors and shifts in consumer preferences that are outside the managers' control, whereas the market-share variance measures how well managers performed relative to their peers.

Be cautious when computing the market-size variance and the market-share variance. Reliable information on market size and market share is not available for all industries. The automobile, computer, and television industries have widely available market-size and market-share statistics. In other industries, such as management consulting and personal financial planning, information about market size and market share is far less reliable.

Exhibit 15-14 presents an overview of the sales-mix, sales-quantity, market-share, and market-size variances for the Provalue Division. These variances can also be calculated in a multiproduct company, in which each individual product has a different contribution margin per unit. The Problem for Self-Study presents such a setting.

DECISION POINT

What are the two components of the sales-volume variance and the two components of the sales-quantity variance?

EXHIBIT 15-14 Overview of Variances for Provalue Division for 2019

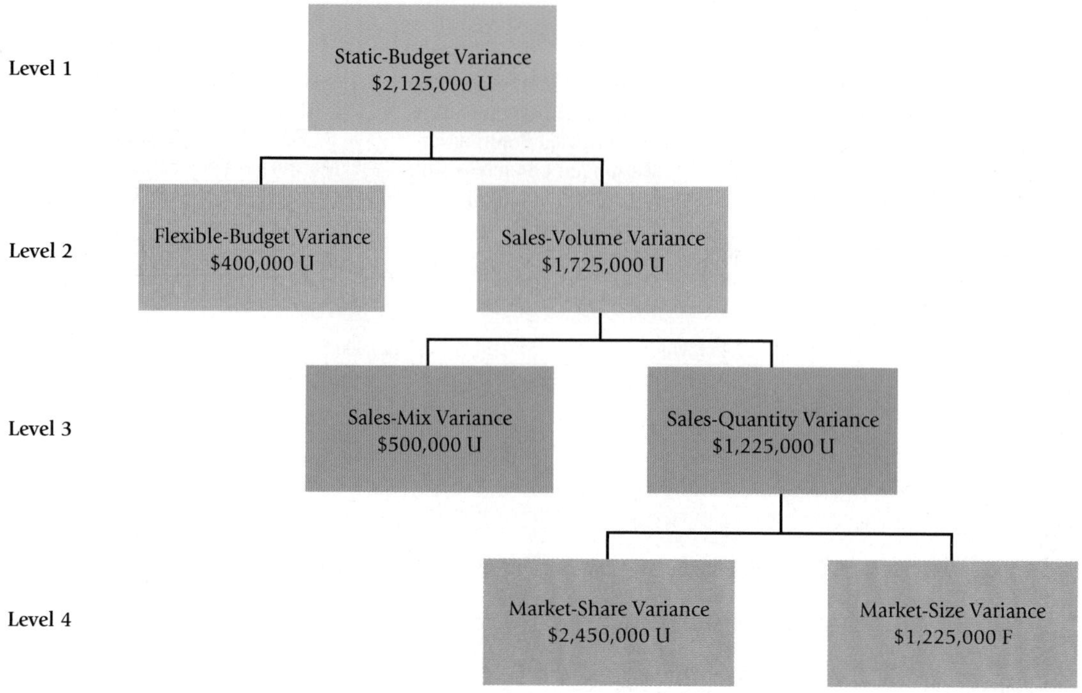

F = favorable effect on operating income; U = unfavorable effect on operating income

TRY IT! 15-5

Forever Corp. buys and sells two types of sunglasses in New York: Duma and Kool. Budgeted and actual results for 2020 are as follows:

	Budget for 2020			Actual for 2020		
Product	Selling Price	Variable Cost per Unit	Units Sold	Selling Price	Variable Cost per Unit	Units Sold
Duma	$23	$19	88,000	$21	$18	90,000
Kool	$29	$24	132,000	$31	$25	110,000

Forever Corp. prepared the budget for 2020 assuming an 11% market share based on total sales of 2,000,000 units in New York. However, actual total sales volume in New York was 2,500,000 units.

Calculate the market-share and market-size variances for Forever Corp. in 2020. Calculate all variances in terms of contribution margin. Comment on the results.

PROBLEM FOR SELF-STUDY

The Payne Company manufactures two types of vinyl flooring. Budgeted and actual operating data for 2020 are as follows:

	Static Budget			Actual Results		
	Commercial	Residential	Total	Commercial	Residential	Total
Unit sales in rolls	20,000	60,000	80,000	25,200	58,800	84,000
Contribution margin	$10,000,000	$24,000,000	$34,000,000	$11,970,000	$24,696,000	$36,666,000

In late 2019, a marketing research firm estimated industry volume for commercial and residential vinyl flooring for 2020 at 800,000 rolls. Actual industry volume for 2020 was 700,000 rolls.

Required

1. Compute the sales-mix variance and the sales-quantity variance by type of vinyl flooring and in total. (Compute all variances in terms of contribution margins.)
2. Compute the market-share variance and the market-size variance.
3. What insights do the variances calculated in requirements 1 and 2 provide about Payne Company's performance in 2020?

Solution

1. Actual sales-mix percentage:

Commercial = 25,200 ÷ 84,000 = 0.30, or 30%

Residential = 58,800 ÷ 84,000 = 0.70, or 70%

Budgeted sales-mix percentage:

Commercial = 20,000 ÷ 80,000 = 0.25, or 25%

Residential = 60,000 ÷ 80,000 = 0.75, or 75%

Budgeted contribution margin per unit:

Commercial = $10,000,000 ÷ 20,000 units = $500 per unit

Residential = $24,000,000 ÷ 60,000 units = $400 per unit

	Actual Units of All Products Sold	×	(Actual Sales-Mix Percentage − Budgeted Sales-Mix Percentage)	×	Budgeted Contribution Margin per Unit	=	Sales-Mix Variance
Commercial	84,000 units	×	(0.30 − 0.25)	×	$500 per unit	=	$2,100,000 F
Residential	84,000 units	×	(0.70 − 0.75)	×	$400 per unit	=	1,680,000 U
Total sales-mix variance							$ 420,000 F

	(Actual Units of All Products Sold − Budgeted Units of All Products Sold)	×	Budgeted Sales-Mix Percentage	×	Budgeted Contribution Margin per Unit	=	Sales-Quantity Variance
Commercial	(84,000 units − 80,000 units)	×	0.25	×	$500 per unit	=	$ 500,000 F
Residential	(84,000 units − 80,000 units)	×	0.75	×	$400 per unit	=	1,200,000 F
Total sales-quantity variance							$1,700,000 F

2. Actual market share = 84,000 ÷ 700,000 = 0.12, or 12%
Budgeted market share = 80,000 ÷ 800,000 units = 0.10, or 10%

Budgeted contribution margin per composite unit of budgeted mix = $34,000,000 ÷ 80,000 units = $425 per unit

Budgeted contribution margin per composite unit of budgeted mix can also be calculated as follows:

Commercial: 500 per unit × 0.25	=	$125
Residential: 400 per unit × 0.75	=	300
Budgeted contribution margin per composite unit	=	$425

Market-share variance = Actual market size in units × (Actual market share − Budgeted market share) × Budgeted contribution margin per composite unit for budgeted mix

= 700,000 units × (0.12 − 0.10) × $425 per unit

= $5,950,000 F

$$\text{Market-size variance} = \left(\begin{matrix}\text{Actual}\\ \text{market size}\\ \text{in units}\end{matrix} - \begin{matrix}\text{Budgeted}\\ \text{market size}\\ \text{in units}\end{matrix}\right) \times \begin{matrix}\text{Budgeted}\\ \text{market}\\ \text{share}\end{matrix} \times \begin{matrix}\text{Budgeted}\\ \text{contribution margin}\\ \text{per composite unit}\\ \text{for budgeted mix}\end{matrix}$$

$$= (700{,}000 \text{ units} - 800{,}000 \text{ units}) \times 0.10 \times \$425 \text{ per unit}$$

$$= \$4{,}250{,}000 \text{ U}$$

Note that the algebraic sum of the market-share variance and the market-size variance is equal to the sales-quantity variance: \$5,950,000 F + \$4,250,000 U = \$1,700,000 F.

3. Both the total sales-mix variance and the total sales-quantity variance are favorable. The favorable sales-mix variance occurred because the actual mix was composed of more of the higher-margin commercial vinyl flooring. The favorable total sales-quantity variance occurred because the actual total quantity of rolls sold exceeded the budgeted amount.

   The company's large favorable market-share variance is due to a 12% actual market share compared with a 10% budgeted market share. The market-size variance is unfavorable because the actual market size was 100,000 rolls less than the budgeted market size. Payne's performance in 2020 is very good. Although overall market size declined, the company sold more units than budgeted and gained market share.

DECISION POINTS

The following question-and-answer format summarizes the chapter's learning objectives. Each decision presents a key question related to a learning objective. The guidelines are the answer to that question.

Decision	Guidelines
1. How can a company's revenues and costs differ across customers?	Revenues differ because of differences in the quantity purchased and price discounts. Costs differ because different customers place different demands on a company's resources in terms of processing sales orders, making deliveries, and customer support.
2. How do customer-profitability profiles help managers?	Companies should be aware of and devote sufficient resources to maintaining and expanding relationships with customers who contribute significantly to operating income and design incentives to change behavior patterns of unprofitable customers. Customer-profitability profiles often highlight that a small percentage of customers contributes a large percentage of operating income.
3. Why do managers prepare cost-hierarchy-based operating income statements?	Cost-hierarchy-based operating income statements allocate only those costs that will be affected by actions at a particular hierarchical level. For example, costs such as sales-order costs and shipment costs are allocated to customers because customer actions can affect these costs, but costs of managing the wholesale channel are not allocated to customers because changes in customer behavior will have no effect on these costs.
4. What criteria should managers use to guide cost-allocation decisions?	Managers should use the cause-and-effect and the benefits-received criteria to guide most cost-allocation decisions. Other criteria are fairness or equity and ability to bear.

Decision	Guidelines
5. What are two key decisions managers must make when collecting and allocating costs in indirect-cost pools?	Two key decisions related to indirect-cost pools are the number of indirect-cost pools to form and the individual cost items to be included in each cost pool to make homogeneous cost pools. Generally, cost pools include both variable costs and allocated fixed costs.
6. What are the two components of the sales-volume variance and the two components of the sales-quantity variance?	The two components of sales-volume variance are (a) the difference between actual sales mix and budgeted sales mix (the sales-mix variance) and (b) the difference between actual unit sales and budgeted unit sales (the sales-quantity variance). The two components of the sales-quantity variance are (a) the difference between the actual market share and the budgeted market share (the market-share variance) and (b) the difference between the actual market size in units and the budgeted market size in units (the market-size variance).

TERMS TO LEARN

The chapter and the Glossary at the end of the text contain definitions of the following important terms:

composite unit (**p. 618**)
customer-cost hierarchy (**p. 598**)
customer-profitability analysis (**p. 597**)
homogeneous cost pools (**p. 614**)
market-share variance (**p. 620**)
market-size variance (**p. 620**)
price discount (**p. 597**)
sales-mix variance (**p. 618**)
sales-quantity variance (**p. 619**)
whale curve (**p. 603**)

ASSIGNMENT MATERIAL

Questions

15-1 "I'm going to focus on the customers of my business and leave cost-allocation issues to my accountant." Do you agree with this comment by a division president? Explain.

15-2 Why is customer-profitability analysis an important topic for managers?

15-3 How can a company track the extent of price discounting on a customer-by-customer basis?

15-4 "A customer-profitability profile highlights those customers a company should drop to improve profitability." Do you agree? Explain.

15-5 Give examples of three different levels of costs in a customer-cost hierarchy.

15-6 What information does the whale curve provide?

15-7 "A company should not allocate all of its corporate costs to its divisions." Do you agree? Explain.

15-8 What criteria might managers use to guide cost-allocation decisions? Which are the dominant criteria?

15-9 "Once a company allocates corporate costs to divisions, these costs should not be reallocated to the indirect-cost pools of the division." Do you agree? Explain.

15-10 "A company should not allocate costs that are fixed in the short run to customers." Do you agree? Explain briefly.

15-11 How should a company decide on the number of cost pools it should use to allocate costs to divisions, channels, and customers?

15-12 Show how managers can gain insight into the causes of a sales-volume variance by subdividing the components of this variance.

15-13 How can the concept of a composite unit be used to explain why an unfavorable total sales-mix variance of contribution margin occurs?

15-14 Explain why a favorable sales-quantity variance occurs.

15-15 How can the sales-quantity variance be decomposed further?

Multiple-Choice Questions

In partnership with:
BECKER
PROFESSIONAL EDUCATION®

15-16 Flexible-budget variance, sales-quantity, market-size, and market-share variance. The actual contribution margin per unit will impact the following sales variance:

a. Flexible-budget variance
b. Market-size variance
c. Market-share variance
d. Sales-quantity variance

15-17 Sales-volume, sales-mix, and sales-quantity variance. Lexota, Inc., an auto manufacturer, reported the following budgeted and actual sales of its vehicles during September, Year 2:

	Budgeted Units	Budgeted Sales	Actual Units	Actual Sales
Power Lex 500	200	$10,000,000	150	$8,000,000
Ota Gas Sipper	200	$ 4,000,000	250	$4,000,000

The budgeted contribution margin is 20% for both vehicle types. Which of the following statements is true concerning the sales variances for Lexota, Inc. for September, Year 2?

a. The sales-volume variance for the company is favorable.
b. The sales-quantity variance for the company is unfavorable.
c. The budgeted variable cost for each vehicle type is the same.
d. The sales-mix variance for the company is unfavorable.

Exercises

15-18 Cost allocation in hospitals, alternative allocation criteria. Dave McKnight vacationed at Lake Tahoe last winter. Unfortunately, he broke his ankle while skiing and spent 2 days at the Sierra University Hospital. McKnight's insurance company received a $4,850 bill for his 2-day stay. One item that caught McKnight's attention was a $11.75 charge for a roll of cotton. McKnight is a salesman for Johnson & Johnson and knows that the cost to the hospital of the roll of cotton is between $2.15 and $2.95. He asked for a breakdown of the $11.75 charge. The accounting office of the hospital sent him the following information:

a. Invoiced cost of cotton roll	$ 2.55
b. Cost of processing of paperwork for purchase	0.56
c. Supplies-room management fee	0.68
d. Operating-room and patient-room handling costs	1.57
e. Administrative hospital costs	1.01
f. University teaching-related costs	0.58
g. Malpractice insurance costs	1.23
h. Cost of treating uninsured patients	3.00
i. Profit component	0.57
Total	$11.75

McKnight believes the overhead charge is outrageous. He comments, "There was nothing I could do about it. When they come in and dab your stitches, it's not as if you can say, 'Keep your cotton roll. I brought my own.'"

Required

1. Compute the overhead rate Sierra University Hospital charged on the cotton roll.
2. What criteria might Sierra use to justify allocation of the overhead items **b–i** in the preceding list? Examine each item separately and use the allocation criteria listed in Exhibit 15-8 (page 608) in your answer.
3. What should McKnight do about the $11.75 charge for the cotton roll?

15-19 Customer profitability, customer-cost hierarchy. Enviro-Tech has only two retail and two wholesale customers. Information relating to each customer for 2020 follows (in thousands):

	Wholesale Customers		Retail Customers	
	North America Wholesaler	South America Wholesaler	Green Energy	Global Power
Revenues at list prices	$375,000	$590,000	$175,000	$130,000
Discounts from list prices	25,800	47,200	8,400	590
Cost of goods sold	285,000	510,000	144,000	95,000
Delivery costs	4,550	6,710	2,230	2,145
Order processing costs	3,820	5,980	2,180	1,130
Costs of sales visits	6,300	2,620	2,620	1,575

Enviro-Tech's annual distribution-channel costs are $33 million for wholesale customers and $12 million for retail customers. The company's annual corporate-sustaining costs, such as salary for top management and general-administration costs are $48 million. There is no cause-and-effect or benefits-received relationship between any cost-allocation base and corporate-sustaining costs. That is, Enviro-Tech could save corporate-sustaining costs only if the company completely shuts down.

Required

1. Calculate customer-level operating income using the format in Exhibit 15-3.
2. Prepare a customer-cost hierarchy report, using the format in Exhibit 15-6.
3. Enviro-Tech's management decides to allocate all corporate-sustaining costs to distribution channels: $38 million to the wholesale channel and $10 million to the retail channel. As a result, distribution channel costs are now $71 million ($33 million + $38 million) for the wholesale channel and $22 million ($12 million + $10 million) for the retail channel. Calculate the distribution-channel-level operating income. On the basis of these calculations, what actions, if any, should Enviro-Tech's managers take? Explain.
4. How might Enviro-Tech use the new cost information from its activity-based costing system to better manage its business?

15-20 Customer profitability, service company. Instant Service (IS) repairs printers and photocopiers for five multisite companies in a tristate area. IS's costs consist of the cost of technicians and equipment that are directly traceable to the customer site and a pool of office overhead. Until recently, IS estimated customer profitability by allocating the office overhead to each customer based on share of revenues. For 2020, IS reported the following results:

	A	B	C	D	E	F	G
1		Avery	Okie	Wizard	Grainger	Duran	Total
2	Revenues	$390,000	$300,000	$483,000	$183,000	$318,000	$1,674,000
3	Technician and equipment cost	273,000	262,500	337,500	160,500	267,000	1,300,500
4	Office overhead allocated	47,789	36,760	59,186	22,423	38,967	205,125
5	Operating income	$ 69,211	$ 740	$ 86,314	$ 77	$ 12,033	$ 168,375

Abby Costa, IS's new controller, notes that office overhead is more than 10% of total costs, so she spends a couple of weeks analyzing the consumption of office overhead resources by customers. She collects the following information:

	I	J	K
1	Activity Area	Cost Driver Rate	
2	Service call handling	$85	per service call
3	Parts ordering	$80	per Web-based parts order
4	Billing and collection	$50	per bill (or reminder)

	A	B	C	D	E	F
8		Avery	Okie	Wizard	Grainger	Duran
9	Number of service calls	225	360	60	180	270
10	Number of Web-based parts orders	180	315	90	225	225
11	Number of bills (or reminders)	45	135	135	90	180

Required

1. Compute customer-level operating income using the new information that Costa has gathered.
2. Prepare exhibits for IS similar to Exhibits 15-4 and 15-5. Comment on the results.
3. What options should IS consider, with regard to individual customers, in light of the new data and analysis of office overhead?

15-21 Customer profitability, distribution. HQ Drugs is a distributor of pharmaceutical products. Its ABC system has five activities:

Activity Area	Cost Driver Rate in 2017
1. Order processing	$44 per order
2. Line-item ordering	$ 2 per line item
3. Store deliveries	$50 per store delivery
4. Carton deliveries	$ 5 per carton
5. Shelf-stocking	$12 per stocking-hour

Rick Flair, the controller of HQ Drugs, wants to use this ABC system to examine individual customer profitability within each distribution market. He focuses first on the Ma and Pa single-store distribution market. Using only two customers helps highlight the insights available with the ABC approach. Data pertaining to these two customers in August 2020 are as follows:

	Albany Pharmacy	Dallas Pharmacy
Total orders	11	12
Average line items per order	6	21
Total store deliveries	7	11
Average cartons shipped per store delivery	23	22
Average hours of shelf-stocking per store delivery	0.25	0.50
Average revenue per delivery	$2,400	$1,800
Average cost of goods sold per delivery	$2,100	$1,550

Required

1. Use the ABC information to compute the operating income of each customer in August 2020. Comment on the results and what, if anything, Flair should do.
2. Flair ranks the individual customers in the Ma and Pa single-store distribution market on the basis of monthly operating income. The cumulative operating income of the top 20% of customers is $55,680. HQ Drugs reports operating losses of $18,290 for the bottom 40% of its customers. Make four recommendations that you think HQ Drugs should consider in light of this new customer-profitability information.

15-22 Cost allocation and decision making. Travel Ready has three divisions: United States, Europe, and Caribbean. Corporate headquarters is in Boston. Travel Ready corporate headquarters incurs costs of $34,000,000 annually, which is an indirect cost of the divisions. Corporate headquarters currently allocates this cost to the divisions based on the revenues of each division. The president has asked each division manager to suggest an allocation base for the corporate headquarters costs from among revenues, division margin, direct costs, and number of employees. The following is relevant information about each division:

	United States	Europe	Caribbean
Revenues	$40,000,000	$34,000,000	$26,000,000
Direct costs	25,000,000	21,000,000	14,000,000
Division margin	$15,000,000	$13,000,000	$12,000,000
Division margin percentage	37.5%	38.2%	46.2%
Number of employees	15,000	20,000	10,000

Required

1. Allocate the corporate headquarters costs of Travel Ready to each of the three divisions using revenues, direct costs, division margin, and number of employees as the allocation bases. Calculate operating margins for each division after allocating headquarters costs.
2. Which method of allocation would you expect each manager to recommend? Explain.
3. What factors would you consider in deciding which allocation base Travel Ready should use?
4. Suppose Travel Ready decides to use number of employees as the allocation base. Should the European division be closed? Why or why not?

15-23 Cost allocation to divisions. Martini Hotel & Casino is situated on beautiful Lake Tahoe in Nevada. The complex includes a 300-room hotel, a casino, and a restaurant. As Martini's new controller, your manager asks you to recommend the basis the hotel should use for allocating fixed overhead costs to the three divisions in 2020. You are presented with the following income statement information for 2019:

	Hotel	Restaurant	Casino
Revenues	$16,925,000	$6,150,000	$12, 400,000
Direct costs	9,700,000	3,924,600	4,493,200
Segment margin	$ 7,225,000	$2,225,400	$ 7,906,800

You are also given the following data on the three divisions:

	Hotel	Restaurant	Casino
Floor space (square feet)	115,000	23,000	92,000
Number of employees	360	90	450

You are told that you may choose to allocate indirect costs based on one of the following: direct costs, floor space, or the number of employees. Total fixed overhead costs for 2019 were $14,660,000.

Required

1. Calculate division margins in percentage terms prior to allocating fixed overhead costs.
2. Allocate indirect costs to the three divisions using each of the three allocation bases suggested. For each allocation base, calculate division operating margins after allocations, in dollars and as a percentage of revenues.
3. Discuss the results. How would you decide how to allocate indirect costs to the divisions? Why?
4. Would you recommend closing any of the three divisions in the short run (and possibly reallocating resources to other divisions) as a result of your analysis? If so, which division would you close and why?

15-24 Cost allocation to divisions. Holbrook Corporation has three divisions: pulp, paper, and fibers. Holbrook's new controller, Paul Mayer, is reviewing the allocation of fixed corporate-overhead costs to the three divisions. He is presented with the following information for each division for 2020:

	Pulp	Paper	Fibers
Revenues	$8,800,000	$16,600,000	$26,800,000
Direct manufacturing costs	3,500,000	8,200,000	10,500,000
Division administrative costs	3,000,000	1,200,000	5,800,000
Division margin	$2,300,000	$ 7,200,000	$10,500,000
Number of employees	160	120	520
Floor space (square feet)	28,800	22,440	68,760

Until now, Holbrook Corporation has allocated fixed corporate-overhead costs to the divisions on the basis of division margins. Mayer asks for a list of costs that comprise fixed corporate overhead and suggests the following new allocation bases:

Fixed Corporate-Overhead Costs		Suggested Allocation Bases
Human resource management	$ 2,100,000	Number of employees
Facility	3,600,000	Floor space (square feet)
Corporate administration	4,600,000	Division administrative costs
Total	$10,300,000	

Required

1. Allocate 2020 fixed corporate-overhead costs to the three divisions using division margin as the allocation base. What is each division's operating margin percentage (division margin minus allocated fixed corporate-overhead costs as a percentage of revenues)?

2. Allocate 2020 fixed costs using the allocation bases suggested by Mayer. What is each division's operating margin percentage under the new allocation scheme?
3. Compare and discuss the results of requirements 1 and 2. If division performance incentives are based on operating margin percentage, which division would be most receptive to the new allocation scheme? Which division would be the least receptive? Why?
4. Which allocation scheme should Holbrook Corporation use? Why? How might Mayer overcome any objections that may arise from the divisions?

15-25 Variance analysis, multiple products. The Chicago Tigers play in the American Ice Hockey League. The Tigers play in the Downtown Arena, which is owned and managed by the City of Chicago. The arena has a capacity of 15,000 seats (5,500 lower-tier seats and 9,500 upper-tier seats). The arena charges the Tigers a per-ticket charge for use of its facility. All tickets are sold by the Reservation Network, which charges the Tigers a reservation fee per ticket. The Tigers' budgeted contribution margin for each type of ticket in 2020 is computed as follows:

	Lower-Tier Tickets	Upper-Tier Tickets
Selling price	$33	$18
Downtown Arena fee	9	6
Reservation Network fee	4	5
Contribution margin per ticket	$20	$ 7

The budgeted and actual average attendance figures per game in the 2020 season are as follows:

	Budgeted Seats Sold	Actual Seats Sold
Lower tier	4,500	3,300
Upper tier	5,500	7,700
Total	10,000	11,000

There was no difference between the budgeted and actual contribution margin for lower-tier or upper-tier seats.

The manager of the Tigers was delighted that actual attendance was 10% above budgeted attendance per game, especially given the depressed state of the local economy in the past 6 months.

Required

1. Compute the sales-volume variance for each type of ticket and in total for the Chicago Tigers in 2020. (Calculate all variances in terms of contribution margins.)
2. Compute the sales-quantity and sales-mix variances for each type of ticket and in total in 2020.
3. Present a summary of the variances in requirements 1 and 2. Comment on the results.

15-26 Variance analysis, working backward. The Hiro Corporation sells two brands of wine glasses: Plain and Chic. Hiro provides the following information for sales in the month of June 2020:

Static-budget total contribution margin	$ 15,525
Budgeted units to be sold of all glasses	2,300 units
Budgeted contribution margin per unit of Plain	$ 5 per unit
Budgeted contribution margin per unit of Chic	$12 per unit
Total sales-quantity variance	$ 2,700 U
Actual sales-mix percentage of Plain	60%

All variances are computed in contribution-margin terms.

Required

1. Calculate the sales-quantity variances for each product for June 2020.
2. Calculate the individual-product and total sales-mix variances for June 2020. Calculate the individual-product and total sales-volume variances for June 2020.
3. Briefly describe the conclusions you can draw from the variances.

15-27 Variance analysis, multiple products. Emcee Inc. manufactures and sells two fruit drinks: Kostor and Limba. Budgeted and actual results for 2020 are as follows:

	Budget for 2020			Actual for 2020		
Product	Selling Price	Variable Cost per Carton	Cartons Sold	Selling Price	Variable Cost per Carton	Cartons Sold
Kostor	$12.00	$7.20	130,000	$12.50	$8.00	132,000
Limba	$15.00	$8.25	120,000	$16.00	$7.75	108,000

Required

1. Compute the total sales-volume variance, the total sales-mix variance, and the total sales-quantity variance. (Calculate all variances in terms of contribution margin.) Show results for each product in your computations.
2. What inferences can you draw from the variances computed in requirement 1?

15-28 Market-share and market-size variances (continuation of 15-27). Emcee Inc. prepared the budget for 2020 assuming a 20% market share based on total sales in the Midwest region of the United States. The total fruit drinks market was estimated to reach sales of 1.25 million cartons in the region. However, actual total sales volume in the western region was 1.5 million cartons.

Required

Calculate the market-share and market-size variances for Emcee Inc. in 2020. (Calculate all variances in terms of contribution margin.) Comment on the results.

Problems

15-29 Purposes of cost allocation. Ashley Miller recently started a job as an administrative assistant in the cost accounting department of Norton Manufacturing. New to the area of cost accounting, Ashley is puzzled by the fact that one of Norton's manufactured products, SR670, has a different cost depending on who asks for it. When the marketing department requested the cost of SR670 in order to determine pricing for the new catalog, Ashley was told to report one amount, but when a request came in the very next day from the financial-reporting department for the cost of SR670, she was told to report a very different cost. Ashley runs a report using Norton's cost accounting system, which produces the following cost elements for one unit of SR670:

Direct materials	$118.00
Direct manufacturing labor	62.20
Variable manufacturing overhead	33.65
Allocated fixed manufacturing overhead	133.20
Research and development costs specific to SR670[a]	25.50
Marketing costs[a]	21.20
Sales commissions[a]	40.60
Allocated administrative costs of corporate headquarters	70.25
Customer service costs[a]	12.49
Distribution costs[a]	30.52

[a]These costs are specific to SR670, but would not be eliminated if SR670 were purchased from an outside supplier. Allocated costs would be reallocated elsewhere in the company should the company cease production of SR670.

Required

1. Explain to Ashley why the cost given to the marketing and financial-reporting departments would be different.
2. Calculate the cost of one unit of SR670 to determine the following:
   a. The selling price of SR670
   b. The cost of inventory for financial reporting
   c. Whether to continue manufacturing SR670 or to purchase it from an outside source (Assume that SR670 is used as a component in one of Norton's other products.)

15-30 Customer profitability. Bracelet Delights is a new company that manufactures custom jewelry. Bracelet Delights currently has six customers referenced by customer number: 01, 02, 03, 04, 05, and 06. Besides the costs of making the jewelry, the company has the following activities:

1. Customer orders. The salespeople, designers, and jewelry makers spend time with the customer. The cost-driver rate is $42 per hour spent with a customer.
2. Customer fittings. Before the jewelry piece is completed, the customer may come in to make sure it looks right and fits properly. Cost-driver rate is $30 per hour.
3. Rush orders. Some customers want their jewelry quickly. The cost-driver rate is $90 per rush order.
4. Number of customer return visits. Customers visit to return jewelry up to 30 days after the pickup of the jewelry to have something refitted or repaired at no charge. The cost-driver rate is $40 per return visit.

Information about the six customers follows. Some customers purchase multiple items. The cost of the jewelry is 60% of the selling price.

Customer number	01	02	03	04	05	06
Sales revenue	$850	$4,500	$280	$2,200	$5,500	$650
Cost of item(s)	$510	$2,700	$168	$1,320	$3,300	$390
Hours spent on customer order	3	10	1	8	17	5
Hours on fittings	1	6	0	0	4	0
Number of rush orders	0	2	1	2	3	0
Number of return visits	0	0	0	0	0	1

Required

1. Calculate the customer-level operating income for each customer. Rank the customers in order of most to least profitable and prepare a customer-profitability analysis, as in Exhibits 15-3 and 15-4.
2. Are any customers unprofitable? What is causing this? What should Bracelet Delights do about these customers?

15-31 Customer profitability, distribution. Green Paper Delivery has decided to analyze the profitability of five new customers. It buys recycled paper at $20 per case and sells to retail customers at a list price of $26 per case. Data pertaining to the five customers are as follows:

	Customer				
	1	2	3	4	5
Cases sold	1,830	6,780	44,500	31,200	1,950
List selling price	$ 26	$ 26	$ 26	$ 26	$ 26
Actual selling price	$ 26	$25.20	$24.30	$25.80	$23.90
Number of purchase orders	10	18	35	16	35
Number of customer visits	3	5	12	4	12
Number of deliveries	12	28	65	25	35
Miles traveled per delivery	14	4	8	6	45
Number of expedited deliveries	0	0	0	0	3

Green Paper Delivery's five activities and their cost drivers are as follows:

Activity	Cost-Driver Rate
Order taking	$ 90 per purchase order
Customer visits	$ 75 per customer visit
Deliveries	$ 3 per delivery mile traveled
Product handling	$ 1.20 per case sold
Expedited deliveries	$250 per expedited delivery

Required

1. Compute the customer-level operating income of each of the five retail customers now being examined (1, 2, 3, 4, and 5). Comment on the results.
2. What insights do managers gain by reporting both the list selling price and the actual selling price for each customer?
3. What factors should managers consider in deciding whether to drop one or more of the five customers?

15-32 Customer profitability in a manufacturing firm. Mississippi Manufacturing makes a component called B2040. This component is manufactured only when ordered by a customer, so Mississippi keeps no inventory of B2040. The list price is $112 per unit, but customers who place "large" orders receive a 10% discount on price. The customers are manufacturing firms. Currently, the salespeople decide whether an order is large enough to qualify for the discount. When the product is finished, it is packed in cases of 10. If the component needs to be exchanged or repaired, customers can come back within 14 days for free exchange or repair.

The full cost of manufacturing a unit of B2040 is $95. In addition, Mississippi incurs customer-level costs. Customer-level cost-driver rates are shown below:

Order taking	$360 per order
Product handling	$15 per case
Rush-order processing	$560 per rush order
Exchange and repair costs	$50 per unit

Information about Mississippi's five biggest customers follows:

	A	B	C	D	E
Number of units purchased	5,400	1,800	1,200	4,400	8,100
Discounts given	10%	10%	0	10%	10% on half the units
Number of orders	8	16	50	20	18
Number of cases	540	180	120	440	810
Number of rush orders	2	7	1	0	8
Number of units exchanged/repaired	18	70	13	50	200

All customers except E ordered units in the same order size. Customer E's order quantity varied, so E got a discount part of the time but not all the time.

Required

1. Calculate the customer-level operating income for these five customers. Use the format in Exhibit 15-3. Prepare a customer-profitability analysis by ranking the customers from most to least profitable, as in Exhibit 15-4.
2. Discuss the results of your customer-profitability analysis. Does Mississippi have unprofitable customers? Is there anything Mississippi should do differently with its five customers?

15-33 Customer-cost hierarchy, customer profitability. Louise Adam Inc. operates two divisions: Architectural Designs, which provides architecture services for homes, and Commercial Interior, which provides interior design service for commercial customers. Architecture Designs serves two customers, Adair and Arsdale, and Commercial Interiors serves two customers, Caleigh and Comet. Louise would like to evaluate the profitability of her four customers, as well as evaluate the profitability of each of the two divisions and the business as a whole. Information about her most recent quarter follow:

	Architecture Designs		Commercial Interiors	
	Adair	Arsdale	Caleigh	Comet
Gross revenue	$480,000	$290,000	$320,000	$310,000
Customer-level costs	225,000	145,000	170,000	130,000

Overhead costs total $750,000. Louise has determined that 45% of her overhead costs relate directly to Architectural Designs, 35% relate directly to Commercial Interiors, and the remaining 20% are corporate overhead costs.

Required

1. Prepare a customer-cost hierarchy report for Louise Adam Inc., using the format in Exhibit 15-6.
2. Prepare a customer-profitability analysis for the four customers, using the format in Exhibit 15-4.
3. Comment on the results of the preceding reports. What recommendations would you give Louise Adam?

15-34 Allocation of corporate costs to divisions. Cathy Carpenter, controller of the Sweet and Salty Snacks, is preparing a presentation to senior executives about the performance of its four divisions. Summary data related to the four divisions for the most recent year are as follows:

	A	B	C	D	E	F
1		DIVISIONS				
2		Candy	Nuts	Crackers	Cookies	Total
3	Revenues	$ 870,000	$ 975,000	$ 654,000	$ 501,000	$ 3,000,000
4	Operating Costs	330,800	378,000	658,000	314,000	1,680,800
5	Operating Income	$ 539,200	$ 597,000	$ (4,000)	$ 187,000	$ 1,319,200
6						
7	Identifiable assets	$1,800,000	$ 2,880,000	$1,440,000	$1,080,000	$ 7,200,000
8	Number of employees	3,600	6,600	2,700	2,100	15,000

Under the existing accounting system, costs incurred at corporate headquarters are collected in a single cost pool ($1.2 million in the most recent year) and allocated to each division on the basis of its actual revenues. The top managers in each division share in a division-income bonus pool. Division income is defined as operating income less allocated corporate costs.

Carpenter has analyzed the components of corporate costs and proposes that corporate costs be collected in four cost pools. The components of corporate costs for the most recent year and Carpenter's suggested cost pools and allocation bases are as follows:

	A	B	C	D	E	F
11	Corporate Cost Category	Amount	Suggested Cost Pool	Suggested Allocation Base		
12	Interest on debt	$ 380,000	Cost Pool 1	Identifiable assets		
13	Corporate salaries	200,000	Cost Pool 2	Division revenues		
14	Accounting and control	160,000	Cost Pool 2			
15	General marketing	170,000	Cost Pool 2			
16	Public affairs	150,000	Cost Pool 3	Positive operating income*		
17	Personnel and payroll	140,000	Cost Pool 4	Number of employees		
18	Total	$1,200,000				
19						
20	*Carpenter proposes that this cost be allocated using the operating income (if positive) of divisions,					
21	with only divisions with positive operating income included in the allocation base.					

Required

1. Discuss two reasons why Sweet and Salty Snacks should allocate corporate costs to each division.
2. Calculate the operating income of each division when all corporate costs are allocated based on revenues of each division.
3. Calculate the operating income of each division when all corporate costs are allocated using the four cost pools.
4. How do you think the division managers will receive the new proposal? What are the strengths and weaknesses of Carpenter's proposal relative to the existing single cost-pool method?

15-35 Cost allocation to divisions. Francisco Bakery makes baked goods for grocery stores and has three divisions: bread, cake, and doughnuts. Each division is run and evaluated separately, but the main headquarters incurs costs that are indirect costs for the divisions. Costs incurred in the main headquarters are as follows:

Human resources (HR) costs	$1,700,000
Accounting department costs	1,300,000
Rent and depreciation	1, 440,000
Other	510,000
Total costs	$4,950,000

The Francisco upper management currently allocates this cost to the divisions equally. One of the division managers has done some research on activity-based costing and proposes the use of different allocation bases for the different indirect costs—number of employees for HR costs, total revenues for accounting department costs, square feet of space for rent and depreciation costs, and equal allocation among the divisions of "other" costs. Information about the three divisions follows:

	Bread	Cake	Doughnuts
Total revenues	$21,300,000	$4,300,000	$13,500,000
Direct costs	14,100,000	2,900,000	7, 550,000
Segment margin	$ 7,200,000	$1,400,000	$ 5,950,000
Number of employees	600	150	250
Square feet of space	18,000	3,000	9,000

Required

1. Allocate the indirect costs of Francisco to each division equally. Calculate division operating income after allocation of headquarter costs.
2. Allocate headquarter costs to the individual divisions using the proposed allocation bases. Calculate the division operating income after allocation. Comment on the allocation bases used to allocate headquarter costs.
3. Which division manager do you think suggested this new allocation. Explain briefly. Which allocation do you think is "better?"

15-36 Cost-hierarchy income statement and allocation of corporate costs to customers. ISPStar offers Internet, phone, and television services to customers in Wyoming. It has two divisions, an Urban Division catering to urban customers and a Rural Division catering to rural customers. Currently, the company allocates corporate overhead on the basis of revenues of the two divisions. Harvey Leonard, ISPStar's president, believes that this method of allocation does not adequately capture the demands that the two divisions put on corporate resources. He proposes developing a cost-hierarchy income statement and also an income statement allocating corporate overhead costs based on the number of service hours used in the two divisions. The Rural Division has a higher number of service hours because service personnel have to travel longer distances to reach customers.

The following information is available for the forthcoming period:

	Urban Division	Rural Division	Total
Revenue	$4,840,000	$3,960,000	$8,800,000
Customer-level costs	2, 800,000	2,700,000	5,500,000
Customer-level operating income	$2,040,000	$1,260,000	$3,300,000
Customer-level operating income percentage	42.15%	31.82%	37.5%
Service-hours worked	6,000 hours	12,000 hours	18,000 hours

In addition to the customer-level costs above, the company expects to incur $2,250,000 of corporate costs.

Required

1. Prepare a cost-hierarchy income statement for ISPStar using the format in Exhibit 15-7. assuming corporate costs are not allocated to each division.
2. Allocate the corporate costs to each division and calculate the income of each division after assigning corporate costs based on revenues of each division.
3. Allocate the corporate costs to each division and calculate the income of each division after assigning corporate costs based on service-hours worked in each division.
4. What are the advantages and disadvantages of ISPStar allocating corporate overhead costs to the two divisions?
5. Based on your answers to requirements 1 through 4, should Leonard close down the Rural Division? Explain.

15-37 Cost-hierarchy income statement and allocation of corporate, division, and channel costs to customers. Sportscast Inc. has two divisions, the Sporting Goods Division and the Memorabilia Division. Recently the company's profitability has decreased. Management would like to analyze the profitability of each division based on the following information for the upcoming period:

	Sporting Goods Division	Memorabilia Division	Total
Revenue	$1,440,000	$1,560,000	$3,000,000
Customer-level costs	880,000	1,120,000	2,000,000
Customer-level operating income	$ 560,000	$ 440,000	$1,000,000
Customer-level operating income as a percentage of revenue	38.9%	28.2%	33.3%

The company allocates marketing and administration costs incurred to support the divisions as follows:

	Total	Allocation basis
Marketing costs	$400,000	Channel revenue
Administration costs	$450,000	Customer-level costs

Based on a special study, the company allocates corporate costs of $200,000 to the two divisions based on the corporate resources demanded by the divisions as follows: Sporting Goods Division, $130,000, and Memorabilia Division, $70,000. If the company were to close a division, none of the corporate costs would be saved.

Required

1. Calculate the operating income for each division as a percentage of revenue after assigning customer-level costs, marketing costs, administration costs, and corporate costs.
2. Should Sportscast Inc. close down any division? Explain briefly including any assumptions that you made.
3. Would you allocate corporate costs to divisions? Why is allocating these costs helpful? What actions would it help you take?

15-38 Variance analysis, sales-mix and sales-quantity variances. Miami Infonautics, Inc., produces Windows phones. Miami Infonautics markets three different handheld models: WinPro is a souped-up version for the executive on the go, WinCE is a consumer-oriented version, and WinKid is a stripped-down version for the young adult market. You are Miami Infonautics' senior vice president of marketing. The chief executive officer (CEO) has discovered that the total contribution margin came in lower than budgeted, and it is your responsibility to explain to him why actual results are different from the budget. Budgeted and actual operating data for the company's third quarter of 2020 are as follows:

Budgeted Operating Data, Third Quarter 2020

	Selling Price	Variable Cost per Unit	Contribution Margin per Unit	Sales Volume in Units
WinPro	$373	$181	$192	10,215
WinCE	270	100	170	38,817
WinKid	140	80	60	53,118
				102,150

Actual Operating Data, Third Quarter 2020

	Selling Price	Variable Cost per Unit	Contribution Margin per Unit	Sales Volume in Units
WinPro	$370	$175	$195	12,360
WinCE	280	96	184	42,230
WinKid	110	76	34	48,410
				103,000

Required

1. Compute the actual and budgeted contribution margins in dollars for each product and in total for the third quarter of 2020.
2. Calculate the actual and budgeted sales mixes for the three products for the third quarter of 2020.
3. Calculate total sales-volume, sales-mix, and sales-quantity variances for the third quarter of 2020. (Calculate all variances in terms of contribution margins.)

4. Given that your CEO gets very angry if actual results differ from budget, you want to be well prepared for this meeting. In order to prepare, write a paragraph or two comparing actual results to budgeted amounts.

15-39 Market-share and market-size variances (continuation of 15-38). Miami Infonautics' senior vice president of marketing prepared his budget at the beginning of the third quarter assuming a 25% market share based on total sales. Foolinstead Research estimated that the total market would reach sales of 408,600 units worldwide in the third quarter. However, actual sales in the third quarter were 515,000 units.

Required

1. Calculate the market-share and market-size variances for Miami Infonautics in the third quarter of 2020 (calculate all variances in terms of contribution margins).
2. Explain what happened based on the market-share and market-size variances.
3. Calculate the actual market size, in units, that would have led to no market-size variance (again using budgeted contribution margin per unit). Use this market-size figure to calculate the actual market share that would have led to a zero market-share variance.

15-40 Variance analysis, multiple products. The Robin's Basket operates a chain of Italian gelato stores. Although the Robin's Basket charges customers the same price for all flavors, production costs vary, depending on the type of ingredients. Budgeted and actual operating data of its Washington, D.C., store for August 2020 are as follows:

Budget for August 2020

	Selling Price per Pint	Variable Cost per Pint	Contribution Margin per Pint	Sales Volume in Pints
Mint chocolate chip	$9.00	$4.80	$4.20	35,000
Vanilla	9.00	3.20	5.80	45,000
Rum raisin	9.00	5.00	4.00	20,000
				100,000

Actual for August 2020

	Selling Price per Pint	Variable Cost per Pint	Contribution Margin per Pint	Sales Volume in Pints
Mint chocolate chip	$9.00	$4.60	$4.40	33,750
Vanilla	9.00	3.25	5.75	56,250
Rum raisin	9.00	5.15	3.85	22,500
				112,500

The Robin's Basket focuses on contribution margin in its variance analysis.

Required

1. Compute the total sales-volume variance for August 2020.
2. Compute the total sales-mix variance for August 2020.
3. Compute the total sales-quantity variance for August 2020.
4. Comment on your results in requirements 1, 2, and 3.

15-41 Market-share and market-size variances (continuation of 15-40). The Robin's Basket's senior vice president of marketing prepared her budget at the beginning of the third quarter assuming a 10% market share based on a budgeted market size of 1,000,000 pints in August. However, actual market size in August was 1,250,000 pints.

Required

1. Calculate the market-share and market-size variances for the Robin's Basket in August 2020 (calculate all variances in terms of contribution margins).
2. Explain what happened based on the market-share and market-size variances.
3. How many pints would the Robin's Basket have to sell in August 2020 for the market share variance to be zero? Calculate the actual market size, in units, that would have led to no market-size variance.

15-42 Customer profitability and ethics. KC Corporation manufactures an air-freshening device called GoodAir, which it sells to six merchandising firms. The list price of a GoodAir is $30, and the full manufacturing costs are $18. Salespeople receive a commission on sales, but the commission is based on number of orders taken, not on sales revenue generated or number of units sold. Salespeople receive a commission of $10 per order (in addition to regular salary).

KC Corporation makes products based on anticipated demand. KC carries an inventory of GoodAir, so rush orders do not result in any extra manufacturing costs over and above the $18 per unit. KC ships finished product to the customer at no additional charge for either regular or expedited delivery. KC incurs significantly higher costs for expedited deliveries than for regular deliveries. Customers occasionally return shipments to KC, and the company subtracts these returns from gross revenue. The customers are not charged a restocking fee for returns.

Budgeted (expected) customer-level cost driver rates follow:

Order taking (excluding sales commission)	$ 15 per order
Product handling	$ 1 per unit
Delivery	$ 1.20 per mile driven
Expedited (rush) delivery	$175 per shipment
Restocking	$ 50 per returned shipment
Visits to customers	$125 per customer

Because salespeople are paid $10 per order, they often break up large orders into multiple smaller orders. This practice reduces the actual order-taking cost by $7 per smaller order (from $15 per order to $8 per order) because the smaller orders are all written at the same time. This lower cost rate is not included in budgeted rates because salespeople create smaller orders without telling management or the accounting department. All other actual costs are the same as budgeted costs.

Information about KC's clients follows:

	AC	DC	MC	JC	RC	BC
Total number of units purchased	225	520	295	110	390	1,050
Number of actual orders	5	20	4	6	9	18
Number of written orders	10	20*	9	12	24	36
Total number of miles driven to deliver all products	360	580	350	220	790	850
Total number of units returned	15	40	0	0	35	40
Number of returned shipments	3	2	0	0	1	5
Number of expedited deliveries	0	8	0	0	3	4

* Because DC places 20 separate orders, its order costs are $15 per order. All other orders are multiple smaller orders and so have actual order costs of $8 each.

Required

1. Classify each of the customer-level operating costs as a customer output unit-level, customer batch-level, or customer-sustaining cost.
2. Using the preceding information, calculate the expected customer-level operating income for the six customers of KC Corporation. Use the number of written orders at $15 each to calculate expected order costs.
3. Recalculate the customer-level operating income using the number of written orders but at their actual $8 cost per order instead of $15 (except for DC, whose actual cost is $15 per order). How will KC Corporation evaluate customer-level operating cost performance this period?
4. Recalculate the customer-level operating income if salespeople had not broken up actual orders into multiple smaller orders. Don't forget to also adjust sales commissions.
5. How is the behavior of the salespeople affecting the profit of KC Corporation? Is their behavior ethical? What could KC Corporation do to change the behavior of the salespeople?

Allocation of Support-Department Costs, Common Costs, and Revenues

16

How a company allocates its overhead and internal support costs—of information systems, production control, and other internal services—to its various production departments or projects can impact the profitability of those departments or projects.

While the allocation may not affect the firm's profit as a whole, the allocation can make the profitability of some departments and projects (and their managers) look better or worse than they should. In other cases, the allocations can affect the decisions of managers and, as the following article shows, competition.

LEARNING OBJECTIVES

1. Distinguish the single-rate method from the dual-rate method
2. Understand how the choice between allocation based on budgeted and actual rates and between budgeted and actual usage can affect the incentives of division managers
3. Allocate multiple support-department costs using the direct method, the step-down method, and the reciprocal method
4. Allocate common costs using the stand-alone method and the incremental method
5. Explain the importance of explicit agreement between contracting parties when the reimbursement amount is based on costs incurred
6. Understand how bundling of products causes revenue allocation issues and the methods managers use to allocate revenues

COST ALLOCATION AND THE UNITED STATES POSTAL SERVICE[1]

In recent years, cost allocation at the United States Postal Service (USPS) has been a hotly contested business and political issue. The dispute centers on how USPS splits its fixed "institutional" costs, such as driver salaries, trucking fees, and other overhead expenses, between its two businesses: the "market dominant" letter business (a government-protected monopoly) and the "competitive" package business (which competes against United Parcel Service [UPS] and FedEx, among others).

In 2017, the "market dominant" business accounted for 97% of USPS volume and 70% of revenue, while the "competitive" business comprised only 3% of volume, but 30% of revenue. USPS is required to cover the costs of its competitive business but how much of fixed costs should be allocated to this business? U.S. law requires USPS to cover at least 5.5% of its fixed costs with revenue from the "competitive" package business (although, based on volume, only 3% of fixed costs would be allocated). UPS and FedEx argue that the "competitive" business should pay a larger share of the fixed costs—approximately 30%, which is in line with USPS package-delivery revenue. They believe that by allocating lower costs to the competitive business, USPS charges lower package shipping rates and unfairly subsidizes the "competitive" business with the monopoly "market dominant" business.

Companies like Amazon want to keep the share at 5.5%, or even eliminate it entirely, because they rely heavily on USPS to ship their orders and would like to keep delivery

dennizn/Shutterstock

---

[1] *Sources:* Eugene Kim, "Amazon and UPS Have Been Quietly Fighting over the Post Office's Cost Structure — Long Before Trump," CNBC.com, April 5, 2018 (https://www.cnbc.com/2018/04/05/amazon-and-ups-disagree-postal-regulatory-commission-public-filings-post-office-cost-structure.html); Helen Edwards and Dave Edwards, "What the US Post Office Really Gets from Amazon," Quartz.com, April 9, 2018 (https://qz.com/1247302/what-the-us-post-office-really-gets-from-amazon/).

prices low. These heavy-shippers argue that cost allocation should be based on volume, not revenue. Some observers believe that increasing the cost allocation and raising shipping prices on Amazon, which accounts for 25% of USPS "competitive" revenue, would encourage Amazon to create its own infrastructure around the so-called "last mile"—that is, putting things directly into the hands of customers—that USPS has had in place for the past century. That would potentially result in a significant drop in the contribution of the "competitive" business to overall USPS revenue.

The same allocation dilemmas apply when costs of corporate support departments are allocated across multiple divisions or operating departments at manufacturing companies such as Nestle, service companies such as Comcast, merchandising companies such as Trader Joe's, and academic institutions such as Auburn University. This chapter focuses on the challenges managers face when allocating costs and revenues and the consequences of those allocations.

Allocating Support Department Costs Using the Single-Rate and Dual-Rate Methods

LEARNING OBJECTIVE 1

Distinguish the single-rate method

... one rate for allocating costs in a cost pool

from the dual-rate method

... two rates for allocating costs in a cost pool—one for variable costs and one for fixed costs

Companies distinguish operating departments (and operating divisions) from support departments. An **operating department**, also called a **production department**, directly adds value to a product or service. Examples are manufacturing departments where products are made. A **support department**, also called a **service department**, provides the services that assist other internal departments (operating departments and other support departments) in the company. Examples of support departments are information systems, production control, materials management, and plant maintenance. Managers face two questions when allocating the costs of a support department to operating departments or divisions: (1) Should fixed costs of support departments, such as the salary of the department manager, be allocated to operating divisions? Most companies believe that fixed costs of support departments should be allocated because these fixed costs are needed to provide operating divisions with the services they require. (2) If fixed costs are allocated, should variable and fixed costs of the support department be allocated in the same way? There are two approaches to allocating support-department costs: the *single-rate cost-allocation method* and the *dual-rate cost-allocation method*.

Single-Rate and Dual-Rate Methods

The **single-rate method** does not distinguish between fixed and variable costs. It allocates costs in each cost pool (support department in this section) to cost objects (operating departments in this section) using the same rate per unit of a single allocation base. By contrast, the **dual-rate method** separates support department costs into a variable-cost pool and a fixed-cost pool, and allocates each pool using a different cost-allocation base. For both the single-rate method and the dual-rate method, managers can use a *budgeted* rate or the eventual *actual* cost rate to allocate support-department costs to operating departments. Using the actual cost rate is neither conceptually preferred nor widely used in practice (we explain why in the next section). Accordingly, we illustrate the single-rate and dual-rate methods using *budgeted* rates.

The Robinson Company manufactures and installs specialized machinery for the paper-making industry. In Chapter 4, Robinson collected all manufacturing overhead costs in a single cost pool and used direct manufacturing labor-hours to allocate manufacturing overhead to jobs. In this chapter, we present a more detailed accounting system to take into account the different operating and service departments within Robinson's manufacturing department.

Robinson has two operating departments—the Machining Department and the Assembly Department—where specialized machinery is produced, and three support departments—Plant Administration, Engineering and Production Control, and Materials Management—that provide services to the operating departments.

- The Plant Administration Department is responsible for managing all activities in the plant. Costs incurred in this department support supervision activities of the other departments.
- The Engineering and Production Control Department costs support all the engineering activity in the other departments.

- The Materials Management Department is responsible for managing and moving materials and components required for different jobs. Each job at Robinson requires small quantities of unique components to be machined and assembled. Materials Management Department costs vary with the number of material-handling labor-hours incurred in a department.

The specialized machinery that Robinson manufactures does not go through the service departments and so the costs of the service departments must be allocated to the operating departments to determine the full cost of making the specialized machinery. Once costs are accumulated in the operating departments, they can be allocated to the different machines manufactured. Different jobs need different amounts of machining and assembly resources. Overhead costs are allocated to machines produced based on machine-hours in the Machining Department and assembly labor-hours in the Assembly Department.

We first focus on the allocation of the Materials Management Department costs to the Machining Department and the Assembly Department. Budgeted and actual information for the Materials Management Department in 2020 follows:

Practical capacity	4,000 hours
Fixed costs of the Materials Management Department in the 3,000 labor-hour to 4,000 labor-hour relevant range	$144,000
Budgeted usage (quantity) of materials management labor-hours required to support the production departments:	
Machining Department	800 hours
Assembly Department	2,800 hours
Total	3,600 hours
Budgeted variable cost per materials-handling labor-hour in the 3,000 labor-hour to 4,000 labor-hour relevant range	$ 30 per hour used
Actual usage (quantity) of materials management labor-hours required to support the production departments:	
Machining Department	1,200 hours
Assembly Department	2,400 hours
Total	3,600 hours

The budgeted rates and allocations of Materials Management Department costs can be computed based on either (1) the demand for (or usage of) materials-handling services or (2) the supply of materials-handling services.

Allocation Based on the Demand for (or Usage of) Materials-Handling Services

We present the single-rate method followed by the dual-rate method.

Single-Rate Method

In this method, a combined budgeted rate is calculated for fixed and variable costs:

Budgeted usage of materials-handling labor-hours	3,600 hours
Budgeted total cost pool: $144,000 + (3,600 hours × $30/hour)	$252,000
Budgeted total rate per hour: $252,000 ÷ 3,600 hours	$ 70 per hour used

The rate of $70 per hour is used to allocate Materials Management Department costs to the Machining and Assembly Departments. Note that the budgeted rate of $70 per hour is substantially higher than the $30 budgeted *variable* cost per hour because it includes an allocated amount of $40 per hour (budgeted fixed costs, $144,000 ÷ budgeted usage, $3,600 hours) for the *fixed* costs of operating the facility.

Departments are charged the budgeted rate for each hour of *actual* use of the central facility. In our example, Robinson allocates Materials Management Department costs based on the $70 per hour budgeted rate and the actual hours the two operating departments use:

Machining Department: $70 per hour × 1,200 hours	$ 84,000
Assembly Department: $70 per hour × 2,400 hours	168,000
Total Materials Management Department costs allocated	$252,000

Dual-Rate Method

In the dual-rate method, managers must choose allocation bases for (1) the variable and (2) the fixed-cost pools of the Materials Management Department. As in the single-rate method, variable costs are assigned based on the *budgeted* variable cost per hour of \$30 for *actual* hours each department uses. However, fixed costs are assigned based on *budgeted* fixed costs per hour and the *budgeted* number of hours for each department. At the budgeted usage of 800 hours for the Machining Department and 2,800 hours for the Assembly Department, the budgeted fixed-cost rate is \$40 per hour (\$144,000 ÷ 3,600 hours). Because this rate is charged on the basis of *budgeted* usage, fixed costs are effectively allocated in advance as a lump sum to the operating departments based on the budgeted use of the materials management facilities.

Under the dual-rate method:

The costs allocated to the Machining Department in 2020 equal:

Fixed costs: \$40 per hour × 800 (budgeted) hours	\$32,000
Variable costs: \$30 per hour × 1,200 (actual) hours	36,000
Total costs	\$68,000

The costs allocated to the Assembly Department in 2020 equal:

Fixed costs: \$40 per hour × 2,800 (budgeted) hours	\$112,000
Variable costs: \$30 per hour × 2,400 (actual) hours	72,000
Total costs	\$184,000
Total Materials Management Department costs allocated (\$68,000 + \$184,000)	\$252,000

Each operating department is charged the same amount for variable costs under the single-rate and dual-rate methods (\$30 per hour multiplied by the actual hours used). However, the total costs assigned are different because the single-rate method allocates fixed costs of the Materials Management Department based on *actual* usage of materials-handling resources by the operating departments, whereas the dual-rate method allocates fixed costs based on *budgeted* usage.

We next consider the alternative approach of allocating Materials Management Department costs based on the capacity of materials-handling services supplied.

Allocation Based on the Supply of Capacity

We illustrate this approach using the 4,000 hours of practical capacity of the Materials Management Department. The budgeted rate is then determined as follows:

Budgeted fixed-cost rate per hour, \$144,000 ÷ 4,000 hours	\$36 per hour
Budgeted variable-cost rate per hour	30 per hour
Budgeted total-cost rate per hour	\$66 per hour

Using the same procedures for the single-rate and dual-rate methods as in the previous section, Materials Management Department costs allocated to operating departments are as follows:

Single-Rate Method	
Machining Department: \$66 per hour × 1,200 (actual) hours	\$ 79,200
Assembly Department: \$66 per hour × 2,400 (actual) hours	158,400
Fixed costs of unused Materials Management Department capacity:	
\$36 per hour × 400 hours[a]	14,400
Total Materials Management Department costs	\$252,000

[a]400 hours = Practical capacity of 4,000 − (1,200 hours used by Machining Department + 2,400 hours used by Assembly Department)

Dual-Rate Method	
Machining Department	
Fixed costs: \$36 per hour × 800 (budgeted) hours	\$ 28,800
Variable costs: \$30 per hour × 1,200 (actual) hours	36,000
Total costs	\$ 64,800

Assembly Department	
Fixed costs: $36 per hour × 2,800 (budgeted) hours	$100,800
Variable costs: $30 per hour × 2,400 (actual) hours	72,000
Total costs	$172,800
Fixed costs of unused Materials Management Department capacity:	
$36 per hour × 400 hours[b]	$ 14,400
Total Materials Management Department costs ($64,800 + $172,800 + $14,400)	$252,000

[b]400 hours = Practical capacity of 4,000 hours − (800 hours budgeted to be used by Machining Department + 2,800 hours budgeted to be used by Assembly Department)

When a company uses practical capacity to allocate costs, the single-rate method allocates only the *actual* fixed-cost resources used by the Machining and Assembly Departments, while the dual-rate method allocates the *budgeted* fixed-cost resources to be used by the operating departments. Cost of unused Materials Management Department resources are highlighted but not allocated to departments.[2]

Using practical capacity to allocate costs focuses management's attention on managing unused capacity (see Chapter 9, pages 339–340, and Chapter 13, pages 542–543). Using practical capacity also avoids burdening the user departments with the cost of unused capacity of the Materials Management Department. In contrast, allocating costs on the basis of the demand for materials-handling services, assigns all $144,000 of budgeted fixed costs, including the cost of unused capacity, to user departments. If costs are used as a basis for pricing, charging user departments for unused capacity could result in the downward demand spiral (see pages 340–341).

Resource consumption accounting (RCA), a management accounting system, employs an allocation procedure similar to a dual-rate system. For each cost/resource pool, cost assignment rates for fixed costs are based on practical capacity supplied, while variable costs of a resource pool use a budgeted rate.[3]

We next discuss advantages and disadvantages of the single-rate and dual-rate methods.

Advantages and Disadvantages of Single-Rate Method

Advantages: (1) The single-rate method is less costly to implement because it avoids the expensive analysis of classifying individual cost items into fixed and variable categories. **(2) It offers user departments some operational control over the charges they bear** by conditioning the final allocations on the actual usage of support services, rather than on uncertain forecasts of expected demand.

Disadvantage: The single-rate method may lead operating department managers to make suboptimal decisions that are in their own best interest but inefficient from the standpoint of the organization as a whole. This occurs because under the single-rate method, allocated fixed costs of the support department appear as variable costs to the operating departments. In the Robinson Company example, each user department is charged $70 per hour (or $66 per hour based on practical capacity) under the single-rate method where $40 (or $36) relates to the allocated fixed costs of the Materials Management Department. Suppose an external provider offers the Machining Department materials-handling labor services at a rate of $55 per hour, at a time when the Materials Management Department has unused capacity. The Machining Department's managers would be tempted to use this vendor because it would lower the department's costs ($55 per hour instead of the $70 per hour internal charge). In the short run, however, fixed costs of the Materials Management Department remain unchanged

[2] In our example, the costs of unused capacity under the single-rate and the dual-rate methods are the same (each equals $14,400). This occurs because the total actual usage of the facility matches the total budgeted usage of 3,600 hours. The budgeted cost of unused capacity (in the dual-rate method) can be either greater or lower than the actual cost of unused capacity (in the single-rate method), depending on whether the total budgeted usage is lower or higher than the actual usage.

[3] Other important features of resource consumption accounting (RCA) include (1) the selective use of activity-based costing, (2) the nonassignment of fixed costs when causal relationships cannot be established, and (3) the depreciation of assets based on their replacement cost. RCA has its roots in the nearly 50-year-old German cost accounting system called Grenzplankostenrechnung (GPK), which is used by organizations such as Mercedes-Benz, Porsche, and Stihl. For further details, as well as illustrations of the use of RCA and GPK in organizations, see Sally Webber and Douglas B. Clinton, "Resource Consumption Accounting Applied: The Clopay Case," *Management Accounting Quarterly* (Fall 2004); and Brian Mackie, "Merging GPK and ABC on the Road to RCA," *Strategic Finance* (November 2006).

in the relevant range (between 3,000 hours of usage and the practical capacity of 4,000 hours). Robinson will incur an additional cost of $25 per hour by accepting this offer—the difference between the $55 per hour external purchase price and the internal variable cost of $30 per hour of the Materials Management Department.

Advantages and Disadvantages of Dual-Rate Method

Advantages: (1) The dual-rate method guides department managers to make decisions that benefit both the organization as a whole and each department because it signals to department managers that variable costs and fixed costs behave differently. By charging the fixed costs of resources budgeted to be used by the operating departments as a lump sum, the dual-rate method succeeds in removing fixed costs from the operating department managers' consideration when making marginal decisions to outsource services. Operating department managers will only use an external provider of material-handling services if it costs less than the $30 variable cost per hour charged by the Materials Management Department. The dual-rate method therefore avoids the potential conflict of interest that can arise under the single-rate method. **(2) Allocating fixed costs based on budgeted usage helps user departments with both short-run and long-run planning because user departments know the costs allocated to them in advance.** Companies commit to infrastructure costs (such as the fixed costs of a support department) on the basis of a long-run planning horizon; budgeted usage measures the long-run demands of the user departments for support-department services.

Disadvantages: (1) The dual-rate method requires managers to distinguish variable costs from fixed costs, which is often a challenging task. (2) The dual-rate method does not measure the cost of fixed support department resources actually used by operating departments because fixed costs are allocated based on budgeted rather than actual usage. For example, the Machining Department manager is allocated fixed costs of the Materials Management Department based on budgeted usage of 800 labor-hours even though the Machining Department actually uses 1,200 labor-hours. **(3) Allocating fixed costs on the basis of budgeted long-run usage may tempt some managers to underestimate budgeted usage.** Underestimating budgeted usage leads to lower allocation of fixed costs (assuming all other operating department managers do not similarly underestimate usage). If all user department managers underestimate usage, it will lead to Robinson underestimating total support department needs. To discourage such underestimates, companies reward managers who make accurate forecasts of long-run usage—the "carrot" approach. Other companies impose cost penalties—the "stick" approach—for underestimating long-run usage by charging a higher cost rate if an operating department exceeds its budgeted usage.

DECISION POINT

When should managers use the dual-rate method over the single-rate method?

TRY IT! 16-1

Amp Corporation has one support department, Engineering Services, and two production departments, Machining and Assembly. The following data relate to the 2020 budget for the Engineering Services Department:

Practical capacity	16,000 hours
Fixed costs of the Engineering Services Department in the12,000 labor-hour to 16,000 labor-hour relevant range	$560,000
Budgeted usage (quantity) of engineering services labor-hours required to support the productions departments:	
Machining department	5,000 hours
Assembly department	9,000 hours
Total	14,000 hours
Budgeted variable cost per engineering services labor-hour in the 12,000 labor-hour to 16,000 labor-hour relevant range	$ 25 per hour used
Actual usage (quantity) of Engineering Services labor-hours required to support the production departments:	
Machining department	4,000 hours
Assembly department	8,000 hours
Total	12,000 hours

1. Using the single-rate method, calculate the cost to be allocated to the Machining and Assembly Departments if the allocation rate is based on budgeted costs and budgeted quantity of Engineering Services and allocated based on actual Engineering Services hours used in each department.
2. Using the dual-rate method, calculate the cost to be allocated to the Machining and Assembly Departments if (a) variable costs are allocated based on the budgeted variable cost per hour for actual hours used in each department and (b) fixed costs are allocated based on budgeted fixed costs per hour and the budgeted number of hours for each department.
3. Using the single-rate method, calculate the cost to be allocated to the Machining and Assembly Departments if the allocation rate is based on budgeted costs and practical capacity of the Engineering Services Department and allocated based on actual Engineering Services hours used in each department.
4. Using the dual-rate method, calculate the cost to be allocated to the Machining and Assembly Departments if (a) variable costs are allocated based on the budgeted variable cost per hour for actual hours used in each department and (b) the fixed-cost allocation rate is based on budgeted costs and practical capacity of Engineering Services Department and fixed costs are allocated based on budgeted Engineering Service hours in each department.

Budgeted Versus Actual Costs and the Choice of Allocation Base

In this section, we examine in greater detail the decision about using actual or budgeted costs, and actual or budgeted usage as the allocation base. These choices have a significant impact on the cost allocated to each operating department and the incentives of the operating department managers.

LEARNING OBJECTIVE 2

Understand how the choice between allocation based on budgeted and actual rates

... budgeted rates provide certainty to users about charges and motivate the support division to control costs

and between budgeted and actual usage can affect the incentives of division managers

... budgeted usage helps in planning and efficient utilization of fixed resources; actual usage controls consumption of variable resources

Budgeted Versus Actual Rates

In both the single-rate and dual-rate methods, Robinson uses budgeted rates to assign support department costs (fixed as well as variable costs) to user departments. An alternative approach would be to use actual rates based on the support costs realized during the period. This method is much less common because it imposes uncertainty on user departments. When allocations are made using budgeted rates, managers of departments to which costs are allocated know with certainty the rates to be used in that budget period. Users can then determine the amount of the service to request and—if company policy allows—whether to use the internal resource or an external vendor. In contrast, when actual rates are used for cost allocation, user department managers do not know the costs allocated to the departments until the end of the budget period.

Budgeted rates also help motivate the manager of the support (or supplier) department to improve efficiency. The support department, not the user departments, bears the cost of any unfavorable variances. User departments do not pay for any costs or inefficiencies of the supplier department that cause actual rates to exceed budgeted rates.

The manager of the supplier department would likely view budgeted rates negatively if unfavorable cost variances occur due to price increases outside his or her control. Some organizations try to identify these uncontrollable factors and do not hold the support department manager responsible for these variances. In other organizations, the supplier department and the user department agree to share the risk (through an explicit formula) of a large, uncontrollable increase in the prices of inputs of the supplier department. This avoids imposing risk completely on the supplier department (when budgeted rates are used) or the user department (when actual rates are used).

For the rest of this chapter, we focus only on allocation methods based on budgeted rates.

Budgeted Versus Actual Usage

In both the single-rate and dual-rate methods, variable costs are assigned on the basis of budgeted rates and actual usage because variable costs are directly and causally linked to usage. Allocating variable costs on the basis of budgeted usage would provide user departments with no incentive to control consumption of support services.

What about fixed costs? Consider the \$144,000 budgeted fixed costs of the Materials Management Department of Robinson Company. Budgeted usage is 800 hours for the Machining Department and 2,800 hours for the Assembly Department. Assume that actual usage of the Machining Department equals budgeted usage. Consider three cases:

Case 1: Actual usage by the Assembly Department equals budgeted usage.

Case 2: Actual usage by the Assembly Department is greater than budgeted usage.

Case 3: Actual usage by the Assembly Department is lower than budgeted usage.

Fixed-Cost Allocation Based on Budgeted Rates and Budgeted Usage

When budgeted usage is the allocation base, regardless of the actual usage of facilities (i.e., whether Case 1, 2, or 3 occurs), user departments receive a preset lump-sum fixed-cost charge as in the dual-rate procedure discussed earlier. If rates are calculated based on budgeted usage at \$40 per hour (\$144,000 ÷ 3,600 hours), the Machining Department is assigned \$32,000 (\$40 per hour × 800 hours) and the Assembly Department, \$112,000 (\$40 per hour × 2,800 hours). If rates are set using practical capacity at \$36 per hour (\$144,000 ÷ 4,000 hours), the Machining Department is charged \$28,800 (\$36 per hour × 800 hours), the Assembly Department is allocated \$100,800 (\$36 per hour × 2,800 hours), and the remaining \$14,400 (\$36 per hour × 400 hours) is the unallocated cost of excess capacity.

Fixed-Cost Allocation Based on Budgeted Rates and Actual Usage

Column 2 of Exhibit 16-1 shows the allocations when the budgeted rate is based on budgeted usage (\$40 per hour), while column 3 shows the allocations when practical capacity is used to derive the budgeted rate (\$36 per hour). Note that each operating department's fixed-cost allocation varies based on its actual usage of support facilities. However, variations in actual usage in one department do not affect the costs allocated to the other department. The Machining Department is allocated either \$32,000 or \$28,800, depending on the budgeted rate chosen, independent of the Assembly Department's actual usage.

This allocation procedure for fixed costs is exactly the same as the allocation procedure under the single-rate method. The procedure therefore shares the advantages of the single-rate method, such as advanced knowledge of budgeted rates, as well as control over the costs charged to the operating departments based on actual usage.[4]

The procedure in column (2) also shares the disadvantages of the single-rate method discussed in the previous section. When the budgeted rate (of \$40 per hour) is calculated based on budgeted usage, user departments are charged for the cost of unused capacity. Consider Case 1 when actual usage equals budgeted usage of 3,600 materials-handling labor-hours and is less than the practical capacity of 4,000 labor-hours. In this case, all \$144,000 (\$32,000 + \$112,000) of fixed costs of the Materials Management Department are allocated to the operating departments even though the Materials Management Department has idle capacity. On the other hand, when actual usage (4,000 labor-hours) is more than the budgeted amount (3,600 labor-hours) as in Case 2, a total of \$160,000 (\$32,000 + \$128,000) is allocated, which is more than the fixed costs of \$144,000. This results in overallocation of fixed costs requiring end-of period adjustments, as discussed in Chapters 4 and 8. If, however, practical capacity is used to calculate the budgeted rate (of \$36 per hour), as in column (3),

[4] The total amount of fixed costs allocated to departments will in general not equal the actual realized costs. Adjustments for overallocations and underallocations would then be made using the methods discussed previously in Chapters 4, 7, and 8.

EXHIBIT 16-1 Effect of Variations in Actual Usage on Fixed-Cost Allocation to Operating Divisions

	(1) Actual Usage		(2) Budgeted Rate Based on Budgeted Usage[a]		(3) Budgeted Rate Based on Practical Capacity[b]		(4) Allocation of Budgeted Total Fixed Cost	
Case	**Mach. Dept.**	**Assmb. Dept.**	**Mach. Dept.**	**Assmb. Dept.**	**Mach. Dept.**	**Assmb. Dept.**	**Mach. Dept.**	**Assmb. Dept.**
1	800 hours	2,800 hours	\$ 32,000	\$ 112,000	\$ 28,800	\$ 100,800	\$ 32,000[c]	\$ 112,000[d]
2	800 hours	3,200 hours	\$ 32,000	\$ 128,000	\$ 28,800	\$ 115,200	\$ 28,800[e]	\$ 115,200[f]
3	800 hours	2,400 hours	\$ 32,000	\$ 96,000	\$ 28,800	\$ 86,400	\$ 36,000[g]	\$ 108,000[h]

[a] $\frac{\$144,000}{(800 + 2,800) \text{ hours}} = \$40 \text{ per hour}$ [b] $\frac{\$144,000}{4,000 \text{ hours}} = \$36 \text{ per hour}$ [c] $\frac{800}{(800 + 2,800)} \times \$144,000$ [d] $\frac{2,800}{(800 + 2,800)} \times \$144,000$

[e] $\frac{800}{(800 + 3,200)} \times \$144,000$ [f] $\frac{3,200}{(800 + 3,200)} \times \$144,000$ [g] $\frac{800}{(800 + 2,400)} \times \$144,000$ [h] $\frac{2,400}{(800 + 2,400)} \times \$144,000$

user departments are only charged for the actual resources of the Materials Management Department used by the operating departments and not for the costs of unused capacity.

As noted earlier, allocating fixed costs based on actual usage induces conflicts of interest when evaluating outsourcing possibilities. The Machining and Assembly Departments can reduce fixed costs allocated to them by reducing the actual usage of Materials Management Department services. That's because the allocated fixed costs of the Materials Management Department appear as variable costs to the operating departments. From the point of view of the company as a whole, however, the fixed costs of the Materials Management Department will not be saved if the operating departments do not use the services of the Materials Management Department. Any variable cost paid to an outside supplier, even if it is lower than the allocated fixed costs, will increase Robinson's total costs.

Allocating Budgeted Fixed Costs Based on Actual Usage

In this case, a budgeted fixed-cost rate is not calculated. Instead, the budgeted fixed costs of \$144,000 of the Materials Management Department are allocated to the Machining and Assembly Departments based on the actual labor-hours used by the Machining and Assembly Departments as shown in Exhibit 16-1, column 4.

- In Case 1, the fixed costs allocated to the Machining Department equal the amount in column 2 calculated based on a budgeted rate and budgeted usage.
- In Case 2, the fixed costs allocated to the Machining Department are \$3,200 less than the amount in column 2 calculated based on a budgeted rate and budgeted usage (\$28,800 versus \$32,000).
- In Case 3, the fixed costs allocated to the Machining Department are \$4,000 more than the amount in column 2 calculated based on a budgeted rate and budgeted usage (\$36,000 versus \$32,000).

Why is the Machining Department allocated \$4,000 more of the fixed costs of the Materials Management Department in Case 3, even though its actual usage equals its budgeted usage? Because total fixed costs of \$144,000 are now spread over 400 fewer hours of actual total usage. The lower usage by the Assembly Department leads to an increase in fixed costs allocated to the Machining Department. When budgeted fixed costs are allocated based on actual usage, user departments will not know their fixed-cost allocations until the end of the budget period. This method shares the same flaw as methods that rely on the use of actual cost rates rather than budgeted cost rates.

To summarize, there are strong economic and motivational reasons for companies to use the dual-rate allocation procedure described in the previous section.

DECISION POINT

What factors should managers consider when deciding between allocation based on budgeted and actual rates and budgeted and actual usage?

Allocating Costs of Multiple Support Departments

LEARNING OBJECTIVE 3

Allocate multiple support-department costs using the direct method,

... allocates support-department costs directly to operating departments

the step-down method,

... partially allocates support-department costs to other support departments

and the reciprocal method

... fully allocates support-department costs to other support departments

In this section, we consider multiple support departments and the cost-allocation problems that arise when two or more support departments provide reciprocal support to each other and to operating departments. An example of reciprocal support of support departments is Robinson's Materials Management Department providing materials-handling labor services to all other departments, including the Engineering and Production Control Department, while also utilizing the services of the Engineering and Production Control Department for managing materials-handling equipment and scheduling materials movement to the production floor. More accurate support-department cost allocations result in more accurate product, service, and customer costs.

Exhibit 16-2, column 6, provides details of Robinson's total budgeted manufacturing overhead costs of $1,120,000 for 2020 (see page 112), for example, supervision salaries, $200,000; depreciation and maintenance, $193,000; indirect labor, $195,000; and rent, utilities, and insurance, $160,000. Robinson allocates the $1,120,000 of total budgeted manufacturing overhead costs to the Machining and Assembly Departments in several steps.

Step A: Trace or Allocate Each Cost to Various Support and Operating Departments. Exhibit 16-2, columns 1 through 5, show calculations for this step. For example, supervision salaries are traced to the departments in which the supervisors work. As described on page 31, supervision costs are an indirect cost of individual jobs because supervisory costs cannot be traced to individual jobs. They are a direct cost of the different departments, however, because

EXHIBIT 16-2 Details of Budgeted Manufacturing Overhead at Robinson Company for 2020 and Allocation of Plant Administration Department Costs

	A	B	C	D	E	F	G
1		Support Departments			Operating Departments		
2	Step A	Plant Administration Department (1)	Engineering and Production Control Department (2)	Materials Management Department (3)	Machining Department (4)	Assembly Department (5)	Total (6)
3	Plant manager's salary	$ 92,000					$ 92,000
4	Supervision salaries (traced to each department)		$ 48,000	$ 40,000	$ 52,000	$ 60,000	200,000
5	Engineering salaries (traced to each department)		110,000	36,000	60,000	24,000	230,000
6	Depreciation and maintenance (traced to each department)		39,000	55,000	79,000	20,000	193,000
7	Indirect materials (traced to each department)		20,000	12,000	11,000	7,000	50,000
8	Indirect labor (traced to each department)		43,000	77,000	37,000	38,000	195,000
9	Rent, utilities, and insurance (allocated to each department based on square feet area; $8[1] × 1,000; 2,000; 3,000; 8,000; 6,000 sq. ft.)	8,000	16,000	24,000	64,000	48,000	160,000
10	Total	$ 100,000	$276,000	$244,000	$303,000	$197,000	$1,120,000
11							
12	Step B						
13	Allocation of plant administration costs 0.50[2] × $48,000; $40,000; $52,000; $60,000	(100,000)	24,000	20,000	26,000	30,000	
14		$ 0	$300,000	$264,000	$329,000	$227,000	
15	[1]$160,000 ÷ 20,000 total square feet area = $8 per square foot						
16	[2]Plant administration cost-allocation rate $= \frac{\text{Total plant administration costs}}{\text{Total supervision salaries}} = \frac{\$100,000}{\$200,000} = 0.50$						

they can be identified with each department in an economically feasible way. Rent, utilities, and insurance costs cannot be traced to each department because these costs are incurred for all of Robinson's manufacturing facility. These costs are therefore allocated to different departments on the basis of the square feet area—the cost driver for rent, utilities, and insurance costs (Row 9).

Step B: Allocate Plant Administration Costs to Other Support Departments and Operating Departments. Plant administration supports supervisors in each department, so plant administration costs are allocated to departments on the basis of supervision costs.

Some companies prefer not to allocate plant administration costs to jobs, products, or customers because these costs are fixed and independent of the level of activity in the plant. However, most companies, like Robinson, allocate plant administration costs to departments and jobs, products, or customers to calculate the full manufacturing costs of products. Robinson calculates the plant administration cost-allocation rate as follows:

$$\frac{\text{Plant administration}}{\text{cost-allocation rate}} = \frac{\text{Total plant administration costs}}{\text{Total supervision salaries}} = \frac{\$100{,}000}{\$200{,}000} = 0.50$$

In Step B of Exhibit 16-2, Robinson uses the 0.50 cost-allocation rate and supervision salaries to allocate plant administration costs to other support and operating departments.

Step C: Allocate Engineering and Production Control and Materials Management Costs to the Machining and Assembly Operating Departments. The two support departments whose costs are being allocated—Engineering and Production Control and Materials Management—provide reciprocal support to each other and to operating departments. That is, the Engineering and Production Control Department serves the Materials Management Department (for example, engineering services for materials-handling equipment and scheduling material movements), while the Materials Management Department serves the Engineering and Production Control Department (for example, delivering materials).

Consider the Materials Management Department. From Exhibit 16-2, the total budgeted cost of the Materials Management Department equals $264,000. We can also calculate this cost using the fixed and variable cost classification of the previous section. The Materials Management Department is budgeted to provide 800 hours of materials-handling labor services to the Machining Department and 2,800 hours of materials-handling labor services to the Assembly Department. In this section, we further assume that the Materials Management Department will provide an additional 400 hours of materials-handling labor services to the Engineering and Production Control Department. Recall from the previous section that the Materials Management Department has budgeted fixed costs (for example, plant administration, depreciation, and rent) of $144,000 and budgeted variable costs (for example, indirect materials, indirect labor, and maintenance) of $30 per labor-hour. Total budgeted costs of the Materials Management Department equals $264,000 [$144,000 + $30 per labor-hour × (800 + 2,800 + 400) labor-hours] as shown in Exhibit 16-2.[5]

Exhibit 16-3 displays the data for budgeted overhead costs from Exhibit 16-2 after allocating Plant Administration Department costs but before any further interdepartment cost allocations for services provided by each support department to other departments. To understand the percentages in this exhibit, consider the Engineering and Production Control Department. This department supports the engineering activity in the other departments and so the budgeted costs of this department are allocated to the other departments based on budgeted engineering salaries— Materials Management Department, $36,000; Machining Department, $60,000; and Assembly Department, $24,000 for a total of $120,000 ($36,000 + $60,000 + $24,000) (see Exhibit 16-3). The Engineering and Production Control Department is budgeted to provide support of 30% ($36,000 ÷ $120,000 = 0.30) to the Materials Management Department, 50% ($60,000 ÷ $120,000 = 0.50) to the Machining Department, and 20% ($24,000 ÷ $120,000 = 0.20) to the Assembly Department. Similarly, the Materials

[5] The previous section assumed that the Materials Management Department only provided services to the Machining and Assembly Departments and not to the Engineering and Production Control Department, resulting in total budgeted costs of $252,000 [$144,000 + $30 per labor-hour × (800 + 2,800) labor-hours].

EXHIBIT 16-3 Data for Allocating Support Department Costs at Robinson Company for 2020

	A	B	C	D	E	F	G
1		SUPPORT DEPARTMENTS			OPERATING DEPARTMENTS		
2		Engineering and Production Control	Materials Management		Machining	Assembly	Total
3	Budgeted overhead costs						
4	before any interdepartment cost allocations	$300,000	$264,000		$329,000	$227,000	$1,120,000
5	Support work furnished:						
6	By Engineering and Production Control						
7	Budgeted engineering salaries	—	$ 36,000		$ 60,000	$ 24,000	$ 120,000
8	Percentage	—	30%		50%	20%	100%
9	By Materials Management						
10	Budgeted material-handling labor-hours	400	—		800	2,800	4,000
11	Percentage	10%	—		20%	70%	100%

Management Department is budgeted to provide a total of 4,000 material handling labor-hours of support work: 10% (400 ÷ 4,000 = 0.10) for the Engineering and Production Control Department, 20% (800 ÷ 4,000 = 0.20) for the Machining Department, and 70% (2,800 ÷ 4,000 = 0.70) for the Assembly Department.

We describe three methods of allocating budgeted overhead costs from the support departments to the operating departments: *direct, step-down*, and *reciprocal*. We use budgeted costs and budgeted hours of the operating and support departments to calculate the budgeted costs of the operating departments (Machining and Assembly) after allocation of support departments' (Materials Management and Engineering and Production Control) costs. The budgeted costs of the Machining Department are divided by the budgeted machine-hours in the Machining Department (the cost driver of Machining Department costs) and the budgeted costs of the Assembly Department are divided by the budgeted direct manufacturing labor-hours in the Assembly Department (the cost driver of Assembly Department costs) to calculate the budgeted overhead allocation rates for each operating department. These overhead rates are used to allocate overhead costs to each job as it passes through an operating department based on actual machine-hours used in the Machining Department and actual direct manufacturing labor-hours used in the Assembly Department. To simplify the explanation and to focus on concepts, we use the single-rate method to allocate the costs of each support department. (The Problem for Self-Study [page 666] illustrates the dual-rate method for allocating reciprocal support-department costs.)

Direct Method

The **direct method** allocates each support-department's budgeted costs directly to only operating departments. Support department costs are not allocated to other support departments. Exhibit 16-4 illustrates this method using the data in Exhibit 16-3. The base used to allocate Engineering and Production Control costs to operating departments is the budgeted engineering salaries in the operating departments: $60,000 + $24,000 = $84,000. This amount excludes the $36,000 of budgeted engineering salaries in the Materials Management Department. The budgeted cost of the Engineering and Production Control Department of $300,000 is allocated to the Machining Department and the Assembly Department in the ratio ($60,000 ÷ $84,000, $24,000 ÷ 84,000) or (5/7, 2/7). The Machining Department is allocated 5/7 × $300,000 = $214,286 and the Assembly Department is allocated

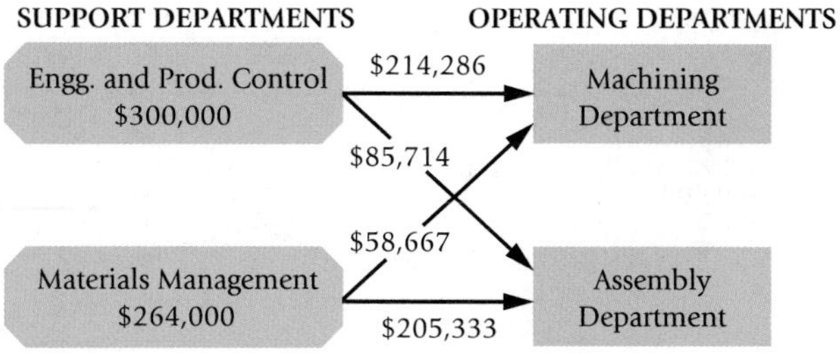

EXHIBIT 16-4

Direct Method of Allocating Support-Department Costs at Robinson Company for 2020

	A	B	C	D	E	F	G
1		SUPPORT DEPARTMENTS			OPERATING DEPARTMENTS		
2		Engineering and Production Control	Materials Management		Machining	Assembly	Total
3	Budgeted overhead costs						
4	before any interdepartment cost allocations	$300,000	$264,000		$329,000	$227,000	$1,120,000
5	Allocation of Engg. And Prod. Control (5/7, 2/7)[a]	(300,000)			214,286	85,714	
6	Allocation of Materials Management (2/9, 7/9)[b]		(264,000)		58,667	205,333	
7							
8	Total budgeted overhead of operating departments	$ 0	$ 0		$601,953	$518,047	$1,120,000
9							
10	[a] Base is ($60,000 + $24,000), or $84,000; $60,000 ÷ $84,000 = 5/7; $24,000 ÷ $84,000 = 2/7.						
11	[b] Base is (800 + 2,800), or 3,600 hours; 800 ÷ 3,600 = 2/9; 2,800 ÷ 3,600 = 7/9.						

2/7 × $300,000 = $85,714. Similarly, the base used to allocate the budgeted cost of the Materials Management Department to the operating departments is 800 + 2,800 = 3,600 budgeted materials-handling labor-hours in the operating departments, excluding the 400 budgeted materials-handling labor-hours in the Engineering and Production Control Department.

An equivalent approach to implementing the direct method is to calculate a budgeted rate for each support department. For example, the budgeted cost rate for the Engineering and Production Control Department is ($300,000 ÷ $84,000), or 357.143%. The Machining Department is then allocated $214,286 (357.143% × $60,000), while the Assembly Department is allocated $85,714 (357.143% × $24,000). For ease of computation and explanation throughout this section, we use the fraction of the support department services used by other departments to allocate support department costs, rather than budgeted cost rates.

The direct method is simple and easy to use. Managers do not need to predict the usage of support department services by other support departments. Its disadvantage is that it ignores information about reciprocal services provided among support departments and can therefore lead to inaccurate estimates of the cost of operating departments. We next examine a second approach, which partially recognizes the services provided among support departments.

Step-Down Method

The **step-down method**—also called the **sequential allocation method**—allocates support-department costs to other support departments and operating departments in a sequential manner that partially recognizes the mutual services provided among support departments.

Exhibit 16-5 shows the step-down method. The Engineering and Production Control budgeted costs of $300,000 are allocated first—30% to the Materials Management Department, 50% to the Machining Department, and 20% to the Assembly Department (see Exhibit 16-3).

EXHIBIT 16-5

Step-Down Method of Allocating Support-Department Costs at Robinson Company for 2020

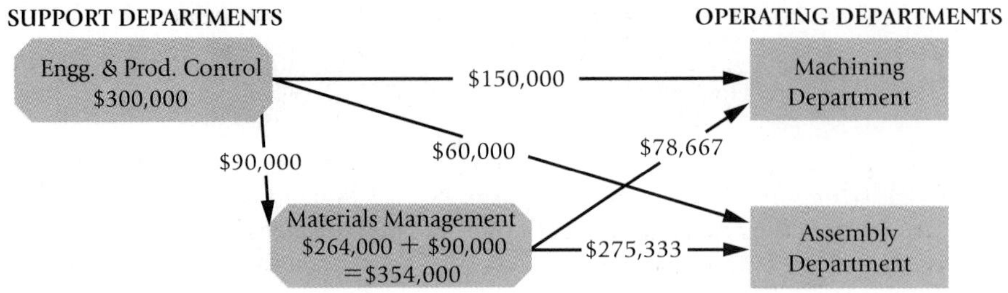

	SUPPORT DEPARTMENTS			OPERATING DEPARTMENTS		
	Engineering and Production Control	**Materials Management**		**Machining**	**Assembly**	**Total**
Budgeted overhead costs before any						
interdepartment cost allocations	$300,000	$264,000		$329,000	$227,000	$1,120,000
Allocation of Engg. and Prod. Control (3/10, 5/10, 2/10)[a]	(300,000)	90,000		150,000	60,000	
		354,000				
Allocation of Materials Management (2/9, 7/9)[b]		(354,000)		78,667	275,333	
Total budgeted overhead of operating departments	$ 0	$ 0		$557,667	$562,333	$1,120,000

[a] Base is ($36,000 + $60,000 + $24,000), or $120,000 ; $36,000 ÷ $120,000 = 3/10; $60,000 ÷ $120,000 = 5/10; $24,000 ÷ $120,000 = 2/10.

[b] Base is (800 + 2,800), or 3,600 hours; 800 ÷ 3,600 = 2/9; 2,800 ÷ 3,600 = 7/9.

Therefore, $90,000 is allocated to Materials Management (30% of $300,000), $150,000 to Machining (50% of $300,000), and $60,000 to Assembly (20% of $300,000). The Materials Management Department budgeted costs now total $354,000: budgeted costs of the Materials Management Department before any interdepartmental cost allocations, $264,000, plus $90,000 from the allocation of Engineering and Production Control Department costs to the Materials Management Department. The $354,000 is then only allocated to the two operating departments in the proportion of 800:2,800 materials-handling labor-hours in the Machining Department and the Assembly Department, respectively (see Exhibit 16-3). The Machining Department is allocated $78,667 (800/3,600 × $354,000) is and the Assembly Department is allocated $275,333 (2,800/3,600 × $354,000).

This method requires managers to rank (sequence) the support departments in the order that the step-down allocation is to proceed. In our example, the budgeted costs of the Engineering and Production Control Department were allocated first. Different sequences will result in different allocations of support-department costs to operating departments, for example, if the Materials Management Department costs had been allocated first and the Engineering and Production Control Department costs second. A popular step-down sequence begins with the support department that renders the highest percentage of its total services to *other support departments*, continues with the department that renders the next-highest percentage, and so on, ending with the support department that renders the lowest percentage.[6] In our example, budgeted costs of the Engineering and Production Control Department

[6] An alternative approach to selecting the sequence of allocations is to begin with the support department that renders the highest dollar amount of services to other support departments. The sequence ends with the allocation of the costs of the department that renders the lowest dollar amount of services to other support departments.

were allocated first because it provides 30% of its services to the Materials Management Department, whereas the Materials Management Department provides only 10% of its services to the Engineering and Production Control Department (see Exhibit 16-3).

Under the step-down method, once a support department's costs have been allocated to other departments, such as the costs of the Engineering and Production Control Department allocated to Materials Management, Machining, and Assembly Departments, no subsequent support-department costs are allocated back to it. The result is that the step-down method does not recognize the total services that support departments provide to *each other*. The reciprocal method fully recognizes all such services, as we will see next.

Reciprocal Method

The **reciprocal method** allocates support-department costs to operating departments by fully recognizing the mutual services provided among all support departments. For example, the reciprocal method fully incorporates the engineering services provided by the Engineering and Production Control Department to the Materials Management Department and the material-handling services provided by the Materials Management Department to the Engineering and Production Control Department.

Exhibit 16-6 presents one way to understand the reciprocal method as an extension of the step-down method. First, Engineering and Production Control Department budgeted costs are allocated to all other departments, including the Materials Management Support Department (Materials Management, 30%; Machining, 50%; Assembly, 20%). The budgeted costs of the Materials Management Department then total $354,000 ($264,000 + $90,000

EXHIBIT 16-6 Reciprocal Method of Allocating Support-Department Costs Using Repeated Iterations at Robinson Company for 2020

	A	B	C	D	E	F	G
1		Engineering and					
2		Production Control	Materials Management		Machining Department	Assembly Department	Total
3	Budgeted overhead costs before any						
4	interdepartment cost allocations	$300,000	$264,000		$329,000	$227,000	$1,120,000
5	1st Allocation of Engg. and Prod. Control (3/10,5/10,2/10)[a]	(300,000)	90,000		150,000	60,000	
6			354,000				
7	1st Allocation of Materials Management (1/10,2/10,7/10)[b]	35,400	(354,000)		70,800	247,800	
8	2nd Allocation of Engg. and Prod. Control (3/10,5/10,2/10)[a]	(35,400)	10,620		17,700	7,080	
9	2nd Allocation of Materials Management (1/10,2/10,7/10)[b]	1,062	(10,620)		2,124	7,434	
10	3rd Allocation of Engg. and Prod. Control (3/10,5/10,2/10)[a]	(1,062)	319		531	212	
11	3rd Allocation of Materials Management (1/10,2/10,7/10)[b]	32	(319)		63	224	
12	4th Allocation of Engg. and Prod. Control (3/10,5/10,2/10)[a]	(32)	10		16	6	
13	4th Allocation of Materials Management (1/10,2/10,7/10)[b]	1	(10)		2	7	
14	5th Allocation of Engg. and Prod. Control (3/10,5/10,2/10)[a]	(1)	0		1	0	
15							
16	Total budgeted overhead of operating departments	$ 0	$ 0		$570,237	$549,763	$1,120,000
17							
18	Total support department amounts allocated and reallocated (the numbers in parentheses in the first two columns):						
19	Engineering and Production Control: $300,000 + $35,400 + $1,062 + $32 + $1 = $336,495						
20	Materials Management: $354,000 + $10,620 + $319 + $10 = $364,949						
21							
22	[a]Base is $36,000 + $60,000 + $24,000 = $120,000; $36,000 ÷ $120,000 = 3/10; $60,000 ÷ $120,000 = 5/10; $24,000 ÷ $120,000 = 2/10						
23	[b]Base is 400 + 800 + 2,800 = 4,000 labor-hours; 400 ÷ 4,000 = 1/10; 800 ÷ 4,000 = 2/10; 2,800 ÷ 4,000 = 7/10						

from the first-round allocation), as in Exhibit 16-5. The $354,000 is then allocated to all other departments that the Materials Management Department supports, including the Engineering and Production Control Support Department—Engineering and Production Control, 10%; Machining, 20%; and Assembly, 70% (see Exhibit 16-3). The Engineering and Production Control Department budgeted costs that had been brought down to $0 now have $35,400 from the Materials Management Department allocation. Engineering and Production Control Department costs are again reallocated to all other departments (Materials Management, 30%; Machining, 50%; Assembly, 20%) as previously allocated. Now the Materials Management Department budgeted costs that had been brought down to $0 have $10,620 from the Engineering and Production Control Department allocations. Materials Management Department costs are again reallocated to all departments (Engineering and Production Control, 10%; Machining, 20%; and Assembly, 70%) as previously allocated. Successive rounds result in smaller and smaller amounts being allocated to and reallocated from the support departments until eventually all support-department costs are allocated to the Machining Department and the Assembly Department.

An alternative way to implement the reciprocal method is to formulate and solve linear equations. This implementation requires three steps.

Step 1: Express Support-Department Budgeted Costs and Reciprocal Relationships in the Form of Linear Equations. Let *EPC* be the *complete reciprocated costs* of the Engineering and Production Control Department and *MM* be the *complete reciprocated costs* of the Materials Management Department. **Complete reciprocated costs** are support department costs plus any interdepartmental cost allocations. We express the data in Exhibit 16-3 as:

$$EPC = \$300{,}000 + 0.1\,MM \qquad (1)$$

$$MM = \$264{,}000 + 0.3\,EPC \qquad (2)$$

The 0.1 *MM* term in equation 1 is the budgeted percentage of the Materials Management Department services *used by* the Engineering and Production Control Department. The 0.3 *EPC* term in equation 2 is the budgeted percentage of Engineering and Production Control Department services *used by* the Materials Management Department. Complete reciprocated costs in equations 1 and 2 are also called **artificial costs** of the support departments.

Step 2: Solve the Set of Linear Equations to Obtain the Complete Reciprocated Budgeted Costs of Each Support Department. Substituting equation 1 into 2:

$$\begin{aligned} MM &= \$264{,}000 + [0.3\,(\$300{,}000 + 0.1\,MM)] \\ MM &= \$264{,}000 + \$90{,}000 + 0.03\,MM \\ 0.97\,MM &= \$354{,}000 \\ MM &= \$364{,}949 \end{aligned}$$

Substituting this into equation 1:

$$\begin{aligned} EPC &= \$300{,}000 + 0.1\,(\$364{,}949) \\ EPC &= \$300{,}000 + \$36{,}495 = \$336{,}495 \end{aligned}$$

The complete reciprocated costs or artificial costs are budgeted to be $364,949 for the Materials Management Department and $336,495 for the Engineering and Production Control Department. The complete-reciprocated-cost figures also appear at the bottom of Exhibit 16-6 as the total amounts allocated and reallocated from the Materials Management Department and the Engineering and Production Control Department. When there are more than two support departments with reciprocal relationships, software programs help calculate the complete reciprocated costs of each support department. Because the calculations involve finding the inverse of a matrix, the reciprocal method is also sometimes referred to as the **matrix method**.[7]

[7] If there are n support departments, then Step 1 will yield n linear equations. Solving the equations to calculate the complete reciprocated costs then requires finding the inverse of an $n \times n$ matrix.

Step 3: Allocate the Complete Reciprocated Budgeted Costs of Each Support Department to All Other Departments (Both Support Departments and Operating Departments) on the Basis of the Budgeted Usage Percentages (Based on Total Units of Service Provided to All Departments). Consider the Materials Management Department. The complete reciprocated budgeted costs of $364,949 are allocated as follows:

To Engineering and Production Control Department (1 / 10) × $364,949	= $ 36,495
To Machining Department (2 / 10) × $364,949	= $ 72,990
To Assembly Department (7 / 10) × $364,949	= $255,464
Total	$364,949

Similarly, the $336,495 in reciprocated budgeted costs of the Engineering and Production Control Department are allocated to the Materials Management Department (3/10), Machining Department (5/10), and Assembly Department (2/10).

Exhibit 16-7 presents summary data based on the reciprocal method.

Robinson's $701,444 complete reciprocated budgeted costs of the support departments exceed the budgeted amount of $564,000.

Support Department	Complete Reciprocated Budgeted Costs	Budgeted Costs	Difference
Engineering and Production Control	$336,495	$300,000	$ 36,495
Materials Management	364,949	264,000	100,949
Total	$701,444	$564,000	$137,444

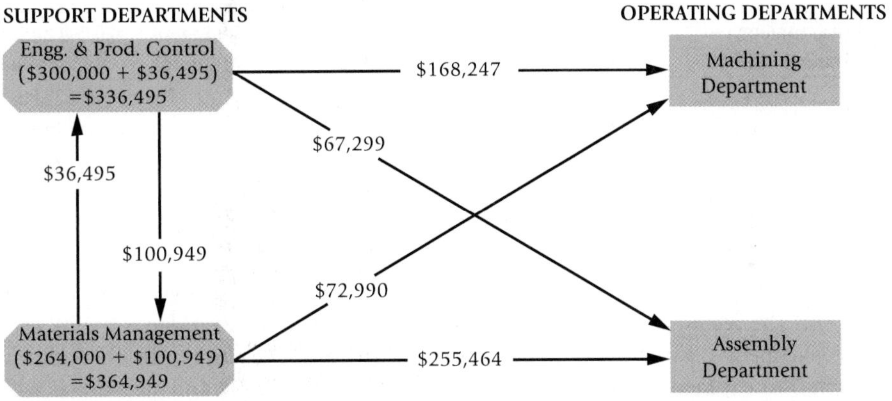

EXHIBIT 16-7

Reciprocal Method of Allocating Support-Department Costs Using Linear Equations at Robinson Company for 2020

	A	B	C	D	E	F	G
1		SUPPORT DEPARTMENTS			OPERATING DEPARTMENTS		
2		Engineering and Production Control	Materials Management		Machining	Assembly	Total
3	Budgeted overhead costs before any						
4	interdepartment cost allocations	$300,000	$264,000		$329,000	$227,000	$1,120,000
5	Allocation of Engg. & Prod. Control (3/10, 5/10, 2/10)[a]	(336,495)	100,949		168,247	67,299	
6	Allocation of Materials Management (1/10, 2/10, 7/10)[b]	36,495	(364,949)		72,990	255,464	
7							
8	Total budgeted overhead of operating departments	$ 0	$ 0		$570,237	$549,763	$1,120,000
9							
10	[a]Base is ($36,000 + $60,000 + $24,000), or $120,000 ; $36,000 ÷ $120,000 = 3/10; $60,000 ÷ $120,000 = 5/10; $24,000 ÷ $120,000 = 2/10.						
11	[b]Base is (400 + 800 + 2,800), or 4,000 hours; 400 ÷ 4,000 = 1/10; 800 ÷ 4,000 = 2/10; 2,800 ÷ 4,000 = 7/10.						

Each support department's complete reciprocated budgeted cost is greater than the budgeted amount because it takes into account that support costs are allocated to all departments using its services and not just to operating departments. This step ensures that the reciprocal method fully recognizes all interrelationships among support departments, as well as relationships between support and operating departments. The difference between complete reciprocated budgeted costs and budgeted costs for each support department reflects the costs allocated among support departments. The total budgeted costs allocated to the operating departments under the reciprocal method are still only $564,000 ($168,247 + $67,299 allocated from the Engineering and Production Control Department and $72,990 + $255,464 allocated from the Materials Management Department, see Exhibit 16-7).

Overview of Methods

Robinson uses the budgeted costs of each operating department (Machining and Assembly) to compute the rate per unit of each cost-allocation base used to allocate the indirect costs to a job (Step 5 in a job-costing system, see Chapter 4). Robinson budgets 20,000 direct manufacturing labor-hours for the Assembly Department (of the 28,000 total budgeted direct manufacturing labor-hours) and 10,000 machine-hours for the Machining Department.

The budgeted overhead allocation rates for each operating department by allocation method are as follows:

	Total Budgeted Overhead Costs After Allocation of All Support-Department Costs		Budgeted Overhead Rate per Hour for Product-Costing Purposes	
Support Department Cost-Allocation Method	Machining	Assembly	Machining (10,000 budgeted machine-hours)	Assembly (20,000 budgeted labor-hours)
Direct	$601,953	$518,047	$60.20	$25.90
Step-down	557,667	562,333	55.77	28.12
Reciprocal	570,237	549,763	57.02	27.49

The amount of budgeted manufacturing overhead costs allocated to the Machining and Assembly Departments differs by the method used to allocate support-department costs. Differences among costs allocated to the operating departments using the three methods increase (1) if the reciprocal allocations are large and (2) if operating departments use each support department's service in different proportions. In our example, the final allocations under the reciprocal method are in between those under the direct and step-down methods (see above). In general, there is no relationship among the costs allocated to the operating departments under the different methods. The method of allocation is particularly important in cost-reimbursement contracts that require allocation of support-department costs. To avoid disputes, managers should always clarify the method to be used. For example, Medicare reimbursements and federal government research contracts with universities that allow for recovery of indirect costs typically mandate the step-down method, with explicit requirements about the order and the costs that can be included in the indirect-cost pools.

The reciprocal method is conceptually the most precise method because it considers the mutual services provided among all support departments. The advantage of the direct and step-down methods is that they are simple for managers to compute and understand relative to the reciprocal method. If the costs allocated to operating departments using the direct or step-down methods closely approximate the costs allocated using the reciprocal method, managers should use the simpler direct or step-down methods. However, as computing power to perform repeated iterations (as in Exhibit 16-6) or to solve sets of simultaneous equations (as on page 654) increases, more companies will find the reciprocal method easier to implement.

Another advantage of the reciprocal method is that it highlights the complete reciprocated costs of support departments and how these costs differ from the budgeted or actual costs of the departments. Knowing the complete reciprocated costs of a support department is a key input for decisions about whether to outsource services that the support department provides.

Suppose all of Robinson's support-department costs are variable costs. Consider a third party's bid to provide all services currently provided by the Materials Management Department. Do not compare the bid to the expected (budgeted) $264,000 costs of the Materials Management Department. The complete reciprocated costs of the Materials Management Department, which include the services the Engineering and Production Control Department provides the Materials Management Department, are $364,949 to deliver 4,000 hours of materials-handling labor to other departments at Robinson. The complete reciprocated cost for materials-handling labor is $91.24 per hour ($364,949 ÷ 4,000 hours). Other things being equal, an external provider's bid to supply the same materials management services as Robinson's internal department at less than $364,949, or $91.24 per hour (even if much greater than $264,000) would improve Robinson's operating income.

To see this point, note that the relevant savings from closing down the Materials Management Department are $264,000 of Materials Management Department costs *plus* $100,949 of expected Engineering and Production Control Department costs (see Exhibit 16-7). By shutting down the Materials Management Department, Robinson will no longer incur the 30% of reciprocated Engineering and Production Control Department costs (equal to $100,949) that were incurred to support the Materials Management Department. Therefore, the total expected cost savings are $364,949 ($264,000 + 100,949).[8] Neither the direct nor the step-down method can provide this relevant information for outsourcing decisions.

Calculating the Cost of Job WPP 298

The next step in a job-costing system (Step 6, see Chapter 4) is to compute the indirect costs allocated to a job. For the WPP 298 job, Robinson actually uses 40 machine-hours in the Machining Department and 55 labor-hours in the Assembly Department (out of 88 direct manufacturing labor-hours). The overhead costs allocated to the WPP 298 job under the three methods would be

Direct:	$3,833 ($60.20 × 40 + $25.90 × 55)
Step-down:	$3,777 ($55.77 × 40 + $28.12 × 55)
Reciprocal:	$3,793 ($57.02 × 40 + $27.49 × 55)

The manufacturing overhead costs allocated to WPP 298 differ only a little under the three methods because the WPP 298 job requires roughly equal amounts of machine-hours and assembly labor-hours. These differences would be larger if a job required many more machine-hours than assembly hours or vice versa.

Using normal costing and multiple cost-allocation bases results in higher indirect manufacturing costs allocated to Job WPP 298, $3,793 (under the reciprocal method) compared to $3,520 allocated using direct manufacturing labor-hours as the sole allocation base in Chapter 4 (page 113). By using two cost-allocation bases—machine-hours and assembly labor-hours—Robinson is better able to model the drivers of manufacturing overhead costs.

The final step (Step 7, see Chapter 4) computes the total cost of the job by adding all direct and indirect costs assigned to the job. Under the reciprocal method, the total manufacturing costs of the WPP 298 job are

Direct manufacturing costs		
Direct materials	$4,606	
Direct manufacturing labor	1,579	$6,185
Manufacturing overhead costs		
Machining Department ($57.02 per machine-hour × 40 machine-hours)	2,281	
Assembly Department ($27.49 per labor-hour × 55 labor-hours)	1,512	3,793
Total manufacturing costs of job WPP 298		$9,978

Note that the costs in Step 7 have four dollar amounts, each corresponding respectively to the two direct-cost and two indirect-cost categories in the costing system.

[8] Technical issues when using the reciprocal method in outsourcing decisions are discussed in Robert S. Kaplan and Anthony A. Atkinson, *Advanced Management Accounting*, 3rd ed. (Upper Saddle River, NJ: Prentice Hall, 1998), pp. 73–81.

DECISION POINT

What methods can managers use to allocate costs of multiple support departments to operating departments?

At the end of the year, actual manufacturing overhead costs of the Machining Department and the Assembly Department would be compared to the manufacturing overhead allocated for each department. To calculate the actual manufacturing overhead costs of the Machining and Assembly Departments, Robinson would need to allocate the *actual* (rather than budgeted) costs of the Materials Management and Engineering and Production Control Departments to the *actual* costs of the Machining and Assembly Departments using the methods described in this chapter. Management accountants would then make end-of-year adjustments (pages 125–130) separately for each cost pool for under- or overallocated overhead costs.

TRY IT! 16-2

Traxx Tours provides guided educational tours to college alumni associations. The company is divided into two operating divisions: domestic tours and world tours. Each of the tour divisions uses the services of the company's two support departments: Administration and Information Technology. Additionally, the Administration and Information Technology departments use the services of each other. Data concerning the past year are as follows:

	Support Departments		Operating Departments		
	Administration	Information Technology	Domestic Tours	World Tours	Total
Budgeted overhead costs before any interdepartment cost allocations	$400,000	$300,000	$1,350,000	$1,860,000	$3,910,0000
Support work furnished:					
By Administration					
Budgeted Administration salaries	—	$ 80,000	$ 50,000	$ 70,000	$ 200,000
Percentage	—	40%	25%	35%	100%
By Information Technology					
Budgeted IT service hours	400	—	2,800	800	4,000
Percentage	10%	—	70%	20%	100%

What are the total overhead costs of the operating departments (domestic and world tours) *after* the support department costs of Administration and Information Technology have been allocated using (1) the direct method, (2) the step-down method (allocate Administration first), (3) the step-down method (allocate Information Technology first), and (4) the reciprocal method using the method of repeated iterations and linear equations?

Allocating Common Costs

LEARNING OBJECTIVE 4

Allocate common costs using the stand-alone method

... uses cost information of each user as a separate entity to allocate common costs

and the incremental method

... allocates common costs primarily to one user and the remainder to other users

Management accountants must sometimes allocate *common costs*. A **common cost** is the cost of operating a facility, activity, or cost object when that facility, activity, or cost object is shared by two or more users. Common costs arise because each user incurs a lower cost by sharing a facility or activity than operating the facility or performing the activity independently. The cost accounting challenge is how to allocate common costs to each user in a reasonable way.

Consider Jason Stevens, a graduating senior in Seattle who has been invited to a job interview with an employer in Albany. The round-trip Seattle–Albany airfare costs $1,200. A week later, Stevens is also invited to an interview with an employer in Chicago. The Seattle–Chicago round-trip airfare costs $800. Stevens decides to combine the two recruiting trips into a Seattle–Albany–Chicago–Seattle trip that will cost $1,500 in airfare. The prospective employers will reimburse Stevens for the airfare. The $1,500 is a common cost that benefits both prospective employers because it is less than the $2,000 ($1,200 + $800) that the employers would have to pay if Stevens interviewed with them independently.

How should Stevens allocate common costs of $1,500 to the two employers? Two methods of allocating common costs are the stand-alone method and the incremental method.

Stand-Alone Cost-Allocation Method

The **stand-alone cost-allocation method** determines the weights for cost allocation by considering each user of the common cost facility or activity as a separate entity. For the common-cost airfare of \$1,500, information about the separate (stand-alone) round-trip airfares (\$1,200 and \$800) is used to determine the allocation weights:

$$\text{Albany employer: } \frac{\$1{,}200}{\$1{,}200 + \$800} \times \$1{,}500 = 0.60 \times \$1{,}500 = \$900$$

$$\text{Chicago employer: } \frac{\$800}{\$800 + \$1{,}200} \times \$1{,}500 = 0.40 \times \$1{,}500 = \$600$$

Advocates of this method often emphasize the fairness or equity criterion described in Exhibit 14-1 (page 565). The method is viewed as reasonable because each employer bears a proportionate share of total costs in relation to the individual stand-alone costs.

Incremental Cost-Allocation Method

The **incremental cost-allocation method** ranks the individual users of a cost object in the order of users most responsible for the common cost and then uses this ranking to allocate cost among those users. The first-ranked user of the cost object is the *primary user* (also called the *primary party*) and is allocated costs up to the costs of the primary user as a stand-alone user. The second-ranked user is the *first-incremental user* (*first-incremental party*) and is allocated the additional cost that arises from two users instead of only the primary user. The third-ranked user is the *second-incremental user* (*second-incremental party*) and is allocated the additional cost that arises from three users instead of two users, and so on.

We illustrate this method for Jason Stevens and his \$1,500 airfare cost. Assume the Albany employer is viewed as the primary party because Stevens's had already committed to go to Albany before accepting the invitation to interview in Chicago. The cost allocations would be

Party	Costs Allocated	Cumulative Costs Allocated
Albany (primary)	\$1,200	\$1,200
Chicago (incremental)	300 (\$1,500 − \$1,200)	\$1,500
Total	\$1,500	

The Albany employer is allocated the full Seattle–Albany airfare. The unallocated part of the total airfare is then allocated to the Chicago employer. If the Chicago employer had been chosen as the primary party, the cost allocations would have been Chicago \$800 (the stand-alone round-trip Seattle–Chicago airfare) and Albany \$700 (\$1,500 − \$800). When there are more than two parties, this method requires them to be ranked from first to last (such as by the date on which each employer invited the candidate to interview).

Under the incremental method, the primary party typically receives the highest allocation of the common costs. The difficulty with the method is that every user prefers to be viewed as the incremental party!

One approach to address this challenge is to use the *Shapley value method*, which considers each party as first the primary party and then the incremental party. From the calculations shown earlier, the Albany employer is allocated \$1,200 as the primary party and \$700 as the incremental party, for an average of \$950 [(\$1,200 + \$700) ÷ 2]. The Chicago employer is allocated \$800 as the primary party and \$300 as the incremental party, for an average of \$550 [(\$800 + 300) ÷ 2]. The Shapley value method allocates, to each employer, the average of the costs allocated as the primary party and as the incremental party: \$950 to the Albany employer and \$550 to the Chicago employer.[9]

[9] For further discussion of the Shapley value method, see Joel S. Demski, "Cost Allocation Games," in *Joint Cost Allocations*, ed. Shane Moriarity (University of Oklahoma Center for Economic and Management Research, 1981); Lech Krus′ and Piotr Bronisz, "Cooperative Game Solution Concepts to a Cost Allocation Problem," *European Journal of Operational Research* 122:2 (April 16, 2000): 258–271.

As our discussion suggests, allocating common costs is not clear-cut and can cause disputes. Whenever feasible, managers should specify the rules for such allocations in advance. If this is not done, then, rather than blindly follow one method or another, managers should exercise judgment when allocating common costs by thinking carefully about allocation methods that are fair to each party. For instance, Stevens must choose an allocation method for his airfare cost that is acceptable to each prospective employer and does not exceed the maximum reimbursable amount of airfare for either employer.

DECISION POINT

What methods can managers use to allocate common costs to two or more users?

TRY IT! 16-3

Travis Inc. and Vilk Inc. are two small clothing companies that are considering leasing a dyeing machine together. The companies estimated that in order to meet production, Travis needs the machine for 1,100 hours and Vilk needs it for 900 hours. If each company rents the machine on its own, the fee will be $80 per hour of usage. If they rent the machine together, the fee will decrease to $75 per hour of usage.

1. Calculate Travis's and Vilk's respective share of fees under the stand-alone cost-allocation method.
2. Calculate Travis's and Vilk's respective share of fees using the incremental cost-allocation method assuming (a) Travis ranked as the primary party and (b) Vilk ranked as the primary party.
3. Calculate Travis's and Vilk's respective share of fees using the Shapley value method.
4. Which method would you recommend Travis and Vilk use to share the fees?

Cost Allocations and Contract Disputes

LEARNING OBJECTIVE 5

Explain the importance of explicit agreement between contracting parties when the reimbursement amount is based on costs incurred

... to avoid disputes regarding allowable cost items and how indirect costs should be allocated

Many commercial contracts include clauses based on cost accounting information and cost allocations. Examples include the following:

- A contract between the Department of Defense and a company designing and assembling a new fighter plane specifies that the price paid for the plane will be based on the contractor's direct and overhead costs plus a fixed fee.
- A contract between a consulting firm and a hospital specifies that the consulting firm receives a fixed fee plus a share of the cost savings that arise from implementing the consulting firm's recommendations.

Contract disputes often arise over cost computations, for example, what costs should be included to calculate the costs specified in the contracts above. Managers can reduce disputes between contracting parties by explicitly writing the "rules of the game" into the contract. Such rules could include the definition of allowable cost items; the definitions of terms used, such as what constitutes direct labor; the permissible cost-allocation bases; and how to account for differences between budgeted and actual costs.

The U.S. government reimburses most contractors in one of two main ways:

1. **The contractor is paid a set price without analysis of actual contract cost data.** This approach is used, for example, when there is competitive bidding, when there is adequate price competition, or when there is an established catalog with prices quoted for items sold in substantial quantities to the general public.
2. **The contractor is paid based on an analysis of actual contract cost data.** In some cases, the nature of the task, for example, a new weapon system, creates great uncertainty about the cost to complete a job. Such contracts, which often involve billions of dollars, are rarely subject to competitive bidding because no contractor is willing to assume all the risk of receiving a fixed price for the contract and subsequently incurring high costs to fulfill it. Setting a fixed price for the contract either will not attract contractors or will require a contract price that is very high to cover uncertain costs. To address this issue, the government typically assumes a major share of the risk of the potentially high costs of completing the contract. Rather than setting selling prices, the government negotiates contracts on the basis of *costs plus a fixed fee*. This arrangement is called a *cost-plus contract*.

CONCEPTS IN ACTION

Contract Disputes Over Reimbursable Costs With the U.S. Government[10]

David Coleman/Have Camera Will Travel North America/ Alamy Stock Photo

The U.S. government spends billions of dollars annually with private companies for health care goods and services. In recent years, the government has pursued cases against several contractors for overcharging against these contracts. The following examples are from cases pursued by the U.S. Department of Justice's Civil Division on behalf of the federal government.

- Mylan, a drug manufacturer, paid $465 million to resolve allegations that it underpaid contractually obligated rebates to the Medicaid program by erroneously classifying its brand-name drug EpiPen as a generic to avoid its obligation to pay higher rebates. From 2010 to 2016, the price of EpiPen increased 400%, yet Mylan only paid a fixed 13% rebate to Medicaid over the same time period based on EpiPen's misclassification as a generic pharmaceutical.
- Hospital chain Health Management Associates agreed to pay $216 million to settle claims that it incorrectly billed government health care programs for more-costly inpatient services that should have been billed as less-costly observation or outpatient services.

[10] *Source:* Press releases from the U.S. Department of Justice, Civil Division (2017–2018).

Cost-plus contracts specify what costs are allowable. An **allowable cost** is a cost that the contract parties agree to include in the costs to be reimbursed. For example, only economy-class airfares are allowable in many U.S. government contracts. Contracts also identify cost categories that are unallowable. For example, the costs of lobbying activities and alcoholic beverages are not allowable costs in U.S. government contracts. However, the set of allowable costs is not always clear-cut. Contract disputes and allegations about overcharging the government arise from time to time across a range of areas including health care (see Concepts in Action: Contract Disputes Over Reimbursable Costs With the U.S. Government).

Some allowable overhead costs, such as supervision costs, support many different contracts and activities. Government regulations stipulate that supervision costs would be allocable to a specific contract on a cause-and-effect or benefits received basis. Other allowable overhead costs, such as general administration costs, support many contracts and are difficult to allocate based on cause-and-effect or benefits received. Nonetheless, the contracting parties may still view it as "reasonable" or "fair" to allocate these costs in some manner to help establish a contract amount. The general rule for government cost-plus contracts is that the reimbursement amount is based on actual allocable costs plus a fixed fee.[11]

All contracts with U.S. government agencies must comply with cost accounting standards issued by the **Cost Accounting Standards Board (CASB)**. For government contracts, the CASB has the exclusive authority to make, put into effect, amend, and rescind cost accounting standards and interpretations. The standards are designed to achieve *uniformity* and *consistency* in the measurement, assignment, and allocation of costs to government contracts within the United States.[12] The standards represent the complex interplay of political considerations and accounting principles. Terms such as *fairness* and *equity*, as well as cause and effect and benefits received, are relevant to and a part of government contracts.

DECISION POINT

How can contract disputes over reimbursement amounts based on costs be reduced?

[11] The Federal Acquisition Regulation, March 2019 (see www.acquisition.gov/far/current/pdf/FAR.pdf) includes the following definition of *allocability* (in FAR 31.201-4): "A cost is allocable if it is assignable or chargeable to one or more cost objectives on the basis of relative benefits received or other equitable relationships. Subject to the foregoing, a cost is allocable to a Government contract if it:
(a) Is incurred specifically for the contract;
(b) Benefits both the contract and other work, and can be distributed to them in reasonable proportion to the benefits received; or
(c) Is necessary to the overall operation of the business, although a direct relationship to any particular cost objective cannot be shown."

[12] Details on the Cost Accounting Standards Board are available at www.whitehouse.gov/omb/procurement/casb.html. The CASB is part of the Office of Federal Procurement Policy, U.S. Office of Management and Budget.

LEARNING OBJECTIVE 6

Understand how bundling of products

... two or more products sold for a single price

causes revenue allocation issues

... need to allocate revenues to each product in the bundle to evaluate managers of individual products

and the methods managers use to allocate revenues

... the stand-alone method, the incremental method, or the Shapley value method

Bundled Products and Revenue Allocation Methods

Revenue allocation issues arise when revenues from multiple products (for example, different software programs or cable and Internet packages) are bundled together and sold at a single price. The methods for revenue allocation parallel those described for common-cost allocations.

Bundling and Revenue Allocation

Revenues are inflows of assets (almost always cash or accounts receivable) received for products or services provided to customers. Similar to cost allocation, **revenue allocation** occurs when revenues are related to a particular *revenue object* but cannot be traced to it in an economically feasible (cost-effective) way. A **revenue object** is anything for which a separate measurement of revenue is desired. Examples of revenue objects include products, customers, and divisions. We illustrate revenue-allocation issues for Dynamic Software Corporation, which develops, sells, and supports three software programs:

1. WordMaster, a word-processing program, released 36 months ago
2. DataMaster, a spreadsheet program, released 18 months ago
3. FinanceMaster, a budgeting and cash-management program, released 6 months ago with a lot of favorable media attention

Dynamic Software sells these three products individually as well as bundled together.

A **bundled product** is a package of two or more products (or services) that is sold for a single price but whose individual components may be sold as separate items at their own "stand-alone" prices. The price of a bundled product is typically less than the sum of the prices of the individual products sold separately. For example, banks often provide individual customers with a bundle of services from its different departments (checking, safe-deposit box, and investment advisory) for a single fee. A resort hotel may offer, for a single amount per customer, a weekend package that includes services from its lodging (the room), food (the restaurant), and recreational (golf and tennis) departments. When department managers have revenue or profit responsibilities for individual products, the bundled revenue must be allocated among the individual products in the bundle.

Dynamic Software allocates revenues from its bundled product sales (called "suite sales") to individual products. Individual-product profitability is used to compensate software engineers and product managers responsible for developing and managing each product.

How should Dynamic Software allocate suite revenues to individual products? Consider information pertaining to the three "stand-alone" and "suite" products in 2020:

	Selling Price	Manufacturing Cost per Unit
Stand-alone		
WordMaster	$125	$18
DataMaster	150	20
FinanceMaster	225	25
Suite		
Word + Data	$220	
Word + Finance	280	
Finance + Data	305	
Word + Finance + Data	380	

Just as we saw in the section on common-cost allocations, the two main revenue-allocation methods are the stand-alone method and the incremental method.

Stand-Alone Revenue-Allocation Method

The **stand-alone revenue-allocation method** uses product-specific information on the products in the bundle as weights for allocating the bundled revenues to the individual products. The term *stand-alone* refers to the product as a separate (nonsuite) item. Consider the Word + Finance suite which sells for $280 and assume Dynamic Software sells equal quantities of WordMaster and FinanceMaster. Three types of weights for the stand-alone method are as follows:

1. **Selling prices.** Using the individual selling prices of \$125 for WordMaster and \$225 for FinanceMaster, the weights for allocating the \$280 suite revenues between the products are as follows:

$$\text{WordMaster: } \frac{\$125}{\$125 + \$225} \times \$280 = 0.357 \times \$280 = \$100$$

$$\text{FinanceMaster: } \frac{\$225}{\$125 + \$225} \times \$280 = 0.643 \times \$280 = \$180$$

2. **Unit costs.** This method uses the costs of the individual products (in this case, manufacturing cost per unit) to determine the weights for the revenue allocations.

$$\text{WordMaster: } \frac{\$18}{\$18 + \$25} \times \$280 = 0.419 \times \$280 = \$117$$

$$\text{FinanceMaster: } \frac{\$25}{\$18 + \$25} \times \$280 = 0.581 \times \$280 = \$163$$

3. **Physical units.** This method gives each product unit in the suite the same weight when allocating suite revenue to individual products. Therefore, with two products in the Word + Finance suite, each product is allocated 50% of the suite revenues.

$$\text{WordMaster: } \frac{1}{1+1} \times \$280 = 0.50 \times \$280 = \$140$$

$$\text{FinanceMaster: } \frac{1}{1+1} \times \$280 = 0.50 \times \$280 = \$140$$

These three approaches to determining weights for the stand-alone method result in very different revenue allocations to the individual products:

Revenue-Allocation Weights	WordMaster	FinanceMaster
Selling prices	\$100	\$180
Unit costs	117	163
Physical units	140	140

Which method do managers prefer? The selling prices method is best because the weights explicitly consider the prices customers are willing to pay for the individual products. Weighting approaches that use revenue information better capture "benefits received" by customers than unit costs or physical units.[13] The physical-units revenue-allocation method is used when managers cannot use any of the other methods (such as when selling prices are unstable or unit costs are difficult to calculate for individual products).[14]

Incremental Revenue-Allocation Method

The **incremental revenue-allocation method** ranks individual products in a bundle according to criteria determined by management and then uses this ranking to allocate bundled revenues

[13] Revenue-allocation issues also arise in external reporting. The AICPA's Statement of Position 97-2 (Software Revenue Recognition) states that with bundled products, revenue allocation "based on vendor-specific objective evidence (VSOE) of fair value" is required. The "price charged when the element is sold separately" is said to be "objective evidence of fair value" (see "Statement of Position 97-2," Jersey City, NJ: AICPA, 1998). In September 2009, the Financial Accounting Standards Board ratified Emerging Issues Task Force Issue 08-1, specifying that with no VSOE or third-party evidence of selling price for all units of accounting in an arrangement, the consideration received for the arrangement should be allocated to the separate units based upon their estimated relative selling prices. Revenue allocation is an important and integral issue in the new revenue recognition standards that became effective in 2018.

[14] If Dynamic Software sells 80,000 units of WordMaster and 20,000 units of FinanceMaster in the most recent quarter and Dynamic Software's managers believe that sales of the Word + Finance suite are four times more likely to be driven by WordMaster than FinanceMaster (80,000 ÷ 20,000), the revenue-allocation methods can be adapted to put four times more weight on WordMaster compared to Finance Master. Using selling prices results in the following allocations:

$$\text{WordMaster: } \frac{\$125 \times 4}{\$125 \times 4 + \$225 \times 1} \times \$280 = 0.690 \times \$280 = \$193$$

$$\text{FinanceMaster: } \frac{\$225 \times 1}{\$125 \times 4 + \$225 \times 1} \times \$280 = 0.310 \times \$280 = \$87$$

Note that the allocations in this case are equivalent to using revenues rather than prices as the weights. Revenues of WordMaster = \$125 × 80,000 units = \$10,000,000 and revenues of FinanceMaster = \$225 × 20,000 units = \$4,500,000.

$$\text{WordMaster: } \frac{\$10,000,000}{\$10,000,000 + \$4,500,000} \times \$280 = 0.690 \times \$280 = \$193$$

$$\text{FinanceMaster: } \frac{\$4,500,000}{\$10,000,000 + \$4,500,000} \times \$280 = 0.310 \times \$280 = \$87$$

to individual products. The first-ranked product is the *primary product* in the bundle. The second-ranked product is the *first-incremental product*, the third-ranked product is the *second-incremental product*, and so on.

How do companies decide on product rankings under the incremental revenue-allocation method? Some organizations survey customers about the importance of each of the individual products in their purchase decision. For example, if one product in the bundle is an established product and the second product in the bundle is a new product, managers would rank the established product as the primary product and the new product as the first-incremental product. Other managers rank products on the basis of the recent stand-alone revenues of the individual products in the bundle. In a third approach, top managers use their knowledge or intuition to decide the rankings.

Consider again the Word + Finance suite and assume Dynamic Software sells equal quantities of WordMaster and FinanceMaster. Assume WordMaster is designated as the primary product and FinanceMaster as the first-incremental product. WordMaster is allocated 100% of its *stand-alone* revenue of \$125 and FinanceMaster is allocated the remaining revenue of \$155 (\$280 − \$125):

Product	**Revenue Allocated**	**Cumulative Revenue Allocated**
WordMaster	\$125	\$125
FinanceMaster	155 (\$280 − \$125)	\$280
Total	\$280	

If the suite price is less than or equal to the stand-alone price of the primary product, the primary product is allocated 100% of the *suite* revenue. All other products in the suite receive no allocation of revenue.

Now suppose FinanceMaster is designated as the primary product and WordMaster as the first-incremental product. Then the incremental revenue-allocation method allocates revenues of the Word + Finance suite as follows:

Product	**Revenue Allocated**	**Cumulative Revenue Allocated**
FinanceMaster	\$225	\$225
WordMaster	\$ 55 (\$280 − \$225)	\$280
Total	\$280	

The Shapley value method allocates to each product the average of the revenues allocated as the primary and first-incremental products:

WordMaster:	(\$125 + \$55) ÷ 2 = \$180 ÷ 2 =	\$ 90
FinanceMaster:	(\$225 + \$155) ÷ 2 = \$380 ÷ 2 =	190
Total		\$280

The incremental revenue-allocation methods can be adapted if Dynamic Software sells many more units of one product relative to another.[15]

When there are more than two products in the suite, the incremental revenue-allocation method allocates suite revenues sequentially. Assume WordMaster is the primary product in Dynamic Software's three-product suite, Word + Finance + Data. FinanceMaster is the first-incremental product, and DataMaster is the second-incremental product and Dynamic Software sells equal quantities of WordMaster, FinanceMaster, and DataMaster. The suite sells for \$380. The allocation of the \$380 suite revenues proceeds as follows:

Product	**Revenue Allocated**	**Cumulative Revenue Allocated**
WordMaster	\$125	\$125
FinanceMaster	155 (\$280 − \$125)	\$280 (price of Word + Finance suite)
DataMaster	\$100 (\$380 − \$280)	\$380 (price of Word + Finance + Data suite)
Total	\$380	

[15] Suppose Dynamic Software sells 80,000 units of WordMaster and 20,000 units of FinanceMaster in the most recent quarter and its managers believe that the sales of the Word + Finance suite are four times more likely to be driven by WordMaster as the primary product. The *weighted Shapley value method* assigns four times as much weight to the revenue allocations when WordMaster is the primary product as when FinanceMaster is the primary product, resulting in the following allocations:

WordMaster:	(\$125 × 4 + \$55 × 1) ÷ (4 + 1) = \$555 ÷ 5 =	\$111
FinanceMaster:	(\$225 × 1 + \$155 × 4) ÷ (4 + 1) = \$845 ÷ 5 =	169
Total		\$280

Now suppose WordMaster is the primary product, DataMaster is the first-incremental product, and FinanceMaster is the second-incremental product.

Product	Revenue Allocated	Cumulative Revenue Allocated
WordMaster	$125	$125
DataMaster	95 ($220 − $125)	$220 (price of Word + Data suite)
FinanceMaster	160 ($380 − $220)	$380 (price of Word + Data + Finance suite)
Total	$380	

The ranking of the individual products in the suite determines the revenues allocated to them. Product managers at Dynamic Software likely would have different views of how their individual products contribute to sales of the suite products. In fact, each product manager would claim to be responsible for the primary product in the Word + Finance + Data suite![16] Because the stand-alone revenue-allocation method does not require rankings of individual products in the suite, this method is less likely to cause debates among product managers.[17]

Revenue allocations are also important for tax reasons. For example, Verizon Communications Inc., the second-largest provider of telecommunications and cable services in the United States, sells each of its services—telephone, cable television, and broadband—separately and in bundled arrangements. State and local tax laws often stipulate that if a bundle is sold and the price for each line item is not split out on the consumer's bill, then all services are taxed as telephone services, which generally carries the highest tax rate. To preclude consumers from paying higher taxes on the entire package, Verizon allocates bundled service revenue to its telephone, cable television, and broadband services based on the stand-alone selling prices of these services. Consumers then pay taxes on the amounts billed for each service. Specialized software packages, such as CCH SureTax, help companies such as Verizon to properly recognize revenue according to the laws of each state.[18]

DECISION POINT

What is product bundling, and how can managers allocate revenues of a bundled product to individual products in the bundle?

16-4 TRY IT!

Axiom Company blends and sells designer fragrances. It has a Men's Fragrances Division and a Women's Fragrances Division, each with different sales strategies, distribution channels, and product offerings. Axiom is now considering the sale of a bundled product called Sync, consisting of one bottle of Him, a men's cologne, and one bottle of Her, a women's perfume, two of Axiom's very successful products. Axiom sells equal quantities of Him and Her perfume. For the most recent year, Axiom reported the following:

Product	Retail Price
Him	$40.00
Her	$60.00
Sync (Him and Her)	$90.00

1. Allocate revenue from the sale of each unit of Sync to Him and Her using the following:
   a. The stand-alone revenue-allocation method based on the selling price of each product
   b. The incremental revenue-allocation method, with Him ranked as the primary product
   c. The incremental revenue-allocation method, with Her ranked as the primary product
   d. The Shapley value method
2. Of the four methods in requirement 1, which one would you recommend for allocating Sync's revenues to Him and Her? Explain.

[16] Calculating the Shapley value method mitigates this problem because each product is considered as a primary, first-incremental, and second-incremental product. Assuming equal weights on all products, the revenue allocated to each product is an average of the revenues calculated for the product under these different assumptions. In the preceding example, the interested reader can verify that this will result in the following revenue allocations: FinanceMaster, $180; WordMaster, $87.50; and DataMaster, $112.50.

[17] To avoid the challenges of revenue allocations and to encourage departments to work together to achieve sales of bundled products, some companies credit all departments with the full revenues from the bundled product when evaluating each department's performance. Besides the problem of double-counting revenues, the issue here is that different departments may have contributed unequally to achieving the bundled revenue, yet will get credit for the same total revenue.

[18] CCH Incorporated, "CCH SureTax Communications," http://www.suretax.com/solutions/suretax-telecom, accessed July 2019; Verizon Communications Inc., 2018 Annual Reports (New York: Verizon Communications Inc., 2019).

PROBLEM FOR SELF-STUDY

This problem illustrates how costs of two corporate support departments are allocated to operating divisions using the dual-rate method. Fixed costs are allocated using budgeted costs and budgeted hours used by other departments. Variable costs are allocated using actual costs and actual hours used by other departments.

Computer Horizons reports the following budgeted and actual amounts for its two central corporate support departments (legal and personnel) that support each other and two manufacturing divisions: the laptop division (LTD) and the work station division (WSD):

	A	B	C	D	E	F	G
1		SUPPORT			OPERATING		
2		Legal Department	Personnel Department		LTD	WSD	Total
3	**BUDGETED USAGE**						
4	Legal (hours)	—	250		1,500	750	2,500
5	(Percentages)	—	10%		60%	30%	100%
6	Personnel (hours)	2,500	—		22,500	25,000	50,000
7	(Percentages)	5%	—		45%	50%	100%
8							
9	**ACTUAL USAGE**						
10	Legal (hours)	—	400		400	1,200	2,000
11	(Percentages)	—	20%		20%	60%	100%
12	Personnel (hours)	2,000	—		26,600	11,400	40,000
13	(Percentages)	5%	—		66.5%	28.5%	100%
14	Budgeted fixed overhead costs before any						
15	interdepartment cost allocations	$360,000	$475,000		—	—	$835,000
16	Actual variable overhead costs before any						
17	interdepartment cost allocations	$200,000	$600,000		—	—	$800,000

Required

What amount of support-department costs for legal and personnel will be allocated to LTD and WSD using (1) the direct method, (2) the step-down method (allocating the legal department costs first), and (3) the reciprocal method using linear equations?

Solution

Exhibit 16-8 presents the computations for allocating the fixed and variable support-department costs. A summary of these costs follows:

	Laptop Division (LTD)	Work Station Division (WSD)
(1) Direct Method		
Fixed costs	$465,000	$370,000
Variable costs	470,000	330,000
	$935,000	$700,000
(2) Step-Down Method		
Fixed costs	$458,053	$376,947
Variable costs	488,000	312,000
	$946,053	$688,947
(3) Reciprocal Method		
Fixed costs	$462,513	$372,487
Variable costs	476,364	323,636
	$938,877	$696,123

EXHIBIT 16-8 Alternative Methods of Allocating Corporate Support-Department Costs to Operating Divisions of Computer Horizons: Dual-Rate Method

Home | Insert | Page Layout | Formulas | Data | Review | View

	A	B	C	D	E	F	G
20		CORPORATE SUPPORT DEPARTMENTS			OPERATING DIVISIONS		
21	Allocation Method	Legal Department	Personnel Department		LTD	WSD	Total
22	**A. DIRECT METHOD**						
23	Fixed costs	$360,000	$475,000				
24	Legal (1,500 ÷ 2,250; 750 ÷ 2,250)	(360,000)			$240,000	$120,000	
25	Personnel (22,500 ÷ 47,500; 25,000 ÷ 47,500)		(475,000)		225,000	250,000	
26	Fixed support dept. cost allocated to operating divisions	$ 0	$ 0		$465,000	$370,000	$835,000
27	Variable costs	$200,000	$600,000				
28	Legal (400 ÷ 1,600; 1,200 ÷ 1,600)	(200,000)			$ 50,000	$150,000	
29	Personnel (26,600 ÷ 38,000; 11,400 ÷ 38,000)		(600,000)		420,000	180,000	
30	Variable support dept. cost allocated to operating divisions	$ 0	$ 0		$470,000	$330,000	$800,000
31	**B. STEP-DOWN METHOD**						
32	(Legal department first)						
33	Fixed costs	$360,000	$475,000				
34	Legal (250 ÷ 2,500; 1,500 ÷ 2,500; 750 ÷ 2,500)	(360,000)	36,000		$216,000	$108,000	
35	Personnel (22,500 ÷ 47,500; 25,000 ÷ 47,500)		(511,000)		242,053	268,947	
36	Fixed support dept. cost allocated to operating divisions	$ 0	$ 0		$458,053	$376,947	$835,000
37	Variable costs	$200,000	$600,000				
38	Legal (400 ÷ 2,000; 400 ÷ 2,000; 1,200 ÷ 2,000)	(200,000)	40,000		$ 40,000	$120,000	
39	Personnel (26,600 ÷ 38,000; 11,400 ÷ 38,000)		(640,000)		448,000	192,000	
40	Variable support dept. cost allocated to operating divisions	$ 0	$ 0		$488,000	$312,000	$800,000
41	**C. RECIPROCAL METHOD**						
42	Fixed costs	$360,000	$475,000				
43	Legal (250 ÷ 2,500; 1,500 ÷ 2,500; 750 ÷ 2,500)	(385,678)[a]	38,568		$231,407	$115,703	
44	Personnel (2,500 ÷ 50,000; 22,500 ÷ 50,000; 25,000 ÷ 50,000)	25,678	(513,568)[a]		231,106	256,784	
45	Fixed support dept. cost allocated to operating divisions	$ 0	$ 0		$462,513	$372,487	$835,000
46	Variable costs	$200,000	$600,000				
47	Legal (400 ÷ 2,000; 400 ÷ 2,000; 1,200 ÷ 2,000)	(232,323)[b]	46,465		$ 46,465	$139,393	
48	Personnel (2,000 ÷ 40,000; 26,600 ÷ 40,000; 11,400 ÷ 40,000)	32,323	(646,465)[b]		429,899	184,243	
49	Variable support dept. cost allocated to operating divisions	$ 0	$ 0		$476,364	$323,636	$800,000
50							
51	[a] FIXED COSTS	[b] VARIABLE COSTS					
52	Letting *LF* = Legal department fixed costs, and *PF* = Personnel department fixed costs, the simultaneous equations for the reciprocal method for fixed costs are	Letting *LV* = Legal department variable costs, and *PV* = Personnel department variable costs, the simultaneous equations for the reciprocal method for variable costs are					
53	$LF = \$360,000 + 0.05\ PF$	$LV = \$200,000 + 0.05\ PV$					
54	$PF = \$475,000 + 0.10\ LF$	$PV = \$600,000 + 0.20\ LV$					
55	$LF = \$360,000 + 0.05\ (\$475,000 + 0.10\ LF)$	$LV = \$200,000 + 0.05\ (\$600,000 + 0.20\ LV)$					
56	$LF = \$385,678$	$LV = \$232,323$					
57	$PF = \$475,000 + 0.10\ (\$385,678) = \$513,568$	$PV = \$600,000 + 0.20\ (\$232,323) = \$646,465$					

DECISION POINTS

The following question-and-answer format summarizes the chapter's learning objectives. Each decision presents a key question related to a learning objective. The guidelines are the answer to that question.

Decision	Guidelines
1. When should managers use the dual-rate method over the single-rate method?	The single-rate method aggregates fixed and variable costs and allocates them to objects using a single allocation base and rate. The dual-rate method groups costs into variable-cost and fixed-cost pools, each with its own cost-allocation base and rate. If costs can be separated into variable and fixed costs, the dual-rate method is preferred because it provides better information for making decisions.
2. What factors should managers consider when deciding between allocation based on budgeted and actual rates and budgeted and actual usage?	Using budgeted rates creates certainty about costs allocated to managers of user departments and insulates them from inefficiencies in the supplier department. Using budgeted variable-cost rates and actual usage charges users for resources consumed and promotes control of resource consumption. Charging fixed-cost rates based on budgeted usage helps user divisions with planning and leads to goal congruence when considering outsourcing decisions.
3. What methods can managers use to allocate costs of multiple support departments to operating departments?	Three methods managers can use are the direct, step-down, and reciprocal methods. The direct method allocates a support department's costs to operating departments without allocating costs to other support departments. The step-down method allocates support-department costs to other support departments and operating departments in a sequential manner that partially recognizes mutual services provided among support departments. The reciprocal method fully recognizes mutual services provided among all support departments.
4. What methods can managers use to allocate common costs to two or more users?	Common costs are the costs of a cost object (such as an activity) that are shared by two or more users. The stand-alone cost-allocation method uses information about each user to determine cost-allocation weights. The incremental cost-allocation method ranks individual users and allocates common costs first to the primary user and then to other incremental users. The Shapley value method considers each user, in turn, as the primary and incremental user.
5. How can contract disputes over reimbursement amounts based on costs be reduced?	Disputes can be reduced by making cost-allocation rules explicit and including them in the contract. These rules should include details such as allowable costs, acceptable cost-allocation bases, and how to account for differences between budgeted and actual costs.
6. What is product bundling, and how can managers allocate revenues of a bundled product to individual products in the bundle?	Bundling occurs when a package of two or more products (or services) is sold for a single price. Revenue allocation of the bundled price is required to evaluate managers of the individual products in the bundle. Revenues can be allocated using the stand-alone method, the incremental method, or the Shapley value method.

TERMS TO LEARN

This chapter and the Glossary at the end of the text contain definitions of the following important terms:

allowable cost (**p. 661**)
artificial costs (**p. 654**)
bundled product (**p. 662**)
common cost (**p. 658**)
complete reciprocated costs (**p. 654**)
Cost Accounting Standards Board (CASB) (**p. 661**)
direct method (**p. 650**)
dual-rate method (**p. 640**)
incremental cost-allocation method (**p. 659**)
incremental revenue-allocation method (**p. 663**)
matrix method (**p. 654**)
operating department (**p. 640**)
production department (**p. 640**)
reciprocal method (**p. 653**)
revenue allocation (**p. 662**)
revenue object (**p. 662**)
service department (**p. 640**)
single-rate method (**p. 640**)
sequential allocation method (**p. 651**)
stand-alone cost-allocation method (**p. 659**)
stand-alone revenue-allocation method (**p. 662**)
step-down method (**p. 651**)
support department (**p. 640**)

ASSIGNMENT MATERIAL

Questions

16-1 Distinguish between the single-rate and the dual-rate methods.

16-2 Describe how the dual-rate method is useful to division managers in decision making.

16-3 How do budgeted cost rates motivate the support-department manager to improve efficiency?

16-4 Give examples of allocation bases used to allocate support-department cost pools to operating departments.

16-5 Why might a manager prefer that budgeted rather than actual cost-allocation rates be used for costs being allocated to his or her department from another department?

16-6 "To ensure unbiased cost allocations, fixed costs should be allocated on the basis of estimated long-run use by user-department managers." Do you agree? Why?

16-7 Distinguish among the three methods of allocating the costs of multiple support departments to operating departments.

16-8 What is conceptually the most defensible method for allocating multiple support-department costs? Why?

16-9 Distinguish between two methods of allocating common costs.

16-10 What are the challenges of using the incremental cost allocation method when allocating common costs and how might they be overcome?

16-11 What role does the Cost Accounting Standards Board play when companies contract with the U.S. government?

16-12 What is one key way to reduce cost-allocation disputes that arise with government contracts?

16-13 Describe why companies are increasingly facing revenue-allocation decisions.

16-14 Distinguish between the stand-alone and the incremental revenue-allocation methods.

16-15 Identify and discuss arguments that individual product managers may put forward to support their preferred revenue-allocation method.

Exercises

16-16 **Single-rate versus dual-rate methods, support department.** The Cincinnati power plant that services all manufacturing departments of Eastern Mountain Engineering has a budget for the coming year. This budget has been expressed in the following monthly terms:

Manufacturing Department	Needed at Practical Capacity Production Level (Kilowatt-Hours)	Average Expected Monthly Usage (Kilowatt-Hours)
Loretta	13,000	10,000
Bently	21,000	9,000
Melboum	14,000	10,000
Eastmoreland	32,000	11,000
Total	80,000	40,000

The expected monthly costs for operating the power plant during the budget year are $20,000: $8,000 variable and $12,000 fixed.

Required

1. Assume that a single cost pool is used for the power plant costs. What budgeted amounts will be allocated to each manufacturing department if (a) the rate is calculated based on practical capacity and costs are allocated based on practical capacity and (b) the rate is calculated based on expected monthly usage and costs are allocated based on expected monthly usage?
2. Assume the dual-rate method is used with separate cost pools for the variable and fixed costs. Variable costs are allocated on the basis of expected monthly usage. Fixed costs are allocated on the basis of practical capacity. What budgeted amounts will be allocated to each manufacturing department? Why might you prefer the dual-rate method?

16-17 Single-rate method, budgeted versus actual costs and quantities. Chocolat Inc. is a producer of premium chocolate based in Palo Alto. The company has a separate division for each of its two products: dark chocolate and milk chocolate. Chocolat purchases ingredients from Wisconsin for its dark chocolate division and from Louisiana for its milk chocolate division. Both locations are the same distance from Chocolat's Palo Alto plant.

Chocolat Inc. operates a fleet of trucks as a cost center that charges the divisions for variable costs (drivers and fuel) and fixed costs (vehicle depreciation, insurance, and registration fees) of operating the fleet. Each division is evaluated on the basis of its operating income. For 2020, the trucking fleet had a practical capacity of 50 round-trips between the Palo Alto plant and the two suppliers. It recorded the following information:

	A	B	C
1		**Budgeted**	**Actual**
2	Costs of truck fleet	$115,000	$96,750
3	Number of round-trips for dark chocolate division (Palo Alto plant—Wisconsin)	30	30
4	Number of round-trips for milk chocolate division (Palo Alto plant—Louisiana)	20	15

Required

1. Using the single-rate method, allocate costs to the dark chocolate division and the milk chocolate division in these three ways.
   a. Calculate the budgeted rate per round-trip and allocate costs based on round-trips budgeted for each division.
   b. Calculate the budgeted rate per round-trip and allocate costs based on actual round-trips used by each division.
   c. Calculate the actual rate per round-trip and allocate costs based on actual round-trips used by each division.
2. Describe the advantages and disadvantages of using each of the three methods in requirement 1. Would you encourage Chocolat Inc. to use one of these methods? Explain and indicate any assumptions you made.

16-18 Dual-rate method, budgeted versus actual costs and quantities (continuation of 16-17). Chocolat Inc. decides to examine the effect of using the dual-rate method for allocating truck costs to each round-trip. At the start of 2020, the budgeted costs were

Variable cost per round-trip	$ 1,350
Fixed costs	$47,500

The actual results for the 45 round-trips made in 2020 were

Variable costs	$58,500
Fixed costs	38,250
	$96,750

Assume all other information to be the same as in Exercise 16-17.

Required

1. Using the dual-rate method, what are the costs allocated to the dark chocolate division and the milk chocolate division when (a) variable costs are allocated using the budgeted rate per round-trip and actual round-trips used by each division and when (b) fixed costs are allocated based on the budgeted rate per round-trip and round-trips budgeted for each division?
2. From the viewpoint of the dark chocolate division, what are the effects of using the dual-rate method rather than the single-rate method?

16-19 Support-department cost allocation; direct and step-down methods. Phoenix Partners provides management consulting services to government and corporate clients. Phoenix has two support departments—administrative services (AS) and information systems (IS)—and two operating departments—government consulting (GOVT) and corporate consulting (CORP). For the first quarter of 2020, Phoenix's cost records indicate the following:

	A	B	C	D	E	F	G
1		SUPPORT			OPERATING		
2		AS	IS		GOVT	CORP	Total
3	Budgeted overhead costs before any						
4	interdepartment cost allocations	$600,000	$2,400,000		$8,756,000	$12,452,000	$24,208,000
5	Support work supplied by AS (budgeted head count)	—	25%		40%	35%	100%
6	Support work supplied by IS (budgeted computer time)	10%	—		30%	60%	100%

Required

1. Allocate the two support departments' costs to the two operating departments using the following methods:
   a. Direct method
   b. Step-down method (allocate AS first)
   c. Step-down method (allocate IS first)
2. Compare and explain differences in the support-department costs allocated to each operating department.
3. What approaches might be used to decide the sequence in which to allocate support departments when using the step-down method?

16-20 Support-department cost allocation, reciprocal method (continuation of 16-19). Refer to the data given in Exercise 16-19.

Required

1. Allocate the two support departments' costs to the two operating departments using the reciprocal method. Use (a) linear equations and (b) repeated iterations.
2. Compare and explain differences in requirement 1 with those in requirement 1 of Exercise 16-19. Which method do you prefer? Why?

16-21 Direct and step-down allocation. E-books, an online book retailer, has two operating departments—corporate sales and consumer sales—and two support departments—human resources and information systems. Each sales department conducts merchandising and marketing operations independently. E-books uses number of employees to allocate human resources costs and processing time to allocate information systems costs. The following data are available for September 2020:

	A	B	C	D	E	F
1		SUPPORT DEPARTMENTS			OPERATING DEPARTMENTS	
2		Human Resources	Information Systems		Corporate Sales	Consumer Sales
3	Budgeted costs incurred before any					
4	interdepartment cost allocations	$72,700	$234,400		$998,270	$489,860
5	Support work supplied by human resources department					
6	Budgeted number of employees	—	21		42	28
7	Support work supplied by information systems department					
8	Budgeted processing time (in minutes)	320	—		1,920	1,600

Required

1. Allocate the support departments' costs to the operating departments using the direct method.
2. Rank the support departments based on the percentage of their services provided to other support departments. Use this ranking to allocate the support departments' costs to the operating departments based on the step-down method.
3. How could you have ranked the support departments differently?

16-22 Reciprocal cost allocation (continuation of 16-21). Consider E-books again. The controller of E-books reads a widely used textbook that states that "the reciprocal method is conceptually the most defensible." He seeks your assistance.

Required

1. Describe the key features of the reciprocal method.
2. Allocate the support departments' costs (human resources and information systems) to the two operating departments using the reciprocal method. Use (a) linear equations and (b) repeated iterations.
3. In the case presented in this exercise, which method (direct, step-down, or reciprocal) would you recommend? Why?

16-23 Allocation of common costs. Evan and Brett are students at Berkeley College. They share an apartment that is owned by Brett. Brett is considering subscribing to an Internet provider that has the following packages available:

Package	Per Month
A. Internet access	$75
B. Phone services	25
C. Internet access + phone services	90

Evan spends most of his time on the Internet ("everything can be found online now"). Brett prefers to spend his time talking on the phone rather than using the Internet ("going online is a waste of time"). They agree that the purchase of the $90 total package is a "win–win" situation.

Required

1. Allocate the $90 between Evan and Brett using (a) the stand-alone cost-allocation method, (b) the incremental cost-allocation method, and (c) the Shapley value method.
2. Which method would you recommend they use and why?

16-24 Allocation of common costs. John Wilkes, a self-employed consultant near Miami, receives an invitation to consult with a client in San Francisco and another client in Chicago. He decides to combine his visits, traveling from Miami to San Francisco, San Francisco to Chicago, and Chicago to Miami.

Wilkes wonders how he should allocate his travel costs between the two clients. He has collected the following data for regular round-trip fares with no stopovers:

Miami to San Francisco	$450
Miami to Chicago	$300

Wilkes paid $600 for his three-leg flight (Miami–San Francisco, San Francisco–Chicago, Chicago–Miami).

Required

1. How should Wilkes allocate the $600 airfare between the clients in San Francisco and Chicago using (a) the stand-alone cost-allocation method, (b) the incremental cost-allocation method, and (c) the Shapley value method?
2. Which method would you recommend Wilkes use and why?

16-25 Revenue allocation, bundled products. Couture Corp sells Samsung 10 cases. It has a Men's Division and a Women's Division. Couture is now considering the sale of a bundled product called Dynamic Duo consisting of Smarty, a men's case, and Sublime, a women's case. For the most recent year, Couture sold equal quantities of Smarty and Sublime and reported the following:

Home Insert Page Layout Formulas

	A	B
1	**Product**	**Retail Price**
2	Smarty	$ 40.00
3	Sublime	$ 60.00
4	Dynamic Duo (Smarty and Sublime)	$ 90.00

Required

1. Allocate revenue from the sale of each unit of Dynamic Duo to Smarty and Sublime using the following:
   a. The stand-alone revenue-allocation method based on selling price of each product
   b. The incremental revenue-allocation method, with Smarty ranked as the primary product
   c. The incremental revenue-allocation method, with Sublime ranked as the primary product
   d. The Shapley value method
2. Of the four methods in requirement 1, which one would you recommend for allocating Couture's revenues to Smarty and Sublime? Explain.

16-26 Allocation of common costs. Jim Dandy Auto Sales uses different media to advertise its products (television, radio, newspaper, Internet, and so on). At the end of 2019, the company president, Jim McKinnley, decided that corporate headquarters would negotiate and pay for all advertising costs and allocate these costs to each of the company's four sales locations based on number of vehicles sold. The managers had already drawn up their advertising plans for 2020 so the corporate plan would do the same advertising for them as they had planned. McKinnley budgeted $1.6 million of total advertising cost for 2020, which was also the actual advertising costs in 2020. If managers had done the same advertising on their own, their advertising costs and the actual number of cars sold would be as follows:

Sales Location	Actual Number of Cars Sold in 2020	Advertising Costs in 2020 if Divisions Had Bought the Advertising
East	5,600	$ 279,500
West	1,440	473,000
North	3,200	580,500
South	5,760	817,000
	16,000	$2,150,000

The manager of the East sales location, Tom Stevens, was not happy. He complained that the new allocation method was unfair and increased his advertising costs significantly. The East location sold high volumes of low-priced used cars and most of the corporate advertising budget related to new car sales.

Required

1. Show the amount of the 2020 advertising cost ($1,600,000) that would be allocated to each of the divisions under the following criteria:
   a. McKinnley's allocation method based on actual number of cars sold
   b. The stand-alone method based on the amounts divisions would have spent on their own advertising
   c. The incremental-allocation method, with divisions ranked on the basis of dollars they would have spent on advertising in 2020
2. Which method do you think is most equitable to the divisional sales managers? What other options might President Jim McKinnley have for allocating the advertising costs?

Problems

16-27 Single-rate, dual-rate, and practical capacity allocation. Henry Jackson, the new controller of United Manufacturing Company (UMC) believes that the company should use the dual rate method of allocating overhead costs of its Materials Management Department to its Machining and Assembly Departments instead of the single rate method, which the company has used since its inception 20 years ago. Jackson's Materials Management Department has an annual capacity of 6,000 labor-hours and a budgeted fixed cost of $240,000. The budgeted variable cost per labor-hour of the Materials Management Department is $20. Jackson gathers the following information:

	Machining Department	Assembly Department	Total
Budgeted usage of Materials Management labor-hours	1,250	3,750	5,000
Actual usage of Materials Management labor-hours	1,200	3,600	4,800

Required

1. Using the single-rate method, allocate Materials Management Department costs to the Machining and Assembly Departments in these three ways:
   a. Calculate the budgeted rate based on the budgeted number of Materials Management Department labor-hours and allocate costs based on the budgeted use of Materials Management labor-hours in the Machining and Assembly Departments.
   b. Calculate the budgeted rate based on the budgeted number of Materials Management Department labor-hours and allocate costs based on actual usage.
   c. Calculate the budgeted rate based on the practical capacity of Materials Management Department labor-hours and allocate costs based on actual usage.
2. Using the dual-rate method, compute the amount allocated to the Machining and Assembly Departments when (a) the budgeted fixed-cost rate is calculated using budgeted fixed costs and practical capacity of the Materials Management Department, (b) fixed costs are allocated based on

the budgeted fixed-cost rate and budgeted usage of Materials Management Department services by the Machining and Assembly Departments, and (c) variable costs are allocated using the budgeted variable-cost rate and actual usage.

3. Comment on your results in requirements 1 and 2. Discuss the advantages of the dual-rate method.

16-28 Revenue allocation. Fang Inc. produces and sells DVDs to businesspeople and students who are planning extended stays in China. It has been very successful with two DVDs: Beginning Mandarin and Conversational Mandarin. The company is introducing a third DVD, Reading Chinese Characters. It has also decided to market its new DVD in two different packages grouping the Reading Chinese Characters DVD with each of the other two language DVDs. Information about the separate DVDs and the packages follow.

DVD	Selling Price
Beginning Mandarin (BegM)	$ 63
Conversational Mandarin (ConM)	$108
Reading Chinese Characters (RCC)	$ 27
BegM + RCC	$ 70
ConM + RCC	$125

Required

1. Using selling prices, allocate revenues from the BegM + RCC package to each DVD in that package using (a) the stand-alone method; and (b) the incremental method, with BegM and RCC in turn as the primary product.
2. Using the selling prices, allocate revenues from the ConM + RCC package to each DVD in that package using (a) the stand-alone method; and (b) the incremental method, with ConM and RCC in turn as the primary product.
3. Which method is most appropriate for allocating revenues among the DVDs? Why?

16-29 Fixed-cost allocation. Central University completed construction of its newest administrative building at the end of 2020. The university's first employees moved into the building on January 1, 2021. The building consists of office space, common meeting rooms (including a conference center), a cafeteria, and even a workout room for its exercise enthusiasts. The total 2021 building space of 250,000 square feet was utilized as follows:

Usage of Space	% of Total Building Space
Office space (occupied)	52%
Vacant office space	8%
Common area and meeting space	17%
Workout room	8%
Cafeteria	15%

The new building cost the university $40 million and was depreciated using the straight-line method over 20 years with zero residual value so $2,000,000 per year. At the end of 2021, three departments occupied the building: executive offices of the president, accounting, and human resources. Each department's usage of its assigned space was as follows:

Department	Actual Office Space Used (sq. ft.)	Planned Office Space (sq. ft.)	Practical Capacity Office Space (sq. ft.)
Executive	29,900	27,500	36,000
Accounting	54,600	50,000	64,500
Human resources	45,500	47,500	49,500

Required

1. How much of the total annual building cost of $2,000,000 will be allocated in 2021 to each of the departments, if the cost is allocated to each department on the basis of the following?
   a. Actual usage of the three departments
   b. Planned office space of the three departments
   c. Practical capacity of the three departments
2. Assume that Central University allocates the total annual building cost of $2,000,000 in the following manner:
   a. All vacant office space is absorbed by the university and is not allocated to the departments.
   b. All occupied office space costs are allocated on the basis of actual square footage used by each department.
   c. All costs of the common area and meeting space, workout room, and cafeteria are allocated on the basis of a department's practical capacity.

   Calculate the cost allocated to each department in 2021 under this plan. Do you think the allocation method used here is appropriate? Explain.

16-30 Allocating costs of support departments; step-down and direct methods. The Eastern Summit Company has prepared department overhead budgets for budgeted-volume levels before allocations as follows:

Support departments:		
Building and grounds	$45,000	
Personnel	7,800	
General plant administration	36,120	
Cafeteria: operating loss	20,670	
Storeroom	18,300	$127,890
Operating departments:		
Machining	$36,000	
Assembly	60,000	96,000
Total for support and operating departments		$223,890

Management has decided that the most appropriate inventory costs are achieved by using individual-department overhead rates. These rates are developed after support-department costs are allocated to operating departments.

Bases for allocation are to be selected from the following:

Department	Direct Manufacturing Labor-Hours	Number of Employees	Square Feet of Floor Space Occupied	Indirect Manufacturing Labor-Hours	Number of Requisitions
Building and grounds	0	0	0	0	0
Personnel[a]	0	0	2,500	0	0
General plant administration	0	40	12,000	0	0
Cafeteria: operating loss	0	10	4,500	3,000	0
Storeroom	0	5	6,000	2,000	0
Machining	10,000	55	22,000	13,000	10,000
Assembly	30,000	140	203,000	26,000	8,300
Total	40,000	250	250,000	44,000	18,300

[a]Basis used is number of employees.

Required

1. Using the step-down method, allocate support-department costs. Develop overhead rates per direct manufacturing labor-hour for machining and assembly. Allocate the costs of the support departments in the order given in this problem. Use the allocation base for each support department you think is most appropriate.
2. Using the direct method, rework requirement 1.
3. Based on the following information about two jobs, determine the total overhead costs for each job by using rates developed in (a) requirement 1 and (b) requirement 2.

	Direct Manufacturing Labor-Hours	
	Machining	Assembly
Job 88	18	8
Job 89	10	20

4. The company evaluates the performance of the operating department managers on the basis of how well they managed their total costs, including allocated costs. As the manager of the Machining Department, which allocation method would you prefer from the results obtained in requirements 1 and 2? Explain.

16-31 Support-department cost allocations; single-department cost pools; direct, step-down, and reciprocal methods. The Martinez Company has two products. Product 1 is manufactured entirely in department X. Product 2 is manufactured entirely in department Y. To produce these two products, the Martinez Company has two support departments: A (a materials-handling department) and B (a power-generating department).

An analysis of the work done by departments A and B in a typical period follows:

	Used by			
Supplied by	A	B	X	Y
A	—	400	1,000	600
B	1,500	—	250	750

The work done in department A is measured by the direct labor-hours of materials-handling time. The work done in department B is measured by the kilowatt-hours of power. The budgeted costs of the support departments for the coming year are as follows:

	Department A (Materials Handling)	Department B (Power Generation)
Variable indirect labor and indirect materials costs	$300,000	$ 30,000
Supervision	90,000	50,000
Depreciation	30,000	100,000
	$420,000	$180,000
	+ Power costs	+ Materials-handling costs

The budgeted costs of the operating departments for the coming year are $2,500,000 for department X and $1,900,000 for department Y.

Supervision costs are salary costs. Depreciation in department B is the straight-line depreciation of power-generation equipment in its 19th year of an estimated 25-year useful life; it is old, but well-maintained, equipment.

Required

1. What are the allocations of costs of support departments A and B to operating departments X and Y using (a) the direct method, (b) the step-down method (allocate department A first), (c) the step-down method (allocate department B first), and (d) the reciprocal method?
2. An outside company has offered to supply all the power needed by the Martinez Company and to provide all the services of the present power department. The cost of this service will be $80 per kilowatt-hour of power. Should Martinez accept this offer? Explain.

16-32 Common costs. Jeana's Cupcake Shop and Jody's Cakes each operate a bakery close to each other in a small town in Florida. If Jeana rents ovens on her own, it will cost $40,000. If Jody rents ovens on her own, it will cost $60,000. If they consolidate baking operations and share ovens, the total cost will be $80,000.

Required

1. Calculate Jeana's and Jody's respective cost of the shared ovens under the stand-alone cost-allocation method.
2. Calculate Jeana's and Jody's respective cost of the shared ovens using the incremental cost-allocation method assuming (a) Jeana is the primary party and (b) Jody is the primary party.
3. Calculate Jeana's and Jody's respective cost of the shared ovens using the Shapley value method.
4. Which method would you recommend Jeana and Jody use to share the cost of the ovens? Why?

16-33 Stand-alone revenue allocation. Marble Company has three departments that sell furniture: the Sofa Department, the Easy Chair Department, and the Coffee Table Department. These products are sold individually and in a bundle. Marble Company sells roughly equal quantities of the three products. Managers of the three departments are evaluated on the performance of their individual departments. The individual selling prices and per unit costs of the products are as follows:

Furniture	Individual Selling Price per Unit	Cost per Unit
Sofas	$1,200	$500
Easy chairs	$ 500	$300
Coffee tables	$ 300	$200
Bundle purchase price	$1,600	

Required

1. Allocate the revenue from the furniture bundle purchase to each of the products using the stand-alone method based on the individual selling price per unit.
2. Allocate the revenue from the furniture bundle purchase to each of the products using the stand-alone method based on cost per unit.
3. Allocate the revenue from the furniture bundle purchase to each of the products using the stand-alone method based on physical units (that is, the number of individual units of product sold per bundle).
4. Which basis of allocation makes the most sense in this situation? Explain your answer.

16-34 Support-department cost allocations; single-department cost pools; direct, step-down, and reciprocal methods. Sportz, Inc., manufactures athletic shoes and athletic clothing for both amateur and professional athletes. The company has two product lines (clothing and shoes), which are produced in separate manufacturing facilities; however, both manufacturing facilities share the same support services for information technology and human resources. The following shows costs (in thousands) for each manufacturing facility and for each support department.

	Variable Costs	Fixed Costs	Total Costs by Department
Information technology (IT)	$ 1,200	$ 4,000	$ 5,200
Human resources (HR)	800	2,000	2,800
Clothing	5,000	16,000	21,000
Shoes	6,000	9,000	15,000
Total costs	$13,000	$31,000	$44,000

The total costs of the support departments (IT and HR) are allocated to the production departments (clothing and shoes) using a single rate based on the following:

Information technology:	Number of IT labor-hours worked by department
Human resources:	Number of employees supported by department

Data on the quantity of the cost-allocation bases, by department, are given as follows:

Department	IT Hours Used	Number of Employees
Clothing	10,080	440
Shoes	7,920	176
Information technology	—	184
Human resources	6,000	—

Required

1. What are the total costs of the production departments (clothing and shoes) *after* the support-department costs of information technology and human resources have been allocated using (a) the direct method, (b) the step-down method (allocate information technology first), (c) the step-down method (allocate human resources first), and (d) the reciprocal method?
2. Assume that all of the work of the IT department could be outsourced to an independent company for $97.50 per hour. If Sportz no longer operated its own IT department, 30% of the fixed costs of the IT department could be eliminated. Should Sportz outsource its IT services?

16-35 Revenue allocation, bundled products. Lintner Hotels (LH) is a five-star hotel with a world-class spa. LH has a decentralized management structure, with three divisions:

- Lodging (rooms, conference facilities)
- Food (restaurants and in-room service)
- Spa

Starting next month, LH will offer a 2-day, two-person "getaway package" for $1,200.

This deal includes the following:

	As Priced Separately
Two nights' stay	$ 900 ($450 per night)
Two spa treatments	360 ($180 per treatment)
Candlelight dinner	240 ($120 per person)
Total package value	$1,500

Christine Maple, president of the spa division, wants to know how her division would share in the $1,200 revenue from the getaway package. The spa is operating at 100% capacity. Currently, anyone booking the package is guaranteed access to a spa appointment. Maple noted that every "getaway" booking would displace $360 of other spa bookings not related to the package. She emphasized that the high demand reflected the work done by her team to keep the spa rated as one of the best spas in the world. The lodging and food divisions were not as busy and had excess capacity that the package would help them fill.

Required

1. Using selling prices, allocate the $1,200 getaway-package revenue to the three divisions using
   a. The stand-alone revenue-allocation method
   b. The incremental revenue-allocation method (with spa first, then lodging, and then food)
2. What are the pros and cons of the two methods in requirement 1?
3. Because the spa division is able to book the spa at 100% capacity, the company chief executive officer has decided to revise the getaway package to only include the lodging and food offerings shown previously. The new package will sell for $950. Allocate the revenue to the lodging and food divisions using the following:
   a. The Shapley value method
   b. The weighted Shapley value method, assuming that lodging is three times as likely to sell as the food

16-36 Support-department cost allocations; direct, step-down, and reciprocal methods. Ballantine Corporation has two operating departments: Eastern Department and Western Department. Each of the operating departments uses the services of the company's two support departments: Engineering and Information Technology. Additionally, the Engineering and Information Technology departments use the services of each other. Data concerning the past year are as follows:

	Support Departments		Operating Departments		
	Engineering	Information Technology	Eastern Department	Western Department	Total
Budgeted overhead costs before any interdepartment cost allocations	$300,000	$250,000	$650,000	$920,000	$2,120,000
Support work furnished:					
By Engineering					
Budgeted Engineering salaries	—	$ 60,000	$ 50,000	$ 90,000	$ 200,000
Percentage	—	30%	25%	45%	100%
By Information Technology					
Budgeted IT service hours	450	—	1,500	1,050	3,000
Percentage	15%	—	50%	35%	100%

Required

1. What are the total overhead costs of the operating departments (Eastern and Western) *after* the support-department costs of Engineering and Information Technology have been allocated using (a) the direct method, (b) the step-down method (allocate Engineering first), (c) the step-down method (allocate Information Technology first), and (d) the reciprocal method?
2. Which method would you recommend that Ballantine Corporation use to allocate service-department costs? Why?

Cost Allocation: Joint Products and Byproducts

17

LEARNING OBJECTIVES

1 Identify the splitoff point in a joint-cost situation and distinguish joint products from byproducts

2 Explain why joint costs are allocated to individual products

3 Allocate joint costs using four methods

4 Identify situations when the sales value at splitoff method is preferred when allocating joint costs

5 Explain why joint costs are irrelevant in a sell-or-process-further decision

6 Account for byproducts using two methods

Many companies, such as petroleum refiners, produce and sell two or more products simultaneously.

For example, ExxonMobil sells petroleum, natural gas, and raw liquefied petroleum gas (LPG), which are produced when the company extracts and refines crude oil. Similarly, health care providers offer multiple services, such as medical treatment, nursing care, and rehabilitation, to patients. The question is "How should these companies allocate costs to 'joint' products and services?" Charitable organizations also have to understand how to allocate joint costs, especially because of increased scrutiny by nonprofit watchdogs.

JOINT-COST ALLOCATION AND THE WOUNDED WARRIOR PROJECT[1]

Around the world, charities raise money from philanthropic donors to fulfil their missions. In the United States, the Wounded Warrior Project (WWP), the largest veteran's charity in the United States, raises money for programs and services for wounded military veterans. However, in 2016, WWP ousted its two top executives over a joint-cost allocation controversy.

U.S. accounting rules allow charities to allocate costs of certain fund-raising mailings as a public-interest service if the solicitations are educational and include a call to action, such as contacting public officials. The mailing costs are joint costs that must be allocated to either programs, fund raising, or administration. In 2015, WWP reported that $308 million, or 78% of its budget, went to veterans' programs—a share that charity watchdogs consider respectable. However, this amount included more than $47 million of fund-raising mailing costs allocated to programs as educational components. Without it, programming and services were only 65% of WWP's budget.

Charities argue that incurring joint costs is efficient because it combines multiple goals in a single campaign. Others argue that joint costs allow charities to overstate the program portion of its work, misleading donors into believing that more is being done for a cause than is really the case.

In 2016, when media reports surfaced WWP's joint-cost allocation and some questionable expenses, including spending

Ricky Fitchett/ZUMA Wire/Alamy Stock Photo

[1] *Sources:* Dave Phillips, "Wounded Warrior Project Spends Lavishly on Itself, Insiders Say," *The New York Times* (January 27, 2016); "Wounded Warrior Veterans Aid Group Fires Executives Over Lavish Spending," *Los Angeles Times* (March 11, 2016); Bennett Weiner, "Can Mail Appeals Also Educate and Advocate?" BBB Wise Giving Alliance, *Wise Giving Guide* (Spring 2013); Mark Hrywna, "Grassley Praises WPP Management Changes," *The NonProfit Times*, May 24, 2017.

hundreds of thousands of dollars on public relations and lobbying campaigns to deflect criticism of its spending and to fight efforts to restrict how much charities such as WPP spend on overhead, WPP fired its chief executive officer and chief operating officer. By 2017, WPP changed the calculation of its program-expense ratio to better reflect its activities.

This chapter examines methods for allocating costs to joint products. We also examine how cost numbers appropriate for one purpose, such as external reporting, may not be appropriate for other purposes, such as decisions about the further processing of joint products.

Joint-Cost Basics

LEARNING OBJECTIVE 1

Identify the splitoff point in a joint-cost situation

. . . the point at which two or more products become separately identifiable

and distinguish joint products

. . . products with high sales values

from byproducts

. . . products with low sales values

Joint costs are the costs of a production process that yields multiple products simultaneously. Distillation of coal yields coke, natural gas, and other products. The costs of distillation are joint costs. The **splitoff point** is the juncture in a joint production process when two or more products become separately identifiable, for example, when coal becomes coke, natural gas, and other products. **Separable costs** are all costs—manufacturing, marketing, distribution, and so on—incurred beyond the splitoff point that are assignable to each of the specific products identified at the splitoff point. At or beyond the splitoff point, decisions relating to the sale or further processing of each identifiable product can be made independently of decisions about the other products.

As the examples in Exhibit 17-1 show, the production processes in many industries simultaneously yield two or more products, either at the splitoff point or after further processing. In each of these examples, no individual product can be produced without the accompanying products appearing, although in some cases the proportions can be varied. Joint costing allocates the joint costs to the individual products that are eventually sold.

The outputs of a joint production process can be classified into two general categories: outputs with a positive sales value and outputs with a zero sales value.[2] For example, offshore processing of hydrocarbons yields oil and natural gas, which have positive sales value; the processing also yields water, which has zero sales value and is recycled back into the ocean. The term **product** describes any output that has a positive total sales value (or an output that

EXHIBIT 17-1

Examples of Joint-Cost Situations

Industry	Separable Products at the Splitoff Point
Agriculture and Food Processing Industries	
Cocoa beans	Cocoa butter, cocoa powder, cocoa drink mix, tanning cream
Lambs	Lamb cuts, tripe, hides, bones, fat
Hogs	Bacon, ham, spare ribs, pork roast
Raw milk	Cream, liquid skim
Lumber	Lumber of varying grades and shapes
Turkeys	Breast, wings, thighs, drumsticks, digest, feather meal, poultry meal
Extractive Industries	
Coal	Coke, gas, benzol, tar, ammonia
Copper ore	Copper, silver, lead, zinc
Petroleum	Crude oil, natural gas
Salt	Hydrogen, chlorine, caustic soda
Chemical Industries	
Raw LPG (liquefied petroleum gas)	Butane, ethane, propane
Crude oil	Gasoline, kerosene, benzene, naphtha
Semiconductor Industry	
Fabrication of silicon-wafer chips	Memory chips of different quality (as to capacity), speed, life expectancy, and temperature tolerance

[2] Some outputs of a joint production process have "negative" revenue when their disposal costs (such as the costs of handling nonsalable toxic substances that require special disposal procedures) are considered. These net costs should be added to the joint production costs that are allocated to joint or main products.

enables a company to avoid incurring costs, such as an intermediate chemical product used as input in another process). The total sales value can be high or low.

When a joint production process yields one product with a high total sales value, compared with the total sales values of other products of the process, that product is called a **main product**. When a joint production process yields two or more products with high total sales values relative to the total sales values of other products, those products are called **joint products**. In contrast, products of a joint production process that have low total sales values relative to the total sales value of the main product or of joint products are called **byproducts**.

Consider some examples. If timber (logs) is processed into standard lumber and wood chips, standard lumber is a main product and wood chips are the byproduct because standard lumber has a high total sales value compared with wood chips. If, however, the logs are processed into fine-grade lumber, standard lumber, and wood chips, fine-grade lumber and standard lumber are joint products and wood chips are the byproduct. That's because both fine-grade lumber and standard lumber have high total sales values relative to wood chips.

Distinctions among main products, joint products, and byproducts are not so clear-cut in practice. Companies use different thresholds for determining whether the relative sales value of a product is high enough for it to be considered a joint product. Consider kerosene, obtained when refining crude oil. Based on a comparison of its sales value to the total sales values of gasoline and other products, some companies classify kerosene as a joint product whereas others classify it as a byproduct. Moreover, the classification of products—main, joint, or byproduct—can change over time, especially for products such as lower-grade semiconductor chips, whose market prices may increase or decrease by 30% or more in a year. When prices of lower-grade chips are high, they are considered joint products together with higher-grade chips; when prices of lower-grade chips fall considerably, they are considered byproducts. In practice, it is important to understand how a specific company chooses to classify its products. Concepts in Action: Big Data Joint Products and Byproducts Create New Business Opportunities describes how companies are categorizing new data-based businesses as joint products or byproducts.

DECISION POINT

What do the terms *joint cost* and *splitoff point* mean, and how do joint products differ from byproducts?

CONCEPTS IN ACTION

Big Data Joint Products and Byproducts Create New Business Opportunities[3]

NiP STUDIO/Shutterstock

Forward-thinking companies are using their data to create new products and business lines as a byproduct of their operations. For some companies, the value of big data is so significant that it is a joint product, not a byproduct.

UnitedHealth, for example, has built a business by reusing the information contained in the insurance claim forms it processes. These aggregated data allow pharmaceutical companies to see how their products are used, how effective they are, and how well they are competing with rival drugs.

Similarly, Toyota created a new business that leverages the GPS navigation devices it installs in cars sold in Japan. It captures the speed and position of cars and sells traffic data to municipal planning departments and corporate delivery fleets at prices that start at $2,000 a month.

Cargill developed a new digital product line to supplement its business of selling crop seeds to farmers. By analyzing its large database of information on how its seeds performed in various types of soil and weather conditions, it built software that gives customized advice to farmers looking to increase their crop yields.

Companies are increasingly leveraging their data to find product enhancements that increase revenue, build services that broaden their customer relationships, and even create new businesses that capitalize on the large quantities of data they are collecting to serve new customers.

[3] *Source:* Alan Lewis and Dan McKone, *Edge Strategy: A New Mindset for Profitable Growth* (Boston, MA: Harvard Business School Press, 2016).

Allocating Joint Costs

LEARNING OBJECTIVE 2

Explain why joint costs are allocated to individual products

...to calculate cost of goods sold and inventory and for reimbursements under cost-plus contracts and other types of claims

Joint costs are allocated to individual products or services for several purposes:

- Computing inventoriable costs and the cost of goods sold for external and internal reporting purposes. Recall from Chapter 9 that absorption costing is required for financial accounting and tax reporting. This necessitates the allocation of joint manufacturing or processing costs to products for calculating ending inventory values.
- Analyzing profitability of divisions and evaluating performance of division managers.
- Reimbursing companies that have some, but not all, of their products or services reimbursed under cost-plus contracts with, say, a government agency. For example, joint costs of removing multiple organs from a single donor need to be allocated to various organ centers because transplants into Medicare patients are reimbursed on a cost-plus basis. Stringent rules typically specify the way to assign joint costs. That said, fraud in cost-plus defense contracts remains one of the most active areas of litigation under the Federal False Claims Act. A common practice is "cross-charging," where a contractor shifts joint costs from "fixed-price" defense contracts to cost-plus contracts.[4]
- Regulating the rates or prices of one or more jointly produced products or services, such as in extractive and energy industries, where output prices are regulated to yield a fixed return on a cost basis that includes joint-cost allocations. In telecommunications, firms have some products subject to price regulation (e.g., wireline services) and others that are unregulated (such as wireless services). In this case, joint costs must be allocated to ensure that costs are not transferred from unregulated services to regulated ones.
- For any commercial litigation or insurance settlement situation in which the costs of joint products or services are key inputs.

DECISION POINT

Why are joint costs allocated to individual products?

Approaches to Allocating Joint Costs

LEARNING OBJECTIVE 3

Allocate joint costs using four methods

...sales value at splitoff, physical measure, net realizable value (NRV), and constant gross-margin percentage NRV

Two approaches are used to allocate joint costs.

- **Approach 1.** Allocate joint costs using *market-based* data such as revenues. This chapter illustrates three methods that use this approach:
  1. Sales value at splitoff method
  2. Net realizable value (NRV) method
  3. Constant gross-margin percentage NRV method
- **Approach 2.** Allocate joint costs using *physical measures*, such as the weight, quantity (physical units), or volume of the joint products.

The cause-and-effect and benefits-received criteria often guide cost-allocation decisions (see Exhibit 15-2, page 599). Joint costs do not have a cause-and-effect relationship with individual products because the production process simultaneously yields multiple products. The benefits-received criterion leads managers to favor methods under approach 1 because revenues are, in general, a better indicator of benefits received than physical measures. Mining companies, for example, receive more benefit from one ton of gold than from 10 tons of coal.

In the simplest joint production process, joint products are sold at the splitoff point without further processing. For this case, Example 1 illustrates two methods: the sales value at splitoff method and the physical-measure method. Sometimes, the joint production process yields products that require further processing beyond the splitoff point. For this case, Example 2 illustrates the NRV method and the constant gross-margin percentage NRV method. To help focus on key concepts, we use numbers and amounts that are smaller than the numbers typically found in practice.

[4] See, for example, www.dodig.mil/iginformation/IGInformationReleases/3eSettlementPR.pdf.

The following symbols distinguish a joint or main product from a byproduct:

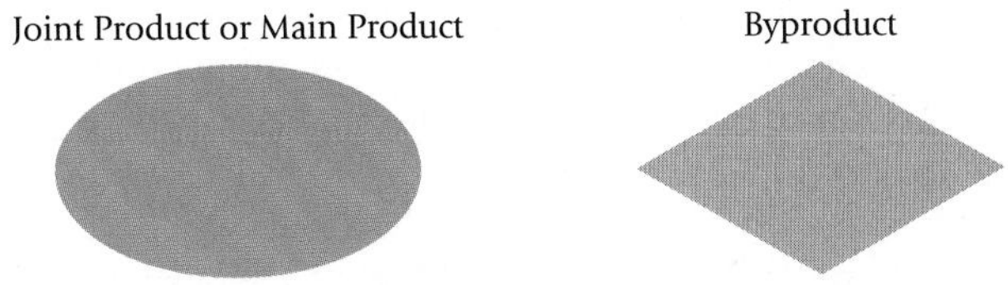

Example 1: Farmland Dairy purchases raw milk from individual farms and processes it until the splitoff point, when two products—cream and liquid skim—emerge. These products are sold to an independent company, which markets and distributes them to supermarkets and other retail outlets.

In May 2020, Farmland Dairy operates at capacity and processes 110,000 gallons of raw milk. During processing, 10,000 gallons are lost due to evaporation and spillage, yielding 25,000 gallons of cream and 75,000 gallons of liquid skim. The data follow:

Home | Insert | Page Layout | Formulas | Data | Review

	A	B	C
1		Joint Costs	
2	Joint costs (costs of 110,000 gallons raw milk and processing to splitoff point)	$400,000	
3			
4		Cream	Liquid Skim
5	Beginning inventory (gallons)	0	0
6	Production (gallons)	25,000	75,000
7	Sales (gallons)	20,000	30,000
8	Ending inventory (gallons)	5,000	45,000
9	Selling price per gallon	$ 8	$ 4

Exhibit 17-2 depicts the basic relationships in this example.

How much of the $400,000 joint costs should be allocated to the cost of goods sold of 20,000 gallons of cream and 30,000 gallons of liquid skim, and how much to the ending inventory of 5,000 gallons of cream and 45,000 gallons of liquid skim? We illustrate the sales value at splitoff method and the physical-measure method.

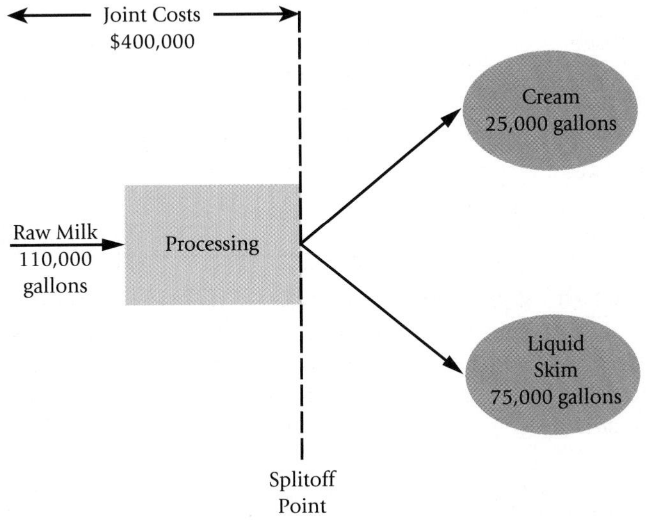

EXHIBIT 17-2

Example 1: Overview of Farmland Dairy

Sales Value at Splitoff Method

The **sales value at splitoff method** allocates joint costs to joint products produced during the accounting period on the basis of the relative total sales value at the splitoff point. Exhibit 17-3, Panel A, shows how joint costs are allocated to individual products to calculate the cost per gallon of cream and liquid skim for valuing ending inventory. This method uses the sales value of the *entire production of the accounting period* (25,000 gallons of cream and 75,000 gallons of liquid skim), not just the quantity sold (20,000 gallons of cream and 30,000 gallons of liquid skim). That's because joint costs were incurred to produce all units, not just the products sold during the current period.[5] Exhibit 17-3, Panel B, presents the product-line income statement using the sales value at splitoff method. The gross-margin percentage for each product is 20% because the sales value at splitoff method allocates joint costs to each product in proportion to the sales value of total production (cream: $160,000 ÷ $200,000 = 80%; liquid skim: $240,000 ÷ $300,000 = 80%). Therefore, the gross-margin percentage for each product manufactured in May 2020 is the same: 20%.[6]

The sales value at splitoff method follows the benefits-received criterion of cost allocation: Costs are allocated to products in proportion to their revenue-generating power (their expected revenues). This method requires selling prices for all products at the splitoff point.

Physical-Measure Method

The **physical-measure method** allocates joint costs to joint products produced during the accounting period on the basis of a *comparable* physical measure, such as the relative weight, quantity, or volume at the splitoff point. Exhibit 17-4, Panel A, shows how the $400,000 of joint costs are allocated to individual products to calculate the cost per gallon of cream and liquid skim based on the 25,000 gallons of cream and 75,000 gallons of liquid skim produced.

Because the physical-measure method allocates joint costs on the basis of the number of gallons, the cost per gallon is the same for both products. Exhibit 17-4, Panel B, presents the product-line income statement using the physical-measure method. The gross-margin percentages are 50% for cream and 0% for liquid skim.

EXHIBIT 17-3 Joint-Cost Allocation and Product-Line Income Statement Using Sales Value at Splitoff Method: Farmland Dairy for May 2020

	A	B	C	D
1	**PANEL A: Allocation of Joint Costs Using Sales Value at Splitoff Method**	**Cream**	**Liquid Skim**	**Total**
2	Sales value of total production at splitoff point			
3	(25,000 gallons × $8 per gallon; 75,000 gallons × $4 per gallon)	$200,000	$300,000	$500,000
4	Weighting ($200,000 ÷ $500,000; $300,000 ÷ 500,000)	0.40	0.60	
5	Joint costs allocated (0.40 × $400,000; 0.60 × $400,000)	$160,000	$240,000	$400,000
6	Joint production cost per gallon			
7	($160,000 ÷ 25,000 gallons; $240,000 ÷ 75,000 gallons)	$ 6.40	$ 3.20	
8				
9	**PANEL B: Product-Line Income Statement Using Sales Value at Splitoff Method for May 2020**	**Cream**	**Liquid Skim**	**Total**
10	Revenues (20,000 gallons × $8 per gallon; 30,000 gallons × $4 per gallon)	$160,000	$120,000	$280,000
11	Cost of goods sold (joint costs):			
12	Production costs (0.40 × $400,000; 0.60 × $400,000)	160,000	240,000	400,000
13	Deduct ending inventory (5,000 gallons × $6.40 per gallon; 45,000 gallons × $3.20 per gallon)	32,000	144,000	176,000
14	Cost of goods sold (joint costs)	128,000	96,000	224,000
15	Gross margin	$ 32,000	$ 24,000	$ 56,000
16	Gross margin percentage ($32,000 ÷ $160,000; $24,000 ÷ $120,000; $56,000 ÷ $280,000)	20%	20%	20%

[5] If Farmland Dairy had excess processing capacity in May 2020, it could choose not to allocate the cost of unused capacity to individual products as discussed in Chapter 16. To simplify exposition, we assume zero excess processing capacity throughout this chapter.

[6] Suppose Farmland Dairy has beginning inventory of cream and liquid milk in May 2020 and when this inventory is sold, Farmland earns a gross margin different from 20%. Then the gross-margin percentage for cream and liquid skim will not be the same. The relative gross-margin percentages will depend on how much of the sales of each product came from beginning inventory and how much came from current-period production.

EXHIBIT 17-4 Joint-Cost Allocation and Product-Line Income Statement Using Physical-Measure Method: Farmland Dairy for May 2020

	A	B	C	D
1	**PANEL A: Allocation of Joint Costs Using Physical-Measure Method**	**Cream**	**Liquid Skim**	**Total**
2	Physical measure of total production (gallons)	25,000	75,000	100,000
3	Weighting (25,000 gallons ÷ 100,000 gallons; 75,000 gallons ÷ 100,000 gallons)	0.25	0.75	
4	Joint costs allocated (0.25 × $400,000; 0.75 × $400,000)	$100,000	$300,000	$400,000
5	Joint production cost per gallon ($100,000 ÷ 25,000 gallons; $300,000 ÷ 75,000 gallons)	$ 4.00	$ 4.00	
6				
7	**PANEL B: Product-Line Income Statement Using Physical-Measure Method for May 2020**	**Cream**	**Liquid Skim**	**Total**
8	Revenues (20,000 gallons × $8 per gallon; 30,000 gallons × $4 per gallon)	$160,000	$120,000	$280,000
9	Cost of goods sold (joint costs):			
10	Production costs (0.25 × $400,000; 0.75 × $400,000)	100,000	300,000	400,000
11	Deduct ending inventory (5,000 gallons × $4 per gallon; 45,000 gallons × $4 per gallon)	20,000	180,000	200,000
12	Cost of goods sold (joint costs)	80,000	120,000	200,000
13	Gross margin	$ 80,000	$ 0	$ 80,000
14	Gross margin percentage ($80,000 ÷ $160,000; $0 ÷ $120,000; $80,000 ÷ $280,000)	50%	0%	28.6%

Under the benefits-received criterion, the physical-measure method is much less desirable than the sales value at splitoff method. Why? Because the physical measures of the individual products may have no relationship to their respective revenue-generating abilities. Consider a mine that extracts ore containing gold, silver, and lead. Using a common physical measure (tons) would result in almost all costs being allocated to lead, the product that weighs the most but has the lowest revenue-generating power. This method of cost allocation is inconsistent with the main reason the mining company is incurring mining costs—to earn revenues from gold and silver, not lead. When using the physical-measure method, products with a high sales value per ton, like gold and silver, show a large "profit," and products with a low sales value per ton, like lead, show sizable losses.

Obtaining comparable physical measures for all products is not always straightforward. Consider the joint costs of producing oil and natural gas; oil is a liquid and gas is a vapor. To use a physical measure, the oil and gas need to be converted to the energy equivalent for oil and gas, British thermal units.

Managers must decide which products of a joint process to include in a physical-measure computation. Outputs with no sales value (such as dirt in gold mining) are always excluded. Although many more tons of dirt than gold are produced, costs are not incurred to produce zero sales value outputs. Byproducts are also often excluded from the physical-measure computation because of their low sales values relative to the joint products or the main product. The general guideline is to include only the physical measures of joint-product outputs in the weighting computations.

17-1 TRY IT!

Merk Chemicals processes resin from fir trees into three products: printing inks, varnishes, and adhesives. During June, the joint costs of processing were $960,000. Additional information is given below:

Product	Units Produced	Sales Value at Splitoff Point
Printing inks	30,000 liters	$240,000
Varnishes	30,000 liters	144,000
Adhesives	15,000 liters	96,000

Determine the amount of joint cost allocated to each product if Merk uses (1) the physical measure method, and (2) the sales value at splitoff method.

Net Realizable Value Method

In many cases, products are processed beyond the splitoff point to bring them to a marketable form or to increase their value above their selling price at the splitoff point. For example, when crude oil is refined, the gasoline, kerosene, benzene, and naphtha must be processed further before they can be sold. To illustrate, let's extend the Farmland Dairy example.

Example 2: Assume the same data as in Example 1 except that both cream and liquid skim can be processed further:

- Cream → Buttercream: 25,000 gallons of cream are further processed to yield 20,000 gallons of buttercream at additional processing costs of $280,000. Buttercream, sells for $25 per gallon.
- Liquid Skim → Condensed Milk: 75,000 gallons of liquid skim are further processed to yield 50,000 gallons of condensed milk at additional processing costs of $520,000. Condensed milk sells for $22 per gallon.
- Sales during May 2020 are 12,000 gallons of buttercream and 45,000 gallons of condensed milk.

Exhibit 17-5, Panel A, depicts how (1) raw milk is converted into cream and liquid skim in the joint production process and (2) how cream is separately processed into buttercream and liquid skim is separately processed into condensed milk. Panel B shows the data for Example 2.

The **net realizable value (NRV) method** allocates joint costs to joint products produced during the accounting period on the basis of their relative NRV—final sales value minus separable costs. The NRV method is typically preferred to the sales value at splitoff method only when selling prices for one or more products at splitoff do not exist. Using the NRV method, Exhibit 17-6, Panel A, allocates joint costs to individual products to calculate cost per gallon of buttercream and condensed milk. Panel B presents the product-line income statement. The gross-margin percentages are 22.0% for buttercream and 26.4% for condensed milk.

The NRV method is often implemented using simplifying assumptions. For example, even when selling prices of joint products vary frequently, companies assume a constant set of selling prices for the accounting period. Similarly, even if companies change post-splitoff processing to adjust to variations in input quality or local conditions, the NRV method assumes a specific constant set of such steps.

EXHIBIT 17-5

Example 2: Overview of Farmland Dairy

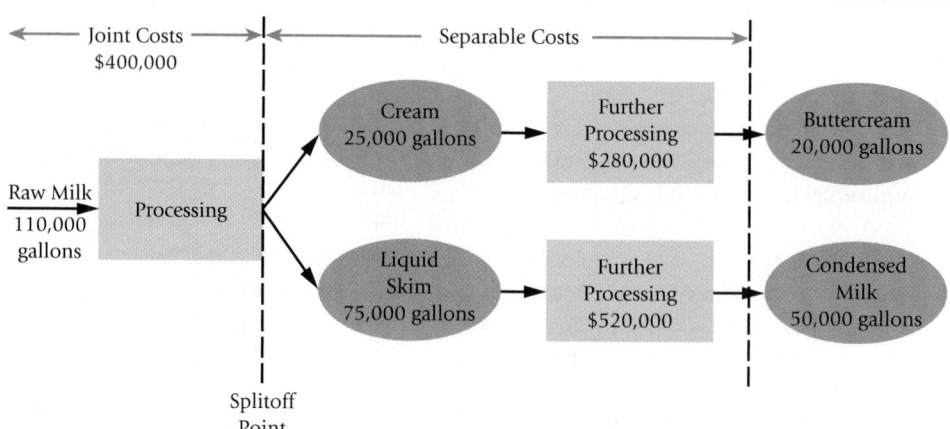

PANEL A: Graphical Presentation of Process for Example 2

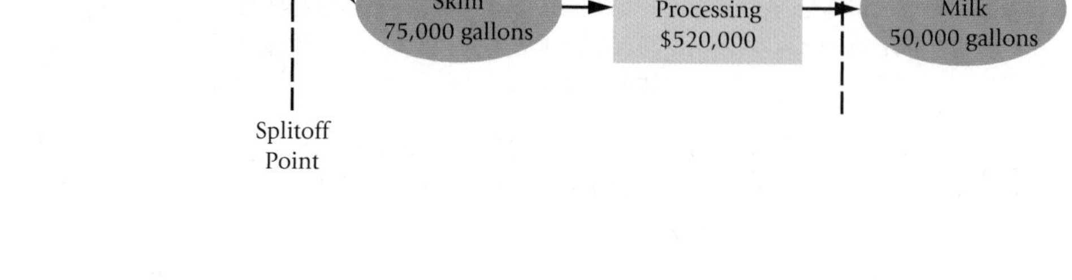

PANEL B: Data for Example 2

EXHIBIT 17-5

Example 2: Overview of Farmland Dairy (*continued*)

	A	B	C	D	E
1		Joint Costs		Buttercream	Condensed Milk
2	Joint costs (costs of 110,000 gallons raw milk and processing to splitoff point)	$400,000			
3	Separable cost of processing 25,000 gallons cream into 20,000 gallons buttercream			$280,000	
4	Separable cost of processing 75,000 gallons liquid skim into 50,000 gallons condensed milk				$520,000
5					
6		Cream	Liquid Skim	Buttercream	Condensed Milk
7	Beginning inventory (gallons)	0	0	0	0
8	Production (gallons)	25,000	75,000	20,000	50,000
9	Transfer for further processing (gallons)	25,000	75,000		
10	Sales (gallons)			12,000	45,000
11	Ending inventory (gallons)	0	0	8,000	5,000
12	Selling price per gallon	$ 8	$ 4	$ 25	$ 22

EXHIBIT 17-6 Joint-Cost Allocation and Product-Line Income Statement Using NRV Method: Farmland Dairy for May 2020

	A	B	C	D
1	**PANEL A: Allocation of Joint Costs Using Net Realizable Value Method**	Buttercream	Condensed Milk	Total
2	Final sales value of total production during accounting period			
3	(20,000 gallons × $25 per gallon; 50,000 gallons × $22 per gallon)	$500,000	$1,100,000	$1,600,000
4	Deduct separable costs	280,000	520,000	800,000
5	Net realizable value at splitoff point	$220,000	$ 580,000	$ 800,000
6	Weighting ($220,000 ÷ $800,000; $580,000 ÷ $800,000)	0.275	0.725	
7	Joint costs allocated (0.275 × $400,000; 0.725 × $400,000)	$110,000	$ 290,000	$ 400,000
8	Production cost per gallon			
9	([$110,000 + $280,000] ÷ 20,000 gallons; [$290,000 + $520,000] ÷ 50,000 gallons)	$ 19.50	$ 16.20	
10				
11	**PANEL B: Product-Line Income Statement Using Net Realizable Value Method for May 2020**	Buttercream	Condensed Milk	Total
12	Revenues (12,000 gallons × $25 per gallon; 45,000 gallons × $22 per gallon)	$300,000	$ 990,000	$1,290,000
13	Cost of goods sold:			
14	Joint costs (0.275 × $400,000; 0.725 × $400,000)	110,000	290,000	400,000
15	Separable costs	280,000	520,000	800,000
16	Production costs	390,000	810,000	1,200,000
17	Deduct ending inventory (8,000 gallons × $19.50 per gallon; 5,000 gallons × $16.20 per gallon)	156,000	81,000	237,000
18	Cost of goods sold	234,000	729,000	963,000
19	Gross margin	$ 66,000	$ 261,000	$ 327,000
20	Gross margin percentage ($66,000 ÷ $300,000; $261,000 ÷ $990,000; $327,000 ÷ $1,290,000)	22.0%	26.4%	25.3%

TRY IT! 17-2

Green Stripe Company processes tomatoes into ketchup, tomato juice, and canned tomatoes. During July 2020, joint costs of processing tomatoes were $4,172,000. The company maintains no inventories. Production and sales information follows:

Product	Cases	Sales Value at Splitoff Point	Separable Costs	Selling Price
Ketchup	200,000	$6 per case	$3 per case	$24 per case
Juice	350,000	8 per case	5 per case	25 per case
Canned	400,000	5 per case	3 per case	10 per case

Determine the amount of joint cost allocated to each product if Green Stripe uses the estimated net realizable value method. What is the cost per case for each product?

Constant Gross-Margin Percentage NRV Method

The **constant gross-margin percentage NRV method** allocates joint costs to joint products produced during the accounting period in such a way that each individual product achieves an identical gross-margin percentage. The method works backward by first computing the overall gross margin. Then, for each product, the gross-margin percentage and any separable costs are deducted from the final sales value of production to back into the joint-cost allocation for that product. Exhibit 17-7, Panel A, shows the three steps for allocating the $400,000 joint costs between buttercream and condensed milk in the Farmland Dairy example using this method. Refer to the panel as we describe each step.

Step 1: Compute the Overall Gross-Margin Percentage. This step calculates the overall gross-margin percentage for all joint products together based on the final sales value of *total production* during the accounting period, not the *total revenues* of the period. Accordingly, Exhibit 17-7, Panel A, uses $1,600,000, the final expected sales value of the entire output of buttercream and condensed milk, not the $1,290,000 in actual sales revenue for the month of May.

Step 2: Compute the Total Production Costs for Each Product. The gross margin (in dollars) for each product is computed by multiplying the overall gross-margin percentage by the product's final sales value of total production. For each product, subtracting the gross margin from the final sales value of total production yields the total production costs of the product.

Step 3: Compute the Allocated Joint Costs. For each product, the total production costs minus separable costs equal the joint cost allocated to that product.

Exhibit 17-7, Panel B, presents the product-line income statement for the constant gross-margin percentage NRV method.

EXHIBIT 17-7 Joint-Cost Allocation and Product-Line Income Statement Using Constant Gross-Margin Percentage NRV Method: Farmland Dairy for May 2020

	A	B	C	D
1	**PANEL A: Allocation of Joint Costs Using Constant Gross-Margin Percentage NRV Method**			
2	**Step 1:**			
3	Final sales value of total production during accounting period: (20,000 gallons × $25 per gallon) + (50,000 gallons × $22 per gallon)	$1,600,000		
4	Deduct joint and separable costs ($400,000 + $280,000 + $520,000)	1,200,000		
5	Gross margin	$ 400,000		
6	Gross margin percentage ($400,000 ÷ $1,600,000)	25%		
7		**Buttercream**	**Condensed Milk**	**Total**
8	**Step 2:**			
9	Final sales value of total production during accounting period: (20,000 gallons × $25 per gallon; 50,000 gallons × $22 per gallon)	$ 500,000	$1,100,000	$1,600,000
10	Deduct gross margin, using overall gross-margin percentage (25% × $500,000; 25% × $1,100,000)	125,000	275,000	400,000
11	Total production costs	375,000	825,000	1,200,000
12	**Step 3:**			
13	Deduct separable costs	280,000	520,000	800,000
14	Joint costs allocated	$ 95,000	$ 305,000	$ 400,000
15				
16	**PANEL B: Product-Line Income Statement Using Constant Gross-Margin Percentage NRV Method for May 2020**	**Buttercream**	**Condensed Milk**	**Total**
17	Revenues (12,000 gallons × $25 per gallon; 45,000 gallons × $22 per gallon)	$ 300,000	$ 990,000	$1,290,000
18	Cost of goods sold:			
19	Joint costs (from Panel A)	95,000	305,000	400,000
20	Separable costs	280,000	520,000	800,000
21	Production costs	375,000	825,000	1,200,000
22	Deduct ending inventory			
23	(8,000 gallons × $18.75 per gallon[a]; 5,000 gallons × $16.50 per gallon[b])	150,000	82,500	232,500
24	Cost of goods sold	225,000	742,500	967,500
25	Gross margin	$ 75,000	$ 247,500	$ 322,500
26	Gross margin percentage ($75,000 ÷ $300,000; $247,500 ÷ $990,000; $322,500 ÷ $1,290,000)	25%	25%	25%
27				
28	[a]Total production costs of buttercream ÷ Total production of buttercream = $375,000 ÷ 20,000 gallons = $18.75 per gallon.			
29	[b]Total production costs of condensed milk ÷ Total production of condensed milk = $825,000 ÷ 50,000 gallons = $16.50 per gallon.			

The constant gross-margin percentage NRV method is the only method where products can receive negative allocations. This may be required to bring gross-margin percentages of relatively unprofitable products up to the overall average. The constant gross-margin percentage NRV method is also the only method that allocates both joint costs and profits—the same gross-margin percentage is allocated to each product to determine the joint-cost allocations. Neither the sales value at splitoff method nor the NRV method takes account of profits earned either before or after the splitoff point when allocating joint costs.

DECISION POINT

What methods can be used to allocate joint costs to individual products?

Consider Green Stripe Company again. With the same information for 2020 as provided in Try It! 17-2, calculate the amount of joint cost allocated to each product if Green Stripe uses the constant gross-margin percentage NRV method.

17-3 TRY IT!

Choosing an Allocation Method

LEARNING OBJECTIVE 4

Identify situations when the sales value at splitoff method is preferred when allocating joint costs

. . . objectively measuring the benefits received by each product

Which method of allocating joint costs should be used? When selling-price data exist at the splitoff, the sales value at splitoff method is preferred, even if further processing is done. The following are the reasons:

1. **Measure of benefits received.** The sales value at splitoff is the best measure of the benefits received by joint products relative to all other methods of allocating joint costs (such as the physical method) because a company incurs joint costs to generate revenues at the splitoff point. Sometimes, increasing or decreasing joint costs affects the physical mix and market value of joint products. In such cases, there is a clear causal link between total cost and sales value at splitoff.[7]
2. **Independent of further processing decisions.** The sales value at splitoff method does not require information on the processing steps after splitoff. In contrast, the NRV and constant gross-margin percentage NRV methods require information on (a) the specific sequence of further processing decisions, (b) the separable costs of further processing, and (c) the point at which individual products will be sold.
3. **Common allocation basis.** As with other market-based approaches, in the sales value at splitoff method, revenue is a convenient common basis for allocating joint costs. In contrast, the physical measure at splitoff method may lack an easily identifiable common basis for cost allocation.
4. **Simplicity.** The sales value at splitoff method is simple. In contrast, the NRV and constant gross-margin percentage NRV methods can be complex for operations with multiple products and multiple splitoff points. This complexity increases when managers make frequent changes to the sequence of post-splitoff processing decisions or to the point at which individual products are sold.

When selling prices of all products at the splitoff point are unavailable, the NRV method is the best alternative. It attempts to approximate the sales values at splitoff by subtracting from final selling prices the separable costs incurred after the splitoff point. The NRV method assumes that all the markup (profit margin) is attributable to the joint process and none to the separable processes and costs. This is unrealistic if, for example, a firm uses special patented technology in its separable process or innovative marketing to generate significant profits. Despite this limitation, the NRV method is commonly used when selling prices at splitoff are not available as it provides a better measure of the benefits received than either the constant gross-margin percentage NRV method or the physical-measure method.

The constant gross-margin percentage NRV method treats the joint products as though they are a single product. It calculates the aggregate gross-margin percentage, applies this percentage to each product, and views the residual after subtracting separable costs as the amount of joint costs assigned to each product. Unlike the NRV method, it does not measure the benefits received by each joint product at the splitoff point. A positive feature of the

[7] In the semiconductor industry, for example, the use of cleaner facilities, higher-quality silicon wafers, and more sophisticated equipment (all of which require higher joint costs) shifts the distribution of output to higher-quality memory devices with more market value. For details, see James F. Gatti and D. Jacque Grinnell, "Joint Cost Allocations: Measuring and Promoting Productivity and Quality Improvements," *Journal of Cost Management* (2000). The authors also demonstrate that joint-cost allocations based on market value are preferable for promoting quality and productivity improvements.

constant gross-margin percentage method is the recognition that the profit margin is attributable to both the joint process and the separable process after splitoff. But its weakness is the assumption that the profit margin (and ratio of costs to revenues) is identical across products. Recall from our discussion of activity-based costing (ABC) in Chapter 5 that such a situation is uncommon when companies offer a diverse set of products.

Although there are difficulties in using the physical-measure method—such as not reflecting benefits-received—there are instances when it may be preferred, such as when prices are volatile or the process after splitoff is long or uncertain, and a comparable physical measure for all products is available. This is the case, for instance, in the chemical and oil refining industries. The physical-measure method is also useful when joint cost allocations are used as the basis for setting market prices, as in rate regulation. It avoids the circular reasoning of using selling prices to allocate costs on which prices (rates) are based.

Not Allocating Joint Costs

Some companies choose to not allocate joint costs to products due to the complexity of their production or extraction processes and the difficulty of gathering a sufficient amount of data to allocate the costs correctly. For example, a survey of nine sawmills in Norway revealed that none of them allocated joint costs. The study's authors noted that the "interviewed sawmills considered the joint cost problem very interesting, but pointed out that the problem is not easily solved."[8]

Rather than allocating joint costs, some companies, such as in the meatpacking, canning, and mining industries, simply subtract joint costs from total revenues in their management accounts and value inventories at NRV. Recording inventories at NRV recognizes income on products *before* they are sold. To deal with this problem, some companies record inventories at NRV minus an estimated operating income margin. When any end-of-period inventories are sold in the next period, the cost of goods sold equals this carrying value. This approach is akin to the "production method" of accounting for byproducts, described later in this chapter.

DECISION POINT

When is the sales value at splitoff method considered preferable for allocating joint costs to individual products, and why?

Why Joint Costs Are Irrelevant for Decision Making

LEARNING OBJECTIVE 5

Explain why joint costs are irrelevant in a sell-or-process-further decision

...because joint costs are the same whether or not further processing occurs

Chapter 12 introduced the concepts of *relevant revenues*, and *relevant costs*, which are expected future revenues and expected future costs that differ among alternative courses of action. We apply these concepts to decide whether a joint product or main product should be sold at the splitoff point or processed further.

Sell-or-Process-Further Decisions

Consider Farmland Dairy's decision to either sell the joint products, cream and liquid skim, at the splitoff point or to further process them into buttercream and condensed milk. In Example 2, it was profitable to further process both cream and liquid skim into buttercream and condensed milk, respectively. The incremental operating income from processing beyond the splitoff point is as follows:

Further Processing Cream into Buttercream	
Incremental revenues	
($25/gallon × 20,000 gallons) − ($8/gallon × 25,000 gallons)	$300,000
Deduct incremental processing costs	280,000
Increase in operating income from buttercream	$ 20,000
Further Processing Liquid Skim into Condensed Milk	
Incremental revenues	
($22/gallon × 50,000 gallons) − ($4/gallon × 75,000 gallons)	$800,000
Deduct incremental processing costs	520,000
Increase in operating income from condensed milk	$280,000

[8] For further details, see Torgrim Tunes, Anders Q. Nyrud, and Birger Eikenes, "Cost and Performance Management in the Sawmill Industry," *Scandinavian Forest Economics* (2006).

In this example, the operating income increases by further processing each product, so the manager decides to process cream into buttercream and liquid skim into condensed milk. *Note that the $400,000 joint costs incurred before the splitoff point are irrelevant in deciding whether to process further.* Why? Because the joint costs of $400,000 are the same whether the products are sold at the splitoff point or processed further. What matters is the incremental income from additional processing.

Incremental costs are the additional costs incurred for an activity, such as further processing. *Do not assume all separable costs in joint-cost allocations are incremental costs.* Some separable costs may be fixed costs, such as the lease cost on buildings where the further processing is done; some separable costs may be sunk costs, such as depreciation on the equipment that converts cream into buttercream; and some separable costs may be allocated costs, such as corporate costs allocated to the condensed milk operations. None of these costs will differ between the alternatives of selling products at the splitoff point or processing further; therefore, they are irrelevant.

Decision Making and Performance Evaluation

The potential conflict between cost concepts used for decision making and cost concepts used for evaluating the performance of managers often arises in sell-or-process-further decisions Continuing with Example 2, suppose the fixed corporate and administrative costs *allocated* to further processing cream into buttercream is $30,000 and that these costs will be allocated to buttercream and to the manager's product-line income statement only if buttercream is produced. How might this policy affect the decision to process further?

As we have seen, on the basis of incremental revenues and incremental costs, Farmland's operating income will increase by $20,000 by processing cream into buttercream. However, producing buttercream results in an additional charge of $30,000 for allocated fixed costs. If the manager is evaluated on a full-cost basis (after allocating all costs), processing cream into buttercream will lower the manager's performance-evaluation measure by $10,000 (incremental operating income, $20,000 − allocated fixed costs, $30,000). Therefore, the manager may be tempted to sell the cream at the splitoff point and not process it into buttercream.

A similar conflict can also arise with joint products. In Example 1, suppose Farmland Dairy can sell raw milk at a profit of $20,000. From a decision-making standpoint, the company maximizes operating income by processing raw milk into cream and liquid skim because total revenues from selling both joint products ($500,000, see Exhibit 17-3, page 684) exceed joint costs ($400,000, page 683) by $100,000, which is greater than the $20,000 profit from selling raw milk. Suppose, however, the cream and liquid-skim product lines are managed by different managers, each evaluated on product-line profitability. If the physical-measure method of joint-cost allocation is used and the selling price per gallon of liquid skim falls below $4.00 per gallon, the liquid-skim product line will show a loss (from Exhibit 17-4, page 685, revenues will be less than $120,000, but cost of goods sold will be unchanged at $120,000). From a performance-evaluation standpoint, the manager of the liquid-skim line will prefer to not produce liquid skim but rather to sell raw milk.

Farmland Dairy's performance-evaluation conflicts will be less severe if it uses market-based methods of joint-cost allocations—sales value at splitoff, NRV, or constant gross-margin percentage NRV—because each of these methods allocates costs using revenues, which generally leads to each joint product having positive income.

Pricing Decisions

Joint costs are allocated to products based on some convenient allocation base rather than a cause-and-effect measure of resources used by each joint product. Therefore, these costs are not a useful basis for pricing decisions. If sales value at splitoff or the net realizable value method is used to allocate joint costs, the selling prices of joint products drive joint-cost allocations, rather than cost allocations serving as the basis for the pricing of joint products! Of course, as we saw in Chapter 14, the joint products must generate a sufficient amount of combined revenue in the long run to cover the joint costs of processing.

DECISION POINT

Are joint costs relevant in a sell-or-process-further decision?

Accounting for Byproducts

LEARNING OBJECTIVE 6

Account for byproducts using two methods

...recognize in financial statements at time of production or at time of sale

Joint production processes can yield not only joint products and main products but also byproducts. Although their total sales values are relatively low, the byproducts in a joint production process can affect the allocation of joint costs. Moreover, byproducts can be quite profitable for a firm. Wendy's, the fast-food chain, uses surplus hamburger patties in its "rich and meaty" chili and, because it cooks meat specifically for the chili only 10% of the time, makes great margins even at a price of $0.99 for an eight-ounce serving of chili.

Let's consider a two-product example of a main product and a byproduct.

Example 3: The Westlake Corporation processes timber into fine-grade lumber and wood chips, which are used as mulch in gardens and lawns.

- Fine-grade lumber (the main product)—sells for $6 per board foot (b.f.)
- Wood chips (the byproduct)—sells for $1 per cubic foot (c.f.)

The data for July 2020 are as follows:

	Beginning Inventory	Production	Sales	Ending Inventory
Fine-grade lumber (b.f.)	0	50,000	40,000	10,000
Wood chips (c.f.)	0	4,000	1,200	2,800

The joint manufacturing costs for these products in July 2020 are $250,000, direct materials, $150,000 and conversion costs, $100,000. Both products are sold at the splitoff point without further processing, as Exhibit 17-8 shows.

We present two methods of byproduct accounting: the production method and the sales method. The production method recognizes byproducts in the financial statements when their production is completed. The sales method recognizes byproducts when they are sold.[9] Exhibit 17-9 presents the income statement of Westlake Corporation under both methods.

Production Method: Byproducts Recognized at Time Production Is Completed

This method recognizes the byproduct in the financial statements—the 4,000 cubic feet of wood chips—in the month it is produced, July 2020. The NRV from the byproduct produced

EXHIBIT 17-8

Example 3: Overview of Westlake Corporation

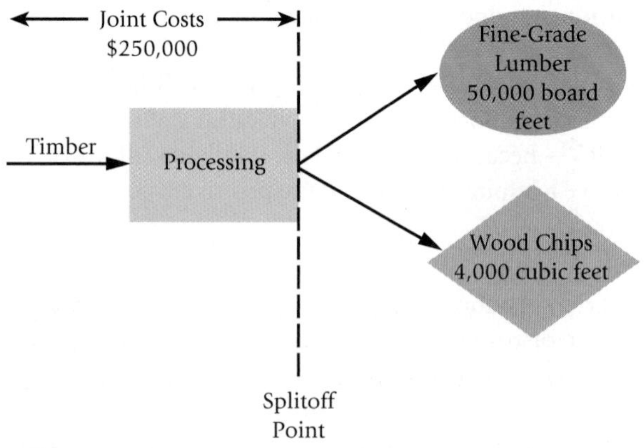

[9] For a discussion of joint-cost allocation and byproduct accounting methods, see P. Douglas Marshall and Robert F. Dombrowski, "A Small Business Review of Accounting for Primary Products, Byproducts and Scrap," *The National Public Accountant* (February/March 2003): 10–13.

EXHIBIT 17-9

Income Statements of Westlake Corporation for July 2020 Using the Production and Sales Methods for Byproduct Accounting

	Production Method	Sales Method
Revenues		
Main product: Fine-grade lumber (40,000 b.f. × $6 per b.f.)	$240,000	$240,000
Byproduct: Wood chips (1,200 c.f. × $1 per c.f.)	—	1,200
Total revenues	240,000	241,200
Cost of goods sold:		
Total manufacturing costs	250,000	250,000
Deduct byproduct revenue and inventory (4,000 c.f. × $1 per c.f.)	(4,000)	—
Net manufacturing costs	246,000	250,000
Deduct main-product inventory	(49,200)[a]	(50,000)[b]
Cost of goods sold	196,800	200,000
Gross margin	$ 43,200	$ 41,200
Gross-margin percentage ($43,200 ÷ $240,000; $41,200 ÷ $241,200)	18.00%	17.08%
Inventoriable costs (end of period):		
Main product: Fine-grade lumber	$ 49,200	$ 50,000
Byproduct: Wood chips (2,800 c.f. × $1 per c.f.)[c]	2,800	0

[a](10,000 ÷ 50,000) × net manufacturing cost = (10,000 ÷ 50,000) × $246,000 = $49,200
[b](10,000 ÷ 50,000) × total manufacturing cost = (10,000 ÷ 50,000) × $250,000 = $50,000
[c]Recorded at selling prices.

offsets the costs of the main product. The following journal entries illustrate the production method:

1. Work in Process	150,000	
Accounts Payable		150,000
To record the direct materials purchased and used in production during July.		
2. Work in Process	100,000	
Various accounts such as Wages Payable and Accumulated Depreciation		100,000
To record the conversion costs in the production process during July; examples include energy, manufacturing supplies, all manufacturing labor, and plant depreciation.		
3. Byproduct Inventory—Wood Chips (4,000 c.f. × $1 per c.f.)	4,000	
Finished Goods—Fine-Grade Lumber ($250,000 − $4,000)	246,000	
Work in Process ($150,000 + $100,000)		250,000
To record the cost of goods completed during July.		
4a. Cost of Goods Sold [(40,000 b.f. ÷ 50,000 b.f.) × $246,000]	196,800	
Finished Goods—Fine-Grade Lumber		196,800
To record the cost of the main product sold during July.		
4b. Cash or Accounts Receivable (40,000 b.f. × $6 per b.f.)	240,000	
Revenues—Fine-Grade Lumber		240,000
To record the sales of the main product during July.		
5. Cash or Accounts Receivable (1,200 c.f. × $1 per c.f.)	1,200	
Byproduct Inventory—Wood Chips		1,200
To record the sales of the byproduct during July.		

The production method reports byproduct inventory of wood chips in the balance sheet at $1 per cubic foot selling price [(4,000 cubic feet − 1,200 cubic feet) × $1 per cubic foot = $2,800].

One variation of this method reports byproduct inventory at its NRV reduced by a normal profit margin, say 20%: $2,800 − 20% × $2,800 = $2,240. When the byproduct inventory is sold in a subsequent period, the income statement will match the selling price, $2,800, with the "cost" reported for the byproduct inventory, $2,240, resulting in a byproduct operating income of $560 ($2,800 − $2,240).[10] The deduction for the byproduct inventory in Exhibit 17-9

[10] One way to implement this variation is to assume all products have the same "normal" profit margin, as in the constant gross-margin percentage NRV method. Alternatively, the company might allow products to have different profit margins based on an analysis of the margins earned by other companies that sell these products individually.

is \$3,200 (80% × \$4,000) so that net manufacturing costs equal \$246,800 (\$250,000 − \$3,200). Cost of goods sold equals \$197,440 [(40,000 b.f. ÷ 50,000 b.f.) × \$246,800].

Sales Method: Byproducts Recognized at Time of Sale

With this method, no journal entries are made for byproducts until they are sold. At that time, byproduct revenues are reported in the income statement as either other income or a deduction from cost of goods sold. In the Westlake Corporation example, byproduct revenues in July 2020 are \$1,200 (1,200 cubic feet × \$1 per cubic foot) based on sales of 1,200 cubic feet of wood chips of the 4,000 cubic feet produced. The journal entries are as follows:

1. and 2.	*Same as for the production method.*		
	Work in Process	150,000	
	Accounts Payable		150,000
	Work in Process	100,000	
	Various accounts such as Wages Payable and Accumulated Depreciation		100,000
3.	Finished Goods—Fine-Grade Lumber	250,000	
	Work in Process		250,000
	To record the cost of the main product completed during July.		
4a.	Cost of Goods Sold [(40,000 b.f. ÷ 50,000 b.f.) × \$250,000]	200,000	
	Finished Goods—Fine-Grade Lumber		200,000
	To record the cost of the main product sold during July.		
4b.	Same as for the production method.		
	Cash or Accounts Receivable (40,000 b.f. × \$6 per b.f.)	240,000	
	Revenues—Fine-Grade Lumber		240,000
5.	Cash or Accounts Receivable	1,200	
	Revenues—Wood Chips		1,200
	To record the sales of the byproduct during July.		

DECISION POINT

What methods can be used to account for byproducts, and which of them is preferable?

Which method should a company use? The production method for accounting for byproducts is consistent with the matching principle and is preferred. The method recognizes byproduct inventory in the accounting period in which it is produced and simultaneously reduces the cost of manufacturing the main or joint products, thereby better matching revenues and expenses from selling the main product. The sales method is simpler and is often used in practice, because the dollar amounts of byproducts are immaterial. The drawback of the sales method is that it allows a firm to "manage" its reported earnings by timing the sale of byproducts. For example, a firm might store byproducts for several periods and sell them when revenues and profits from the main product or joint products are low.

TRY IT! 17-4

Canyon Resources, Inc., mines copper. Its smelting process also yields a byproduct, molybdenum, that can be sold for industrial use. Both products are sold at the splitoff point.

Canyon Resources started November 2020 with no inventories and spent \$600,000 on operations that month. Production and sales information for November are given below:

	Production (in tons)	Sales (in tons)	Selling Price per ton
Copper	26,000	20,800	\$32
Molybdenum	4,250	3,250	\$10

What is the gross margin for Canyon Resources, Inc., under the production method and the sales method of accounting for byproducts?

PROBLEM FOR SELF-STUDY

Inorganic Chemicals (IC) processes salt into various industrial products. In July 2020, IC incurred joint costs of $100,000 to purchase salt and convert it into two products: caustic soda and chlorine. Although there is an active outside market for chlorine, IC processes all 800 tons of chlorine into 500 tons of PVC (polyvinyl chloride), which is then sold. There were no beginning or ending inventories of salt, caustic soda, chlorine, or PVC in July. Information for July 2020 production and sales follows:

	A	B	C	D
1		Joint Costs		PVC
2	Joint costs (costs of salt and processing to splitoff point)	$100,000		
3	Separable cost of processing 800 tons of chlorine into 500 tons of PVC			$20,000
4				
5		Caustic Soda	Chlorine	PVC
6	Beginning inventory (tons)	0	0	0
7	Production (tons)	1,200	800	500
8	Transfer for further processing (tons)		800	
9	Sales (tons)	1,200		500
10	Ending inventory (tons)	0	0	0
11	Selling price per ton in active outside market (for products not actually sold)		$ 75	
12	Selling price per ton for products sold	$ 50		$ 200

Required

1. Allocate the joint costs of $100,000 between caustic soda and PVC under (a) the sales value at splitoff method and (b) the physical-measure method.
2. Allocate the joint costs of $100,000 between caustic soda and PVC under the NRV method.
3. Under the three allocation methods in requirements 1 and 2, what is the gross-margin percentage of (a) caustic soda and (b) PVC?
4. Lifetime Swimming Pool Products offers to purchase 800 tons of chlorine in August 2020 at $75 per ton. Assume all other production and sales data are the same for August as they were for July. This sale of chlorine to Lifetime would mean that no PVC would be produced by IC in August. How would accepting this offer affect IC's August 2020 operating income?

Solution

The following picture provides a visual illustration of the main facts in this problem.

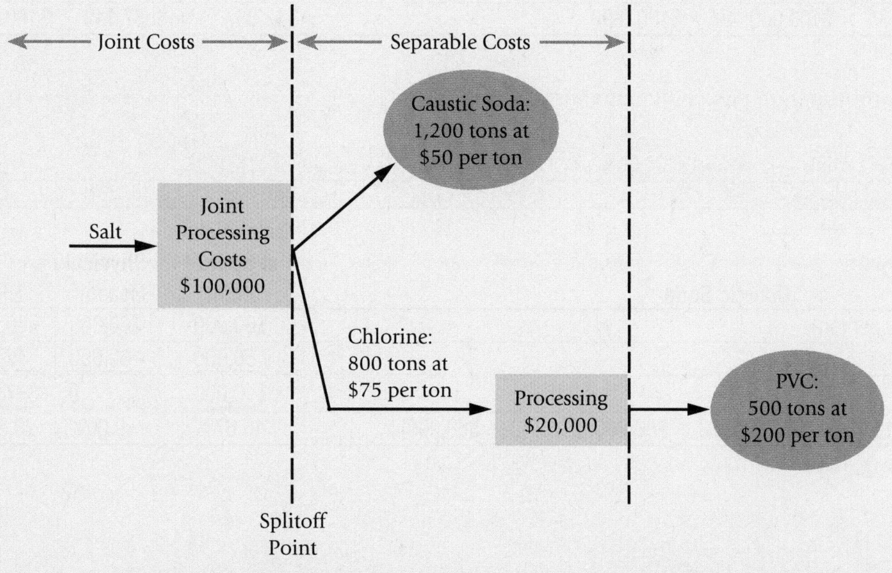

Note that caustic soda is sold as is, while chlorine, despite having a market value at splitoff, is sold in processed form as PVC. The goal is to allocate the joint costs of $100,000 to the final products—caustic soda and PVC. However, because PVC exists only in the form of chlorine at the splitoff point, we use chlorine's sales value and physical measure to allocate joint costs to PVC under the sales value at splitoff and physical measure at splitoff methods.

1a. Sales value at splitoff method

	A	B	C	D
1	**Allocation of Joint Costs Using Sales Value at Splitoff Method**	**Caustic Soda**	**PVC/Chlorine**	**Total**
2	Sales value of total production at splitoff point			
3	(1,200 tons × $50 per ton; 800 × $75 per ton)	$60,000	$60,000	$120,000
4	Weighting ($60,000 ÷ $120,000; $60,000 ÷ $120,000)	0.50	0.50	
5	Joint costs allocated (0.50 × $100,000; 0.50 × $100,000)	$50,000	$50,000	$100,000

1b. Physical-measure method

	A	B	C	D
8	**Allocation of Joint Costs Using Physical-Measure Method**	**Caustic Soda**	**PVC/Chlorine**	**Total**
9	Physical measure of total production (tons)	1,200	800	2,000
10	Weighting (1,200 tons ÷ 2,000 tons; 800 tons ÷ 2,000 tons)	0.60	0.40	
11	Joint cost allocated (0.60 × $100,000; 0.40 × $100,000)	$60,000	$40,000	$100,000

2. Net realizable value (NRV) method

	A	B	C	D
14	**Allocation of Joint Costs Using Net Realizable Value Method**	**Caustic Soda**	**PVC**	**Total**
15	Final sales value of total production during accounting period			
16	(1,200 tons × $50 per ton; 500 tons × $200 per ton)	$60,000	$100,000	$160,000
17	Deduct separable costs to complete and sell	0	20,000	20,000
18	Net realizable value at splitoff point	$60,000	$ 80,000	$140,000
19	Weighting ($60,000 ÷ $140,000; $80,000 ÷ $140,000)	3/7	4/7	
20	Joint costs allocated (3/7 × $100,000; 4/7 × $100,000)	$42,857	$ 57,143	$100,000

3a. Gross-margin percentage of caustic soda

	A	B	C	D
23	**Caustic Soda**	**Sales Value at Splitoff Point**	**Physical Measure**	**NRV**
24	Revenues (1,200 tons × $50 per ton)	$60,000	$60,000	$60,000
25	Cost of goods sold (joint costs)	50,000	60,000	42,857
26	Gross margin	$10,000	$ 0	$17,143
27	Gross margin percentage ($10,000 ÷ $60,000; $0 ÷ $60,000; $17,143 ÷ $60,000)	16.67%	0.00%	28.57%

3b. Gross-margin percentage of PVC

	A	B	C	D
30	PVC	Sales Value at Splitoff Point	Physical Measure	NRV
31	Revenues (500 tons × \$200 per ton)	\$100,000	\$100,000	\$100,000
32	Cost of goods sold:			
33	Joint costs	50,000	40,000	57,143
34	Separable costs	20,000	20,000	20,000
35	Cost of goods sold	70,000	60,000	77,143
36	Gross margin	\$ 30,000	\$ 40,000	\$ 22,857
37	Gross margin percentage (\$30,000 ÷ \$100,000; \$40,000 ÷ \$100,000; \$22,857 ÷ \$100,000)	30.00%	40.00%	22.86%

4. Sale of chlorine versus processing into PVC

	A	B
40	Incremental revenue from processing 800 tons of chlorine into 500 tons of PVC	
41	(500 tons × \$200 per ton) – (800 tons × \$75 per ton)	\$40,000
42	Incremental cost of processing 800 tons of chlorine into 500 tons of PVC	20,000
43	Incremental operating income from further processing	\$20,000

If IC sells 800 tons of chlorine to Lifetime Swimming Pool Products instead of further processing it into PVC, its August 2020 operating income will reduce by \$20,000.

DECISION POINTS

The following question-and-answer format summarizes the chapter's learning objectives. Each decision presents a key question related to a learning objective. The guidelines are the answer to that question.

Decision	Guidelines
1. What do the terms *joint cost* and *splitoff point* mean, and how do joint products differ from byproducts?	A joint cost is the cost of a single production process that yields multiple products simultaneously. The splitoff point is the juncture in a joint production process when the products become separately identifiable. Joint products have high total sales values at the splitoff point. A byproduct has a low total sales value at the splitoff point relative to the total sales value of a joint or main product.
2. Why are joint costs allocated to individual products?	The purposes for allocating joint costs to products include inventory costing for financial accounting and internal reporting, cost reimbursement, insurance settlements, rate regulation, and product-cost litigation.
3. What methods can be used to allocate joint costs to individual products?	The methods to allocate joint costs to products are the sales value at splitoff, physical-measure, NRV, and constant gross-margin percentage NRV methods.

Decision	Guidelines
4. When is the sales value at splitoff method considered preferable for allocating joint costs to individual products, and why?	The sales value at splitoff method is preferred when market prices exist at splitoff because using revenues is consistent with the benefits-received criterion; moreover, the method is simple and does not depend on subsequent decisions made about further processing.
5. Are joint costs relevant in a sell-or-process-further decision?	No, joint costs and how they are allocated are irrelevant because they are the same regardless of whether further processing occurs.
6. What methods can be used to account for byproducts, and which of them is preferable?	The production method recognizes byproducts in financial statements at the time of their production, whereas the sales method recognizes byproducts in financial statements at the time of their sale. The production method is conceptually superior, but the sales method is often used in practice because the dollar amounts of byproducts are immaterial.

TERMS TO LEARN

This chapter and the Glossary at the end of the text contain definitions of the following important terms:

byproducts (**p. 681**)
constant gross-margin percentage NRV method (**p. 688**)
joint costs (**p. 680**)
joint products (**p. 681**)
main product (**p. 681**)
net realizable value (NRV) method (**p. 686**)
physical-measure method (**p. 684**)
product (**p. 680**)
sales value at splitoff method (**p. 684**)
separable costs (**p. 680**)
splitoff point (**p. 680**)

ASSIGNMENT MATERIAL

Questions

17-1 Give two examples of industries in which joint costs are found. For each example, what are the individual products at the splitoff point?

17-2 What is a joint cost? What is a separable cost?

17-3 Distinguish between a joint product and a byproduct.

17-4 Why might the number of products in a joint-cost situation differ from the number of outputs? Give an example.

17-5 Provide three reasons for allocating joint costs to individual products or services.

17-6 Why does the sales value at splitoff method use the sales value of the total production in the accounting period and not just the revenues from the products sold?

17-7 Describe a situation in which the sales value at splitoff method cannot be used but the NRV method can be used for joint-cost allocation.

17-8 Distinguish between the sales value at splitoff method and the NRV method.

17-9 Give two limitations of the physical-measure method of joint-cost allocation.

17-10 How might a company simplify its use of the NRV method when final selling prices can vary sizably in an accounting period and management frequently changes the point at which it sells individual products?

17-11 Why is the constant gross-margin percentage NRV method sometimes called a "joint-cost-allocation and a profit-allocation" method?

17-12 "Managers must decide whether a product should be sold at splitoff or processed further. The sales value at splitoff method of joint-cost allocation is the best method for generating the information managers need for this decision." Do you agree? Explain.

17-13 "Managers should consider only additional revenues and separable costs when making decisions about selling at splitoff or processing further." Do you agree? Explain.

17-14 Describe two major methods to account for byproducts.

17-15 Why might managers seeking a monthly bonus based on attaining a target operating income prefer the sales method of accounting for byproducts rather than the production method?

Multiple-Choice Questions

In partnership with:
BECKER
PROFESSIONAL EDUCATION®

17-16 Select Manufacturing Co. produces three joint products and one organic waste byproduct. Assuming the byproduct can be sold to an outside party, what is the correct accounting treatment of the byproduct proceeds received by the firm?

a. Apply sale proceeds on a prorated basis to the joint products' sales.
b. Use the sale proceeds to reduce the common costs in the joint production process.
c. Apply the sale proceeds to the firm's miscellaneous income account.
d. Either "b" or "c" can be used.

17-17 Joint costs of $8,000 are incurred to process X and Y. Upon splitoff, $4,000 and $6,000 in costs are incurred to produce 200 units of X and 150 units of Y, respectively. In order to justify processing further at the splitoff point, revenues for product:

a. X must exceed $12,000.
b. Y must exceed $14,000.
c. X must be greater than $60 per unit.
d. Y must be greater than $40 per unit.

17-18 Houston Corporation has two products, Astros and Texans, with the following volume information:

	Volume
Product Astros	20,000 gal
Product Texans	10,000 gal
Total	30,000 gal

The joint cost to produce the two products is $120,000. What portion of the joint cost will each product be allocated if the allocation is performed by volume?

1. $100,000 and $0
2. $80,000 and $40,000
3. $40,000 and $80,000
4. $50,000 and $50,000

17-19 Dallas Company produces joint products, TomL and JimmyJ, each of which incurs separable production costs after the splitoff point. Information concerning a batch produced at a $200,000 joint cost before splitoff follows:

Product	**Separable Costs**	**Sales Value**
TomL	$10,000	$ 80,000
JimmyJ	20,000	50,000
	$30,000	$130,000

What is the joint cost assigned to TomL if costs are assigned using relative net realizable value?

1. $60,000
2. $140,000
3. $48,000
4. $200,000

17-20 Earl's Hurricane Lamp Oil Company produces both A-1 Fancy and B Grade Oil. There are approximately $9,000 in joint costs that Earl may allocate using the relative sales value at splitoff or the net realizable value approach. At splitoff, A-1 sells for $20,000 while B grade sells for $40,000. After an additional investment of $10,000 after splitoff, $3,000 for B grade and $7,000 for A-1, both the products sell for $50,000. What is the difference in allocated costs for the A-1 product assuming applications of the net realizable value and the sales value at splitoff approach?

1. A-1 Fancy has $1,300 more joint costs allocated to it under the net realizable value approach than the sales value at splitoff approach.
2. A-1 Fancy has $1,300 less joint costs allocated to it under the net realizable value approach than the sales value at splitoff approach.
3. A-1 Fancy has $1,500 more joint costs allocated to it under the net realizable value approach than the sales value at splitoff approach.
4. A-1 Fancy has $1,500 less joint costs allocated to it under the net realizable value approach than the sales value at splitoff approach.

Exercises

17-21 Joint-cost allocation, insurance settlement. Quality Chicken grows and processes chickens. Each chicken is disassembled into five main parts. Information pertaining to production in July 2020 follows:

Parts	Pounds of Product	Wholesale Selling Price per Pound When Production Is Complete
Breasts	100	$0.55
Wings	20	0.20
Thighs	40	0.35
Bones	80	0.10
Feathers	10	0.05

Joint cost of production in July 2020 was $50.

A special shipment of 40 pounds of breasts and 15 pounds of wings has been destroyed in a fire. Quality Chicken's insurance policy provides reimbursement for the cost of the items destroyed. The insurance company permits Quality Chicken to use a joint-cost-allocation method. The splitoff point is assumed to be at the end of the production process.

Required

1. Compute the cost of the special shipment destroyed using the following:
   a. Sales value at splitoff method
   b. Physical-measure method (pounds of finished product)
2. What joint-cost-allocation method would you recommend Quality Chicken use? Explain.

17-22 Joint products and byproducts (continuation of 17-21). Quality Chicken is computing the ending inventory values for its July 31, 2020, balance sheet. Ending inventory amounts on July 31 are 15 pounds of breasts, 4 pounds of wings, 6 pounds of thighs, 5 pounds of bones, and 2 pounds of feathers.

Quality Chicken's management wants to use the sales value at splitoff method. However, management wants you to explore the effect on ending inventory values of classifying one or more products as a byproduct rather than a joint product.

Required

1. Assume Quality Chicken classifies all five products as joint products. What are the ending inventory values of each product on July 31, 2020?
2. Assume Quality Chicken uses the production method of accounting for byproducts. What are the ending inventory values for each joint product on July 31, 2020, assuming breasts and thighs are the joint products and wings, bones, and feathers are byproducts?
3. Comment on differences in the results in requirements 1 and 2.

17-23 Net realizable value method. Sweeney Company is one of the world's leading corn refiners. It produces two joint products—corn syrup and corn starch—using a common production process. In July 2020, Sweeney reported the following production and selling-price information:

	A	B	C	D
1		**Corn Syrup**	**Corn Starch**	**Joint Costs**
2	Joint costs (costs of processing corn to splitoff point)			$321,000
3	Separable cost of processing beyond splitoff point	$430,560	$94,740	
4	Beginning inventory (cases)	0	0	
5	Production and Sales (cases)	12,900	6,500	
6	Ending inventory (cases)	0	0	
7	Selling price per case	$ 52	$ 25	

Allocate the $321,000 joint costs using the NRV method.

Required

17-24 Alternative joint-cost-allocation methods, further-process decision. The Tempura Spirits Company produces two products—methanol (wood alcohol) and turpentine—by a joint process. Joint costs amount to $124,000 per batch of output. Each batch totals 9,500 gallons: 25% methanol and 75% turpentine. Both products are processed further without gain or loss in volume. Separable processing costs are methanol, $4 per gallon, and turpentine, $2 per gallon. Methanol sells for $22 per gallon. Turpentine sells for $16 per gallon.

Required

1. How much of the joint costs per batch will be allocated to methanol and to turpentine, assuming that joint costs are allocated based on the number of gallons at splitoff point?
2. If joint costs are allocated on an NRV basis, how much of the joint costs per batch will be allocated to methanol and to turpentine?
3. Prepare product-line income statements per batch for requirements 1 and 2. Assume no beginning or ending inventories.
4. The company has discovered an additional process by which the methanol (wood alcohol) can be made into a pleasant-tasting alcoholic beverage. The selling price of this beverage would be $55 a gallon. Additional processing would increase separable costs $12 per gallon (in addition to the $4 per gallon separable cost required to yield methanol). The company would have to pay excise taxes of 20% on the selling price of the beverage. Assuming no other changes in cost, what is the joint cost applicable to the wood alcohol (using the NRV method)? Should the company produce the alcoholic beverage? Show your computations.

17-25 Alternative methods of joint-cost allocation, ending inventories. The Cook Company operates a simple chemical process to convert a single material into three separate items, referred to here as X, Y, and Z. All three end products are separated simultaneously at a single splitoff point.

Products X and Y are ready for sale immediately upon splitoff without further processing or any other additional costs. Product Z, however, is processed further before being sold. There is no available market price for Z at the splitoff point.

During 2020, the selling prices of the items and the total amounts sold were as follows:

- X—68 tons sold for $1,200 per ton
- Y—480 tons sold for $900 per ton
- Z—672 tons sold for $600 per ton

The total joint manufacturing costs for the year were $580,000. Cook spent an additional $200,000 to finish product Z.

There were no beginning inventories of X, Y, or Z. At the end of the year, the following inventories of completed units were on hand: X, 132 tons; Y, 120 tons; Z, 28 tons. There was no beginning or ending work in process.

Required

1. Compute the cost of inventories of X, Y, and Z for balance sheet purposes and the cost of goods sold for income statement purposes as of December 31, 2020, using the following joint-cost-allocation methods:
   a. NRV method
   b. Constant gross-margin percentage NRV method
2. Compare the gross-margin percentages for X, Y, and Z using the two methods given in requirement 1.

17-26 Joint-cost allocation, process further. Sinclair Oil & Gas, a large energy conglomerate, jointly processes purchased hydrocarbons to generate three nonsalable intermediate products: ICR8, ING4, and XGE3. These intermediate products are further processed separately to produce crude oil, natural gas liquids, and natural gas (measured in liquid equivalents). An overview of the process and results for August 2020 are shown here. (Note: The numbers are small to keep the focus on key concepts.)

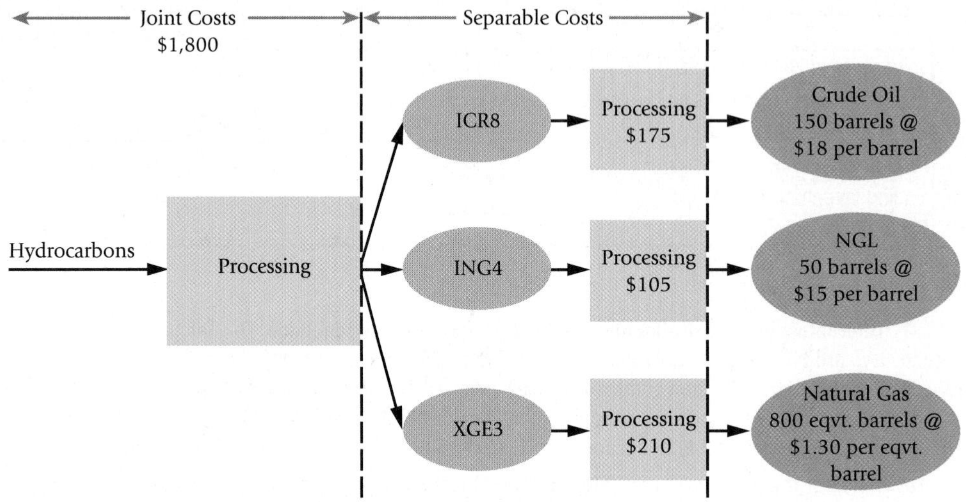

A federal law that has recently been passed taxes crude oil at 30% of operating income. No new tax is to be paid on natural gas liquids or natural gas. Starting August 2020, Sinclair Oil & Gas must report a separate product-line income statement for crude oil. One challenge facing Sinclair Oil & Gas is how to allocate the joint cost of producing the three separate saleable outputs. Assume no beginning or ending inventory.

Required

1. Allocate the August 2020 joint cost among the three products using the following:
   a. Physical-measure method
   b. NRV method
2. Show the operating income for each product using the methods in requirement 1.
3. Discuss the pros and cons of the two methods to Sinclair Oil & Gas for making decisions about product emphasis (pricing, sell-or-process-further decisions, and so on).
4. Draft a letter to the taxation authorities on behalf of Sinclair Oil & Gas that justifies the joint-cost-allocation method you recommend Sinclair use.

17-27 Joint-cost allocation, sales value, physical measure, NRV methods. Tasty Foods produces two types of microwavable products: beef-flavored ramen and shrimp-flavored ramen. The two products share common inputs such as noodle and spices. The production of ramen results in a waste product referred to as stock, which Tasty dumps at negligible costs in a local drainage area. In June 2020, the following data were reported for the production and sales of beef-flavored and shrimp-flavored ramen:

	A	B	C
1		Joint Costs	
2	Joint costs (costs of noodles, spices, and other inputs and processing to splitoff point)	$380,000	
3			
4		Beef Ramen	Shrimp Ramen
5	Beginning inventory (tons)	0	0
6	Production (tons)	9,000	11,000
7	Sales (tons)	9,000	11,000
8	Selling price per ton	$ 15	$ 35

Due to the popularity of its microwavable products, Tasty decides to add a new line of products that targets dieters. These new products are produced by adding a special ingredient to dilute the original ramen and are to be sold under the names Special B and Special S, respectively. Following are the monthly data for all the products:

	A	B	C	D	E
11		Joint Costs		Special B	Special S
12	Joint costs (costs of noodles, spices, and other inputs and processing to splitoff point)	$380,000			
13	Separable costs of processing 9,000 tons of Beef Ramen into 12,000 tons of Special B			$36,000	
14	Separable cost of processing 11,000 tons of Shrimp Ramen into 17,000 tons of Special S				$136,000
15					
16		Beef Ramen	Shrimp Ramen	Special B	Special S
17	Beginning inventory (tons)	0	0	0	0
18	Production (tons)	9,000	11,000	12,000	17,000
19	Transfer for further processing (tons)	9,000	11,000		
20	Sales (tons)			12,000	17,000
21	Selling price per ton	$ 15	$ 35	$ 20	$ 47

Required

1. Calculate Tasty's gross-margin percentage for Special B and Special S when joint costs are allocated using the following:
   a. Sales value at splitoff method
   b. Physical-measure method
   c. Net realizable value method
2. Recently, Tasty discovered that the stock it is dumping can be sold to cattle ranchers at $5 per ton. In a typical month with the production levels shown, 3,000 tons of stock are produced and can be sold by incurring marketing costs of $11,100. Sabrina Donahue, a management accountant, points out that treating the stock as a joint product and using the sales value at splitoff method, the stock product would lose about $6,754 each month, so it should not be sold. How did Donahue arrive at that final number, and what do you think of her analysis? Should Tasty sell the stock?

17-28 Joint-cost allocation: Sell immediately or process further. Nervana Soy Products (NSP) buys soybeans and processes them into other soy products. Each ton of soybeans that NSP purchases for $350 can be converted for an additional $210 into 650 pounds of soy meal and 100 gallons of soy oil. A pound of soy meal can be sold at splitoff for $1.32 and soy oil can be sold in bulk for $4.50 per gallon.

NSP can process the 650 pounds of soy meal into 750 pounds of soy cookies at an additional cost of $300. Each pound of soy cookies can be sold for $2.32 per pound. The 100 gallons of soy oil can be packaged at a cost of $230 and made into 400 quarts of Soyola. Each quart of Soyola can be sold for $1.15.

Required

1. Allocate the joint cost to the soy cookies and the Soyola using the following:
   a. Sales value at splitoff method
   b. NRV method
2. Should NSP have processed each of the products further? What effect does the allocation method have on this decision?

17-29 Accounting for a main product and a byproduct. (Cheatham and Green, adapted) Crispy, Inc., is a producer of potato chips. A single production process at Crispy, Inc., yields potato chips as the main product as well as a byproduct that can be sold as a snack. Both products are fully processed by the splitoff point, and there are no separable costs.

For September 2020, the cost of operations is $520,000. Production and sales data are as follows:

	Production (in pounds)	Sales (in pounds)	Selling Price per Pound
Potato chips	46,000	34,960	$26
Byproduct	8,200	5,000	$ 5

There were no beginning inventories on September 1, 2020.

Required

1. What is the gross margin for Crispy, Inc., under the production method and the sales method of byproduct accounting?
2. What are the inventory costs reported in the balance sheet on September 30, 2020, for the main product and byproduct under the two methods of byproduct accounting in requirement 1?
3. Prepare the journal entries to record the byproduct activities under (a) the production method and (b) the sales method. Briefly discuss the effects on the financial statements.

17-30 Joint costs and decision making. Jack Bibby is a prospector in the Texas Panhandle. He has also been running a side business for the past couple of years. Based on the popularity of shows such as "Rattlesnake Nation," there has been a surge of interest from professionals and amateurs to visit the northern counties of Texas to capture snakes in the wild. Jack has set himself up as a purchaser of these captured snakes.

Jack purchases rattlesnakes in good condition from "snake hunters" for an average of $11 per snake. Jack produces canned snake meat, cured skins, and souvenir rattles, although he views snake meat as his primary product. At the end of the recent season, Jack Bibby evaluated his financial results:

	Meat	Skins	Rattles	Total
Sales revenues	$33,000	$8,800	$2,200	$44,000
Share of snake cost	19,800	5,280	1,320	26,400
Processing expenses	6,600	990	660	8,250
Allocated overhead	4,400	660	440	5,500
Income (loss)	$ 2,200	$1,870	$ (220)	$ 3,850

The cost of snakes is assigned to each product line using the *relative* sales value of meat, skins, and rattles (i.e., the percentage of total sales generated by each product). Processing expenses are directly traced to each product line. Overhead costs are allocated to each product line on the basis of processing expenses.

Jack has a philosophy of every product line paying for itself and is determined to cut his losses on rattles.

Required

1. Should Jack Bibby drop rattles from his product offerings? Support your answer with computations.
2. An old miner has offered to buy every rattle "as is" for $0.60 per rattle (note: "as is" refers to the situation where Jack only removes the rattle from the snake and no processing costs are incurred). Assume that Jack expects to process the same number of snakes each season. Should he sell rattles to the miner? Support your answer with computations.

17-31 Joint costs and byproducts. (W. Crum adapted) Royston, Inc., is a large food-processing company. It processes 150,000 pounds of peanuts in the peanuts department at a cost of $180,000 to yield 12,000 pounds of product A, 65,000 pounds of product B, and 16,000 pounds of product C.

- Product A is processed further in the salting department at a cost of $27,000. It yields 12,000 pounds of salted peanuts, which are sold for $12 per pound.
- Product B (raw peanuts) is sold without further processing at $3 per pound.
- Product C is considered a byproduct and is processed further in the paste department at a cost of $12,000. It yields 16,000 pounds of peanut butter, which are sold for $6 per pound.

The company wants to make a gross margin of 10% of revenues on product C and needs to allow 20% of revenues for marketing costs on product C. An overview of operations follows:

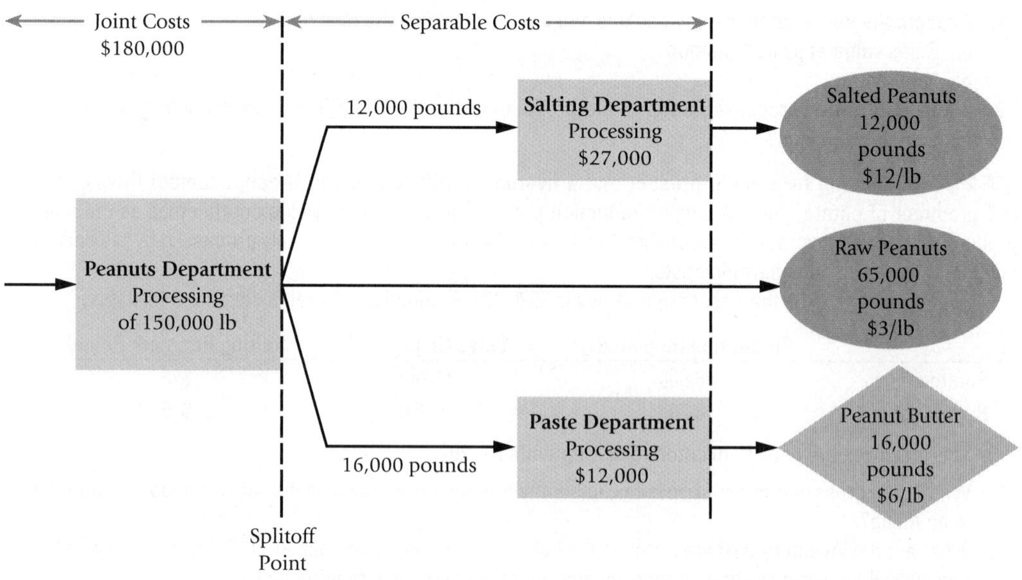

Required

1. Compute unit costs per pound for products A, B, and C, treating C as a byproduct. Use the NRV method for allocating joint costs. Deduct the NRV of the byproduct produced from the joint cost of products A and B.
2. Compute unit costs per pound for products A, B, and C, treating all three as joint products and allocating joint costs by the NRV method.

Problems

17-32 Methods of joint-cost allocation, ending inventory. Garden Labs produces a drug used for the treatment of arthritis. The drug is produced in batches. Chemicals costing $50,000 are mixed and heated, then a unique separation process extracts the drug from the mixture. A batch yields a total of 3,000 gallons of the drug. The first 2,500 gallons are sold for human use while the last 500 gallons, which contain impurities, are sold to veterinarians.

The costs of mixing, heating, and extracting the drug amount to $155,000 per batch. The output sold for human use is pasteurized at a total cost of $130,000 and is sold for $600 per gallon. The product sold to veterinarians is irradiated at a cost of $20 per gallon and is sold for $450 per gallon.

In March, Garden, which had no opening inventory, processed one batch of chemicals. It sold 2,000 gallons of product for human use and 300 gallons of the veterinarian product. Garden uses the net realizable value method for allocating joint production costs.

Required

1. How much in joint costs does Garden allocate to each product?
2. Compute the cost of ending inventory for each of Garden's products.
3. If Garden were to use the constant gross-margin percentage NRV method instead, how would it allocate its joint costs?
4. Calculate the gross margin on the sale of the product for human use in March under the constant gross-margin percentage NRV method.
5. Suppose that the separation process also yields 300 pints of a toxic byproduct. Garden currently pays a hauling company $6,000 to dispose of this byproduct. Garden is contacted by a firm interested in purchasing a modified form of this byproduct for a total price of $7,000. Garden estimates that it will cost about $35 per pint to make the required modification. Should Garden accept the offer?

17-33 Alternative methods of joint-cost allocation, product-mix decisions. The Chicago Oil Company buys crude vegetable oil. Refining this oil results in four products at the splitoff point: A, B, C, and D. Product C is fully processed by the splitoff point. Products A, B, and D can individually be further refined into Super A, Super B, and Super D. In the most recent month (November), the output at the splitoff point was as follows:

- Product A, 550,000 gallons
- Product B, 200,000 gallons
- Product C, 150,000 gallons
- Product D, 100,000 gallons

The joint costs of purchasing and processing the crude vegetable oil were $210,000. Chicago had no beginning or ending inventories. Sales of product C in November were $90,000. Products A, B, and D were further refined and then sold. Data related to November follow:

	Separable Processing Costs to Make Super Products	Revenues
Super A	$480,000	$750,000
Super B	120,000	300,000
Super D	90,000	150,000

Chicago had the option of selling products A, B, and D at the splitoff point. This alternative would have yielded the following revenues for the November production:

- Product A, $150,000
- Product B, $125,000
- Product D, $135,000

Required

1. Compute the gross-margin percentage for each product sold in November, using the following methods for allocating the $210,000 joint costs:
   a. Sales value at splitoff
   b. Physical measure
   c. NRV
2. Could Chicago Oil have increased its November operating income by making different decisions about the further processing of products A, B, or D? Show the effect on operating income of any changes you recommend.

17-34 Comparison of alternative joint-cost-allocation methods, further-processing decision, chocolate products. The Rich and Creamy Edibles Factory manufactures and distributes chocolate products. It purchases cocoa beans and processes them into two intermediate products: chocolate-powder liquor base and milk-chocolate liquor base. These two intermediate products become separately identifiable at a single splitoff point. Every 600 pounds of cocoa beans yields 20 gallons of chocolate-powder liquor base and 60 gallons of milk-chocolate liquor base.

The chocolate-powder liquor base is further processed into chocolate powder. Every 20 gallons of chocolate-powder liquor base yield 680 pounds of chocolate powder. The milk-chocolate liquor base is further processed into milk chocolate. Every 60 gallons of milk-chocolate liquor base yield 1,100 pounds of milk chocolate.

Production and sales data for August 2020 are as follows (assume no beginning inventory):

- Cocoa beans processed, 27,600 pounds
- Costs of processing cocoa beans to splitoff point (including purchase of beans), $70,000

	Production	Sales	Selling Price	Separable Processing Costs
Chocolate powder	31,280 pounds	6,800 pounds	$8 per pound	$46,035
Milk chocolate	50,600 pounds	14,400 pounds	$9 per pound	$55,085

Rich and Creamy Edibles Factory fully processes both of its intermediate products into chocolate powder or milk chocolate. There is an active market for these intermediate products. In August 2020, Rich and Creamy Edibles Factory could have sold the chocolate-powder liquor base for $21 a gallon and the milk-chocolate liquor base for $28 a gallon.

Required

1. Calculate how the joint costs of $70,000 would be allocated between chocolate powder and milk chocolate under the following methods:
   a. Sales value at splitoff
   b. Physical measure (gallons)
   c. NRV
   d. Constant gross-margin percentage NRV
2. What are the gross-margin percentages of chocolate powder and milk chocolate under each of the methods in requirement 1?
3. Could Rich and Creamy Edibles Factory have increased its operating income by a change in its decision to fully process both of its intermediate products? Show your computations.

17-35 Joint-cost allocation, process further or sell. (CMA, adapted) Liverpool Sawmill, Inc. (LSI) purchases logs from independent timber contractors and processes the logs into three types of lumber products:

- Studs for residential buildings (walls, ceilings)
- Decorative pieces (fireplace mantels, beams for cathedral ceilings)
- Posts used as support braces (mine support braces, braces for exterior fences on ranch properties)

These products are the result of a joint sawmill process that involves removal of bark from the logs, cutting the logs into a workable size (ranging from 8 to 16 feet in length), and then cutting the individual products from the logs.

The joint process results in the following costs of products for a typical month:

Direct materials (rough timber logs)	$ 480,000
Debarking (labor and overhead)	50,000
Sizing (labor and overhead)	220,000
Product cutting (labor and overhead)	260,000
Total joint costs	$1,010,000

Product yields and average sales values on a per-unit basis from the joint process are as follows:

Product	Monthly Output of Materials at Splitoff Point	Fully Processed Selling Price
Studs	78,000 units	$ 5
Decorative pieces	4,000 units	85
Posts	28,000 units	26

The studs are sold as rough-cut lumber after emerging from the sawmill operation without further processing by Liverpool Sawmill. Also, the posts require no further processing beyond the splitoff point. The decorative pieces must be planed and further sized after emerging from the sawmill. This additional processing costs $90,000 per month and normally results in a loss of 10% of the units entering the process. Without this planing and sizing process, there is still an active intermediate market for the unfinished decorative pieces in which the selling price averages $55 per unit.

Required

1. Based on the information given for Liverpool Sawmill, allocate the joint processing costs of $1,010,000 to the three products using:
   a. Sales value at splitoff method
   b. Physical-measure method (volume in units)
   c. NRV method
2. Prepare an analysis for Liverpool Sawmill that compares processing the decorative pieces further, as it currently does, with selling them as a rough-cut product immediately at splitoff.
3. Assume Liverpool Sawmill announced that in 6 months it will sell the unfinished decorative pieces at splitoff due to increasing competitive pressure. Identify at least three types of likely behavior that will be demonstrated by the skilled labor in the planing-and-sizing process as a result of this announcement. Include in your discussion how this behavior could be influenced by management.

17-36 Joint-cost allocation. SW Flour Company buys whole wheat flour and mills it into Bread Flour and All-Purpose White Flour (APWF). In 2020, SW bought 300,000 pounds of whole wheat flour for $70,000. SW spent an additional $50,000 to process the whole wheat flour into Bread Flour and All-Purpose White Flour, so total joint costs equal $120,000.

SW Flour Company reported the following production and sales information for 2020:

	Bread Flour	APWF
Production and sales (in pounds)	60,000	240,000
Selling price per pound	$0.85	$0.50

SW can also put the All-Purpose White Flour through a second process and convert it into Cake Flour. This process costs an additional $50,000 but 20,000 pounds of flour are lost and thus yields only 220,000 pounds of Cake Flour. The Cake Flour sells for $1 per pound.

Required

1. Allocate the $120,000 joint cost to the All-Purpose White Flour and the Bread Flour using the following:
   a. Physical-measure method (using pounds)
   b. Sales value at splitoff method
   c. NRV method
   d. Constant gross-margin percentage NRV method
2. Each of these measures has advantages and disadvantages; what are they?
3. Some managers claim that the sales value at splitoff method is the best method to use. Discuss the logic behind this claim.

17-37 Further processing decision (continuation of 17-36). SW Flour Company has decided that their bread flour may sell better if it was marketed for gourmet baking and sold with infused spices. This would involve additional cost for the spices of $1.70 per pound. Each pound could be sold for $2.50.

Required

1. If SW uses the sales value at splitoff method, what combination of products should SW sell to maximize profits?
2. If SW uses the physical-measure method, what combination of products should SW sell to maximize profits?
3. Explain the effect that the different cost-allocation methods have on the decision to sell the products at splitoff or to process them further.

17-38 Accounting for a main product and a byproduct. (Cheatham and Green, adapted) Holy Cow is a producer of milk and by products. A single production process at Holy Cow yields milk as the main product, as well as ghee, a byproduct of milk production, that can be sold. Both products are fully processed by the splitoff point, and there are no separable costs.

For the month of October 2020, the cost of operations is $380,000. Production and sales data are as follows:

	Production (in gallons)	Sales (in gallons)	Selling Price per Gallon
Milk	540,000	523,800	$0.80
Ghee, byproduct	12,000	11,400	$0.70

There were no beginning inventories on October 1, 2020.

Required

1. What is the gross margin for Holy Cow under the production method and the sales method of byproduct accounting?
2. What are the inventory costs reported in the balance sheet on October 31, 2020, for the main product and byproduct under the two methods of byproduct accounting in requirement 1?

17-39 Byproduct-costing journal entries (continuation of 17-38). The accountant for Holy Cow needs to record the information about the joint and byproducts in the general journal, but is not sure what the entries should be. The company has hired you as a consultant to help the accountant.

Required

1. Show journal entries at the time of production and at the time of sale assuming Holy Cow accounts for the byproduct using the production method.
2. Show journal entries at the time of production and at the time of sale assuming Holy Cow accounts for the byproduct using the sales method.

17-40 Alternative joint-cost-allocation methods, further-process decision. The Palm Company produces two products—coconut and coconut water—by a joint process. Joint costs amount to $14,000 per batch of output. Each batch totals 4,000 pounds of coconut and 6,000 pounds of coconut water. Both products are processed further without a gain or loss in volume. Separable processing costs for the coconut are $1.47 per pound and for the coconut water are $2.02 per pound. Coconut sells for $6.30 per pound and the coconut water sells for $5.80 per pound.

Required

1. How much of the joint costs per batch will be allocated to coconut and to coconut water, assuming that joint costs are allocated based on the number of pounds at the splitoff point?
2. If joint costs are allocated on an NRV basis, how much of the joint costs will be allocated to the coconut and to the coconut water?
3. Prepare product-line income statements per batch for requirements 1 and 2. Assume no beginning or ending inventories of either product.
4. The company has the option of processing the coconut further and producing coconut slices. The selling price of the coconut slices would be $8 per pound after incurring additional processing costs of $0.3875 per pound. Assuming no other changes in cost, what is the joint cost allocated to coconut slices (using the NRV method)? Should the company produce the coconut slices? Show your computations.

17-41 Process further or sell, byproduct. (CMA, adapted) Newcastle Mining Company (NMC) mines coal, puts it through a one-step crushing process, and loads the bulk raw coal onto river barges for shipment to customers.

NMC's management is currently evaluating the possibility of further processing the raw coal by sizing and cleaning it and selling it to an expanded set of customers at higher prices. The option of building a new sizing and cleaning plant is ruled out as being financially infeasible. Instead, Amy Kimbell, a mining engineer, is asked to explore outside-contracting arrangements for the cleaning and sizing process. Kimbell puts together the following summary:

	A	B	C
1	Selling price of raw coal	$ 30	per ton
2	Cost of producing raw coal	$ 21	per ton
3	Selling price of sized and cleaned coal	$ 34	per ton
4	Annual raw coal output	9,000,000	tons
5	Percentage of material wasted in sizing/cleaning coal	6%	
6			
7		Incremental Costs of Sizing & Cleaning Processes	
8	Direct labor	$ 790,000	per year
9	Supervisory personnel	$ 190,000	per year
10	Heavy equipment: rental, operating, maintenance costs	$ 35,000	per month
11	Contract sizing and cleaning	$ 3.30	per ton of raw coal
12	Outbound rail freight	$ 250	per 600-ton rail car
13			
14	Percentage of sizing/cleaning waste that can be salvaged for coal fines	75%	
15	Range of costs per ton for preparing coal fine for sale	$ 3	$ 5
16	Range of coal fine selling prices (per ton)	$ 14	$25

Kimbell also learns that 75% of the material waste that occurs in the cleaning and sizing process can be salvaged as coal fines, which can be sold to steel manufacturers for their furnaces. The sale of coal fines is erratic. The selling price of coal fines ranges from $14 to $25 per ton, and costs of preparing coal fines for sale range from $3 to $5 per ton.

Required

1. Prepare an analysis to show whether it is more profitable for NMC to continue selling raw bulk coal or to process it further through sizing and cleaning. (Ignore coal fines in your analysis.)
2. How would your analysis be affected if the cost of producing raw coal could be held down to $20 per ton?
3. Now consider the potential value of the coal fines and prepare an addendum that shows how their value affects the results of your analysis prepared in requirement 1.

17-42 Joint-cost allocation: Sell immediately or process further. Forrest Products buys cut trees and processes them into wood products. Each batch of trees that Forrest purchases for $500 can be converted for an additional $400 into 2,000 ft of rough sawn lumber and 200 bundles of bulk firewood. Rough sawn lumber can be sold at splitoff for $0.90 per foot, and the bulk firewood can be sold for $0.50 per bundle.

Forrest can process the 2,000 ft of rough sawn lumber into 1,720 ft of dried, treated lumber for an additional cost of $800, and the firewood can be split into smaller pieces and bundled into 180 bundles for an additional cost of $200. Dried, treated lumber can be sold for $1.50 per foot. The 180 bundles of firewood can be sold for $2.50. per bundle.

Required

1. Allocate the joint cost to the dried, treated lumber and the processed firewood bundles using the following:
   a. Sales value at splitoff method
   b. NRV method
2. Should Forrest process each of the products further or sell at spittoff? What effect does the allocation method have on this decision?

17-43 Methods of joint-cost allocation, comprehensive. Kardash Cosmetics purchases flowers in bulk and processes them into perfume. From a certain mix of petals, the firm uses Process A to generate Seduction, its high-grade perfume, as well as a certain residue. The residue is then further treated, using Process B, to yield Romance, a medium-grade perfume. An ounce of residue typically yields an ounce of Romance.

In July, the company used 25,000 pounds of petals. Costs involved in Process A, i.e., reducing the petals to Seduction and the residue, were

Direct Materials – $440,000; Direct Labor – $220,000; Overhead Costs – $110,000.

The additional costs of producing Romance in Process B were

Direct Materials – $22,000; Direct Labor – $50,000; Overhead Costs – $40,000.

During July, Process A yielded 7,000 ounces of Seduction and 49,000 ounces of residue. From this, 5,000 ounces of Seduction were packaged and sold for $109.50 an ounce. Also, 28,000 ounces of Romance were processed in Process B and then packaged and sold for $31.50 an ounce. The other 21,000 ounces remained as residue. Packaging costs incurred were $137,500 for Seduction and $196,000 for Romance. The firm has no beginning inventory on July 1.

If it so desired, the firm could have sold unpackaged Seduction for $56 an ounce and the residue from Process A for $24 an ounce.

Required

1. What is the joint cost of the firm to be allocated to Seduction and Romance?
2. Under the physical measure method, how would the joint costs be allocated to Seduction and Romance?
3. Under the sales value at splitoff method, what portion of the joint costs would be allocated to Seduction and Romance, respectively?
4. What is the estimated net realizable value per ounce of Seduction and Romance?
5. Under the net realizable value method, what portion of the joint costs would be allocated to Seduction and Romance, respectively?
6. What is the gross margin percentage for the firm as a whole?
7. Allocate the joint costs to Seduction and Romance under the constant gross-margin percentage NRV method.
8. If you were the manager of Kardash Cosmetics, would you continue to process the petal residue into Romance perfume? Explain your answer.

18 Process Costing

LEARNING OBJECTIVES

1. Identify the situations in which process-costing systems are appropriate
2. Understand the basic concepts of process costing and compute average unit costs
3. Describe the five steps in process costing and calculate equivalent units
4. Use the weighted-average method and the first-in, first-out (FIFO) method of process costing
5. Apply process-costing methods to situations with transferred-in costs
6. Understand the need for hybrid-costing systems such as operation costing

Many companies use mass-production techniques to produce identical or similar units of a product or service:

Apple (smartphones), Coca-Cola (soft drinks), Chevron (gasoline), JPMorgan Chase (processing of checks), and Novartis (pharmaceuticals). These companies use a method of accounting called process costing to value inventory and calculate cost of goods sold. As you learned in financial accounting, there are several methods to value inventory; the choice of method results in different operating income and affects the taxes a company pays and the performance evaluation of managers. When prices are volatile, as has been the case recently with commodities, the impact of using a particular method of inventory valuation can be substantial.

CRYPTOCURRENCY AND FIFO VERSUS LIFO ACCOUNTING[1]

In 2018, Goldman Sachs established the first institutional cryptocurrency trading operation on Wall Street. Fidelity Investments and others soon followed. With banks trading Bitcoin and other digital currencies for the first time, an important question emerged: How should profits on cryptocurrencies be calculated and taxed?

Each Bitcoin is very similar to another. The default rule for determining gain or loss on securities—which many accounting experts consider cryptocurrencies to be—is the first-in, first-out (FIFO) method. Under FIFO, the oldest cryptoasset is recorded as sold, regardless of whether that specific asset was sold. This method can trigger higher taxes, as older cryptocurrencies often have the lowest cost basis. Others argue that the last-in, first-out (LIFO) valuation method is more accurate. Under LIFO, the most recently acquired cryptoasset, which often has the highest cost, is regarded as sold, lowering profits and taxes. The FIFO versus LIFO choice is a significant decision for managers and regulators.

icemanphotos/Shutterstock

This chapter describes how companies, such as Kellogg (cereals) and AB InBev (beer), that produce many identical or similar units of a product using mass-production techniques use process-costing methods to value inventory and cost of goods sold.

[1] *Sources:* Nathaniel Popper, "Goldman Sachs to Open a Bitcoin Trading Operation," *The New York Times*, May 2, 2018 (https://www.nytimes.com/2018/05/02/technology/bitcoin-goldman-sachs.html); Kate Rooney, "Fidelity just made it easier for hedge funds and other pros to invest in cryptocurrencies," CNBC.com, October 15, 2018 (https://www.cnbc.com/2018/10/15/fidelity-launches-trade-execution-and-custody-for-cryptocurrencies.html); Tyson Cross, "Are Crypto Taxes Giving You A Headache? Keep These Tips in Mind To Make Next Year Go Smoother," Forbes.com, January 28, 2019 (https://www.forbes.com/sites/tysoncross/2019/01/28/are-crypto-taxes-giving-you-a-headache-keep-these-tips-in-mind-to-make-next-year-go-smoother/).

Illustrating Process Costing

LEARNING OBJECTIVE 1

Identify the situations in which process-costing systems are appropriate

. . . when masses of identical or similar units are produced

Before examining process costing in detail, let's briefly review the distinction between job costing and process costing explained in Chapter 4. Job-costing and process-costing systems are best viewed as ends of a continuum:

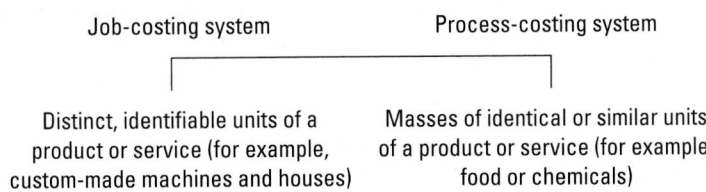

Job-costing system	Process-costing system
Distinct, identifiable units of a product or service (for example, custom-made machines and houses)	Masses of identical or similar units of a product or service (for example, food or chemicals)

In a process-costing system, the unit cost of a product or service is obtained by assigning total costs to many identical or similar units of output. Unit cost equals total costs divided by the number of units of output from the production process. In a manufacturing process-costing setting, each unit receives the same or similar amounts of direct material costs, direct manufacturing labor costs, and indirect manufacturing costs (manufacturing overhead).

The main difference between process costing and job costing is the *extent of averaging* used to compute unit costs. In job-costing, individual jobs use *different* quantities of resources, so it is incorrect to cost each job at the same average production cost. In contrast, when *identical* or *similar* units of products or services are mass-produced, process costing calculates an average production cost for all units produced. Some processes, such as clothes manufacturing, have aspects of both process costing (the cost per unit of each operation, such as cutting or sewing, is identical) and job costing (different materials are used in different batches of clothing, say, wool versus cotton). The final section in this chapter describes "hybrid" costing systems that combine elements of both job and process costing.

Consider the following example: Pacific Electronics manufactures a cell phone, model SG-40. The phones are assembled in the assembly department. Upon completion, units are transferred to the testing department. All units of SG-40 are identical. The process-costing system for SG-40 in the assembly department has a single direct-cost category—direct materials—and a single indirect-cost category—conversion costs. Conversion costs are all manufacturing costs other than direct material costs, including manufacturing labor, energy, plant depreciation, and so on. Direct materials, such as a phone's processor, image sensors, and microphone, are added at the beginning of the assembly process. Conversion costs are added evenly during assembly.

The following graphic represents these facts:

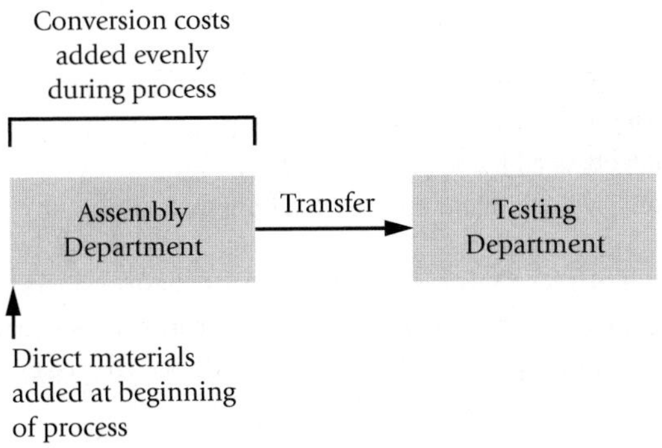

Process-costing systems separate costs into cost categories according to *when costs are introduced into the process*. Often, as in our Pacific Electronics example, only two cost classifications—direct materials and conversion costs—are necessary to assign costs to products. Why only two? Because *all* direct materials are added to the process at one time and all conversion costs generally are added to the process evenly through time. Sometimes the situation is different.

1. If two different direct materials—such as the processor and digital camera—are added to the process at different times, two different direct materials categories would be needed to assign these costs to products.

2. If manufacturing labor costs are added to the process at a different time compared to other conversion costs, an additional cost category—direct manufacturing labor costs—would be needed to assign these costs to products.

We illustrate process costing using three cases of increasing complexity:

- **Case 1**—Process costing with zero beginning and zero ending work-in-process inventory of SG-40 (all units are started and fully completed within the accounting period). *This case presents the most basic concepts of process costing and illustrates the averaging of costs.*
- **Case 2**—Process costing with zero beginning work-in-process inventory and some ending work-in-process inventory of SG-40. (That is, some units of SG-40 started during the accounting period are incomplete at the end of the period.) *This case introduces the five steps of process costing and the concept of equivalent units.*
- **Case 3**—Process costing with some beginning and some ending work-in-process inventory of SG-40. *This case adds more complexity and illustrates the effects the weighted-average and first-in, first-out (FIFO) methods have on the cost of units completed and the cost of work-in-process inventory.*

DECISION POINT
Under what conditions is a process-costing system used?

Case 1: Process Costing With Zero Beginning or Ending Work-in-Process Inventory

LEARNING OBJECTIVE 2
Understand the basic concepts of process costing and compute average unit costs
...divide total costs by total units in a given accounting period

On January 1, 2020, there was no beginning inventory of SG-40 units in the assembly department. During the month of January, Pacific Electronics started, completely assembled, and transferred 400 units to the testing department.

Data for the assembly department for January 2020 follow:

Physical Units for January 2020	
Work in process, beginning inventory (January 1)	0 units
Started during January	400 units
Completed and transferred out during January	400 units
Work in process, ending inventory (January 31)	0 units

Physical units refer to the number of output units, whether complete or incomplete. In January 2020, all 400 physical units started were completed.

Total Costs for January 2020	
Direct materials costs added during January	$32,000
Conversion costs added during January	24,000
Total assembly department costs added during January	$56,000

Pacific Electronics records direct materials costs and conversion costs in the assembly department as these costs are incurred. The cost per unit equals total costs incurred in a given accounting period divided by total units produced in that period. So, the assembly department cost of SG-40 is $56,000 ÷ 400 units = $140 per unit:

Direct materials cost per unit ($32,000 ÷ 400 units)	$ 80
Conversion costs per unit ($24,000 ÷ 400 units)	60
Assembly department cost per unit	$140

Case 1 applies whenever a company produces a homogeneous product or service but has no incomplete units when each accounting period ends. This is a common situation in service-sector organizations. For example, banks adopt this process-costing approach to compute the unit cost of processing 100,000 customer deposits made in a month because each deposit is processed in the same way regardless of the amount of the deposit.

DECISION POINT
How are average unit costs computed when no inventories are present?

Case 2: Process Costing With Zero Beginning and Some Ending Work-in-Process Inventory

In February 2020, Pacific Electronics places another 400 units of SG-40 into production. Recall there is no beginning inventory of partially completed units in the assembly department on February 1. Of the 400 units started in February, only 175 units are completed and transferred to the testing department. Data for the assembly department for February 2020 follow:

	A	B	C	D	E
1		Physical Units (SG-40s) (1)	Direct Materials (2)	Conversion Costs (3)	Total Costs (4) = (2) + (3)
2	Work in process, beginning inventory (February 1)	0			
3	Started during February	400			
4	Completed and transferred out during February	175			
5	Work in process, ending inventory (February 28)	225			
6	Degree of completion of ending work in process		100%	60%	
7	Total costs added during February		$32,000	$18,600	$50,600

LEARNING OBJECTIVE 3

Describe the five steps in process costing

...to assign total costs to units completed and to units in work in process

and calculate equivalent units

...output units adjusted for incomplete units

The 225 partially assembled units as of February 29 2020, are fully processed for direct materials because all direct materials in the assembly department are added at the beginning of the assembly process. Conversion costs, however, are added evenly during assembly. An assembly department supervisor estimates that the partially assembled units are, on average, 60% complete with respect to conversion costs.

The accuracy of the completion estimate depends on the care, skill, and experience of the estimator and the nature of the conversion process. Estimating degree of completion is usually easier for direct materials costs than for conversion costs because the quantity of direct materials needed for a completed unit and the quantity of direct materials in a partially completed unit can be measured more accurately. In contrast, the conversion sequence usually consists of a number of operations, each for a specified period of time, at various steps in the production process.[2] The degree of completion for conversion costs depends on the proportion of total conversion costs needed to complete one unit (or a batch of production) that has already been incurred on units still in process.

Department supervisors and line managers often estimate completion rates for conversion costs because they are most familiar with the conversion process. However, in some industries, such as semiconductor manufacturing, no exact estimate is possible because manufacturing occurs inside sealed environments that can only be opened when the process is complete. In other industries, such as textiles, vast quantities of unfinished products, such as shirts and pants, make the task of estimation too costly. In these cases, to calculate conversion costs, managers assume that all work in process in a department is complete to some preset degree (for example, one-third, one-half, or two-thirds).

Because some units are fully assembled and some are only partially assembled, a common metric, called *equivalent units*, is needed to compare the work that's been done on them and, more importantly, obtain a total measure of the work done. We will explain this concept in greater detail next as part of the set of five steps required to calculate (1) the cost of fully assembled units in February 2020 and (2) the cost of partially assembled units still in process at the end of that month, for Pacific Electronics. The five steps of process costing are shown below:

Step 1: Summarize the flow of physical units of output.

Step 2: Compute output in terms of equivalent units.

[2] For example, consider the conventional tanning process for converting hide to leather. Obtaining 250–300 kg of leather requires putting one metric ton of raw hide through as many as 15 steps: from soaking, liming, and pickling to tanning, dyeing, and fatliquoring, the step in which oils are introduced into the skin before the leather is dried.

Step 3: Summarize total costs to account for.

Step 4: Compute cost per equivalent unit.

Step 5: Assign total costs to units completed and to units in ending work-in-process inventory.

Summarizing the Physical Units and Equivalent Units (Steps 1 and 2)

In **Step 1**, managers track the physical units of output. Physical units are the number of output units, whether complete or incomplete. The physical-units column of Exhibit 18-1 tracks where the physical units came from (0 units from beginning inventory and 400 units started) and where they went (175 units completed and transferred out and 225 units in ending inventory).

In **Step 2**, managers compute output in *equivalent units*, not in *physical units*. **Equivalent units** are a derived measure of output calculated by (1) taking the quantity of each input (factor of production) in units completed and in incomplete units of work in process and (2) converting the quantity of input into the amount of completed output units that could be produced with that quantity of input. To see what is meant by equivalent units, suppose that during a month, 50 physical units were started but not completed. These 50 units in ending inventory are 70% complete for conversion costs. Suppose all conversion costs represented in these units were used to make fully completed units instead. How many completed units could be made? The answer: 35 units. Why? Because conversion costs incurred to produce 50 units that are each 70% complete could have instead produced 35 (0.70×50) units that are 100% complete. The 35 units are called *equivalent units* of output. That is, in terms of the work done on them, the 50 partially completed units are considered equivalent to 35 completed units. Note that equivalent units of output are calculated separately for each input (such as direct materials and conversion costs). Moreover, every completed unit, by definition, is composed of one equivalent unit of each input required to make it.

When calculating equivalent units in Step 2, focus on quantities. Disregard dollar amounts until after equivalent units are computed. In the Pacific Electronics example, all 400 physical units—the 175 fully assembled units and the 225 partially assembled units—are 100% complete with respect to direct materials because all direct materials are added at the start of the process. Therefore, Exhibit 18-1 shows 400 *equivalent units* of output for direct materials: 175 equivalent units for the 175 physical units assembled and transferred out and 225 equivalent units for the 225 physical units in ending work-in-process inventory.

The 175 fully assembled units have incurred 100% of conversion costs. The 225 partially assembled units in ending work in process are 60% complete (on average). Therefore, their conversion costs are *equivalent* to conversion costs incurred by 135 fully assembled units ($225 \times 60\% = 135$). Hence, Exhibit 18-1 shows 310 ($175 + 135$) *equivalent units* of output for conversion costs: 175 equivalent units for the 175 physical units assembled

EXHIBIT 18-1

Summarize the Flow of Physical Units and Compute Output in Equivalent Units for the Assembly Department for February 2020

	A	B	C	D
1		(Step 1)	(Step 2)	
2			Equivalent Units	
3	Flow of Production	Physical Units	Direct Materials	Conversion Costs
4	Work in process, beginning	0		
5	Started during current period	400		
6	To account for	400		
7	Completed and transferred out during current period	175	175	175
8	Work in process, ending[a]	225		
9	(225 × 100%; 225 × 60%)		225	135
10	Accounted for	400		
11	Equivalent units of work done in current period		400	310
12				
13	[a]Degree of completion in this department: direct materials, 100%; conversion costs, 60%.			

and transferred out and 135 equivalent units for the 225 physical units in ending work-in-process inventory.

This chapter focuses on manufacturing settings, but equivalent-unit calculations are also used in nonmanufacturing settings. For example, universities convert part-time student enrolments into "full-time student equivalents" to get a better measure of faculty–student ratios over time. Part-time students take fewer academic courses and do not need the same number of instructors as full-time students. Without this adjustment, an increase in part-time students would give a misleading picture of a lower faculty–student ratio.

Calculating Product Costs (Steps 3, 4, and 5)

Exhibit 18-2 shows Steps 3, 4, and 5. Together, they are called the *production cost worksheet*.

Step 3 summarizes total costs to account for. Because the beginning balance of work-in-process inventory is zero on February 1, total costs to account for (that is, total charges or debits to Work in Process—Assembly account) consist only of costs added during February: $32,000 in direct materials and $18,600 in conversion costs, for a total of $50,600.

In **Step 4**, managers calculate the cost per equivalent unit separately for direct materials costs and conversion costs. This is done by dividing direct material costs and conversion costs added during February by their related quantities of equivalent units of work done in February (calculated in Exhibit 18-1).

To understand the relevance of equivalent unit calculations, compare conversion costs for January and February 2020. The $18,600 in total conversion costs for the 400 units worked on during February are lower than the $24,000 in total conversion costs for the 400 units worked on in January. However, the conversion costs to fully assemble a unit are the same: $60 per unit in both January and February. Total conversion costs are lower in February because fewer equivalent units of conversion-costs work were done (310 in February versus 400 in January). Note that using physical units instead of equivalent units would have resulted in a conversion cost per unit of just $46.50 ($18,600 ÷ 400 units) for February versus $60 in January. This incorrect costing would mislead managers to conclude that the assembly department had achieved efficiencies when in fact conversion cost per unit was the same.

EXHIBIT 18-2 Summarize Total Costs to Account For, Compute Cost per Equivalent Unit, and Assign Costs to Units Completed and Units in Ending Work-in-Process Inventory for the Assembly Department for February 2020

	A	B	C	D	E	F
1			Total Production Costs	Direct Materials		Conversion Costs
2	(Step 3)	Costs added during February	$50,600	$32,000	+	$18,600
3		Total costs to account for	$50,600	$32,000	+	$18,600
4						
5	(Step 4)	Costs added in current period		$32,000		$18,600
6		Divide by equivalent units of work done in current period (Exhibit 18-1)		÷ 400		÷ 310
7		Cost per equivalent unit		$ 80		$ 60
8						
9	(Step 5)	Assignment of costs:				
10		Completed and transferred out (175 units)	$24,500	(175[a] × $80)	+	(175[a] × $60)
11		Work in process, ending (225 units)	26,100	(225[b] × $80)	+	(135[b] × $60)
12		Total costs accounted for	$50,600	$32,000	+	$18,600
13						
14	[a] Equivalent units completed and transferred out from Exhibit 18-1, Step 2.					
15	[b] Equivalent units in ending work in process from Exhibit 18-1, Step 2.					

Step 5 assigns total direct materials and conversion costs to units completed and transferred out and to units still in process at the end of February 2020. As Exhibit 18-2 shows, this is done for each input by multiplying the equivalent output units by the cost per equivalent unit. For example, total costs (direct materials and conversion costs assigned to the 225 physical units in ending work-in-process inventory) are as follows:

Direct material costs of 225 equivalent units (calculated in Step 2) × $80 cost per equivalent unit of direct materials (calculated in Step 4)	$18,000
Conversion costs of 135 equivalent units (calculated in Step 2) × $60 cost per equivalent unit of conversion costs (calculated in Step 4)	8,100
Total cost of ending work-in-process inventory	$26,100

Total costs to account for in Step 3 ($50,600) equal total costs accounted for in Step 5.

Journal Entries

Journal entries in process-costing systems are similar to entries made in job-costing systems with respect to direct materials and conversion costs. The main difference is that in process costing there is one Work in Process account for each process. In our example, there are two accounts: (1) Work in Process—Assembly and (2) Work in Process—Testing. Pacific Electronics purchases direct materials as needed, with materials being delivered directly to the assembly department. Using amounts from Exhibit 18-2, summary journal entries for February are as follows:

1.	Work in Process—Assembly	32,000	
	Accounts Payable Control		32,000
	To record direct materials purchased and used in production in February.		
2.	Work in Process—Assembly	18,600	
	Various accounts such as Wages Payable Control and Accumulated Depreciation		18,600
	To record conversion costs for February; examples include energy, manufacturing supplies, all manufacturing labor, and plant depreciation.		
3.	Work in Process—Testing	24,500	
	Work in Process—Assembly		24,500
	To record cost of goods completed and transferred from assembly to testing in February.		

Exhibit 18-3 shows a general framework for the flow of costs through T-accounts. Notice how entry 3 for $24,500 follows the physical transfer of goods from the assembly to the testing department. The T-account Work in Process—Assembly shows February 2020's ending balance of $26,100, which is the beginning balance of Work in Process—Assembly in March 2020.

Earlier, we discussed the importance of accurately estimating the completion percentages for conversion costs. What if Pacific Electronics' managers overestimate the degree of completion for conversion costs to be 80% instead of 60%. The computations would change as follows:

- Exhibit 18-1, Step 2
  Equivalent units of conversion costs in ending Work in Process—Assembly = 80% × 225 = 180
  Equivalent units of conversion costs for work done in the current period = 175 + 180 = 355
- Exhibit 18-2, Step 4
  Cost per equivalent unit of conversion costs = $18,600 ÷ 355 = $52.39
  Cost per equivalent unit of direct materials is unchanged, $80
- Exhibit 18-2, Step 5
  Cost of 175 units of goods completed and transferred out = 175 × $80 + 175 × $52.39 = $23,168.25

EXHIBIT 18-3 Flow of Costs in a Process-Costing System for the Assembly Department for February 2020

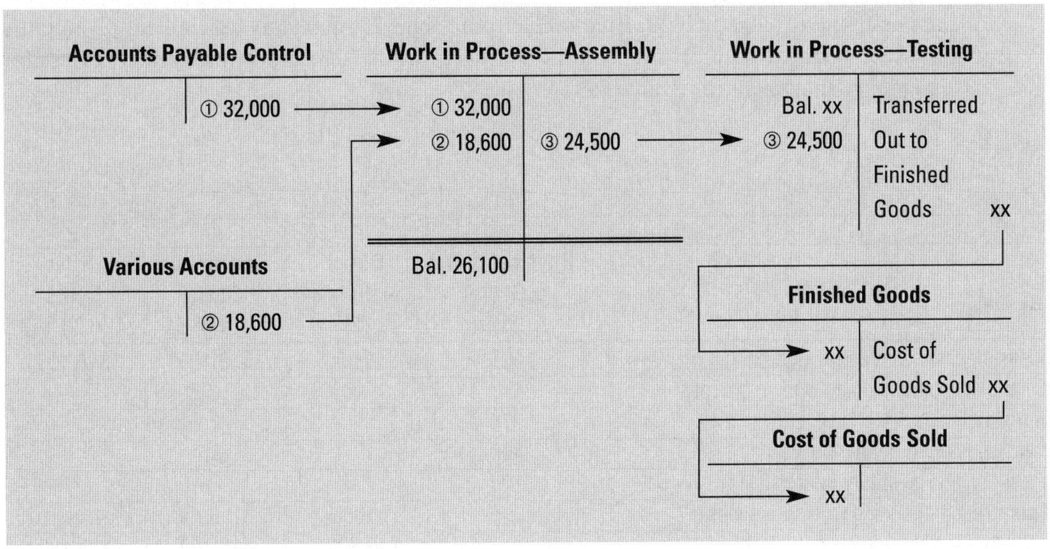

This amount is lower than the $24,500 of costs assigned to goods completed and transferred out in Exhibit 18-2. Overestimating the degree of completion decreases the costs assigned to goods transferred out and eventually to cost of goods sold and increases operating income.

Managers must ensure that department supervisors avoid introducing personal biases into estimates of degrees of completion. To show better performance, for example, a department supervisor might report a higher degree of completion resulting in overstated operating income. If performance for the period is very good, the department supervisor may be tempted to report a lower degree of completion, increasing cost of goods sold and lowering operating income in the current period. It would also reduce costs of ending inventory and the following period's beginning inventory, resulting in higher operating income in the following period. In other words, estimates of degree of completion can help smooth earnings from one period to the next.

To guard against possible bias, managers should ask supervisors specific questions about the process of preparing estimates. Top management should always emphasize acting ethically and obtaining the correct answer, regardless of how it affects reported performance.

DECISION POINT

What are the five steps in a process-costing system, and how are equivalent units calculated?

18-1 TRY IT!

SemiCom Corporation produces a semiconductor chip used in communications. The direct materials are added at the start of the production process, while conversion costs are added uniformly throughout the production process. SemiCom had no inventory at the start of June. During the month, it incurred direct materials costs of $950,000 and conversion costs of $4,620,000. SemiCom started 500,000 chips and completed 200,000 of them in June. Ending inventory was 50% complete as to conversion costs.

Compute (a) the equivalent units of work done in June and (b) the total manufacturing cost per chip. Allocate the total costs between the completed chips and those in ending inventory.

Case 3: Process Costing With Some Beginning and Some Ending Work-in-Process Inventory

At the beginning of March 2020, Pacific Electronics had 225 partially assembled SG-40 units in the assembly department. It started production of another 275 units in March. The data for the assembly department for March follow:

	A	B	C	D	E
1		Physical Units (SG-40s) (1)	Direct Materials (2)	Conversion Costs (3)	Total Costs (4) = (2) + (3)
2	Work in process, beginning inventory (March 1)	225	$18,000[a]	$ 8,100[a]	$26,100
3	Degree of completion of beginning work in process		100%	60%	
4	Started during March	275			
5	Completed and transferred out during March	400			
6	Work in process, ending inventory (March 31)	100			
7	Degree of completion of ending work in process		100%	50%	
8	Total costs added during March		$19,800	$16,380	$36,180
9					
10					
11	[a]Work in process, beginning inventory (equals work in process, ending inventory for February)				
12	Direct materials: 225 physical units × 100% completed × $80 per unit = $18,000				
13	Conversion costs: 225 physical units × 60% completed × $60 per unit = $8,100				

LEARNING OBJECTIVE 4

Use the weighted-average method

...assign costs based on total costs and equivalent units completed to date

and the first-in, first-out (FIFO) method

...assign costs based on costs and equivalent units of work done in the current period

of process costing

Pacific Electronics has incomplete units in both beginning work-in-process inventory and ending work-in-process inventory for March 2020. We use the five steps described earlier to assign costs to (1) the cost of units completed and transferred out and (2) the cost of ending work-in-process inventory. To do so, we first need to choose an inventory-valuation method. We describe the five-step approach for two key methods—the *weighted-average method* and the *first-in, first-out method*. The different valuation methods generally produce different costs for units completed and for ending work-in-process inventory.

Weighted-Average Method

The **weighted-average process-costing method** calculates the cost per equivalent unit of all *work done to date* (regardless of the accounting period in which it was done) and assigns this cost to equivalent units completed and transferred out of the process and to equivalent units in ending work-in-process inventory. The weighted-average cost is the total of all costs entering the Work in Process account (whether the costs are from beginning work in process or from work started during the current period) divided by total equivalent units of work done to date. We describe the weighted-average method using the five-step procedure from pages 713–714.

Step 1: Summarize the Flow of Physical Units of Output. The physical-units column in Exhibit 18-4 shows where the units came from—225 units from beginning inventory and 275 units started during the current period—and where the units went—400 units completed and transferred out and 100 units in ending inventory.

Step 2: Compute Output in Terms of Equivalent Units. We use the relationship shown in the following equation:

$$\begin{matrix}\text{Equivalent units} \\ \text{in beginning work} \\ \text{in process}\end{matrix} + \begin{matrix}\text{Equivalent units} \\ \text{of work done in} \\ \text{current period}\end{matrix} = \begin{matrix}\text{Equivalent units} \\ \text{completed and transferred} \\ \text{out in current period}\end{matrix} + \begin{matrix}\text{Equivalent units} \\ \text{in ending work} \\ \text{in process}\end{matrix}$$

EXHIBIT 18-4

Summarize the Flow of Physical Units and Compute Output in Equivalent Units Using the Weighted-Average Method for the Assembly Department for March 2020

	A	B	C	D
1		(Step 1)	(Step 2)	
2			Equivalent Units	
3	Flow of Production	Physical Units	Direct Materials	Conversion Costs
4	Work in process, beginning (given, p. 718)	225		
5	Started during current period (given, p. 718)	275		
6	To account for	500		
7	Completed and transferred out during current period	400	400	400
8	Work in process, ending[a] (given, p. 718)	100		
9	(100 × 100%; 100 × 50%)		100	50
10	Accounted for	500		
11	Equivalent units of work done to date		500	450
12				
13	[a]Degree of completion in this department: direct materials, 100%; conversion costs, 50%.			

Although we are interested in calculating the left side of the preceding equation, it is easier to calculate this sum using the equation's right side: (1) the equivalent units completed and transferred out in the current period plus (2) the equivalent units in ending work in process. *Note that the stage of completion of the current-period beginning work in process is not used in this computation.*

The equivalent-units columns in Exhibit 18-4 show the equivalent units of work done to date: 500 equivalent units of direct materials and 450 equivalent units of conversion costs. All completed and transferred-out units are 100% complete with regard to both direct materials and conversion costs. Partially completed units in ending work in process are 100% complete with regard to direct materials costs (because direct materials are introduced at the beginning of the process) and 50% complete with regard to conversion costs, based on estimates from the assembly department manager.

Step 3: Summarize Total Costs to Account For. Exhibit 18-5 presents Step 3. The total costs to account for in March 2020 are described in the example data on page 718:

Beginning work in process (direct materials, \$18,000 + conversion costs, \$8,100)	\$26,100
Costs added during March (direct materials, \$19,800 + conversion costs, \$16,380)	36,180
Total costs to account for in March	\$62,280

Step 4: Compute Cost per Equivalent Unit. Exhibit 18-5, Step 4, computes the weighted-average cost per equivalent unit for direct materials and conversion costs by dividing the sum of the costs for beginning work in process plus the costs for work done in the current period by the total equivalent units of work done to date. The weighted-average conversion cost per equivalent unit in Exhibit 18-5 follows:

Total conversion costs (beginning work in process, \$8,100 + work done in current period, \$16,380)	\$24,480
Divided by the total equivalent units of work done to date (equivalent units of conversion costs in beginning work in process and in work done in current period)	450
Weighted-average cost per equivalent unit	\$ 54.40

Step 5: Assign Costs to Units Completed and to Units in Ending Work-in-Process Inventory. Step 5 in Exhibit 18-5 assigns dollar amounts to the equivalent units completed and transferred out and the equivalent units in ending work in process (calculated in Exhibit 18-4, Step 2) using the weighted-average cost per equivalent unit for direct materials and conversion costs

EXHIBIT 18-5 Summarize Total Costs to Account For, Compute Cost per Equivalent Unit, and Assign Costs to Units Completed and to Units in Ending Work-in-Process Inventory Using the Weighted-Average Method for the Assembly Department for March 2020

Home Insert Page Layout Formulas Data Review View

	A	B	C	D	E	F
1			Total Production Costs	Direct Materials		Conversion Costs
2	(Step 3)	Work in process, beginning (given, p. 718)	$26,100	$18,000	+	$ 8,100
3		Costs added in current period (given, p. 718)	36,180	19,800	+	16,380
4		Total costs to account for	$62,280	$37,800	+	$24,480
5						
6	(Step 4)	Costs incurred to date		$37,800		$24,480
7		Divide by equivalent units of work done to date (Exhibit 18-4)		÷ 500		÷ 450
8		Cost per equivalent unit of work done to date		$ 75.60		$ 54.40
9						
10	(Step 5)	Assignment of costs:				
11		Completed and transferred out (400 units)	$52,000	(400[a] × $75.60)	+	(400[a] × $54.40)
12		Work in process, ending (100 units)	10,280	(100[b] × $75.60)	+	(50[b] × $54.40)
13		Total costs accounted for	$62,280	$37,800	+	$24,480
14						
15	[a]Equivalent units completed and transferred out from Exhibit 18-4, Step 2.					
16	[b]Equivalent units in ending work in process from Exhibit 18-4, Step 2.					

calculated in Step 4. For example, total costs of the 100 physical units in ending work in process are shown below:

Direct materials:	
100 equivalent units × weighted-average cost per equivalent unit of $75.60	$ 7,560
Conversion costs:	
50 equivalent units × weighted-average cost per equivalent unit of $54.40	2,720
Total costs of ending work in process	$10,280

The following table summarizes total costs to account for ($62,280) and how they are accounted for in Exhibit 18-5. The arrows indicate that costs of units completed and transferred out and units in ending work in process are calculated using weighted-average total costs obtained after merging costs of beginning work in process and costs added in the current period.

Costs to Account For		→	Costs Accounted for Calculated on a Weighted-Average Basis	
Beginning work in process	$26,100	→	Completed and transferred out	$52,000
Costs added in current period	36,180	→	Ending work in process	10,280
Total costs to account for	$62,280		Total costs accounted for	$62,280

Before proceeding, review Exhibits 18-4 and 18-5 to check your understanding of the weighted-average method. Note: Exhibit 18-4 deals with only physical and equivalent units, not costs. Exhibit 18-5 shows the cost amounts.

Summary journal entries under the weighted-average method for March 2020 (see Exhibit 18-5) are shown below:

1.	Work in Process—Assembly	19,800	
	Accounts Payable Control		19,800
	To record direct materials purchased and used in production in March.		
2.	Work in Process—Assembly	16,380	
	Various accounts such as Wages Payable Control and Accumulated Depreciation		16,380
	To record conversion costs for March; examples include energy, manufacturing supplies, all manufacturing labor, and plant depreciation.		
3.	Work in Process—Testing	52,000	
	Work in Process—Assembly		52,000
	To record cost of goods completed and transferred from assembly to testing in March.		

The T-account Work in Process—Assembly, under the weighted-average method, is:

Work in Process—Assembly

Beginning inventory, March 1	26,100	③ Completed and transferred out to Work in Process—Testing	52,000
① Direct materials	19,800		
② Conversion costs	16,380		
Ending inventory, March 31	10,280		

18-2 TRY IT!

The Sutton Processing Company had work in process at the beginning and end of March 2020 in its Painting Department as follows:

		Percentage of Completion	
		Direct Materials	**Conversion Costs**
March 1	(5,000 units)	40%	10%
March 31	(2,000 units)	80%	40%

The company completed 33,000 units during March. Manufacturing costs incurred during March were direct materials costs of $179,300 and conversion costs of $333,000. Inventory at March 1 was carried at a cost of $20,990 (direct materials, $7,540 and conversion costs, $13,450).

Assuming Sutton uses weighted-average costing, determine the equivalent units of work done in March, and calculate the cost of units completed and the cost of units in ending inventory.

First-In, First-Out Method

The **first-in, first-out (FIFO) process-costing method** (1) assigns the cost of the previous accounting period's equivalent units in beginning work-in-process inventory to the first units completed and transferred out of the process and (2) assigns the cost of equivalent units worked on during the *current* period first to complete the beginning inventory, next to start and complete new units, and finally to units in ending work-in-process inventory. The FIFO method assumes that the earliest equivalent units in work in process are completed first.

A distinctive feature of the FIFO process-costing method is that work done on the beginning inventory before the current period is kept separate from work done in the current period. The costs incurred and units produced in the current period are used to calculate the cost per equivalent unit of work done in the current period. In contrast, the equivalent-unit and cost-per-equivalent-unit calculations under the weighted-average method *merge* the units and costs in beginning inventory with the units and costs of work done in the current period.

We now describe the FIFO method using the five-step procedure from pages 713–714.

Step 1: Summarize the Flow of Physical Units of Output. Exhibit 18-6, Step 1, traces the flow of physical units of production and explains how they are calculated under the FIFO method.

- The first physical units assumed to be completed and transferred out during the period are 225 units from beginning work-in-process inventory.
- There are 400 physical units completed during March (see page 718). The FIFO method assumes that of these 400 units, 175 units (400 units − 225 units from beginning work-in-process inventory) were started and completed during March.
- The ending work-in-process inventory consists of 100 physical units—the 275 physical units started minus the 175 units that were started and completed.
- The physical units "to account for" equal the physical units "accounted for" (500 units).

Step 2: Compute Output in Terms of Equivalent Units. Exhibit 18-6 also presents the computations for Step 2 under the FIFO method. *The equivalent-unit calculations for each cost category focus on equivalent units of work done in the current period (March) only.*

Under the FIFO method, equivalent units of work done in March on beginning work-in-process inventory equal 225 physical units times *the remaining percentage of work done in March to complete these units*: 0% for direct materials, because beginning work in process is 100% complete for direct materials, and 40% for conversion costs, because beginning work in process is 60% complete for conversion costs. The results are 0 (0% × 225) equivalent units of work done in March for direct materials and 90 (40% × 225) equivalent units of work done in March for conversion costs.

The equivalent units of work done in March on the 175 physical units started and completed equals 175 units times 100% for both direct materials and conversion costs because all work on these units is done in the current period.

EXHIBIT 18-6

Summarize the Flow of Physical Units and Compute Output in Equivalent Units Using the FIFO Method for the Assembly Department for March 2020

Home Insert Page Layout Formulas Data Review View

	A	B	C	D
1		(Step 1)	(Step 2)	
2			Equivalent Units	
3	**Flow of Production**	**Physical Units**	**Direct Materials**	**Conversion Costs**
4	Work in process, beginning (given, p. 718)	225	(work done before current period)	
5	Started during current period (given, p. 718)	275		
6	To account for	500		
7	Completed and transferred out during current period:			
8	From beginning work in process[a]	225		
9	[225 × (100% – 100%); 225 × (100% – 60%)]		0	90
10	Started and completed	175[b]		
11	(175 × 100%; 175 × 100%)		175	175
12	Work in process, ending[c] (given, p. 718)	100		
13	(100 × 100%; 100 × 50%)		100	50
14	Accounted for	500		
15	Equivalent units of work done in current period		275	315
16				
17	[a] Degree of completion in this department: direct materials, 100%; conversion costs, 60%.			
18	[b] 400 physical units completed and transferred out minus 225 physical units completed and			
19	transferred out from beginning work-in-process inventory.			
20	[c] Degree of completion in this department: direct materials, 100%; conversion costs, 50%.			

The equivalent units of work done in March on the 100 units of ending work in process equal 100 physical units times 100% for direct materials (because all direct materials for these units are added in the current period) and 50% for conversion costs (because 50% of the conversion-costs work on these units is done in the current period).

Step 3: Summarize Total Costs to Account For. Exhibit 18-7 presents Step 3 and summarizes the $62,280 in total costs to account for in March 2020 (the costs of beginning work in process, $26,100, and costs added in the current period, $36,180).

Step 4: Compute Cost per Equivalent Unit. Exhibit 18-7 shows the Step 4 computation of the cost per equivalent unit of *work done in the current period only* for direct materials and conversion costs. For example, the conversion cost per equivalent unit of $52 is obtained by dividing current-period conversion costs of $16,380 by current-period conversion-costs equivalent units of 315.

Step 5: Assign Costs to Units Completed and to Units in Ending Work-in-Process Inventory. Exhibit 18-7 shows the assignment of costs under the FIFO method. The costs of work done in the current period are assigned (1) first to the additional work done to complete beginning work-in-process inventory, then (2) to work done on units started and completed during the current period, and finally (3) to ending work-in-process inventory. *Step 5 takes each quantity of equivalent units calculated in Exhibit 18-6, Step 2, and assigns dollar amounts to them (using the cost-per-equivalent-unit calculations in Step 4).*

EXHIBIT 18-7 Summarize Total Costs to Account For, Compute Cost per Equivalent Unit, and Assign Costs to Units Completed and to Units in Ending Work-in-Process Inventory Using the FIFO Method for the Assembly Department for March 2020

Home Insert Page Layout Formulas Data Review View

	A	B	C	D	E	F
1			Total Production Costs	Direct Materials		Conversion Costs
2	**(Step 3)**	Work in process, beginning (given, p. 718)	$26,100	$18,000	+	$ 8,100
3		Costs added in current period (given, p. 718)	36,180	19,800	+	16,380
4		Total costs to account for	$62,280	$37,800	+	$24,480
5						
6	**(Step 4)**	Costs added in current period		$19,800		$16,380
7		Divide by equivalent units of work done in current period (Exhibit 18-6)		÷ 275		÷ 315
8		Cost per equivalent unit of work done in current period		$ 72		$ 52
9						
10	**(Step 5)**	Assignment of costs:				
11		Completed and transferred out (400 units):				
12		Work in process, beginning (225 units)	$26,100	$18,000	+	$ 8,100
13		Costs added to beginning work in process in current period	4,680	(0[a] × $72)	+	(90[a] × $52)
14		Total from beginning inventory	30,780			
15		Started and completed (175 units)	21,700	(175[b] × $72)	+	(175[b] × $52)
16		Total costs of units completed and transferred out	52,480			
17		Work in process, ending (100 units)	9,800	(100[c] × $72)	+	(50[c] × $52)
18		Total costs accounted for	$62,280	$37,800	+	$24,480
19						
20	[a] Equivalent units used to complete beginning work in process from Exhibit 18-6, Step 2.					
21	[b] Equivalent units started and completed from Exhibit 18-6, Step 2.					
22	[c] Equivalent units in ending work in process from Exhibit 18-6, Step 2.					

Of the 400 completed units, 225 units are from beginning inventory and 175 units are started and completed during March. The FIFO method first assigns costs of beginning work-in-process inventory of $26,100 to the first units completed and transferred out. As we saw in Step 2, an additional 90 equivalent units of conversion costs are needed to complete these units in the current period. The current-period conversion cost per equivalent unit is $52, so $4,680 (90 equivalent units × $52 per equivalent unit) of additional costs are incurred to complete the beginning inventory. The total production costs for units in beginning inventory are therefore $26,100 + $4,680 = $30,780. The 175 units started and completed in the current period consist of 175 equivalent units of direct materials and 175 equivalent units of conversion costs. These units are costed at the cost per equivalent unit in the current period (direct materials, $72, and conversion costs, $52) for a total production cost of $21,700 [175 × ($72 + $52)].

Under FIFO, the ending work-in-process inventory comes from units that were started but not fully completed during the current period. The total costs of the 100 partially assembled physical units in ending work in process are shown below:

Direct materials:	
100 equivalent units × $72 cost per equivalent unit in March	$7,200
Conversion costs:	
50 equivalent units × $52 cost per equivalent unit in March	2,600
Total cost of work in process on March 31	$9,800

The following table summarizes the total costs to account for ($62,280) and how they are accounted for under FIFO in Exhibit 18-7. Notice how the FIFO method keeps separate the layers of the beginning work-in-process costs and the costs added in the current period. The arrows indicate where the costs in each layer go—that is, to units completed and transferred out or to ending work in process. Be sure to include the costs of beginning work-in-process inventory ($26,100) when calculating costs of units completed.

Costs to Account For		Costs Accounted for Calculated on a FIFO Basis	
		Completed and transferred out:	
Beginning work in process	$26,100	→ Beginning work in process	$26,100
Costs added in current period	36,180	→ Used to complete beginning work in process	4,680
		→ Started and completed	21,700
		Completed and transferred out	52,480
		→ Ending work in process	9,800
Total costs to account for	$62,280	Total costs accounted for	$62,280

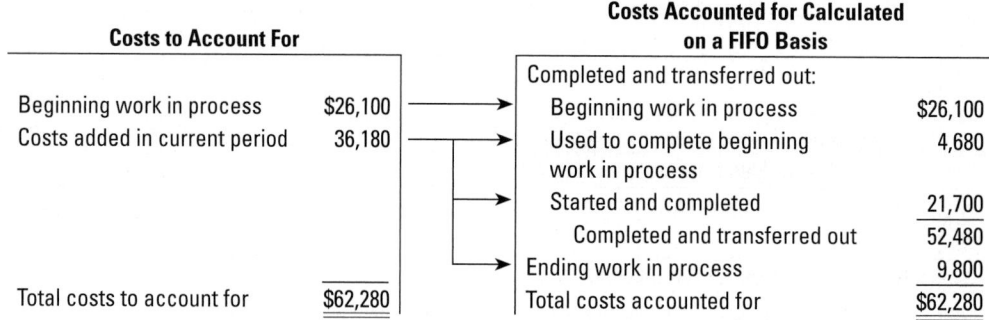

Before proceeding, review Exhibits 18-6 and 18-7 to check your understanding of the FIFO method. Note: Exhibit 18-6 deals with only physical and equivalent units, not costs. Exhibit 18-7 shows the cost amounts.

The journal entries under the FIFO method are identical to the journal entries under the weighted-average method except for one difference. The entry to record the cost of goods completed and transferred out is $52,480 under the FIFO method instead of $52,000 under the weighted-average method.

Using a strict FIFO assumption, the 225 units completed from beginning inventory would be transferred to the testing department at a cost of $136.80 per unit ($30,780 ÷ 225 units). The 175 units started and completed during March would be transferred at a cost of $124 per unit ($21,700 ÷ 175 units). As a practical matter, however, units *transferred in* during a given period usually are carried at a single average unit cost. The testing department would carry all the units transferred in during March (which consist of costs incurred in both February and March) in one layer at a single average unit cost of $131.20 ($52,480 ÷ 400 units). If this averaging were not done, the attempt to track costs on a pure FIFO basis throughout a series of processes would be cumbersome. As a result, the FIFO method should really be called a *modified* or *department* FIFO method.

Consider Sutton Processing Company again. With the same information for 2020 as provided in Try It! 18-2, redo the problem assuming Sutton uses FIFO costing instead.

18-3 TRY IT!

Comparing the Weighted-Average and FIFO Methods

Consider the summary of the costs assigned to units completed and to units still in process under the weighted-average and FIFO process-costing methods in our example for March 2020:

	Weighted Average (from Exhibit 18-5)	FIFO (from Exhibit 18-7)	Difference
Cost of units completed and transferred out	$52,000	$52,480	+$480
Work in process, ending	10,280	9,800	−$480
Total costs accounted for	$62,280	$62,280	

The weighted-average ending inventory is higher than the FIFO ending inventory by $480, or 4.9% ($\$480 \div \$9,800 = 0.049$, or 4.9%). This would be a significant difference when aggregated over the many thousands of products Pacific Electronics makes. When completed units are sold, the weighted-average method in our example leads to lower cost of goods sold and, therefore, higher operating income than the FIFO method. To see why, recall the data on page 718. For the beginning work-in-process inventory, direct materials cost per equivalent unit is $80 and conversion cost per equivalent unit is $60. The cost per equivalent unit of work done during the current period is $72 for direct materials and $52 for conversion costs. The current-period costs could be lower because of lower prices of direct materials and conversion-cost inputs or as a result of process efficiencies resulting in smaller quantities of inputs being used per unit of output or both.

FIFO assumes that (1) all the higher-cost units from the previous period in beginning work in process are the first to be completed and transferred out of the process and (2) the ending work in process consists of only the lower-cost current-period units. The weighted-average method smooths out the cost per equivalent unit by assuming that (1) more of the lower-cost units from the current period are completed and transferred out and (2) some of the higher-cost units from beginning inventory are placed in ending work in process.

Managers use information from process-costing systems to make pricing and product-mix decisions and for managing costs. FIFO provides managers with information about costs per unit in the current and previous periods. Managers can use these data to adjust selling prices based on current conditions (for example, based on the $72 direct materials cost and the $52 conversion cost in March). Managers can also more easily evaluate the firm's cost performance relative to a budget or the previous period. By focusing on the work done and the costs of work done during the current period, the FIFO method provides valuable information for these planning and control purposes.

The weighted-average method merges unit costs from different accounting periods, obscuring period-to-period comparisons. For example, the weighted-average method would lead managers at Pacific Electronics to make decisions based on the $75.60 direct materials and $54.40 conversion costs, rather than the $72 and $52 costs prevailing in the current period. Its advantage is that it is relatively easy to compute and results in a more-representative average unit cost when input prices fluctuate from month to month.

The weighted-average and FIFO methods result in materially different cost of units completed and operating income when (1) direct materials or conversion cost per equivalent unit differs significantly from period to period and (2) physical-inventory levels of work in process are large relative to total number of units transferred out of the process. As changes in unit costs and inventory levels across periods decrease, the difference in the costs of units completed under the weighted-average and FIFO methods also decreases.[3]

[3] For example, suppose the beginning work-in-process inventory for March was 125 physical units (instead of 225), and suppose the costs per equivalent unit of work done in the current period (March) were direct materials, $75, and conversion costs, $55. Assume that all other data for March are the same as in our example. In this case, the cost of units completed and transferred out would be $52,833 under the weighted-average method and $53,000 under the FIFO method. The work-in-process ending inventory would be $10,417 under the weighted-average method and $10,250 under the FIFO method (calculations not shown). These differences are much smaller than in the chapter example. The weighted-average ending inventory is higher than the FIFO ending inventory by only $167 ($\$10,417 - \$10,250$), or 1.6% ($\$167 \div \$10,250 = 0.016$), compared with 4.9% higher in the chapter example.

When the cost of units completed under the weighted-average and FIFO methods differs substantially, which method should a manager choose? In a period of falling prices, as in the Pacific Electronics case, the higher cost of goods sold under the FIFO method will lead to lower operating income and lower tax payments, saving the company cash and increasing the company's value. FIFO is the preferred choice, but managers may not make this choice. If the manager's compensation, for instance, is based on operating income, the manager may prefer the weighted-average method, which increases operating income even though it results in higher tax payments. Boards and top managers must design compensation plans to encourage managers to take actions that increase a company's value, for example, by rewarding after-tax cash flow in addition to operating income, to align decision making and performance evaluation.

Other factors can also affect the choice of a process-costing method. Suppose that by using FIFO and reporting a lower income, a company would violate its debt covenants (such as its debt to income ratio) resulting in its loans coming due. In this case, a manager may prefer the weighted-average income-increasing method even though it results in higher taxes to avoid being forced to repay its loans.

In a period of rising prices, the weighted-average method will decrease taxes because more of the higher costs of the current period will be included in cost of goods sold, lowering operating income. Readers familiar with the last-in, first-out (LIFO) method (not presented in this chapter) will recognize that with rising prices, the LIFO method reduces operating income and taxes even more than the weighted-average method.

DECISION POINT

What are the weighted-average and first-in, first-out (FIFO) methods of process costing? Under what conditions will they yield different levels of operating income?

We close with comments on the use of activity-based costing and standard costing in process costing. Each process—assembly, testing, and so on—can be considered a different (production) activity. However, no additional activities need to be identified within each process. That's because products are homogeneous and, in contrast to job-costing environments, use the resources of each process in a uniform way. This uniform use of resources makes it easier to establish standard costs of products. *The appendix illustrates the use of the standard costing method for the assembly department.*

Transferred-In Costs in Process Costing

LEARNING OBJECTIVE 5

Apply process-costing methods to situations with transferred-in costs

. . . using weighted-average and FIFO methods

Many process-costing systems have two or more departments or processes in the production cycle. As units move from department to department, the related costs are also transferred by monthly journal entries. **Transferred-in costs** (also called **previous-department costs**) are costs incurred in previous departments that are carried forward as the product's costs when it moves to a subsequent process in the production cycle.

We now extend our Pacific Electronics example to the testing department. As the assembly process is completed, the assembly department of Pacific Electronics transfers SG-40 units to the testing department. Conversion costs are added evenly during the testing department's process. At the *end of the testing process*, the units receive additional direct materials, including crating and other packing materials. As units are completed in testing, they are transferred to Finished Goods. The testing department costs consist of transferred-in costs, as well as direct materials and conversion costs added during testing.

The following diagram represents these facts:

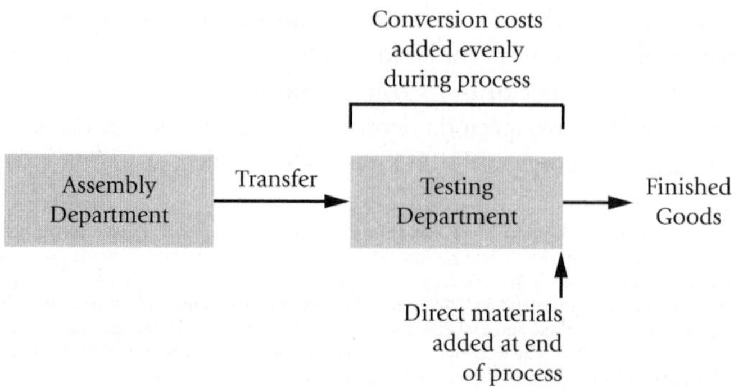

The data for the testing department for March 2020 are as follows:

	A	B	C	D	E
1		**Physical Units (SG-40s)**	**Transferred-In Costs**	**Direct Materials**	**Conversion Costs**
2	Work in process, beginning inventory (March 1)	240	$33,600	$ 0	$18,000
3	Degree of completion, beginning work in process		100%	0%	62.5%
4	Transferred-in during March	400			
5	Completed and transferred out during March	440			
6	Work in process, ending inventory (March 31)	200			
7	Degree of completion, ending work in process		100%	0%	80%
8	Total costs added during March:				
9	Direct materials and conversion costs			$13,200	$48,600
10	Transferred-in (Weighted-average from Exhibit 18-5)[a]		$52,000		
11	Transferred-in (FIFO from Exhibit 18-7)[a]		$52,480		
12					
13	[a]The transferred-in costs during March are different under the weighted-average method (Exhibit 18-5) and the FIFO method (Exhibit 18-7). In our example, beginning work-in-process inventory, $51,600 ($33,600 + $0 + $18,000) is the same under both the weighted-average and FIFO inventory methods because we assume costs per equivalent unit to be the same in both January and February. If costs per equivalent unit had been different in the two months, work-in-process inventory at the end of February (beginning of March) would be costed differently under the weighted-average and FIFO methods. The basic approach to process costing with transferred-in costs, however, would still be the same as what we describe in this section.				

Transferred-in costs are treated as if they are a separate type of direct materials added at the beginning of the process. The transferred-in costs represent assembly department costs, which are always 100% complete at the beginning of the testing department process. When successive departments are involved, the transferred units from one department become all or a part of the direct materials of the next department; however, they are called transferred-in costs, not direct materials costs.

Transferred-In Costs and the Weighted-Average Method

To examine the weighted-average process-costing method with transferred-in costs, we use the five-step procedure described earlier (pages 713–714) to assign costs of the testing department to units completed and transferred out and to units in ending work in process.

Exhibit 18-8 shows Steps 1 and 2. The computations are similar to the calculations of equivalent units under the weighted-average method for the assembly department in Exhibit 18-4. The one difference is that we have transferred-in costs as an additional input. All units, whether completed and transferred out during the period or in ending work in process, are always 100% complete with respect to transferred-in costs. In contrast, the direct materials costs have a zero degree of completion in both beginning and ending work-in-process inventories because, in the testing department, direct materials are introduced at the *end* of the process.

Exhibit 18-9 describes Steps 3, 4, and 5 for the weighted-average method. Beginning work in process and work done in the current period are combined for the purposes of computing the cost per equivalent unit for the transferred-in costs, direct materials costs, and conversion costs.

The journal entry for the transfer from testing to Finished Goods (see Exhibit 18-9) is shown below:

Finished Goods Control	120,890	
Work in Process—Testing		120,890
To record cost of goods completed and transferred from testing to Finished Goods.		

EXHIBIT 18-8 Summarize the Flow of Physical Units and Compute Output in Equivalent Units Using the Weighted-Average Method for the Testing Department for March 2020

	A	B	C	D	E
1		(Step 1)		(Step 2)	
2				Equivalent Units	
3	Flow of Production	Physical Units	Transferred-In Costs	Direct Materials	Conversion Costs
4	Work in process, beginning (given, p. 727)	240			
5	Transferred-in during current period (given, p. 727)	400			
6	To account for	640			
7	Completed and transferred out during current period	440	440	440	440
8	Work in process, ending[a] (given, p. 727)	200			
9	(200 × 100%; 200 × 0%; 200 × 80%)		200	0	160
10	Accounted for	640			
11	Equivalent units of work done to date		640	440	600
12					
13	[a] Degree of completion in this department: transferred-in costs, 100%; direct materials, 0%; conversion costs, 80%.				

EXHIBIT 18-9 Summarize Total Costs to Account For, Compute Cost per Equivalent Unit, and Assign Costs to Units Completed and to Units in Ending Work-in-Process Inventory Using the Weighted-Average Method for the Testing Department for March 2020

	A	B	C	D	E	F	G	H
1			Total Production Costs	Transferred-In Costs		Direct Materials		Conversion Costs
2	(Step 3)	Work in process, beginning (given, p. 727)	$ 51,600	$33,600	+	$ 0	+	$18,000
3		Costs added in current period (given, p. 727)	113,800	52,000	+	13,200	+	48,600
4		Total costs to account for	$165,400	$85,600	+	$13,200	+	$66,600
5								
6	(Step 4)	Costs incurred to date		$85,600		$13,200		$66,600
7		Divide by equivalent units of work done to date (Exhibit 18-8)		÷ 640		÷ 440		÷ 600
8		Cost per equivalent unit of work done to date		$133.75		$ 30.00		$111.00
9								
10	(Step 5)	Assignment of costs:						
11		Completed and transferred out (440 units)	$120,890	(440[a] × $133.75)	+	(440[a] × $30)	+	(440[a] × $111)
12		Work in process, ending (200 units)	44,510	(200[b] × $133.75)	+	(0[b] × $30)	+	(160[b] × $111)
13		Total costs accounted for	$165,400	$85,600	+	$13,200	+	$66,600
14								
15	[a] Equivalent units completed and transferred out from Exhibit 18-8, Step 2.							
16	[b] Equivalent units in ending work in process from Exhibit 18-8, Step 2.							

Entries in the Work in Process—Testing account (see Exhibit 18-9) are as follows:

Work in Process—Testing

Beginning inventory, March 1	51,600	Transferred out	120,890
Transferred-in costs	52,000		
Direct materials	13,200		
Conversion costs	48,600		
Ending inventory, March 31	44,510		

Transferred-In Costs and the FIFO Method

To examine the FIFO process-costing method with transferred-in costs, we again use the five-step procedure. Exhibit 18-10 shows Steps 1 and 2. Other than accounting for transferred-in costs, computing the equivalent units is the same as under the FIFO method for the assembly department (see Exhibit 18-6).

Exhibit 18-11 describes Steps 3, 4, and 5. In Step 3, the $165,880 in total costs to account for under the FIFO method differ from the total costs under the weighted-average method, which are $165,400. This is because of the difference in the costs of completed units transferred in from the assembly department under the two methods—$52,480 under FIFO and $52,000 under the weighted-average method. The cost per equivalent unit for the current period in Step 4 is calculated on the basis of costs transferred in and work done in the current period only. Step 5 then accounts for the total costs of $165,880 by assigning them to the units transferred out and those in ending work-in-process inventory. Again, other than considering transferred-in costs, the calculations mirror those under the FIFO method for the assembly department (in Exhibit 18-7).

Remember that in a series of interdepartmental transfers, each department is regarded as separate and distinct for accounting purposes. The journal entry for the transfer from testing to Finished Goods (see Exhibit 18-11) is shown below:

Finished Goods Control	122,360	
Work in Process—Testing		122,360
To record the cost of goods completed and transferred from testing to Finished Goods.		

The entries in the Work in Process—Testing account (see Exhibit 18-11) are as follows:

Work in Process—Testing

Beginning inventory, March 1	51,600	Transferred out	122,360
Transferred-in costs	52,480		
Direct materials	13,200		
Conversion costs	48,600		
Ending inventory, March 31	43,520		

EXHIBIT 18-10 Summarize the Flow of Physical Units and Compute Output in Equivalent Units Using the FIFO Method for the Testing Department for March 2020

Home Insert Page Layout Formulas Data Review View

	A	B	C	D	E
1		(Step 1)	(Step 2)		
2			Equivalent Units		
3	Flow of Production	Physical Units	Transferred-In Costs	Direct Materials	Conversion Costs
4	Work in process, beginning (given, p. 727)	240	(work done before current period)		
5	Transferred in during current period (given, p. 727)	400			
6	To account for	640			
7	Completed and transferred out during current period:				
8	From beginning work in process[a]	240			
9	[240 × (100% − 100%); 240 × (100% − 0%); 240 × (100% − 62.5%)]		0	240	90
10	Started and completed	200[b]			
11	(200 × 100%; 200 × 100%; 200 × 100%)		200	200	200
12	Work in process, ending[c] (given, p. 727)	200			
13	(200 × 100%; 200 × 0%; 200 × 80%)		200	0	160
14	Accounted for	640			
15	Equivalent units of work done in current period		400	440	450
16					
17	[a]Degree of completion in this department: Transferred-in costs, 100%; direct materials, 0%; conversion costs, 62.5%.				
18	[b]440 physical units completed and transferred out minus 240 physical units completed and transferred out from beginning				
19	work-in-process inventory.				
20	[c]Degree of completion in this department: Transferred-in costs, 100%; direct materials, 0%; conversion costs, 80%.				

EXHIBIT 18-11

Summarize Total Costs to Account For, Compute Cost per Equivalent Unit, and Assign Costs to Units Completed and to Units in Ending Work-in-Process Inventory Using the FIFO Method for the Testing Department for March 2020

Home Insert Page Layout Formulas Data Review View

	A	B	C	D	E	F	G	H
1			Total Production Costs	Transferred-In Cost		Direct Materials		Conversion Costs
2	(Step 3)	Work in process, beginning (given, p. 727)	$ 51,600	$33,600	+	$ 0	+	$18,000
3		Costs added in current period (given, p. 727)	114,280	52,480	+	13,200	+	48,600
4		Total costs to account for	$165,880	$86,080	+	$13,200	+	$66,600
5								
6	(Step 4)	Costs added in current period		$52,480		$13,200		$48,600
7		Divide by equivalent units of work done in current period (Exhibit 18-10)		÷ 400		÷ 440		÷ 450
8		Cost per equivalent unit of work done in current period		$131.20		$ 30		$ 108
9								
10	(Step 5)	Assignment of costs:						
11		Completed and transferred out (440 units):						
12		Work in process, beginning (240 units)	$ 51,600	$33,600	+	$0	+	$18,000
13		Costs added to beginning work in process in current period	16,920	(0[a] × $131.20)	+	(240[a] × $30)	+	(90[a] × $108)
14		Total from beginning inventory	68,520					
15		Started and completed (200 units)	53,840	(200[b] × $131.20)	+	(200[b] × $30)	+	(200[b] × $108)
16		Total costs of units completed and transferred out	122,360					
17		Work in process, ending (200 units)	43,520	(200[c] × $131.20)	+	(0[c] × $30)	+	(160[c] × $108)
18		Total costs accounted for	$165,880	$86,080	+	$13,200	+	$66,600
19								
20	[a]Equivalent units used to complete beginning work in process from Exhibit 18-10, Step 2.							
21	[b]Equivalent units started and completed from Exhibit 18-10, Step 2.							
22	[c]Equivalent units in ending work in process from Exhibit 18-10, Step 2.							

Points to Remember About Transferred-In Costs

Some points to remember when accounting for transferred-in costs are:

1. Be sure to include the transferred-in costs from previous departments in your calculations.
2. When calculating the costs to be transferred using the FIFO method, do not overlook costs assigned in the previous period to units that were in process at the beginning of the current period but are now included in the units transferred. For example, do not overlook the $51,600 in Exhibit 18-11.
3. Unit costs may fluctuate between periods. Therefore, transferred units may contain batches accumulated at different unit costs. For example, the 400 units transferred in at $52,480 in Exhibit 18-11 using the FIFO method consist of units that have different unit costs of direct materials and conversion costs when these units were worked on in the assembly department (see Exhibit 18-7). Remember, however, that when these units are transferred to the testing department, they are costed at *one average unit cost* of $131.20 ($52,480 ÷ 400 units), as in Exhibit 18-11.
4. Units may be measured in different denominations in different departments. Consider each department separately. For example, unit costs could be based on kilograms in the first department and liters in the second department. Accordingly, as units are received in the second department, their measurements must be converted to liters.

DECISION POINT

How are the weighted-average and FIFO process-costing methods applied to transferred-in costs?

Hybrid Costing Systems

Product-costing systems do not always fall neatly into either job-costing or process-costing categories. Many production systems are hybrid systems in which both mass production and customization occur. Consider Ford Motor Company. Automobiles are manufactured in a continuous flow (suited to process costing), but individual units may be customized with different engine sizes, transmissions, music systems, and so on (which requires job costing). A **hybrid-costing system** blends characteristics from both job-costing and process-costing systems. Managers must design product-costing systems to fit the particular characteristics of different production systems.

LEARNING OBJECTIVE 6

Understand the need for hybrid-costing systems such as operation costing

. . . when product-costing does not fall into job-costing or process-costing categories

Firms that manufacture closely related standardized products (for example, various types of televisions, dishwashers, washing machines, and shoes) tend to use hybrid-costing systems. They use process costing to account for conversion costs and job costing for material and customizable components. Consider Nike, which has a message for shoppers looking for the hottest new shoe design: Just do it... yourself! Nike is making it possible for customers to design their own shoes and clothing. Using the Internet and mobile applications, Nike's customers can personalize with their own colors and patterns for Jordan-brand sneakers and other apparel. Concepts in Action: Hybrid Costing for Adidas Customized 3D Printed Shoes describes customization and the use of a hybrid-costing system at one of Nike's rivals, Adidas. The next section explains *operation costing*, a common type of hybrid-costing system.

Overview of Operation-Costing Systems

An **operation** is a standardized method or technique performed repetitively, often on different materials, resulting in different finished goods. Multiple operations are often performed within a department. For instance, a suit maker may have a cutting operation and a hemming operation within a single department. The term *operation*, however, is used loosely. It may be a synonym for a department or process. For example, some companies may call their finishing department a finishing process or a finishing operation.

An **operation-costing system** is a hybrid-costing system applied to batches of similar, but not identical, products. Each batch of products is often a variation of a single design, and it proceeds through a sequence of operations. Within each operation, all product units are treated exactly alike, using identical amounts of the operation's resources. A key point in the operation system is that each batch does not necessarily move through the same operations as other batches. Batches are also called production runs.

CONCEPTS IN ACTION: Hybrid Costing for Adidas Customized 3D Printed Shoes[4]

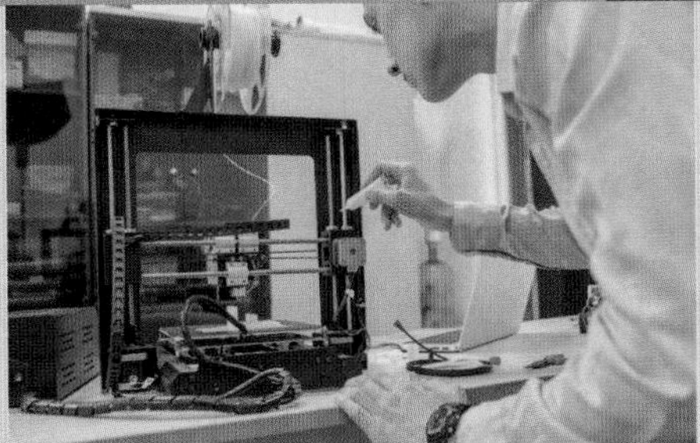
Westend61 GmbH/Alamy Stock Photo

In 2018, Adidas overtook Nike's Jordan brand to become the second largest sneaker maker in the United States. Known for its iconic three-stripe logo and partnerships with NBA superstar James Harden and rapper Kanye West, the company is embracing cutting-edge manufacturing and 3D printing to create customized shoes for its customers.

Adidas' Futurecraft 4D running shoes feature a standard 3D-printed midsole. But new versions of the sneakers will feature customized midsoles engineered and printed based on the biomechanical data of each customer. To accomplish this, Adidas computers will make a three-dimensional scan of a customer's feet and measure the load and torque in their running stride. From there, the single-piece customized midsoles will be 3D-printed using digital light synthesis and incorporated into the knit Futurecraft 4D shoes. The result will be a customized pair of running shoes tailored to each person's unique feet and running style.

Customized 3D-printed shoes, like the Futurecraft 4D, use a hybrid-costing system. Accounting for the 3D printing of the midsoles requires job costing, but the similar process used to make the shoes they are stitched into lends itself to process costing.

Along with athletic shoes, 3D printing is letting people create personalized jewelry, headphones, and mobile phone cases. Adoption of 3D printing is growing rapidly, and by 2023 the market for 3D printing is expected to eclipse $32 billion.

[4] *Sources:* Andria Cheng, "How Adidas Plans to Bring 3D Printing to the Masses," Forbes.com, May 22, 2018 (https://www.forbes.com/sites/andriacheng/2018/05/22/with-adidas-3d-printing-may-finally-see-its-mass-retail-potential/); Isabel Flower, "Is Mass Customization the Future of Footwear?" *The Wall Street Journal*, October 24, 2017 (https://www.wsj.com/articles/is-mass-customization-the-future-of-footwear-1508850000); Anna Wiener, "Inside Adidas' Robot-Powered, On-Demand Sneaker Factory," *Wired*, November 29, 2017 (https://www.wired.com/story/inside-speedfactory-adidas-robot-powered-sneaker-factory/); No author, *3D Printing Market* (Chicago, IL: Markets and Markets, 2017).

In a company that makes suits, managers may select a single basic design for every suit to be made, but depending on specifications, each batch of suits varies somewhat from other batches. Batches may vary with respect to the material used or the type of stitching. Semiconductors, textiles, and shoes are also manufactured in batches and may have similar variations from batch to batch.

An operation-costing system uses work orders that specify the needed direct materials and step-by-step operations. Product costs are compiled for each work order. Direct materials that are unique to different work orders are specifically identified with the appropriate work order, as in job costing. However, each unit is assumed to use an identical amount of conversion costs for a given operation, as in process costing. A single average conversion cost per unit is calculated for each operation by dividing total conversion costs for that operation by the number of units that pass through it. This average cost is then assigned to each unit passing through the operation. Units that do not pass through an operation are not allocated any costs for that operation.

Illustrating an Operation-Costing System

The Baltimore Clothing Company, a clothing manufacturer, produces two lines of blazers: those made of wool and those made of polyester. Wool blazers use better-quality materials and undergo more operations than polyester blazers. The operations information on Work Order 423 for 50 wool blazers and Work Order 424 for 100 polyester blazers follows:

	Work Order 423	Work Order 424
Direct materials	Wool	Polyester
	Satin full lining	Rayon partial lining
	Bone buttons	Plastic buttons
Operations		
1. Cutting cloth	Use	Use
2. Checking edges	Use	Do not use
3. Sewing body	Use	Use
4. Checking seams	Use	Do not use
5. Machine sewing of collars and lapels	Do not use	Use
6. Hand sewing of collars and lapels	Use	Do not use

The cost data for these work orders, started and completed in March 2020, are as follows:

	Work Order 423	Work Order 424
Number of blazers	50	100
Direct materials costs	$ 6,000	$3,000
Conversion costs allocated:		
Operation 1	580	1,160
Operation 2	400	—
Operation 3	1,900	3,800
Operation 4	500	—
Operation 5	—	875
Operation 6	700	—
Total manufacturing costs	$10,080	$8,835

As in process costing, all product units in any work order are assumed to consume identical amounts of conversion costs of a particular operation. Baltimore's operation-costing system uses a budgeted rate to calculate the conversion costs of each operation. The budgeted rate for Operation 1 (amounts assumed) is shown below:

$$\text{Operation 1 budgeted conversion-cost rate for 2020} = \frac{\text{Operation 1 budgeted conversion costs for 2020}}{\text{Operation 1 budgeted product units for 2020}}$$

$$= \frac{\$232{,}000}{20{,}000 \text{ units}}$$

$$= \$11.60 \text{ per unit}$$

The budgeted conversion costs of Operation 1 include labor, power, repairs, supplies, depreciation, and other overhead of this operation. If some units have not been completed (so all units in Operation 1 have not received the same amounts of conversion costs), the conversion-cost rate is computed by dividing the budgeted conversion costs by the *equivalent units* of the conversion costs, as in process costing.

As the company manufactures blazers, managers allocate conversion costs to work orders processed in Operation 1 by multiplying the $11.60 conversion cost per unit by the number of units processed. Conversion costs of Operation 1 for 50 wool blazers (Work Order 423) are $11.60 per blazer × 50 blazers = $580 and for 100 polyester blazers (Work Order 424) are $11.60 per blazer × 100 blazers = $1,160. When equivalent units are used to calculate the conversion-cost rate, costs are allocated to work orders by multiplying the conversion cost per equivalent unit by the number of equivalent units in the work order. The direct materials costs of $6,000 for the 50 wool blazers (Work Order 423) and $3,000 for the 100 polyester blazers (Work Order 424) are specifically identified with each order, as in job costing. The basic point of operation costing is this: Operation unit costs are assumed to be the same regardless of the work order, but direct materials costs vary across orders when the materials for each work order vary.

Journal Entries

The actual conversion costs for Operation 1 in March 2020—assumed to be $24,400, including the actual costs incurred for Work Order 423 and Work Order 424—are entered into a Conversion Costs Control account:

1. Conversion Costs Control	24,400	
Various accounts (such as Wages Payable Control and Accumulated Depreciation)		24,400

Summary journal entries for assigning costs to polyester blazers (Work Order 424) follow. Entries for wool blazers are similar. Of the $3,000 of direct materials for Work Order 424, $2,975 are used in Operation 1, and the remaining $25 of materials are used in another operation. The journal entry to record direct materials used for the 100 polyester blazers is shown below:

2. Work in Process, Operation 1	2,975	
Materials Inventory Control		2,975

The journal entry to record the allocation of conversion costs to products uses the budgeted rate of $11.60 per blazer times the 100 polyester blazers processed, or $1,160:

3. Work in Process, Operation 1	1,160	
Conversion Costs Allocated		1,160

The journal entry to record the transfer of 100 polyester blazers (at a cost of $2,975 + $1,160) from Operation 1 to Operation 3 (polyester blazers do not go through Operation 2) is as follows:

4. Work in Process, Operation 3	4,135	
Work in Process, Operation 1		4,135

After posting these entries, the Work in Process, Operation 1, account appears as follows:

Work in Process, Operation 1

② Direct materials	2,975	④ Transferred to Operation 3	4,135
③ Conversion costs allocated	1,160		
Ending inventory, March 31	0		

The costs of the blazers are transferred through the operations in which blazers are worked on and then to finished goods in the usual manner. Costs are added throughout the fiscal year in the Conversion Costs Control account and the Conversion Costs Allocated account. Any overallocation or underallocation of conversion costs is disposed of in the same way as overallocated or underallocated manufacturing overhead in a job-costing system, that is, using either the adjusted allocation-rate, proration, or writeoff to cost of goods sold approach (see pages 126–130).

DECISION POINT

What is an operation-costing system, and when is it a better approach to product costing?

Managers find operation costing useful in cost management because operation costing focuses on control of physical processes, or operations, of a given production system. For example, in clothing manufacturing, managers are concerned with fabric waste, how many fabric layers can be cut at one time, and so on. Operation costing measures, in financial terms, how well managers have controlled physical processes.

TRY IT! 18-4

Modern Bakery sells dinner rolls and multigrain bread. The company needs to determine the cost of two work orders for the month of July. Work Order 215 is for 3,600 packages of dinner rolls and Work Order 216 is for 4,000 loaves of multigrain bread. The following information shows the different operations used by the two work orders:

	Work Order 215	Work Order 216
Operations		
1. Bake	Use	Use
2. Shape loaves	Do not use	Use
3. Cut rolls	Use	Do not use

For July, Modern Bakery budgeted that it would make 10,000 packages of dinner rolls and 15,000 of multigrain loaves (with associated direct materials costs of \$8,000 and \$15,000, respectively). Budgeted conversion costs for each operation in July were Baking, \$20,500; Shaping, \$2,100; and Cutting, \$2,000.

a. Using the budgeted number of packages as the denominator, calculate the budgeted conversion-cost rates for each operation.
b. Using the information in requirement (a), calculate the budgeted cost of goods manufactured for the two July work orders.

PROBLEM FOR SELF-STUDY

Allied Chemicals operates an assembly process as the second of three processes at its plastics plant. Conversion costs are added evenly during the process, while direct materials are added at the end. The following data pertain to the assembly department for June 2020:

	A	B	C	D	E
1		Physical Units	Transferred-In Costs	Direct Materials	Conversion Costs
2	Work in process, beginning inventory	50,000			
3	Degree of completion, beginning work in process		100%	0%	80%
4	Transferred in during current period	200,000			
5	Completed and transferred out during current period	210,000			
6	Work in process, ending inventory	?			
7	Degree of completion, ending work in process		100%	0%	40%

Required

Compute equivalent units under (1) the weighted-average method and (2) the FIFO method.

Solution

1. The weighted-average method uses equivalent units of work done to date to compute cost per equivalent unit. The calculations of equivalent units follow:

	A	B	C	D	E
1		(Step 1)	(Step 2)		
2			Equivalent Units		
3	Flow of Production	Physical Units	Transferred-In Costs	Direct Materials	Conversion Costs
4	Work in process, beginning (given)	50,000			
5	Transferred-in during current period (given)	200,000			
6	To account for	250,000			
7	Completed and transferred out during current period	210,000	210,000	210,000	210,000
8	Work in process, ending[a]	40,000[b]			
9	(40,000 × 100%; 40,000 × 0%; 40,000 × 40%)		40,000	0	16,000
10	Accounted for	250,000			
11	Equivalent units of work done to date		250,000	210,000	226,000
12					
13	[a]Degree of completion in this department: Transferred-in costs, 100%; direct materials, 0%; conversion costs, 40%.				
14	[b]250,000 physical units to account for minus 210,000 physical units completed and transferred out.				

2. The FIFO method uses equivalent units of work done in the current period only to compute cost per equivalent unit. The calculations of equivalent units follow:

	A	B	C	D	E
1		(Step 1)	(Step 2)		
2			Equivalent Units		
3	Flow of Production	Physical Units	Transferred-In Costs	Direct Materials	Conversion Costs
4	Work in process, beginning (given)	50,000			
5	Transferred-in during current period (given)	200,000			
6	To account for	250,000			
7	Completed and transferred out during current period:				
8	From beginning work in process[a]	50,000			
9	[50,000 × (100% − 100%); 50,000 × (100% − 0%); 50,000 × (100% − 80%)]		0	50,000	10,000
10	Started and completed	160,000[b]			
11	(160,000 × 100%; 160,000 × 100%; 160,000 × 100%)		160,000	160,000	160,000
12	Work in process, ending[c]	40,000[d]			
13	(40,000 × 100%; 40,000 × 0%; 40,000 × 40%)		40,000	0	16,000
14	Accounted for	250,000			
15	Equivalent units of work done in current period		200,000	210,000	186,000
16					
17	[a]Degree of completion in this department: Transferred-in costs, 100%; direct materials, 0%; conversion costs, 80%.				
18	[b]210,000 physical units completed and transferred out minus 50,000 physical units completed and transferred out from beginning work-in-process inventory.				
19	[c]Degree of completion in this department: Transferred-in costs, 100%; direct materials, 0%; conversion costs, 40%.				
20	[d]250,000 physical units to account for minus 210,000 physical units completed and transferred out.				

DECISION POINTS

The following question-and-answer format summarizes the chapter's learning objectives. Each decision presents a key question related to a learning objective. The guidelines are the answer to that question.

Decision	Guidelines
1. Under what conditions is a process-costing system used?	A process-costing system is used to determine cost of a product or service when masses of identical or similar units are produced. Industries using process-costing systems include the food, textiles, and oil-refining industries.
2. How are average unit costs computed when no inventories are present?	Average unit costs are computed by dividing the total costs in a given accounting period by the total units produced in that period.
3. What are the five steps in a process-costing system, and how are equivalent units calculated?	The five steps in a process-costing system are (a) summarize the flow of physical units of output, (b) compute output in terms of equivalent units, (c) summarize total costs to account for, (d) compute cost per equivalent unit, and (e) assign total costs to units completed and to units in ending work-in-process inventory. An equivalent unit is a derived measure of output that (a) takes the quantity of each input (factor of production) in units completed or in incomplete units in work in process and (b) converts the quantity of input into the amount of completed output units that could be made with that quantity of input.
4. What are the weighted-average and first-in, first-out (FIFO) methods of process costing? Under what conditions will they yield different levels of operating income?	The weighted-average method computes cost per equivalent unit by dividing total costs in the work-in-process account by total equivalent units completed to date and assigns this average cost to units completed and to units in ending work-in-process inventory. The first-in, first-out (FIFO) method computes cost per equivalent unit based on costs incurred during the current period and equivalent units of work done in the current period. Operating income can differ materially between the two methods when (a) direct material or conversion cost per equivalent unit varies significantly from period to period and (b) physical-inventory levels of work in process are large in relation to the total number of units transferred out of the process.
5. How are the weighted-average and FIFO process-costing methods applied to transferred-in costs?	The weighted-average method computes transferred-in costs per equivalent unit by dividing the total transferred-in costs to date by the total equivalent transferred-in units completed to date and assigns this average cost to units completed and to units in ending work-in-process inventory. The FIFO method computes the transferred-in costs per equivalent unit based on the costs transferred in during the current period and equivalent units of transferred-in costs of work done in the current period. The FIFO method assigns transferred-in costs in the beginning work-in-process inventory to units completed; it assigns costs transferred in during the current period to start and complete new units, and then to units in ending work-in-process inventory.
6. What is an operation-costing system, and when is it a better approach to product costing?	Operation costing is a hybrid-costing system that blends characteristics from both job-costing (for direct materials) and process-costing systems (for conversion costs). It is a better approach to product costing when production systems share some features of custom-order manufacturing and other features of mass-production manufacturing.

APPENDIX

Standard-Costing Method of Process Costing

Chapter 7 described accounting in a standard-costing system. Recall that this involves making entries using standard costs and then isolating variances from these standards in order to support management control. This appendix describes how the principles of standard costing can be employed in process-costing systems.

Benefits of Standard Costing

Companies that use process-costing systems produce masses of identical or similar units of output. In such companies, it is fairly easy to budget for the quantities of inputs needed to produce a unit of output. Standard cost per input unit can then be multiplied by input quantity standards to develop a standard cost per output unit.

The weighted-average and FIFO methods become very complicated when used in process industries, such as textiles, ceramics, paints, and packaged food, that produce a wide variety of similar products. For example, a steel-rolling mill uses various steel alloys and produces sheets of varying sizes and finishes. The different types of direct materials used and the operations performed are few, but used in various combinations, they yield a wide variety of products. In these cases, if the broad averaging procedure of *actual* process costing were used, the result would be inaccurate costs for each product. Therefore, managers in these industries typically use the standard-costing method of process costing.

Under the standard-costing method, teams of design and process engineers, operations personnel, and management accountants work together to determine *separate* standard costs per equivalent unit on the basis of different technical processing specifications for each product. Identifying standard costs for each product overcomes the disadvantage of costing all products at a single average amount, as under actual costing.

Computations Under Standard Costing

We present standard costing for the assembly department of Pacific Electronics using the five-step procedure introduced on pages 713–714. We assume the same standard costs apply in February and March 2020. Data for the assembly department follow:

	A	B	C	D	E
1		Physical Units (SG-40s) (1)	Direct Materials (2)	Conversion Costs (3)	Total Costs (4) = (2) + (3)
2	Standard cost per unit		$ 74	$ 54	
3	Work in process, beginning inventory (March 1)	225			
4	Degree of completion of beginning work in process		100%	60%	
5	Beginning work-in-process inventory at standard costs		$16,650[a]	$ 7,290[a]	$23,940
6	Started during March	275			
7	Completed and transferred out during March	400			
8	Work in process, ending inventory (March 31)	100			
9	Degree of completion of ending work in process		100%	50%	
10	Actual total costs added during March		$19,800	$16,380	$36,180
11					
12	[a]Work in process, beginning inventory at standard costs:				
13	Direct materials: 225 physical units × 100% completed × $74 per unit = $16,650				
14	Conversion costs: 225 physical units × 60% completed × $54 per unit = $7,290				

Exhibit 18-12 presents Steps 1 and 2. These steps are identical to the steps described for the FIFO method in Exhibit 18-6 because, as in FIFO, the standard-costing method also assumes

EXHIBIT 18-12

Summarize the Flow of Physical Units and Compute Output in Equivalent Units Using the Standard-Costing Method for the Assembly Department for March 2020

	A	B	C	D
1		(Step 1)	(Step 2)	
2			Equivalent Units	
3	Flow of Production	Physical Units	Direct Materials	Conversion Costs
4	Work in process, beginning (given, p. 737)	225		
5	Started during current period (given, p. 737)	275		
6	To account for	500		
7	Completed and transferred out during current period:			
8	From beginning work in process[a]	225		
9	[225 × (100% – 100%); 225 × (100% – 60%)]		0	90
10	Started and completed	175[b]		
11	(175 × 100%; 175 × 100%)		175	175
12	Work in process, ending[c] (given, p. 737)	100		
13	(100 × 100%; 100 × 50%)		100	50
14	Accounted for	500		
15	Equivalent units of work done in current period		275	315
16				
17	[a]Degree of completion in this department: direct materials, 100%; conversion costs, 60%.			
18	[b]400 physical units completed and transferred out minus 225 physical units completed and transferred out from beginning work-in-process inventory.			
19	[c]Degree of completion in this department: direct materials, 100%; conversion costs, 50%.			

that the earliest equivalent units in beginning work in process are completed first. Work done in the current period for direct materials is 275 equivalent units. Work done in the current period for conversion costs is 315 equivalent units.

Exhibit 18-13 describes Steps 3, 4, and 5. In Step 3, total costs to account for (that is, the total debits to Work in Process—Assembly) differ from total debits to Work in Process—Assembly under the actual-cost-based weighted-average and FIFO methods. That's because, as in all standard-costing systems, the debits to the Work in Process account are at standard costs, rather than actual costs. These standard costs total \$61,300 in Exhibit 18-13. In Step 4, costs per equivalent unit are standard costs: direct materials, \$74, and conversion costs, \$54. *Therefore, costs per equivalent unit do not have to be computed as they were for the weighted-average and FIFO methods.*

Exhibit 18-13, Step 5, assigns total costs to units completed and transferred out and to units in ending work-in-process inventory, as in the FIFO method. Step 5 assigns amounts of standard costs to equivalent units calculated in Exhibit 18-12: (1) first to complete beginning work-in-process inventory, (2) next to start and complete new units, and (3) finally to start new units that are in ending work-in-process inventory. Note how the \$61,300 total costs accounted for in Step 5 of Exhibit 18-13 equal total costs to account for.

Accounting for Variances

Process-costing systems using standard costs record actual direct materials costs in Direct Materials Control and actual conversion costs in Conversion Costs Control (similar to Variable and Fixed Overhead Control in Chapter 8). In the journal entries that follow, the first two record these *actual costs*. In entries 3 and 4a, the Work-in-Process—Assembly account

EXHIBIT 18-13 Summarize Total Costs to Account For, Compute Cost per Equivalent Unit, and Assign Costs to Units Completed and to Units in Ending Work-in-Process Inventory Using the Standard-Costing Method for the Assembly Department for March 2020

Home Insert Page Layout Formulas Data Review View

	A	B	C	D	E	F	G
1			Total Production Costs	Direct Materials		Conversion Costs	
2	(Step 3)	Work in process, beginning	$23,940	(225 × $74)	+	(135 × $54)	
3		Costs added in current period at standard costs	37,360	(275 × $74)	+	(315 × $54)	
4		Total costs to account for	$61,300	$37,000	+	$ 24,300	
5							
6	(Step 4)	Standard cost per equivalent unit (given, p. 737)	$ 128	$ 74	+	$ 54	
7							
8	(Step 5)	Assignment of costs at standard costs:					
9		Completed and transferred out (400 units):					
10		Work in process, beginning (225 units)	$23,940	(225 × $74)	+	(135 × $54)	
11		Costs added to beginning work in process in current period	4,860	(0[a] × $74)	+	(90[a] × $54)	
12		Total from beginning inventory	28,800				
13		Started and completed (175 units)	22,400	(175[b] × $74)	+	(175[b] × $54)	
14		Total costs of units completed and transferred out	51,200				
15		Work in process, ending (100 units)	10,100	(100[c] × $74)	+	(50[c] × $54)	
16		Total costs accounted for	$61,300	$37,000	+	$24,300	
17							
18	Summary of variances for current performance:						
19	Costs added in current period at standard costs[d]			$20,350		$17,010	
20	Actual costs incurred (given, p. 737)			$19,800		$16,380	
21	Variance			$ 550	F	$ 630	F
22							
23	[a]Equivalent units used to complete beginning work in process from Exhibit 18-12, Step 2.						
24	[b]Equivalent units started and completed from Exhibit 18-12, Step 2.						
25	[c]Equivalent units in ending work in process from Exhibit 18-12, Step 2.						
26	[d]From Step 3 above: Direct Materials: (275 × $74); Conversion Costs: (315 × $54)						

accumulates direct materials costs and conversion costs at *standard costs*. Entries 3 and 4b isolate total variances. The final entry transfers out completed goods at standard costs.

1. Assembly Department Direct Materials Control (at actual costs)	19,800	
Accounts Payable Control		19,800
To record direct materials purchased and used in production during March. This cost control account is debited with actual costs.		
2. Assembly Department Conversion Costs Control (at actual costs)	16,380	
Various accounts such as Wages Payable Control and Accumulated Depreciation		16,380
To record assembly department conversion costs for March. This cost control account is debited with actual costs.		
Entries 3, 4, and 5 use standard cost amounts from Exhibit 18-13.		
3. Work in Process—Assembly (at standard costs)	20,350	
Direct Materials Variances		550
Assembly Department Direct Materials Control		19,800
To record standard costs of direct materials assigned to units worked on and total direct materials variances.		

4a.	Work in Process—Assembly (at standard costs)	17,010	
	Assembly Department Conversion Costs Allocated		17,010
	To record conversion costs allocated at standard costs to the units worked on during March.		
4b.	Assembly Department Conversion Costs Allocated	17,010	
	Conversion Costs Variances		630
	Assembly Department Conversion Costs Control		16,380
	To record total conversion costs variances.		
5.	Work in Process—Testing (at standard costs)	51,200	
	Work in Process—Assembly (at standard costs)		51,200
	To record standard costs of units completed and transferred out from assembly to testing.		

Variances arise under standard costing, as in entries 3 and 4b. That's because the standard costs assigned to products on the basis of work done in the current period do not equal actual costs incurred in the current period. Recall that variances that result in higher income (or lower costs) than the standard are favorable, while those that reduce income are unfavorable. In journal entries, favorable cost variances are credits, while unfavorable variances are debits. In our example, both direct materials and conversion cost variances are favorable, as indicated by the "F" designations in Exhibit 18-13.

Variances can be analyzed in little or great detail for planning and control purposes, as described in Chapters 7 and 8. Sometimes direct materials price variances are isolated at the time direct materials are purchased and only efficiency variances are computed in entry 3. Exhibit 18-14 shows how costs flow through the general-ledger accounts under standard costing.

EXHIBIT 18-14 Flow of Standard Costs in a Process-Costing System for the Assembly Department for March 2020

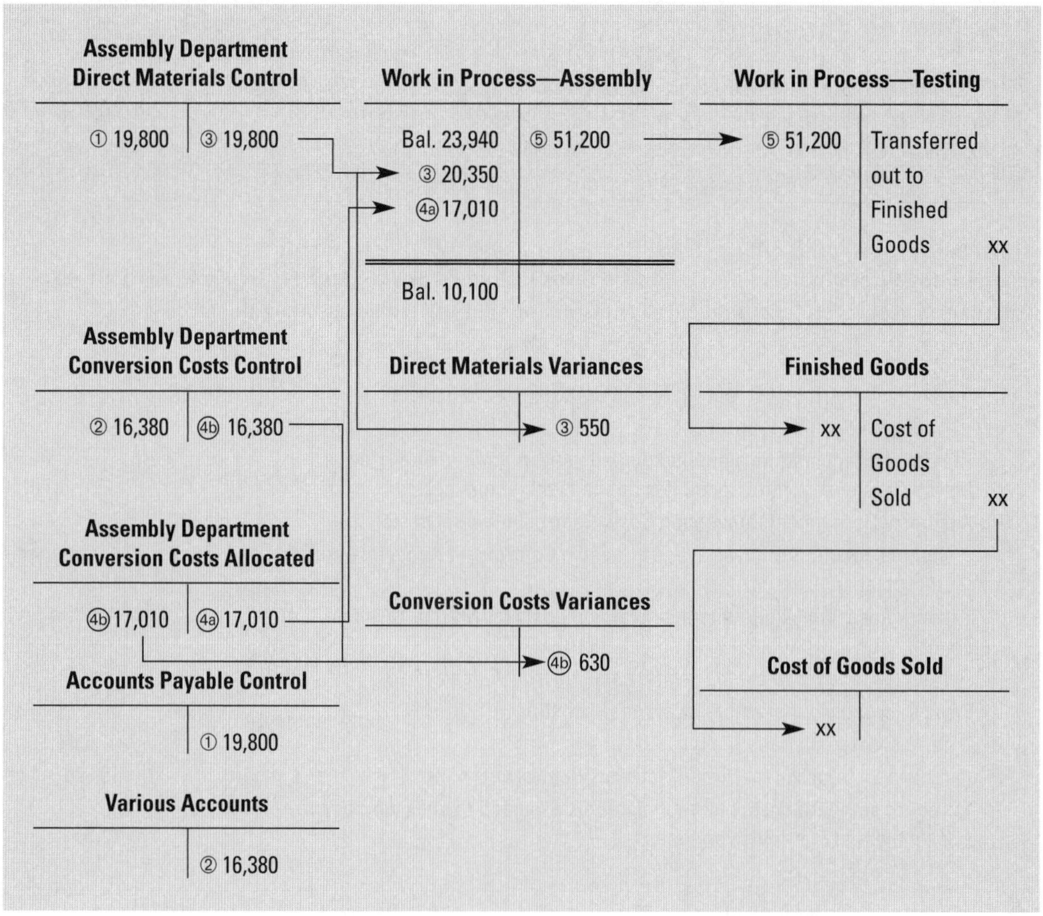

TERMS TO LEARN

This chapter and the Glossary at the end of the text contain definitions of the following important terms:

equivalent units (**p. 714**)
first-in, first-out (FIFO) process-costing method (**p. 721**)
hybrid-costing system (**p. 731**)
operation (**p. 731**)
operation-costing system (**p. 731**)
previous-department costs (**p. 726**)
transferred-in costs (**p. 726**)
weighted-average process-costing method (**p. 718**)

ASSIGNMENT MATERIAL

Questions

18-1 Give three examples of industries that use process-costing systems.

18-2 In process costing, why are costs often divided into two main classifications?

18-3 Explain equivalent units. Why are equivalent-unit calculations necessary in process costing?

18-4 What problems might arise in estimating the degree of completion of semiconductor chips in a semiconductor plant?

18-5 Name the five steps in process costing when equivalent units are computed.

18-6 Name the three inventory methods commonly associated with process costing.

18-7 Describe the distinctive characteristic of weighted-average computations in assigning costs to units completed and to units in ending work in process.

18-8 Describe the distinctive characteristic of FIFO computations in assigning costs to units completed and to units in ending work in process.

18-9 Why should the FIFO method be called a modified or department FIFO method?

18-10 Identify a major advantage of the FIFO method for purposes of planning and control.

18-11 Identify the main difference between journal entries in process costing and job costing.

18-12 "The standard-costing method is particularly applicable to process-costing situations." Do you agree? Why?

18-13 Why should the accountant distinguish between transferred-in costs and additional direct materials costs for each subsequent department in a process-costing system?

18-14 "Transferred-in costs are those costs incurred in the preceding accounting period." Do you agree? Explain.

18-15 "There's no reason for me to get excited about the choice between the weighted-average and FIFO methods in my process-costing system. I have long-term contracts with my materials suppliers at fixed prices." Do you agree with this statement made by a plant controller? Explain.

Multiple-Choice Questions

In partnership with: BECKER PROFESSIONAL EDUCATION

18-16 Assuming beginning work in process is zero, the equivalent units of production computed using FIFO versus weighted average will have the following relationship:

1. FIFO equivalent units will be greater than weighted-average equivalent units.
2. FIFO equivalent units will be less than weighted-average equivalent units.
3. Weighted-average equivalent units are always greater than FIFO equivalent units.
4. Weighted-average equivalent units will be equal to FIFO equivalent units.

18-17 The following information concerns Westheimer Corporation's equivalent units in May 20X1:

	Units
Beginning work in process (50% complete)	4,000
Units started during May	16,000
Units completed and transferred	14,000
Ending work in process (80% complete)	6,000

Using the weighted-average method, what were Westheimer's May 20X1 equivalent units?

1. 14,000 **2.** 18,800
3. 20,000 **4.** 39,000

18-18 Sepulveda Corporation uses a process costing system to manufacture laptop PCs. The following information summarizes operations for its VeryLite model during the quarter ending March 31, Year 1:

	Units	Direct Materials
Work-in-process inventory, January 1	100	$ 60,000
Started during the quarter	500	
Completed during the quarter	400	
Work-in-process inventory, March 31	200	
Costs added during the quarter		$840,000

Beginning work-in-process inventory was 50% complete for direct materials. Ending work-in-process inventory was 75% complete for direct materials. What were the equivalent units for direct materials for the quarter using the FIFO method?

1. 450 **2.** 500
3. 550 **4.** 600

18-19 Penn Manufacturing Corporation uses a process-costing system to manufacture printers for PCs. The following information summarizes operations for its NoToner model during the quarter ending September 30, Year 1:

	Units	Direct Manufacturing Labor
Work-in-process inventory, July 1	100	$ 50,000
Started during the quarter	500	
Completed during the quarter	400	
Work-in-process inventory, September 30	200	
Costs added during the quarter		$775,000

Beginning work-in-process inventory was 50% complete for direct manufacturing labor. Ending work-in-process inventory was 75% complete for direct manufacturing labor. What is the total value of the direct manufacturing labor in the ending work-in-process inventory using the weighted-average method?

1. $183,000 **2.** $194,000
3. $225,000 **4.** $210,000

18-20 Kimberly Manufacturing uses a process-costing system to manufacture Dust Density Sensors for the mining industry. The following information pertains to operations for the month of May, Year 5.

	Units
Beginning work-in-process inventory, May 1	16,000
Started in production during May	100,000
Completed production during May	92,000
Ending work-in-process inventory, May 31	24,000

The beginning inventory was 60% complete for direct materials and 20% complete for conversion costs. The ending inventory was 90% complete for direct materials and 40% complete for conversion costs.

Costs pertaining to the month of May are as follows:

- Beginning inventory costs are direct materials, $54,560; direct manufacturing labor $20,320; and manufacturing overhead, $15,240.
- Costs incurred during May are direct materials used, $468,000; direct manufacturing labor, $182,880; and manufacturing overhead, $391,160.

Using the weighted-average method, the equivalent-unit conversion cost for May is

1. $5.65 2. $5.83
3. $6.00 4. $6.41

Exercises

18-21 Equivalent units, zero beginning inventory. Panagra, Inc. manufactures digital cameras. It has two departments: assembly and testing. In January 2020, the company incurred $775,000 on direct materials and $816,000 on conversion costs, for a total manufacturing cost of $1,591,000.

Required

1. Assume there was no beginning inventory of any kind on January 1, 2020. During January, 10,000 cameras were placed into production and all 10,000 were fully completed at the end of the month. What is the unit cost of an assembled camera in January?
2. Assume that during February 10,000 cameras are placed into production. Further assume the same total assembly costs for January are also incurred in February, but only 9,000 cameras are fully completed at the end of the month. All direct materials have been added to the remaining 1,000 cameras. However, on average, these remaining 1,000 cameras are only 60% complete as to conversion costs. (a) What are the equivalent units for direct materials and conversion costs and their respective costs per equivalent unit for February? (b) What is the unit cost of an assembled camera in February 2020?
3. Explain the difference in your answers to requirements 1 and 2.

18-22 Journal entries (continuation of 18-21). Refer to requirement 2 of Exercise 18-21. Prepare summary journal entries for the use of direct materials and incurrence of conversion costs. Also prepare a journal entry to transfer out the cost of goods completed. Show the postings to the work-in-process account.

Required

18-23 Zero beginning inventory, materials introduced in middle of process. Castle Cakes uses a mixing department and a baking department in producing its cake. Its process-costing system in the mixing department has two direct materials cost categories (cake mix and flavorings) and one conversion cost pool. The following data pertain to the mixing department for April 2020:

Work in process, April 1	0
Started in April	13,000 pounds
Completed and transferred to baking	10,900 pounds
Costs:	
Cake mix	$32,500
Flavorings	$ 6,540
Conversion costs	$22,850

The cake mix is introduced at the start of operations in the mixing department, and the flavorings are added when the product is 50% completed in the mixing department. Conversion costs are added evenly during the process. The ending work in process in the mixing department is 25% complete.

Required

1. Compute the equivalent units in the mixing department for April 2020 for each cost category.
2. Compute (a) the cost of goods completed and transferred to the baking department during April and (b) the cost of work in process as of April 30, 2020.

18-24 Weighted-average method, equivalent units. The assembly division of Quality Time Pieces, Inc. uses the weighted-average method of process costing. Consider the following data for May 2020:

	Physical Units (Watches)	Direct Materials	Conversion Costs
Beginning work in process (May 1)[a]	100	$ 459,888	$ 142,570
Started in May 2020	510		
Completed during May 2020	450		
Ending work in process (May 31)[b]	160		
Total costs added during May 2020		$3,237,000	$1,916,000

[a] Degree of completion: direct materials, 80%; conversion costs, 35%.
[b] Degree of completion: direct materials, 80%; conversion costs, 40%.

Required

Compute equivalent units for direct materials and conversion costs. Show physical units in the first column of your schedule.

18-25 Weighted-average method, assigning costs (continuation of 18-24).

Required

For the data in Exercise 18-24, summarize total costs to account for, calculate cost per equivalent unit for direct materials and conversion costs, and assign costs to units completed (and transferred out) and to units in ending work-in-process inventory.

18-26 FIFO method, equivalent units. Refer to the information in Exercise 18-24. Suppose the assembly division at Quality Time Pieces, Inc. uses the FIFO method of process costing instead of the weighted-average method.

Required

Compute equivalent units for direct materials and conversion costs. Show physical units in the first column of your schedule.

18-27 FIFO method, assigning costs (continuation of 18-26).

Required

For the data in Exercise 18-24, use the FIFO method to summarize total costs to account for, calculate cost per equivalent unit for direct materials and conversion costs, and assign costs to units completed (and transferred out) and to units in ending work-in-process inventory.

18-28 Operation costing. The Carter Furniture Company needs to determine the cost of two work orders for December 2020. Work Order 1200A is for 250 painted, unassembled chests and Work Order 1250A is for 400 stained, assembled chests. The following information pertains to these two work orders:

	Work Order 1200A	Work Order 1250A
Number of chests	250	400
Operations		
1. Cutting	Use	Use
2. Painting	Use	Do not use
3. Staining	Do not use	Use
4. Assembling	Do not use	Use
5. Packaging	Use	Use

Selected budget information for December follows:

	Unassembled Chests	Assembled Chests	Total
Chests	800	1,500	2,300
Direct materials costs	$52,000	$180,000	$232,000

Budgeted conversion costs for each operation for December follow:

Cutting	$41,400
Painting	6,400
Staining	24,000
Assembling	33,000
Packaging	11,500

Required

1. Using budgeted number of chests as the denominator, calculate the budgeted conversion-cost rates for each operation.
2. Using information in requirement 1, calculate the budgeted cost of goods manufactured for the two December work orders.
3. Calculate the cost per unassembled chest and assembled chest for Work Order 1200A and Work Order 1250A, respectively.

18-29 Weighted-average method, assigning costs. ZanyBrainy Corporation makes interlocking children's blocks in a single processing department. Direct materials are added at the start of production. Conversion costs are added evenly throughout production. ZanyBrainy uses the weighted-average method of process costing. The following information for October 2020 is available.

		Equivalent Units	
	Physical Units	Direct Materials	Conversion Costs
Work in process, October 1	12,000[a]	12,000	9,600
Started in October	48,000		
Completed and transferred out during October	55,000	55,000	55,000
Work in process, October 31	5,000[b]	5,000	1,500

[a] Degree of completion: direct materials, 100%; conversion costs, 80%.
[b] Degree of completion: direct materials, 100%; conversion costs, 30%.

Total Costs for October 2020		
Work in process, beginning		
Direct materials	$ 5,760	
Conversion costs	14,825	$ 20,585
Direct materials added during October		25,440
Conversion costs added during October		58,625
Total costs to account for		$104,650

Required

1. Calculate cost per equivalent unit for direct materials and conversion costs.
2. Summarize total costs to account for and assign them to units completed (and transferred out) and to units in ending work-in-process inventory.

18-30 FIFO method, assigning costs (continuation of 18-29).

Required

1. Do Exercise 18-29 using the FIFO method.
2. ZanyBrainy's management seeks to have a more consistent cost per equivalent unit. Which method of process costing should the company choose and why?

18-31 Transferred-in costs, weighted-average method. Trendy Clothing, Inc. is a manufacturer of winter clothes. It has a knitting department and a finishing department. This exercise focuses on the finishing department. Direct materials are added at the end of the process. Conversion costs are added evenly during the process. Trendy uses the weighted-average method of process costing. Information for June 2020 follows:

Home Insert Page Layout Formulas Data Review View

	A	B	C	D	E
1		Physical Units (tons)	Transferred-In Costs	Direct Materials	Conversion Costs
2	Work in process, beginning inventory (June 1)	60	$ 60,000	$ 0	$24,000
3	Degree of completion, beginning work in process		100%	0%	50%
4	Transferred-in during June	100			
5	Completed and transferred out during June	120			
6	Work in process, ending inventory (June 30)	40			
7	Degree of completion, ending work in process		100%	0%	75%
8	Total costs added during June		$117,000	$27,000	$62,400

Required

1. Calculate equivalent units of transferred-in costs, direct materials, and conversion costs.
2. Summarize total costs to account for and calculate cost per equivalent unit for transferred-in costs, direct materials, and conversion costs.
3. Assign costs to units completed (and transferred out) and to units in ending work in process.

18-32 Transferred-in costs, FIFO method (continuation of 18-31). Refer to the information in Exercise 18-31. Suppose Trendy uses the FIFO method instead of the weighted-average method in all its departments. The only changes to Exercise 18-31 under the FIFO method are that total transferred-in costs of beginning work in process on June 1 are $45,000 (instead of $60,000) and total transferred-in costs added during June are $114,000 (instead of $117,000).

Required

Do Exercise 18-31 using the FIFO method. Note that you first need to calculate equivalent units of work done in the current period (for transferred-in costs, direct materials, and conversion costs) to complete beginning work in process, to start and complete new units, and to produce ending work-in-process inventory.

18-33 Operation costing. Egyptian Spa produces two different spa products: Relax and Refresh. The company uses three operations to manufacture the products: mixing, blending, and packaging. Relax is produced in powder form in the mixing department, then transferred to the blending department, and finally to packaging. Refresh undergoes no mixing; It is produced in liquid form in the blending department and then transferred to packaging.

In the mixing department, Egyptian Spa applies conversion costs based on labor-hours. It takes 3 minutes to mix the ingredients for a container of Relax. In the blending department, conversion costs are applied based on the number of containers and in the packaging department, on the basis of machine-hours. It takes 0.5 minutes of machine time to fill a container, regardless of the product.

The budgeted number of containers and budgeted direct materials cost for each product in May are:

	Relax	Refresh
Number of containers	24,000	18,000
Direct materials cost	$17,160	$13,140

The budgeted conversion costs for each department for May are as follows:

Department	Allocation of Conversion Costs	Budgeted Conversion Cost
Mixing	Direct labor-hours	$11,760
Blending	Number of containers	$20,160
Packaging	Machine-hours	$ 2,800

Required

1. Calculate the conversion cost rates for each department.
2. Calculate the budgeted cost of goods manufactured for Relax and Refresh for the month of May.
3. Calculate the cost per container for each product for the month of May.

18-34 Standard-costing with beginning and ending work in process. Tiger Company is a manufacturer of paint for consumer use. Tiger uses process costing to account for production. Costs and output figures for October are as follows:

Tiger Company's Process Costing for the Month Ended October 31, 2020

	Gallons	Direct Materials	Conversion Costs
Standard cost per gallon		$ 6.00	$ 12.00
Work in process, beginning inventory (Oct. 1)	8,000	48,000	$ 19,200
Degree of completion of beginning work in process		100%	20%
Started in October	70,000		
Completed and transferred out	75,000		
Work in process, ending inventory (Oct. 31)	3,000		
Degree of completion of ending work in process		100%	60%
Total costs added during October		$421,600	$900,000

Required

1. Compute equivalent units for direct materials and conversion costs. Show physical units (gallons) in the first column of your schedule.
2. Compute the total standard costs of paint transferred out in October and the total standard costs of the October 31 inventory of work in process.
3. Compute the total October variances for direct materials and conversion costs.
4. Prepare summarized journal entries to record both the actual costs and standard costs for direct materials and conversion costs, including the variances for both production costs.

Problems

18-35 Equivalent units, comprehensive. Imperial Bakery supplies cupcakes to a national grocery chain for their private label. The cupcakes must meet specific requirements of the grocery chain. Imperial uses a specific process to produce the cupcakes to the grocery chain's specifications.

The cupcakes are baked, filled and frosted, in that sequence. Materials are added as follows:

1. The basic ingredients for the cupcakes are added at the start of the **baking** process.
2. The **filling** is inserted into the cupcakes when cupcakes are 90% complete.
3. The **frosting** is added at the end of the process.

Of the total conversion costs, 70% are incurred during the baking process when cupcakes are 80% complete, an additional 10% are incurred at the start of the filling process when the cupcakes are 90% complete, and the remaining 20% are incurred when the frosting is done at the end of the process.

On May 1, 2020, Imperial had 500 dozen cupcakes in inventory. These cupcakes were 90% complete and ready for filling and frosting. During May, 1,500 dozen cupcakes were put into production. At the end of May, Imperial had 200 dozen cupcakes that had been baked and filled and ready for frosting.

Required

1. Using the weighted-average method of process costing, compute equivalent units of work done for (a) baking materials, (b) filling materials, (c) frosting materials, and (d) conversion costs for the month of May.
2. Using the FIFO method of process costing, compute equivalent units of work done for (a) baking materials, (b) filling materials, (c) frosting materials, and (d) conversion costs for the month of May.

18-36 Weighted-average method. Hoffman Company manufactures car seats in its Boise plant. Each car seat passes through the assembly department and the testing department. This problem focuses on the assembly department. The process-costing system at Hoffman Company has a single direct-cost category (direct materials) and a single indirect-cost category (conversion costs). Direct materials are added at the beginning of the process. Conversion costs are added evenly during the process. When the assembly department finishes work on each car seat, it is immediately transferred to testing.

Hoffman Company uses the weighted-average method of process costing. Data for the assembly department for October 2020 are as follows:

	Physical Units (Car Seats)	Direct Materials	Conversion Costs
Work in process, October 1[a]	4,000	$1,248,000	$ 241,650
Started during October 2020	22,500		
Completed during October 2020	26,000		
Work in process, October 31[b]	500		
Total costs added during October 2020		$4,635,000	$2,575,125

[a] Degree of completion: direct materials,?%; conversion costs, 45%.
[b] Degree of completion: direct materials,?%; conversion costs, 65%.

Required

1. For each cost category, compute equivalent units in the assembly department. Show physical units in the first column of your schedule.
2. What issues should the manager focus on when reviewing the equivalent-unit calculations?
3. For each cost category, summarize total assembly department costs for October 2020 and calculate cost per equivalent unit.
4. Assign costs to units completed and transferred out and to units in ending work in process.

18-37 Journal entries (continuation of 18-36).
Prepare a set of summarized journal entries for all October 2020 transactions affecting Work in Process—Assembly. Set up a T-account for Work in Process—Assembly and post your entries to it.

Required

18-38 FIFO method (continuation of 18-36).

Required

1. Do Problem 18-36 using the FIFO method of process costing. Explain any difference between cost per equivalent unit in the assembly department under the weighted-average method and the FIFO method.
2. Should Hoffman's managers choose the weighted-average method or the FIFO method? Explain briefly.

18-39 Transferred-in costs, weighted-average method (related to 18-36 to 18-38). Hoffman Company, as you know, is a manufacturer of car seats. Each car seat passes through the assembly and testing departments. This problem focuses on the testing department. Direct materials are added when the testing department process is 90% complete. Conversion costs are added evenly during the testing department's process. As work in assembly is completed, each unit is immediately transferred to testing. As each unit is completed in testing, it is immediately transferred to Finished Goods.

Hoffman Company uses the weighted-average method of process costing. Data for the testing department for October 2020 are as follows:

	Physical Units (Car Seats)	Transferred-In Costs	Direct Materials	Conversion Costs
Work in process, October 1[a]	5,500	$2,931,000	$ 0	$ 499,790
Transferred in during October 2020	?			
Completed during October 2020	29,800			
Work in process, October 31[b]	1,700			
Total costs added during October 2020		$8,094,000	$10,877,000	$ 4,696,260

[a] Degree of completion: transferred-in costs,?%; direct materials,?%; conversion costs, 65%.
[b] Degree of completion: transferred-in costs,?%; direct materials,?%; conversion costs, 45%.

Required

1. What is the percentage of completion for transferred-in costs and direct materials in (a) beginning work-in-process inventory and (b) ending work-in-process inventory?
2. For each cost category, compute equivalent units in the testing department. Show physical units in the first column of your schedule.
3. For each cost category, summarize total testing department costs for October 2020, calculate cost per equivalent unit, and assign costs to units completed (and transferred out) and to units in ending work-in-process inventory.
4. Prepare journal entries for October transfers from the assembly department to the testing department and from the testing department to Finished Goods.

18-40 Transferred-in costs, FIFO method (continuation of 18-39). Refer to the information in Problem 18-39. Suppose that Hoffman Company uses the FIFO method instead of the weighted-average method in all its departments. The only changes to Problem 18-39 under the FIFO method are that total transferred-in costs of beginning work in process on October 1 are $2,879,000 (instead of $2,931,000) and that total transferred-in costs added during October are $9,048,000 (instead of $8,094,000).

Required

Do Problem 18-39 using the FIFO process-costing method.

18-41 Weighted-average method. McKnight Handcraft is a manufacturer of picture frames for large retailers. Every picture frame passes through two departments: the assembly department and the finishing department. This problem focuses on the assembly department. The process-costing system at McKnight has a single direct-cost category (direct materials) and a single indirect-cost category (conversion costs). Direct materials are added when the assembly department process is 10% complete. Conversion costs are added evenly during the assembly department's process.

McKnight uses the weighted-average method of process costing. Consider the following data for the assembly department in April 2020:

	Physical Unit (Frames)	Direct Materials	Conversion Costs
Work in process, April 1[a]	60	$ 1,530	$ 156
Started during April 2020	510		
Completed during April 2020	450		
Work in process, April 30[b]	120		
Total costs added during April 2020		$17,850	$11,544

[a] Degree of completion: direct materials, 100%; conversion costs, 40%.
[b] Degree of completion: direct materials, 100%; conversion costs, 15%.

Required

1. Summarize total assembly department costs for April 2020, and assign them to units completed (and transferred out) and to units in ending work-in-process inventory.
2. What issues should a manager focus on when reviewing the equivalent units calculation?

18-42 FIFO method (continuation of 18-41).

Required

1. Complete Problem 18-41 using the FIFO method of process costing.
2. If you did Problem 18-41, explain any difference between the cost of work completed and transferred out and the cost of ending work-in-process inventory in the assembly department under the weighted-average method and the FIFO method. Should McKnight's managers choose the weighted-average method or the FIFO method? Explain briefly.

18-43 Transferred-in costs, weighted-average method. Spelling Sports produces basketballs in two departments: cutting and stitching. Each department has one direct-cost category (direct materials) and one indirect-cost category (conversion costs). This problem focuses on the stitching department.

After cutting, basketballs are immediately transferred to the stitching department. Direct material is added when the stitching process is 70% complete. Conversion costs are added evenly during stitching operations. After stitching is completed, basketballs are immediately transferred to Finished Goods.

Spelling Sports uses the weighted-average method of process costing. The following is a summary of the March 2020 operations of the stitching department:

Home Insert Page Layout Formulas Data Review View

	A	B	C	D	E
1		Physical Units (basketballs)	Transferred-In Costs	Direct Materials	Conversion Costs
2	Beginning work in process, March 1	17,500	$ 45,360	$ 0	$17,660
3	Degree of completion, beginning work in process		100%	0%	60%
4	Transferred in during March 2020	56,000			
5	Completed and transferred out during March 2020	52,000			
6	Ending work in process, March 31	21,500			
7	Degree of completion, ending work in process		100%	0%	20%
8	Total costs added during March		$154,560	$28,080	$89,310

Required

1. Summarize total stitching department costs for March 2020 and assign these costs to units completed (and transferred out) and to units in ending work-in-process inventory.
2. Prepare journal entries for March transfers from the cutting department to the stitching department and from the stitching department to Finished Goods.

18-44 Transferred-in costs, FIFO method (continuation of 18-43). Refer to the information in Problem 18-43. Suppose Spelling Sports uses the FIFO method instead of the weighted-average method. Assume that all other information, including the cost of beginning work in process, is unchanged.

Required

1. Do Problem 18-43 using the FIFO process-costing method.
2. If you did Problem 18-43, explain any difference between the cost of work completed and transferred out and the cost of ending work in process in the stitching department under the weighted-average method and the FIFO method.

18-45 Standard costing, journal entries. The Tiffenex Company manufactures reproductions of expensive earrings. Tiffenex uses the standard-costing method of process costing to account for production of earrings. All materials are added at the beginning of production. The costs and output of earrings (pairs) for May 2020 are:

	Physical Units	Percent Completion for Conversion Costs	Direct Materials	Conversion Costs
Work in process, beginning	8,000	30%	$ 16,000	$ 7,200
Started during May	72,000			
Completed and transferred out	75,000			
Work in process, ending	5,000	80%		
Standard cost per unit			$ 2.00	$ 3.00
Costs added during May			$145,200	$226,500

Required

1. Compute equivalent units for direct materials and conversion costs. Show physical units of earrings (pairs) in the first column of your schedule.
2. Compute the total standard costs of earrings (pairs) transferred out in May and the total standard costs of the May 31 inventory of work in process.
3. Compute the total May variances for direct materials and conversion costs.
4. Prepare summarized journal entries to record both actual costs and standard costs for direct materials and conversion costs, including variances for both direct materials and conversion costs.

18-46 Multiple processes or operations, costing. The Sedona Company is dedicated to making products that meet the needs of customers in a sustainable manner. Sedona is best known for its KLN water bottle, which is a BPA-free, dishwasher-safe, bubbly glass bottle in a soft silicone sleeve.

The production process consists of three basic operations. In the first operation, the glass is formed by remelting cullets (broken or refuse glass). In the second operation, the glass is assembled with the silicone gasket and sleeve. The resulting product is finished in the final operation with the addition of the polypropylene cap.

Consulting studies have indicated that of the total conversion costs required to complete a finished unit, the forming operation requires 60%, the assembly 30%, and the finishing 10%.

The following data are available for March 2020 (there is no beginning inventory of any kind):

Cullets purchased	$67,500
Silicone purchased	$24,000
Polypropylene used	$ 6,000
Total conversion costs incurred	$68,850
Ending inventory, cullets	$ 4,500
Ending inventory, silicone	$ 3,000
Number of bottles completed and transferred	12,000
Inventory in process at the end of the month:	
Units formed but not assembled	4,000
Units assembled but not finished	2,000

Required

1. What is the cost per equivalent unit for conversion costs for KLN bottles in March 2020?
2. Compute the cost per equivalent unit with respect to each of the three materials: cullets, silicone, and polypropylene.
3. What is the cost of goods completed and transferred out?
4. What is the cost of goods formed but not assembled?
5. What is the cost of goods assembled but not finished?

18-47 Benchmarking, ethics. Brown Industries operates several laminate flooring plants. Given the competitive pricing for flooring, Brown's managers pay close attention to costs. Each plant uses a process-costing system, and at the end of every quarter, each plant manager submits a production report and a production-cost report. The production report includes the plant manager's estimate of the percentage of completion of the ending work in process as to direct materials and conversion costs, as well as the quantity (sheets) of laminate flooring completed. The corporate controller uses these estimates to compute the cost per equivalent unit of work done for each input for the quarter. Plants are ranked, and the two plants with the lowest cost per equivalent unit for direct materials and conversion costs are each given a bonus and recognized in the company newsletter.

The corporate controller has been pleased with the success of the company's benchmarking program. However, the corporate controller has recently received anonymous e-mails that a plant manager has been manipulating his quarterly estimates of percentage of completion in an attempt to obtain the bonus.

The plant in question provided the following data:

Summary of the Flow of Physical Units and Output in Equivalent Units; Weighted-Average Method of Process Costing, Plant C of Brown Industries for Quarter 4, 2020

		Equivalent Units	
	Physical Units	Direct Materials	Conversion Costs
Completed and transferred out during current period	30,000	30,000	30,000
Work in process, ending[a] (given)	10,000		
10,000 × 100%; 10,000 × 70%		10,000	7,000
Accounted for	40,000		
Equivalent units of work done to date		40,000	37,000

[a] Degree of completion reported in this plant: direct materials, 100%; conversion costs, 70%.

Summary of Cost per Equivalent Unit and Costs Assigned to Units Completed and to Units in Ending Work-in-Process Inventory; Weighted-Average Method of Process Costing, Plant C of Brown Industries for Quarter 4, 2020

	Total Production Costs	Direct Materials	Conversion Costs
Costs incurred to date		$114,000	$225,700
Divide by equivalent units of work done to date		÷ 40,000	÷ 37,000
Cost per equivalent unit of work done to date		$2.85	$6.10
Assignment of costs:			
Completed and transferred out (30,000 units)	$268,500	(30,000 × $2.85)	(30,000 × $6.10)
Work in process, ending (10,000 units)	71,200	(10,000 × $2.85)	(7,000 × $6.10)
Total costs accounted for	$339,700	$114,000	$225,700

Required

1. Recalculate the cost per equivalent unit, assuming the actual percentage of completion of ending work in process was 80% for direct materials and 50% for conversion costs.
2. Based on the correct percentage of completion computed in requirement 1, recalculate cost of goods completed and transferred out and the cost of ending work in process inventory.
3. Why might managers manipulate their quarterly estimates of percentage of completion? Explain.
4. What is the ethical responsibility of each plant controller?
5. What should the corporate controller do?
6. How might the corporate controller learn whether the data provided by particular plants are being manipulated?

Spoilage, Rework, and Scrap

19

When a product doesn't meet specification but is subsequently repaired and sold, it is called rework.

Companies try to minimize rework, as well as spoilage and scrap, during production. Why? Because higher-than-normal levels of spoilage and scrap can have a significant negative effect on a company's profits. Rework can also cause companies to incur substantial costs, as the following article about Tesla shows.

LEARNING OBJECTIVES

1. Understand the definitions of spoilage, rework, and scrap
2. Identify the differences between normal and abnormal spoilage
3. Account for spoilage in process costing using the weighted-average method and the first-in, first-out (FIFO) method
4. Account for spoilage at various stages of completion in process costing
5. Account for spoilage in job costing
6. Account for rework in job costing
7. Account for scrap

REWORK HAMPERS TESLA MODEL 3 PRODUCTION[1]

When Tesla unveiled its Model 3 electric car, more than 400,000 people paid $1,000 for a spot on the waiting list to purchase one of the sedans. To meet this unprecedented demand, Tesla quickly ramped up Model 3 production. The goal: produce 5,000 new cars per week by June 30, 2018.

As that deadline neared, Tesla encountered significant production woes with high levels of raw materials waste and rework required on parts made at its Gigafactory in Nevada. Out of the 5,000 Model 3s produced per week, nearly 4,300 required some rework. Tesla did the rework at its offsite remanufacturing facility rather than onsite, as is standard industry practice.

Along with increased materials costs, the rework added more than 2,600 additional labor-hours per week to the manufacturing process. In early 2019, Tesla was forced to cut its full-time workforce by 7% to cut costs and bolster Model 3 profitability amid its rocky launch.

For Tesla and other companies, the costs of producing defective output can be enormous. Firms in industries as varied as construction (Skanska), aeronautics (Lockheed Martin), product development software (Dassault Systemes), and specialty food (Tate & Lyle) have set zero-defects goals. Reducing defects and waste is also a key element of sustainability programs at many enlightened organizations and government bodies.

In this chapter, we focus on three types of costs that arise as a result of defects—spoilage, rework, and scrap—and ways to account for them. We also describe how to determine (1) the cost of products, (2) cost of goods sold, and (3) inventory values when spoilage, rework, and scrap occur.

The Washington Post/Mason Trinca

[1] *Sources:* Linette Lopez, "Internal Documents Reveal the Grueling Way Tesla Hit Its 5,000 Model 3 Target," *Business Insider,* August 21, 2018 (https://www.businessinsider.com/tesla-hit-model-3-target-by-reworking-thousands-of-cars-2018-8); Lora Kolodny, "Tesla Factories Reportedly Struggling With High Scrap Volume, and Low Vehicle Production Rate per Employee," CNBC.com, June 5, 2018 (https://www.cnbc.com/2018/06/05/tesla-factories-have-struggled-with-scrap-production-rate-reports.html); Lora Kolodny, "Tesla Employees Say Automaker Is Churning Out a High Volume of Flawed Parts Requiring Costly Rework," CNBC.com, March 14, 2018 (https://www.cnbc.com/2018/03/14/tesla-manufacturing-high-volume-of-flawed-parts-employees.html).

Defining Spoilage, Rework, and Scrap

LEARNING OBJECTIVE 1

Understand the definitions of spoilage,

... unacceptable units of production

rework,

... unacceptable units of production subsequently repaired

and scrap

... leftover material

The following terms used in this chapter may seem familiar to you, but be sure you understand them in the context of management accounting.

Spoilage refers to units of production—whether fully or partially completed—that do not meet the specifications required by customers for good units and are discarded or sold at reduced prices. Some examples of spoilage are defective shirts, jeans, shoes, and carpeting sold as "seconds" and defective aluminum cans sold to aluminum manufacturers for remelting to produce other aluminum products.

Rework refers to units of production that do not meet the specifications required by customers but that are subsequently repaired and sold as good finished units. For example, defective units of products (such as smartphones, tablets, and laptops) detected during or after the production process but before the units are shipped to customers can sometimes be reworked and sold as good products.

Scrap is residual material that results from manufacturing a product. Examples are short lengths from woodworking operations, edges from plastic molding operations or from cutting sheet metals, and frayed cloth and end cuts from suit-making operations. Scrap can sometimes be sold for relatively small amounts. In that sense, scrap is similar to byproducts, which we studied in Chapter 17. The difference is that scrap arises as a residual from the manufacturing process and is not a product targeted for manufacture or sale by the firm.

A certain amount of spoilage, rework, or scrap is inherent in many production processes. For example, semiconductor manufacturing is so complex and delicate that some spoiled units are inevitable due to dust adhering to wafers in the wafer production process and crystal defects in the silicon substrate. Usually, spoiled units cannot be reworked. In the manufacture of high-precision machine tools, spoiled units can be reworked to meet standards, but only at considerable cost. And in the mining industry, companies process ore that contains varying amounts of valuable metals and rock. Some amount of rock, which is scrap, is inevitable.

DECISION POINT

What are spoilage, rework, and scrap?

Two Types of Spoilage

LEARNING OBJECTIVE 2

Identify the differences between normal spoilage

... spoilage inherent in an efficient production process

and abnormal spoilage

... spoilage that would not arise under efficient operation

Accounting for spoilage includes determining the magnitude of spoilage costs and distinguishing between the costs of normal and abnormal spoilage.[2] To manage, control, and reduce spoilage costs, companies need to highlight them, not bury them as an unidentified part of the costs of good units manufactured.

To illustrate normal and abnormal spoilage, consider Mendoza Plastics, which uses plastic injection molding to make casings for the iMac desktop computer. In January 2020, Mendoza incurs costs of $3,075,000 to produce 20,500 units. Of these 20,500 units, 20,000 are good units and 500 are spoiled units. Mendoza has no beginning inventory and no ending inventory that month. Of the 500 spoiled units, 400 units are spoiled because injection molding machines cannot manufacture good casings 100% of the time. These units are spoiled despite machines being run carefully and efficiently. The remaining 100 units are spoiled as a result of machine breakdowns and operator errors.

Normal Spoilage

Normal spoilage is spoilage inherent in a particular production process. In particular, it arises even when the process is carried out in an efficient manner. The costs of normal spoilage are included as a component of the costs of good units manufactured because good units cannot be made without also making some defective units. For this reason, normal spoilage costs are

[2] The helpful suggestions of Samuel Laimon, University of Saskatchewan, are gratefully acknowledged.

inventoried and included in the cost of the good units completed. Mendoza Plastics accounts for the cost of the 400 units of normal spoilage as follows:

Manufacturing cost per unit, $3,075,000 ÷ 20,500 units = $150	
Manufacturing costs of good units alone, $150 per unit × 20,000 units	$3,000,000
Normal spoilage costs, $150 per unit × 400 units	60,000
Manufacturing costs of good units completed (includes normal spoilage)	$3,060,000

$$\text{Manufacturing cost per good unit} = \frac{\$3,060,000}{20,000 \text{ units}} = \$153$$

Normal spoilage rates are computed by dividing the units of normal spoilage by total *good units completed*, not total *actual units started* in production. At Mendoza Plastics, the normal spoilage rate is 400 ÷ 20,000 = 2%. There is often a tradeoff between speed of production and normal spoilage rate. Managers choose how many units to produce per hour with the understanding that, at the chosen rate, a certain level of spoilage is unavoidable.

Abnormal Spoilage

Abnormal spoilage is spoilage that is not inherent in a particular production process and would not arise under efficient operating conditions. At Mendoza, the 100 units spoiled due to machine breakdowns and operator errors are abnormal spoilage. Abnormal spoilage is regarded as avoidable and controllable. Line operators and other plant personnel generally can decrease or eliminate abnormal spoilage by identifying the reasons for machine breakdowns, operator errors, and so forth, and by taking steps to prevent them from recurring. To highlight abnormal spoilage costs, companies record the cost of abnormal spoilage in a Loss from Abnormal Spoilage account, which appears as a separate line item in the income statement. That is, unlike normal spoilage, the costs of abnormal spoilage are not considered inventoriable and are written off as a period expense. At Mendoza, the loss from abnormal spoilage is $15,000 ($150 per unit × 100 units).

Issues about accounting for spoilage arise in both process-costing and job-costing systems. We discuss both instances next, beginning with spoilage in process costing.

DECISION POINT

What is the distinction between normal and abnormal spoilage?

Spoilage in Process Costing Using Weighted-Average and FIFO

LEARNING OBJECTIVE 3

Account for spoilage in process costing using the weighted-average method

... spoilage cost based on total costs and equivalent units completed to date

and the first-in, first-out (FIFO) method

... spoilage cost based on costs of current period and equivalent units of work done in current period

We first consider normal spoilage. The following example illustrates how to count normal spoilage units when computing physical and equivalent output units in a process-costing system.

Count All Spoilage

Example 1: Chipmakers, Inc., manufactures computer chips for television sets. All direct materials are added at the beginning of the production process. We assume there is no beginning inventory and focus only on direct materials costs. The following data are for May 2020.

	A	B	C
1		Physical Units	Direct Materials
2	Work in process, beginning inventory (May 1)	0	
3	Started during May	10,000	
4	Good units completed and transferred out during May	5,000	
5	Units spoiled (all normal spoilage)	1,000	
6	Work in process, ending inventory (May 31)	4,000	
7	Direct materials costs added in May		$270,000

Spoilage is detected upon completion of the process and has zero net disposal value.

EXHIBIT 19-1

Using Equivalent Units to Account for the Direct Materials Costs of Good and Spoiled Units for Chipmakers, Inc., for May 2020

	A	B
1		**Approach Counting Spoiled Units When Computing Output in Equivalent Units**
2	Costs to account for	$270,000
3	Divide by equivalent units of output	÷10,000
4	Cost per equivalent unit of output	$ 27
5	Assignment of costs:	
6	Good units completed (5,000 units × $27 per unit)	$135,000
7	Add normal spoilage (1,000 units × $27 per unit)	27,000
8	Total costs of good units completed and transferred out	162,000
9	Work in process, ending (4,000 units × $27 per unit)	108,000
10	Costs accounted for	$270,000

An **inspection point** is the stage of the production process at which products are examined to determine whether they are acceptable or unacceptable units. Spoilage is assumed to occur at the stage of completion where inspection occurs. In our example, spoiled units are 100% complete with respect to direct materials.

Exhibit 19-1 calculates and assigns the cost of direct materials used to produce both good units and normal spoilage units. Overall, Chipmakers generated 10,000 equivalent units of output: 5,000 equivalent units in good units completed (5,000 physical units × 100%), 4,000 units in ending work in process (4,000 physical units × 100%), and 1,000 equivalent units in normal spoilage (1,000 physical units × 100%). Equivalent-unit cost is $27 (total direct materials costs, $270,000 ÷ 10,000 equivalent units). The total cost of good units completed and transferred out, which includes the cost of normal spoilage, is $162,000 (6,000 equivalent units × $27). The ending work in process is $108,000 (4,000 equivalent units × $27).

Notice that the 4,000 units in ending work in process are not assigned any costs of normal spoilage because they have not yet been inspected. Undoubtedly some units in ending work in process will be found to be spoiled after they are completed and inspected in the next accounting period. At that time, their costs will be assigned to the good units completed in that period. Note that Exhibit 19-1 identifies normal spoilage costs of $27,000 to highlight and focus attention on the potential economic benefits of reducing spoilage.

Five-Step Procedure for Process Costing With Spoilage

Example 2: Anzio Company manufactures a recycling container in its forming department. Direct materials are added at the beginning of the production process. Conversion costs are added evenly during the production process. Some units are spoiled and are detected only when finished units are inspected. Normal spoilage is 10% of the finished output of good units (one unit of normal spoilage for every 10 good units produced). Summary data for July 2020 are shown on the next page:

	A	B	C	D	E
1		Physical Units (1)	Direct Materials (2)	Conversion Costs (3)	Total Costs (4) = (2) + (3)
2	Work in process, beginning inventory (July 1)	1,500	$12,000	$ 9,000	$ 21,000
3	Degree of completion of beginning work in process		100%	60%	
4	Started during July	8,500			
5	Good units completed and transferred out during July	7,000			
6	Work in process, ending inventory (July 31)	2,000			
7	Degree of completion of ending work in process		100%	50%	
8	Total costs added during July		$76,500	$89,100	$165,600
9	Normal spoilage as a percentage of good units	10%			
10	Degree of completion of normal spoilage		100%	100%	
11	Degree of completion of abnormal spoilage		100%	100%	

We slightly modify the five-step procedure for process costing used in Chapter 18 to include the costs of Anzio Company's spoilage.

Step 1: Summarize the Flow of Physical Units of Output. Identify the number of units of both normal and abnormal spoilage.

$$\text{Total Spoilage} = \left(\begin{array}{c}\text{Units in beginning}\\ \text{work-in-process inventory}\end{array} + \begin{array}{c}\text{Units}\\ \text{started}\end{array}\right) - \left(\begin{array}{c}\text{Good units}\\ \text{completed and}\\ \text{transferred out}\end{array} + \begin{array}{c}\text{Units in ending}\\ \text{work-in-process inventory}\end{array}\right)$$

$$= (1{,}500 + 8{,}500) - (7{,}000 + 2{,}000)$$

$$= 10{,}000 - 9{,}000$$

$$= 1{,}000 \text{ units}$$

Normal spoilage equals 10% of 7,000 units of *good* output, or 700 units. Hence,

$$\text{Abnormal spoilage} = \text{Total spoilage} - \text{Normal spoilage}$$

$$= 1{,}000 \text{ units} - 700 \text{ units}$$

$$= 300 \text{ units}$$

Step 2: Compute Output in Equivalent Units. Equivalent units for spoilage are computed the same way as equivalent units for good units. All spoiled units are included in the computation of output units. Because Anzio's inspection point is at the completion of production, the amount of work done on each spoiled and each completed good unit is the same.

Step 3: Summarize Total Costs to Account For. The total costs to account for are all costs debited to Work in Process. The details for this step are similar to Step 3 in Chapter 18.

Step 4: Compute Cost per Equivalent Unit. This step is similar to Step 4 in Chapter 18.

Step 5: Assign Costs to Units Completed, Spoiled Units, and to Units in Ending Work-in-Process Inventory. This step computes the cost of spoiled units and good units.

We illustrate these five steps of process costing for the weighted-average and FIFO methods next. *The appendix to this chapter illustrates the standard-costing method.*

Weighted-Average Method and Spoilage

Exhibit 19-2, Panel A, presents Steps 1 and 2 to calculate equivalent units of work done to date, including equivalent units of normal and abnormal spoilage. Exhibit 19-2, Panel B, presents Steps 3, 4, and 5 (together called the production-cost worksheet).

EXHIBIT 19-2 Weighted-Average Method of Process Costing With Spoilage for the Forming Department for July 2020

PANEL A: Summarize the Flow of Physical Units and Compute Output in Equivalent Units

	A	B	C	D	E
1			(Step 1)	(Step 2)	
2				Equivalent Units	
3		Flow of Production	Physical Units	Direct Materials	Conversion Costs
4		Work in process, beginning (given, p. 755)	1,500		
5		Started during current period (given, p. 755)	8,500		
6		To account for	10,000		
7		Good units completed and transferred out during current period	7,000	7,000	7,000
8		Normal Spoilage[a]	700		
9		(700 × 100%; 700 × 100%)		700	700
10		Abnormal Spoilage[b]	300		
11		(300 × 100%; 300 × 100%)		300	300
12		Work in process, ending[c] (given, p. 755)	2,000		
13		(2,000 × 100%; 2,000 × 50%)		2,000	1,000
14		Accounted for	10,000		
15		Equivalent units of work done to date		10,000	9,000
16					
17	[a]Normal spoilage is 10% of good units transferred out; 10% × 7,000 = 700 units. Degree of completion of normal spoilage				
18	in this department: direct materials, 100%; conversion costs, 100%.				
19	[b]Abnormal spoilage = Total spoilage − Normal spoilage = 1,000 − 700 = 300 units. Degree of completion of abnormal spoilage				
20	in this department: direct materials, 100%; conversion costs, 100%.				
21	[c]Degree of completion in this department: direct materials, 100%; conversion costs, 50%.				

PANEL B: Summarize the Total Costs to Account For, Compute the Cost per Equivalent Unit, and Assign Costs to the Units Completed, Spoiled Units, and Units in Ending Work-in-Process Inventory

			Total Production Costs	Direct Materials		Conversion Costs
23						
24	(Step 3)	Work in process, beginning (given, p. 755)	$ 21,000	$12,000	+	$ 9,000
25		Costs added in current period (given, p. 755)	165,600	76,500	+	89,100
26		Total costs to account for	$186,600	$88,500	+	$98,100
27	(Step 4)	Costs incurred to date		$88,500		$98,100
28		Divide by equivalent units of work done to date (Panel A)		÷10,000		÷9,000
29		Cost per equivalent unit		$ 8.85		$ 10.90
30	(Step 5)	Assignment of costs:				
31		Good units completed and transferred out (7,000 units):				
32		Costs before adding normal spoilage	$138,250	(7,000[d] × $8.85)	+	(7,000[d] × $10.90)
33		Normal spoilage (700 units)	13,825	(700[d] × $8.85)	+	(700[d] × $10.90)
34	(A)	Total costs of good units completed and transferred out	152,075			
35	(B)	Abnormal spoilage (300 units)	5,925	(300[d] × $8.85)	+	(300[d] × $10.90)
36	(C)	Work in process, ending (2,000 units)	28,600	(2,000[d] × $8.85)	+	(1,000[d] × $10.90)
37	(A) + (B) + (C)	Total costs accounted for	$186,600	$88,500	+	$98,100
38						
39	[d]Equivalent units of direct materials and conversion costs calculated in Step 2 in Panel A.					

In Step 3, managers summarize total costs to account for. In Step 4, they calculate cost per equivalent unit using the weighted-average method. Note how, for each cost category, the costs of beginning work in process and the costs of work done in the current period are totaled and divided by equivalent units of all work done to date to calculate the weighted-average cost per equivalent unit. In the final step, managers assign total costs to completed units, normal and abnormal spoiled units, and ending inventory by multiplying the equivalent units calculated in Step 2 by the cost per equivalent unit calculated in Step 4. The \$13,825 costs of normal spoilage are added to the costs of good units completed and transferred out.

$$\text{Cost per good unit completed and transferred out of the process} = \frac{\text{Total costs transferred out (including normal spoilage)}}{\text{Number of good units produced}}$$

$$= \$152{,}075 \div 7{,}000 \text{ good units} = \$21.725 \text{ per good unit}$$

This amount is not equal to \$19.75 per good unit (\$8.85 cost per equivalent unit of direct materials plus \$10.90 cost per equivalent unit of conversion costs). That's because the cost per good unit equals \$19.75, plus a charge for normal spoilage cost per good unit, \$1.975 (\$13,825 ÷ 7,000 good units), equal to \$21.725 per good unit. The \$5,925 costs of abnormal spoilage are charged to Loss from Abnormal Spoilage account and are not part of the costs of good units.[3]

19-1 TRY IT!

Tensor Textiles Company makes silk banners and uses the weighted-average method of process costing. Direct materials are added at the beginning of the process, and conversion costs are added evenly during the process. Spoilage is detected upon inspection at the completion of the process. Spoiled units are disposed of at zero net disposal value.

	Physical Units (Banners)	Direct Materials	Conversion Costs
Work in process, July 1[a]	2,000	\$ 2,000	\$ 840
Started in July 2020	?		
Good units completed and transferred out in July	10,750		
Normal spoilage	200		
Abnormal spoilage	50		
Work in process, July 31[b]	1,000		
Total costs added during July 2020		\$16,000	\$31,930

[a]Degree of completion: direct materials, 100%; conversion costs, 50%.
[b]Degree of completion: direct materials, 100%; conversion costs, 30%.

Determine the equivalent units of work done in July, and calculate the cost of units completed and transferred out (including normal spoilage), the cost of abnormal spoilage, and the cost of units in ending inventory.

FIFO Method and Spoilage

Exhibit 19-3, Panel A, presents Steps 1 and 2 using the FIFO method, which focuses on equivalent units of work done in the current period. Exhibit 19-3, Panel B, presents Steps 3, 4, and 5. When assigning costs, the FIFO method keeps costs of beginning work in process separate and distinct from costs of work done in the current period. All spoilage costs are assumed to be related to units completed during the period, using unit costs of the current period.[4]

[3] The actual costs of spoilage (and rework) are often greater than the costs recorded in the accounting system because the opportunity costs of disruption of the production line, storage, and lost contribution margins are not recorded in accounting systems. Chapter 20 discusses these opportunity costs from the perspective of cost management.

[4] To simplify calculations under FIFO, spoiled units are accounted for as if they were started in the current period. Although some of the beginning work in process probably did spoil, all spoilage is treated as if it came from current production.

EXHIBIT 19-3 First-In, First-Out (FIFO) Method of Process Costing With Spoilage for the Forming Department for July 2020

PANEL A: Summarize the Flow of Physical Units and Compute Output in Equivalent Units

Home Insert Page Layout Formulas Data Review View

	A	B	C	D	E
1			(Step 1)	(Step 2)	
2				Equivalent Units	
3		Flow of Production	Physical Units	Direct Materials	Conversion Costs
4		Work in process, beginning (given, p. 755)	1,500		
5		Started during current period (given, p. 755)	8,500		
6		To account for	10,000		
7		Good units completed and transferred out during current period			
8		From beginning work in process[a]	1,500		
9		[1,500 × (100% − 100%); 1,500 × (100% − 60%)]		0	600
10		Started and completed	5,500[b]		
11		(5,500 × 100%; 5,500 × 100%)		5,500	5,500
12		Normal Spoilage[c]	700		
13		(700 × 100%; 700 × 100%)		700	700
14		Abnormal Spoilage[d]	300		
15		(300 × 100%; 300 × 100%)		300	300
16		Work in process, ending[e] (given, p. 755)	2,000		
17		(2,000 × 100%; 2,000 × 50%)		2,000	1,000
18		Accounted for	10,000		
19		Equivalent units of work in current period		8,500	8,100
20					
21	[a]Degree of completion in this department: direct materials, 100%; conversion costs, 60%.				
22	[b]7,000 physical units completed and transferred out minus 1,500 physical units completed and transferred out from beginning work-in-process inventory.				
23	[c]Normal spoilage is 10% of good units transferred out; 10% × 7,000 = 700 units. Degree of completion of normal spoilage in this department: direct materials, 100%; conversion costs, 100%.				
24	[d]Abnormal spoilage = Total spoilage − Normal spoilage = 1,000 − 700 = 300 units. Degree of completion of abnormal spoilage in this department: direct materials, 100%; conversion costs, 100%.				
25	[e]Degree of completion in this department: direct materials, 100%; conversion costs, 50%.				

PANEL B: Summarize the Total Costs to Account For, Compute the Cost per Equivalent Unit, and Assign Costs to the Units Completed, Spoiled Units, and Units in Ending Work-in-Process Inventory

			Total Production Costs	Direct Materials		Conversion Costs
26						
27	(Step 3)	Work in process, beginning (given, p. 755)	$ 21,000	$12,000	+	$ 9,000
28		Costs added in current period (given, p. 755)	165,600	76,500	+	89,100
29		Total costs to account for	$186,600	$88,500	+	$98,100
30	(Step 4)	Costs added in current period		$76,500		$89,100
31		Divide by equivalent units of work done in current period (Panel A)		÷ 8,500		÷ 8,100
32		Cost per equivalent unit		$ 9		$ 11
33	(Step 5)	Assignment of costs:				
34		Good units completed and transferred out (7,000 units):				
35		Work in process, beginning (1,500 units)	$ 21,000	$12,000		$ 9,000
36		Costs added to beginning work in process in current period	6,600	(0[f] × $9)	+	(600[f] × $11)
37		Total from beginning inventory before normal spoilage	27,600			
38		Started and completed before normal spoilage (5,500 units)	110,000	(5,500[f] × $9)	+	(5,500[f] × $11)
39		Normal spoilage (700 units)	14,000	(700[f] × $9)	+	(700[f] × $11)
40	(A)	Total costs of good units completed and transferred out	151,600			
41	(B)	Abnormal spoilage (300 units)	6,000	(300[f] × $9)	+	(300[f] × $11)
42	(C)	Work in process, ending (2,000 units)	29,000	(2,000[f] × $9)	+	(1,000[f] × $11)
43	(A) + (B) + (C)	Total costs accounted for	$186,600	$88,500	+	$98,100
44						
45	[f]Equivalent units of direct materials and conversion costs calculated in Step 2 in Panel A.					

TRY IT! 19-2 Consider Tensor Textiles Company again. With the same information for July 2020 as provided in Try It 19-1, redo the problem assuming Tensor uses FIFO costing instead.

Chapter 18 highlighted taxes, performance evaluation, and information for making decisions as some of the factors influencing the choice between the FIFO and weighted-average methods. It also stressed the importance of carefully estimating degrees of completion to avoid misstating operating income. These same considerations apply when there is spoilage. In addition, the normal spoilage percentage must be estimated in an unbiased manner. Categorizing more spoilage as normal leads to higher income by reducing the amount written off as loss from abnormal spoilage. Senior managers must stress the importance of consistent and unbiased estimates of completion and normal spoilage percentages and the need for ethical actions when reporting income.

Journal Entries

The following journal entries record the transfer of good units completed to finished goods and the loss from abnormal spoilage based on information in Panel B in Exhibits 19-2 and 19-3.

	Weighted-Average		FIFO	
Finished Goods	152,075		151,600	
Work in Process—Forming		152,075		151,600
To record the transfer of good units completed in July.				
Loss from Abnormal Spoilage	5,925		6,000	
Work in Process—Forming		5,925		6,000
To record the abnormal spoilage detected in July.				

DECISION POINT

How do the weighted-average and FIFO methods of process costing calculate the costs of good units and spoilage?

Inspection Points and Allocating Costs of Normal Spoilage

LEARNING OBJECTIVE 4

Account for spoilage at various stages of completion in process costing

... spoilage costs vary based on the point at which inspection is carried out

Spoilage might occur at various stages of a production process, but it is detected only at one or more inspection points. The cost of spoiled units equals all costs incurred on them up to the point of inspection. When spoiled goods have a disposal value (for example, carpeting sold as "seconds"), the net cost of spoilage is the cost of the spoiled goods minus the disposal value.

The unit costs of normal and abnormal spoilage are the same when the two are detected at the same inspection point as in our Anzio Company example, where inspection occurs only upon completion of the units. However, in some situations abnormal spoilage occurs at a different point than normal spoilage. Consider shirt manufacturing. Normal spoilage in the form of defective shirts is identified upon inspection at the *end* of the production process. Now suppose a faulty machine produces defective shirts at the *halfway point* of the production process. These defective shirts are abnormal spoilage that occurs at a different point in the production process than normal spoilage. The per-unit cost of abnormal spoilage is then based on costs incurred up to the halfway point of the production process, while the per-unit cost of normal spoilage is based on costs incurred through the end of the production process.

How should normal spoilage costs be allocated between completed units and ending work-in-process inventory? *The general approach is to presume that normal spoilage occurs at the inspection point in the production cycle and to therefore allocate its cost over all units that have passed that point during the accounting period.*

Anzio Company inspects units only at the end of the production process. So, units in ending work-in-process inventory have not been inspected and are not assigned any costs of normal spoilage. Suppose Anzio were to inspect units at an earlier stage. Then, if units in ending work in process passed the inspection point, the costs of normal spoilage would be allocated to units in ending work in process as well as to completed units. For example, if the inspection point is at the halfway point of production, any ending work in process that is at least 50% complete are allocated normal spoilage costs based on costs incurred up to the inspection point. However, if ending work-in-process inventory is less than 50% complete, no normal spoilage costs are allocated to it.

Suppose Anzio Company inspects units at various stages in the forming department. Recall that direct materials are added at the start of production, whereas conversion costs are added evenly during the process.

Consider three different cases: Inspection occurs at (1) the 20%, (2) the 55%, or (3) the 100% completion stage. The last option is the one we have analyzed so far. A total of 1,000 units are spoiled in all three cases. Normal spoilage is 10% of the *good units* that pass the inspection point *during the current period*. The following data are for July 2020. Note how the number of units of normal and abnormal spoilage changes depending on when inspection occurs.

	A	B	C	D
1		**Physical Units: Stage of Completion at Which Inspection Occurs**		
2	**Flow of Production**	**20%**	**55%**	**100%**
3	Work in process, beginning[a]	1,500	1,500	1,500
4	Started during July	8,500	8,500	8,500
5	To account for	10,000	10,000	10,000
6	Good units completed and transferred out			
7	(10,000 – 1,000 spoiled – 2,000 ending)	7,000	7,000	7,000
8	Normal Spoilage	750[c]	550[d]	700[e]
9	Abnormal Spoilage (1,000 – normal spoilage)	250	450	300
10	Work in process, ending[b]	2,000	2,000	2,000
11	Accounted for	10,000	10,000	10,000
12				
13	[a]Degree of completion in this department: direct materials, 100%; conversion costs, 60%.			
14	[b]Degree of completion in this department: direct materials, 100%; conversion costs, 50%.			
15	[c]10% × (8,500 units started – 1,000 units spoiled), because only the units started passed the 20% completion			
16	inspection point in the current period. Beginning work in process is excluded from this calculation because,			
17	being 60% complete at the start of the period, it passed the inspection point in the previous period.			
18	[d]10% × (8,500 units started – 1,000 units spoiled – 2,000 units in ending work in process). Both beginning and			
19	ending work in process are excluded since neither was inspected this period.			
20	[e]10% × 7,000, because 7,000 units are fully completed and inspected in the current period.			

The following diagram shows the flow of physical units for July and explains normal spoilage calculations in the preceding table. Note that 7,000 good units are completed and transferred out—1,500 from beginning work in process and 5,500 started and completed during the period—while 2,000 units are in ending work in process.

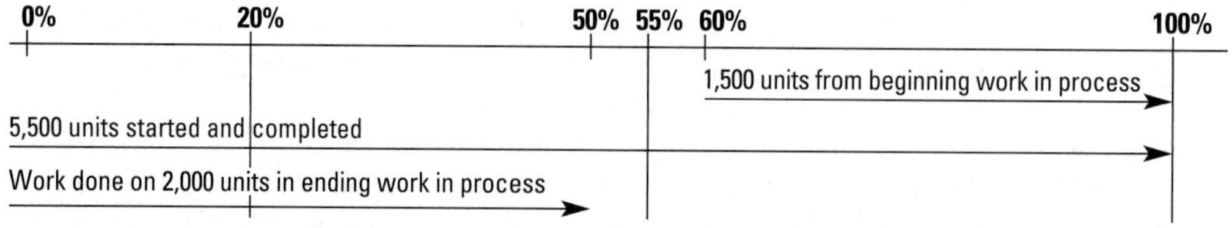

To see the number of units passing each inspection point, consider in the diagram the vertical lines at the 20%, 55%, and 100% inspection points. The vertical line at 20% crosses two horizontal lines—5,500 good units started and completed and 2,000 units in ending work in process—for a total of 7,500 good units. (The 20% vertical line does not cross the line representing work done on the 1,500 good units completed from beginning work in process because these units are already 60% complete at the start of the period and, hence, are not inspected this period.) Normal spoilage equals 10% of 7,500 = 750 units. The vertical line at the 55% point crosses just the second horizontal line so only 5,500 good units pass this point. Normal spoilage equals 10% of 5,500 = 550 units. At the 100% point, normal spoilage is 10% of 7,000 (1,500 + 5,500) good units = 700 units.

EXHIBIT 19-4

Computing Equivalent Units With Spoilage Using the Weighted-Average Method of Process Costing With Inspection at 20% of Completion for the Forming Department for July 2020

	A	B	C	D
1		(Step 1)	(Step 2)	
2			Equivalent Units	
3	Flow of Production	Physical Units	Direct Materials	Conversion Costs
4	Work in process, beginning[a]	1,500		
5	Started during current period	8,500		
6	To account for	10,000		
7	Good units completed and transferred out	7,000	7,000	7,000
8	Normal Spoilage	750		
9	(750 × 100%; 750 × 20%)		750	150
10	Abnormal Spoilage	250		
11	(250 × 100%; 250 × 20%)		250	50
12	Work in process, ending[b]	2,000		
13	(2,000 × 100%; 2,000 × 50%)		2,000	1,000
14	Accounted for	10,000		
15	Equivalent units of work done to date		10,000	8,200
16				
17	[a]Degree of completion: direct materials, 100%; conversion costs, 60%.			
18	[b]Degree of completion: direct materials, 100%; conversion costs, 50%.			

Exhibit 19-4 shows how equivalent units are computed under the weighted-average method if units are inspected at the 20% completion stage. The calculations depend on the direct materials and conversion costs incurred to get the units to this inspection point. The spoiled units have 100% of direct materials costs and 20% of conversion costs. Because ending work-in-process inventory has passed the inspection point, these units are assigned normal spoilage costs, just like units that have been completed and transferred out. Conversion costs of units completed and transferred out equal conversion costs for (1) 7,000 good units produced plus (2) $20\% \times (10\% \times 5{,}500) = 110$ equivalent units of normal spoilage. *We multiply by 20% to obtain the equivalent units of normal spoilage because conversion costs are only 20% complete at the inspection point.* Conversion costs of ending work-in-process inventory equal conversion costs of (1) 50% of $2{,}000 = 1{,}000$ equivalent good units plus (2) $20\% \times (10\% \times 2{,}000) = 40$ equivalent units of normal spoilage. Thus, equivalent units of normal spoilage accounted for equal 110 equivalent units related to units completed and transferred out plus 40 equivalent units related to units in ending work in process, for a total of 150 equivalent units, as Exhibit 19-4 shows.

Early inspections help prevent further costs being wasted on units that are already spoiled. For example, suppose units can be inspected when they are 70% complete rather than 100% complete. If spoilage occurs prior to the 70% point, a company can avoid incurring the final 30% of conversion costs on spoiled units or direct materials added after the 70% stage. The downside to conducting inspections too early is that units spoiled at later stages of the process may go undetected. For these reasons, firms often conduct multiple inspections and also empower workers to identify and resolve defects on a timely basis.

DECISION POINT

How does inspection at various stages of completion affect the amount of normal and abnormal spoilage?

19-3 TRY IT!

Normal spoilage is 7% of good units passing inspection in a forging process. In March, a total of 13,000 units were spoiled. Other data include units started during March, 140,000; work in process, beginning, 17,000 units (20% completed for conversion costs); and work in process, ending, 14,000 units (70% completed for conversion costs). Compute the normal and abnormal spoilage in units, assuming the inspection point is at (a) the 15% stage of completion, (b) the 40% stage of completion, and (c) the 100% stage of completion.

Job Costing and Spoilage

LEARNING OBJECTIVE 5

Account for spoilage in job costing

... normal spoilage assigned directly or indirectly to job; abnormal spoilage written off as a loss of the period

The concepts of normal and abnormal spoilage also apply to job-costing systems. Normal spoilage costs in job-costing systems—as in process-costing systems—are inventoriable costs, although increasingly companies are tolerating only small amounts of spoilage as normal. The costs of abnormal spoilage are not inventoriable costs and are written off as costs of the accounting period in which the abnormal spoilage is detected. When assigning costs, job-costing systems distinguish among *normal spoilage attributable to a specific job, normal spoilage common to all jobs*, and *abnormal spoilage*.

We describe accounting for spoilage in job costing using the following example.

Example 3: In the Hull Machine Shop, 5 aircraft parts out of a job lot of 50 aircraft parts are spoiled. The costs assigned prior to the inspection point are $2,000 per part. When the spoilage is detected, the spoiled goods are inventoried at $600 per part, the net disposal value. How should Hull account for the spoiled parts under different production assumptions?

Normal Spoilage Attributable to a Specific Job

When normal spoilage occurs because of the specifications of a particular job, that job bears the cost of spoilage minus the disposal value of the spoilage. The journal entry to recognize the disposal value follows (items in parentheses indicate subsidiary ledger postings):

Materials Control (spoiled goods at current net disposal value): 5 units × $600 per unit	3,000	
Work-in-Process Control (specific job): 5 units × $600 per unit		3,000

Note that the Work-in-Process Control (for the specific job) has already been debited (charged) $10,000 for the spoiled parts (5 spoiled parts × $2,000 per part). So, the net cost of normal spoilage is $7,000 ($10,000 − $3,000), which is an additional cost of the 45 (50 − 5) good units produced. Therefore, total cost of the 45 good units is $97,000: $90,000 (45 units × $2,000 per unit) incurred to produce the good units plus the $7,000 net cost of normal spoilage. Cost per good unit is $2,155.56 ($97,000 ÷ 45 good units).

Normal Spoilage Common to All Jobs

In some cases, spoilage may be considered a normal characteristic of the production process. The spoilage inherent in production will, of course, occur when a specific job is being worked on. However, the spoilage is not attributable to, and hence is not charged directly to, the specific job. Instead, the spoilage is allocated indirectly to the job as manufacturing overhead because the spoilage is common to all jobs. The journal entry is as follows:

Materials Control (spoiled goods at current disposal value): 5 units × $600 per unit	3,000	
Manufacturing Overhead Control (normal spoilage): ($10,000 − $3,000)	7,000	
Work-in-Process Control (specific job): 5 units × $2,000 per unit		10,000

When normal spoilage is common to all jobs, the budgeted manufacturing overhead rate includes a provision for normal spoilage cost. The normal spoilage cost is spread, through overhead allocation, over all jobs rather than being allocated to a specific job.[5] For example, if Hull produced 140 good units from all jobs in a given month, the $7,000 of normal spoilage overhead costs would be allocated at the rate of $50 per good unit ($7,000 ÷ 140 good units). Normal spoilage overhead costs allocated to the 45 good units in the current job would be $2,250 ($50 × 45 good units). The total cost of the 45 good units is $92,250: $90,000 (45 units × $2,000 per unit) incurred to produce the good units plus $2,250 of normal spoilage overhead costs. The cost per good unit is $2,050 ($92,250 ÷ 45 good units).

[5] Note that costs already assigned to products are charged back to Manufacturing Overhead Control, which generally accumulates only costs incurred, not both costs incurred and costs already assigned.

Abnormal Spoilage

If the spoilage is abnormal, the net loss is charged to the Loss from Abnormal Spoilage account. Unlike normal spoilage costs, abnormal spoilage costs are not included as a part of the cost of good units produced. The total cost of the 45 good units is $90,000 (45 units × $2,000 per unit). The cost per good unit is $2,000 ($90,000 ÷ 45 good units).

Materials Control (spoiled goods at current disposal value): 5 units × $600 per unit	3,000	
Loss from Abnormal Spoilage ($10,000 − $3,000)	7,000	
Work-in-Process Control (specific job): 5 units × $2,000 per unit		10,000

Even though, for external reporting purposes, abnormal spoilage costs are written off in the accounting period and are not linked to specific jobs or units, companies often identify the particular reasons for abnormal spoilage and, when appropriate, link it with specific jobs or units for cost management purposes.

The accounting treatment described above highlights the potential impact of misclassifying the nature of the spoilage. Normal spoilage costs are inventoriable and are added to the cost of good units produced, while abnormal spoilage costs are expensed in the accounting period in which they occur. So, when inventories are present, classifying spoilage as normal rather than abnormal results in an increase in current operating income. In the above example, if the 45 parts remain unsold at the end of the period, such misclassification would boost income for that period by $7,000. As with our discussion of completion percentages, it is important for managers to verify that spoilage rates and spoilage categories are not manipulated by department supervisors for short-term benefits.

DECISION POINT

How do job-costing systems account for spoilage?

Job Costing and Rework

LEARNING OBJECTIVE 6

Account for rework in job costing

... normal rework assigned directly or indirectly to job; abnormal rework written off as a loss of the period

Rework refers to units of production that are inspected, determined to be unacceptable, repaired, and sold as acceptable finished goods. We again distinguish (1) normal rework attributable to a specific job, (2) normal rework common to all jobs, and (3) abnormal rework.

Consider the Hull Machine Shop data in Example 3 on page 762. Assume the five spoiled parts are reworked. The journal entry for the $10,000 of total costs (the details of these costs are assumed) assigned to the five spoiled units before considering rework costs is as follows:

Work-in-Process Control (specific job)	10,000	
Materials Control		4,000
Wages Payable Control		4,000
Manufacturing Overhead Allocated		2,000

Assume the rework costs equal $3,800 ($800 in direct materials, $2,000 in direct manufacturing labor, and $1,000 in manufacturing overhead).

Normal Rework Attributable to a Specific Job

If the rework is normal but occurs because of the requirements of a specific job, the rework costs are charged to that job. The journal entry is as follows:

Work-in-Process Control (specific job)	3,800	
Materials Control		800
Wages Payable Control		2,000
Manufacturing Overhead Allocated		1,000

Normal Rework Common to All Jobs

The costs of rework when it is normal and not attributable to a specific job are charged to manufacturing overhead and are spread, through overhead allocation, over all jobs.

Manufacturing Overhead Control (rework costs)	3,800	
Materials Control		800
Wages Payable Control		2,000
Manufacturing Overhead Allocated		1,000

Abnormal Rework

If rework is abnormal, it is charged to a loss account.

Loss from Abnormal Rework	3,800	
Materials Control		800
Wages Payable Control		2,000
Manufacturing Overhead Allocated		1,000

Accounting for rework in a process-costing system also distinguishes abnormal rework from normal rework. Process costing accounts for abnormal rework in the same way as job costing. Accounting for normal rework follows the accounting described for normal rework common to all jobs (units) because masses of identical or similar units are being manufactured.

Costing rework focuses managers' attention on the resources wasted on activities that would not have to be undertaken if the product had been made correctly. The cost of rework prompts managers to seek ways to reduce rework, for example, by redesigning products or processes, training workers, or investing in new machines. To eliminate rework and to simplify the accounting, some companies set a standard of zero rework. All rework is then treated as abnormal and written off as a cost of the current period.

DECISION POINT

How do job-costing systems account for rework?

TRY IT! 19-4

Danner Corporation manufactures a sophisticated controller that is compatible with a variety of gaming consoles. Excluding rework costs, the cost of manufacturing one controller is $300. This consists of $190 in direct materials, $22 in direct manufacturing labor, and $88 in manufacturing overhead. Maintaining a reputation for quality is critical to Danner. Any defective units identified at the inspection point are sent back for rework. It costs Danner $70 to rework each defective controller, $21 in direct materials, $17 in direct manufacturing labor, and $32 in manufacturing overhead.

In August 2020, Danner manufactured 3,000 controllers, 86 of which required rework. Of these 86 controllers, 58 were considered normal rework common to all jobs and the other 28 were considered abnormal rework.

a. Prepare journal entries to record the accounting for both the normal and abnormal rework.
b. What were the total rework costs of controllers in August 2020?
c. Suppose instead that the normal rework is attributable entirely to Job #9, for 200 controllers intended for Australia. In this case, what are the total and unit costs of the good units produced for that job in August 2020? Prepare journal entries for the manufacture of the 200 controllers, as well as the normal rework costs.

Accounting for Scrap

LEARNING OBJECTIVE 7

Account for scrap

... reduces cost of job either at time of sale or at time of production

Scrap is residual material that results from manufacturing a product; it has low total sales value compared with the total sales value of the product. No distinction is made between normal and abnormal scrap because no cost is assigned to scrap. The only distinction made is between scrap attributable to a specific job and scrap common to all jobs.

There are two aspects of accounting for scrap:

1. Planning and control, including physical tracking
2. Inventory costing, including when and how scrap affects operating income

Initial entries to scrap records are commonly expressed in physical terms. In various industries, companies quantify items such as stamped-out metal sheets or edges of molded plastic parts by weighing, counting, or some other measure. Scrap records not only help measure efficiency, but also help keep track of scrap, and so reduce the chances of theft. Companies use scrap records to prepare periodic summaries of actual scrap versus budgeted or standard amounts. Scrap is either sold or disposed of quickly or stored for later sale, disposal, or reuse.

To carefully track scrap, many companies maintain a distinct account for scrap costs somewhere in their accounting system. The issues here are similar to the issues in Chapter 17 for accounting for byproducts:

- When should the value of scrap be recognized in the accounting records—at the time scrap is produced or at the time scrap is sold?
- How should the revenues from scrap be accounted for?

To illustrate, we extend our Hull example. Assume the manufacture of aircraft parts generates scrap and that the scrap from a job has a net sales value of $900.

Recognizing Scrap at the Time of Its Sale

When the dollar amount of the scrap is immaterial, it is simplest to record the physical quantity of scrap returned to the storeroom and to regard the revenues from the sale of scrap as a separate line item in the income statement. The only journal entry is shown below:

Sale of scrap:	Cash or Accounts Receivable	900	
	Scrap Revenues		900

When the dollar amount of the scrap is material and it is sold quickly after it is produced, the accounting depends on whether scrap is attributable to a specific job or is common to all jobs.

Scrap Attributable to a Specific Job

Job-costing systems sometimes trace scrap revenues to the jobs that yielded the scrap. This method is used only when the tracing can be done in an economically feasible way. For example, the Hull Machine Shop and its customers, such as the U.S. Department of Defense, may reach an agreement that provides for charging specific jobs with all rework or spoilage costs and then crediting these jobs with all scrap revenues that arise from the jobs. The journal entry is as follows:

Scrap returned to storeroom:	No journal entry. [Notation of quantity received and related job entered in the inventory record]		
Sale of scrap:	Cash or Accounts Receivable	900	
	Work-in-Process Control		900
	Posting made to specific job cost record.		

Unlike spoilage and rework, no cost is assigned to scrap, so no distinction is made between normal and abnormal scrap. All scrap revenues, whatever the amount, are credited to the specific job. Scrap revenues reduce the costs of the job.

Scrap Common to All Jobs

The journal entry in this case is as follows:

Scrap returned to storeroom:	No journal entry. [Notation of quantity received and related job entered in the inventory record]		
Sale of scrap:	Cash or Accounts Receivable	900	
	Manufacturing Overhead Control		900
	Posting made to subsidiary ledger—"Sales of Scrap" column on department cost record.		

Because scrap is not linked with a particular job or product, all products bear its costs. Expected scrap revenues reduce budgeted manufacturing overhead costs and the budgeted manufacturing overhead rate used to allocate manufacturing overhead costs to jobs. This method of accounting for scrap is also used in process costing because scrap is common to the manufacture of identical or similar units (and cannot be identified with specific units).

Recognizing Scrap at the Time of Its Production

Our preceding illustrations assume that scrap returned to the storeroom is sold quickly and so is not assigned an inventory cost figure. Sometimes, as in the case with edges of molded plastic parts, the value of the scrap is material, and market conditions may cause the time between storing it and selling or reusing it to be long and unpredictable. In these situations, the company assigns an inventory cost to scrap at a conservative estimate of its net realizable value to recognize production costs and related scrap revenues in the same accounting period. If scrap prices are volatile, as in the case of scrap metal, a "reasonable inventory value" is not easy to determine.

Scrap Attributable to a Specific Job

The journal entry in the Hull example is as follows:

Scrap returned to storeroom:	Materials Control	900	
	Work-in-Process Control		900

Scrap Common to All Jobs

The journal entry in this case is:

Scrap returned to storeroom:	Materials Control	900	
	Manufacturing Overhead Control		900

Notice that Materials Control account is debited in place of Cash or Accounts Receivable. When scrap is sold, the journal entry is as follows:

Sale of scrap:	Cash or Accounts Receivable	900	
	Materials Control		900

Scrap is sometimes reused as direct material rather than sold. In this case, Materials Control is debited at its estimated net realizable value and then credited when scrap is reused. For example, when scrap is common to all jobs, the entries are as follows:

Scrap returned to storeroom:	Materials Control	900	
	Manufacturing Overhead Control		900
Reuse of scrap:	Work-in-Process Control	900	
	Materials Control		900

When scrap is reused as direct materials in a process costing system, the accounting is similar to accounting under job costing when scrap is common to all jobs. Why? Because scrap is common to the manufacture of identical or similar units.

Managers are constantly seeking ways to reduce the cost of scrap. For example, General Motors has redesigned its plastic injection molding processes to reduce scrap. General Motors also regrinds and reuses plastic scrap saving direct material costs. Concepts in Action: Google's Zero Waste to Landfill Initiative shows how a firm deeply committed to principles of environmental sustainability minimizes waste and scrap.

DECISION POINT

How is scrap accounted for?

CONCEPTS IN ACTION

Google's Zero Waste to Landfill Initiative[6]

Benny Marty/Alamy Stock Photo

In 2016, Google introduced its Zero Waste to Landfill initiative for its global data center operations. The goal: ensure that 100% of waste is diverted away from landfills toward a sustainable pathway.

Google has 14 data centers on four continents that power digital services such as Gmail, YouTube, and Android. Each data center houses thousands of servers, hard drives, networking equipment, and cooling systems.

Google uses four strategies to keep data-center waste away out of landfills:

- *Maintain*: Use refurbished parts from old Google servers for repairs and upgrades.
- *Refurbish*: Custom build and remanufacture servers with refurbishing in mind, for example, dismantling hard drives into separate components.
- *Reuse*: Resell excess machines on the secondary market so they can be reused by other organizations.
- *Recycle*: Maximize the recycling of all data center materials such as clean hard drives that cannot be resold; reuse wastewater from sewage treatment plants.

To date, Google's data centers are diverting 91% of waste away from landfills. Google's other sustainability efforts include avoiding food waste and being the world's largest corporate purchaser of renewable energy.

[6] *Sources:* Adele Peters, "Google Is Planning For A Zero-Waste, Circular Economy," *Fast Company*, October 7, 2015 (https://www.fastcompany.com/3051869/google-is-planning-for-a-zero-waste-circular-economy); Rachel Futrell, "Six Google Data Centers Are Diverting 100% of Waste From Landfill," The Keyword (blog), Google, September 14, 2016 (https://blog.google/outreach-initiatives/environment/six-google-data-centers-diverting-100/); Google, Inc., "Environment Projects: Once is Never Enough," https://sustainability.google/projects/circular-economy/, accessed January 2019. Google, Inc., Google Environmental Report 2018, Mountain View, CA: Google, Inc., 2018.

PROBLEM FOR SELF-STUDY

Burlington Textiles has spoiled goods with an assigned cost of $40,000 and zero net disposal value.

Prepare a journal entry for each of the following conditions under (1) process costing (department A) and (2) job costing:

Required

1. Abnormal spoilage of $40,000
2. Normal spoilage of $40,000 regarded as common to all operations
3. Normal spoilage of $40,000 regarded as attributable to specifications of a particular job

Solution

	(1) Process Costing			(2) Job Costing		
1.	Loss from Abnormal Spoilage	40,000		Loss from Abnormal Spoilage	40,000	
	Work in Process—Dept. A		40,000	Work-in-Process Control (specific job)		40,000
2.	No entry until units are completed and transferred out. Then normal spoilage costs are transferred as part of cost of good units.			Manufacturing Overhead Control	40,000	
				Work-in-Process Control (specific job)		40,000
	Work in Process—Dept. B	40,000				
	Work in Process—Dept. A		40,000			
3.	Not applicable			No entry. Normal spoilage cost remains in Work-in-Process Control (specific job)		

DECISION POINTS

The following question-and-answer format summarizes the chapter's learning objectives. Each decision presents a key question related to a learning objective. The guidelines are the answer to that question.

Decision	Guidelines
1. What are spoilage, rework, and scrap?	Spoilage refers to units of production that do not meet the specifications required by customers for good units and that are discarded or sold at reduced prices. Rework refers to unacceptable units that are subsequently repaired and sold as acceptable finished goods. Scrap is residual material that results from manufacturing a product; it has low total sales value compared with the total sales value of the product.
2. What is the distinction between normal and abnormal spoilage?	Normal spoilage is inherent in a particular production process and arises when the process is done in an efficient manner. Abnormal spoilage is not inherent in a particular production process and would not arise under efficient operating conditions. Abnormal spoilage is usually regarded as avoidable and controllable.
3. How do the weighted-average and FIFO methods of process costing calculate the costs of good units and spoilage?	The weighted-average method combines costs of beginning inventory with costs of the current period when determining costs of good units, which include normal spoilage, and costs of abnormal spoilage, which are written off as a loss of the accounting period. The FIFO method keeps costs of beginning inventory separate from costs of the current period when determining costs of good units (which include normal spoilage) and costs of abnormal spoilage, which are written off as a loss of the accounting period.
4. How does inspection at various stages of completion affect the amount of normal and abnormal spoilage?	The cost of spoiled units is assumed to equal all costs incurred in producing spoiled units up to the point of inspection. Spoilage costs therefore vary based on different inspection points.
5. How do job-costing systems account for spoilage?	Normal spoilage specific to a job is assigned to that job or, when common to all jobs, is allocated as part of manufacturing overhead. The cost of abnormal spoilage is written off as a loss in the accounting period.
6. How do job-costing systems account for rework?	Normal rework specific to a job is assigned to that job or, when common to all jobs, is allocated as part of manufacturing overhead. Cost of abnormal rework is written off as a loss of the accounting period.
7. How is scrap accounted for?	Scrap is recognized in a firm's accounting records either at the time of sale or at the time of production. If scrap is immaterial, it is recognized as revenue when sold. If material, the net realizable value of scrap reduces the cost of a specific job or, when common to all jobs, reduces Manufacturing Overhead Control.

APPENDIX

Standard-Costing Method and Spoilage

The standard-costing method simplifies the computations for normal and abnormal spoilage. To illustrate, we return to the Anzio Company example in the chapter. Suppose Anzio develops the following standard costs per unit for work done in the forming department in July 2020:

Direct materials	$ 8.50
Conversion costs	10.50
Total manufacturing cost	$19.00

Assume the same standard costs per unit also apply to the beginning inventory: 1,500 (1,500 × 100%) equivalent units of direct materials and 900 (1,500 × 60%) equivalent units of conversion costs. Hence, the beginning inventory at standard costs is shown below:

Direct materials, 1,500 units × $8.50 per unit	$12,750
Conversion costs, 900 units × $10.50 per unit	9,450
Total manufacturing costs	$22,200

Exhibit 19-5, Panel A, presents Steps 1 and 2 for calculating physical and equivalent units. These steps are the same as for the FIFO method described in Exhibit 19-3. Exhibit 19-5, Panel B, presents Steps 3, 4, and 5.

EXHIBIT 19-5 Standard-Costing Method of Process Costing With Spoilage for the Forming Department for July 2020

PANEL A: Summarize the Flow of Physical Units and Compute Output in Equivalent Units

	A	B	C	D	E
1			(Step 1)	(Step 2)	
2				Equivalent Units	
3		Flow of Production	Physical Units	Direct Materials	Conversion Costs
4		Work in process, beginning (given, p. 755)	1,500		
5		Started during current period (given, p. 755)	8,500		
6		To account for	10,000		
7		Good units completed and transferred out during current period			
8		From beginning work in process[a]	1,500		
9		[1,500 × (100% – 100%); 1,500 × (100% – 60%)]		0	600
10		Started and completed	5,500[b]		
11		(5,500 × 100%; 5,500 × 100%)		5,500	5,500
12		Normal Spoilage[c]	700		
13		(700 × 100%; 700 × 100%)		700	700
14		Abnormal Spoilage[d]	300		
15		(300 × 100%; 300 × 100%)		300	300
16		Work in process, ending[e] (given, p. 755)	2,000		
17		(2,000 × 100%; 2,000 × 50%)		2,000	1,000
18		Accounted for	10,000		
19		Equivalent units of work done in current period		8,500	8,100
20					

21 [a]Degree of completion in this department: direct materials, 100%; conversion costs, 60%.
22 [b]7,000 physical units completed and transferred out minus 1,500 physical units completed and transferred out from beginning
23 work-in-process inventory.
24 [c]Normal spoilage is 10% of good units transferred out; 10% × 7,000 = 700 units. Degree of completion of normal spoilage in this
25 department: direct materials, 100%; conversion costs, 100%.
26 [d]Abnormal spoilage = Actual spoilage – Normal spoilage = 1,000 – 700 = 300 units. Degree of completion of abnormal spoilage in this
27 department: direct materials, 100%; conversion costs, 100%.
28 [e]Degree of completion in this department: direct materials, 100%; conversion costs, 50%.

EXHIBIT 19-5

Standard-Costing Method of Process Costing With Spoilage for the Forming Department for July 2020 *(continued)*

PANEL B: Summarize the Total Costs to Account For, Compute the Cost per Equivalent Unit, and Assign Costs to the Units Completed, Spoiled Units, and Units in Ending Work-in-Process Inventory

	A	B	C	D	E	F
30			Total Production Costs	Direct Materials		Conversion Costs
31	(Step 3)	Work in process, beginning (given, p. 755)	$ 22,200	(1,500 × $8.50)	+	(900 × $10.50)
32		Costs added in current period at standard costs	157,300	(8,500 × $8.50)	+	(8,100 × $10.50)
33		Total costs to account for	$179,500	$85,000	+	$94,500
34	(Step 4)	Standard costs per equivalent unit (given, p. 755)	$ 19.00	$ 8.50		$ 10.50
35	(Step 5)	Assignment of costs:				
36		Good units completed and transferred out (7,000 units):				
37		Work in process, beginning (1,500 units)	$ 22,200	(1,500 × $8.50)	+	(900 × $10.50)
38		Costs added to beginning work in process in current period	6,300	(0^f × $8.50)	+	(600^f × $10.50)
39		Total from beginning inventory before normal spoilage	28,500			
40		Started and completed before normal spoilage (5,500 units)	104,500	($5{,}500^f$ × $8.50)	+	($5{,}500^f$ × $10.50)
41		Normal spoilage (700 units)	13,300	(700^f × $8.50)	+	(700^f × $10.50)
42	(A)	Total costs of good units completed and transferred out	146,300			
43	(B)	Abnormal spoilage (300 units)	5,700	(300^f × $8.50)	+	(300^f × $10.50)
44	(C)	Work in process, ending (2,000 units)	27,500	($2{,}000^f$ × $8.50)	+	($1{,}000^f$ × $10.50)
45	(A) + (B) + (C)	Total costs accounted for	$179,500	$85,000	+	$94,500
46						
47	[f]Equivalent units of direct materials and conversion costs calculated in Step 2 in Panel A.					

The costs to account for in Step 3 are at standard costs and, hence differ from the costs to account for under the weighted-average and FIFO methods, which are at actual costs. In Step 4, cost per equivalent unit is simply the standard cost: $8.50 per unit for direct materials and $10.50 per unit for conversion costs. The standard-costing method simplifies process costing because there is no need to calculate equivalent-unit costs. In Step 5, managers assign standard costs to units completed (including normal spoilage), to abnormal spoilage, and to ending work-in-process inventory by multiplying the equivalent units calculated in Step 2 by the standard costs per equivalent unit in Step 4. Managers measure and analyze variances as described in the appendix to Chapter 18 (pages 738–740).[7]

Journal entries corresponding to the amounts calculated in Step 5 are:

Finished Goods	146,300	
Work in Process—Forming		146,300
To record transfer of good units completed in July.		
Loss from Abnormal Spoilage	5,700	
Work in Process—Forming		5,700
To record abnormal spoilage detected in July.		

[7] For example, from Exhibit 19-5, Panel B, standard costs for July are direct materials used, 8,500 × 8.50 = $72,250, and conversion costs, 8,100 × $10.50 = $85,050. From page 755, actual costs added during July are direct materials, $76,500, and conversion costs, $89,100, resulting in a direct materials variance of $72,250 − $76,500 = $4,250 U and a conversion costs variance of $85,050 − $89,100 = $4,050 U. These variances can be subdivided further as in Chapters 7 and 8; abnormal spoilage is part of the efficiency variance.

TERMS TO LEARN

This chapter and the Glossary at the end of the text contain definitions of the following important terms:

abnormal spoilage (**p. 753**)
inspection point (**p. 754**)
normal spoilage (**p. 752**)
rework (**p. 752**)
scrap (**p. 752**)
spoilage (**p. 752**)

ASSIGNMENT MATERIAL

Questions

19-1 Why is there an unmistakable trend in manufacturing to improve quality?

19-2 Distinguish among spoilage, rework, and scrap.

19-3 "Normal spoilage is planned spoilage." Discuss.

19-4 "Costs of abnormal spoilage are losses." Explain.

19-5 "What has been regarded as normal spoilage in the past is not necessarily acceptable as normal spoilage in the present or future." Explain.

19-6 "Units of abnormal spoilage are inferred rather than identified." Explain.

19-7 "In accounting for spoiled units, we are dealing with cost assignment rather than cost incurrence." Explain.

19-8 "Normal spoilage rate is computed by dividing the units of normal spoilage by total actual units started in production." Do you agree? Explain.

19-9 "The inspection point is key to the allocation of spoilage costs." Do you agree? Explain.

19-10 "The unit cost of normal spoilage is the same as the unit cost of abnormal spoilage." Do you agree? Explain.

19-11 "In job costing, the costs of normal spoilage that occur while a specific job is being done are charged to the specific job." Do you agree? Explain.

19-12 "The costs of rework are always charged to the specific jobs in which the defects were originally discovered." Do you agree? Explain.

19-13 "Abnormal rework costs should be charged to a loss account, not to manufacturing overhead." Do you agree? Explain.

19-14 When is a company justified in inventorying scrap?

19-15 How do managers use information about scrap?

Multiple-Choice Questions

In partnership with:

BECKER PROFESSIONAL EDUCATION®

19-16 All of the following are accurate regarding the treatment of normal or abnormal spoilage by a firm with the exception of

a. Abnormal spoilage is excluded in the standard cost of a manufactured product.
b. Normal spoilage is capitalized as part of inventory cost.
c. Abnormal spoilage has no financial statement impact.
d. Normal and abnormal spoilage units affect the equivalent units of production.

19-17 Which of the following is a TRUE statement regarding the treatment of scrap by a firm?

a. Scrap is always allocated to a specific job.
b. Scrap is separated between normal and abnormal scrap.
c. When scrap is material and specific to a job, the accounting for scrap lowers the total costs for that job.
d. There are costs assigned to scrap.

19-18 Healthy Dinners Co. produces frozen dinners for the health conscious consumer. During the quarter ended September 30, the company had the following cost data:

Dinner ingredients	$3,550,000
Preparation labor	900,000
Sales and marketing costs	125,000
Plant production overhead	50,000
Normal food spoilage	60,000
Abnormal food spoilage	40,000
General and administrative expenses	75,000

Based on the above, what is the total amount of period expenses reflected in the company's income statement for the quarter ended September 30?

a. $200,000 **b.** $240,000
c. $290,000 **d.** $300,000

19-19 Fresh Products, Inc. incurred the following costs during December related to the production of its 162,500 frozen ice cream cone specialty items:

Food product labor	$175,000
Ice cream cone ingredients	325,000
Sales and marketing costs	10,000
Factory (manufacturing) overhead	16,000
Normal food spoilage	4,000
Abnormal spoilage	3,000

What is the December per-unit inventory cost allocated to the company's frozen ice cream cone specialty items?

a. $3.18 **b.** $3.20
c. $3.22 **d.** $3.26

Exercises

19-20 Normal and abnormal spoilage in units. The following data, in physical units, describe a grinding process for January:

Work in process, beginning	19,300
Started during current period	145,400
To account for	164,700
Spoiled units	12,000
Good units completed and transferred out	128,000
Work in process, ending	24,700
Accounted for	164,700

Inspection occurs at the 100% completion stage. Normal spoilage is 5% of the good units passing inspection.

Required

1. Compute the normal and abnormal spoilage in units.
2. Assume that the equivalent-unit cost of a spoiled unit is $8. Compute the amount of potential savings if all spoilage were eliminated, assuming that all other costs would be unaffected. Comment on your answer.

19-21 Weighted-average method, spoilage, equivalent units. (CMA, adapted) Consider the following data for November 2020 from MacLean Manufacturing Company, which makes silk pennants and uses a process-costing system. All direct materials are added at the beginning of the process and conversion costs are added evenly during the process. Spoilage is detected upon inspection at the completion of the process. Spoiled units are disposed of at zero net disposal value. MacLean Manufacturing Company uses the weighted-average method of process costing.

	Physical Units (Pennants)	Direct Materials	Conversion Costs
Work in process, November 1[a]	1,350	$ 966	$ 711
Started in November 2020	?		
Good units completed and transferred out during November 2020	8,800		
Normal spoilage	80		
Abnormal spoilage	50		
Work in process, November 30[b]	1,700		
Total costs added during November 2020		$10,302	$30,055

[a]Degree of completion: direct materials, 100%; conversion costs, 45%.
[b]Degree of completion: direct materials, 100%; conversion costs, 35%.

Required

Compute equivalent units for direct materials and conversion costs. Show physical units in the first column.

19-22 Weighted-average method, assigning costs (continuation of 19-21).
For the data in Exercise 19-21, summarize total costs to account for; calculate cost per equivalent unit for direct materials and conversion costs; and assign costs to units completed and transferred out (including normal spoilage), to abnormal spoilage, and to units in ending work-in-process inventory.

Required

19-23 FIFO method, spoilage, equivalent units (continuation of 19-21). Refer to the information in Exercise 19-21. Suppose MacLean Manufacturing Company uses the FIFO method of process costing instead of the weighted-average method.

Required

Compute equivalent units for direct materials and conversion costs. Show physical units in the first column.

19-24 FIFO method, assigning costs (continuation of 19-23).
For the data in Exercise 19-21, use the FIFO method to summarize total costs to account for; calculate cost per equivalent unit for direct materials and conversion costs; and assign costs to units completed and transferred out (including normal spoilage), to abnormal spoilage, and to units in ending work in process inventory.

Required

19-25 Weighted-average method, spoilage. LaCroix Company produces handbags from leather of moderate quality. It distributes the product through outlet stores and department store chains. At LaCroix's facility in northeast Ohio, direct materials (primarily leather hides) are added at the beginning of the process, while conversion costs are added evenly during the process. Spoiled units are detected upon inspection at the end of the process and are discarded at a net disposal value of zero.

LaCroix uses the weighted-average method of process costing. Summary data for April 2020 are shown below:

	A	B	C	D
1		**Physical Units**	**Direct Materials**	**Conversion Costs**
2	Work in process, beginning inventory (April 1)	2,400	$21,240	$ 13,332
3	Degree of completion of beginning work in process		100%	50%
4	Started during April	12,000		
5	Good units completed and transferred out during April	10,800		
6	Work in process, ending inventory (April 30)	2,160		
7	Degree of completion of ending work in process		100%	75%
8	Total costs added during April		$97,560	$111,408
9	Normal spoilage as a percentage of good units	10%		
10	Degree of completion of normal spoilage		100%	100%
11	Degree of completion of abnormal spoilage		100%	100%

Required

1. For each cost category, calculate equivalent units. Show physical units in the first column.
2. Summarize total costs to account for; calculate cost per equivalent unit for each cost category; and assign costs to units completed and transferred out (including normal spoilage), to abnormal spoilage, and to units in ending work in process inventory.

19-26 FIFO method, spoilage (continuation of 19-25).

Required

1. Do Exercise 19-25 using the FIFO method.
2. What are the managerial issues involved in selecting or reviewing the percentage of spoilage considered normal? How would your answer to requirement 1 differ if all spoilage were viewed as normal?

19-27 Spoilage, journal entries. Mason produces small machined parts. Mason uses a job-costing system. The nature of its process is such that management expects normal spoilage at a rate of 2% of good parts. Data for last quarter are shown below:

Production (units)	100,000
Good parts produced	97,000
Direct material cost/unit	$ 1.00

The spoiled parts were identified after 100% of the direct material cost was incurred. The disposal value is $0.20/part.

Required

1. Record the journal entries if the spoilage was (a) job specific or (b) common to all jobs.
2. Comment on the differences arising from the different treatment for these two scenarios.

19-28 Recognition of loss from spoilage. Southwest Toys manufactures globes at its San Fernando facility. The company uses job costing and provides you with the following information regarding operations for April 2020:

Total globes manufactured	35,000
Globes rejected as spoiled units	850
Total manufacturing cost	$700,000

Assume the spoiled units have no disposal value.

Required

1. What is the unit cost of making the 35,000 globes?
2. What is the total cost of the 850 spoiled units?
3. If the spoilage is considered normal, what is the increase in the unit cost of good globes manufactured as a result of the spoilage?
4. If the spoilage is considered abnormal, prepare the journal entries for the spoilage incurred.

19-29 Weighted-average method, spoilage. LogicCo is a fast-growing manufacturer of computer chips. Direct materials are added at the start of the production process. Conversion costs are added evenly during the process. Some units of this product are spoiled as a result of defects not detectable before inspection of finished goods. Spoiled units are disposed of at zero net disposal value. LogicCo uses the weighted-average method of process costing.

Summary data for September 2020 are shown below:

Home Insert Page Layout Formulas Data Review View

	A	B	C	D
1		Physical Units (Computer Chips)	Direct Materials	Conversion Costs
2	Work in process, beginning inventory (September 1)	900	$125,766	$ 10,368
3	Degree of completion of beginning work in process		100%	30%
4	Started during September	2,754		
5	Good units completed and transferred out during September	2,500		
6	Work in process, ending inventory (September 30)	490		
7	Degree of completion of ending work in process		100%	10%
8	Total costs added during September		$619,650	$253,098
9	Normal spoilage as a percentage of good units	15%		
10	Degree of completion of normal spoilage		100%	100%
11	Degree of completion of abnormal spoilage		100%	100%

Required

1. For each cost category, compute equivalent units. Show physical units in the first column.
2. Summarize total costs to account for; calculate cost per equivalent unit for each cost category; and assign costs to units completed and transferred out (including normal spoilage), to abnormal spoilage, and to units in ending work in process inventory.

19-30 FIFO method, spoilage (continuation of 19-29). Refer to the information in Exercise 19-29.

Required

1. Do Exercise 19-29 using the FIFO method of process costing.
2. Should LogicCo's managers choose the weighted-average method or the FIFO method? Explain.

19-31 Standard-costing method, spoilage (continuation of 19-29). Refer to the information in Exercise 19-29. Suppose LogicCo determines standard costs of $215 per equivalent unit for direct materials and $92 per equivalent unit for conversion costs for both beginning work in process and work done in the current period.

Required

1. Do Exercise 19-29 using the standard-costing method.
2. What issues should the manager focus on when reviewing the equivalent units calculations?

19-32 Spoilage and job costing. (L. Bamber) Barrett Kitchens produces a variety of items in accordance with special job orders from hospitals, plant cafeterias, and university dormitories. An order for 2,100 cases of mixed vegetables costs $9 per case: direct materials, $4; direct manufacturing labor, $3; and manufacturing overhead allocated, $2. The manufacturing overhead rate includes a provision for normal spoilage. Consider each requirement independently.

Required

1. Assume that a laborer dropped 420 cases. Suppose part of the 420 cases could be sold to a nearby prison for $420 cash. Prepare a journal entry to record this event. Calculate and explain briefly the unit cost of the remaining 1,680 cases.
2. Refer to the original data. Tasters at the company reject 420 of the 2,100 cases. The 420 cases are disposed of for $840. Assume that this rejection rate is considered normal. Prepare a journal entry to record this event, and do the following:
   a. Calculate the unit cost if the rejection is attributable to exacting specifications of this particular job.
   b. Calculate the unit cost if the rejection is characteristic of the production process and is not attributable to this specific job.
   c. Are unit costs the same in requirements 2a and 2b? Explain your reasoning briefly.
3. Refer to the original data. Tasters rejected 420 cases that had insufficient salt. The product can be placed in a vat, salt can be added, and the product can be reprocessed into jars. This operation, which is considered normal, will cost $420. Prepare a journal entry to record this event and do the following:
   a. Calculate the unit cost of all the cases if this additional cost was incurred because of the exacting specifications of this particular job.
   b. Calculate the unit cost of all the cases if this additional cost occurs regularly because of difficulty in seasoning.
   c. Are unit costs the same in requirements 3a and 3b? Explain your reasoning briefly.

19-33 Reworked units, costs of rework. Heyer Appliances assembles dishwashers at its plant in Tuscaloosa, Alabama. In February 2020, 60 circulation motors that cost $110 each (from a new supplier that subsequently went bankrupt) were defective and had to be disposed of at zero net disposal value. Heyer Appliances was able to rework all 60 dishwashers by substituting new circulation motors purchased from one of its existing suppliers. Each replacement motor cost $125.

Required

1. What alternative approaches are there to account for the materials cost of reworked units?
2. Should Heyer Appliances use the $110 circulation motor or the $125 motor to calculate the cost of materials reworked? Explain.
3. What other costs might Heyer Appliances include in its analysis of the total costs of rework due to the circulation motors purchased from the (now) bankrupt supplier?

19-34 Scrap, job costing. The Russell Company has an extensive job-costing facility that uses a variety of metals. Consider each requirement independently.

Required

1. Job 372 uses a particular metal alloy that is not used for any other job. Assume that scrap is material in amount and sold for $480 quickly after it is produced. Prepare the journal entry.
2. The scrap from Job 372 consists of a metal that can be used by many other jobs. No record is maintained of the scrap generated by individual jobs. Scrap is accounted for at the time of its sale. Scrap totaling $4,500 is sold. Prepare two alternative journal entries that could be used to account for the sale of scrap.
3. Suppose the scrap generated in requirement 2 is returned to the storeroom for future use, and a journal entry is made to record the scrap. A month later, the scrap is reused as direct material on a subsequent job. Prepare the journal entries to record these transactions.

Problems

19-35 Weighted-average method, spoilage. World Class Steaks is a meat-processing firm based in Texas. It uses the weighted-average method of process costing and has two departments: preparation (prep) and shipping. For the prep department, conversion costs are added evenly during the process, and direct materials are added at the beginning of the process. Spoiled units are detected upon inspection at the end of the prep process and are disposed of at zero net disposal value. All completed work is transferred to the shipping department. Summary data for May follow on the next page:

	A	B	C	D
1	World Class Steaks: Preparation (Prep) Department	Physical Units	Direct Materials	Conversion Costs
2	Work in process, beginning inventory (May 1)	7,200	$ 10,632	$ 2,778
3	Degree of completion of beginning work in process		100%	50%
4	Started during May	60,000		
5	Good units completed and transferred out during May	49,200		
6	Work in process, ending inventory (May 31)	10,080		
7	Degree of completion of ending work in process		100%	25%
8	Total costs added during May		$111,000	$89,664
9	Normal spoilage as a percentage of good units	10%		
10	Degree of completion of normal spoilage		100%	100%
11	Degree of completion of abnormal spoilage		100%	100%

Required

For the prep department, summarize total costs to account for and assign those costs to units completed and transferred out (including normal spoilage), to abnormal spoilage, and to units in ending work in process inventory. (Problem 19-37 explores additional facets of this problem.)

19-36 FIFO method, spoilage (continuation of 19-35). Refer to the information in Problem 19-35.

Required

Do Problem 19-35 using the FIFO method of process costing. (Problem 19-38 explores additional facets of this problem.)

19-37 Weighted-average method, shipping department (continuation of 19-35). In the shipping department of World Class Steaks, conversion costs are added evenly during the process and direct materials are added at the end of the process. Spoiled units are detected upon inspection at the end of the process and are disposed of at zero net disposal value. The transferred-in costs for May equal the total cost of good units completed and transferred out in May from the prep department, calculated in Problem 19-35 using the weighted-average method of process costing. Summary data for May follow:

	A	B	C	D	E
1	World Class Steaks: Shipping Department	Physical Units	Transferred-In Costs	Direct Materials	Conversion Costs
2	Work in process, beginning inventory (May 1)	25,200	$67,397	$ 0	$46,950
3	Degree of completion of beginning work in process		100%	0%	70%
4	Started during May	49,200			
5	Good units completed and transferred out during May	52,800			
6	Work in process, ending inventory (May 31)	16,800			
7	Degree of completion of ending work in process		100%	0%	40%
8	Total costs added during May		?	$11,520	$81,690
9	Normal spoilage as a percentage of good units	7%			
10	Degree of completion of normal spoilage			100%	100%
11	Degree of completion of abnormal spoilage			100%	100%

Required

For the shipping department, use the weighted-average method to summarize total costs to account for and assign those costs to units completed and transferred out (including normal spoilage), to abnormal spoilage, and to units in ending work in process inventory.

19-38 FIFO method, shipping department (continuation of 19-36). Refer to the information in Problem 19-37 except that transferred-in costs of beginning work in process on May 1 are $66,180 (instead of $67,397). Transferred-in costs for May equal the total cost of good units completed and transferred out in May from the prep department, as calculated in Problem 19-36 using the FIFO method of process costing.

Required

For the shipping department, use the FIFO method to summarize total costs to account for and assign those costs to units completed and transferred out (including normal spoilage), to abnormal spoilage, and to units in ending work in process inventory.

19-39 Physical units, inspection at various levels of completion, weighted-average process costing. Jiminy Jacks produces jacks that are used in many types of automobiles. In the assembly department, materials are added at the beginning of the process and conversion costs are added evenly during the process.

At the start of April 2020, Jiminy Jacks assembly department had 2,500 jacks in beginning work-in-process inventory that were 100% complete for materials and 50% complete for conversion costs.

An additional 14,000 jacks were started in April and 3,500 remain in work-in-process at the end of the month. The unfinished units are 100% complete for materials and 80% complete for conversion costs.

The assembly department had 2,000 spoiled units in April. The rate of normal spoilage is 10% of good units.

Required

1. Using the format on page 760, compute the normal and abnormal spoilage in units for April, assuming the inspection point is at (a) the 40% stage of completion, (b) the 70% stage of completion, and (c) the 100% stage of completion.
2. Refer to your answer in requirement 1. Why are there different amounts of normal and abnormal spoilage at different inspection points?

19-40 Spoilage in job costing. Paradise Bay Shop is a manufacturer of golf carts.

Peter Cranston, the plant manager of Paradise Bay, obtains the following information for Job #22 in August 2020. A total of 23 units were started, and 3 spoiled units were detected and rejected at final inspection, yielding 20 good units. The spoiled units were considered to be normal spoilage. Costs assigned prior to the inspection point are $1,300 per unit. The current disposal price of the spoiled units is $215 per unit. When the spoilage is detected, the spoiled goods are inventoried at $215 per unit.

Required

1. What is the normal spoilage rate?
2. Prepare the journal entries to record the normal spoilage, assuming the following:
   a. The spoilage is related to a specific job.
   b. The spoilage is common to all jobs.
   c. The spoilage is considered to be abnormal spoilage.

19-41 Rework in job costing, journal entry (continuation of 19-40). Assume that the 3 spoiled units of Paradise Bay Shop's Job #22 can be reworked for a total cost of $2,200. A total cost of $3,900 associated with these units has already been assigned to Job #22 before the rework.

Prepare the journal entries for the rework, assuming the following:

Required

a. The rework is related to a specific job.
b. The rework is common to all jobs.
c. The rework is considered to be abnormal.

19-42 Scrap at time of sale or at time of production, journal entries (continuation of 19-40). Assume that Job #22 of Paradise Bay Shop generates scrap with a total sales value of $400 (it is assumed that scrap returned to the storeroom is sold quickly).

Prepare journal entries for the recognition of scrap, assuming the following:

Required

a. The value of scrap is immaterial and scrap is recognized at the time of sale.
b. The value of scrap is material, is related to a specific job, and is recognized at the time of sale.
c. The value of scrap is material, is common to all jobs, and is recognized at the time of sale.
d. The value of scrap is material, is recognized as inventory at the time of production, and is recorded at its net realizable value.

19-43 Physical units, inspection at various stages of completion. Chemet manufactures chemicals in a continuous process. The company combines various materials in a machine at the beginning of the process, and conversion costs are added evenly during the process. Occasionally, the chemical reactions among the materials do not work as expected and the output is spoiled. Normal spoilage is 4% of good units that pass inspection. The following information pertains to March 2020:

Beginning inventory	2,500 units (100% complete for materials; 25% complete for conversion costs)
Units started	30,000
Units in ending work in process	2,100 (100% complete for materials; 70% complete for conversion costs)

Chemet had 1,900 spoiled units in March 2020.

Required

Using the format on page 760, compute normal and abnormal spoilage in units, assuming the inspection point is at the (1) 20% stage of completion, (2) 45% stage of completion, and (3) 100% stage of completion.

19-44 Weighted-average method, inspection at 80% completion. (A. Atkinson) The Horsheim Company manufactures furniture in two departments: molding and finishing. The company uses the weighted-average method of process costing. August data for the finishing department are as follows:

Units of beginning work-in-process inventory	25,000
Percentage completion of beginning work-in-process units	25%
Units started	175,000
Units completed	125,000
Units in ending inventory	50,000
Percentage completion of ending work-in-process units	95%
Spoiled units	25,000
Total costs added during current period:	
Direct materials	$1,638,000
Direct manufacturing labor	$1,589,000
Manufacturing overhead	$1,540,000
Work in process, beginning:	
Transferred-in costs	$ 207,250
Conversion costs	$ 105,000
Cost of units transferred in during current period	$1,618,750

Conversion costs are added evenly during the process. Direct material costs are added when production is 90% complete. The inspection point is at the 80% stage of production. Normal spoilage is 10% of all good units that pass inspection. Spoiled units are disposed of at zero net disposal value.

Required

1. For August, summarize total costs to account for and assign these costs to units completed and transferred out (including normal spoilage), to abnormal spoilage, and to units in ending work in process inventory.
2. What are the managerial issues involved in determining the percentage of spoilage considered normal? How would your answer to requirement 1 differ if all spoilage were treated as normal?

19-45 Job costing, classifying spoilage, ethics. Flextron Company is a contract manufacturer for a variety of pharmaceutical and over-the-counter products. Lynn Sanger, one of Flextron's quality control managers, obtains the following information for Job No. M102. The order was completed recently, just before the close of Flextron's fiscal year. The units will be delivered early in the next accounting period. A total of 128,500 units were started, and 6,000 spoiled units were rejected at final inspection, yielding 122,500 good units. Normal spoilage is 2,500 units. Spoiled units were sold at $4 per unit. Sanger indicates that all spoilage was related to this specific job.

The total costs for all 128,500 units of Job No. M102 follow. The job has been completed, but the costs are yet to be transferred to Finished Goods.

Direct materials	$ 979,000
Direct manufacturing labor	840,000
Manufacturing overhead	1,650,500
Total manufacturing costs	$3,469,500

Required

1. Calculate the unit quantities of normal and abnormal spoilage.
2. Prepare journal entries to account for Job No. M102, including spoilage, disposal of spoiled units, and transfer of costs to the Finished Goods account.
3. Flextron's controller, Vince Chadwick, tells Marta Suarez, the management accountant responsible for Job No. M102, the following: "This was an unusual job. I think all 6,000 spoiled units should be considered normal." Suarez knows that the work involved in Job No. M102 was typical and that normal spoilage is 2,500 units. She feels Chadwick made these comments because he wants to show a higher operating income for the year.
   a. Prepare journal entries, similar to requirement 2, to account for Job No. M102 if all spoilage were considered normal. How will operating income be affected if all spoilage is considered normal?
   b. What should Suarez do in response to Chadwick's comment?

Balanced Scorecard: Quality and Time

20

To satisfy ever-increasing customer expectations, managers at companies such as General Electric, Sony, Texas Instruments, and Toyota find cost-effective ways to continuously improve the quality of their products and services and shorten response times.

Managers balance the costs of achieving these improvements against the benefits from higher performance. Improving quality and decreasing customer-response times are hard work. When managers fail to deliver on these dimensions, the losses can be substantial, as the following article about the Volkswagen Group shows.

LEARNING OBJECTIVES

1. Explain the four cost categories in a costs-of-quality program
2. Develop nonfinancial measures and methods to improve quality
3. Use costs-of-quality measures to make decisions
4. Use financial and nonfinancial measures to evaluate quality
5. Describe customer-response time and on-time performance and why delays occur
6. Determine the costs of delays
7. Use financial and nonfinancial measures of time

"DIESELGATE" DERAILS VOLKSWAGEN'S GRAND AMBITIONS[1]

Volkswagen, the German automaker, had a longstanding goal to become the world's largest and most profitable automaker by 2018. To help meet this audacious goal, VW—one of the largest producers of fuel-efficient and hybrid-power-train vehicles—introduced its new "clean diesel" line of cars in 2009. Long renowned for its high-quality environmentally friendly vehicles, the company struggled to manufacture the new "clean diesel" engine, leading to the largest scandal in the history of the automotive industry.

In 2015, the United States Environmental Protection Agency revealed that VW had installed illegal software in hundreds of thousands of so-called "clean diesel" engines since 2009. The software helped make the cars meet exhaust pollution standards when monitored in tests, but in real life their emissions exceeded the limits. A few days later, VW admitted that some 11 million diesel vehicles worldwide, including 8.5 million in Europe and 600,000 in the United States, had been fitted with the illegal software. Investigators found that some VW cars emitted up to 40 times more harmful nitrogen oxide—which has been linked to respiratory and cardiovascular disease—than legally allowed.

Since 2015, fallout from the "Dieselgate" scandal has cost VW more than $30 billion in fines, compensation, and buybacks, mainly in the United States. Several former company executives were criminally convicted and given prison terms for their role in the fraud. Further, VW's reputation for quality took a significant hit. Sales in the United States have plummeted, and the company is now focused on the production of electric cars, which do not have the same manufacturing challenges as diesel-engine cars.

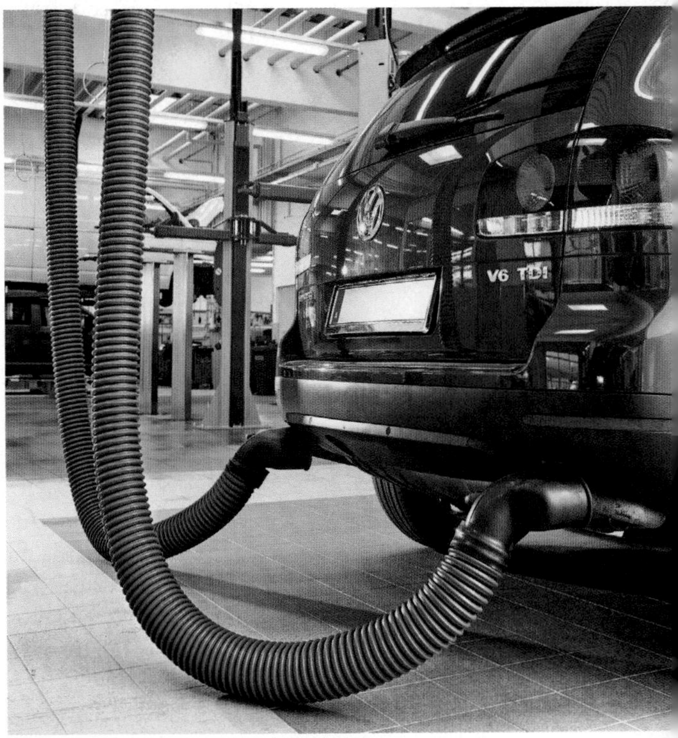

Christian Vorhofer/imageBROKER/Shutterstock

[1] *Sources:* Geoffrey Smith and Roger Parloff, "Hoaxwagen," *Fortune*, March 7, 2016 (http://fortune.com/inside-volkswagen-emissions-scandal/); Phys.org, "Five Things to Know About VW's 'Dieselgate' Scandal," June 18, 2018 (https://phys.org/news/2018-06-vw-dieselgate-scandal.html).

Quality as a Competitive Tool

LEARNING OBJECTIVE 1

Explain the four cost categories in a costs-of-quality program

...prevention, appraisal, internal failure, and external failure costs

The American Society for Quality defines **quality** as the total features and characteristics of a product or a service made or performed according to specifications to satisfy customers at the time of purchase and during use. Many companies throughout the world—like Cisco Systems, Motorola, British Telecom, Fujitsu, and Honda—see quality as an important source of strategic competitive advantage. Focusing on the quality of a product or service builds expertise in producing it, lowers the costs of providing it, creates higher satisfaction for customers using it, and generates higher future revenues for the company selling it. Several high-profile awards, such as the Malcolm Baldrige National Quality Award in the United States, the Deming Prize in Japan, and the Premio Nacional de Calidad in Mexico, recognize quality excellence.

International quality standards have also emerged. ISO 9000, developed by the International Organization for Standardization, is a set of standards for quality management adopted by more than 170 countries. The standards help companies monitor, document, and certify the elements of their production processes that lead to quality. To ensure their suppliers deliver high-quality products at competitive costs, companies such as DuPont and General Electric require their suppliers to obtain ISO 9001 certification. ISO 9001 certification has become a necessary condition for competing in the global marketplace.

Companies are also using quality management and measurement practices to find cost-effective ways to reduce the environmental and economic costs of air pollution, wastewater, oil spills, and hazardous waste disposal. ISO 14000, also developed by the International Organization for Standardization, is a set of standards designed to encourage organizations to develop (1) environmental management systems to reduce environmental costs and (2) environmental auditing and performance-evaluation systems to review and monitor their progress toward their environmental goals. Quality and environmental issues came together in a major way when British Petroleum's Deepwater Horizon platform exploded in the Gulf of Mexico in 2010 while drilling for oil. Eleven workers died as a result of the explosion, and over the course of approximately 3 months, nearly 5 million gallons of oil spilled out into the Gulf, causing an environmental catastrophe.

Product quality can also be an important engine for environmental progress. For example, Stonyfield Farm, the world's leading organic yogurt company, provides high-quality, all-natural products while educating customers and suppliers about sustainable farming and protecting the environment. As Stonyfield Farm transitioned to organic production, it developed quality control capabilities, performing more than 900 quality checks daily to ensure that its yogurt justified the higher costs of organic milk, fruit, and sugar. Automated systems accomplish quality compliance electronically. Plant processes are interlocked so elements of production cannot move forward unless the product passes inspection at every stage of the process. The quality focus has allowed Stonyfield to grow at over 20% annually for two decades, while its use of organic ingredients has kept more than 180,000 farm acres free of pesticides and chemical fertilizers.

In this chapter, we focus on two key aspects of quality: design quality and conformance quality. **Design quality** refers to how closely the characteristics of a product or service meet the needs and wants of customers. **Conformance quality** is the performance of a product or service relative to its design and product specifications. Apple Inc. has built a reputation for design quality by developing innovative products such as the iPod, iPhone, and iPad that have uniquely met customers' music, telephone, entertainment, and business needs. Apple's products have also generally had excellent conformance quality; rarely do the products fail to do what they are supposed to do. In the case of the MacBook, however, reports of sticky keyboards were an example of good design quality but poor conformance quality because the narrower profile of butterfly keyboards and the resulting thinner laptops were features desired by customers but the keyboards themselves did not perform according to their specifications. The following diagram illustrates that actual performance can fall short of customer satisfaction because of design-quality failure or because of conformance-quality failure.

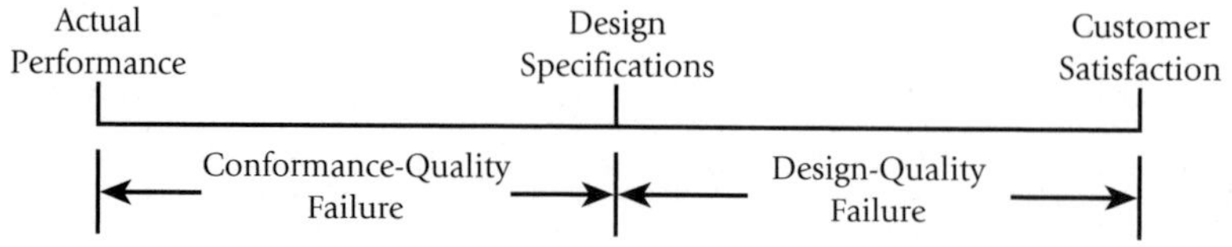

We illustrate the issues in managing quality—computing the costs of quality, identifying quality problems, and taking actions to improve quality—using Formrob Corporation. While Formrob makes many products, we focus only on Formrob's 3D printers, which earned an operating income of $24 million on revenues of $300 million (from sales of 20,000 3D printers) in 2019.

Quality has both financial and nonfinancial components relating to customer satisfaction, improving internal quality processes, reducing defects, and the training and empowering of workers. To provide some structure, we discuss quality from the four perspectives of the balanced scorecard: financial, in the next section, and customer, internal-business-process, and learning-and-growth in the following section.

The Financial Perspective: The Costs of Quality

Financial measures include measures affected by quality, such as revenues. The most direct and comprehensive financial measure of quality is called *costs of quality*. The **costs of quality (COQ)** are the costs incurred to prevent the production of a low-quality product or the costs arising as a result of such products. These costs are classified into the following four categories. Examples for each category are listed in Exhibit 20-1.

1. **Prevention costs**—costs incurred to prevent the production of products that do not conform to specifications
2. **Appraisal costs**—costs incurred to detect which individual units of products do not conform to specifications
3. **Internal failure costs**—costs incurred on defective products *before* they are shipped to customers
4. **External failure costs**—costs of defective products *after* they have been shipped to customers

The costs in Exhibit 20-1 arise in all business functions of the value chain, and they are broader than the internal failure costs of spoilage, rework, and scrap described in Chapter 19.

Formrob determines the COQ of its 3D printers by adapting the seven-step activity-based costing approach described in Chapter 5.

Step 1: Identify the Chosen Cost Object. The cost object is the quality of the 3D printer that Formrob made and sold in 2019. Formrob's goal is to calculate the total costs of quality of these 20,000 machines.

Step 2: Identify the Direct Costs of Quality of the Product. The 3D printers have no direct costs of quality because no resources, such as inspection or repair workers, are dedicated to managing the quality of the 3D printers.

Step 3: Select the Activities and Cost-Allocation Bases to Use for Allocating the Indirect Costs of Quality to the Product. Column 1 of Exhibit 20-2, Panel A, classifies the activities that contribute to prevention, appraisal, and internal and external failure costs of quality at Formrob

EXHIBIT 20-1 Items Pertaining to Costs-of-Quality Reports

Prevention Costs	Appraisal Costs	Internal Failure Costs	External Failure Costs
Design engineering Process engineering Supplier evaluations Preventive equipment maintenance Quality training Testing of new materials	Inspection Online product manufacturing and process inspection Product testing	Spoilage Rework Scrap Machine repairs Manufacturing/ process engineering on internal failures	Customer support Manufacturing/ process engineering for external failures Warranty repair costs Liability claims

EXHIBIT 20-2 Analysis of Activity-Based Costs of Quality (COQ) for 3D Printers at Formrob Corporation

Home Insert Page Layout Formulas Data Review View

	A	B	C	D	E	F	G
1	**PANEL A: ACCOUNTING COQ REPORT**						**Percentage of**
2		**Cost Allocation**		**Quantity of Cost**		**Total**	**Revenues**
3	**Cost of Quality and Value-Chain Category**	**Rate[a]**		**Allocation Base**		**Costs**	**(5) = (4) ÷**
4	**(1)**	**(2)**		**(3)**		**(4) = (2) × (3)**	**$300,000,000**
5	*Prevention costs*						
6	Design engineering (R&D/Design)	$ 80	per hour	40,000	hours	$ 3,200,000	1.1%
7	Process engineering (R&D/Design)	$ 60	per hour	45,000	hours	2,700,000	0.9%
8	Total prevention costs					5,900,000	2.0%
9	*Appraisal costs*						
10	Inspection (Manufacturing)	$ 40	per hour	240,000	hours	9,600,000	3.2%
11	Total appraisal costs					9,600,000	3.2%
12	*Internal failure costs*						
13	Rework (Manufacturing)	$100	per hour	100,000	hours	10,000,000	3.3%
14	Total internal failure costs					10,000,000	3.3%
15	*External failure costs*						
16	Customer support (Marketing)	$ 50	per hour	12,000	hours	600,000	0.2%
17	Transportation (Distribution)	$240	per load	3,000	loads	720,000	0.2%
18	Warranty repair (Customer service)	$110	per hour	120,000	hours	13,200,000	4.4%
19	Total external failure costs					14,520,000	4.8%
20	Total costs of quality					$40,020,000	13.3%
21							
22	[a]Calculations not shown.						
23							
24	**PANEL B: OPPORTUNITY COST ANALYSIS**						
25						**Total Estimated**	**Percentage**
26						**Contribution**	**of Revenues**
27	**Cost of Quality Category**					**Margin Lost**	**(3) = (2) ÷**
28	**(1)**					**(2)**	**$300,000,000**
29	*External failure costs*						
30	Estimated forgone contribution margin						
31	and income on lost sales					$12,000,000[b]	4.0%
32	Total external failure costs					$12,000,000	4.0%
33							
34	[b]Calculated as total revenues minus all variable costs (whether output-unit, batch, product-sustaining, or facility-sustaining) on						
35	lost sales in 2019. If poor quality causes Photon to lose sales in subsequent years as well, the opportunity costs will be						
36	even greater.						

Corporation and the business functions of the value chain where these costs occur. For example, the quality-inspection activity results in appraisal costs and occurs in the manufacturing function. Formrob identifies the total number of inspection-hours (across all products) as the cost-allocation base for the inspection activity. (To avoid details not needed to explain the concepts here, we do not show the total quantities of each cost-allocation base.)

Step 4: Identify the Indirect Costs of Quality Associated with Each Cost-Allocation Base. These are the total costs (variable and fixed) identified with each of the costs-of-quality activities, such as inspections, across all of Formrob's products. (To avoid details not needed to understand the points described here, we do not present these total costs.)

Step 5: Compute the Rate per Unit of Each Cost-Allocation Base. For each activity, the total costs (identified in Step 4) are divided by the total quantity of the cost-allocation base (calculated in Step 3) to compute the rate per unit of each cost-allocation base. Column 2 in Exhibit 20-2, Panel A, shows these rates (without supporting calculations).

Step 6: Compute the Indirect Costs of Quality Allocated to the Product. The indirect costs of quality of the 3D printers, shown in Exhibit 20-2, Panel A, column 4, equal the cost-allocation rate from Step 5 (column 2) multiplied by the total quantity of the cost-allocation base used by the 3D printers for each activity (column 3). For example, the inspection costs for the 3D printers are $9,600,000 ($40 per hour × 240,000 inspection-hours).

Step 7: Compute the Total Costs of Quality by Adding All Direct and Indirect Costs of Quality Assigned to the Product. Formrob's total costs of quality in the COQ report for 3D printers is $40.02 million (Exhibit 20-2, Panel A, column 4), or 13.3% of current revenues (column 5).

As we have seen in Chapter 12, opportunity costs are not recorded in financial accounting systems. Yet an important component of costs of quality is the opportunity cost of the contribution margin and income forgone from lost sales, lost production, and lower prices resulting from poor design and conformance quality. Formrob's market research department estimates that design and conformance quality problems experienced by some customers resulted in lost sales of 2,000 3D printers in 2019 and forgone contribution margin and operating income of $12 million (Exhibit 20-2, Panel B). The total costs of quality, including opportunity costs, therefore, equal $52.02 million ($40.02 million recorded in the accounting system and shown in Panel A plus $12 million of opportunity costs shown in Panel B), or 17.3% of current revenues. Opportunity costs account for 23.1% ($12 million ÷ $52.02 million) of Formrob's total costs of quality.

We turn next to the leading indicators of the costs of quality, the nonfinancial quality measures for Formrob's 3D printers.

DECISION POINT

What are the four cost categories of a costs-of-quality program?

20-1 TRY IT!

Costs-of-Quality Analysis

Benson Company makes tables for the outdoors. The company has been working on improving quality over the last year and wants to evaluate how well it has done on costs-of-quality (COQ) measures. Here are the results:

Annual COQ Report, Benson Company

	2019	2020
Process engineering	$ 11,000	$ 9,500
Scrap	$ 19,000	$ 10,300
Warranty repair costs	$ 17,350	$ 17,450
Design engineering	$ 7,850	$ 10,450
Inspection	$ 4,000	$ 7,800
Rework	$ 20,340	$ 12,340
Total COQ	$ 79,540	$ 67,840
Total Revenue	$ 900,000	$1,050,000

1. Identify the COQ category (prevention, appraisal, internal failure, and external failure) for each of these costs.
2. Prepare a COQ Report by calculating the costs of quality for each category and the ratio of each COQ category to revenues and total quality costs.

Using Nonfinancial Measures to Evaluate and Improve Quality

Companies such as Unilever, FedEx, and U-Haul use nonfinancial measures to manage quality. The first step is to look at quality through the eyes of customers. Managers then turn their attention inward toward their organizations to develop processes that help improve quality and corporate cultures that help sustain it.

LEARNING OBJECTIVE 2

Develop nonfinancial measures

...customer satisfaction measures such as number of customer complaints, internal-business-process measures such as percentage of defective and reworked products, and learning-and-growth measures such as employee empowerment and training

and methods to improve quality

...control charts, Pareto diagrams, and cause-and-effect diagrams

The Customer Perspective: Nonfinancial Measures of Customer Satisfaction

Formrob's managers track the following measures of customer satisfaction:

- Market research information on customer preferences for and customer satisfaction with specific product features (as measures of design quality)
- Market share
- Percentage of highly satisfied customers
- Number of defective units shipped to customers as a percentage of total units shipped
- Number of customer complaints (Companies estimate that for every customer who actually complains, there are 10 to 20 others who have had bad experiences with the product or service but did not complain.)
- Percentage of products that fail soon after they have been delivered to customers
- Average delivery delays (difference between the scheduled delivery date and the date requested by the customer)
- On-time delivery rate (percentage of shipments delivered on or before the scheduled delivery date)

Formrob's managers monitor these numbers over time. Higher customer satisfaction should lead to lower external failure costs, lower costs of quality, and higher future revenues due to greater customer retention, loyalty, and positive word-of-mouth advertising. Lower customer satisfaction is indicative of higher future external failure costs and costs of quality. We next discuss internal business processes to identify and analyze quality problems that help to improve quality and increase customer satisfaction.

The Internal-Business-Process Perspective: Analyzing Quality Problems and Improving Quality

We present three techniques for identifying and analyzing quality problems: control charts, Pareto diagrams, and cause-and-effect diagrams.

Control Charts

Statistical quality control (SQC), also called statistical process control, is a formal means of distinguishing between random and nonrandom variations in an operating process. Random variations occur, for example, when chance fluctuations in the speed of equipment cause defective products to be produced, such as 3D printers that produce objects that have small holes in them or objects with uneven color. Nonrandom variations occur when defective products are produced as a result of a systematic problem such as an incorrect speed setting, a flawed part design, or the mishandling of a component part. A **control chart**, an important SQC tool, is a graph of a series of successive observations of a particular step, procedure, or operation taken at regular intervals of time. Each observation is plotted relative to specified ranges that represent the limits within which observations are expected to fall when caused by random events. Observations that fall outside the ranges are regarded as nonrandom and worth investigating.

Exhibit 20-3 presents control charts for the daily defect rates (defective 3D printers divided by the total number of 3D printers produced) at Formrob's three 3D printer production lines. The defect rates in the prior 60 days for each production line provide a basis upon which to calculate the distribution of daily defect rates. The arithmetic mean (μ, read as "mu") and standard deviation (σ, read as "sigma," how much an observation deviates from the mean) are the two parameters of the distribution that are used in the control charts in Exhibit 20-3. On the basis of experience, the company decides that managers should investigate any observation outside the $\mu \pm 2\sigma$ range. For example, if the average defect rate is $\mu = 10\%$ or 0.1, and the standard deviation is $\sigma = 2\%$ or 0.02, the company will investigate all observations when the defect rate is greater than 14% $[10\% + (2 \times 2\%)]$ or less than 6% $[10\% - (2 \times 2\%)]$.[2]

[2] Companies such as General Electric, Honeywell, and Motorola aim to set both μ and σ sufficiently low that they can use a control limit of $\mu \pm 6\sigma$^. The implication of controlling a process at this "Six Sigma" level is that the process produces only 3.4 defects per million products produced.

EXHIBIT 20-3 Statistical Quality Control Charts: Daily Defect Rate for 3D Printers at Formrob Corporation

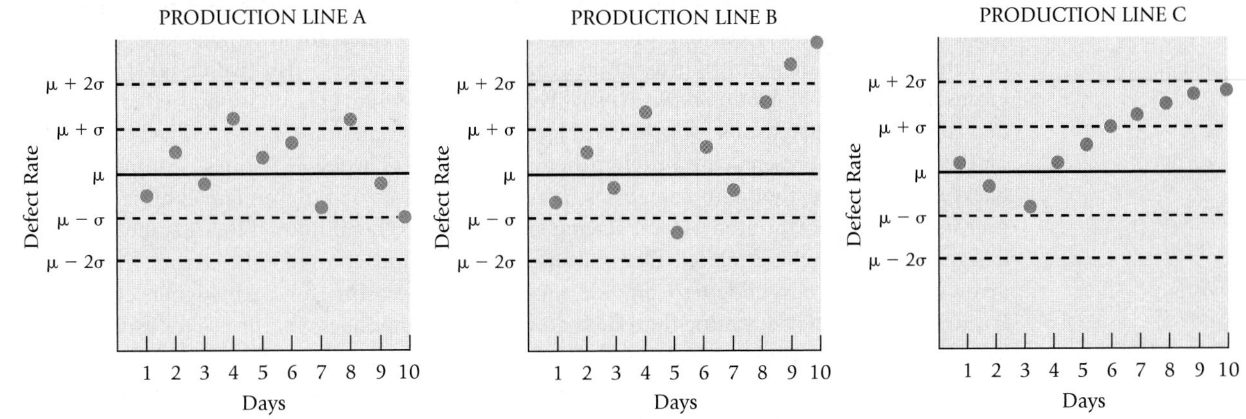

For production line A, all observations are within the range of $\mu \pm 2\sigma$, so managers believe no investigation is necessary. For production line B, the last two observations signal that a higher-than-expected percentage of 3D printers are not performing as they should, indicating that the problem is probably because of a nonrandom, out-of-control occurrence such as an incorrect speed setting or mishandling of a component part. Given the $\pm\ 2\sigma$ rule, both observations would be investigated. Production line C illustrates a process that would not prompt an investigation under the $\pm\ 2\sigma$ rule but that may well be out of control. Why? Because the last eight observations show a clear pattern: Over the last 7 days, the percentage of defective 3D printers increased and got further and further away from the mean. The pattern could be due to, for example, the tooling on a machine wearing out, resulting in poorly machined parts. As the tooling deteriorates further, the trend in producing defective 3D printers is likely to persist; the defect rate is expected to move beyond the random range. Statistical procedures have been developed using the trend as well as the variation to evaluate whether a process is out of control.

Pareto Diagrams

Observations outside control limits serve as inputs for Pareto diagrams. A **Pareto diagram** is a chart that indicates how frequently each type of defect occurs, ordered from the most frequent to the least frequent. Exhibit 20-4 presents a Pareto diagram of quality problems for all observations outside the control limits at the final inspection point in 2019. 3D printers that produce printed objects that have small holes in them are the most frequently recurring problem. They result in high rework costs, high warranty and repair costs, and low customer satisfaction.

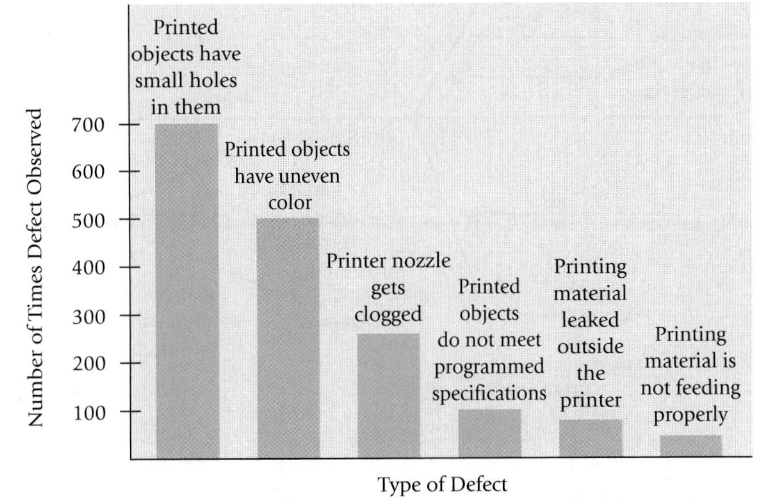

EXHIBIT 20-4

Pareto Diagram for 3D Printers at Formrob Corporation

Cause-and-Effect Diagrams

The most frequently recurring and costly problems identified by the Pareto diagram are analyzed using cause-and-effect diagrams. A **cause-and-effect diagram** identifies potential causes of defects using a diagram that resembles the bone structure of a fish (which is why the diagrams are also called *fishbone diagrams*).[3] Exhibit 20-5 presents the cause-and-effect diagram describing potential reasons for printed objects that have small holes in them. The "backbone" of the diagram represents the problem being examined. The large "bones" coming off the backbone represent the main categories of potential causes of failure. The exhibit identifies four main causes for printed objects having small holes in them: human factors, methods and design factors, machine-related factors, and materials and components factors. Additional arrows, or bones, are added to provide more detailed reasons for each higher-level cause. Formrob's engineers determine that the materials and components factor is a plausible reason for the printed objects to have small holes in them and that two potential causes of the material and component problems are incorrect component specifications and variations of the purchased components from the specifications. The engineers quickly determine that Formrob's component specifications are correct. They then begin to explore reasons for variations in the purchased components. They discover that the aluminum frame (which holds in place various components of the 3D printer such as the printing bed, extruders, and motor) is mishandled and fractionally bent while being transported from the manufacturer to the shop floor. The resulting misalignment of components causes printed objects to have small holes in them.

Manufacturers use automated equipment and computers to record the number and types of defects and the operating parameters when defects occur. Using these inputs, computer programs simultaneously and iteratively prepare control charts, Pareto diagrams, and cause-and-effect diagrams with the goal of continuously reducing the mean defect rate, μ, and the standard deviation, σ.

Nonfinancial Measures of Internal-Business-Process Quality

Companies routinely use nonfinancial measures to track the quality improvements they are making. Formrob's managers use the following nonfinancial measures of internal-business-process quality:

- Percentage of defective products manufactured
- Percentage of reworked products
- Number of different types of defects analyzed using control charts, Pareto diagrams, and cause-and-effect diagrams
- Number of design and process changes made to improve design quality or reduce the costs of quality

EXHIBIT 20-5

Cause-and-Effect Diagram for Printed Objects Having Small Holes in Them at Formrob Corporation

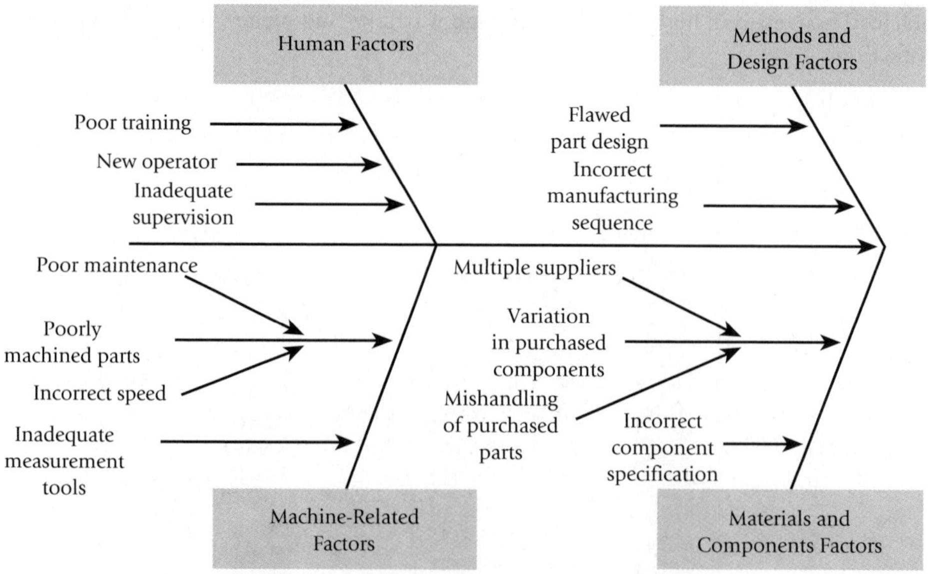

[3] See Timothy J. Clark, "Getting the Most from Cause-and-Effect Diagrams," *Quality Progress* 33:6 (June 2000).

Formrob's managers believe that improving these measures will lead to greater customer satisfaction, lower costs of quality, and better financial performance.

The Learning-and-Growth Perspective: Quality Improvements

What are the learning-and-growth drivers that improve internal-business-process quality? Formrob's managers identify the following drivers: (1) recruiting outstanding design engineers, (2) training employees in quality management techniques, (3) lowering employee turnover, (4) increasing employee empowerment and satisfaction, and (5) creating a quality-first culture of identifying and eliminating the root causes of defects. Formrob measures the following factors in the learning-and-growth perspective in the balanced scorecard:

- Experience and qualifications of design engineers
- Employee training (percentage of employees trained in different quality-enhancing methods)
- Employee turnover (ratio of number of employees who leave the company to the average total number of employees)
- Employee empowerment (ratio of the number of processes in which employees have the authority to make decisions without consulting supervisors to the total number of processes)
- Employee satisfaction (ratio of employees indicating high satisfaction to the total number of employees surveyed)

DECISION POINT

What nonfinancial measures and methods can managers use to improve quality?

Weighing the Costs and Benefits of Improving Quality

LEARNING OBJECTIVE 3

Use costs-of-quality measures to make decisions

...identify relevant incremental costs and benefits and opportunity costs to evaluate tradeoffs

Recall from the analysis of the cause-and-effect diagram that mishandling of the aluminum frame during transportation from a supplier's warehouse to Formrob's warehouse and then to the production line results in printed objects that have small holes in them. The frame must meet very precise specifications or else the 3D printer components (such as the printing bed, extruders, and motor) will not align exactly on the frame.

A team of engineers offers two solutions: (1) electronically inspect and test the frames before production starts or (2) redesign and strengthen the frames and their shipping containers to withstand mishandling during transportation. The cost structure of the costs of quality for 2020 is expected to be the same as the cost structure for 2019 presented in Exhibit 20-2.

To evaluate each alternative versus the status quo, managers focus on the relevant costs and benefits for each solution in 2020. *How will total costs and total revenues change under each alternative*? The relevant-cost and relevant-revenue analysis ignores all allocated costs (see Chapter 12).

Formrob uses a 1-year time horizon (2020) for the analysis because it plans to introduce a completely new line of 3D printers at the end of 2020. The new line is so different that the choice of either the inspection or the redesign alternative will have no effect on the sales of 3D printers in future years.

Exhibit 20-6 shows the relevant costs and benefits for each alternative.

1. **Estimated incremental costs:** \$400,000 for the inspection alternative; \$660,000 for the redesign alternative (\$300,000 for process engineering, \$160,000 for design engineering, and \$200,000 for the frames).
2. **Cost savings from lower rework, customer support, and repairs:** Exhibit 20-6, line 10, shows that reducing rework saves \$40 per hour of rework. However, Exhibit 20-2, Panel A, column 2, line 13, shows that the total rework cost per hour is \$100, not \$40. Why the difference? Because as it improves quality, Formrob will save only the \$40 variable cost per rework-hour, not the \$60 in fixed cost per rework-hour. Exhibit 20-6, line 10, shows Formrob will save a total of \$960,000 (\$40 per hour × 24,000 rework-hours saved) if it inspects the frames versus \$1,280,000 (\$40 per rework-hour × 32,000 rework-hours saved) if it redesigns the frames. Exhibit 20-6 also shows Formrob's expected variable-cost savings for customer support (line 11), transportation (line 12), and warranty repair (line 13) for the two alternatives.

EXHIBIT 20-6 Estimated Effects of Quality-Improvement Actions on Costs of Quality for 3D Printers at Formrob Corporation

Home Insert Page Layout Formulas Data Review View

	A	B	C	D	E	F	G	H	I	J
1				Relevant Costs and Benefits of						
2				Further Inspecting Incoming Frames				Redesigning Frames		
3	Relevant Items	Relevant Benefit per Unit		Quantity		Total Benefits		Quantity		Total Benefits
4	(1)	(2)		(3)		(4)		(5)		(6)
5	Additional inspection and testing costs					$ (400,000)				
6	Additional process engineering costs									$ (300,000)
7	Additional design engineering costs									(160,000)
8	Additional cost of frames $10 per frame × 20,000 frames									(200,000)
9						(2) × (3)				(2) × (5)
10	Savings in rework costs	$ 40	per hour	24,000	hours	960,000		32,000	hours	1,280,000
11	Savings in customer-support costs	$ 20	per hour	2,000	hours	40,000		2,800	hours	56,000
12	Savings in transportation costs for repair parts	$ 180	per load	500	loads	90,000		700	loads	126,000
13	Savings in warranty repair costs	$ 45	per hour	20,000	hours	900,000		28,000	hours	1,260,000
14	Total contribution margin from additional sales	$6,000	per copier	250	copiers	1,500,000		300	copiers	1,800,000
15										
16	Net cost savings and additional contribution margin					$3,090,000				$3,862,000
17										
18	Difference in favor of redesigning frames (J16) – (F16)						$772,000			

3. **Increased contribution margin from higher sales as a result of building a reputation for quality and performance:** Exhibit 20-6, line 14, shows $1,500,000 in higher contribution margins from selling 250 more 3D printers under the inspection alternative and $1,800,000 in higher contribution margins from selling 300 more 3D printers under the redesign alternative. Management should always look for opportunities to generate higher revenues, not just cost reductions, from quality improvements.

Exhibit 20-6 shows that both the inspection and the redesign alternatives yield net benefits relative to the status quo. However, consistent with value engineering, design for manufacturing, and Kaizen or continuous improvement that emphasize eliminating the root causes of defects, Formrob expects the net benefits from the redesign alternative to be $772,000 greater than the inspection alternative. Toyota has a similar philosophy emphasizing defect prevention ("front of the pipe solutions") over defect inspection ("back of the pipe solutions").

Note how quality improvements affect the costs of quality. Redesigning the frame increases Formrob's prevention costs (the costs of process engineering, design engineering, and the cost of the frames themselves), but decreases the firm's internal failure costs (rework) and external failure costs (customer-support costs, transportation costs, and warranty repairs). Improving quality also results in greater sales and higher contribution margins. COQ reports provide insight into quality improvements, allowing managers to compare trends over time. In successful quality programs, costs of quality and, in particular, internal and external failure costs as a percentage of revenues decrease over time. Many companies, such as Hewlett-Packard, go further and believe they should eliminate all failure costs and have zero defects.

DECISION POINT

How do managers identify the relevant costs and benefits of quality-improvement programs?

TRY IT! 20-2

Quality Improvement, Relevant Costs, Relevant Revenues

Cell Glam produces cell phone covers for all makes and models of cell phones. Cell Glam sells 1,020,000 units each year at a price of $8 per unit and a contribution margin of 20%.

A survey of Cell Glam customers over the past 12 months indicates that customers were very satisfied with the products but a number of customers were disappointed because the products they purchased did not fit their phones. The customers then had to hassle with returns and replacements.

Cell Glam's managers want to modify their production processes to develop products that more closely match Cell Glam's specifications because the quality control in place to prevent poor-quality products from reaching customers is not working very well.

The current costs of quality are as follows:

Prevention costs	$220,000
Appraisal costs	$ 50,000
Internal failure costs	
Rework	$440,000
Scrap	$ 20,000
External failure costs	
Product replacements	$319,000
Lost sales from customer returns	$800,000

The QC manager and controller have forecast the following additional costs to modify the production process:

CAD design improvement	$140,000
Machine calibration improvement to meet specifications	$140,250

If the improvements result in a 30% decrease in product replacement cost and a 50% decrease in customer returns, what is the impact on the overall COQ and the company's operating income? What should Cell Glam do? Explain.

Evaluating a Company's Quality Performance

LEARNING OBJECTIVE 4

Use financial and nonfinancial measures to evaluate quality

...nonfinancial measures are leading indicators of future costs of quality

To evaluate the firm's quality performance, Formrob's managers use both financial (COQ) and nonfinancial measures. That's because each measure offers different advantages.

Advantages of COQ Measures

- COQ measures focus managerial attention on the effects of poor quality on operating income.
- Total costs of quality help managers evaluate the costs and benefits of incurring prevention and appraisal costs to eliminate internal and external failure costs.
- COQ measures assist in problem solving by comparing costs and benefits of different quality-improvement programs and by setting priorities for cost reduction.

Advantages of Nonfinancial Measures of Quality

- Nonfinancial measures of quality are often easy to quantify and understand.
- Nonfinancial measures direct attention to physical processes that help managers identify the precise problem areas that need improvement.
- Nonfinancial measures such as number of defects provide immediate short-run feedback on whether quality-improvement efforts are succeeding.
- Nonfinancial measures such as measures of customer satisfaction and employee satisfaction are useful indicators of long-run quality performance.

COQ measures and nonfinancial measures complement each other. Without financial quality measures, companies could be spending more money on improving nonfinancial quality measures than the effort is worth. Without nonfinancial quality measures, quality problems might not be identified until it is too late. Most organizations use both types of measures to gauge their quality performance and to evaluate if improvements in nonfinancial quality measures eventually translate to financial gains. McDonald's pays "mystery shoppers" to score individual restaurants on quality, cleanliness, service, and value measures. The company uses these scores to evaluate each restaurant's performance across these dimensions over time and against other restaurants.

DECISION POINT

How do managers use financial and nonfinancial measures to evaluate quality?

Time as a Competitive Tool

LEARNING OBJECTIVE 5

Describe customer-response time

...time between receipt of customer order and product delivery

and on-time performance

...delivery of product at the time it is scheduled

and why delays occur

...uncertainty about the timing of customer orders and limited capacity

In addition to quality, companies increasingly view time as a driver of strategy. For example, Capital One has increased the business on its Web site by promising home-loan approval decisions in 30 minutes or less. Companies such as Amazon and Zara attribute not only higher revenues but also lower costs to doing things faster and on time. These firms claim, for example, that they need to carry fewer inventories because they are able to respond rapidly to customer demands.

Managers need to measure time to manage it properly. In this section, we focus on two *operational measures of time: customer-response time*, which reveals how quickly companies respond to customers' demands for their products and services, and *on-time performance*, which indicates how reliably companies meet their scheduled delivery dates. We also show how managers measure the causes and costs of delays.

Customer-Response Time and On-Time Performance

Customer-response time is the time it takes from the point when a customer places an order for a product or service to the point when the product or service is delivered to the customer. Quickly responding to customers is strategically important in many industries, including the construction, banking, car-rental, and fast-food industries. Some companies, such as Airbus, have to pay penalties to compensate their customers (airline companies) for lost revenues and profits (from being unable to operate flights) as a result of delays in delivering aircraft to them.

Exhibit 20-7 describes the components of customer-response time. *Receipt time* is how long it takes the marketing department to specify to the manufacturing department the exact requirements of the customer's order. **Manufacturing cycle time** (also called **manufacturing lead time**) is how long it takes from the time an order is received by manufacturing to the time a finished good is produced. Manufacturing cycle time is the sum of waiting time and manufacturing time for an order. For example, an aircraft order received by Airbus's manufacturing department may need to wait for components before the plane can be assembled. *Delivery time* is how long it takes to deliver a completed order to a customer.

Some companies evaluate their response time improvement efforts using a measure called **manufacturing cycle efficiency (MCE)**:

$$\text{MCE} = (\text{Value-added manufacturing time} \div \text{Manufacturing cycle time})$$

Value-added manufacturing activities (see Chapter 14) are activities that customers perceive as adding value or utility to a product. The time spent efficiently assembling the product is value-added manufacturing time. The rest of the manufacturing cycle time, such as the time a product spends waiting for parts or for the next stage in the production process or being repaired, is non-value-added manufacturing time. Identifying and minimizing the sources of non-value-added manufacturing time increases a firm's responsiveness to its customers and reduces its costs.

Similar measures apply to service-sector companies. Consider a 40-minute doctor's office visit. Suppose a patient spends 9 of those minutes on administrative tasks such as filling out forms, 20 minutes waiting in the reception area and examination room, and 11 minutes with a nurse or doctor. The service cycle efficiency for this visit equals 11 ÷ 40, or 0.275. In other words, only 27.5% of the 40 minutes added value to the patient/customer. Minimizing

EXHIBIT 20-7

Components of Customer-Response Time

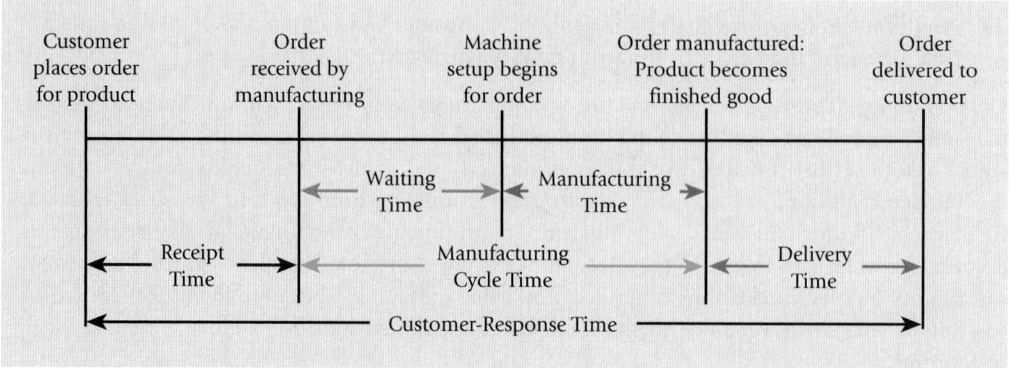

their non-value-added service times has allowed hospitals such as Alle-Kiski Medical Center in Pennsylvania to treat more patients in less time.

On-time performance is the delivery of a product or service by the time it is scheduled to be delivered. Consider FedEx, which specifies a price per package and a next-day delivery time of 10:30 a.m. for its overnight courier service. FedEx measures the on-time performance of the service based on how often the firm meets that standard. Commercial airlines gain loyal passengers as a result of consistent on-time service. But there is a tradeoff between a customer's desire for a shorter response time and better on-time performance. Scheduling longer customer-response times, such as airlines lengthening scheduled arrival times, displeases customers on the one hand but increases customer satisfaction on the other hand by improving the airline's on-time performance.

Time Drivers and Bottlenecks

Managing customer-response time and on-time performance requires managers to understand the causes and costs of delays, for example, at a machine in a manufacturing plant or at a checkout counter in a store. A **time driver** is any factor that causes a change in the speed of an activity when the factor changes. Two time drivers are described below:

1. **Uncertainty about when customers will order products or services.** For example, the more randomly Airbus receives orders for its airplanes, the more likely queues will form and delays will occur.
2. **Bottlenecks due to limited capacity.** A **bottleneck** occurs in an operation when the work to be performed approaches or exceeds the capacity available to do it. For example, a bottleneck results and causes delays when products that must be processed at a particular machine arrive while the machine is being used to process other products. Bottlenecks also occur on the Internet, for example, when many users try to operate wireless mobile devices at the same time (see Concepts in Action: Facebook Works to Overcome Mobile Data Bottlenecks).

Many banks, such as Bank of China; grocery stores, such as Kroger; and entertainment parks, such as Disneyland, actively work to reduce queues and delays to better serve their customers.

Consider again Formrob Corporation, which uses one turning machine to convert steel bars into a heating block for its 3D printers. The heating block is the only product the company makes on the turning machine. Formrob makes and sells the heating blocks as spare parts for its 3D printers after receiving orders from wholesalers. Each order is for 750 heating blocks.

Formrob's managers are examining opportunities to produce and sell other products to increase the firm's profits without sacrificing its short customer-response times. The managers examine these opportunities using the five-step decision-making process introduced in Chapter 1.

1. **Identify the problem and uncertainties.** Formrob's managers are considering introducing a second product, a motor front panel, which will use the same turning machine currently used to make heating blocks. The primary uncertainty is how the introduction of a second product will affect the manufacturing cycle times for heating blocks. (We focus on Formrob's manufacturing cycle time because the receipt time and delivery time for the heating blocks and motor front panels are minimal.)

2. **Obtain information.** Managers gather data on the number of past orders for heating blocks, the time it takes to manufacture them, the available capacity, and their average manufacturing cycle time. Formrob typically receives 30 orders for heating blocks each year, but it could receive 10, 30, or 50 orders. Each order is for 750 units and takes 100 hours of manufacturing time (8 hours of setup time to clean and prepare the machine that makes the heating blocks and 92 hours of processing time). The annual capacity of the machine is 4,000 hours.

3. **Make predictions about the future.** If Formrob only makes heating blocks in 2020, it expects to receive 30 orders of 750 units each requiring 100 hours of manufacturing time. The total amount of manufacturing time required on the machine is 3,000 hours (100 hours per order × 30 orders), which is less than the available machine capacity of 4,000 hours. Queues and delays will still occur because wholesalers can place their orders at any time, while the machine is processing an earlier order.

CONCEPTS IN ACTION

Facebook Works to Overcome Mobile Data Bottlenecks[4]

Wachiwit/Shutterstock

Facebook is the world's largest social networking company. More than 2.6 billion people around the world use its core Facebook, Messenger, Instagram, and WhatsApp services to communicate with each other every month. Forty-seven percent of users globally access Facebook via mobile phones, including 68% in the United States. As a result, Facebook consumes a large amount of mobile data.

Ensuring ample mobile bandwidth is critical to Facebook's success. The more people access Facebook services on their phones, the more they see Facebook ads, which are the company's primary sources of income. But Facebook contends for mobile bandwidth with everything from competing services such as Twitter and WeChat to personal and industrial devices connected as part of the Internet of Things. With data traffic from mobile devices increasing by an estimated 53% per year, the demand for mobile bandwidth is fast outstripping the best efforts of providers like Facebook to supply it.

Aware of this challenge, Facebook actively works behind the scenes to alleviate mobile data bottlenecks that slow the delivery of its content. In recent years, Facebook has deployed various strategies to overcome mobile bottlenecks that affect the delivery of its content:

- Facebook spends billions of dollars annually operating geographically distributed data centers. By 2018, Facebook had nearly 15 million square feet of data center space completed or under construction around the world storing replicas of its data to route queries from mobile devices to the closest server. Content cached at these data centers is what allows viewers to fast-forward video as if the file were stored on a home device.
- Facebook is also experimenting with new ways to improve mobile network access around the world. From testing the use of drones to deploy mobile bandwidth in hard-to-reach places to using high-frequency radio waves to speed up networks in dense urban areas, the company is constantly investing in new technologies to help clear mobile traffic jams and keep the multimedia content (and ads) flowing to its billions of users.

Looking ahead, Facebook will continue to invest in new technologies to help overcome mobile bandwidth bottlenecks, as well as continuously improve the underlying technical infrastructure of its own apps to increase efficiency—for example, by unifying the code used for its WhatsApp, Instagram, and Messenger apps—to help overcome mobile data choke points and meet the ever-growing demand for its services around the world.

[4] *Sources:* Stephen Shankland, "Facebook Takes On Global Internet Bottlenecks," Cnet.com, April 13, 2016 (https://www.cnet.com/news/facebook-tries-to-speed-internet-access-with-aries-and-terragraph/); Jeff Hecht, "The Bandwidth Bottleneck That Is Throttling The Internet," *Nature*, August 10, 2016 (https://www.scientificamerican.com/article/the-bandwidth-bottleneck-that-is-throttling-the-internet/); Artyom Dogtiev, "Facebook Revenue and Usage Statistics (2018)," Business of Apps.com, May 4, 2018 (http://www.businessofapps.com/data/facebook-statistics/); Kaushik Veeraraghaven et al., "Kraken: Leveraging Live Traffic Tests to Identify and Resolve Resource Utilization Bottlenecks in Large Scale Web Services," Facebook, Inc. working paper, November 2016 (https://research.fb.com/wp-content/uploads/2016/11/kraken_leveraging_live_traf_c_tests_to_identify_and_resolve_resource_utilization_bottlenecks_in_large_scale_web_services.pdf); Mike Isaac, "Zuckerberg Plans to Integrate WhatsApp, Instagram and Facebook Messenger," *The New York Times*, January 25, 2019 (https://www.nytimes.com/2019/01/25/technology/facebook-instagram-whatsapp-messenger.html).

Average waiting time, the average amount of time that an order waits in line before the machine is set up and the order is processed, equals[5]

$$\frac{\text{Annual average number of orders for heating blocks} \times \left(\text{Manufacturing time per order for heating blocks}\right)^2}{2 \times \left[\text{Annual machine capacity} - \left(\text{Annual average number of orders for heating blocks} \times \text{Manufacturing time per order for heating blocks}\right)\right]}$$

$$= \frac{30 \times 100^2}{2 \times [4{,}000 - (30 \times 100)]} = \frac{30 \times 10{,}000}{2 \times (4{,}000 - 3{,}000)} = \frac{300{,}000}{2 \times 1{,}000} = \frac{300{,}000}{2{,}000}$$

$$= 150 \text{ hours per order (for heating blocks)}$$

[5] The technical assumptions are (1) that customer orders for the product follow a Poisson distribution with a mean equal to the expected number of orders (30 in our example) and (2) that orders are processed on a first-in, first-out (FIFO) basis. The Poisson arrival pattern for customer orders has been found to be reasonable in many real-world settings. The FIFO assumption can be modified. Under the modified assumptions, the basic queuing and delay effects will still occur, but the precise formulas will be different.

Therefore, the average manufacturing cycle time for an order is 250 hours (150 hours of average waiting time + 100 hours of manufacturing time). Note that manufacturing time per order is a squared term in the numerator. The squared term indicates the disproportionately large impact that manufacturing time has on the waiting time. As the manufacturing time lengthens, there is a much greater chance that the machine will be in use when an order arrives, leading to longer delays. The denominator in this formula is a measure of the unused capacity, or cushion. As the unused capacity becomes smaller, the chance that the machine is processing an earlier order becomes more likely, leading to greater delays.

The formula describes only the *average* waiting time. A particular order might arrive when the machine is free, in which case manufacturing will start immediately. In another situation, Formrob may receive an order while two other orders are waiting to be processed, which means the delay will be longer than 150 hours.

If Formrob makes heating blocks and motor front panels in 2020, it expects to receive the following:

- Heating blocks: 30 orders of 750 units each requiring 100 hours of manufacturing time per order.
- Motor front panels: 10 orders for motor panels of 800 units each requiring 50 hours of manufacturing time per order, composed of 3 hours for setup and 47 hours of processing.
- The expected demand for heating blocks will be unaffected by whether Formrob produces and sells motor front panels.

If Formrob makes both heating blocks and motor panels, the average waiting time *before* the machine setup begins is expected to be as follows (the formula is an extension of the preceding formula for the single-product case):

$$\frac{\left[\begin{array}{c}\text{Annual average number}\\ \text{of orders for heating blocks}\end{array} \times \left(\begin{array}{c}\text{Manufacturing}\\ \text{time per order}\\ \text{for heating blocks}\end{array}\right)^2\right] + \left[\begin{array}{c}\text{Annual average number}\\ \text{of orders for motor panels}\end{array} \times \left(\begin{array}{c}\text{Manufacturing}\\ \text{time per order}\\ \text{for motor panels}\end{array}\right)^2\right]}{2 \times \left[\begin{array}{c}\text{Annual machine}\\ \text{capacity}\end{array} - \left(\begin{array}{c}\text{Annual average number}\\ \text{of orders for heating blocks}\end{array} \times \begin{array}{c}\text{Manufacturing}\\ \text{time per order}\\ \text{for heating blocks}\end{array}\right) - \left(\begin{array}{c}\text{Annual average number}\\ \text{of orders for motor panels}\end{array} \times \begin{array}{c}\text{Manufacturing}\\ \text{time per order}\\ \text{for motor panels}\end{array}\right)\right]}$$

$$= \frac{[30 \times (100)^2] + [10 \times (50)^2]}{2 \times [4{,}000 - (30 \times 100) - (10 \times 50)]} = \frac{(30 \times 10{,}000) + (10 \times 2{,}500)}{2 \times (4{,}000 - 3{,}000 - 500)}$$

$$= \frac{300{,}000 + 25{,}000}{2 \times 500} = \frac{325{,}000}{1{,}000} = 325 \text{ hours per order (for heating blocks and motor panels)}$$

Producing motor panels will cause the average waiting time for an order to more than double, from 150 hours to 325 hours. The waiting time increases because the production of motor panels will cause the machine's unused capacity to shrink, increasing the probability that new orders will arrive while current orders are being manufactured or waiting to be manufactured. The average waiting time is very sensitive to the shrinking of unused capacity.

If Formrob's managers decide to make motor panels as well as heating blocks, the average manufacturing cycle time will be 425 hours for a heating block order (325 hours of average waiting time + 100 hours of manufacturing time) and 375 hours for a motor panel order (325 hours of average waiting time + 50 hours of manufacturing time). A heating block order will, on average, spend 76.5% (325 hours ÷ 425 hours) of its manufacturing cycle time just waiting for its manufacturing to start!

4. **Make decisions by choosing among alternatives.** Should Formrob produce motor panels, given how much it would slow down the manufacturing cycle time for heating blocks? To help the company's managers make a decision, the management accountant identifies and analyzes the relevant revenues and relevant costs of producing motor panels and, in particular, the cost of delays on all products. The next section focuses on this step.

DECISION POINT

What is customer-response time, and what are the reasons for delays?

Relevant Revenues and Costs of Delays

LEARNING OBJECTIVE 6

Determine the costs of delays

. . . lower revenues and higher inventory carrying costs

To determine the relevant revenues and costs of producing motor panels under Step 4, the management accountant prepares the following additional information:

		Average Selling Price per Order If the Average Manufacturing Cycle Time per Order Is			
Product	**Annual Average Number of Orders**	**Less Than 300 Hours**	**More Than 300 Hours**	**Direct Materials Cost per Order**	**Inventory Carrying Cost per Order per Hour**
Heating Blocks	30	$22,000	$21,500	$16,000	$1.00
Motor Panels	10	10,000	9,600	8,000	0.50

Manufacturing cycle times affect both revenues and costs. Revenues are affected because customers are willing to pay a higher price for faster delivery. On the cost side, direct materials costs and inventory carrying costs are the only relevant costs of introducing motor panels (all other costs are unaffected and therefore irrelevant). Inventory carrying costs equal the opportunity costs of the investment tied up in inventory (see Chapter 12, pages 481–482) and the relevant costs of storage, such as space rental, spoilage, deterioration, and materials handling. Usually, companies calculate inventory carrying costs on a per-unit, per-year basis. To simplify the calculations, the management accountant calculates inventory carrying costs on a per-order, per-hour basis. Also, Formrob acquires direct materials at the time the order is received by manufacturing and, therefore, calculates inventory carrying costs for the duration of the manufacturing cycle time.

Exhibit 20-8 presents expected relevant revenues and relevant costs for the "introduce motor panels" and "do not introduce motor panels" alternatives. Based on the analysis, Formrob's managers decide not to introduce motor panels, even though they have a positive contribution margin of $1,600 ($9,600 − $8,000) per order and Formrob has the capacity to make them. If it produces motor panels, Formrob will, on average, use only 3,500 (Heating blocks: 100 hours per order × 30 orders + Motor panels: 50 hours per order × 10 orders) of the available 4,000 machine-hours. So why is Formrob better off not introducing motor panels? *Because of the*

EXHIBIT 20-8

Determining Expected Relevant Revenues and Relevant Costs for Formrob's Decision to Introduce Motor Panels

Relevant Items	Alternative 1: Introduce Motor Panels (1)	Alternative 2: Do Not Introduce Motor Panels (2)	Difference (3) = (1) − (2)
Expected revenues	$741,000[a]	$660,000[b]	$ 81,000
Expected variable costs	560,000[c]	480,000[d]	(80,000)
Expected inventory carrying costs	14,625[e]	7,500[f]	(7,125)
Expected total costs	574,625	487,500	(87,125)
Expected revenues minus expected costs	$166,375	$172,500	$ (6,125)

[a]($21,500 × 30) + ($9,600 × 10) = $741,000; average manufacturing cycle time will be more than 300 hours.

[b]($22,000 × 30) = $660,000; average manufacturing cycle time will be less than 300 hours.

[c]($16,000 × 30) + ($8,000 × 10) = $560,000.

[d]$16,000 × 30 = $480,000.

[e](Average manufacturing cycle time for heating blocks × Carrying cost per order per hour for heating blocks × Expected number of orders for heating blocks) + (Average manufacturing cycle time for motor panels × Carrying cost per order per hour for motor panels × Expected number of orders for motor panels) = (425 × $1.00 × 30) + (375 × $0.50 × 10) = $12,750 + $1,875 = $14,625.

[f]Average manufacturing cycle time for heating blocks × Carrying cost per order per hour for heating blocks × Expected number of orders for heating blocks = 250 × $1.00 × 30 = $7,500.

negative effects that producing them will have on the existing product, heating blocks. The following table presents the *costs of time*, the expected loss in revenues and expected increase in carrying costs as a result of the delays caused by manufacturing motor panels.

	Effect of Increasing Average Manufacturing Cycle Time		
Product	**Expected Loss in Revenues for Heating Blocks (1)**	**Expected Increase in Carrying Costs for All Products (2)**	**Expected Loss in Revenues Plus Expected Increase in Carrying Costs of Introducing Motor Panels**
Heating Blocks	$15,000[a]	$5,250[b]	$20,250
Motor Panels	—	1,875[c]	1,875
Total	$15,000	$7,125	$22,125

[a] ($22,000 − $21,500) per order × 30 expected orders = $15,000.
[b] (425 − 250) hours × $1.00 per order per hour × 30 expected orders = $5,250.
[c] (375 − 0) hours × $0.50 per order per hour × 10 expected orders = $1,875.

Introducing motor panels will cause the average manufacturing cycle time of heating blocks to increase from 250 hours to 425 hours. Longer manufacturing cycle times will increase the inventory carrying costs of heating blocks and decrease heating block revenues (the average manufacturing cycle time for heating blocks will exceed 300 hours, so the average selling price per order will decrease from $22,000 to $21,500). Together with the inventory carrying cost of the motor panels, the expected cost of introducing the motor panels, $22,125, will exceed the expected contribution margin of $16,000 ($1,600 per order × 10 expected orders) from selling motor panels by $6,125 (the difference calculated in Exhibit 20-8).

This example illustrates that when demand uncertainty is high, some unused capacity is desirable.[6] Increasing the capacity of a bottleneck resource reduces manufacturing cycle times and delays. One way to increase capacity is to reduce the time it takes for setups and processing. Another way to increase capacity is to invest in new equipment, such as flexible manufacturing systems that can be programmed to switch quickly from producing one product to producing another. Delays can also be reduced by carefully scheduling production, such as by batching similar jobs together for processing.

DECISION POINT
What are relevant revenues and costs of delays?

20-3 TRY IT!

Waiting Times, Manufacturing Cycle Times, Relevant Revenues, and Relevant Costs

The Sandstone Corporation uses an injection molding machine to make a plastic product, Z39, after receiving firm orders from its customers. Sandstone estimates that it will receive 60 orders for Z39 during the coming year. Each order of Z39 will take 100 hours of machine time. The annual machine capacity is 8,000 hours.

1. Calculate (a) the average amount of time that an order for Z39 will wait in line before it is processed and (b) the average manufacturing cycle time per order for Z39.
2. Sandstone is considering introducing a new product, Y28. The company expects it will receive 30 orders of Y28 in the coming year. Each order of Y28 will take 40 hours of machine time. Assuming the demand for Z39 will not be affected by the introduction of Y28, calculate (a) the average waiting time for an order received and (b) the average manufacturing cycle time per order for each product, if Sandstone introduces Y28.

[6] Other complexities, such as analyzing a network of machines, priority scheduling, and allowing for uncertainty in processing times, are beyond the scope of this text. In these cases, the basic queuing and delay effects persist, but the precise formulas are more complex.

3. Sandstone is debating whether it should introduce Y28. The following table provides information on selling prices, variable costs, and inventory carrying costs for Z39 and Y28:

Product	Annual Average Number of Orders	Selling Price per Order If Average Manufacturing Cycle Time per Order Is Less Than 395 Hours	Selling Price per Order If Average Manufacturing Cycle Time per Order Is More Than 395 Hours	Variable Cost per Order	Inventory Carrying Cost per Order per Hour
Z39	60	$21,000	$20,500	$11,550	$0.70
Y28	30	9,200	6,520	5,520	0.30

Using the average manufacturing cycle times calculated in requirement 2, should Sandstone manufacture and sell Y28?

Balanced Scorecard and Time-Based Measures

LEARNING OBJECTIVE 7

Use financial and nonfinancial measures of time

. . . nonfinancial measures are leading indicators of future financial effects of delays

In this section, we focus on the final step of the five-step decision-making process—**implement the decision, evaluate performance, and learn**—by tracking changes in time-based measures, evaluating and learning whether these changes affect financial performance, and modifying decisions and plans to achieve the company's goals. We use the structure of the balanced scorecard perspectives—financial, customer, internal business processes, and learning and growth—to summarize how financial and nonfinancial measures of time relate to one another, reduce delays, and increase the output of bottleneck operations.

Financial measures

Revenue gains or price increases from fewer delays

Carrying cost of inventories

Customer measures

Customer-response time (the time it takes to fulfill a customer order)

On-time performance (delivering a product or service by the scheduled time)

Internal-business-process measures

Average manufacturing time for key products

Manufacturing cycle efficiency for key processes

Defective units produced at bottleneck operations

Average reduction in setup time and processing time at bottleneck operations

Learning-and-growth measures

Employee satisfaction

Number of employees trained to manage bottlenecks

To see the cause-and-effect linkages across these balanced scorecard perspectives, consider the example of the Bell Group, a designer and manufacturer of equipment for the jewelry industry. A key financial measure is to achieve a higher profit margin on a specific product line. In the customer-measure category, the company sets a goal of a 2-day turnaround time on all orders for the product. To achieve this goal, an internal-business-process measure requires a bottleneck machine to be operated 22 hours per day, 6 days a week. Finally, in the learning-and-growth measures category, the company trains new employees to carry out nonbottleneck operations to free experienced employees to operate the bottleneck machine. The Bell Group's emphasis on time-related measures in its balanced scorecard has allowed the company to substantially increase manufacturing throughput and decrease customer-response times, leading to higher revenues and increased profits.

Managers use both financial and nonfinancial measures to manage the performance of their firms along the time dimension. Nonfinancial measures help managers evaluate how well they have done on goals such as improving manufacturing cycle times and customer-response times. Revenue and cost measures help managers evaluate the financial effects of increases or decreases in nonfinancial measures, such as manufacturing cycle time and customer-response times.

DECISION POINT

What financial and nonfinancial measures of time can managers use in the balanced scorecard?

PROBLEM FOR SELF-STUDY

The Sloan Moving Corporation transports household goods from one city to another within the continental United States. Managers measure quality of service in terms of (1) time required to transport goods, (2) on-time delivery (within 2 days of agreed-upon delivery date), and (3) number of lost or damaged items. Sloan is considering investing in a new scheduling-and-tracking system costing $160,000 per year, which should help it improve performance for items (2) and (3). The following information describes Sloan's current performance and the expected performance if the new system is implemented:

	Current Performance	Expected Future Performance
On-time delivery performance	85%	95%
Variable cost per carton lost or damaged	$ 60	$ 60
Number of cartons lost or damaged per year	3,000 cartons	1,000 cartons

Sloan expects each percentage point increase in on-time performance to increase revenue by $20,000 per year. Sloan's contribution margin percentage is 45%.

1. Should Sloan acquire the new system? Show your calculations.
2. Sloan is very confident about the cost savings from fewer lost or damaged cartons as a result of introducing the new system but unsure about the increase in revenues. Calculate the minimum amount of increase in revenues needed to make it worthwhile for Sloan to invest in the new system.

Solution

1. Additional costs of the new scheduling-and-tracking system are $160,000 per year. Additional annual benefits of the new scheduling-and-tracking system are as follows:

Additional annual revenues from a 10% improvement in on-time performance, from 85% to 95%, $20,000 per 1% × 10 percentage points	$200,000
45% contribution margin from additional annual revenues (0.45 × $200,000)	$ 90,000
Decrease in variable costs per year from fewer cartons lost or damaged [$60 per carton × (3,000 − 1,000) cartons]	120,000
Total additional benefits	$210,000

Because the benefits of $210,000 exceed the costs of $160,000, Sloan should invest in the new system.

2. As long as Sloan earns a contribution margin of $40,000 (to cover incremental costs of $160,000 minus relevant variable-cost savings of $120,000) from additional annual revenues, investing in the new system is beneficial. This contribution margin corresponds to additional revenues of $40,000 ÷ 0.45 = $88,889.

DECISION POINTS

The following question-and-answer format summarizes the chapter's learning objectives. Each decision presents a key question related to a learning objective. The guidelines are the answer to that question.

Decision	Guidelines
1. What are the four cost categories of a costs-of-quality program?	Four cost categories in a costs-of-quality program are prevention costs (costs incurred to prevent the production of products that do not conform to specifications), appraisal costs (costs incurred to detect which of the individual units of products do not conform to specifications), internal failure costs (costs incurred on defective products before they are shipped to customers), and external failure costs (costs incurred on defective products after they are shipped to customers).
2. What nonfinancial measures and methods can managers use to improve quality?	Nonfinancial quality measures managers can use include customer satisfaction measures such as the number of customer complaints and percentage of defective units shipped to customers, internal-business-process measures such as the percentage of defective and reworked products, and learning-and-growth measures such as the percentage of employees trained in and empowered to use quality principles. Three methods to identify quality problems and to improve quality are (a) control charts to distinguish random from nonrandom variations in an operating process; (b) Pareto diagrams to indicate how frequently each type of failure occurs; and (c) cause-and-effect diagrams to identify and respond to potential causes of failure.
3. How do managers identify the relevant costs and benefits of quality-improvement programs?	The relevant costs of quality-improvement programs are the expected incremental costs to implement the program. The relevant benefits are the cost savings and the estimated increase in contribution margin from the higher revenues expected from quality improvements.
4. How do managers use financial and nonfinancial measures to evaluate quality?	Financial measures help managers evaluate the tradeoffs among prevention costs, appraisal costs, and failure costs. Nonfinancial measures identify problem areas that need improvement and serve as indicators of future financial performance.
5. What is customer-response time, and what are the reasons for delays?	Customer-response time is how long it takes from the time a customer places an order for a product or service to the time the product or service is delivered to the customer. Delays occur because of (a) uncertainty about when customers will order products or services and (b) bottlenecks due to limited capacity. Bottlenecks are operations at which the work to be performed approaches or exceeds available capacity.
6. What are relevant revenues and costs of delays?	Relevant revenues and costs of delays include lower revenues as a result of delays and higher inventory carrying costs.
7. What financial and nonfinancial measures of time can managers use in the balanced scorecard?	Examples of financial and nonfinancial measures managers can use in the balanced scorecard to evaluate a company's performance related to time are revenue losses from delays, customer-response time, on-time performance, average manufacturing cycle time, and number of employees trained to manage bottleneck operations.

TERMS TO LEARN

This chapter and the Glossary at the end of the text contain definitions of the following important terms:

appraisal costs **(p. 781)**
average waiting time **(p. 792)**
bottleneck **(p. 791)**
cause-and-effect diagram **(p. 786)**
conformance quality **(p. 780)**
control chart **(p. 784)**
costs of quality (COQ) **(p. 781)**
customer-response time **(p. 790)**
design quality **(p. 780)**
external failure costs **(p. 781)**
internal failure costs **(p. 781)**
manufacturing cycle efficiency (MCE) **(p. 790)**
manufacturing cycle time **(p. 790)**
manufacturing lead time **(p. 790)**
on-time performance **(p. 791)**
Pareto diagram **(p. 785)**
prevention costs **(p. 781)**
quality **(p. 780)**
time driver **(p. 791)**

ASSIGNMENT MATERIAL

Questions

20-1 Describe two benefits of improving quality.
20-2 How does conformance quality differ from design quality? Explain.
20-3 Name two items classified as prevention costs.
20-4 Give two examples of appraisal costs.
20-5 Distinguish between internal failure costs and external failure costs.
20-6 Describe three methods that companies use to identify quality problems.
20-7 "Companies should focus on financial measures of quality because these are the only measures of quality that can be linked to bottom-line performance." Do you agree? Explain.
20-8 Give two examples of nonfinancial measures of customer satisfaction relating to quality.
20-9 Give two examples of nonfinancial measures of internal-business-process quality.
20-10 "When evaluating alternative ways to improve quality, managers need to consider the fully allocated costs of quality." Do you agree? Explain.
20-11 Distinguish between customer-response time and manufacturing cycle time.
20-12 "There is no tradeoff between customer-response time and on-time performance." Do you agree? Explain.
20-13 Give two reasons why delays occur.
20-14 "When evaluating a company's performance on the time dimension, managers should only consider financial measures." Do you agree? Explain.
20-15 What are the advantages of nonfinancial measures of quality?

Multiple-Choice Questions

In partnership with:
BECKER PROFESSIONAL EDUCATION®

20-16 Rector Corporation is examining its quality control program. Which of the following statements is/are correct?

I. Rework costs should be regarded as a cost of quality when the rework is caused by internal failure.
II. Prevention costs are costs that are incurred to prevent the sale and production of defective units.
III. Internal failure costs are costs of failure of machinery on the production line.

1. I, II, and III are correct.
2. II only is correct.
3. I and III only are correct.
4. I only is correct.

Exercises

20-17 Costs of quality. (CMA, adapted) Osborn, Inc., produces cell phone equipment. Amanda Westerly, Osborn's president, implemented a quality-improvement program that has now been in operation for 2 years. The cost report shown here has recently been issued.

Semi-Annual COQ Report, Osborn, Inc. (in thousands)

	6/30/2019	12/31/2019	6/30/2020	12/31/2020
Prevention costs				
Machine maintenance	$ 480	$ 480	$ 440	$ 290
Supplier training	21	90	45	35
Design reviews	30	218	198	196
Total prevention costs	531	788	683	521
Appraisal costs				
Incoming inspections	109	124	89	55
Final testing	327	327	302	202
Total appraisal costs	436	451	391	257
Internal failure costs				
Rework	226	206	166	115
Scrap	127	124	68	65
Total internal failure costs	353	330	234	180
External failure costs				
Warranty repairs	182	89	70	67
Customer returns	594	510	263	186
Total external failure costs	776	599	333	253
Total quality costs	$2,096	$2,168	$1,641	$1,211
Total revenues	$8,220	$9,180	$9,260	$9,050

Required

1. For each period, calculate the ratio of each COQ category to revenues and to total quality costs.
2. Based on the results of requirement 1, would you conclude that Osborn's quality program has been successful? Prepare a short report to present your case.
3. Based on the 2018 survey, Amanda Westerly believed that Osborn had to improve product quality. In making her case to Osborn management, how might Westerly have estimated the opportunity cost of not implementing the quality-improvement program?

20-18 Costs of quality analysis. Teton Company makes chairs for outside living spaces. The company has been working on improving quality over the last year and wants to evaluate how well it has done on costs-of-quality (COQ) measures. Here are the results:

Annual COQ Report, Teton Company

	2019	2020
Supplier evaluation	$ 3,000	$ 5,800
Scrap	7,400	5,800
Warranty repair costs	9,950	7,740
Design engineering	4,050	6,740
Inspection	3,700	5,100
Rework	8,850	5,400
Total COQ	$ 36,950	$ 36,580
Total Revenue	$650,000	$775,000

Required

1. Identify the costs-of-quality category (prevention, appraisal, internal failure, and external failure) for each of these costs.
2. Prepare a COQ report by calculating the costs of quality for each category and the ratio of each COQ category to revenues and total quality costs.
3. Based on the results of requirement 2, would you conclude that Teton's quality program has been successful? Prepare a short report to present your case.

20-19 Costs-of-quality analysis. Safe Travel produces car seats for children from newborn to 2 years old. Safe Travel's only problem with its car seats was stitching in the straps. The problem can usually be detected and repaired during an internal inspection. Inspection costs $5.00 per car seat, and repairs cost $1.00 per car seat. All 200,000 car seats were inspected last year, and 5% were found to have problems with the stitching. Another 1% of the 200,000 car seats had problems with the stitching, but the internal inspection did not discover them. Defective units that were sold and shipped to customers are shipped back to Safe Travel and repaired. Shipping costs are $8.00 per car seat, and repair costs are $1.00 per car seat. Negative publicity will result in a loss of future contribution margin of $100 for each external failure.

Required

1. Identify total costs of quality by category (appraisal, internal failure, and external failure).
2. Safe Travel is concerned with the high up-front cost of inspecting all 200,000 units. Managers are considering an alternative internal inspection plan that will cost only $3.00 per car seat inspected. During the internal inspection, the alternative technique will detect only 3.5% of the 200,000 car seats that have stitching problems. The other 2.5% will be detected after the car seats are sold and shipped. What are the total costs of quality for the alternative technique?
3. What factors other than cost should Safe Travel consider before changing inspection techniques?

20-20 Costs of quality, quality improvement. iCover produces bags for carrying laptop computers. iCover sells 1,000,000 units each year at a price of $20 per unit and a contribution margin of 40%.

To respond to customer complaints, iCover's mangers want to modify the production processes to produce higher-quality products.

The current costs of quality are as follows:

Prevention costs	$400,000
Appraisal costs	$150,000
Internal failure costs	
Rework	$325,000
Scrap	$ 75,000
External failure costs	
Product repair costs	$400,000
Lost sales from customer returns	$650,000

The management accountant has forecast the following additional costs to modify the production process.

Design changes	$125,000
Process engineering	$210,000

Required

1. Which costs-of-quality category are managers focusing on? Why?
2. If the improvements result in a 55% decrease in product repair costs and a 70% decrease in lost sales from customer returns, what is the impact on the overall COQ and the company's operating income? What should iCover do? Explain.
3. Calculate prevention, appraisal, internal failure, and external failure costs as a percentage of total quality costs and as a percentage of sales before and after the change in the production process. Comment briefly on your results.

20-21 Quality improvement, relevant costs, relevant revenues. SpeedPrint manufactures and sells 18,000 high-technology printing presses each year. The variable and fixed costs of rework and repair are as follows:

	Variable Cost	Fixed Cost	Total Cost
Rework cost per hour	$ 79	$115	$194
Repair costs			
Customer support cost per hour	35	55	90
Transportation cost per load	350	115	465
Warranty repair cost per hour	89	150	239

SpeedPrint's current presses have a quality problem that causes variations in the shade of some colors. Its engineers suggest changing a key component in each press. The new component will cost $70 more than the old one. In the next year, however, SpeedPrint expects that with the new component it will (1) save 14,000 hours of rework, (2) save 850 hours of customer support, (3) move 225 fewer loads, (4) save 8,000 hours of warranty repairs, and (5) sell an additional 140 printing presses, for a total contribution margin of $1,680,000. SpeedPrint believes that even as it improves quality, it will not be able to save any of the fixed costs of rework or repair. SpeedPrint uses a 1-year time horizon for this decision because it plans to introduce a new press at the end of the year.

Required

1. Should SpeedPrint change to the new component? Show your calculations.
2. Suppose the estimate of 140 additional printing presses sold is uncertain. What is the minimum number of additional printing presses that SpeedPrint needs to sell to justify adopting the new component?
3. What other factors should managers at SpeedPrint consider when making their decision about changing to a new component?

20-22 Quality improvement, relevant costs, relevant revenues. Bloom Floral offers a special-priced arrangement for holidays and business increases significantly during these specials. Cathy, the owner of Bloom, guarantees customer satisfaction and charges $50 for these arrangement specials.

Bloom receives orders for 1,000 of these arrangement specials for Mother's Day. Typically, 30% of these arrangements have to be reworked by Cathy to assure customer satisfaction. Each rework by Cathy costs approximately $8 per arrangement.

Cathy believes that the rework problem could be significantly reduced if she holds a short training before each special-priced arrangement holiday. The expected cost of this training would be $100 per holiday. Cathy expects this training would reduce sales by 20 arrangements but would reduce Cathy's rework to only 5% of the arrangements.

Required

1. Should Bloom Floral implement Cathy's idea? Show your calculations.
2. What nonfinancial and qualitative factors should Bloom Floral consider in deciding whether to implement the new plan?

20-23 Waiting time. It's a Dog's World (IDW) makes toys for big-breed puppies. IDW's managers have recently learned that they can calculate the average waiting time for an order from the time an order is received till the time manufacturing starts. They have asked for your help and have provided the following information.

Expected number of orders for the product: 3,200

Manufacturing time per order: 5 hours

Annual machine capacity in hours: 18,000

Required

1. Calculate the average waiting time per order.
2. After learning about the average waiting time, IDW's managers are confused. They do not understand why, if annual machine capacity is greater than the average number of orders for the product, there would be any waiting time at all. Write a memo to clarify the situation.
3. The managers have asked for your suggestions on what they can do to minimize or eliminate waiting time. How would you respond?

20-24 Waiting time, service industry. The registration advisors at a small Midwestern college (SMC) help 6,000 students develop their class schedules and register for classes each semester. Each advisor works for 10 hours a day during the registration period. SMC currently has 15 advisors. While advising an individual student can take anywhere from 2 to 30 minutes, it takes an average of 12 minutes per student. During the registration period, the 15 advisors see an average of 500 students a day on a first-come, first-served basis.

Required

1. Using the formula on page 792, calculate how long the average student will have to wait in the advisor's office before being advised.
2. The head of the registration advisors would like to increase the number of students seen each day because at 500 students a day it would take 12 working days to see all of the students. This is a problem because the registration period lasts for only 2 weeks (10 working days). If the advisors could advise 600 students a day, it would take only 2 weeks (10 days). However, the head advisor wants to make sure that the waiting time is not excessive. What would be the average waiting time if 600 students were seen each day?
3. SMC wants to know the effect of reducing the average advising time on the average wait time. If SMC can reduce the average advising time to 10 minutes, what would be the average waiting time if 600 students were seen each day?

20-25 Waiting time, cost considerations, customer satisfaction (continuation of 20-24). Refer to the information presented in Exercise 20-24. The head of the registration advisors at SMC has decided that the advisors must finish their advising in 2 weeks (10 working days) and therefore must advise 600 students a day. However, the average waiting time, given a 12-minute advising period, will result in student complaints, as will reducing the average advising time to 10 minutes. SMC is considering two alternatives:

a. Hire two more advisors for the 2-week (10-working-day) advising period. This will increase the available number of advisors to 17 and therefore lower the average waiting time.
b. Increase the number of days that the advisors will work during the 2-week registration period to 6 days a week. If SMC increases the number of days worked to 6 per week, then the 15 advisors need only see 500 students a day to advise all of the students in 2 weeks.

Required

1. What would the average wait time be under alternative A and under alternative B?
2. If advisors earn $100 per day, which alternative would be cheaper for SMC (assume that if advisors work 6 days in a given workweek, they will be paid time and a half for the sixth day)?
3. From a student satisfaction point of view, which of the two alternatives would be preferred? Why?

20-26 Nonfinancial measures of quality and time. For the past 2 years, Worldwide Cell Phones has been working to improve the quality of its phones. Data for 2019 and 2020 follows (in thousands of phones):

	2019	2020
Cell phones produced and shipped	2,500	10,000
Number of defective units shipped	125	400
Number of customer complaints	190	250
Units reworked before shipping	150	700
Manufacturing cycle time	13 days	14 days
Average customer-response time	28 days	26 days

Required

1. For each year, 2019 and 2020, calculate the following:
   a. Percentage of defective units shipped
   b. Customer complaints as a percentage of units shipped
   c. Percentage of units reworked during production
   d. Manufacturing cycle time as a percentage of total time from order to delivery
2. Referring to the information computed in requirement 1, explain whether Worldwide Cell Phones' quality and timeliness have improved.

20-27 Nonfinancial measures of quality, manufacturing cycle efficiency. (CMA, adapted) Turnkey Manufacturing evaluates the performance of its production managers based on a variety of factors, including cost, quality, and cycle time. The following are nonfinancial measures for quality and time for 2019 and 2020 for its only product:

Nonfinancial Quality Measures	2019	2020
Number of returned goods	500	1,000
Number of defective units reworked	2,500	2,000
Annual hours spent on quality training per employee	36	54
Number of units delivered on time	20,000	34,000

Annual Totals	2019	2020
Units of finished goods shipped	25,000	40,000
Average total hours worked per employee	1,800	1,800

The following information relates to the average amount of time needed to complete an order:

Time to Complete an Order	2019	2020
Wait time		
From customer placing order to order being received by production	14	10
From order received by production to machine being set up for production	9	7
Inspection time	5	3
Process time	4	4
Move time	2	2

Required

1. Compute the manufacturing cycle efficiency for an order for 2019 and 2020.
2. For each year, 2019 and 2020, calculate the following:
   a. Percentage of goods returned
   b. Defective units reworked as a percentage of units shipped
   c. Percentage of on-time deliveries
   d. Percentage of hours spent by each employee on quality training
3. Evaluate management's performance on quality and timeliness in 2019 and 2020.

Problems

20-28 Statistical quality control. Harvest Cereals produces a wide variety of breakfast products. The company's three best-selling breakfast cereals are Double Bran Bits, Honey Wheat Squares, and Sugar King Pops. Each box of a particular type of cereal is required to meet predetermined weight specifications, so that no single box contains more or less cereal than another. The company measures the mean weight per production run to determine whether there are variances over or under the company's specified upper- and lower-level control limits. A production run that falls outside of the specified control limit does not meet quality standards and is investigated further by management to determine the cause of the variance. The three Harvest breakfast cereals had the following weight standards and production run data for the month of March:

Quality Standard: Mean Weight per Production Run		
Double Bran Bits	Honey Wheat Squares	Sugar King Pops
17.97 ounces	14 ounces	16.02 ounces

Actual Mean Weight per Production Run (Ounces)

Production Run	Double Bran Bits	Honey Wheat Squares	Sugar King Pops
1	18.23	14.11	15.83
2	18.14	14.13	16.11
3	18.22	13.98	16.24
4	18.30	13.89	15.69
5	18.10	13.91	15.95
6	18.05	14.01	15.50
7	17.84	13.94	15.86
8	17.66	13.99	16.23
9	17.60	14.03	16.15
10	17.52	13.97	16.60
Standard Deviation	**0.28**	**0.16**	**0.21**

Required

1. Using the $\mu \pm 2\sigma$ rule, what variance investigation decisions would be made?
2. Present control charts for each of the three breakfast cereals for March. What inferences can you draw from the charts?
3. What are the costs of quality in this example?

20-29 Quality improvement, Pareto diagram, cause-and-effect diagram. Pauli's Pizza has recently begun collecting data on the quality of its customer order processing and delivery. Pauli's made 1,800 deliveries during the first quarter of 2020. The following quality data pertain to first-quarter deliveries:

Type of Quality Failure	Quality Failure Incidents, First Quarter 2020
Late delivery	50
Damaged or spoiled product delivered	5
Incorrect order delivered	12
Service complaints by customer of delivery personnel	8
Failure to deliver incidental items with order (drinks, side items, etc.)	18

Required

1. Draw a Pareto diagram of the quality failures experienced by Pauli's Pizza.
2. Give examples of prevention activities that could reduce the failures experienced by Pauli's.
3. Draw a cause-and-effect diagram of possible causes for late deliveries.

20-30 Quality improvement, relevant costs, and relevant revenues. The Brady Corporation sells 375,000 V262 valves to the automobile and truck industry. Brady has a capacity of 210,000 machine-hours and can produce two valves per machine-hour. V262's contribution margin per unit is $9. Brady sells only 375,000 valves because 45,000 valves (12% of the good valves) need to be reworked. It takes one machine-hour to rework two valves, so 22,500 hours of capacity are used in the rework process. Brady's rework costs are $315,000. Rework costs consist of the following:

- Direct materials and direct rework labor (variable costs): $3 per unit
- Fixed costs of equipment, rent, and overhead allocation: $4 per unit

Brady's process designers have developed a modification that would maintain the speed of the process and ensure 100% quality and no rework. The new process would cost $523,000 per year. The following additional information is available:

- The demand for Brady's V262 valves is 440,000 per year.
- The Mason Corporation has asked Brady to supply 19,000 T971 valves (another product) if Brady implements the new design. The contribution margin per T971 valve is $9. Brady can make one T971 valve per machine-hour with 100% quality and no rework.

Required

1. Suppose Brady's designers implement the new design. Should Brady accept Mason's order for 19,000 T971 valves? Show your calculations.
2. Should Brady implement the new design? Show your calculations.
3. What nonfinancial and qualitative factors should Brady consider in deciding whether to implement the new design?

20-31 Quality improvement, relevant costs, and relevant revenues. The Azure Corporation uses multicolor molding to make plastic lamps. The molding operation has a capacity of 220,000 units per year. The demand for lamps is very strong. Azure will be able to sell whatever output quantities it can produce at $35 per lamp.

Azure can start only 220,000 units into production in the molding department because of capacity constraints on the molding machines. If a defective unit is produced at the molding operation, it must be scrapped at a net disposal value of zero. Of the 220,000 units started at the molding operation, 44,000 defective units (20%) are produced. The cost of a defective unit, based on total (fixed and variable) manufacturing costs incurred up to the molding operation, equals $26 per unit, as follows:

Direct materials (variable)	$17 per unit
Direct manufacturing labor, setup labor, and materials-handling labor (variable)	3 per unit
Equipment, rent, and other allocated overhead, including inspection and testing costs on scrapped parts (fixed)	6 per unit
Total	$26 per unit

Azure's designers have determined that adding a different type of material to the existing direct materials would result in no defective units being produced, but it would increase the variable costs by $11 per lamp in the molding department.

Required

1. Should Azure use the new material? Show your calculations.
2. What nonfinancial and qualitative factors should Azure consider in making the decision?

20-32 Waiting times, manufacturing cycle times. The Shipley Corporation uses an injection molding machine to make a plastic product, P25, after receiving firm orders from its customers. Shipley estimates that it will receive 100 orders for P25 during the coming year. Each order of P25 will take 80 hours of machine time. The annual machine capacity is 9,000 hours.

Required

1. Calculate (a) the average amount of time that an order for P25 will wait in line before it is processed and (b) the average manufacturing cycle time per order for P25.
2. Shipley is considering introducing a new product, Q19. The company expects it will receive 25 orders of Q19 in the coming year. Each order of Q19 will take 20 hours of machine time. Assuming the demand for P25 will not be affected by the introduction of Q19, calculate (a) the average waiting time for an order received and (b) the average manufacturing cycle time per order for each product, if Shipley introduces Q19.

20-33 Waiting times, relevant revenues, and relevant costs (continuation of 20-32). Shipley is still debating whether it should introduce Q19. The following table provides information on selling prices, variable costs, and inventory carrying costs for P25 and Q19:

		Selling Price per Order If Average Manufacturing Cycle Time per Order Is			
Product	**Annual Average Number of Orders**	**Less Than 640 Hours**	**More Than 640 Hours**	**Variable Cost per Order**	**Inventory Carrying Cost per Order per Hour**
P25	100	$21,000	$20,500	$11,550	$0.75
Q19	25	8,500	8,000	5,100	0.20

Required

Using the average manufacturing cycle times calculated in Problem 20-32, should Shipley manufacture and sell Q19? Show your calculations and briefly explain your reasoning.

20-34 Manufacturing cycle times, relevant revenues, and relevant costs. The DJ Corporation makes custom specified wire harnesses for the trucking industry only upon receiving firm orders from its customers. DJ has recently purchased a new machine to make two types of wire harnesses, one for Peterbilt and the other for Kenworth. The annual capacity of the new machine is 5,000 hours. The following information is available for next year:

			Selling Price per Order If Average Manufacturing Cycle Time per Order Is			
Customer	**Annual Average Number of Orders**	**Manufacturing Time Required**	**Less Than 200 Hours**	**More Than 200 Hours**	**Variable Cost per Order**	**Inventory Carrying Cost per Order per Hour**
Peterbilt	100	40 hours	$14,000	$13,400	$9,000	$0.50
Kenworth	10	50 hours	12,500	11,960	8,000	0.45

Required

1. Calculate the average manufacturing cycle times per order (a) if DJ manufactures only Peterbilt and (b) if DJ manufactures both Peterbilt and Kenworth.
2. Even though Kenworth has a positive contribution margin, DJ's managers are evaluating whether DJ should (a) make and sell only Peterbilt or (b) make and sell both Peterbilt and Kenworth. Which alternative will maximize DJ's operating income? Show your calculations.
3. What other factors should DJ consider in choosing between the alternatives in requirement 2?

20-35 Quality improvement, relevant costs, relevant revenues. American Electronics manufactures 200,000 55-inch 4K TVs each year. The variable and fixed costs of rework and repair for the TVs are as follows:

		Repair Costs		
	Rework cost per hour	Customer support cost per hour	Transportation cost per load	Warranty repair cost per hour
Variable cost	$ 75	$ 25	$275	$105
Fixed cost	$100	$ 50	$150	$ 75
Total cost	$175	$ 75	$425	$180

American Electronics' 55-inch 4K TVs have a quality problem that causes shadows in the picture. Its engineers suggest changing a key component in each TV. The new component will cost $22 more than the old one. In the next year, however, American Electronics expects that with the new component it will (1) save 10,000 hours of rework, (2) save 1,000 hours of customer support, (3) move 300 fewer loads, (4) save 10,000 hours of warranty repairs, and (5) sell an additional 2,000 4K TVs, for a total additional contribution margin of $2,200,000. American Electronics believes that even as it improves quality, it will not be able to save any of the fixed costs of rework or repair. American Electronics uses a 1-year time horizon for this decision because it plans to introduce a 5K TV at the end of the year.

Required

1. Should American Electronics change to the new component? Show your calculations.
2. Suppose the estimate of 2,000 additional TVs sold is uncertain. What is the minimum number of additional TVs that American Electronics needs to sell to justify adopting the new component?
3. What other factors should managers at American Electronics consider when making their decision about changing to a new component?

20-36 Ethics and quality. Outmark Corporation manufactures computer processors for leading computer makers. Joe Agent is the management accountant for one of Outmark's largest manufacturing plants. His bonus is based on the plant's revenues. The plant's general manager, Chris Levine, has just returned from a meeting at corporate headquarters where quality expectations were outlined for 2020. Chris calls Joe into his office to relay the corporate objective to minimize quality costs and that total quality costs will not exceed 8% of total revenues by plant under any circumstances. Chris asks Joe to provide him with a list of options for meeting corporate headquarters' quality objective. The plant's initial budgeted revenues and quality costs for 2020 are as follows:

Revenues	$8,675,000
Quality costs:	
Inspection of raw materials	$ 1,825
Raw material scrap	25,950
Customer support	37,400
Quality design engineering	83,000
Engineering redesign of failed parts	72,800
Rework of failed parts	64,075
Product inspection	182,125
Warranty repairs	172,850
Quality control training for production staff	80,000

For each processor sold at the current price, the contribution margin is positive. Prior to receiving the new corporate quality objective, Joe had collected information for all of the plant's possible options for improving both product quality and costs of quality. He was planning to introduce the idea of reengineering the manufacturing process at a one-time cost of $135,000, which would decrease product inspection costs by approximately 28% per year and is expected to reduce warranty repairs and customer support by an estimated 46% per year. It would also allow the plant to produce and sell 5% more units.

After seeing the new corporate objective, Joe crunches the numbers again and comes up with another idea. By increasing the cost-of-quality control training for production staff by $35,000 per year, the plant would reduce product inspection costs by 16% annually and reduce warranty repairs and customer support costs by 28% per year as well. However, under this option, the plant wouldn't be able to increase its production and sales.

Required

1. Calculate the ratio of each budgeted costs-of-quality category (prevention, appraisal, internal failure, and external failure) to budgeted revenues for 2020. Are the budgeted total costs of quality as a percentage of budgeted revenues currently less than 8%?
2. Which of the two quality options should Joe propose to the general manager, Chris Levine? Show the impact on quality costs and revenues for the two options: (a) reengineer the manufacturing process for $135,000 and (b) increase quality training expenditure by $35,000 per year. Do the calculations using a 1-year time horizon.
3. Suppose Joe decides not to present the quality training option to Chris. Is Joe's action unethical? Explain.

20-37 Quality improvement. Dover Corporation makes printed cloth in two departments: weaving and printing. Currently, all product first moves through the weaving department and then through the printing department before it is sold to retail distributors for $2,800 per roll. Dover provides the following information:

	Weaving	Printing
Monthly capacity	20,000 rolls	30,000 rolls
Monthly production	19,000 rolls	17,100 rolls
Direct material cost per roll of cloth processed at each operation	$ 1,200	$ 300
Fixed operating costs	$11,400,000	$1,710,000

Dover can start only 20,000 rolls of cloth in the weaving department because of capacity constraints of the weaving machines. Of the 20,000 rolls of cloth started in the weaving department, 1,000 (5%) defective rolls are scrapped at zero net disposal value. The good rolls from the weaving department (called gray cloth) are sent to the printing department. Of the 19,000 good rolls started at the printing operation, 1,900 (10%) defective rolls are scrapped at zero net disposal value. The Dover Corporation's total monthly sales of printed cloth equal the printing department's output.

Required

1. The printing department is considering buying 10,000 additional rolls of gray cloth from an outside supplier at $2,000 per roll, which is much higher than Dover's cost of weaving the roll. The printing department expects that 10% of the rolls obtained from the outside supplier will result in defective products. Should the printing department buy the gray cloth from the outside supplier? Show your calculations.
2. Dover's engineers have developed a method that would lower the printing department's rate of defective products to 6% at the printing operation. Implementing the new method would cost $1,400,000 per month. Should Dover implement the change? Show your calculations.
3. The design engineering team has proposed a modification that would lower the weaving department's rate of defective products to 3%. The modification would cost the company $700,000 per month. Should Dover implement the change? Show your calculations.

Inventory Management, Just-in-Time, and Simplified Costing Methods

21

Suppose you could receive a large quantity discount for a product that you regularly use, but the discount requires you to buy several months' supply of it and make a large up-front payment.

Would you take the quantity discount? Companies face similar decisions because firms pay a price for tying up money in inventory sitting on their shelves or elsewhere. Selecting the right products to sell, understanding customers deeply, and pricing products smartly helps companies keep their inventories low as the following example from Target indicates.

LEARNING OBJECTIVES

1. Identify six categories of costs associated with goods for sale
2. Balance ordering costs with carrying costs using the economic-order-quantity (EOQ) decision model
3. Identify the effect of errors that can arise when using the EOQ decision model and ways to reduce conflicts between the EOQ model and models used for performance evaluation
4. Describe why companies are using just-in-time (JIT) purchasing
5. Distinguish materials requirements planning (MRP) systems from just-in-time (JIT) systems for manufacturing
6. Identify the features and benefits of a just-in-time production system
7. Describe different ways backflush costing can simplify traditional inventory-costing systems
8. Understand the principles of lean accounting

TARGET LEVERAGES THE INTERNET OF THINGS TO RESPOND TO THE CHANGING RETAIL LANDSCAPE[1]

The retail business is changing every day. Customers are no longer seeing a distinction between online and offline shopping, so retailers are reconfiguring how they quickly get products into the hands of customers wherever they are. Many forward-thinking retailers like Target are turning to the Internet of Things (IoT) for help.

The IoT connects computers, networks, and equipment systems that can communicate and share data in real time without human interaction. At Target, stores and warehouses are being equipped with innovative technologies that help the company better track its inventory to avoid in-store stockouts and help fulfill orders from its growing e-commerce business.

For example, Target increasingly uses smart shelves with radio-frequency identification (RFID) chips. When customers purchase a product, updated inventory data is sent to the warehouse. Alerts inform employees when they need to restock shelves and order more product. Because of this technology, Target is able to replenish its inventory more quickly, which reduces the amount of item storage space the company needs while simultaneously keeping shelves stocked and ready for business.

This new approach also allows Target to speed up delivery of online orders by filling them with merchandise from stores close to a customer's home, cutting down on

auremar/Shutterstock

[1] *Sources:* Julianne Slovak, "Target Experiments With Faster Supply Chain," *Forbes,* May 14, 2018 (https://www.forbes.com/sites/julianneslovak/2018/05/14/target-experiments-with-faster-supply-chain/#136a48322a4f); Edwin Lopez, "Why 2018 Is the Year of Modernization for Target," *Supply Chain Dive,* June 4, 2018 (https://www.supplychaindive.com/news/data-target-optimizes-supply-chain-inventory-logic/524971/); Christopher Schroeder, "Retail IoT: How to Streamline Inventory Supply Chains," *Digitalist Magazine,* May 17, 2018 (https://www.digitalistmag.com/digital-supply-networks/2018/05/17/retail-iot-streamline-inventory-supply-chains-06166681).

shipping time and costs. Since its stores are restocked quickly, there are no concerns about not having enough inventory to supply both in-store and online shoppers.

These IoT innovations have had a profound impact on Target's supply chain efficiency, sales, and profitability. RFID-enabled stores have decreased back-room inventories to a fraction of previous levels, reduced stockouts by 40%, and increased sales by 4%. Additionally, during the 2018 holiday season, Target filled nearly 70% of online orders through its retail stores.

Inventory Management in Retail Organizations

LEARNING OBJECTIVE 1

Identify six categories of costs associated with goods for sale

... purchasing, ordering, carrying, stockout, quality, and shrinkage

Inventory management includes planning, coordinating, and controlling activities related to the flow of inventory into, through, and out of an organization. Consider this breakdown of operations for three major retailers for which cost of goods sold constitutes their largest cost item.

	Costco	Kroger	Walmart
Revenues	100.0%	100.0%	100.0%
Deduct costs:			
Cost of goods sold	87.0%	78.3%	74.9%
Selling and administration costs	9.8%	17.5%	20.8%
Other costs, interest, and taxes	1.0%	1.6%	3.0%
Total costs	97.8%	97.4%	98.7%
Net income	2.2%	2.6%	1.3%

The low percentages of net income to revenues mean that improving the purchase and management of goods for sale can cause dramatic percentage increases in net income.

Costs Associated With Goods for Sale

In addition to the costs of the actual goods purchased, there are a number of different types of costs associated with inventory. These costs fall into the following six categories:

1. **Purchasing costs** are the costs of goods acquired from suppliers, including incoming freight costs. These costs usually make up the largest cost category of goods in inventory. Discounts for large purchase-order sizes and faster supplier payment terms reduce purchasing costs.
2. **Ordering costs** are the costs of preparing and issuing purchase orders, receiving and inspecting the items included in the orders, and matching invoices received, purchase orders, and delivery records to make payments. Ordering costs include the cost of obtaining purchase approvals, as well as other special processing costs.
3. **Carrying costs** are costs that arise while goods are being held in inventory. Carrying costs include the opportunity cost of the investment tied up in inventory (see Chapter 12, pages 481–482) and the costs associated with storage, such as space rental, insurance, and obsolescence.
4. **Stockout costs** are costs that arise when a company runs out of a particular item for which there is customer demand, a *stockout*. The company must act quickly to replenish inventory to meet that demand or suffer the costs of not meeting it. A company may respond to a stockout by expediting an order from a supplier, which can be expensive because of additional ordering and manufacturing costs plus any associated transportation costs. Or the company may lose sales due to the stockout. In this case, the opportunity cost of the stockout includes the lost contribution margin on the sale not made plus any contribution margin lost on future sales due to customer ill will.
5. Costs of quality are the costs incurred to prevent and appraise, or that arise as a result of, quality issues. Quality problems arise, for example, because products get spoiled or broken or are mishandled while being moved in and out of the warehouse. There are four

categories of quality costs (also discussed in Chapter 20): prevention costs, appraisal costs, internal failure costs, and external failure costs.

6. **Shrinkage costs** result from theft by outsiders, embezzlement by employees, and misclassification or misplacement of inventory. Shrinkage is measured by the difference between (a) the cost of inventory recorded on the books (after correcting errors) and (b) the cost of inventory when physically counted. Shrinkage can often be an important measure of management performance. Consider, for example, the grocery business, where operating income hovers around 2% of sales. With such small margins, it is easy to see why one of a store manager's prime responsibilities is controlling inventory shrinkage. A \$1,000 increase in shrinkage will erase the operating income from sales of \$50,000 (2% × \$50,000 = \$1,000). Because shrinkage costs generally increase when a firm's inventory increases, most firms try not to hold more inventory than necessary.

Note that not all inventory costs are captured in financial accounting systems. For example, opportunity costs are not recorded in financial accounting systems but are a significant component in several of the inventory cost categories.

Information-gathering technology increases the reliability and timeliness of inventory information and reduces the costs related to inventory. For example, barcoding technology allows a scanner to record individual units purchased and sold. As soon as a unit is scanned, a record of its movement is created, which helps a firm better manage its purchasing, carrying, and stockout costs. In the next several sections, we consider how relevant costs are computed for different inventory-related decisions in merchandising companies.

DECISION POINT

What are the six categories of costs associated with goods for sale?

The Economic-Order-Quantity Decision Model

LEARNING OBJECTIVE 2

Balance ordering costs with carrying costs using the economic-order-quantity (EOQ) decision model

... choose the inventory quantity per order to minimize these costs

How much should a firm order of a given product? The **economic order quantity (EOQ)** is a decision model that calculates the optimal quantity of inventory to order, given the following set of assumptions:

- Under the simplest version of the EOQ model, there are only ordering and carrying costs, the most common costs of inventory.
- The same quantity is ordered at each reorder point.
- Demand, ordering costs, and carrying costs are known with certainty. The **purchase-order lead time**, the time between placing an order and its delivery, is also known with certainty.
- The purchasing cost per unit is unaffected by the order quantity. This assumption makes purchasing costs irrelevant to determining the EOQ because the purchase price is the same, whatever the order size.
- No stockouts occur. The basis for this assumption is that the costs of stockouts are so high that managers maintain adequate inventory to prevent them.
- When deciding on the size of a purchase order, managers consider the costs of quality and shrinkage costs only to the extent that these costs affect ordering or carrying costs.

Note that EOQ analysis ignores purchasing costs, stockout costs, costs of quality, and shrinkage costs. Also recall from Chapter 12 that managers only consider relevant costs when making decisions. In a later section, we will discuss how to identify the relevant ordering and carrying costs. At this point, we simply note that EOQ is the order quantity that minimizes the sum of a company's relevant ordering and carrying costs. The sum of the costs is the firm's *relevant total ordering and carrying cost* of inventory. The relevant total costs are calculated as follows:

$$\text{Relevant total costs} = \text{Relevant ordering costs} + \text{Relevant carrying costs}$$

We use the following notations:

$$D = \text{Demand in units for a specified period (one year in this example)}$$

$$Q = \text{Size of each order (order quantity)}$$

$$\text{Number of purchase orders per period (one year)} = \frac{\text{Demand in units for a period (one year)}}{\text{Size of each order (order quantity)}} = \frac{D}{Q}$$

Average inventory in units $= \frac{Q}{2}$, because each time the inventory goes down to 0, an order for Q units is received. The inventory varies from Q to 0, so the average inventory is $\frac{0 + Q}{2}$.

P = Relevant ordering cost per purchase order

C = Relevant carrying cost of one unit in stock for the time period used for D (one year)

For any order quantity, Q,

$$\text{Annual relevant ordering costs} = \left(\begin{array}{c}\text{Number of}\\ \text{purchase orders}\\ \text{per year}\end{array} \times \begin{array}{c}\text{Relevant ordering}\\ \text{cost per}\\ \text{purchase order}\end{array}\right) = \left(\frac{D}{Q} \times P\right)$$

$$\text{Annual relevant carrying costs} = \left(\begin{array}{c}\text{Average inventory}\\ \text{in units}\end{array} \times \begin{array}{c}\text{Annual}\\ \text{relevant carrying}\\ \text{cost per unit}\end{array}\right) = \left(\frac{Q}{2} \times C\right)$$

$$\text{Annual relevant total costs} = \begin{array}{c}\text{Annual}\\ \text{relevant ordering}\\ \text{costs}\end{array} + \begin{array}{c}\text{Annual}\\ \text{relevant carrying}\\ \text{costs}\end{array} = \left(\frac{D}{Q} \times P\right) + \left(\frac{Q}{2} \times C\right)$$

The order quantity that minimizes annual relevant total costs is

$$EOQ = \sqrt{\frac{2DP}{C}}$$

The EOQ model is solved using calculus, but the key intuition is that relevant total costs are minimized when relevant ordering costs equal relevant carrying costs. If carrying costs are lower (greater) than ordering costs, the total costs can be reduced by increasing (decreasing) the order quantity. To solve for EOQ, we set

$$\left(\frac{Q}{2} \times C\right) = \left(\frac{D}{Q} \times P\right)$$

$$\text{Multiplying both sides by } \frac{2Q}{C}, \text{ we get } Q^2 = \frac{2DP}{C}$$

$$Q = \sqrt{\frac{2DP}{C}}$$

The formula indicates that EOQ increases with higher demand and/or higher ordering costs and decreases with higher carrying costs.

Let's see how EOQ analysis works. Glare Shade sells sunglasses. This problem focuses on Glare Shade's basic sunglasses, UX1. Glare Shade purchases the UX1s from Rytek at $14 a unit. Rytek pays for all incoming freight. No inspection is necessary at Glare Shade because Rytek supplies quality merchandise. Glare Shade's annual demand is 13,000 units of UX1s, at a rate of 250 units per week. Glare Shade requires a 15% annual rate of return on its investment. Relevant ordering cost per purchase order is $200.

The relevant carrying cost per unit per year is as follows:

Required annual return on investment, 0.15 × $14	$2.10
Relevant costs of insurance, materials handling, breakage, shrinkage, and so on, per year	3.10
Total	$5.20

What is the EOQ for ordering UX1 sunglasses?

Substituting D = 13,000 units per year, P = $200 per order, and C = $5.20 per unit per year, in the EOQ formula, we get

$$EOQ = \sqrt{\frac{2 \times 13{,}000 \times 200}{\$5.20}} = \sqrt{1{,}000{,}000} = 1{,}000 \text{ units}$$

Purchasing 1,000 units per order minimizes total relevant ordering and carrying costs. Therefore, the number of deliveries each period (1 year in this example) is as follows:

$$\frac{D}{EOQ} = \frac{13{,}000}{1{,}000} = 13 \text{ deliveries}$$

Recall the annual relevant total costs (RTC) $= \left(\frac{D}{Q} \times P\right) + \left(\frac{Q}{2} \times C\right)$

For $Q = 1{,}000$ units,

$$RTC = \frac{13{,}000 \times \$200}{1{,}000} + \frac{1{,}000 \times \$5.20}{2}$$

$$= \$2{,}600 + \$2{,}600 = \$5{,}200$$

Exhibit 21-1 graphs the annual relevant total costs of ordering (DP/Q) and carrying inventory ($QC/2$) under various order sizes (Q), and it illustrates the tradeoff between these two types of costs. The larger the order quantity, the lower the annual relevant ordering costs but the higher the annual relevant carrying costs. *The annual relevant total costs are at a minimum at the* EOQ *at which the relevant ordering and carrying costs are equal.*

When to Order, Assuming Certainty

The second decision that Glare Shade's managers face is *when to order* the units. The **reorder point** is the quantity level of inventory on hand that triggers a new purchase order. The reorder point is simplest to compute when both demand and the purchase-order lead time are known with certainty:

$$\text{Reorder point} = \frac{\text{Number of units sold}}{\text{per time period}} \times \frac{\text{Purchase-order}}{\text{lead time}}$$

Suppose the purchase-order lead time for UX1s is 2 weeks:

Economic order quantity	1,000 units
Number of units sold per week	250 units per week (13,000 units ÷ 52 weeks)
Purchase-order lead time	2 weeks

$$\text{Reorder point} = 250 \text{ units per week} \times 2 \text{ weeks} = 500 \text{ units}$$

EXHIBIT 21-1 Graphic Analysis of Ordering Costs and Carrying Costs for UX1 Sunglasses at Glare Shade

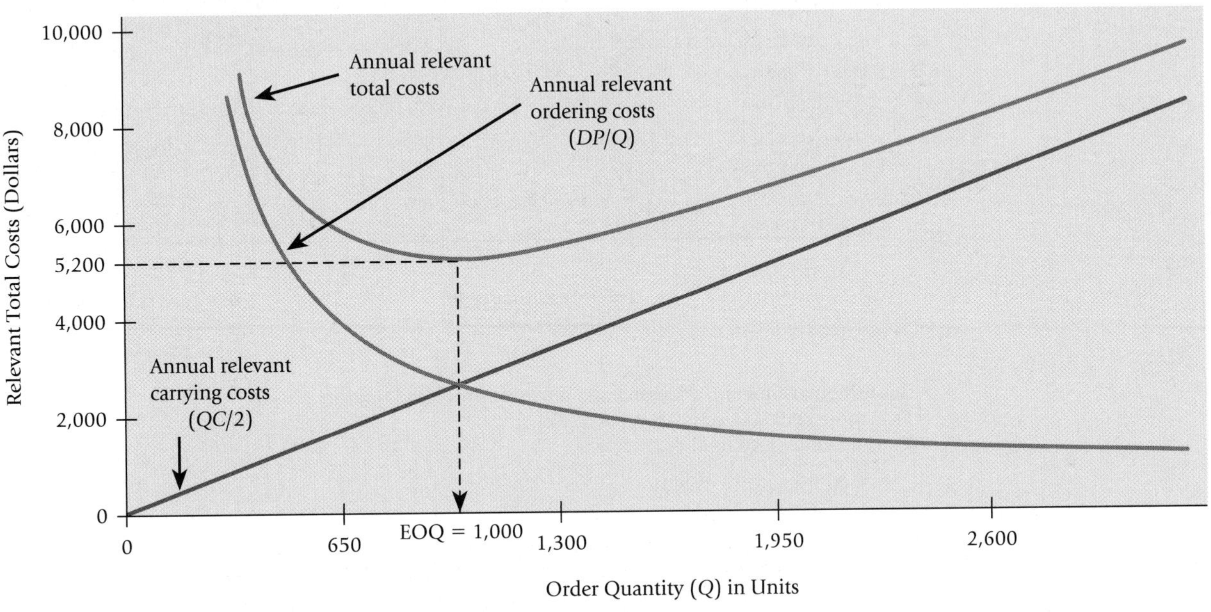

TRY IT! 21-1

Wantage Corporation sells 55,000 iPhone covers each year. These covers are sold evenly throughout the year. Ordering costs are $180 per order, and carrying costs are $2.20 per unit per year.

1. What is the economic order quantity (EOQ) for ordering the covers?
2. What is the relevant total cost?
3. If the purchase-order lead time is 1 week, what is the reorder point?

Glare Shade will order 1,000 units of UX1s each time its inventory falls to 500 units.[2] Exhibit 21-2 shows the behavior of the inventory level of UX1 units, assuming demand occurs uniformly during each week. If the purchase-order lead time is 2 weeks, a new order will be placed when the inventory level falls to 500 units, so the 1,000 units ordered will be received at the precise time that inventory reaches zero.

Safety Stock

If Glare Shade's managers are uncertain about demand or the purchase-order lead time or if they are uncertain about the quantities of UX1s Rytek can provide, they will hold safety stock. **Safety stock** is inventory held at all times regardless of the quantity of inventory ordered using the EOQ model. Companies use safety stock as a buffer against unexpected increases in demand, uncertainty about lead time, and unavailability of stock from suppliers. Suppose Glare Shade's managers are uncertain about demand. They expect the demand for UX1s to be 250 units per week, but it could be as high as 400 units per week or as low as 100 units per week. If stockout costs are very high, the managers will want to hold a safety stock of 300 units and incur higher carrying costs. The 300 units equal the maximum excess demand of 150(400 − 250) units per week times the 2 weeks of purchase-order lead time. If stockout costs are minimal, no safety stock will be held to avoid incurring the additional carrying costs. But if stockout costs are moderate (neither very high nor very low), managers need to balance the benefits of reducing stockouts with the extra cost of carrying safety-stock inventory.

EXHIBIT 21-2

Inventory Level of UX1 Sunglasses at Glare Shade[a]

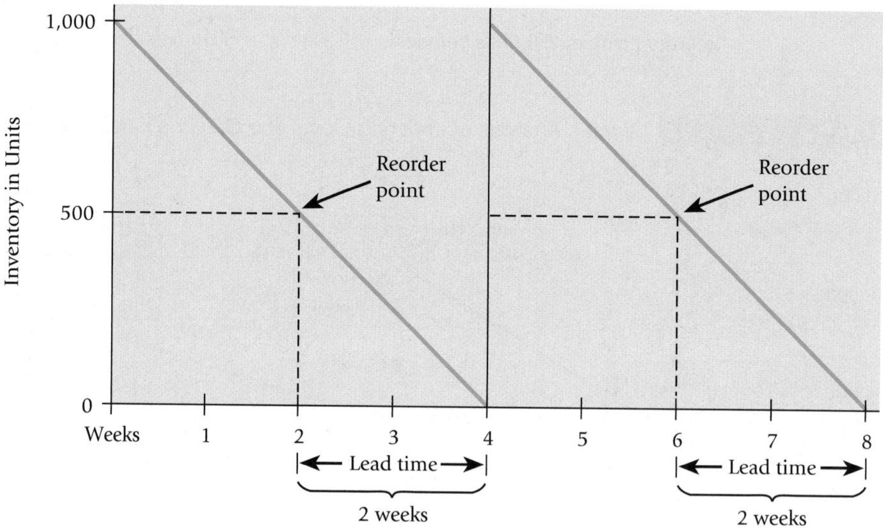

[a] This exhibit assumes that demand and purchase-order lead time are certain:
Demand = 250 UX1 sunglasses per week
Purchase-order lead time = 2 weeks

[2] This handy but special formula does not apply when receipt of the order fails to increase inventory to the reorder-point quantity (for example, when lead time is 3 weeks and the order is a 1-week supply). In these cases, orders will overlap.

Managers use a frequency distribution based on prior daily or weekly levels of demand to compute safety-stock levels. Assume that one of the following levels of demand for UX1s will occur over the 2-week purchase-order lead time.

Total Demand for 2 Weeks	200 Units	300 Units	400 Units	500 Units	600 Units	700 Units	800 Units
Probability (sums to 1.00)	0.06	0.09	0.20	0.30	0.20	0.09	0.06

We see that 500 units is the most likely level of demand for 2 weeks because it has the highest probability of occurrence. We see also a 0.35 probability that demand will be 600, 700, or 800 units (0.20 + 0.09 + 0.06 = 0.35).

If a customer wants to buy UX1s and the store has none in stock, Glare Shade can "rush" them to the customer at an additional cost to Glare Shade of $4 per unit. The relevant stockout costs in this case are $4 per unit. The optimal safety-stock level is the quantity of safety stock that minimizes the sum of annual relevant stockout and carrying costs. Note that Glare Shade will place 13 orders per year for UX1s and will incur the same ordering costs whatever level of safety stock it chooses. Therefore, ordering costs are irrelevant for the safety-stock decision. Recall that the relevant carrying cost for UX1s is $5.20 per unit per year.

Exhibit 21-3 tabulates the annual relevant total stockout and carrying costs when the reorder point is 500 units. Over the 2-week purchase-order lead time, stockouts can occur if demand is 600, 700, or 800 units because these levels exceed the 500 units in stock at the time Glare Shade places the purchase orders. Consequently, Glare Shade only evaluates safety stock levels of 0, 100, 200, and 300 units of UX1s. If the safety stock is 0 units, Glare Shade will incur stockout costs if demand is 600, 700, or 800 units but will have no additional carrying costs. At the other extreme, if the safety stock is 300 units, Glare Shade will never incur stockout costs but will have higher carrying costs. As Exhibit 21-3 shows, the firm's annual relevant total stockout and carrying costs are lowest ($1,352) when a safety stock of 200 units of UX1s is maintained. Therefore, 200 units is the optimal safety-stock level. The 200 units of safety stock is the extra stock that Glare Shade always maintains. For example, Glare Shade's total inventory of UX1s at the time of reordering its EOQ of 1,000 units would be 700 units (the reorder point of 500 units plus safety stock of 200 units).

DECISION POINT

What does the EOQ decision model help managers do, and how do managers decide on the safety-stock levels?

EXHIBIT 21-3 Computation of Safety Stock for Glare Shade When Reorder Point Is 500 Units

	A	B	C	D	E	F	G	H	I
1–4	Safety Stock Level in Units	Demand Levels Resulting in Stockouts	Stockout in Units[a]	Probability of Stockout	Relevant Stockout Costs[b]	Number of Orders per Year[c]	Expected Stockout Costs[d]	Relevant Carrying Costs[e]	Relevant Total Costs
5	(1)	(2)	(3) = (2) − 500 − (1)	(4)	(5) = (3) × $4	(6)	(7) = (4) × (5) × (6)	(8) = (1) × $5.20	(9) = (7) + (8)
6	0	600	100	0.20	$ 400	13	$1,040		
7		700	200	0.09	800	13	936		
8		800	300	0.06	1,200	13	936		
9							$2,912	$ 0	$2,912
10	100	700	100	0.09	400	13	$ 468		
11		800	200	0.06	800	13	624		
12							$1,092	$ 520	$1,612
13	200	800	100	0.06	400	13	$ 312	$1,040	$1,352
14	300	-	-	-	-	-	$ 0[f]	$1,560	$1,560

[a]Demand level resulting in stockouts – Inventory available during lead time (excluding safety stock), 500 units – Safety stock.

[b]Stockout in units × Relevant stockout costs of $4.00 per unit.

[c]Annual demand, 13,000 ÷ 1,000 EOQ = 13 orders per year.

[d]Probability of stockout × Relevant stockout costs × Number of orders per year.

[e]Safety stock × Annual relevant carrying costs of $5.20 per unit (assumes that safety stock is on hand at all times and that there is no overstocking caused by decreases in expected usage).

[f]At a safety stock level of 300 units, no stockout will occur and, hence, expected stockout costs = $0.

Companies are getting increasingly sophisticated at understanding customers using techniques such as design thinking and data analytics. This deeper understanding reduces the uncertainties about demand that companies face and the need to hold large quantities of safety stocks.

Estimating Inventory-Related Relevant Costs and Their Effects

LEARNING OBJECTIVE 3

Identify the effect of errors that can arise when using the EOQ decision model

... errors in predicting parameters have a small effect on costs

and ways to reduce conflicts between the EOQ model and models used for performance evaluation

... by making the two models congruent

How do Glare Shade's managers calculate the annual relevant inventory-related costs, such as the relevant carrying, stockout, and ordering costs?

We start by discussing the relevant inventory carrying costs of $5.20 per unit per year, which consist of the *relevant incremental costs* plus the *relevant opportunity cost of capital*. What are the *relevant incremental costs* of carrying inventory? Only those costs, such as warehouse rent, warehouse workers' salaries, costs of obsolescence, costs of shrinkage, costs of breakage, and costs of insurance, that change with the quantity of inventory held. The salaries paid to clerks, stock keepers, and materials handlers are irrelevant if they are unaffected by changes in inventory levels. Suppose, however, that as inventories increase (decrease), total salary costs increase (decrease) as clerks, stock keepers, and materials handlers are added (transferred to other activities or laid off). In this case, the salaries paid are relevant costs of carrying inventory. Similarly, costs of storage space owned that cannot be used for other profitable purposes when inventories decrease are irrelevant. But if the space has other profitable uses or if total rental cost is tied to the amount of space occupied, storage costs are relevant costs of carrying inventory.

What is the *relevant opportunity cost of capital*? It is the return forgone by investing capital in inventory rather than elsewhere. It is calculated as the required rate of return multiplied by the per-unit costs of acquiring inventory, such as the purchase price of units, incoming freight, and incoming inspection. Opportunity costs are also computed on investments (say, in equipment) if these investments are affected by changes in inventory levels.

In the case of stockouts, the relevant incremental cost is the cost of expediting an order from a supplier. The relevant opportunity cost is (1) the lost contribution margin on sales forgone because of the stockout and (2) the lost contribution margin on future sales forgone as a result of customer ill will.

The relevant ordering costs are only those ordering costs that change with the number of orders placed (for example, the costs of preparing and issuing purchase orders and receiving and inspecting materials).

Cost of a Prediction Error

Predicting relevant costs is difficult and seldom flawless, which raises the question, "What is the cost when actual relevant costs differ from the estimated relevant costs used for decision making?"

Suppose Glare Shade's relevant ordering costs per purchase order for UX1s are $200, but the manager predicts them to be $100 when calculating the order quantity. We can calculate the cost of this "prediction" error using a three-step approach.

Step 1: Compute the Monetary Outcome from the Best Action That Could Be Taken, Given the *Actual* Amount of the Cost Input (Cost per Purchase Order). This is the benchmark—the decision the manager would have made if the manager had known the correct ordering cost. Using $D = 13{,}000$ units of UX1 per year, $P = \$200$, and $C = \$5.20$ per unit per year, the best action is to purchase 1,000 units in each order (page 812).

Glare Shade's annual relevant total costs when the $EOQ = 1{,}000$ units are

$$RTC = \frac{DP}{Q} + \frac{QC}{2}$$

$$= \frac{13{,}000 \times \$200}{1{,}000} + \frac{1{,}000 \times \$5.20}{2}$$

$$= \$2{,}600 + \$2{,}600 = \$5{,}200$$

Step 2: Compute the Monetary Outcome From the Best Action Based on the Incorrect *Predicted* Amount of the Cost Input (Cost per Purchase Order). In this step, the manager calculates the order quantity based on the prediction (that later proves to be wrong) that the ordering cost is \$100. Using $P = \$100$, $D = 13{,}000$ units of UX1 per year, and $C = \$5.20$ per unit per year, the economic order quantity is as follows:

$$EOQ = \sqrt{\frac{2DP}{C}}$$

$$= \sqrt{\frac{2 \times 13{,}000 \times \$100}{\$5.20}} = \sqrt{500{,}000}$$

$$= 707 \text{ units (rounded)}$$

However, the actual cost of the purchase order is \$200. Consequently, the actual annual relevant total costs when $D = 13{,}000$ units per year, $Q = 707$ units, $P = \$200$, and $C = \$5.20$ per unit per year are as follows:

$$RTC = \frac{13{,}000 \times 200}{707} + \frac{707 \times \$5.20}{2}$$

$$= \$3{,}678 + \$1{,}838 = \$5{,}516$$

Step 3: Compute the Difference Between the Monetary Outcomes From Step 1 and Step 2.

	Monetary Outcome
Step 1	\$5,200
Step 2	5,516
Difference	\$ (316)

The cost of the prediction error, \$316, is 6% of the relevant total costs of \$5,200. Note that the annual relevant-total-costs curve in Exhibit 21-1 is somewhat flat over the range of order quantities from 700 to 1,300 units. That is, the annual relevant cost is roughly the same even if misestimating the relevant carrying and ordering costs results in an EOQ quantity of 1,000 plus 30% (1,300) or 1,000 minus 30% (700). *The square root in the EOQ model diminishes the effect of estimation errors because it results in the effects of the incorrect numbers becoming smaller.*

In the next section, we consider a planning-and-control and performance-evaluation issue that frequently arises when managing inventory.

21-2 TRY IT!

Wantage Corporation sells 55,000 iPhone covers each year. These covers are sold evenly throughout the year. Ordering costs are \$180 per order, and carrying costs are \$2.20 per unit per year. Suppose the manager predicts ordering costs to be \$125 instead of the actual \$180 when calculating the order quantity.

What is the cost of the prediction error?

Conflicts Between the EOQ Decision Model and Managers' Performance Evaluation

What happens if the order quantity based on the EOQ decision model differs from the order quantity managers would choose to make their own performance look best? Consider, for example, opportunity costs. As we have seen, the EOQ model takes into account opportunity costs because these costs are relevant costs when calculating inventory carrying costs. However, managers evaluated on financial accounting numbers, which is often the case, will ignore opportunity costs. Why? Because financial accounting only records actual transactions, not the costs of opportunities forgone (see Chapter 12). Managers interested in making their own performance look best will only focus on measures used to evaluate their performance. Conflicts will then arise between the EOQ model's optimal order quantity and the order quantity that managers regard as optimal.

As a result of ignoring some of the carrying costs (the opportunity costs), managers will be inclined to purchase larger lot sizes of materials than the lot sizes calculated according to the EOQ model, particularly if larger lot sizes result in lower purchase prices. As we discussed in the previous section, the cost of these suboptimal choices is small if the quantities purchased are close to the EOQ. However, if the lot sizes become much greater, the cost to the company can be quite large. Moreover, if we consider other costs, such as costs of quality and shrinkage of holding large inventories, the cost to the company of purchasing in large lot sizes is even greater. To achieve congruence between the EOQ decision model and managers' performance evaluations, companies such as Walmart design performance-evaluation systems that charge managers responsible for managing inventory levels with carrying costs that include a required return on investment.

DECISION POINT

How do errors in predicting the parameters of the EOQ model affect costs? How can companies reduce the conflict between the EOQ decision model and models used for performance evaluation?

Just-in-Time Purchasing

LEARNING OBJECTIVE 4

Describe why companies are using just-in-time (JIT) purchasing

... high carrying costs, costs of quality, and shrinkage costs; low ordering costs, high-quality suppliers, and reliable supply chains

Just-in-time (JIT) purchasing is the purchase of materials (or goods) so that they are delivered just as needed for production (or sale). Consider Hewlett-Packard's (HP's) JIT purchasing: HP has long-term agreements with suppliers of the major components of its printers. Each supplier is required to make frequent deliveries of small orders directly to the production floor, based on the production schedules HP provides them. The suppliers work hard to keep their commitments because any failure on their part will result in HP's assembly plant not meeting its scheduled deliveries of printers.

JIT Purchasing and EOQ Model Parameters

Suppose Glare Shade's managers believe that the current purchasing policies might result in the carrying costs of the company's inventories (parameter *C* in the EOQ model) being much greater than what they had estimated because of higher warehousing, handling, insurance, and equipment costs. Suppose they also believe that the cost of placing a purchase order (parameter *P* in the EOQ model) is likely to decrease because of the following:

- Glare Shade is establishing long-term purchasing agreements that define the price and quality terms it has with its suppliers over an extended period. No additional negotiations need to take place before supplies can be ordered.
- New electronic systems allow Glare Shade to place purchase orders, tally delivery records, and make payments to suppliers more cost effectively.
- Glare Shade is using purchase-order cards (similar to consumer credit cards such as VISA and MasterCard). As long as purchasing personnel stay within preset total and individual-transaction dollar limits, traditional labor-intensive procurement-approval procedures are not required.

Exhibit 21-4 tabulates the sensitivity of the EOQ (page 819) to changes in carrying and ordering costs of UX1s. Exhibit 21-4 supports moving toward JIT purchasing because, as the company's relevant carrying costs increase and relevant ordering costs per purchase order decrease, the EOQ decreases and ordering frequency increases.

Relevant Costs of JIT Purchasing

JIT purchasing is not guided solely by the EOQ model because that model only emphasizes the tradeoff between relevant carrying and ordering costs. Inventory management, however, also includes accounting for a company's purchasing costs, stockout costs, costs of quality, and shrinkage costs. Glare Shade's managers are concerned that ordering and storing large quantities of UX1 units have contributed to defective and broken units and shrinkage. So, the company begins implementing JIT purchasing by asking the supplier of UX1 units to make more frequent deliveries of smaller sizes. Glare Shade has recently established an online business-to-business purchase-order link with its supplier, Rytek. Glare Shade triggers a purchase order for UX1s by a single computer entry. Payments are made electronically for batches of deliveries, rather than for each individual delivery. These changes reduce the company's ordering costs

EXHIBIT 21-4

Sensitivity of EOQ to Variations in Relevant Ordering and Carrying Costs for UX1 Sunglasses

	A	B	C	D	E	F	G
1				Economic Order Quantity in Units			
2				at Different Ordering and Carrying Costs			
3	Annual Demand (D) =	13,000	units				
4							
5	Relevant Carrying Costs			Relevant Ordering Costs per Purchase Order (P)			
6	Per unit per Year (C)			$ 200	$150	$100	$ 30
7	$ 5.20			1,000	866	707	387
8	7.00			862	746	609	334
9	10.00			721	624	510	279
10	15.00			589	510	416	228

from $200 to only $2 per purchase order! Glare Shade will use the online purchase-order link whether or not it shifts to JIT purchasing. We next evaluate the effect JIT purchasing has on quality and costs.

Description of Item	Current Purchasing Practice	JIT Purchasing Practice
Deliveries	1,000 units purchased 13 times per year	100 units purchased 130 times per year (5 times every 2 weeks)
Purchasing costs	$14 per unit	$14.02 per unit (Note: Many companies do not pay a higher price for more frequent deliveries.)
Inspection of units	Units not inspected at the time of receipt because Rytek ensures delivery of high-quality UX1 sunglasses.	Units not inspected because Rytek ensures that high-quality UX1 sunglasses are delivered to support Glare Shade's JIT purchasing.
Required rate of return on investment	15%	15%
Relevant carrying cost of insurance, materials handling, storage, etc.	$3.10 per unit of average inventory per year	$3.00 per unit of average inventory per year (lower insurance, materials handling, and storage rates)
Customer return costs	$10 for shipping and processing a unit returned by a customer. The high quality of units supplied by Rytek will result in no units being returned by customers.	$10 for shipping and processing a unit returned by a customer. The high quality of units supplied by Rytek will result in no units being returned by customers.
Stockout costs	No stockout costs because demand and purchase-order lead times during each 4-week period (52 weeks ÷ 13 deliveries) are known with certainty.	More stockouts because demand variations and delays in supplying units are more likely in the short time intervals between orders under JIT purchasing. Glare Shade expects to incur stockout costs on 150 units of UX1 per year under the JIT purchasing policy. When a stockout occurs, Glare Shade must rush-order units at an additional cost of $4 per unit.

Should Glare Shade implement the JIT purchasing option of 130 deliveries of UX1 per year? Exhibit 21-5 compares Glare Shade's relevant total costs under the current purchasing policy and the JIT policy. It shows net cost savings of $1,251 per year by shifting to a JIT purchasing policy. The benefits of JIT purchasing arise from lower carrying costs. JIT purchasing also gives Glare Shade's managers immediate feedback about quality problems by reducing the "safety net" large quantities of inventory provide.

EXHIBIT 21-5 Annual Relevant Costs of Current Purchasing Policy and JIT Purchasing Policy for UX1 Sunglasses

	A	B	C	D	E	F	G	H	I	J
1		Relevant Costs Under								
2		Current Purchasing Policy					JIT Purchasing Policy			
3	Relevant Items	Relevant Cost per Unit		Quantity per Year	Total Costs		Relevant Cost per Unit		Quantity per Year	Total Costs
4	(1)	(2)		(3)	(4) = (2) × (3)		(5)		(6)	(7) = (5) × (6)
5	Purchasing costs	$14.00	per unit	13,000	$182,000		$14.02	per unit	13,000	$182,260
6	Ordering costs	$ 2.00	per order	13	26		$ 2.00	per order	130	260
7	Inspection costs	-	per unit	-	-		$ -	per unit	-	-
8	Opportunity carrying costs	$ 2.10[a]	per unit of average inventory per year	500[b]	1,050		$ 2.10[a]	per unit of average inventory per year	50[c]	105
9	Other carrying costs (insurance, materials handling, etc.)	$ 3.10	per unit of average inventory per year	500[b]	1,550		$ 3.00	per unit of average inventory per year	50[c]	150
10	Customer return costs	$10.00	per unit returned	0	0		$10.00	per unit returned	0	0
11	Stockout costs	$ 4.00	per unit	0	0		$ 4.00	per unit	150	600
12	Total annual relevant costs				$184,626					$183,375
13	Annual difference in favor of JIT Purchasing					$1,251				
14										
15	[a]Purchasing cost per unit × 0.15 per year									
16	[b]Order quantity/2 = 1,000/2 = 500 units									
17	[c]Order quantity/2 = 100/2 = 50 units									

Supplier Evaluation and Relevant Costs of Quality and Timely Deliveries

Companies that implement JIT purchasing choose their suppliers carefully and develop long-term supplier relationships. Some suppliers are better positioned than others to support JIT purchasing. For example, the corporate strategy of Frito-Lay, a supplier of potato chips and other snack foods, emphasizes service, consistency, freshness, and the quality of the products the company delivers. As a result, Frito-Lay makes deliveries to retail outlets more frequently than many of its competitors.

What are the relevant total costs when choosing suppliers? Consider again the UX1 units purchased by Glare Shade. Denton Corporation, another supplier of UX1 sunglasses, offers to supply all the units that Glare Shade needs. Glare Shade requires the supplier to deliver 100 units 130 times per year (5 times every 2 weeks). Glare Shade will establish an online purchase-order link with whichever supplier it chooses, trigger a purchase order for UX1 units by a single computer entry, and make payments electronically for batches of deliveries, rather than for each individual delivery. As discussed earlier, the company's ordering costs will be only $2 per purchase order. The following table provides information about Denton versus Rytek. Rytek charges a higher price than Denton but also supplies higher-quality UX1s. The information about Rytek is the same as that presented earlier under JIT purchasing in Exhibit 21-5.

Description of Item	Purchasing Terms From Rytek	Purchasing Terms From Denton
Purchasing costs	$14.02 per unit	$13.80 per unit
Inspection of UX1s	Glare Shade has bought UX1s from Rytek in the past and knows that it will deliver quality UX1s on time. UX1s supplied by Rytek require no inspection.	Denton does not enjoy a sterling reputation for quality, so Glare Shade plans to inspect UX1s at a cost of $0.05 per UX1.
Required rate of return on investment	15%	15%
Relevant carrying cost of insurance, materials handling, storage, etc.	$3.00 per unit per year	$2.90 per unit per year because of lower purchasing costs

Description of Item	Purchasing Terms From Rytek	Purchasing Terms From Denton
Customer return costs	Glare Shade estimates $10 for shipping and processing a UX1 unit returned by a customer. Fortunately, the high quality of units supplied by Rytek will result in no units being returned by customers.	Glare Shade estimates $10 for shipping and processing a UX1 unit returned by a customer and product returns of 2.5% of all units sold.
Stockout costs	Glare Shade expects to incur stockout costs on 150 UX1 units each time, resulting in a rush-order at a cost of $4 per unit.	Denton has less control over its processes, so Glare Shade expects to incur stockout costs on 360 UX1 units each time, initiating rush orders at a cost of $4 per unit.

Exhibit 21-6 shows the relevant total costs of purchasing from Rytek and Denton. Even though Denton is offering a lower price per unit, there is a net cost savings of $1,873 per year by purchasing UX1s from Rytek because of lower inspection, customer returns, and stockout costs. The benefit of purchasing from Rytek could be even greater if purchasing high-quality UX1s from Rytek enhances Glare Shade's reputation and increases customer goodwill, leading to higher sales and profitability in the future.

21-3 TRY IT!

The Buxhaven Corporation is an automotive supplier that uses automatic turning machines to manufacture precision parts from steel bars. Buxhaven's inventory of raw steel averages $380,000. The steel supplier is willing to supply steel in smaller lots at no additional charge. Helena Frank, Buxhaven's controller, identifies the following effects of adopting a JIT inventory program to virtually eliminate steel inventory:

- Without scheduling any overtime, lost sales due to stockouts would increase by 33,000 units per year. However, by incurring overtime premiums of $17,000 per year, the increase in lost sales could be reduced to 18,000 units per year. This would be the maximum amount of overtime that would be feasible for Buxhaven.
- Two warehouses currently used for steel bar storage would no longer be needed. Buxhaven rents one warehouse from another company under a cancelable leasing arrangement at an annual cost of $38,000. The other warehouse is owned by Buxhaven and contains 14,000 square feet. Three-fourths of the space in the owned warehouse could be rented for $0.50 per square foot per year. Insurance and property tax costs totaling $5,000 per year would be eliminated.

Buxhaven's required rate of return on investment is 20% per year. Buxhaven's budgeted income statement for the year ending December 31, 2020, (in thousands) is

Revenues (880,000 units)		$ 4,400
Cost of goods sold		
Variable costs	$2,200	
Fixed costs	825	
Total costs of goods sold		3,025
Gross margin		1,375
Marketing and distribution costs		
Variable costs	$ 440	
Fixed costs	775	
Total marketing and distribution costs		1,215
Operating income		$ 160

Calculate the estimated dollar savings (loss) for the Buxhaven Corporation that would result in 2020 from the adoption of JIT purchasing.

EXHIBIT 21-6 Annual Relevant Costs of JIT Purchasing for UX1 Sunglasses From Rytek and Denton

	A	B	C	D	E	F	G	H	I	J
1					Relevant Cost of JIT Purchasing From					
2			Rytek					Denton		
3	Relevant Items	Relevant Cost per Unit		Quantity per Year	Total Costs		Relevant Cost per Unit		Quantity per Year	Total Costs
4	(1)	(2)		(3)	(4) = (2) × (3)		(5)		(6)	(7) = (5) × (6)
5	Purchasing costs	$14.02	per unit	13,000	$182,260		$13.80	per unit	13,000	$179,400
6	Ordering costs	$ 2.00	per order	130	260		2.00	per order	130	260
7	Inspection costs	-	per unit	-	-		0.05	per unit	13,000	650
8	Opportunity carrying costs	$ 2.10[a]	per unit of average inventory per year	50[b]	105		2.07[a]	per unit of average inventory per year	50[b]	103
9	Other carrying costs (insurance, materials handling, etc.)	$ 3.00	per unit of average inventory per year	50[b]	150		2.90	per unit of average inventory per year	50[b]	145
10	Customer return costs	$10.00	per unit returned	0	0		10.00	per unit returned	325[c]	3,250
11	Stockout costs	$ 4.00	per unit	150	600		4.00	per unit	360	1,440
12	Total annual relevant costs				$183,375					$185,248
13	Annual difference in favor of Rytek					$1,873				
14										
15	[a]Purchasing cost per unit × 0.15 per year									
16	[b]Order quantity ÷ 2 = 100 ÷ 2 = 50 units									
17	[c]2.5% of units returned × 13,000 units									

JIT Purchasing, Planning and Control, and Supply-Chain Analysis

Retailers' inventory levels depend on the demand patterns of their customers and supply relationships with their distributors and manufacturers, the suppliers to their manufacturers, and so on. The *supply chain* describes the flow of goods, services, and information from the initial sources of materials and services to the delivery of products to consumers, regardless of whether those activities occur in the same company or in other companies. Retailers can purchase inventories on a JIT basis only if activities throughout the supply chain are properly planned, coordinated, and controlled.

Procter and Gamble's (P&G's) experience with its Pampers product illustrates the gains from supply-chain coordination. Retailers selling Pampers found that the weekly demand for the product varied because families purchased disposable diapers randomly. Anticipating even more demand variability and lacking information about available inventory with P&G, retailers' orders to P&G became more variable. This, in turn, increased variability of orders at P&G's suppliers, resulting in high levels of inventory at all stages in the supply chain.

How did P&G respond to these problems? By sharing information and planning and coordinating activities throughout the supply chain among retailers, P&G, and P&G's suppliers. Sharing sales information reduced the level of uncertainty that P&G and its suppliers had about retail demand for the product and led to (1) fewer stockouts at the retail level, (2) reduced manufacturing of Pampers not immediately needed by retailers, (3) fewer manufacturing orders that had to be "rushed" or "expedited," and (4) lower inventories held by each company in the supply chain. The benefits of supply-chain coordination at P&G have been so great that retailers such as Walmart have contracted with P&G to manage their inventories on a just-in-time basis. This practice is called *supplier- or vendor-managed inventory*. Coordinating supply chains, however, can be difficult because supply-chain partners don't always share accurate and timely information about their sales, inventory levels, and sales forecasts with one another. Some of the reasons for these challenges are communication problems, trust issues between the companies, incompatible information systems, and limited people and financial resources.

DECISION POINT

Why are companies using just-in-time (JIT) purchasing?

Inventory Management, MRP, and JIT Production

We now turn our attention from purchasing to managing the production inventories of manufacturing companies. Two of the most widely used systems to plan and implement inventory activities within plants are materials requirements planning (MRP) and just-in-time (JIT) production.

LEARNING OBJECTIVE 5

Distinguish materials requirements planning (MRP) systems

... manufacturing products based on demand forecasts

from just-in-time (JIT) systems for manufacturing

... manufacturing products only upon receiving customer orders

Materials Requirements Planning

A **materials requirements planning (MRP) system** is a "push-through" system that manufactures finished goods for inventory on the basis of demand forecasts. Companies such as Guidant, which manufactures medical devices, and Philips, which makes consumer electronic products, use MRP systems. To determine outputs at each stage of production, MRP uses (1) the demand forecasts for final products; (2) a bill of materials detailing the materials, components, and subassemblies for each final product; and (3) information about a company's inventories of materials, components, and products. Taking into account the lead time required to purchase materials and to manufacture components and finished products, a master production schedule specifies the quantity and timing of each item to be produced. Once production starts as scheduled, the output of each department is pushed through the production line.

Maintaining accurate inventory records and costs is critical in an MRP system. For example, after becoming aware of the full costs of carrying finished-goods inventory in its MRP system, National Semiconductor (now a division of Texas Instruments) contracted with FedEx to airfreight its microchips from a central location in Singapore to customer sites worldwide instead of storing the chips at geographically dispersed warehouses.

Just-in-Time (JIT) Production

In contrast, JIT production is a "demand-pull" approach, which is used by companies such as Toyota in the automobile industry, Acer in the computer industry, and Miele in the appliance industry. **Just-in-time (JIT) production**, which is also called **lean production**, is a "demand-pull" manufacturing system that manufactures each component in a production line as soon as, and only when, needed by the next step in the production line. Demand triggers each step of the production process, starting with customer demand for a finished product at the end of the process and working all the way back to the demand for direct materials at the beginning of the process. In this way, demand pulls an order through the production line. The demand-pull feature of JIT production systems results in close coordination among workstations and smooths the flow of goods, despite low quantities of inventory. JIT production systems help companies meet the demand for high-quality products on time and at the lowest possible cost.

As customer information systems get increasingly sophisticated and computing power allows companies to process and analyze large quantities of data at rapid speed, companies are able to develop deep insights into the needs of customers. As a result, many companies are combining the best features of MRP and JIT systems—anticipating demand changes to some extent but continuing to operate flexible production systems to quickly respond to fluctuations in demand.

DECISION POINT

How do materials requirements planning (MRP) systems differ from just-in-time (JIT) production systems?

Features of JIT Production Systems

LEARNING OBJECTIVE 6

Identify the features and benefits of a just-in-time production system

... for example, organizing work in manufacturing cells, improving quality, and reducing manufacturing lead time to reduce costs and earn higher margins

A JIT production system has these features:

- Production is organized in **manufacturing cells**, which are work areas with different types of equipment grouped together to make related products. Materials move from one machine to another, and various operations are performed in sequence, minimizing materials-handling costs.
- Workers are hired and trained to be multiskilled and capable of performing a variety of operations and tasks, including minor repairs and routine equipment maintenance.

- Defects are aggressively eliminated. Because of the tight links between workstations and the minimal inventories at each workstation, defects arising at one workstation quickly affect other workstations in the line. JIT creates an urgency for solving problems immediately and eliminating the root causes of defects as quickly as possible. Low levels of inventories allow workers to trace problems to and solve problems at earlier workstations in the production process, where the problems likely originated.
- The *setup time*, the time required to get equipment, tools, and materials ready to start the production of a component or product, and the *manufacturing cycle time*, the time from when an order is received by manufacturing until it becomes a finished good, are reduced. Setup costs correspond to the ordering costs P in the EOQ model. Reducing the setup time and its costs makes production in smaller batches economical, which in turn reduces inventory levels. Reducing the manufacturing cycle time enables a company to respond faster to changes in customer demand (see also Concepts in Action: Just-in-Time Live Concert Recordings).
- Suppliers are selected on the basis of their ability to deliver quality materials in a timely manner. Most companies implementing *JIT production* also implement *JIT purchasing*. JIT plants expect JIT suppliers to make timely deliveries of high-quality goods directly to the production floor.

We next present a relevant-cost analysis for deciding whether to implement a JIT production system.

CONCEPTS IN ACTION

Just-in-Time Live Concert Recordings[3]

dwphotos/Shutterstock

Live concerts are big business. In 2018, the concert-touring industry grossed $8 billion in North America alone. With music sales declining for nearly two decades, musicians big and small rely on live shows for more than half of their revenue. This includes merchandise sales, which is why artists always have plenty of T-shirts for sale at their concerts.

These days, when fans stop by the merchandise stand after the show ends, many artists—ranging from The Avett Brothers and Rob Thomas to Bruce Springsteen and Pearl Jam—offer another option: a processional recording of the concert they just saw. Just-in-time production, enabled by advances in technology, now allows fans to relive the live concert experience just a few minutes after the final note is played.

Several upstart companies, including Aderra, VNUE, and Exit Live, use microphones, state-of-the-art recording and audio mixing hardware and software, and an army of high-speed computers to produce concert recordings during the show. As soon as each song is complete, engineers burn that track onto flash drives and microSD cards. At the end of the show, they only have to burn one last song. Once completed, the recordings are rushed to merchandise stands throughout the venue for instant sale. Many artists also sell the recordings via online download, creating another revenue stream from fans already heading for the exits or those who were not at the show.

With artists and music publishers starting to crack down on unauthorized concert bootlegs posted on YouTube and elsewhere, just-in-time recordings allow musicians to provide fans high-quality memories of their concerts while creating another revenue stream in today's music business.

[3] *Sources:* Neil Shah, "On the Concert Circuit, Rock Is King," *The Wall Street Journal*, October 4, 2018 (https://www.wsj.com/articles/rap-is-huge-but-on-the-concert-circuit-rock-is-king-1538575751); Steve Knopper, "Nine Ways Musicians Actually Make Money Today," *Rolling Stone*, August 28, 2012 (www.rollingstone.com/music/lists/9-ways-musicians-actually-make-money-today-20120828/instant-concert-recordings-19691231); Rachel Stilwell and Makenna Cox, "Phone Recordings of Concerts Are More Than Just Annoying, They're Potentially Illegal: Guest Post," *Billboard*, March 17, 2017 (https://www.billboard.com/articles/business/7724330/phone-recordings-concerts-illegal-federal-bootlegging-laws); Cherie Hu, "VNUE Acquires Live Music Distribution Platform Set.fm From PledgeMusic," *Billboard*, October 17, 2017 (https://www.billboard.com/articles/business/8005727/vnue-acquires-set-fm-from-pledge-music); Buddy Iahn, "Rob Thomas Offering Instant Live Recordings via VNUE," The Music Universe.com, January 3, 2018 (https://themusicuniverse.com/rob-thomas-offering-instant-live-recordings-via-vnue/Nugs.net, http://nugs.net, accessed February 2019; Aderra.net, http://aderra.net/, accessed February 2019.

Costs and Benefits of JIT Production

As we have seen, JIT production clearly lowers a company's carrying costs of inventory. But there are other benefits of lower inventories: heightened emphasis on improving quality by eliminating the specific causes of rework, scrap, and waste, and lower manufacturing cycle times. It is important, therefore, when computing the relevant benefits and costs of reducing inventories in JIT production systems for managers to take into account all benefits and all costs.

Consider Hudson Corporation, a manufacturer of brass fittings. Hudson is considering implementing a JIT production system. To do so, Hudson must incur $100,000 in annual tooling costs to reduce setup times. Hudson expects that JIT production will reduce its average inventory by $500,000 and that the relevant costs of insurance, storage, materials handling, and setups will decline by $30,000 per year. The company's required rate of return on its inventory investments is 10% per year. Should Hudson implement a JIT production system? On the basis of the information provided, we would be tempted to say "no" because the annual relevant total cost savings amount to $80,000 [(10% of $500,000) + $30,000)], which is less than the additional annual tooling costs of $100,000.

Our analysis, however, is incomplete. We have not considered the other benefits of lower inventories associated with JIT production. Hudson estimates that implementing JIT will improve quality and reduce rework on 500 units each year, resulting in savings of $50 per unit. Also, better quality and faster delivery will allow Hudson to charge $2 more per unit on the 20,000 units that it sells each year.

The annual relevant benefits and costs from implementing JIT equal the following:

Incremental savings in insurance, storage, materials handling, and setup	$ 30,000
Incremental savings in inventory carrying costs (10% × $500,000)	50,000
Incremental savings from reduced rework ($50 per unit × 500 units)	25,000
Additional contribution margin from better quality and faster delivery ($2 per unit × 20,000 units)	40,000
Incremental annual tooling costs	(100,000)
Net incremental benefit	$ 45,000

Therefore, Hudson *should* implement a JIT production system.

JIT in Service Industries

JIT purchasing and production methods can be used in service industries as well. For example, inventories and supplies, and the associated labor costs to manage them, represent more than a third of the costs in most hospitals. By implementing a JIT purchasing and distribution system, Eisenhower Memorial Hospital in Palm Springs, California, reduced its inventories and supplies by 90% in 18 months. McDonald's has adapted JIT production practices to making hamburgers.[4] Before, McDonald's precooked a batch of hamburgers that were placed under heat lamps to stay warm until ordered. If the hamburgers didn't sell within a specified period of time, they were discarded, resulting in high inventory holding costs and spoilage costs. Moreover, the quality of hamburgers deteriorated the longer they sat under the heat lamps. A customer placing a special order for a hamburger (such as a hamburger with no cheese) had to wait for it to be cooked. Now McDonald's cooks hamburgers only when they are ordered. By increasing the quality of hamburgers and reducing the time needed for special orders, JIT has led to greater customer satisfaction. Responding to the needs of younger customers at the time, McDonald's introduced customizable burgers in 2013 with its "Create Your Taste" line that let customers customize their burgers by choosing the meat, cheese, toppings, and sauce. However, the line produced challenges for the company in the form of longer preparation times and higher prices. McDonald's downgraded the program to the semicustomizable "Signature Crafted Recipe" line in 2016 and ultimately eliminated offering customizable burgers altogether in 2019.[5]

We next turn our attention to planning and control of production systems.

---

[4] Charles Atkinson, "McDonald's, A Guide to the Benefits of JIT," *Inventory Management Review,* November 8, 2005. (http://www.inventorymanagementreview.org/2005/11/mcdonalds_a_gui.html.)

[5] https://www.restaurantbusinessonline.com/financing/mcdonalds-cuts-its-signature-crafted-line

Enterprise Resource Planning (ERP) Systems[6]

Enterprise resource planning systems are frequently used in conjunction with JIT production. An **enterprise resource planning (ERP) system** is an integrated set of software modules covering a company's accounting, distribution, manufacturing, purchasing, human resources, and other functions. Real-time information is collected in a single database and simultaneously fed into all of the software applications, giving personnel greater visibility into the company's end-to-end business processes. For example, using an ERP system, a salesperson can generate a contract for a customer in Germany, verify the customer's credit limits, and place a production order. The system will then use this same information to schedule manufacturing in, say, Brazil, requisition materials from inventory, order components from suppliers, and schedule shipments. Simultaneously the system credits the salesperson with his or her commission and records all the costing and financial accounting information. An ERP system also allows a company to shift its manufacturing and distribution plans rapidly in response to changes in supply and demand.

Companies believe that an ERP system is essential to support JIT initiatives because of the effect it has on lead times. For example, using an ERP system, Autodesk, a maker of computer-aided design software, reduced order lead time from 2 weeks to 1 day. Fujitsu, an information technology company, reduced its lead time from 18 days to 1.5 days.

In recent years, providers of ERP systems such as SAP and Oracle have increasingly been offering cloud-based products and providing the software as a service. For example, Oracle expanded its cloud offering with the acquisition of Netsuite in 2016. Cloud-based products require less upfront investment and can be adapted more easily than previous generations of ERP systems, which required customers to purchase licenses and to make hardware investments.

Performance Measures and Control in JIT Production

In addition to their personal observations, managers use financial and nonfinancial measures to evaluate and control JIT production. We now describe these measures and indicate the effect JIT systems are expected to have on these measures.

1. Financial performance measures, such as the inventory turnover ratio (cost of goods sold ÷ average inventory), which is expected to increase
2. Nonfinancial performance measures of inventory, quality, and time such as the following:
   - Number of days of inventory on hand, expected to decrease
   - Units produced per hour, expected to increase
   - $\frac{\text{Number of units scrapped or requiring rework}}{\text{Total number of units started and completed}}$, expected to decrease
   - Manufacturing cycle time, expected to decrease
   - $\frac{\text{Total setup time for machines}}{\text{Total manufacturing time}}$, expected to decrease

Personal observation and nonfinancial performance measures provide the most timely, intuitive, and easy-to-understand measures of manufacturing performance. Rapid, meaningful feedback is critical because the lack of inventories in a demand-pull system makes it urgent for managers to detect and solve problems quickly.

Effect of JIT Systems on Product Costing

By reducing materials handling, warehousing, and inspection, JIT systems reduce overhead costs. JIT systems also aid in the direct tracing of some costs usually classified as indirect. For example, the use of manufacturing cells makes it cost-effective to trace materials handling, machine operating, and inspection costs to specific products or product families made in these

[6] For an excellent discussion, see Thomas H. Davenport, "Putting the Enterprise Into the Enterprise System," *Harvard Business Review* (July–August 1998); also see A. Cagilo, "Enterprise Resource Planning Systems and Accountants: Towards Hybridization?" *European Accounting Review* (May 2003).

cells. These costs then become direct costs of those products or product families. Also, the use of multiskilled workers in these cells allows the costs of setup, maintenance, and quality inspection to be traced as direct costs. These changes have prompted some companies using JIT to adopt simplified product-costing methods that dovetail with JIT production and that are less costly to operate than the traditional costing systems described in Chapters 4, 7, 8, and 18. We examine two of these methods next: backflush costing and lean accounting.

DECISION POINT

What are the features and benefits of a just-in-time (JIT) production system?

Backflush Costing

LEARNING OBJECTIVE 7

Describe different ways backflush costing can simplify traditional inventory-costing systems

... for example, by not recording journal entries for work-in-process, purchase of materials, or production of finished goods

Organizing manufacturing in cells, reducing defects and manufacturing cycle times, and ensuring the timely delivery of materials enable a company's purchasing, production, and sales to occur in quick succession with minimal inventories. The absence of inventories makes choices about cost-flow assumptions (such as weighted average or first-in, first-out) or inventory-costing methods (such as absorption or variable costing) unimportant: All manufacturing costs of the accounting period flow directly into cost of goods sold. The rapid conversion of direct materials into finished goods that are immediately sold greatly simplifies the costing system.

Simplified Normal or Standard-Costing Systems

Traditional normal or standard-costing systems (Chapters 4, 7, 8, and 18) use **sequential tracking**, which is a costing system in which the recording of the journal entries occurs in the same order as actual purchases and progress in production. Costs are tracked sequentially as products pass through each of the following four stages:

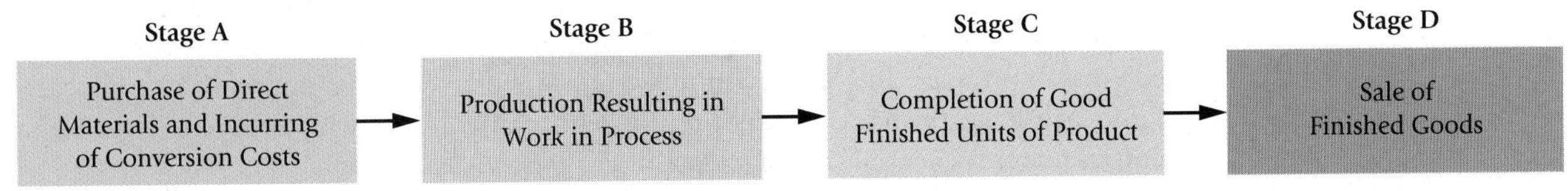

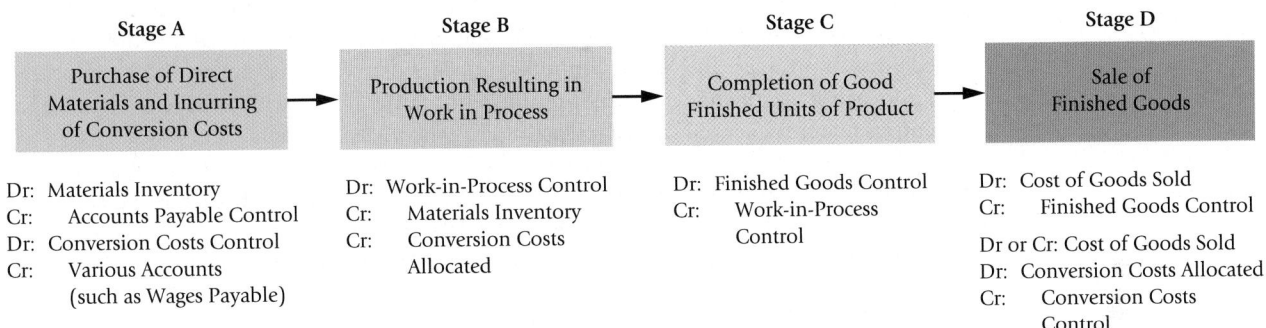

Stage A	Stage B	Stage C	Stage D
Dr: Materials Inventory Cr: Accounts Payable Control Dr: Conversion Costs Control Cr: Various Accounts (such as Wages Payable)	Dr: Work-in-Process Control Cr: Materials Inventory Cr: Conversion Costs Allocated	Dr: Finished Goods Control Cr: Work-in-Process Control	Dr: Cost of Goods Sold Cr: Finished Goods Control Dr or Cr: Cost of Goods Sold Dr: Conversion Costs Allocated Cr: Conversion Costs Control

A sequential-tracking costing system has four *trigger points*, corresponding to Stages A, B, C, and D. A **trigger point** is a stage in the cycle, from the purchase of direct materials and incurring of conversion costs (Stage A) to the sale of finished goods (Stage D), at which journal entries are made in the accounting system. The journal entries (with Dr. representing debits and Cr. representing credits) for each stage are displayed below the box for that stage (as described in Chapter 4).

An alternative approach to sequential tracking is backflush costing. **Backflush costing** is a costing system that omits recording some of the journal entries relating to the stages from the purchase of direct materials to the sale of finished goods. When journal entries for one or more stages are omitted, the journal entries for a subsequent stage use normal or standard costs to work backward to "flush out" the costs in the cycle for which journal entries were *not* made. When inventories are minimal, as in JIT production systems, backflush costing simplifies costing systems without losing much information.

Consider the following data for the month of April for Silicon Valley Computer (SVC), which produces keyboards for personal computers.

- There are no beginning inventories of direct materials and no beginning or ending work-in-process inventories.
- SVC has only one direct manufacturing cost category (direct materials) and one indirect manufacturing cost category (conversion costs). All manufacturing labor costs are included in conversion costs.

- From its bill of materials and an operations list (description of operations to be undergone), SVC determines that the standard direct materials cost per keyboard unit is $19 and the standard conversion cost is $12.
- SVC purchases $1,950,000 of direct materials. To focus on the basic concepts, we assume SVC has no direct materials variances. Actual conversion costs equal $1,260,000. SVC produces 100,000 good keyboard units and sells 99,000 units.
- Any underallocated or overallocated conversion costs are written off to cost of goods sold at the end of April.

We use three examples to illustrate backflush costing. *They differ in the number and placement of trigger points.*

Example 1: The three trigger points for journal entries are Purchase of direct materials (Stage A), Completion of good finished units of product (Stage C), and Sale of finished goods (Stage D).

Note that there is no journal entry for Production resulting in work in process (Stage B) because this method is used when work-in-process inventory is minimal (units started are quickly converted to finished goods).

SVC records two inventory accounts:

Type	Account Title
Combined materials inventory and materials in work in process	Materials and In-Process Inventory Control
Finished goods	Finished Goods Control

Exhibit 21-7, Panel A, summarizes the journal entries for Example 1 with three trigger points: Purchase of direct materials and incurring of conversion costs, Completion of good finished units of product, and Sale of finished goods (and recognizing under- or overallocated costs). For each stage, the backflush costing entries for SVC are shown on the left. The comparable entries under sequential tracking (costing) are shown on the right.

Consider first the entries for the purchase of direct materials and incurring of conversion costs (Stage A). As described earlier, the inventory account under backflush costing combines direct materials and work in process. When materials are purchased, these costs increase (are debited to) the Materials and In-Process Inventory Control account. Under the sequential tracking approach, the direct materials and work-in-process accounts are separate, so the purchase of direct materials is debited to Materials Inventory Control. Actual conversion costs are recorded as incurred under backflush costing, just as in sequential tracking, and they increase (are debited to) Conversion Costs Control.

Next consider the entries for production resulting in work in process (Stage B). Recall that 100,000 units were started into production in April and that the standard cost for the units produced is $31 ($19 direct materials + $12 conversion costs) per unit. Under backflush costing, no entry is recorded in Stage B because work-in-process inventory is minimal and all units are quickly converted to finished goods. Under sequential tracking, work-in-process inventory is increased as manufacturing occurs and later decreased as manufacturing is completed and the product becomes a finished good.

The entries to record the completion of good finished units (Stage C) give backflush costing its name. The costs have not been recorded sequentially with the flow of the product along its production route through work in process and finished goods. Instead, the output trigger point reaches *back* and pulls ("*flushes*") the standard direct material costs from Materials and In-Process Inventory Control and the standard conversion costs for manufacturing the finished goods. Under the sequential tracking approach, Finished Goods Control is debited (increased) and Work-in-Process Control is credited (decreased) as manufacturing is completed and finished goods are produced. The net effect of Stages B and C under sequential tracking is the same as the effect under backflush costing (except for the name of the inventory account).

Finally consider the entries to record the sale of finished goods (and under- or overallocated conversion costs) (Stage D). The standard cost of 99,000 units sold in April equals $3,069,000 (99,000 units × $31 per unit). The entries to record the cost of finished goods sold are exactly the same under backflush costing and sequential tracking.

EXHIBIT 21-7 Journal Entries and General Ledger Overview for Backflush Costing and Journal Entries for Sequential Tracking With Three Trigger Points: Purchase of Direct Materials, Completion of Good Finished Units of Product, and Sale of Finished Goods (Example 1)

PANEL A: Journal Entries

Entry	Backflush Costing			Sequential Tracking		
Stage A: Record Purchase of Direct Materials and Incurring of Conversion Costs						
1. Record Direct Materials Purchased						
Entry (A1)	Materials and In-Process Inventory Control	1,950,000		Materials Inventory Control	1,950,000	
	Accounts Payable Control		1,950,000	Accounts Payable Control		1,950,000
2. Record Conversion Costs Incurred						
Entry (A2)	Conversion Costs Control	1,260,000		Conversion Costs Control	1,260,000	
	Various accounts (such as Wages Payable Control)		1,260,000	Various accounts (such as Wages Payable Control)		1,260,000
Stage B: Record Production Resulting in Work in Process						
Entry (B1)	No Entry Recorded			Work-in-Process Control	3,100,000	
				Materials Inventory Control		1,900,000
				Conversion Costs Allocated		1,200,000
Stage C: Record Cost of Good Finished Units Completed						
Entry (C1)	Finished Goods Control	3,100,000		Finished Goods Control	3,100,000	
	Materials and In-Process Inventory Control		1,900,000	Work-in-Process Control		3,100,000
	Conversion Costs Allocated		1,200,000			
Stage D: Record Cost of Finished Goods Sold (and Under- or Overallocated Conversion Costs)						
1. Record Cost of Finished Goods Sold						
Entry (D1)	Cost of Goods Sold	3,069,000		Cost of Goods Sold	3,069,000	
	Finished Goods Control		3,069,000	Finished Goods Control		3,069,000
2. Record Underallocated or Overallocated Conversion Costs						
Entry (D2)	Conversion Costs Allocated	1,200,000		Conversion Costs Allocated	1,200,000	
	Cost of Goods Sold	60,000		Cost of Goods Sold	60,000	
	Conversion Costs Control		1,260,000	Conversion Costs Control		1,260,000

PANEL B: General Ledger Overview for Backflush Costing

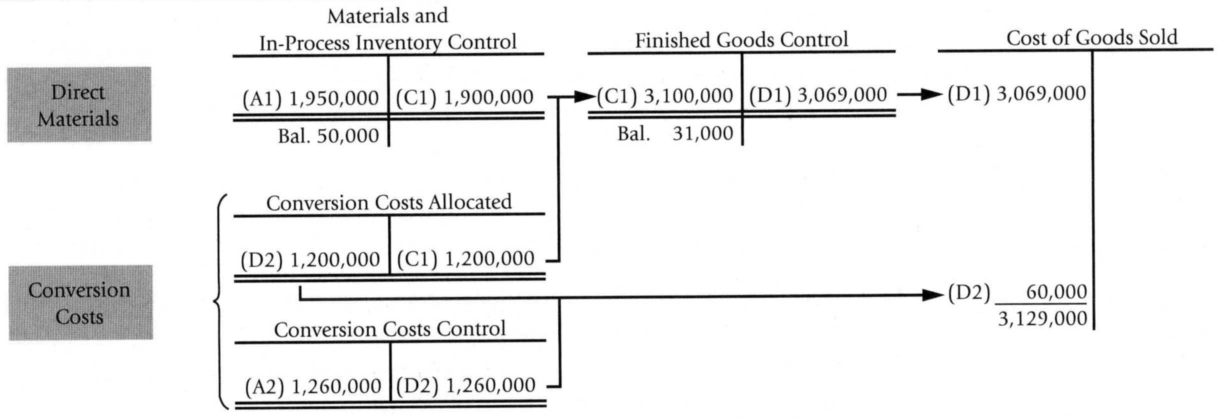

The coding that appears in parentheses for each entry indicates the stage in the production process that the entry relates to as presented in the text.

Actual conversion costs may be underallocated or overallocated in an accounting period. Chapter 4 (pages 125–130) discussed various ways to dispose of underallocated or overallocated manufacturing overhead costs. Companies that use backflush costing typically have low inventories, so prorating underallocated or overallocated conversion costs between work in process, finished goods, and cost of goods sold is seldom necessary. Generally, companies write off underallocated or overallocated conversion costs to cost of goods sold only at the end of the fiscal year. Other companies, like SVC, record the write-off monthly. The journal entry to dispose of the difference between actual conversion costs incurred and standard conversion costs allocated is exactly the same under backflush costing and sequential tracking.

The April 30 ending inventory balances under backflush costing are as follows:

Materials and In-Process Inventory Control ($1,950,000 − $1,900,000)	$50,000
Finished Goods Control 1,000 units × $31/unit (or $3,100,000 − $3,069,000)	31,000
Total	$81,000

The April 30 ending inventory balances under sequential tracking would be exactly the same except that the inventory account would be Materials Inventory Control. Exhibit 21-7, Panel B (page 829), provides a general-ledger overview of this version of backflush costing.

The elimination of the typical Work-in-Process Control account reduces the amount of detail in the accounting system. Units on the production line may still be tracked in physical terms, but there is "no assignment of costs" to specific work orders while they are in the production cycle. In fact, there are no work orders or labor-time records in the accounting system.

The three trigger points to make journal entries in Example 1 will lead SVC's backflush costing system to report costs that are similar to the costs reported under sequential tracking when SVC has minimal work-in-process inventory. In Example 1, any inventories of direct materials or finished goods are recognized in SVC's backflush costing system when they are acquired or produced (as would be done in a costing system using sequential tracking). International Paper Company uses a method similar to Example 1 in its specialty papers plant.

Accounting for Variances

Accounting for variances between actual and standard costs is basically the same under all standard-costing systems. The procedures are described in Chapters 7 and 8. Suppose that in Example 1, SVC had an unfavorable direct materials price variance of $42,000. Then the journal entry would be as follows:

Materials and In-Process Inventory Control	1,950,000	
Direct Materials Price Variance	42,000	
Accounts Payable Control		1,992,000

Direct materials costs are often a large proportion of total manufacturing costs, sometimes as much as 60%. Consequently, many companies measure the direct materials efficiency variance in total by physically comparing what remains in direct materials inventory against what should remain based on the output of finished goods for the accounting period. In our example, suppose that such a comparison showed an unfavorable materials efficiency variance of $30,000. The journal entry would be as follows:

Direct Materials Efficiency Variance	30,000	
Materials and In-Process Inventory Control		30,000

The underallocated or overallocated conversion costs are split into various overhead variances (spending variance, efficiency variance, and production-volume variance), as explained in Chapter 8. Each variance is closed to the Cost of Goods Sold account, if it is immaterial in amount.

Example 2: The two trigger points are Purchase of direct materials (Stage A) and Sale of finished goods (Stage D).

This example uses the SVC data to illustrate a backflush costing that differs more from sequential tracking than the backflush costing in Example 1. This example and Example 1 have the same first trigger point, purchase of direct materials and incurring of conversion costs. But the second trigger point in Example 2 is the sale, not the completion, of finished goods. *Note that there is no journal entry for Production resulting in work in process (Stage B) and Completion of good finished units of product (Stage C) because this method is used when there are minimal work-in-process and finished-goods inventories (units started are quickly converted into finished goods that are immediately sold).*

In this example, there is only one inventory account: direct materials, whether the materials are in storerooms, in process, or in finished goods.

Type	Account Title
Combines direct materials inventory and any direct materials in work-in-process and finished-goods inventories	Inventory Control

Exhibit 21-8, Panel A, summarizes the journal entries for Example 2 with two trigger points: Purchase of direct materials and incurring of conversion costs and Sale of finished goods (and recognizing under- or overallocated costs). As in Example 1, for each stage, the backflush costing entries for SVC are shown on the left. The comparable entries under sequential tracking are shown on the right.

The entries for direct materials purchased and conversion costs incurred (Stage A) are the same as in Example 1, except that the inventory account is called Inventory Control. As in Example 1, no entry is made to record the production of work-in-process inventory (Stage B) because the work-in-process inventory is minimal. When finished goods are completed (Stage C), no entry is recorded because the completed units are expected to be sold quickly and the finished-goods inventory is expected to be minimal. As finished goods are sold (Stage D), the cost of goods sold is calculated as 99,000 units sold × \$31 per unit = \$3,069,000, which is composed of direct materials costs (99,000 units × \$19 per unit = \$1,881,000) and conversion costs allocated (99,000 units × \$12 per unit = \$1,188,000). This is the same Cost of Goods Sold calculated under sequential tracking as described in Example 1.

Under this method of backflush costing, conversion costs are not inventoried because no entries are recorded when finished goods are produced in Stage C. That is, compared with sequential tracking, Example 2 does not assign \$12,000 (\$12 per unit × 1,000 units) of conversion costs to finished-goods inventory produced but not sold. Of the \$1,260,000 in conversion costs, \$1,188,000 is allocated at standard cost to the units sold. The remaining \$72,000 (\$1,260,000 − \$1,188,000) of conversion costs is underallocated compared to \$60,000 under sequential tracking. Entry (D2) presents the journal entry if SVC, like many companies, writes off these underallocated costs monthly as additions to the Cost of Goods Sold account.

The April 30 ending balance of the Inventory Control account is \$69,000 (\$1,950,000 − \$1,881,000). This balance represents the \$50,000 direct materials still on hand + \$19,000 direct materials embodied in the 1,000 finished units manufactured but not sold during the period. Finished-goods inventory under sequential tracking is: direct materials, \$19,000 + conversion costs, \$12,000 for a total of \$31,000. Exhibit 21-8, Panel B, provides a general-ledger overview of Example 2. The approach described in Example 2 closely approximates the costs computed using sequential tracking when a company holds minimal work-in-process and finished-goods inventories.

Toyota's cost accounting system at its Kentucky plant is similar to this example. Two advantages of this system are (1) it removes the incentive for managers to produce for inventory because conversion costs are recorded as period costs instead of inventoriable costs and (2) it focuses managers on sales.

Example 3: The two trigger points are Completion of good finished units of product (Stage C) and Sale of finished goods (Stage D).

This example has two trigger points. In contrast to Example 2, the first trigger point in Example 3 is delayed until Stage C, SVC's completion of good finished units of product. *Note that there are no journal entries for Purchase of direct materials and incurring of conversion costs (Stage A) and Production resulting in work in process (Stage B) because this method is used when there are minimal direct materials and work-in-process inventories (direct materials purchased are quickly placed into production and then quickly converted into finished goods).*

Exhibit 21-9, Panel A, summarizes the journal entries for Example 3 with two trigger points: Completion of good finished units of product and Sale of finished goods (and

EXHIBIT 21-8 Journal Entries and General Ledger Overview for Backflush Costing and Journal Entries for Sequential Tracking With Two Trigger Points: Purchase of Direct Materials and Sale of Finished Goods (Example 2)

PANEL A: Journal Entries

	Backflush Costing			Sequential Tracking		
Stage A: Record Purchase of Direct Materials and Incurring of Conversion Costs						
1. Record Direct Materials Purchased						
Entry (A1)	Inventory: Control	1,950,000		Materials Inventory Control	1,950,000	
	Accounts Payable Control		1,950,000	Accounts Payable Control		1,950,000
2. Record Conversion Costs Incurred						
Entry (A2)	Conversion Costs Control	1,260,000		Conversion Costs Control	1,260,000	
	Various accounts (such as Wages Payable Control)		1,260,000	Various accounts (such as Wages Payable Control)		1,260,000
Stage B: Record Production Resulting in Work in Process						
Entry (B1)	No Entry Recorded			Work-in-Process Control	3,100,000	
				Materials Inventory Control		1,900,000
				Conversion Costs Allocated		1,200,000
Stage C: Record Cost of Good Finished Units Completed						
Entry (C1)	No Entry Recorded			Finished Goods Control	3,100,000	
				Work-in-Process Control		3,100,000
Stage D: Record Cost of Finished Goods Sold (and Under- or Overallocated Conversion Costs)						
1. Record Cost of Finished Goods Sold						
Entry (D1)	Cost of Goods Sold	3,069,000		Cost of Goods Sold	3,069,000	
	Inventory Control		1,881,000	Finished Goods Control		3,069,000
	Conversion Costs Allocated		1,188,000			
2. Record Underallocated or Overallocated Conversion Costs						
Entry (D2)	Conversion Costs Allocated	1,188,000		Conversion Costs Allocated	1,200,000	
	Cost of Goods Sold	72,000		Cost of Goods Sold	60,000	
	Conversion Costs Control		1,260,000	Conversion Costs Control		1,260,000

PANEL B: General Ledger Overview for Backflush Costing

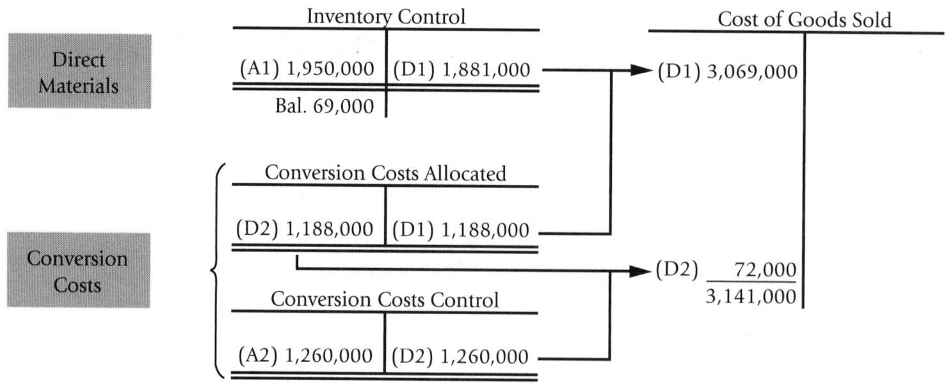

The coding that appears in parentheses for each entry indicates the stage in the production process that the entry relates to as presented in the text.

EXHIBIT 21-9 Journal Entries and General Ledger Overview for Backflush Costing and Journal Entries for Sequential Tracking With Two Trigger Points: Completion of Good Finished Units of Product and Sale of Finished Goods (Example 3)

PANEL A: Journal Entries

Entry	Backflush Costing			Sequential Tracking		
Stage A: Record Purchase of Direct Materials and Incurring of Conversion Costs						
1. Record Direct Materials Purchased						
Entry (A1)	No Entry Recorded			Materials Inventory Control	1,950,000	
				Accounts Payable Control		1,950,000
2. Record Conversion Costs Incurred						
Entry (A2)	Conversion Costs Control	1,260,000		Conversion Costs Control	1,260,000	
	Various accounts (such as Wages Payable Control)		1,260,000	Various accounts (such as Wages Payable Control)		1,260,000
Stage B: Record Production Resulting in Work in Process						
Entry (B1)	No Entry Recorded			Work-in-Process Control	3,100,000	
				Materials Inventory Control		1,900,000
				Conversion Costs Allocated		1,200,000
Stage C: Record Cost of Good Finished Units Completed						
Entry (C1)	Finished Goods Control	3,100,000		Finished Goods Control	3,100,000	
	Accounts Payable Control		1,900,000	Work-in-Process Control		3,100,000
	Conversion Costs Allocated		1,200,000			
Stage D: Record Cost of Finished Goods Sold (and Under- or Overallocated Conversion Costs)						
1. Record Cost of Finished Goods Sold						
Entry (D1)	Cost of Goods Sold	3,069,000		Cost of Goods Sold	3,069,000	
	Finished Goods Control		3,069,000	Finished Goods Control		3,069,000
2. Record Underallocated or Overallocated Conversion Costs						
Entry (D2)	Conversion Costs Allocated	1,200,000		Conversion Costs Allocated	1,200,000	
	Cost of Goods Sold	60,000		Cost of Goods Sold	60,000	
	Conversion Costs Control		1,260,000	Conversion Costs Control		1,260,000

PANEL B: General Ledger Overview for Backflush Costing

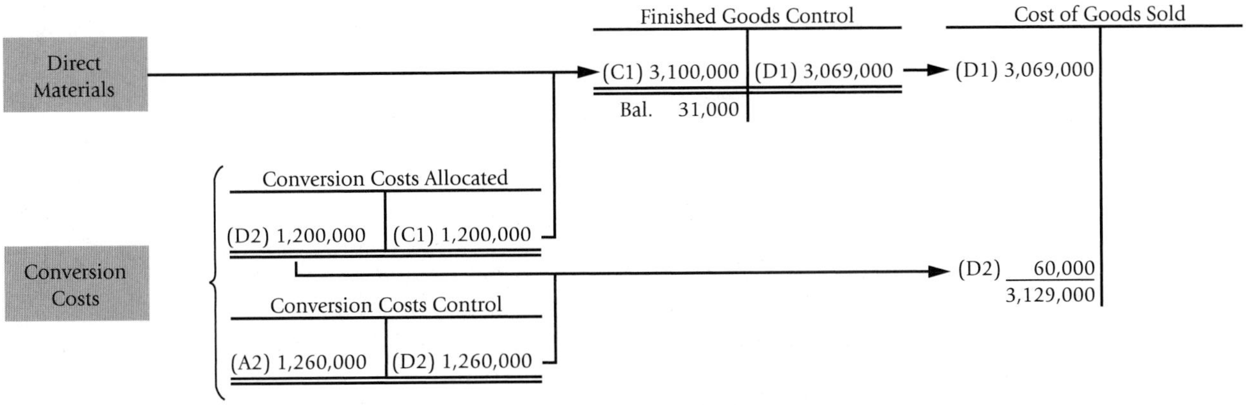

The coding that appears in parentheses for each entry indicates the stage in the production process that the entry relates to as presented in the text.

recognizing under- or overallocated costs). As in Examples 1 and 2, for each stage, the backflush costing entries for SVC are shown on the left. The comparable entries under sequential tracking are shown on the right.

No entry is made for direct materials purchases of $1,950,000 (Stage A) because the acquisition of direct materials is not a trigger point in this form of backflush costing. As in Examples 1 and 2, actual conversion costs are recorded as incurred and no entry is made to record production resulting in work-in-process inventory (Stage B). The cost of 100,000 good finished units completed (Stage C) is recorded at standard cost of $31 ($19 direct materials + $12 conversion costs) per unit as in Example 1 except that Accounts Payable Control is credited (instead of Materials and In-Process Inventory Control) because no entry had been made when direct materials were purchased in Stage A. Note that at the end of April, $50,000 of direct materials purchased have not yet been placed into production ($1,950,000 − $1,900,000 = $50,000), nor have the cost of those direct materials been entered into the inventory-costing system. The Example 3 version of backflush costing is suitable for a JIT production system in which both direct materials inventory and work-in-process inventory are minimal. As finished goods are sold (Stage D), the cost of goods sold is calculated as 99,000 units sold × $31 per unit = $3,069,000. This is the same Cost of Goods sold calculated under sequential tracking. The Finished Goods Control account has a balance of $31,000 under both this form of backflush costing and sequential tracking. The journal entry to dispose of the difference between the actual conversion costs incurred and standard conversion costs allocated is the same under backflush costing and sequential tracking. The only difference between this form of backflush costing and sequential tracking is that direct materials inventory of $50,000 (and the corresponding Accounts Payable Control) is not recorded, which is no problem if direct materials inventories are minimal. Exhibit 21-9, Panel B, provides a general-ledger overview of Example 3.

DECISION POINT

How does backflush costing simplify traditional inventory costing?

Extending Example 3, backflush costing systems could use the sale of finished goods as the only trigger point. This version of backflush costing is most suitable for a JIT production system with minimal direct materials, work-in-process, and finished-goods inventories. That's because this backflush costing system maintains no inventory accounts.

TRY IT! 21-4

The Spark Corporation manufactures electrical meters. Spark uses a JIT production system. For August, there were no beginning inventories of direct materials and no beginning or ending work in process.

Spark's August standard cost per meter is direct materials, $26, and conversion cost, $19. Spark has no direct materials variances. The following data apply to August manufacturing:

Direct materials purchased	$545,000	Number of finished units manufactured	20,000
Conversion costs incurred	$430,000	Number of finished units sold	18,000

1. Assume Spark uses a backflush costing system with three trigger points for making entries in the accounting system:
   - Purchase of direct materials
   - Completion of good finished units of product
   - Sale of finished goods

   a. Prepare summary journal entries for August (without disposing of under- or overallocated conversion costs). Assume no direct materials variances.
   b. Post the entries in requirement 1a to T-accounts for Materials and In-Process Inventory Control, Finished Goods Control, Conversion Costs Control, Conversion Costs Allocated, and Cost of Goods Sold.
2. Now assume Spark uses a JIT production system and backflush costing with two trigger points for making entries in the accounting system:
   - Purchase of direct materials
   - Sale of finished goods

Also, the inventory account is confined solely to direct materials, whether these materials are in a storeroom, in work in process, or in finished goods. No conversion costs are inventoried. They are allocated to the units sold at standard costs. Any under- or overallocated conversion costs are written off monthly to Cost of Goods Sold.

a. Prepare summary journal entries for August, including the disposition of under- or overallocated conversion costs. Assume no direct materials variances.

b. Post the entries in requirement 2a to T-accounts for Inventory Control, Conversion Costs Control, Conversion Costs Allocated, and Cost of Goods Sold.

3. Next assume Spark uses a JIT production system and backflush costing with two trigger points for making entries in the accounting system:

- Completion of good finished units of product
- Sale of finished goods

The inventory account is confined solely to finished goods. Any under- or overallocated conversion costs are written off monthly to Cost of Goods Sold.

a. Prepare summary journal entries for August, including the disposition of under- or overallocated conversion costs. Assume no direct materials variances.

b. Post the entries in requirement 3a to T-accounts for Finished Goods Control, Conversion Costs Control, Conversion Costs Allocated, and Cost of Goods Sold.

Lean Accounting

LEARNING OBJECTIVE 8

Understand the principles of lean accounting

. . . focus on costing value streams rather than products and limit arbitrary allocations

Another simplified product costing system that can be used with JIT (or lean production) systems is *lean accounting*. When a company utilizes JIT production, it has to focus on the entire value chain of business functions (from suppliers to manufacturing to customers) in order to reduce inventories, lead times, and waste. The resulting improvements in the value chain have led some JIT companies, such as Toyota, to develop organizational structures and costing systems that focus on **value streams**—all value-added activities needed to design, manufacture, and deliver a given product or product line to customers. For example, a value stream can include the activities needed to develop and engineer products, advertise and market those products, process orders, purchase and receive materials, manufacture and ship orders, bill customers, and collect payments. The use of manufacturing cells in JIT systems helps keep a company focused on its value streams.

Lean accounting is a costing method that focuses on value streams, as distinguished from individual products or departments, thereby eliminating waste in the accounting process.[7] If a company makes multiple, related products in a single value stream, it does not compute product costs for the individual products. Instead, it traces many actual costs directly to the value stream. More costs can be traced as direct costs to value streams because companies using lean accounting often dedicate resources to individual value streams. We now illustrate lean accounting for Manuela Corporation.

Manuela Corporation manufactures toner cartridges and ink cartridges for use with its printers. It makes two models of toner cartridges in one manufacturing cell and two models of ink cartridges in another manufacturing cell. The following table lists revenues, operating costs, operating income, and other information for the different products.

[7] See Bruce L. Baggaley, "Costing by Value Stream," *Journal of Cost Management* (May–June 2003).

	Toner Cartridges		Ink Cartridges	
	Model A	Model B	Model C	Model D
Revenues	$600,000	$700,000	$800,000	$550,000
Direct materials (a)	340,000	400,000	410,000	270,000
Direct manufacturing labor	70,000	78,000	105,000	82,000
Manufacturing overhead costs (e.g., equipment lease, supervision, and unused facility costs)	112,000	130,000	128,000	103,000
Rework costs	15,000	17,000	14,000	10,000
Design costs	20,000	21,000	24,000	18,000
Marketing and sales costs	30,000	33,000	40,000	28,000
Total costs (b)	587,000	679,000	721,000	511,000
Operating income	$ 13,000	$ 21,000	$ 79,000	$ 39,000
Unused facility costs	$ 22,000	$ 38,000	$ 18,000	$ 15,000
Direct materials purchased (c)	$350,000	$420,000	$430,000	$285,000
Excess of direct materials purchased over direct materials used (d) = (c) − (a)	$ 10,000	$ 20,000	$ 20,000	$ 15,000
Total costs based on direct materials purchased rather than direct materials used (e) = (b) + (d)	$597,000	$699,000	$741,000	$526,000

Using lean accounting principles, Manuela's managers calculate the value-stream operating costs and operating income for toner cartridges and ink cartridges, not individual models, as follows:

	Toner Cartridges	Ink Cartridges
Revenues ($600,000 + $700,000; $800,000 + $550,000)	$1,300,000	$1,350,000
Direct materials used ($340,000 + $400,000; $410,000 + $270,000)	740,000	680,000
Direct manufacturing labor ($70,000 + $78,000; $105,000 + $82,000)	148,000	187,000
Manufacturing overhead (after deducting unused facility costs) ($112,000 − $22,000) + ($130,000 − $38,000); ($128,000 − $18,000) + ($103,000 − $15,000)	182,000	198,000
Design costs ($20,000 + $21,000; $24,000 + $18,000)	41,000	42,000
Marketing and sales costs ($30,000 + $33,000; $40,000 + $28,000)	63,000	68,000
Total value-stream operating costs	1,174,000	1,175,000
Value-stream operating income	$ 126,000	$ 175,000

To gain insights, Manuela's lean accounting system, like many lean accounting systems, compares value-stream costs against costs that include costs of all purchased materials. Doing so keeps the company focused on reducing its direct materials and work-in-process inventory.

Manuela allocates its facility costs (such as depreciation, property taxes, and leases) to value streams based on the square footage each value stream uses. This encourages managers to use less space for production and for holding and moving inventory. Note that Manuela excludes unused facility costs when calculating the manufacturing overhead costs of value streams because unused facility costs do not add value to value streams. Instead, it flags these costs as plant or business unit expenses. Increasing the visibility of unused capacity costs creates incentives to reduce these costs or to find alternative uses for the company's capacity.

Manuela also excludes rework costs when calculating its value-stream costs and operating income because these costs are non-value-added costs. Companies also exclude from value-stream costs common costs such as corporate or support-department costs that cannot reasonably be assigned to value streams.

The total cost of the toner cartridges based on direct materials purchases rather than direct materials used from line (e) of the preceding table and including unused capacity costs and rework costs is \$1,296,000 (\$597,000 + \$699,000). The value-stream cost using lean accounting is \$1,174,000 (which is 90.6% × \$1,296,000). The difference of \$122,000 (\$1,296,000 − \$1,174,000) represents the opportunities for improving the company's profitability by reducing unused facility and rework costs and by purchasing direct materials only as needed for production. Making improvements is particularly important because Manuela's current operating income for toner cartridges is only 2.6% [(\$13,000 + \$21,000) ÷ 1,300,000] of its revenues. Manuela's ink cartridges portray a different picture. The total cost for ink cartridges based on direct materials purchases rather than direct materials used from line (e) of the preceding table and including unused capacity costs and rework costs is \$1,267,000 (\$741,000 + \$526,000). The value-stream cost using lean accounting is \$1,175,000 (which is 92.7% × \$1,267,000). The ink cartridges value stream has lower unused facility and rework costs but its direct materials purchases are much higher than the direct materials it needs and uses. Moreover, Manuela's current operating income from ink cartridges even after taking into account non-value-added costs is 8.7% [(\$79,000 + \$39,000) ÷ 1,350,000]. Of course, Manuela's managers would like to reduce non-value-added costs for both value streams.

Lean accounting is much simpler than traditional product costing. Why? Because calculating actual product costs by value streams requires less overhead allocation. Consistent with JIT and lean production, lean accounting emphasizes improvements in the value chain from suppliers to customers. Lean accounting encourages practices—such as reducing direct materials and work-in-process inventories, improving quality, using less space, and eliminating unused capacity—that reflect the goals of JIT production.

Critics of lean accounting charge that it does not compute the costs of individual products, which makes it less useful for making decisions. Proponents of lean accounting argue that the lack of individual product costs is not a problem because most decisions are made at the product line level rather than the individual product level and that pricing decisions are based on the value created for the customer (market prices) and not product costs.

Another criticism of lean accounting is that it excludes certain support costs and unused capacity costs. As a result, decisions based on lower value-stream costs may cause managers to underprice products. Proponents of lean accounting argue that the method overcomes this problem by adding a larger markup on value-stream costs to compensate for some of these excluded costs. Moreover, in a competitive market, prices will eventually settle at a level that represents a reasonable markup above a product's value-stream costs because customers will be unwilling to pay for non-value-added costs. The goal must therefore be to eliminate non-value-added costs.

A final criticism of lean accounting is that, like backflush costing, it does not correctly value inventories under Generally Accepted Accounting Principles (GAAP). However, the method's proponents are quick to point out that in lean accounting environments, work-in-process and finished-goods inventories are immaterial from an accounting perspective.

DECISION POINT

How is lean accounting different from traditional costing systems?

PROBLEMS FOR SELF-STUDY

Problem 1

Lee Company has a Singapore plant that manufactures Blu-Ray players. One component is an XT chip. Expected demand is for 5,200 of these chips in March 2020. Lee estimates the ordering cost per purchase order to be $250. The monthly carrying cost for one unit of XT in stock is $5.

Required

1. Compute the EOQ for the XT chip.
2. Compute the number of deliveries of XT in March 2020.

Solution

$$EOQ = \sqrt{\frac{2 \times 5{,}200 \times 250}{5}}$$
$$= 721 \text{ chips (rounded)}$$

$$\text{Number of deliveries} = \frac{5{,}200}{721}$$
$$= 8 \text{ (rounded)}$$

Problem 2

Littlefield Company uses a backflush costing system with three trigger points:

- Purchase of direct materials
- Completion of good finished units of product
- Sale of finished goods

There are no beginning inventories. Information for April 2020 is as follows:

Direct materials purchased	$880,000	Conversion costs allocated	$ 400,000
Direct materials used	$850,000	Costs transferred to finished goods	$1,250,000
Conversion costs incurred	$422,000	Cost of goods sold	$1,190,000

Required

1. Prepare journal entries for April (without disposing of under- or overallocated conversion costs). Assume there are no direct materials variances.
2. Under an ideal JIT production system, how would the amounts in your journal entries differ from the journal entries in requirement 1?

Solution

1. Journal entries for April are as follows:

Entry (A1)	Materials and In-Process Inventory Control	880,000	
	Accounts Payable Control		880,000
	(direct materials purchased)		
Entry (A2)	Conversion Costs Control	422,000	
	Various Accounts (such as Wages Payable Control)		422,000
	(conversion costs incurred)		
Entry (C1)	Finished Goods Control	1,250,000	
	Materials and In-Process Inventory Control		850,000
	Conversion Costs Allocated		400,000
	(standard cost of finished goods completed)		
Entry (D1)	Cost of Goods Sold	1,190,000	
	Finished Goods Control		1,190,000
	(standard costs of finished-goods sold)		

2. Under an ideal JIT production system, if the manufacturing lead time per unit is very short, there would be zero inventories at the end of each day. Entry (C1) would be for $1,190,000 finished-goods production [to match finished-goods sold in entry (D1)], not $1,250,000. If the marketing department could only sell goods costing $1,190,000, the JIT production system would call for direct materials purchases and conversion costs of lower than $880,000 and $422,000, respectively, in entries (A1) and (A2).

DECISION POINTS

The following question-and-answer format summarizes the chapter's learning objectives. Each decision presents a key question related to a learning objective. The guidelines are the answer to that question.

Decision	Guidelines
1. What are the six categories of costs associated with goods for sale?	The six categories are purchasing costs (costs of goods acquired from suppliers), ordering costs (costs of preparing a purchase order and receiving goods), carrying costs (costs of holding inventory of goods for sale), stockout costs (costs arising when a customer demands a unit of product and that unit is not on hand), costs of quality (prevention, appraisal, internal failure, and external failure costs), and shrinkage costs (the costs resulting from theft by outsiders, embezzlement by employees, misclassification or misplacement of inventory).
2. What does the EOQ decision model help managers do, and how do managers decide on the safety-stock levels?	The economic-order-quantity (EOQ) decision model helps managers to calculate the optimal quantity of inventory to order by balancing ordering costs and carrying costs. The larger the order quantity, the higher the annual carrying costs and the lower the annual ordering costs. The EOQ model includes costs recorded in the financial accounting system as well as opportunity costs of carrying inventory that are not recorded in the financial accounting system. Managers choose a level of safety stock to minimize the stockout costs and the carrying costs of holding more inventory.
3. How do errors in predicting the parameters of the EOQ model affect costs? How can companies reduce the conflict between the EOQ decision model and models used for performance evaluation?	The cost of prediction errors when using the EOQ model is small. The square root in the EOQ model reduces the effect of estimation errors. To reduce the conflict between the EOQ decision model and the performance evaluation model, companies should include the opportunity cost of investment in inventory when evaluating managers. The opportunity cost of investment tied up in inventory is a key input in the EOQ decision model that is often ignored in the performance-evaluation model.
4. Why are companies using just-in-time (JIT) purchasing?	Just-in-time (JIT) purchasing is making purchases in small order quantities just as needed for production (or sales). JIT purchasing is a response to high carrying costs and low ordering costs. JIT purchasing increases the focus of companies and suppliers on quality and timely deliveries. Companies coordinate their activities and reduce inventories throughout the supply chain, from the initial sources of materials and services to the delivery of products to consumers.
5. How do materials requirements planning (MRP) systems differ from just-in-time (JIT) production systems?	Materials requirements planning (MRP) systems use a "push-through" approach whereby finished goods are manufactured on the basis of demand forecasts. Just-in-time (JIT) production systems use a "demand-pull" approach in which goods are manufactured only after receiving customer orders.

Decision	Guidelines
6. What are the features and benefits of a just-in-time (JIT) production system?	JIT production systems (a) organize production in manufacturing cells, (b) hire and train multiskilled workers, (c) emphasize total quality management, (d) reduce manufacturing lead time and setup time, and (e) build strong supplier relationships. The benefits of JIT production include lower costs and higher margins from better flow of information, higher quality, and faster delivery as well as simpler accounting systems.
7. How does backflush costing simplify traditional inventory costing?	Traditional inventory-costing systems use sequential tracking, in which recording of the journal entries occurs in the same order as actual purchases and progress in production. Most backflush costing systems do not record journal entries for the work-in-process stage of production. Some backflush costing systems also do not record entries for either the purchase of direct materials or the completion of finished goods.
8. How is lean accounting different from traditional costing systems?	Lean accounting assigns costs to value streams rather than to products. Non-value-added costs, unused capacity costs, and costs of direct materials inventory are not assigned to value streams to indicate how much current profitability could be improved. Moreover, costs that cannot be easily traced to value streams are not allocated but instead expensed.

TERMS TO LEARN

This chapter and the Glossary at the end of the text contain definitions of the following important terms:

backflush costing **(p. 827)**
carrying costs **(p. 810)**
economic order quantity (EOQ) **(p. 811)**
enterprise resource planning (ERP) system **(p. 826)**
inventory management **(p. 810)**
just-in-time (JIT) production **(p. 823)**
just-in-time (JIT) purchasing **(p. 818)**
lean accounting **(p. 835)**
lean production **(p. 823)**
manufacturing cells **(p. 823)**
materials requirements planning (MRP) system **(p. 823)**
ordering costs **(p. 810)**
purchase-order lead time **(p. 811)**
purchasing costs **(p. 810)**
reorder point **(p. 813)**
safety stock **(p. 814)**
sequential tracking **(p. 827)**
shrinkage costs **(p. 811)**
stockout costs **(p. 810)**
trigger point **(p. 827)**
value streams **(p. 835)**

ASSIGNMENT MATERIAL

Questions

21-1 Why do better decisions regarding the purchasing and managing of goods for sale frequently cause dramatic percentage increases in net income?

21-2 Name six cost categories that are important in managing goods for sale in a retail company.

21-3 What assumptions are made when using the simplest version of the economic-order-quantity (EOQ) decision model?

21-4 Give examples of costs included in annual carrying costs of inventory when using the EOQ decision model.

21-5 Give three examples of opportunity costs that typically are not recorded in accounting systems, although they are relevant when using the EOQ model in the presence of demand uncertainty.

21-6 What are the steps in computing the cost of a prediction error when using the EOQ decision model?
21-7 Why might goal-congruence issues arise when managers use an EOQ model to guide decisions on how much to order?
21-8 "JIT purchasing has many benefits but also some risks." Do you agree? Explain briefly.
21-9 What are three factors causing reductions in the cost to place purchase orders for materials?
21-10 "You should always choose the supplier that offers the lowest price per unit." Do you agree? Explain.
21-11 What is supply-chain analysis, and how can it benefit manufacturers and retailers?
21-12 What are the main features of JIT production, and what are its benefits and costs?
21-13 Distinguish inventory-costing systems using sequential tracking from those using backflush costing.
21-14 Describe three different versions of backflush costing.
21-15 Discuss the differences between lean accounting and traditional cost accounting.

Multiple-Choice Questions

In partnership with: BECKER PROFESSIONAL EDUCATION®

21-16 The order size associated with the economic-order-quantity (EOQ) model will necessarily decline if

a. Ordering costs rise.
b. Storage costs rise.
c. Insurance costs for materials in storage fall.
d. Stockout costs rise.

21-17 Jack's Tracks sells 24,000 custom-designed GoKarts per year. These GoKarts are sold evenly throughout the year. The manufacturer charges Jack a $50 processing cost per order, and Jack incurs a carrying cost of $240 per year including storing each GoKart at a local warehouse. What is the economic order quantity for ordering materials?

a. 100 **b.** 1,000
c. 2,000 **d.** 10,000

21-18 Jill's Custom Bags manufacturers and sells 12,000 customer designer bags per year, each requiring three yards of a specially manufactured fabric. These bags are sold evenly throughout the year. The materials for these bags require 2 months' lead time. Jill wants to maintain a safety stock of sufficient material to meet 1 month's demand. What is Jill's reorder point?

a. 3,000 **b.** 6,000
c. 9,000 **d.** 12,000

21-19 Lyle Co. has only one product line. For that line, the reorder point is 500 units, the lead time for production is 3 weeks, and the sales volume is estimated at 50 units per week. Lyle has established which of the following amounts as its safety stock?

a. 150 **b.** 350
c. 500 **d.** 650

21-20 Just-in-time inventory assumes all of the following, except

1. Zero defects.
2. Resources will only be introduced as they are needed.
3. Just-in-time inventory presumes first-in, first-out costing.
4. Production of components only occurs when requested further downstream in the manufacturing cycle.

Exercises

21-21 Economic order quantity for retailer. Wonder Line (WL) operates a megastore featuring sports merchandise. It uses an EOQ decision model to make inventory decisions. It is now considering inventory decisions for its Los Angeles Galaxy soccer jerseys product line. This is a highly popular item. Data for 2020 are as follows:

Expected annual demand for Galaxy jerseys	9,000
Ordering cost per purchase order	$250
Carrying cost per year	$8 per jersey

Each jersey costs WL $50 and sells for $100. The $8 carrying cost per jersey per year consists of the required return on investment of $5.00 (10% × $50 purchase price) plus $3.00 in relevant insurance, handling, and storage costs. The purchasing lead time is 5 days. WL is open 365 days a year.

Required

1. Calculate the EOQ.
2. Calculate the number of orders that will be placed each year.
3. Calculate the reorder point.

21-22 Economic order quantity, effect of parameter changes (continuation of 21-21). Sportsman Textiles (ST) manufactures the Galaxy jerseys that Wonder Line (WL) sells to its customers. ST has recently installed computer software that enables its customers to conduct "one-stop" purchasing using state-of-the-art Web site technology. WL's ordering cost per purchase order will be $40 using this new technology.

Required

1. Calculate the EOQ for the Galaxy jerseys using the revised ordering cost of $40 per purchase order. Assume all other data from Exercise 21-21 are the same. Comment on the result.
2. Suppose ST proposes to "assist" WL. ST will allow WL customers to order directly from the ST Web site. ST would ship directly to these customers. ST would pay $12 to WL for every Galaxy jersey purchased by one of WL's customers. Comment qualitatively on how this offer would affect inventory management at WL. What factors should WL consider in deciding whether to accept ST's proposal?

21-23 EOQ for a retailer. The Cloth Bonanza sells fabrics to a wide range of industrial and consumer users. One of the products it carries is denim cloth, used in the manufacture of jeans and carrying bags. The supplier for the denim cloth pays all incoming freight. No incoming inspection of the denim is necessary because the supplier has a track record of delivering high-quality merchandise. The purchasing officer of the Cloth Bonanza has collected the following information:

Annual demand for denim cloth	29,250 yards
Ordering cost per purchase order	$195
Carrying cost per year	20% of purchase costs
Safety-stock requirements	None
Cost of denim cloth	$15 per yard

The purchasing lead time is 2 weeks. The Cloth Bonanza is open 250 days a year (50 weeks for 5 days a week).

Required

1. Calculate the EOQ for denim cloth.
2. Calculate the number of orders that will be placed each year.
3. Calculate the reorder point for denim cloth.

21-24 EOQ for a manufacturer. Sk8 Company produces skateboards and purchases 20,000 units of a wheel bearing each year at a cost of $1 per unit. Sk8 requires a 15% annual rate of return on investment. In addition, the relevant carrying cost (for insurance, materials handling, breakage, etc.) is $0.17 per unit per year. The relevant ordering cost per purchase order is $38.40.

Required

1. Calculate Sk8's EOQ for the wheel bearing.
2. Calculate Sk8's annual relevant ordering costs for the EOQ calculated in requirement 1.
3. Calculate Sk8's annual relevant carrying costs for the EOQ calculated in requirement 1.
4. Assume that demand is uniform throughout the year and known with certainty so there is no need for safety stocks. The purchase-order lead time is half a month. Calculate Sk8's reorder point for the wheel bearing.

21-25 Sensitivity of EOQ to changes in relevant ordering and carrying costs, cost of prediction error. Alpha Company's annual demand for its only product, XT-590, is 10,000 units. Alpha is currently analyzing possible combinations of relevant carrying cost per unit per year and relevant ordering cost per purchase order, depending on the company's choice of supplier and average levels of inventory. This table presents three possible combinations of carrying and ordering costs.

Relevant Carrying Cost per Unit per Year	Relevant Ordering Cost per Purchase Order
$10	$400
$20	$200
$40	$100

Required

1. For each of the relevant ordering and carrying-cost alternatives, determine (a) EOQ and (b) annual relevant total costs.
2. How does your answer to requirement 1 give insight into the impact of changes in relevant ordering and carrying costs on EOQ and annual relevant total costs? Explain briefly.
3. Suppose the relevant carrying cost per unit per year was $20 and the relevant ordering cost per purchase order was $200. Suppose further that Alpha calculates EOQ after incorrectly estimating relevant carrying cost per unit per year to be $10 and relevant ordering cost per purchase order to be $400. Calculate the annual relevant total costs of Alpha's EOQ decision. Compare this cost to the annual relevant total costs that Alpha would have incurred if it had correctly estimated the relevant carrying cost per unit per year of $20 and the relevant ordering cost per purchase order of $200 that you have already calculated in requirement 1. Calculate and comment on the cost of the prediction error.

21-26 JIT production, relevant benefits, relevant costs. The Knot manufactures men's neckwear at its Spartanburg plant. The Knot is considering implementing a JIT production system. The following are the estimated costs and benefits of JIT production:

a. Additional annual tooling costs of $250,000.
b. Average inventory would decline by 80% from the current level of $1,000,000.
c. Insurance, space, materials-handling, and setup costs, which currently total $400,000 annually, would decline by 20%.
d. The emphasis on quality inherent in JIT production would reduce rework costs by 25%. The Knot currently incurs $160,000 in annual rework costs.
e. Improved product quality under JIT production would enable The Knot to raise the price of its product by $2 per unit. The Knot sells 100,000 units each year.

The Knot's required rate of return on inventory investment is 15% per year.

Required

1. Calculate the net benefit or cost to The Knot if it adopts JIT production at the Spartanburg plant.
2. What nonfinancial and qualitative factors should The Knot consider when making the decision to adopt JIT production?
3. Suppose The Knot implements JIT production at its Spartanburg plant. Give examples of performance measures The Knot could use to evaluate and control JIT production. What would be the benefit of The Knot implementing an enterprise resource planning (ERP) system?

21-27 Backflush costing, two trigger points, incentives. Raymore, a unit of Outdoor UnPlugged, manufactures a line of electric, cordless, lawn mowers. Senior management of Outdoor UnPlugged has noticed that Raymore has been producing more lawn mowers than it has been selling, and that the unit's inventory has been steadily increasing. Senior management of Outdoor UnPlugged suspects that the bonus plan in place for the head of Raymore is behind this practice. Senior management of Outdoor UnPlugged is contemplating to switch from the current sequential tracking to a backflush costing system in order to stop the overproduction at Raymore. Specifically, senior management of Outdoor UnPlugged is considering a backflush costing system with the following two trigger points:

- Purchase of direct materials
- Sale of finished goods

Each mower takes 2 hours to assemble. There are no beginning inventories of materials or finished goods and no beginning or ending work-in-process inventories. The following data are for Raymore for March 2020:

Direct materials purchased	$1,550,000	Conversion costs incurred	$901,000
Direct materials used	$1,530,000	Conversion costs allocated	$884,000

Raymore records direct materials purchased and conversion costs incurred at actual costs. It has no direct materials variances. When finished goods are sold, the backflush costing system "pulls through" standard direct materials cost ($90 per unit) and standard conversion cost ($52 per unit). Raymore produced 17,000 finished units in March 2020 and sold 16,800 units. The actual direct materials cost per unit in March 2020 was $90, and the actual conversion cost per unit was $53. Any under- or overallocated conversion costs are written off monthly to Cost of Goods Sold.

Required

1. Following Exhibit 21-8, prepare summary journal entries for March 2020 and post the entries to applicable T-accounts for both methods the current sequential tracking and the backflush costing that senior management of Outdoor UnPlugged is considering.
2. Refer to your answer in requirement 1. How is operating income going to differ under backflush costing compared to the current sequential tracking?
3. Do you think that switching to the backflush costing system is going to accomplish the goal of Outdoor UnPlugged's senior management to stop the overproduction at Raymore?

21-28 Backflush costing, two trigger points, operating income (continuation of 21-27). Refer to Exercise 21-27. Jose, the unit manager of Raymore, is concerned that switching to the backflush costing system will lower the operating income of his unit. The senior management at Outdoor UnPlugged tells Jose that this will only be the case if the standard costs continue to be imprecise estimates of actual costs and that income will remain the same under the proposed backflush costing system if his team can better estimate standard costs.

Required

1. Assume that Jose correctly estimates the standard conversion costs to be $53 and that conversion costs incurred and conversion costs allocated are both equal to $901,000; otherwise assume the same facts as in 21-27. Following Exhibit 21-8 prepare summary journal entries for March 2020 and post the entries to applicable T-accounts for both methods the current sequential tracking and the backflush costing that senior management of Outdoor UnPlugged is considering.
2. Is the claim of the senior management at Outdoor UnPlugged correct that Raymore's operating income will remain the same under the proposed backflush costing system as long as the standard costs are estimated correctly?

21-29 Backflush costing. Silicon Valley Computer (SVC), the producer of keyboards for personal computers, which is discussed in the chapter, is a subsidiary of El Camino Corporation. Each year, headquarters of El Camino provides a capital budget to each of their subsidiaries, the amount of which is determined by the size of the subsidiary's balance sheet. The senior management of SVC is considering to simplify their accounting and to move to one of the backflush costing systems in Exhibits 21-7, 21-8, or 21-9.

Required

Refer to exhibits 21-7, 21-8, and 21-9. Which of the backflush costing systems should the senior management of SVC choose if they want to maximize the capital budget that they receive from headquarters? Show your calculations.

Problems

21-30 EOQ, uncertainty, safety stock, reorder point. Maynard Shoe Co. produces and sells an excellent-quality walking shoe. After production, the shoes are distributed to 20 warehouses around the country. Each warehouse services approximately 100 stores in its region. Maynard uses an EOQ model to determine the number of pairs of shoes to order for each warehouse from the factory. Annual demand for warehouse OR2 is approximately 132,000 pairs of shoes. The ordering cost is $264 per order. The annual carrying cost of a pair of shoes is $2.50 per pair.

Required

1. Use the EOQ model to determine the optimal number of pairs of shoes per order.
2. Assume each month consists of approximately 4 weeks. If it takes 1 week to receive an order, at what point should warehouse OR2 reorder shoes?
3. Although OR2's average weekly demand is 2,750 pairs of shoes (132,000 ÷ 12 months ÷ 4 weeks), demand each week may vary with the following probability distribution:

Total demand for 1 week	2,000 pairs	1,950 pairs	2,750 pairs	2,970 pairs	3,260 pairs
Probability (sums to 1.00)	0.02	0.10	0.76	0.10	0.02

If a store wants shoes and OR2 has none in stock, OR2 can "rush" them to the store at an additional cost of $4 per pair. How much safety stock should warehouse OR2 hold? How will this affect the reorder point and reorder quantity?

21-31 EOQ, uncertainty, safety stock, reorder point. Phillips Corporation is a major manufacturer of food processors. It purchases motors from Viking Corporation. Annual demand is 52,000 motors per year or 1,000 motors per week. The ordering cost is $360 per order. The annual carrying cost is $6.50 per motor. It currently takes 2 weeks to supply an order to the assembly plant.

Required

1. What is the optimal number of motors that Phillips' managers should order according to the EOQ model?
2. At what point should managers reorder the motors, assuming that both demand and purchase-order lead time are known with certainty?
3. Now assume that demand can vary during the 2-week purchase-order lead time. The following table shows the probability distribution of various demand levels:

Total Demand for Motors for 2 Weeks	Probability of Demand (sums to 1)
1,600	0.05
1,800	0.20
2,000	0.50
2,200	0.20
2,400	0.05

If Phillips runs out of stock, it would have to rush order the motors at an additional cost of $5 per motor. How much safety stock should the assembly plant hold? How will this affect the reorder point and reorder quantity?

21-32 MRP, EOQ, and JIT. Gadgets Galore Corp. produces J-Pods, music players that can download thousands of songs. Gadgets Galore forecasts that demand in 2020 will be 22,800 J-Pods. The variable production cost of each J-Pod is $52. In its MRP system, due to the large $19,000 cost per setup, Gadgets Galore plans to produce J-Pods once a month in batches of 1,900 units. The carrying cost of a unit in inventory is $15 per year.

Required

1. Using the MRP system, what is the annual cost of producing and carrying J-Pods in inventory? (Assume that, on average, half of the units produced in a month are in inventory.)
2. A new manager at Gadgets Galore has suggested that the company use the EOQ model to determine the optimal batch size to produce. (To use the EOQ model, Gadgets Galore needs to treat the setup cost in the same way it would treat ordering cost in a traditional EOQ model.) Determine the optimal batch size and number of batches. Round up the number of batches to the nearest whole number. What would be the annual cost of producing and carrying J-Pods in inventory if it uses the optimal batch size? Compare this cost to the cost calculated in requirement 1. Comment briefly.
3. Gadgets Galore is also considering switching from its MRP system to a JIT system. This will result in producing J-Pods in batch sizes of 300 J-Pods and will reduce obsolescence, improve quality, and result in a higher selling price. Gadgets Galore will reduce setup time and setup cost. The new setup cost will be $200 per setup. What is the annual cost of producing and carrying J-Pods in inventory under the JIT system?
4. Compare the models analyzed in the previous parts of the problem. What are the advantages and disadvantages of each?

21-33 Effect of management evaluation criteria on EOQ model. Rugged Outfitters purchases one model of mountain bike at a wholesale cost of $520 per unit and resells it to end consumers. The annual demand for the company's product is 49,000 units. Ordering costs are $500 per order and carrying costs are $100 per bike per year, including $40 opportunity cost of holding inventory.

Required

1. Compute the optimal order quantity using the EOQ model.
2. Compute (a) the number of orders per year and (b) the annual relevant total cost of ordering and carrying inventory.
3. Assume that when evaluating the manager, the company excludes the opportunity cost of carrying inventory. If the manager makes the EOQ decision excluding the opportunity cost of carrying inventory, the relevant carrying cost would be $60, not $100. How would this affect the EOQ amount and the actual annual relevant cost of ordering and carrying inventory?
4. What is the cost impact on the company of excluding the opportunity cost of carrying inventory when making EOQ decisions? Why do you think the company currently excludes the opportunity costs of carrying inventory when evaluating the manager's performance? What could the company do to encourage the manager to make decisions more congruent with the goal of reducing total inventory costs?

21-34 JIT purchasing, relevant benefits, relevant costs. (CMA, adapted) The Gibson Corporation is a manufacturing company that uses automatic stamping machines to manufacture garage doors from rolled sheets of raw steel. Gibson's inventory of raw steel averages $600,000. Juan Sanchez, president of Gibson, and Jane Anderson, Gibson's controller, are concerned about the costs of carrying inventory. The steel supplier is willing to supply steel in smaller lots at no additional charge. Anderson identifies the following effects of adopting a JIT inventory program to virtually eliminate steel inventory:

- Without scheduling any overtime, lost sales due to stockouts would increase by 700 units per year. However, by incurring overtime premiums of $90,000 per year, the increase in lost sales could be reduced to 300 units per year. This would be the maximum amount of overtime that would be feasible for Gibson.
- Two warehouses currently used for rolled steel storage would no longer be needed. Gibson rents one warehouse from another company under a cancelable leasing arrangement at an annual cost of $80,000. The other warehouse is owned by Gibson and contains 20,000 square feet. Three-fourths of the space in the owned warehouse could be rented for $2.50 per square foot per year. Insurance and property tax costs totaling $16,000 per year would be eliminated.

Gibson's required rate of return on investment is 15% per year. Gibson's budgeted income statement for the year ending December 31, 2020, (in thousands) is as follows:

Revenues (20,000 units)		$16,000
Cost of goods sold		
Variable costs	$8,450	
Fixed costs	3,280	
Total costs of goods sold		11,730
Gross margin		4,270
Marketing and distribution costs		
Variable costs	$1,045	
Fixed costs	890	
Total marketing and distribution costs		1,935
Operating income		$ 2,335

Required

1. Calculate the estimated dollar savings (loss) for the Gibson Corporation that would result in 2020 from the adoption of JIT purchasing.
2. Identify and explain other factors that Gibson should consider before deciding whether to adopt JIT purchasing.

21-35 Supply-chain effects on total relevant inventory cost. Peach Co. outsources the production of motherboards for its computers. It is currently deciding which of two suppliers to use: Alpha or Beta. Due to differences in the product failure rates in the two companies, 5% of motherboards purchased from Alpha will be inspected and 25% of motherboards purchased from Beta will be inspected. The following data refer to costs associated with Alpha and Beta:

	Alpha	Beta
Number of orders per year	50	50
Annual motherboards demanded	10,000	10,000
Price per motherboard	$ 108	$ 105
Ordering cost per order	$ 13	$ 10
Inspection cost per unit	$ 6	$ 6
Average inventory level	100 units	100 units
Expected number of stockouts	100	300
Stockout cost (cost of rush order) per stockout	$ 4	$ 6
Units returned by customers for replacing motherboards	50	500
Cost of replacing each motherboard	$ 30	$ 30
Required annual return on investment	10%	10%
Other carrying cost per unit per year	$ 3.50	$ 3.50

Required

1. What is the relevant cost of purchasing from Alpha and Beta?
2. What factors other than cost should Peach consider?

21-36 Supply-chain effects on total relevant inventory cost. Couture Jeans orders high-quality denim fabric from two different suppliers: Designer Fabrics and Cannon Cotton. Couture would like to use only one of the suppliers in the future. Due to variations in quality, Couture would need to inspect 20% of Designer's 30-yard bolts (rolls) and 30% of Cannon's. The following data refer to costs associated with the two suppliers.

	Designer	Cannon
Number of orders per year	50	50
Annual bolts demanded	2,000	2,000
Price per bolt	$ 200	$ 195
Ordering cost per order	$ 150	$ 200
Inspection cost per bolt	$ 30	$ 30
Average inventory level	20	20
Expected number of stockouts	10	10
Stockout cost of rush order	$ 20	$ 15
Estimated number of jeans returned by customers because of defective fabric	100	200
Cost of fixing jeans returned by customers because of defective fabric	$ 25	$ 25
Opportunity cost of investment	15%	15%
Other carrying costs per bolt per year	$ 10	$ 10

Required

1. What is the relevant cost of purchasing from Designer Fabrics and Cannon Cotton?
2. What factors other than cost should Couture Jeans consider?

21-37 Backflush costing and JIT production. The Rippel Corporation manufactures electrical meters. For August, there were no beginning inventories of direct materials and no beginning or ending work in process. Rippel uses a JIT production system and backflush costing with three trigger points for making entries in the accounting system:

- Purchase of direct materials
- Completion of good finished units of product
- Sale of finished goods

Rippel's August standard cost per meter is direct materials, $23, and conversion cost, $17. Rippel has no direct materials variances. The following data apply to August manufacturing:

Direct materials purchased	$535,000	Number of finished units manufactured	18,000
Conversion costs incurred	$420,000	Number of finished units sold	16,000

Required

1. Prepare summary journal entries for August (without disposing of under- or overallocated conversion costs).
2. Post the entries in requirement 1 to T-accounts for Materials and In-Process Inventory Control, Finished Goods Control, Conversion Costs Control, Conversion Costs Allocated, and Cost of Goods Sold.

21-38 Backflush, two trigger points, materials purchase and sale (continuation of 21-37). Assume the same facts for Rippel Corporation as in Problem 21-37, except that now assume Rippel uses a JIT production system and backflush costing with two trigger points for making entries in the accounting system:

- Purchase of direct materials
- Sale of finished goods

The inventory account is confined solely to direct materials, whether these materials are in a storeroom, in work in process, or in finished goods. No conversion costs are inventoried. They are allocated to the units sold at standard costs. Any under- or overallocated conversion costs are written off monthly to Cost of Goods Sold.

Required

1. Prepare summary journal entries for August, including the disposition of under- or overallocated conversion costs.
2. Post the entries in requirement 1 to T-accounts for Inventory Control, Conversion Costs Control, Conversion Costs Allocated, and Cost of Goods Sold.

21-39 Backflush, two trigger points, completion of production and sale (continuation of 21-37). Assume the same facts for Rippel Corporation as in Problem 21-37, except that now assume Rippel uses a JIT production system and backflush costing with two trigger points for making entries in the accounting system:

- Completion of good finished units of product
- Sale of finished goods

The inventory account is confined solely to finished goods. Any under- or overallocated conversion costs are written off monthly to Cost of Goods Sold.

Required

1. Prepare summary journal entries for August, including the disposition of under- or overallocated conversion costs.
2. Post the entries in requirement 1 to T-accounts for Finished Goods Control, Conversion Costs Control, Conversion Costs Allocated, and Cost of Goods Sold.

21-40 Lean accounting. Flight Security Devices (FSD) has introduced a just-in-time production process and is considering adopting lean accounting principles to support its new production philosophy. The company has two product lines: Mechanical Devices and Electronic Devices. Two individual products are made in each line. Product-line manufacturing overhead costs are traced directly to product lines and then allocated to the two individual products in each line. The company's traditional cost accounting system allocates all plant-level facility costs and some corporate overhead costs to individual products. The latest accounting report using traditional cost accounting methods included the following information (in thousands of dollars):

	Mechanical Devices		Electronic Devices	
	Product A	Product B	Product C	Product D
Sales	$790	$500	$990	$440
Direct material (based on quantity used)	225	115	255	75
Direct manufacturing labor	140	95	230	85
Manufacturing overhead (equipment lease, supervision, production control)	100	140	220	100
Allocated plant-level facility costs	35	45	70	15
Design and marketing costs	93	46	106	38
Allocated corporate overhead costs	32	4	29	32
Operating income	$165	$ 55	$ 80	$ 95

FSD has determined that each of the two product lines represents a distinct value stream. It has also determined that out of the $165,000 ($35,000 + $45,000 + $70,000 + $15,000) plant-level facility costs, product A occupies 25% of the plant's square footage, product B occupies 15%, product C occupies 25%, and product D occupies 25%. The remaining 10% of square footage is not being used. Finally, FSD has decided that in order to identify inefficiencies, direct material should be expensed in the period it is purchased, rather than when the material is used. According to purchasing records, direct material purchase costs during the period were as follows:

	Mechanical Devices		Electronic Devices	
	Product A	Product B	Product C	Product D
Direct material (purchases)	$205	$150	$255	$90

Required

1. What are the cost objects in FSD's lean accounting system?
2. Compute operating income for the cost objects identified in requirement 1 using lean accounting principles. What would you compare this operating income against? Comment on your results.

21-41 JIT production, relevant benefits, relevant costs, ethics. Galveston Pump Corporation is considering implementing a JIT production system. The new system would reduce current average inventory levels of $2,000,000 by 75%, but it would require a much greater dependency on the company's core suppliers for on-time deliveries and high-quality inputs. The company's operations manager, Frank Griswold, is opposed to the idea of a new JIT system because he is concerned that the new system (1) will be too costly to manage; (2) will result in too many stockouts; and (3) will lead to the layoff of his employees, several of whom are currently managing inventory. He believes that these layoffs will affect the morale of his entire production department. The management accountant, Bonnie Barrett, is in favor of the new system because of its likely cost savings. Frank wants Bonnie to rework the numbers because he is concerned that top management will give more weight to financial factors and not give due consideration to nonfinancial factors such as employee morale. In addition to the reduction in inventory described previously, Bonnie has gathered the following information for the upcoming year regarding the JIT system:

- Annual insurance and warehousing costs for inventory would be reduced by 60% of the current budgeted level of $350,000.
- Payroll expenses for current inventory management staff would be reduced by 15% of the budgeted total of $600,000.
- Additional annual costs for JIT system implementation and management, including personnel costs, would equal $220,000.
- The additional number of stockouts under the new JIT system is estimated to be 5% of the total number of shipments annually. Ten thousand shipments are budgeted for the upcoming year. Each stockout would result in an average additional cost of $250.
- Galveston's required rate of return on inventory investment is 10% per year.

Required

1. From a financial perspective, should Galveston adopt the new JIT system?
2. Should Bonnie Barrett rework the numbers?
3. How should she manage Frank Griswold's concerns?

Capital Budgeting and Cost Analysis

22

Should Toyota open a new plant in China or India?

Should Bose invest in developing the next generation of in-home smart speakers? Should Under Armour discontinue its children's shoe line and expand its women's golf clothing line? Working closely with accountants, top executives have to figure out how and when to best allocate the firm's financial resources among alternative opportunities to create future value for the company. Because it's hard to know what the future holds and how much projects will ultimately cost, this can be a challenging task, but it's one that managers must constantly confront. To meet this challenge, companies such as Target and Chevron have developed special groups to make project-related capital budgeting decisions. This chapter explains the different methods organizations (and individuals) use to get the "biggest bang for the buck" in terms of the projects they invest in or undertake.

LEARNING OBJECTIVES

1 Understand the five stages of capital budgeting for a project

2 Use and evaluate the two main discounted cash flow (DCF) methods: the net present value (NPV) method and the internal rate-of-return (IRR) method

3 Use and evaluate the payback and discounted payback methods

4 Use and evaluate the accrual accounting rate-of-return (AARR) method

5 Identify relevant cash inflows and outflows for capital budgeting decisions

6 Understand issues involved in implementing capital budgeting decisions and evaluating managerial performance

7 Explain how managers can use capital budgeting to achieve their firms' strategic goals

NPV AND CALIFORNIA'S NEW RESIDENTIAL SOLAR PANEL RULES[1]

Starting in 2020, virtually all new homes in California will be required to have rooftop solar panels—a historic development for clean energy in the United States. While this new California Energy Commission rule will increase the cost of building a new house by around $9,500, officials concluded that homeowners will save nearly double that, $19,000, in lower energy and maintenance costs over 30 years.

The Commission used net present value (NPV) to determine the long-term financial benefit to homeowners. On average, if a homeowner buys a new solar-equipped house with a 30-year mortgage, the added mortgage cost will be $40 per month and the energy savings $80 per month. This results in $28,800 in energy savings over 30 years. Using a 3% discount rate, the NPV of the future energy savings is still $19,000, a pretty advantageous deal for California homebuyers.

With more than 100,000 new homes built in California every year, the Commission's new rule is expected to reduce home energy use in the Golden State by 53% compared to the current rule, saving Californians $1.7 billion in energy costs over the next 30 years.

kostasgr/Shutterstock

[1] *Sources:* Justin Fox, "Let's Talk About Net Present Value and Solar Panels," Bloomberg.com, May 13, 2018 (https://www.bloomberg.com/opinion/articles/2018-05-13/california-solar-panels-and-understanding-net-present-value); Julia Pyper, "It's Official. All New California Homes Must Incorporate Solar," GreenTechMedia.com, May 9, 2018 (https://www.greentechmedia.com/articles/read/solar-mandate-all-new-california-homes#gs.WvI9ItwG).

Stages of Capital Budgeting

LEARNING OBJECTIVE 1

Understand the five stages of capital budgeting for a project

... identify projects; obtain information; make predictions; make decisions; and implement the decision, evaluate performance, and learn

Capital budgeting is the process of making long-run planning decisions for investments in projects. In much of accounting, income is calculated on a period-by-period basis. In choosing investments, however, managers select from among multiple projects, each of which may span several periods. Exhibit 22-1 illustrates these two different yet intersecting dimensions of cost analysis: (1) horizontally across, as the *project dimension*, and (2) vertically upward, as the *accounting-period dimension*. Each project is represented as a horizontal rectangle starting and ending at different times and stretching over time spans longer than 1 year. The vertical rectangle for the 2021 accounting period, for example, represents the dimensions of income determination and routine annual planning and control that cut across all projects that are ongoing that year.

To make capital budgeting decisions, managers analyze each project by considering all the life-span cash flows from its initial investment through its termination. This process is analogous to life-cycle budgeting and costing (Chapter 14, pages 578–580). For example, when Honda considers producing a new model of automobile, it begins by estimating all potential revenues from the project as well as any costs that will be incurred during its life cycle, which may be as long as 10 years. Only after examining the potential costs and benefits across all of the business functions in the value chain, from research and development (R&D) to customer service, across the entire life span of the new-car project does Honda decide whether the new model is a wise investment.

Managers use capital budgeting as a decision-making and a control tool. Like the five-step decision-making process that we have emphasized throughout this text, there are five stages to the capital budgeting process:

Stage 1: Identify Projects. *Identify potential capital investments that agree with the organization's strategy.* For example, Nike, an industry leader in product differentiation, makes significant investments in product innovation, engineering, and design, hoping to develop the next generation of high-quality sportswear. Alternatively, managers could promote products that improve productivity and efficiency as a cost-leadership strategy. For example, Lenovo's strategy of cost leadership includes outsourcing certain components to lower-cost contract manufacturing facilities located overseas. Identifying which types of capital projects to invest in is largely the responsibility of a firm's top managers.

Stage 2: Obtain Information. *Gather information from all parts of the value chain to evaluate alternative projects.* Returning to the new car example at Honda, in this stage, the firm's top managers ask the company's marketing managers for potential revenue numbers, plant managers for assembly times, and suppliers for prices and the availability of key components.

Lower-level managers are asked to validate the data provided and to explain the assumptions underlying them. The goal is to encourage open and honest communication that results in accurate estimates so that the best investment decisions can be made. Some projects will be rejected at this stage. For example, suppose Honda learns that the car cannot be built using existing plants. It may then opt to cancel the project altogether. At AkzoNobel, a global paints and coating company, the chief sustainability officer reviews projects against a set of environmental criteria and has the power to reject projects that do not meet the criteria or lack an acceptable explanation for why the company's sustainability factors were not considered.

EXHIBIT 22-1

The Project and Time Dimensions of Capital Budgeting

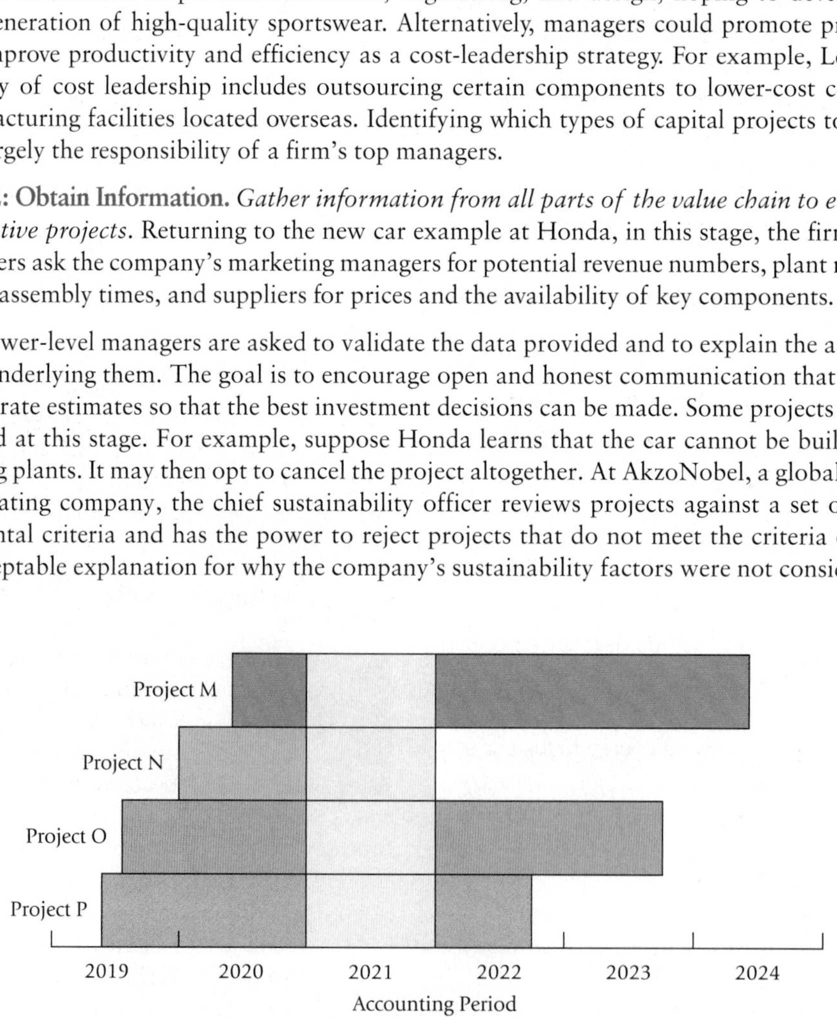

Stage 3: Make Predictions. *Forecast all potential cash flows attributable to the alternative projects.* A new project generally requires a firm to make a substantial initial outlay of capital, which is recouped over time through annual cash inflows and the disposal value of the project's assets after it is terminated. Consequently, investing in a new project requires the firm to forecast its cash flows several years into the future. BMW, for example, estimates yearly cash flows and sets its investment budgets accordingly using a 12-year planning horizon. Because of the significant uncertainty associated with these predictions, firms typically analyze a wide range of alternate circumstances. In the case of BMW, the marketing group is asked to estimate a band of possible sales figures within a 90% confidence interval. Firms also attempt to ensure that estimates, especially for the later years of a project, are grounded in realistic scenarios. It is tempting for managers to introduce biases into these projections in order to drive the outcome of the capital budgeting process to their preferred choice. This effect is exacerbated by the fact that managers may not expect to be employed at the firm during those later years and therefore cannot be held accountable for their estimates.

Stage 4: Make Decisions by Choosing Among Alternatives. *Determine which investment yields the greatest benefit and the least cost to the organization.* Using the quantitative information obtained in Stage 3, the firm uses any one of several capital budgeting methodologies to determine which project best meets organizational goals. While capital budgeting calculations are typically limited to financial information, managers use their judgment and intuition to factor in qualitative information and strategic considerations as well. For example, even if a proposed new line of cars meets its financial targets on a standalone basis, Honda might decide not to pursue the line if it is not aligned with the strategic imperatives of the company on matters such as brand positioning, industry leadership in safety and technology, and fuel consumption. Considerations of environmental sustainability might also favor certain projects that currently appear unprofitable. Freight and logistics giant UPS relaxes the company's minimum rate of return on vehicles that have the potential to reduce fuel use and costs. Similarly, Sealed Air is willing to accept projects with a lower projected return if they look promising with regard to reducing greenhouse gas emissions. For another example, see Concepts in Action: AkzoNobel Integrates Sustainability Into Capital Budgeting. Finally, managers spend a significant amount of time assessing the risks of a project, in terms of both the uncertainty of the estimated cash flows as well as the potential downside risks of the project (including to the firm as a whole) if the worst-case scenario were to occur.

Stage 5: Implement the Decision, Evaluate Performance, and Learn. Given the complexities of capital investment decisions and their long time horizons, this stage can be separated into two phases:

- **Obtain funding and make the investments selected in Stage 4.** The sources of funding include internally generated cash as well as equity and debt securities sold in capital markets. Making capital investments is often an arduous task, laden with the purchase of many different goods and services. If Honda opts to build a new car, it must order steel, aluminum, paint, and so on. If some of the materials are unavailable, managers must determine the economic feasibility of using alternative inputs.
- **Track realized cash flows, compare against estimated numbers, and revise plans if necessary.** As the cash outflows and inflows begin to accumulate, managers can verify whether the predictions made in Stage 3 agree with the actual flows of cash from the project. Snap Inc. saw disappointing advertising revenues and monthly active users in 2018 due to its ill-received app redesign and loss of market share to Facebook Inc.'s Instagram Stories. As a result, Snap introduced a suite of new products and services, including an ad-supported gaming platform.

  It is equally important for a company to abandon projects that are performing poorly relative to expectations. Managers have a natural bias to escalate their commitment to a project they chose to implement for fear of revealing they made an incorrect capital budgeting decision. It is in the firm's and the managers' long-term interest, however, to acknowledge the mistake when it is clear that the project is not financially sustainable. For example, in July 2017, a consortium of companies cancelled the $29 billion Pacific Northwest LNG project to build a natural gas liquefaction and export facility in British

CONCEPTS IN ACTION

AkzoNobel Integrates Sustainability Into Capital Budgeting[2]

Kristoffer Tripplaar/Alamy Stock Photo

AkzoNobel is a major producer of specialty chemicals in the global paints and coating industry. Over time, the Netherlands-based company has factored sustainability into its strategy and management processes as part of its company-wide "Planet Possible" environmental strategy. This includes integrating sustainability into its capital budgeting processes.

AkzoNobel implemented a program called the "Sustainability Assessment of Investments" to ensure sustainability was being factored into decision making for capital allocation for investments in infrastructure and new facilities. This program requires that any capital budget request over $5 million analyze sustainability impacts and answer critical questions such as the following:

- Where can AkzoNobel locate a new facility to improve access to sustainable transport options for product distribution and minimize the company's carbon and water footprint?
- Where should AkzoNobel locate a new facility so it has greater access to renewable energy sources?
- What are the cleanest sources of power generation that can be used at AkzoNobel facilities? How can the options be evaluated in the most transparent manner?

AkzoNobel's chief sustainability officer has the power to veto capital budget requests that are found to have insufficiently addressed sustainability considerations, even if approved by the company's controller. This incentivizes business units to perform both a high-quality financial analysis and a sustainability analysis to ensure that their projects are approved.

These processes have helped AkzoNobel make significant progress towards its goal of reducing carbon emissions across the value chain by 25–30% by 2020. The proportion of renewable energy used in company operations has also increased to 45%. Additionally, AkzoNobel has invested in creating more environmentally-sustainable products such as chemical additives that allow asphalt to be mixed at lower temperatures and marine coatings that help ships reduce fuel consumption and cut emissions.

[2] *Sources:* Alexander Perera et al., "Aligning Profit and Environmental Sustainability: Stories From Industry," World Resources Institute working paper, February 2013 (https://www.wri.org/publication/aligning-profit-and-environmental-sustainability); Akzo Nobel N.V., "Sustainability," https://www.akzonobel.com/en/about-us/what-we-do/sustainability, accessed February 2019.

Columbia, Canada. Petronas, the Malaysian energy company, led the project with a 62% stake and lost an estimated $800 million for work already done. The project was cancelled due to low natural gas prices and changes in the energy market.

To illustrate capital budgeting, consider Vector Transport. Vector operates bus lines throughout the United States, often providing transportation services on behalf of local transit authorities. Several of Vector's buses are nearing the end of their useful lives and now require increased operating and maintenance costs. Customers have also complained that the buses lack adequate storage, flexible seating configurations, and newer amenities such as wireless Internet access and personal entertainment systems. The firm has made a commitment to act in an environmentally responsible manner and will only pursue projects that do minimal harm to the ecosystem. Accordingly, in Stage 1, Vector's managers decide to look for replacement buses that generate low emissions. In the information-gathering stage (Stage 2), the company learns that as early as 2020, it could feasibly begin purchasing and using diesel-electric hybrid buses that have Wi-Fi and also offer greater comfort and storage. After collecting additional data, Vector begins to forecast its future cash flows if it invests in the new buses (Stage 3). Vector estimates that it can purchase a hybrid bus with a useful life of 5 years for a net after-tax initial investment of $648,900, which is calculated as follows:[3]

[3] For the purposes of exposition, we study the capital budgeting problem for replacing one bus rather than a fleet of buses.

Cost of new hybrid bus	$660,000
Investment in working capital	30,000
Cash flow from disposing of existing bus (after-tax)	(41,100)
Net initial investment for new bus	$648,900

Working capital refers to the difference between current assets and current liabilities. New projects often require additional investments in current assets such as inventories and receivables. In the case of Vector, the purchase of the new bus is accompanied by an incremental outlay of $30,000 for supplies, replacement batteries, and spare parts inventory. At the end of the project, the $30,000 in current assets is liquidated, resulting in a cash inflow. However, because of the rapid nature of improvements in hybrid technology, the bus itself is believed to have no terminal disposal value after 5 years.

Managers estimate that by introducing the new hybrid buses, operating cash inflows (cash revenues minus cash operating costs) will increase by $180,000 (after tax) in the first 4 years and by $150,000 in year 5. This arises from higher ticket prices and increases in ridership due to new customers who are drawn to the amenities of the hybrid bus, as well as savings in fuel, maintenance, and operating costs. To simplify the analysis, suppose that all cash flows occur at the end of each year. Note that cash flow at the end of the fifth year also increases by $180,000 − $150,000 in operating cash inflows and $30,000 in working capital. Management next calculates the costs and benefits of the proposed project (Stage 4). This chapter discusses four capital budgeting methods to analyze financial information: (1) net present value (NPV), (2) internal rate-of-return (IRR), (3) payback, and (4) accrual accounting rate-of-return (AARR). Both the net present value (NPV) and internal rate-of-return (IRR) methods use *discounted cash flows*, which we discuss in the next section.

DECISION POINT

What are the five stages of capital budgeting?

Discounted Cash Flow

LEARNING OBJECTIVE 2

Use and evaluate the two main discounted cash flow (DCF) methods: the net present value (NPV) method and the internal rate-of-return (IRR) method

... to explicitly consider all project cash flows and the time value of money

Discounted cash flow (DCF) methods measure all expected future cash inflows and outflows of a project discounted back to the present point in time. The key feature of DCF methods is the **time value of money**, which means that a dollar (or any other monetary unit) received today is worth more than a dollar received at any future time. The reason is that $1 received today can be invested at, say, 10% per year so that it grows to $1.10 at the end of 1 year. The time value of money is the opportunity cost (the return of $0.10 forgone per year) from not having the money today. In this example, $1 received 1 year from now is worth $1 ÷ 1.10 = $0.9091 today. Similarly, $100 received 1 year from now will be weighted by 0.9091 to yield a discounted cash flow of $90.91, which is today's value of that $100 next year. In this way, discounted cash flow methods explicitly measure cash flows in terms of the time value of money. Note that DCF focuses exclusively on cash inflows and outflows rather than on operating income as calculated under accrual accounting. The compound interest tables and formulas used in DCF analysis are in Appendix A, pages 960–967. If you are unfamiliar with compound interest, do not proceed until you have studied Appendix A, as the tables in Appendix A will be used frequently in this chapter.

The two DCF methods we describe are the net present value (NPV) method and the internal rate-of-return (IRR) method. Both DCF methods use the **required rate of return (RRR)**, the minimum acceptable annual rate of return on an investment. The RRR is set internally by the organization, usually by upper management, and typically represents the return that an organization could expect to receive elsewhere for an investment of comparable risk. The RRR is also called the **discount rate**, **hurdle rate**, **cost of capital**, or **opportunity cost of capital**. Let's suppose the chief financial officer (CFO) at Vector has set the required rate of return for the firm's investments at 8% per year.

Net Present Value Method

The **net present value (NPV) method** calculates the expected monetary gain or loss from a project by discounting all expected future cash inflows and outflows back to the present point in time using the required rate of return. To use the NPV method, apply the following three steps:

Step 1: Draw a Sketch of Relevant Cash Inflows and Outflows. The right side of Exhibit 22-2 shows arrows that depict the cash flows of the new hybrid bus. The sketch helps the decision maker visualize and organize the data in a systematic way. *Note that parentheses denote relevant cash outflows throughout all of the exhibits in this chapter.* Exhibit 22-2 includes the outflow for the acquisition of the new bus at the start of year 1 (also referred to as end of year 0) and the inflows over the subsequent 5 years. The NPV method specifies cash flows regardless of their source, such as operations, the purchase or sale of equipment, or an investment in or recovery of working capital. However, accrual-accounting concepts such as sales made on credit or noncash expenses are not included because the focus of the NPV method is on *cash* inflows and outflows.

Step 2: Discount the Cash Flows Using the Correct Compound Interest Table From Appendix A and Sum the Discounted Cash Flows. In the Vector example, the cash inflows all have the same dollar value and thus constitute an annuity, which is a series of equal cash flows at equal time intervals. So, we can compute the present value of an annuity using Table 4. Alternatively, we can discount each year's cash flow separately using Table 2. (Both tables are in Appendix A.) If we use Table 2, we find the discount factors for periods 1–5 under the 8% column. Approach 1 in Exhibit 22-2 uses the five discount factors. To obtain the present

EXHIBIT 22-2 Net Present Value Method: Vector's Hybrid Bus

Home Insert Page Layout Formulas Data Review View

	A	B	C	D	E	F	G	H	I
1			Net initial investment	$648,900					
2			Useful life	5 years					
3			Annual cash flow	$180,000					
4			Required rate of return	8%					
5									
6		Present Value	Present Value of	Sketch of Relevant Cash Flows at End of Each Year					
7		of Cash Flow	$1 Discounted at 8%	0	1	2	3	4	5
8	Approach 1: Discounting Each Year's Cash Flow Separately[a]								
9	Net initial investment	$(648,900) ←	1.000 ←	$(648,900)					
10		166,680 ←	0.926 ←		$180,000				
11		154,260 ←	0.857 ←			$180,000			
12	Annual cash inflow	142,920 ←	0.794 ←				$180,000		
13		132,300 ←	0.735 ←					$180,000	
14		122,580 ←	0.681 ←						$180,000
15	NPV if new bus purchased	$ 69,840							
16									
17	Approach 2: Using Annuity Table[b]								
18	Net initial investment	$(648,900) ←	1.000 ←	$(648,900)					
19					$180,000	$180,000	$180,000	$180,000	$180,000
20									
21	Annual cash inflow	718,740 ←	3.993 ←						
22	NPV if new bus purchased	$ 69,840							
23									
24	*Note:* Parentheses denote relevant cash outflows throughout all exhibits in Chapter 22.								
25	[a] Present values from Table 2, Appendix A, at the end of the text. For example, $0.857 = 1 \div (1.08)^2$.								
26	[b] Annuity present value from Table 4, Appendix A. The annuity value of 3.993 is the sum of the individual discount rates, 0.926 + 0.857 + 0.794 + 0.735 + 0.681.								

value amount, multiply each discount factor by the corresponding amount represented by the arrow on the right in Exhibit 22-2 (−$648,900 × 1.000; $180,000 × 0.926; and so on to $180,000 × 0.681). Because the investment in the new bus produces an annuity, we may also use Table 4. Under Approach 2, we find that the annuity factor for five periods under the 8% column is 3.993, which is the sum of the five discount factors used in Approach 1. We multiply the uniform annual cash inflow by this factor to obtain the present value of the inflows ($718,740 = $180,000 × 3.993). Subtracting the initial investment then yields the NPV of the project as $69,840 ($69,840 = $718,740 − $648,900).

Step 3: Make the Project Decision on the Basis of the Calculated NPV. An NPV that is zero or positive suggests that from a financial standpoint, the company should accept the project because its expected rate of return equals or exceeds the required rate of return. If the NPV is negative, the company should reject the project because its expected rate of return is below the required rate of return.

Exhibit 22-2 calculates an NPV of $69,840 at the required rate of return of 8% per year. The project is acceptable based on financial information. The cash flows from the project are adequate to (1) recover the net initial investment in the project and (2) earn a return greater than 8% per year on the investment tied up in the project over its useful life.

Managers must also weigh nonfinancial factors such as the effect that purchasing the bus will have on Vector's brand. The financial benefits that accrue from Vector's brand are difficult to estimate. Nevertheless, managers must consider brand effects before reaching a final decision. Suppose, for example, that the NPV of the hybrid bus is negative. Vector's managers might still decide to buy the bus if it maintains Vector's technological image and reputation for environmental responsibility. These are factors that could increase Vector's financial outcomes in the future, such as by attracting more riders or generating additional contracts from government transit agencies. For example, Unilever, the consumer goods corporation, recognized customers' growing taste for sustainable products and acquired the sustainable cleaning products company Seventh Generation in 2016.

Pause here. Do not proceed until you understand what you see in Exhibit 22-2. Compare Approach 1 with Approach 2 in Exhibit 22-2 to see how Table 4 in Appendix A merely aggregates the present value factors of Table 2. That is, the fundamental table is Table 2. Table 4 just simplifies calculations when there is an annuity.

Internal Rate-of-Return Method

The **internal rate-of-return (IRR) method** calculates the discount rate at which an investment's present value of all expected cash inflows equals the present value of its expected cash outflows. That is, the IRR is the discount rate that makes NPV = $0. Exhibit 22-3 shows the cash flows and the NPV of Vector's hybrid project using a 12% annual discount rate. At a 12% discount rate, the NPV of the project is $0. Therefore, the IRR is 12% per year.

Managers or analysts solving capital budgeting problems typically use a calculator or computer program to determine the internal rate of return. The following trial-and-error approach can also provide the answer.

Step 1: Use a discount rate and calculate the project's NPV.

Step 2: If the calculated NPV is less than zero, use a lower discount rate. (A *lower* discount rate will *increase* the NPV. Remember that we are trying to find a discount rate for which the NPV = $0.) If the NPV exceeds zero, use a higher discount rate to lower the NPV. Keep adjusting the discount rate until the NPV does equal $0. In the Vector example, a discount rate of 8% yields an NPV of +$69,840 (see Exhibit 22-2). A discount rate of 14% yields an NPV of −30,960 (3.433, the present value annuity factor from Table 4, × $180,000 minus $648,900). Therefore, the discount rate that makes the NPV equal to $0 must lie between 8% and 14%. We use 12% and get NPV = $0. Hence, the IRR is 12% per year.

EXHIBIT 22-3 Internal Rate-of-Return Method: Vector's Hybrid Bus[a]

	A	B	C	D	E	F	G	H	I
1			Net initial investment	$648,900					
2			Useful life	5 years					
3			Annual cash flow	$180,000					
4			Annual discount rate	12%					
5									
6		Present Value	Present Value of		Sketch of Relevant Cash Flows at End of Each Year				
7		of Cash Flow	$1 Discounted at 12%	0	1	2	3	4	5
8	**Approach 1: Discounting Each Year's Cash Flow Separately[b]**								
9	Net initial investment	$(648,900)	1.000	$(648,900)					
10		160,740	0.893		$180,000				
11		143,460	0.797			$180,000			
12	Annual cash inflow	128,160	0.712				$180,000		
13		114,480	0.636					$180,000	
14		102,060	0.567						$180,000
15	NPV if new bus purchased	$ 0							
16	(the zero difference proves that								
17	the internal rate of return is 12%)								
18									
19	**Approach 2: Using Annuity Table[c]**								
20	Net initial investment	$(648,900)	1.000	$(648,900)					
21					$180,000	$180,000	$180,000	$180,000	$180,000
22									
23	Annual cash inflow	648,900	3.605						
24	NPV if new bus purchased	$ 0							
25									
26	[a]The internal rate of return is computed by methods explained on pp. 855–856.								
27	[b]Present values from Table 2, Appendix A, at the end of the text.								
28	[c]Annuity present value from Table 4, Appendix A. The annuity value of 3.605 is the sum of the individual discount rates 0.893 + 0.797 + 0.712 + 0.636 + 0.567.								

Computing the IRR is easier when the cash inflows are constant, as in our Vector example. The information in Exhibit 22-3 can be expressed as follows:

$$\$648{,}900 = \text{Present value of annuity of } \$180{,}000 \text{ at } X\% \text{ per year for 5 years}$$

Or, what factor F in Table 4 (in Appendix A) will satisfy this equation?

$$\$648{,}900 = \$180{,}000F$$

$$F = \$648{,}900 \div \$180{,}000 = 3.605$$

On the five-period line of Table 4, find the percentage column that is closest to 3.605. It is exactly 12%. If the factor (F) falls between the factors in two columns, straight-line interpolation is used to approximate the IRR. This interpolation is illustrated in the Problem for Self-Study (pages 871–872).

Managers accept a project only if its IRR equals or exceeds the firm's RRR (required rate of return). In the Vector example, the hybrid bus has an IRR of 12%, which is greater than the RRR of 8%. On the basis of financial factors, Vector should invest in the new bus. In general, the NPV and IRR decision rules result in consistent project acceptance or rejection decisions. If the IRR exceeds the RRR, then the project has a positive NPV (favoring acceptance). If the IRR equals the RRR, then NPV equals $0, so the company is indifferent between accepting and rejecting the project. If the IRR is less than the RRR, the NPV is negative (favoring rejection). Obviously, managers prefer projects with higher IRRs to projects with lower IRRs, if all other things are equal. The IRR of 12% means the cash inflows from the project are adequate to (1) recover the net initial investment in the project and (2) earn a return of exactly 12% on the investment tied up in the project over its useful life.

22-1 TRY IT!

Elegant Home Company operates a number of home improvement stores in a metropolitan area. Elegant Home's management estimates that if it invests $300,000 in a new computer system, it can save $69,000 in annual cash operating costs. The system has an expected useful life of 8 years and no terminal disposal value. The required rate of return is 10%. Ignore income tax issues and assume all cash flows occur at year-end except for initial investment amounts.

Calculate the following for the new computer system:

a. Net present value
b. Internal rate of return (using the interpolation method)

Comparing the Net Present Value and Internal Rate-of-Return Methods

The NPV method leads to shareholder value maximization and is preferable to the IRR technique for several reasons.[4] One advantage of the NPV method is that it's expressed in dollars, not in percentages. Therefore, we can sum NPVs of individual projects to calculate an NPV of a combination or portfolio of projects. In contrast, the IRRs of individual projects cannot be added or averaged to represent the IRR of a combination of projects.

A second advantage of NPV is that it can be expressed as a unique number. From the sign and magnitude of this number, the firm can then make an accurate assessment of the financial consequences of accepting or rejecting the project. Under the IRR method, it is possible that more than one IRR may exist for a given project. In other words, there may be multiple discount rates that equate the NPV of a set of cash flows to zero. This is the case, for example, when the signs of the cash flows switch over time; that is, when there are outflows, followed by inflows, followed by additional outflows, and so forth. In such cases, it is difficult to know which of the IRR estimates should be compared to the firm's required rate of return.

A third advantage of the NPV method is that it can be used when the RRR varies over the life of a project. Suppose Vector's management sets an RRR of 10% per year in years 1 and 2 and 14% per year in years 3, 4, and 5. Total present value of the cash inflows can be calculated as $633,780 (computations not shown). It is not possible to use the IRR method in this case. That's because different RRRs in different years mean there is no single RRR that the IRR (a single figure) can be compared against to decide if the project should be accepted or rejected.

Finally, in some situations, the IRR method is prone to indicating erroneous decisions. This can occur when mutually exclusive projects with unequal lives or unequal levels of initial investment are being compared to one another. The reason is that the IRR method implicitly assumes that project cash flows can be reinvested at the *project's* rate of return. The NPV method, in contrast, accurately assumes that project cash flows can only be reinvested at the *company's* required rate of return.

Despite its limitations, the IRR method is widely used.[5] Why? Probably because managers find the percentage return computed under the IRR method easy to understand and compare. Moreover, in most instances where a single project is being evaluated, their decisions would likely be unaffected by the choice of using IRR or NPV.

Sensitivity Analysis

To present the basics of the NPV and IRR methods, we have assumed that the expected values of cash flows will occur *for certain*. In reality, there is much uncertainty associated with predicting future cash flows. To examine how a result will change if the predicted financial outcomes are not achieved or if an underlying assumption changes, managers use *sensitivity analysis*, also called "what if" technique, introduced in Chapter 3.

---

[4] More detailed explanations of the preeminence of the NPV criterion can be found in corporate finance texts.

[5] In a survey, John Graham and Campbell Harvey found that 75.7% of CFOs always or almost always used IRR for capital budgeting decisions, while a slightly smaller number, 74.9%, always or almost always used the NPV criterion.

EXHIBIT 22-4

Net Present Value Calculations for Vector's Hybrid Bus Under Different Assumptions of Annual Cash Flows and Required Rates of Return[a]

	A	B	C	D	E	F
1	**Required**	**Annual Cash Flows**				
2	**Rate of Return**	**$ 140,000**	**$160,000**	**$180,000**	**$200,000**	**$220,000**
3	8%	$ (89,880)	$ (10,020)	$ 69,840	$149,700	$229,560
4	10%	$(118,160)	$ (42,340)	$ 33,480	$109,300	$185,120
5	12%	$(144,200)	$ (72,100)	$ 0	$ 72,100	$144,200
6						
7	[a]All calculated amounts assume the project's useful life is 5 years.					

A common way to apply sensitivity analysis to capital budgeting decisions is to vary each of the inputs to the NPV calculation by a certain percentage and assess the effect on the project's NPV. Sensitivity analysis can take on other forms as well. Suppose a manager at Vector believes the firm's forecasted cash flows are difficult to predict. She asks, "What are the minimum annual cash inflows that make the investment in a new hybrid bus acceptable—that is, what inflows lead to an NPV = $0?" For the data in Exhibit 22-2, let A = annual cash flow and let the NPV = $0. The net initial investment is $648,900, and the present value factor at the 8% required annual rate of return for a 5-year annuity of $1 is 3.993. Then

$$\text{NPV} = \$0$$
$$3.993A - \$648{,}900 = \$0$$
$$3.993A = \$648{,}900$$
$$A = \$162{,}509$$

At the discount rate of 8% per year, the annual (after-tax) cash inflows can decrease to $162,509 (a decline of $180,000 − $162,509 = $17,491) before the NPV falls to $0. If the manager believes she can attain annual cash inflows of at least $162,509, she can justify investing in the hybrid bus on financial grounds.

DECISION POINT

What are the two primary discounted cash flow (DCF) methods for project evaluation?

Exhibit 22-4 shows that variations in the annual cash inflows or the RRR significantly affect the NPV of the hybrid bus project. NPVs can also vary with different useful lives of a project. Sensitivity analysis helps managers to focus on decisions that are most sensitive to different assumptions and to worry less about decisions that are not as sensitive. It is also an important risk-management tool because it provides information to managers about the downside risks of projects as well as their potential impact on the health of the overall firm.

Payback Method

LEARNING OBJECTIVE 3

Use and evaluate the payback and discounted payback methods

... to calculate the time it takes to recoup the investment

We now consider the third method for analyzing the financial aspects of projects. The **payback method** measures the time it will take to recoup, in the form of expected future cash flows, the net initial investment in a project. Like the NPV and IRR methods, the payback method does not distinguish among the sources of cash flows, such as those from operations, purchase or sale of equipment, or investment or recovery of working capital. As you will see, the payback method is simpler to calculate when a project has uniform cash flows than when cash flows are uneven over time.

Uniform Cash Flows

The hybrid bus Vector is considering buying costs $648,900 and generates a *uniform* $180,000 cash inflow every year of its 5-year expected useful life. The payback period is calculated as follows:

$$\text{Payback period} = \frac{\text{Net initial investment}}{\text{Uniform increase in annual future cash flows}}$$
$$= \frac{\$648{,}900}{\$180{,}000} = 3.6 \text{ years}^{6}$$

[6] Cash inflows from the new hybrid bus occur uniformly *throughout* the year, but for simplicity in calculating NPV and IRR, we assume they occur at the *end* of each year. A literal interpretation of this assumption would imply a payback of 4 years because Vector will only recover its investment when cash inflows occur at the end of year 4. The calculations shown in the chapter, however, better approximate Vector's payback on the basis of uniform cash flows throughout the year.

The payback method highlights liquidity, a factor that often plays a role in capital budgeting decisions, particularly when the investments are large. Managers prefer projects with shorter payback periods (projects that are more liquid) to projects with longer payback periods, if all other things are equal. Projects with shorter payback periods give an organization more flexibility because funds for other projects become available sooner. Also, managers are less confident about cash flow predictions that stretch far into the future, again favoring shorter payback periods.

Unlike the NPV and IRR methods where managers select an RRR, under the payback method, managers choose a cutoff period for the project. Projects with payback periods that are shorter than the cutoff period are considered acceptable, and those with payback periods that are longer than the cutoff period are rejected. Japanese companies favor the payback method over other methods and use cutoff periods ranging from 3 to 5 years, depending on the risks involved with the project.[7] In general, modern risk management calls for using shorter cutoff periods for riskier projects. If Vector's cutoff period under the payback method is 3 years, it will reject the new bus.

The payback method is easy to understand. As in DCF methods, the payback method is not affected by accrual accounting conventions such as depreciation. Payback is a useful measure when (1) preliminary screening of many proposals is necessary, (2) interest rates are high, and (3) the expected cash flows in later years of a project are highly uncertain. Under these conditions, companies give much more weight to cash flows in the early periods of a capital budgeting project and to recovering the investments they have made, thereby making the payback criterion especially relevant.

Two weaknesses of the payback method are that (1) it fails to explicitly incorporate the time value of money and (2) it does not consider a project's cash flows after the payback period. Consider an alternative to the $648,900 hybrid bus. Another hybrid bus, one with a 3-year useful life and no terminal disposal value, requires only a $504,000 net initial investment and will also result in cash inflows of $180,000 per year. First, compare the payback periods:

$$\text{Bus 1} = \frac{\$648{,}900}{\$180{,}000} = 3.6 \text{ years}$$

$$\text{Bus 2} = \frac{\$504{,}000}{\$180{,}000} = 2.8 \text{ years}$$

The payback criterion favors bus 2, which has a shorter payback. If the cutoff period were 3 years, bus 1 would fail to meet the payback criterion.

Consider next the NPV of the two investment options using Vector's 8% required rate of return for the hybrid bus investment. At a discount rate of 8%, the NPV of bus 2 is −$40,140 (2.577, the present value annuity factor for 3 years at 8% per year from Table 4, times $180,000 = $463,860, minus net initial investment of $504,000). Bus 1, as we know, has a positive NPV of $69,840 (from Exhibit 22-2). The NPV criterion suggests Vector should acquire bus 1. Bus 2, which has a negative NPV, would fail to meet the NPV criterion.

The payback method gives a different answer from the NPV method in this example because the payback method ignores cash flows after the payback period and ignores the time value of money. Another problem with the payback method is that choosing too short a cutoff period can lead to projects with high short-run cash flows being selected. Projects with long-run, positive NPVs will tend to be rejected. Despite these differences, companies find it useful to look at both NPV and payback when making capital investment decisions.

Nonuniform Cash Flows

When cash flows are not uniform, the payback computation takes a cumulative form: The cash flows over successive years are accumulated until the amount of net initial investment is recovered. Suppose Venture Law Group is considering purchasing videoconferencing equipment for

---

[7] A 2010 survey of Japanese firms found that 50.2% of them often or always used the payback method to make capital budgeting decisions. The NPV method came in a distant second at 30.5% (see Tomonari Shinoda, "Capital Budgeting Management Practices in Japan," *Economic Journal of Hokkaido University* 39 (2010): 39–50).

$150,000. The equipment is expected to provide total cash savings of $340,000 over the next 5 years, due to reduced travel costs and more effective use of associates' time. The cash savings occur uniformly throughout each year but are not uniform across years.

Year	Cash Savings	Cumulative Cash Savings	Net Initial Investment Unrecovered at End of Year
0	—	—	$150,000
1	$50,000	$ 50,000	100,000
2	55,000	105,000	45,000
3	60,000	165,000	—
4	85,000	250,000	—
5	90,000	340,000	—

The chart shows that payback occurs during the third year. Straight-line interpolation within the third year reveals that the final $45,000 needed to recover the $150,000 investment (that is, $150,000 − $105,000 recovered by the end of year 2) will be achieved three-quarters of the way through year 3, during which $60,000 of cash savings occur:

$$\text{Payback period} = 2 \text{ years} + \left(\frac{\$45{,}000}{\$60{,}000} \times 1 \text{ year}\right) = 2.75 \text{ years}$$

It is relatively simple to adjust the payback method to incorporate the time value of money by using a similar cumulative approach. The **discounted payback method** calculates the amount of time required for the discounted expected future cash flows to recoup the net initial investment in a project. For the videoconferencing example, we can modify the preceding chart by discounting the cash flows at the 8% required rate of return.

Year (1)	Cash Savings (2)	Present Value of $1 Discounted at 8% (3)	Discounted Cash Savings (4) = (2) × (3)	Cumulative Discounted Cash Savings (5)	Net Initial Investment Unrecovered at End of Year (6)
0	—	1.000	—	—	$150,000
1	$50,000	0.926	$46,300	$ 46,300	103,700
2	55,000	0.857	47,135	93,435	56,565
3	60,000	0.794	47,640	141,075	8,925
4	85,000	0.735	62,475	203,550	—
5	90,000	0.681	61,290	264,840	—

The fourth column shows the present values of the future cash savings. It is evident from the chart that discounted payback occurs between years 3 and 4. At the end of the third year, $8,925 of the initial investment is still unrecovered. Comparing this to the $62,475 in present value of savings achieved in the fourth year, straight-line interpolation reveals that the discounted payback period is exactly one-seventh of the way into the fourth year:

$$\text{Discounted payback period} = 3 \text{ years} + \left(\frac{\$8{,}925}{\$62{,}475} \times 1 \text{ year}\right) = 3.14 \text{ years}$$

The discounted payback does incorporate the time value of money, but is still subject to the other criticism of the payback method—that cash flows beyond the discounted payback period are ignored, resulting in a bias toward projects with high short-run cash flows. Companies such as Hewlett-Packard value the discounted payback method (Hewlett-Packard refers to it as "breakeven time") because they view longer-term cash flows as inherently unpredictable in high-growth industries, such as technology.

Finally, the videoconferencing example has a single cash outflow of $150,000 in year 0. When a project has multiple cash outflows occurring at different points in time, these outflows are first aggregated to obtain a total cash-outflow figure for the project. For computing the payback period, the cash flows are simply added, with no adjustment for the time value of money. For calculating the discounted payback period, the present values of the outflows are added instead.

DECISION POINT

What are the payback and discounted payback methods? What are their main weaknesses?

22-2 TRY IT!

Consider Elegant Home Company. With the same information as provided in Try It! 22-1, calculate the following for the new computer system:

a. Payback period
b. Discounted payback period

Accrual Accounting Rate-of-Return Method

LEARNING OBJECTIVE 4

Use and evaluate the accrual accounting rate-of-return (AARR) method

... after-tax operating income divided by investment

We now consider a fourth method for analyzing the financial aspects of capital budgeting projects. The **accrual accounting rate-of-return (AARR) method** divides the average annual (accrual accounting) income of a project by a measure of the investment in it. We illustrate this method for Vector using the project's net initial investment as the amount in the denominator:

$$\text{Accrual accounting rate of return} = \frac{\text{Increase in expected average annual after-tax operating income}}{\text{Net initial investment}}$$

If Vector purchases the new hybrid bus, its net initial investment is $648,900. The increase in the expected average annual after-tax operating cash inflows is $174,000. This amount is the expected after-tax total operating cash inflows of $870,000 ($180,000 for 4 years and $150,000 in year 5), divided by the time horizon of 5 years. Suppose that the new bus results in additional depreciation deductions of $120,000 per year ($132,000 in annual depreciation for the new bus, relative to $12,000 per year on the existing bus).[8] The increase in the expected average annual after-tax income is therefore $54,000 (the difference between the cash flow increase of $174,000 and the depreciation increase of $120,000). The AARR on net initial investment is computed as

$$\text{AARR} = \frac{\$174{,}000 - \$120{,}000}{\$648{,}900} = \frac{\$54{,}000 \text{ per year}}{\$648{,}900} = 0.083, \text{ or } 8.3\% \text{ per year}$$

The 8.3% figure for AARR indicates the average rate at which a dollar of investment generates after-tax operating income. The new hybrid bus has a low AARR for two reasons: (1) the use of the net initial investment as the denominator and (2) the use of income as the numerator, which necessitates deducting depreciation charges from the annual operating cash flows. To mitigate the first issue, many companies calculate AARR using an average level of investment. This alternative procedure recognizes that the book value of the investment declines over time. In its simplest form, average investment for Vector is calculated as the arithmetic mean of the net initial investment of $648,900 and the net terminal cash flow of $30,000 (terminal disposal value of hybrid bus of $0, plus the terminal recovery of working capital of $30,000):

$$\text{Average investment over 5 years} = \frac{\text{Net initial investment} + \text{Net terminal cash flow}}{2}$$

$$= \frac{\$648{,}900 + \$30{,}000}{2} = \$339{,}450$$

[8] We provide further details on these numbers in the next section; see page 863.

The AARR on average investment is then calculated as follows:

$$\text{AARR} = \frac{\$54{,}000}{\$339{,}450} = 0.159\text{, or } 15.9\% \text{ per year}$$

Companies vary in how they calculate the AARR. There is no uniformly preferred approach. Be sure you understand how the AARR is defined in each individual situation. Projects with AARRs that exceed a specific required rate of return are regarded as acceptable (the higher the AARR, the better the project is considered to be).

The AARR method is similar to the IRR method in that both calculate a rate-of-return percentage. The AARR method calculates the return using operating-income numbers after considering accruals and taxes, whereas the IRR method calculates the return using after-tax cash flows and the time value of money. Because cash flows and time value of money are central to capital budgeting decisions, the IRR method is regarded as better than the AARR method.

AARR computations are easy to understand, and they use numbers reported in the financial statements. The AARR gives managers an idea of how the accounting numbers they will report in the future will be affected if a project is accepted. Unlike the payback method, which ignores cash flows after the payback period, the AARR method considers income earned *throughout* a project's expected useful life. Unlike the NPV method, the AARR method uses accrual accounting income numbers, it does not track cash flows, and it ignores the time value of money. Critics of the AARR method argue that these are its drawbacks.

DECISION POINT

What are the strengths and weaknesses of the accrual accounting rate-of-return (AARR) method for evaluating long-term projects?

Overall, keep in mind that companies frequently use multiple methods for evaluating capital investment decisions. When different methods lead to different rankings of projects or different decisions regarding individual projects, more weight should be given to the NPV method because the assumptions underlying the NPV method are most consistent with decision making that maximizes a company's shareholder value.

TRY IT! 22-3

Consider Elegant Home Company again, and assume the same information as provided in Try It! 22-1 about its proposed new computer system. Elegant Home uses straight-line depreciation.

a. What is the project's accrual accounting rate of return based on net initial investment?
b. What is the project's accrual accounting rate of return based on average investment?
c. What other factors should Elegant Home consider in deciding whether to purchase the new computer system?

Relevant Cash Flows in Discounted Cash Flow Analysis

LEARNING OBJECTIVE 5

Identify relevant cash inflows and outflows for capital budgeting decisions

... the differences in expected future cash flows resulting from the investment

So far, we have examined methods for evaluating long-term projects in settings where the expected future cash flows of interest were assumed to be known. One of the biggest challenges in capital budgeting, particularly DCF analysis, however, is determining which cash flows are relevant in making an investment selection. Relevant cash flows are the differences in expected future cash flows as a result of making the investment. In the Vector example, the relevant cash flows are the differences in expected future cash flows that will result from continuing to use one of the firm's old buses versus purchasing a new hybrid bus. *When reading this section, focus on identifying expected future cash flows and the differences in expected future cash flows.*

To illustrate relevant cash flow analysis, consider a more complex version of the Vector example with these additional assumptions:

- Vector is a profitable company. The income tax rate is 40% of operating income each year.
- The before-tax additional operating cash inflows from the hybrid bus are $220,000 in years 1–4 and $170,000 in year 5.

- For tax purposes, Vector uses the straight-line depreciation method and assumes there is no terminal disposal value of the bus.
- Gains or losses on the sale of depreciable assets are taxed at the same rate as ordinary income.
- The tax effects of cash inflows and outflows occur at the same time that the cash inflows and outflows occur.
- Vector uses an 8% required rate of return for discounting after-tax cash flows.

The data for the buses follow:

	Old Bus	New Hybrid Bus
Purchase price	—	$660,000
Current book value	$60,000	—
Current disposal value	28,500	Not applicable
Terminal disposal value 5 years from now	0	0
Annual depreciation	12,000[a]	132,000[b]
Working capital required	6,000	36,000

[a] $60,000 ÷ 5 years = $12,000 annual depreciation.
[b] $660,000 ÷ 5 years = $132,000 annual depreciation.

Relevant After-Tax Flows

We use the concepts of differential cost and differential revenue introduced in Chapter 12. We compare (1) the after-tax cash outflows as a result of replacing the old bus with (2) the additional after-tax cash inflows generated from using the new bus rather than the old bus.

As Benjamin Franklin said, "Two things in life are certain: death and taxes." Income taxes are a fact of life for most corporations and individuals. It is important to understand how income taxes affect cash flows in each year. Exhibit 22-5 shows how investing in the new bus will affect Vector's cash flow from operations and its income taxes in year 1. Recall that Vector

EXHIBIT 22-5

Effect on Cash Flow From Operations, Net of Income Taxes, in Year 1 for Vector's Investment in the New Hybrid Bus

PANEL A: Two Methods Based on the Income Statement

C	Operating cash inflows from investment in bus	$220,000
D	Additional depreciation deduction	120,000
OI	Increase in operating income	100,000
T	Income taxes (Income tax rate $t \times OI$) = 40% × $100,000	40,000
NI	Increase in net income	$ 60,000

Increase in cash flow from operations, net of income taxes:
Method 1: $C - T$ = $220,000 − $40,000 = $180,000; or
Method 2: $NI + D$ = $60,000 + $120,000 = $180,000

PANEL B: Item-by-Item Method

	Effect of cash operating flows:	
C	Operating cash inflows from investment in bus	$220,000
$t \times C$	Deduct income tax cash outflow at 40%	88,000
$C \times (1 - t)$	After-tax cash flow from operations (excluding the depreciation effect)	$132,000
	Effect of depreciation:	
D	Additional depreciation deduction, $120,000	
$t \times D$	Income tax cash savings from additional depreciation deduction at 40% × $120,000	48,000
$C \times (1 - t) + t \times D$	Cash flow from operations, net of income taxes	$180,000

will generate \$220,000 in before-tax additional operating cash inflows by investing in the new bus (page 862), but it will record additional depreciation of \$120,000 (\$132,000 − \$12,000) for tax purposes.

Panel A shows, using two methods based on the income statement, that the year 1 cash flow from operations, net of income taxes, equals \$180,000. The first method focuses on cash items only, the \$220,000 operating cash inflows minus income taxes of \$40,000. The second method starts with the \$60,000 increase in net income (calculated after subtracting the \$120,000 additional depreciation deductions for income tax purposes) and adds back the \$120,000 because depreciation is an operating cost that reduces net income but is a noncash item itself.

Panel B of Exhibit 22-5 describes a third method frequently used to compute the cash flow from operations, net of income taxes. The easiest way to interpret the third method is to think of the government as a 40% (equal to the tax rate) partner in Vector. Each time Vector obtains operating cash inflows, *C*, its income is higher by *C*, so it will pay 40% of the operating cash inflows (0.40*C*) in taxes. This results in additional after-tax cash operating flows of *C* − 0.40*C*, which in this example is \$220,000 − (0.40 × \$220,000) = \$132,000, or \$220,000 × (1 − 0.40) = \$132,000.

To achieve the higher operating cash inflows, *C*, Vector incurs higher depreciation charges, *D*, from investing in the new bus. Depreciation costs do not directly affect cash flows because depreciation is a noncash cost, but a higher depreciation cost *lowers* Vector's taxable income by *D*, saving income tax cash outflows of 0.40*D*, which in this example is 0.40 × \$120,000 = \$48,000.

Letting t = tax rate, cash flow from operations, net of income taxes, in this example equals the operating cash inflows, *C*, minus the tax payments on these inflows, $t \times C$, plus the tax savings on depreciation deductions, $t \times D$: \$220,000 − (0.40 × \$220,000)+ (0.40 × \$120,000) = \$220,000 − \$88,000 + \$48,000 = \$180,000.

By the same logic, each time Vector has a gain on the sale of assets, *G*, it will show tax outflows, $t \times G$; and each time Vector has a loss on the sale of assets, *L*, it will show tax benefits or savings of $t \times L$.

Categories of Cash Flows

A capital investment project typically has three categories of cash flows: (1) the net initial investment in the project, which includes the acquisition of assets and any associated additions to working capital, minus the after-tax cash flow from the disposal of existing assets; (2) the after-tax cash flow from operations (including income tax cash savings from annual depreciation deductions) each year; and (3) the after-tax cash flow from disposing of an asset and recovering any working capital invested at the termination of the project. We use the Vector example to discuss these three categories.

As you work through the cash flows in each category, refer to Exhibit 22-6. This exhibit sketches the relevant cash flows for Vector's decision to purchase the new bus as described in items 1–3 here. Note that the total relevant cash flows for each year equal the relevant cash flows used in Exhibits 22-2 and 22-3 to illustrate the NPV and IRR methods.

1. **Net Initial Investment.** Three components of net-initial-investment cash flows in the Vector example are (a) the cash outflow to purchase the hybrid bus, (b) the cash outflow for working capital, and (c) the after-tax cash inflow from the current disposal of the old bus.

   1a. *Initial bus investment.* These outflows, made for purchasing plant and equipment, occur at the beginning of the project's life and include cash outflows for transporting and installing the equipment. In the Vector example, the \$660,000 cost (including transportation and initial preparation) of the hybrid bus is an outflow in year 0. These cash flows are relevant to the capital budgeting decision because they will be incurred only if Vector decides to purchase the new bus.

   1b. *Initial working-capital investment.* Initial investments in plant and equipment are usually accompanied by additional investments in working capital. These additional investments take the form of current assets, such as accounts receivable and inventories, minus current liabilities, such as accounts payable. Working-capital investments are

EXHIBIT 22-6 Relevant Cash Inflows and Outflows for Vector's Hybrid Bus

Home Insert Page Layout Formulas Data Review View

	A	B	C	D	E	F	G	H
1			**Sketch of Relevant Cash Flows at End of Each Year**					
2			**0**	**1**	**2**	**3**	**4**	**5**
3	**1a.**	Initial hybrid bus investment	$(660,000)					
4	**1b.**	Initial working-capital investment	(30,000)					
5	**1c.**	After-tax cash inflow from current disposal						
6		of old bus	41,100					
7	Net initial investment		(648,900)					
8	**2a.**	Annual after-tax cash flow from operations						
9		(excluding the depreciation effect)		$ 132,000	$132,000	$ 132,000	$ 132,000	$102,000
10	**2b.**	Income tax savings from annual						
11		depreciation deductions		48,000	48,000	48,000	48,000	48,000
12	**3a.**	After-tax cash flow from terminal disposal						
13		of bus						0
14	**3b.**	After-tax cash flow from recovery of						
15		working capital						30,000
16	Total relevant cash flows,							
17		as shown in Exhibits 22-2 and 22-3	$(648,900)	$ 180,000	$180,000	$ 180,000	$ 180,000	$180,000
18								

similar to plant and equipment investments in that they require cash. The magnitude of the investment generally increases as a function of the level of additional sales generated by the project. However, the exact relationship varies based on the nature of the project and the operating cycle of the industry. For a given dollar of sales, a maker of heavy equipment, for example, would require more working-capital support than Vector, which in turn has to invest more in working capital than a retail grocery store.

The Vector example assumes a $30,000 additional investment in working capital if the hybrid bus is acquired. The additional working-capital investment is the difference between the working capital required to operate the new bus ($36,000) and that required to operate the old bus ($6,000). The $30,000 additional investment, a consequence of the higher cost of replacement batteries and spare parts for the technologically advanced new bus, is a cash outflow in year 0 and is returned, that is, becomes a cash inflow, at the end of year 5.

1c. *After-tax cash flow from current disposal of old bus.* Any cash received from disposal of the old bus is a relevant cash inflow (in year 0) because it is a cash flow that differs between the alternatives of investing and not investing in the new bus. Vector will dispose of the old bus for $28,500 only if it invests in the new hybrid bus. Recall from Chapter 12 (pages 491–493) that the book value (which is original cost minus accumulated depreciation) of the old equipment is generally irrelevant to the decision because it is a past, or sunk, cost. However, when tax considerations are included, the book value does play a role because it determines the gain or loss on the sale of the bus and, therefore, the taxes paid (or saved) on the transaction.

Consider the tax consequences of disposing of the old bus. We first have to compute the gain or loss on disposal:

Current disposal value of old bus (given, page 863)	$ 28,500
Deduct current book value of old bus (given, page 863)	60,000
Loss on disposal of bus	$(31,500)

Any loss on the sale of assets lowers taxable income and results in tax savings. The after-tax cash flow from disposal of the old bus is as follows:

Current disposal value of old bus	$28,500
Tax savings on loss (0.40 × $31,500)	12,600
After-tax cash inflow from current disposal of old bus	$41,100

The sum of items **1a, 1b,** and **1c** appears in Exhibit 22-6 as the year 0 net initial investment for the new hybrid bus. It equals $648,900 (initial bus investment, $660,000, plus additional working-capital investment, $30,000, minus the after-tax cash inflow from current disposal of the old bus, $41,100).[9]

2. **Cash Flow From Operations.** This category includes the difference between each year's cash flow from operations under the two alternatives. Organizations make capital investments to generate future cash inflows. These inflows may result from producing and selling additional goods or, as in the case of Vector, from savings in fuel, maintenance, and operating costs and the additional revenue from higher ticket prices as well as new customers who wish to take advantage of the greater comfort and accessibility of the hybrid bus. The annual cash flow from operations can be net outflows in some years. For example, Chevron periodically upgrades its oil extraction equipment, and when it does, the cash flow from operations tends to be negative for the site being upgraded. However, in the long run, the upgrades are NPV positive. Always focus on the cash flow from operations, not on revenues and expenses under accrual accounting.

   Vector's additional operating cash inflows—$220,000 in each of the first 4 years and $170,000 in the fifth year—are relevant because they are expected future cash flows that will differ depending on whether the firm purchases the new bus. The after-tax effects of these cash flows are described next.

2a. *Annual after-tax cash flow from operations (excluding the depreciation effect).* The 40% tax rate reduces the benefit of the $220,000 additional operating cash inflows for years 1 through 4 with the new hybrid bus. The after-tax cash flow (excluding the depreciation effect) is

Annual cash flow from operations with new bus	$220,000
Deduct income tax payments (0.40 × $220,000)	88,000
Annual after-tax cash flow from operations	$132,000

For year 5, the after-tax cash flow (excluding the depreciation effect) is as follows:

Annual cash flow from operations with new bus	$170,000
Deduct income tax payments (0.40 × $170,000)	68,000
Annual after-tax cash flow from operations	$102,000

Exhibit 22-6, item **2a**, shows that the after-tax cash flows are $132,000 in each of years 1 through 4 and $102,000 for year 5.

To reinforce the idea about focusing on cash flows, consider the following additional fact about Vector. Suppose its total administrative costs will not change whether the company purchases a new bus or keeps the old one. The administrative costs are allocated to individual buses—Vector has several—on the basis of the costs of operating each bus. Because the new hybrid bus would have lower operating costs, the administrative costs allocated to it would be $25,000 less than the amount allocated to the bus it would replace. How should Vector incorporate the $25,000 decrease in allocated administrative costs in the relevant cash flow analysis?

To answer that question, we need to ask, "Do *total* administrative costs decrease at Vector Transport as a result of acquiring the new bus?" In our example, they do not.

[9] To illustrate the case when there is a gain on disposal, suppose that the old bus could be sold for $70,000 instead. Then the firm would record a gain on disposal of $10,000 ($70,000 less the book value of $60,000), resulting in additional tax payments of $4,000 (0.40 tax rate × $10,000 gain). The after-tax cash inflow from current disposal would then equal $66,000 (the disposal value of $70,000, less the tax payment of $4,000).

They remain the same whether or not the new bus is acquired. *Only the administrative costs allocated to individual buses change*. The administrative costs allocated to the new bus are $25,000 less than the amount allocated to the bus it would replace. This $25,000 difference in costs would be allocated to *other* buses in the company. That is, no cash flow savings in total costs would occur. Therefore, the $25,000 should not be included as part of the annual cash savings from operations.

Next consider the effects of depreciation. *The depreciation line item is itself irrelevant in a DCF analysis*. That's because depreciation is a noncash allocation of costs, whereas DCF is based on inflows and outflows of *cash*. If a DCF method is used, the initial cost of equipment is regarded as a *lump-sum* outflow of cash in year 0. Deducting depreciation expenses from operating cash inflows would result in counting the lump-sum amount twice. *However, depreciation results in income tax cash savings. These tax savings are a relevant cash flow*.

2b. *Income tax cash savings from annual depreciation deductions*. Tax deductions for depreciation, in effect, partially offset the cost of acquiring the new hybrid bus. By purchasing the new bus, Vector is able to deduct $132,000 in depreciation each year, relative to the $12,000 depreciation on the old bus. The additional annual depreciation deduction of $120,000 results in incremental income tax cash savings of $120,000 × 0.4, or $48,000 annually. Exhibit 22-6, item **2b**, shows these $48,000 amounts for years 1 through 5.[10]

For economic-policy reasons, usually to encourage (or in some cases, discourage) investments, tax laws specify which depreciation methods and which depreciable lives are permitted. Suppose the government permitted accelerated depreciation to be used, allowing for higher depreciation deductions in earlier years. Should Vector then use accelerated depreciation? Yes, because there is a general rule in tax planning for profitable companies such as Vector: When there is a legal choice, take the depreciation (or any other deduction) sooner rather than later. Doing so causes the (cash) income tax savings to occur earlier, which increases a project's NPV.

3. **Terminal Disposal of Investment.** The disposal of an investment generally increases cash inflow of a project at its termination. An error in forecasting the disposal value is seldom critical for a long-duration project because the present value of the amounts to be received in the distant future is usually small. For Vector, the two components of the terminal disposal value of the investment are (a) the after-tax cash flow from the terminal disposal of buses and (b) the after-tax cash flow from recovery of working capital.

3a. *After-tax cash flow from terminal disposal of buses*. At the end of the useful life of the project, the bus's terminal disposal value is usually considerably less than the net initial investment (and sometimes zero). The relevant cash inflow is the difference in the expected after-tax cash inflow from terminal disposal at the end of 5 years under the two alternatives. Disposing of both the existing and the new bus will result in a zero after-tax cash inflow in year 5. Hence, there is no difference in the disposal-related after-tax cash inflows of the two alternatives.

Because both the existing and the new bus have disposal values that equal their book values at the time of their disposal (in each case, this value is $0), there are no tax effects for either alternative. What if either the existing or the new bus had a terminal value that differed from its book value at the time of disposal? In that case, the approach for computing the terminal inflow is identical to that for calculating the after-tax cash flow from current disposal illustrated earlier in item **1c**.

3b. *After-tax cash flow from terminal recovery of working-capital investment*. The initial investment in working capital is usually fully recouped when the project is terminated. At that time, inventories and accounts receivable necessary to support the project are no longer needed. Vector receives cash equal to the book value of its working capital.

---

[10] If Vector were a nonprofit foundation not subject to income taxes, cash flow from operations would equal $220,000 in years 1 through 4 and $170,000 in year 5. The revenues would not be reduced by 40% nor would there be income tax cash savings from the depreciation deduction.

Thus, there is no gain or loss on working capital and, hence, no tax consequences. The relevant cash inflow is the difference in the expected working capital recovered under the two alternatives. At the end of year 5, Vector recovers $36,000 cash from working capital if it invests in the new hybrid bus versus $6,000 if it continues to use the old bus. The relevant cash inflow at the end of year 5 if Vector invests in the new bus is thus $30,000 ($36,000 − $6,000).

Some capital investment projects *reduce* working capital. Assume that a computer-integrated manufacturing (CIM) project with a 7-year life will reduce inventories and, hence, working capital by $20 million from, say, $50 million to $30 million. This reduction will be represented as a $20 million cash *inflow* for the project in year 0. At the end of 7 years, the recovery of working capital will show a relevant incremental cash *outflow* of $20 million. That's because, at the end of year 7, the company recovers only $30 million of working capital under CIM, rather than the $50 million of working capital it would have recovered had it not implemented CIM.

DECISION POINT

What are the relevant cash inflows and outflows for capital budgeting decisions? How should accrual accounting concepts be considered?

Exhibit 22-6 shows items **3a** and **3b** in the "year 5" column. The relevant cash flows in Exhibit 22-6 serve as inputs for the four capital budgeting methods described earlier in the chapter.

TRY IT! 22-4

Long-lasting Tire Company needs to overhaul its auto lift system or purchase a new one. The facts have been gathered:

	Current Machine	New Machine
Purchase price, new	$122,750	$165,800
Current book value	37,100	
Overhaul needed now	30,500	
Annual cash operating costs	69,700	53,800
Current salvage value	46,000	
Salvage value in 9 years	9,000	40,500

Which alternative is the most desirable with a current required rate of return of 16%? Show computations, and assume no taxes.

Project Management and Performance Evaluation

LEARNING OBJECTIVE 6

Understand issues involved in implementing capital budgeting decisions and evaluating managerial performance

... the importance of post-investment audits and the correct choice of performance measures

We have so far looked at ways to identify relevant cash flows and techniques for analyzing them. The final stage (Stage 5) of capital budgeting begins with implementing the decision and managing the project.[11] This includes management control of the investment activity itself, as well as the project as a whole.

Capital budgeting projects, such as purchasing a hybrid bus or videoconferencing equipment, are easier to implement than projects involving building shopping malls or manufacturing plants. The building projects are more complex, so monitoring and controlling the investment schedules and budgets are critical to successfully completing the investment activity. This leads to the second dimension of Stage 5 in the capital budgeting process: evaluate performance and learn.

Post-Investment Audits

A post-investment audit provides managers with feedback about the performance of a project so they can compare the actual results to the costs and benefits expected at the time the project was selected. Suppose the actual outcomes (such as the additional operating cash flows from Vector's purchase of a new hybrid bus) are much lower than expected. Managers must then determine if this result occurred because the original estimates were overly optimistic or because of implementation problems. Either of these explanations is a concern.

Optimistic estimates can result in managers accepting a project they should have rejected. To discourage unrealistic forecasts, companies such as DuPont maintain records comparing

[11] In this section, we do not consider the different options for financing a project (refer to a text on corporate finance for details).

the actual results of the firm's projects to the estimates individual managers either made or signed off on when seeking approval for capital investments. Post-investment audits prevent managers from overstating the expected cash inflows from projects and accepting projects they should reject. Implementation problems, such as weak project management, poor quality control, or inadequate marketing, are also a concern. Post-investment audits help to alert senior management to these problems so they can be quickly corrected.

Companies should perform post-investment audits with thought and care, and only after the outcomes of projects are fully known. Performing audits too early can be misleading. In addition, obtaining actual results to compare against estimates is often difficult. For example, in any particular period, macroeconomic factors, such as the weather and changes in fuel prices, can greatly affect the ridership on buses and the costs of running them. Consequently, the overall additional net revenues from Vector's new hybrid bus may not be immediately comparable to the estimated revenues. A better evaluation would look at the average revenues across a couple of seasons.

Performance Evaluation

As the preceding discussion suggests, ideally one should evaluate managers on a project-by-project basis and look at how well managers achieve the amounts and timing of forecasted cash flows. In practice, however, companies often evaluate managers based on aggregate information, especially when multiple projects are under way at any given point in time. It is important then for companies to ensure that the method of evaluation does not conflict with the use of the NPV method for making capital budgeting decisions. For example, suppose Vector uses the accrual accounting rate of return generated in each period to assess its managers. We know that the managers should purchase the hybrid bus because it has a positive NPV of $69,840. However, they may reject the project if the AARR of 8.3% on the net initial investment is lower than the minimum accounting rate of return Vector requires them to achieve.

There is an inconsistency between promoting the NPV method as best for capital budgeting decisions and then using a different method to evaluate performance. Even though the NPV method is best for capital budgeting decisions, managers will be tempted to make capital budgeting decisions based on the method on which they are evaluated. The temptation becomes more pronounced if managers are frequently transferred (or promoted) or if their bonuses are affected by the level of year-to-year income earned under accrual accounting.

Other conflicts between decision making and performance evaluation persist even if a company uses similar measures for both purposes. If the AARR on the hybrid bus exceeds the minimum required AARR but is below Vector's current AARR in the region, the manager may still be tempted to reject purchase of the hybrid bus because the lower AARR of the hybrid bus will reduce the AARR of the entire region and thus hurt the manager's reported performance. Or consider an example where the cash inflows from the hybrid bus occur mostly in the later years of the project. Then, even if the project's AARR exceeds the current AARR of the projects overseen by the manager (as well as the minimum required return), the manager may still reject the purchase because for the first few years it will have a negative effect on the rate of return earned under accrual accounting. In Chapter 24, we study these conflicts in greater depth and describe how performance evaluation models such as economic value added (EVA) help lessen these conflicts.

DECISION POINT

What conflicts can arise between using DCF methods for capital budgeting decisions and accrual accounting for performance evaluation? How can these conflicts be reduced?

Strategic Considerations in Capital Budgeting

LEARNING OBJECTIVE 7

Explain how managers can use capital budgeting to achieve their firms' strategic goals

... make critical investments aligned with the firm's objectives but whose benefits are uncertain or difficult to estimate

Managers consider a company's strategic goals when making capital budgeting decisions. Strategic decisions by Apple, FedEx, Starbucks, and Starwood Hotels & Resorts to expand in Europe and Asia required a capital investments in several countries. The strategic decision by Verizon to enter the videoconferencing market required a capital investment in the form of the acquisition of BlueJeans. Amazon's desire to enter the healthcare market led to its purchase of PillPack, Inc., as well as its entering into a collaboration with JP Morgan Chase and Berkshire Hathaway, called Haven. Gilead Sciences' decision to develop Harvoni as a patented drug for the treatment of hepatitis C led to major investments in R&D and marketing. Porsche's decision to offer an electric vehicle, the Porsche Taycan, required start-up investments to form an electric division and ongoing investments to fund the division's research efforts.

Capital investment decisions that are strategic in nature require managers to consider a broad range of factors that may be difficult to estimate. Consider some of the difficulties of justifying investments made by companies such as General Motors, Google, and Uber in autonomous vehicle technology. Quantifying a potential benefit from these investments requires assumptions around ultimate robustness of the technology, regulatory approval, legal liability, change in consumer demand, and overall future direction of the transportation industry in light of the ongoing climate crisis. The potential benefit of this emerging technology is still difficult to assess. Managers must develop judgment and intuition to make these decisions.

Investment in Research and Development

Companies such as GlaxoSmithKline, in the pharmaceutical industry, and Intel, in the semiconductor industry, regard R&D projects as important strategic investments. The distant payoffs from R&D investments, however, are more uncertain than other investments such as new equipment purchases. On the positive side, R&D investments are often staged: As time unfolds, companies can increase or decrease the resources committed to a project based on how successful it has been up to that point. This feature, called real options, is an important aspect of R&D investments. It increases the NPV of these investments because a company can limit its losses when things are going badly and take advantage of new opportunities when things are going well. As an example, a pharmaceutical company can increase or decrease its investment in an R&D joint venture based on the progress of the clinical trials of new drugs being developed by the venture.

Customer Value and Capital Budgeting

Finally, note that managers can use the framework described in this chapter to both evaluate investment projects and to make strategic decisions regarding which customers to invest in. Consider Potato Supreme, which makes potato products for sale to retail outlets. It is currently analyzing two of its customers: Shine Stores and Always Open. Potato Supreme predicts the following cash flow from operations, net of income taxes (in thousands), from each customer account for the next 5 years:

	2020	2021	2022	2023	2024
Shine Stores	$1,450	$1,305	$1,175	$1,058	$ 950
Always Open	690	1,160	1,900	2,950	4,160

Which customer is more valuable to Potato Supreme? Looking at only the current period, 2020, Shine Stores provides more than double the cash flow compared to Always Open ($1,450 versus $690). A different picture emerges, however, if you look at the entire 5-year horizon. Potato Supreme anticipates Always Open's orders to increase; meanwhile, it expects Shine Stores' orders to decline. Using Potato Supreme's 10% RRR, the NPV of the Always Open customer is $7,610, compared with $4,591 for Shine Stores (computations not shown). Note how NPV captures in its estimate of customer value the future growth of Always Open. Potato Supreme uses this information to allocate more resources and salespeople to service the Always Open account. Potato Supreme can also use NPV calculations to examine the effects of alternative ways of increasing customer loyalty and retention, such as introducing frequent-purchaser cards.

A comparison of year-to-year changes in customer NPV estimates highlights whether managers have been successful in maintaining long-run profitable relationships with their customers. Suppose the NPV of Potato Supreme's customer accounts declines by 15% in a year. The firm's managers can then examine the reasons for the decline, such as aggressive pricing by competitors, and devise new-product development and marketing strategies for the future.

DECISION POINT

How can managers use capital budgeting to achieve strategic goals?

Capital One, a financial-services company, uses NPV to estimate the value of different credit-card customers. Cellular telephone companies such as Sprint and Verizon Wireless attempt to sign up customers for multiple years of service. The objective is to prevent "customer churn"—that is, customers switching frequently from one company to another. The higher the probability is of a customer switching, the lower the customer's NPV.

PROBLEM FOR SELF-STUDY

Part A

Returning to the Vector hybrid bus project, assume that Vector is a *nonprofit organization* and that the expected additional operating cash inflows are $240,000 in years 1 through 4 and $210,000 in year 5. Using data from page 863, the net initial investment is $661,500 (new bus, $660,000, plus additional working capital, $30,000, minus current disposal value of old bus, $28,500). All other facts are unchanged: a 5-year useful life, no terminal disposal value, and an 8% RRR. Year 5 cash inflows are $240,000, which includes a $30,000 recovery of working capital.

Required

Calculate the following:

1. Net present value
2. Internal rate of return
3. Payback period
4. Accrual accounting rate of return on net initial investment

Solution

1. NPV = ($240,000 × 3.993) − $661,500
   = $958,320 − $661,500 = $296,820

2. There are several approaches to computing IRR. One is to use a calculator with an IRR function. This approach gives an IRR of 23.8%. Another approach is to use Table 4 in Appendix A at the end of the text:

$$\$661{,}500 = \$240{,}000F$$

$$F = \frac{\$661{,}500}{\$240{,}000} = 2.756$$

On the five-period line of Table 4, the column closest to 2.756 is 24%. To obtain a more-accurate number, use straight-line interpolation:

	Present Value Factors	
22%	2.864	2.864
IRR	—	2.756
24%	2.745	—
Difference	0.119	0.108

$$\text{IRR} = 22\% + \frac{0.108}{0.119}(2\%) = 23.8\% \text{ per year}$$

3. $$\text{Payback period} = \frac{\text{Net initial investment}}{\text{Uniform increase in annual future cash flows}}$$
   = $661,500 ÷ $240,000 = 2.76 years

4. $$\text{AARR} = \frac{\text{annual operating income}}{\text{Net initial investment}}$$

Increase in expected average annual operating cash inflows = [($240,000 × 4) + $210,000] ÷ 5 years
= $1,170,000 ÷ 5 = $234,000

Increase in annual depreciation = $120,000 ($132,000 − $12,000, see p. 863)

Increase in expected average annual operating income = $234,000 − $120,000 = $114,000

$$AARR = \frac{\$114{,}000}{\$661{,}500} = 17.2\% \text{ per year}$$

Part B

Assume that Vector is subject to income tax at a 40% rate. All other information from Part A is unchanged. Compute the NPV of the new hybrid bus project.

Solution

To save space, Exhibit 22-7 shows the calculations using a format slightly different from the format used in this chapter. Item **2a** is where the new cash flow assumptions affect the NPV analysis (compared with Exhibit 22-6). All other amounts in Exhibit 22-7 are identical to the corresponding amounts in Exhibit 22-6. For years 1 through 4, after-tax cash flow (excluding the depreciation effect) is as follows:

Annual cash flow from operations with new bus	$240,000
Deduct income tax payments (0.40 × $240,000)	96,000
Annual after-tax cash flow from operations	$144,000

For year 5, after-tax cash flow (excluding the depreciation effect) is as follows:

Annual cash flow from operations with new bus	$210,000
Deduct income tax payments (0.40 × $210,000)	84,000
Annual after-tax cash flow from operations	$126,000

The NPV in Exhibit 22-7 is $125,928. As computed in Part A, the NPV when there are no income taxes is $296,820. The difference in these two NPVs illustrates the impact of income taxes in capital budgeting analysis.

EXHIBIT 22-7 Net Present Value Method Incorporating Income Taxes: Vector's Hybrid Bus With Revised Annual Cash Flow From Operations

Home Insert Page Layout Formulas Data Review View

	A	B	C	D	E	F	G	H	I	J
1			Present Value	Present Value of		Sketch of Relevant Cash Flows at End of Year				
2			of Cash Flow	$1 Discounted at 8%	0	1	2	3	4	5
3	1a.	Initial hybrid bus investment	$(660,000) ←	1.000 ←	$(660,000)					
4										
5	1b.	Initial working-capital investment	(30,000) ←	1.000 ←	$ (30,000)					
6	1c.	After-tax cash inflow from current disposal								
7		of old bus	41,100 ←	1.000 ←	$ 41,100					
8	Net initial investment		(648,900)							
9	2a.	Annual after-tax cash flow from operations								
10		(excluding the depreciation effect)								
11		Year 1	133,344 ←	0.926 ←		$144,000				
12		Year 2	123,408 ←	0.857 ←			$144,000			
13		Year 3	114,336 ←	0.794 ←				$144,000		
14		Year 4	105,840 ←	0.735 ←					$144,000	
15		Year 5	85,806 ←	0.681 ←						$126,000
16	2b.	Income tax cash savings from annual								
17		depreciation deductions								
18		Year 1	44,448 ←	0.926 ←		$ 48,000				
19		Year 2	41,136 ←	0.857 ←			$ 48,000			
20		Year 3	38,112 ←	0.794 ←				$ 48,000		
21		Year 4	35,280 ←	0.735 ←					$ 48,000	
22		Year 5	32,688 ←	0.681 ←						$ 48,000
23	3.	After-tax cash flow from recovery of								
24		a. Terminal disposal of bus	0 ←	0.681 ←						$ 0
25		b. Recovery of working capital	20,430 ←	0.681 ←						$ 30,000
26	NPV if new hybrid bus purchased		$ 125,928							
27										

DECISION POINTS

The following question-and-answer format summarizes the chapter's learning objectives. Each decision presents a key question related to a learning objective. The guidelines are the answer to that question.

Decision	Guidelines
1. What are the five stages of capital budgeting?	Capital budgeting is long-run planning for proposed investment projects. The five stages of capital budgeting are: (1) Identify projects: Identify potential capital investments aligned with the organization's strategy; (2) Obtain information: Gather information from all parts of the value chain to evaluate alternative projects; (3) Make predictions: Forecast all potential cash flows attributable to the alternative projects; (4) Choose among alternatives: Determine which investment yields the greatest benefit and the least cost to the organization; and (5) Implement the decision, evaluate performance, and learn: Obtain funding and make the investments selected in Stage 4; track the realized cash flows, compare them against estimated numbers, and revise plans if necessary.
2. What are the two primary discounted cash flow (DCF) methods for project evaluation?	The two main DCF methods are the net present value (NPV) method and the internal rate-of-return (IRR) method. The NPV method calculates the expected net monetary gain or loss from a project by discounting to the present all expected future cash inflows and outflows, using the required rate of return. A project is acceptable in financial terms if it has a positive NPV. The IRR method computes the rate of return (also called the discount rate) at which a project's present value of expected cash inflows equals the present value of its expected cash outflows. A project is acceptable in financial terms if its IRR exceeds the required rate of return. The DCF method is the best approach to capital budgeting because it explicitly includes all project cash flows and recognizes the time value of money. The NPV method is the preferred DCF method.
3. What are the payback and discounted payback methods? What are their main weaknesses?	The payback method measures the time it will take to recoup, in the form of cash inflows, the total cash amount invested in a project. The payback method neglects the time value of money and ignores cash flows beyond the payback period. The discounted payback method measures the time it takes for the present value of cash inflows to equal the present value of cash outflows. It adjusts for the time value of money but overlooks cash flows after the discounted payback period.
4. What are the strengths and weaknesses of the accrual accounting rate-of-return (AARR) method for evaluating long-term projects?	The accrual accounting rate-of-return (AARR) method divides an accrual accounting measure of average annual income from a project by an accrual accounting measure of its investment. The AARR gives managers an idea of how accepting a project will affect a firm's future reported accounting profitability. However, the AARR uses accrual accounting income numbers, does not track cash flows, and ignores the time value of money.
5. What are the relevant cash inflows and outflows for capital budgeting decisions? How should accrual accounting concepts be considered?	Relevant cash inflows and outflows in a DCF analysis are the differences in expected future cash flows as a result of making the investment. Only cash inflows and outflows matter; accrual accounting concepts are irrelevant for DCF methods. For example, the income taxes saved as a result of depreciation deductions are relevant because they decrease cash outflows, but the depreciation itself is a noncash item.

Decision	Guidelines
6. What conflicts can arise between using DCF methods for capital budgeting decisions and accrual accounting for performance evaluation? How can these conflicts be reduced?	Using accrual accounting to evaluate the performance of a manager may create conflicts with the use of DCF methods for capital budgeting. Frequently, the decision made using a DCF method will not report good "operating income" results in the project's early years under accrual accounting. For this reason, managers are tempted to not use DCF methods even though the decisions based on them would be in the best interests of the company as a whole over the long run. This conflict can be reduced by evaluating managers on a project-by-project basis and by looking at their ability to achieve the amounts and timing of forecasted cash flows.
7. How can managers use capital budgeting to achieve strategic goals?	A company's strategy is the source of its strategic capital budgeting decisions. Such decisions require managers to consider a broad range of factors that may be difficult to estimate. Managers must develop judgment and intuition to make these decisions. R&D projects, for example, are important strategic investments, with distant and usually highly uncertain payoffs.

APPENDIX

Capital Budgeting and Inflation

The Vector example (Exhibits 22-2 to 22-6) does not include adjustments for inflation in the relevant revenues and costs. **Inflation** is the decline in the general purchasing power of the monetary unit, such as dollars. An inflation rate of 10% per year means that an item bought for $100 at the beginning of the year will cost $110 at the end of the year.

Why is it important to account for inflation in capital budgeting? Because declines in the general purchasing power of the monetary unit will inflate future cash flows above what they would have been in the absence of inflation. These inflated cash flows will cause the project to look better than it really is unless the analyst recognizes that the inflated cash flows are measured in dollars that have less purchasing power than the dollars that were initially invested. When analyzing inflation, distinguish real rate of return from nominal rate of return:

Real rate of return is the rate of return demanded to cover investment risk if there is no inflation. The real rate is made up of two elements: (1) a risk-free element (the pure rate of return on risk-free long-term government bonds when there is no expected inflation) and (2) a business-risk element (the risk premium demanded for bearing risk).

Nominal rate of return is the rate of return demanded to cover investment risk and the decline in general purchasing power of the monetary unit as a result of expected inflation. The nominal rate is made up of three elements: (1) a risk-free element when there is no expected inflation, (2) a business-risk element, and (3) an inflation element. Items 1 and 2 make up the real rate of return to cover investment risk. The inflation element is the premium above the real rate. The rates of return earned in the financial markets are nominal rates because investors want to be compensated both for the investment risks they take and for the expected decline in the general purchasing power, as a result of inflation, of the money they get back.

Assume that the real rate of return for investments in high-risk cellular data-transmission equipment at Network Communications is 20% per year and that the expected inflation rate is 10% per year. Nominal rate of return is as follows:

$$\begin{aligned}\text{Nominal rate} &= (1 + \text{Real rate})\,(1 + \text{Inflation rate}) - 1\\ &= (1 + 0.20)\,(1 + 0.10) - 1\\ &= (1.20 \times 1.10) - 1 = 1.32 - 1 = 0.32, \text{ or } 32\%\end{aligned}$$

Nominal rate of return is related to the real rate of return and the inflation rate:

Real rate of return	0.20
Inflation rate	0.10
Combination (0.20 × 0.10)	0.02
Nominal rate of return	0.32

Note the nominal rate, 0.32, is slightly higher than 0.30, the real rate (0.20) plus the inflation rate (0.10). That's because the nominal rate recognizes that inflation of 10% also decreases the purchasing power of the real rate of return of 20% earned during the year. The combination component represents the additional compensation investors seek for the decrease in the purchasing power of the real return earned during the year because of inflation.[12]

Net Present Value Method and Inflation

When incorporating inflation into the NPV method, the key is *internal consistency*. There are two internally consistent approaches:

1. **Nominal approach**—predicts cash inflows and outflows in nominal monetary units *and* uses a nominal rate as the required rate of return
2. **Real approach**—predicts cash inflows and outflows in real monetary units *and* uses a real rate as the required rate of return

We will limit our discussion to the simpler nominal approach. Consider an investment that is expected to generate sales of 100 units and a net cash inflow of $1,000 ($10 per unit) each year for 2 years *absent inflation*. Assume cash flows occur at the end of each year. If inflation of 10% is expected each year, net cash inflows from the sale of each unit would be $11 ($10 × 1.10) in year 1 and $12.10 ($11 × 1.10, or $10 × $(1.10)^2$) in year 2, resulting in net cash inflows of $1,100 in year 1 and $1,210 in year 2. The net cash inflows of $1,100 and $1,210 are nominal cash inflows because they include the effects of inflation. *Nominal cash flows are the cash flows that are recorded in the accounting system.* The cash inflows of $1,000 each year are real cash flows. The accounting system does not record these cash flows. The nominal approach is easier to understand and apply because it uses nominal cash flows from accounting systems and nominal rates of return from financial markets.

Assume that Network Communications can purchase equipment to make and sell an Ethernet blade switch for a net initial investment of $750,000. The equipment is expected to have a 4-year useful life and no terminal disposal value. An annual inflation rate of 10% is expected over this 4-year period. Network Communications requires an after-tax nominal rate of return of 32% (see page 874). The following table presents the predicted amounts of real (that's assuming no inflation) and nominal (that's after considering cumulative inflation) net cash inflows from the equipment over the next 4 years (excluding the $750,000 investment in the equipment and before any income tax payments):

Year (1)	Before-Tax Cash Inflows in Real Dollars (2)	Cumulative Inflation Rate Factor[a] (3)	Before-Tax Cash Inflows in Nominal Dollars (4) = (2) × (3)
1	$500,000	$(1.10)^1 = 1.1000$	$550,000
2	600,000	$(1.10)^2 = 1.2100$	726,000
3	600,000	$(1.10)^3 = 1.3310$	798,600
4	300,000	$(1.10)^4 = 1.4641$	439,230

[a] 1.10 = 1.00 + 0.10 inflation rate.

[12] The real rate of return can be expressed in terms of the nominal rate of return as follows:

$$\text{Real rate} = \frac{1 + \text{Nominal rate}}{1 + \text{Inflation rate}} - 1 = \frac{1 + 0.32}{1 + 0.10} - 1 = 0.20, \text{ or } 20\%$$

EXHIBIT 22-8 Net Present Value Method Using Nominal Approach to Inflation for Network Communication's New Equipment

	A	B	C	D	E	F	G	H	I	J	K	L
1						Present	Present Value					
2						Value of	Discount Factor[a] at	Sketch of Relevant Cash Flows at End of Each Year				
3						Cash Flow	32%	0	1	2	3	4
4	1.	Net initial investment										
5		Year	Investment Outflows									
6		0	$(750,000)			$(750,000)	← 1.000 ←	$(750,000)				
7	2a.	Annual after-tax cash flow from										
8		operations (excluding the depreciation effect)										
9			Annual		Annual							
10			Before-Tax	Income	After-Tax							
11			Cash Flow	Tax	Cash Flow							
12		Year	from Operations	Outflows	from Operations							
13		(1)	(2)	(3) = 0.40 × (2)	(4) = (2) − (3)							
14		1	$550,000	$220,000	$330,000	250,140	← 0.758 ←		$330,000			
15		2	726,000	290,400	435,600	250,034	← 0.574 ←			$435,600		
16		3	798,600	319,440	479,160	208,435	← 0.435 ←				$479,160	
17		4	439,230	175,692	263,538	86,704	← 0.329 ←					$263,538
18						795,313						
19	2b.	Income tax cash savings from annual										
20		depreciation deductions										
21		Year	Depreciation	Tax Cash Savings								
22		(1)	(2)	(3) = 0.40 × (2)								
23		1	$187,500[b]	$75,000		56,850	← 0.758 ←		$ 75,000			
24		2	187,500	75,000		43,050	← 0.574 ←			$ 75,000		
25		3	187,500	75,000		32,625	← 0.435 ←				$ 75,000	
26		4	187,500	75,000		24,675	← 0.329 ←					$ 75,000
27						157,200						
28												
29	NPV if new equipment purchased					$ 202,513						
30												
31	[a]The nominal discount rate of 32% is made up of the real rate of return of 20% and the inflation rate of 10%: [(1 + 0.20) (1 + 1.10)] − 1 = 0.32.											
32	[b]$750,000 ÷ 4 = $187,500											

We continue to make the simplifying assumption that cash flows occur at the end of each year. The income tax rate is 40%. For tax purposes, the cost of the equipment will be depreciated using the straight-line method.

Exhibit 22-8 shows the calculation of NPV using cash flows in nominal dollars and using a nominal discount rate. The calculations in Exhibit 22-8 include the net initial bus investment, annual after-tax cash flows from operations (excluding the depreciation effect), and income tax cash savings from annual depreciation deductions. The NPV is $202,513, and, based on financial considerations alone, Network Communications should purchase the equipment.

TERMS TO LEARN

This chapter and the Glossary at the end of the text contain definitions of the following important terms:

accrual accounting rate-of-return (AARR) method (**p. 861**)
capital budgeting (**p. 850**)
cost of capital (**p. 853**)
discount rate (**p. 853**)
discounted cash flow (DCF) methods (**p. 853**)
discounted payback method (**p. 860**)
hurdle rate (**p. 853**)
inflation (**p. 874**)
internal rate-of-return (IRR) method (**p. 855**)
net present value (NPV) method (**p. 854**)
nominal rate of return (**p. 874**)
opportunity cost of capital (**p. 853**)
payback method (**p. 858**)
real rate of return (**p. 874**)
required rate of return (RRR) (**p. 853**)
time value of money (**p. 853**)

ASSIGNMENT MATERIAL

Questions

22-1 "Capital budgeting has the same focus as accrual accounting." Do you agree? Explain.

22-2 List and briefly describe each of the five stages in capital budgeting.

22-3 What is the essence of the discounted cash flow methods?

22-4 "Only quantitative outcomes are relevant in capital budgeting analyses." Do you agree? Explain.

22-5 How can sensitivity analysis be incorporated in DCF analysis?

22-6 What is the payback method? What are its main strengths and weaknesses?

22-7 Describe the accrual accounting rate-of-return method. What are its main strengths and weaknesses?

22-8 "The trouble with discounted cash flow methods is that they ignore depreciation." Do you agree? Explain.

22-9 "Let's be more practical. DCF is not the gospel. Managers should not become so enchanted with DCF that strategic considerations are overlooked." Do you agree? Explain.

22-10 "All overhead costs are relevant in NPV analysis." Do you agree? Explain.

22-11 Bill Watts, president of Western Publications, accepts a capital budgeting project proposed by division X. This is the division in which the president spent his first 10 years with the company. On the same day, the president rejects a capital budgeting project proposal from division Y. The manager of division Y is incensed. She believes that the division Y project has an internal rate of return at least 10 percentage points higher than the division X project. She comments, "What is the point of all our detailed DCF analysis? If Watts is panting over a project, he can arrange to have the proponents of that project massage the numbers so that it looks like a winner." What advice would you give the manager of division Y?

22-12 Distinguish different categories of cash flows to be considered in an equipment-replacement decision by a taxpaying company.

22-13 Describe three ways income taxes can affect the cash inflows or outflows in a motor-vehicle-replacement decision by a taxpaying company.

22-14 How can capital budgeting tools assist in evaluating a manager who is responsible for retaining customers of a cellular telephone company?

22-15 Distinguish the nominal rate of return from the real rate of return.

Multiple-Choice Questions

In partnership with:

BECKER PROFESSIONAL EDUCATION®

22-16 A company should accept for investment all positive NPV investment alternatives when which of the following conditions is true?

- **a.** The company has extremely limited resources for capital investment.
- **b.** The company has excess cash on its balance sheet.
- **c.** The company has virtually unlimited resources for capital investment.
- **d.** The company has limited resources for capital investment but is planning to issue new equity to finance additional capital investment.

22-17 Which of the following items describes a weakness of the internal rate-of-return method?

- **a.** The internal rate of return is difficult to calculate and requires a financial calculator or spreadsheet tool such as Excel to calculate efficiently.
- **b.** Cash flows from the investment are assumed in the IRR analysis to be reinvested at the internal rate of return.
- **c.** The IRR calculation ignores time value of money.
- **d.** The IRR calculation ignores project cash flows occurring after the initial investment is recovered.

22-18 Which of the following statements is true if the NPV of a project is −$4,000 (negative $4,000) and the required rate of return is 5%?

- **a.** The project's IRR is less than 5%.
- **b.** The required rate of return is lower than the IRR.
- **c.** The NPV assumes cash flows are reinvested at the IRR.
- **d.** The NPV would be positive if the IRR was equal to 5%.

22-19 The following information pertains to the January 2, year 2 transaction replacing a print machine for Hidden Creek Enterprises, Inc.

Net book value – old print machine $20,000
Total cost of new machine $180,000
Down payment on new machine $35,000
Sale price of old machine $30,000
Tax rate 30%

What is the net total of relevant costs on January 2, year 2?

a. $173,000 **b.** $153,000
c. $28,000 **d.** $8,000.

22-20 Nick's Enterprises has purchased a new machine tool that will allow the company to improve the efficiency of its operations. On an annual basis, the machine will produce 20,000 units with an expected selling price of $10, prime costs of $6 per unit, and a fixed cost allocation of $3 per unit. Annual depreciation on the machine is $12,000, and the tax rate of the company is 25%.
What is the annual cash flow generated from the new machine?

a. $63,000 **b.** $51,000
c. $18,000 **d.** $6,000

Exercises

22-21 Exercises in compound interest, no income taxes. To be sure that you understand how to use the tables in Appendix A at the end of this text, solve the following exercises. Ignore income tax considerations. The correct answers, rounded to the nearest dollar, appear on page 886.

Required

1. You have just won $50,000. How much money will you accumulate at the end of 5 years if you invest it at 6% compounded annually? At 12%?
2. Twelve years from now, the unpaid principal of the mortgage on your house will be $249,600. How much do you need to invest today at 6% interest compounded annually to accumulate the $249,600 in 12 years?
3. If the unpaid mortgage on your house in 12 years will be $249,600, how much money do you need to invest at the end of each year at 6% to accumulate exactly this amount at the end of the 12th year?
4. You plan to save $4,800 of your earnings at the end of each year for the next 8 years. How much money will you accumulate at the end of the eighth year if you invest your savings compounded at 4% per year?
5. You have just turned 65 and an endowment insurance policy has paid you a lump sum of $400,000. If you invest the sum at 6%, how much money can you withdraw from your account in equal amounts at the end of each year so that at the end of 7 years (age 72), there will be nothing left?
6. You have estimated that for the first 6 years after you retire you will need a cash inflow of $48,000 at the end of each year. How much money do you need to invest at 4% at your retirement age to obtain this annual cash inflow? At 6%?
7. The following table shows two schedules of prospective operating cash inflows, each of which requires the same net initial investment of $18,000 now:

	Annual Cash Inflows	
Year	**Plan A**	**Plan B**
1	$ 2,000	$ 3,000
2	3,000	5,000
3	4,000	9,000
4	7,000	5,000
5	9,000	3,000
Total	$25,000	$25,000

The required rate of return is 6% compounded annually. All cash inflows occur at the end of each year. In terms of net present value, which plan is more desirable? Show your computations.

22-22 Capital budgeting methods, no income taxes. Heavenly Candy Company is considering purchasing a second chocolate dipping machine in order to expand its business. The information Heavenly has accumulated regarding the new machine is

Cost of the machine	$90,000
Increased annual contribution margin	$19,000
Life of the machine	9 years
Required rate of return	12%

Heavenly estimates it will be able to produce more candy using the second machine and thus increase its annual contribution margin. It also estimates there will be a small disposal value of the machine but the cost of removal will offset that value. Ignore income tax issues in your answers. Assume all cash flows occur at year-end except for initial investment amounts.

Required

1. Calculate the following for the new machine:
   a. Net present value
   b. Payback period
   c. Discounted payback period
   d. Internal rate of return (using the interpolation method)
   e. Accrual accounting rate of return based on the net initial investment (assume straight-line depreciation)
2. What other factors should Heavenly Candy consider in deciding whether to purchase the new machine?

22-23 Capital budgeting methods, no income taxes. City Hospital, a nonprofit organization, estimates that it can save $28,000 a year in cash operating costs for the next 10 years if it buys a special-purpose eye-testing machine at a cost of $110,000. No terminal disposal value is expected. City Hospital's required rate of return is 14%. Assume all cash flows occur at year-end except for initial investment amounts. City Hospital uses straight-line depreciation.

Required

1. Calculate the following for the special-purpose eye-testing machine:
   a. Net present value
   b. Payback period
   c. Internal rate of return
   d. Accrual accounting rate of return based on net initial investment
   e. Accrual accounting rate of return based on average investment
2. What other factors should City Hospital consider in deciding whether to purchase the special-purpose eye-testing machine?

22-24 Capital budgeting, income taxes. Assume the same facts as in Exercise 22-23 except that City Hospital is a taxpaying entity. The income tax rate is 30% for all transactions that affect income taxes.

Required

1. Complete requirement 1 of Exercise 22-23 taking the income tax rate of 30% into account.
2. How would your computations in requirement 1 be affected if the special-purpose machine had a $10,000 terminal disposal value at the end of 10 years? Assume depreciation deductions are based on the $110,000 purchase cost and zero terminal disposal value using the straight-line method. Answer briefly in words without further calculations.

22-25 Capital budgeting with uneven cash flows, no income taxes. Eastern Cola is considering the purchase of a special-purpose bottling machine for $70,000. It is expected to have a useful life of 4 years with no terminal disposal value. The plant manager estimates the following savings in cash operating costs:

Year	Amount
1	$30,000
2	25,000
3	20,000
4	15,000
Total	$90,000

Eastern Cola uses a required rate of return of 20% in its capital budgeting decisions. Ignore income taxes in your analysis. Assume all cash flows occur at year-end except for initial investment amounts.
Calculate the following for the special-purpose bottling machine:

Required

1. Net present value
2. Payback period
3. Discounted payback period
4. Internal rate of return (using the interpolation method)
5. Accrual accounting rate of return based on net initial investment (Assume straight-line depreciation. Use the average annual savings in cash operating costs when computing the numerator of the accrual accounting rate of return.)

22-26 Comparison of projects, no income taxes. (CMA, adapted) New Med Corporation is a rapidly growing biotech company that has a required rate of return of 12%. It plans to build a new facility in Santa Clara County. The building will take 2 years to complete. The building contractor offered New Med a choice of three payment plans, as follows:

- **Plan I:** Payment of $150,000 at the time of signing the contract and $4,575,000 upon completion of the building. The end of the second year is the completion date.
- **Plan II:** Payment of $1,775,000 at the time of signing the contract and $1,775,000 at the end of each of the two succeeding years.
- **Plan III:** Payment of $450,000 at the time of signing the contract and $1,575,000 at the end of each of the three succeeding years.

Required

1. Using the net present value method, calculate the comparative cost of each of the three payment plans being considered by New Med.
2. Which payment plan should New Med choose? Explain.
3. Discuss the financial factors, other than the cost of the plan, and the nonfinancial factors that should be considered in selecting an appropriate payment plan.

22-27 Payback and NPV methods, no income taxes. (CMA, adapted) Lulus Construction is analyzing its capital expenditure proposals for the purchase of equipment in the coming year. The capital budget is limited to $12,000,000 for the year. Lyssa Bickerson, staff analyst at Lulus, is preparing an analysis of the three projects under consideration by Caden Lulus, the company's owner.

Home Insert Page Layout Formulas Data Review View

	A	B	C	D
1		**Project A**	**Project B**	**Project C**
2	**Projected cash outflow**			
3	Net initial investment	$6,000,000	$4,000,000	$8,000,000
4				
5	**Projected cash inflows:**			
6	Year 1	$2,050,000	$1,100,000	$4,700,000
7	Year 2	$2,050,000	2,300,000	$4,700,000
8	Year 3	$2,050,000	700,000	50,000
9	Year 4	$2,050,000		25,000
10				
11	Required rate of return	8%	8%	8%

Required

1. Because the company's cash is limited, Lulus thinks the payback method should be used to choose between the capital budgeting projects.
   a. What are the benefits and limitations of using the payback method to choose between projects?
   b. Calculate the payback period for each of the three projects. Ignore income taxes. Using the payback method, which projects should Lulus choose?
2. Bickerson thinks that projects should be selected based on their NPVs. Assume all cash flows occur at the end of the year except for initial investment amounts. Calculate the NPV for each project. Ignore income taxes.
3. Which projects, if any, would you recommend funding? Briefly explain why.

22-28 DCF, accrual accounting rate of return, working capital, evaluation of performance, no income taxes. Green Lab plans to purchase a new centrifuge machine for its Florida facility. The machine costs $437,000 and is expected to have a useful life of 8 years, with a terminal disposal value of $42,000. Savings in cash operating costs are expected to be $85,000 per year. However, additional working capital is needed to keep the machine running efficiently. The working capital must continually be replaced, so an investment of $15,000 needs to be maintained at all times, but this investment is fully recoverable (will be "cashed in") at the end of the useful life. Green Lab's required rate of return is 8%. Ignore income taxes in your analysis. Assume all cash flows occur at year-end except for initial investment amounts. Green Lab uses straight-line depreciation for its machines.

Required

1. Calculate net present value.
2. Calculate internal rate of return.

3. Calculate accrual accounting rate of return based on net initial investment.
4. Calculate accrual accounting rate of return based on average investment.
5. You have the authority to make the purchase decision. Why might you be reluctant to base your decision on the DCF methods?

22-29 New equipment purchase, income taxes. Jenna's Bakery plans to purchase a new oven for its store. The oven has an estimated useful life of 4 years. The estimated pretax cash flows for the oven are as shown in the table that follows, with no anticipated change in working capital. Jenna's Bakery has an 8% after-tax required rate of return and a 34% income tax rate. Assume depreciation is calculated on a straight-line basis for tax purposes using the initial investment in the oven and its estimated terminal disposal value. Assume all cash flows occur at year-end except for initial investment amounts.

Home Insert Page Layout Formulas Data Review View

	A	B	C	D	E	F
1		Relevant Cash Flows at End of Each Year				
2		0	1	2	3	4
3	Initial oven investment	($70,000)				
4	Annual cash flow from operations (excluding the depreciation effect)		$24,000	$24,000	$24,000	$24,000
5	Cash flow from terminal disposal of oven					$ 7,000

Required

1. Calculate (a) net present value, (b) payback period, and (c) internal rate of return.
2. Calculate accrual accounting rate of return based on net initial investment.

22-30 New equipment purchase, income taxes. Captain Inc. is considering the purchase of new equipment that will automate production and thus reduce labor costs. Captain made the following estimates related to the new machinery:

Cost of the equipment	$ 128,000
Reduced annual labor costs	$ 35,000
Estimated life of equipment	10 years
Terminal disposal value	$ 0
After-tax cost of capital	8%
Tax rate	30%

Assume depreciation is calculated on a straight-line basis for tax purposes. Assume all cash flows occur at year-end except for initial investment amounts.

Required

1. Calculate (a) net present value, (b) payback period, (c) discounted payback period, and (d) internal rate of return.
2. Compare and contrast the capital budgeting methods in requirement 1.

22-31 Project choice, taxes. Klein Dermatology is contemplating purchasing new laser therapy equipment. This new equipment would cost $300,000 to purchase and $20,000 for installation. Klein estimates that this new equipment would yield incremental margins of $98,000 annually due to new client services but would require incremental cash maintenance costs of $10,000 annually. Klein expects the life of this equipment to be 5 years and estimates a terminal disposal value of $20,000.

Klein has a 25% income tax rate and depreciates assets on a straight-line basis (to terminal value) for tax purposes. The required rate of return on investments is 10%.

Required

1. What is the expected increase in annual net income from investing in the new equipment?
2. Calculate the accrual accounting rate of return based on average investment.
3. Is the new equipment worth investing in from an NPV standpoint?
4. Suppose the tax authorities are willing to let Klein depreciate the new equipment down to zero over its useful life. If Klein plans to liquidate the equipment in 5 years, should it take this option? Quantify the impact of this choice on the NPV of the new equipment.

22-32 Customer value. Ortel Telecom sells telecommunication products and services to a variety of small businesses. Two of Ortel's key clients are Square and Cloudburst, both fast-growing technology start-ups located in New York City. Ortel has compiled information regarding its transactions with Square and Cloudburst for 2020, as well as its expected transactions with them over the next 3 years:

	A	B	C	D	E
1		Expected Annual Percentage Increase		2020	
2		Square	Cloudburst	Square	Cloudburst
3	Sales Revenues	6%	5.5%	$567,000	$3,510,000
4	Cost of Sales	5%	4.5%	$364,800	$3,060,000
5	Net cash flow			$202,200	$ 450,000

Ortel's transactions with Square and Cloudburst are in cash. Assume that they occur at year-end. Ortel is headquartered in the Cayman Islands and pays no income taxes. The owners of Ortel insist on a required rate of return of 12%.

Required

1. What is the expected net cash flow from Square and Cloudburst for the next 3 years?
2. Based on the net present value from cash flows over the next 3 years, is Cloudburst or Square a more valuable customer for Ortel?
3. Cloudburst threatens to switch to another supplier unless Ortel gives a 10% price reduction on all sales starting in 2021. Calculate the 3-year NPV of Cloudburst after incorporating the 10% discount. Should Ortel continue to transact with Cloudburst? What other factors should Ortel consider before making its final decision?

22-33 Selling a plant, income taxes. (CMA, adapted) The Platinum Company is a national mattress manufacturer. Its Marion plant will become idle on December 31, 2020. Nina Simon, the corporate controller, has been asked to look at three options regarding the plant:

- **Option 1:** The plant can be leased to the Coil Corporation, one of Platinum's suppliers, for 3 years. Under the lease terms, Coil would pay Platinum $220,000 rent per year (payable at year-end) and would grant Platinum a $64,000 annual discount from the normal price of coils purchased by Platinum. (Assume that the discount is received at year-end for each of the 3 years.) Coil would bear all of the plant's ownership costs. Platinum expects to sell this plant for $320,000 at the end of the 3-year lease.
- **Option 2:** The plant could be used for 3 years to make mattress covers as an accessory to be sold with a mattress. Fixed overhead costs (a cash outflow) before any equipment upgrades are estimated to be $18,000 annually for the 3-year period (assume the fixed costs occur at year-end). The covers are expected to sell for $25 each and variable cost per unit is expected to be $10. The following production and sales of the mattress covers are expected: 2021, 22,000 units; 2022, 18,000 units; 2023, 20,000 units. In order to manufacture the mattress covers, some of the plant equipment would need to be upgraded at an immediate cost of $120,000. The equipment would be depreciated using the straight-line depreciation method and zero terminal disposal value over the 3 years it would be in use. Because of the equipment upgrades, Platinum could sell the plant for $360,000 at the end of 3 years. No change in working capital would be required.
- **Option 3:** The plant, which has been fully depreciated for tax purposes, can be sold immediately for $800,000.

Platinum Company uses an after-tax required rate of return of 10%. Platinum is subject to a 25% tax rate on all income, including capital gains.

Required

1. Calculate net present value of each of the options and determine which option Platinum should select using the NPV criterion.
2. What nonfinancial factors should Platinum consider before making its choice?

Problems

22-34 Equipment replacement, no income taxes. Dublin Chips is a manufacturer of prototype chips based in Dublin, Ireland. Next year, in 2021, Dublin Chips expects to deliver 615 prototype chips at an average price of $95,000. Dublin Chips' marketing vice president forecasts growth of 65 prototype chips per year through 2027. That is, demand will be 615 in 2021, 680 in 2022, 745 in 2023, and so on.

The plant cannot produce more than 585 prototype chips annually. To meet future demand, Dublin Chips must either modernize the plant or replace it. The old equipment is fully depreciated and can be sold for $4,200,000 if the plant is replaced. If the plant is modernized, the costs to modernize it are to be capitalized and depreciated over the useful life of the modernized plant. The old equipment is retained as part of the "modernize" alternative. The following data on the two options are available:

	Modernize	Replace
Initial investment in 2021	$35,300,000	$66,300,000
Terminal disposal value in 2027	$ 7,500,000	$16,000,000
Useful life	7 years	7 years
Total annual cash operating costs per prototype chip	$ 78,500	$ 66,000

Dublin Chips uses straight-line depreciation, assuming zero terminal disposal value. For simplicity, we assume no change in prices or costs in future years. The investment will be made at the beginning of 2021, and all transactions thereafter occur on the last day of the year. Dublin Chips' required rate of return is 14%.

There is no difference between the "modernize" and "replace" alternatives in terms of required working capital. Dublin Chips has a special waiver on income taxes until 2027.

Required

1. Sketch the cash inflows and outflows of the "modernize" and "replace" alternatives over the 2021–2027 period.
2. Calculate the payback period for the "modernize" and "replace" alternatives.
3. Calculate the net present value of the "modernize" and "replace" alternatives.
4. What factors should Dublin Chips consider in choosing between the alternatives?

22-35 Equipment replacement, income taxes (continuation of 22-34). Assume the same facts as in Problem 22-34, except that the plant is located in Buffalo, New York. Dublin Chips has no special waiver on income taxes. It pays a 35% tax rate on all income. Proceeds from sales of equipment above book value are taxed at the same 35% rate.

Required

1. Sketch the after-tax cash inflows and outflows of the "modernize" and "replace" alternatives over the 2021–2027 period.
2. Calculate the net present value of the "modernize" and "replace" alternatives.
3. Suppose Dublin Chips is planning to build several more plants. It wants to have the most advantageous tax position possible. Dublin Chips has been approached by Spain, Malaysia, and Australia to construct plants in their countries. Use the data in Problem 22-34 and this problem to briefly describe in qualitative terms the income tax features that would be advantageous to Dublin Chips.

22-36 NPV, IRR, and sensitivity analysis. Jeong Natural Snacks is contemplating an expansion. The finance manager is looking at buying a second machine that would cost $62,000 and last for 10 years, with no disposal value at the end of that time. Jeong expects the increase in cash revenues from the expansion at $28,000 per year, with additional annual cash costs of $18,000. Jeong's cost of capital is 8%, and the company pays no taxes because of its location in a special economic zone.

Required

1. Calculate the net present value and internal rate of return for this investment.
2. Assume the finance manager of Jeong is unsure about the cash revenues and costs. The revenues could be anywhere from 10% higher to 10% lower than predicted. Assume cash costs are still $18,000 per year. What are NPV and IRR at the high and low points for revenue?
3. The finance manager thinks that costs will vary with revenues, and if the revenues are 10% higher, the costs will be 7% higher. If the revenues are 10% lower, the costs will be 10% lower. Recalculate the NPV and IRR at the high and low revenue points with this new cost information.
4. The finance manager has decided that the company should earn 2% more than the cost of capital on any project. Recalculate the original NPV in requirement 1 using the new discount rate and evaluate the investment opportunity.
5. Discuss how the changes in assumptions have affected the decision to expand.

22-37 NPV and AARR, goal-congruence issues. Paulina Jones, a manager for the Carpenter Manufacturing Company, has the opportunity to upgrade the equipment in the Midwest division by replacing and upgrading some of its machinery. The cost of the upgraded machinery will be $840,000 and will be depreciated using the straight-line method. The machinery is expected to have a useful life of 12 years and no residual value at the end the 12 years. The firm requires a minimum after-tax rate of return of 10% on investments. Paulina estimates annual net cash operating savings for this equipment of $150,000 before taxes and an investment in working capital at the beginning of the project of $10,000 that will be returned at the project's end. Carpenter's tax rate is 25%.

Required

1. Calculate the net present value of this equipment.
2. Calculate the accrual accounting rate of return based on net initial investment for this equipment.
3. Should Paulina accept the project? Will Paulina accept the project if her bonus depends on achieving an accrual accounting rate of return of 10%? How can this conflict be resolved?

22-38 Payback methods, even and uneven cash flows. Bobwhite Laundromat is trying to enhance the services it provides to customers, mostly college students. It is looking into the purchase of new high-efficiency washing machines that will allow for the laundry's status to be checked via smartphone.

Bobwhite estimates the cost of the new equipment at $178,000. The equipment has a useful life of 9 years. Bobwhite expects cash fixed costs of $87,000 per year to operate the new machines, as well as cash variable costs in the amount of 10% of revenues. Bobwhite evaluates investments using a cost of capital of 6%.

Required

1. Calculate the payback period and the discounted payback period for this investment, assuming Bobwhite expects to generate $190,000 in incremental revenues every year from the new machines.
2. Assume instead that Bobwhite expects the following uneven stream of incremental cash revenues from installing the new washing machines:

	A	B	C	D	E	F	G	H	I	J
1	**Year**	**1**	**2**	**3**	**4**	**5**	**6**	**7**	**8**	**9**
2	**Projected Revenue**	$85,000	$130,000	$140,000	$170,000	$180,000	$170,000	$140,000	$150,000	$185,000

Based on this estimated revenue stream, what are the payback and discounted payback periods for the investment?

22-39 Replacement of a machine, income taxes, sensitivity. (CMA, adapted) The Kuhl Brothers own a frozen custard ice cream shop. The brothers currently are using a machine that has been in use for the last 4 years. On January 1, 2020, the Kuhl Brothers are considering buying a new machine to make their frozen custard. The Kuhl Brothers have two options: (1) continue using the old freezing machine or (2) sell the old machine and purchase a new freezing machine. The seller of the new machine is not interested in a trade-in of Kuhl's old machine. The following information has been obtained:

	A	B	C
1		**Old Machine**	**New Machine**
2	Initial cost of machines	$180,000	$225,000
3	Useful life from acquisition date (years)	9	5
4	Terminal disposal value at the end of useful life on Dec. 31, 2024 (for depreciation purposes)	$ 13,500	$ 20,000
5	Expected annual cash operating costs:		
6	Variable cost per serving	$ 0.50	$ 0.40
7	Total fixed costs	$ 12,000	$ 8,000
8	Depreciation method for tax purposes	Straight line	Straight line
9	Estimated disposal value of machines:		
10	January 1, 2020	$ 75,000	$225,000
11	December 31, 2024	$ 10,000	$ 18,000
12	Expected servings made and served	240,000	240,000

The Kuhl Brothers are subject to a 25% income tax rate. Any gain or loss on the sale of machines is treated as an ordinary tax item and will affect the taxes paid by the Kuhl Brothers in the year in which it occurs. The Kuhl Brothers have an after-tax required rate of return of 8%. Assume all cash flows occur at year-end except for initial investment amounts.

Required

1. The Kuhl Brothers ask you whether they should buy the new machine. To help in your analysis, calculate the following:
   a. One-time after-tax cash effect of disposing of the old machine on January 1, 2020
   b. Annual recurring after-tax cash operating savings from using the new machine (variable and fixed)
   c. Cash tax savings due to differences in annual depreciation of the old machine and the new machine
   d. Difference in after-tax cash flow from terminal disposal of new machine and old machine
2. Use your calculations in requirement 1 and the net present value method to determine whether the Kuhl Brothers should continue to use the old machine or acquire the new machine.

3. How much more or less would the recurring after-tax cash operating savings of the new machine need to be for the Kuhl Brothers to earn exactly the 8% after-tax required rate of return? Assume that all other data about the investment do not change.

22-40 Recognizing cash flows for capital investment projects. Johnny Buster owns Entertainment World, a place that combines fast food, innovative beverages, and arcade games. Worried about the shifting tastes of younger audiences, Johnny contemplates bringing in new simulators and virtual reality games to maintain customer interest.

As part of this overhaul, Johnny is also looking at replacing his old Guitar Hero equipment with a Rock Band Pro machine. The Guitar Hero setup was purchased for $25,200 and has accumulated depreciation of $23,000, with a current trade-in value of $2,700. It currently costs Johnny $600 per month in utilities and another $5,000 a year in maintenance to run the Guitar Hero equipment. Johnny estimates that the equipment could be kept in service for another 11 years, after which it would have no salvage value.

The Rock Band Pro machine is more energy efficient and durable. It would reduce the utilities costs by 30% and cut the maintenance cost in half. The Rock Band Pro costs $49,000 and has an expected disposal value of $5,000 at the end of its useful life of 11 years.

Johnny charges an entrance fee of $5 per hour for customers to play an unlimited number of games. He does not believe that replacing Guitar Hero with Rock Band Pro will have an impact on this charge or materially change the number of customers who will visit Entertainment World.

Required

1. Johnny decides to evaluate the Rock Band Pro purchase using capital budgeting techniques. To help him, read through the problem and separate the cash flows into four groups: (1) net initial investment cash flows, (2) cash flow savings from operations, (3) cash flows from terminal disposal of investment, and (4) cash flows not relevant to the capital budgeting problem.
2. Assuming a tax rate of 40%, a required rate of return of 8%, and straight-line depreciation over the remaining useful life of equipment, should Johnny purchase Rock Band Pro?

22-41 NPV, inflation and taxes. TriMart is considering replacing 20 of their checkout registers with new self-checkout equipment. The equipment currently being used is fully depreciated and has no disposal value. The new equipment will cost a total of $220,000. Because the new equipment is self-serve, TriMart will have annual incremental cash savings in labor costs of $60,000 per year. The equipment will have a 5-year useful life and no terminal disposal value. The equipment will be depreciated using the straight-line method. TriMart requires a 4% real rate of return.

Required

1. Given the preceding information, what is the net present value (NPV) of the new equipment? Ignore taxes.
2. Assume the $60,000 cost savings are in current real dollars and the inflation rate is 2%. Recalculate the NPV of the project.
3. Based on your answers to requirements 1 and 2, should TriMart buy the new checkout equipment?
4. Now assume that the company's tax rate is 20%. Calculate the NPV of the equipment assuming no inflation.
5. Again assuming that the company faces a 20% tax rate, calculate the NPV of the equipment under an inflation rate of 2%.
6. Based on your answers to requirements 4 and 5, should TriMart buy the new checkout equipment?

22-42 Recognizing cash flows for capital investment projects, NPV. Shalie Manufacturing makes several thousand different metal products, including building materials, tools, and furniture parts. The manager of the furniture parts division has proposed that his division expand into bicycle parts. The furniture parts division currently generates cash revenues of $5,000,000 and incurs cash costs of $3,550,000, with an investment in assets of $12,050,000. One-fourth of the cash costs are direct labor.

The manager estimates that the expansion of the business will require an investment in working capital of $25,000. Because the company already has a facility, there would be no additional rent or purchase costs for a building, but the project would require an additional $390,000 in annual cash overhead. Moreover, the manager expects annual materials cash costs for bicycle parts to be $1,300,000, and labor for the bicycle parts to be about the same as the labor cash costs for furniture parts.

The controller of Shalie, working with various managers, estimates that the expansion would require the purchase of equipment with a $2,575,000 cost and an expected disposal value of $370,000 at the end of its 7-year useful life. Depreciation would occur on a straight-line basis.

The CFO of Shalie determines the firm's cost of capital as 14%. The CFO's salary is $150,000 per year. Adding another division will not change that. The chief executive officer asks for a report on expected revenues for the project, and is told by the marketing department that it might be able to achieve cash revenues of $3,372,500 annually from bicycle parts. Shalie Manufacturing has a tax rate of 35%.

Required

1. Separate the cash flows into four groups: (a) net initial investment cash flows, (b) cash flows from operations, (c) cash flows from terminal disposal of investment, and (d) cash flows not relevant to the capital budgeting problem.
2. Calculate the NPV of the expansion project and comment on your analysis.

Answers to Exercises in Compound Interest (Exercise 22-21)

The general approach to these exercises centers on a key question: Which of the four basic tables in Appendix A should be used? No computations should be made until this basic question has been answered with confidence.

1. **From Table 1.** The $50,000 is the present value P of your winnings. Their future value S in 5 years will be as follows:

$$S = P(1 + r)^n$$

The conversion factor, $(1 + r)^n$, is on line 5 of Table 1.

$$\text{Substituting at 6\%}: S = \$50{,}000\ (1.338) = \$66{,}900$$
$$\text{Substituting at 12\%}: S = \$50{,}000\ (1.762) = \$88{,}100$$

2. **From Table 2.** The $249,600 is a future value. You want the present value of that amount, $P = S \div (1 + r)^n$. The conversion factor, $1 \div (1 + r)^n$, is on line 12 of Table 2. Substituting,

$$P = \$249{,}600(.497) = \$124{,}051.20$$

3. **From Table 3.** The $249,600 is a future value. You are seeking the uniform amount (annuity) to set aside annually. Note that $1 invested each year for 12 years at 6% has a future value of $16.870 after 12 years, from line 12 of Table 3.

$$\$249{,}600/16.870 = \$14{,}795.49$$

4. **From Table 3.** You need to find the future value of an annuity of $4,800 per year. Note that $1 invested each year for 8 years at 4% has a future value of $9.214 after 8 years.

$$\$4{,}800(9.214) = \$44{,}227.20$$

5. **From Table 4.** When you reach age 65, you will get $400,000, the present value at that time. You need to find the annuity that will exactly exhaust the $400,000 in 7 years. To pay yourself $1 each year for 7 years when the interest rate is 6% requires you to have $5.582 today, from line 7 of Table 4.

$$\$400{,}000\,/\,5.582 = \$71{,}658.90$$

6. **From Table 4.** You need to find the present value of an annuity for 6 years at 4% and at 6%:

$$4\%\!: \$48{,}000(5.242) = \$251{,}616$$
$$6\%\!: \$48{,}000(4.917) = \$236{,}016$$

7. **From Table 2.** Plans A and B both have positive net present values because the present value of their cash inflows exceeds their outflow of $18,000. If only one plan can be chosen, Plan B is preferable because the NPV of plan B exceeds that of plan A by $857.

		Plan A		Plan B	
Year	**PV Factor at 6%**	**Cash Inflows**	**PV of Cash Inflows**	**Cash Inflows**	**PV of Cash Inflows**
1	.943	$2,000	$ 1,886	$3,000	$ 2,829
2	.890	$3,000	$ 2,670	$5,000	$ 4,450
3	.840	$4,000	$ 3,360	$9,000	$ 7,560
4	.792	$7,000	$ 5,544	$5,000	$ 3,960
5	.747	$9,000	$ 6,723	$3,000	$ 2,241
			$20,183		$21,040

Even though plans A and B have the same initial outflow and the same total cash inflows over the 5 years, plan B is preferred because it has greater cash inflows occurring earlier.

Management Control Systems, Transfer Pricing, and Multinational Considerations

23

Transfer pricing is the price one subunit of a company charges for the services it provides another subunit of the same company.

At Ford, for example, automotive components, vehicles, and assembly services are bought and sold internally across divisions. The intellectual property patents of many pharmaceutical companies, such as Merck, are usually held by foreign subsidiaries, making the transfer price to these subsidiaries a critical factor in how much income is recognized in various tax jurisdictions.

Firms use transfer prices (1) to focus managers' attention on the performance of their own subunits and (2) to plan and coordinate the actions of different subunits to maximize the company's income as a whole. Transfer prices can lead to disagreements, however, because managers of different subunits often have very different preferences about how transfer prices should be set. For example, some managers prefer the prices be based on market prices. Others prefer the prices be based on costs alone. Controversies also arise when multinational corporations seek to reduce their overall income tax burden by charging high transfer prices to units located in countries with high tax rates. Many jurisdictions, including the European Union, attempt to restrict this practice, as the following article shows.

Ken Wolter/Shutterstock

APPLE FORCED TO PAY IRELAND €14.3 BILLION IN TAX SETTLEMENT[1]

For many years, companies have used controversial transfer-pricing techniques to shift their profits from higher-tax countries to lower-tax jurisdictions. In 2016, the European

LEARNING OBJECTIVES

1. Describe a management control system and its three key properties
2. Describe the benefits and costs of decentralization
3. Explain transfer prices and the four criteria managers use to evaluate them
4. Calculate transfer prices using three methods
5. Illustrate how market-based transfer prices promote goal congruence in perfectly competitive markets
6. Understand how to avoid making suboptimal decisions when transfer prices are based on full cost plus a markup
7. Describe the range of feasible transfer prices when there is unused capacity and alternative methods for arriving at the eventual hybrid price
8. Apply a general guideline for determining a minimum transfer price
9. Incorporate income tax considerations in multinational transfer pricing

[1] *Sources:* Sean Farrell and Henry McDonald, "Apple Ordered to Pay €13bn After EU Rules Ireland Broke State Aid Laws," *The Guardian,* August 30, 2016 (https://www.theguardian.com/business/2016/aug/30/apple-pay-back-taxes-eu-ruling-ireland-state-aid); Cliff Taylor, "Apple's Irish Company Structure Key to EU Tax Finding," *The Irish Times,* September 2, 2016 (https://www.irishtimes.com/business/economy/apple-s-irish-company-structure-key-to-eu-tax-finding-1.2775684); No author, "Ireland Collects More Than €14bn in Taxes and Interest from Apple," *The Guardian,* September 18, 2018 (https://www.theguardian.com/world/2018/sep/18/ireland-collects-more-than-14bn-disputed-taxes-from-apple).

Union (EU) ordered Apple to pay €13.1 billion in back taxes plus €1.2 billion in interest to Ireland for unpaid taxes on €111 billion of profits from 2004 to 2014. This was the largest corporate tax fine ever.

The EU concluded that Apple booked almost all the profit generated from its sales of iPhones and other products across Europe between 1991 and 2015 to a "head office," Apple Sales International, in Ireland that only existed on paper. From there, Apple Inc., the corporate parent, levied a heavy charge on those profits to account for the subsidiary's use of its intellectual property, which reduced the tax owed Ireland to extremely low levels. The EU found that the deal allowed Apple to pay a maximum annual tax rate of just 1%. Often, it paid far less. In 2014, for example, the company paid a mere 0.005% of its profits in tax.

For its part, Apple rejected the EU ruling and filed an appeal. Tim Cook, Apple's chief executive officer (CEO), said the EU was rewriting Apple's history in Ireland and disrupting the international tax system. He said Apple chose the Irish city of Cork as its European base in the 1980s, and it had expanded to almost 6,000 workers in Ireland. The appeal is still under review.

Though not all companies face multinational tax concerns, transfer-pricing issues are common to many companies. In these companies, transfer pricing is part of the larger management control system. This chapter discusses the links among a firm's strategy, organizational structure, management control systems, and accounting information. We'll examine the benefits and costs of centralized and decentralized organizational structures and look at the pricing of products or services transferred between subunits of the same company. We emphasize how accounting data, such as costs, budgets, and prices, help in planning and coordinating actions of subunits.

Management Control Systems

LEARNING OBJECTIVE 1

Describe a management control system

... gathers information for planning and control decisions

and its three key properties

... aligns with strategy, supports organizational responsibility of managers, and motivates employees

A **management control system** is a means of gathering and using information to aid and coordinate the planning and control decisions throughout an organization and to guide the behavior of its managers and other employees. Some companies design their management control system around the concept of the balanced scorecard. For example, ExxonMobil's management control system contains financial and nonfinancial information in each of the four perspectives of the balanced scorecard (see Chapter 13 for details). Well-designed management control systems use information both from within the company, such as its net income and levels of employee satisfaction, and from outside the company, such as its stock price and customer-satisfaction data.

Formal and Informal Systems

Management control systems consist of formal and informal control systems. The formal management control system of a company includes explicit rules, procedures, performance measures, and incentive plans that guide the behavior of its managers and other employees. The formal control system is composed of several systems, such as the following:

- The management accounting systems, which provide information about the firm's costs, revenues, and income
- The human resources systems, which provide information about the recruiting and training of employees, absenteeism, and accidents
- The quality system, which provides information about yields, defective products, and late deliveries to customers

The informal management control system includes the shared values, loyalties, and mutual commitments among members of the organization, the company's culture, and the unwritten norms about acceptable behavior for managers and other employees. Examples of company slogans that reinforce values and loyalties are "Levi's, Quality Never Goes Out of Style" and "Walmart, Save Money, Live Better."

Effective Management Control

To be effective, management control systems should be closely aligned with the organization's strategies and goals. Two examples of strategies at ExxonMobil are (1) providing innovative products and services to increase the company's market share in key customer segments (by targeting customers who are willing to pay more for faster service, better facilities, and well-stocked convenience stores) and (2) reducing costs and targeting price-sensitive customers. Suppose ExxonMobil decides to pursue the former strategy. The management control system must then reinforce this goal, and ExxonMobil should tie managers' rewards to achieving the targeted measures.

Management control systems should also be designed to support the organizational responsibilities of individual managers. Different levels of management at ExxonMobil need different kinds of information to perform their tasks. For example, top managers need stock-price information to evaluate how much shareholder value the company has created. The stock price, however, is less important for line managers supervising individual refineries. Those managers are more concerned with obtaining information about the firm's on-time delivery of gasoline, equipment downtime, product quality, number of days lost to accidents and environmental problems, cost per gallon of gasoline, and employee satisfaction. Similarly, marketing managers are more concerned with information about the service at gas stations, customer satisfaction, and market share.

Effective management control systems should also motivate managers and other employees. **Motivation** is the desire to attain a selected goal (the *goal-congruence* aspect) combined with the resulting pursuit of that goal (the *effort* aspect).

Goal congruence exists when individuals and groups work toward achieving the organization's goals—that is, managers working in their own best interest take actions that align with the overall goals of top management. Suppose the goal of ExxonMobil's top management is to maximize operating income. If the management control system evaluates refinery managers *only* on the basis of costs, the managers may be tempted to make decisions that minimize costs but overlook product quality or timely delivery to retail stations. This oversight probably won't maximize the operating income of the company as a whole. In this case, the management control system will not achieve goal congruence.

Effort is the extent to which managers strive or endeavor in order to achieve a goal. Effort goes beyond physical exertion, such as a worker producing at a faster rate, to include mental actions as well. For example, effort includes the diligence or acumen with which a manager gathers and analyzes data before authorizing a new investment. It is impossible to directly observe or reward effort. As a result, management control systems motivate employees to exert effort by rewarding them for the achievement of tangible goals, such as profit targets or stock returns. This induces managers to exert effort because higher levels of effort increase the likelihood that the goals are achieved. The rewards can be monetary (such as cash, shares of company stock, use of a company car, or membership in a club) or nonmonetary (such as a better title, greater responsibility, or authority over a larger number of employees).

Management control systems must be aligned with an organization's structure. An organization with a decentralized structure will have different issues to consider when designing its management control system than a firm with a centralized structure.

DECISION POINT

What is a management control system, and how should it be designed?

Decentralization

LEARNING OBJECTIVE 2

Describe the benefits

... responsiveness to customers, faster decision making, management development

and costs of decentralization

... loss of control, duplication of activities

Until the mid-20th century, many firms were organized in a centralized, hierarchical fashion. Centralization is an organizational structure in which power is concentrated at the top and there is relatively little freedom for managers at the lower levels to make decisions. Perhaps the most famous example of a highly centralized structure is the Soviet Union, prior to its collapse in the late 1980s.

Today, organizations are largely decentralized and many companies have pushed decision-making authority down to subunit managers. **Decentralization** is an organizational structure that gives managers at lower levels the freedom to make decisions. **Autonomy** is the degree of freedom to make decisions. The greater the freedom, the greater the autonomy. As we discuss the issues of decentralization and autonomy, we use the term *subunit* to refer to any part of an organization below the top. A subunit may be a large division, such as the refining division of ExxonMobil, or a small group, such as a two-person advertising department of a local clothing chain.

Examples of firms with decentralized structures include Nucor, the U.S. steel giant, which gives the general managers of its plants a substantial amount of operational autonomy, and Tesco, Britain's largest retailer, which offers great latitude to its store managers. Of course, no firm is completely decentralized. Nucor's top managers are still responsible for the firm's overall strategic planning, financing, setting of base salary levels and bonus targets, and so on. How much decentralization is optimal? Companies try to choose the degree of decentralization that maximizes benefits over costs. We next discuss the key benefits and costs of decentralization.

Benefits of Decentralization

Proponents of decentralizing decision making argue that granting responsibilities to managers of subunits has the following benefits:

1. **Creates greater responsiveness to the needs of a subunit's customers, suppliers, and employees.** Good decisions cannot be made without good information. Compared with top managers, subunit managers are better informed about their units' competitors, suppliers, and employees, as well as about local factors that affect performance, such as ways to decrease costs, improve quality, and better respond to customers. Flex, a global supply chain solutions company, uses decentralization to reduce bureaucracy and increase responsiveness. Managers can use the company's worldwide information technology to solve a local customer's problem or send a project to other managers without going through red tape.
2. **Leads to gains from faster decision making by subunit managers.** Decentralization speeds decision making, creating a competitive advantage over centralized organizations. Centralization slows down decision making because decisions must be pushed upward through layer after layer of management before they are finalized. Interlake Mecalux, a leading provider of materials-handling solutions and storage products, cites this benefit of decentralization: "We have distributed decision-making powers more broadly to the cutting edge of product and market opportunity." Interlake's storage system solutions must often be customized to fit the needs of customers. Delegating decision making to the sales force allows Interlake to respond faster to changing customer requirements.
3. **Assists management development and learning.** Subunit managers are more motivated and committed when they can exercise initiative. Moreover, giving managers more responsibility helps a company develop an experienced pool of talent to fill higher-level management positions and weed out people unlikely to be successful top managers. According to Tektronix, an electronics company based in Oregon, "Decentralized units provide a training ground for general managers and a visible field of combat where product champions can fight for their ideas."
4. **Sharpens the focus of subunit managers and broadens the reach of top management.** In a decentralized setting, the manager of a subunit has a concentrated focus. The head of Facebook Indonesia, for example, can develop country-specific knowledge and expertise (about local advertising trends, cultural norms, payment forms, and so on) and focus on maximizing Facebook's profits in Indonesia. At the same time, this relieves Facebook's senior executives at its Menlo Park, California, headquarters from the burden of controlling day-to-day operating decisions in Indonesia. They can spend more time and effort on strategic planning for the entire organization.

Costs of Decentralization

Advocates of more-centralized decision making argue that decentralizing is costly for the following reasons:

1. **Leads to suboptimal decision making.** If subunit managers do not have the necessary expertise or talent to make major decisions, the company, as a whole, is worse off because its top managers have relinquished their responsibility for doing so. Even if subunit

managers are sufficiently skilled, **suboptimal decision making**—also called **incongruent decision making** or **dysfunctional decision making**—occurs when a decision's benefit to one subunit is more than offset by the costs to the organization as a whole. This is most prevalent when the subunits of the company are highly interdependent, such as when the end product of one subunit is used or sold by another subunit. For example, suppose Sony's marketing group receives a rush order for additional PS4 Pro PlayStation systems in Australia following the release of popular new games. A manufacturing manager in Japan who is evaluated on the basis of costs may be unwilling to arrange this rush order because altering production schedules invariably increases manufacturing costs. From Sony's viewpoint, however, supplying the consoles may be optimal, both because the Australian customers are willing to pay a premium price and because the current shipment is expected to stimulate future orders for other Sony games and devices.

2. **Leads to unhealthy competition.** In a decentralized setting, subunit managers may regard themselves as competing with managers of other subunits in the same company as if they were external rivals. This pushes them to view the relative performance of the subunit as more important than the goals of the overall company. Consequently, managers may be unwilling to assist other subunits (as in the Sony example) or share important information. The 2010 congressional hearings on the recall of Toyota vehicles revealed that it was common for Toyota's Japan unit to not share information about engineering problems or reported defects between its United States, Asian, and European operations. Toyota has since asserted that it will change this dysfunctional behavior.
3. **Results in duplication of output.** If subunits provide similar products or services, their internal competition could lead to failure in the external markets. The reason is that divisions may find it easier to steal market share from one another by mimicking each other's successful products, rather than those of competing firms. Eventually, this leads to confusion in the minds of customers and the loss of each division's distinctive strengths. A classic example is General Motors, which eventually dissolved its Oldsmobile, Pontiac, and Saturn divisions. Similarly, Condé Nast Publishing's initially distinct food magazines *Bon Appétit* and *Gourmet* eventually ended up chasing the same readers and advertisers, to the detriment of both. *Gourmet* magazine stopped publication in November 2009.[2]
4. **Results in duplication of activities.** Even if the subunits operate in distinct markets, several individual subunits of the company may undertake the same activity separately. In a highly decentralized company, each subunit may have personnel to carry out staff functions such as human resources or information technology. Centralizing these functions helps to streamline and use fewer resources for these activities and eliminates wasteful duplication. For example, ABB of Switzerland, a global leader in power and automation technology, is decentralized but has generated significant cost savings by centralizing its sourcing decisions across business units for parts, such as pipe pumps and fittings, as well as engineering and erection services. Having subunits share services such as information technology and human resources is becoming popular with companies because it saves 30–40% of the cost of having each subunit purchase these services on its own.

Comparing Benefits and Costs

Top managers must compare the benefits and costs of decentralization, often on a function-by-function basis, when choosing an organizational structure. Surveys of U.S. and European companies report that the decisions made most frequently at the decentralized level are related to product mix and advertising. In these areas, subunit managers develop their own operating plans and performance reports and make faster decisions based on local information. Decisions related to the type and source of long-term financing are made least frequently at the decentralized level. Corporate managers have better information about financing terms in different markets and can obtain the best terms. Likewise, centralizing its income tax strategies

[2] For an intriguing comparison of the failure of decentralization in these disparate settings, see Jack Shafer's article "How Condé Nast Is Like General Motors: The Magazine Empire as Car Wreck," *Slate* (October 5, 2009), www.slate.com/id/2231177/.

allows the organization to optimize across subunits, for example by offsetting the income in one subunit with losses in others.

Decentralization in Multinational Companies

Multinational companies—companies that operate in multiple countries—are often decentralized because centralizing the control of their subunits around the world can be physically and practically impossible. Also, language, customs, cultures, business practices, rules, laws, and regulations vary significantly across countries. Decentralization enables managers in different countries to make decisions that exploit their knowledge of local business and political conditions and enables them to deal with uncertainties in their individual environments. For example, Coca-Cola maintains a global brand strategy and architecture but delegates major decisions to overseas markets, including franchise relations with bottlers, new product launches, and locally relevant communication, pricing, and packaging. Multinational corporations often rotate managers between foreign locations and corporate headquarters. Job rotation combined with decentralization helps develop the ability of managers to operate in the global environment.

There are drawbacks to decentralizing multinational companies. One of the most important is the lack of control and the resulting risks. In 1995, Barings PLC, a British investment banking firm, went bankrupt and had to be sold when one of its traders in Singapore caused the firm to lose more than £1 billion on unauthorized trades that went undetected. Similarly, in 2011, a London trader working for UBS, Switzerland's largest bank, circumvented the bank's risk controls and made unauthorized trades that resulted in a $2.3 billion loss for the company. UBS's CEO and other top managers resigned because of the scandal. Multinational corporations that implement decentralized decision making usually design their management control systems to measure and monitor the performance of divisions. Information and communications technology help the flow of information for reporting and control.

Choices About Responsibility Centers

Recall (from Chapter 6) that a responsibility center is a segment or subunit of the organization whose manager is accountable for a specified set of activities. To measure the performance of subunits in centralized or decentralized companies, the management control system uses one or a mix of the four types of responsibility centers:

1. *Cost center*—the manager is accountable for costs only.
2. *Revenue center*—the manager is accountable for revenues only.
3. *Profit center*—the manager is accountable for revenues and costs.
4. *Investment center*—the manager is accountable for revenues, costs, and investments.

Each type of responsibility center can be found in either centralized or decentralized companies.

A common misconception is that *profit center*—and, in some cases, *investment center*—is a synonym for a decentralized subunit and *cost center* is a synonym for a centralized subunit. *Profit centers can be coupled with a highly centralized organization, and cost centers can be coupled with a highly decentralized organization.* For example, managers in a division organized as a profit center may have little freedom in making decisions. They may need to obtain approval from corporate headquarters for introducing new products and services or to make expenditures over some preset limit. When Michael Eisner ran Walt Disney Company, the giant media and entertainment conglomerate, from 1984 until 2005, the firm's strategic-planning division scrutinized business proposals so closely that managers were reluctant to pitch new ideas.[3] In other companies, divisions such as information technology may be organized as cost centers, but their managers may have great latitude to make capital expenditures and purchase materials and services. In short, the labels *profit center* and *cost center* are independent of the degree of centralization or decentralization in a company.

DECISION POINT

What are the benefits and costs of decentralization?

[3] When Robert Iger replaced Eisner as CEO in 2005, one of his first acts was to disassemble the strategic-planning division, thereby giving more authority to Disney's business units (parks and resorts, consumer products, and media networks).

23-1 TRY IT!

For each of the following, identify whether they can be found in a centralized organization, a decentralized organization, or both types of organizations.

a. Freedom for managers at lower organizational levels to make decisions
b. Greater responsiveness to user needs
c. Maximum constraints and minimum freedom for managers at lowest levels
d. Maximization of benefits over costs
e. Minimization of duplicate functions
f. Minimum of suboptimization
g. Multiple responsibility centers with various reporting units
h. Profit centers

Transfer Pricing

LEARNING OBJECTIVE 3

Explain transfer prices

... price one subunit charges another for product

and the four criteria managers use to evaluate them

... goal congruence, management effort, subunit performance evaluation, and subunit autonomy

In a decentralized organization, much of the decision-making power resides in its individual subunits. Often, the subunits interact by supplying goods or services to one another. In these cases, top management uses *transfer prices* to coordinate the actions of the subunits and to evaluate the performance of their managers.

A **transfer price** is the price one subunit (department or division) charges for a product or service supplied to another subunit within the same organization. If, for example, a car manufacturer like BMW or Ford has separate divisions for manufacturing engines and assembling cars, the transfer price is the price the engine division charges when it transfers engines to the car assembly division. The transfer price creates revenues for the selling subunit (the engine division in our example) and costs for the buying subunit (the assembly division in our example), affecting each subunit's operating income. These operating incomes can be used to evaluate the subunits' performances and to motivate their managers. The product or service transferred between subunits of an organization is called an **intermediate product**. The receiving unit (the assembly division in the engine example) may work on the product further or the product may be transferred from production to marketing and sold directly on the external market.

In one sense, transfer pricing is a curious phenomenon. Activities within an organization are clearly nonmarket in nature; products and services are not bought and sold as they are in open-market transactions. Yet establishing prices for transfers among subunits of a company has a distinctly market flavor. The rationale for transfer prices is that they allow subunit managers (such as the manager of the engine division) to focus only on the performance of their subunits when making decisions without having to evaluate how their decisions affect company-wide performance. In this sense, transfer prices ease the subunit managers' information-processing and decision-making tasks. In a well-designed transfer-pricing system, managers focus on maximizing the performance of their subunits and in doing so optimize the performance of the company as a whole.

Criteria for Evaluating Transfer Prices

To help a company achieve its goals, transfer prices should meet four key criteria:

1. Promote goal congruence, so that division managers acting in their own interest will take actions that are aligned with the objectives of top management.
2. Induce managers to exert a high level of effort. Subunits selling a product or service should be motivated to hold down their costs; subunits buying the product or service should be motivated to acquire and use inputs efficiently.
3. Help top managers evaluate the performance of individual subunits.
4. Preserve autonomy of subunits if top managers favor a high degree of decentralization. A subunit manager seeking to maximize the operating income of the subunit should have the freedom to transact with other subunits of the company (on the basis of transfer prices) or to transact with external parties.

DECISION POINT

What are transfer prices, and what criteria do managers use to evaluate them?

Calculating Transfer Prices

LEARNING OBJECTIVE 4

Calculate transfer prices using three methods

... (1) market based, (2) cost based, or (3) hybrid, each of which yields different operating incomes for the subunits

There are three broad categories of methods top managers can use to determine transfer prices:

1. **Market-based transfer prices.** Top managers may choose to use the price of a similar product or service publicly listed on, say, a trade association's website. Or they may select the external price a subunit charges outside customers.
2. **Cost-based transfer prices.** Top managers may choose a transfer price based on the cost of producing the product being transferred. Examples include the variable production cost, variable and fixed production costs, and full cost of the product. The full cost of the product includes all production costs plus costs from other business functions (research and development, design, marketing, distribution, and customer service). The cost used in cost-based transfer prices can be actual cost or budgeted cost. Sometimes, the cost-based transfer price includes a markup or profit margin that represents a return on subunit investment.
3. **Hybrid transfer prices.** Hybrid transfer prices take into account both cost and market information. Top managers may set the prices by specifying a transfer price that is an average of the cost of producing and transporting the product internally and the market price for comparable products. At other times, a hybrid transfer price may allow for the revenue recognized by the selling unit to differ from the cost recognized by the buying unit. The most common form of hybrid prices arises via negotiation—the subunit managers are asked to negotiate the transfer price between them and to decide whether to buy and sell internally or deal with external parties. Negotiated transfer prices are often employed when market prices are volatile. Thus, managers need current information about the costs and prices of products to participate in the bargaining process.

Under what circumstances should each of these options be used? To answer this question, we next demonstrate how each of the three transfer-pricing methods works and highlight the differences among them. We examine transfer pricing at Horizon Petroleum against the four criteria of promoting goal congruence, motivating management effort, evaluating subunit performance, and preserving subunit autonomy.

An Illustration of Transfer Pricing

Horizon Petroleum has two divisions, each operating as a profit center. The transportation division purchases crude oil in Matamoros, Mexico, and transports it from Matamoros to Houston, Texas. The refining division processes crude oil into gasoline. For simplicity, we assume gasoline is the only salable product the Houston refinery makes and that it takes two barrels of crude oil to yield one barrel of gasoline.

The variable costs of each division are associated with a single cost driver: barrels of crude oil transported by the transportation division and barrels of gasoline produced by the refining division. The fixed cost per unit is based on the budgeted annual fixed costs and practical capacity of crude oil that can be transported by the transportation division, as well as the budgeted annual fixed costs and practical capacity of gasoline that can be produced by the refining division. Horizon Petroleum reports all costs and revenues of its non-U.S. operations in U.S. dollars using the prevailing exchange rate.

- The transportation division has obtained rights to certain oil fields in the Matamoros area. It has a long-term contract to purchase crude oil extracted from these fields at $72 per barrel. The division transports the oil to Houston and then "sells" it to the refining division. The pipeline from Matamoros to Houston can transport 40,000 barrels of crude oil per day.
- The refining division has been operating at capacity (30,000 barrels of crude oil a day), using oil supplied by Horizon's transportation division (an average of 10,000 barrels per day) and oil bought from another producer and delivered to the Houston refinery (an average of 20,000 barrels per day at $85 per barrel).
- The refining division sells the gasoline it produces to outside parties at $190 per barrel.

EXHIBIT 23-1 Operating Data for Horizon Petroleum

	A	B	C	D	E	F	G	H
1								
2				**Transportation Division**				
3				Variable cost per barrel of crude oil	$ 1			
4	Contract price per barrel of crude oil supplied in Matamoros =	$72	→	Fixed cost per barrel of crude oil	3			
5				Full cost per barrel of crude oil	$ 4			
6								
7				↓				
8				Barrels of crude oil transferred				
9								
10				↓				
11				**Refining Division**				
12				Variable cost per barrel of gasoline	$ 8			
13	Market price per barrel of crude oil supplied to Houston refinery =	$85	→	Fixed cost per barrel of gasoline	6	→	Market price per barrel of gasoline sold to external parties =	$190
14				Full cost per barrel of gasoline	$14			
15								

Exhibit 23-1 summarizes Horizon Petroleum's variable and fixed costs per barrel of crude oil in the transportation division and variable and fixed costs per barrel of gasoline in the refining division, the external market price of buying crude oil, and the external market price of selling gasoline. What's missing in the exhibit is the actual transfer price paid by the refining division to the transportation division. This transfer price will vary depending on the transfer-pricing method used. The transfer prices paid by the refining division to the transportation division under each of the three methods are as follows:

1. A market-based transfer price of $85 per barrel of crude oil based on the competitive market price in Houston.
2. A cost-based transfer price at, say, 105% of full cost, where the full cost is the cost of the crude oil purchased in Matamoros plus the transportation division's own variable and fixed costs (from Exhibit 23-1): 1.05 × ($72 + $1 + $3) = $79.80.
3. A hybrid transfer price of, say, $82 per barrel of crude oil, which is between the market-based and cost-based transfer prices. We describe later in this section the various ways in which hybrid prices can be determined.

Exhibit 23-2 presents division operating incomes for 100 barrels of crude oil purchased under each transfer-pricing method. Transfer prices create income for the selling division and corresponding costs for the buying division that cancel out when divisional results are consolidated for the company as a whole. The exhibit assumes all three transfer-pricing methods yield transfer prices that are in a range that does not cause division managers to change the business relationships shown in Exhibit 23-1. That is, Horizon Petroleum's total operating income from purchasing, transporting, and refining the 100 barrels of crude oil and selling the 50 barrels of gasoline is the same ($1,200) *regardless of the internal transfer prices used.*

Total operating income = Revenues − Cost of crude oil purchases in Matamoros − Transportation Division costs − Refining Division costs

= ($190 × 50 barrels of gasoline) − ($72 × 100 barrels of crude oil) − ($4 × 100 barrels of crude oil) − ($14 × 50 barrels of gasoline)

= $9,500 − $7,200 − $400 − $700 = $1,200

Under all three methods, summing the two division operating incomes equals Horizon Petroleum's total operating income of $1,200. By keeping the total operating income the same,

EXHIBIT 23-2 Division Operating Income of Horizon Petroleum for 100 Barrels of Crude Oil Under Alternative Transfer-Pricing Methods

	A	B	C	D	E	F	G	H
1	**Production and Sales Data**							
2	Barrels of crude oil transferred = 100							
3	Barrels of gasoline sold = 50							
4								
5		**Internal Transfers at**			**Internal Transfers at**		**Internal Transfers at**	
6		**Market Price =**			**105% of Full Cost =**		**Hybrid Price =**	
7		**$85 per Barrel**			**$79.80 per Barrel**		**$82 per Barrel**	
8	**Transportation Division**							
9	Revenues, $85, $79.80, $82 × 100 barrels of crude oil	$8,500			$7,980		$8,200	
10	Costs:							
11	Crude oil purchase costs, $72 × 100 barrels of crude oil	7,200			7,200		7,200	
12	Division variable costs, $1 × 100 barrels of crude oil	100			100		100	
13	Division fixed costs, $3 × 100 barrels of crude oil	300			300		300	
14	Total division costs	7,600			7,600		7,600	
15	Division operating income	$ 900			$ 380		$ 600	
16								
17	**Refining Division**							
18	Revenues, $190 × 50 barrels of gasoline	$9,500			$9,500		$9,500	
19	Costs:							
20	Transferred-in costs, $85, $79.80, $82 × 100 barrels of crude oil	8,500	←		7,980	←	8,200	←
21	Division variable costs, $8 × 50 barrels of gasoline	400			400		400	
22	Division fixed costs, $6 × 50 barrels of gasoline	300			300		300	
23	Total division costs	9,200			8,680		8,900	
24	Division operating income	$ 300			$ 820		$ 600	
25								
26	Operating income of both divisions together	$1,200			$1,200		$1,200	

we focus attention on the effects different transfer-pricing methods have on the operating income of each division. Subsequent sections of this chapter show that the choice of transfer-pricing method can cause managers to take actions that lead to different total operating incomes for the company as a whole.

Consider the two methods in columns B and E of Exhibit 23-2. The operating income of the transportation division is $520 more ($900 – $380) if transfer prices are based on market prices rather than on 105% of the full cost. Correspondingly, the operating income of the refining division is $520 lower ($820 – $300) if transfer prices are based on market prices rather than 105% of the full cost. If the transportation division's sole criterion were to maximize its own operating income, it would favor transfer prices at market prices. In contrast, the refining division would prefer transfer prices at 105% of full cost to maximize its own operating income. The hybrid transfer price of $82 is between the 105% of full cost and market-based transfer prices. It splits the $1,200 of operating income equally between the divisions. This price could arise as a result of negotiations between the transportation and refining division managers.

It's not surprising that subunit managers, especially those whose compensation or promotion directly depends on subunit operating income, take considerable interest in setting transfer prices. To reduce the excessive focus of subunit managers on their own divisions, many companies compensate subunit managers on the basis of both the operating income earned by their respective divisions and the company as a whole.

DECISION POINT

What are alternative ways of calculating transfer prices?

We next examine market-based, cost-based, and hybrid transfer prices in more detail. We show how the choice of transfer-pricing method can determine the size of the total company-wide operating-income pie.

Market-Based Transfer Prices

LEARNING OBJECTIVE 5

Illustrate how market-based transfer prices promote goal congruence in perfectly competitive markets

... division managers transacting internally are motivated to take the same actions as if they were transacting externally

Transferring products or services at market prices generally leads to optimal decisions when three conditions are satisfied: (1) The market for the intermediate product is perfectly competitive, (2) the interdependencies of subunits are minimal, and (3) there are no additional costs or benefits to the company as a whole from buying or selling on the external market instead of transacting internally.

Perfect Competition

A **perfectly competitive market** exists when there is a homogeneous product with buying prices equal to selling prices and no individual buyers or sellers can affect those prices by their own actions. By using market-based transfer prices in perfectly competitive markets, a company can (1) promote goal congruence, (2) motivate management effort, (3) evaluate the performance of subunits, and (4) preserve their autonomy.

Consider Horizon Petroleum again. Assume there is a perfectly competitive market for crude oil in the Houston area. As a result, the transportation division can sell and the refining division can buy as much crude oil as each wants at $85 per barrel. Horizon would prefer its managers to buy or sell crude oil internally. Think about the decisions that Horizon's division managers would make if each had the autonomy to sell or buy crude oil externally. If the transfer price between Horizon's transportation and refining divisions is set below $85, the manager of the transportation division will be motivated to sell all crude oil to external buyers in the Houston area at $85 per barrel. If the transfer price is set above $85, the manager of the refining division will be motivated to purchase all crude oil from external suppliers. Only an $85 transfer price will motivate the transportation division and the refining division to buy and sell internally. That's because neither division profits by buying or selling on the external market.

Suppose Horizon evaluates its division managers on the basis of their individual division's operating income. The transportation division will sell, either internally or externally, as much crude oil as it can profitably transport, and the refining division will buy, either internally or externally, as much crude oil as it can profitably refine. An $85-per-barrel transfer price results in goal congruence—the actions that maximize each division's operating income are also the actions that maximize the operating income of Horizon Petroleum as a whole. Furthermore, because the transfer price is not based on costs, it motivates each division manager to maximize his or her own division's operating income. Market prices also serve to evaluate the economic viability and profitability of each division individually. For example, Koch Industries, the second-largest private company in the United States, uses market-based pricing for all internal transfers. As its CFO, Steve Feilmeier, noted, "We believe that the alternative for any given asset should always be considered in order to best optimize the profitability of the asset. If you simply transfer price between two different divisions at cost, then you may be subsidizing your whole operation and not know it." Returning to our Horizon example, suppose that under market-based transfer prices, the refining division consistently shows small or negative profits. Then Horizon may consider shutting down the refining division and simply transport and sell the oil to other refineries in the Houston area.

Imperfect Competition

If markets are not perfectly competitive, selling prices affect the quantity of product sold. Consider an auto dealer: In order to sell more new or used cars, the dealer has to reduce the price of the vehicles. A similar situation applies to industries ranging from toilet paper and toothpaste to software. Faced with an imperfectly competitive market, the manager of the selling division will choose a price and quantity combination for the intermediate product that maximizes the division's operating income. If the transfer price is set at this price, the buying division may find that acquiring the product is too costly and results in a loss and decide not to purchase the product. Yet, from the point of view of the company as a whole, it may well be that profits are maximized if the selling division transfers the product to the buying division for further processing and sale. For this reason, when the market for the

DECISION POINT

Under what market conditions do market-based transfer prices promote goal congruence?

intermediate good is imperfectly competitive, the transfer price must generally be set below the external market price (but above the selling division's variable cost) in order to induce efficient transfers.[4]

Cost-Based Transfer Prices

LEARNING OBJECTIVE 6

Understand how to avoid making suboptimal decisions when transfer prices are based on full cost plus a markup

... buying divisions should not regard the fixed costs and the markup as variable costs

Cost-based transfer prices are helpful when market prices are unavailable, inappropriate, or too costly to obtain. This can occur, for example, when markets are not perfectly competitive, when the product is specialized, or when the internal product is different from the products available externally in terms of its quality and the customer service provided for it.

Full-Cost Bases

In practice, many companies use transfer prices based on a product's full cost. To approximate market prices, cost-based transfer prices are sometimes set at the full cost plus a margin. These transfer prices, however, can lead to suboptimal decisions. Suppose Horizon Petroleum makes internal transfers at 105% of the full cost. Recall that the refining division purchases, on average, 20,000 barrels of crude oil per day from a local Houston supplier, who delivers the crude oil to the refinery at a price of $85 per barrel. To reduce its crude oil costs, the refining division has located an independent producer in Matamoros—Gulfmex Corporation—that is willing to sell 20,000 barrels of crude oil per day at $79 per barrel, delivered to Horizon's pipeline in Matamoros. Given Horizon's organizational structure, the transportation division would purchase the 20,000 barrels of crude oil in Matamoros from Gulfmex, transport it to Houston, and then sell it to the refining division. The pipeline has unused capacity and can ship the 20,000 barrels per day at its variable cost of $1 per barrel without affecting the shipment of the 10,000 barrels of crude oil per day acquired under its existing long-term contract arrangement. Will Horizon Petroleum incur lower costs by purchasing crude oil from Gulfmex in Matamoros or by purchasing crude oil from the Houston supplier? Will the refining division show lower crude oil purchasing costs by acquiring oil from Gulfmex or by acquiring oil from its current Houston supplier?

The following analysis shows that Horizon Petroleum's operating income would be maximized by purchasing oil from Gulfmex. The analysis compares the incremental costs in both divisions under the two alternatives. The analysis assumes the fixed costs of the transportation division will be the same regardless of the alternative chosen. That is, the transportation division cannot save any of its fixed costs if it does not transport Gulfmex's 20,000 barrels of crude oil per day.

- **Alternative 1:** Buy 20,000 barrels from the Houston supplier at $85 per barrel. The total costs to Horizon Petroleum are 20,000 barrels × $85 per barrel = $1,700,000.
- **Alternative 2:** Buy 20,000 barrels from Gulfmex at $79 per barrel and transport them from Matamoros to Houston at a variable cost of $1 per barrel. The total costs to Horizon Petroleum are 20,000 barrels × ($79 + $1) per barrel = $1,600,000.

There is a reduction in total costs to Horizon Petroleum of $100,000 ($1,700,000 − $1,600,000) by acquiring oil from Gulfmex.

[4] Consider a firm where division S produces the intermediate product. S has a capacity of 15 units and a variable cost per unit of $2. The imperfect competition is reflected in a downward-sloping demand curve for the intermediate product—if S wants to sell Q units, it has to lower the market price to $P = 20 - Q$. The division's profit function is therefore given by $Q \times (20 - Q) - 2Q = 18Q - Q^2$. Simple calculus reveals that it is optimal for S to sell nine units of the intermediate product at a price of $11, thereby making a profit of $81. Now, suppose that division B in the same firm can take the intermediate product, incur an additional variable cost of $4, and sell it in the external market for $12. Because S has surplus capacity (it only uses 9 of its 15 units of capacity), it is clearly in the firm's interest to have S make additional units and transfer them to B. The firm makes an incremental profit of $12 − $2 − $4 = $6 for each transferred unit. However, if the transfer price for the intermediate product were set equal to the market price of $11, B would reject the transaction because it would lose money on it ($12 − $11 − $4 = −$3 per unit).

To resolve this conflict, the transfer price should be set at a suitable *discount* to the external price in order to induce the buying division to seek internal transfers. In our example, the selling price must be greater than S's variable cost of $2, but less than B's contribution margin of $8. That is, the transfer price has to be discounted relative to the market price ($11) by a minimum of $3. We explore the issue of feasible transfer-pricing ranges further in the section on hybrid transfer prices.

Suppose the transfer price paid by the refining division to the transportation division is 105% of the full cost of the transportation division. The refining division will see its reported division costs increase if the crude oil is purchased from Gulfmex:

$$\text{Transfer price} = 1.05 \times \left(\begin{array}{c}\text{Purchase price}\\ \text{from}\\ \text{Gulfmex}\end{array} + \begin{array}{c}\text{Variable cost per unit}\\ \text{of Transportation}\\ \text{Division}\end{array} + \begin{array}{c}\text{Fixed cost per unit}\\ \text{to Transportation}\\ \text{Division}\end{array}\right)$$

$$= 1.05 \times (\$79 + \$1 + \$3) = 1.05 \times \$83 = \$87.15 \text{ per barrel}$$

- **Alternative 1:** Buy 20,000 barrels from Houston supplier at $85 per barrel. The total costs to the refining division are 20,000 barrels × $85 per barrel = $1,700,000.
- **Alternative 2:** Buy 20,000 barrels from the transportation division of Horizon Petroleum that were purchased from Gulfmex. The total costs to the refining division are 20,000 barrels × $87.15 per barrel = $1,743,000.

As a profit center, the refining division can maximize its short-run division operating income by purchasing from the Houston supplier.

The refining division looks at each barrel that it obtains from the transportation division as a variable cost of $87.15 per barrel; if 10 barrels are transferred, it costs the refining division $871.50; if 100 barrels are transferred, it costs $8,715. In fact, the variable cost per barrel is $80 ($79 to purchase the oil from Gulfmex plus $1 to transport it to Houston). The remaining $7.15 ($87.15 − $80) per barrel is the transportation division's fixed cost and markup. *The full cost plus a markup transfer-pricing method causes the refining division to regard the fixed cost (and the 5% markup) of the transportation division as a variable cost and leads to goal incongruence.*

Should Horizon's top managers interfere and force the refining division to buy from the transportation division? Doing so would undercut the philosophy of decentralization, so Horizon's top managers would probably view the decision by the refining division to purchase crude oil from external suppliers as an inevitable cost of decentralization and not interfere. Of course, some interference may occasionally be necessary to prevent costly blunders. But recurring interference would simply transform Horizon from a decentralized company into a centralized company.

What transfer price will promote goal congruence for both the transportation and refining divisions? The minimum transfer price is $80 per barrel. A transfer price below $80 does not provide the transportation division with an incentive to purchase crude oil from Gulfmex in Matamoros because it is below the transportation division's incremental costs. The maximum transfer price is $85 per barrel. A transfer price above $85 will cause the refining division to purchase crude oil from the external market in Houston rather than from the transportation division. A transfer price between the minimum and maximum transfer prices of $80 and $85 will promote goal congruence: Each division will increase its own reported operating income while increasing Horizon Petroleum's operating income if the refining division purchases crude oil from Gulfmex in Matamoros.

When using transfer prices based on costs rather than market prices, Horizon's top managers cannot easily determine the profitability of the investment made in the transportation division and hence whether Horizon should keep or sell the pipeline. Furthermore, if transfer prices are based on the actual costs of the transportation division, it would provide the division with no incentive to control costs. That's because all cost inefficiencies of the transportation division would get passed along as part of the actual full-cost transfer price. In fact, every additional dollar of cost arising from wastefulness in the transportation division would generate an additional $0.05 in profit for the division under the "105% of full cost" rule!

Surveys by accounting firms and researchers indicate that, despite its limitations, managers generally prefer to use full-cost-based transfer prices because (1) they represent relevant costs for long-run decisions, (2) they facilitate external pricing based on variable and fixed costs, and (3) they are the least costly to administer. However, full-cost transfer pricing does raise many issues. How are each subunit's indirect costs allocated to products? Have the correct activities, cost pools, and cost-allocation bases been identified? Should the chosen fixed-cost rates be actual or budgeted? The issues here are similar to the issues related to allocating fixed costs, discussed in Chapter 15. Many companies determine the transfer price based on budgeted rates and practical capacity because it overcomes the problem of inefficiencies in actual costs and costs of unused capacity getting passed along to the buying division.

Variable-Cost Bases

Transferring 20,000 barrels of crude oil from the transportation division to the refining division at the variable cost of $80 per barrel achieves goal congruence, as shown in the preceding section. The refining division would buy from the transportation division because the transportation division's variable cost is less than the $85 price charged by external suppliers. Setting the transfer price equal to the variable cost has other benefits. Knowing the variable cost per barrel of crude oil helps the refining division make many decisions such as the short-run pricing decisions discussed in Chapter 12. However, at the $80-per-barrel transfer price, the transportation division would record an operating loss and the refining division would show a large profit because it would be charged only for the variable costs of the transportation division. One approach to addressing this problem is to have the refining division make a lump-sum transfer payment to cover the fixed costs and generate some operating income for the transportation division while the transportation division continues to make transfers at the variable cost. The fixed payment is the price the refining division pays for using the capacity of the transportation division. The income earned by each division can then be used to evaluate the performance of each division and its manager.

DECISION POINT

What problems can arise when full cost plus a markup is used as the transfer price?

TRY IT! 23-2

True North Corporation has two divisions. The Mining division makes Toldine, which is then transferred to the Metals division. Toldine is further processed by the Metals division and is sold to customers at a price of $190 per unit. The Mining division is currently required by True North to transfer its total yearly output of 250,000 units of Toldine to the Metals division at 120% of full manufacturing cost. Unlimited quantities of Toldine can be purchased and sold on the outside market at $95 per unit.

The following table gives the manufacturing cost per unit in the Mining and Metals divisions for 2020:

	Mining Division	Metals Division
Direct materials cost	$14	$12
Direct manufacturing labor cost	24	29
Variable manufacturing overhead cost	13	15
Fixed manufacturing overhead cost	29	12
Total manufacturing cost per unit	$80	$68

1. Calculate the operating incomes for the Mining and Metals divisions for the 250,000 units of Toldine transferred under the following transfer-pricing methods: (a) market price and (b) 120% of full manufacturing cost.
2. Which transfer-pricing method does the manager of the Mining division prefer? What arguments might he make to support this method?

LEARNING OBJECTIVE 7

Describe the range of feasible transfer prices when there is unused capacity

... from variable cost to market price of the product transferred

and alternative methods for arriving at the eventual hybrid price

... proration, negotiation between divisions, and dual pricing

Hybrid Transfer Prices

Consider again Horizon Petroleum. As we saw earlier, the transportation division has unused capacity it can use to transport oil from Matamoros to Houston at an incremental cost of $80 per barrel. Horizon Petroleum, as a whole, maximizes its operating income if the refining division purchases crude oil from the transportation division rather than from the Houston market (the incremental cost per barrel is $80 versus the price per barrel of $85). Both divisions would be interested in transacting with each other (and the firm achieves goal congruence) if the transfer price is between $80 and $85.

For any internal transaction, there is generally a minimum transfer price the selling division will not go below, based on its cost structure. In the Horizon Petroleum example, the minimum price acceptable to the transportation division is $80. There is also a maximum price the buying division will not wish to exceed, which is determined by the lower of two quantities—the eventual contribution the division generates from an internal transaction and the price of purchasing a comparable intermediate product from an outside party. For the refining division, each barrel of gasoline sold to external parties generates $182 in contribution (the $190 price less the $8 variable cost of refining). Because it takes two barrels of crude oil to generate a barrel of gasoline, this is equivalent to a contribution of $91 per barrel of crude oil. For any price higher than $91, the refining division would lose money for each barrel of crude oil it buys from the transportation division. On the other hand, the refining division can purchase crude oil on the open market for $85 rather than having it transported internally. The maximum feasible transfer price is thus the lower of $91 and $85, or $85 in this instance. We saw previously that a transfer price between the minimum price ($80) and the maximum ($85) would promote goal congruence. We now describe three different ways in which firms attempt to determine the specific transfer price within these bounds.

Prorating the Difference Between Maximum and Minimum Transfer Prices

One approach that Horizon Petroleum could pursue is to choose a transfer price that splits, on some fair basis, the $5 difference between the $85-per-barrel market-based maximum price the refining division is willing to pay and the $80-per-barrel variable cost-based minimum price the transportation division wants to receive. An easy solution is to split the difference equally, resulting in a transfer price of $82.50. However, this solution ignores the relative costs incurred by the two divisions and might lead to disparate profit margins on the work contributed by each division to the final product. As an alternative approach, Horizon Petroleum could allocate the $5 difference on the basis of the variable costs of the two divisions. Using the data in Exhibit 23-1 (page 895), variable costs are as follows:

Transportation division's variable costs to transport 100 barrels of crude oil ($1 × 100)	$100
Refining division's variable costs to refine 100 barrels of crude oil and produce 50 barrels of gasoline ($8 × 50)	400
Total variable costs	$500

Of the $5 difference, the transportation division gets to keep ($100 ÷ $500) × $5.00 = $1.00, and the refining division gets to keep ($400 ÷ $500) × $5.00 = $4.00. That is, the transfer price is $81 per barrel of crude oil ($79 purchase cost + $1 variable cost + $1 that the transportation division gets to keep). In effect, this approach results in a budgeted variable-cost-plus transfer price.

To decide on the $1 and $4 allocations of the $5 incremental benefit to the company's total operating income per barrel, the divisions must share information about their variable costs. In effect, each division does not operate (at least for this transaction) in a totally decentralized manner. Furthermore, each division has an incentive to overstate its variable costs to receive a more-favorable transfer price. In the preceding example, suppose the transportation division claims it costs $2 per barrel to ship crude oil from Gulfmex to Houston. This increased cost raises the variable cost-based minimum price to $79 + $2 = $81 per barrel; the maximum price remains $85. Of the $4 difference between the minimum and maximum, the transportation division now gets to keep ($200 ÷ ($200 + $400)) × $4.00 = $1.33, resulting in a higher transfer price of $82.33. The refining division similarly benefits from asserting that its variable cost to refine 100 barrels of crude oil is greater than $400. As a consequence, proration methods either require a high degree of trust and exchange of information among divisions or include provisions for objective audits of cost information in order to be successful.

Negotiated Pricing

Negotiated pricing is the most common hybrid method. Under this approach, top managers do not administer a specific split of the eventual profits across the transacting divisions. Rather, the eventual transfer price results from a bargaining process between the selling and buying subunits. In Horizon Petroleum's case, for example, the transportation division and the refining division would be free to negotiate a price that is acceptable to both.

Recall that the minimum and maximum feasible transfer prices are \$80 and \$85, respectively, per barrel of crude oil. Where in this interval will the transfer price per barrel be set? Under a negotiated transfer price, the answer depends on several things: the bargaining strengths of the two divisions; information the transportation division has about the price minus the incremental marketing costs of supplying crude oil to outside refineries; and the information the refining division has about its other available sources of crude oil. The negotiations become particularly sensitive when each division's performance is evaluated on the basis of its operating income. The price negotiated by the two divisions will, in general, have no specific relationship to either costs or the market price. But the cost and price information is often the starting point in the negotiation process.

Consider the following situation: Suppose the refining division receives an order to supply specially processed gasoline. The incremental cost to purchase and supply crude oil is still \$80 per barrel. However, suppose the refining division will profit from this order only if the transportation division can supply crude oil at a price not exceeding \$82 per barrel.[5] In this case, the transfer price that would benefit both divisions must be greater than \$80 but less than \$82. Negotiations would allow the two divisions to achieve an acceptable transfer price. By contrast, a rule-based transfer price, such as a market-based price of \$85 or a 105% of full-cost-based price of \$87.15, would result in Horizon passing up a profitable opportunity.

A negotiated transfer price strongly preserves the autonomy of divisions, and the division managers are motivated to put forth effort to increase the operating income of their respective divisions. Surveys have found that approximately 15–20% of firms set transfer prices based on negotiation. Firms that do not use negotiated prices believe the time and energy spent by managers haggling over transfer prices make the method too costly.

Dual Pricing

There is seldom a single transfer price that simultaneously meets all the criteria we have discussed (achieving goal congruence, motivating managerial effort, evaluating the performance of subunits, and preserving their autonomy). As a result, some companies choose **dual pricing**, which uses two separate transfer-pricing methods to price each transfer from one subunit to another. An example of dual pricing arises when the selling division receives a full-cost-based price and the buying division pays the market price for the internally transferred products. Assume Horizon Petroleum purchases crude oil from Gulfmex in Matamoros at \$79 per barrel. One way to record the journal entry for the transfer between the transportation division and the refining division is as follows:

1. Debit the refining division (the buying division) with the market-based transfer price of \$85 per barrel of crude oil.
2. Credit the transportation division (the selling division) with the 105%-of-full-cost transfer price of \$87.15 per barrel of crude oil.
3. Debit a corporate cost account for the \$2.15 (\$87.15 − \$85) per barrel difference between the two transfer prices.

The dual-pricing system promotes goal congruence because it makes the refining division no worse off if it purchases the crude oil from the transportation division rather than from the external supplier at \$85 per barrel. The transportation division receives a corporate subsidy. As a result, the operating income for Horizon Petroleum as a whole under dual pricing is less than the sum of the operating incomes of the divisions.

Dual pricing is not widely used. One concern with dual pricing is that it leads to disputes about which price should be used when computing the taxable income of subunits located in different tax jurisdictions, such as in our example, where the transportation division is taxed in Mexico while the refining division is taxed in the United States. A second concern is that dual pricing insulates managers from the realities of the marketplace because costs, not market prices, affect the revenues of the supplying division.

DECISION POINT

Within a range of feasible transfer prices, what are alternative ways for firms to arrive at the eventual hybrid price?

[5] For example, suppose a barrel of specially processed gasoline could be sold for \$200 but also required a higher variable cost of refining of \$36 per barrel. In this setting, the incremental contribution to the refining division is \$164 per barrel of gasoline, which implies that it will pay at most \$82 for a barrel of crude oil (because two barrels of crude are required for one barrel of gasoline).

A General Guideline for Transfer-Pricing Situations

LEARNING OBJECTIVE 8

Apply a general guideline for determining a minimum transfer price

... incremental cost plus opportunity cost of supplying division

Exhibit 23-3 summarizes the properties of market-based, cost-based, and negotiated transfer-pricing methods using the criteria we have described in this chapter. As the exhibit indicates, it is difficult for a transfer-pricing method to meet all the criteria. The transfer price a company will eventually choose depends on the economic circumstances and the decision being made. Surveys by Ernst & Young as well as those sponsored by the Institute of Management Accountants indicate that full-cost-based transfer pricing is generally the most frequently used method around the world, followed by market-based and negotiated transfer pricing methods.[6]

Our discussion so far highlights that, barring settings in which a perfectly competitive market exists for the intermediate product, there is typically a range of possible transfer prices that would promote goal congruence. The following formula provides a general guideline for determining the minimum price in that range:

$$\text{Minimum transfer price} = \begin{array}{c}\text{Incremental cost} \\ \text{per unit} \\ \text{incurred up} \\ \text{to the point of transfer}\end{array} + \begin{array}{c}\text{Opportunity cost} \\ \text{per unit} \\ \text{to the selling subunit}\end{array}$$

The incremental cost in the formula is the additional cost of producing and transferring the product or service. The opportunity cost is the maximum contribution margin forgone by the selling subunit if the product or service is transferred internally. For example, if the selling subunit is operating at capacity, the opportunity cost of transferring a unit internally rather than selling it externally is equal to the market price minus the variable cost. That's because by transferring a unit internally, the subunit forgoes the contribution margin it could have

EXHIBIT 23-3 Comparison of Different Transfer-Pricing Methods

Criteria	Market-Based	Cost-Based	Negotiated
Achieves goal congruence	Yes, when markets are competitive	Often, but not always	Yes
Motivates management effort	Yes	Yes, when based on budgeted costs; less incentive to control costs if transfers are based on actual costs	Yes
Useful for evaluating subunit performance	Yes, when markets are competitive	Difficult unless transfer price exceeds full cost and even then is somewhat arbitrary	Yes, but transfer prices are affected by bargaining strengths of the buying and selling divisions
Preserves subunit autonomy	Yes, when markets are competitive	No, because it is rule-based	Yes, because it is based on negotiations between subunits
Other factors	Market may not exist, or markets may be imperfect or in distress	Useful for determining full cost of products and services; easy to implement	Bargaining and negotiations take time and may need to be reviewed repeatedly as conditions change

[6] See, for example, *Current Trends and Corporate Cases in Transfer Pricing* by Roger Tang with IMA Foundation for Applied Research, Institute of Management Accountants (Westport, CT: Quorum Books, 2002).

obtained by selling the unit in the external market. We distinguish the incremental cost from the opportunity cost because financial accounting systems record incremental cost but do not record opportunity cost. The guideline measures a *minimum* transfer price because it represents the selling unit's cost of transferring the product. We illustrate the general guideline in some specific situations using data from Horizon Petroleum.

1. **A perfectly competitive market for the intermediate product exists, and the selling division has no unused capacity.** If the market for crude oil in Houston is perfectly competitive, the transportation division can sell all the crude oil it transports to the external market at \$85 per barrel, and it will have no unused capacity. The transportation division's incremental cost (as shown in Exhibit 23-1, page 895) is \$73 per barrel (the purchase cost of \$72 per barrel plus the variable transportation cost of \$1 per barrel) for oil purchased under the long-term contract or \$80 per barrel (the purchase cost of \$79 plus the variable transportation cost of \$1) for oil purchased at current market prices from Gulfmex. The transportation division's opportunity cost per barrel of transferring the oil internally is the contribution margin per barrel forgone by not selling the crude oil in the external market: \$12 for oil purchased under the long-term contract (the market price, \$85, minus the variable cost, \$73) and \$5 for oil purchased from Gulfmex (the market price, \$85, minus the variable cost, \$80). In either case,

$$\begin{aligned}\text{Minimum transfer price per barrel} &= \text{Incremental cost per barrel} + \text{Opportunity cost per barrel}\\ &= \$73 + \$12 = \$85\\ &\text{or}\\ &= \$80 + \$5 = \$85\end{aligned}$$

2. **An intermediate market exists that is not perfectly competitive, and the selling division has unused capacity.** In markets that are not perfectly competitive, companies can increase their capacity utilization only by decreasing their prices. Unused capacity exists because decreasing prices is often not worthwhile—it decreases operating income.

   If the transportation division at Horizon Petroleum has unused capacity, its opportunity cost of transferring the oil internally is zero because the division does not forgo any external sales or contribution margin from internal transfers. In this case,

$$\text{Minimum transfer price per barrel} = \text{Incremental cost per barrel} = \begin{array}{c}\text{\$73 per barrel for oil purchased under the}\\ \text{long-term contract or \$80 per barrel for}\\ \text{oil purchased from Gulfmex in Matamoros}\end{array}$$

   In general, when markets are not perfectly competitive, the impact of prices on demand (and operating income) complicates the measurement of opportunity costs. The transfer price depends on constantly changing levels of supply and demand. There is not just one transfer price. Rather, the transfer prices for various quantities supplied and demanded depend on the incremental costs and opportunity costs of the units transferred.

3. **No market exists for the intermediate product.** This situation would occur if the crude oil transported by the transportation division could be used only by the Houston refinery (due to, say, its high tar content) and would not be wanted by external parties. Here the opportunity cost of supplying crude oil internally is zero because it can't be sold externally, so no contribution margin is forgone. For the transportation division, the minimum transfer price under the general guideline is the incremental cost per barrel (either \$73 or \$80). As in the previous case, any transfer price between the incremental cost and \$85 will achieve goal congruence.

DECISION POINT

What is the general guideline for determining a minimum transfer price?

23-3 TRY IT!

Emerge Aeronautics, which sells aircraft, has two profit centers, Systems and Assembly. Systems makes navigation equipment and transfers them to Assembly, which then puts together the aircraft for external sale. Systems can make up to 150 units a year at a variable cost of \$3 million each. Assembly has variable costs of \$11 million per aircraft. Assembly receives an order for 7 planes at a price of \$22 million each.

Suppose that Systems has no ability to sell its output externally and has excess capacity.

1. Would the top management of Emerge want the divisions to take the order?
2. What range of transfer prices would induce the managers of Systems and Assembly to take the decision you identified in requirement 1?

Now suppose that Systems can sell any navigation systems it makes externally for \$4.5 million per unit. The division incurs advertising and distribution costs of \$150,000 per system for external sales.

3. Would the top management of Emerge want the divisions to take the order?
4. What range of transfer prices would induce the managers of Systems and Assembly to take the decision you identified in requirement 3?

How Multinationals Use Transfer Pricing to Minimize Their Income Taxes

LEARNING OBJECTIVE 9

Incorporate income tax considerations in multinational transfer pricing

... set transfer prices to minimize tax payments to the extent permitted by tax authorities

Transfer pricing is an important accounting priority for managers around the world. A 2010 Ernst & Young survey of multinational enterprises in 25 countries found that 74% of parent firms and 76% of subsidiary respondents believed that transfer pricing was "absolutely critical" or "very important" to their organizations. The reason is that parent companies can save large sums of money in income taxes depending on the transfer-pricing methods they use. As noted in the vignette at the start of this chapter, firms such as Apple place their intellectual property in locations with low tax rates (e.g., Ireland). They then charge a high royalty fee to the units that generate sales revenue in higher tax areas (e.g., the United Kingdom), thereby minimizing or even eliminating the profits in those regions. Facebook, IBM, and Microsoft have used similar transfer-pricing practices, with names like "Double Irish" and "Dutch Sandwich." Such profit-shifting arrangements are estimated to save companies billions of dollars annually.[7]

Consider the Horizon Petroleum data in Exhibit 23-2 (page 896). Assume that the transportation division based in Mexico pays a Mexican tax rate of 30% on its operating income and that the refining division based in the United States pays a U.S. income tax rate of 20% on its operating income. Horizon Petroleum would minimize its total income tax payments with the 105%-of-full-cost transfer-pricing method, as shown in the following table, because this method minimizes the income reported in Mexico, where income is taxed at a higher rate than in the United States.

	Operating Income for 100 Barrels of Crude Oil			Income Tax on 100 Barrels of Crude Oil		
Transfer-Pricing Method	Transportation Division (Mexico) (1)	Refining Division (United States) (2)	Total (3) = (1) + (2)	Transportation Division (Mexico) (4) = 0.30 × (1)	Refining Division (United States) (5) = 0.20 × (2)	Total (6) = (4) + (5)
Market price	\$900	\$300	\$1,200	\$270	\$ 60	\$330
105% of full costs	380	820	1,200	114	164	278
Hybrid price	600	600	1,200	180	120	300

[7] Before the 2017 Tax Cuts and Jobs Act (TCJA), American companies paid no taxes to the IRS until profits were repatriated back to the United States. As a result, the incentive for top management was to generate and reinvest cash overseas. As of 2015, U.S. corporations accumulated more than \$2.6 trillion of earnings in foreign subsidiaries, according to the Joint Committee on Taxation. Pursuant to the TCJA, the United States now generally exempts the earnings of a U.S. firm from active businesses of foreign subsidiaries, even if the earnings are repatriated. But, as a transition to the new system and to avoid a potential windfall for corporations that had accumulated unrepatriated earnings abroad, the new law taxes these earnings as if they were repatriated but at preferred lower rates (either 8% or 15.5%). The tax revenue raised by this transition tax on earnings accumulated abroad is estimated at \$340 billion over the 10 years from 2018 to 2027.

CONCEPTS IN ACTION

IRS Accuses Medtronic of Unfair Tax Deal[8]

Kristoffer Tripplaar/Alamy Stock Photo

For years, the U.S. Internal Revenue Service (IRS) and Medtronic have been embroiled in a dispute over how much of the medical device maker's profit should be taxed by low-tax Puerto Rico and how much should face higher U.S. federal taxes. While Medtronic contends that its transfer pricing arrangement with its Puerto Rican subsidiary is tallied at an arm's-length, as required by tax law, the IRS describes Medtronic's actions as the "classic case" of artificially lowering the company's U.S. tax obligations to boost its after-tax profits.

While Puerto Rico is part of the United States, companies based there are considered foreign corporations for U.S. income-tax purposes. This means companies pay a low local tax rate and are not subject to higher federal taxes until they bring the money back to the United States. This is why Medtronic transferred $2.2 billion worth of intellectual property (IP) licenses to its Puerto Rican manufacturing affiliate for the tax years 2005 and 2006. The Puerto Rican affiliate then paid Medtronic royalties of 26–44% for the IP used to make medical devices on the island. The IRS says Medtronic significantly undervalued the royalties paid to it by the affiliate, which lowered the company's taxable profit in the United States. As a result, the IRS issued a deficiency notice to Medtronic alleging that the licensing of the IP to its Puerto Rican affiliate wasn't arm's-length in 2005 and 2006 and reallocated $1.4 billion in income to the company for those years. Medtronic made a $1.1 billion payment to the IRS to cover its revised tax bill, but it also sued the IRS arguing it applied the wrong transfer-pricing methodology in determining the company's royalty rates. As of early 2020, the lawsuit remained under litigation in the U.S. tax court.

The Medtronic case is one of many examples of governments around the world investigating companies' use of transfer pricing to avoid paying taxes. In the United States, the IRS has taken action against Coca-Cola, Facebook, and Intel in recent years. Across Europe, companies including Fiat, McDonald's, and Microsoft have had related-party transfer-pricing arrangements ruled to be illegal. Margrethe Vestager, the European Union's competition commissioner, summarized the argument against tax avoidance: "Paying one's fair share of tax should be firmly integrated in a company's corporate social responsibility."

[8] *Sources:* Harvey Poniachek, "INSIGHT: Medtronic Appeals Court Requires Transparent, Replicative Application of Tax Regulations," Transfer Pricing Report, October 2, 2018 (https://www.bna.com/insight-medtronic-appeals-n73014482979/); Lynnley Browning and Sony Kassam, "Facebook, Coke Could Face Tax Hit After Ruling Against Medtronic," BloombergQuint, August 20, 2018 (https://www.bloombergquint.com/business/facebook-coke-could-face-tax-hit-after-ruling-against-medtronic#gs.oK4bCg1F); Sara-Jane Tovey, "Eighth Circuit Vacates and Remands Tax Court's Transfer Pricing Decision in 'Medtronic,'" PWC Tax Insights from Transfer Pricing, August 29, 2018 (https://thesuite.pwc.com/insights/eighth-circuit-vacates-and-remands-tax-court-s-transfer-pricing-decision-in-medtronic); Vanessa Houlder, Christian Oliver, and Jim Brunsden, "Multinationals Seek Cover as EU Begins Tax Avoidance Battle," *The Financial Times*, October 21, 2015 (https://www.ft.com/content/b4b66986-77fa-11e5-933d-efcdc3c11c89).

Minimizing a firm's income taxes can sometimes conflict with the other objectives the firm's top managers hope to achieve via transfer pricing. Suppose the market for crude oil in Houston is perfectly competitive. In this case, the market-based transfer price achieves goal congruence, provides incentives for management effort, and helps Horizon evaluate the economic profitability of the transportation division. But this transfer price is costly from the perspective of income taxes. For tax reporting purposes, Horizon would favor using 105% of the full cost as the transfer price. But the tax laws in the United States and Mexico constrain this option. Mexico's tax authorities would challenge any attempt by Horizon to shift income to the refining division through an unreasonably low transfer price (see also Concepts in Action: IRS Accuses Medtronic of Unfair Tax Deal).

Section 482 of the U.S. Internal Revenue Code governs how multinationals can set transfer prices for tax purposes. Section 482 requires that transfer prices between a company and its foreign division or subsidiary, for both tangible and intangible property, equal the price that would be charged by an unrelated third party in a comparable transaction. Regulations related to Section 482 recognize that transfer prices can be market-based or cost-plus-based, where the plus represents margins on comparable transactions.[9]

[9] See John Henshall and Roy Donegan, *Global Transfer Pricing: Principles and Practice* (Bloomsbury Professional, 4th edition, 2019).

Consequently, if the market for crude oil in Houston is perfectly competitive, Horizon would be required to calculate its taxes using the market price of $85 for transfers from the transportation division to the refining division. Horizon might successfully argue that the transfer price should be set below the market price because the transportation division incurs no marketing and distribution costs when selling crude oil to the refining division. For example, if marketing and distribution costs equal $2 per barrel, Horizon could set the transfer price at $83 ($85 − $2) per barrel, the selling price net of marketing and distribution costs.

Transfer pricing has long been an important issue for tax directors and government authorities. It is now firmly on the agenda of world leaders, who have been driven by a search for tax revenues, as well as media scrutiny on transfer pricing, to impose tighter rules. Countries such as Canada, Greece, India, and Turkey have focused on intellectual-property values, the costs of back-office functions, and losses of any type. Countries rich in minerals and natural resources, including Australia, Chile, and Indonesia, have introduced new tax policies and transfer-pricing guidelines aimed at increasing the local tax base, especially in the area of outbound commodities. There is also coordinated action by governments, best illustrated by the Organisation for Economic Co-operation and Development's (OECD's) project on base erosion and profit shifting, which produced a 15-point action plan in October 2015. Today, over 130 countries and jurisdictions are collaborating on the implementation of these measures to tackle tax avoidance, improve the coherence of international tax rules and ensure a more transparent tax environment.

In the United States, the IRS has made a substantial investment in transfer-pricing resources. In 2011, the IRS named its first director of transfer pricing and subsequently raised inquiries or disputes with a variety of technology firms, including Amazon, Adobe, Juniper Networks, and Yahoo. In July 2016, the IRS delivered a "notice of deficiency" to Facebook for $3 billion to $5 billion, plus interest and penalties, following an audit of the value at which Facebook transferred its intellectual property to its Irish entity.

The tariffs and customs duties governments levy on imports of products into a country also affect the transfer-pricing practices of multinationals. The issues here are similar to income tax considerations. Companies are motivated to lower the transfer prices of products they are exporting into a country to reduce the tariffs and customs duties charged on those products. The restrictions some countries place on dividend- or income-related payments to parties outside their national borders also affect how firms set their transfer prices. By increasing the prices of goods or services transferred into divisions in these countries, companies can increase the cash paid out of these countries without violating dividend- or income-related restrictions.

23-4 TRY IT!

Generation Electronics makes solar panels at its plant in Akron, Ohio. Its variable cost per panel is $90 and the full manufacturing cost is $250. Generation ships 300,000 panels to a division in Madrid, Spain. Net of marketing and distribution costs, the Madrid division sells the panels throughout the European Union at an average price of $500. Generation pays a 25% tax on the U.S. division's income. Spain levies a 30% tax rate on income in the Madrid division. Both tax authorities only permit transfer prices that are between the full manufacturing cost per unit and a market price of $375, based on comparable imports into Spain.

1. What transfer price should Generation select to minimize the company's tax liability?

   In an effort to protect local manufacturers, Spain introduces customs duties on solar panel imports. A 17% customs duty is now levied on the price at which panels are transferred into the country. The duty is a deductible expense for calculating Spanish income for the purposes of income tax.
2. Calculate the after-tax operating income earned by the U.S. and Spanish divisions from transferring 300,000 solar panels (a) at the full manufacturing cost per unit and (b) at the market price of comparable imports.
3. In the presence of the customs duty, what transfer price should Generation select to minimize the company's tax liability? Explain your reasoning.

Transfer Prices Designed for Multiple Objectives

At times, one transfer price will not satisfy all of a firm's objectives, such as minimizing its income taxes, achieving goal congruence, and motivating managers' effort. As a result, a company may choose to keep one set of accounting records for tax reporting and a second set for internal management reporting. Of course, it is costly to maintain two sets of books. Some companies, such as CNH Industrial, a world leader in the agricultural and construction equipment business, have opposed doing so based on the principle that statutory and internal reporting systems must reflect the same information. However, a survey by the AnswerThink Consulting Group of large companies (more than $2 billion in revenues) found that 77% of companies considered to follow "best practices" used separate reporting systems to track internal pricing information, compared with about 25% of companies outside that group.

Microsoft, for example, believes in "delinking" transfer prices and employs an internal measurement system (Microsoft Accounting Principles) that uses a separate set of company-designed rules and accounts.[10] A key aspect of management control at Microsoft is holding product and division managers accountable for the profitability of products and establishing appropriate sales and marketing spending levels for every product line. To set these sales and spending levels, the firm creates a profitability statement for every product in each region and allocates research and development and administrative costs across sales divisions in ways that aren't necessarily the most tax efficient.

Even if a company does not have separate reporting systems, a firm can still informally adjust its transfer prices to satisfy the tradeoff between minimizing its taxes and incentivizing its managers. Consider a multinational firm that makes semiconductor products that it sells through its sales organization in a higher-tax country. To minimize the firm's taxes, the parent company sets a high transfer price, thereby lowering the operating income of the foreign sales organization. It would be inappropriate to penalize the country sales manager for this low income because the sales organization has no say in determining the transfer price. As an alternative, the company can evaluate the sales manager on the direct contribution (revenues minus marketing costs) incurred in the country. That is, the transfer price incurred to acquire the semiconductor products is omitted for performance-evaluation purposes. Of course, this is not a perfect solution. By ignoring the cost of acquiring the products, the sales manager has an incentive to overspend on local marketing relative to what would be optimal from the firm's perspective. If the dysfunctional effects are suitably large, corporate managers must then step in, evaluate the situation, and dictate specific operational decisions and goals for the manager. More generally, when a firm adopts a tax-compliant transfer-pricing policy, it needs nonfinancial performance indicators (such as production yields, number of on-time deliveries, or customer-response times) at lower management levels in order to better evaluate and reward performance.[11]

DECISION POINT

How do income tax considerations affect transfer pricing in multinationals?

[10] For further details, see I. Springsteel, "Separate but Unequal," *CFO Magazine* (August 1999).

[11] M. Cools et al., "Management Control in the Transfer Pricing Tax Compliant Multinational Enterprise," *Accounting, Organizations and Society* (August 2008) provides an illustrative case study of this issue in the context of a semiconductor product division of a multinational firm.

PROBLEM FOR SELF-STUDY

The Pillercat Corporation is a highly decentralized company. Each division manager has full authority for sourcing decisions and selling decisions. The machining division of Pillercat has been the major supplier of the 2,000 crankshafts the tractor division needs each year.

The tractor division, however, has just announced that it plans to purchase all its crankshafts in the forthcoming year from two external suppliers at $200 per crankshaft. The machining division of Pillercat recently increased its selling price for the forthcoming year to $220 per unit (from $200 per unit in the current year).

Juan Gomez, manager of the machining division, views the 10% price increase as justified. It results from a higher depreciation charge on some new specialized equipment used to manufacture crankshafts and an increase in labor costs. Gomez wants the president of Pillercat Corporation to force the tractor division to buy all its crankshafts from the machining division at the price of $220. The following table summarizes the key data.

	A	B
1	Number of crankshafts purchased by tractor division	2,000
2	External supplier's market price per crankshaft	$ 200
3	Variable cost per crankshaft in machining division	$ 190
4	Fixed cost per crankshaft in machining division	$ 20

Required

1. Compute the advantage or disadvantage of Juan Gomez's proposal in terms of annual operating income to the Pillercat Corporation as a whole if the tractor division buys crankshafts internally from the machining division under each of the following cases:
   a. The machining division has no alternative use for the facilities used to manufacture crankshafts.
   b. The machining division can use the facilities for other production operations, which will result in annual cash operating savings of $29,000.
   c. The machining division has no alternative use for its facilities, and the external supplier drops the price to $185 per crankshaft.
2. As the president of Pillercat, how would you respond to Juan Gomez's request that you force the tractor division to purchase all of its crankshafts from the machining division? Would your response differ according to the three cases described in requirement 1? Explain.

Solution

1. Computations for the tractor division buying crankshafts internally for 1 year under cases **a**, **b**, and **c** are as follows:

	A	B	C	D
1			Case	
2		a	b	c
3	Number of crankshafts purchased by tractor division	2,000	2,000	2,000
4	External supplier's market price per crankshaft	$ 200	$ 200	$ 185
5	Variable cost per crankshaft in machining division	$ 190	$ 190	$ 190
6	Opportunity costs of the machining division supplying crankshafts to the tractor division	-	$ 29,000	-
7				
8	Total purchase costs if buying from an external supplier			
9	(2,000 shafts × $200, $200, $185 per shaft)	$400,000	$400,000	$370,000
10	Incremental cost of buying from the machining division			
11	(2,000 shafts × $190 per shaft)	380,000	380,000	380,000
12	Total opportunity costs of the machining division	-	29,000	-
13	Total relevant costs	380,000	409,000	380,000
14	Annual operating income advantage (disadvantage) to			
15	Pillercat of internal transfer from the machining division	$ 20,000	$ (9,000)	$ (10,000)

The general guideline that was introduced in the chapter (page 903) as a first step in setting a transfer price can be used to highlight the alternatives:

	A	B	C	D	E	F	G
1	**Case**	**Incremental Cost per Unit Incurred to Point of Transfer**	**+**	**Opportunity Cost per Unit to the Supplying Division**	**=**	**Transfer Price**	**External Market Price**
2	a	$190	+	$ 0	=	$190.00	$200
3	b	$190	+	$14.50[a]	=	$204.50	$200
4	c	$190	+	$ 0	=	$190.00	$185
5							
6	[a]Opportunity cost per unit = Total opportunity costs ($29,000) ÷ Number of crankshafts (2,000) = $14.50						

Comparing transfer price to external-market price, the tractor division will maximize annual operating income of Pillercat Corporation as a whole by purchasing from the machining division in case **a** and by purchasing from the external supplier in cases **b** and **c**.

2. Pillercat Corporation is a highly decentralized company. If no forced transfer were made, the tractor division would use an external supplier, a decision that would be in the best interest of the company as a whole in cases **b** and **c** of requirement 1 but not in case **a**.

   Suppose in case **a**, the machining division refuses to meet the price of $200. This decision means that the company will be $20,000 worse off in the short run. Should top management interfere and force a transfer at $200? This interference would undercut the philosophy of decentralization. Many top managers would not interfere because they would view the $20,000 as an inevitable cost of a suboptimal decision that can occur under decentralization. But how high must this cost be before the temptation to interfere would be irresistible? $30,000? $40,000?

   Any top management interference with lower-level decision making weakens decentralization. Of course, Pillercat's management may occasionally interfere to prevent costly mistakes. But recurring interference and constraints would hurt Pillercat's attempts to operate as a decentralized company.

DECISION POINTS

The following question-and-answer format summarizes the chapter's learning objectives. Each decision presents a key question related to a learning objective. The guidelines are the answer to that question.

Decision	Guidelines
1. What is a management control system, and how should it be designed?	A management control system is a means of gathering and using information to aid and coordinate the planning and control decisions throughout the organization and to guide the behavior of managers and other employees. Effective management control systems (a) are closely aligned to the organization's strategy, (b) support the organizational responsibilities of individual managers, and (c) motivate managers and other employees to give effort to achieve the organization's goals.

Decision	Guidelines
2. What are the benefits and costs of decentralization?	The benefits of decentralization include (a) greater responsiveness to local needs, (b) gains from faster decision making, (c) greater management development and learning, and (d) sharpened focus of subunit managers. The costs of decentralization include (a) suboptimal decision making, (b) excessive focus on the subunit rather than the company as a whole, (c) increased costs of information gathering, and (d) duplication of activities.
3. What are transfer prices, and what criteria do managers use to evaluate them?	A transfer price is the price one subunit charges for a product or service supplied to another subunit of the same organization. Transfer prices seek to (a) promote goal congruence, (b) motivate management effort, (c) help evaluate subunit performance, and (d) preserve subunit autonomy (if desired).
4. What are alternative ways of calculating transfer prices?	Transfer prices can be (a) market based, (b) cost based, or (c) hybrid. Different transfer-pricing methods produce different revenues and costs for individual subunits and, thus, different operating incomes for the subunits.
5. Under what market conditions do market-based transfer prices promote goal congruence?	In perfectly competitive markets, there is no unused capacity, and division managers can buy and sell as much of a product or service as they want at the market price. In such settings, using the market price as the transfer price motivates division managers to transact internally and to take exactly the same actions as they would if they were transacting in the external market.
6. What problems can arise when full cost plus a markup is used as the transfer price?	A transfer price based on the full cost plus a markup may lead to suboptimal decisions because it leads the buying division to regard the fixed costs and the markup of the selling division as a variable cost. The buying division may then purchase products from an external supplier and expect cost savings that will not occur.
7. Within a range of feasible transfer prices, what are alternative ways for firms to arrive at the eventual hybrid price?	When there is unused capacity, the transfer-price range lies between the minimum price at which the selling division is willing to sell (its variable cost per unit) and the maximum price the buying division is willing to pay (the lower of its contribution margin or the price at which the product is available from external suppliers). Methods for arriving at a price in this range include proration (such as splitting the difference equally or on the basis of relative variable costs), negotiation between divisions, and dual pricing.
8. What is the general guideline for determining a minimum transfer price?	The general guideline states that the minimum transfer price equals the incremental cost per unit incurred up to the point of transfer plus the opportunity cost per unit to the selling division.
9. How do income tax considerations affect transfer pricing in multinationals?	A firm can use transfer pricing to lower its income tax payments by reporting more income in low-tax-rate countries and less income in high-tax-rate countries. However, the tax regulations of different countries restrict the transfer prices that companies can use.

TERMS TO LEARN

This chapter and the Glossary at the end of the text contain definitions of the following important terms:

autonomy (**p. 889**)
decentralization (**p. 889**)
dual pricing (**p. 902**)
dysfunctional decision making (**p. 891**)
effort (**p. 889**)
goal congruence (**p. 889**)
incongruent decision making (**p. 891**)
intermediate product (**p. 893**)
management control system (**p. 888**)
motivation (**p. 889**)
perfectly competitive market (**p. 897**)
suboptimal decision making (**p. 891**)
transfer price (**p. 893**)

ASSIGNMENT MATERIAL

Questions

23-1 What is a management control system?

23-2 Describe three criteria you would use to evaluate whether a management control system is effective.

23-3 What is the relationship among motivation, goal congruence, and effort?

23-4 Name three benefits and two costs of decentralization.

23-5 "Organizations typically adopt a consistent decentralization or centralization philosophy across all their business functions." Do you agree? Explain.

23-6 "Transfer pricing is confined to profit centers." Do you agree? Explain.

23-7 What are the three methods for determining transfer prices?

23-8 What properties should transfer-pricing systems have?

23-9 "All transfer-pricing methods give the same division operating income." Do you agree? Explain.

23-10 Under what conditions is a market-based transfer price optimal?

23-11 What is one potential limitation of full-cost-based transfer prices?

23-12 Give two reasons why the dual-pricing system of transfer pricing is not widely used.

23-13 "Cost and price information play no role in negotiated transfer prices." Do you agree? Explain.

23-14 "Under the general guideline for transfer pricing, the minimum transfer price will vary depending on whether the supplying division has unused capacity." Do you agree? Explain.

23-15 How should managers consider income tax issues when choosing a transfer-pricing method?

Exercises

23-16 **Cost centers, profit centers, decentralization, transfer prices.** Fenster Corporation manufactures windows with wood and metal frames. Fenster has three departments: glass, wood, and metal. The glass department makes the window glass and sends it to either the wood or metal department where the glass is framed. The window is then sold. Upper management sets the production schedules for the three departments and evaluates them on output quantity, cost variances, and product quality.

Required

1. Are the three departments cost centers, revenue centers, or profit centers?
2. Are the three departments centralized or decentralized?
3. Can a centralized department be a profit center? Why or why not?
4. Suppose the upper management of Fenster Corporation decides to let the three departments set their own production schedules, buy and sell products in the external market, and have the wood and metal departments negotiate with the glass department for the glass panes using a transfer price.
   a. Will this decision change your answers to requirements 1 and 2?
   b. How would you recommend upper management evaluate the three departments if this change is made?

23-17 Transfer-pricing methods, goal congruence. Vancouver Lumber has a raw lumber division and a finished lumber division. The variable costs are as follows:

- Raw lumber division: $120 per 100 board-feet of raw lumber
- Finished lumber division: $145 per 100 board-feet of finished lumber

Assume that there is no board-feet loss in processing raw lumber into finished lumber. Raw lumber can be sold at $170 per 100 board-feet. Finished lumber can be sold at $370 per 100 board-feet.

Required

1. Should Vancouver Lumber process raw lumber into its finished form? Show your calculations.
2. Assume that internal transfers are made at 130% of variable cost. Will each division maximize its division operating-income contribution by adopting the action that is in the best interest of Vancouver Lumber as a whole? Explain.
3. Assume that internal transfers are made at market prices. Will each division maximize its division operating-income contribution by adopting the action that is in the best interest of Vancouver Lumber as a whole? Explain.

23-18 Transfer price, proration. Chocfix produces hot cocoa mix. The company has two divisions, each operating as a profit center. The transportation division purchases raw cocoa in the Ivory Coast and transports it to the mixing division in Atlanta, Georgia. The mixing division processes the raw cocoa into the cocoa mix. It takes two pounds of raw cocoa to yield one pound of cocoa mix. Variable and fixed costs per pound of raw cocoa in the transportation division and variable and fixed costs per pound of cocoa mix in the mixing division area as follows:

Transportation Division	
Price per pound of raw cocoa supplied in the Ivory Coast	$10
Variable transportation costs per pound of raw cocoa	$ 1
Fixed transportation costs per pound of raw cocoa	$ 1

Mixing Division	
Variable mixing costs per pound of cocoa mix	$ 4
Fixed mixing costs per pound of cocoa mix	$ 4

The market price for a pound of raw cocoa supplied to the mixing division in Atlanta is $14. Chocfix can sell each pound of hot cocoa mix for $42.

Required

1. What are the minimum and maximum transfer prices per pound of raw cocoa transported to the mixing division at which both divisions are willing to transact with each other? Assume the transportation division has unused capacity to transport raw cocoa to the mixing division.
2. Refer to your answer in requirement 1. The management of Chocfix is trying to decide on the specific transfer price within the bounds identified in requirement 1. James Ladell, Chocfix's CEO, is suggesting to split the difference between the maximum and the minimum transfer price evenly. What is the transfer price under this scenario? What is the contribution margin per pound of raw cocoa for the transportation division? What is the contribution margin per pound of cocoa mix for the mixing division?
3. Leila Brown, Chocfix's CFO, disagrees with James Ladell's suggestion to split the difference evenly. She argues that the difference between the maximum and minimum transfer price should be prorated based on the value of the work contributed by each of the divisions to the final product.
   a. What is the value of the work contributed by each of the divisions towards a pound of cocoa mix? Ignore fixed costs.
   b. What is the transfer price if the difference between the maximum and the minimum transfer price (identified in requirement 1) is prorated based on the relative value of the work contributed by each of the divisions (identified in requirement 3a)? What is the contribution margin per pound of raw cocoa for the transportation division? What is the contribution margin per pound of cocoa mix for the mixing division?
   c. Which transfer price, the one identified in requirement 2 or the one identified in requirement 3b, do you think Chocfix should use?

23-19 Transfer pricing, dual pricing. Jose Martinez is the CEO of ShakeIt, a producer of premium ice cream. ShakeIt has two divisions, the supplying division and the processing division. The supplying division supplies milk, the main ingredient, to the processing division. Jose is an ambitious entrepreneur, and he is hoping to soon sell ShakeIt, which is a private company, to one of the larger competitors. The supplying division buys milk from local farmers for $5 per 10 gallons, and incurs $1 of variable costs per 10 gallons transported to the processing division (the supplying division doesn't incur any material fixed costs). The processing division could buy milk of the same high quality for $8 per 10 gallons on the outside market. Jose is trying to "whip his company into shape" by implementing a transfer pricing system that he views as providing very strong incentives for the two divisions to work hard: The supplying division will get reimbursed for its incremental costs of supplying the milk to the processing division; the processing division is charged the price that it would have to pay on the open market.

Required

1. What is the profit for the supplying division of supplying 10 gallons of milk to the processing division under Jose's transfer pricing system? Do you think that the transfer pricing system incentivizes the managers of the supplying division to work hard, as Jose intends?
2. In the back of Jose's mind is that one of the larger competitors may be interested in buying only one of the divisions, and not his entire company. He is patting himself on the back for choosing the transfer pricing system since, in his view, it makes the profitability of each of the two divisions look very good. Do you agree with Jose?

23-20 Multinational transfer pricing, effect of alternative transfer-pricing methods, global income tax minimization. People Able Computer, Inc., with headquarters in San Francisco, manufactures and sells a desktop computer. People Able has three divisions, each of which is located in a different country:

a. China division—manufactures memory devices and keyboards
b. South Korea division—assembles desktop computers using locally manufactured parts, along with memory devices and keyboards from the China division
c. U.S. division—packages and distributes desktop computers

Each division is run as a profit center. The costs for the work done in each division for a single desktop computer are as follows:

China division:	Variable cost	= 1,000 yuan
	Fixed cost	= 1,800 yuan
South Korea division:	Variable cost	= 360,000 won
	Fixed cost	= 480,000 won
U.S. division:	Variable cost	= \$100
	Fixed cost	= \$200

- Chinese income tax rate on the China division's operating income: 40%
- South Korean income tax rate on the South Korea division's operating income: 20%
- U.S. income tax rate on the U.S. division's operating income: 28%

Each desktop computer is sold to retail outlets in the United States for \$3,200. Assume that the current foreign exchange rates are as follows:

8 yuan = \$1 U.S.
1,200 won = \$1 U.S.

Both the China and the South Korea divisions sell part of their production under a private label. The China division sells the comparable memory/keyboard package used in each People Able desktop computer to a Chinese manufacturer for 3,600 yuan. The South Korea division sells the comparable desktop computer to a South Korean distributor for 1,560,000 won.

Required

1. Calculate the after-tax operating income per unit earned by each division under the following transfer-pricing methods: (a) market price, (b) 200% of full cost, and (c) 300% of variable cost. (Income taxes are not included in the computation of the cost-based transfer prices.)
2. Which transfer-pricing method(s) will maximize the after-tax operating income per unit of People Able Computer?

23-21 Transfer pricing, general guideline, goal congruence. (CMA, adapted). Watson Motors, Inc., operates as a decentralized multidivision company. The Vadner division of Watson Motors purchases most of its airbags from the airbag division. The airbag division's incremental cost for manufacturing the airbags is \$160 per unit. The airbag division is currently working at 80% of capacity. The current market price of the airbags is \$200 per unit.

Required

1. Using the general guideline presented in the chapter, what is the minimum price at which the airbag division would sell airbags to the Vadner division?
2. Suppose that Watson Motors requires that whenever divisions with unused capacity sell products internally, they must do so at the incremental cost. Evaluate this transfer-pricing policy using the criteria of goal congruence, evaluating division performance, motivating management effort, and preserving division autonomy.
3. If the two divisions were to negotiate a transfer price, what is the range of possible transfer prices? Evaluate this negotiated transfer-pricing policy using the criteria of goal congruence, evaluating division performance, motivating management effort, and preserving division autonomy.

4. Instead of allowing negotiation, suppose that Watson specifies a hybrid transfer price that "splits the difference" between the minimum and maximum prices from the divisions' standpoint. What would be the resulting transfer price for airbags?

23-22 Multinational transfer pricing, global tax minimization. The Burton Company manufactures chainsaws at its plant in Sandusky, Ohio. The company has marketing divisions throughout the world. A Burton marketing division in Lille, France, imports 200,000 chainsaws annually from the United States. The following information is available:

U.S. income tax rate on the U.S. division's operating income	40%
French income tax rate on the French division's operating income	45%
French import duty	20%
Variable manufacturing cost per chainsaw	\$100
Full manufacturing cost per chainsaw	\$175
Selling price (net of marketing and distribution costs) in France	\$300

Suppose the United States and French tax authorities only allow transfer prices that are between the full manufacturing cost per unit of \$175 and a market price of \$250, based on comparable imports into France. The French import duty is charged on the price at which the product is transferred into France. Any import duty paid to the French authorities is a deductible expense for calculating French income taxes.

Required

1. Calculate the after-tax operating income earned by the United States and French divisions from transferring 200,000 chainsaws (a) at full manufacturing cost per unit and (b) at market price of comparable imports. (Income taxes are not included in the computation of the cost-based transfer prices.)
2. Which transfer price should the Burton Company select to minimize the total of company import duties and income taxes? Remember that the transfer price must be between the full manufacturing cost per unit of \$175 and the market price of \$250 of comparable imports into France. Explain your reasoning.

23-23 Multinational transfer pricing, goal congruence (continuation of 23-22). Suppose that the U.S. division could sell as many chainsaws as it makes at \$225 per unit in the U.S. market, net of all marketing and distribution costs.

Required

1. From the viewpoint of the Burton Company as a whole, would after-tax operating income be maximized if it sold the 200,000 chainsaws in the United States or in France? Show your computations.
2. Suppose division managers act autonomously to maximize their division's after-tax operating income. Will the transfer price calculated in requirement 2 of Exercise 23-22 result in the U.S. division manager taking the actions determined to be optimal in requirement 1 of this exercise? Explain.
3. What is the minimum transfer price that the U.S. division manager would agree to? Does this transfer price result in the Burton Company as a whole paying more import duty and taxes than under the answer to requirement 2 of Exercise 23-22? If so, by how much?

23-24 Transfer-pricing dispute. The Jill-Farley Corporation, manufacturer of tractors and other heavy farm equipment, is organized along decentralized product lines, with each manufacturing division operating as a separate profit center. Each division manager has been delegated full authority on all decisions involving the sale of that division's output both to outsiders and to other divisions of Jill-Farley. Division C has in the past always purchased its requirement of a particular tractor-engine component from division A. However, when informed that division A is increasing its selling price to \$145, division C's manager decides to purchase the engine component from external suppliers.

Division C can purchase the component for \$120 per unit in the open market. Division A insists that, because of the recent installation of some highly specialized equipment and the resulting high depreciation charges, it will not be able to earn an adequate return on its investment unless it raises its price. Division A's manager appeals to top management of Jill-Farley for support in the dispute with division C and supplies the following operating data:

C's annual purchases of the tractor-engine component	1,800 units
A's variable cost per unit of the tractor-engine component	\$ 110
A's fixed cost per unit of the tractor-engine component	\$ 20

Required

1. Assume that there are no alternative uses for internal facilities of division A. Determine whether the company as a whole will benefit if division C purchases the component from external suppliers for \$120 per unit. What should the transfer price for the component be set at so that division managers acting in their own divisions' best interests take actions that are also in the best interest of the company as a whole?

2. Assume that internal facilities of division A would not otherwise be idle. By not producing the 1,800 units for division C, division A's equipment and other facilities would be used for other production operations that would result in annual cash-operating savings of $21,000. Should division C purchase from external suppliers? Show your computations.
3. Assume that there are no alternative uses for division A's internal facilities and that the price from outsiders drops by $20. Should division C purchase from external suppliers? What should the transfer price for the component be set at so that division managers acting in their own divisions' best interests take actions that are also in the best interest of the company as a whole?

23-25 Transfer-pricing problem (continuation of 23-24). Refer to Exercise 23-24. Assume that division A can sell the 1,800 units to other customers at $153 per unit, with variable marketing costs of $8 per unit.

Required

Determine whether Jill-Farley will benefit if division C purchases the 1,800 units from external suppliers at $120 per unit. Show your computations.

Problems

23-26 General guideline, transfer pricing. The Aqua Company manufactures and sells television sets. Its assembly division (AD) buys television screens from the screen division (SD) and assembles the TV sets. The SD, which is operating at capacity, incurs an incremental manufacturing cost of $60 per screen. The SD can sell all its output to the outside market at a price of $110 per screen, after incurring a variable marketing and distribution cost of $10 per screen. If the AD purchases screens from outside suppliers at a price of $110 per screen, it will incur a variable purchasing cost of $8 per screen. Aqua's division managers can act autonomously to maximize their own division's operating income.

Required

1. What is the minimum transfer price at which the SD manager would be willing to sell screens to the AD?
2. What is the maximum transfer price at which the AD manager would be willing to purchase screens from the SD?
3. Now suppose that the SD can sell only 80% of its output capacity of 10,000 screens per month on the open market. Capacity cannot be reduced in the short run. The AD can assemble and sell more than 10,000 TV sets per month.
   a. What is the minimum transfer price at which the SD manager would be willing to sell screens to the AD?
   b. From the point of view of Aqua's management, how much of the SD output should be transferred to the AD?
   c. If Aqua mandates the SD and AD managers to "split the difference" on the minimum and maximum transfer prices they would be willing to negotiate over, what would be the resulting transfer price? Does this price achieve the outcome desired in requirement 3b?

23-27 Pertinent transfer price, perfect and imperfect markets. Chicago, Inc., has two divisions, A and B, that manufacture expensive bicycles. Division A produces the bicycle frame, and division B assembles the rest of the bicycle onto the frame. There is a market for both the subassembly and the final product. Each division has been designated as a profit center. The transfer price for the subassembly has been set at the long-run average market price. The following data are available for each division:

Selling price for final product	$360
Long-run average selling price for intermediate product	275
Incremental cost per unit for completion in division B	120
Incremental cost per unit in division A	150

The manager of division B has made the following calculation:

Selling price for final product		$360
Transferred-in cost per unit (market)	$275	
Incremental cost per unit for completion	120	395
Contribution (loss) on product		$ (35)

Required

1. Should transfers be made to division B if there is no unused capacity in division A? Is the market price the correct transfer price? Show your computations.
2. Assume that division A's maximum capacity for this product is 1,200 units per month and sales to the intermediate market are now 900 units. Assume that for a variety of reasons, division A will maintain the $275 selling price indefinitely. That is, division A is not considering lowering the price to outsiders even if idle capacity exists. Should 300 units be transferred to division B? At what transfer price?

3. Suppose division A quoted a transfer price of $240 for up to 300 units. What would be the contribution to the company as a whole if a transfer were made? As manager of division B, would you be inclined to buy at $240? Explain.
4. Suppose the manager of division A has the option of (a) cutting the external price to $270, with the certainty that sales will rise to 1,200 units, or (b) maintaining the external price of $275 for the 900 units and transferring the 300 units to division B at a price that would produce the same operating income for division A. What transfer price would produce the same operating income for division A? Is that price consistent with that recommended by the general guideline in the chapter so that the resulting decision would be desirable for the company as a whole?

23-28 Effect of alternative transfer-pricing methods on division operating income. Cranfuel Products is a cranberry cooperative that operates two divisions, a harvesting division and a processing division. Currently, all of harvesting's output is converted into cranberry juice by the processing division, and the juice is sold to large beverage companies that produce cranberry juice blends. The processing division has a yield of 500 gallons of juice per 1,000 pounds of cranberries. Cost and market price data for the two divisions are as follows:

	A	B	C	D	E
1	**Harvesting Division**			**Processing Division**	
2	Variable cost per pound of cranberries	$0.08		Variable processing cost per gallon of juice produced	$0.30
3	Fixed cost per pound of cranberries	$0.32		Fixed cost per gallon of juice produced	$0.50
4	Selling price per pound of cranberries in outside market	$0.60		Selling price per gallon of juice	$2.40

Required

1. Compute Cranfuel's operating income from harvesting 520,000 pounds of cranberries during June 2020 and processing them into juice.
2. Cranfuel rewards its division managers with a bonus equal to 4% of operating income. Compute the bonus earned by each division manager in June 2020 for each of the following transfer-pricing methods:
   a. 175% of full cost
   b. Market price
3. Which transfer-pricing method will each division manager prefer? How might Cranfuel resolve any conflicts that may arise on the issue of transfer pricing?

23-29 Goal-congruence problems with cost-plus transfer-pricing methods, dual-pricing system (continuation of 23-28). Refer to Problem 23-28. Assume that Pat Borges, CEO of Cranfuel, had mandated a transfer price equal to 175% of full cost. Now he decides to decentralize some management decisions and sends around a memo that states: "Effective immediately, each division of Cranfuel is free to make its own decisions regarding the purchase of direct materials and the sale of finished products."

Required

1. Give an example of a goal-congruence problem that will arise if Cranfuel continues to use a transfer price of 175% of full cost and Borges's decentralization policy is adopted.
2. Borges feels that a dual transfer-pricing policy will improve goal congruence. He suggests that transfers out of the harvesting division be made at 175% of full cost and transfers into the processing division be made at market price. Compute the operating income of each division under this dual transfer-pricing method when 520,000 pounds of cranberries are harvested during June 2020 and processed into juice.
3. Why is the sum of the division operating incomes computed in requirement 2 different from Cranfuel's operating income from harvesting and processing 520,000 pounds of cranberries in requirement 1 of Problem 23-38?
4. Determine two problems that may arise if Cranfuel implements the dual transfer prices described in requirement 2.

23-30 Multinational transfer pricing, global tax minimization. Rapid Grow Inc., based in Des Moines, Iowa, sells high-end fertilizers. Rapid Grow has two divisions:

- North Italy mining division, which mines potash in northern Italy
- U.S. processing division, which uses potash in manufacturing top-grade fertilizer

The processing division's yield is 50%: It takes 2 tons of raw potash to produce 1 ton of top-grade fertilizer. Although all of the mining division's output of 15,000 tons of potash is sent for processing in the United States, there is also an active market for potash in Italy. The foreign exchange rate is 0.80 Euro = 1 U.S. The following information is known about the two divisions:

	A	B	C
1	**North Italy Mining Division**		
2	Variable cost per ton of raw potash	92	EURO
3	Fixed cost per ton of raw potash	104	EURO
4	Market price per ton of raw potash	304	EURO
5	Tax rate	30%	
6			
7	**U.S. Processing Division**		
8	Variable cost per ton of fertilizer	49	U.S. dollars
9	Fixed cost per ton of fertilizer	121	U.S. dollars
10	Market price per ton of fertilizer	1,170	U.S. dollars
11	Tax rate	35%	

Required

1. Compute the annual pretax operating income, in U.S. dollars, of each division under the following transfer-pricing methods: (a) 150% of full cost and (b) market price.
2. Compute the after-tax operating income, in U.S. dollars, for each division under the transfer-pricing methods in requirement 1. (Income taxes are not included in the computation of cost-based transfer price, and Rapid Grow does not pay U.S. income tax on income already taxed in Italy.)
3. If the two division managers are compensated based on after-tax division operating income, which transfer-pricing method will each prefer? Which transfer-pricing method will maximize the total after-tax operating income of Rapid Grow?
4. In addition to tax minimization, what other factors might Rapid Grow consider in choosing a transfer-pricing method?

23-31 Transfer pricing, external market, goal congruence. Ballantine Corp. produces and sells lead crystal glassware. The firm consists of two divisions, commercial and specialty. The commercial division manufactures 300,000 glasses per year. It incurs variable manufacturing costs of $8 per unit and annual fixed manufacturing costs of $900,000. The commercial division sells 100,000 units externally at a price of $12 each, mostly to department stores. It transfers the remaining 200,000 units internally to the specialty division, which modifies the units, adds an etched design, and sells them directly to consumers online.

Ballantine Corp. has adopted a market-based transfer-pricing policy. For each glass it receives from the commercial division, the specialty division pays the weighted-average external price the commercial division charges its customers outside the company. The current transfer price is accordingly set at $12.

Eileen McCarthy, the manager of the commercial division, receives an offer from Home Décor, a chain of upscale home furnishings stores. Home Décor offers to buy 20,000 glasses at a price of $9 each, knowing that the entire lead crystal industry (including Ballantine Corp.) has excess capacity at this time. The variable manufacturing cost to the commercial division for the units Home Décor is requesting is $8, and there are no additional costs associated with this offer. Accepting Home Décor's offer would not affect the current price of $12 charged to existing external customers.

Required

1. Calculate the commercial division's current annual level of profit (without the new order).
2. Compute the change in the commercial division's profit if it accepts Home Décor's offer. Will Eileen McCarthy accept this offer if her aim is to maximize the commercial division's profit?
3. Would the top management of Ballantine Corp. want the commercial division to accept the offer? Compute the change in firm-wide profit associated with Home Décor's offer.

23-32 International transfer pricing, taxes, goal congruence. Beacon, a division of Libra Corporation, is located in the United States. Its effective income tax rate is 30%. Another division of Libra, Falcon, is located in Canada, where the income tax rate is 40%. Falcon manufactures, among other things, an intermediate product for Beacon called XPS-2022. Falcon operates at capacity and makes 15,000 units of XPS-2022 for

Beacon each period, at a variable cost of $28 per unit. Assume that there are no outside customers for XPS-2022. Because the XPS-2022 must be shipped from Canada to the United States, it costs Falcon an additional $4 per unit to ship the XPS-2022 to Beacon. There are no direct fixed costs for XPS-2022. Falcon also manufactures other products.

A product similar to XPS-2022 that Beacon could use as a substitute is available in the United States for $38.50 per unit.

Required

1. What are the minimum and maximum transfer prices that would be acceptable to Beacon and Falcon for XPS-2022, and why?
2. What transfer price would minimize income taxes for Libra Corporation as a whole? Would Beacon and Falcon want to be evaluated on operating income using this transfer price?
3. Suppose Libra uses the transfer price from requirement 2 and each division is evaluated on its own after-tax division operating income. Now suppose Falcon has an opportunity to sell 8,000 units of XPS-2022 to an outside customer for $31 each. Falcon will not incur shipping costs because the customer is nearby and offers to pay for shipping. Assume that if Falcon accepts the special order, Beacon will have to buy 8,000 units of the substitute product in the United States at $38.50 per unit.
   a. Will accepting the special order maximize after-tax operating income for Libra Corporation as a whole?
   b. Will Beacon want Falcon to accept this special order? Why or why not?
   c. Will Falcon want to accept this special order? Explain.
   d. Suppose Libra Corporation wants to operate in a decentralized manner. What transfer price should Libra set for XPS-2022 so that each division acting in its own best interest takes actions with respect to the special order that are in the best interest of Libra Corporation as a whole?

23-33 Transfer pricing, goal congruence, ethics. Jeremiah Industries manufactures high-grade aluminum luggage made from recycled metal. The company operates two divisions: metal recycling and luggage fabrication. Each division operates as a decentralized entity. The metal recycling division is free to sell sheet aluminum to outside buyers, and the luggage fabrication division is free to purchase recycled sheet aluminum from other sources. Currently, however, the recycling division sells all of its output to the fabrication division, and the fabrication division does not purchase materials from any outside suppliers.

Aluminum is transferred from the recycling division to the fabrication division at 110% of full cost. The recycling division purchases recyclable aluminum for $0.50 per pound. The division's other variable costs equal $2.80 per pound, and fixed costs at a monthly production level of 50,000 pounds are $1.50 per pound. During the most recent month, 50,000 pounds of aluminum were transferred between the two divisions. The recycling division's capacity is 70,000 pounds.

Due to increased demand, the fabrication division expects to use 60,000 pounds of aluminum next month. Metalife Corporation has offered to sell 10,000 pounds of recycled aluminum next month to the fabrication division for $5.00 per pound.

Required

1. Calculate the transfer price during the most recent month per pound of recycled aluminum. Assuming that each division is considered a profit center, would the fabrication manager choose to purchase 10,000 pounds next month from Metalife?
2. Is the purchase in the best interest of Jeremiah Industries? Show your calculations. What is the cause of this goal incongruence?
3. The fabrication division manager suggests that $5.00 is now the market price for recycled sheet aluminum, and that this should be the new transfer price. Jeremiah Industries' corporate management tends to agree. The metal recycling manager is suspicious. Metalife's prices have always been considerably higher than $5.00 per pound. Why the sudden price cut? After further investigation by the recycling division manager, it is revealed that the $5.00 per pound price was a one-time-only offer made to the fabrication division due to excess inventory at Metalife. Future orders would be priced at $5.50 per pound. Comment on the validity of the $5.00 per pound market price and the ethics of the fabrication manager. Would changing the transfer price to $5.00 matter to Jeremiah Industries?

23-34 Transfer pricing, goal congruence. The Croydon division of CC Industries supplies the Hauser division with 100,000 units per month of an infrared LED that Hauser uses in a remote control device it sells. The transfer price of the LED is $8, which is the market price. However, Croydon does not operate at or near capacity. The variable cost to Croydon of the LED is $4.80, while Hauser incurs variable costs (excluding the transfer price) of $12 for each remote control. Hauser's selling price is $32.

Hauser's manager is considering a promotional campaign. The market research department of Hauser has developed the following estimates of additional monthly volume associated with additional monthly promotional expenses.

Additional Monthly Promotional Expenses:	$80,000	$120,000	$160,000
Additional Monthly Volume (Units)	10,000	15,000	18,000

Required

1. What level of additional promotional expenses would the Hauser division manager choose?
2. As the manager of the Croydon division, what level of additional promotional expenses would you like to see the Hauser division manager select?
3. As the president of CC Industries, what level of spending would you like the Hauser division manager to select?
4. What is the maximum transfer price that would induce the Hauser division to spend the optimal additional promotional expense from the standpoint of the firm as a whole?

23-35 Transfer pricing, perfect and imperfect markets. Letang Company has three divisions (R, S, and T), organized as decentralized profit centers. Division R produces the basic chemical Ranbax, in multiples of 1,000 pounds, and transfers it to divisions S and T. Division S processes Ranbax into the final product Syntex, and division T processes Ranbax into the final product Termix. No material is lost during processing.

Division R has no fixed costs. The variable cost per pound of Ranbax is $0.18. Division R has a capacity limit of 10,000 pounds. Divisions S and T have capacity limits of 4,000 and 6,000 pounds, respectively. Divisions S and T sell their final product in separate markets. The company keeps no inventories of any kind.

The *cumulative* net revenues (i.e., total revenues – total processing costs) for divisions S and T at various output levels are summarized below.

Division S

Pounds of Ranbax processed in S	1,000	2,000	3,000	4,000
Total net revenues ($) from sale of Syntex	$ 500	$ 850	$1,100	$1,200

Division T

Pounds of Ranbax processed in T	1,000	2,000	3,000	4,000	5,000	6,000
Total net revenues ($) from sale of Termix	$ 600	$1,200	$1,800	$2,100	$2,250	$2,350

Required

1. Suppose there is no external market for Ranbax. What quantity of Ranbax should the Letang Company produce to maximize overall income? How should this quantity be allocated between the two processing divisions?
2. What range of transfer prices will motivate divisions S and T to demand the quantities that maximize overall income (as determined in requirement 1), as well as motivate division R to produce the sum of those quantities?
3. Suppose that division R can sell any quantity of Ranbax in a perfectly competitive market for $0.33 a pound. To maximize Letang's income, how many pounds of Ranbax should division R transfer to divisions S and T, and how much should it sell in the external market?
4. What range of transfer prices will result in divisions R, S, and T taking the actions determined as optimal in requirement 3? Explain your answer.

23-36 Transfer pricing, full cost and market-based transfer prices. Compost Systems, Inc. (CSI) operates a composting service business and produces organic fertilizer that it sells to farmers in the Midwest. CSI operates with two divisions, collection and composting. The collection division contracts with universities, hospitals, and other large institutions to provide compostable waste collection bins in their dining service areas, and hauls the waste away daily. The waste providers pay the collection division a monthly fee for this service, and the collection division in turn charges the composting division for the compostable materials at a full-cost transfer price of $200 per ton. Monthly, CSI collects and transfers 1,000 tons of waste.

The composting division processes the waste, places it in bins, adds microbes to break down the organic material, and ultimately delivers the fertilizer it produces to farmers for use in their fields. After the removal of water, 1,000 tons of waste produces 500 tons of fertilizer. Demand for the fertilizer has risen steeply as consumer demand for organic produce has increased in recent years.

Below are key data related to CSI's monthly operations:

Collection Division	
Revenues:	
Revenues from waste providers (monthly fees)	$ 50,000
Revenues from transfer of materials to composting division, 1,000 tons × $200/ton	200,000
Total revenues	$250,000
Costs:	
Variable costs, 1,000 tons × $150/ton	$150,000
Fixed costs	50,000
Total costs	200,000
Divisional operating income	$ 50,000
Composting Division	
Revenues, 500 tons × $550/ton	$275,000
Costs:	
Transfer price of compostable materials, 1,000 tons × $200/ton	$200,000
Other variable costs, 500 tons × $50/ton	25,000
Fixed costs	20,000
Total costs	245,000
Divisional operating income	30,000
Operating income of both divisions together	$ 80,000

The composting division has demand for an additional 200 tons of fertilizer per month. To provide the 400 tons of compostable waste necessary to meet the increased demand, the collection division will have to invest in additional marketing and equipment that will increase monthly fixed costs by $28,000. Estimated additional monthly revenue to the collection division from waste providers is $10,000.

Required

1. Compute the new full-cost transfer price if it is applied to all waste transferred to the composting division.
2. Compute the new full-cost transfer price if it is applied to just the additional 400 tons.
3. What difficulties do you see in using a full-cost transfer-pricing system in the future?
4. The composting division has identified a source of additional compostable waste at a price of $205 per ton. What would be the impact on the company as a whole if the 400 tons of material is purchased from the outside supplier? As a decentralized unit, what decision would the composting division make regarding the additional material?
5. Would a market-based transfer price be agreeable to both divisional managers?

23-37 Transfer pricing, utilization of capacity. (J. Patell, adapted) Sierra Inc. consists of a semiconductor division and a process-control division, each of which operates as an independent profit center. The semiconductor division employs craftsmen who produce two different electronic components: the new high-performance Xcel-chip and an older product called the Dcel-chip. These products have the following cost characteristics:

	Xcel-chip	Dcel-chip
Direct materials	$ 10	$ 8
Direct manufacturing labor: 4 hours × $25; 2 hours × $25	100	50

Due to the high skill level necessary for the craftsmen, the semiconductor division's capacity is set at 55,000 hours per year.

Maximum demand for the Xcel-chip is 13,750 units annually, at a price of $130 per chip. There is unlimited demand for the Dcel-chip at $65 per chip.

The process-control division produces only one product, a process-control unit, with the following cost structure:

- Direct materials (circuit board): $80
- Direct manufacturing labor (3.5 hours × $10): $35

The current market price for the control unit is $125 per unit.

A joint research project has just revealed that a single Xcel-chip could be substituted for the circuit board currently used to make the process-control unit. The direct manufacturing labor cost of the process-control unit would be unchanged. The improved process-control unit could be sold for $185.

Required

1. Calculate the contribution margin per direct labor-hour of selling Xcel-chip and Dcel-chip. If no transfers of Xcel-chip are made to the process-control division, how many Xcel-chips and Dcel-chips should the semiconductor division manufacture and sell? What would be the division's annual contribution margin? Show your computations.
2. The process-control division expects to sell 1,250 process-control units this year. From the viewpoint of Sierra Inc. as a whole, should 1,250 Xcel-chips be transferred to the process-control division to replace circuit boards? Show your computations.
3. What transfer price, or range of prices, would ensure goal congruence among the division managers? Show your calculations.
4. If labor capacity in the semiconductor division were 60,000 hours instead of 55,000, would your answer to requirement 3 differ? Show your calculations.

Performance Measurement, Compensation, and Multinational Considerations

24

When you complete this course, you'll receive a grade that represents a measure of your performance in it.

Your grade will likely consist of four elements—homework, quizzes, exams, and class participation. Do some of these elements better reflect your knowledge of the material than others? Would the relative weights placed on the various elements in determining your final grade influence how much effort you expend to improve your performance on the different elements?

Would it be fair if you received a good grade regardless of your performance? The following article about chief executives at General Electric examines that very situation in a corporate context.

LEARNING OBJECTIVES

1. Select financial and nonfinancial performance measures to use in a balanced scorecard
2. Examine accounting-based measures for evaluating a business unit's performance, including return on investment (ROI), residual income (RI), and economic value added (EVA)
3. Analyze the key measurement choices in the design of each performance measure
4. Study the choice of performance targets and design of feedback mechanisms
5. Indicate the difficulties that occur when the performance of divisions operating in different countries is compared
6. Understand the roles of salaries and incentives when rewarding managers
7. Describe the four levers of control and why they are necessary

CEO COMPENSATION AT GENERAL ELECTRIC[1]

General Electric (GE) was once the most valuable company in the United States, worth nearly $600 billion at the turn of the century. After famed chief executive officer (CEO) Jack Welch retired in 2001, the company began a long, steep decline resulting in a smaller company today worth around one-tenth what it was back in 2000.

While GE's performance significantly declined over the years, compensation for then-CEOs Jeff Immelt and John Flannery did not. During his 16-year run as CEO, Immelt earned nearly $211 million in salary and incentive compensation. In 2016, while the company's stock price remained flat, Immelt took home a $3.8 million salary, $4.3 million performance bonus, and nearly $1.2 million in miscellaneous compensation, including $257,639 for his use of GE's private jet.

When Immelt retired under shareholder pressure in 2017, he left with at least another $112 million, mostly in supplemental pension plans and early vesting of stock options. His replacement, John Flannery, earned $5.8 million during his 14-month tenure as CEO. During his short time at the helm, GE's stock price fell nearly 50%.

Sundry Photography/Shutterstock

Companies measure and reward performance to motivate managers to work toward organizational goals. As the GE example illustrates, if rewards are inappropriate or not connected to sustained performance, managers can increase their compensation without supporting the company's objectives. This chapter discusses the design, implementation, and uses of performance measures, which are part of the final step in the decision-making process.

[1] *Sources:* Thomas Gryta and Ted Mann, "Burned Out," *The Wall Street Journal*, December 15, 2018 (https://www.wsj.com/articles/ge-powered-the-american-centurythen-it-burned-out-11544796010); Alicia Ritcey and Anders Melin, "GE's Immelt to Receive at Least $112 Million as CEO Steps Down," Bloomberg.com, June 12, 2017 (https://www.bloomberg.com/news/articles/2017-06-12/ge-s-immelt-to-receive-at-least-112-million-as-ceo-steps-down); Ed Crooks, "Immelt Had 72% Pay Cut After Plunging Profits Hit GE," *The Financial Times,* March 12, 2018 (https://www.ft.com/content/597e9832-2648-11e8-b27e-cc62a39d57a0).

Financial and Nonfinancial Performance Measures

LEARNING OBJECTIVE 1

Select financial performance measures

... such as return on investment and residual income

and nonfinancial performance measures

... such as customer satisfaction and number of defects

to use in a balanced scorecard

As you have learned, many organizations record financial and nonfinancial performance measures for their subunits on a *balanced scorecard*. The scorecards of different organizations emphasize different measures, but the measures are always derived from a company's strategy. Consider the case of Hospitality Inns, a chain of hotels. Hospitality Inns' strategy is to provide excellent customer service and to charge a higher room rate than its competitors. Hospitality Inns uses the following measures in its balanced scorecard:

1. **Financial perspective**—the firm's stock price, net income, return on sales, return on investment, and residual income
2. **Customer perspective**—market share in different geographic locations, customer satisfaction, brand image, and average number of repeat visits
3. **Internal-business-process perspective**—customer-service time for making reservations, check-in, and restaurant services; cleanliness of the hotels and rooms; time taken to clean rooms; room-service and restaurant quality; reductions in waste output and energy and water consumption; number of new services, such as wireless Internet, provided to customers; and the time taken to plan and build new hotels
4. **Learning-and-growth perspective**—the education, skills, and satisfaction levels of the firm's employees; employee turnover and hours of employee training; and the company's achievement of ISO 14001:2015 certification for environmental management

As in all balanced scorecard implementations, the goal is to make improvements in the learning-and-growth perspective that will lead to enhancements in the internal-business-process perspective that, in turn, will result in gains in the customer and financial perspectives. Hospitality Inns also uses balanced scorecard measures to evaluate and reward the performance of its managers.

Some performance measures, such as the time it takes to plan and build new hotels, have a long time horizon. Other measures, such as check-in time or quality of room service, have a short time horizon. In this chapter, we focus on *organization subunits'* most widely used performance measures that cover an intermediate to long time horizon. These are internal financial measures based on accounting numbers routinely reported by organizations. In later sections, we describe why companies use both financial and nonfinancial measures to evaluate performance.

Designing accounting-based performance measures requires several steps:

Step 1: Choose Performance Measures That Align With the Firm's Financial Goals. For example, is operating income, net income, return on assets, or revenue the best measure of a subunit's financial performance?

Step 2: Choose the Details of Each Performance Measure in Step 1. Once a firm has chosen a specific performance measure, it must make a variety of decisions about the precise way in which various components of the measure are to be calculated. For example, if the chosen performance measure is return on assets, should it be calculated for 1 year or for a multiyear period? Should assets be defined as total assets or net assets (total assets minus total liabilities)? Should assets be measured at historical cost or current cost?

Step 3: Choose a Target Level of Performance and Feedback Mechanism for Each Performance Measure in Step 1. For example, should all subunits have identical targets, such as the same required rate of return on assets? Should performance reports be sent to top managers daily, weekly, or monthly?

The decisions made in these steps don't have to be sequential. The issues considered in each step are interdependent, and top managers will often iterate through these steps several times before deciding on one or more accounting-based performance measures. At each step, the answers to the questions raised depend on top management's beliefs about how well each measure fulfills the criteria of promoting goal congruence, motivating management effort, evaluating subunit performance, and preserving subunit autonomy (see Chapter 23).

DECISION POINT

What financial and nonfinancial performance measures do companies use in their balanced scorecards?

Accounting-Based Measures for Business Units

LEARNING OBJECTIVE 2

Examine accounting-based measures for evaluating a business unit's performance, including return on investment (ROI),

... return on sales times investment turnover

residual income (RI),

... income minus a dollar amount for required return on investment

and economic value added (EVA)

... a variation of residual income

Companies commonly use four financial measures to evaluate the economic performance of their subunits. We illustrate these measures for Hospitality Inns.

Hospitality Inns owns and operates three hotels: one each in San Francisco, Chicago, and New Orleans. Exhibit 24-1 summarizes data for each hotel for 2020. At present, Hospitality Inns does not allocate the total long-term debt of the company to the three separate hotels. The exhibit indicates that the New Orleans hotel generates the highest operating income, $510,000, compared with Chicago's $300,000 and San Francisco's $240,000. But does this comparison mean the New Orleans hotel is the most "successful"? The main weakness of comparing operating incomes alone is that it ignores the differences in *the size of the investment* in each hotel. **Investment** refers to the resources or assets used to generate income. The real question is whether a division generates sufficient operating income relative to the investment made to earn it.

Three of the approaches to measuring subunit financial performance include a measure of investment: return on investment, residual income, and economic value added. A fourth approach, return on sales, does not measure investment.

Return on Investment

Return on investment (ROI) is an accounting measure of income divided by an accounting measure of investment.

$$\text{Return on investment} = \frac{\text{Income}}{\text{Investment}}$$

Return on investment is the most popular approach to measuring performance for two reasons: (1) It blends all the ingredients of profitability—revenues, costs, and investment—into

EXHIBIT 24-1 Financial Data for Hospitality Inns for 2020 (in thousands)

Home Insert Page Layout Formulas Data Review View

	A	B	C	D	E
1		San Francisco Hotel	Chicago Hotel	New Orleans Hotel	Total
2	Hotel revenues	$1,200,000	$1,400,000	$3,185,000	$5,785,000
3	Hotel variable costs	310,000	375,000	995,000	1,680,000
4	Hotel fixed costs	650,000	725,000	1,680,000	3,055,000
5	Hotel operating income	$ 240,000	$ 300,000	$ 510,000	1,050,000
6	Interest costs on long-term debt at 10%				450,000
7	Income before income taxes				600,000
8	Income taxes at 30%				180,000
9	Net income				$ 420,000
10	Net book value at the end of 2020:				
11	Current assets	$ 400,000	$ 500,000	$ 660,000	$1,560,000
12	Long-term assets	600,000	1,500,000	2,340,000	4,440,000
13	Total assets	$1,000,000	$2,000,000	$3,000,000	$6,000,000
14	Current liabilities	$ 50,000	$ 150,000	$ 300,000	$ 500,000
15	Long-term debt				4,500,000
16	Stockholders' equity				1,000,000
17	Total liabilities and stockholders' equity				$6,000,000
18					

a single percentage and (2) it can be compared with the rate of return on opportunities elsewhere, inside or outside the company. As with any single performance measure, however, managers should use ROI cautiously and in conjunction with other measures.

ROI is also called the *accounting rate of return* or the *accrual accounting rate of return* (Chapter 22, pages 861–862). Managers usually use the term *ROI* when evaluating the performance of an organization's subunit and the term *accrual accounting rate of return* when using an ROI measure to evaluate a project. Companies vary in the way they define income in the numerator and investment in the denominator of the ROI calculation. Some companies use operating income for the numerator; others prefer to calculate ROI on an after-tax basis and use net income. Some companies use total assets in the denominator; others prefer to focus on only those assets financed by long-term debt and stockholders' equity and use total assets minus current liabilities.

Consider the ROIs of each of the three Hospitality hotels in Exhibit 24-1. For our calculations, we use the operating income of each hotel for the numerator and the total assets of each hotel for the denominator.

Using these ROI figures, the San Francisco hotel appears to make the best use of its total assets.

Hotel	Operating Income	÷	Total Assets	=	ROI
San Francisco	$240,000	÷	$1,000,000	=	24%
Chicago	$300,000	÷	$2,000,000	=	15%
New Orleans	$510,000	÷	$3,000,000	=	17%

Each manager can increase his or her hotel's ROI by increasing its revenues or decreasing its costs (each of which increases the numerator) or by decreasing the investment in the hotel (which decreases the denominator). Even when a hotel's operating income falls, the manager can increase its ROI by reducing its total assets by a greater percentage. Suppose, for example, that the operating income of the Chicago hotel decreases by 4% from $300,000 to $288,000 and its total assets decrease by 10% from $2,000,000 to $1,800,000. The ROI of the Chicago hotel would then increase from 15% to 16% ($288,000 ÷ $1,800,000).

ROI can provide additional insight into performance when it is represented as two components:

$$\frac{\text{Income}}{\text{Investment}} = \frac{\text{Income}}{\text{Revenues}} \times \frac{\text{Revenues}}{\text{Investment}}$$

which is also written as

$$ROI = \text{Return on sales} \times \text{Investment turnover}$$

This approach is known as the *DuPont method of profitability analysis*. The DuPont method recognizes the two basic ingredients in profit making: increasing the income per dollar of revenues and using assets to generate more revenues. An improvement in either ingredient, even without changing the other, increases the ROI.

Assume Hospitality Inns' top managers adopt a 30% target ROI for the San Francisco hotel. How can this return be attained? Using the DuPont method, the following example shows three alternative ways the managers of the hotel can increase its ROI from 24% to 30%.

	Operating Income (1)	Revenues (2)	Total Assets (3)	Operating Income / Revenues (4) = (1) ÷ (2)	×	Revenues / Total Assets (5) = (2) ÷ (3)	=	Operating Income / Total Assets (6) = (4) × (5)
Current ROI	$240,000	$1,200,000	$1,000,000	20%	×	1.2	=	24%
Alternatives								
A. Decrease assets (such as receivables), keeping revenues and operating income per dollar of revenue constant	$240,000	$1,200,000	$ 800,000	20%	×	1.5	=	30%

	Operating Income (1)	Revenues (2)	Total Assets (3)	Operating Income / Revenues (4) = (1) ÷ (2)	×	Revenues / Total Assets (5) = (2) ÷ (3)	=	Operating Income / Total Assets (6) = (4) × (5)
B. Increase revenues (via higher occupancy rate), keeping assets and operating income per dollar of revenue constant	$300,000	$1,500,000	$1,000,000	20%	×	1.5	=	30%
C. Decrease costs (via, say, efficient maintenance) to increase operating income per dollar of revenue, keeping revenue and assets constant	$300,000	$1,200,000	$1,000,000	25%	×	1.2	=	30%

Other alternatives, such as increasing the selling price per room, could increase both the revenues per dollar of total assets and the operating income per dollar of revenues.

ROI makes clear the benefits managers can obtain by reducing their investment in current or long-term assets. Most managers know they need to boost revenues and control costs, but pay less attention to reducing their investment base. Reducing the investment base involves decreasing idle cash, managing credit judiciously, determining proper inventory levels, and spending carefully on long-term assets.

Residual Income

Residual income (RI) is an accounting measure of income minus a dollar amount for required return on an accounting measure of investment.

$$\text{Residual income } (RI) = \text{Income} - (\text{Required rate of return} \times \text{Investment})$$

The required rate of return multiplied by the investment is the *imputed cost of the investment.* The **imputed cost** of the investment is a cost recognized in particular situations but not recorded in financial accounting systems because it is an opportunity cost. In this situation, the imputed cost refers to the return Hospitality Inns could have obtained by making an alternative investment with similar risk characteristics.

Assume that each hotel faces similar risks and that Hospitality Inns has a required rate of return of 12%. The RI for each hotel is calculated as the operating income minus the required rate of return of 12% of total assets:

Hotel	Operating Income	–	Required Rate of Return	×	Investment	=	Residual Income
San Francisco	$240,000	–	(12%	×	$1,000,000)	=	$120,000
Chicago	$300,000	–	(12%	×	$2,000,000)	=	$ 60,000
New Orleans	$510,000	–	(12%	×	$3,000,000)	=	$150,000

Note that the New Orleans hotel has the best RI. In general, RI is influenced by size: For a given level of performance, larger divisions generate higher RI.

Some companies favor the RI measure because managers will concentrate on maximizing an absolute amount, such as dollars of RI, rather than a percentage, such as ROI. The objective of maximizing RI means that as long as a subunit earns a return in excess of the required return for investments, that subunit should continue to invest.

The objective of maximizing ROI may give managers of highly profitable subunits the incentive to reject projects that, from the viewpoint of the company as a whole, should be accepted. Suppose Hospitality Inns is considering upgrading room features and furnishings at the San Francisco hotel. The upgrade will increase the operating income of the San Francisco hotel by \$70,000 and increase its total assets by \$400,000. The ROI for the expansion is 17.5% (\$70,000 ÷ \$400,000), which is attractive to Hospitality Inns because it exceeds the required rate of return of 12%. By making this expansion, however, the San Francisco hotel's ROI will decrease:

$$\text{Pre-upgrade } ROI = \frac{\$240{,}000}{\$1{,}000{,}000} = 0.24, \text{ or } 24\%$$

$$\text{Post-upgrade } ROI = \frac{\$240{,}000 + \$70{,}000}{\$1{,}000{,}000 + \$400{,}000} = \frac{\$310{,}000}{\$1{,}400{,}000} = 0.221, \text{ or } 22.1\%$$

The annual bonus paid to the San Francisco manager may decrease if ROI impacts the bonus calculation and the upgrading option is selected. Consequently, the manager may not support the expansion. In contrast, if the annual bonus is a function of RI, the San Francisco manager will favor the expansion:

$$\text{Pre-upgrade } RI = \$240{,}000 - (0.12 \times \$1{,}000{,}000) = \$120{,}000$$

$$\text{Post-upgrade } RI = \$310{,}000 - (0.12 \times \$1{,}400{,}000) = \$142{,}000$$

So, it is more likely that a firm will achieve goal congruence if it uses RI rather than ROI to measure the subunit manager's performance.

To see that this is a general result, notice that the post-upgrade ROI is a weighted average of the pre-upgrade ROI and the ROI of the project under consideration. Therefore, whenever a new project has a return higher than the required rate of return (12% in our example) but below the current ROI of the division (24% in our example), the division manager is tempted to reject it even though it is a project shareholders would like to pursue.[2] On the other hand, RI is a measure that aggregates linearly, that is, the post-upgrade RI always equals the pre-upgrade RI plus the RI of the project under consideration. To verify this in the preceding example, observe that the project's RI is \$70,000 − (12% × \$400,000) = \$22,000, which is the difference between the post-upgrade and pre-upgrade RI amounts. As a result, a manager who is evaluated on residual income will choose a new project only if it has a positive RI. But this is exactly the criterion shareholders want the manager to employ; in other words, RI achieves goal congruence.

TRY IT! 24-1

Front Investments has two divisions. Each division's required rate of return is 12%. Planned operating results for 2020 are as follows:

Division	Operating income	Investment
A	\$ 9,800,000	\$70,000,000
B	\$12,000,000	\$60,000,000

a. What is the current ROI for each division?
b. What is the current residual income for each division?

Front is planning an expansion that will require each division to increase its investment by \$30,000,000 and its income by \$5,000,000.

c. Assuming the managers are evaluated on either ROI or residual income, which division (if either) is pleased with the expansion?

[2] Analogously, the manager of an underperforming division with an ROI of 7%, say, may wish to accept projects with returns between 7% and 12% even though these opportunities do not meet the shareholders' required rate of return.

Economic Value Added

Economic value added (EVA) is a variation of RI used by many companies.[3] It is calculated as follows:

$$\text{Economic value added (EVA)} = \text{After-tax operating income} - \left[\text{Weighted average cost of capital} \times \left(\text{Total assets} - \text{Current liabilities}\right)\right]$$

That is, EVA substitutes the following numbers in the RI calculation:

1. Income: After-tax operating income
2. Required rate of return: (After-tax) weighted-average cost of capital
3. Investment: Total assets minus current liabilities, or, equivalently, long-term assets plus working capital[4]

We use the Hospitality Inns' data in Exhibit 24-1 to illustrate the basic EVA calculations. The weighted-average cost of capital (WACC) equals the *after-tax* average cost of all the long-term funds Hospitality Inns uses. The company has two sources of long-term funds: (1) long-term debt with a market value and book value of \$4.5 million issued at an interest rate of 10%, and (2) equity capital that also has a market value of \$4.5 million (but a book value of \$1 million).[5] Because interest costs are tax-deductible and the income tax rate is 30%, the after-tax cost of debt financing is $0.10 \times (1 - \text{Tax rate}) = 0.10 \times (1 - 0.30) = 0.07$, or 7%. The cost of equity capital is the opportunity cost to investors of not investing their capital in another investment that is similar in risk to Hospitality Inns. Hospitality Inns' cost of equity capital is 14%.[6] The WACC computation, which uses market values of debt and equity, is as follows:

$$WACC = \frac{(7\% \times \text{Market value of debt}) + (14\% \times \text{Market value of equity})}{\text{Market value of debt} + \text{Market value of equity}}$$

$$= \frac{(0.07 \times \$4{,}500{,}000) + (0.14 \times \$4{,}500{,}000)}{\$4{,}500{,}000 + \$4{,}500{,}000}$$

$$= \frac{\$945{,}000}{\$9{,}000{,}000} = 0.105, \text{ or } 10.5\%$$

The company applies the same WACC to all its hotels because each hotel faces similar risks.

After-tax hotel operating income is

$$\text{Hotel operating income} \times (1 - \text{Tax rate}) = \text{Hotel operating income} \times (1 - 0.30) = \text{Hotel operating income} \times 0.70$$

[3] Stephen F. O'Byrne and S. David Young, *EVA and Value-Based Management: A Practical Guide to Implementation* (New York: McGraw-Hill, 2000); Joel M. Stern, John S. Shiely, and Irwin Ross, *The EVA Challenge: Implementing Value Added Change in an Organization* (New York: John Wiley and Sons, 2001).

[4] When implementing EVA, companies make several adjustments to the operating income and asset numbers reported under Generally Accepted Accounting Principles (GAAP). For example, when calculating EVA, costs such as R&D, restructuring costs, and leases that have long-run benefits are recorded as assets (which are then amortized) rather than as current operating costs. The goal of these adjustments is to obtain a better representation of the economic assets, particularly intangible assets, used to earn income. Of course, the specific adjustments applicable to a company will depend on its individual circumstances.

[5] The market value of Hospitality Inns' equity exceeds book value because book value, based on historical cost, does not measure the current value of the company's assets and because various intangible assets, such as the company's brand name, are omitted in the balance sheet under GAAP.

[6] In practice, the most common method of calculating the cost of equity capital is by applying the capital asset pricing model. For details, see Jonathan Berk and Peter DeMarzo, *Corporate Finance*, 4th ed. (Boston, MA: Pearson, 2017).

EVA calculations for Hospitality Inns are as follows:

Hotel	After-Tax Operating Income	−	[WACC × (Total Assets − Current Liabilities)]	=	EVA
San Francisco	$240,000 × 0.70	−	[10.50% × ($1,000,000 − $ 50,000)]	=	$68,250
Chicago	$300,000 × 0.70	−	[10.50% × ($2,000,000 − $150,000)]	=	$15,750
New Orleans	$510,000 × 0.70	−	[10.50% × ($3,000,000 − $300,000)]	=	$73,500

The New Orleans hotel has the highest EVA. Economic value added, like residual income, charges managers for the cost of their investments in long-term assets and working capital. Value is created only if the subunit's after-tax operating income exceeds the cost of investing the capital. To improve EVA, managers can, for example, (1) earn more after-tax operating income with the same amount of capital, (2) use less capital to earn the same after-tax operating income, or (3) invest capital in high-return projects.[7]

Companies such as Briggs and Stratton (a leading producer of gasoline engines), Coca-Cola, Eli Lilly, and Infosys Limited use EVA to guide their decisions. CSX, a railroad company, credits EVA for decisions such as to run trains with three locomotives instead of four and to schedule arrivals just in time for unloading rather than having trains arrive at their destination several hours in advance. The result? Higher income because of lower fuel costs and lower capital investments in locomotives. Division managers find EVA helpful because it allows them to incorporate the cost of capital, which is generally only available at the company-wide level, into the decisions they make.

TRY IT! 24-2

Performance City supplies helicopters to corporate clients. Performance City has two sources of funds: long-term debt with a market and book value of $34 million issued at an interest rate of 10% and equity capital that has a market value of $12 million (book value of $7 million). The cost of equity capital for Performance City is 16%, and its tax rate is 40%. Performance City has divisions in two cities that operate autonomously. The company's results for 2020 are as follows:

	Operating Income	Assets	Current Liabilities
New York	$2,250,000	$12,000,000	$2,400,000
Chicago	$2,900,000	$10,500,000	$3,600,000

a. What is Performance City's weighted average cost of capital?
b. Compute each division's Economic Value Added.

Return on Sales

The income-to-revenues ratio (or sales ratio), often called the *return on sales* (*ROS*), is a frequently used financial performance measure. As we have seen, ROS is one component of ROI in the DuPont method of profitability analysis. To calculate the ROS for each of Hospitality Inns' hotels, we divide operating income by revenues:

Hotel	Operating Income	÷	Revenues (Sales)	=	ROS
San Francisco	$240,000	÷	$1,200,000	=	20.0%
Chicago	$300,000	÷	$1,400,000	=	21.4%
New Orleans	$510,000	÷	$3,185,000	=	16.0%

The Chicago hotel has the highest ROS, but its performance is rated worse than the other hotels using measures such as ROI, RI, and EVA.

[7] Observe that the sum of the divisional after-tax operating incomes used in the EVA calculation, ($240,000 + $300,000 + $510,000) × 0.7 = $735,000, exceeds the firm's net income of $420,000. The difference is due to the firm's after-tax interest expense on its long-term debt, which amounts to 450,000 × 0.7 = $315,000. Because the EVA measure includes a charge for the weighted-average cost of capital, which includes the after-tax cost of debt, the income figure used to compute EVA should reflect the after-tax profit before interest payments on debt are considered. After-tax operating income (often referred to in practice as NOPAT, or net operating profit after taxes) is thus the relevant measure of divisional profit for EVA calculations.

Comparing Performance Measures

The following table summarizes the performance of each hotel and ranks it (in parentheses) under each of the four performance measures:

Hotel	ROI	RI	EVA	ROS
San Francisco	24% (1)	$120,000 (2)	$68,250 (2)	20.0% (2)
Chicago	15% (3)	$ 60,000 (3)	$15,750 (3)	21.4% (1)
New Orleans	17% (2)	$150,000 (1)	$73,500 (1)	16.0% (3)

The RI and EVA rankings are the same. They differ from the ROI and ROS rankings. Consider the ROI and RI rankings for the San Francisco and New Orleans hotels. The New Orleans hotel has a smaller ROI, indicating that its assets are being used relatively less efficiently. Although its operating income is only slightly more than twice the operating income of the San Francisco hotel—$510,000 versus $240,000—its total assets are three times as large—$3 million versus $1 million. However, the New Orleans hotel has a higher RI because it earns a higher income after covering the required rate of return on investment of 12%. Even though each dollar invested in the New Orleans hotel does not yield the same return as the San Francisco hotel, this large investment creates considerable value because its return exceeds the required rate of return. The Chicago hotel has the highest ROS but the lowest ROI. The high ROS indicates that the Chicago hotel has the lowest cost structure per dollar of revenues of all of Hospitality Inns' hotels. Chicago has a low ROI because it generates very low revenues per dollar of assets invested.

Is any method better than the others for measuring performance? No, because each method evaluates a different aspect of performance. ROS measures how effectively costs are managed. To evaluate a unit's overall aggregate performance, however, ROI, RI, or EVA measures are more appropriate than ROS because they consider both income and investment. ROI indicates which investment yields the highest return. RI and EVA overcome some of the goal-congruence problems of ROI. Some managers favor EVA because of the accounting adjustments related to the capitalization of investments in intangibles. Other managers favor RI because it is easier to calculate and because, in most cases, it leads to the same conclusions as EVA does. Generally, companies use multiple financial measures to evaluate performance.

DECISION POINT

What are the relative merits of return on investment (ROI), residual income (RI), and economic value added (EVA) as performance measures for subunit managers?

Choosing the Details of the Performance Measures

LEARNING OBJECTIVE 3

Analyze the key measurement choices in the design of each performance measure

... choice of time horizon, alternative definitions, and measurement of assets

It is not sufficient for a company to identify the set of performance measures it wishes to use. The company has to decide how to compute the measures. This includes deciding on the time frame over which the measures are computed, defining key terms such as *investment*, and agreeing on how to calculate the components of each performance measure.

Alternative Time Horizons

An important element in designing accounting-based performance measures is choosing the time horizon of the performance measures. The ROI, RI, EVA, and ROS calculations represent the results for a single period, 1 year in our example. Managers could take actions that cause short-run increases in these measures but that conflict with the long-run interest of the company. For example, managers might curtail research and development (R&D) and plant maintenance spending in the last 3 months of a fiscal year to achieve a target level of annual operating income. For this reason, many companies evaluate subunits on the basis of ROI, RI, EVA, and ROS over *multiple* years.

Another reason to evaluate subunits over multiple years is that the benefits of actions taken in the current period may not show up in short-run performance measures, such as the current year's ROI or RI. For example, an investment in a new hotel may adversely affect ROI and RI in the short run but positively affect them in the long run.

A multiyear analysis highlights another advantage of the RI measure: The net present value of all cash flows over the life of an investment equals the net present value of the RIs.[8] This means that if managers use the net present value method to make investment decisions (as Chapter 22 advocates), then using a multiyear RI to evaluate managers' performances achieves goal congruence.

Another way to motivate managers to take a long-run perspective is by compensating them on the basis of changes in the market price of the company's stock because stock prices incorporate the expected future effects of a firm's current decisions.

Alternative Definitions of Investment

Companies use a variety of definitions to measure the investments made in their divisions. Four common alternative definitions used in the construction of accounting-based performance measures are as follows:

1. **Total assets available**—includes all assets, regardless of their intended purpose.
2. **Total assets employed**—total assets available minus the sum of idle assets and assets purchased for future expansion. For example, if the New Orleans hotel in Exhibit 24-1 has unused land set aside for potential expansion, the total assets employed (used) by the hotel would exclude the cost of that land.
3. **Total assets employed minus current liabilities**—total assets employed, excluding assets financed by short-term creditors. One negative feature of defining investment in this way is that it may encourage subunit managers to use an excessive amount of short-term debt because short-term debt reduces the amount of investment.
4. **Stockholders' equity**—calculated by assigning liabilities to subunits and deducting these amounts from the total assets of each subunit. One drawback of this method is that it combines the operating decisions made by hotel managers with the financing decisions made by top management.

Companies that use ROI or RI generally define investment as the total assets available. When a firm directs a subunit manager to carry extra or idle assets, the total assets employed can be more informative than total assets available. Companies that use EVA define investment as the total assets employed minus current liabilities. The rationale for using this definition is that it captures total investment as measured by the sum of working capital (current assets minus current liabilities) and the long-term assets employed in the subunit. Managers are responsible for generating an adequate return on both components.

Alternative Asset Measurements

To design accounting-based performance measures, we must consider different ways to measure the assets included in the investment calculations. Should the assets be measured at

[8] This equivalence, referred to as the "conservation property" of residual income, was first articulated by Gabriel Preinreich in 1938. To see the equivalence, suppose the \$400,000 investment in the San Francisco hotel increases its operating income by \$70,000 per year as follows: Increase in operating cash flows of \$150,000 each year for 5 years minus depreciation of \$80,000 (\$400,000 ÷ 5) per year, assuming straight-line depreciation and \$0 terminal disposal value. Depreciation reduces the investment amount by \$80,000 each year. Assuming a required rate of return of 12%, the net present values of cash flows and residual incomes are as follows:

Year		0	1	2	3	4	5	Net Present Value
(1)	Cash flow		\$150,000	\$150,000	\$150,000	\$150,000	\$150,000	
(2)	Present value of \$1 discounted at 12%	1	0.89286	0.79719	0.71178	0.63552	0.56743	
(3)	Present value:		\$133,929	\$119,578	\$106,767	\$ 95,328	\$ 85,114	\$140,716
(4)	Operating income		\$ 70,000	\$ 70,000	\$ 70,000	\$ 70,000	\$ 70,000	
(5)	Assets at start of year		\$400,000	\$320,000	\$240,000	\$160,000	\$ 80,000	
(6)			\$ 48,000	\$ 38,400	\$ 28,800	\$ 19,200	\$ 9,600	
(7)			\$ 22,000	\$ 31,600	\$ 41,200	\$ 50,800	\$ 60,400	
(8)			\$ 19,643	\$ 25,191	\$ 29,325	\$ 32,284	\$ 34,273	\$140,716

historical cost or current cost? Should gross book value (that is, original cost) or net book value (original cost minus accumulated depreciation) be used for depreciable assets?

Current Cost

Current cost is the cost of purchasing an asset today identical to the one currently held or the cost of purchasing an asset that provides services like the one currently held if an identical asset cannot be purchased. Of course, measuring assets at current costs will result in different ROIs than the ROIs calculated on the basis of historical costs.

We illustrate the current-cost ROI calculations using the data for Hospitality Inns (Exhibit 24-1) and then compare current-cost-based ROIs and historical-cost-based ROIs. Consider the following additional information about the long-term assets of each hotel:

	San Francisco	Chicago	New Orleans
Age of facility in years (at end of 2020)	8	4	2
Gross book value (original cost)	$1,400,000	$2,100,000	$2,730,000
Accumulated depreciation	$ 800,000	$ 600,000	$ 390,000
Net book value (at end of 2020)	$ 600,000	$1,500,000	$2,340,000
Depreciation for 2020	$ 100,000	$ 150,000	$ 195,000

Hospitality Inns assumes its facilities have a 14-year estimated useful life and zero terminal disposal value and uses straight-line depreciation.

An index of construction costs indicating how the cost of construction has changed over the 8-year period Hospitality Inns has been operating (2012 year-end = 100) is as follows:

Year	2013	2014	2015	2016	2017	2018	2019	2020
Construction cost index	110	122	136	144	152	160	174	180

Earlier in this chapter, we computed an ROI of 24% for San Francisco, 15% for Chicago, and 17% for New Orleans (page 926). One possible explanation for the high ROI for the San Francisco hotel is that its long-term assets are expressed in 2012 construction-price levels—prices that prevailed 8 years ago—and the long-term assets for the Chicago and New Orleans hotels are expressed in terms of higher, more recent construction-price levels, which depress ROIs for these two hotels.

Exhibit 24-2 illustrates a step-by-step approach for incorporating current-cost estimates of long-term assets and depreciation expense into the ROI calculation. We make these calculations to approximate what it would cost today to obtain assets that would produce the same expected operating income the subunits currently earn. (For RI and EVA calculations, similar adjustments to represent the current costs of capital and depreciation expense can be made.) The current-cost adjustment reduces the ROI of the San Francisco hotel by more than half.

	Historical-Cost ROI	Current-Cost ROI
San Francisco	24%	10.8%
Chicago	15%	11.1%
New Orleans	17%	14.7%

Adjusting assets to recognize current costs negates differences in the investment base caused solely by differences in construction-price levels. The current-cost ROI better measures the current economic returns from the investment than the historical-cost ROI does. If Hospitality Inns were to invest in a new hotel today, investing in one like the New Orleans hotel offers the best ROI.

Current-cost estimates can be difficult to obtain for some assets. Why? Because the estimate requires a company to consider, in addition to increases in price levels, technological advances and process improvements that could reduce the current cost of assets needed to earn today's operating income.

EXHIBIT 24-2 ROI for Hospitality Inns: Computed Using Current-Cost Estimates as of the End of 2020 for Depreciation Expense and Long-Term Assets

Home Insert Page Layout Formulas Data Review View

	A	B	C	D	E	F	G	H	I	J
1	**Step 1:** Restate long-term assets from gross book value at historical cost to gross book value at current cost as of the end of 2020.									
2		**Gross book value of long-term assets at historical cost**	×	**(Construction cost index in 2020**	÷	**Construction cost index in year of construction)**	=	**Gross book value of long-term assets at current cost at end of 2020**		
3	San Francisco	$1,400,000	×	(180	÷	100)	=	$2,520,000		
4	Chicago	$2,100,000	×	(180	÷	144)	=	$2,625,000		
5	New Orleans	$2,730,000	×	(180	÷	160)	=	$3,071,250		
6										
7	**Step 2:** Derive net book value of long-term assets at current cost as of the end of 2020. (Assume estimated useful life of each hotel is 14 years.)									
8		**Gross book value of long-term assets at current cost at end of 2020**	×	**(Estimated remaining useful life**	÷	**Estimated total useful life)**	=	**Net book value of long-term assets at current cost at end of 2020**		
9	San Francisco	$2,520,000	×	(6	÷	14)	=	$1,080,000		
10	Chicago	$2,625,000	×	(10	÷	14)	=	$1,875,000		
11	New Orleans	$3,071,250	×	(12	÷	14)	=	$2,632,500		
12										
13	**Step 3:** Compute current cost of total assets in 2020. (Assume current assets of each hotel are expressed in 2020 dollars.)									
14		**Current assets at end of 2020 (from Exhibit 24-1)**	+	**Long-term assets from Step 2**	=	**Current cost of total assets at end of 2020**				
15	San Francisco	$400,000	+	$1,080,000	=	$1,480,000				
16	Chicago	$500,000	+	$1,875,000	=	$2,375,000				
17	New Orleans	$660,000	+	$2,632,500	=	$3,292,500				
18										
19	**Step 4:** Compute current-cost depreciation expense in 2020 dollars.									
20		**Gross book value of long-term assets at current cost at end of 2020 (from Step 1)**	÷	**Estimated total useful life**	=	**Current-cost depreciation expense in 2020 dollars**				
21	San Francisco	$2,520,000	÷	14	=	$180,000				
22	Chicago	$2,625,000	÷	14	=	$187,500				
23	New Orleans	$3,071,250	÷	14	=	$219,375				
24										
25	**Step 5:** Compute 2020 operating income using 2020 current-cost depreciation expense.									
26		**Historical-cost operating income**	–	**(Current-cost depreciation expense in 2020 dollars (from Step 4)**	–	**Historical-cost depreciation expense)**	=	**Operating income for 2020 using current-cost depreciation expense in 2020 dollars**		
27	San Francisco	$240,000	–	($180,000	–	$100,000)	=	$160,000		
28	Chicago	$300,000	–	($187,500	–	$150,000)	=	$262,500		
29	New Orleans	$510,000	–	($219,375	–	$195,000)	=	$485,625		
30										
31	**Step 6:** Compute ROI using current-cost estimates for long-term assets and depreciation expense.									
32		**Operating income for 2020 using current-cost depreciation expense in 2020 dollars (from Step 5)**	÷	**Current cost of total assets at end of 2020 (from Step 3)**	=	**ROI using current-cost estimate**				
33	San Francisco	$160,000	÷	$1,480,000	=	10.8%				
34	Chicago	$262,500	÷	$2,375,000	=	11.1%				
35	New Orleans	$485,625	÷	$3,292,500	=	14.7%				

Long-Term Assets: Gross or Net Book Value?

The historical cost of assets is often used to calculate ROI. There has been much discussion about whether managers should use gross book value or net book value of assets. Using the data in Exhibit 24-1 (page 925), we calculate ROI using net and gross book values of plant and equipment:

	Operating Income (from Exhibit 24-1) (1)	Net Book Value of Total Assets (from Exhibit 24-1) (2)	Accumulated Depreciation (from page 933) (3)	Gross Book Value of Total Assets (4) = (2) + (3)	2020 ROI Using Net Book Value of Total Assets Calculated Earlier (5) = (1) ÷ (2)	2020 ROI Using Gross Book Value of Total Assets (6) = (1) ÷ (4)
San Francisco	$240,000	$1,000,000	$800,000	$1,800,000	24%	13.3%
Chicago	$300,000	$2,000,000	$600,000	$2,600,000	15%	11.5%
New Orleans	$510,000	$3,000,000	$390,000	$3,390,000	17%	15.0%

Using gross book value, the 13.3% ROI of the older San Francisco hotel is lower than the 15.0% ROI of the newer New Orleans hotel. Those who favor using gross book value claim it enables a firm to compare ROI across its subunits more accurately. For example, when using gross-book-value calculations, the return on the original plant-and-equipment investment is higher for the newer New Orleans hotel than for the older San Francisco hotel. This difference probably reflects the decline in earning power of the San Francisco hotel. Using the net book value masks this decline in earning power because the constantly decreasing investment base results in a higher ROI for the San Francisco hotel—24% in this example. This higher rate may mislead decision makers into thinking that the earning power of the San Francisco hotel has not decreased.

The proponents of using net book value as an investment base maintain that it is less confusing because (1) it is consistent with the amount of total assets shown in the conventional balance sheet, and (2) it is consistent with income computations that include deductions for depreciation expense. Surveys report that the net book value is the measure of assets most commonly used by companies for internal performance evaluation.

DECISION POINT

Over what time frame should companies measure performance, and what are the alternative choices for calculating the components of each performance measure?

24-3 TRY IT!

Sangoma Products, which exports processed palm oil, operates in a variety of West African countries. The following information relates to its Nigerian division for 2020:

Sales revenues	$1,430,000
Plant depreciation	210,000
Other operating costs	700,000
Operating income	$ 520,000

The division has current assets of $450,000 and one long-term asset (the plant) with a net book value of $1,890,000. The plant is 3 years old at the end of 2020 and has an estimated useful life of 12 years. The straight-line method is used for depreciation and no salvage value is assumed.

Over the 10-year period Sangoma has been operating, the index of construction costs in Nigeria is as follows

2010	2017	2020
100	150	180

a. What is the ROI for the Nigerian division using historical-cost measures?
b. What is the ROI for the Nigerian division using current-cost estimates for depreciation expense and long-term assets?

LEARNING OBJECTIVE 4

Study the choice of performance targets and design of feedback mechanisms

. . . carefully crafted budgets and sufficient feedback for timely corrective action

Target Levels of Performance and Feedback

Now that we have covered the different types of measures and how to choose them, let us turn our attention to how mangers set and measure target levels of performance.

Choosing Target Levels of Performance

Historical-cost-based accounting measures are usually inadequate for evaluating economic returns on new investments and, in some cases, create disincentives for expansion. Despite these problems, managers can use historical-cost ROIs to evaluate current performance by establishing meaningful *target* ROIs. For Hospitality Inns, we need to recognize that the hotels were built in different years, which means they were built at different construction-price levels. The firm could adjust the target historical-cost-based ROIs accordingly, say, by setting San Francisco's ROI at 26%, Chicago's at 21%, and New Orleans' at 19%.

This useful alternative of comparing actual results with targeted, or budgeted, results is often overlooked, but should not be. *Companies should tailor and negotiate a budget for a particular subunit, a particular accounting system, and a particular performance measure while keeping in mind the pitfalls of using historical-cost accounting.* For example, many problems related to valuing assets and measuring income can be resolved if top managers can get subunit managers to focus on what is attainable in the forthcoming budget period—whether ROI, RI, or EVA is used and whether the financial measures are based on historical costs or some other measure, such as current costs.

A popular way to establish targets is to set continuous improvement targets. If a company is using EVA as a performance measure, the firm can evaluate operations on the year-to-year changes in EVA, rather than on absolute measures of EVA. Evaluating performance on the basis of *improvements* in EVA makes the initial method of calculating the measure less important.

Companies using balanced scorecards establish targets for financial performance measures, while simultaneously setting targets in the customer, internal-business-process, and learning-and-growth perspectives. For example, Hospitality Inns will establish targets for employee training and satisfaction, customer-service times for reservations and check-in, the quality of room service, and customer satisfaction levels that each hotel must reach to achieve its ROI and EVA targets.

Choosing the Timing of Feedback

A final step in designing accounting-based performance measures is the timing of performance feedback, which depends largely on (1) how critical the information is for the success of the organization, (2) the management level receiving the feedback, and (3) the sophistication of the organization's information technology. For example, hotel managers responsible for room sales want information on the number of rooms sold (rented) on a daily or weekly basis because a large percentage of hotel costs are fixed costs. Achieving high room sales and taking quick action to reverse any declining sales trends are critical to the financial success of each hotel. The company's top managers, however, might look at information about daily room sales only on a monthly basis unless there is a problem, like the low sales-to-total-assets ratio the Chicago hotel has. In this case, the managers might ask for the information weekly.

DECISION POINT

What targets should companies use, and when should they give feedback to managers regarding their performance relative to these targets?

Similarly, human resources managers at each hotel measure employee satisfaction annually because satisfaction is best measured over a longer horizon. However, housekeeping department managers measure the quality of room service over much shorter time horizons, such as a week, because poor levels of performance in these areas for even a short period of time can harm a hotel's reputation for a long period. Moreover, managers can detect and resolve housekeeping problems over a short time period.

LEARNING OBJECTIVE 5

Indicate the difficulties that occur when the performance of divisions operating in different countries is compared

... adjustments needed for differences in inflation rates and changes in exchange rates

Performance Measurement in Multinational Companies

Our discussion so far has focused on performance evaluation of different divisions of a company operating within a single country. We next discuss the additional difficulties created when managers compare the performance of divisions of a company operating in different countries. Several issues arise.[9]

[9] See M. Zafar Iqbal, *International Accounting: A Global Perspective* (Cincinnati: South-Western College Publishing, 2002).

- The economic, legal, political, social, and cultural environments differ significantly across countries. Operating a division in an open economy like Australia is very different from operating in a closed economy such as Venezuela, where the government controls prices and threatens to nationalize industries.
- Import quotas and tariffs range widely from country to country, and it's not unusual for countries to impose custom duties to restrict the imports of certain goods.
- The availability of materials and skilled labor as well as the costs of materials, labor, and infrastructure (power, transportation, and communication) also differ significantly across countries. Companies operating in Indonesia, for example, must spend 30% of their total production costs on transportation, whereas these costs account for just 12% of total spending in China.
- Divisions operating in different countries account for their performance in different currencies, and inflation and fluctuations in foreign-currency exchange rates affect performance measurement. For example, economies such as Argentina, Myanmar, and Nigeria suffer from double-digit inflation, which dampens the performance of divisions in those countries when their results are measured in dollars.

As a result of these differences, adjustments need to be made to accurately compare the performance of divisions in different countries.

Calculating a Foreign Division's ROI in the Foreign Currency

Suppose Hospitality Inns invests in a hotel in Mexico City. The investment consists mainly of the costs of buildings and furnishings. Also assume the following:

- The exchange rate at the time of Hospitality Inns' investment on December 31, 2019, is 20 pesos = $1.
- During 2020, the Mexican peso continues its steady decline in its value. The exchange rate on December 31, 2020, is 30 pesos = $1.
- The average exchange rate during 2020 is $[(20 + 30) \div 2] = 25$ pesos = $1.
- The investment (total assets) in the Mexico City hotel is 30,000,000 pesos.
- The operating income of the Mexico City hotel in 2020 is 6,000,000 pesos.

What is the historical-cost-based ROI for the Mexico City hotel in 2020?

To answer this question, Hospitality Inns' managers first have to determine whether they should calculate the ROI in pesos or in dollars. If they calculate the ROI in dollars, what exchange rate should they use? The managers may also be interested in how the ROI of Hospitality Inns Mexico City (HIMC) compares with the ROI of Hospitality Inns New Orleans (HINO), which is also a relatively new hotel of approximately the same size. The answers to these questions yield information that will be helpful when making future investment decisions.

$$\text{HIMC's } ROI \text{ (calculated using pesos)} = \frac{\text{Operating income}}{\text{Total assets}} = \frac{6{,}000{,}000 \text{ pesos}}{30{,}000{,}000 \text{ pesos}} = 0.20, \text{ or } 20\%$$

HIMC's ROI of 20% is higher than HINO's ROI of 17% (page 926). Does this mean that HIMC outperformed HINO based on the ROI criterion? Not necessarily. That's because HIMC operates in a very different economic environment than HINO.

The peso has declined in value relative to the dollar in 2020. This decline has led to higher inflation in Mexico than in the United States. As a result of the higher inflation in Mexico, HIMC will charge higher prices for its hotel rooms, which will increase HIMC's operating income and lead to a higher ROI. Inflation clouds the real economic returns on an asset and makes historical-cost-based ROI higher. Differences in inflation rates between the two countries make a direct comparison of HIMC's peso-denominated ROI with HINO's dollar-denominated ROI misleading.

Calculating a Foreign Division's ROI in U.S. Dollars

One way to make a comparison of historical-cost-based ROIs more meaningful is to restate HIMC's performance in U.S. dollars. But what exchange rate should the managers use to make the comparison meaningful? Assume HIMC's operating income was earned evenly throughout 2020. Hospitality Inns' managers should use the average exchange rate of 25 pesos = \$1 to convert the operating income from pesos to dollars: 6,000,000 pesos ÷ 25 pesos per dollar = \$240,000. The effect of dividing the operating income in pesos by the higher pesos-to-dollar exchange rate prevailing during 2020, rather than the 20 pesos = \$1 exchange rate on December 31, 2019, is that any increase in operating income in pesos as a result of inflation during 2020 is eliminated when converting back to dollars.

At what rate should HIMC's total assets of 30,000,000 pesos be converted? They should be converted at the 20 pesos = \$1 exchange rate, which was the exchange rate when the assets were acquired on December 31, 2019. Why? Because HIMC's assets are recorded in pesos at the December 31, 2019, cost, and the assets are not revalued as a result of inflation in Mexico in 2020. Since the subsequent inflation does not affect the cost of assets in HIMC's financial accounting records, managers should use the exchange rate prevailing on the date the assets were acquired to convert the assets into dollars. Using exchange rates after December 31, 2019, would be incorrect because these exchange rates incorporate the higher inflation in Mexico in 2020. HIMC's total assets are therefore \$1,500,000 (30,000,000 pesos ÷ 20 pesos per dollar).

Then

$$\text{HIMC's } ROI \text{ (calculated using dollars)} = \frac{\text{Operating income}}{\text{Total assets}} = \frac{\$240{,}000}{\$1{,}500{,}000} = 0.16, \text{ or } 16\%$$

With these adjustments, the historical-cost-based ROIs of the Mexico City and New Orleans hotels are comparable because they negate the effects of differential inflation rates in the two countries. Now HIMC's ROI is less than HINO's (16% versus HINO's ROI of 17%).

Calculating residual income in pesos poses the same problems as calculating the ROI in pesos does. Calculating HIMC's RI in dollars adjusts for changes in exchange rates and makes for more-meaningful comparisons with Hospitality's other hotels:

DECISION POINT

How can companies compare the performance of divisions operating in different countries?

$$\begin{aligned}\text{HIMC's } RI &= \$240{,}000 - (0.12 \times \$1{,}500{,}000)\\ &= \$240{,}000 - \$180{,}000 = \$60{,}000\end{aligned}$$

which is also less than HINO's RI of \$150,000.

Keep in mind that HIMC's and HINO's ROIs and RIs are historical-cost-based calculations. However, both hotels are relatively new, so this is less of a concern.

TRY IT! 24-4

Vinci Corporation has a division in the United States and another in France. The investment in the French assets was made when the exchange rate was \$1.36 per euro. The average exchange rate for the year was \$1.43 per euro. The exchange rate at the end of the fiscal year was \$1.50 per euro. Income and investment for the two divisions are as follows:

	United States	France
Investment in assets	\$3,500,000	€2,900,000
Income for current year	\$ 472,500	€ 394,400

The required return for Vinci is 11%. Calculate ROI and RI for the two divisions in their local currencies. For the French division, also calculate these measures in dollars. Which division is doing better?

Distinguishing the Performance of Managers From the Performance of Their Subunits[10]

LEARNING OBJECTIVE 6

Understand the roles of salaries and incentives when rewarding managers

...balancing risk and performance-based rewards

Our focus has been on how to evaluate the performance of a subunit of a company, such as a division. If the subunit performed well, does it mean the manager performed well? In this section, we argue that a company should distinguish between the performance evaluation of a *manager* and the performance evaluation of that manager's *subunit*. For example, companies often put their most skillful manager in charge of the division producing the poorest economic return in an attempt to improve it. But turning around a subunit may take years, and the relative underperformance of the division during that time is no reflection of the performance of the manager.

As another example, consider again the Hospitality Inns Mexico City (HIMC) hotel. Suppose, despite the high inflation in Mexico, HIMC could not increase its room prices due to price-control regulations imposed by the government. HIMC's performance in dollar terms would be poor because of the decline in the value of the peso. But should top managers conclude that the HIMC manager performed poorly? Probably not. The poor performance of HIMC is largely the result of regulatory and economic factors beyond the manager's control.

In the following sections, we show the basic principles for evaluating the performance of an individual subunit manager. Later sections consider the principles that apply to rank-and-file employees and those that apply to top executives. We illustrate these principles using the RI performance measure.

The Basic Tradeoff: Creating Incentives Versus Imposing Risk

How companies measure and evaluate the performance of managers and other employees typically affects their compensation. Compensation arrangements range from a flat salary with no performance-based incentive (or bonus), as in the case of many government employees, to rewards based solely on performance, as in the case of real estate agents who are paid only via commissions on the properties they sell. The total compensation for most managers includes some combination of salary and performance-based incentive. In designing compensation arrangements, we need to consider the *tradeoff between creating incentives and imposing risk.* We illustrate this tradeoff in the context of our Hospitality Inns example.

Indra Chungi owns the Hospitality Inns chain of hotels. Roger Brett manages the Hospitality Inns San Francisco (HISF) hotel. Assume Chungi uses RI to measure performance. To improve the hotel's RI, Chungi would like Brett to increase its sales, control its costs, provide prompt and courteous customer service, and reduce the hotel's working capital. But even if Brett did all those things, a high RI is not guaranteed. HISF's RI is affected by many factors beyond Chungi's and Brett's control, such as road construction near the hotel that would make it difficult for customers to get to it or an earthquake in the San Francisco Bay Area that would make people reluctant to travel to the region.

As an entrepreneur, Chungi expects to bear risk. But Brett does not like being subjected to risk. One way of "insuring" Brett against risk is to pay him a flat salary, regardless of the actual amount of RI the San Francisco hotel earns. Chungi would then bear all of the risk. This arrangement creates a problem, however, because Brett's effort is difficult to monitor. The absence of performance-based compensation means that Brett has no direct incentive to work harder or to undertake extra physical and mental effort beyond what is necessary to hold on to his job.

Moral hazard describes a situation in which an employee prefers to exert less effort compared with the effort the owner desires because the owner cannot accurately monitor and enforce the employee's effort.[11] Moral hazard also occurs when an employee reports inaccurate or distorted information for personal benefit because the owner cannot monitor the validity

[10] The presentations here draw (in part) from teaching notes prepared by S. Huddart, N. Melumad, and S. Reichelstein.

[11] The term *moral hazard* originated in insurance contracts to represent situations in which insurance coverage caused insured parties to take less care of their properties than they might otherwise. One response to moral hazard in insurance contracts is the system of deductibles (that is, the insured parties pay for damages below a specified amount).

of the reported information. Repetitive jobs, as in electronic assembly, are relatively straightforward to monitor and so are less subject to moral hazard. However, a manager's job, which is to gather and interpret information and exercise judgment on the basis of the information obtained, is more difficult to monitor.

Paying no salary and rewarding Brett *only* on the basis of some performance measure—RI in our example—raises different concerns. In this case, Brett would be motivated to strive to increase the hotel's RI because his rewards would increase. But compensating Brett on RI also subjects him to risk because HISF's RI depends not only on Brett's effort, but also on factors such as local economic conditions over which Brett has no control.

Brett does not like being subjected to risk. To compensate Brett for taking risk, Chungi must pay him extra compensation. That is, using performance-based bonuses will cost Chungi more money, *on average*, than paying Brett a flat salary. Why "on average"? Because Chungi's compensation payment to Brett will vary with RI outcomes. When averaged over these outcomes, the RI-based compensation will cost Chungi more than paying Brett a flat salary. The motivation for having some salary and some performance-based compensation is to balance the benefit of incentives against the extra cost of imposing risk on a manager.

Intensity of Incentives and Financial and Nonfinancial Measurements

What affects the intensity of incentives? That is, how large should the incentive component of a manager's compensation be relative to the salary component? To answer these questions, we need to understand how much the performance measure is affected by the actions the manager takes to further the owner's objectives.

Preferred performance measures are those that are sensitive to or that change significantly with the manager's performance. They do not change much with changes in factors that are beyond the manager's control. Sensitive performance measures motivate the manager and limit the manager's exposure to risk, thereby reducing the cost of providing incentives. Less-sensitive performance measures are not affected by the manager's performance and fail to induce the manager to exert effort. The more owners have access to sensitive performance measures, the more they can rely on incentive compensation for their managers.

The salary component of compensation dominates when performance measures that are sensitive to managers' actions are not available. This is the case, for example, for some corporate staff and government employees. A high salary component, however, does not mean incentives are completely absent. Promotions and salary increases do depend on some overall measure of performance, but the incentives are less direct. The incentive component of compensation is high when sensitive performance measures are available and when directly monitoring the employee's effort is difficult, such as in real estate agencies.

To evaluate Brett, Chungi uses measures from multiple perspectives of the balanced scorecard because nonfinancial measures in the scorecard—employee satisfaction and the time taken for check-in, cleaning rooms, and providing room service—are more sensitive to Brett's actions. Financial measures such as RI are less sensitive to Brett's actions because they are affected by external factors, such as local economic conditions, beyond Brett's control. Residual income may capture the economic viability of the hotel, but it is only a partial measure of Brett's performance.

In addition to considerations of sensitivity and risk, another reason for using nonfinancial measures is that these measures follow Hospitality Inns' strategy and are drivers of future performance. Evaluating managers on these nonfinancial measures motivates them to take actions that will sustain the long-run financial performance of the firm's hotels while meeting the company's environmental and social goals. Therefore, evaluating performance in all four perspectives of the balanced scorecard promotes actions aimed at both the short and the long run. The relative weight placed on the various measures in the scorecard is ideally aimed at achieving congruence between the extent to which the manager is motivated to maximize each performance metric and its importance in generating the long-run objective the firm wishes to achieve. The tradeoff between considerations of sensitivity and risk, on the one hand, and the congruence of goals, on the other, determines the effective intensity of incentives placed on each measure of performance. Concepts in Action: Performance Measurement at Unilever illustrates the use of multiple measures to motivate a CEO to balance financial and nonfinancial (health and environmental sustainability) goals.

CONCEPTS IN ACTION: Performance Measurement at Unilever[12]

Kristoffer Tripplaar/Alamy Stock Photo

Managers and boards of directors are often pushed to focus intently on a single measure of success, such as shareholder value or profit, and then do everything they can to maximize it. As a result, they can overlook other important measures, which can do long-term damage to a company.

Unilever, the Anglo-Dutch manufacturer of Axe body spray and Lipton tea, has taken a different approach under chief executive officer Paul Polman. On Polman's first day as CEO, Unilever did away with earnings guidance and quarterly reporting in order to refocus the company's metrics on the long-term needs of a full range of stakeholders. And in 2012, Unilever launched an ambitious plan to double revenue by 2020 while halving the company's environmental impact.

Dubbed the Unilever Sustainable Living Plan, the company is working to decouple financial growth from its impact on the environment and global health. Unilever's ambitious goals include improving financial performance while slashing its environmental footprint by 50%, sourcing 100% of its raw materials sustainably, and helping more than a billion people improve their health and well-being. Assessing the impact of its commitment means Unilever not only measures success based on its financial performance—including annual revenue, year-over-year revenue growth, and operating margin—but also how many calories it cuts from its ice cream products and how much of its energy use is derived from renewable sources.

Initially, investors took a dim view of Unilever's shift in perspective, punishing the stock price. But it quickly rebounded, after analysts and shareholders accepted Polman's wider lens. When Polman retired at the end of 2018, the company had more than 160,000 employees worldwide, had annual revenue of €51 billion, and delivered a total shareholder return of 290% during his tenure.

[12] *Sources:* Graham Kenny, "The False Promise of the Single Metric," HBR.org, August 26, 2015 (https://hbr.org/2015/08/the-false-promise-of-the-single-metric); Adi Ignatius, "Captain Planet," *Harvard Business Review*, June 2012 (https://hbr.org/2012/06/captain-planet); Graham Ruddick, "Unilever CEO Paul Polman–The Optimistic Pessimist," *The Guardian*, January 25, 2016 (https://www.theguardian.com/business/2016/jan/25/unilever-ceo-paul-polman-the-optimistic-pessimist); Andy Boynton and Margareta Barchan, "Unilever's Paul Polman: CEOs Can't Be 'Slaves' to Shareholders," Forbes.com, July 20, 2015 (https://www.forbes.com/sites/andyboynton/2015/07/20/unilevers-paul-polman-ceos-cant-be-slaves-to-shareholders/#33e41372561e); "Unilever CEO Announcement: Paul Polman to Retire; Alan Jope Appointed as Successor," Unilever PLC press release, London, United Kingdom/Rotterdam, Netherlands, November 29, 2018 (https://www.unilever.com/news/press-releases/2018/unilever-ceo-announcement.html.

Benchmarks and Relative Performance Evaluation

Owners often use financial and nonfinancial benchmarks to evaluate the performance of their managers. The benchmarks, which correspond to the best practices of organizations, may be available inside or outside of the organization. For HISF, the benchmarks could be from similar hotels, either within or outside of the Hospitality Inns chain. Suppose Brett is responsible for HISF's revenues, costs, and investments. To evaluate Brett's performance, Chungi would want to benchmark a similar-sized hotel—one affected by the same uncontrollable factors, such as location, demographic trends, or economic conditions, that affect HISF. If all these factors were the same or very similar, the *differences* in the performances of the two hotels could, for the most part, be attributed to the differences in the two managers' performances. Benchmarking, which is also called *relative performance evaluation*, filters out the effects of common uncontrollable factors.

Can the performance of two managers responsible for running similar operations within a company be benchmarked against each other? Yes, but this approach could create a problem: It could reduce the managers' incentives to help one another. When managers do not cooperate, the company suffers. In this case, using internal benchmarks for performance evaluation may not lead to goal congruence.

Performance Measures at the Individual Activity Level

Managers face two challenges when designing measures to evaluate the performance of individual employees: (1) designing performance measures for activities that require multiple tasks and (2) designing performance measures for team activities.

Performing Multiple Tasks

Most employees perform more than one task as part of their jobs. Marketing representatives sell products, provide customer support, and gather market information. Manufacturing workers are responsible for both the quantity and quality of their output. Employers want employees to allocate their time and effort intelligently among various tasks or aspects of their jobs.

Consider mechanics at an auto repair shop. Their jobs have two distinct aspects: repair work—performing more repair work generates more revenues for the shop—and customer satisfaction—the higher the quality of the job, the more likely the customer will be pleased. If the employer wants an employee to focus on both aspects, then the employer must measure and compensate performance on both aspects.

Suppose the employer can easily measure the quantity, but not the quality, of auto repairs. If the employer rewards workers on a by-the-job rate, which pays workers only on the basis of the number of repairs actually performed, mechanics will likely increase the number of repairs they make and quality will suffer. Sears Auto Center experienced this problem when it introduced by-the-job rates for its mechanics. To resolve the problem, Sears took three steps to motivate workers to balance both quantity and quality: (1) The company dropped the by-the-job rate system and paid mechanics an hourly salary, a step that de-emphasized the quantity of repairs. Managers determined mechanics' bonuses, promotions, and pay increases by assessing each mechanic's overall quantity and quality of repairs. (2) Sears evaluated employees, in part, using the number of dissatisfied customers, the number of customer complaints, and data gathered from customer satisfaction surveys. (3) Finally, Sears used staff from an independent outside agency to randomly monitor whether the repairs performed were of high quality.

Team-Based Compensation Arrangements

Many manufacturing, marketing, and design problems can be resolved when employees with multiple skills, knowledge, experiences, and perceptions pool their talents. A team achieves better results than individual employees acting alone.[13] Many companies reward employees on teams based on how well their teams perform. Team-based incentives encourage individuals to help one another as they strive toward a common goal.

The specific forms of team-based compensation vary across companies. Colgate-Palmolive rewards teams based on each team's performance. Novartis, the Swiss pharmaceutical company, rewards teams based on the company's overall performance; some team-based bonuses are paid only if the company reaches certain goals. Whether team-based compensation is desirable depends, to a large extent, on the culture and management style of a particular organization. One criticism of team-based compensation is that it diminishes the incentives of individual employees, which can harm a firm's overall performance. Another problem is how to manage team members who are not productive contributors to the team's success but who, nevertheless, share in the team's rewards. Survey evidence suggests that a majority of employees are not motivated by team-based bonuses once team size surpasses five. Familiarity with team members is also important in sustaining the value of team-based compensation.

Executive Performance Measures and Compensation

The principles of performance evaluation described in the previous sections also apply to executive compensation plans. These plans are based on both financial and nonfinancial performance measures and consist of a mix of (1) base salary; (2) annual incentives, such as a cash bonus based on achieving a target annual RI; (3) long-run incentives, such as stock options (described later in this section) based on a stock's performance over, say, a 4-year period; and (4) other benefits, such as medical benefits, pension plans, and life insurance.

Well-designed plans use a compensation mix that balances risk (the effect of uncontrollable factors on the performance measures and hence compensation) with short-run and long-run incentives. For example, an evaluation based on a firm's annual EVA sharpens an executive's short-run focus. Using EVA and stock option plans over, say, 4 years motivates the executive to take a long-run view as well.

---

[13] *Teams That Click: The Results-Driven Manager Series* (Boston: Harvard Business School Press, 2004).

Stock options give executives the right to buy company stock at a specified price (called the exercise price) within a specified period. Suppose that on July 1, 2019, Hospitality Inns gave its CEO the option to buy 200,000 shares of the company's stock at any time between June 30, 2023 and June 30, 2026, at the July 1, 2019, market price of $49 per share. Let's say Hospitality Inns' stock price rises to $69 per share on March 24, 2024, and the CEO exercises options on all 200,000 shares. The CEO would earn $20 per share ($69 − $49) on 200,000 shares, or $4 million. Alternatively, if Hospitality Inns' stock price stays below $49 during the entire 7-year period, the CEO will simply forgo the right to buy the shares. By linking CEO compensation to increases in the company's stock price, the stock option plan motivates the CEO to improve the company's long-run performance and stock price.

The Securities and Exchange Commission (SEC) requires detailed disclosures of the compensation arrangements of top-level executives. For example, in 2019, Hyatt Hotels Corporation, one of the world's leading hospitality companies, disclosed a compensation table showing the salaries, bonuses, stock options, stock awards, and other compensation earned by its top five executives during the 2016, 2017, and 2018 fiscal years. Hyatt also disclosed the peer companies it uses to set the pay for its executives and conduct performance comparisons. These companies include competitors in the hospitality industry such as Hilton, Marriott, and Wyndham. The list also includes companies with similar revenues, brand strength, global presence, or business models, as well as firms with which Hyatt competes for executive talent. Examples are Carnival, Starbucks, and Wendy's. Investors use this information to evaluate the relationship between compensation and performance across companies generally and across companies operating in similar industries.

SEC rules require companies to disclose the principles underlying their executive compensation plans. In its financial statements, Hyatt describes some of its compensation principles. They include motivating through the alignment of total rewards with performance goals; offering compelling opportunities in order to attract, retain and develop talent globally; and staying cost effective and financially sustainable over time. The SEC also compels companies to disclose the performance criteria—such as a firm's profitability, revenue growth, and market share—used to reward executives. Hyatt uses adjusted earnings before interest, tax, depreciation, and amortization (EBITDA), relative to goal, as the primary basis for annual incentive pay, and performance on metrics tied to four strategic priorities as the secondary basis. The Compensation Committee of the board of directors then reviews each executive's contributions on individual metrics related to areas of responsibility in setting the final pay award. Hyatt also provides long-term equity-based incentives tied directly to both the company's stock price performance (e.g., grants of restricted stock) and multiyear adjusted EBITDA goals. For fiscal years starting in 2017, the SEC has mandated an additional disclosure for public companies—the ratio of the CEO's annual total compensation to that of the median employee. For 2018, Hyatt reported a ratio of 356 (the average ratio across the S&P 500 was 287 to 1).

The Dodd-Frank law was passed in 2010 in response to the financial crisis of 2007–2009 and requires companies to provide shareholders with an advisory (nonbinding) vote on executive compensation. These "say-on-pay" votes must be held at least once every 3 years. This law has reshaped the way companies create, disclose, and communicate their executive compensation policies. To date, however, they have not slowed down growth in executive pay or indicated much shareholder dissatisfaction with compensation plans. In 2018, a record 2.5% of the Russell 3000 companies failed their say-on-pay votes. However, this number is still relatively small, and over 76% of companies received greater than 90% support.

DECISION POINT

Why are managers compensated based on a mix of salary and incentives?

LEARNING OBJECTIVE 7

Describe the four levers of control and why they are necessary

... boundary, belief, and interactive control systems counterbalance diagnostic control systems

Strategy and Levers of Control[14]

Financial and nonfinancial performance-evaluation measures help managers track their progress toward achieving a company's strategic goals. Because these measures help diagnose whether a company is performing to expectations, they are collectively called **diagnostic control systems**. Companies motivate managers by holding them accountable for and by rewarding them for

[14] For a more detailed discussion, see Robert Simons, *Levers of Control: How Managers Use Innovative Control Systems to Drive Strategic Renewal* (Boston: Harvard Business School Press, 1995).

meeting these goals. It's not unusual for managers to cut corners and misreport numbers to make their performance look better than it is, as happened at companies such as Enron, WorldCom, Tyco, and Health South. To prevent unethical and outright fraudulent behavior, companies need to balance the push for performance resulting from diagnostic control systems, the first of four levers of control, with three other levers: *boundary systems, belief systems*, and *interactive control systems*. This will ensure that proper business ethics, inspirational values, and attention to future threats and opportunities are not sacrificed while achieving business results.

Boundary Systems

Boundary systems describe standards of behavior and codes of conduct expected of all employees, especially actions that are off-limits. Ethical behavior on the part of managers is paramount. In particular, numbers that subunit managers' report should not be tainted by "cooking the books." The books should be free of, for example, overstated assets, understated liabilities, fictitious revenues, and understated costs.

Codes of business conduct signal appropriate and inappropriate individual behaviors. The following are excerpts from Caterpillar's "Code of Conduct":

> While we conduct our business within the framework of applicable laws and regulations, for us, compliance with the law is not enough. We strive for more than that.... We must not engage in activities that create, or even appear to create, conflict between our personal interests and the interests of the company.

Division managers who fail to adhere to legal or ethical accounting policies and procedures often rationalize their behavior by claiming they were under enormous pressure from top managers "to make the budget." A healthy amount of motivational pressure is desirable, as long as the "tone from the top" and the firm's code of conduct simultaneously communicate the absolute need for all managers to behave ethically at all times. Managers should also train employees to behave ethically. They should promptly and severely reprimand unethical conduct, regardless of the benefits that might accrue to the company from unethical actions. Some companies, such as Lockheed Martin, emphasize ethical behavior by routinely evaluating employees against the firm's code of ethics.

Many organizations also set explicit boundaries precluding actions that harm the environment. Environmental violations (such as water and air pollution) carry heavy fines and prison terms under the laws of the United States and other countries.

In many companies, the environmental responsibilities of employees extend beyond legal requirements. Some companies, such as DuPont, make environmental performance a line item on every employee's salary appraisal report. Duke Power Company appraises employees on measures such as reducing solid waste, cutting emissions and discharges, and implementing environmental plans. Socially responsible companies such as Best Buy, Campbell Soup, and Intel set aggressive environmental goals and measure and report their performance against them. German, Swiss, and Scandinavian companies report on environmental performance as part of a larger set of social responsibility disclosures (such as employee welfare and community development activities). Dutch financial services giant ING incorporates social, ethical, and environmental objectives as part of its top management's pay structure. Other firms in the Netherlands—including chemical company AkzoNobel, life sciences group DSM, and mail operator TNT—also tie executive compensation to environmental improvement.

More broadly, there is growing awareness of the empirical business case for embedding sustainability into corporate operations. As a result, companies are integrating sustainability into traditional governance practices, including board oversight, and through corporate policies and management systems. About a quarter of companies link executive pay to some sustainability metrics, with a smaller percent making explicit links between compensation practices and publicly disclosed sustainability targets. At materials company Alcoa, 30% of executive compensation is tied to safety, environmental stewardship (including greenhouse gas reductions), energy efficiency, and diversity goals. Energy provider Exelon has an innovative long-term performance share award that, among other nonfinancial goals, rewards executives for engaging stakeholders to help shape the company's public policy positions. Xcel Energy ties compensation to goals achieved in "demand-side management," that is, reductions in energy consumption by its customers.

Belief Systems

Belief systems articulate the mission, purpose, and core values of a company. They describe the accepted norms and patterns of behavior expected of all managers and other employees when interacting with one another, shareholders, customers, and communities. For example, Johnson & Johnson describes its values and norms in a credo statement that is intended to inspire all managers and other employees to do their best.[15] Belief systems play to employees' *intrinsic motivation*, the desire to achieve self-satisfaction for performing well regardless of external rewards such as bonuses or promotion. Intrinsic motivation comes from being given greater responsibility, doing interesting and creative work, having pride in doing that work, making a commitment to the organization, and developing personal bonds with one's coworkers. High intrinsic motivation enhances a firm's performance because managers and workers feel a sense of achievement in doing something important, feel satisfied with their jobs, and see opportunities for personal growth.

Interactive Control Systems

Interactive control systems are formal information systems managers use to focus the company's attention and learning on key strategic issues. Managers use interactive control systems to create an ongoing dialogue around these key issues and to personally involve themselves in the decision-making activities of subordinates. An excessive focus on diagnostic control systems and critical performance variables can cause an organization to ignore emerging threats and opportunities—changes in technology, customer preferences, regulations, and competitors that can undercut a business. Interactive control systems help prevent this problem by highlighting and tracking strategic uncertainties businesses face, such as the emergence of digital imaging in the case of Kodak and Fujifilm, airline deregulation in the case of American Airlines, and the shift in customer preferences toward open-source Android operating systems in the case of BlackBerry. The key to this control lever is frequent face-to-face communications among managers and employees regarding these critical uncertainties. The result is ongoing discussion and debate about assumptions and action plans. New strategies emerge from the dialogue and debate surrounding the interactive process. Interactive control systems force busy managers to step back from the actions needed to manage the business today and to shift their focus forward to positioning the organization for the opportunities and threats of tomorrow.

DECISION POINT

What are the four levers of control, and why does a company need to implement them?

[15] A full statement of the credo can be accessed at www.jnj.com/about-jnj/jnj-credo.

PROBLEM FOR SELF-STUDY

The baseball division of Home Run Sports manufactures and sells baseballs. Assume production equals sales. Budgeted data for February 2020 are as follows:

Current assets	$ 400,000
Long-term assets	600,000
Total assets	$1,000,000
Production output	200,000 baseballs per month
Target ROI (Operating income ÷ Total assets)	30%
Fixed costs	$ 400,000 per month
Variable cost	$ 4 per baseball

1. Compute the minimum selling price per baseball necessary to achieve the target ROI of 30%.
2. Using the selling price from requirement 1, separate the target ROI into its two components using the DuPont method.

3. Compute the RI of the baseball division for February 2020, using the selling price from requirement 1. Home Run Sports uses a required rate of return of 12% on total division assets when computing division RI.
4. In addition to her salary, Amanda Kelly, the division manager, receives 3% of the monthly RI of the baseball division as a bonus. Compute Kelly's bonus. Why do you think Kelly is rewarded using both salary and a performance-based bonus? Kelly does not like bearing risk.

Solution

1.

$$\text{Target operating income} = 30\% \text{ of } \$1{,}000{,}000 \text{ of total assets}$$
$$= \$300{,}000$$
$$\text{Let } P = \text{Selling price}$$
$$\text{Revenues} - \text{Variable costs} - \text{Fixed costs} = \text{Operating income}$$
$$200{,}000P - (200{,}000 \times \$4) - \$400{,}000 = \$300{,}000$$
$$200{,}000P = \$300{,}000 + \$800{,}000 + \$400{,}000$$
$$= \$1{,}500{,}000$$
$$P = \$7.50 \text{ per baseball}$$

Proof:	Revenues, 200,000 baseballs × $7.50/baseball	$1,500,000
	Variable costs, 200,000 baseballs × $4/baseball	800,000
	Contribution margin	700,000
	Fixed costs	400,000
	Operating income	$ 300,000

2. The DuPont method describes ROI as the product of two components: return on sales (income ÷ revenues) and investment turnover (revenues ÷ investment).

$$\frac{\text{Income}}{\text{Revenues}} \times \frac{\text{Revenues}}{\text{Investment}} = \frac{\text{Income}}{\text{Investment}}$$

$$\frac{\$300{,}000}{\$1{,}500{,}000} \times \frac{\$1{,}500{,}000}{\$1{,}000{,}000} = \frac{\$300{,}000}{\$1{,}000{,}000}$$

$$0.2 \times 1.5 = 0.30, \text{ or } 30\%$$

3.

$$RI = \text{Operating income} - \text{Required return on investment}$$
$$= \$300{,}000 - (0.12 \times \$1{,}000{,}000)$$
$$= \$300{,}000 - \$120{,}000$$
$$= \$180{,}000$$

4.

$$\text{Kelly's bonus} = 3\% \text{ of } RI$$
$$= 0.03 \times \$180{,}000 = \$5{,}400$$

The baseball division's RI is affected by many factors, such as general economic conditions, beyond Kelly's control. These uncontrollable factors make the baseball division's profitability uncertain and risky. Because Kelly does not like bearing risk, paying her a flat salary, regardless of RI, would shield her from this risk. But there is a moral-hazard problem with this compensation arrangement. Because Kelly's effort is difficult to monitor, the absence of performance-based compensation will provide her with no incentive to undertake extra physical and mental effort beyond what is necessary to retain her job or to uphold her personal values.

Paying no salary and rewarding Kelly only on the basis of RI provides her with incentives to work hard but also subjects her to excessive risk because of uncontrollable factors that will affect RI and hence Kelly's compensation. A compensation arrangement based only on RI would be costlier for Home Run Sports because it would have to compensate Kelly for taking on uncontrollable risk. A compensation arrangement that consists of both a salary and an RI-based performance bonus balances the benefits of incentives against the extra costs of imposing uncontrollable risk.

DECISION POINTS

The following question-and-answer format summarizes the chapter's learning objectives. Each decision presents a key question related to a learning objective. The guidelines are the answer to that question.

Decision	Guidelines
1. What financial and nonfinancial performance measures do companies use in their balanced scorecards?	Financial measures such as return on investment and residual income measure aspects of the performance of organizations and their subunits, managers, and employees. In many cases, financial measures are supplemented with nonfinancial measures of performance based on the customer, internal-business-process, and learning-and-growth perspectives of the balanced scorecard—for example, customer satisfaction, quality of products and services, employee satisfaction, and the achievement of environmental objectives.
2. What are the relative merits of return on investment (ROI), residual income (RI), and economic value added (EVA) as performance measures for subunit managers?	Return on investment (ROI) is the product of two components: income divided by revenues (return on sales) and revenues divided by investment (investment turnover). Managers can increase ROI by increasing revenues, decreasing costs, and decreasing the investment. But ROI may induce the managers of highly profitable divisions to reject projects in the firm's best interest because accepting the project reduces the ROI for their divisions. Residual income (RI) is income minus a dollar amount of required return on investment. RI is more likely than ROI to promote goal congruence. Evaluating managers on RI is also consistent with using the net present value method to choose long-term projects. Economic value added (EVA) is a variation of the RI calculation. It equals after-tax operating income minus the product of the (after-tax) weighted-average cost of capital and total assets minus current liabilities.
3. Over what time frame should companies measure performance, and what are the alternative choices for calculating the components of each performance measure?	A multiyear measure gives managers the incentive to consider the long-term consequences of their actions and prevents a myopic focus on short-run profits. When constructing accounting-based performance measures, firms must first define what constitutes investment. They must also choose whether the assets included in the investment calculations are measured at historical cost or current cost and whether depreciable assets are calculated at gross or net book value.
4. What targets should companies use, and when should they give feedback to managers regarding their performance relative to these targets?	Companies should tailor a budget to a particular subunit, a particular accounting system, and a particular performance measure. In general, asset valuation and income measurement problems can be overcome by emphasizing budgets and targets that stress continuous improvement. Timely feedback enables managers to implement actions that correct deviations from the target performance.
5. How can companies compare the performance of divisions operating in different countries?	Comparing the performance of divisions operating in different countries is difficult because of legal, political, social, economic, and currency differences. ROI and RI calculations for subunits operating in different countries need to be adjusted for differences in inflation between the two countries and changes in exchange rates.
6. Why are managers compensated based on a mix of salary and incentives?	Companies create incentives by rewarding managers on the basis of performance. But managers face risk because factors beyond their control may also affect their performance. Owners choose a mix of salary and incentive compensation to trade off the incentive benefit against the cost of imposing risk.

Decision	Guidelines
7. What are the four levers of control, and why does a company need to implement them?	The four levers of control are diagnostic control systems, boundary systems, belief systems, and interactive control systems. Implementing the four levers of control helps a company simultaneously strive for performance, behave ethically, inspire employees, and respond to strategic threats and opportunities.

TERMS TO LEARN

This chapter and the Glossary at the end of the text contain definitions of the following important terms:

belief systems (**p. 945**)
boundary systems (**p. 944**)
current cost (**p. 933**)
diagnostic control systems (**p. 943**)
economic value added (EVA) (**p. 929**)
imputed cost (**p. 927**)
interactive control systems (**p. 945**)
investment (**p. 925**)
moral hazard (**p. 939**)
residual income (RI) (**p. 927**)
return on investment (ROI) (**p. 925**)

ASSIGNMENT MATERIAL

Questions

24-1 Give examples of financial and nonfinancial performance measures that can be found in each of the four perspectives of the balanced scorecard.
24-2 What are the three steps in designing accounting-based performance measures?
24-3 What factors affecting ROI does the DuPont method of profitability analysis highlight?
24-4 "RI is not identical to ROI, although both measures incorporate income and investment into their computations." Do you agree? Explain.
24-5 Describe EVA.
24-6 Give three definitions of investment used in practice when computing ROI.
24-7 Distinguish between measuring assets based on current cost and historical cost.
24-8 What special problems arise when evaluating performance in multinational companies?
24-9 Why is it important to distinguish between the performance of a manager and the performance of the organization subunit for which the manager is responsible? Give an example.
24-10 Describe moral hazard.
24-11 "Managers should be rewarded only on the basis of their performance measures. They should be paid no salary." Do you agree? Explain.
24-12 Explain the role of benchmarking in evaluating managers.
24-13 Explain the incentive problems that can arise when employees must perform multiple tasks as part of their jobs.
24-14 Describe two disclosures required by the SEC with respect to executive compensation.
24-15 Describe the four levers of control.

Multiple-Choice Questions

In partnership with: BECKER PROFESSIONAL EDUCATION

24-16 During the current year, a strategic business unit (SBU) within Roke Inc. saw costs increase by $2 million, revenues increase by $4 million, and assets decrease by $1 million. SBUs are set up by Roke as follows:

I. Cost SBU
II. Revenue SBU
III. Profit SBU
IV. Investment SBU

Given the preceding numbers, an SBU manager will receive a favorable performance review if she is responsible for

a. I or IV only.
b. II or III only.
c. I, II, or IV only.
d. II, III, or IV only.

24-17 Assuming an increase in price levels over time, which of the following asset valuations will produce the highest return on assets?

a. Net book value
b. Gross book value
c. Replacement cost
d. Depreciated replacement cost

24-18 If ROI is used to evaluate a manager's performance for a relatively new division, which of the following measures for assets (or investment) will increase ROI?

a. Gross book value used instead of net book value.
b. Net book value using accelerated rather than straight-line depreciation.
c. Gross book value used instead of replacement cost, if gross book value is higher.
d. Replacement cost used instead of liquidation value, if replacement cost is higher.

24-19 The Long Haul Trucking Company is developing metrics for its drivers. The company computes variable costs of each load based upon miles driven and allocates fixed costs based upon time consumed. Load costing standards consider safe driving speeds and Department of Transportation regulations on hours of service (the amount of time the driver can be on duty or drive). The most effective metric for driver performance would likely be

a. Contribution per mile driven.
b. Gross margin per mile driven.
c. Achievement of delivered loads in allowed times.
d. Percentage increase in delivered loads below standard.

24-20 ABC Inc. wants to maintain a capital structure of 80% equity and 20% debt. They currently have an effective tax rate of 30%. The company's cost of equity capital is 12%. To obtain their debt financing, they issue bonds with an interest rate of 10%. What is the company's weighted average cost of capital?

a. 8.0%
b. 10.4%
c. 11.0%
d. 11.6%

Exercises

24-21 ROI, comparisons of three companies. (CMA, adapted) Return on investment (ROI) is often expressed as follows:

$$\frac{\text{Income}}{\text{Investment}} = \frac{\text{Income}}{\text{Revenues}} \times \frac{\text{Revenues}}{\text{Investment}}$$

Required

1. What advantages are there in the breakdown of the computation into two separate components?
2. Fill in the blanks for the following table:

	Companies in the Same Industry		
	A	B	C
Revenues	$1,600,000	$1,300,000	?
Income	$ 96,000	$ 78,000	?
Investment	$ 800,000	?	$2,600,000
Income as a percentage of revenues	?	?	1.5%
Investment turnover	?	?	2.0
ROI	?	3%	?

After filling in the blanks, comment on the relative performance of these companies as thoroughly as the data permit.

24-22 Analysis of return on invested assets, comparison of two divisions, DuPont method. Online Learning, Inc. has two divisions: Test Preparation and Language Arts. Results (in millions) for the past 3 years are partially displayed here:

	A	B	C	D	E	F	G
1		Operating Income	Operating Revenues	Total Assets	Operating Income/ Operating Revenues	Operating Revenues/ Total Assets	Operating Income/ Total Assets
2	Test Preparation Division						
3	2018	$ 720	$ 9,000	$1,800	?	?	?
4	2019	840	?	?	10%	?	48%
5	2020	1,110	?	?	13%	4	?
6	Language Arts Division						
7	2018	$ 660	$ 3,000	$2,000	?	?	?
8	2019	?	4,000	2,500	20.5%	?	?
9	2020	?	?	2,950	?	1.6	20%
10	Online Learning Inc.						
11	2018	$1,380	$12,000	$3,800	?	?	?
12	2019	?	?	?	?	?	?
13	2020	?	?	?	?	?	?

Required

1. Complete the table by filling in the blanks.
2. Use the DuPont method of profitability analysis to explain changes in the operating-income-to-total-assets ratios over the 2018–2020 period for each division and for Online Learning as a whole. Comment on the results.

24-23 ROI and RI. (D. Kleespie, adapted) The Quality Athletics Company produces a wide variety of sports equipment. Its newest division, Golf Technology, manufactures and sells a single product—AccuDriver, a golf club that uses global positioning satellite technology to improve the accuracy of golfers' shots. The demand for AccuDriver is relatively insensitive to price changes. The following data are available for Golf Technology, which is an investment center for Quality Athletics:

Total annual fixed costs	$32,000,000
Variable cost per AccuDriver	$ 700
Number of AccuDrivers sold each year	165,000
Average operating assets invested in the division	$55,000,000

Required

1. Compute Golf Technology's ROI if the selling price of AccuDrivers is $930 per club.
2. If management requires an ROI of at least 25% from the division, what is the minimum selling price that the Golf Technology Division should charge per AccuDriver club?
3. Assume that Quality Athletics judges the performance of its investment centers on the basis of RI rather than ROI. What is the minimum selling price that Golf Technology should charge per AccuDriver if the company's required rate of return is 20%?

24-24 ROI, RI, measurement of assets. Carter Corporation recently announced a bonus plan to be awarded to the manager of its most profitable division. The three division managers are to choose whether ROI or RI will be used to measure profitability. In addition, they must decide whether investment will be measured using gross book value or net book value of assets. Carter defines income as operating income and investment as total assets. The following information is available for the year just ended:

Division	Gross Book Value of Assets	Accumulated Depreciation	Operating Income
Rosemont	$1,200,000	$645,000	$142,050
Evanston	1,140,000	615,000	137,550
Marietta	750,000	420,000	92,100

Carter uses a required rate of return of 10% on investment to calculate RI.

Required

Each division manager has selected a method of bonus calculation that ranks his or her division number one. Identify the method for calculating profitability that each manager selected, supporting your answer with appropriate calculations. Comment on the strengths and weaknesses of the methods chosen by each manager.

24-25 ROI and RI with manufacturing costs. Fabulous Motor Company makes electric model cars and has two products, the Simplegreen and the Fabulousgreen. To produce the Simplegreen, Fabulous Motor employed assets of $11,250,000 at the beginning of 2020 and $4,790,000 of assets at the end of 2020. Other costs to manufacture the Simplegreen include the following:

Direct materials	$2,000 per unit
Setup	$ 800 per setup-hour
Production	$ 290 per machine-hour

General administration and selling costs for Simplegreen total $6,230,000 in 2020. During the year, Fabulous Motor produced 16,000 Simplegreen cars using 5,000 setup-hours and 178,500 machine-hours. It sold these cars for $6,000 each.

Required

1. Assuming that Fabulous Motor defines investment as average assets during the period, what is the return on investment for the Simplegreen division?
2. Calculate the residual income for Simplegreen if Fabulous Motor has a required rate of return of 8% on investments.

24-26 ROI, RI, EVA. Hamilton Corp. is a reinsurance and financial services company. Hamilton strongly believes in evaluating the performance of its stand-alone divisions using financial metrics such as ROI and residual income. For the year ended December 31, 2020, Hamilton's chief financial officer (CFO) received the following information about the performance of the property/casualty division:

Sales revenues	$ 900,000
Operating income	225,000
Total assets	1,500,000
Current liabilities	300,000
Debt (interest rate: 5%)	400,000
Common equity (book value)	500,000

For the purposes of divisional performance evaluation, Hamilton defines investment as total assets and income as operating income (that is, income before interest and taxes). The firm pays a flat rate of 25% in taxes on its income.

Required

1. What was the net income after taxes of the property/casualty division?
2. What was the division's ROI for the year?
3. Based on Hamilton's required rate of return of 8%, what was the property/casualty division's residual income for 2020?
4. Hamilton's CFO has heard about EVA and is curious about whether it might be a better measure to use for evaluating division managers. Hamilton's four divisions have similar risk characteristics. Hamilton's debt trades at book value while its equity has a market value approximately 150% that of its book value. The company's cost of equity capital is 10%. Calculate each of the following components of EVA for the property/casualty division, as well as the final EVA figure:
   a. Net operating profit after taxes
   b. Weighted-average cost of capital
   c. Investment, as measured for EVA calculations

24-27 ROI, loss-making division. Mary Jane is an upscale retailer for women's clothing with stores in many high-end shopping centers across the United States. In recent years, sales in most of the stores, especially the company's flagship store in the midtown of Manhattan, have been declining since Mary Jane is increasingly selling its clothing through its website. Not willing to give up on its flagship store, senior management at headquarters hired Susan Marcos 2 years ago to turn around the New York City store. The company is currently evaluating all its division managers using return on investment. The flagship store's financial performance in 2019 and 2020 was as follows (in thousands):

Operating Income		Revenues		Total Assets	
2019	2020	2019	2020	2019	2020
–$5,000	–$2,000	$30,000	$35,000	$40,000	$45,000

Required

1. Calculate the flagship store's ROI for 2020.
2. The company has a corporate-wide policy of not paying out a bonus when a division's ROI is negative. Do you think that the company is making a mistake by not paying Susan Marcos a bonus for 2020?
3. How could the company change its bonus program so that Susan Marcos could receive a bonus for 2020?

24-28 Goal incongruence and ROI. McCall Corporation manufactures furniture in several divisions, including the patio furniture division. The manager of the patio furniture division plans to retire in 2 years. The manager receives a bonus based on the division's ROI, which is currently 15%.

One of the machines that the patio furniture division uses to manufacture the furniture is rather old, and the manager must decide whether to replace it. The new machine would cost $30,000 and would last 10 years. It would have no salvage value. The old machine is fully depreciated and has no trade-in value. McCall uses straight-line depreciation for all assets. The new machine, being new and more efficient, would save the company $6,000 per year in cash operating costs. The only difference between cash flow and net income is depreciation. The internal rate of return of the project is approximately 15%. McCall Corporation's weighted-average cost of capital is 6%. McCall is not subject to any income taxes.

Required

1. Should McCall Corporation replace the machine? Why or why not?
2. Assume that "investment" is defined as average net long-term assets (that is, after depreciation) during the year. Compute the project's ROI for each of its first 5 years. If the patio furniture manager is interested in maximizing his bonus, would he replace the machine before he retires? Why or why not?
3. What can McCall do to entice the manager to replace the machine before retiring?

24-29 ROI, RI, EVA. Accelerate Auto Company operates a new car division (that sells high-performance sports cars) and a performance parts division (that sells performance-improvement parts for family cars). Some division financial measures for 2020 are as follows:

	A	B	C
1		New Car Division	Performance Parts Division
2	Total assets	$35,000,000	$32,312,500
3	Current liabilities	$ 6,100,000	$ 8,700,000
4	Operating income	$ 2,450,000	$ 2,585,000
5	Required rate of return	12%	12%

Required

1. Calculate return on investment (ROI) for each division using operating income as a measure of income and total assets as a measure of investment.
2. Calculate residual income (RI) for each division using operating income as a measure of income and total assets minus current liabilities as a measure of investment.
3. William Abraham, the new car division manager, argues that the performance parts division has "loaded up on a lot of short-term debt" to boost its RI. Calculate an alternative RI for each division that is not sensitive to the amount of short-term debt taken on by the performance parts division. Comment on the result.
4. Accelerate Auto Company, whose tax rate is 30%, has two sources of funds: long-term debt with a market value of $16,000,000 at an interest rate of 10% and equity capital with a market value of $9,000,000 and a cost of equity of 14%. Applying the same weighted-average cost of capital (WACC) to each division, calculate EVA for each division.
5. Use your preceding calculations to comment on the relative performance of each division.

24-30 Capital budgeting, RI. Ryan Alcoa, a new associate at Jonas Partners, has compiled the following data for a potential investment for the firm:

Investment: $300,000

Annual sales revenues = $180,000

Annual cash costs = $80,000

4-year useful life, no salvage value

Jonas Partners faces a 30% tax rate on income and is aware that the tax authorities will only permit straight-line depreciation for tax purposes. The firm has an after-tax required rate of return of 8%.

Required

1. Based on net present value considerations, is this a project Jonas Partners would want to take?
2. Jonas Partners uses straight-line depreciation for internal accounting and measures investment as the net book value of assets at the start of the year. Calculate the residual income in each year if the project were adopted.
3. Demonstrate that the conservation property of residual income, as described on page 932, holds in this example.
4. If Ryan Alcoa is evaluated on the residual income of the projects he undertakes, would he take this project? Explain.

24-31 Multinational performance measurement, ROI, RI. The Mountainside Corporation manufactures similar products in the United States and Norway. The U.S. and Norwegian operations are organized as decentralized divisions. The following information is available for 2020; ROI is calculated as operating income divided by total assets:

	U.S. Division	Norwegian Division
Operating income	?	7,140,000 kroner
Total assets	$10,000,000	70,000,000 kroner
ROI	16.00%	?

Both investments were made on December 31, 2019. The exchange rate at the time of Mountainside's investment in Norway on December 31, 2019, was 8 kroner = $1. During 2020, the Norwegian kroner decreased steadily in value so that the exchange rate on December 31, 2020, is 9 kroner = $1. The average exchange rate during 2020 is $[(8 + 9) \div 2] = 8.5$ kroner = $1.

Required

1. **a.** Calculate the U.S. division's operating income for 2020.
   b. Calculate the Norwegian division's ROI for 2020 in kroner.
2. Top management wants to know which division earned a better ROI in 2020. What would you tell them? Explain your answer.
3. Which division do you think had the better RI performance? Explain your answer. The required rate of return on investment (calculated in U.S. dollars) is 12%.

24-32 ROI, RI, EVA, and performance evaluation. Isla Manufacturing makes fashion products and competes on the basis of quality and leading-edge designs. The company has two divisions, clothing and cosmetics. Isla has $2,500,000 invested in assets in its clothing division. After-tax operating income from sales of clothing this year is $550,000. The cosmetics division has $11,000,000 invested in assets and an after-tax operating income this year of $1,650,000. The weighted-average cost of capital for Isla is 8%. The CEO of Isla has told the manager of each division that the division that "performs best" this year will get a bonus.

Required

1. Calculate the ROI and residual income for each division of Isla Manufacturing, and briefly explain which manager will get the bonus. What are the advantages and disadvantages of each measure?
2. The CEO of Isla Manufacturing has recently heard of another measure similar to residual income called EVA. The CEO has the accountant calculate adjusted incomes for clothing and cosmetics, and finds that the adjusted after-tax operating incomes are $401,400 and $2,067,200, respectively. Also, the clothing division has $270,000 of current liabilities, while the cosmetics division has only $120,000 of current liabilities. Using the preceding information, calculate the EVA for each division and discuss which manager will get the bonus.
3. What nonfinancial measures could Isla use to evaluate divisional performances?

24-33 Risk sharing, incentives, benchmarking, multiple tasks. Estancia, Inc. is a large company that owns restaurants and has a wine division and a frozen food division. Management of the company gives its division managers autonomy in running their divisions for both operating and investment decisions. Estancia is considering how it should compensate Mr. Jim Beam, the general manager of the frozen food division.

- Proposal 1 calls for paying Beam a fixed salary.
- Proposal 2 calls for paying Beam no salary and compensating him only on the basis of the division's RI, calculated based on operating income before any bonus payments.
- Proposal 3 calls for paying Beam some salary and some bonus based on RI.

Required

1. Evaluate the three proposals, specifying the advantages and disadvantages of each.
2. Estancia competes against Starship Industries in the frozen food business. Starship is approximately the same size as Estancia's frozen food division and operates in a similar business environment. Top management of Estancia is considering evaluating Beam on the basis of his division's RI minus Starship's RI. Of course, Beam complains that this approach is unfair because the performance of another company, over which he has no control, is included in his performance evaluation measure. Is Beam's complaint valid? Why or why not?

3. Now suppose that Beam has no authority for making capital-investment decisions. Corporate management makes these decisions. Is RI a good performance measure to use to evaluate Beam? Is RI a good measure to evaluate the economic viability of the frozen food division? Explain.
4. The salespeople for the frozen food division of Estancia, Inc. are responsible for selling and for providing customer service and support. Sales are easy to measure. Although customer service is important to the frozen food division in the long run, the division has not yet implemented customer-service measures. Beam wants to compensate his sales force only on the basis of sales commissions paid for each unit of product sold. He cites two advantages to this plan:
   a. It creates strong incentives for the sales force to work hard.
   b. The company pays salespeople only when the company itself is earning revenues.

   Do you agree with this plan? Why or why not?

Problems

24-34 Residual income and EVA; timing issues. Doorharmony Company makes doorbells. It has a weighted-average cost of capital of 7% and total assets of $5,630,000. Doorharmony has current liabilities of $750,000. Its operating income for the year was $620,000. Doorharmony does not have to pay any income taxes. One of the expenses for accounting purposes was a $150,000 advertising campaign run in early January. The entire amount was deducted this year, although the Doorharmony CEO believes the beneficial effects of this advertising will last 4 years.

Required

1. Calculate residual income, assuming Doorharmony defines investment as total assets.
2. Calculate EVA for the year. Adjust both the year-end assets and operating income for advertising assuming that for the purposes of economic value added the advertising is capitalized and amortized on a straight-line basis over 4 years.
3. Discuss the difference between the outcomes of requirements 1 and 2. Which measure would you recommend, and why?

24-35 ROI performance measures based on historical and current cost. Blue Fish owns and operates coffee shops in three large cities on the West Coast: Seattle, San Francisco, and Los Angeles. The three geographic areas are considered separate divisions. Each division owns the buildings of the coffee shops, which are considered long-term assets. The buildings are all 10 years old and have a total useful life of 20 years. Current assets are considered negligible in each division. Division managers at Blue Fish are evaluated on the basis of ROI, which traditionally has been calculated as the ratio of operating income divided by the net book value of assets, measured at historical costs. The following information refers to the three divisions at the end of 2020:

	Seattle	San Francisco	Los Angeles
Revenues	$1,500,000	$1,750,000	$1,250,000
Operating costs (excluding building depreciation)	800,000	900,000	550,000
Building depreciation expense	100,000	150,000	80,000
Operating income	$ 600,000	$ 700,000	$ 620,000
Gross book value of long-term assets	$2,000,000	$3,000,000	$1,600,000
Accumulated depreciation	1,000,000	1,500,000	800,000
ROI based on historical costs	60%	46.67%	77.5%

Senior management at Blue Fish wants to switch to calculating ROI based on current costs. Costs of new constructions have exploded all along the West Cost and would now be twice as expensive as they were 10 years ago. In other words, the construction cost index has doubled in all three cities. (The useful life of new constructions is still 20 years).

Required

1. Explain how the numerator of the ROI measure, operating income, has to be adjusted to reflect current costs and do the calculation for the three divisions (see Exhibit 24-2).
2. Explain how the denominator of the ROI measure, net book value of assets, has to be adjusted to reflect current costs and do the calculations for the three divisions (see Exhibit 24-2).
3. Calculate ROI based on current costs for the three divisions and compare to the ROI measures based on historical costs (see Exhibit 24-2).

24-36 ROI performance measures based on historical cost and current cost. Natural Bounty Corporation operates three divisions that process and bottle natural fruit juices. The historical-cost accounting system reports the following information for 2020:

	Passion Fruit Division	Kiwi Fruit Division	Mango Fruit Division
Revenues	$1,300,000	$2,000,000	$2,550,000
Operating costs (excluding plant depreciation)	500,000	890,000	1,200,000
Plant depreciation	240,000	220,000	230,000
Operating income	$ 560,000	$ 890,000	$1,120,000
Current assets	$ 300,000	$ 500,000	$ 600,000
Long-term assets—plant	480,000	1,760,000	2,300,000
Total assets	$ 780,000	$2,260,000	$2,900,000

Natural Bounty estimates the useful life of each plant to be 12 years, with no terminal disposal value. The straight-line depreciation method is used. At the end of 2020, the passion fruit plant is 10 years old, the kiwi fruit plant is 4 years old, and the mango fruit plant is 2 years old. An index of construction costs over the 10-year period that Natural Bounty has been operating (2010 year-end = 100) is as follows:

2010	2016	2018	2020
100	150	175	195

Given the high turnover of current assets, management believes that the historical-cost and current-cost measures of current assets are approximately the same.

Required

1. Compute the ROI ratio (operating income to total assets) of each division using historical-cost measures. Comment on the results.
2. Use the approach in Exhibit 24-2 (page 934) to compute the ROI of each division, incorporating current-cost estimates as of 2020 for depreciation expenses and long-term assets. Comment on the results.
3. What advantages might arise from using current-cost asset measures as compared with historical-cost measures for evaluating the performance of the managers of the three divisions?

24-37 Multinational firms, differing risk, comparison of profit, ROI, and RI. Newmann, Inc. has divisions in the United States, France, and Australia. The U.S. division is the oldest and most established of the three and has a cost of capital of 6%. The French division was started 4 years ago when the exchange rate for the euro was €1 = $1.34 USD. The French division has a cost of capital of 8%. The division in Australia was started this year, when the exchange rate was 1 Australian Dollar (AUD) = $0.87 USD. Its cost of capital is 11%. Average exchange rates for the current year are €1 = $1.07 USD and 1 AUD = $0.74 USD. Other information for the three divisions includes the following:

	United States	France	Australia
Long-term assets	$22,048,000	€11,422,761	8,798,851 AUD
Operating revenues	$31,826,170	€ 7,023,860	4,509,628 AUD
Operating expenses	$26,738,330	€ 4,980,290	3,216,892 AUD
Income-tax rate	35%	30%	20%

Required

1. Translate the French and Australian information into dollars to make the divisions comparable. Find the after-tax operating income for each division and compare the profits.
2. Calculate ROI using after-tax operating income. Compare among divisions.
3. Use after-tax operating income and the individual cost of capital of each division to calculate residual income and compare.
4. Redo requirement 2 using pretax operating income instead of net income. Why is there a big difference, and what does this mean for performance evaluation?

24-38 ROI, RI, DuPont method, investment decisions, balanced scorecard. News Report Group has two major divisions: print and Internet. Summary financial data (in millions) for 2019 and 2020 are as follows:

	A	B	C	D	E	F	G	H	I
1		Operating Income			Revenues			Total Assets	
2		2019	2020		2019	2020		2019	2020
3	Print	$3,720	$4,500		$18,700	$22,500		$18,200	$25,000
4	Internet	525	690		25,000	23,000		11,150	10,000

The two division managers' annual bonuses are based on division ROI (defined as operating income divided by total assets). If a division reports an increase in ROI from the previous year, its management is automatically eligible for a bonus; however, the management of a division reporting a decline in ROI has to present an explanation to the News Report Group board and is unlikely to get any bonus.

Carol Mays, manager of the print division, is considering a proposal to invest $2,580 million in a new computerized news reporting and printing system. It is estimated that the new system's state-of-the-art graphics and ability to quickly incorporate late-breaking news into papers will increase 2021 division operating income by $360 million. News Report Group uses a 10% required rate of return on investment for each division.

Required

1. Use the DuPont method of profitability analysis to explain differences in 2020 ROIs between the two divisions. Use 2020 total assets as the investment base.
2. Why might Mays be less than enthusiastic about accepting the investment proposal for the new system despite her belief in the benefits of the new technology?
3. John Mendenhall, CEO of News Report Group, is considering a proposal to base division executive compensation on division RI.
   a. Compute the 2020 RI of each division.
   b. Would adoption of an RI measure reduce Mays' reluctance to adopt the investment proposal for the new computerized system?
4. Mendenhall is concerned that the focus on annual ROI could have an adverse long-run effect on News Report Group's customers. What other measurements, if any, do you recommend that Mendenhall use? Explain briefly.

24-39 Division managers' compensation, levers of control (continuation of 24-38). John Mendenhall seeks your advice on revising the existing bonus plan for division managers of News Report Group. Assume division managers do not like bearing risk. Mendenhall is considering three ideas:

- Make each division manager's compensation depend on division RI.
- Make each division manager's compensation depend on company-wide RI.
- Use benchmarking and compensate division managers on the basis of their division's RI minus the RI of the other division.

Required

1. Evaluate the three ideas Mendenhall has put forth using performance-evaluation concepts described in this chapter. Indicate the positive and negative features of each proposal.
2. Mendenhall is concerned that the pressure for short-run performance may cause managers to cut corners. What systems might Mendenhall introduce to avoid this problem? Explain briefly.
3. Mendenhall is also concerned that the pressure for short-run performance might cause managers to ignore emerging threats and opportunities. What system might Mendenhall introduce to prevent this problem? Explain briefly.

24-40 Executive compensation, balanced scorecard. Kroger Company recently introduced a new bonus plan for its corporate executives. The company believes that current profitability and customer satisfaction levels are equally important to the company's long-term success. As a result, the new plan awards a bonus equal to 0.5% of salary for each 1% increase in business unit net income or 1% increase in the business unit's customer satisfaction index. For example, increasing net income from $1 million to $1.1 million (or 10% from its initial value) leads to a bonus of 5% of salary, while increasing the business unit's customer satisfaction index from 50 to 60 (or 20% from its initial value) leads to a bonus of 10% of salary. There is no bonus penalty when net income or customer satisfaction declines. In 2019 and 2020, Kroger's three business units reported the following performance results:

	Retail Sales		Online Sales		Wholesale Sales	
	2019	2020	2019	2020	2019	2020
Net income	$750,000	$816,300	$1,256,000	$1,576,628	$1,062,910	$1,148,674
Customer satisfaction	79	85	79.5	78	68.5	74.7

Required

1. Compute the bonus as a percent of salary earned by each business unit executive in 2020.
2. What factors might explain the differences between improvement rates for net income and those for customer satisfaction in the three units? Are increases in customer satisfaction likely to result in increased net income right away?
3. Kroger's board of directors is concerned that the 2020 bonus awards may not accurately reflect the executives' overall performance. In particular, the board is concerned that executives can earn large bonuses by doing well on one performance dimension but underperforming on the other. What changes can it make to the bonus plan to prevent this from happening in the future? Explain briefly.

24-41 Financial and nonfinancial performance measures, goal congruence. (CMA, adapted) Precision Equipment specializes in the manufacture of medical equipment, a field that has become increasingly competitive. Approximately 2 years ago, Pedro Mendez, president of Precision, decided to revise the bonus plan (based, at the time, entirely on operating income) to encourage division managers to focus on areas that were important to customers and that added value without increasing cost. In addition to a profitability incentive, the revised plan includes incentives for reduced rework costs, reduced sales returns, and on-time deliveries. The company calculates and rewards bonuses semiannually on the following basis: A base bonus is calculated at 2% of operating income; this amount is then adjusted as follows:

a. (i) Reduced by excess of rework costs over and above 2% of operating income

(ii) No adjustment if rework costs are less than or equal to 2% of operating income

b. (i) Increased by $4,000 if more than 98% of deliveries are on time and by $1,500 if 96–98% of deliveries are on time

(ii) No adjustment if on-time deliveries are below 96%

c. (i) Increased by $2,500 if sales returns are less than or equal to 1.5% of sales

(ii) Decreased by 50% of excess of sales returns over 1.5% of sales

If the calculation of the bonus results in a negative amount for a particular period, the manager simply receives no bonus, and the negative amount is not carried forward to the next period.

Results for Precision's Central division and Western division for 2020, the first year under the new bonus plan, follow. In 2019, under the old bonus plan, the Central division manager earned a bonus of $20,295 and the Western division manager received a bonus of $15,830.

	Central Division		Western Division	
	Jan. 1, 2020, to June 30, 2020	July 1, 2020, to Dec. 31, 2020	Jan. 1, 2020, to June 30, 2020	July 1, 2020, to Dec. 31, 2020
Revenues	$3,150,000	$3,300,000	$2,137,500	$2,175,000
Operating income	$ 346,500	$ 330,000	$ 256,500	$ 304,500
On-time delivery	95.4%	97.3%	98.2%	94.6%
Rework costs	$ 8,625	$ 8,250	$ 4,500	$ 6,000
Sales returns	$ 63,000	$ 52,500	$ 33,560	$ 31,875

Required

1. Why did Mendez need to introduce these new performance measures? That is, why does Mendez need to use these performance measures in addition to the operating-income numbers for the period?
2. Calculate the bonus earned by each manager for each 6-month period and for 2020 overall.
3. What effect did the change in the bonus plan have on each manager's behavior? Did the new bonus plan achieve what Mendez wanted? What changes, if any, would you make to the new bonus plan?

24-42 Ethics, levers of control. Channels is a manufacturer of flatware that is grade-rolled rather than stamped. The flatware is sold in upscale stores as a high-quality item. The company sells the goods that are within specifications at regular prices to the stores. If a piece doesn't pass inspection, it is put through a second inspection, and if useable, is sold at a highly discounted price to low-end stores.

In recent years, the company's average yield as been 93% of first-quality products. Last year, the company put in place a performance-evaluation system that utilizes both profit numbers vs. budget and budgeted yield, which had been set at 93% based on recent year history.

When Fannie May, the company controller, was reviewing the performance evaluation results, she noted that the yield percentage was 96% in the year just ended, which resulted in significantly better than budgeted profits. Ms. May decided to investigate.

The supervisor in the quality control department was happy to show Ms. May what changes were made that resulted in the improved yield percentage. In short, the supervisor of the department, following the manager's instructions, had changed the measuring procedure to determine what was "within specification" such that more pieces were in compliance than before. Ms. May worried that the customers would be unhappy with the lower quality of the pieces they would be receiving.

Required

1. What should Ms. May do? You may want to refer to the *IMA Statement of Ethical Professional Practice*, page 17.
2. Which lever of control is Channels emphasizing? What changes, if any, should be made?

24-43 RI, EVA, measurement alternatives, goal congruence. Refresh Resorts, Inc., operates health spas in Key West, Florida; Phoenix, Arizona; and Carmel, California. The Key West spa was the company's first and opened in 1994. The Phoenix spa opened in 2007, and the Carmel spa opened in 2016. Refresh Resorts has previously evaluated divisions based on RI, but the company is considering changing to an EVA approach. All spas are assumed to face similar risks. Data for 2020 are shown below:

	A	B	C	D	E
1		**Key West**	**Phoenix**	**Carmel**	**Total**
2	Revenues	$4,100,000	$4,380,000	$3,230,000	$11,710,000
3	Variable costs	1,600,000	1,630,000	955,000	4,185,000
4	Fixed costs	1,280,000	1,560,000	980,000	3,820,000
5	Operating income	1,220,000	1,190,000	1,295,000	3,705,000
6	Interest costs on long-term debt at 8%	368,000	416,000	440,000	1,224,000
7	Income before taxes	852,000	774,000	855,000	2,481,000
8	Net income after 35% taxes	553,800	503,100	555,750	1,612,650
9					
10	Net book value at 2020 year-end:				
11	Current assets	$1,280,000	$ 850,000	$ 600,000	$ 2,730,000
12	Long-term assets	4,875,000	5,462,000	6,835,000	17,172,000
13	Total assets	6,155,000	6,312,000	7,435,000	19,902,000
14					
15	Current liabilities	330,000	265,000	84,000	679,000
16	Long-term debt	4,600,000	5,200,000	5,500,000	15,300,000
17	Stockholders' equity	1,225,000	847,000	1,851,000	3,923,000
18	Total liabilities and stockholders' equity	6,155,000	6,312,000	7,435,000	19,902,000
19					
20	Market value of debt	$4,600,000	$5,200,000	$5,500,000	$15,300,000
21	Market value of equity	2,400,000	2,660,000	2,590,000	7,650,000
22	Cost of equity capital				14%
23	Required rate of return				11%
24	Accumulated depreciation on long-term assets	$2,200,000	$1,510,000	$ 220,000	

Required

1. Calculate RI for each of the spas based on operating income and using total assets as the measure of investment. Suppose that the Key West spa is considering adding a new group of saunas from Finland that will cost $225,000. The saunas are expected to bring in operating income of $22,000. What effect would this project have on the RI of the Key West spa? Based on RI, would the Key West manager accept or reject this project? Without resorting to calculations, would the other managers accept or reject the project? Why?
2. Why might Refresh Resorts want to use EVA instead of RI for evaluating the performance of the three spas?
3. Refer back to the original data. Calculate the WACC for Refresh Resorts.
4. Refer back to the original data. Calculate EVA for each of the spas, using net book value of long-term assets. Calculate EVA again, this time using gross book value of long-term assets. Comment on the differences between the two methods.
5. How does the selection of asset measurement method affect goal congruence?

Appendix A

Notes on Compound Interest and Interest Tables

Interest is the cost of using money. It is the rental charge for funds, just as renting a building and equipment entails a rental charge. When the funds are used for a period of time, it is necessary to recognize interest as a cost of using the borrowed ("rented") funds. This requirement applies even if the funds represent ownership capital and if interest does not entail an outlay of cash. Why must interest be considered? Because the selection of one alternative automatically commits a given amount of funds that could otherwise be invested in some other alternative.

Interest is generally important, even when short-term projects are under consideration. Interest looms correspondingly larger when long-run plans are studied. The rate of interest has significant enough impact to influence decisions regarding borrowing and investing funds. For example, \$100,000 invested now and compounded annually for 10 years at 8% will accumulate to \$215,900; at 20%, the \$100,000 will accumulate to \$619,200.

Interest Tables

Many computer programs and calculators are available that handle computations involving the time value of money. You may also turn to the following four basic tables to compute interest.

Table 1—Future Amount of \$1

Table 1 shows how much \$1 invested now will accumulate in a given number of periods at a given compounded interest rate per period. Consider investing \$1,000 now for three years at 8% compound interest. A tabular presentation of how this \$1,000 would accumulate to \$1,259.70 follows:

Year	Interest per Year	Cumulative Interest Called Compound Interest	Total at End of Year
0	\$—	\$—	\$1,000.00
1	80.00 (0.08 × \$1,000)	80.00	1,080.00
2	86.40 (0.08 × \$1,080)	166.40	1,166.40
3	93.30 (0.08 × \$1,166.40)	259.70	1,259.70

This tabular presentation is a series of computations that could appear as follows, where S is the future amount and the subscripts 1, 2, and 3 indicate the number of time periods.

$$S_1 = \$1{,}000\,(1.08)^1 = \$1{,}080$$

$$S_2 = \$1{,}080\,(1.08) = \$1{,}000\,(1.08)^2 = \$1{,}166.40$$

$$S_3 = \$1{,}166.40\,(1.08) = \$1{,}000\,(1.08)^3 = \$1{,}259.70$$

The formula for the "future amount of $P," often called the "future value of $P," or "compound amount of $P," can be written as follows:

$$S = P(1 + r)^n$$

S is the future value amount; *P* is the present value, *r* is the rate of interest; and *n* is the number of time periods.

When $P = \$1{,}000$, $n = 3$, $r = 0.08$, $S = \$1{,}000(1 + .08)^3 = \$1{,}259.70$.

Fortunately, tables make key computations readily available. A facility in selecting the *proper* table will minimize computations. Check the accuracy of the preceding answer using Table 1, page 964.

Table 2—Present Value of $1

In the previous example, if $1,000 compounded at 8% per year will accumulate to $1,259.70 in three years, then $1,000 must be the present value of $1,259.70 due at the end of three years. The formula for the present value can be derived by reversing the process of *accumulation* (finding the future amount) that we just finished.

If

$$S = P(1 + r)^n$$

then

$$P = \frac{S}{(1 + r)^n}$$

In our example, $S = \$1{,}259.70$, $n = 3$, $r = 0.08$, so

$$P = \frac{\$1{,}259.70}{(1.08)^3} = \$1{,}000$$

Use Table 2, page 965, to check this calculation.

When accumulating, we advance or roll forward in time. The difference between our original amount and our accumulated amount is called *compound interest*. When discounting, we retreat or roll back in time. The difference between the future amount and the present value is called *compound discount*. Note the following formulas:

$$\text{Compound interest} = P[(1 + r)^n - 1]$$

In our example, $P = \$1{,}000$, $n = 3$, $r = 0.08$, so

$$\text{Compound interest} = \$1{,}000[(1.08)^3 - 1] = \$259.70$$

$$\text{Compound discount} = S\left[1 - \frac{1}{(1 + r)^n}\right]$$

In our example, $S = \$1{,}259.70$, $n = 3$, $r = 0.08$, so

$$\text{Compound discount} = \$1{,}259.70\left[1 - \frac{1}{(1.08)^3}\right] = \$259.70$$

Table 3—Compound Amount (Future Value) of Annuity of $1

An (ordinary) *annuity* is a series of equal payments (receipts) to be paid (or received) at the end of successive periods of equal length. Assume that $1,000 is invested at the end of each of three years at 8%:

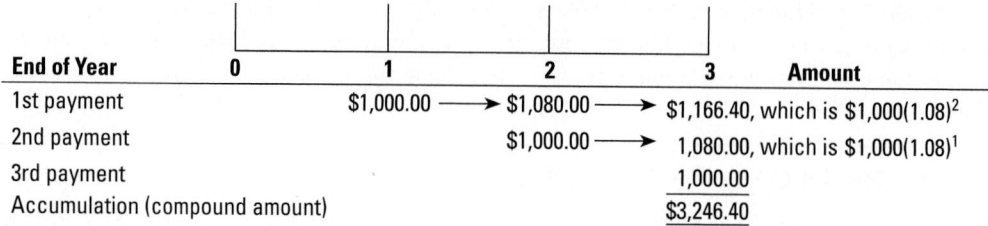

End of Year	0	1	2	3 Amount
1st payment		$1,000.00 →	$1,080.00 →	$1,166.40, which is $1,000(1.08)^2
2nd payment			$1,000.00 →	1,080.00, which is $1,000(1.08)^1
3rd payment				1,000.00
Accumulation (compound amount)				$3,246.40

The preceding arithmetic may be expressed algebraically as the future value of an ordinary annuity of $1,000 for 3 years = $1,000(1 + r)^2 + $1,000(1 + r)^1 + $1,000.

We can develop the general formula for S_n, the future value of an ordinary annuity of $1, by using the preceding example as a basis where $n = 3$ and $r = 0.08$:

1. $S_3 = 1 + (1 + r)^1 + (1 + r)^2$
2. Substitute $r = 0.08$: $S_3 = 1 + (1.08)^1 + (1.08)^2$
3. Multiply (2) by $(1 + r)$: $(1.08)\,S_3 = (1.08)^1 + (1.08)^2 + (1.08)^3$
4. Subtract (2) from (3): Note that all terms on the right-hand side are removed except $(1.08)^3$ in equation (3) and 1 in equation (2). $1.08S_3 - S_3 = (1.08)^3 - 1$
5. Factor (4): $S_3(1.08 - 1) = (1.08)^3 - 1$
6. Divide (5) by $(1.08 - 1)$: $$S_3 = \frac{(1.08)^3 - 1}{1.08 - 1} = \frac{(1.08)^3 - 1}{0.08} = \frac{0.2597}{0.08} = 3.246$$
7. The general formula for the future value of an ordinary annuity of $1 becomes: $$S_n = \frac{(1 + r)^n - 1}{r} \text{ or } \frac{\text{Compound interest}}{\text{Rate}}$$

This formula is the basis for Table 3, page 966. Check the answer in the table.

Table 4—Present Value of an Ordinary Annuity of $1

Using the same example as for Table 3, we can show how the formula of P_n, *the present value of an ordinary annuity*, is developed.

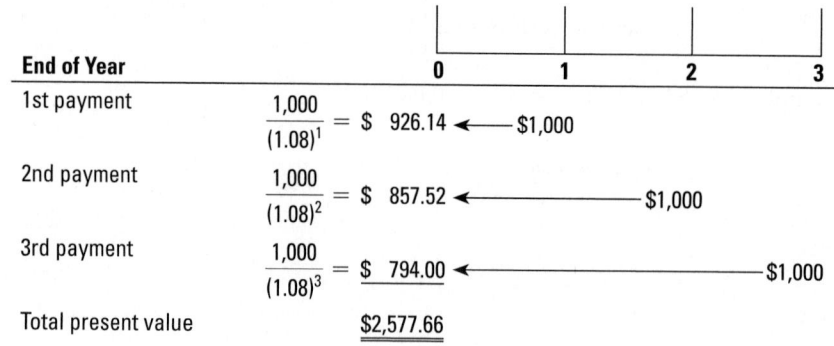

End of Year		0	1	2	3
1st payment	$\frac{1,000}{(1.08)^1}$ =	$ 926.14 ←	$1,000		
2nd payment	$\frac{1,000}{(1.08)^2}$ =	$ 857.52 ←		$1,000	
3rd payment	$\frac{1,000}{(1.08)^3}$ =	$ 794.00 ←			$1,000
Total present value		$2,577.66			

We can develop the general formula for P_n by using the preceding example as a basis where $n = 3$ and $r = 0.08$:

1. $$P_3 = \frac{1}{1+r} + \frac{1}{(1+r)^2} + \frac{1}{(1+r)^3}$$

2. Substitute $r = 0.08$: $$P_3 = \frac{1}{1.08} + \frac{1}{(1.08)^2} + \frac{1}{(1.08)^3}$$

3. Multiply (2) by $\frac{1}{1.08}$: $$P_3\frac{1}{1.08} = \frac{1}{(1.08)^2} + \frac{1}{(1.08)^3} + \frac{1}{(1.08)^4}$$

4. Subtract (3) from (2): $$P_3 - P_3\frac{1}{1.08} = \frac{1}{1.08} - \frac{1}{(1.08)^4}$$

5. Factor (4): $$P_3\left(1 - \frac{1}{1.08}\right) = \frac{1}{1.08}\left[1 - \frac{1}{(1.08)^3}\right]$$

6. or $$P_3\left(\frac{0.08}{1.08}\right) = \frac{1}{1.08}\left[1 - \frac{1}{(1.08)^3}\right]$$

7. Multiply (6) by $\frac{1.08}{0.08}$: $$P_3 = \frac{1}{0.08}\left[1 - \frac{1}{(1.08)^3}\right] = \frac{0.2062}{0.08} = 2.577$$

The general formula for the present value of an annuity of \$1.00 is as follows:

$$P_n = \frac{1}{r}\left[1 - \frac{1}{(1+r)^n}\right] = \frac{\text{Compound discount}}{\text{Rate}}$$

The formula is the basis for Table 4, page 967. Check the answer in the table. The present value tables, Tables 2 and 4, are used most frequently in capital budgeting.

The tables for annuities are not essential. With Tables 1 and 2, compound interest and compound discount can readily be computed. It is simply a matter of dividing either of these by the rate to get values equivalent to those shown in Tables 3 and 4.

TABLE 1

Compound Amount of $1.00 (The Future Value of $1.00)

$S = P(1 + r)^n$. In this table $P = \$1.00$

Periods	2%	4%	6%	8%	10%	12%	14%	16%	18%	20%	22%	24%	26%	28%	30%	32%	40%	Periods
1	1.020	1.040	1.060	1.080	1.100	1.120	1.140	1.160	1.180	1.200	1.220	1.240	1.260	1.280	1.300	1.320	1.400	1
2	1.040	1.082	1.124	1.166	1.210	1.254	1.300	1.346	1.392	1.440	1.488	1.538	1.588	1.638	1.690	1.742	1.960	2
3	1.061	1.125	1.191	1.260	1.331	1.405	1.482	1.561	1.643	1.728	1.816	1.907	2.000	2.097	2.197	2.300	2.744	3
4	1.082	1.170	1.262	1.360	1.464	1.574	1.689	1.811	1.939	2.074	2.215	2.364	2.520	2.684	2.856	3.036	3.842	4
5	1.104	1.217	1.338	1.469	1.611	1.762	1.925	2.100	2.288	2.488	2.703	2.932	3.176	3.436	3.713	4.007	5.378	5
6	1.126	1.265	1.419	1.587	1.772	1.974	2.195	2.436	2.700	2.986	3.297	3.635	4.002	4.398	4.827	5.290	7.530	6
7	1.149	1.316	1.504	1.714	1.949	2.211	2.502	2.826	3.185	3.583	4.023	4.508	5.042	5.629	6.275	6.983	10.541	7
8	1.172	1.369	1.594	1.851	2.144	2.476	2.853	3.278	3.759	4.300	4.908	5.590	6.353	7.206	8.157	9.217	14.758	8
9	1.195	1.423	1.689	1.999	2.358	2.773	3.252	3.803	4.435	5.160	5.987	6.931	8.005	9.223	10.604	12.166	20.661	9
10	1.219	1.480	1.791	2.159	2.594	3.106	3.707	4.411	5.234	6.192	7.305	8.594	10.086	11.806	13.786	16.060	28.925	10
11	1.243	1.539	1.898	2.332	2.853	3.479	4.226	5.117	6.176	7.430	8.912	10.657	12.708	15.112	17.922	21.199	40.496	11
12	1.268	1.601	2.012	2.518	3.138	3.896	4.818	5.936	7.288	8.916	10.872	13.215	16.012	19.343	23.298	27.983	56.694	12
13	1.294	1.665	2.133	2.720	3.452	4.363	5.492	6.886	8.599	10.699	13.264	16.386	20.175	24.759	30.288	36.937	79.371	13
14	1.319	1.732	2.261	2.937	3.797	4.887	6.261	7.988	10.147	12.839	16.182	20.319	25.421	31.691	39.374	48.757	111.120	14
15	1.346	1.801	2.397	3.172	4.177	5.474	7.138	9.266	11.974	15.407	19.742	25.196	32.030	40.565	51.186	64.359	155.568	15
16	1.373	1.873	2.540	3.426	4.595	6.130	8.137	10.748	14.129	18.488	24.086	31.243	40.358	51.923	66.542	84.954	217.795	16
17	1.400	1.948	2.693	3.700	5.054	6.866	9.276	12.468	16.672	22.186	29.384	38.741	50.851	66.461	86.504	112.139	304.913	17
18	1.428	2.026	2.854	3.996	5.560	7.690	10.575	14.463	19.673	26.623	35.849	48.039	64.072	85.071	112.455	148.024	426.879	18
19	1.457	2.107	3.026	4.316	6.116	8.613	12.056	16.777	23.214	31.948	43.736	59.568	80.731	108.890	146.192	195.391	597.630	19
20	1.486	2.191	3.207	4.661	6.727	9.646	13.743	19.461	27.393	38.338	53.358	73.864	101.721	139.380	190.050	257.916	836.683	20
21	1.516	2.279	3.400	5.034	7.400	10.804	15.668	22.574	32.324	46.005	65.096	91.592	128.169	178.406	247.065	340.449	1171.356	21
22	1.546	2.370	3.604	5.437	8.140	12.100	17.861	26.186	38.142	55.206	79.418	113.574	161.492	228.360	321.184	449.393	1639.898	22
23	1.577	2.465	3.820	5.871	8.954	13.552	20.362	30.376	45.008	66.247	96.889	140.831	203.480	292.300	417.539	593.199	2295.857	23
24	1.608	2.563	4.049	6.341	9.850	15.179	23.212	35.236	53.109	79.497	118.205	174.631	256.385	374.144	542.801	783.023	3214.200	24
25	1.641	2.666	4.292	6.848	10.835	17.000	26.462	40.874	62.669	95.396	144.210	216.542	323.045	478.905	705.641	1033.590	4499.880	25
26	1.673	2.772	4.549	7.396	11.918	19.040	30.167	47.414	73.949	114.475	175.936	268.512	407.037	612.998	917.333	1364.339	6299.831	26
27	1.707	2.883	4.822	7.988	13.110	21.325	34.390	55.000	87.260	137.371	214.642	332.955	512.867	784.638	1192.533	1800.927	8819.764	27
28	1.741	2.999	5.112	8.627	14.421	23.884	39.204	63.800	102.967	164.845	261.864	412.864	646.212	1004.336	1550.293	2377.224	12347.670	28
29	1.776	3.119	5.418	9.317	15.863	26.750	44.693	74.009	121.501	197.814	319.474	511.952	814.228	1285.550	2015.381	3137.935	17286.737	29
30	1.811	3.243	5.743	10.063	17.449	29.960	50.950	85.850	143.371	237.376	389.758	634.820	1025.927	1645.505	2619.996	4142.075	24201.432	30
35	2.000	3.946	7.686	14.785	28.102	52.800	98.100	180.314	327.997	590.668	1053.402	1861.054	3258.135	5653.911	9727.860	16599.217	130161.112	35
40	2.208	4.801	10.286	21.725	45.259	93.051	188.884	378.721	750.378	1469.772	2847.038	5455.913	10347.175	19426.689	36118.865	66520.767	700037.697	40

TABLE 2 *(Place a clip on this page for your reference.)*

Present Value of $1.00

$P = \frac{S}{(1 + r)^n}$. In this table $S = \$1.00$.

Periods	2%	4%	6%	8%	10%	12%	14%	16%	18%	20%	22%	24%	26%	28%	30%	32%	40%	Periods
1	0.980	0.962	0.943	0.926	0.909	0.893	0.877	0.862	0.847	0.833	0.820	0.806	0.794	0.781	0.769	0.758	0.714	1
2	0.961	0.925	0.890	0.857	0.826	0.797	0.769	0.743	0.718	0.694	0.672	0.650	0.630	0.610	0.592	0.574	0.510	2
3	0.942	0.889	0.840	0.794	0.751	0.712	0.675	0.641	0.609	0.579	0.551	0.524	0.500	0.477	0.455	0.435	0.364	3
4	0.924	0.855	0.792	0.735	0.683	0.636	0.592	0.552	0.516	0.482	0.451	0.423	0.397	0.373	0.350	0.329	0.260	4
5	0.906	0.822	0.747	0.681	0.621	0.567	0.519	0.476	0.437	0.402	0.370	0.341	0.315	0.291	0.269	0.250	0.186	5
6	0.888	0.790	0.705	0.630	0.564	0.507	0.456	0.410	0.370	0.335	0.303	0.275	0.250	0.227	0.207	0.189	0.133	6
7	0.871	0.760	0.665	0.583	0.513	0.452	0.400	0.354	0.314	0.279	0.249	0.222	0.198	0.178	0.159	0.143	0.095	7
8	0.853	0.731	0.627	0.540	0.467	0.404	0.351	0.305	0.266	0.233	0.204	0.179	0.157	0.139	0.123	0.108	0.068	8
9	0.837	0.703	0.592	0.500	0.424	0.361	0.308	0.263	0.225	0.194	0.167	0.144	0.125	0.108	0.094	0.082	0.048	9
10	0.820	0.676	0.558	0.463	0.386	0.322	0.270	0.227	0.191	0.162	0.137	0.116	0.099	0.085	0.073	0.062	0.035	10
11	0.804	0.650	0.527	0.429	0.350	0.287	0.237	0.195	0.162	0.135	0.112	0.094	0.079	0.066	0.056	0.047	0.025	11
12	0.788	0.625	0.497	0.397	0.319	0.257	0.208	0.168	0.137	0.112	0.092	0.076	0.062	0.052	0.043	0.036	0.018	12
13	0.773	0.601	0.469	0.368	0.290	0.229	0.182	0.145	0.116	0.093	0.075	0.061	0.050	0.040	0.033	0.027	0.013	13
14	0.758	0.577	0.442	0.340	0.263	0.205	0.160	0.125	0.099	0.078	0.062	0.049	0.039	0.032	0.025	0.021	0.009	14
15	0.743	0.555	0.417	0.315	0.239	0.183	0.140	0.108	0.084	0.065	0.051	0.040	0.031	0.025	0.020	0.016	0.006	15
16	0.728	0.534	0.394	0.292	0.218	0.163	0.123	0.093	0.071	0.054	0.042	0.032	0.025	0.019	0.015	0.012	0.005	16
17	0.714	0.513	0.371	0.270	0.198	0.146	0.108	0.080	0.060	0.045	0.034	0.026	0.020	0.015	0.012	0.009	0.003	17
18	0.700	0.494	0.350	0.250	0.180	0.130	0.095	0.069	0.051	0.038	0.028	0.021	0.016	0.012	0.009	0.007	0.002	18
19	0.686	0.475	0.331	0.232	0.164	0.116	0.083	0.060	0.043	0.031	0.023	0.017	0.012	0.009	0.007	0.005	0.002	19
20	0.673	0.456	0.312	0.215	0.149	0.104	0.073	0.051	0.037	0.026	0.019	0.014	0.010	0.007	0.005	0.004	0.001	20
21	0.660	0.439	0.294	0.199	0.135	0.093	0.064	0.044	0.031	0.022	0.015	0.011	0.008	0.006	0.004	0.003	0.001	21
22	0.647	0.422	0.278	0.184	0.123	0.083	0.056	0.038	0.026	0.018	0.013	0.009	0.006	0.004	0.003	0.002	0.001	22
23	0.634	0.406	0.262	0.170	0.112	0.074	0.049	0.033	0.022	0.015	0.010	0.007	0.005	0.003	0.002	0.002	0.000	23
24	0.622	0.390	0.247	0.158	0.102	0.066	0.043	0.028	0.019	0.013	0.008	0.006	0.004	0.003	0.002	0.001	0.000	24
25	0.610	0.375	0.233	0.146	0.092	0.059	0.038	0.024	0.016	0.010	0.007	0.005	0.003	0.002	0.001	0.001	0.000	25
26	0.598	0.361	0.220	0.135	0.084	0.053	0.033	0.021	0.014	0.009	0.006	0.004	0.002	0.002	0.001	0.001	0.000	26
27	0.586	0.347	0.207	0.125	0.076	0.047	0.029	0.018	0.011	0.007	0.005	0.003	0.002	0.001	0.001	0.001	0.000	27
28	0.574	0.333	0.196	0.116	0.069	0.042	0.026	0.016	0.010	0.006	0.004	0.002	0.002	0.001	0.001	0.000	0.000	28
29	0.563	0.321	0.185	0.107	0.063	0.037	0.022	0.014	0.008	0.005	0.003	0.002	0.001	0.001	0.000	0.000	0.000	29
30	0.552	0.308	0.174	0.099	0.057	0.033	0.020	0.012	0.007	0.004	0.003	0.002	0.001	0.001	0.000	0.000	0.000	30
35	0.500	0.253	0.130	0.068	0.036	0.019	0.010	0.006	0.003	0.002	0.001	0.001	0.000	0.000	0.000	0.000	0.000	35
40	0.453	0.208	0.097	0.046	0.022	0.011	0.005	0.003	0.001	0.001	0.000	0.000	0.000	0.000	0.000	0.000	0.000	40

TABLE 3

Compound Amount of Annuity of $1.00 in Arrears* (Future Value of Annuity)

$$S_n = \frac{(1 + r)^n - 1}{r}$$

Periods	2%	4%	6%	8%	10%	12%	14%	16%	18%	20%	22%	24%	26%	28%	30%	32%	40%	Periods
1	1.000	1.000	1.000	1.000	1.000	1.000	1.000	1.000	1.000	1.000	1.000	1.000	1.000	1.000	1.000	1.000	1.000	1
2	2.020	2.040	2.060	2.080	2.100	2.120	2.140	2.160	2.180	2.200	2.220	2.240	2.260	2.280	2.300	2.320	2.400	2
3	3.060	3.122	3.184	3.246	3.310	3.374	3.440	3.506	3.572	3.640	3.708	3.778	3.848	3.918	3.990	4.062	4.360	3
4	4.122	4.246	4.375	4.506	4.641	4.779	4.921	5.066	5.215	5.368	5.524	5.684	5.848	6.016	6.187	6.362	7.104	4
5	5.204	5.416	5.637	5.867	6.105	6.353	6.610	6.877	7.154	7.442	7.740	8.048	8.368	8.700	9.043	9.398	10.946	5
6	6.308	6.633	6.975	7.336	7.716	8.115	8.536	8.977	9.442	9.930	10.442	10.980	11.544	12.136	12.756	13.406	16.324	6
7	7.434	7.898	8.394	8.923	9.487	10.089	10.730	11.414	12.142	12.916	13.740	14.615	15.546	16.534	17.583	18.696	23.853	7
8	8.583	9.214	9.897	10.637	11.436	12.300	13.233	14.240	15.327	16.499	17.762	19.123	20.588	22.163	23.858	25.678	34.395	8
9	9.755	10.583	11.491	12.488	13.579	14.776	16.085	17.519	19.086	20.799	22.670	24.712	26.940	29.369	32.015	34.895	49.153	9
10	10.950	12.006	13.181	14.487	15.937	17.549	19.337	21.321	23.521	25.959	28.657	31.643	34.945	38.593	42.619	47.062	69.814	10
11	12.169	13.486	14.972	16.645	18.531	20.655	23.045	25.733	28.755	32.150	35.962	40.238	45.031	50.398	56.405	63.122	98.739	11
12	13.412	15.026	16.870	18.977	21.384	24.133	27.271	30.850	34.931	39.581	44.874	50.895	57.739	65.510	74.327	84.320	139.235	12
13	14.680	16.627	18.882	21.495	24.523	28.029	32.089	36.786	42.219	48.497	55.746	64.110	73.751	84.853	97.625	112.303	195.929	13
14	15.974	18.292	21.015	24.215	27.975	32.393	37.581	43.672	50.818	59.196	69.010	80.496	93.926	109.612	127.913	149.240	275.300	14
15	17.293	20.024	23.276	27.152	31.772	37.280	43.842	51.660	60.965	72.035	85.192	100.815	119.347	141.303	167.286	197.997	386.420	15
16	18.639	21.825	25.673	30.324	35.950	42.753	50.980	60.925	72.939	87.442	104.935	126.011	151.377	181.868	218.472	262.356	541.988	16
17	20.012	23.698	28.213	33.750	40.545	48.884	59.118	71.673	87.068	105.931	129.020	157.253	191.735	233.791	285.014	347.309	759.784	17
18	21.412	25.645	30.906	37.450	45.599	55.750	68.394	84.141	103.740	128.117	158.405	195.994	242.585	300.252	371.518	459.449	1064.697	18
19	22.841	27.671	33.760	41.446	51.159	63.440	78.969	98.603	123.414	154.740	194.254	244.033	306.658	385.323	483.973	607.472	1491.576	19
20	24.297	29.778	36.786	45.762	57.275	72.052	91.025	115.380	146.628	186.688	237.989	303.601	387.389	494.213	630.165	802.863	2089.206	20
21	25.783	31.969	39.993	50.423	64.002	81.699	104.768	134.841	174.021	225.026	291.347	377.465	489.110	633.593	820.215	1060.779	2925.889	21
22	27.299	34.248	43.392	55.457	71.403	92.503	120.436	157.415	206.345	271.031	356.443	469.056	617.278	811.999	1067.280	1401.229	4097.245	22
23	28.845	36.618	46.996	60.893	79.543	104.603	138.297	183.601	244.487	326.237	435.861	582.630	778.771	1040.358	1388.464	1850.622	5737.142	23
24	30.422	39.083	50.816	66.765	88.497	118.155	158.659	213.978	289.494	392.484	532.750	723.461	982.251	1332.659	1806.003	2443.821	8032.999	24
25	32.030	41.646	54.865	73.106	98.347	133.334	181.871	249.214	342.603	471.981	650.955	898.092	1238.636	1706.803	2348.803	3226.844	11247.199	25
26	33.671	44.312	59.156	79.954	109.182	150.334	208.333	290.088	405.272	567.377	795.165	1114.634	1561.682	2185.708	3054.444	4260.434	15747.079	26
27	35.344	47.084	63.706	87.351	121.100	169.374	238.499	337.502	479.221	681.853	971.102	1383.146	1968.719	2798.706	3971.778	5624.772	22046.910	27
28	37.051	49.968	68.528	95.339	134.210	190.699	272.889	392.503	566.481	819.223	1185.744	1716.101	2481.586	3583.344	5164.311	7425.699	30866.674	28
29	38.792	52.966	73.640	103.966	148.631	214.583	312.094	456.303	669.447	984.068	1447.608	2128.965	3127.798	4587.680	6714.604	9802.923	43214.343	29
30	40.568	56.085	79.058	113.263	164.494	241.333	356.787	530.312	790.948	1181.882	1767.081	2640.916	3942.026	5873.231	8729.985	12940.859	60501.081	30
35	49.994	73.652	111.435	172.317	271.024	431.663	693.573	1120.713	1816.652	2948.341	4783.645	7750.225	12527.442	20188.966	32422.868	51869.427	325400.279	35
40	60.402	95.026	154.762	259.057	442.593	767.091	1342.025	2360.757	4163.213	7343.858	12936.535	22728.803	39792.982	69377.460	120392.883	207874.272	1750091.741	40

*Payments (or receipts) at the end of each period.

TABLE 4 (*Place a clip on this page for your reference.*)

Present Value of Annuity $1.00 in Arrears*

$$P_n = \frac{1}{r}\left[1 - \frac{1}{(1+r)^n}\right]$$

Periods	2%	4%	6%	8%	10%	12%	14%	16%	18%	20%	22%	24%	26%	28%	30%	32%	40%	Periods
1	0.980	0.962	0.943	0.926	0.909	0.893	0.877	0.862	0.847	0.833	0.820	0.806	0.794	0.781	0.769	0.758	0.714	1
2	1.942	1.886	1.833	1.783	1.736	1.690	1.647	1.605	1.566	1.528	1.492	1.457	1.424	1.392	1.361	1.331	1.224	2
3	2.884	2.775	2.673	2.577	2.487	2.402	2.322	2.246	2.174	2.106	2.042	1.981	1.923	1.868	1.816	1.766	1.589	3
4	3.808	3.630	3.465	3.312	3.170	3.037	2.914	2.798	2.690	2.589	2.494	2.404	2.320	2.241	2.166	2.096	1.849	4
5	4.713	4.452	4.212	3.993	3.791	3.605	3.433	3.274	3.127	2.991	2.864	2.745	2.635	2.532	2.436	2.345	2.035	5
6	5.601	5.242	4.917	4.623	4.355	4.111	3.889	3.685	3.498	3.326	3.167	3.020	2.885	2.759	2.643	2.534	2.168	6
7	6.472	6.002	5.582	5.206	4.868	4.564	4.288	4.039	3.812	3.605	3.416	3.242	3.083	2.937	2.802	2.677	2.263	7
8	7.325	6.733	6.210	5.747	5.335	4.968	4.639	4.344	4.078	3.837	3.619	3.421	3.241	3.076	2.925	2.786	2.331	8
9	8.162	7.435	6.802	6.247	5.759	5.328	4.946	4.607	4.303	4.031	3.786	3.566	3.366	3.184	3.019	2.868	2.379	9
10	8.983	8.111	7.360	6.710	6.145	5.650	5.216	4.833	4.494	4.192	3.923	3.682	3.465	3.269	3.092	2.930	2.414	10
11	9.787	8.760	7.887	7.139	6.495	5.938	5.453	5.029	4.656	4.327	4.035	3.776	3.543	3.335	3.147	2.978	2.438	11
12	10.575	9.385	8.384	7.536	6.814	6.194	5.660	5.197	4.793	4.439	4.127	3.851	3.606	3.387	3.190	3.013	2.456	12
13	11.348	9.986	8.853	7.904	7.103	6.424	5.842	5.342	4.910	4.533	4.203	3.912	3.656	3.427	3.223	3.040	2.469	13
14	12.106	10.563	9.295	8.244	7.367	6.628	6.002	5.468	5.008	4.611	4.265	3.962	3.695	3.459	3.249	3.061	2.478	14
15	12.849	11.118	9.712	8.559	7.606	6.811	6.142	5.575	5.092	4.675	4.315	4.001	3.726	3.483	3.268	3.076	2.484	15
16	13.578	11.652	10.106	8.851	7.824	6.974	6.265	5.668	5.162	4.730	4.357	4.033	3.751	3.503	3.283	3.088	2.489	16
17	14.292	12.166	10.477	9.122	8.022	7.120	6.373	5.749	5.222	4.775	4.391	4.059	3.771	3.518	3.295	3.097	2.492	17
18	14.992	12.659	10.828	9.372	8.201	7.250	6.467	5.818	5.273	4.812	4.419	4.080	3.786	3.529	3.304	3.104	2.494	18
19	15.678	13.134	11.158	9.604	8.365	7.366	6.550	5.877	5.316	4.843	4.442	4.097	3.799	3.539	3.311	3.109	2.496	19
20	16.351	13.590	11.470	9.818	8.514	7.469	6.623	5.929	5.353	4.870	4.460	4.110	3.808	3.546	3.316	3.113	2.497	20
21	17.011	14.029	11.764	10.017	8.649	7.562	6.687	5.973	5.384	4.891	4.476	4.121	3.816	3.551	3.320	3.116	2.498	21
22	17.658	14.451	12.042	10.201	8.772	7.645	6.743	6.011	5.410	4.909	4.488	4.130	3.822	3.556	3.323	3.118	2.498	22
23	18.292	14.857	12.303	10.371	8.883	7.718	6.792	6.044	5.432	4.925	4.499	4.137	3.827	3.559	3.325	3.120	2.499	23
24	18.914	15.247	12.550	10.529	8.985	7.784	6.835	6.073	5.451	4.937	4.507	4.143	3.831	3.562	3.327	3.121	2.499	24
25	19.523	15.622	12.783	10.675	9.077	7.843	6.873	6.097	5.467	4.948	4.514	4.147	3.834	3.564	3.329	3.122	2.499	25
26	20.121	15.983	13.003	10.810	9.161	7.896	6.906	6.118	5.480	4.956	4.520	4.151	3.837	3.566	3.330	3.123	2.500	26
27	20.707	16.330	13.211	10.935	9.237	7.943	6.935	6.136	5.492	4.964	4.524	4.154	3.839	3.567	3.331	3.123	2.500	27
28	21.281	16.663	13.406	11.051	9.307	7.984	6.961	6.152	5.502	4.970	4.528	4.157	3.840	3.568	3.331	3.124	2.500	28
29	21.844	16.984	13.591	11.158	9.370	8.022	6.983	6.166	5.510	4.975	4.531	4.159	3.841	3.569	3.332	3.124	2.500	29
30	22.396	17.292	13.765	11.258	9.427	8.055	7.003	6.177	5.517	4.979	4.534	4.160	3.842	3.569	3.332	3.124	2.500	30
35	24.999	18.665	14.498	11.655	9.644	8.176	7.070	6.215	5.539	4.992	4.541	4.164	3.845	3.571	3.333	3.125	2.500	35
40	27.355	19.793	15.046	11.925	9.779	8.244	7.105	6.233	5.548	4.997	4.544	4.166	3.846	3.571	3.333	3.125	2.500	40

*Payments (or receipts) at the end of each period.

Glossary

Abnormal spoilage. Spoilage that would not arise under efficient operating conditions; it is not inherent in a particular production process. (753)

Absorption costing. Method of inventory costing in which all variable manufacturing costs and all fixed manufacturing costs are included as inventoriable costs. (323)

Account analysis method. Approach to cost function estimation that classifies various cost accounts as variable, fixed, or mixed with respect to the identified level of activity. Typically, qualitative rather than quantitative analysis is used when making these cost-classification decisions. (372)

Accrual accounting rate-of-return (AARR) method. Capital budgeting method that divides an accrual accounting measure of average annual income of a project by an accrual accounting measure of its investment. See also *return on investment (ROI)*. (861)

Activity. An event, task, or unit of work with a specified purpose. (157)

Activity-based budgeting (ABB). Budgeting approach that focuses on the budgeted cost of the activities necessary to produce and sell products and services. (205)

Activity-based costing (ABC). Approach to costing that focuses on individual activities as the fundamental cost objects. It uses the costs of these activities as the basis for assigning costs to other cost objects such as products or services. (157)

Activity-based management (ABM). Method of management decision making that uses activity-based costing information to improve customer satisfaction and profitability. (170)

Actual cost. Cost incurred (a historical or past cost), as distinguished from a budgeted or forecasted cost. (29)

Actual costing. A costing system that traces direct costs to a cost object by using the actual direct-cost rates times the actual quantities of the direct-cost inputs and allocates indirect costs based on the actual indirect-cost rates times the actual quantities of the cost-allocation bases. (108)

Actual indirect-cost rate. Actual total indirect costs in a cost pool divided by the actual total quantity of the cost-allocation base for that cost pool. (116)

Adjusted allocation-rate approach. Restates all overhead entries in the general ledger and subsidiary ledgers using actual cost rates rather than budgeted cost rates. (126)

Allowable cost. Cost that the contract parties agree to include in the costs to be reimbursed. (661)

Appraisal costs. Costs incurred to detect which of the individual units of products do not conform to specifications. (781)

Artificial costs. See *complete reciprocated costs*. (654)

Autonomy. The degree of freedom to make decisions. (889)

Average cost. See *unit cost*. (37)

Average waiting time. The average amount of time that an order will wait in line before the machine is set up and the order is processed. (792)

Backflush costing. Costing system that omits recording some of the journal entries relating to the stages from purchase of direct materials to the sale of finished goods. (827)

Balanced scorecard. A framework for implementing strategy that translates an organization's mission and strategy into a set of performance measures. (520)

Batch-level costs. The costs of activities related to a group of units of products or services rather than to each individual unit of product or service. (160)

Belief systems. Lever of control that articulates the mission, purpose, norms of behaviors, and core values of a company intended to inspire managers and other employees to do their best. (945)

Benchmarking. The continuous process of comparing the levels of performance in producing products and services and executing activities against the best levels of performance in competing companies or in companies having similar processes. (262)

Book value. The original cost minus accumulated depreciation of an asset. (491)

Bottleneck. An operation where the work to be performed approaches or exceeds the capacity available to do it. (791)

Boundary systems. Lever of control that describes standards of behavior and codes of conduct expected of all employees, especially actions that are off-limits. (944)

Breakeven point (BEP). Quantity of output sold at which total revenues equal total costs; that is, where the operating income is zero. (72)

Budget. Quantitative expression of a proposed plan of action by management for a specified period and an aid to coordinating what needs to be done to execute that plan. (10)

Budgetary slack. The practice of underestimating budgeted revenues, or overestimating budgeted costs, to make budgeted targets easier to achieve. (216)

Budgeted cost. Predicted or forecasted cost (future cost) as distinguished from an actual or historical cost. (29)

Budgeted indirect-cost rate. Budgeted annual indirect costs in a cost pool divided by the budgeted annual quantity of the cost-allocation base. (110)

Budgeted performance. Expected performance or a point of reference to compare actual results. (246)

Bundled product. A package of two or more products (or services) that is sold for a single price, but whose individual components may be sold as separate items at their own "stand-alone" prices. (662)

Business function costs. The sum of all costs (variable and fixed) in a particular business function of the value chain. (470)

Byproducts. Products from a joint production process that have low total sales values compared with the total sales value of the main product or of joint products. (681)

Capital budgeting. The process of making long-run planning decisions for investments in projects. (850)

Carrying costs. Costs that arise while holding inventory of goods for sale. (810)

Cash budget. Schedule of expected cash receipts and disbursements. (223)

Cause-and-effect diagram. Diagram that identifies potential causes of defects. Four categories of potential causes of failure are human factors, methods and design factors, machine-related factors, and materials and components factors. Also referred to as a *fishbone diagram*. (786)

Chief financial officer (CFO). Executive responsible for overseeing the financial operations of an organization. Also called *finance director*. (14)

Choice criterion. Objective that can be quantified in a decision model. (89)

Coefficient of determination (r^2). Measures the percentage of variation in a dependent variable explained by one or more independent variables. (393)

Collusive pricing. Companies in an industry conspire in their pricing and production decisions to achieve a price above the competitive price and so restrain trade. (581)

Common cost. Cost of operating a facility, activity, or like cost object that is shared by two or more users. (658)

Complete reciprocated costs. The support department's own costs plus any interdepartmental cost allocations. Also called the *artificial costs* of the support department. (654)

Composite unit. Hypothetical unit with weights based on the mix of individual units. (618)

Conference method. Approach to cost function estimation on the basis of analysis and opinions about costs and their drivers gathered from various departments of a company (purchasing, process engineering, manufacturing, employee relations, and so on). (372)

Conformance quality. Refers to the performance of a product or service relative to its design and product specifications. (780)

Confusion matrix. A matrix that shows the predicted versus actual classifications, for example, defaults and repay loans, at a given threshold value. (443)

Constant. The component of total cost that, within the relevant range, does not vary with changes in the level of the activity. Also called *intercept*. (368)

Constant gross-margin percentage NRV method. Method that allocates joint costs to joint products produced during the accounting period in such a way that the overall gross-margin percentage is identical for the individual products. (687)

Constraint. A mathematical inequality or equality that must be satisfied by the variables in a mathematical model. (499)

Continuous budget. See *rolling budget*. (199)

Contribution income statement. Income statement that groups costs into variable costs and fixed costs to highlight the contribution margin. (68)

Contribution margin. Total revenues minus total variable costs. (67)

Contribution margin per unit. Selling price minus the variable cost per unit. (67)

Contribution margin percentage. Contribution margin divided by revenues. Also called *contribution margin ratio*. (68)

Contribution margin ratio. See *contribution margin percentage*. (68)

Control. Taking actions that implement the planning decisions, evaluating past performance, and providing feedback and learning that will help future decision making. (10)

Control chart. Graph of a series of successive observations of a particular step, procedure, or operation taken at regular intervals of time. Each observation is plotted relative to specified ranges that represent the limits within which observations are expected to fall. (784)

Controllability. Degree of influence that a specific manager has over costs, revenues, or related items for which he or she is responsible. (214)

Controllable cost. Any cost that is primarily subject to the influence of a given responsibility center manager for a given period. (214)

Controller. The financial executive primarily responsible for management accounting and financial accounting. Also referred to as *chief accounting officer*. (14)

Conversion costs. All manufacturing costs other than direct materials costs. (46)

Cost. Monetary value of resources sacrificed or forgone to achieve a specific objective. (29)

Cost accounting. Measures, analyzes, and reports financial and nonfinancial information relating to the costs of acquiring or using resources in an organization. It provides information for both management accounting and financial accounting. (3)

Cost Accounting Standards Board (CASB). Government agency that has the exclusive authority to make, put into effect, amend, and rescind cost accounting standards and interpretations thereof designed to achieve uniformity and consistency in regard to measurement, assignment, and allocation of costs to government contracts within the United States. (661)

Cost accumulation. Collection of cost data in some organized way by means of an accounting system. (29)

Cost allocation. Assignment of indirect costs to a particular cost object. (30)

Cost-allocation base. A factor that links in a systematic way an indirect cost or group of indirect costs to a cost object. (105)

Cost assignment. General term that encompasses both (1) tracing accumulated costs that have a direct relationship to a cost object and (2) allocating accumulated costs that have an indirect relationship to a cost object. (30)

Cost–benefit approach. Approach to decision making and resource allocation based on a comparison of the expected benefits from attaining company goals and the expected costs. (12)

Cost center. Responsibility center where the manager is accountable for costs only. (213)

Cost driver. A variable, such as the level of activity or volume, that causally affects costs over a given time span. (35)

Cost estimation. The attempt to measure a past relationship based on data from past costs and the related level of an activity. (370)

Cost function. Mathematical description of how a cost changes with changes in the level of an activity relating to that cost. (367)

Cost hierarchy. Categorization of indirect costs into different cost pools on the basis of the different types of cost drivers, or cost-allocation bases, or different degrees of difficulty in determining cause-and-effect (or benefits received) relationships. (159)

Cost incurrence. Describes when a resource is consumed (or a benefit is forgone) to meet a specific objective. (571)

Cost leadership. Organization's ability to achieve lower costs relative to competitors through productivity and efficiency improvements, elimination of waste, and tight cost control. (519)

Cost management. The approaches and activities of managers to use resources to increase value to customers and to achieve organizational goals. (3)

Cost object. Anything for which a measurement of costs is desired. (29)

Cost of capital. See *required rate of return (RRR)*. (853)

Cost of goods manufactured. Cost of goods brought to completion, whether they were started before or during the current accounting period. (43)

Cost pool. A grouping of individual cost items. (105)

Cost predictions. Forecasts about future costs. (370)

Cost tracing. Describes the assignment of direct costs to a particular cost object. (30)

Costs of quality (COQ). Costs incurred to prevent, or the costs arising as a result of, the production of a low-quality product. (781)

Cost–volume–profit (CVP) analysis. Examines the behavior of total revenues, total costs, and operating income as changes occur in the units sold, the selling price, the variable cost per unit, or the fixed costs of a product. (66)

Cross-validation. The process of comparing predictions and choosing among different (data science) models on a new set of data for which the actual outcomes are already known. (435)

Cumulative average-time learning model. Learning curve model in which the cumulative average time per unit declines by a constant percentage each time the cumulative quantity of units produced doubles. (384)

Current cost. Asset measure based on the cost of purchasing an asset today identical to the one currently held, or, if an identical asset cannot be purchased, the cost of purchasing an asset that provides services like the one currently held. (933)

Customer-cost hierarchy. Hierarchy that categorizes costs related to customers into different cost pools on the basis of different types of cost drivers, or cost-allocation bases, or different degrees of difficulty in determining cause-and-effect or benefits-received relationships. (598)

Customer life-cycle costs. Focuses on the total costs incurred by a customer to acquire, use, maintain, and dispose of a product or service. (580)

Customer-profitability analysis. The reporting and analysis of revenues earned from customers and the costs incurred to earn those revenues. (597)

Customer relationship management (CRM). A strategy that integrates people and technology in all business functions to deepen relationships with customers, partners, and distributors. (6)

Customer-response time. Duration from the time a customer places an order for a product or service to the time the product or service is delivered to the customer. (790)

Customer service. Providing after-sale support to customers. (5)

Data science. Use of data analytics to draw conclusions from data. (420)

Decentralization. The freedom for managers at lower levels of the organization to make decisions. (889)

Decision model. Formal method for making a choice, often involving both quantitative and qualitative analyses. (467)

Decision table. Summary of the alternative actions, events, outcomes, and probabilities of events in a decision model. (90)

Decision tree. A data science technique for segmenting the target variable into different regions based on a set of rules. (425)

Degree of operating leverage. Contribution margin divided by operating income at any given level of sales. (81)

Denominator level. The denominator in the budgeted fixed overhead rate computation. (285)

Denominator-level variance. See *production-volume variance*. (292)

Dependent variable. The cost to be predicted. (374)

Design of products and processes. The detailed planning, engineering, and testing of products and processes. (5)

Design quality. Refers to how closely the characteristics of a product or service meet the needs and wants of customers. (780)

Designed-in costs. See *locked-in costs*. (571)

Diagnostic control systems. Lever of control that monitors critical performance variables that help managers track progress toward achieving a company's strategic goals. Managers are held accountable and rewarded for meeting these goals. (943)

Differential cost. Difference in total cost between two alternatives. (476)

Differential revenue. Difference in total revenue between two alternatives. (476)

Direct costing. See *variable costing*. (323)

Direct costs of a cost object. Costs related to the particular cost object that can be unambiguously traced to that object in an economically feasible (cost-effective) way. (29)

Direct manufacturing labor costs. Include the compensation of all manufacturing labor that can be easily traced to the cost object (work in process and then finished goods) in an economically feasible way. (39)

Direct manufacturing labor mix variance. The difference between (1) budgeted cost for actual mix of the actual total quantity of direct manufacturing labor used and (2) budgeted cost of budgeted mix of the actual total quantity of direct manufacturing labor used. (267)

Direct manufacturing labor yield variance. The difference between (1) budgeted cost of direct manufacturing labor based on the actual total quantity of direct manufacturing labor used and (2) flexible-budget cost of direct manufacturing labor based on the budgeted total quantity of direct manufacturing labor allowed for actual output produced. (267)

Direct materials costs. Acquisition costs of all materials that eventually become part of the cost object (work in process and then finished goods), and that can be easily traced to the cost object in an economically feasible way. (39)

Direct materials inventory. Direct materials in stock and awaiting use in the manufacturing process. (39)

Direct method. Cost allocation method that directly allocates each support department's costs to operating departments only. (650)

Discount rate. See *required rate of return (RRR)*. (853)

Discounted cash flow (DCF) methods. Capital budgeting methods that measure all expected future cash inflows and outflows of a project as if they occurred at the present point in time. (853)

Discounted payback method. Capital budgeting method that calculates the amount of time required for the discounted expected future cash flows to recoup the net initial investment in a project. (860)

Distribution. Processing orders and delivering products or services to customers. (5)

Downsizing. An integrated approach of configuring processes, products, and people to match costs to the activities that need to be performed to operate effectively and efficiently in the present and future. Also called *rightsizing*. (542)

Downward demand spiral. Pricing context where prices are raised to spread capacity costs over a smaller number of output units, resulting in lower demand for products when the prices of competitors' products are not met; as output drops further, higher and higher unit costs result in higher prices and ever lower demand. (340)

Dual pricing. Approach to transfer pricing using two separate transfer prices to price each transfer from one subunit to another. (902)

Dual-rate method. Allocation method that classifies costs in each cost pool into two pools (a variable-cost pool and a fixed-cost pool) with each pool using a different cost-allocation base. (640)

Dumping. Under U.S. laws, it occurs when a non-U.S. company sells a product in the United States at a price below the market value in the country where it is produced, and this lower price materially injures or threatens to materially injure an industry in the United States. (582)

Dysfunctional decision making. See *suboptimal decision making*. (891)

Economic order quantity (EOQ). Decision model that calculates the optimal quantity of inventory to order under a set of assumptions to minimize the sum of ordering and carrying costs. (811)

Economic value added (EVA). After-tax operating income minus the (after-tax) weighted-average cost of capital multiplied by total assets minus current liabilities. (929)

Efficiency variance. The difference between actual input quantity used and budgeted input quantity allowed for actual output, multiplied by budgeted price. Also called *usage variance*. (254)

Effort. Exertion toward achieving a goal. (889)

Enterprise resource planning (ERP) system. An integrated set of software modules covering a company's accounting, distribution, manufacturing, purchasing, human resources, and other functions. (826)

Equivalent units. Derived amount of output units that (1) takes the quantity of each input (factor of production) in units completed and in incomplete units of work in process and (2) converts the quantity of input into the amount of completed output units that could be produced with that quantity of input. (714)

Event. A possible relevant occurrence in a decision model. (89)

Expected monetary value. See *expected value*. (91)

Expected value. Weighted average of the outcomes of a decision with the probability of each outcome serving as the weight. Also called *expected monetary value*. (91)

Experience curve. Function that measures the decline in cost per unit in various business functions of the value chain, such as manufacturing, marketing, distribution, and so on, as the amount of these activities increases. (384)

External failure costs. Costs incurred on defective products after they are shipped to customers. (781)

Facility-sustaining costs. The costs of activities that cannot be traced to individual products or services but support the organization as a whole. (160)

Factory overhead costs. See *indirect manufacturing costs*. (39)

False negatives (FN). Actual positives (for example, default loans) in a classification model incorrectly predicted as negatives (repay loans) at a given threshold value. (444)

False positive rate. Fraction of actual negatives (for example, repay loans) in a classification model incorrectly predicted as positives (default loans) at a given threshold value. (442)

False positives (FP). Actual negatives (for example, repay loans) in a classification model incorrectly predicted as positives (default loans) at a given threshold value. (444)

Favorable variance. Variance that has the effect of increasing operating income relative to the budgeted amount. Denoted F. (248)

Finance director. See *chief financial officer (CFO)*. (14)

Financial accounting. Measures and records business transactions and provides financial statements that are based on generally accepted accounting principles. It focuses on reporting to external parties such as investors and banks. (2)

Financial budget. Part of the master budget that focuses on how operations and planned capital outlays affect cash. It is made up of the capital expenditures budget, the cash budget, the budgeted balance sheet, and the budgeted statement of cash flows. (200)

Financial planning models. Mathematical representations of the relationships among operating activities, financial activities, and other factors that affect the master budget. (211)

Finished-goods inventory. Goods completed but not yet sold. (39)

First-in, first-out (FIFO) process-costing method. Method of process costing that assigns the cost of the previous accounting period's equivalent units in beginning work-in-process inventory to the first units completed and transferred out of the process, and assigns the cost of equivalent units worked on during the current period first to complete beginning inventory, next to start and complete new units, and finally to units in ending work-in-process inventory. (721)

Fixed cost. Cost that remains unchanged in total for a given time period, despite wide changes in the related level of total activity or volume. (32)

Fixed overhead flexible-budget variance. The difference between actual fixed overhead costs and fixed overhead costs in the flexible budget. (290)

Fixed overhead spending variance. Same as the fixed overhead flexible-budget variance. The difference between actual fixed overhead costs and fixed overhead costs in the flexible budget. (291)

Flexible budget. Budget developed using budgeted revenues and budgeted costs based on the actual output in the budget period. (248)

Flexible-budget variance. The difference between an actual result and the corresponding flexible-budget amount based on the actual output level in the budget period. (250)

Full costs of the product. The sum of all variable and fixed costs in all business functions of the value chain (R&D, design, production, marketing, distribution, and customer service). (470)

Gini impurity. A metric in decision tree analysis to measure the purity of a collection of observations in a tree branch. (428)

Goal congruence. Exists when individuals and groups work toward achieving the organization's goals. Managers working in their own best interest take actions that align with the overall goals of top management. (889)

Gross margin percentage. Gross margin divided by revenues. (87)

Growth component. Change in operating income attributable solely to the change in the quantity of output sold between one period and the next. (535)

High-low method. Method used to estimate a cost function that uses only the highest and lowest observed values of the cost driver within the relevant range and their respective costs. (375)

Homogeneous cost pools. Cost pools in which all the costs have the same or a similar cause-and-effect or benefits-received relationship with the cost-allocation base. (614)

Hurdle rate. See *required rate of return (RRR)*. (853)

Hybrid-costing system. Costing system that blends characteristics from both job-costing systems and process-costing systems. (731)

Hyperparameter. A parameter that cannot be learned by running a decision model but must be chosen prior to building the model. (439)

Idle time. Wages paid for unproductive time caused by lack of orders, machine breakdowns, delays, poor scheduling, and the like. (46)

Imputed cost. Costs recognized in particular situations but not recorded in financial accounting systems. (927)

Incongruent decision making. See *suboptimal decision making*. (891)

Incremental cost. Additional total cost incurred for an activity. (476)

Incremental cost-allocation method. Method that ranks the individual users of a cost object in the order of users most responsible for the common cost and then uses this ranking to allocate cost among those users. (659)

Incremental revenue. Additional total revenue from an activity. (476)

Incremental revenue-allocation method. Method that ranks individual products in a bundle according to criteria determined by management (for example, sales), and then uses this ranking to allocate bundled revenues to the individual products. (669)

Incremental unit-time learning model. Learning curve model in which the incremental time needed to produce the last unit declines by a constant percentage each time the cumulative quantity of units produced doubles. (385)

Independent variable. Level of activity or cost driver used to predict the dependent variable (costs) in a cost estimation or prediction model. (374)

Indirect costs of a cost object. Costs related to the particular cost object that cannot be traced unambiguously to that object in an economically feasible (cost-effective) way. (30)

Indirect manufacturing costs. All manufacturing costs that are related to the cost object (work in process and then finished goods) but that cannot be traced to that cost object in an economically feasible way. Also called *manufacturing overhead costs* and *factory overhead costs*. (39)

Industrial engineering method. Approach to cost function estimation that analyzes the relationship between inputs and outputs in physical terms. Also called *work-measurement method*. (371)

Inflation. The decline in the general purchasing power of a monetary unit, such as dollars. (874)

Insourcing. Process of producing goods or providing services within the organization rather than purchasing those same goods or services from outside vendors. (474)

Inspection point. Stage of the production process at which products are examined to determine whether they are acceptable or unacceptable units. (754)

Interactive control systems. Formal information systems that managers use to focus organization attention and learning on key strategic issues. (945)

Intercept. See *constant*. (368)

Intermediate product. Product transferred from one subunit to another subunit of an organization. This product may be either further worked on by the receiving subunit or sold to an external customer. (893)

Internal failure costs. Costs incurred on defective products before they are shipped to customers. (781)

Internal rate-of-return (IRR) method. Capital budgeting discounted cash flow (DCF) method that calculates the discount rate at which the present value of expected cash inflows from a project equals the present value of its expected cash outflows. (855)

Inventoriable costs. All costs of a product that are considered as assets in the balance sheet when they are incurred and that become cost of goods sold only when the product is sold. (39)

Inventory management. Planning, coordinating, and controlling activities related to the flow of inventory into, through, and out of an organization. (810)

Investment. Resources or assets used to generate income. (925)

Investment center. Responsibility center where the manager is accountable for investments, revenues, and costs. (213)

Job. A unit or multiple units of a distinct product or service. (106)

Job-cost record. Source document that records and accumulates all the costs assigned to a specific job, starting when work begins. Also called *job-cost sheet*. (110)

Job-cost sheet. See *job-cost record*. (110)

Job-costing system. Costing system in which the cost object is a unit or multiple units of a distinct product or service called a job. (106)

Joint costs. Costs of a production process that yields multiple products simultaneously. (680)

Joint products. Two or more products that have high total sales values compared with the total sales values of other products yielded by a joint production process. (681)

Just-in-time (JIT) production. Demand-pull manufacturing system in which each component in a production line is produced as soon as, and only when, needed by the next step in the production line. Also called *lean production*. (823)

Just-in-time (JIT) purchasing. The purchase of materials (or goods) so that they are delivered just as needed for production (or sales). (818)

Kaizen budgeting. Budgetary approach that explicitly incorporates continuous improvement anticipated during the budget period into the budget numbers. (218)

Labor-time sheet. Source document that contains information about the amount of labor time used for a specific job in a specific department. (110)

Lean accounting. Costing method that supports creating value for the customer by costing the entire value stream, not individual products or departments, thereby eliminating waste in the accounting process. (835)

Lean production. See *just-in-time (JIT) production.* (823)

Learning. Involves managers examining past performance and systematically exploring alternative ways to make better-informed decisions and plans in the future. (11)

Learning curve. Function that measures how labor-hours per unit decline as units of production increase because workers are learning and becoming better at their jobs. (383)

Life-cycle budgeting. Budget that estimates the revenues and business function costs of the value chain attributable to each product from initial R&D to final customer service and support. (578)

Life-cycle costing. System that tracks and accumulates business function costs of the value chain attributable to each product from initial R&D to final customer service and support. (578)

Line management. Managers (for example, in production, marketing, or distribution) who are directly responsible for attaining the goals of the organization. (13)

Linear cost function. Cost function in which the graph of total costs versus the level of a single activity related to that cost is a straight line within the relevant range. (367)

Linear programming (LP). Optimization technique used to maximize an objective function (for example, contribution margin of a mix of products) when there are multiple constraints. (499)

Locked-in costs. Costs that have not yet been incurred but, based on decisions that have already been made, will be incurred in the future. Also called *designed-in costs.* (571)

Main product. Product from a joint production process that has a high total sales value compared with the total sales values of all other products of the joint production process. (681)

Make-or-buy decisions. Decisions about whether a producer of goods or services will insource (produce goods or services within the firm) or outsource (purchase them from outside vendors). (474)

Management accounting. Measures, analyzes, and reports financial and nonfinancial information that helps managers make decisions to fulfill the goals of an organization. It focuses on internal reporting. (2)

Management by exception. Practice of focusing management attention on areas not operating as expected and giving less attention to areas operating as expected. (246)

Management control system. Means of gathering and using information to aid and coordinate the planning and control decisions throughout an organization and to guide the behavior of its managers and employees. (888)

Manufacturing cells. Grouping of all the different types of equipment used to make a given product. (823)

Manufacturing cycle efficiency (MCE). Value-added manufacturing time divided by manufacturing cycle time. (790)

Manufacturing cycle time. See *manufacturing lead time.* (790)

Manufacturing lead time. Duration between the time an order is received by manufacturing to the time a finished good is produced. Also called *manufacturing cycle time.* (790)

Manufacturing overhead allocated. Amount of manufacturing overhead costs allocated to individual jobs (or products or services) based on the budgeted rate multiplied by the actual quantity of the cost-allocation base used for each job. Also called *manufacturing overhead applied.* (120)

Manufacturing overhead applied. See *manufacturing overhead allocated.* (120)

Manufacturing overhead costs. See *indirect manufacturing costs.* (39)

Manufacturing-sector companies. Companies that purchase materials and components and convert them into various finished goods. (38)

Margin of safety. Amount by which budgeted (or actual) revenues exceed breakeven revenues. (79)

Marketing. Promoting and selling products or services to customers or prospective customers. (5)

Market-share variance. The difference in budgeted contribution margin for actual market size in units caused solely by actual market share being different from budgeted market share. (620)

Market-size variance. The difference in budgeted contribution margin at the budgeted market share caused solely by actual market size in units being different from budgeted market size in units. (620)

Master budget. Expression of management's operating and financial plans for a specified period (usually a fiscal year) including a set of budgeted financial statements. Also called *pro forma statements.* (196)

Master-budget capacity utilization. The expected level of capacity utilization for the current budget period (typically 1 year). (337)

Materials requirements planning (MRP) system. Push-through system that manufactures finished goods for inventory on the basis of demand forecasts. (823)

Materials-requisition record. Source document that contains information about the cost of direct materials used on a specific job and in a specific department. (110)

Matrix method. See *reciprocal method.* (654)

Merchandising-sector companies. Companies that purchase and then sell tangible products without changing their basic form. (38)

Mixed cost. A cost that has both fixed and variable elements. Also called a *semivariable cost.* (368)

Moral hazard. Describes situations in which an employee prefers to exert less effort (or to report distorted information) compared with the effort (or accurate information) desired by the owner because the employee's effort (or validity of the reported information) cannot be accurately monitored and enforced. (939)

Motivation. The desire to attain a selected goal (the goal-congruence aspect) combined with the resulting pursuit of that goal (the effort aspect). (889)

Multicollinearity. Exists when two or more independent variables in a multiple regression model are highly correlated with each other. (401)

Multiple regression. Regression model that estimates the relationship between the dependent variable and two or more independent variables. (377)

Net income. Operating income plus nonoperating revenues (such as interest revenue) minus nonoperating costs (such as interest cost) minus income taxes. (75)

Net present value (NPV) method. Capital budgeting discounted cash flow (DCF) method that calculates the expected monetary gain or loss from a project by discounting all expected future cash inflows and outflows to the present point in time, using the required rate of return. (854)

Net realizable value (NRV) method. Method that allocates joint costs to joint products on the basis of final sales value minus separable costs of total production of the joint products during the accounting period. (686)

Nominal rate of return. Made up of three elements: (1) a risk-free element when there is no expected inflation, (2) a business-risk element, and (3) an inflation element. (874)

Nonlinear cost function. Cost function in which the graph of total costs based on the level of a single activity is not a straight line within the relevant range. (382)

Non-value-added cost. A cost that, if eliminated, would not reduce the actual or perceived value or utility (usefulness) customers obtain from using the product or service. (571)

Normal capacity utilization. The level of capacity utilization that satisfies average customer demand over a period (say, 2 to 3 years) that includes seasonal, cyclical, and trend factors. (337)

Normal costing. A costing system that traces direct costs to a cost object by using the actual direct-cost rates times the actual quantities of the direct-cost inputs and that allocates indirect costs based on the budgeted indirect-cost rates times the actual quantities of the cost-allocation bases. (110)

Normal spoilage. Spoilage inherent in a particular production process that arises even under efficient operating conditions. (752)

Objective function. Expresses the objective to be maximized (for example, operating income) or minimized (for example, operating costs) in a decision model (for example, a linear programming model). (498)

On-time performance. Delivering a product or service by the time it is scheduled to be delivered. (791)

One-time-only special order. Orders that have no long-run implications. (470)

Operating budget. Budgeted income statement (for operations) and its supporting budget schedules. (199)

Operating department. Department that directly adds value to a product or service. Also called a *production department* in manufacturing companies. (640)

Operating income. Total revenues from operations minus cost of goods sold and operating (period) costs (excluding interest expense and income taxes). (44)

Operating-income volume variance. The difference between static-budget operating income and the operating income based on budgeted profit per unit and actual units of output. (300)

Operating leverage. Effects that fixed costs have on changes in operating income as changes occur in units sold and contribution margin. (81)

Operation. A standardized method or technique that is performed repetitively, often on different materials, resulting in different finished goods. (731)

Operation-costing system. Hybrid-costing system applied to batches of similar, but not identical, products. Each batch of products is often a variation of a single design, and proceeds through a sequence of operations, but each batch does not necessarily move through the same operations as other batches. Within each operation, all product units use identical amounts of the operation's resources. (731)

Opportunity cost. The contribution to operating income that is forgone or rejected by not using a limited resource in its next-best alternative use. (478)

Opportunity cost of capital. See *required rate of return (RRR).* (853)

Ordering costs. Costs of preparing and issuing purchase orders; receiving and inspecting the items included in the orders; and matching invoices received, purchase orders, and delivery records to make payments. (810)

Organization structure. Arrangement of lines of responsibility within the organization. (213)

Outcomes. Predicted economic results of the various possible combinations of actions and events in a decision model. (90)

Output unit–level costs. The costs of activities performed on each individual unit of a product or service. (160)

Outsourcing. Process of purchasing goods and services from outside vendors rather than producing the same goods or providing the same services within the organization. (474)

Overabsorbed indirect costs. See *overallocated indirect costs.* (125)

Overallocated indirect costs. Allocated amount of indirect costs in an accounting period is greater than the actual (incurred) amount in that period. Also called *overapplied indirect costs* and *overabsorbed indirect costs.* (125)

Overapplied indirect costs. See *overallocated indirect costs.* (125)

Overfitting. Occurs when a data science model adheres too closely to the specific details of a training dataset such that, in addition to signal, the model captures noise from random chance. The model does a poor job of predicting on new data sets. (433)

Overtime premium. Wage rate paid to workers (for both direct labor and indirect labor) in excess of their straight-time wage rates. (46)

Pareto diagram. Chart that indicates how frequently each type of defect occurs, ordered from the most frequent to the least frequent. (785)

Partial productivity. Measures the quantity of output produced divided by the quantity of an individual input used. (548)

Payback method. Capital budgeting method that measures the time it will take to recoup, in the form of expected future cash flows, the net initial investment in a project. (858)

Peak-load pricing. Practice of charging a higher price for the same product or service when the demand for it approaches the physical limit of the capacity to produce that product or service. (582)

Perfectly competitive market. Exists when there is a homogeneous product with buying prices equal to selling prices and no individual buyers or sellers can affect those prices by their own actions. (897)

Period costs. All costs in the income statement other than cost of goods sold. (40)

Physical-measure method. Method that allocates joint costs to joint products on the basis of the relative weight, volume, or other physical measure at the splitoff point of total production of these products during the accounting period. (684)

Planning. Selecting organization goals, predicting results under various alternative ways of achieving those goals, deciding how to attain the desired goals, and communicating the goals and how to achieve them to the entire organization. (10)

Practical capacity. The level of capacity that reduces theoretical capacity by unavoidable operating interruptions such as scheduled maintenance time, shutdowns for holidays, and so on. (337)

Predatory pricing. Company deliberately prices below its costs in an effort to drive out competitors and restrict supply, and then recoups its losses by raising prices or enlarging demand. (581)

Predictive modeling. A data science technique used to make predictions based on past or current data. (420)

Prevention costs. Costs incurred to preclude the production of products that do not conform to specifications. (781)

Previous-department costs. See *transferred-in costs*. (726)

Price discount. Reduction in selling price below list selling price to encourage increases in customer purchases. (597)

Price discrimination. Practice of charging different customers different prices for the same product or service. (581)

Price-recovery component. Change in operating income attributable solely to changes in prices of inputs and outputs between one period and the next. (535)

Price variance. The difference between actual price and budgeted price multiplied by actual quantity of input. Also called *rate variance*. (254)

Prime costs. All direct manufacturing costs. (46)

Pro forma statements. Budgeted financial statements. See also *master budget*. (196)

Probability. Likelihood or chance that an event will occur. (89)

Probability distribution. Describes the likelihood (or the probability) that each of the mutually exclusive and collectively exhaustive set of events will occur. (89)

Process-costing system. Costing system in which the cost object is masses of identical or similar units of a product or service. (106)

Product. Any output that has a positive total sales value (or an output that enables an organization to avoid incurring costs). (680)

Product cost. Sum of the costs assigned to a product for a specific purpose. (47)

Product-cost cross-subsidization. Costing outcome where one undercosted (overcosted) product results in at least one other product being overcosted (undercosted). (151)

Product differentiation. Organization's ability to offer products or services perceived by its customers to be superior and unique relative to the products or services of its competitors. (519)

Product life cycle. Spans the time from initial R&D on a product to when customer service and support is no longer offered for that product. (578)

Product-mix decisions. Decisions about which products to sell and in what quantities. (482)

Product overcosting. A product consumes a low level of resources but is reported to have a high cost per unit. (150)

Product-sustaining costs. The costs of activities undertaken to support individual products regardless of the number of units or batches in which products are produced. (160)

Product undercosting. A product consumes a high level of resources but is reported to have a low cost per unit. (150)

Production. Acquiring, storing, coordinating, and assembling resources to produce a product or deliver a service. (5)

Production department. See *operating department*. (640)

Production-volume variance. The difference between budgeted fixed overhead and fixed overhead allocated on the basis of actual output produced. Also called *denominator-level variance*. (291)

Productivity. Measures the relationship between actual inputs used (both quantities and costs) and actual outputs produced; the lower the inputs for a given quantity of outputs or the higher the outputs for a given quantity of inputs, the higher the productivity. (547)

Productivity component. Change in costs attributable to a change in the quantity of inputs used in the current period relative to the quantity of inputs that would have been used in the prior period to produce the quantity of current period output. (535)

Profit center. Responsibility center where the manager is accountable for revenues and costs. (213)

Proration. The spreading of underallocated manufacturing overhead or overallocated manufacturing overhead among ending work in process, finished goods, and cost of goods sold. (126)

Pruning. A technique in which a decision tree is not grown to its full size but instead is only allowed to grow to a certain depth. (433)

Purchase-order lead time. The time between placing an order and its delivery. (811)

Purchasing costs. Cost of goods acquired from suppliers, including incoming freight or transportation costs. (810)

PV graph. Shows how changes in the quantity of units sold affect operating income. (75)

Qualitative factors. Outcomes that are difficult to measure accurately in numerical terms. (469)

Quality. The total features and characteristics of a product made or a service performed according to specifications to satisfy customers at the time of purchase and during use. (780)

Quantitative factors. Outcomes that are measured in numerical terms. (469)

Rate variance. See *price variance.* (254)

Real rate of return. The rate of return demanded to cover investment risk (with no inflation). It has a risk-free element and a business-risk element. (874)

Receiver operating characteristic (ROC) curve. A graph of the false positive rate on the x-axis and the true positive rate on the y-axis in data science analyses. (443)

Reciprocal method. Cost allocation method that fully recognizes the mutual services provided among all support departments. Also called *matrix method.* (653)

Refined costing system. Costing system that reduces the use of broad averages for assigning the cost of resources to cost objects (jobs, products, services) and provides better measurement of the costs of indirect resources used by different cost objects, no matter how differently various cost objects use indirect resources. (155)

Regression analysis. Statistical method that measures the average amount of change in the dependent variable associated with a unit change in one or more independent variables. (377)

Relevant costs. Expected future costs that differ among alternative courses of action being considered. (467)

Relevant range. Band of normal activity level or volume in which there is a specific relationship between the level of activity or volume and the cost in question. (35)

Relevant revenues. Expected future revenues that differ among alternative courses of action being considered. (467)

Reorder point. The quantity level of inventory on hand that triggers a new purchase order. (813)

Required rate of return (RRR). The minimum acceptable annual rate of return on an investment. Also called the *discount rate, hurdle rate, cost of capital,* or *opportunity cost of capital.* (853)

Research and development (R&D). Generating and experimenting with ideas related to new products, services, or processes. (5)

Residual income (RI). An accounting measure of income minus a dollar amount for required return on an accounting measure of investment. (927)

Residual term. The vertical difference or distance between actual cost and estimated cost for each observation in a regression model. (377)

Responsibility accounting. System that measures the plans, budgets, actions, and actual results of each responsibility center. (213)

Responsibility center. Part, segment, or subunit of an organization whose manager is accountable for a specified set of activities. (213)

Return on investment (ROI). An accounting measure of income divided by an accounting measure of investment. See also *accrual accounting rate-of-return method.* (925)

Revenue allocation. The allocation of revenues that are related to a particular revenue object but cannot be traced to it in an economically feasible (cost-effective) way. (662)

Revenue center. Responsibility center where the manager is accountable for revenues only. (213)

Revenue driver. A variable, such as volume, that causally affects revenues. (71)

Revenue object. Anything for which a separate measurement of revenue is desired. (662)

Revenues. Inflows of assets (usually cash or accounts receivable) received for products or services provided to customers. (39)

Rework. Units of production that do not meet the specifications required by customers for finished units that are subsequently repaired and sold as good finished units. (752)

Rightsizing. See *downsizing.* (542)

Rolling budget. Budget or plan that is always available for a specified future period by adding a period (month, quarter, or year) to the period that just ended. Also called *continuous budget* or *rolling forecast.* (199)

Rolling forecast. See *rolling budget.* (199)

Safety stock. Inventory held at all times regardless of the quantity of inventory ordered using the EOQ model. (814)

Sales mix. Quantities of various products or services that constitute total unit sales. (83)

Sales-mix variance. The difference between (1) budgeted contribution margin for the actual sales mix, and (2) budgeted contribution margin for the budgeted sales mix. (618)

Sales-quantity variance. The difference between (1) budgeted contribution margin based on actual units sold of all products at the budgeted mix and (2) contribution margin in the static budget (which is based on the budgeted units of all products to be sold at the budgeted mix). (619)

Sales value at splitoff method. Method that allocates joint costs to joint products on the basis of the relative total sales value at the splitoff point of the total production of these products during the accounting period. (684)

Sales-volume variance. The difference between a flexible-budget amount and the corresponding static-budget amount. (250)

Scrap. Residual material left over when making a product. (752)

Selling-price variance. The difference between the actual selling price and the budgeted selling price multiplied by the actual units sold. (251)

Semivariable cost. See *mixed cost.* (368)

Sensitivity analysis. A what-if technique that managers use to examine how an outcome will change if the original predicted data are not achieved or if an underlying assumption changes. (78)

Separable costs. All costs (manufacturing, marketing, distribution, and so on) incurred beyond the splitoff point that are assignable to each of the specific products identified at the splitoff point. (680)

Sequential allocation method. See *step-down method.* (651)

Sequential tracking. Approach in a product-costing system in which recording of the journal entries occurs in the same order as actual purchases and progress in production. (827)

Service department. See *support department.* (640)

Service-sector companies. Companies that provide services or intangible products to their customers. (38)

Service-sustaining costs. The costs of activities undertaken to support individual services regardless of the number of units or batches in which services are provided. (160)

Shrinkage costs. Costs that result from theft by outsiders, embezzlement by employees, and misclassifications or misplacement of inventory. (811)

Simple regression. Regression model that estimates the relationship between the dependent variable and one independent variable. (377)

Single-rate method. Allocation method that allocates costs in each cost pool to cost objects using the same rate per unit of a single allocation base without distinguishing fixed from variable costs. (640)

Slope coefficient. Coefficient term in a cost estimation model that indicates the amount by which total cost changes when a one-unit change occurs in the level of activity within the relevant range. (367)

Source document. An original record that supports journal entries in an accounting system. (110)

Specification analysis. Testing of the assumptions of regression analysis. (396)

Splitoff point. The juncture in a joint-production process when two or more products become separately identifiable. (680)

Spoilage. Units of production that do not meet the specifications required by customers for good units and that are discarded or sold at reduced prices. (752)

Staff management. Staff (such as management accountants and human resources managers) who provide advice, support, and assistance to line management. (13)

Stand-alone cost-allocation method. Method that uses information pertaining to each user of the common cost facility or activity as a separate entity to determine the cost-allocation weights. (659)

Stand-alone revenue-allocation method. Method that uses product-specific information on the products in the bundle as weights for allocating the bundled revenues to the individual products. (662)

Standard. A carefully determined price, cost, or quantity that is used as a benchmark for judging performance. It is usually expressed on a per-unit basis. (253)

Standard cost. A carefully determined cost of a unit of output. (253)

Standard costing. Costing system that traces direct costs to output produced by multiplying the standard prices or rates by the standard quantities of inputs allowed for actual outputs produced and allocates overhead costs on the basis of the standard overhead-cost rates times the standard quantities of the allocation bases allowed for the actual outputs produced. (284)

Standard error of the estimated coefficient. Regression statistic that indicates how much the estimated value of the coefficient is likely to be affected by random factors. (394)

Standard error of the regression. Statistic that measures the standard deviation of residuals in a regression analysis. (394)

Standard input. A carefully determined quantity of input required for one unit of output. (253)

Standard price. A carefully determined price that a company expects to pay for a unit of input. (253)

Static budget. Budget based on the level of output planned at the start of the budget period. (247)

Static-budget variance. Difference between an actual result and the corresponding budgeted amount in the static budget. (247)

Step cost function. A cost function in which the cost remains the same over various ranges of the level of activity, but the cost increases by discrete amounts (that is, increases in steps) as the level of activity changes from one range to the next. (382)

Step-down method. Cost allocation method that allocates support department costs to other support departments and to operating departments in a sequential manner that partially recognizes the mutual services provided among all support departments. Also called *sequential allocation method*. (651)

Stockout costs. Costs that result when a company runs out of a particular item for which there is customer demand. The company must act to meet that demand or suffer the costs of not meeting it. (810)

Strategic cost management. Describes cost management that specifically focuses on strategic issues. (4)

Strategy. Specifies how an organization matches its own capabilities with the opportunities in the marketplace to accomplish its objectives. (4)

Strategy map. A diagram that describes how an organization creates value by connecting strategic objectives in explicit cause-and-effect relationships with each other in the financial, customer, internal business process, and learning and growth perspectives. (521)

Suboptimal decision making. Decisions in which the benefit to one subunit is more than offset by the costs or loss of benefits to the organization as a whole. Also called *incongruent decision making* or *dysfunctional decision making*. (891)

Sunk costs. Past costs that are unavoidable because they cannot be changed no matter what action is taken. (468)

Super-variable costing. See *throughput costing*. (334)

Supply chain. The flow of goods, services, and information from the initial sources of materials and services to the delivery of products to consumers, regardless of whether those activities occur in the same organization or in other organizations. (6)

Support department. Department that provides the services that assist other internal departments (operating departments and other support departments) in the company. Also called a *service department*. (640)

Sustainability. The development and implementation of strategies to achieve long-term financial, social, and environmental goals. (7)

Target cost per unit. Estimated long-run cost per unit of a product or service that enables the company to achieve its target operating income per unit when selling at the target price. Target cost per unit is derived by subtracting the target operating income per unit from the target price. (569)

Target leakage. Refers to data that are not available at the time of making a decision and should be excluded from the model-building analyses. (424)

Target operating income per unit. Operating income that a company aims to earn per unit of a product or service sold. (569)

Target price. Estimated price for a product or service that potential customers will pay. (569)

Target rate of return on investment. The target annual operating income that an organization aims to achieve divided by invested capital. (576)

Theoretical capacity. The level of capacity based on producing at full efficiency all the time. (337)

Theory of constraints (TOC). Describes methods to maximize operating income when faced with some bottleneck and some non-bottleneck operations. (484)

Throughput costing. Method of inventory costing in which only variable direct material costs are included as inventoriable costs. Also called *super-variable costing.* (334)

Throughput margin. Revenues minus the direct material costs of the goods sold. (484)

Time driver. Any factor in which a change in the factor causes a change in the speed of an activity. (791)

Time value of money. Recognition of the fact that a dollar (or any other monetary unit) received today is worth more than a dollar received at any future time. (853)

Total factor productivity (TFP). The ratio of the quantity of output produced to the costs of all inputs used, based on current period prices. (549)

Total-overhead variance. The sum of the flexible-budget variance and the production-volume variance. (298)

Total quality management (TQM). An integrative philosophy of management for continuously improving the quality of products and processes. (7)

Transfer price. Price one subunit (department or division) charges for a product or service supplied to another subunit of the same organization. (893)

Transferred-in costs. Costs incurred in previous departments that are carried forward as the product's costs when it moves to a subsequent process in the production cycle. Also called *previous department costs.* (726)

Trigger point. Refers to a stage in the cycle from purchase of direct materials to sale of finished goods at which journal entries are made in the accounting system. (827)

True negatives (TN). Actual negatives (for example, repay loans) in a classification model correctly predicted as negatives at a given threshold value. (444)

True positive rate. Fraction of actual positives (for example, default loans) in a classification model correctly predicted as positives at a given threshold value. (442)

True positives (TP). Actual positives (for example, default loans) in a classification model correctly predicted as positives at a given threshold value. (444)

Uncertainty. The possibility that an actual amount will deviate from an expected amount. (80)

Underabsorbed indirect costs. See *underallocated indirect costs.* (125)

Underallocated indirect costs. Allocated amount of indirect costs in an accounting period is less than the actual (incurred) amount in that period. Also called *underapplied indirect costs* or *underabsorbed indirect costs.* (125)

Underapplied indirect costs. See *underallocated indirect costs.* (125)

Unfavorable variance. Variance that has the effect of decreasing operating income relative to the budgeted amount. Denoted U. (248)

Unit cost. Cost computed by dividing total cost by the number of units. Also called *average cost.* (37)

Unused capacity. The amount of productive capacity available over and above the productive capacity employed to meet consumer demand in the current period. (542)

Usage variance. See *efficiency variance.* (254)

Value-added cost. A cost that, if eliminated, would reduce the actual or perceived value or utility (usefulness) customers obtain from using the product or service. (571)

Value chain. The sequence of business functions by which a product is made progressively more useful to customers. (5)

Value engineering. Systematic evaluation of all aspects of the value chain, with the objective of reducing costs and achieving a quality level that satisfies customers. (571)

Value streams. All valued-added activities needed to design, manufacture, and deliver a given product or product line to customers. (835)

Variable cost. Cost that changes in total in proportion to changes in the related level of total activity or volume. (32)

Variable costing. Method of inventory costing in which only all variable manufacturing costs are included as inventoriable costs. Also called *direct costing.* (323)

Variable overhead efficiency variance. The difference between the actual quantity of variable overhead cost-allocation base used and budgeted quantity of variable overhead cost-allocation base that should have been used to produce actual output, multiplied by budgeted variable overhead cost per unit of cost-allocation base. (287)

Variable overhead flexible-budget variance. The difference between actual variable overhead costs incurred and flexible-budget variable overhead amounts. (286)

Variable overhead spending variance. The difference between actual variable overhead cost per unit and budgeted variable overhead cost per unit of the cost-allocation base, multiplied by actual quantity of variable overhead cost-allocation base used for actual output. (288)

Variance. The difference between actual result and expected performance. (246)

Weighted-average process-costing method. Method of process costing that assigns the equivalent-unit cost of all work done to date (regardless of the accounting period in which it was done) to equivalent units completed and transferred out of the process and to equivalent units in ending work-in-process inventory. (718)

Whale curve. A typically backward-bending curve that represents the results from customer profitability analysis by first ranking customers from best to worst and then plotting their cumulative profitability level. (603)

Work-in-process inventory. Goods partially worked on but not yet completed. Also called *work in progress.* (39)

Work in progress. See *work-in-process inventory.* (39)

Work-measurement method. See *industrial engineering method.* (371)

Index

Figures are indicated by page numbers followed by *f*.
Notes are indicated by page numbers followed by *n*.

Author

Company

Subject

D

E

O